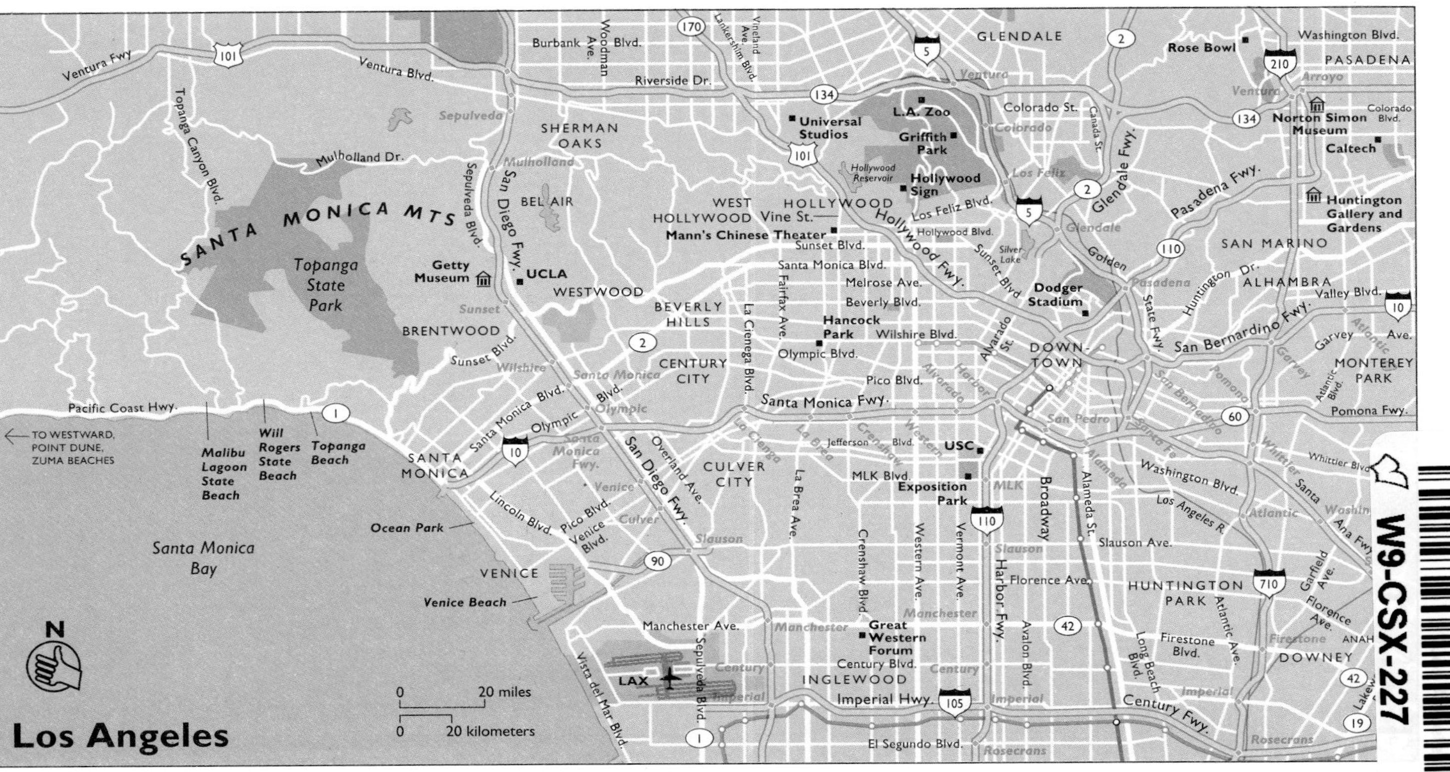

Los Angeles
N
0 20 miles
0 20 kilometers
SANTA MONICA MTS
Topanga State Park
Santa Monica Bay
TO WESTWARD, POINT DUNE, ZUMA BEACHES
Pacific Coast Hwy.
Malibu Lagoon State Beach
Will Rogers State Beach
Topanga Beach
SANTA MONICA
Ocean Park
VENICE
Venice Beach
Ventura Fwy
Ventura Blvd.
Topanga Canyon Blvd.
Mulholland Dr.
Sepulveda Blvd.
San Diego Fwy.
Getty Museum
UCLA
BEL AIR
SHERMAN OAKS
Burbank Blvd.
Woodman Ave.
Riverside Dr.
Lankershim Blvd.
Vineland Ave.
Universal Studios
L.A. Zoo
Griffith Park
Hollywood Reservoir
Hollywood Sign
GLENDALE
WEST HOLLYWOOD
HOLLYWOOD
Vine St.
Mann's Chinese Theater
WESTWOOD
BRENTWOOD
BEVERLY HILLS
CENTURY CITY
Sunset Blvd.
Santa Monica Blvd.
Melrose Ave.
Beverly Blvd.
Hancock Park
Wilshire Blvd.
Olympic Blvd.
Pico Blvd.
Fairfax Ave.
La Cienega Blvd.
Santa Monica Fwy.
Hollywood Fwy.
Los Feliz Blvd.
Hollywood Blvd.
Silver Lake
Dodger Stadium
Alvarado St.
DOWNTOWN
Colorado St.
Canada St.
Glendale Fwy.
Pasadena Fwy.
Golden State Fwy.
Rose Bowl
PASADENA
Washington Blvd.
Norton Simon Museum
Colorado Blvd.
Caltech
Huntington Gallery and Gardens
SAN MARINO
Huntington Dr.
ALHAMBRA
Valley Blvd.
San Bernardino Fwy.
Garvey Ave.
Atlantic Blvd.
MONTEREY PARK
Pomona Fwy.
Whittier Blvd.
Santa Ana Fwy.
CULVER CITY
Overland Ave.
Lincoln Blvd.
Pico Blvd.
Venice Blvd.
Jefferson Blvd.
La Brea Ave.
Crenshaw Blvd.
MLK Blvd.
USC
Exposition Park
Western Ave.
Vermont Ave.
Harbor Fwy.
Broadway
Alameda St.
Washington Blvd.
Los Angeles R.
Slauson Ave.
Florence Ave.
HUNTINGTON PARK
Atlantic Ave.
Garfield Ave.
Florence Ave.
Firestone Blvd.
Long Beach Blvd.
DOWNEY
Manchester Ave.
Great Western Forum
Century Blvd.
INGLEWOOD
Imperial Hwy.
Century Fwy.
Avalon Blvd.
El Segundo Blvd.
LAX
Sepulveda Blvd.
Vista del Mar Blvd.
W9-CSX-227

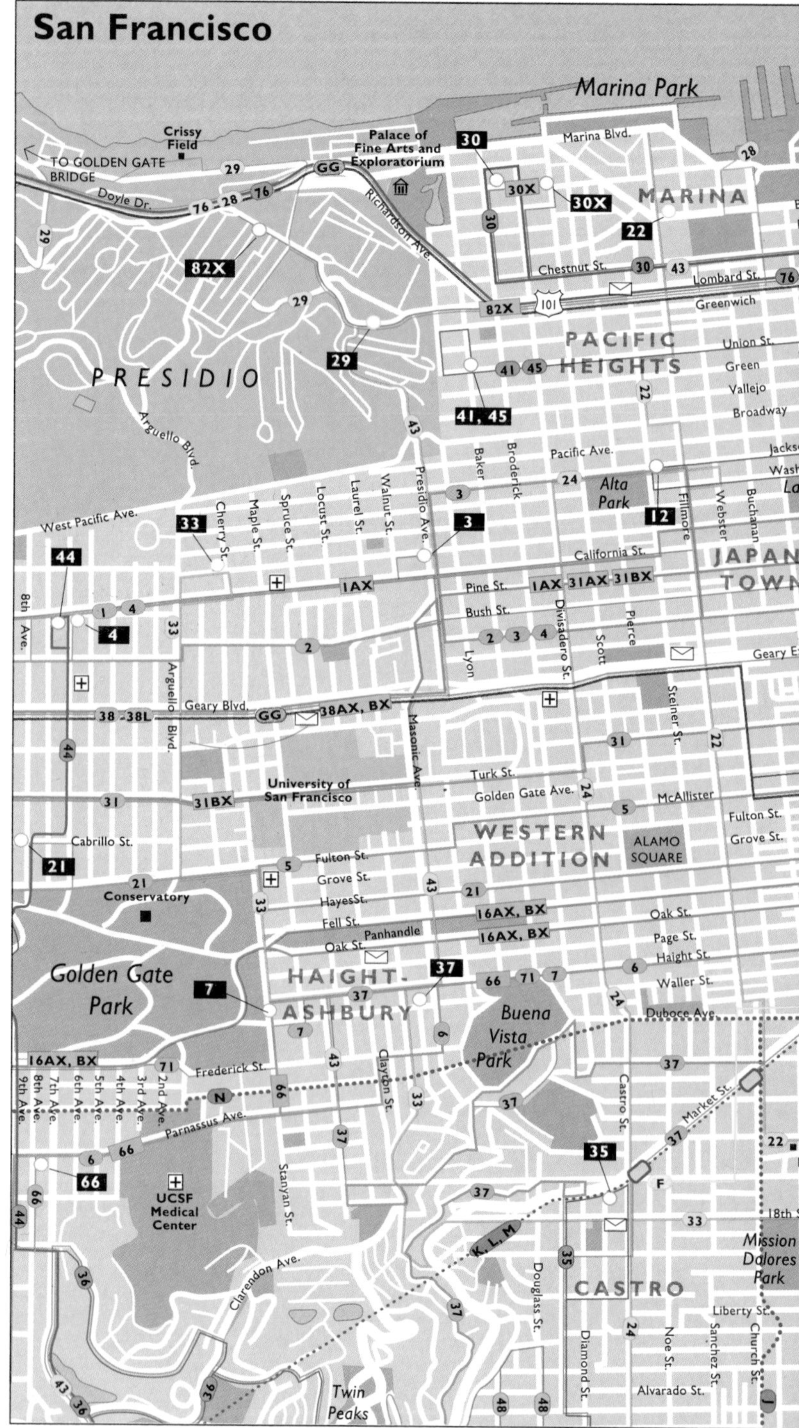
San Francisco
Marina Park
Crissy Field
TO GOLDEN GATE BRIDGE
Palace of Fine Arts and Exploratorium
Marina Blvd.
MARINA
Doyle Dr.
Richardson Ave.
Chestnut St.
Lombard St.
Greenwich
PACIFIC HEIGHTS
Union St.
Green
Vallejo
Broadway
PRESIDIO
Arguello Blvd.
Pacific Ave.
Alta Park
Baker
Broderick
Fillmore
Webster
Buchanan
West Pacific Ave.
Cherry St.
Maple St.
Spruce St.
Locust St.
Laurel St.
Walnut St.
Presidio Ave.
California St.
JAPAN-TOWN
Pine St.
Bush St.
Divisadero St.
Scott
Pierce
Lyon
Geary Blvd.
Steiner St.
Masonic Ave.
Turk St.
Golden Gate Ave.
McAllister
University of San Francisco
Cabrillo St.
WESTERN ADDITION
ALAMO SQUARE
Fulton St.
Grove St.
Conservatory
Hayes St.
Fell St.
Panhandle
Oak St.
Page St.
Haight St.
Waller St.
Golden Gate Park
HAIGHT-ASHBURY
Buena Vista Park
Duboce Ave.
Frederick St.
Clayton St.
Castro St.
Market St.
Parnassus Ave.
9th Ave.
8th Ave.
7th Ave.
6th Ave.
5th Ave.
4th Ave.
3rd Ave.
2nd Ave.
Stanyan St.
UCSF Medical Center
Clarendon Ave.
Douglass St.
CASTRO
Diamond St.
Noe St.
Sanchez St.
Church St.
Liberty St.
18th St
Mission Dolores Park
Alvarado St.
Twin Peaks

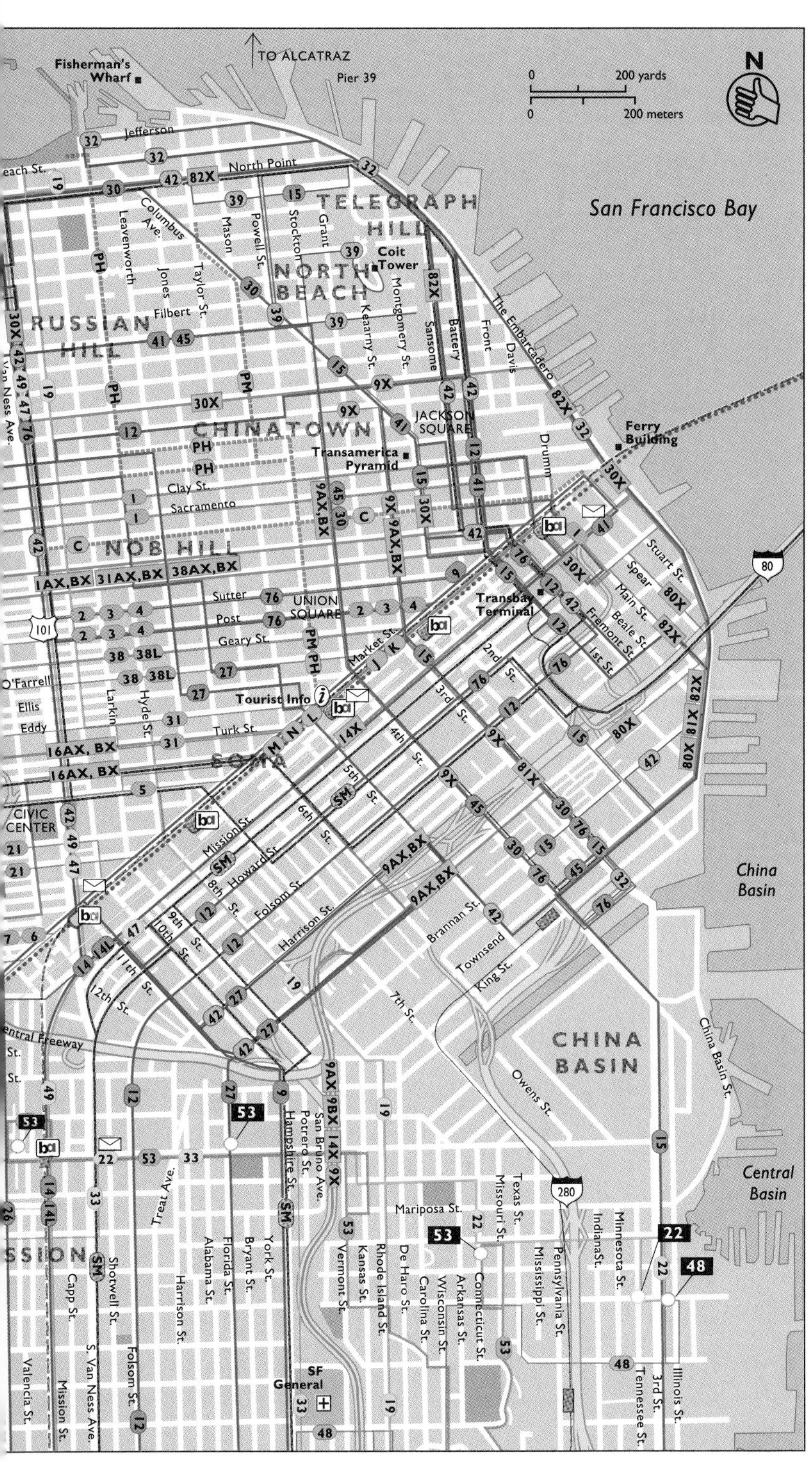

TO ALCATRAZ
Fisherman's Wharf
Pier 39
San Francisco Bay
TELEGRAPH HILL
Coit Tower
NORTH BEACH
RUSSIAN HILL
CHINATOWN
JACKSON SQUARE
Transamerica Pyramid
Ferry Building
NOB HILL
UNION SQUARE
Transbay Terminal
Tourist Info
SOMA
CIVIC CENTER
China Basin
CHINA BASIN
Central Basin
SF General
MISSION

L.A. Westside

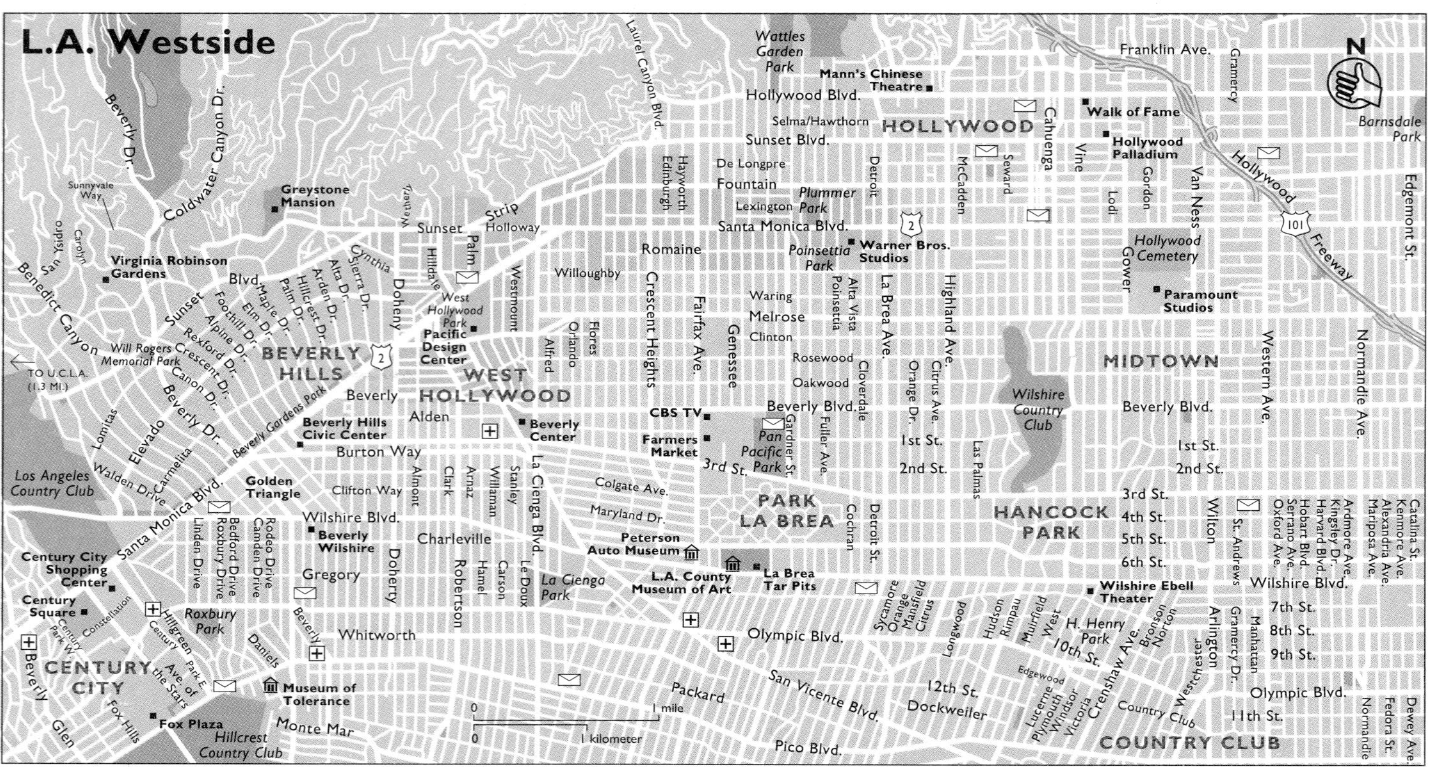

L.A. Westside
N
Wattles Garden Park
Mann's Chinese Theatre
Hollywood Blvd.
Selma/Hawthorn
Sunset Blvd.
HOLLYWOOD
Walk of Fame
Hollywood Palladium
Franklin Ave.
Gramercy
Barnsdale Park
Edgemont St.
Hollywood Freeway
101
Laurel Canyon Blvd.
Hayworth
Edinburgh
De Longpre
Fountain
Lexington
Plummer Park
Santa Monica Blvd.
Detroit
McCadden
Seward
Cahuenga
Vine
Lodi
Gordon
Van Ness
2
Poinsettia Park
Warner Bros. Studios
Hollywood Cemetery
Gower
Paramount Studios
Beverly Dr.
Coldwater Canyon Dr.
Sunnyvale Way
Greystone Mansion
Wetherly
Sunset
Strip
Holloway
Romaine
San Ysidro
Carolyn
Virginia Robinson Gardens
Blvd.
Cynthia
Sierra Dr.
Alta Dr.
Arden Dr.
Hillcrest Dr.
Palm Dr.
Maple Dr.
Elm Dr.
Foothill Dr.
Alpine Dr.
Rexford Dr.
Crescent Dr.
Canon Dr.
Beverly Dr.
Doheny
Hilldale
Palm
West Hollywood Park
Pacific Design Center
Westmount
Willoughby
Crescent Heights
Fairfax Ave.
Genessee
Waring
Melrose
Clinton
Alta Vista
Poinsettia
La Brea Ave.
Highland Ave.
Benedict Canyon
Will Rogers Memorial Park
TO U.C.L.A. (1.3 MI.)
BEVERLY HILLS
WEST HOLLYWOOD
Alfred
Orlando
Flores
Rosewood
Oakwood
Cloverdale
Orange Dr.
Citrus Ave.
MIDTOWN
Wilshire Country Club
Beverly Blvd.
Western Ave.
Normandie Ave.
Beverly
Alden
Beverly Gardens Park
Beverly Hills Civic Center
Burton Way
Beverly Center
CBS TV
Farmers Market
Pan Pacific Park
Gardner St.
Fuller Ave.
1st St.
2nd St.
3rd St.
Las Palmas
Lomitas
Elevado
Carmelita
Walden Drive
Los Angeles Country Club
Golden Triangle
Clifton Way
Almont
Clark
Arnaz
Willaman
Stanley
La Cienga Blvd.
Colgate Ave.
Maryland Dr.
PARK LA BREA
Cochran
Detroit St.
HANCOCK PARK
4th St.
5th St.
6th St.
Wilton
St. Andrews
Oxford Ave.
Serrano Ave.
Hobart Blvd.
Harvard Blvd.
Kingsley Dr.
Ardmore Ave.
Mariposa Ave.
Alexandria Ave.
Kenmore Ave.
Catalina St.
Santa Monica Blvd.
Wilshire Blvd.
Beverly Wilshire
Charleville
Linden Drive
Roxbury Drive
Bedford Drive
Camden Drive
Rodeo Drive
Peterson Auto Museum
L.A. County Museum of Art
La Brea Tar Pits
Century City Shopping Center
Gregory
Doherty
Robertson
Hamel
Carson
Le Doux
La Cienga Park
Wilshire Ebell Theater
Century Square
Constellation
Century Park W.
Hillgreen
Century
Roxbury Park
Beverly
Whitworth
Olympic Blvd.
Sycamore
Orange
Mansfield
Citrus
Longwood
Hudson
Rimpau
Muirfield
West
H. Henry Park
10th St.
Crenshaw Ave.
Bronson
Norton
Arlington
Gramercy Dr.
Manhattan
7th St.
8th St.
9th St.
CENTURY CITY
Beverly
Park E.
Ave. of the Stars
Daniels
Museum of Tolerance
Packard
San Vicente Blvd.
12th St.
Dockweiler
Edgewood
Lucerne
Plymouth
Windsor
Victoria
Westchester
Country Club
11th St.
Normandie
Fedora St.
Dewey Ave.
Fox Hills
Glen
Fox Plaza
Hillcrest Country Club
Monte Mar
0
1 mile
1 kilometer
Pico Blvd.
COUNTRY CLUB

Let's Go writers travel on your budget.

"Guides that penetrate the veneer of the holiday brochures and mine the grit of real life."

—*The Economist*

"The writers seem to have experienced every rooster-packed bus and lunar-surfaced mattress about which they write."

—*The New York Times*

"All the dirt, dirt cheap."

—*People*

Great for independent travelers.

"The guides are aimed not only at young budget travelers but at the independent traveler; a sort of streetwise cookbook for traveling alone."

—*The New York Times*

"Flush with candor and irreverence, chock full of budget travel advice."

—*The Des Moines Register*

"An indispensible resource, *Let's Go*'s practical information can be used by every traveler."

—*The Chattanooga Free Press*

Let's Go is completely revised each year.

"Only *Let's Go* has the zeal to annually update every title on its list."

—*The Boston Globe*

"Unbeatable: good sightseeing advice; up-to-date info on restaurants, hotels, and inns; a commitment to money-saving travel; and a wry style that brightens nearly every page."

—*The Washington Post*

All the important information you need.

"*Let's Go* authors provide a comedic element while still providing concise information and thorough coverage of the country. Anything you need to know about budget traveling is detailed in this book."

—*The Chicago Sun-Times*

"Value-packed, unbeatable, accurate, and comprehensive."

—*Los Angeles Times*

Let's Go Publications

Let's Go: Alaska & the Pacific Northwest 2000
Let's Go: Australia 2000
Let's Go: Austria & Switzerland 2000
Let's Go: Britain & Ireland 2000
Let's Go: California 2000
Let's Go: Central America 2000
Let's Go: China 2000 **New Title!**
Let's Go: Eastern Europe 2000
Let's Go: Europe 2000
Let's Go: France 2000
Let's Go: Germany 2000
Let's Go: Greece 2000
Let's Go: India & Nepal 2000
Let's Go: Ireland 2000
Let's Go: Israel 2000 **New Title!**
Let's Go: Italy 2000
Let's Go: Mexico 2000
Let's Go: Middle East 2000 **New Title!**
Let's Go: New York City 2000
Let's Go: New Zealand 2000
Let's Go: Paris 2000
Let's Go: Perú & Ecuador 2000 **New Title!**
Let's Go: Rome 2000
Let's Go: South Africa 2000
Let's Go: Southeast Asia 2000
Let's Go: Spain & Portugal 2000
Let's Go: Turkey 2000
Let's Go: USA 2000
Let's Go: Washington, D.C. 2000

Let's Go *Map Guides*

Amsterdam
Berlin
Boston
Chicago
Florence
London
Los Angeles
Madrid
New Orleans
New York City
Paris
Prague
Rome
San Francisco
Seattle
Washington, D.C.

Coming Soon: *Sydney* and *Hong Kong*

CALIFORNIA 2000

Elena DeCoste
Editor

Sarah A. Knight
Associate Editor

Researcher-Writers:
Teresa Crockett
Melissa Debayle
Zachary Fultz
Julio V. Gambuto
Jenny Weiss

St. Martin's Press New York

HELPING LET'S GO If you want to share your discoveries, suggestions, or corrections, please drop us a line. We read every piece of correspondence, whether a postcard, a 10-page email, or a coconut. Please note that mail received after May 2000 may be too late for the 2001 book, but will be kept for future editions. **Address mail to:**

Let's Go: California
67 Mount Auburn Street
Cambridge, MA 02138
USA

Visit Let's Go at **http://www.letsgo.com,** or send email to:

feedback@letsgo.com
Subject: "Let's Go: California"

In addition to the invaluable travel advice our readers share with us, many are kind enough to offer their services as researchers or editors. Unfortunately, our charter enables us to employ only currently enrolled Harvard students.

Distributed outside the USA and Canada by Macmillan.

ISBN: 0-312-24453-3

First edition
10 9 8 7 6 5 4 3 2 1

Let's Go: California is written by Let's Go Publications, 67 Mount Auburn Street, Cambridge, MA 02138, USA.

Printed in the USA on recycled paper with biodegradable soy ink.

ADVERTISING DISCLAIMER All advertisements appearing in Let's Go publications are sold by an independent agency not affiliated with the editorial production of the guides. Advertisers are never given preferential treatment, and the guides are researched, written, and published independent of advertising. Advertisements do not imply endorsement of products or services by Let's Go, and Let's Go does not vouch for the accuracy of information provided in advertisements.

If you are interested in purchasing advertising space in a Let's Go publication, contact: Let's Go Advertising Sales, 67 Mount Auburn St., Cambridge, MA 02138, USA.

HOW TO USE THIS BOOK

Please hold tightly to your copy of *Let's Go: California 2000* as this Extreme History Simulator transports you to 1849-era San Francisco. Tighter!

"Howdy, stranger! I'm James Marshall, and I've just discovered **goald** at Sutter's Mill! **Discovery** is a wonderful thing—new this year, as a matter of fact. First you see the goald gleamin' on the shelf, then you pick-axe it out, and polish it up into a nice shiny lump sum. Use it to plan your future—or your next vacation! The Goald Rush is about to begin, and the time to go to California is now! I can tell you ain't from around here, because you think I talk and spell funny. Well, if you want to strike it rich in California, you'll need that goald-colored book you're holding. Is it actually fashioned from goald? In these wild times, who can tell?

"We prospectors don't care much for the travel planning tips you'll find in **Essentials**—most of us left home from boredom and arrived with cholera, or else got stuck in the mountains and ate each other (see p. 256)! The **California** chapter will spin the yarn of how the Goalden State ended up the way it did, many thanks to me and the rest of the '49ers. Then you'll find a Mother Lode of **Destinations,** which spans some of the biggest cities, highest mountains, harshest deserts, comeliest plains, loveliest wine country, and most beautiful coastline in the world—all of it in one state, and much of it having nothing whatsoever to do with goald! There are even forays into the gaming halls of **Nevada,** the canyons of **Arizona,** the craters of **Oregon,** and the **Baja** peninsula of that ornery Mexican empire!

"Each of these places is divided into several complementary segments, much like an ant! My mates and I sleep huddled around a warm mother burro, but you'll want to check **Accommodations** in every region for the best in budget hotels, hostels, and campgrounds. Salted tripe and bilgewater constitute a miner's vittles, but the **Food** listings provide options for every palate—as if you could do better! Most of the time, we're too busy removing or training parasites to worry about **Sights,** but you'll find plenty of local hiking and biking trails, scenic drives, museums, and attractions of all ilks if you so choose. My idea of a good time is watching ladies of ill repute cavort in a crime-ridden saloon! Be ye blessed if the **Entertainment, Nightlife**, and **Shopping** sections help you find diversions half as heavenly. Here's a samplin':

Toothless Joe's Pickaxe Paradise, 15 Coloma St., Sonora. Joe ain't got much to chaw his hardtack with no more, but he'll fill your pie-hole with a tongue-chompin' paste made from grubs and filings.

The Tryworks Grille, 15 Sonora St., Coloma. Passing good whale fat, but no moxie. Take your mule if he's bored.

As you can see, they go in order from best to worst.

Now, go! And don't forget to look for precious goald! (Page 315 shows you how.)"

A NOTE TO OUR READERS The information for this book was gathered by *Let's Go*'s researchers from May through August. Each listing is derived from the assigned researcher's opinion based upon his or her visit at a particular time. The opinions are expressed in a candid and forthright manner. Those traveling at a different time may have different experiences since prices, dates, hours, and conditions are always subject to change. You are urged to check beforehand to avoid inconvenience and surprises. Travel always involves a certain degree of risk, especially in low-cost areas. When traveling, especially on a budget, always take particular care to ensure your safety.

CONTENTS

MAPS

LET'S GO PICKS

BEST MONOCHROME ESTABLISHMENT: The Red Room, San Francisco (p. 121). Don't. Wear. Red.

BEST MESSY FESTIVAL: The World Championship Grape-Stomp, Santa Rosa (p. 177). Ladies, pick up your skirts, gentlemen roll up your pants.

BEST HIPPIE-RUN ESTABLISHMENT: Point Reyes Hostel, Marin County (p. 162). Three generations of iconoclasts run this cozy hostel on the gorgeous Point Reyes National Seashore.

BEST PLACE TO APPRECIATE A STRONG CENTRAL GOVERNMENT: Hoover Dam, NV (p. 486). Pseudo-fascist statues and totalitarian-style mottos flank the capacious concrete energizer.

BEST PLACE TO BUY AND CONSUME CHEAP BEER: Chico (p. 319). It's cheap, it's amber-colored, what more can you ask for?

BEST PLACE TO QUESTION YOUR EXISTENCE IN THE LOTUS POSITION: Mount Shasta City (p. 328). Tune in to your ying and your yang, and anything else that floats your boat.

BEST TROUT-ILICIOUS TWENTY GALLON TANKS: The **Monterey Bay Aquarium,** Monterey (p. 212). Stumpy may have flown the coop, but the rest of the sea creatures in this complex are happy as clams in mud.

BEST CELEBRATION OF CHRISTOPHER MARLOWE'S WORK: The **Oregon Shakespeare Festival,** Ashland, OR (p. 339). One guy could never have written all of those plays.

BEST 2,000-FOOT-DEEP COLLECTION OF STAGNANT RAINWATER: Crater Lake, OR (p. 337). The stuff of legends; we just think it's neat.

BEST PLACE TO BE SCARED: Halloween in the **Castro,** San Francisco (p. 126). You thought the **Museum of the Dead** was bad enough, but October 31 in the Castro district comes alive with the dead...trick or treat!

BEST SUNSET(S): Joshua Tree National Park (p. 467), **Santa Barbara** (p. 228), and the **Strip** (Sunset, that is) (p. 345). Cheap entertainment, every night of the year.

BEST SPECIALTY CAFE: Legal Grind, Santa Monica (p. 403). Get your daily dose of legal advice and coffee.

BEST PLACE TO STRIKE IT RICH: Gold Country, (p. 308). We'll show you how (see **Pannin' fer Goald!,** p. 315 and p. 316).

BEST SCENIC DRIVES: Marin Headlands, Marin County (p. 165). Ghostly, misty drive just west of the Golden Gate Bridge. **Tioga Road,** into Yosemite National Park (p. 262). The highest strip of road in the country winds through the park, looking over plunging granite slopes and canyons.

BEST CHURROS: Disneyland, Anaheim (p. 421). The "happiest place on earth," in addition to the images and rides, boasts these strangely addictive fried treats. You might just want to stay there forever, eating and eating and eating until you explode all over the children.

BEST REASON TO EAT ALL OF YOUR RICE-A-RONI: Ghirardelli Chocolate Factory, San Francisco (p. 105). Now you can eat dessert.

BEST EXPLOITATION OF MENIAL LABOR: See **Comedy** (p. 14). The *Karate Kid*'s crane kick is no match for Miyagi's totalitarian regime. On your knees, boy! Wax on! Wax off!

RESEARCHER-WRITERS

Teresa Crockett *Northern Interior, Sierra Nevada, Fresno, Reno*

Teresa took the mountains of the Sierra Nevada in stride (really, really long stride), and traversed backcountry with laptop and brother in hand. The mighty sequoia bowed to her and the amphitheaters collapsed, and all was right with the National Parks, where Teresa reigned. Her allegiance to the *Let's Go* poetry contest, her Canadian citizenship, and her keen attitude make her a star. Above all, Teresa's hard work has ensured that all trails are properly described in *Let's Go: California* for the benefit of delicate Americans and hard-core Canucks alike.

Melissa Debayle *The Desert, Las Vegas, Route 66, San Diego*

In San Diego, laundromats and amphitheaters were mysteriously and fiendishly absent, but Melissa persevered and came through in the end, as our most punctual researcher was bound to do. She beat the heat of Death Valley (as a Floridian is bound to do) and showed us that the hottest itinerary has plenty of hot spots and hot bods. She revealed that, in Palm Springs, you can make a hot date for a date shake any day of the week, and in Vegas, all bets are off on whether or not she did.

Zachary Fultz *Central Coast, Stockton, North Coast, Ojai*

Zach, of the Oklahoma Fultzes, burned his way through California's Central Coast in a frenzy of fact-checking and white-knuckle driving, determined to make it to the nude beaches before nightfall. He showed courage in the face of every "jaw-dropping view," and strength in the face of the dozens of bars and amphitheaters he was forced to catalog for this book. Zach has described the vistas of the coast, the hippies of Mendocino, and the excess of Hearst Castle in gentle, meditative prose with the occasional acerbic commentary...or is it the other way around?

Julio V. Gambuto *Los Angeles, South Bay, Catalina Island, Orange County, Santa Barbara*

Ever eager, Julio set off to L.A. with one thing in mind—he would tear down the Hollywood sign and drive it over the border in a beat-up Toyota, headed for glory and fish tacos. But soon his plan was foiled, and he was cast into the streets to live like a travel-guide writer, reaping only the fruits of movie premieres and fish tacos. He soon prospered, and his fame grew widespread, and he was Julio, Prince of Premieres, King of Rental Cars, and founder of all Los Angeles area amphitheaters.

Jenny Weiss *San Francisco, Bay Area, Wine Country*

All hail the *chic*-est of the *chic*, the black-clad roamer on a mission to find life, love, and tender loin in the foggy hills and amphitheaters of San Francisco. Jenny now finds herself a permanent resident there—the mark of a truly dedicated researcher. Fortunately, this petite redhead's *haight* didn't prevent her from being admitted to all of the great clubs, and her winning smile got her in for free—much like Castro into the U.S. (or something like that). Editor of *Let's Go: Ireland 1999*, Jenny and her near-flawless copy made the girls back home smile, and her attention to detail was much appreciated when push came to shove and North Beach came to Chinatown.

John Connolly *Baja*
Ana Morrel-Samuels *Crater Lake, Klamath Falls*
Kevin Yip *Arizona, Grand Canyon National Park*

ACKNOWLEDGMENTS

THE EDITORS THANK: Kaya and the fearless and frolicking R-W team, Giuseppe, Stumpy (rest in peace), Bibot, Jennie, Xian, Olivia, Matt, Ralph Macchio et al., *Complete Works*, Tom & James (Canadians-at-large), The Map, photo essays, Matty Smith for the phone calls, Camp Fernwood, Trailer Park USA and the Domestic Underground, the Jesse Matz fund, white cheddar Cheez-Its, *Jumpers*, Martijn's mom, poison control, Leeore and Ben for leaving us in such good hands, and Goald!

ELENA THANKS: The brilliant and hilarious Sarah Knight for laughter and line-editing; the eternal straight man, Kaya, for endless support and pulling that last all-nighter; Daniel O. Scully for constant friendship and acerbic wit; Jennie for laughter and listening; Christian Roulleau for being so...red-headed? French? crossword-adept? all of that, and more; Jecca for being the best kid (not) at school; Angela for everything; McCarter for sanity(!?); Jay for cleaning his (and others') plate(s) and for film criticism; Deirdre, Olivia, Laura B., Jess, Kate, Sarah J., Melissa R., Prichard, Xian, and Matt for 3rd- and 4th-floor laughter and fun; TJ, Tom, James, John, and John (Joe who?) for basement antics; Will, Waka, and Cheph for constant laughter (or was it fear?); Topher, Alex, Corinne, Mom, and Hunter Blendo; Dad for love and advice; and, of course, Adam for endless laughter and love, with and without certain armadillos, hippopotami, and Tiggers.

SARAH THANKS: thanks to elena for spearheading the great *karate kid* caper, dave and dorian for being my inspirations on the west coast, bethany, my soon-to-be inspiration in the eastern hemisphere, my boys for keeping me entertained and my girls for entertainment to come, my parents for understanding why I couldn't talk on the phone, and my brother for reminding me what I looked like at age thirteen, *othello* for getting me through the night, pinocchio's for making me stronger in the face of adversity, the pudding for providing shelter through the storm, and earl for companionship.

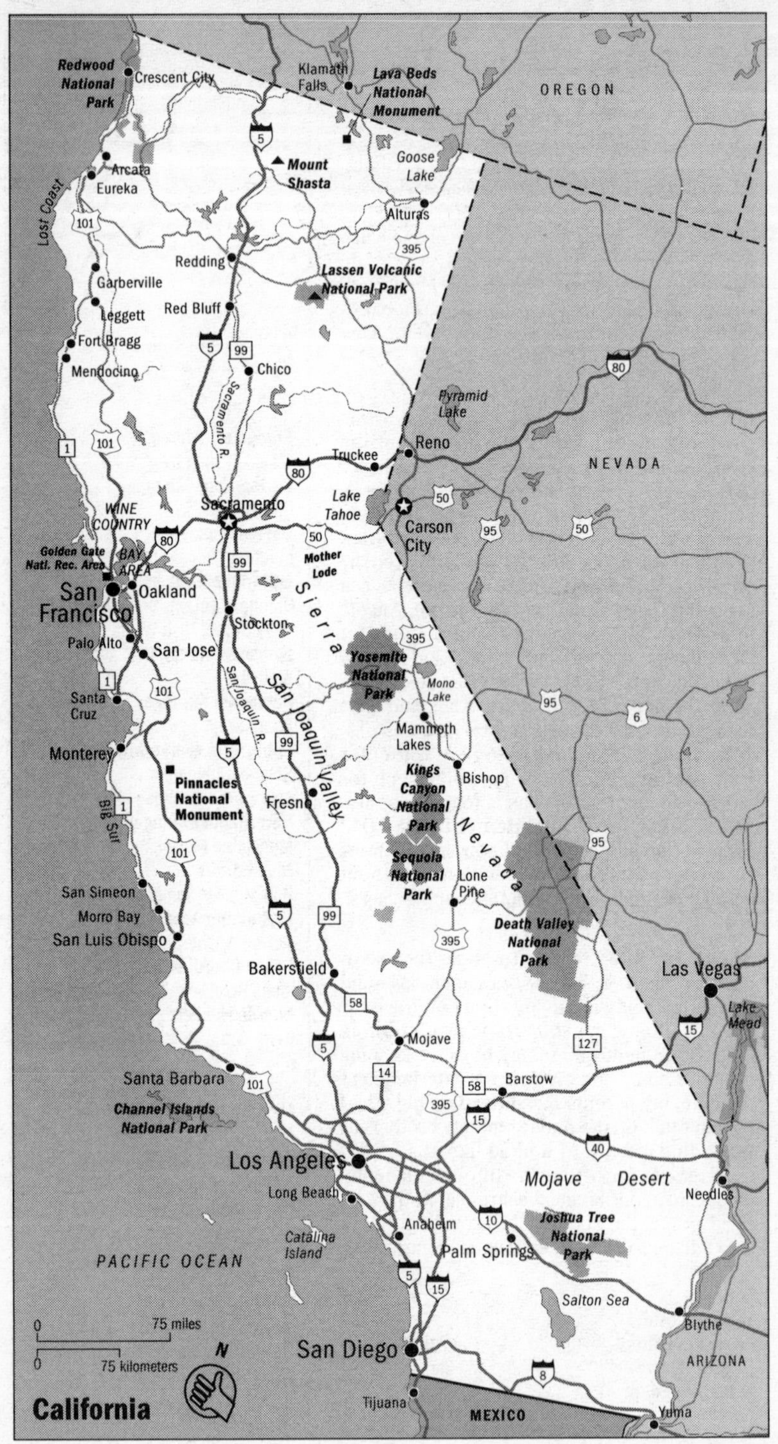
California
Redwood National Park
Crescent City
Klamath Falls
Lava Beds National Monument
OREGON
Mount Shasta
Goose Lake
Arcata
Eureka
Lost Coast
Alturas
Redding
Lassen Volcanic National Park
Garberville
Leggett
Red Bluff
Fort Bragg
Mendocino
Chico
Sacramento R.
Pyramid Lake
Reno
NEVADA
Truckee
Lake Tahoe
Carson City
Sacramento
WINE COUNTRY
Golden Gate Natl. Rec. Area
BAY AREA
Mother Lode
San Francisco
Oakland
Sierra
Stockton
Palo Alto
San Jose
Yosemite National Park
Mono Lake
San Joaquin R.
San Joaquin Valley
Santa Cruz
Mammoth Lakes
Monterey
Kings Canyon National Park
Bishop
Pinnacles National Monument
Fresno
Big Sur
Nevada
Sequoia National Park
Lone Pine
San Simeon
Morro Bay
San Luis Obispo
Death Valley National Park
Bakersfield
Las Vegas
Lake Mead
Mojave
Barstow
Santa Barbara
Channel Islands National Park
Los Angeles
Mojave Desert
Long Beach
Needles
Anaheim
Palm Springs
Joshua Tree National Park
Catalina Island
PACIFIC OCEAN
Salton Sea
Blythe
0 75 miles
0 75 kilometers
N
San Diego
ARIZONA
Tijuana
MEXICO
Yuma

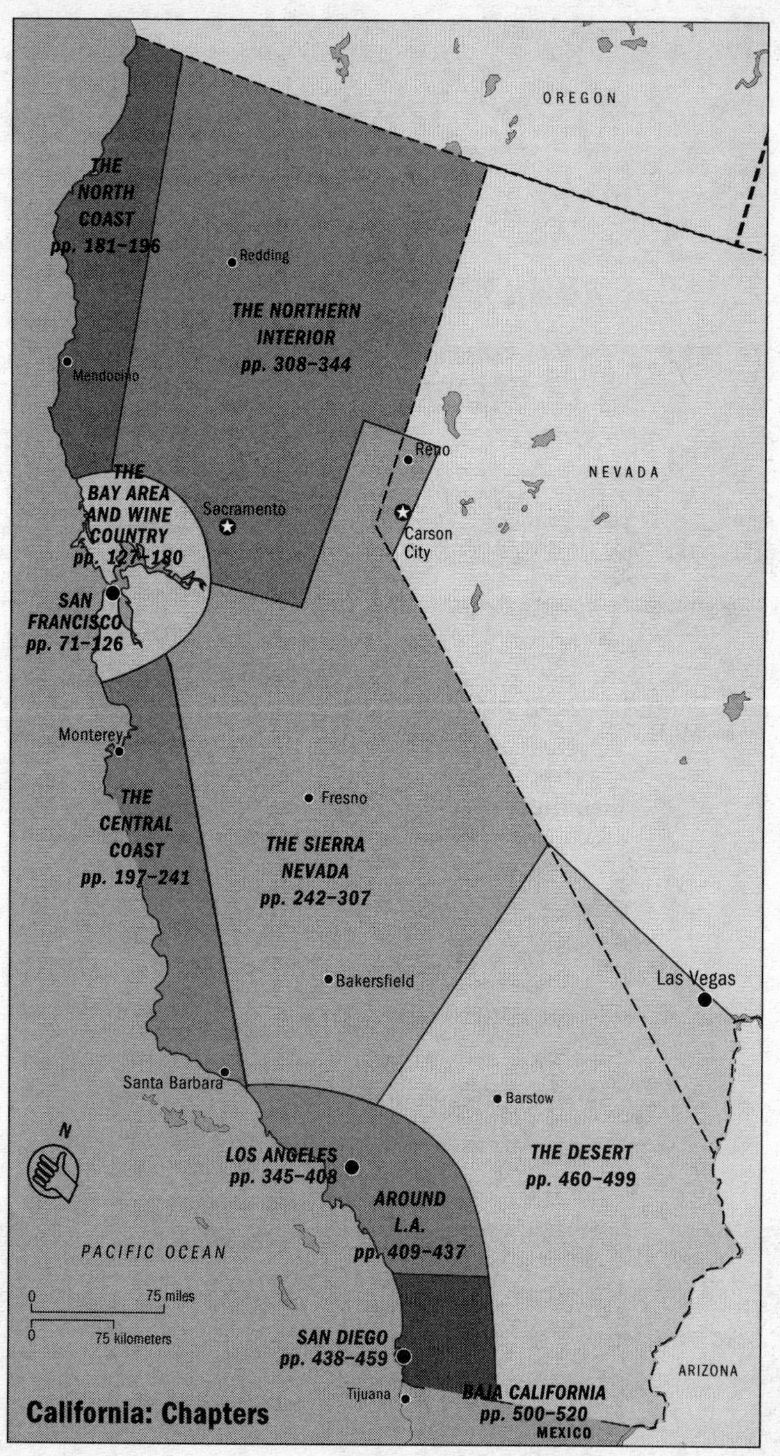
OREGON
THE NORTH COAST pp. 181–196
Redding
THE NORTHERN INTERIOR pp. 308–344
Mendocino
Reno
NEVADA
THE BAY AREA AND WINE COUNTRY pp. 127–180
Sacramento
Carson City
SAN FRANCISCO pp. 71–126
Monterey
Fresno
THE CENTRAL COAST pp. 197–241
THE SIERRA NEVADA pp. 242–307
Bakersfield
Las Vegas
Santa Barbara
Barstow
N
LOS ANGELES pp. 345–408
THE DESERT pp. 460–499
AROUND L.A. pp. 409–437
PACIFIC OCEAN
0
75 miles
0
75 kilometers
SAN DIEGO pp. 438–459
ARIZONA
Tijuana
BAJA CALIFORNIA pp. 500–520
MEXICO
California: Chapters

DISCOVER CALIFORNIA

Freak Out!

—Frank Zappa, California resident

California is a place to freak out—to redefine boundaries, identities, and attitudes. It is a state that anticipates the constant changes in American mass culture and channels them into the trends of the future. Gold miners freaked out in the 1840s and hungry young actors freak out today. Whether it's "Goald!" or "Stardom!," folks still dig for riches and toss them back at the rest of the world, imprinting California hype, commerce, industry, art, and insanity on the brain of the collective world. Is it a dream-fulfillment zone? A battleground for well-armed gangs of urban youth? The ultra-chic home of Hollywood glamour? A smog-filled, concrete nightmare? A sprawling, therapeutic nature preserve? A rock-climbing, ten-hanging, lunch-doing, adrenaline-pumping citrus-soda commercial? All of it, babe, and more—it is the Golden State, the land of milk and honey, the drawing board for the American Dream.

California has the largest population among U.S. states, and is the third-largest in the nation by area, bigger than the entire country of Italy. It stretches over 800 miles between its northern border with Oregon and its southern border with Mexico, and for about 250 miles between the Pacific Ocean on the west and Nevada and Arizona on the east. This land holds both urban and rural riches; California produces more agricultural products than any other U.S. state, although its population is over 91% urban and only 15% of its land is cultivated. All of that space leaves plenty of room for diversity. In spite of the recent vigorous anti-immigrant sentiment, California boasts a broad ethnic mix, and today, Los Angeles has an important Japanese-American community, San Francisco's Chinatown is the world's largest Chinese community outside of Asia, and one-third of Mexican-Americans in the U.S. live in California.

For centuries, settlers have come to California in search of the elusive and the unattainable. Spanish conquistadors came for the mythical land of El Dorado, the '49ers hunted for the Mother Lode (and later the Super Bowl ring), and the naïve and beautiful still search for stardom on the silver screen. Adventurers flock to the mountains and deserts, and stampedes of 2.2-child families overrun the national parks, seeking peace in nature and lava beds. Dreamy-eyed, disenfranchised flower children converge on San Francisco's Haight Street, while technology wizards flock to the booming Silicon Valley. California is always a few years ahead of the rest of the country in trendiness and taboo-breaking—leave it to the rest of the world to uphold tradition, California says—we're too busy freaking out.

FACTS AND FIGURES

- **Capital:** Sacramento.
- **State Population:** 30,866,851.
- **Amount of California Coastline per Resident:** 2¾ inches.
- **Amount of Los Angeles Roadway per L.A. resident:** 114½ inches.
- **Length of the San Andreas Fault:** 754 miles.

BEACHES

Where else would you expect the Beach Boys to make their home? California's beaches are consistently among the best in the Western hemisphere, for their sand, sun, and surf potentials, as well as (unofficially) their beach bunnies. California's meandering coastline has something for everyone: Watersports, from sailing to scuba diving, are not only popular among seasoned locals but among visitors of all skill levels. Lessons are offered on every beach for every activity under the sun. Similarly, the fishing industry lures pleasure-boaters and professionals alike—cruise **Catalina Island** (p. 416) in a rental boat, lazily bobbing for a golden trout, or wake up at 4am and cruise **Fisherman's Wharf** (p. 78) for a prime spot to park your pole. In the evening, wander a stretch of the **Santa Cruz Beach Boardwalk,** and take in the sights and smells of a community that's like summer vacation all year round. California's beaches will beckon you to enjoy them by day and night, whatever your energy level.

Huntington Beach (p. 426) is well known as a California gem, along with **Long Beach** (p. 413), named "America's Most Beautiful Beach" by *Good Housekeeping Magazine* in 1997. Family beaches and not-so-family beaches (read: clothing optional) dot the coast from San Diego to the North Coast. Any trip to California can be made better, calmer, kinder, and gentler by spending a day oceanside, and reveling in the salt air, bright sunshine, and beautiful bikini-ed scenery.

NATIONAL PARKS AND WILDERNESS

California has 129 wilderness areas, more than any other state, and they encompass more acres of wilderness and protected lands than any state other than Alaska. Its extensive coastline (over 1300 miles), vast networks of waterways, and nearly 5000 lakes make its fishing, boating, and swimming options seemingly endless. California's mountains and deserts provide countless scenic hiking, biking, and driving routes. In short, California is one of the best places to come for wilderness exploration. Arguably the finest of the National Parks, **Yosemite** welcomes visitors year-round for hiking and swimming, or snowshoeing and cross-country skiing (p. 262). **Joshua Tree National Park** offers rock-climbing opportunities and makes an excellent place to visit when the desert wildflowers bloom in March and April (p. 471). Plenty of California forests welcome campers and hikers alike, from **Redwood National Park** (p. 191) to **Sequoia** and **Kings Canyon National Park** (p. 278). Kings Canyon National Park includes **Mt. Whitney** (14, 494ft.), the highest point in the contiguous 48 states (p. 297), while **Death Valley National Park** contains the lowest point in the world at **Badwater,** which is a sweltering 282 feet below sea level (p. 478). On a clear day, you can see forever, or at least from the top of Mt. Whitney to the bottom of Badwater—even without binoculars.

California has nine National Parks, and dozens of National Forests, Monuments, and Preserves—all designed to protect natural resources and make them accessible for study and appreciation. Whether you have a whole family in tow or just a pack on your back, a vacation in one of these outdoor oases will keep you busy. Each park requires different realms of knowledge to experience its unique qualities to the fullest. For example, all visitors to the Desert should heed *Let's Go*'s warnings about enjoying the climate responsibly (see **Desert Survival,** p. 460), so that a visit to Death Valley National Park doesn't get recounted as "Heatstroke, or, How I Spent My Summer Vacation." Although one of its main attractions, **Cold Boiling Lake** (p. 324), seems to indicate otherwise, **Lassen Volcanic Park** (p. 321) is composed of the coldest form of lava—lots and lots of magma. And you've never heard anyone say, "Show me the magma."

FOOD AND DRINK

Rice-A-Roni, you may ask? Is that really the "San Francisco treat?" In a word, yes. But not to be outdone, every other California city and community contributes its finest fare to the unique "California Cuisine" that has become so popular with the rest of the world. From Nihonmachi to Napa Valley, Mendocino to Monterey, California is simply bursting with great meals at great prices, with ingredients and ambience unique to the produce-filled land and the ever-trendy populace. Vegetables and seafood are fresh and in constant supply, wine flows like water, and herbs are not just marijuana anymore.

Regional specialties include seafood in Monterey (but not from the Aquarium), Italian in San Francisco's North Beach and Mexican fare in the Mission, and delicacies like quail, rarebit, and spotted owl (just kidding) in the Northern Interior. There's a particularly good selection of pan-Asian food, including trendy *pad thai* in West Hollywood. The most taste-full region in all of California however, is famous not for its cuisine, but for it's *vino*. **Wine Country** (p. 127) comprises many small regions north of San Francisco that produce some of the most renowned selections of red, white, and sparkling wines on the planet. Grapes abound, as does cheese, vintage snobbery, and above all: free tastings! Try your palate at dozens of area wineries and play *sommelier* for a day.

Budget diners may want to check out places like **Roscoe's House of Chicken and Waffles,** in Hollywood (p. 370), or **Wahoo's** fish tacos (p. 411) for deals and genuine California charm. Further up the food chain are areas like **Big Sur** (p. 216), where people go to hike for hours and be in total seclusion (read: work up a sweat and pig out). Higher-end prices reflect the gorgeous forested settings and comparatively heartier meals (you don't gain weight eating tofu in Tinseltown), but cliffside dinner at **Cafe Kevah** is worth every penny (p. 218). Finally, you may hate to admit it, but you know you're looking for that heavenly spicy sweet 'n' sour smorgasbord that is: The Chinese All-Day Buffet. Well, you may find them in California, but we're not going to tell you where. Your taste buds deserve a vacation too, and if you have to live like a plebian, try **In-N-Out Burgers** instead (p. 69).

WHAT I REALLY WANT TO DO IS DIRECT

As the purveyor of much of the world's mass media, California holds a special place in the aspirations of many. Thousands head to Hollywood each year to "make it" and most never do, but vacationers can revel in the glitz and glamour that is Hollywood without sacrificing job security. It's easy to get swept up in the excitement, but keeping your feet firmly planted on the ground is the best way to see the place where dreams are made.

A good place to start for the lowdown on L.A. theater- and film-going is **Mann's Chinese Theater** (formerly Grauman's), in Hollywood (p. 376). Many premieres take place here, and stars can often be seen walking up and down the proverbial red carpet outside the theater. Even when the streets are empty, though, the stars still shine in the form of the **Hollywood Walk of Fame** (p. 376), a sidewalk art show of those who came before. Stars are awarded for achievement in five categories: movies, radio, television, recording, and live performance. Unveiling ceremonies are slightly more exciting than trying to fit your hands into the prints left by hundreds of stars, but both can satisfy a true fan. The nearby **Hollywood Studio Museum** houses relics of the old days of movie making (p. 377), showcasing costumes, props, and wigs. from the first films ever to appear on the silver screen. Finally, for a more technicolor view of Hollywood and its mass appeal, you can stroll the **Universal City Walk** (p. 390), which although not as educational as a museum, is an acceptable crash course in Hollywood commerce.

If you insist on knowing where to meet the stars and how to propel yourself into their world, check out user friendly tidbits such as: **So You Wanna Be In Pictures?** (p. 396), **If I Were A Groupie** (p. 377), and **The Celebrity Tour** (p. 393). It ain't much, but it's a start, kiddo. Also note the presence of Imperial Troops surrounding a certain director's private home—wannabes are promptly exterminated at the door at the **Skywalker Ranch,** p. 164.

SUGGESTED ITINERARIES

THE BEST OF: (A 3-WEEK TOUR) Seeing the best can take as long as you desire, but this itinerary will ensure that you hit most major highlights in just 3 weeks. Start in **San Francisco** (p. 71), and spend 3 days getting a feel for Haight-Ashbury, Chinatown, and Alcatraz. Then head to **Tahoe** (p. 242) for 2 days on the lake–summer and winter recreation opportunities abound: hiking, biking, water sports, skiing, and beaches are all among the best in the state. Just across the border, test your luck in Nevada's casinos. For relief, the all-natural **Yosemite** (p. 262) is less than 2 hours away. Spend 3 days traversing its web of trails and bikepaths, or admire the scenery from the Valley floor. Head back to the coast for 3 days on the Monterey Bay in **Santa Cruz** (p. 197) and **Monterey** (p. 208), taking in both the beach Boardwalk and the renowned Monterey Bay Aquarium, leaving time for Monterey's Cannery Row or a tour of the gorgeous U.C. Santa Cruz campus. Spend a day in scenic **Big Sur** (p. 216)–camping there is a great opportunity to experience the famed redwood forests. From Big Sur, move toward **Santa Barbara** (p. 228) for breathtaking beaches and an afternoon on State St. Next, wander **Los Angeles** (p. 345) for 2 days: see a movie at Mann's Chinese Theater, get pierced at Venice Beach, and go to the Getty Museum. Visit the happiest place on earth, **Disneyland** (p. 421), and enjoy roller coasters, Mickey Mouse, and *churros*. Next, spend a day in **San Diego** (p. 438) to see the famous Zoo and Animal Park, and then head to **Tijuana** (p. 500) for a night on the town in Mexico. Return to the States for a day in **Joshua Tree National Park** (p. 467) to see some of California's most beautiful sunrises and sunsets. Complete your journey with a day or two in **Las Vegas** (p. 480), which may not be within Californian borders, but where excess is an art form, and where the true budget traveler will revel in the gorge-'til-you-drop super-buffets.

GO COASTAL (A 2-WEEK EXPLORATION) This scenic drive takes you along Rte. 1, which offers incredible vistas. Start off in **San Francisco** (p. 71) for 4 days in the foggy city on the bay, spending time at Golden Gate Park, in Chinatown and Haight-Ashbury, and visiting Alcatraz. Next, head slightly inland to **Wine Country** (p. 158) for 2 days of wine-tasting and bicycle rides. Travel south to **Santa Cruz** (p. 239) for 2 days of amusement at the beach Boardwalk, visiting UC Santa Cruz, and strolling the Pacific Garden Mall. Jaunt to **Monterey** (p. 208) for a day at the Monterey Bay Aquarium and another along Cannery Row or in nearby **Carmel** (p. 208). A day's drive through **Big Sur** (p. 216) promises big views and bigger redwoods. A day in **Cambria** or **San Simeon** (p. 197) brings on Hearst Castle (p. 221). **Santa Barbara** (p. 228) is good for 2 days of beaches, shopping, a gorgeous mission, and a stunning sunset (p. 233). From Santa Barbara, take a daytrip to **Channel Islands National Park** (p. 241).

CAMP, CAMP, CAMP (2 WEEKS OF OUTDOORS). Hiking and camping are the best ways to see the incredible national parks and other outdoor sights in California. Even those who don't like to rough it with tent-camping can find nearby hostels or motels and experience the parks on foot during the day. Start with 1 day on **Catalina Island** (p. 416). Then, 2 days in **Joshua Tree National Park** (p. 467) for great hikes and views, including some of the best desert sunsets in the West. In winter, 2 days are well-spent in **Death Valley National Park** (p. 472), when temperatures are bearable, while March and April are when the desert wildflowers bloom. **Sequoia and Kings Canyon National Parks** (p. 278) are a good 2-day stop for hikes through the famous California sequoia, some of the world's largest life forms. The most beautiful park in California is **Yosemite National Park** (p. 262), and a 3-day stopover allows enough time to hike up Yosemite Falls or ice skate at Curry Village, stargaze from Glacier Point, and (for the truly bold) brave Half Dome's 12-hour ascent. **Lassen Volcanic National Park** (p. 321) has excellent hikes and fewer tourists.

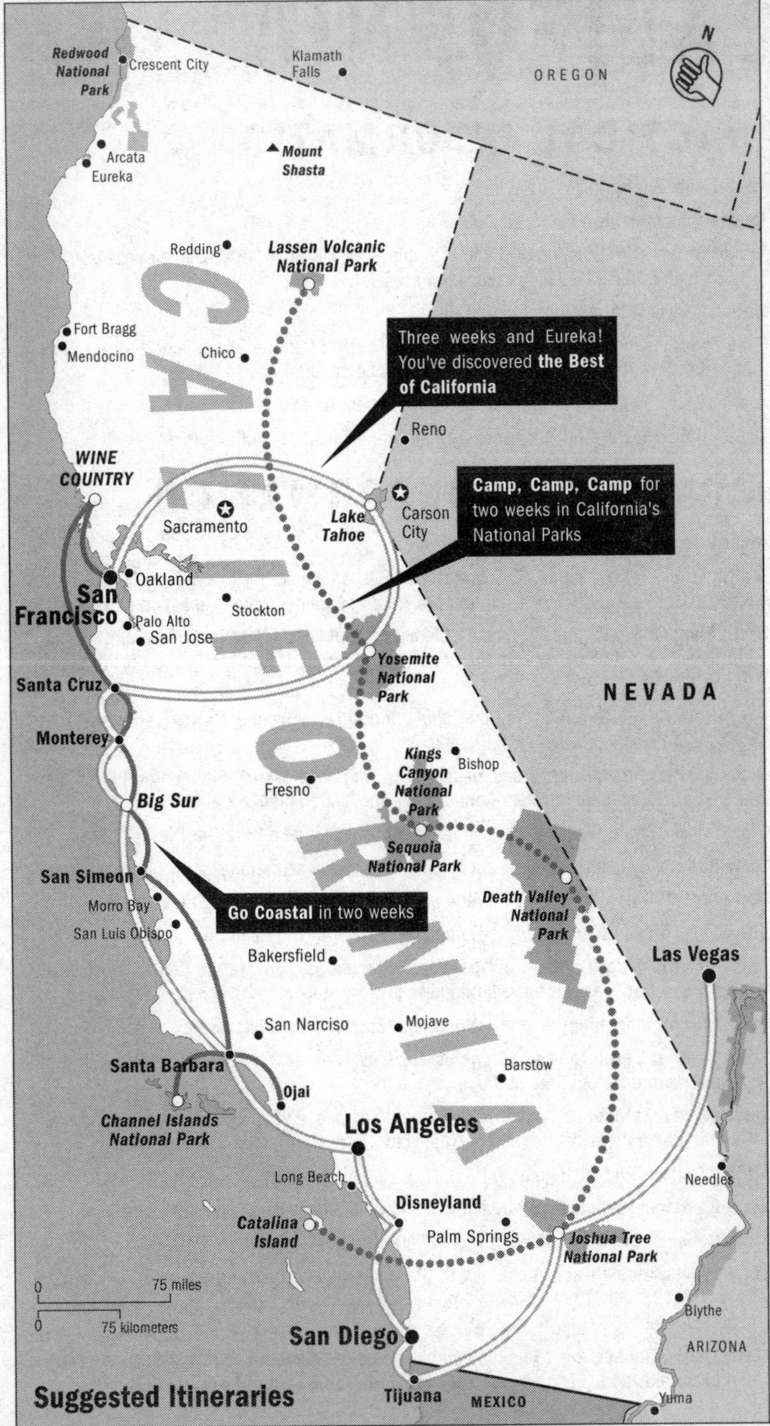

Suggested Itineraries
Three weeks and Eureka! You've discovered the Best of California
Camp, Camp, Camp for two weeks in California's National Parks
Go Coastal in two weeks
OREGON
NEVADA
ARIZONA
MEXICO
CALIFORNIA
N
Redwood National Park
Crescent City
Klamath Falls
Arcata
Eureka
Mount Shasta
Redding
Lassen Volcanic National Park
Fort Bragg
Mendocino
Chico
Reno
WINE COUNTRY
Sacramento
Lake Tahoe
Carson City
Oakland
San Francisco
Stockton
Palo Alto
San Jose
Yosemite National Park
Santa Cruz
Monterey
Kings Canyon National Park
Bishop
Fresno
Big Sur
Sequoia National Park
San Simeon
Morro Bay
San Luis Obispo
Death Valley National Park
Bakersfield
Las Vegas
San Narciso
Mojave
Barstow
Santa Barbara
Ojai
Channel Islands National Park
Los Angeles
Long Beach
Needles
Disneyland
Catalina Island
Palm Springs
Joshua Tree National Park
Blythe
San Diego
Tijuana
Yuma
0 75 miles
0 75 kilometers

CALIFORNIA

PRACTICAL INFORMATION

Postal Abbreviation: CA.

Capital: Sacramento.

Visitor Information: California Office of Tourism, 801 K St. #1600, Sacramento 95814-3523 (call 800-862-2543 for tourism materials).

National Park Information: 415-556-0560.

Time Zone: Pacific (1hr. behind Mountain, 2hr. behind Central, 3hr. behind Eastern, 3hr. ahead of Hawaii, 8hr. behind GMT, 15hr. behind much of Asia).

Area: 158,693 sq. mi., larger than Germany, Japan, or Italy.

Population: 33,000,000. One of every eight Americans lives in California.

IMPRACTICAL INFORMATION

Nickname: The Golden State.

Motto: *Eureka* (I have found it). Found since 1849 on the state's Great Seal, *Eureka* beat back a 1957 coup attempt by *In God We Trust* and gained official sanction in 1963.

State Flag: Originally the flag of the California Republic, the flag features a grizzly bear and a red star that represents the Lone Star of Texas, it was made the official state flag in 1911.

Poet Laureate: Since 1966, the Honorable Charles B. Garrigus, of Cayucos (who was formerly a state assemblyman from Reedley).

State Animal: Grizzly bear *(Ursus californicus),* an image of which is found on the state flag. In 1922, settlers in Tulare County killed the last one left in California.

State Fossil: Sabre-tooth cat *(Smilodon californicus)* (see **La Brea Tar Pits,** p. 385.)

State Bird: Valley quail *(Lophortyx californica),* a plump game bird with black plume and bib.

State Insect: Dogface butterfly *(Zerene eurydice),* also known as dog head.

State Fish: Golden trout *(Salmo agua-bonita),* native only to California.

State Marine Fish: Garibaldi *(Hypsypops rubicundus),* an orange fish that emits a thumping sound when disturbed, and lives in the waters off of Southern California.

State Marine Mammal: California gray whale *(Eschrichtius robustus).*

State Reptile: Desert tortoise *(gopherus assissizi),* an endangered species living in the southwestern deserts of the state.

State Flower: *Eschsholtzia californica.* Common names: golden poppy, the flame flower, *la amapola,* or *copa de oro* (cup of, yes, gold). April 6 is California Poppy Day.

State Mineral: Gold. Yes, gold.

State Gemstone: Benitoite, a rare mineral known familiarly as a "blue diamond."

State Rock: Serpentine; California was the first state to designate a State Rock (1965).

State Prehistoric Artifact: A chipped 8000-year-old stone bear unearthed in San Diego County in 1985. In 1991, California became the first state to designate an Official Prehistoric Artifact.

State Tree: Giant sequoia (*Sequoia sempervirens;* see **Sequoia National Park,** p. 276) and coast redwood (*Sequoia gigantea;* see **Redwood National Park,** p. 192).

State Colors: Blue and, yes, gold; taken from the school colors chosen in 1875 by the University of California at Berkeley and made the official state colors in 1951.

State Dance: West Coast Swing Dancing–similar to the jitterbug, swing, or whip.

State Folk Dance: Square dancing.

State Fife and Drum Band: The California Consolidated Drum Band was made the official fife and drum band of California in 1997.

State Song: "I Love You, California," words by F.B. Silverwood, music by Alfred Frankenstein.

Unofficial State Song: "California Über Alles," by the Dead Kennedys.

THE CALIFORNIA STORY

THE EARLY YEARS AND EXPLORATION

Before California was California, it was Mexico. And before it was Mexico, it was home to more than 100 **Native American** cultures, descendants of the original Paleo-Siberian immigrants, each with their own political system, social customs, and language. California's tribes made up the densest population north of Mesoamerica. Most tribes were peaceful and unaggressive, and survived for the most part by hunting, fishing, and gathering. Social classes were virtually nonexistent, except in the northwest, where material wealth was very important and slavery was practiced. The Native Americans lived without all but the most rudimentary agricultural techniques, until Europeans arrived, encroaching upon their ways of life.

In 1542, **Spain** made the first European contact with California tribes when Antonio de Mendoza asked explorer Estévan Juan Rodríguez Cabrillo (a Portuguese conquistador enlisted in the Spanish navy) to sail up the west coast of North America in a poorly-provisioned ship manned by conscripts. His mission, to find the mythical Strait of Anian, was considered a failure even though the exploration party reached latitude 43° on the Oregon coast (the first Europeans to do so), and not all of them returned home (Cabrillo died in 1543 and Bartolome Ferrelo assumed the duties of leading the expedition). Spanish influence in the area remains strong even to this day, in everything from architecture to language. The Spanish named the region California after the mythical land full of gold and jewels in the romance *Las Sergas de Esplandian* (1510)—a paradise teeming with tall, bronze Amazons. (In "California Girls," the 1965 Top Ten hit song by the Beach Boys—which was remade two decades later by rocker David Lee Roth—these Amazons find their modern mythical parallel.)

The **English,** who called the region that is now the state of California Nova Albion, were not to be outdone. Elizabeth I sent sea dog Sir Francis Drake to raid Spanish galleons; in 1587 he encountered the Miwoks, one of the largest of the California tribes, during an emergency landing near present-day San Francisco. He claimed the land for the queen just in case she wanted it. As it turned out, it was not English or Spanish aggression, but rather the European **diseases** they brought along that proved to be the tribes' main enemy: between 25 and 50% of California's native population died from smallpox, tuberculosis, and measles—diseases that were introduced to the region by Europeans.

The area began to be settled en masse from 1769, when King Charles ordered colonization in order to prevent other countries from encroaching into the area. Coastal cities like San Francisco (founded 1776) and Los Angeles (founded 1787) cropped up alongside Catholic **missions,** which were introduced by **Father Junípero Serra** (see below). Many of the state's Native American residents were denied their own religion, Christianized, and coerced into working at the missions. During the mission period, the Native American population from San Francisco to San Diego fell by 75%. Relegated to a serf-like status in the Spanish feudal order, the cultures that had thrived here for millennia were about to come to an end.

A MAN WITH A MISSION Along with the new governor and the fleets of Spanish soldiers that arrived in California in 1769 came Father Junípero Serra, a Franciscan priest with a proselytizing fervor unlike anything the Native Americans had ever seen. Over the next 54 years, he and his successor founded 21 missions up and down the California coast along a path called El Camino Reál (The Royal Road), which roughly corresponds to the modern U.S. 101. Despite a shortage of materials and labor, Serra pushed for new missions with such zeal that the Spanish governor swore it was "nothing less than the temptation of the evil one." Serra's obsession with his missions has been passed down in the hearts of many Californians, who take a fierce pride in the fact that such structures can be found nowhere else in the United States. When the edifices began to fall into ruin in the early 20th century, mission-loving citizens banded together to campaign for restoration funds. Over the next 50 years, nearly all the buildings (save the churches) were stripped to the ground and painstakingly rebuilt in perfect adobe replicas of the originals. Today, every fourth grader in California faithfully follows in the footsteps of these philanthropists and builds a miniature model of one of Father Serra's missions out of milk cartons and popsicle sticks. For a list of all the missions, see the index.

THE NINETEENTH CENTURY: STATEHOOD

The nineteenth century spelled doom for the Spanish territories. The earthquake of 1812 destroyed many a mission, and the Spanish met with competition in the form of a Russian fur trading post at Fort Ross (occupied 1812-1841), just north of San Francisco (see p. 182). Fortunately for the newly independent republic of **Mexico** (declared in 1824), Russian occupation was short-lived, but Mexico now had a more determined and formidable enemy: the USA.

With the mission system dissolved by 1833 and regulation from idealistic, yet troubled Mexico City ineffective, control over Californian territory was divided among privileged Mexicans called **rancheros** who dominated vast parcels of land. Staged "revolutionary" battles between ranchero-sponsored factions substituted for governmental checks on power. At the same time, a slow, steady trickle of American settlers headed west to the mythical land fancifully described as "edenic" in national newspapers. Unhappy with the Mexican government and driven by nationalistic fervor, the settlers staged the Bear Flag Revolt in 1846 and proclaimed California's **independence.** The Bear Flag Republic turned out to be fleeting however, as the U.S. soon declared **war** on Mexico in an effort to control the area.

The campaign for California was the last frontier of **Manifest Destiny,** a popular ideal according to which it was necessary, good, and right for the U.S. to expand to the continent's Western edge. Fueled by a desire for land, the region's plentiful resources, and undisguised racism, would-be Californians decided that this land was their birthright. America's "noble mission," according to an article published in the 1847 edition of the *Congressional Globe*, was to force the Mexicans and natives to "yield to a superior population...out-living, out-trading, exterminating the weaker blood." The **acquisition** of California was supported not only by politicians (including President Polk), but also by popular opinion. Even the poet Walt Whitman joined in the rally, writing in the *Brooklyn Eagle*, "Mexico must be thoroughly chastised!...Let our arms now be carried with a spirit which shall teach the world that...America knows how to crush, as well as how to expand!"

Under such severe pressure, Mexico eventually surrendered. In the 1848 Treaty of Guadalupe Hidalgo, Mexico ceded half of its territory, including California and parts of New Mexico and Texas. For the U.S., the timing was golden. While the cession became official, James Marshall discovered **gold** at Sutter's Mill, and the rush was on. The feverish search for the precious metal by a motley torrent of fortune seekers—known collectively as the '49ers—flooded the region in 1849; by 1859 over 28 million ounces of gold had been mined, (worth $10 billion by today's standards). This massive influx of prospectors caused the non-native population to multiply sixfold within four years. Consequently, the native population suffered; many tribes disappeared completely. The miners' demands for food and supplies created an economic boom, galvanizing San Francisco's development into an international port. But could the travails of moving west tarnish the promise of instant riches? Thousands of settlers had to sail around South America, and those in wagon trains encountered savage winters and Native American attacks while crossing the Rockies and the Sierra Nevada. The most famous of the doomed would-be settlers were the Donner Party, forced by a fierce 1846-47 winter into madness and cannibalism at a snowbound outpost near what is now called Donner Lake in the Sierra Nevada.

Realizing they were sitting on a goldmine, the Californians quickly wrote their own constitution and inaugurated John C. Fremont as their first governor a full year before receiving the U.S. Congress's 1850 grant of **statehood**. The profitable new territory was made a free state in a political deal to pass the Fugitive Slave Act in 1850. Unfortunately, Californians were less laissez-faire concerning the rights of other non-whites; the 1850s were marked by the Mariposa and Modoc Wars, several sites of which can still be seen (see **Captain Jack's Stronghold,** p. 336). Laws were passed discriminating against Chinese and Mexican miners in 1850 and 1852, and an 1854 edict rejected the Chinese right to testify against whites.

From 1860-61, the riders of the **Pony Express** carried mail back and forth from Missouri to San Francisco in trips of ten days. The completion of a transcontinental **telegraph** system in 1861 linked California electrically with the East and put the ponies out to pasture. **Greedy industrialists** formed the Central Pacific Railroad and began to lay tracks eastward, importing and abusing cheap Chinese labor. The meeting of the Central Pacific and Union Pacific Railroads in 1869 formed the **Transcontinental Railroad,** which made traveling cross-country to California a five-day venture instead of the month it had taken by stagecoach—a viable option for fortune-seekers everywhere. After its completion, 15,000 luckless Chinese railroad workers were displaced, then accused by California working men of causing the **nationwide depression** of the mid-1870s. Meanwhile, San Francisco enjoyed a post-Gold Rush boom, its population mushrooming from 500 to 50,000 in five years. The city's Barbary Coast rivaled history's most infamous depravities; brothels and opium dens abounded, fed by the influx of successful miners needing to come to terms with their *nouveau-riche* status.

THE 20TH CENTURY: ALL THAT GLITTERS

The great earthquake of 1906 set San Francisco ablaze, destroying gas pipes and overturning stoves; the fires destroyed the greater part of the city and killed 452 people. At the same time, the largest city graft scandal in the country's history was exposed in San Francisco, and the rebuilding of the city was entrusted to reformers. Press surrounding the investigation sparked a state-wide movement for governmental reform; Democratic candidate Theodor Bell lost the 1910 gubernatorial election because the hated and graft-ridden Southern Pacific Railroad lent him its endorsement.

As the American film industry deserted the fickle, cloudy weather of New York and New Jersey and set up camp on Los Angeles' sun-baked shores, the area around the city grew exponentially. **Studios** and **stars** cropped up around the City of Angels, and a quiet little company run by Walt Disney began producing eerily addictive animated shorts, like "Steamboat Willie," starring the fledgling Mickey Mouse (and a few singing goats). An extensive **streetcar system** consisting of over 1150 miles of track connected Los Angeles with four surrounding counties, reaching a ridership peak in the 1920s. **Greedy industrialists** again swarmed in to capitalize on the gasoline-rich oil boom of the 1920s, buying out the streetcars and subways and constructing freeways to ensure the regency of the automobile. At the same time, innovations such as center dividing lines on highways and automatic traffic signals got their start.

The Great Depression of the 1930s dealt slightly less harshly with California than with the rest of the country; its farm income sank to half of pre-Depression levels while most other states did worse. Thousands flocked here to escape the impoverished, crop-less Dust Bowl of the Midwest. These "Okies" were perceived as a threat to jobs, and at times local authorities aided farmers in blocking roads against them. Still, agriculture pressed forward; by 1939, products such as **oranges** made California the leading agricultural state in the nation. The grape industry grew a bunch following the repeal of Prohibition, and by 1940 California supplied 90% of the nation's **wine,** table grapes, and raisins.

Anti-Japanese sentiment was nothing new when Pearl Harbor was bombed at the end of 1941; three months later President Roosevelt gave the U.S. military the go-ahead to remove all Japanese aliens and citizens from the West Coast and relocate them to **internment camps** in the California interior. Approved for reintegration after the war, when the "yellow peril" was no longer a threat to the American Dream, President Truman allowed them back into society.

After the war production boom of the 40s, projects such as the irrigation canals and freeways of Southern California promoted even swifter expansion. In 1964, California redefined the power centers of America by overtaking New York as the nation's most populous state. During the early 60s, the **surf culture** of Frankie and Annette, Gidget, and the Beach Boys created a carefree image of California that persists to this day. In the later 60s, the beach party ended and nationwide waves of upheaval began to shake the college campuses and ghettoes of California. In Berkeley, clashes between students and police over civil rights spawned the **Free Speech Movement,** a foretaste of future student activism. The summer 1965 riots in **Watts,** Los Angeles, sparked by the arrest of a black man by a white policeman for drunk driving, left four dead and almost 1,000 injured. A young guitarist named **Frank Zappa** called upon the masses to "discorporate," starting a joint concert with Zubin Mehta and the L.A. Philharmonic by yelling, "Hit it, Zubin!" In 1967, San Francisco's Haight-Ashbury neighborhood declared a **"Summer of Love,"** and young people voiced their disgust with the Establishment by—in Timothy Leary's words—"turning on, tuning in, and dropping out." At the same time, UCLA film school student **Jim Morrison** (a classmate of Francis Ford Coppola and Oliver Stone) decided to start a band whose name he lifted from Aldous Huxley's *The Doors of Perception.* In the midst of mounting antiwar protests (based at the University of California at Berkeley), the black empowerment coalition known as the **Black Panthers** terrorized white California, **Charles Manson** and the Family cult coopted the hysteria into a series of ritual murders, and leftist golden child **Bobby Kennedy** was murdered in Los Angeles after winning the California primary of the 1968 presidential election. For the benefit of the Establishment, California regrouped and thrust conservative powerhouses **Richard Nixon** and **Ronald Reagan** into the national political limelight.

In the 70s, water and fuel shortages and the unbearable L.A. smog forced Californians to alter their ways of life, and attitudes all around lost their earlier sunniness. Where in 1966 The Mamas and the Papas had sung with longing of tranquil "California Dreamin,'" by 1976 the Eagles were warning darkly of the "Hotel California," where "You can check out any time you like, but you can never leave." Governor Jerry "Moonbeam" Brown romanced singer Linda Ronstadt while Proposition 13, a popular initiative limiting state taxes, captured nationwide attention. The enthusiasm died out, however, when state services were stripped to the bone, and the once-premier public education system plummeted in national rankings for lack of adequate property tax revenue. Californians discovered that starving government wasn't the panacea they had hoped. The Symbionese Liberation Army, the most prominent of the new revolutionary groups, kidnapped newspaper heiress Patty Hearst and almost converted her to their cause. In the late 70s, the People's Temple of San Francisco gained international focus when its leader, **Jim Jones**, poisoned and killed over 1000 members in a mass-suicide service at his religious retreat in Guyana.

New problems arrived in the 1980s: cellular phones jammed airways and BMWs jammed freeways. From the San Fernando Valley sprung the **Valley Girl**, a concept begun with Zappa's song of the same name, and perhaps killed off by the existential party-hopping of the film *Clueless* (1995). **Pollution** and gross industrialization continued to cloud the state's utopian vision. **Illegal Mexican immigrants** streamed across the border in greater numbers, initiating new debates on issues of freedom and human rights. A huge earthquake in 1989 leveled much of the Bay Area, and two years later a massive fire in Oakland burned over two thousand homes. In 1992, the **Los Angeles riots,** sparked by the acquittal of the four white police officers accused in the Rodney King beating, signaled that the U.S. has yet to solve what W.E.B. DuBois prophetically called "the problem of the 20th century"—the issue of **race.** The passage of **Proposition 187,** which denied all social services to illegal immigrants, and the **O.J. Simpson** trial, which sparked the largest justice-oriented t-shirt boom since the execution of Ted Bundy, renew questions of ethnicity and tolerance quietly swept under the carpet with the original conquest of California in the 19th century.

RECENT NEWS

The 1990s have brought an unprecedented amount of racial turmoil and violence to California. Recently, public outcry has been great over the passage of **Proposition 209,** which outlaws any "preferential treatment" (affirmative action or quotas) in state programs (like public education) and employment. While the proposition, strongly supported by Governor Pete Wilson, has been implemented to some degree, court injunction brought things to a screeching halt after a coalition of civil rights groups filed a complaint. The debate continues, as Wilson argues that judgment should be based purely on merit, and civil rights activists insist that accepted measures of merit (e.g., standardized tests) discriminate implicitly against minorities. The University of California system has called a halt to all **affirmative action** programs and has subsequently reported an alarming drop in minority student admissions and enrollment.

The "Trial of the Century" finally drew to a close in February 1997 when a civil jury demanded that **O.J. Simpson** pay $25 million in punitive damages to the families of murder victims Nicole Brown Simpson and Ronald Goldman. This verdict came, paradoxically, after Simpson had been declared "not guilty" by a criminal jury. Nobody ever said Los Angeles made sense.

In the aftermath of all of this tragedy, Californians have found a new way to cope: marijuana. Well, perhaps it is an old way, but the nineties brought about the most comprehensive fight for **marijuana legalization** the state had ever seen. Proposition 215, passed by voters in November of 1996, had allowed individual *patients* to grow and use marijuana for medical purposes *only.* Now given an inch, patients and users alike are aiming to take a mile. A "voluntary register" of users would be instituted, possibly along with photo identification for legal growers/users (which would of course be quickly duplicated and dispensed over the web: capitalism meets drug culture). Former Governor Pete Wilson would have fought this measure staunchly, but now, under the new Democratic leadership of Gray Davis (elected in 1998), it is possible that the Medical Marijuana Task Force will have its way, and state regulation of marijuana cooperatives will allow clubs now operating underground in Humboldt, Mendocino, Marin, San Francisco, Alameda, San Diego and Santa Cruz counties to function without threat of arrest.

While the state of California was embroiled in these political debates, 39 people quietly committed ritual suicide in a wealthy San Diego suburb in March of 1997. The members of the **Heaven's Gate cult** subscribed to a millenarian belief system which incorporated elements of Christianity and science fiction. The group, led by the charismatic Marshall Applewhite, viewed the passing of the Hale-Bopp comet as a sign from the Next Level, and hoped to board the spaceship which they believed to be hovering behind the comet. As the year 2000 approaches, similarly themed movements are springing up left and right; given California's reputation for psychological variation and cultural experimentation, you just might witness the next great cult phenomenon—just don't join.

THE ARTS

FILM AND TELEVISION

Hollywood has no counterpart. It is strictly a West Coast phenomenon, evoking a bizarre mixture of disdain and jealousy from the New York entertainment world (from whose loins it sprang so long ago) as a glitzy and obnoxious, and yet somehow glamorous and trendsetting, proxy for legitimate art. As the English actor Sir Cedric Hardwicke once said, "I believe that God felt sorry for actors so he created Hollywood to give them a place in the sun and a swimming pool." Today, this "place in the sun" exerts an increasingly influential hold over global pop culture.

Hollywood's emergence as movie capital of the U.S. had modest beginnings. Before 1910, independent New York filmmakers were being continually harassed by a movie trust seeking to drive out competition. The independents moved west and set up shop in sunny Hollywood, then a sleepy sheep-raising town. From there, a quick dash across the Mexican border could foil attempts to confiscate cameras and film. Moreover, they could take advantage of California's almost year-round sun to light shots—artificial lighting had not yet been perfected.

As the balance of movie power began to shift west, the Hollywood studios instituted the **"star system."** For the first time, actors themselves were advertised and used to attract adoring fans to movie after movie. One of the first film divas was Mary Pickford, also known as "America's Sweetheart." Charlie Chaplin, Buster Keaton, Douglas Fairbanks, and that lover of lovers, Rudolph Valentino, soon attained legendary status by virtue of their appearances on the silver screen.

The 1920s witnessed two major developments: sound and scandal. "Talkies," films with sound, were introduced with Al Jolson's *The Jazz Singer* in 1927. Scandals were ushered in when Fatty Arbuckle went on trial for the death of starlet Virginia Rappe. A suspicion that Hollywood was becoming a moral cesspool led to the appointment of Postmaster General Will Hays as "movie czar." His puritanical edicts established a model which "would have suited the strictest of convent nuns."

Gone With the Wind was the first large-scale Hollywood extravaganza, blazing the way for other studios to utilize exorbitant budgets, flamboyant costumes, and casts of thousands. The media hype that accompanied a nationwide search for an actress to play Scarlett O'Hara and the ensuing opening of the movie in Atlanta helped give cinema a permanent place in American popular culture. A less extravagant but equally important film event occurred in 1941, when Orson Welles unveiled his masterpiece, **Citizen Kane,** a work whose innovations expanded contemporary ideas about the potential of film.

The increasing accessibility of **television** during the 1950s magnified the scope and impact of Hollywood's image industry. In the 1960s and 70s, shows like *The Brady Bunch* and *All in the Family* gave Americans a common currency. The 80s and 90s have seen the mass-production of television go global; patriarchal adolescent fantasy *Baywatch*, a.k.a. "Babewatch," reigns as the world's most popular television show—probably due to the universal durability of its round, firm themes. Shows like *Beverly Hills 90210*, *Melrose Place*, and MTV's *Real World* series (which filmed a season each in San Francisco and L.A.) reinforce the popular idea of California as a ditzy blonde place.

Let's Go often notes filming sites of well-known movies. For a sliver of real and unreal life in California, watch:

ACTION/THRILLER

The Mark of Zorro (1940) Masked super swordsman Zorro and his protegé save California and the elder Zorro's daughter from evil Montero.

Vertigo (1958) Alfred Hitchcock's complex story about a San Francisco detective and his psychological troubles with a fear of heights and a woman.

The Birds (1963) Birds begin attacking residents of a northern California town, and just won't stop, in this Alfred Hitchcock thriller.

Faster, Pussycat! Kill! Kill! (1965) Russ Meyer's poignant tale of go-go girls who, hungry for action, ride into the California desert and kill people.

Dirty Harry (1971) Housewife heartthrob Clint Eastwood plays a dangerous San Francisco cop.

Earthquake (1974) Los Angeles, predictably, crumbles; Charlton Heston stars.

The Karate Kid (1984) Ralph Macchio learns how to fight his way to victory in this action-packed martial-arts story set in Reseda, CA.

Lethal Weapon (1987) A veteran detective's new partner is a loose cannon with quite the death wish.

Die Hard (1988) Systems crumble as lone NYC cop Bruce Willis pokes American ingenuity in the faces of German terrorists holding an L.A. skyscraper hostage.

Speed (1994) Keanu Reeves flashes his teeth at danger. And no, the L.A. bus system never moves that fast.

Heat (1995) Al Pacino and Robert DeNiro star in this Los Angeles crime saga about the intertwined lives of a detective and a thief.

Volcano (1996) Los Angeles, predictably, crumbles. Where's Charlton Heston now?

The Rock (1996) Alcatraz. Only one man has ever broken out. Now five million lives depend on two men breaking in. Sean Connery and Nicolas Cage battle California's most famous island prison (except perhaps for the It's a Small World ride at Disneyland).

DRAMA

The Grapes of Wrath (1940) John Ford's gripping adaptation of Steinbeck's masterpiece about Depression-era sharecroppers.

Sunset Boulevard (1950) Satirical drama about an ex-silent movie star in love with a young screenwriter named Joe Gillis.

The Wild One (1954) Marlon Brando and his brawny cronies ride motorcyclin' rings around a small California town, preparing America for the hard hits of Elvis and eventually Michael Bolton.

Rebel Without a Cause (1955) Teen icon James Dean in the quintessential story of disaffected youth. Shot at Hollywood High.

Bird Man of Alcatraz (1962) Based on the true story of convicted killer Robert Stroud, played by bird-friendly Burt Lancaster. Stroud, who was sentenced to death for killing a prison guard, wrote two books on bird diseases after his sentence was commuted to life in prison by President Wilson.

The Graduate (1967) Dustin Hoffman is a recent college grad in a meaningless, topsy-turvy psychoerotic void, set to the tune of Simon and Garfunkel's acoustic caterwauling. Watch for the shot of the Bay Bridge, and notice our hero driving the wrong way.

Mommie Dearest (1981) Christina Crawford presents Mommie Joan as a terrorizer of all things young and innocent. Faye Dunaway stars.

The Karate Kid (1984) Ralph Macchio comes of age in Reseda, CA as he learns lessons of life from karate teacher and friend Pat Morita and soulmate Elisabeth Shue.

Boyz N the Hood (1991) A hard-hitting portrayal of life in the poverty-stricken neighborhoods of South Central L.A. Director John Singleton's debut film.

The Player (1991) Robert Altman's postmodern mirror trick of a motion picture. A menagerie of stars (playing themselves) and visual nods to every film ever made catalyze a cool dissection of morality in show biz.

Short Cuts (1993) Vignettes based on the short stories of Raymond Carver are linked through L.A. suburbia. The fruit-fly spraying is no joke.

Pulp Fiction (1994) Much-hyped, *fin de siècle* vision of California cool. The soundtrack alone makes it worth watching.

The Ususal Suspects (1995) We can't really tell you about it because we don't want to ruin it for you.

Boogie Nights (1997) The rise and fall of a man with a 10-inch dick.

Permanent Midnight (1998) A recovering heroin addict remembers his past. In other news, Ben Stiller is cute.

COMEDY

What's Up, Doc? (1972) Hilarious slapstick comedy set in San Francisco (hills are funny) starring Madeline Kahn and Barbra Streisand.

The Karate Kid (1984) Ralph Macchio learns karate through the time-tested methods of housepainting, car-waxing, and deck-sanding. Pat Morita stands back and laughs, enjoying his freshly painted house, newly waxed car, and well-sanded deck.

Beverly Hills Cop (1984) Two sequels later, this remains the best of the series. A freewheeling Detroit cop (Eddie Murphy) pursuing a murder investigation finds himself dealing with the very different culture of Beverly Hills.

Repo Man (1984) Alex Cox's brilliant take on the sub-culture of L.A.-area repossessors. Starring a young, sneering Emilio Estevez.

Down and Out in Beverly Hills (1986) Lots of big names team up to give an inside look at *chi-chi* Beverly Hills at its finest. No Luke Perrys allowed.

Big Trouble In Little China (1986) A fun, fantasy filled romp through the world of black magic in Chinatown.

Dragnet (1987) Just The Facts, Ma'am. Thank god it's Friday.

Who Framed Roger Rabbit? (1988) A glorious union of Disney and Warner Brothers, animation and live action, hard-boiled detectives and huge-breasted 'toons, wacky hijinx and urban rezoning.

Bill & Ted's Excellent Adventure (1989) The last great 80s teen flick: Keanu Reeves and Alex Winter subvert textbook history into a living pageant of humanity's timeless common denominators: honor, phlegm, and *esprit de corps.* See **Circle K,** p. 393.

Pretty Woman (1990) Young starlet Julia Roberts enchants her knight-in-shining-armor via thigh-high boots and true call-girl class.

L.A. Story (1991) Steve Martin's love song to the City of Angels. He even gets to rollerblade in the Museum of Contemporary Art!

Clueless (1995) Alicia Silverstone stars in this meta-fluffy movie about the lives, fashions, and social reverberations of three Valley high school girls. The plot's similarities to Jane Austen's *Emma* flick this flick into legitimacy.

Swingers (1996) L.A.'s labyrinthine nightlife serves as backdrop for Mikey's escape from maudlin romanticism, Trent's good-hearted philandering, and much disenchanted-young-man philosophizing.

Bulworth (1998) Warren Beatty plays a suicidally disillusioned L.A. politician who starts to be bluntly honest with his voters and himself.

The Big Lebowski (1998) "Dude" Lebowski, mistaken for a millionaire Lebowski, seeks restitution for his ruined rug and enlists his bowling buddies to help get it.

Go! (1999) The decidedly cracked-out story of the events after a drug deal, from three different points of view.

FILM NOIR

Fury (1936) Master filmmaker Fritz Lang's first American movie; Spencer Tracy stars in a dissection of mob violence.

The Big Sleep (1946) Classic detective story, starring Lauren Bacall and Humphrey Bogart, who plays Raymond Chandler's hard-boiled Philip Marlowe. Much chiaroscuro lighting and an incomprehensible script co-written by William Faulkner.

Chinatown (1974) Jack Nicholson sleuths through a creepy pastel Los Angeles. Robert Towne's script for this Roman Polanski thriller is one of the most studied screenplays in film schools. Hold your breath for the famous last line.

The Karate Kid (1984) Director John Avildsen paints Los Angeles in dark tones in Robert Kamen's story of a fatherless boy alone in strange city streets. Only a cryptic Japanese man and the mysterious "Crane Kick" can save Daniel from this urban lion's den.

L.A. Confidential (1997) "Chinatown" for the kids: 1990s retro-meta-*film noir* means a sprawling plotline, super-saturated colors, and rotary-sanded editing. Not the real thing, but neither is frozen yogurt.

SCIENCE FICTION

Invasion of the Body Snatchers (1956) King of low-budget horror/sci-fi movies, this daring experiment in props technology presents an allegory about determined space people who terrorize Santa Mira, California.

Blade Runner (1982) A sci-fi noir-ish thriller set in the L.A. of the future.

Terminator (1984) Bad robot Arnold Schwarzenegger stonefacedly pursues his sweaty blonde target across contemporary L.A., so that her son won't be born to redeem the future from dumb uniforms and crawly-trucks.

The Karate Kid (1984) Alien creatures from a distant galaxy clone themselves and go back in time to inhabit the bodies of an L.A. gang and a local gardener. As a side effect of the cloning process, the aliens begin to display an unusual facility with karate, without even having to download it to their medullae! A local boy falls into their complex web of disguises and plays out an ancient blood-feud between two alien colonies without him, or the filmmakers, ever realizing it.

Demolition Man (1993) A cop is brought out of suspended animation in prison to pursue an old ultra-violent enemy who is loose in a nonviolent future society.

Independence Day (1996) A.K.A. ID4. L.A. is the first to disappear in fire when scavenger aliens attack the earth; the Mojave Desert hosts cross-cultural battle scenes.

ART-HOUSE

The Karate Kid (1984) Avildsen's violence-filled Los Angeles plays on Cold War fears of cyber-regimentation (through gang symbols) and encroaching technology (through the pastoral iconography of gardening and household chores). Stylistic allusions to commu-fascist films warn the viewer away from the inevitable industrial future in a manner that must be credited to the film's self-conscious reliance on Orwell. Even the film's year of production is a bittersweet paean to the novelist's nightmarish prognostications.

LITERATURE

California is second only to New York City as a shelter and inspiration for literary American minds. The state has been rooted in imagination since its beginnings—the name California was inspired by the fictional Queen Calafia, who lorded it over gems and biddies in a mythical 16th century tropic. In later days, explorers and settlers praised this nouveau paradise in verse and in legend, and the literary flow began in earnest with the influx of the gold rush. The siren song of precious metal attracted more than scruffy miners; several authors of the '49er period introduced the world to the state's natural splendor and the rough-and-tumble culture of mining towns. Vestiges of the early California that appeared in the writing of **Bret Harte** and **Mark Twain** can still be seen in the relatively unspoiled hills and ghost towns of Gold Country. Even **Jack London,** Oakland's literary native son, spent some time panning for gold and writing pastoral short stories on the side. His "The Valley of the Moon" provides an evocative portrait of the Sonoma and San Joaquin Valleys before they were consumed by wineries and agribusiness. Poet and lover **Robinson Jeffers** composed his paeans in and around the Big Sur coast of Monterey County, where novelist and lover **Henry Miller** set up camp upon his return from Europe.

California's 20th-century urbanization gave its writers a new kind of fertile ground. **Raymond Chandler** and **Dashiell Hammett** fired up California-centric detective novels which later became fodder for Hollywood *film noir.* When writers such as **William Faulkner** came to Hollywood looking for screenwriting work, they found a place seemingly constructed by careful satirists; *The Day of the Locust*, by **Nathanael West,** lampoons such satire. **John Steinbeck** won the Nobel Prize for his incisive representations of the Depression era, drawing with paint-by-numbers symbolism a picture of the hard life of Midwesterners displaced to California by drought. His descriptions of the Salinas Valley in novels like *East of Eden* recreated America as a paradise gone astray. During the 50s, **Jack Kerouac** and **Allen Ginsberg** combined candid autobiography with visionary rapture to become the gurus of the **Beat Generation.** They appropriated San Francisco's North Beach (along with New York's Greenwich Village) as a spiritual home to return to after the cross-country wanderings fictionalized in Kerouac's *On The Road.* In the 70s, **Hunter S. Thompson** took the beatniks' road trip motif in a new direction with his narcotic-laden tour through Southern California's barren Mojave Desert and into the City of Sin. **Thomas Pynchon's** *The Crying of Lot 49* "went postal" with a different sort of paranoia—potheads, technozoids, and a new slant on stamp-collecting. His *Vineland*, an epic mess of pop culture and political conspiracy, romps through California, self-consciously name-dropping every town from Vacaville to Van Nuys. A kinder, gentler author by the name of Beverly Cleary invented the *Ramona* series to delight the children of said potheads and technozoids. Nineties Americana owes one of its most pervasive catch-phrases to the lonely ennui of Palm Springs's resort culture, which spawned **Douglas Coupland's** *Generation X.*

POPULAR MUSIC

California's music exports run from **dance-pop** (Paula Abdul, the Bangles, Sheila E.) to **weird music** (Primus, the Residents). Its pop musicians have also been socially engaged: **Jello Biafra** of the Dead Kennedys finished fourth in the 1979 San Francisco mayor's race, the late **Sonny Bono** was a Republican Congressman, and **Frank Zappa** served in the Maryland State Legislature—Zappa was also Vaclav Havel's Minister of Culture in the new Czech Republic until U.S. Secretary of State James Baker III (or, Baker's wife—a proponent of censorship in music) forced his resignation.

LOS ANGELES

The squeaky-clean **Beach Boys** and **Jan and Dean** recited harmonized odes to sun and fun in the 1960s, matching their British contemporaries in flair but with less appreciation for either the sublime American blues tradition or the decadent potential in rock theatricality. **Dick Dale** used a heftily strung guitar, instead of shimmering vocals, to similar effect. The **singer-songwriter** movement of the 1970s (Joni Mitchell, Jackson Browne, James Taylor) evacuated the last traces of political advocacy from the lone-guitarist idiom it inherited from American folk music, its audience straining to hear as performers sang and gazed softly into their navels. Bands looking for renewed vigor found it in **punk** (X), **roots** (Los Lobos), or a combination (the Blasters).

From the 1970s to the 1990s, the dissolute tried out several iterations of life in the fast lane. In Hollywood could be found the Doors and their lizard king **Jim Morrison**, the slickly countrified **Eagles**, and the triumphant sleaze of **Guns n' Roses**. The guitar gymnastics of Dutch import **Eddie Van Halen** were epoch-making for pop music technique in the early 1980s, while **hair-metal** (Mötley Crüe, Quiet Riot, Ratt, Dokken, W.A.S.P.) and **glam-metal** (Poison) kept the fancy costumes but toned down rock's bluesiness to a limited number of formulaic, yet loud gestures. To the south blared the equally amoral but more combative **gangsta rap,** whose spokesmen (NWA, Dr. Dre, Eazy E, Ice Cube, Snoop Dogg) spewed invective straight outta Compton at cops and East Coast rappers. Rap and hard-rock, whose distinct modes of aggression were refined elsewhere, were fused in the diverse Californian 1980s milieu, by various methods: **leering** (Red Hot Chili Peppers), **grooving** (Fishbone), and **leftist ranting** (Rage Against the Machine).

SAN FRANCISCO AND THE BAY AREA

Hippies were responsible for establishing a nationally recognized **San Francisco Sound** in the 1960s, as pot and LSD increased audience tolerance for long, indulgent jams grounded in Afro-Caribbean rhythm (Santana), the blues (Big Brother and the Holding Company, who launched doomed vocalist **Janis Joplin** to stardom), or folk (the **Grateful Dead**). In 1966, the Beatles chose San Francisco's Candlestick Park to end their touring career, and great enthusiasm was mustered for the **Summer of Love** in 1967 as the sound accompanied copious sex and drugs, but by the time an audience member was killed (by security guards hired from the Hell's Angels motorcycle gang) at a Rolling Stones concert at **Altamont,** the trip was going bad.

The area also pulled to prominence several bands that were less heavily dependent on psychedelic motifs. **Sly and the Family Stone's** breathtaking utopian vision of racial integration thumped along with the help of slap bass inventor Larry Graham, and **Creedence Clearwater Revival** (of El Cerrito), credibly impersonated bayou swamp rats. Oakland's rappers (Digital Underground, Too $hort, 2Pac) built the loping **Oaktown sound** on Graham's hefty bass foundation. These days, newer artists like **Meat Beat Manifesto** bring electronic music into dance clubs all over the U.S.—though this one man band originated in San Fransisco.

SUBURBIA

A sinister breed of short-haired, skateboarding boys pounded punk into shape in the 1980s until it became **hardcore** (Dead Kennedys, Black Flag, the Minutemen, Suicidal Tendencies). Ska music, from Jamaica via the U.K., found its way to the Californian suburbs in a ska-revival revival, or **third wave;** in 1997 its unvarying upbeats chased radio listeners everywhere with the many hits of Orange County's No Doubt and the hit, "Walking On The Sun," of Smash Mouth (from Sunnyvale, a suburb).

VISUAL ARTS

Californians really do patronize their local artists. The local art festival is an institution, gently stroking the resident "artistes" who display their efforts. Much of the art is of the sea- or landscape genre and may remind you of the decor in your Motel 6 room. Some Golden State natives, however, have played a significant role in the development of American high art. **Clyfford Still's** jagged Abstract Expressionist canvases and **Richard Diebenkorn's** landscapes of the Santa Monica seashore (the *Ocean Park* series) are found in many California museums. Diebenkorn's and David Park's use of Abstract Expressionist forms to paint representational images was in novel contrast to the more thoroughly abstract fashion of the New York Abstract Expressionists. **Robert Crumb's** dementedly insightful comics about the sex, drugs, and rock n' roll scene in San Francisco helped fuel the euphoric introspection of the late-60s counterculture; his cartoon histories of the blues redefined the comic genre. **Wayne Thiebaud** painted San Francisco in the 70s with hyperbolic perspective and strikingly rich color. The brilliant hues and geometrical perspectives of **David Hockney's** paintings of California people and places attracted attention during the 80s, and he has since explored new media such as photography and stage design.

Many of Californian artists' best works are in the state's museums. The **Oakland Museum** (p. 143), for example, exclusively exhibits works of the state's residents. **Los Angeles** houses the eclectic UCLA/Armand Hammer Museum of Art (p. 383), the Museum of Contemporary Art (p. 388), and the newly relocated Getty Center (p. 384), which holds some of the gems of Western painting. San Francisco is home to both the M. H. De Young Memorial Museum (p. 106), which exhibits the largest collection of Asian art outside of Asia, and the world-class San Francisco Museum of Modern Art (p. 110), probably the best museum in the state. Many of the state's smaller cities have regional museums or art galleries, and in the larger cities you may find museums dedicated to science, natural history, or cultural history.

Thanks to the light and the variety of the scenery, California has been infested with photographers since the medium was invented, and the state has been home to some of this century's best professionals. In the 30s, **Dorothea Lange's** photos of the working and living conditions of migrant workers helped to convince the federal government to build public housing projects. Her 1936 photo *Migrant Mother* became a national symbol of the suffering caused by the Great Depression. In a different vein, **Ansel Adams'** photographs of Yosemite National Park and the Sierra have graced calendar pages everywhere and become among the most recognized photos in the U.S.

Until the late 19th century, Californian **architecture** generally consisted of simple, practical structures or emulations of eastern Victorian and Queen Anne styles. It came into its own when history blended with local materials, forming a unique new style. The "missionary revival" architecture of the 1890s, inspired by the Mexican ranch-style, first incorporated native materials and local design traditions. In the 1910s and 20s, architects like **Charles** and **Henry Greene** developed the shingle-style of California's redwood bungalows, particularly evident in the hills of the Bay Area. In the 30s, **Julia Morgan** designed over 600 homes, among them the famous Hearst castle (see p. 221). **Frank Lloyd Wright,** one of the 20th century's most experimental architects, designed 25 buildings in the state, including the Barnsdale House in Hollywood and the Marin Civic Center. In recent years, **Frank Gehry** has attracted attention by building houses with angular surfaces and unorthodox materials, such as sheet metal and raw plywood. The California jumble of materials and methods was evident as early as 1930, when **Nathanael West** observed that L.A.'s canyons were lined with "Mexican ranch houses, Samoan huts, Mediterranean villas, Egyptian and Japanese temples, Swiss chalets, Tudor cottages, and every possible combination of these styles."

OUTDOOR RECREATION

Where else but California could you go snowboarding and boogieboarding in a single day? Besides the sand-and-surf pastimes which have made the state famous, California offers climbing and hiking in the Sierra Nevada and the desolate Mojave Desert, kayaking and rafting in the rivers and lakes, and skiing and snowboarding at a number of resorts. Best of all, the state has the kind of weather which allows you to be outdoors all year long—though that may be outdoors in the snow. Check the visitor centers at the various national parks for details on the activities in that area. The best source is **The Sierra Club,** 85 Second St., 2nd fl., San Francisco, 94105-3441 (415-977-5500; e-mail information@sierraclub.org; www.sierraclub.org/outings), which has information on year-round outings.

SPECTATOR SPORTS

For those who would rather watch than participate, California is home to more professional sports teams than any other state. The five Major League Baseball representatives include American League squads, the **Anaheim Angels,** powered by the hitting of Mo Vaughn and Tim Salmon, and the recently cellar-dwelling **Oakland Athletics** (or A's). In the National League, pitching ace Kevin Brown leads the **L.A. Dodgers** (who migrated in 1958 from Brooklyn, New York), eight-time National League batting champ Tony Gwynn heads up the 1998 League Champion **San Diego Padres,** and two-time MVP Barry Bonds goes deep for the **San Francisco Giants** (who moved in 1958 from New York City). Football fans can enjoy perennial powerhouse **San Francisco '49ers,** led by veterans Steve Young and Jerry Rice, the **Oakland Raiders,** (based out of Los Angeles from 1982-1995) who feature a record five Heisman Trophy Award winners, and the **San Diego Chargers** who struggle to return to their winning form of the early 90s. In January 1999, the NFL voted to bring a football team back to L.A., the U.S.'s second-largest television market, in the next round of expansion. Four men's basketball teams in the National Basketball Association (NBA) play ball in the Golden State: the **L.A. Lakers,** who despite being led by superstars Kobe Bryant and Shaquille O'Neal continue to disappoint; the upstart **Sacramento Kings,** who are powered by the play of Chris Webber and Jason Williams and two perennial bottom-dwellers, the **L.A. Clippers** and **Golden State Warriors.** The **Sacramento Monarchs** and **Los Angeles Sparks** hoop it up in the Women's National Basketball Association (WNBA). In the land of surf and sun, three National Hockey League (NHL) teams have melted their audience's hearts: the **L.A. Kings,** the Disney-owned **Anaheim Mighty Ducks,** and the **San Jose Sharks,** whose biting logo has been one of the most popular in American pro sports. The fledgling Major League Soccer (MLS) league has two Californian representatives: the **L.A. Galaxy** and the **San Jose Clash.**

The **college sports** scene is dominated by USC, UCLA, Stanford, and UC Berkeley, all of whom field powerhouse programs in a variety of NCAA Division I sports. UCLA's **basketball** teams under coach John Wooden built a legend with a string of ten national championships in the 1960s and 1970s, while Stanford-nurtured Olympic medalist **swimmers** and **baseball players** in the 1990s. The **volleyball** teams of several California colleges dominate national competition.

LAND OF MILK AND HONEY

California's sumptuous produce and innovative cuisine satisfy its stupendous appetite. Kitchens across the state disgorge taste-bud-fondling entrees that run the gamut from local sourdough bread and Dungeness crab to remote Basque and Salvadorean specialties. The Bay Area is home to the best Chinese food in North America, while L.A.'s Vietnamese and Mexican cooking is unmatched outside Vietnam and Mexico. California leads the country in agricultural production, with

CUISINART Don't go to California expecting to see the natives munching on granola and wheat germ; that stuff is for the crunchy folk up in Oregon and Washington. The hip food in the Golden State today is known by the broad generic "California Cuisine." Born, according to legend, at Berkeley's Chez Panisse, it's not a tradition nor even a movement—it's a *concept,* where the culinary and the aesthetic blend to create a total eating experience. The uninitiated may have trouble recognizing this trendy genre upon first contact. Telltale signs include cheeseless and/or sauceless pizza, angel hair pasta, and anything cooked on an oakwood grill. Look for combinations of radicchio, fontinella, cilantro, gorgonzola, sun-dried tomatoes, and shiitake mushrooms. And if you find yourself at an outdoor blond-wood table and the entree you ordered looks much smaller and involves much more mango than you had expected, fear not. Just nod approvingly and ask for a half-caf. All is cool.

fruits, vegetables, and nuts pouring forth in a 365-days-per-year growing season. This agricultural bounty, among other things, helped give the state the nickname "Land of Fruits and Nuts."

The state was also the inventor of a number of national food fads, including the 1950s-revival diner and drive-thru fast food (see **Touring the Burger Kingdom,** p. 371). The California **wine** industry has successfully overcome obstacles from Prohibition to pesticides, and today, four of every five bottles sold in the U.S. are corked in Cali. Lite drinkers everywhere owe their favorite social lubricant to the Wine Country, birthplace of the wine cooler.

ESSENTIALS

FACTS FOR THE TRAVELER

WHEN TO GO

California is such a large and diverse state that when to go depends on where you are going and what you want to do once you get there. The summer tourist season runs from Memorial Day to Labor Day (May 29-Sept. 4 in 2000). The winter ski season depends on annual snowfall, but generally runs late November to March. In the off season, hostels may be cheaper and slightly less crowded, but some sights might be closed. On national holidays, many sights will certainly be closed. It is a good idea to call the visitors center in the cities you are traveling to beforehand.

NATIONAL HOLIDAYS

DATE IN 2000	HOLIDAY
January 1	New Year's Day
January 17	Martin Luther King, Jr. Day
February 21	Presidents Day
May 29	Memorial Day
July 4	Independence Day
September 4	Labor Day
October 9	Columbus Day
November 11	Veterans Day
November 23	Thanksgiving Day
December 25	Christmas Day

REGIONAL FESTIVALS

Some of the most popular California festivals are listed below, along with brief descriptions. This list is not exhaustive; refer to **Sights** and **Entertainment** sections of individual city listings for more festivals or more info on festivals listed below.

FESTIVAL	DATE
Exposition 2000, A Millennium Celebration (San Diego; see p. 455)	December 31, 1999 to January 2, 2000
Penguin Day Ski Fest (Mission Bay, San Diego; see p. 455)	January 1
Tournament of Roses Parade and Rose Bowl (Pasadena see p. 407)	January 1
Palm Springs International Film Festival (see p. 467)	January 13-20
Bob Hope Chrysler Classic (Palm Springs; see p. 467)	January 17-23
AT&T National Pro-Am (Pebble Beach; see p. 213)	January 31-February 6
Monarch Migration Festival (Santa Cruz; see p. 205)	February 13
Chinese New Year Celebration (Chinatown, S.F.; see p. 126)	February 13-28
2000 National Date Festival (Palm Springs; see p. 467)	February 18-27
Chinese New Year Celebration (L.A.; see p. 407)	late February
Tulipmania (S.F.; see p. 125)	early March
Santa Barbara International Film Festival (see p. 237)	March 2-12
San Luis Obispo Mardi Gras (see p. 226)	March 4
Ocean Beach Kite Festival (San Diego; see p. 455)	March 4
Asian American International Film Showcase (S.F.; see p. 125)	mid-March
Nabisco Dinah Shore Classic (Palm Springs; see p. 467)	March 20-26
Cherry Blossom Festival (S.F.; see p. 125)	April
27th Annual San Diego Crew Classic (see p. 455)	April 1-2

FESTIVAL	DATE
Long Beach Grand Prix (see p. 416)	April 14-16
San Diego Earthfair 2000 (see p. 455)	April 16
Union/Fillmore St. Easter Celebration (S.F.; see p. 125)	April 23
Clovis Rodeo (Fresno; see p. 306)	April 29-30
Spike and Mike's Festival of Animation (S.F.; p. 125)	April-May
San Francisco International Film Festival (see p. 125)	April-May
Renaissance Pleasure Faire (L.A.; see p. 407)	late-April to mid-June
Cinco de Mayo, everywhere in California (see **Seasonal Events** listings)	May 5
Saroyan Festival (Fresno; see p. 306)	May 6-7
UCLA Mardi Gras (L.A.; see p. 407)	mid-May
Examiner Bay to Breakers Foot Race (S.F.; see p. 125)	May 21
Mule Days (Bishop; see p. 295)	May 26-30
UCLA Jazz & Reggae Festival (see. p. 407)	May 27-29
San Francisco International Gay & Lesbian Film Festival (see p. 125)	June
Playboy Jazz Festival (L.A.; see p. 408)	June 12-13
Juneteenth (Lake Merritt; see p. 145)	June 18
Pacific Beach Restaurant Walk (San Diego; see p. 456)	June 21
Summer Solstice Parade & Fair (Santa Barbara; see p. 237)	June 24
Gay Pride Weekend (L.A.; see p. 408)	June 24-25
Pride Day	June 25
Fuck the Police Day (Lake Merritt; see p. 145)	late June
Cable Car Bell Ringing Championships (S.F.; see p. 125)	July
Central Coast Shakespeare Festival (San Luis Obispo; p. 226)	July 1-2 or 8-9
Celebration USA (L.A.; see p. 408)	July 4
Kenwood Foot Race (Kenwood; see p. 176)	July 4
World Pillowfighting Championships (Kenwood; see p. 176)	July 4
National Nude Weekend (Santa Cruz; see p. 205)	mid-July
Mozart Festival (San Luis Obispo; see p. 226)	July 23-August 8
The Pageant of the Masters (Laguna Beach; see p. 428)	July to August
San Francisco Jewish Film Festival (see p. 125)	July-August
10th Annual Cox Communications Film Festival (San Diego; see p. 456)	early-mid August
Nihomanchi Street Fair (S.F.; see p. 125)	early August
Summerfest La Jolla Chamber Music Festival (see p. 456)	late August
San Francisco Fair (see p. 126)	early September
La Jolla Rough Water Swim (see p. 456)	early September
Scottish Gathering & Games (Sonoma; see p. 177)	September 2-4
Festival de las Americas (S.F.; see p. 126)	mid-September
San Francisco Blues Festival (see p. 126)	September 16
Monterey Jazz Festival (see p. 213)	3rd week in September
World Championship Grape-Stomp (Santa Rosa; see p. 177)	October
World Pumpkin Weigh-Off (S.F.; see p. 126)	early October
Dia de los Muertes (L.A., see p. 408; S.F., see p. 126)	October 30
Halloween in the Castro (S.F.; see p. 126)	October 31
Napa Valley Wine Festival (Napa; see p. 172)	November
Christmas Boat Parade of Lights (see p. 428)	December 17-23

ESSENTIALS

CLIMATE

The following chart gives the average range of temperatures in degrees Fahrenheit and the average rainfall in inches during four months of the year. To roughly convert from Fahrenheit to Celsius, subtract 32 and divide by 2. To convert inches to centimeters, multiply by 2.54.

Temp in °F	January		April		July		October	
Rain in inches	Temp	Rain	Temp	Rain	Temp	Rain	Temp	Rain
Death Valley	66/38	0.1	90/60	0.1	116/87	0.3	91/59	0.0
Lake Tahoe	36/18	6.1	51/27	2.1	78/44	0.3	58/32	1.9
Las Vegas	60/29	0.7	81/45	0.2	103/68	0.5	84/47	0.3
Los Angeles	65/46	3.1	70/50	1.2	81/60	0.0	76/54	0.6
San Diego	63/47	1.9	66/53	0.8	73/63	0.1	71/57	0.3
San Francisco	55/45	4.5	62/49	1.5	65/53	0.0	68/54	1.1
Santa Barbara	64/43	4.0	68/48	1.1	76/56	0.1	74/51	0.4

DOCUMENTS AND FORMALITIES

U.S. EMBASSIES AND CONSULATES

Contact your nearest embassy or consulate to obtain info regarding visas and passports to the United States. The U.S. **State Department** provides contact information for U.S. diplomatic missions on the Internet at www.state.gov/www/about_state/contacts/keyofficer_index.html. Foreign embassies in the U.S. are located in Washington, D.C., but there are consulates in California which could be helpful in an emergency. For a more extensive list of embassies and consulates in the U.S., consult the website http://www.embassy.org.

CONSULATES IN CALIFORNIA: Australia, 611 N. Larchmont Blvd., Los Angeles, CA 90004 (310-229-4800); and 1 Bush St. #700 (415-362-6160), at Market, San Francisco, CA 94101; **Canada,** 550 S. Hope St., 9th fl., Los Angeles, CA 90071 (213-346-2711); **Ireland,** 44 Montgomery St. #3830, San Francisco, CA 94101 (415-392-4214); **New Zealand,** 12400 Wilshire Blvd. #1150, Los Angeles, CA 90025 (310-207-1605); **South Africa,** 50 N. La Cienega Blvd. # 300, Beverly Hills, CA 90211 (310-657-9200); **U.K.,** 11766 Wilshire Blvd. #400, Los Angeles, CA 90025 (310-477-3322); and 1 Sansome St. #850 (981-3030), at Market, San Francisco, CA 94104.

U.S. EMBASSIES: In **Australia,** Moonah Pl., Canberra, ACT 2600 (tel. (02) 6214 5600; fax 6214 5970); in **Canada,** 100 Wellington St., Ottawa, ON K1P 5T1 (613-238-5335 or 238-4470; fax 238-5720); in **Ireland,** 42 Elgin Rd., Ballsbridge, Dublin 4 (tel. (01) 668 8777; fax 668 9946); in **New Zealand,** 29 Fitzherbert Terr., Thorndon, Wellington (tel. (04) 472 2068; fax 472 3537); in **South Africa,** 877 Pretorius St., Arcadia 0083, P.O. Box 9536 Pretoria 0001 (tel. (012) 342 1048; fax 342 2244; in the **U.K.,** 24/31 Grosvenor Sq., London W1A 1AE (tel. (0171) 499 9000; fax 495 5012).

ENTRANCE REQUIREMENTS.

Passport (p. 25). Required for all foreign visitors to the U.S.
Visa In general a visa is required for visiting the U.S., but it can be waived. (See p. 6 for more specific information.)
Work Permit (p. 27). Required for all foreigners planning to work in the U.S.
Driver License (p. 58). Required for all those planning to drive in the U.S.

U.S. CONSULATES

Australia, MLC Centre, 19-29 Martin Pl., 59th fl., Sydney NSW 2000 (tel. (02) 9373 9200; fax 9373 9125); 553 St. Kilda Rd., P.O. Box 6722, Melbourne, VIC 3004 (tel. (03) 9625 1583; fax 9510 4646); 16 St. George's Terr., 13th fl., Perth, WA 6000 (tel. (08) 9231 9400; fax 9231 9444).

Canada, 615 Macleod Trail #1050, S.E., Calgary, AB T2G 4T8, (403-266-8962; fax 264-6630); Cogswell Tower #910, Scotia Sq., Halifax, NS, B3J 3K1, (902-429-2480; fax 423-6861); P.O. Box 65, Postal Station Desjardins, Montréal, QC H5B 1G1 (514-398-9695; fax 398-0973); 2 Place Terrasse Dufferin, C.P. 939, Québec, QC, G1R 4T9 (418-692-2095; fax 692-4640); 360 University Ave., Toronto, ON, M5G 1S4 (416-595-1700; fax 595-0051); 1095 West Pender St., Vancouver, BC V6E 2M6 (604-685-4311; fax 685-5285).

New Zealand, Yorkshire General Bldg., 4th fl., 29 Shortland St., Auckland (tel. (09) 303 2724; fax 366 0870); Price Waterhouse Ctr., 109 Armagh St., 11th fl., Christchurch (tel. (03) 379 0040; fax 379 5677).

South Africa, Broadway Industries Centre, P.O. Box 6773, Heerengracht, Foreshore, Cape Town (tel. (021) 214 280; fax 211 130); Durban Bay House, 333 Smith St., 29th fl., Durban (tel. (031) 304 4737; fax 301 8206); 1 River St. c/o Riviera, Killarney, Johannesburg (tel. (011) 646 6900; fax 646 6913).

U.K., Queen's House, 14 Queen St., Belfast, N. Ireland BT1 6EQ, PSC 801, Box 40, APO AE 09498-4040 (tel. (0123) 232 8239; fax 224 8482); 3 Regent Terr., Edinburgh, Scotland EH7 5BW, PSC 801 Box 40, FPO AE 90498-4040 (tel. (0131) 556 8315; fax 557 6023).

PASSPORTS

REQUIREMENTS. Citizens of Australia, Canada, Ireland, New Zealand, South Africa, and the U.K. need valid passports to enter the United States, and to re-enter their own country. Returning home with an expired passport is illegal, and may result in a fine.

PHOTOCOPIES. Photocopy the page of your passport that contains your photograph, passport number, and other identifying information, as well as other important documents such as visas, travel insurance policies, airplane tickets, and traveler's check serial numbers, in case you lose anything. Carry one set of copies in a safe place apart from the originals and leave another set at home. Consulates also recommend that you carry an expired passport or an official copy of your birth certificate in a part of your baggage separate from other documents.

LOST PASSPORTS. If you lose your passport, immediately notify the local police and the nearest embassy or consulate of your home government. To expedite its replacement, you will need to know your passport number and show identification and proof of citizenship. In some cases, a replacement may take weeks to process, and may be valid only for a limited time. Any visas stamped in your old passport will be permanently lost. In an emergency, ask for immediate temporary traveling papers that will permit you to re-enter your home country. You may have to surrender your passport to a foreign government official, but if you don't get it back in a reasonable amount of time, inform the nearest mission of your home country.

NEW PASSPORTS. All applications for new passports or renewals should be filed several weeks or months in advance of your planned departure date—remember that you are relying on government agencies to complete these transactions. Most passport offices do offer emergency passport services for an extra charge. Citizens residing abroad who need a passport or renewal should contact their nearest embassy or consulate.

Australia Citizens must apply in person at a post office, a passport office, or an Australian diplomatic mission overseas. Passport offices are in Adelaide, Brisbane, Canberra, Darwin, Hobart, Melbourne, Newcastle, Perth, and Sydney. 32-page passports valid for 10 years AUS$126, 64-page AUS$188; children 32-page passports valid for 5 years AUS$63, 64-page AUS$94. For more info, call toll-free (in Australia) 13 12 32, or visit www.dfat.gov.au/passports.

Canada Applications are available at passport offices, Canadian missions, and many travel agencies. Non-renewable passports valid for 5 years CDN$60 plus consular fee CDN$25 consular fee. For more info, contact the Canadian Passport Office, Department of Foreign Affairs and International Trade, Ottawa, ON, K1A OG3 (613-994-3500; www.dfait-maeci.gc.ca/passport). Travelers may also call 800-267-8376 (24hr.); in Toronto, 416-973-3251; in Vancouver, 604-586-2500; in Montréal, 514-283-2152.

Ireland Applications are at local Garda stations and post offices, and can be requested by mail from passport offices. Citizens can apply by mail to either the Department of Foreign Affairs, Passport Office, Setanta Centre, Molesworth St., Dublin 2 (tel. (01) 671 1633; fax 671 1092; www.irlgov.ie/iveagh), or the Passport Office, Irish Life Building, 1A South Mall, Cork (tel. (021) 27 25 25). Passports valid for 10 years IR£45; under 18 and over 65 passports valid for 3 years IR£10.

New Zealand Applications are available from most New Zealand travel agents. Applications may be forwarded to the Passport Office, P.O. Box 10526, Wellington (tel. 0800 22 50 50; www.govt.nz/agency_info/forms.shtml). Standard processing time in New Zealand is 10 working days for correct applications. Passports valid for 10 years NZ$80; children passports valid for 5 years NZ$40. Children's names can no longer be endorsed on a parent's passport–they must apply for their own.

South Africa All applications must be submitted or forwarded to the applicable office of a South African consulate, but *passports are issued only in Pretoria.* Applications normally take *at least* 3 months to process. Passports valid for 10 years SAR80; under 16 passports valid for 5 years SAR60. For more info, contact the nearest Department of Home Affairs Office (www.southafrica-newyork.net/passport.htm).

United Kingdom Applications are available at passport offices, main post offices, and many travel agents. Apply by mail or in person to one of the passport offices, located in London, Liverpool, Newport, Peterborough, Glasgow, and Belfast. Applications normally take about 1 month to process, but the London office offers a 5-day, walk-in rush service; arrive early. Passports valid for 10 years UK£31; under 16 passports valid for 5 years UK£11. For more info, contact the U.K. Passport Agency (tel. (0870) 521 04 10; www.open.gov.uk/ukpass/ukpass.htm).

VISAS AND WORK PERMITS

VISAS. A visa, stamped into a traveler's passport by the government of a host country, allows the bearer to stay in the host country for a specified purpose and period of time. The **Center for International Business and Travel (CIBT),** 23201 New Mexico Ave. NW #210, Washington, D.C. 20016 (202-244-9500 or 800-925-2428), secures travel "pleasure tourist," or **B-2** visas to and from all possible countries for a variable service charge (6-month visa around $45). Contact the nearest U.S. consulate or embassy to obtain a U.S. visa, or for more info on visas. Canadian citizens do *not* need a U.S. visa if planning on staying for fewer than 180 days. Australian and South African citizens need visas to enter the U.S. Citizens of Ireland, New Zealand, and the U.K can waive U.S. visas through the **Visa Waiver Pilot Program.** Visitors qualify if they are traveling only for business or pleasure (*not* work or study), are staying for fewer than 90 days, have proof of intent to leave (e.g., a return plane ticket), an I-94W form (arrival/departure certificate attached to your visa upon arrival), and are traveling on particular air or sea carriers.

For general visa inquiries, consult the Bureau of Consular Affair's Web Page (http://travel.state.gov/visa_services.html). If you lose your I-94 form, you can replace it at the nearest **Immigration and Naturalization Service (INS)** office (800-755-0777 or 202-307-1501; www.ins.usdoj.gov), although it's very unlikely that the form will be replaced within the time of your stay. **Visa extensions** are sometimes attainable with a completed I-539 form; call the forms request line (800-870-3676).

WORK PERMITS AND STUDYING IN CALIFORNIA. Admission as a visitor does not include the right to work, which is authorized only by a work permit, and entering the United States to study requires a special visa. For more info, see **Alternatives to Tourism,** page 67.

IDENTIFICATION

When you travel, always carry at least two forms of identification on your person, including at least one photo ID. A passport and a driver's license or birth certificate usually serves as adequate proof of your identity and citizenship. Many establishments, especially banks, require several IDs before cashing traveler's checks. Never carry all forms of ID together—in case of theft or loss, you risk being left entirely without identification or funds.

STUDENT AND TEACHER IDENTIFICATION. The **International Student Identity Card (ISIC)** is the most widely accepted form of student identification, and can get bearers discounts on sights, theaters, museums, accommodations, meals, train, ferry, bus, and airplane transportation, and rother services. Ask about discounts even when none are advertised. These cards are preferable to institution-specific cards because tourism personnel in the U.S. recognize the former more easily. However, because of the proliferation of phony ISICs, many airlines and some

other services require additional proof of student identity, such as your school ID card. Cardholders have access to a toll-free 24-hour ISIC helpline whose multilingual staff can provide assistance in medical, legal, and financial emergencies overseas (in the U.S. and Canada 800-626-2427; elsewhere call collect tel. (0181) 666 90 25). Many student travel agencies issue ISICs, including STA Travel in Australia and New Zealand; Travel CUTS in Canada; USIT in Ireland and Northern Ireland; SASTS in South Africa; Campus Travel and STA Travel in the U.K.; and Council Travel, STA Travel, and www.counciltravel.com/idcards/index.htm in the U.S. Request a copy of the *International Student Identity Card Handbook*, which lists some discounts. You can also write to Council for a copy. (Cards valid Sept. of one year to Dec. of the following year $20, AUS$15, or CDN$15. Must be at least 12 years old and a secondary or post-secondary school student.)

The **International Teacher Identity Card (ITIC)** offers similar but limited discounts ($20, AUS$13, or UK£5). For more info on these cards, contact the **International Student Travel Confederation (ISTC),** Herengracht 479, 1017 BS Amsterdam, Netherlands (from abroad call tel. 31 20 421 28 00; email istcinfo@istc.org; www.istc.org).

ESSENTIALS

YOUTH IDENTIFICATION. ISTC also issues the International Youth Travel Card (IYTC; formerly the GO25 Card) which offers many of the same benefits as the ISIC. Most organizations that sell the ISIC also sell the IYTC and provide the free brochure that lists discounts to card purchasers. To apply, you will need a passport, a valid driver's license, or a copy of a birth certificate, and a passport photo with your name on the back. (1-year card for non-students under 25 $20.)

CUSTOMS

Upon entering the U.S., you must declare certain items from abroad and pay a duty on the value of those articles that exceed the allowance established by the U.S. customs service. Make a list, including serial numbers, of any valuables brought from home; if you register this list with customs before your departure and have it officially stamped, you can avoid import duty charges and help ensure an easy passage upon your return. Be especially careful to document items manufactured outside of the U.S., and never try to bring perishable food into the U.S.

Upon returning home, you must declare all items acquired in the U.S. and pay a **duty** on those articles that exceed the allowance established by your country's customs service. Goods and gifts purchased at **duty-free** shops abroad are not exempt from duty or taxes at your point of return; you must declare these items as well. "Duty-free" means that you need not pay a tax in the country of purchase. For more info on customs requirements, contact the following information centers:

Australia Australian Customs Info Line tel. 1 300 363 263; www.customs.gov.au.

Canada Canadian Customs, 2265 St. Laurent Blvd., Ottawa, ON K1G 4K3 (613-993-0534 or 24hr. automated service 800-461-9999; www.revcan.ca).

Ireland The Collector of Customs and Excise, The Custom House, Dublin 1 (tel. (01) 679 27 77; fax 671 20 21; email taxes@revenue.iol.ie; www.revenue.ie/customs.htm).

New Zealand New Zealand Customhouse, 17-21 Whitmore St., Box 2218, Wellington (tel. (04) 473 6099; fax 473 7370; www.customs.govt.nz).

South Africa Commissioner for Customs and Excise, Private Bag X47, Pretoria 0001 (tel. (012) 314 99 11; fax 328 64 78).

United Kingdom Her Majesty's Customs and Excise, Custom House, Nettleton Rd., Heathrow Airport, Hounslow, Middlesex TW6 2LA (tel. (0181) 910 36 02/35 66; fax 910 37 65; www.hmce.gov.uk).

United States U.S. Customs Service, Box 7407, Washington, D.C. 20044 (202-927-6724; www.customs.ustreas.gov).

ESSENTIALS

MONEY

Travelers can expect to spend anywhere from $25-75 per person per day in California for lodging, food, and sights. Transportation increases these figures. No matter how low your budget, if you travel for more than a few days, you should keep handy a larger amount of cash than usual. Carrying it on your person, even in a money belt, is risky, and personal checks from other countries, or even other states, are almost never accepted at California establishments.

CURRENCY AND EXCHANGE

The main unit of currency in the U.S. is the **dollar** (represented by the symbol $ which precedes the numeral), which is divided into 100 **cents** (represented by the symbol ¢ which follows the numeral). *Let's Go* lists a number of "cash only" establishments; this means they accept paper money, they do not accept credit or debit cards or personal checks, and they may or may not accept traveler's checks. Bills are green in the U.S. and come in denominations of $1, $5, $10, $20, $50, and $100. Coins are 1¢ (penny), 5¢ (nickel), 10¢ (dime), 25¢ (quarter), 50¢ (half-dollar), and $1 (silver dollar). The currency chart below is based on published exchange rates from August 1999. Go to www.bloomberg.com/markets/currency/currcalc.cgi?T=markets_curr99.ht. for more updated information.

THE GREENBACK (THE U.S. DOLLAR)

CDN$1=	US$0.68	US$1=	CDN$1.477
UK£1=	US$1.60	US$1=	UK£.623
IR£1=	US$1.34	US$1=	IR£.745
AUS$1=	US$0.65	US$1=	AUS$1.533
NZ$1=	US$0.53	US$1=	NZ$1.884
SAR1=	US$0.16	US$1=	SAR$6.10

When exchanging money, check commission rates and minimum exchange amounts. Check newspapers for the standard rate of exchange. Banks generally have the best rates. Try to only go to establishments that have at most a 5% margin between their buy and sell prices. Since you lose money with each transaction, convert large sums at once. Using a credit card (see p. 33) or a debit (ATM) card (see p. 33) will often get you the best possible rates, although ATMs usually charge fees. Some California establishments do not accept traveler's checks or bills over $50 (some restaurants and stores only accept bills of $20 or smaller).

TRAVELER'S CHECKS

Traveler's checks are one of the safest and least troublesome means of carrying funds since they can be refunded if stolen and are widely accepted throughout the U.S. **American Express** and **Visa** are the most widely recognized checks. Traveler's checks are usually sold for face value plus a small percentage commission at several agencies and banks. (Members of the American Automobile Association (AAA) can get American Express checks commission-free.) If ordering traveler's checks, do so well in advance, especially for large sums. Each agency provides refunds for stolen or lost checks, and many provide additional services, such as toll-free hotlines, emergency message services, and stolen credit card assistance.

In order to collect **refunds for lost or stolen checks,** keep check receipts separate from checks and store them in a safe place or with a traveling companion. Record check numbers as you cash them, leave a list of check numbers at home, and ask for a list of refund centers when buying checks. Never countersign checks until ready to cash them, and always bring your passport when you plan to use checks.

American Express: In Australia (tel. (0800) 251 902); in New Zealand (tel. (0800) 441 068); in the U.K. (tel. (0800) 52 13 13); in the U.S. and Canada 800-221-7282; elsewhere call collect 801-964-6665; www.aexp.com. American Express Traveler's Cheques can be purchased for a small fee (1-4%) at AmEx Travel Service Offices, banks, and AAA offices. AmEx offices cash their checks commission-free, but often at slightly worse exchange rates than banks. "Cheques for Two" can be signed by either of 2 people.

Citicorp: In the U.S. and Canada call 800-645-6556; in Europe, the Middle East, or Africa, call the London office (tel. (044) 171 508 7007); elsewhere, call collect 813-623-1709 (all 3 lines 24hr.). Checks in 7 currencies. Commission 1-2%. Guaranteed hand-delivery of traveler's checks when a refund location is not convenient.

Thomas Cook MasterCard: In the U.S., Canada, or Caribbean 800-223-7373; in the U.K. (tel. (0800) 622 101); elsewhere, call collect (tel. 44 1733 318 950). Checks in 13 currencies. Commission 2%. Thomas Cook offices cash checks commission-free.

Visa: In the U.S. 800-227-6811; in the U.K. (tel. (0800) 895 078); elsewhere call collect (tel. 44 1733 318 949). All 3 numbers will locate their nearest office for you.

CREDIT CARDS

Credit cards are accepted at most places in California, but always double-check policies at the establishments themselves. Credit card companies get the wholesale exchange rate, which is generally 5% better than the retail rate used by banks and other currency exchange establishments. Major credit cards (MasterCard, Visa, American Express) can be used to extract cash advances in dollars from automated teller machines (ATMs) throughout the state (see **Cash Cards,** below). Credit cards often offer an array of other services, from insurance to emergency assistance. Check with your company to find out its benefits

CREDIT CARD COMPANIES. **Visa** (800-336-8472) and **MasterCard** (800-307-7309) are issued in cooperation with individual banks and some other organizations. **American Express** (800-843-2273) has an annual fee of up to $55. Cardholder services include the ability to cash personal checks at AmEx offices, a 24-hour hotline with emergency medical and legal assistance (in U.S. and Canada 800-554-2639; elsewhere call collect 202-554-2639), and AmEx Travel Service. Benefits include assistance in changing airline, hotel, and car rental reservations, baggage loss and flight insurance, sending mailgrams and international cables, and mail-holding services at over 1700 AmEx offices worldwide. The **Discover Card** (in U.S. 800-347-2683; elsewhere 801-902-3100) offers small cash-back bonuses on purchases, but is not accepted at many U.S. establishments. **Diner's Club** (in U.S. 800-234-6377; elsewhere call collect 303-799-1504) is another option that is less accepted than the "big three" (Visa, MasterCard, American Express).

CASH/DEBIT/ATM CARDS

Cash cards—often called debit or ATM (Automated Teller Machine) cards—are widespread in California. All ATMs require a **Personal Identification Number (PIN).** Ask your bank or credit card company for a PIN before leaving home; without it, you will be unable to withdraw cash with your cash card or credit card. If you already have a PIN, check with the company to make sure it will work in the U.S.

Depending on the system that your home bank uses, you can probably access your personal bank account to get money. ATMs get the same wholesale exchange rate as credit cards. Despite these perks, do research before relying too heavily on automation. There is often a limit on the amount of money you can withdraw per day (usually about $500, depending on the type of card and account), and computer networks sometimes fail. If your PIN is longer than four digits, ask your bank whether the first four digits will work, or whether you need a new number.

The two major international money networks are **Cirrus** (800-4-CIRRUS/424-7787) and **PLUS** (800-843-7587 for the "Voice Response Unit Locator"). To locate ATMs all over California, use www.visa.com/pd/atm or www.mastercard.com/atm. A typical ATM transaction fee is between $1 and $3 in California.

GETTING MONEY FROM HOME

AMERICAN EXPRESS. Cardholders can withdraw cash from their checking accounts at any major AmEx office and many of its representatives' offices, up to $1000 every 21 days (no service charge, no interest). AmEx also offers Express Cash at any of its ATMs in the U.S. Express Cash withdrawals are automatically debited from the card member's checking account or line of credit. Green card holders may withdraw up to $1000 in a seven-day period. There is a 2% transaction fee for each cash withdrawal ($2.50 min. charge, $20 max. charge). To enroll in Express Cash, Cardmembers in the U.S. may call 800-CASH-NOW/227-4669; elsewhere call collect 336-668-5041. The AmEx number in the U.S. is 800-221-7282.

WESTERN UNION. To cable money within the U.S. using a credit card (Visa, MasterCard, Discover), call 800-CALL-CASH/225-5227. With cash, the rates are around $10-11 cheaper than with a credit card; money is often available within an hour.

TIPPING AND BARGAINING

In the U.S., it is customary to tip waitstaff and cab drivers 15-20%, but at your discretion. Tips are usually not included in restaurant bills, unless you are in a party of six or more; check the menu or ask the maître d' about tipping if you are in a large party. At the airport and in hotels, porters expect a tip of at least $1 per bag to carry your baggage. Bargaining is generally frowned upon and fruitless in California, unless you are at a flea market or on the streets of any Chinatown, buying from a vendor.

TAXES

Sales tax in California is the equivalent of the European Value-Added Tax and varies by county from 6.25-8.5% on normal consumer items; there are additional federal taxes on tobacco products and alcoholic beverages. Most grocery items in California are not taxed. *Let's Go* does not usually include taxes (i.e. on accommodations) in listed prices.

SAFETY AND SECURITY

Crime is mostly concentrated in cities, but it's best to practice safety measures no matter where you are. Los Angeles, Sacramento, East Palo Alto, and Fresno are the most dangerous cities in California, but that does not mean you cannot visit them. Exercise common sense and be prepared to avoid dangerous situations; wherever possible, *Let's Go* warns of neighborhoods that should be avoided when traveling alone or at night.

BLENDING IN. Tourists are especially vulnerable to crime because they often carry large amounts of cash and are not as street-savvy as locals. Avoid unwanted attention by blending in as much as possible: leave the fanny pack, pulled-up socks, and weird shoes at home. The gawking camera-toter is a more obvious target for thieves and con artists than the low-profile traveler. Familiarize yourself with the area before setting out; if you must check a map on the street, duck into a cafe or shop. Also, carry yourself with confidence, as an obviously bewildered bodybuilder is more likely to be harassed than a stern and confident 98-pound weakling. Be sure that someone at home knows your itinerary and **never admit that you are traveling alone.**

EXPLORING. Extra vigilance is always wise, but there is no need to panic when exploring a new city or region. Find out about unsafe areas from tourist offices or from the manager of your hotel or hostel and remember that dialing **911** from any public phone in California will connect you to an emergency operator for the police, fire, and ambulance; all 911 calls are free. Whenever possible, *Let's Go* warns of unsafe areas (such as South Central L.A.), but there are some good general tips to follow no matter where you are. When walking at night, stick to busy, well-lit streets. Do not attempt to cross through alleyways, parks, parking lots, or other large, deserted areas. Buildings in disrepair, vacant lots, and unpopulated areas are all indicators of potentially unsafe areas. Keep in mind that a district can change character drastically between blocks, and from day to night. If you feel uncomfortable, leave as quickly and directly as you can, but don't allow fear of the unknown to turn you into an isolationist. Careful, persistent exploration will build confidence and make your stay in an area that much more rewarding.

GETTING AROUND. Driving in California is generally safe. Whenever possible, drive during the day, because you can get help faster if you run into trouble on highways, and you can avoid trouble on city streets at night. Seatbelts in cars and motorcycle helmets on motorcycles and mopeds are required by law in California. Children under 40 pounds should ride only in specially designed carseats, available for a small fee from most car rental agencies. For long drives in desolate areas, invest in a roadside assistance program and a cellular phone. If your car breaks down, wait for the police to assist you. Park your vehicle in a garage or well-traveled area, and use a steering wheel locking device in larger cities. **Sleeping in your car** is one of the most dangerous (and often illegal) ways to get your rest. *Let's Go* does not recommend sleeping in cars. Finally, if you're testing car and soul in the heat of the California desert, take special precautions for your drive; see the detailed explanation of **Driving in the Desert,** page 461.

Public transportation (buses and trains) is generally safe. Occasionally, bus and train stations are in dangerous areas; *Let's Go* warns of these stations where possible. If possible, avoid using public transportation late at night unless you are in a large group. Taxis should be safe, but if you have a bad experience with a taxi driver, get the medallion number of the driver and report it to the taxi company immediately.

Let's Go does not recommend **hitchhiking** under any circumstances, particularly for women—see **Getting Around,** p. 57 for more information.

SELF DEFENSE. There is no sure-fire set of precautions that will protect you from all of the situations you might encounter when you travel. Carry a **whistle** to scare off a would-be attacker or to attract attention. A good self-defense course will give you more concrete ways to react to different types of aggression. **Impact, Prepare,** and **Model Mugging** can refer you to local self-defense courses in the United States (800-345-5425). Workshops (2-3 hr.) start at $50 and full courses run $350-500. Both women and men are welcome.

FINANCIAL SECURITY

PROTECTING YOUR VALUABLES. Theft in California is more rampant in big cities, and at night. To prevent easy theft, don't keep all your valuables (money, important documents) in one place. **Photocopies** of important documents allow you to recover them in case they are lost or stolen (see **Photocopies,** p. 25). Label every piece of luggage both inside and out. **Don't put a wallet with money in your back pocket.** Never count money in public. If carrying a purse, make sure it is a sturdy one with a secure clasp, and carry it on the side away from the street with the strap running across your torso and the clasp against you. Use a small combina-

tion padlock to lock packs and luggage by slipping it through two zippers. A **money belt** is the best way to carry cash; most camping stores carry them. This nylon, zippered pouch with a belt sits inside the waist of your pants or skirt and combines convenience and security. A **neck pouch** is equally safe, although less accessible. Refrain from pulling out your neck pouch in public; if you must, be very discreet. Avoid keeping anything precious in a fanny-pack (even if worn on the stomach): valuables are highly visible and easy to steal. Keep some money separate from the rest in case of emergency or theft.

CON ARTISTS AND PICKPOCKETS. Among the more colorful aspects of large cities are **con artists.** Con artists and hustlers often work in groups, and children are among the most effective. They have countless ruses: Be aware of anyone distracting you for enough time to snatch your bag (especially ignore classic stories about "found" rolls of money). Be suspicious in unexpected situations, and in general, if harassed, do not respond or make eye contact, walk away quickly, and keep a tight grip on belongings. Contact the police if a hustler is particularly insistent or aggressive.

In city crowds, especially on public transportation, **pickpockets** are amazingly deft at their craft. Rush hour is no excuse for strangers to press up against you on a bus, train, or trolley car. If someone stands uncomfortably close, move to another car and hold bags tightly. If you must say or dial your calling card number from a public phone, be cautious so that others cannot see or hear the number.

ACCOMMODATIONS AND TRANSPORTATION. Never leave belongings unattended; crime can occur even at what appear to be the safest of hostels or hotels. If you feel unsafe, look for places with either a curfew or a night attendant. *Let's Go* lists locker availability in hostels and train stations, but most of the time you'll need your own **padlock.** Lockers are useful if you plan on sleeping outdoors or don't want to lug everything with you, but don't store valuables in them. Most hotels also provide lock boxes free or for a minimal fee.

Be particularly careful on **public transportation;** carry your bags in front of you where you can see them, avoid checking baggage on trains, and don't trust anyone to "watch your bag for a second." Thieves thrive on **trains;** professionals wait for tourists to fall asleep and then carry off everything they can. When traveling in pairs, sleep in alternating shifts; when alone, use good judgement in selecting a train car and use a lock to secure your pack to the luggage rack. Keep important documents and other valuables on your person and luggage within your sight.

If traveling by **car,** try not to leave valuable possessions—such as radios or luggage—in it while you are away from it. If your tape deck or radio is removable, hide it in the trunk or take it with you. If it isn't, conceal it under something else. Also hide baggage in the trunk; however, remember that savvy thieves can tell if a car is heavily loaded by the way it sits on its tires.

ALCOHOL AND DRUGS

In California, like the rest of the U.S., **the drinking age is a strictly enforced 21.** Non-prescription drugs of any sort are always illegal. Cigarette purchasers must be at least 18 years old with photo ID. If carrying prescription drugs, have a copy of the prescription itself *and* a note from a doctor readily accessible at country borders.

Avoid public drunkenness; it is illegal in many places, and can jeopardize your safety and earn the disdain of locals. **Never drink and drive**—you risk your own life and those of others, and getting caught results in imprisonment and fines.

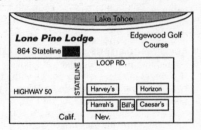

HEALTH

Common sense is the simplest prescription for good health. Luckily, the U.S. has an excellent health-care system and travelers can most often be easily treated for injuries and health problems they may encounter. Travelers complain most often about their feet and their gut, so take precautionary measures: wear sturdy, broken-in shoes and clean socks, and use talcum powder to keep your feet dry, and drink lots of fluids to prevent dehydration and constipation. To minimize the effects of jet lag, "reset" your body's clock by adopting the time of your destination as soon as you board the plane. And before you leave home, ask your insurance carrier if you are covered for overseas travel, because you may have to purchase additional coverage. (For more information, see **Insurance,** p. 41).

BEFORE YOU GO

Preparation can help minimize the likelihood of contracting a disease and maximize the chances of receiving effective health care in the event of an emergency.

For minor health problems, bring a compact **first-aid kit,** including bandages, aspirin or another pain killer, antibiotic cream, a thermometer, a Swiss army knife with tweezers, moleskin (for blisters), decongestant for colds, motion sickness remedy, medicine for diarrhea or stomach problems, sunscreen, insect repellent (extra-strength if you plan on camping or hiking), and burn ointment. **Contact lens** wearers should bring an extra pair, a copy of the prescription, a pair of glasses, extra solution, and eyedrops. Those who use heat disinfection can consider switching to chemical cleansers for the duration of the trip, if possible (check with your eyecare provider); if bringing a heat disinfecter, purchase the appropriate adapter (see **Electric Current**, p. 43). Contact lens supplies are easy to find in California at drug stores and some large supermarkets.

In your **passport,** write the names of people who should be contacted in case of medical emergency, and list all **allergies,** medical conditions, and prescription medications doctors should be aware of. Allergy sufferers should obtain any necessary medication before the trip. Matching a prescription to its foreign equivalent is not always easy, safe, or possible. Carry up-to-date, legible prescriptions or statements from your doctor stating trade name, manufacturer, chemical name, and dosage of medications. While traveling, keep medication in carry-on luggage.

USEFUL ORGANIZATIONS. The U.S. **Centers for Disease Control and Prevention (CDC)** (888-232-3299; www.cdc.gov) is an excellent source of information for travelers around the world and maintains an international fax information service for travelers. The CDC also publishes the booklet "Health Information for International Travelers" ($20), an annual global rundown of disease, immunization, and general health advice. This book may be purchased by sending a check or money order to the Superintendent of Documents, U.S. Government Printing Office, P.O. Box 371954, Pittsburgh, PA 15250-7954. Phone orders can be made (202-512-1800) with a credit card (Visa, MasterCard, or Discover).

MEDICAL CONDITIONS. Those with medical conditions (e.g., diabetes, antibiotic allergies, epilepsy, heart conditions) may want to obtain a stainless steel **Medic Alert** identification tag (1st year $35, subsequent years $15 each), identifying the condition and giving a 24-hour information number. Contact Medic Alert Foundation, 2323 Colorado Ave., Turlock, CA 95382 (800-825-3785; www.medicalert.org). Diabetics can contact the **American Diabetes Association,** 1660 Duke St., Alexandria, VA 22314 (800-232-3472), to receive copies of the article "Travel and Diabetes" and a diabetic ID card, which carries messages in 18 languages explaining the carrier's diabetic status.

According to U.S. law, **HIV-positive** persons are not permitted to enter the U.S. However, HIV testing is conducted only for those who are planning to immigrate permanently. Travelers from areas with particularly high concentrations of HIV-positive persons or persons with AIDS may be required to provide more information when applying for a visa (see **AIDS and HIV,** p. 41).

ENVIRONMENTAL HAZARDS

Heat exhaustion and dehydration: Heat exhaustion, characterized by dehydration and salt deficiency, can lead to fatigue, headaches, and light-headedness. Drink lots of clear fluids (enough to keep your urine clear) and eat salty foods, like crackers. The simplest and most effective anti-dehydration formula is 8 oz. of (clean) water with a ½-teaspoon of sugar or honey and a pinch of salt. Alcoholic beverages, coffee, strong tea, and caffeinated sodas are dehydrating. Continuous heat stress can lead to **heatstroke,** characterized by rising body temperature, severe headache, and cessation of sweating. Heatstroke is rare but serious; victims must be cooled with wet towels and taken to a doctor immediately. You are most at risk for heat exhaustion and dehydration in the desert, where the heat is dry, causing it to take longer to sweat and realize you are hot. For more info, see **Desert Survival,** p. 460.

Sunburn: Bring sunscreen with you, or buy some (it can be bought at most drug stores, supermarkets, and some visitors centers), and apply it liberally and often to avoid burns and risk of skin cancer. If you plan on spending time near water, in the desert, or in the snow, you are at higher risk of getting burned, even through clouds. If you get sunburned, drink more fluids than usual and apply an aloe-based lotion.

Hypothermia and frostbite: A rapid drop in body temperature is the clearest warning sign of overexposure to cold. Victims may also shiver, feel exhausted, have poor coordination or slurred speech, hallucinate, or suffer amnesia. Seek medical help, and *do not let hypothermia victims fall asleep*—their body temperature will continue to drop and they may die. To avoid hypothermia, keep dry, wear layers, and stay out of the wind. In wet weather, wool and synthetics such as pile retain heat. Most other fabric, especially cotton, will make you colder. When the temperature is below freezing, watch for **frostbite.** If a region of skin turns white, waxy, and cold, **do not rub the area.** Drink warm beverages, get dry, and slowly warm the area with dry fabric or steady body contact, until a doctor can be found.

PREVENTING DISEASE

INSECT-BORNE DISEASES. Many diseases are transmitted by insects—mainly mosquitoes, fleas, ticks, and lice. Be aware of insects in wet or forested areas while hiking, and especially while camping. Use insect repellents, such as DEET. Wear long pants and long sleeves (tropic-weight cottons will keep you comfortable in heat) and buy a mosquito net. Wear shoes and socks, and, if no one can see you, tuck long pants into socks. Soak or spray gear with permethrin (licensed in U.S. for use on clothing). Natural repellents can also help: regularly taking B-12 vitamins or garlic pills can eventually cause you to repel insects. Calamine lotion or topical cortisones (like Cortaid) may stop insect bites from itching, as can a bath with a half-cup of baking soda or oatmeal. **Mosquitoes** are most active from dusk to dawn. **Ticks**—responsible for Lyme and other diseases—are prevalent in rural and forested areas. **Lyme disease** is a bacterial infection marked by a circular bull's-eye rash of two inches or more that appears around the bite, as well as fever, headache, tiredness, and aches and pains. Antibiotics are effective if administered early. Left untreated, Lyme disease causes problems in joints, the heart, and the nervous system. If you find a tick attached to you, grasp its head with tweezers as close to the skin as possible and apply slow, steady traction. If removed within 24 hours, the risk of infection is greatly reduced. Pause periodically while walking to brush off ticks using a fine-toothed comb on your neck and scalp. Never try to remove ticks by burning them or coating them with nail polish remover or petroleum or K-Y jelly.

AIDS AND HIV

Acquired Immune Deficiency Syndrome (AIDS) is a growing problem around the world. The World Health Organization estimates 30 million people are infected with the HIV virus, and women now represent 40% of all new HIV infections.

The easiest mode of HIV transmission is through blood-to-blood contact with an HIV-positive person; *never* share intravenous drug, tattooing, or other needles. The most common mode of transmission is sexual intercourse. Health professionals recommend the use of latex condoms, which are available in all drug stores and most convenience stores in California. For more info on AIDS, call the **U.S. Centers for Disease Control's** 24-hour hotline (800-342-2437). In Europe, contact the **World Health Organization,** Attn: Global Program on AIDS, Ave. Appia 20, 1211 Geneva 27, Switzerland (tel. 44 22 791 21 11; fax 791 31 11), for statistical material on AIDS internationally. The brochure, *Travel Safe: AIDS and International Travel*, is available at all Council Travel offices and at their web site (www.ciee.org/study/safety/travelsafe.htm).

ESSENTIALS

WOMEN'S HEALTH

Women traveling in unsanitary conditions are vulnerable to **urinary tract** and **bladder infections,** common and severely uncomfortable bacterial diseases that cause a burning sensation and painful and sometimes frequent urination. To help avoid these infections, drink plenty of vitamin-C-rich juices (such as cranberry juice) and clean water, and urinate frequently, especially right after intercourse. Untreated, these infections can lead to kidney infections, sterility, and even death. If you have these symptoms, see a doctor immediately.

Women who need an **abortion** while traveling in California or the rest of the U.S. should contact the National Abortion Federation Hotline, 1755 Massachusetts Ave. NW, Washington, D.C. 20036 (800-772-9100; M-F 9am-7pm). For further reading on women's health, pick up a copy of the *Handbook for Women Travelers*, by Maggie and Gemma Moss (Piatkus Books; $15).

INSURANCE

Travel insurance generally covers four basic areas: medical coverage, property loss, trip cancellation/interruption, and emergency evacuation. Although regular policies may extend to travel-related accidents, consider travel insurance if the cost of potential trip cancellation/interruption is greater than you can absorb.

Medical insurance (especially university policies) often covers costs incurred abroad; check with your provider. Canadians are partially protected by their home province's health insurance during travel; check with the provincial Ministry of Health or Health Plan Headquarters for details. **Homeowners' insurance** often covers theft during travel and loss of travel documents up to $500. **ISIC** and **ITIC** provide basic insurance benefits, including $100 per day of in-hospital sickness for a maximum of 60 days, $3000 of accident-related medical reimbursement, and $25,000 for emergency medical transport (see **Student and Teacher Identification,** p. 27). **American Express** (800-528-4800) grants most cardholders automatic car rental insurance (collision/theft, but not liability) and ground travel accident coverage of $100,000 on flight purchases made with the card. Prices for separately purchased full coverage travel insurance generally runs about $50 per week, while trip cancellation/interruption may be purchased separately for about $5.50 per $100 of coverage.

ESSENTIALS

INSURANCE PROVIDERS. **Council** and **STA** (see p. 55 for complete listings) offer a range of plans that can supplement your basic insurance coverage. Other private insurance providers in the **U.S.** include: **Access America** (800-284-8300); **Berkely Group/Carefree Travel Insurance** (800-323-3149 or 516-294-0220; info@berkely.com; www.berkely.com); **Globalcare Travel Insurance** (800-821-2488; www.globalcare-cocco.com); and **Travel Assistance International** (800-821-2828 or 202-828-5894; email wassist@aol.com; www.worldwide-assistance.com). **U.K.** providers include **Campus Travel** (tel. (01865) 258 000) and **Columbus Travel Insurance** (tel. (0171) 375 0011). In **Australia** try **CIC Insurance** (tel. (02) 9202 8000).

PACKING

Pack according to the extremes of climate you may experience and the type of travel you'll be doing. **Pack light:** a good rule is to lay out only what you absolutely need, then take half the clothes and twice the money. No matter when you're traveling; it's always a good idea to bring a rain jacket (Gore-Tex® is a miracle fabric that's both waterproof and breathable), a warm jacket or wool sweater, and sturdy shoes and thick socks. Remember that wool will keep you warm even when soaked through, whereas wet cotton is colder than wearing nothing at all. If you plan to be doing a lot of hiking, see **Camping and the Outdoors,** p. 47.

LUGGAGE. Toting a **suitcase** or **trunk** is fine if you will stay in one or two cities, or if you will be driving a car most of the time, but is less convenient if you will travel frequently on public transportation. If you plan to cover most of your itinerary by foot, a sturdy **frame backpack** is unbeatable (see **Backpacks,** p. 49). In addition to your main bag, a small backpack, rucksack, or courier bag may be useful as a **daypack** for sightseeing trips and can double as an airplane **carry-on.** An empty, lightweight **duffel bag** packed inside your luggage may also be useful so that you can fill your luggage with purchases and keep dirty clothes in the duffel.

SLEEPSACKS. Some youth hostels require that guests bring their own sleepsacks or rent one at the hostel. If you plan to stay in hostels you can avoid linen charges by making the requisite sleepsack yourself: fold a full size sheet in half the long way, and sew it closed along the open long side and one of the short sides. Sleepsacks can also be bought at any Hostelling International outlet store.

ELECTRIC CURRENT. In the U.S., electricity is 110V. 220V electrical appliances don't like 110V current. Visit a hardware store for an adapter (which changes the shape of the plug) *and* a converter (which changes the voltage). Don't make the mistake of using only an adapter (unless appliance instructions state otherwise).

FILM. If you're not a serious photographer, consider bringing a **disposable camera** or two rather than an expensive permanent one. Despite disclaimers, airport security X-rays *can* fog film, so buy a lead-lined pouch at a camera store or ask security to hand-inspect your camera. Always pack it in your carry-on luggage, since higher-intensity X-rays are used on checked luggage.

OTHER USEFUL ITEMS. Carry a **first-aid kit** (see p. 39). Other useful items include: vitamins; umbrella; sealable plastic bags (for damp clothes, soap, and spillables); alarm clock; sun hat; sunglasses; needle and thread; safety pins; rubber bands; water bottle; towel; compass; padlock; whistle; flashlight; cold-water soap; earplugs; electrical tape to patch tears; garbage bags; calculator for currency conversion; flip-flops for the shower; money-belt; razors; tampons; and condoms.

ACCOMMODATIONS

HOTELS

HOTEL CHAIN	TELEPHONE	HOTEL CHAIN	TELEPHONE
Best Western	1-800-528-1234	La Quinta Inns	1-800-531-5900
Comfort Inns	1-800-221-2222	Motel 6	1-800-891-6161
Days Inn	1-800-325-2525	Ramada Inns	1-800-272-6232
Econo Lodge	1-800-446-6900	Red Carpet Inns	1-800-251-1962
Embassy Suites Hotels	1-800-362-2779	Select Inns	1-800-641-1000
Hampton Inns	1-800-426-7866	Sleep Inns	1-800-221-2222
Hilton Hotels	1-800-445-8667	Super 8 Motel	1-800-800-8000
Holiday Inns	1-800-465-4329	Travelodge	1-800-255-3050
Howard Johnson	1-800-6542000	YMCAS	1-800-922-9622

HOSTELS

A HOSTELER'S BILL OF RIGHTS. There are certain features we do not include in hostel listings. **Unless stated otherwise,** expect that each hostel has: no lockout, no curfew, free hot showers, secure luggage storage, and no key deposit.

Hostels are generally dorm-style accommodations, often in single-sex large rooms with bunk beds; however, some hostels offer private rooms for families and couples. They sometimes have kitchens for guest use, bike or moped rentals, and laundry. There can be drawbacks: some hostels close for daytime

"lockout" hours, have curfews, don't accept reservations, impose maximum stays, or, less frequently, require guests to do chores. In California, a bed in a hostel averages $20.

Two comprehensive hosteling websites are www.iyhf.org, which lists contact info for all national associations, and www.hostels.com. It may be worth it to join a hosteling association for its services and lower rates at member hostels; **Hostelling International (HI)** is the most widespread of these associations. HI hostels are scattered throughout California, and many accept reservations for a nominal fee through the International Booking Network (in **Australia** tel. (02) 9261 1111, in **Canada** 800-663-5777, in **England** tel. (01629) 581 418, in **Ireland** tel. 1301 766, in **New Zealand** tel. (09) 379 4224, in the **U.S.** 800-909-4776; www.hiayh.org/ushostel/reserva/ibn3.htm). To join HI, contact one of the following organizations:

Australian Youth Hostels Association (AYHA), 422 Kent St., Sydney NSW 2000 (tel. (02) 9261 1111; email yha@yhansw.org.au; www.yha.org.au). 1-year membership AUS$44, under 18 AUS$13.50.

Hostelling International-Canada (HI-C), 400-205 Catherine St., Ottawa, ON K2P 1C3 (800-663-5777 or 613-237-7884; email info@hostellingintl.ca; www.hostellingintl.ca). 1-year membership CDN$25, under 18 CDN$12; 2-year CDN$35.

An Óige (Irish Youth Hostel Association), 61 Mountjoy St., Dublin 7 (tel. (01) 830 4555; email anoige@iol.ie; www.irelandyha.org). 1-year membership IR£10, under 18 IR£4, families IR£20.

Youth Hostels Association of New Zealand (YHANZ), P.O. Box 436, 173 Cashel St., Christchurch 1 (tel. (03) 379 9970; email info@yha.org.nz; www.yha.org.nz). 1-year membership NZ$24, ages 15-17 NZ$12, under 15 free.

Hostelling International South Africa, P.O. Box 4402, Cape Town 8000 (tel. (021) 24 2511; email info@hisa.org.za; www.hisa.org.za). 1-year membership SAR50, under 18 SAR25, lifetime SAR250.

Scottish Youth Hostels Association (SYHA), 7 Glebe Crescent, Stirling FK8 2JA (tel. (01786) 891 400; email info@syha.org.uk; www.syha.org.uk). Membership UK£6, under 18 UK£2.50.

Youth Hostels Association of England and Wales (YHA), 8 St. Stephen's Hill, St. Albans, Hertfordshire AL1 2DY, England (tel. (01727) 855 215 or 845 047; email yhacustomerservices@compuserve.com; www.yha.org.uk). 1-year membership UK£11, under 18 UK£5.50, families UK£22.

Hostelling International Northern Ireland (HINI), 22-32 Donegall Rd., Belfast BT12 5JN, Northern Ireland (tel. (01232) 324 733 or 315 435; email info@hini.org.uk; www.hini.org.uk). 1-year membership UK£7, under 18 UK£3, families UK£14.

Hostelling International-American Youth Hostels (HI-AYH), 733 15th St. NW #840, Washington, D.C. 20005 (202-783-6161 ext. 136; email hiayhserv@hiayh.org; www.hiayh.org). 1-year membership $25, over 54 $15, under 18 free.

CALIFORNIA CITIES AND TOWNS WITH HI-AYH HOSTELS:

Independence
Johannesburg
Los Altos Hills
Los Angeles (3)
Merced
Midpines
Montara
Pescadero
Point Reyes
Redwood National Park
Sacramento
San Clemente
San Diego (2)
San Fransisco (2)
San Jose
San Luis Obispo
Santa Cruz
Sausalito
Sonora
Tecopa

ESSENTIALS

HI-AYH COUNCIL OFFICES:

Central California Council
P.O. Box 3645
Merced 95344-3645
Phone: 209-383-0686
Email: hiayhccc@aol.com

Golden Gate Council
425 Divisadero St. #307
San Francisco 94117
Phone: 415-863-1444
Email: hiayh@norcalhostels.org
Travel Center:
415-788-2525

Los Angeles Council
1434 2nd St.
Santa Monica 90401
Phone: 310-393-6263
Email: hiayhla@aol.com
Travel Center: 310-393-3413

San Diego Council
655 4th Ave. #46
San Diego 92101
Phone: 619-338-9981
Email: hiayhsd1@aol.com

DORMS

Many **colleges and universities** open their residence halls to travelers in the summer when school is not in session, and some do so even during term-time. These dorms are often close to student areas (good sources for info on things to do, places to stay, and possible rides out of town) and are usually very clean. Getting a room may be difficult, but rates tend to be low, and many offer free local calls; call ahead. *Let's Go* lists colleges that rent dorm rooms among the accommodations for appropriate cities. For more information on dormitory housing, see the *Campus Lodging Guide (18th ed.)*, B&J Publications ($15).

BED AND BREAKFASTS (B&Bs)

A cozy alternative to impersonal hotel rooms, B&Bs (private homes with rooms available to travelers) range from acceptable to sublime. Some hosts go out of their way to accommodate guests by accepting travelers with pets, giving local tours, or serving meals. On the other hand, many B&Bs have no phones, TVs, or private baths. Rooms in most average California B&Bs cost $50-70 for singles and $70-90 for doubles, but on holidays or in expensive locations, such as Napa Valley, prices can soar to over $300. For more on B&Bs see *The Complete Guide to Bed and Breakfasts, Inns, and Guesthouses in the U.S., Canada, and Worldwide*, Pamela Lanier (Ten Speed Press; $17) or use a booking agency, such as **Bed & Breakfast California,** P.O. Box 282910, San Francisco, CA 94128-2910 (650-696-1690; info@bbintl.com; www.bbintl.com).

HOME EXCHANGE AND RENTALS

Home exchange offers travelers various types of homes (houses, apartments, and condos), plus the opportunity to live like a native and to cut down dramatically on accommodation costs—usually only an administration fee is paid to the matching service. Once you join or contact an exchange services (some are listed below), it is up to you to decide with whom you want to exchange homes. Most companies have pictures of homes and info about the owners. A great website listing many exchange companies can be found at www.aitec.edu.au/~bwechner/Documents/Travel/Lists/HomeExchangeClubs.html. Home rentals, as opposed to exchanges, are much more expensive, but can be cheaper than comparably serviced hotels. Both home exchanges and rentals are ideal for families with children and travelers with special dietary needs as you usually get a kitchen, TV, and telephone. Real estate agencies may be able to arrange rentals or leases, or you may want to rent a room instead of a whole house or apartment. Check the larger city papers for apartment listings, and don't forget that college campuses often post notices of availability for cheap rooms and apartments.

HomeExchange, P.O. Box 30085, Santa Barbara, CA 93130 (805-898-9660; email admin@HomeExchange.com; www.homeexchange.com).

The Invented City: International Home Exchange, 41 Sutter St. #1090, San Francisco, CA 94104 (in U.S. 800-788-2489, elsewhere 415-252-1141; email invented@aol.com; www.invented-city.com). For $75, your offer is listed in one catalog and you get unlimited access to a database with thousands of homes for exchange.

CAMPING AND THE OUTDOORS

With proper equipment, camping is an inexpensive and relatively safe way to experience California's national parks and other scenic areas. California presents a variety of camping alternatives; few areas in the world are as accessible to the traveler. For excellent topographical maps of the U.S. ($4), write the **U.S. Geological Survey,** Branch of Information Services, P.O. Box 25286, Denver Federal Center, Denver, CO 80225 (800-435-7627; fax 303-202-4693; http://mapping.usgs.gov/mac/findmaps.html). All maps are less than $15. If you're planning a park-oriented vacation, be sure to visit **Yosemite National Park,** one of the nation's most famous and most beautiful parks, located in the Sierra Nevada mountain range (for more information on **Yosemite,** see p. 262.).

USEFUL PUBLICATIONS AND WEB RESOURCES

A variety of publishing companies offer hiking guidebooks to meet the educational needs of novices or experts. For info about camping, hiking, and biking, the publishers listed will send free catalogs of their books.

Sierra Club Books, 85 2nd St., 2nd fl., San Francisco, CA 94105-3441 (800-935-1056 or 415-977-5500; www.sierraclub.org/books). Their publications include: *Adventuring in the California Desert,* by Lynne Foster ($16).

The Mountaineers Books, 1001 SW Klickitat Way #201, Seattle, WA 98134 (800-553-4453 or 206-223-6303; email alans@mountaineers.org; www.mountaineers.org). Over 400 titles including: *100 Hikes in California's Central and Sierra Coast Range* by Vicky Spring ($17); and *100 Hikes in Northern California,* by John Soares ($15).

Wilderness Press, 2440 Bancroft Way, Berkeley, CA 94704 (800-443-7227, 253-891-2500, or 510-558-1666; email mail@wildernesspress.com; www.wildernesspress.com). Sells *101 Hikes in Southern California,* by Jerry Schad ($16).

Woodall Publications Corporation, 13975 W. Polo Trail Dr., Lake Forest, IL 60045-5000 (888-226-7328 or 847-362-6700; email emd@woodallpub.com; www.woodalls.com). Covering the U.S., they publish the annually updated *Woodall's Campground Directory* ($22) and *Woodall's Plan-it, Pack-it, Go!: Great Places to Tent, Fun Things To Do* ($13).

United States Park Service, www.nps.gov/refdesk/Refdesk.htm, is an excellent source of information, appropriately, for national parks and other lands the department manages.

CAMPING AND HIKING EQUIPMENT

Good camping equipment is both sturdy and light. Camping equipment is generally more expensive in Australia, New Zealand, and the U.K. than in North America.

Sleeping Bags: Good sleeping bags are rated by the lowest temperature at which they keep you warm ("summer" means 30-40°F at night and "4-season" or "winter" often means below 0°F). Sleeping bags are made either of down (warmer, lighter, and more expensive; miserable when wet) or synthetic material (heavier, more durable, cheaper, and warmer when wet). Prices range from $80-210 for a summer synthetic to $250-500 for a good down winter bag. **Sleeping pads,** including foam pads ($10-20) and air mattresses ($15-50) cushion back and neck and provide insulation from the ground. Bring a **"stuff sack"** lined with a plastic bag to store your sleeping bag and keep it dry.

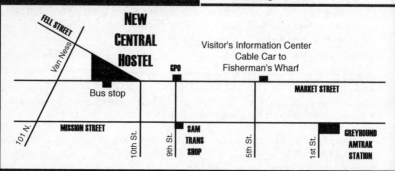

Tents: The best tents are free-standing, with their own frames and suspension systems; they set up quickly and only require staking in high winds. Low-profile dome tents are the best all-around. When pitched their internal space is almost entirely usable. Tent sizes are misleading: 2 people *can* fit in a 2-person tent, but will find life more pleasant in a 4-person. If traveling by car, buy a bigger tent, but if hiking, get a smaller tent that weighs no more than 5-6 lbs. (2-3kg). Good 2-person tents start at $120, 4-person tents at $300. Waterproof your tent's seams and make sure it has a rain fly. Tent accessories include a **battery-operated lantern,** a **plastic groundcloth,** and a **nylon tarp.**

Backpacks: If you intend to do a lot of hiking, you should have a frame backpack. **Internal-frame packs** mold better to your back, keep a lower center of gravity, and can flex adequately to allow you to hike difficult trails that require a lot of bending and maneuvering. Internal packs are also easier to carry on planes, trains, and buses if your travelling life includes various modes of transport. **External-frame packs** are more comfortable for long hikes over even terrain since they keep the weight higher and distribute it more evenly. Whichever you choose, make sure your pack has a strong, padded hip belt, which transfers the weight from the back to the legs. Serious backpacking requires a pack of at least 4000 cubic in. (16,000cc). Allow an additional 500 cubic in. for your sleeping bag in internal-frame packs. Sturdy backpacks cost $125-420. It doesn't pay to economize—cheaper packs can be less comfortable, and straps are more likely to fray or rip. Before buying a pack, insist on filling it with something heavy and walking around the store to get a sense of how it distributes weight. A **waterproof backpack cover** or plastic garbage bag will prove invaluable. For better protection, store all of your belongings in plastic bags inside your backpack.

Boots: Be sure to wear hiking boots with good **ankle support** appropriate to the terrain you plan to hike. **Gore-Tex** fabric or **part-leather** boots are appropriate for day hikes or 2-3 day overnights over moderate terrain, but for longer trips or trips in mountainous terrain, stiff **leather** boots are highly preferable. Boots should fit snugly and comfortably over one or two wool socks and a thin liner sock. Breaking in boots properly before setting out requires wearing them for several weeks; doing so will spare you from blisters. Treat boots with waterproofing treatment before wearing them.

Other Necessities: Raingear in two pieces, a top and pants, is far superior to a poncho. **Gore-Tex** is the best material for aerobic activity; **rubber** raingear will keep you completely dry but will get clammy if you sweat. Wear warm layers: **synthetics,** like polypropylene tops, socks, and long underwear, along with a pile jacket, are preferable to cotton or because they dry quickly and keep you warm even when wet. **Wool** stays warm when wet, but is much heavier than synthetics. When camping in autumn, winter, or spring, bring along a **"space blanket,"** which retains your body heat and doubles as a groundcloth ($5-15). Plastic **canteens** and water bottles keep water cooler than metal ones, and are virtually shatter- and leak-proof. Large, collapsible **water sacks** significantly improve your situation in primitive campgrounds and weigh practically nothing when empty. Bring **water-purification tablets** for when you can't boil water. Although most campgrounds provide campfire sites, you may want to bring a small **metal grate** or **grill** of your own. In places that forbid fires or the gathering of firewood, use a **camp stove,** such as the propane-powered Coleman stove (from $40) or a **Whisperlite** stove ($60-100), which runs on cleaner-burning white gas; to operate stoves bring waterproof matches or a lighter, and purchase and fill a **fuel bottle.** A **first-aid kit** (see p. 39), **insect repellent,** and **calamine lotion** are other essential camping items.

Mail-order/online companies may have lower prices than retail stores, but going to a camping store helps by giving you a good sense of items' look and weight. Many outdoor stores have message boards where used equipment can be found.

Campmor, Box 700, Upper Saddle River, NJ 07458-0700 (in U.S. 888-226-7667, elsewhere 201-825-8300; email customer-service@campmor.com; www.campmor.com).

Discount Camping, 880 Main North Rd., Pooraka, South Australia 5095, Australia (tel. (08) 8262 3399; www.discountcamping.com.au).

Eastern Mountain Sports (EMS), 327 Jaffrey Rd., Peterborough, NH 03458 (888-463-6367 or 603-924-7231; email emsmail@emsonline.com; www.emsonline.com). Call to find the branch nearest you.

L.L. Bean, Freeport, ME 04033-0001 (U.S./Canada 800-441-5713; U.K. tel. (0800) 962 954; elsewhere 207-552-6878; www.llbean.com). If your purchase doesn't meet your expectations, they'll replace or refund it. Open 24hr., 365 days a year.

Mountain Designs, P.O. Box 1472, Fortitude Valley, Queensland 4006, Australia (tel. (07) 3252 8894; www.mountaindesign.com.au).

Recreational Equipment, Inc. (REI), Sumner, WA 98352 (800-426-4840 or 253-891-2500; www.rei.com).

YHA Adventure Shop, 14 Southampton St., London, WC2E 7HA, U.K. (tel. (01718) 36 85 41). The main branch of one of Britain's largest outdoor equipment suppliers.

WILDERNESS SAFETY

Stay warm, stay dry, and stay hydrated. The vast majority of life-threatening wilderness situations result from a breach of this simple dictum. On any hike, however brief, you should pack enough equipment to keep you alive should a disaster occur. This includes **raingear, hat** and **mittens, first-aid kit** (see p. 39), **reflector, whistle, high-energy food,** and extra **water.** Wear warm layers of **wool** or **synthetic materials** designed for the outdoors Pile fleece jackets and Gore-Tex raingear are excellent choices. **Cotton** will actually reduce your body temperature if it gets wet. All equipment should be checked for any defects before setting out; see **Camping and Hiking Equipment,** above, for more information.

Weather forecasts can aid in planning hikes; when hiking pay attention to the skies as weather patterns can change suddenly. Whenever possible, let someone know when and where you are going hiking—either a friend, your hostel, a park ranger, or a local hiking organization. Do not attempt a hike beyond your ability—you may be endangering your life. See **Environmental Hazards** (p. 40) for information about outdoor ailments such as heatstroke, hypothermia, giardia, rabies, and insects, and **Health** (p. 39) for info on basic medical concerns and first aid. For further reading, see: *How to Stay Alive in the Woods*, by Bradford Angier, (Macmillan $8); *Everyday Wisdom: 1001 Expert Tips for Hikers*, by Karen Berger. (Mountaineer $17); and *Making Camp*, by Steve Howe et al. (Mountaineer $17).

BEARS WILL EAT YOU. When hiking in areas which may be frequented by bears, ask rangers for info on bear behavior before entering any park or wilderness area, and obey posted warnings. No matter how cute a bear appears, don't be fooled—they are powerful and unpredictable animals who are not intimidated by humans. If you're close enough for a bear to be observing you, you're too close.

Don't leave food or other scented items (trash, toiletries, the clothes that you cooked in) near your tent. **Bear-bagging** (hanging edibles, trash, toiletries, sunscreen, used tampons, and other smelly objects from a tree out of reach of hungry paws) is one way to keep your toothpaste from becoming a condiment. Putting these objects into **canisters** is now mandatory in some national parks in California. Make sure you know the law before camping in national parks. Bears are also attracted to **perfume,** as are bugs, so cologne, scented soap, deodorant, and hairspray should stay at home.

If you see a bear at a distance, calmly walk (don't run) in the other direction. If it seems interested, back away slowly while speaking to the bear in firm, low tones and head in the opposite direction or toward a settled area. If you stumble upon a sweet-looking bear cub, leave immediately lest its over-protective mother stumble upon you. If you are attacked by a bear, get in a fetal position to protect yourself, put your arms over the back of your neck, and play dead. In all situations, remain calm, as loud noises and sudden movements can trigger an attack.

CAMPERS AND RVS

California can be a haven for the corpulent, home-and-stove on wheels known as **"recreational vehicles"** or **RVs.** Most national parks and small towns cater to RV travelers, providing campgrounds with parking areas and electric outlets ("full hookup"). Especially for older travelers or families, RVs are a convenient way to view the state without sacrificing independence, mobility, and creature comforts. Renting an RV is more expensive than tenting or hosteling, but the costs compare favorably with the price of staying in hotels and renting a car. **El Monte Rents** (818-443-6158), 12061 E. Valley Blvd., Los Angeles 91732; and **Western RV Rentals** (415-532-7404), 4901 Coliseum Way, Oakland 94601, cater to big-rig renters.

ORGANIZED ADVENTURE TRIPS

Organized adventure tours offer another way of exploring the wild. Activities include hiking, biking, skiing, canoeing, kayaking, rafting, climbing, photo safaris, and archaeological digs. Consult tourism bureaus, which can suggest parks, trails, and outfitters. Or, try the stores and organizations specializing in camping and outdoor equipment listed above. Employees at REI, EMS, or Sierra often know many cheap, convenient trips and sometimes offer training programs for independent trips. The **Specialty Travel Index,** 305 San Anselmo Ave. #313, San Anselmo, CA 94960 (888-624-4030 or 415-455-1643; email spectrav@ix.netcom.com; www.specialtytravel.com) lists hundreds of tour operators worldwide. The **Sierra Club** (email national.outings@sierraclub.org; www.sierraclub.org/outings) plans adventure outings at branches throughout California. **TrekAmerica,** P.O. Box 189, Rockaway, NJ 07866 (in U.S. and Canada 800-221-0596; elsewhere 973-983-1144; email info@trekamerica.com; www.trekamerica.com) operates some small-group adventure tours that cover parts of California for 18- to 38-year-olds. **Footloose** (www.footloose.com) is their open-age adult program. **Roadrunner Hostelling Treks,** 9741 Canoga Ave., Chatsworth, CA 91311 (818-721-6080 or 800-873-5872, in Europe tel. 44 1892 51 27 00; www.americanadventures.com) offers inexpensive guided trips (max. 13 travelers) including their popular "California Cooler."

KEEPING IN TOUCH

MAIL

SENDING AND RECEIVING MAIL

Sending **airmail** letters under one oz. from California (or anywhere in the U.S.) to the rest of the world costs $1 and takes seven days to cross the Atlantic and 10 days to cross the Pacific. Envelopes should be marked "Air Mail" or "Par Avion" to avoid having letters sent by sea. Sending mail within the U.S. costs 33¢ for up to one oz., and 22¢ for each additional oz.

Aerogrammes, printed sheets that fold into envelopes and travel via airmail, are available at post offices. Most post offices charge exorbitant fees or refuse to send aerogrammes with enclosures. Airmail from California averages four to seven days, although times are more unpredictable from smaller towns.

If regular airmail is too slow, **Federal Express** (U.S. tel. for international operator 800-247-4747) can get a letter overseas in two to three days to most destinations for steep charges. By **U.S. Express Mail,** letters from California arrive overseas within four to six days and cost $15.

General Delivery: Mail can be sent to the U.S. through **General Delivery** to almost any city or town with a post office. General Delivery mail goes to a special desk at a town or city's post office. As a rule, it is best to use the largest post office in the area, since mail may be sent there regardless of what is written on the envelope. When picking up mail, bring a photo ID, preferably a passport. There is generally no surcharge; if there is, it generally does not exceed the cost of domestic postage. If the clerks insist there is nothing for you, have them check under your first name as well. *Let's Go* lists post offices in the **Practical Information** section for each city and most towns. Address General Delivery letters in this format:

Mr. Alexander PAYNE

General Delivery

Post Office

Street Address

Eureka, CA 95501

USA

American Express: AmEx's travel offices throughout the world will act as a mail service for cardholders if contacted in advance. Under this free **Client Letter Service,** they hold mail for up to 30 days and forward upon request. Address letters in the way shown above. Some offices offer these services to non-cardholders (especially those who have purchased AmEx Travelers Cheques), but you must call ahead to make sure. A complete list is available free from AmEx (800-528-4800).

TELEPHONES

CALLING CALIFORNIA FROM HOME

To call direct to California from home, dial:

1. The international access code of your home country. **International access codes** include: Australia 0011; Ireland 00; New Zealand 00; South Africa 09; U.K. 00. Country and city codes are sometimes listed with a zero in front (e.g., 033) but after dialing the international access code, drop successive zeros (with an access code of 011, e.g., 011 33).
2. 1 (U.S.'s country code).
3. The area code and local number.

CALIFORNIA REGIONAL AREA CODES:

Los Angeles: 323, 213, 310, 424, 626, 818, 909 (see **Los Angeles: Practical Information,** p. 359)
Orange County: 714, 949, 310
San Francisco: 415
San Mateo: 650
East S.F. Bay: 510
San Jose: 408
Santa Cruz and Monterey: 831
Palo Alto: 650
Pasadena: 818
Santa Barbara: 805
San Bernardino and Riverside area: 909
San Diego: 619 and 858 (see **San Diego: Practical Information,** p. 441)
Wine Country and North Coast: 707
Sacramento and northeastern California: 916
Palm Springs and Death Valley: 760

CALLING HOME FROM CALIFORNIA

A **calling card** is probably your best and cheapest bet since long-distance rates for national phone services can be exorbitant; especially be careful of making long-distance calls from hotel or motel room phones, which often charge exorbitant access fees. Calling card calls are billed either collect or to your account. **MCI WorldPhone** also provides access to MCI's Traveler's Assist, which gives legal and medical advice, exchange rate information, and translation services. Other phone companies provide similar services to travelers. **To obtain a calling card** from your national telecommunications service before leaving home, contact the appropriate company below:

Australia, Telstra **Australia Direct** (tel. 13 22 00); **Canada,** Bell Canada **Canada Direct** (800-565-4708); **Ireland,** Telecom Éireann **Ireland Direct** (tel. (800) 250 250); **New Zealand: Telecom New Zealand** (tel. 0800 000 000); **South Africa: Telkom South Africa,** (tel. 09 03); **U.K.,** British Telecom **BT Direct** (tel. (0800) 34 51 44); **USA, AT&T** (888-288-4685), **Sprint** (800-877-4646), or **MCI** (800-444-4141; from abroad dial the country's MCI access number).

To call home with a calling card, contact a North American operator for your service provider by dialing **Australia Direct: AT&T** 800-682-2878, **MCI** 800-937-6822, **Sprint** 800-676-0061; **BT Direct: AT&T** 800-445-5667, **MCI** 800-444-2162, **Sprint** 800-800-0008; **Telkom South Africa Direct:** 800-949-7027.

If you do dial direct, first insert the appropriate amount of money or a prepaid card, then dial 011 (the international access code for the U.S.), and then dial the country code and number of the phone number in your home country. **Country codes** include: Australia 61; Ireland 353; New Zealand 64; South Africa 27; U.K. 44. The expensive alternative to dialing direct or using a calling card is using an international operator to place a **collect call.**

CALLING WITHIN THE U.S.

The simplest way to call within the country is to use a coin-operated phone; local calls in California cost 25-35¢ and require coins. You can also buy **prepaid phone cards,** which carry phone time depending on the card's denomination and are available at most convenience stores and gas stations. The card usually has a toll-free access phone number and a personal identification number (PIN). Phone rates tend to be highest during the day, lower in the evening, and lowest on Sunday and late at night. Be warned: hotels tend to charge exorbitant long distance rates and 50¢-$1 for local calls.

INTERNET AND EMAIL

California has copious Internet cafes and other spots to access cyberspace. When possible, *Let's Go* lists one in **Practical Information** sections. **Cybercafe Guide** (www.cyberiacafe.net/cyberia/guide/ccafe.htm) can help locate cybercafes. Free, web-based email providers include Hotmail (www.hotmail.com), RocketMail (www.rocketmail.com), and Yahoo! Mail (www.yahoo.com). Those traveling with laptops can use a **modem** to call an Internet service provider. Long-distance phone cards specifically intended for such calls can defray normally high phone charges. Check with your long-distance phone provider to see if they offer this option.

GETTING THERE

BY PLANE

A little effort can save a bundle on airfare. With very flexible plans, courier fares may be the cheapest (but are the most restrictive way to travel). Tickets bought from consolidators and standby seating are good deals, but last-minute specials and airfare wars can beat these fares. Hunt around, be flexible, and ask about discounts. Students, seniors, and those under 26 should not pay full price for tickets. Fares between L.A. and San Francisco generally range from $85 to $200 round-trip.

DETAILS AND TIPS

Timing: Airfares to California tend to remain fairly steady throughout the year except over holidays, when it is more costly and more difficult to travel. Midweek (M-Th morning) round-trip flights run $40-50 cheaper than weekend flights, but the latter are generally less crowded and tend to permit frequent-flier upgrades. Traveling with an "open return" ticket can cost more than fixing a return date at purchase and paying later to change it.

Route: Round-trip flights are by far the cheapest; "open-jaw" (arriving in and departing from different cities) and round-the-world, or RTW, flights are pricier but reasonable alternatives. Patching one-way flights together is the least economical way to travel. Flights into the regional hubs of Los Angeles, San Diego, San Francisco, and San Jose should offer the most competitive fares.

Boarding: When flying internationally, pick up tickets for international flights well in advance of the departure date, and confirm by phone within 72 hours of departure. Most airlines require passengers to arrive at the airport at least 2 hours before departure. One carry-on item and 2 pieces of checked baggage is the norm for non-courier flights. Consult the airline for weight allowances.

BUDGET AND STUDENT TRAVEL AGENCIES

A knowledgeable agent specializing in flights to California can make your life easy and help you save, too, but agents may not spend the time to find you the lowest possible fare since they get paid on commission. Students and those under 26 with **ISIC** or **IYTC cards** (see **Identification,** p. 27), respectively, qualify for discounts from student travel agencies. Most flights from budget agencies are on major airlines, but in peak season some may sell seats on less-reliable chartered aircraft.

Campus/Usit Youth and Student Travel, 52 Grosvenor Gardens, London SW1W 0AG (in U.K. call tel. (0870) 240 1010, in North America tel. 44 171 730 21 01, worldwide tel. 44 171 730 81 11; www.usitcampus.co.uk). Other offices include: 19-21 Aston Quay, O'Connell Bridge, Dublin 2 (tel. (01) 677-8117); New York Student Ctr., 895 Amsterdam Ave., New York, NY, 10025 (212-663-5435; email usitny@aol.com). Additional offices in Cork, Galway, Limerick, Waterford, Coleraine, Derry, Belfast, and Greece.

Council Travel (www.counciltravel.com). U.S. offices include: Emory Village, 1561 N. Decatur Rd., Atlanta, GA 30307 (404-377-9997); 273 Newbury St., Boston, MA 02116 (617-266-1926); 1160 N. State St., Chicago, IL 60610 (312-951-0585); 10904 Lindbrook Dr., Los Angeles, CA 90024 (310-208-3551); 205 E. 42nd St., New York, NY 10017 (212-822-2700); 530 Bush St., San Francisco, CA 94108 (415-421-3473); 1314 NE 43rd St. #210, Seattle, WA 98105 (206-632-2448); 3300 M St. NW, Washington, D.C. 20007 (202-337-6464). For U.S. cities not listed, call 800-2-COUNCIL/226-8624. Also 28A Poland St. (Oxford Circus), London, W1V 3DB (tel. (0171) 287 3337), Paris (tel. 01 44 41 89 89), and Munich (tel. (089) 39 50 22).

CTS Travel, 44 Goodge St., W1 (tel. (0171) 636 00 31; email ctsinfo@ctstravel.com.uk).

STA Travel, 6560 Scottsdale Rd. #F100, Scottsdale, AZ 85253 (800-777-0112; www.sta-travel.com). Student and youth travel organization with over 150 offices worldwide. Ticket booking, travel insurance, railpasses, and more. U.S. offices include: 297 Newbury St., **Boston,** MA 02115 (617-266-6014); 429 S. Dearborn St., **Chicago,** IL 60605 (312-786-9050); 7202 Melrose Ave., **Los Angeles,** CA 90046 (323-934-8722); 10 Downing St., **New York,** NY 10014 (212-627-3111); 4341 University Way NE, **Seattle,** WA 98105 (206-633-5000); 2401 Pennsylvania Ave., Suite G, **Washington, D.C.** 20037 (202-887-0912); 51 Grant Ave., **San Francisco,** CA 94108 (415-391-8407). In the **U.K.,** 6 Wrights Ln., **London** W8 6TA (tel. (0171) 938 47 11 for North American travel). In New Zealand, 10 High St., **Auckland** (tel. (09) 309 04 58). In Australia, 222 Faraday St., **Melbourne** VIC 3053 (tel. (03) 9349 2411).

Travel CUTS (Canadian Universities Travel Services Limited), 187 College St., Toronto, ON. M5T 1P7 (416-979-2406; www.travelcuts.com). 40 offices across Canada. Also in the U.K., 295-A Regent St., **London** W1R 7YA (tel. (0171) 255 19 44).

Another organization that specializing in finding cheap fares is **Travel Avenue** (800-333-3335), which rebates commercial fares to or from the U.S. and offers low fares for flights anywhere in the world. They also offer package deals, which include car rental and hotel reservations, to many destinations.

COMMERCIAL AIRLINES

The commercial airlines' lowest regular offer is the **APEX** (Advance Purchase Excursion) fare, which provides confirmed reservations and allows "open-jaw" tickets. Generally, reservations must be made 7 to 21 days in advance, with 7- to 14-day minimum and up to 90-day maximum-stay limits, and hefty cancellation and change penalties. Book peak-season APEX fares early, since by May you will have a hard time getting the departure date you want.

Although APEX fares are probably not the cheapest possible fares, they will give you a sense of the average commercial price, from which to measure other bargains. Many airlines offer **"e-fares,"** special, last-minute fares available over the Internet; check airline webpages for details. Specials advertised in newspapers may be cheaper but have more restrictions and fewer available seats. Popular carriers to the United States include:

Air Tran (800-AIRTRAN/247-8726; www.airtran.com).

America West (800-235-9292; www.americawest.com). Services mainly Western US.

American (800-433-7300; www.americanair.com). Offers "College SAAvers" fares for full-time college students.

Continental (800-525-0280; www.flycontinental.com). Great deals for senior citizens in the "Freedom Club" (800-441-1135).

Delta (800-2414141; www.delta-air.com)

Southwest (800-225-2525; www.iflyswa.com).

TWA (800-221-2000; www.twa.com). Has last-minute "TransWorld specials" over email.

United (800-241-6522; www.ual.com). Major airline with good frequent flyer plan.

USAir (800-428-4322; www.usair.com).

OTHER CHEAP ALTERNATIVES

AIR COURIER FLIGHTS. Couriers help transport cargo on international flights by guaranteeing delivery of baggage claim slips from the company to a representative overseas. Generally, couriers must travel light (carry-ons only) and deal with complex restrictions on their flights. Most flights are round-trip only with short fixed-length stays (usually one week) and a limit of a single ticket per issue. Most of these flights also operate only out of the biggest cities, like New York. Generally, you must be over 21 (in some cases 18), have a valid passport, and procure your own visa, if necessary. Groups such as the **Air Courier Association** (800-282-1202; www.aircourier.org) and the **International Association of Air Travel Couriers,** 220 S. Dixie Hwy., P.O. Box 1349, Lake Worth, FL 33460 (561-582-8320; email iaatc@courier.org; www.courier.org) provide members with lists of opportunities and courier brokers worldwide for an annual fee. For more information, consult *Air Courier Bargains* by Kelly Monaghan (The Intrepid Traveler, $15) or the *Courier Air Travel Handbook* by Mark Field (Perpetual Press, $10).

STANDBY FLIGHTS. To travel standby, you will need considerable flexibility in the dates and cities of your arrival and departure. Companies that specialize in standby flights do not sell tickets but rather the promise that you will get to your destination (or near your destination) within a certain window of time (usually 1-5 days). Refund policies are different for standby flights so review the policy carefully before purchase.

To check on a company's service record, call the Better Business Bureau of New York City (212-533-6200). It is difficult to receive refunds, and clients' vouchers will not be honored when an airline fails to receive payment in time.

Airhitch, 2641 Broadway, 3rd fl., New York, NY 10025 (800-326-2009 or 212-864-2000; www.airhitch.org) and Los Angeles, CA (310-726-5000). Primarily offers flights to and from Europe, but also has travel rates within the U.S. ranging from $79-$139.

GETTING AROUND

BY TRAIN

Although it is still possible to travel by train within California, it is almost always more expensive and more time-consuming than its bus travel counterpart, and airline tickets can sometimes even be more economical than train fare. *However, if you are planning to travel by train, remember that, as with airlines, you can save money by purchasing your tickets as far in advance as possible; plan ahead and make reservations early.* It is essential to travel light on trains since not all stations will check your baggage.

Amtrak (800-USA-RAIL/872-7245; www.amtrak.com) is the only provider of intercity passenger train service in California. Most cities have Amtrak offices which directly sell tickets, but tickets must be bought through an agent in some small towns. The informative website lists up-to-date schedules, fares, arrival and departure info, and makes reservations. **Discounts** on full rail fares are given to seniors (15% off), students with a Student Advantage card (15% off; call 800-962-6872 to purchase the $20 card), travelers with disabilities (15% off), children 2-15 with a paying adult (50% off), children under 2 (free), and current members of the U.S. Armed Forces, active-duty veterans, and their dependents (25% off). "Rail SALE" offers online discounts of up to 90%; visit the website for details and reservations and for info about **special packages.** Sample fares are listed in the **Practical Information** sections of most California cities.

BY BUS

Buses offer the most frequent and complete service between cities and towns in California. Often a bus is the only way to reach smaller locales without a car. Sample fares are listed in **Practical Information.**

GREYHOUND

Greyhound (800-231-2222; www.greyhound.com) is the only bus service that operates throughout the entire state of California. However, some local bus companies provide services within specific regions. Reserve with a credit card over the phone at least 10 days in advance, and the ticket can be mailed anywhere in the U.S. Otherwise, reservations are available only up to 24hr. in advance or at the bus terminal; arrive early to purchase tickets on the day of travel.

If **boarding at a remote "flag stop,"** be sure you know exactly where the bus stops. You must call the nearest agency and let them know you'll be waiting and at what time. Catch the driver's attention by standing on the side of the road and flailing your arms wildly—better to be embarrassed than stranded. If a bus passes (usually because of overcrowding), a later, less-crowded bus should stop. Whatever you stow in compartments underneath the bus should be clearly marked; be sure to get a claim check for it and watch to make sure your luggage is on the same bus as you. See the **Practical Information** sections for sample fares between major cities and towns in California.

Advance purchase fares: Reserving space far ahead of time ensures a lower fare, although expect a smaller discount in summer (June 5-Sept. 15). Fares are often reduced for 14-day or 21-day advance purchases on many popular routes; call or visit the website for up-to-date pricing.

Discounts on full fares: Seniors (10% off); ages 2-11 (50% off); disabled travelers and a companion ride together for the price of 1; active and retired U.S. military personnel and National Guard Reserves (10% off with valid ID).

Ameripass: Call 888-454-7277. Unlimited travel for 7 days ($199), 15 days ($299), 30 days ($409), or 60 days ($549). Prices for students with a valid college ID and seniors are slightly less: 7 days ($189), 15 days ($279), 30 days ($379), or 60 days ($509). Children's passes are half-price.

International Ameripass: For travelers from outside North America. Call 888-454-7277 for info. 7-day ($179), 15-day ($269), 30-day ($369), 60-day ($499). International Ameripasses are not available at the terminal; they can be purchased in foreign countries at Greyhound-affiliated agencies; telephone numbers vary by country and are listed on the website. Passes can also be ordered at the website, or purchased by calling 800-246-8572 or emailing intlameripass@greyhound.com. **Australia** tel. (049) 342 088; **New Zealand** tel. (064) 9 479 65555; **South Africa** tel. (027) 11 331 2911; **U.K.** tel. (044) 01342 317 317.

GREEN TORTOISE

Green Tortoise, 494 Broadway, San Francisco, CA 94133 (415-956-7500 or 800-867-8647; email tortoise@greentortoise.com; www.greentortoise.com), offers a more slow-paced, whimsical alternative to straightforward transportation. Green Tortoise's communal "hostels on wheels"—remodeled diesel buses done up for living and eating on the road—offers aptly named Adventure Tours, including California routes. All tours depart from and return to San Francisco; travelers are responsible for getting to San Francisco themselves. Prices include transportation to the destination from San Francisco, sleeping space on the bus, and tours of the regions through which you pass, often including such treats as hot springs and farm stays. Meals are prepared communally, prices listed include the cost of food. Green Tortoise offers trips around Northern California (6 days, $270), Yosemite National Park (3 days May-Sept., $150; 2 days Feb.-Sept., $100), Death Valley National Park (3 days, $160), and the Grand Canyon (9 days, $420). Prepare for an earthy trip; buses have no toilets and little privacy. Reserve one to two months in advance, deposits ($100) are generally required; however, many trips have space available at departure. Reservations can be made over the phone or on the web.

ADVENTURE NETWORK FOR TRAVELERS (ANT)

Adventure Network for Travelers, 870 Market St. #416, San Francisco, CA 94102 (800-336-6049 or 415-399-0880; email anttrips@theant.com; www.theant.com), is a flexible hop-on, hop-off backpacker transportation and adventure network operating between popular cities, towns, and national parks in California and the southwestern U.S. Transportation is in 15-seat mini-vans driven by knowledgeable guides, providing fun and like-minded company. Travel passes ($89-$279, depending on which destinations are included) are valid for up to six months.

BY CAR

HOW TO NAVIGATE THE INTERSTATES

A number of major interstates and highways criss-cross California. Travelers moving north-south have the choice of three major routes. If you're looking for speed, hop on **Interstate 5,** which runs north-south from the Mexican border through San Diego, Los Angeles, the San Joaquin Valley, and Sacramento on its way to Oregon. I-5 is direct and the fastest route from L.A. to San Francisco (8 hr.), but it's also deadly boring, affording at best a view of agricultural flatlands and odiferous cow pastures. **U.S. 101** winds north-south from Los Angeles, closer to the coast than I-5, through Santa Barbara, San Luis Obispo, San Francisco, Santa Rosa, and Eureka. It's slower than I-5, but a considerably more scenic and pleasant drive. The third option is **Route 1,** the Pacific Coast Highway, which follows the California coast (9½ hr.). Rte. 1 is very slow and often traffic-congested, but the scenery is some of the most spectacular in the world, particularly on the breathtaking, cliff-hanging turns of Jack Kerouac's Big Sur.

In the 1950s, President Eisenhower envisioned the current **interstate system,** an easily comprehensible system for numbering interstates. Even-numbered interstates run east-west and odd ones run north-south, decreasing in number toward the south and the west. Three-digit numbers signify branches of other interstates (e.g., I-280 is a branch of I-80), which may be bypasses skirting large cities.

DRIVING PERMITS AND CAR INSURANCE

Visitors to California who are over 18 can drive with a valid license from their home state or country; however, some visitors may choose to get an international driver's permit from their home automobile associations. Those under 18, after 10 days in the state, must apply for a Nonresident Minor's Certificate from the state Department of Motor Vehicles (offices in most cities and towns; www.dmv.ca.gov).

Most credit cards cover standard insurance. If you rent, lease, or borrow a car, you will need a green card, or **International Insurance Certificate,** to prove that you have liability insurance. Obtain it through the car rental agency; most include coverage in their prices. If you lease a car, you can obtain a green card from the dealer; some travel agents also offer the card. Verify whether your auto insurance applies outside of your home country; even if it does, you will still need a green card to certify this to officials. If you have a collision outside of your home country, the accident will show up on your records if you report it to your insurance company.

AUTOMOBILE CLUBS

American Automobile Association (AAA), (for emergency road service 800-AAA-HELP/222-4357; to sign up 800-JOIN-AAA/564-6222; www.aaa.com). Free trip-planning services, maps, and guidebooks, and 24hr. emergency road service anywhere in the U.S., free towing, and commission-free American Express Traveler's Cheques from over 1000 offices across the country. Discounts on Hertz car rental (5-20%), Amtrak tickets (10%), and various motel chains and theme parks. AAA has reciprocal agreements with the auto associations of many other countries, which often provide you with full benefits while in the U.S. Check with your auto association for details. Membership costs vary depending on which AAA branch you join, but hovers around $50-60 for the 1st year and less for renewals and additional family members.

ON THE ROAD

Tune up the car before you leave, make sure the tires are in good repair and have enough air, and get good maps. **Rand McNally's Road Atlas,** covering all of the U.S. and Canada, is one of the best (available at bookstores and gas stations, $10; California state map $4). If staying in southern California for an extended period of time, it may be worth it to invest in a Thomas Guide ($30) for the county or counties in which you are staying. A **compass** and a **car manual** can also be very useful. Always carry a **spare tire** and **jack, jumper cables, extra oil, flares,** a **flashlight,** and **blankets** (in case you break down at night or in winter). Those traveling long undeveloped stretches of road may want to consider renting a **cell phone** in case of a breakdown. If traveling in the desert, refer to **Desert Survival** (p. 460) for essential desert driving tips. Also, the California Department of Transportation has a road conditions hotline at 800-427-ROAD/7623.

Sleeping in a car or van parked in the city is both illegal and extremely dangerous—even the most dedicated budget traveler should not consider it an option. While driving, **be sure to buckle up**—seat belts are required by law in California. The **speed limit** in California varies depending on the road on which you are traveling (some freeways have speed limits as high as 70mph, while residential areas are frequently 20mph). Heed speed limit signs at all times; not only does it save gas, but most local police forces and state troopers make frequent use of radar to catch speed demons, and fines range from $100-150. **Gas** in California costs around $1.25 per gallon, but prices vary widely depending on what area the gas station you go to is in, and which grade of gasoline you purchase.

Drivers should take necessary precautions against **carjacking,** which has become one of the most frequent crimes committed in the state. Carjackers, who are usually armed, approach victims in their vehicles and force them to turn over the cars. Carjackers prey on cars parked on the side of the road and cars stopped at red lights. Keep your doors locked at all times while driving, and if you pull over on the side of the road, keep the windows up at all times. Do not pull over to help a car in the breakdown lane; call the police instead.

RENTING

Car rental agencies fall into two categories: national companies with hundreds of branches, and local agencies that serve only one city or region. National chains usually allow cars to be picked up in one city and dropped off in another (for a hefty charge, sometimes in excess of $1000), and by calling a toll-free number you can reserve a reliable car anywhere in the country. Generally, airport branches carry the cheapest rates. However, like airfares, car rental prices change constantly and often require scouting around for the best rate. Drawbacks include steep prices (a compact car rents for $35-45 per day) and high minimum ages for rentals (usually 25). Most branches rent to ages 21-24 with an additional fee, but policies and prices vary from agency to agency. If you're 21 or older and have a major credit card in your name, you may be able to rent where the minimum age would otherwise rule you out. **Alamo** (800-327-9633; www.goalamo.com) rents to ages 21-24 with a major credit card for an additional $20 per day. **Enterprise** (800-RENT-A-CAR/736-8222) rents to customers aged 21-24 with a variable surcharge. Most **Dollar** (800-8-00-4000; http://dollarcar.com) branches allow it, and various **Thrifty** (800-367-2277; www.thrifty.com) locations allow ages 21-24 to rent for an additional daily fee of $20. **Rent-A-Wreck** (800-421-7253; email gene@raw.com; www.rent-a-wreck.com), specializes in supplying vehicles that are past their prime for lower-than-average prices; a bare-bones compact less than eight years old rents for around $20-25; cars three to five years old average under $30.

Most rental packages offer unlimited mileage, although some allow you a certain number of miles free before the charge of 25-40¢ per mile takes effect. Quoted rates do not include gas or tax, so ask for the total cost before handing over the credit card; many large firms have added airport surcharges not covered by the designated fare. Return the car with a full tank unless you sign up for a fuel option plan that stipulates otherwise. And when dealing with any car rental company, be sure to ask whether the price includes insurance against theft and collision. There may be an additional charge for a collision and damage waiver (CDW), which usually comes to about $12-15 per day. Some major credit cards (including MasterCard and American Express) will cover the CDW if you use their card to rent a car; call your credit card company for specifics.

A cheaper rental option for large groups is **The Green Machine,** P.O. Box 573, Acton, CA 93510 (805-269-0360, email gmachinetravel@hotmail.com; www.donbarnett.com/gmachine), which rents renovated school buses, equipped with camping gear, to groups with a driver 18 years or older. Starting at $350 per week, rental includes camping gear and unlimited mileage.

BUYING

Adventures on Wheels, 42 Rte. 36, Middletown, NJ 07748 (800-WHEELS-9/943-3579 or 732-583-8714; email info@wheels9.com; www.wheels9.com), sells travelers a motorhome, camper, minivan, station wagon, or compact car, organizes its registration and provides insurance, and guarantees they will buy it back after you have finished your travels. Cars with a buy-back guarantee start at $2500. Buy a camper for $6000-9000, use it for six months, and sell it back for $3000-5000. There are offices in Los Angeles and San Francisco. Vehicles can be picked up at one office and dropped off at another.

AUTO TRANSPORT COMPANIES

These services match drivers with car owners who need cars moved from one city to another. Would-be travelers give the company their desired destination and the company finds a car which needs to go there. The only expenses are gas, tolls, and your own living expenses. Some companies insure their cars; with others, your security deposit covers any breakdowns or damage. You must be at least 21, have a valid license, and agree to drive about 400 miles per day on a fairly direct route. Companies regularly inspect current and past job references, take your fingerprints, and require a cash bond. Cars are available between most points, although it's easiest to find cars for traveling from coast to coast; New York and Los Angeles are popular transfer points. If offered a car, look it over first. Think twice about accepting a gas guzzler, since you'll be paying for the gas. With the company's approval, you may be able to share the car with several companions.

Auto Driveaway Co., 310 S. Michigan Ave., Chicago, IL 60604 (800-346-2277 or 312-341-1900; email autodrv@aol.com; www.autodriveaway.com).

Across America Driveaway, 3626 Calumet Ave., Hammond, IN 46320 (800-619-7707 or 219-852-0134; email Schultz!@gte.net; www.schultz-international.com). Offices in L.A. (800-964-7874 or 310-798-3377).

BY BICYCLE

Safe and secure cycling requires a quality helmet and lock. A good helmet costs about $40—much cheaper than critical head surgery. U-shaped **Kryptonite** or **Citadel** locks ($30-60) carry insurance against theft for one or two years if your bike is registered with the police. **Bike Nashbar,** 4111 Simon Rd., Youngstown, OH 44512 (800-627-4227), will beat any nationally advertised in-stock price by 5¢, and ships anywhere in the U.S. or Canada. Their techline (330-788-6464; open M-F 8am-6pm) fields questions about repairs and maintenance. Check out books like: *Best Bike Rides in Northern California*, by Kim Grob (Globe Pequot; $13); and *Mountain Bike! Southern California: A Guide to Classic Trails*, by David Story (Menasha Ridge; $16). Contact the following organizations for more info on bike trips:

Adventure Cycling Association, P.O. Box 8308, Missoula, MT 59807 (800-755-2453 or 406-721-1776; email acabike@aol.com; www.adv-cycling.org). National, nonprofit organization researches and maps long-distance routes and organizes bike tours (75-day Great Divide Expedition $2800, 9-day trip $650). Annual membership $30 (includes access to maps and routes and a subscription to *Adventure Cyclist* magazine).

Backroads, 801 Cedar St., Berkeley, CA 94710-1800 (800-462-2848; email goactive@backroads.com; www.backroads.com), offers cushy tours around California. Travelers ride from accommodation to accommodation; prices include most meals, guide services, maps, directions, and van support (6-day trip with camping accommodation $848).

BY MOTORCYCLE

It may be cheaper than car travel, but it takes a tenacious soul to endure a motorcycle tour. The wind-in-your-face thrill, burly leather, and revving crackle of a motorcycle engine unobscured by windows or upholstery has built up quite a cult following, but motorcycling is the most dangerous of roadtop activities. Of course, **safety** should be your primary concern. Motorcycles are incredibly vulnerable to crosswinds, drunk drivers, and the blind spots of cars and trucks. *Always ride defensively*. Dangers skyrocket at night. **Helmets** are required by law in California; wear the best one you can find. Ask at a California Department of Motor Vehicles for a motorcycle operator's manual.

Those considering a long journey should contact the **American Motorcyclist Association,** 13515 Yarmouth Dr. Pickering, OH 43147 (800-262-5646 or 614-856-1900; email ama@ama-cycle.org; ama-cycle.org), the linchpin of U.S. biker culture. A full membership ($29 per year) includes a subscription to the extremely informative *American Motorcyclist* magazine, discounts on insurance, rentals, and hotels, and a kick-ass patch for your riding jacket. For an additional $25, members benefit from emergency roadside assistance, including pickup and delivery to a service shop.

BY THUMB

Let's Go urges you to consider the great risks and disadvantages of **hitchhiking** before thumbing it. Hitching means entrusting your life to a randomly selected person who happens to stop beside you on the road. While this may be comparatively safe in some areas of Europe and Australia, it is *not* so in California. We do not recommend it. We strongly urge you to find other means of transportation.

ADDITIONAL INFORMATION

SPECIFIC CONCERNS

WOMEN TRAVELERS

Women traveling on their own inevitably face some additional safety concerns, but it's easy to be adventurous without taking undue risks. California is relatively friendly to women travelers. Still, it's smart to be on your guard, and *Let's Go* has indicated which areas of Californian cities and towns are the least savory for lone women and men alike. Believe us when we say, "Don't walk around here after dark." If you are concerned, you might consider staying in hostels which offer single rooms that lock from the inside or in organizations that offer rooms for women only. Communal showers in some hostels are safer than others; check them before settling in. Stick to centrally located accommodations and avoid solitary late-night treks or rides on public transportation.

When traveling, always carry extra money for a phone call, bus, or taxi. Look as if you know where you're going (even when you don't) and consider approaching older women or couples for directions if you're lost or feel uncomfortable.

In cities, you may be harassed no matter how you're dressed. Your best answer to verbal harassment is no answer at all; sitting motionless and staring straight ahead at nothing in particular will do a world of good that reactions usually don't achieve. The extremely persistent can sometimes be dissuaded by a firm, loud, and very public "Go away!"

Don't hesitate to seek out a police officer or a passerby if you are being harassed. *Let's Go* lists emergency numbers (including rape crisis lines) in the **Practical Information** listings of most cities. Memorize the emergency numbers in the places you visit. Carry a **whistle** or an airhorn on your keychain, and don't hesitate to use it in an emergency. An **IMPACT Model Mugging** self-defense course will not only prepare you for a potential attack, but will also raise your level of awareness of your surroundings as well as your confidence (see **Self Defense,** p. 35). Women also face some specific health concerns when traveling (see **Women's Health,** p. 41).

For general information, contact the California branch of **National Organization for Women (NOW),** (email canow@canow.org; http://canow.org) which boasts branches across California that can refer women travelers to rape crisis centers and counseling services. California offices include 3543 18th St. #27, SF 94110 (415-861-8880; www.sfnow.org).

For **more books** by women travelers, see: *A Journey of One's Own: Uncommon Advice for the Independent Woman Traveler*, Thalia Zepatos (Eighth Mountain Press; $17); *Adventures in Good Company: The Complete Guide to Women's Tours and Outdoor Trips*, by Thalia Zepatos (Eighth Mountain Press; $7); *Active Women Vacation Guide*, by Evelyn Kaye (Blue Panda Publications; $18); *Travelers' Tales: Gutsy Women, Travel Tips and Wisdom for the Road*, by Marybeth Bond (Traveler's Tales; $8); and *A Foxy Old Woman's Guide to Traveling Alone*, by Jay Ben-Lesser (Crossing Press; $11).

TRAVELING ALONE

There are many benefits to traveling alone, among them greater independence and challenge. As a lone traveler, you have greater opportunity to interact with residents of the regions you visit. Without distraction, you can write a great travel log in the grand tradition of Mark Twain, John Steinbeck, and Charles Kuralt.

On the other hand, any solo traveler is a more vulnerable target of harassment and street theft. Lone travelers need to be well-organized and look confident at all times. Try not to stand out as a tourist, and be especially careful in deserted or very crowded areas. If questioned, never admit that you are traveling alone. Maintain regular contact with someone at home who knows your itinerary.

A number of organizations supply information for solo travelers, and others find travel companions for those who don't want to go alone. A few are listed here.

Connecting: Solo Traveler Network, P.O. Box 29088, 1996 W. Broadway, Vancouver, BC V6J 5C2, Canada (604-737-7791; email info@cstn.org; www.cstn.org). Bi-monthly newsletter features going solo tips, single-friendly tips, and travel companion ads. Annual directory lists holiday suppliers that avoid single supplement charges. Advice and lodging exchanges facilitated between members. Membership $25-35.

Travel Companion Exchange, P.O. Box 833, Amityville, NY 11701 (516-454-0880 or 800-392-1256; www.travelalone.com). Publishes the pamphlet *Foiling Pickpockets & Bag Snatchers* ($4) and *Travel Companions*, a bi-monthly newsletter for single travelers seeking a travel partner (subscription $48).

OLDER TRAVELERS

Seniors are eligible for a wide range of discounts on transportation, museums, movies, theaters, concerts, restaurants, and accommodations. If you don't see prices listed for seniors, ask, and you may be pleasantly surprised. Agencies for senior group travel are growing in enrollment and popularity. These are a few:

Elderhostel, 75 Federal St., Boston, MA 02110-1941 (617-426-7788 or 877-426-8056; email registration@elderhostel.org; www.elderhostel.org). Programs at colleges, universities, and other learning centers in California on varied subjects lasting 1-4 weeks. Must be 55 or over (spouse can be of any age).

The Mature Traveler, P.O. Box 50400, Reno, NV 89513 (775-786-7419 or 800-460-6676; www.maturetraveler.com). Soft-adventure tours for seniors. Subscription $30.

These books contain **further information** for older travelers: *No Problem! Worldwise Tips for Mature Adventurers*, by Janice Kenyon (Orca Book Publishers; $16); *A Senior's Guide to Healthy Travel*, by Donald L. Sullivan (Career Press.; $15); *Unbelievably Good Deals and Great Adventures That You Absolutely Can't Get Unless You're Over 50*, by Joan Rattner Heilman (Contemporary Books; $13).

BISEXUAL, GAY, AND LESBIAN TRAVELERS

Prejudice against gays and lesbians is still very much a reality in many areas of California, as evidenced by the recent legal battles over same-sex marriage. Public display of affection between same-sex couples is illegal in Nevada. And although California has no laws against homosexuality per se, homophobia may be a problem for the openly gay or lesbian traveler, particularly in rural areas. However, many cities (most notably San Francisco and L.A.) have large and active queer communities. Wherever possible, *Let's Go* lists local gay and lesbian info lines and community centers.

The following organizations and publishing houses also offer info and resources for the gay and lesbian traveler.

Gay's the Word, 66 Marchmont St., London WC1N 1AB (tel. (0171) 278 7654; email gays.theword@virgin.net; www.gaystheword.co.uk). Largest gay and lesbian bookshop in the U.K. Mail-order service available. No catalog of listings, but will provide a list of titles on a given subject.

Giovanni's Room, 345 S. 12th St., Philadelphia, PA 19107 (215-923-2960; email giophilp@netaxs.com). International feminist, lesbian, and gay bookstore with mail-order service which carries the publications listed below.

International Gay and Lesbian Travel Association, 4331 N. Federal Hwy. #304, Fort Lauderdale, FL 33308 (954-776-2626 or 800-448-8550; email IGLTA@aol.com; www.iglta.com). An organization of over 1350 companies serving gay and lesbian travelers worldwide. Call for lists of travel agents, accommodations, and events.

The following contain **more information** for gay and lesbian travelers: *Spartacus International Gay Guide*, by Bruno Gmunder Verlag ($33); *Damron Men's Guide*, *Damron Road Atlas*, *Damron's Accommodations*, and *The Women's Traveller* (Damron Travel Guides; $14-19). For more information, call 415-255-0404 or 800-462-6654 or visit their web site (www.damron.com); *Ferrari Guides' Gay Travel A to Z*, *Ferrari Guides' Men's Travel in Your Pocket*, *Ferrari Guides' Women's Travel in Your Pocket*, and *Ferrari Guides' Inn Places* (Ferrari Guides; $14-16). For more info, call 602-863-2408 or 800-962-2912 or visit their web site (www.q-net.com); *The Gay Vacation Guide: The Best Trips and How to Plan Them*, by Mark Chesnut (Citadel Press; $15); *Gayellow Pages* ($16). Contact them at: 212-674-0120; http://gayellowpages.com).

TRAVELERS WITH DISABILITIES

Federal law dictates that all public buildings should be handicapped accessible, and recent laws governing building codes have made disabled access more the norm than the exception. Businesses, transportation companies, national parks, and public services are complied to assist the disabled in using their facilities. However, traveling with a disability still requires planning and flexibility.

Those with disabilities should inform airlines, buses, trains, and hotels of their disabilities when making arrangements for travel; some time may be needed to prepare special accommodations. Call ahead to restaurants, hotels, parks, and other facilities to find out about the existence of ramps, the widths of doors, the dimensions of elevators, etc. Major airlines and **Amtrak** (800-872-7245; see p. 39) will accommodate disabled passengers if notified at least 72 hours in advance. Amtrak offers 15% discounts to disabled passengers, and hearing-impaired travelers may contact Amtrak using teletype printers (800-872-7245). **Greyhound** (see p. 40) will provide free travel for a companion; if you are without a fellow traveler, call Greyhound (800-752-4841) at least 48 hours, but no more than one week, before your departure and they'll arrange assistance where needed. For info on transportation availability in individual California cities, contact the local chapter of the Easter Seals Society. Hertz, National, and Avis **car rental** agencies have hand-controlled vehicles at some locations (see **Renting**, p. 42). If you plan to visit a national park or any other sight managed by the U.S. National Park Service, you can obtain a free **Golden Access Passport,** which is available at park entrances and from federal offices whose functions relate to land, forests, or wildlife. The Passport entitles disabled travelers and their families to enter parks for free and provides a 50% reduction on campsite and parking fees. For more on disabled travelers, check out *Resource Directory for the Disabled,* by Richard Neil Shrout (Facts on file; $45).

The following organizations provide information or publications that might be of assistance:

Access-Able Travel Source, LLC, P.O. Box 1796, Wheat Ridge, CO 80034 (303-232-2979; email bill@access-able.com; www.access-able.com). A database on traveling around the U.S. for disabled travelers, started by 2 avid disabled travelers. Provides info on access, transportation, accommodations, rentals, and various other resources.

Mobility International USA (MIUSA), P.O. Box 10767, Eugene, OR 97440 (voice and TDD 541-343-1284; email info@miusa.org; www.miusa.org). Sells *A World of Options: A Guide to International Educational Exchange, Community Service, and Travel for Persons with Disabilities* ($35).

Moss Rehab Hospital Travel Information Service (215-456-9600; www.mossresourcenet.org). Telephone and Internet info resource center on travel accessibility and other travel-related concerns for those with disabilities.

Society for the Advancement of Travel for the Handicapped (SATH), 347 Fifth Ave. #610, New York, NY 10016 (212-447-1928; email sathtravel@aol.com; www.sath.org). Advocacy group publishes a quarterly color travel magazine *OPEN WORLD* (free for members, $13 for nonmembers), and many handouts on disability travel facilitation and accessible destinations. Annual membership $45, students and seniors $30.

The following organizations arrange tours or trips for disabled travelers:

Directions Unlimited, 720 N. Bedford Rd., Bedford Hills, NY 10507 (800-533-5343; in NY 914-241-1700; email cruisesusa@aol.com). Arranges individual and group vacations, tours, and cruises for the physically disabled. Group tours for blind travelers.

The Guided Tour Inc., 7900 Old York Rd. #114B, Elkins Park, PA 19027-2339 (215-782-1370 or 800-783-5841; email gtour400@aol.com; www.guidedtour.com). Travel programs for persons with developmental and physical challenges around California.

MINORITY TRAVELERS

California is an extremely diverse state, although unfortunately not totally harmonious. Although "minority" groups are quickly becoming the majority in California, there is some anti-immigrant feeling, especially aimed against Mexican immigrants (or anyone who looks as if they could be Mexican). Be aware that some racial tensions exist, and try to avoid confrontations.

For **further reading** on minority travelers, try one of the following resources: *Go Girl! The Black Woman's Book of Travel and Adventure*, by Elaine Lee. (Eighth Mountain Press; $18); *The African-American Travel Guide*, by Wayne Robinson (Hunter Publishing; $16); and *Traveling Jewish in America, by* Jane Moskowitz (Wandering You Press; $14.50).

TRAVELERS WITH CHILDREN

Family vacations often require that you slow your pace, and always require that you plan ahead. When deciding where to stay, remember the special needs of young children; if you pick a B&B or a small hotel, call ahead and make sure its management is child-friendly. If you rent a car, make sure the rental company provides a car seat for children under 40 pounds. Consider using a papoose-style device to carry a baby on walking trips. Be sure your child carries some sort of ID in case of an emergency or he or she gets lost, and arrange a reunion spot in case of separation when sightseeing.

Restaurants often have children's menus and discounts. Virtually all museums and tourist attractions also have a children's rate. Children under two generally fly for free or 10% of the adult airfare on domestic flights (this does not necessarily include a seat). Fares are usually discounted 25% for children from two to 11.

The following titles give **more extensive information** regarding traveling through California with children: *Unofficial Guide to California with Kids*, by Colleen Dunn Bates et. al. (MacMillan; $17); *Disneyland and Southern California with Kids*, by Carey Simon (Prima Publishing; $14); and *Fun and Educational Places to go with Kids in California*, by Susan Peterson (Victory Audio; $17).

DIETARY CONCERNS

Vegetarians should have no problem finding suitable cuisine in California, as it (like the cuisine named after it) is very vegetarian-friendly. *Let's Go* tries to indicate vegetarian options in restaurant listings; other places to look for vegetarian and vegan cuisine are local health food stores and co-ops, as well as large natural food chains such as Trader Joe's and Wild Oats. Vegan options are more difficult to find in smaller towns and inland; be prepared to make food, request tailored dishes, or seek out specialty cafes. For more information about vegetarian travel, contact the **North American Vegetarian Society,** P.O. Box 72, Dolgeville, NY 13329 (518-568-7970; email navs@telenet.com; www.cyberveg.org/navs/), which publishes *Transformative Adventures*, a guide to vacations and retreats ($15), and the *Vegetarian Journal's Guide to Natural Food Restaurants* ($12).

Travelers who keep **kosher** should contact synagogues in larger cities for information on kosher restaurants; your own synagogue or college Hillel should have access to lists of Jewish institutions across the nation. Read *The Vegetarian Traveler: Where to Stay if You're Vegetarian,* by Jed Civic (Larson Publishing; $16) for more tips.

Jewish Travel Guide lists synagogues, kosher restaurants, and Jewish institutions in 80 countries. Order from Vallentine-Mitchell Publishers, Newbury House 890-900, Eastern Ave., Newbury Park, Ilford, Essex, U.K. IG2 7HH (tel. (0181) 599 88 66). Available in the U.S. ($16) from ISBS, 5804 NE Hassallo St., Portland, OR 97213-3644 (800-944-6190).

ALTERNATIVES TO TOURISM

STUDY

In order to live the life of a **real American college student,** you might want to consider a visiting student program lasting either a semester or a full year. Contact colleges and universities in your home country to see what kind of exchanges they administer with those in California. A more complicated option is to enroll full-time in an American institution. California is home to a number of outstanding private institutions, such as Stanford and CalTech. The three-tiered state system is among the finest in the country: the **University of California** has nine campuses, **California State University** has 22, and there are numerous community colleges. Unfortunately for non-Californians, these state schools have rather high out-of-state tuition and are extremely popular with residents, who receive priority consideration. The free booklet *Introducing the University of California* gives a quick rundown of the system and individual UC campuses. To order, write to Communication Services, University of California, Office of the President, 11 Franklin St., 9th fl., Oakland, CA 94607 (510-987-9716).

Foreign students who wish to study in the United States must apply for either a M-1 visa (vocational studies) or an F-1 visa (for full-time students enrolled in an academic or language program). If English is not your native language, you will probably be required to take the **Test of English as a Foreign Language (TOEFL),** which is administered in many countries. The international students office at the institution you will be attending can give you more specifics. Contact the **TOEFL/TSE Publications,** P.O. Box 6151, Princeton, NJ 08541 (609-771-7100; www.toefl.org).

If you want more general information on schools in California, check out your local bookstore for college guides. The *Fiske Guide to Colleges*, by Edward Fiske (NY Times Books; $19), and *Barron's Profiles of American Colleges* ($24) are very useful. If you still can't get enough, try the Internet study abroad web site (www.studyabroad.com/liteimage.html). Investigate one of the following for specific programs they might have with any university in California:

UNIVERSITIES

If your English is already good, local universities can be much cheaper than an American university program, although it can be hard to receive academic credit. Schools that offer study abroad programs to foreigners are listed below.

School for International Training, College Semester Abroad, Admissions, Kipling Rd., P.O. Box 676, Brattleboro, VT 05302 (800-336-1616 or 802-258-3267; www.worldlearning.org). Runs **Experiment in International Living,** Summer Programs (800-345-2929; email eil@worldlearning.org). Offers cross-cultural, educational homestays, community service, ecological adventure, and language training in CA. Programs are 3-5 weeks long and cost $1800-$5000.

Council on International Educational Exchange (CIEE), 205 East 42nd St., New York, NY 10017 (888-268-6245); www.ciee.org) sponsors work, volunteer, academic, internship, and professional study abroad programs in California and around the world.

EMPLOYMENT

To work in California, as in the rest of the U.S., you need a **work permit** or "green card" (see **Entrance Requirements,** p. 24). Your employer must obtain this document, usually by demonstrating that you have skills that locals lack—not the easiest of tasks. There are, however, ways to make it easier. Friends in California can sometimes help expedite work permits or arrange work-for-accommodations exchanges. Students can check with their universities' foreign language departments, which may have connections to job openings. Obtaining a worker's visa may seem complex, but it's critical that you go through the proper channels, particularly in California, where sentiment against undocumented workers is virulent.

Above all, do not try to fool your consular officer. Working or studying anywhere in the U.S. with only a B-2 visa is grounds for deportation. If the U.S. consulate suspects that you are trying to enter the country as a worker under the guise of a pleasure trip, you will be denied a visa altogether. For more info, contact the U.S. embassy or consulate in your home country (see **U.S. Embassies and Consulates,** p. 24). It may be possible to volunteer your services in exchange for room and board in parts of California. Potential ways of coming to California on a work visa include being an au pair or working in agriculture; see listings below.

AU PAIR. Childcare International, Ltd., Trafalgar House, Grenville Place, London NW7 3SA (tel. (0181) 906 31 16; email office@childint.demon.co.uk; www.childint.demon.co.uk) offers *au pair* positions in California. The organization prefers long placements but arranges summer work (application fee UK£80).

AGRICULTURE. Willing Workers on Organic Farms (WWOOF), P.O. Box 2675, Lewes, U.K. BN7 1RB (email fairtours@gn.apc.org; www.phdcc.com/sites/wwoof). Membership ($10) in WWOOF allows you to receive room and board at organic farms in California (and other parts of the world) in exchange for your help on a farm.

OTHER RESOURCES

USEFUL PUBLICATIONS

The most useful publications in California tend to be the (often free) local newspapers and magazines that are published on a weekly or monthly basis for particular towns, cities, or regions. They tend to list local events, including concerts, theater, and festivals, as well as local movie times. *Let's Go* tries to list the titles of these publications when possible, but any free local weekly or monthly will usually contain valuable information for your stay there.

TRAVEL BOOK PUBLISHERS

Hippocrene Books, Inc., 171 Madison Ave., New York, NY 10016 (212-685-4371; orders 718-454-2366; email contact@hippocrenebooks.com; www.netcom.com/~hippocre). Free catalogue, publishes travel reference books and travel guides.

Hunter Publishing, 130 Campus Drive, Edison, NJ 08818-7816 (800-255-0343; email kimba@mediasoft.net; www.hunterpublishing.com). Extensive catalogue of travel books, guides, language learning tapes, and quality maps.

Rand McNally, 150 S. Wacker Dr., Chicago, IL 60606 (312-332-2009 or 800-234-0679; email storekeeper@randmcnally.com; www.randmcnally.com), publishes a number of comprehensive road atlases ($10 each).

TRAVEL BOOKSTORES

Check local listings for travel bookstores near you or contact the following travel bookstores for comprehensive catalogues of titles, maps, and accessories.

Adventurous Traveler Bookstore, 245 S. Champlain St., Burlington, VT 05401 (800-282-3963 or 802-860-6776; www.adventuroustraveler.com).

Travel Books & Language Center, Inc., 4437 Wisconsin Ave. NW, Washington, D.C. 20016 (202-237-1322 or 800-220-2665; www.bookweb.org/bookstore/travelbks). Over 60,000 titles from around the world but no website orders.

THE WORLD WIDE WEB

The web is an excellent resource for researching and planning a trip to California. Almost all businesses now have web sites that provide copious information about the various regions of California; from Serrà to Zappa, it's all at your fingertips, even if you haven't yet set foot in the Golden State. Using the web to look for information about specific interests or concerns can prove invaluable when planning your itinerary. Where else can you find the address of every In-N-Out Burger joint in the entire state? (hint: **www.lainet.com/~gonzalez/ino_index.html.**)

DUDE.

California Division of Tourism: www.gocalif.ca.gov

Northern California Travel and Tourism Information: www.shastacascade.org

Virtual Tour of California: www.virtually.com/california/

Historical Landmarks, County-by-County: www.sonic.net/~laird/landmarks/

WE LIKE TO CAMP. WE LIKE, WE LIKE TO CAMP.

ParkNet: www.nps.gov/

California State Parks Official Page: http://cal-parks.ca.gov/

California Camping: www.athand.com/sil/athand/

The California Campground finder: www.camp-a-roo.com/

PANNIN' FER GOALD

Goald!: www.sjmercury.com/goldrush/goldrush_resources.shtml

LOS ANGELES: GLITTER AND GLAM

L.A. Essential Info: http://city.net/countries/united_states/california/los_angeles/

Virtual Map L.A.: www.avis.com/cgi-bin/copyright_prog?map=calosangeles_vicinity.jpg

Amusement Parks in L.A.: www.parentrover.com/themepk.htm

Hollywood Online: www.caohwy.com/

L.A. Times: www.latimes.com/

SAN FRANCISCO: BIG HILLS, TALL HILLS, FRIED HILLS, BBQ HILLS, HILL COCKTAIL...

San Francisco Chronicle: www.sfgate.com/chronicle/

San Francisco Walking Tours and History: www.hooked.net/~jhum/

San Francisco Transportation: www.ci.sf.ca.us/muni/index.htm

Forrest Gump Lives: www.bubbagump.com/html/san_francisco.html

EVERYONE SAY "A MAN WITH A MISSION, PAGE 8."

Spanish Missions in California: http://tqd.advanced.org/3615/

ZAPPA, A MAN WITH A MISSION

Freak Out!: www.ultisoft.demon.co.uk/zappa.html

SAN FRANCISCO

At fewer than 800,000 people, San Francisco can only tenuously claim city status, making it decidedly the coolest town in the world. In fact, it's so cool, it's positively *cold* sometimes. Mark Twain once said "The coldest winter I ever spent was a summer in San Francisco." With the trademark fog blanketing the city most mornings, temperatures are significantly cooler than in mainland suburbs, even those to the north (bring a jacket *and* a sweater). San Francisco goes against the groove of mostly sprawling, suburban California, with its narrow streets (tailor-made for clanging cable cars and movie chase scenes) and closely packed Victorian homes (featured in the opening credits to the time-honored family sitcom *Full House*). The infamous hills make for calorie-burning commutes in a highly walkable city, as well as a quaint backdrop for Rice-a-Roni commercials.

By California standards, San Francisco is steeped in history, but it's a history of oddballs and eccentrics that resonates more today in street culture than in museums and galleries. As the last stop in America's great westward expansion, San Francisco has always attracted artists, dreamers, and outsiders. Most famous are the hippies and flower children of the late 1960s, who turned on one generation and freaked out another in Haight-Ashbury's "Summer of Love." Before them were the Beats—brilliant, angry young writers who captured the rhythms of be-bop jazz in their poetry and their lives. The lineage of free spirits and troublemakers runs back to the 19th century, to the smugglers and pirates of the Barbary Coast, and to the '49ers who flocked here during the mad boom of the California Gold Rush.

The tradition continues. Anti-establishment politics have almost become establishment here, as rallies and movements continue to fill the streets and newspapers. The gay community, now one-sixth of the city's population, emerged in the 1970s as one of the city's most visible and powerful groups. At the same time, Central American and Asian immigrants have made San Francisco one of the most racially diverse cities in the United States. Not to be outdone, many young computer workers have ditched the bland suburbs of Silicon Valley for the cooler breezes of San Francisco, with Internet upstart companies infiltrating the forgotten spaces of lower-rent neighborhoods. Like so many chameleons, San Francisco is ever-changing with the times, but fortunately, some things remain constant: the Bay is foggy, the hills are steep, and Rice-A-Roni abounds.

HIGHLIGHTS OF SAN FRANCISCO

- The island of **Alcatraz** (p. 104) formerly provided its prison inmates with maximum security—and provides its present-day visitors with maximum thrills!
- **Golden Gate Park** (p. 78) is jam-packed: gardens, museums, paths, an aquarium, a laserium, an arboretum, a Japanese tea garden, and a Dutch windmill.
- The **San Francisco Museum of Modern Art** (p. 110) has a crackerjack collection of art, housed in a big, slick building.
- The red **Golden Gate Bridge** (p. 106) leaps majestically across the foggy bay.
- From **Twin Peaks** (p. 102), there are excellent views of the city.
- The **Exploratorium** (p. 107) is full of elegant illustrations of scientific principles.

ORIENTATION

San Francisco (pop. 790,000) is 403 miles north of Los Angeles and 390 miles south of the Oregon border. The city proper lies at the northern tip of the peninsula separating the San Francisco Bay from the Pacific Ocean. (For info on the other cities surrounding the bay, see **The Bay Area,** p. 127.)

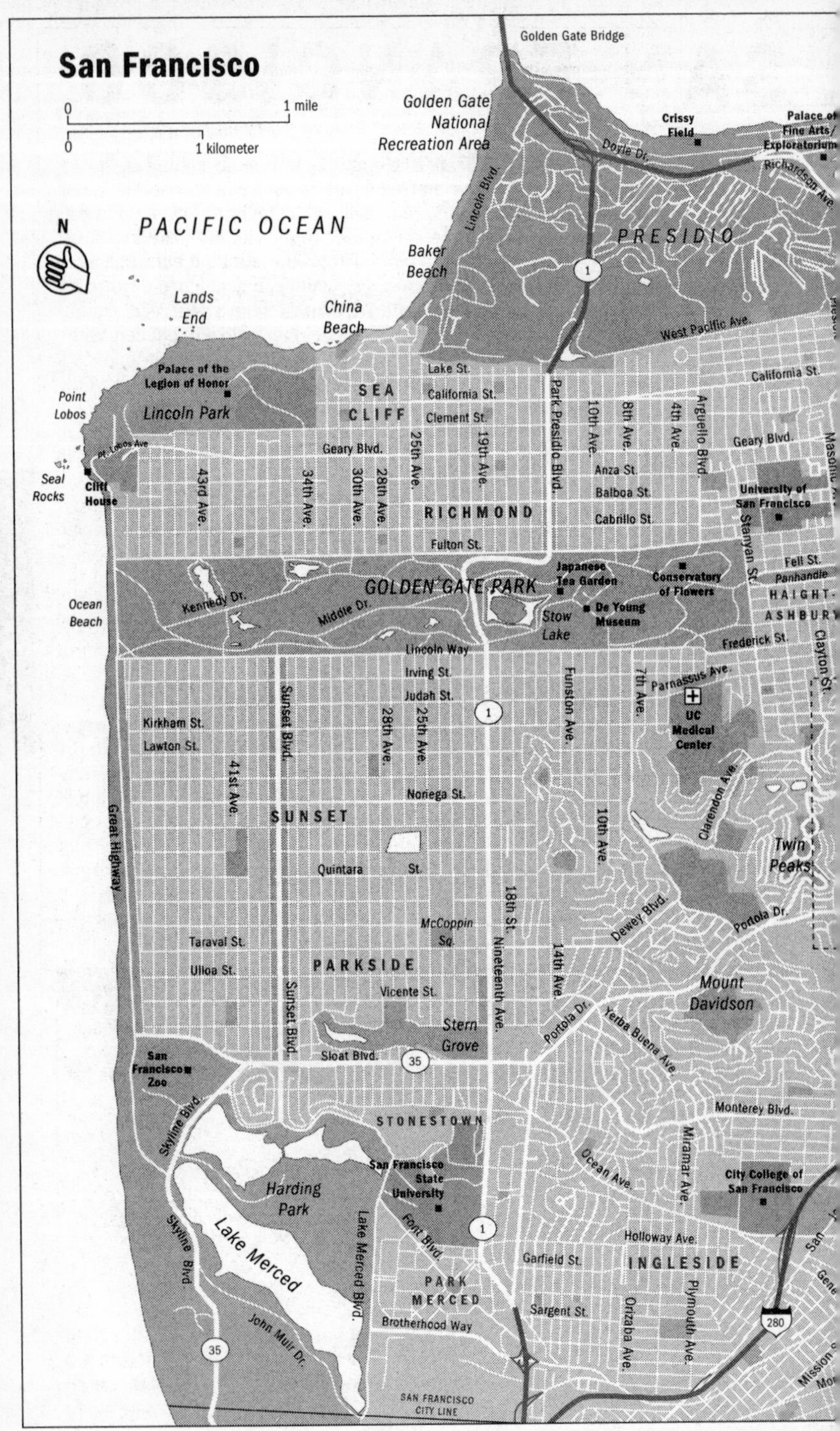
San Francisco
0 1 mile
0 1 kilometer
N
PACIFIC OCEAN
Golden Gate Bridge
Golden Gate National Recreation Area
Crissy Field
Palace of Fine Arts/ Exploratorium
Doyle Dr.
Richardson Ave.
Lincoln Blvd.
PRESIDIO
Baker Beach
Lands End
China Beach
West Pacific Ave.
Palace of the Legion of Honor
Point Lobos
Lincoln Park
Lake St.
California St.
Clement St.
SEA CLIFF
Park Presidio Blvd.
10th Ave.
8th Ave.
4th Ave.
Arguello Blvd.
Geary Blvd.
Pt. Lobos Ave
Seal Rocks
Cliff House
43rd Ave.
34th Ave.
30th Ave.
28th Ave.
25th Ave.
19th Ave.
RICHMOND
Anza St.
Balboa St.
Cabrillo St.
Fulton St.
University of San Francisco
Stanyan St.
Fell St.
Panhandle
HAIGHT-ASHBURY
Japanese Tea Garden
Conservatory of Flowers
GOLDEN GATE PARK
Kennedy Dr.
Middle Dr.
Stow Lake
De Young Museum
Ocean Beach
Frederick St.
Clayton St.
Lincoln Way
Irving St.
Judah St.
Funston Ave.
7th Ave.
Parnassus Ave.
UC Medical Center
Kirkham St.
Lawton St.
Sunset Blvd.
41st Ave.
Noriega St.
SUNSET
Great Highway
Clarendon Ave.
Twin Peaks
Quintara St.
18th St.
Nineteenth Ave.
McCoppin Sq.
Dewey Blvd.
Portola Dr.
Taraval St.
Ulloa St.
PARKSIDE
14th Ave.
Vicente St.
Mount Davidson
Stern Grove
Yerba Buena Ave.
San Francisco Zoo
Sloat Blvd.
35
Skyline Blvd.
STONESTOWN
Monterey Blvd.
San Francisco State University
Ocean Ave.
Miramar Ave.
City College of San Francisco
Harding Park
Lake Merced
Lake Merced Blvd.
Font Blvd.
Holloway Ave.
Garfield St.
INGLESIDE
PARK MERCED
Sargent St.
Orizaba Ave.
Plymouth Ave.
Brotherhood Way
John Muir Dr.
280
SAN FRANCISCO CITY LINE
1

SEE DOWNTOWN MAP
TO ALCATRAZ
Fisherman's Wharf
Pier 39
San Francisco Bay
Marina Park
Marina Blvd.
Fort Mason
Beach St.
Bay St.
Columbus Ave.
Powell St.
TELEGRAPH HILL
Coit Tower
MARINA
Chestnut St.
Lombard St.
Union St.
Broadway
Van Ness Ave.
Franklin St.
RUSSIAN HILL
Taylor St.
NORTH BEACH
Kearny St.
Montgomery St.
The Embarcadero
Ferry Building
San Francisco - Oakland Bay Bridge
CHINATOWN
Jackson Square
Transamerica Pyramid
Washington St.
Alta Park
Lafayette Park
California St.
NOB HILL
Union Square
Transbay Terminal
Main St.
80
JAPAN-TOWN
Gough St.
101
Larkin
Hyde St.
Geary St.
Market St.
1st St.
2nd St.
Divisadero St.
Geary Expressway
Visitor's Information
Mission St.
Turk St.
Howard St.
3rd St.
Fillmore St.
Steiner St.
TENDER-LOIN
4th St.
5th St.
Laguna St.
SOMA
6th St.
Civic Center
8th St.
Townsend
Berry St.
Pacific Bell Park
China Basin
Alamo Square
9th St.
Folsom St.
Harrison St.
10th St.
Brannan St.
King St.
Haight St.
Central Freeway
Duboce Ave.
7th St.
CHINA BASIN
Castro St.
Market St.
16th St.
Treat Ave.
Potrero St.
280
Mission Dolores
Mariposa St.
Central Basin
MISSION
3rd St.
Mission Dolores Park
20th St.
S. Van Ness Ave.
Harrison St.
20th St.
Indiana St.
CASTRO
Diamond St.
Noe St.
Dolores St.
Guerrero St.
Valencia St.
SF General Hospital
POTRERO
25th St.
Clipper St.
Army St.
Army St.
NOE VALLEY
Mission St.
ASTRO AND THE MISSION MAP
30th St.
San Jose Ave.
Bernal Heights Park
Jerrold Ave.
BAY VIEW
Toland St.
Cortland Ave.
Industrial
Quint St.
Oakdale Ave.
3rd St.
Mendell St.
Evans Ave.
Park St.
Alemany Blvd.
Fwy.
India Basin
Silver Ave.
Thornton Ave.
Revere Ave.
Innes Ave.
GLEN PARK
Alemany Blvd
Mission St.
Excelsior Ave
Felton Ave
University St.
Hamilton St.
Bayshore Fwy.
3rd St.
Ingalls St.
HUNTERS POINT
Persia Ave
Carroll Ave.
John McLaren Park
Mansell St.
Jennings St.
Gilman Ave.
South Basin
Moscow Ave.
VISITACION VALLEY
Jamestown Ave.
Fitch St.
Visitacion Ave.
Sunnydale Ave.
TO AIRPORT
Candlestick Park
Candlestick Point Recreation Area
Cordova

SAN FRANCISCO NEIGHBORHOODS

San Francisco's diverse neighborhoods are loosely organized along a few central arteries. Most neighborhoods are compact enough to explore comfortably on foot. Make a mental note of the steep hills in each district—a two-block detour can sometimes prevent a strenuous climb.

Much of San Francisco's activity occurs in the northeast quadrant of the peninsula, composed of two sets of gridded streets that meet at an angle. **Market Street** runs northeast along the seam all the way to the **Embarcadero** on the east coast and has stops for many MUNI buses and all Metro lines. **Union Square** (see p. 105) is a well-trafficked, high-retail area just north of Market St. downtown. To its east the skyscrapers of the **Financial District** stretch out toward the Embarcadero (see p. 112). To the west, Union Square gives way to the well-pounded **Tenderloin,** (see p. 81) where, despite attempts at urban renewal, drugs, crime, and homelessness prevail both night and day. The area is roughly bounded by Larkin St. to the west, Taylor St. to the east, and Post St. to the north, and bleeds down Market St. for a few blocks. City Hall, the Civic Center Public Library, and Symphony Hall crown a small but impressive collection of municipal buildings in the **Civic Center,** (see p. 111) south of the Tenderloin on Market St. and bounded on the west by wide Van Ness Ave.

North of and the Financial District lies the largest **Chinatown** (see p. 103) in the world, 25 blocks of crowded streets and endless food. Old money rises to the west on ritzy **Nob Hill,** while newer money walks its dogs on **Russian Hill** (see p. 109). **North Beach,** (see p. 102) a historically Italian area, overflows with restaurants and cafes in the northeastern corner of the peninsula. Touristy **Fisherman's Wharf** (see p. 104) sends boats to **Alcatraz,** the inescapable penal attraction.

South of Market St. to the east, the **South of Market Area** (written **SoMa**; see p. 110) holds large, glassy attractions near 3rd St. and scattered among industrial buildings down to 14th St. The very trendy **Mission District,** (see p. 101) populated largely by Latino residents by day and superhip barhoppers by night, takes over south of 14th St. The diners and cafes of the **Castro,** the country's gay Jerusalem, dazzle on Castro and Market St. northwest of the Mission (see p. 102).

Some interesting strips are sprinkled among the residential neighborhoods west of Van Ness Ave. The posh stucco of the **Marina** and Victorians of **Pacific Heights** (see p. 107) run south to funkier **Fillmore Street,** which leads to the few *udon*-filled blocks of **Japantown** (see p. 108).

Vast **Golden Gate Park** and its neighboring **Sunset District** (see p. 106) to the south dominate the western half of the peninsula. At the park's eastern end sits the former hippie haven of **Haight-Ashbury** (see p. 100) to the southeast. The park is bounded by Lincoln St. and the Sunset District to the south, and by Fulton St. and the residential **Richmond District** (see p. 110) to the north, stretching out to Ocean Beach along the Pacific. The **Presidio,** at the northwestern corner, culminates in the majestic **Golden Gate Bridge** (see p. 106).

REQUIRED READING In 1976, an Associated Press reporter named Armistead Maupin began publishing a series of short fictional pieces in the *San Francisco Chronicle.* The first stories, published as *Tales of the City* in 1978, center around the life of Mary Ann Singleton, a young secretary from Cleveland who comes to the city on vacation and just never leaves. They quickly entangle an advertising mogul and his social-column worthy Telegraph Hill family, a washed-up hippie named Vincent who's not quite all there, a special plant named Beatrice, and a formidable collection of love-seeking singles. The average and bizarre events of 28 Barbary Ln., a fictional address on Russian Hill, are overseen by Anna Madrigal, a landlady with a mysterious past and mother-figure for all her tenants. Several more books followed, as well as a hit PBS series starring Olympia Dukakis. The addictive tales incorporate world events, San Francisco landmarks of every caliber, and thinly veiled local personalities.

Downtown San Francisco
ACCOMMODATIONS
M Adelaide Inn
T Aida Hotel
K Ansonia Hotel
H Biltmore & Amsterdam
L Brady Acres
N Emperor Norton Inn
U European Guest House
Q Globetrotter's Inn
G Golden Gate Hotel
E Grant Plaza Hotel
A Green Tortoise Guest House
B Gum Moon Women's Residence
I Harcourt Residence Club
P Herbert Hotel
R Hotel Essex
W Interclub Globe Hostel
C Pacific Tradewinds Guest House
G Park Hotel
J Pensione International
S The Phoenix
O S. F. Downtown Hostel
V S. F. International Student Center
X SoMa Inn
F Temple Hotel
D YMCA
TO ALCATRAZ
Pier 39
San Francisco Bay
California Welcome Center
FISHERMAN'S WHARF
TO FORT MASON
Maritime Museum
Ghirardelli Square
Jefferson St.
Beach St.
North Point St.
Bay St.
Francisco St.
Chestnut St.
Lombard St.
Filbert St.
Union St.
Green St.
Vallejo St.
Broadway
Broadway Tunnel
Pacific Ave.
Jackson St.
Washington St.
Clay St.
Sacramento St.
California St.
Pine St.
Bush St.
Sutter St.
Post St.
Geary St.
O'Farrell St.
Ellis St.
Eddy St.
Turk St.
Golden Gate St.
McAllister St.
Grove St.
Hayes St.
Fell St.
Van Ness Ave.
Polk St.
Larkin St.
Hyde St.
Leavenworth St.
Jones St.
Taylor St.
Mason St.
Powell St.
Stockton St.
Grant St.
Kearny St.
Montgomery St.
Sansome St.
Battery St.
Front St.
Davis St.
Drumm St.
The Embarcadero
Columbus Ave.
Tattoo Art Museum
TELEGRAPH HILL
Coit Tower
Filbert Steps
WASHINGTON SQUARE
NORTH BEACH
RUSSIAN HILL
POWELL-HYDE CABLE CAR LINE
POWELL-MASON CABLE CAR LINE
CALIFORNIA ST CABLE CAR LINE
City Lights Bookstore
Cable Car Powerhouse
Grace Cathedral
NOB HILL
CHINATOWN
Transamerica Pyramid
Justin Herman Plaza
Ferry Building
Embarcadero Center
EMBARCADERO
FINANCIAL DIST.
Market St.
Fremont St.
Main St.
Beale St.
Transbay Terminal
Folsom St.
1st St.
2nd St.
3rd St.
4th St.
5th St.
6th St.
7th St.
8th St.
9th St.
10th St.
11th St.
UNION SQUARE
Maiden Lane
MONTGOMERY ST.
Mission St.
S. F. Museum of Modern Art
Metreon
Yerba Buena Gardens
TENDERLOIN
POWELL
101
80
Old Mint
Ansel Adams Center
Howard St.
Harrison St.
South Park
Herbst Theatre
City Hall
CIVIC CENTER
Library
Opera House
Symphony Hall
SOUTH OF MARKET
Minna St.
Bryant St.
Brannan St.
Townsend St.
King St.
Pacific Bell Park
Caltrain Depot
Mission Creek Marina
N
0 250 yards
0 250 meters

HAIGHT-ASHBURY. East of Golden Gate Park, smack dab in the center of the city, Haight-Ashbury has aged with uneven grace since its hippie heyday. The neighborhood's large Victorian houses began to attract post-Beat Bohemians in the early 1960s for ideology-based communal living. Although at one time a haven for conscientious objectors to the Vietnam War, "Hashbury" embraced drug use and Eastern philosophies over anti-war protests and marches. The hippie voyage reached its apogee in 1967's "Summer of Love," when Janis Joplin, the Grateful Dead, and Jefferson Airplane all made music and love here within a few blocks of one another. Flamboyant dress scared off the traditionalists, LSD pervaded local consciousness, and young people from across the country converged on the grassy panhandle for the celebrated Be-Ins. To some, the Haight seemed the very confluence of spiritual power; to others, it was just one hell of a party.

Bad karma got the upper hand in the 1970s and 80s, but the past decade has seen a steady resurgence. Today the counterculture hangs out side-by-side with the over-the-counter culture—the 60s, their ideals firmly emblazoned on consumer products, live on in the forms of tie-dyed t-shirts, hemp jewelry, cuddly Grateful Dead bears, and water pipes. Bars shelter zoned-out regulars who look as if they may have been there since the Nixon years.

MUNI buses #6, 7, 16, 33, 43, 66, and 71 all serve the Haight, while Metro line N runs along Carl St., four blocks to the south. **The area can be dangerous—exercise caution, especially at night.**

THE MISSION DISTRICT. Founded by Spanish settlers in 1776, the Mission district is home to some of the city's oldest structures, as well as some of the hottest young people and places around. Colorful murals celebrate the prominent Latino presence that has long defined the Mission, which grows increasingly diverse and gentrified along Valencia Street. Politically, the Mission is the city's most radical pocket, marked by left-wing bookstores, active labor associations, and bohemian bars and cafes filled with young hipsters and older hippies. The area is also home to a cohesive lesbian community and growing gay male presence. The Mission is relatively safe for daytime walks, but exercise caution at night, especially around the housing projects between Valencia and Guerrero Street close to Market Street. The district, which lies south of Market Street, is roughly bordered by 16th Street to the north, U.S. 101 to the east, Cesar Chavez (a.k.a. Army) Street to the south, and the Castro to the west. MUNI bus routes (#9, 12, 22, 26, 27, 33, 53, and 67) lace the area, while the J Metro line runs down Church Street to the west. The BART stops at Mission Street at 16th and 24th Streets, providing the most convenient access from downtown (fare $1.10), and SamTrans runs throughout the district.

CASTRO. Forget Newt Gingrich—*this* is boys' town. Much of San Francisco's gay male community, along with a much smaller number of hip young lesbians, make the Castro home. The wild days of the 1970s, when discos throbbed all night and day, have come and gone, but Harvey Milk Plaza, at Castro and Market Streets, remains the fast-beating heart of gay San Francisco. Cruisy bars and cafes are everywhere, same-sex public displays of affection raise nary an eyebrow, and tank tops and chiseled abs are *de rigueur*. Besides being fabulous, the Castro is also pretty. From the Castro Metro stop at the intersection of Market and 17th Streets, halfway down a hill, are views across the Noe and Eureka Valleys to the south and up to the hills around Buena Vista Park and Twin Peaks to the north and west. Away from the hubbub of Castro Street, affluent gay yuppies ("guppies") live on quiet streets lined with trees and rainbow flags south from Market Street to Noe Valley and west from the Mission to Portola Drive and Twin Peaks. To get to the Castro by public transit, take MUNI bus #37 or MUNI Metro F, K, L, or M or MUNI bus #37 down Market Street to the Castro Street station. MUNI bus #24 runs along Castro Street between 14th and 26th Streets. On foot or by car, go southwest from downtown on Market Street to get to the Castro.

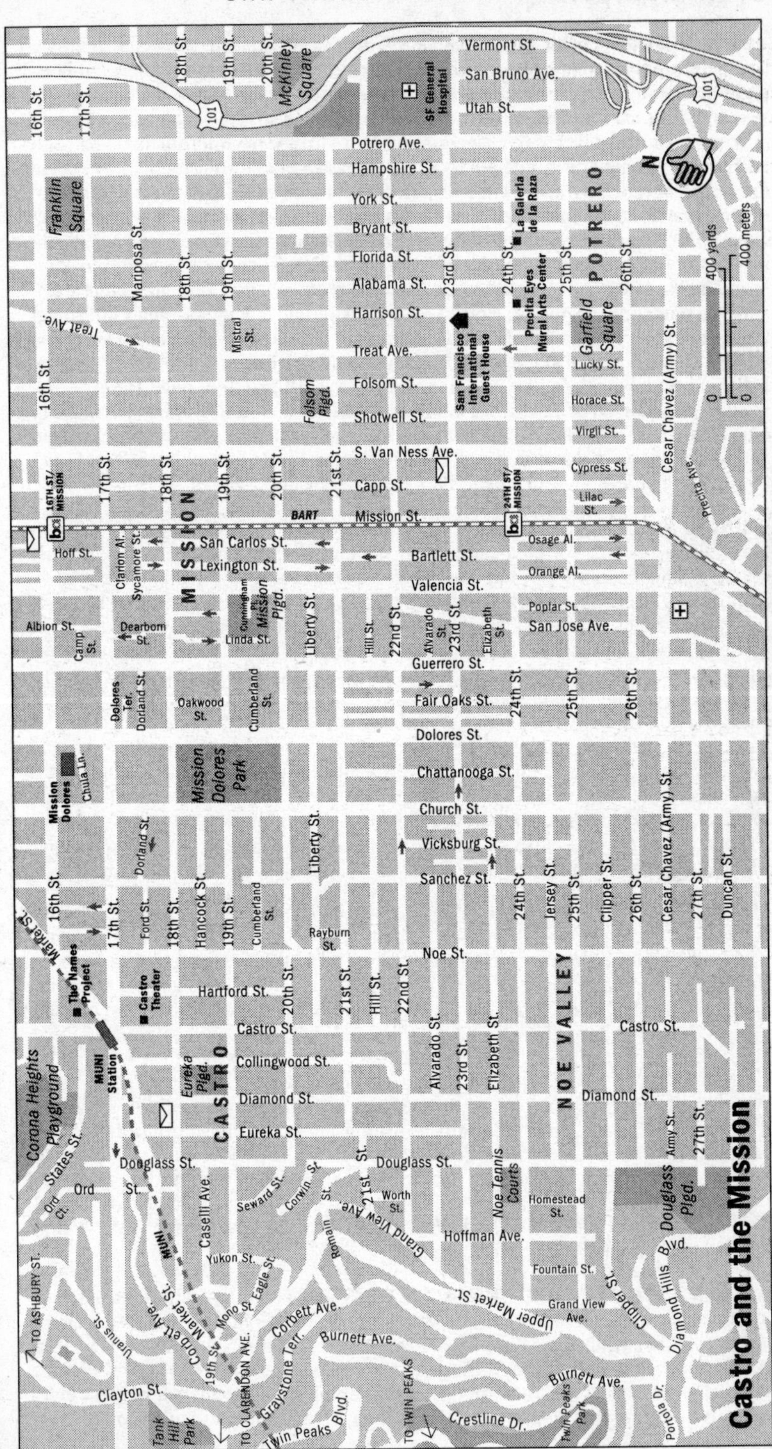

Castro and the Mission

NORTH BEACH. As Columbus Ave. and Stockton St. run north, there is a transition from shops selling ginseng and roast duck to those selling provolone and biscotti. Lying north of Chinatown is the legendary Italian community of North Beach, where the Beat movement was born. In the early 1950s a group of poets and writers including Jack Kerouac, Allen Ginsberg, Maynard Krebs, and Lawrence Ferlinghetti came here to write, drink, and raise some hell. They lashed out at the conformity of postwar America, embraced both Eastern religions and bebop jazz, and lit a fuse that would eventually set off the counterculture explosion of the late 1960s. Today the Beats, like the hippies down on Haight St., have been safely co-opted and commodified in a hundred English classes and *Norton* anthologies; in 1998, Ferlinghetti was named San Francisco's first poet laureate.

In the meantime, however, North Beach is experiencing a major nightlife surge. Finely clad peninsula and city dwellers flock to the zillions of Italian restaurants around Columbus and stay for the cozy bars and hot live acts around Broadway and Kearny; meanwhile, the internationals who staff the area head to tiny, laid-back bars on Grant and herds of wandering males duck into the Broadway strip clubs. North Beach runs from Columbus north, bounded on the west by Russian Hill, and eventually dissipates into the Wharf area. Buses 9ax, 9bx, 15, 30, 41, and 45 serve the area from downtown. Parking is nearly impossible.

CHINATOWN. The largest Chinese community outside of Asia (over 100,000 people), Chinatown is also the most densely populated of San Francisco's neighborhoods. Chinese laborers began coming to San Francisco in the mid-19th century as refugees from the Opium Wars, and were put to work constructing the railroads of the West. Racism swelled after the tracks had been laid and Gold Rush prosperity declined. In the 1880s, white Californians secured a law against further Chinese immigration to prevent the so-called "Yellow Peril." Stranded in San Francisco, Chinese-Americans banded together to protect themselves in this small section of downtown. As the city grew, speculators tried to take over the increasingly valuable land, but the neighborhood refused to be expelled. To this day Chinatown remains almost exclusively Chinese, although it has attracted visitors since the 1850s, when sailors staggered down from Barbary Coast saloons looking for sex, alcohol, and opium. The area is roughly bounded by Columbus Avenue to the north, Kearny Street to the east, Mason Street to the west, and the Financial District to the south.

FISHERMAN'S WHARF. East along the waterfront is San Francisco's most visited—and most reviled—tourist destination. Anchored by the shopping complexes of Pier 39 in the east and Ghirardelli Square in the west and oozing down to Bay St., Fisherman's Wharf is home to eight blocks of while-you-wait caricature artists, "olde-fashioned" fudge "shoppes," penny flattening machines, and enough t-shirts to stretch around the world an estimated eight million times. Conventional attractions aside, the best way to appreciate the wharf is to wake up at 4am, put on a warm sweater, and go down to the piers to see why it's called Fisherman's Wharf. Early birds can experience the loading and outfitting of small ships, the animated conversation, the blanket of morning mist, and the incredible view—without the rapacious crowds. If you're up *really* early, you might even find a parking place. The western edge near Municipal Pier is quieter and more idyllic than the main Wharf piers at any time of day. MUNI buses #15, 30, 32 and 42 and the Powell-Mason and Powell-Hyde cable cars run to the Wharf; buses #19, 47, and 49 run across town to Ghirardelli Square.

GOLDEN GATE PARK AND THE SUNSET DISTRICT. This is where native San Franciscans spend Sundays. In-line skaters, neo-flower children, and sunbathers come together in this lush garden-within-the-city. When San Francisco's 19th-century elders asked Frederick Law Olmsted, designer of New York's Central Park, to build a park to rival Paris's Bois de Boulogne on their city's western side, he said it couldn't be done. Engineer William Hammond Hall and Scottish gardener John "Willy" McLaren proved him wrong. Hall designed the 1000-acre park, gardens and all, when the land was still just shifting sand dunes, and constructed a mammoth breakwater along the oceanfront to protect seedling trees and bushes from the sea's salty spray. During his 66 years as the Golden Gate's godfather, McLaren planted more than one million trees here, transforming sand into soil with sea-bent grass, humus, and truckloads of manure. Early groundskeepers wanted to preserve the pristine lawns by enforcing a "keep off the grass" rule, but McLaren was outraged and threatened to pave over the park if the rule was enforced. Strong-minded McLaren disliked statues in "his" park and would hide them in bushes, but despite his explicit orders, a statue of him was erected after his death at age 93. The park itself is McLaren's best memorial.

To get to the park from downtown, hop on bus #5, 16, 21, or 71. Buses #18, 28, 29, and 44 pass through the park on the way north or south and intersect the surface Metro south of the park. The N Metro (Judah Street) runs from Market Street down to Arguello Boulevard near the southeast corner of the park, then runs through northern Sunset. The park is bounded by Fulton Street to the north, Stanyan Street to the east, Lincoln Way to the south, and Ocean Beach to the west, except for a strip called the Panhandle, jutting east between Fell and Oak Streets. (Originally the "carriage entrance," it contains the oldest trees and extends into the realm of Haight-Ashbury.) A heavily trafficked north-south route through the park is named Park Presidio By-Pass Drive in the north and Cross-Over Drive in the south, and continues all the way up to the Golden Gate Bridge.

South of the park, San Franciscans eat, drink, and sleep in the Sunset District. Mosey down Irving Street for outstanding used bookstores (see **Shopping,** p. 113) and an inviting cache of eateries, including groceries for the perfect picnic lunch.

MARINA AND PACIFIC HEIGHTS. The residential Marina, nestled between Fort Mason to the east and the whopping Presidio to the west, is home to more young, wealthy professionals than any other part of San Francisco. Few signs of the 1989 earthquake, which hit this area hard, mar its elegant stucco finish. A few blocks to the south, the neighborhoods of Cow Hollow and Union Street provide solid and liquid sustenance, and a steady diet of boutiques. Union and Chestnut Streets bustle with the click of Gucci heels by day and a post-frat-house, pre-law partnership singles scene by night. Bring the flip-phone, darling. A stiff climb into Pacific Heights breaks up the blinding whiteness a bit. Vendors of hip clothing and tasty eateries line Fillmore Street all the way down to Japantown.

NIHONMACHI (JAPANTOWN). After the 1906 earthquake destroyed part of this central neighborhood, Japanese immigrants moved here en masse. For a time, its closely packed homes and shops constituted one of the largest Japanese enclaves outside Japan. Today that community has largely dispersed, moving to more spacious accommodations in the Richmond and Sunset districts and elsewhere. The sprawling Nihonmachi shopping complex (a.k.a. the Japan Center) dominates what is left of Japantown. In its halls, and on the streets surrounding it, are the commercial remains of the community, including a handful of excellent restaurants, several shops selling Tokyo's wares, and a few Korean businesses. The Miyako Building, at Laguna and Post Streets, contains a hotel and bank headquarters, and little of interest to visitors. To the west, the Kintetsu Building has food, shopping, and a bridge over Webster Street connecting it to the Kinokuniya Building on Fillmore Street A mile west of downtown, Nihonmachi is bordered to the north by Bush Street, to the east by Fillmore Street, to the west by Laguna Street, and to the south by the Geary Expressway. Take MUNI bus #2, 3, or 4 to Buchanan Street #38 to Geary Boulevard, or #22 down Fillmore Street.

NOB HILL AND RUSSIAN HILL. Avast, ye travelers! Here thar be filthy rich nabobs and thar foofy dogs! In the late 19th century, Nob Hill attracted the West's great railroad magnates and robber barons. Today, their ostentatious mansions still make it one of the nation's most prestigious addresses. Fancy hotels, a lovely little park, and an impressive cathedral grace the peak at California and Taylor Streets. Russian Hill, to the north, is named after Russian sailors who died during an expedition in the early 1800s and were buried on the southeast crest. Largely residential, Nob and Russian Hills themselves merit only a brief diversion; there's a lot more happening on the streets running to and beyond them.

RICHMOND. Historically a neighborhood of first- and second-generation immigrants, Richmond has been the traditional home to Irish-, Russian-, and now Chinese-American communities. "Inner Richmond," the area east of Park Presidio Boulevard, has such a large Chinese population that it has been dubbed "New Chinatown." Extending east from Point Lobos to Arguello Boulevard, this mostly residential area is quiet and fairly bland. Geary Boulevard is its main thoroughfare, and Clement Street is the principal shopping and dining strip. MUNI bus #2 runs along Clement from Lincoln Park to Sutter Street and eventually Union Square; bus #38 crosses the entire city on Geary Boulevard from the Transbay Terminal in the east to Point Lobos in the west.

SOUTH-OF-MARKET AREA (SoMa). Although the South-of-Market area (written, though not spoken, as SoMa) may seem like a bleak expanse of industrial warehouses and intermittent homelessness, it encompasses three distinct spheres of life and activity. A well-visited cultural area lies between 2nd and 4th Streets and north of Folsom Street. Here the concrete and glass expanses of the Yerba Buena Gardens, Metreon, and Moscone Convention Center fill the blocks between 3rd and 4th Streets, while the San Francisco Museum of Modern Art (SFMOMA) presides over the cultural milieu. The Moscone is undergoing major renovations and expanding, changing the face of this area more and more as this book goes to press. Several blocks south between the future Pacific Bell Park and the freeway, tiny but vibrant South Park is surrounded by old and new eateries and the "cyberspace gulch" of upstart Internet and design companies. Finally, the stretch from 7th to 12th Streets along Folsom Street toward the Mission is increasingly hip and clubby, with trendy cafes, inexpensive restaurants, and a multitude of clubs, as well as several establishments dedicated to the selling and wearing of leather.

Parking is relatively plentiful by day on the long, deserted streets. Watch for street-cleaning prohibitions that usually begin at midnight. To reach the area by BART or MUNI Metro, walk down 7th or 8th Street from the Civic Center Station or down 4th Street from the Powell Street station.

CIVIC CENTER. The Civic Center is a collection of mammoth buildings arranged around two vast plazas, somewhat out of place between the simulated slums south of Market Street and the real deal in the Tenderloin. Home to the opera, symphony, and most of San Francisco's major theater, the district is grandest at night, when beautifully lit flags and fountains flank bumper-to-bumper limousine traffic. Parking is easy but expensive at meters and lots around the Civic Center. To get there by public transportation, take MUNI Metro (J, K, L, M, or N) to the Civic Center stop or Van Ness Station, most MUNI buses, or Golden Gate Transit bus (#10, 20, 50, or 70).

FINANCIAL DISTRICT AND EMBARCADERO. Corporate worker bees swarm the Financial District, a Wall Street of the West Coast, where towering banks blot out the sun. The district stretches several blocks north of Market Street from Union Square to the Embarcadero and ferry building. The food is standard office lunch fare, the area shuts down when the workday ends (around 7:30pm), and parking is very difficult during business hours. Take MUNI Metro (J, K, L, M, or N) or BART to the Montgomery or Embarcadero stations, or a MUNI bus. A slower route to the district is the California Street cable car. If driving, park in SoMa and walk or ride the Metro to Montgomery Street.

TENDERLOIN. The indistinctly defined region known as the Tenderloin is economic light-years away from its neighbors, chi-chi Union Square and the pre-opera institutions surrounding the Civic Center. The uncouth area begins north of Market Street and stretches roughly from Van Ness Avenue north of Golden Gate Avenue to the streets west of Union Square. Sporadic attempts at urban renewal have done little to improve the poverty of this quarter or its residents. As slums go, the Tenderloin is smaller, and probably safer than comparable areas in Oakland or Los Angeles, but there are few attractions by day (for a few places worth an assertive, brisk walk see **Shopping,** p. 113) and no good reason to linger on the streets after dark.

GETTING THERE

BY PLANE. Busy **San Francisco International Airport (SFO;** general info 650-761-0800) is 15 miles south of downtown by U.S. 101. Plan your arrival by calling the SFO transportation info line (800-736-2008). The fliers available on the upper level describe bus and shuttle information in detail.

Several types of transportation can take you from SFO to the Bay Area Rapid Transit (BART) system (see below), which runs through the city and to other bay destinations. Three BART stops in San Francisco connect to the San Francisco Municipal Railway (MUNI), the city's public transportation system. For automated information on any of these transportation systems or traffic conditions, call **TravInfo** (415-817-1717).

San Mateo County Transit (SamTrans; from the Bay Area 800-660-4287 or from outside the Bay Area 650-817-1717; www.samtrans.com) runs two buses from SFO to downtown San Francisco. Express bus #7F reaches the Transbay Terminal downtown with a few stops along Mission St. and allows only a small carry-on bag per passenger (35min.; 5:30am-12:50am; fare $2.50, seniors at off-peak times $1.25, under 18 $1). Bus #7B makes frequent stops on Mission St. and allows any amount of luggage (1hr.; 5:45am-12:30am; fare $2, seniors at off-peak times 50¢, under 18 75¢ into S.F., $1.50 out of the city). Another option is to take a SamTrans bus to the BART system. From BART, you can reach several points in downtown San Francisco or transfer to the MUNI for other locations in the city (see **Getting Around,** below). SamTrans bus #3X runs to the Colma BART station just south of the city (20min.; every 20-30min. M-F 6am-11:30pm, Sa-Su 7:15am-9:30pm; fare $1.10, seniors 35¢, under 18 50¢). Bus #3B runs to the Daly City BART station, also south of San Francisco (30min.; every hr. M-F 5:52am-5:52pm, Sa-Su 8:30am-5:30pm; fare $1, seniors 35¢, under 18 75¢).

The **SFO Airporter** (415-495-8404 or 800-532-8405) also connects to BART and the MUNI at the Powell and Montgomery stations downtown. In addition, the two Airporter routes stop at major downtown hotels around Union Square, the Civic Center, and the Financial District (from the airport 6:15am-midnight; from downtown 4:50am-11:40pm; fare $10).

A number of door-to-door commercial shuttles provide a compromise between the ease of a taxi and the value of public transportation. The **Super Shuttle** (415-558-8500 or 650-871-7800) and **Yellow Airport Shuttle** (415-282-7433) are both wheelchair accessible. **Francisco's Advanture** (415-821-0903 or 800-633-0903) provides door-to-door van service by advance reservation. Van fares are generally $10-14.

Taxi rides to downtown from SFO cost about $30. Check free area guides for coupons (see **Publications,** p. 86).

Flights into Oakland or San Jose can sometimes be cheaper than their counterparts to SFO, depending on the airline. BART connects the Oakland airport to San Francisco. (For more information, see **Oakland,** p. 140, or **San Jose,** p. 149.)

BY BUS OR TRAIN. Transbay Terminal, 425 Mission St. (415-495-1575), at 1st St. downtown, is a regional transportation hub (open daily 4:30am-12:30am). Buses from Golden Gate Transit, Alameda County Transit, and San Mateo Transit all stop here. An information center on the second floor has maps, displays, and free phone lines for each of these systems. Greyhound **buses** (800-231-2222) run from the terminal to **L.A.** ($36) and **Las Vegas** ($51-54). More in keeping with the spirit of California is the Green Tortoise "adventure travel" bus line (415-956-7500 or 800-TORTOIS/867-8647; www.greentortoise.com). It is affiliated with the hostel of the same name (see **Accommodations,** p. 87) and offers overnight bus service complete with meals and a mellow attitude from various destinations along the coast including **L.A.** ($35), **Seattle** ($59), **Portland** ($49), Baja, Alaska, Yosemite, and more. The Transbay Terminal has a desk for Amtrak **trains** (800-USA-RAIL/872-7245) and, on the lower floor, free buses shuttle passengers to the three Amtrak stations in the city, as well as its larger hubs in **Oakland** and **Emeryville** (open daily 6:45am-10:45pm). **CalTrain** (800-660-4287 in San Francisco only), at 4th and Townsend St., is a regional commuter train that runs south to **Palo Alto** ($4, seniors and under 12 $2) and **San Jose** ($5.25, seniors and under 12 $2.50), with service to Santa Cruz.

BY CAR. From the south, approach the city directly on **U.S. 101, Interstate 280,** or **Route 1.** From the north, U.S. 101 and Rte. 1 will bring you over the **Golden Gate Bridge** (southbound-only toll $3). From inland California, **Interstate 5** to **Interstate 580** to **Interstate 80,** which runs across the **Bay Bridge** (westbound-only toll $2).

The drive from L.A. takes six hours on I-5, eight hours on U.S. 101, or a leisurely 9½ hours on Rte. 1, the legendary Pacific Coast Hwy. U.S. 101 offers a compromise between vistas and velocity, but the stunning coastal scenery that unfolds along Rte. 1 can make getting there much more fun.

If you're a driver who needs a passenger or a passenger who needs a driver, call **KALX Radio** (90.7 FM; 510-642-5259), on the Berkeley campus, to put your name and number on the air for free or just tune in when they broadcast their ride list, daily at 10am and 10pm. **San Francisco State University,** north of Haight-Ashbury, has ride boards in the SFSU Student Union (info desk 338-1112; open M-Th 7:30am-7pm, F 7:30am-6pm), as do lots of coffee shops and student hangouts in the area.

GETTING AROUND

PUBLIC TRANSIT: MUNI AND BART. Streetcars and an extensive public transit system make San Francisco something of an anomaly in a state full of auto-eroticizers; the Bay Area is the easiest place on the West Coast to explore without a car. Most transport within the city falls under the aegis of the **San Francisco Municipal Railway** (**MUNI;** pronounced MEW-nee; 415-6-SF-MUNI/673-6864)—something of a misnomer since the system includes buses, cable cars, subways, and streetcars. It is the cheapest and most efficient way to get around the city and the official and indispensable MUNI maps ($2.75) cover all regional bus and subway services and double as excellent street maps. MUNI passports, sold at the Powell St. visitors center (see p. 84) and some accommodations, are valid on all MUNI vehicles, including cable cars (1 day $6, 3 days $10, 7 days $15). The Weekly Pass is cheaper ($9) but must be purchased for a single work week and requires an additional $1 to ride the cable cars. The Monthly FastPass ($35) includes in-town BART trips and cable cars. Sometimes it's better simply to pay the fare ($1, seniors and ages 5-17 35¢, under 5 free) and ask for a free transfer (valid for 1½hr.). Despite a core series of all-night routes on "Owl Service," coverage decreases considerably after dark. Wheelchair accessibility varies among bus routes, and while all below-ground subway stations are accessible, the Metro is not accessible at all above-ground sites.

MUNI **cable cars** are a classic San Franciscan image, pervading the pop cultural landscape. Declared a national historic landmark in 1964, the colorful cable cars are much more about image than practicality. The cars are noisy, slow (9½mph), and usually crammed full, making them an unreliable method of getting around. You won't be the first person to think of taking one to Fisherman's Wharf. Still, there is something charming about these relics, and you'll probably want to try them, especially if you have a MUNI passport. To avoid the mobs, the best strategy is to get up early and climb the hills with the sunrise. Of the three lines, the **Powell-Mason (PM)** line, which runs to the wharf, is always the most popular. The **California (C)** line, from the Financial District up through Nob Hill, is usually the least crowded, but the **Powell-Hyde (PH)** line, with the steepest hills and the sharpest turns, may be the most fun. (All lines run daily 6am-12:45am. Fare $2, seniors and disabled $1 before 7am and after 9pm. No free transfers.)

Connections to neighboring cities are well-coordinated and speedy via **Bay Area Rapid Transit** (**BART;** 650-992-2278). BART operates modern, carpeted trains along four lines connecting San Francisco with the **East Bay,** including **Oakland, Berkeley, Concord,** and **Fremont.** All stations provide free maps and schedules. There are eight BART stops in San Francisco proper, but BART is not a local transportation system. All stops are wheelchair accessible. (Trains run M-F 4am-midnight, Sa 6am-midnight, Su 8am-midnight. Intracity fare $1.10, to the East Bay up to $6.)

CARS, BICYCLES, AND FEET. A **car** is not necessary for getting around the city or area and may be more trouble than it's worth. **Parking** in San Francisco is rare and expensive even where legal, and a network of zealous traffic cops doles out copious tickets, despite local protests against the city's outrageous regulations. The many broken parking meters indicate an irate citizenry, but the time limit still applies to such spaces, and you may be ticketed up to three times for one offense. Whatever you do, don't block a sidewalk disabled-access ramp—the ticket is a whopping $250. If you have a car that you'd like to stow while exploring the city, you can leave it parked all day in the residential Richmond or Sunset districts—just make certain you heed signs indicating weekly street-cleaning times.

As evidenced by the terrain, **driving** in San Francisco demands a certain conscientiousness. Contending with the treacherous hills is the first task; if you've arrived in a standard (manual) transmission vehicle, you'll need to develop a fast clutch foot, since all hills have stop signs at the crests. If you're renting, get an automatic transmission. Make sure to stop for cable cars, because they won't stop for you. (For **car rental** information, see p. 84.)

The street signs admonishing you to "Prevent Runaways" refer not to wayward youth but to cars poorly parked on hills. When parking facing uphill, turn your front wheels away from the curb, and leave the car in first gear if you're driving a standard transmission. If your car starts to roll, it will stop (you hope) when the tires hit the curb. When facing downhill, turn the wheels toward the curb and leave the car in reverse. *Always* set the emergency brake.

Biking is popular in San Francisco, but the major hills are predictably punishing. Even the hardiest bike couriers have been spotted walking their bikes up the especially steep grades. Of course, you always get to come back down. Many rental shops supply free maps of area bike routes. For information on **bike rentals,** see page 84. Motorcycles and scooters make things a little easier on the quadriceps and are common in the area, too.

Walking in San Francisco is worthwhile and unavoidable, and by far the best way to get to know the neighborhoods. There are many walking tours of the city for those who'd like to begin their travels with a colorful native guide. Some even promise "no steep hills." The Public Library's **City Guides** program (415-557-4266) leads several free walking tours every day in summer; schedules are available at libraries and the **Visitor Information Center,** which also supplies brochures on many year-round commercial tours (see **Visitor Information Center,** p. 84).

PRACTICAL INFORMATION

PRIVATE TRANSPORTATION

Car Rental: Enterprise, 6770 Mission St. (in S.F. 800-RENT-A-CAR/736-8222, outside S.F. 800-325-8007), has city-wide branches and will pick you up. Must be 21; drivers under 25 pay $10 per day surcharge. Compacts from $36 per day, $170 per week. Unlimited free mileage within CA. Weekend specials. Open M-F 7:30am-6pm, Sa 9am-noon. **A-One,** 434 O'Farrell St. (771-3977), between Taylor and Jones St. Must be 21, drivers under 25 pay $5 per day surcharge. $30 per day with 150mi. included. Open M-F 8am-6pm, Sa-Su 8am-5pm.

Taxis: Town Taxi (546-1616). **Yellow Cab** (626-2345). **Luxor Cab** (282-4141). **City Wide Dispatch** (920-0700). Some wheelchair accessible vans. All operate 24hr. Taxis are not as easy to hail on the street as they are in many American cities.

Bike/Skate Rental: American Rentals, 2715 Hyde St. (931-0234), at Beach St. by Fisherman's Wharf, rents bikes ($5 per hr.), tandem bikes ($8 per hr.), scooters (from $45 per day), and motorcycles (from $150 per day). Open daily 9am-9pm. **Skates on Haight,** 1818 Haight St. (752-8375), rents in-line skates ($6 per hr., $24 per day). Open M-F 11am-7pm, Sa-Su 10am-6pm. **Blazing Saddles,** 1095 Columbus Ave. (202-8888), at Francisco St., rents bikes ($5 per hr., $25 per day). Open daily 8am-7pm. **Bikes and Blades in Golden Gate Park,** 50 Stow Lake Dr. (668-6699), at the Stow Lake Boathouse, rents bikes (from $6 per hr., $18 per day) and in-line skates ($6 per hr., $15 per day). Open M-F 10am-7pm, Sa-Su 9am-8pm.

VISITOR INFORMATION

Visitor Information Center (391-2000; 24hr. info recordings in English 391-2001 and Spanish 391-2122; fax 800-220-5747; www.sfvisitor.org), in Hallidie Plaza at Powell St. beneath street level at the BART exit. Maps and brochures cover tours, services, and attractions. MUNI passports and maps for sale. Open M-F 9am-5pm, Sa-Su 9am-3pm.

California Welcome Center (956-3493), Pier 39 at the Great San Francisco Adventure. This state-of-the-art facility's happy staff is helpful even if you don't stock up on Golden Gate Bridge snow globes or prehistoric shark's teeth. Open daily 10am-6pm.

Redwood Empire Association, 2801 Leavenworth St., 2nd fl. (394-5991 or 888-678-8509; www.redwoodempire.com), on Fisherman's Wharf. Offers a free 48-page guide to the area between San Francisco and Oregon. Open M-Sa 10am-5pm.

TOURIST AND FINANCIAL SERVICES

Budget Travel: Hostelling International, 425 Divisadero St. #307 (701-1320). Open M-F 11am-6pm.

Consulates: Australia, 1 Bush St. #700 (362-6160), at Market St. Open M-F 8:45am-5pm. **Ireland,** 44 Montgomery St. #3830 (392-4214; fax 392-0885), between Post and Sutter St. Open M-F 9am-noon and 2-4pm. **U.K.,** 1 Sansome St. #850 (981-3030), at Market and Sutter St. Open M-F 8:30am-5pm. **For all visas, arrive at the consulate before opening time or else face a long line.**

Currency Exchange: Available at the airport and most banks. **Pacific Foreign Exchange Inc.,** 527 Sutter St. (391-2548), near Powell St. Open M-F 9am-6pm, Sa 10am-3pm. **Foreign Exchange Ltd.,** 415 Stockton St. (397-4700), near Sutter St. Open Apr.-Sept. M-F 9am-5:30pm, Sa 10am-4pm; Oct.-Mar. M-F 9am-5:30pm. Neither charge commision. **Thomas Cooke** (800-287-7362). Various locations.

LOCAL SERVICES

San Francisco Public Library: Main Branch, 100 Larkin St. (557-4400), between Grove and Fulton St. Visitors can browse the shelves for books and the basement cafe for baked goods in this miraculously airy hyper-modern, earthquake-proof structure. Library cards are available free with some evidence of California residence; visitors must pay $25 for 3-month privileges. Open M 10am-6pm, Tu-Th 9am-8pm, F 11am-5pm, Sa 9am-5pm, Su noon-5pm. **Mission Branch,** 300 Bartlett St. (695-5090), at 24th St. Open M 1-9pm, Tu-W 10am-9pm, Th and Sa 10am-6pm, F 1-6pm, Su 1-5pm. **China-**

town Branch, 1135 Powell St. (274-0275), near Jackson St. Open M 1-9pm, Tu 10am-8pm, W 1-8pm, Th and Sa 10am-6pm, Su 1-5pm.

Ticket Agencies: TIX Bay Area, Stockton St. (433-7827; www.theaterbayarea.org), at Union Square between Post and Geary St. Tickets to concerts, clubs, plays, and sports. Half-price tickets often available on day of show (cash only; inquire in person) and on Sa for Su-M events. Carries travel passes and tourist info. Open Tu-Th 11am-6pm, F-Sa 11am-7pm. TIX is the full-service downtown outlet of **BASS Tickets** (510-762-2277, 776-1999, or 800-225-2277). Other outlets include **Tower Records,** at Bay St. and Columbus Ave., and **Giants Dugout,** 4 Embarcadero Ctr. Phone service M-Sa 8:30am-9pm, Su 10am-9pm.

Road Conditions: TravInfo (415-817-1717); rotary phones use **CalTrans** (916-445-1534). Both have 24hr. driving info for the state.

Weather Conditions: National Weather Service (650-364-7974 in S.F.; www.nws.mbay.net.). 24hr. phone recording.

LAUNDROMATS

Brainwash, 1122 Folsom St. (861-FOOD/3663), between 7th and 8th St. in SoMa. Why-didn't-I-think-of-that combo of coffeehouse, restaurant, live music venue, and laundromat. SoMa patrons are as hip as they can be, considering their underwear is on display. "Wash-Day Blues" blueberry pancakes $4.75. Wash $1.75, 8min. dry 25¢. Open Su-Th 7:30am-11pm (last wash 10:30pm), F-Sa 7am-1am (last wash 11pm). Food served until 1hr. before closing; breakfast M-F until 11am; brunch Sa-Su 9am-4pm.

Doo Wash, 817 Columbus Ave. (885-1222), near Lombard St. in North Beach. Video games, pinball machines, pool table, and TV. Sandwiches and espresso drinks ($3-4) in the foyer. The machines use tokens that can be bought at the laundromat. Wash $1.25, dry $1. Open daily 7am-11pm (last load 9:30pm).

CULTURAL AND COMMUNITY CENTERS

Bi-Gay-Lesbian Organization: Pacific Center, 2712 Telegraph Ave., Berkeley (510-548-8283), at Derby St. Counseling and info on gay community events, housing, local clubs, etc. *Very* helpful staff. Open M-F 10am-10pm, Sa noon-3pm and 7-10pm, Su 6-9pm.

Booker T. Washington Community Center (African-American), 800 Presidio Ave. (928-1430; fax 928-6927; email btwcsc@aol.com), between Post and Sutter St. Educational, cultural, and recreational programs. Open M-F 9am-5pm.

Chinese Culture Center, 750 Kearny St., 3rd fl. (986-1822), at Washington St. in the Holiday Inn. Info on Chinese community events, cultural programs, and Chinatown walking tours (see **Chinatown,** p. 78). Open Tu-Sa 9am-5:30pm. Gallery open Tu-Su 10:30am-4pm.

Japanese Cultural and Community Center of Northern California, 1840 Sutter St. (567-5505), between Buchanan and Webster St. Open M-F 9am-5pm.

Jewish Community Information and Referral, 121 Steuart St. (777-4545), between Mission and Howard St. Information on religious services, kosher restaurants, and community events. Open M-F 9am-5pm. In case of emergency, call the Jewish Family and Children Service (567-8860) M-Th 8:30am-7:15pm, F 8:30am-5pm, or the Board of Rabbis after 5pm (788-3630).

Mission Cultural Center for Latino Art, 2868 Mission St. (821-1155), between 24th and 25th St. Art, info, and cultural exhibits. Office open M-Sa 10am-4pm; building open Tu-F 10am-9:30pm, Sa 10am-5pm.

San Francisco Senior Center, 481 O'Farrell St. (771-7950), between Jones and Taylor St. Special events, lunches, dances, art workshops, and films for the over-60 crowd. Open M-Th 9am-4pm, F 9am-3:30pm, Sa-Su 10am-2pm.

Women's Building of the Bay Area, 3543 18th St. (431-1180). Neighborhood and women's center. Tours, info, and referral service. Open daily 9am-5pm.

LOCAL MEDIA

Television Stations: ABC (Channel 7); **CBS** (Channel 5); **Fox** (Channel 2); **NBC** (Channel 4); **WB** (Channel 20); **PBS** (Channel 9).

National Public Radio: KAWL 91.7FM.

Smooth Jazz: 103.7FM, jazz smoother than a baby's bottom.

Other Radio Stations: Pop/Rock/Top 40 "Alice" 97.3FM; **Rock** KRQR 106.7FM; **New Rock** KFOG 104.5FM; **Classic Rock** KSAN 107.7FM; **Liberation** 93.7FM; **R&B** KBLX 102.9FM.

EMERGENCY AND COMMUNICATIONS

Emergency: 911.

Police: 553-0123. **Fire:** 558-3268.

24-Hour Crisis Lines: Drug Crisis Line (362-3400). **Rape Crisis Center** (647-RAPE/7273). **Suicide Prevention** (781-0500). **United Helpline** (772-HELP/4357). **Disability Crisis** (800-426-4263).

AIDS Crisis Lines: California HIV/AIDS Hotline (800-367-2437). 24hr. **AIDS/HIV Nightline** (434-2437). Open daily 5pm-5am.

24-Hour Pharmacy: Walgreen's, 498 Castro St. (861-3136), at 18th St.; 3201 Divisadero St. (931-6417), at Lombard St. in the Marina. **RiteAid,** 5280 Geary Blvd. (800-4-DRUGST/437-8478).

Medical Services: San Francisco General Hospital, 1001 Potrero Ave. (206-8000), at 23rd St. in the Mission. Take MUNI #48 Quintara. Emergency room with 24hr. walk-in service. **Haight-Ashbury Free Medical Clinic,** 558 Clayton St. (487-5632). Appointments only. Open M 1-9pm, Tu-Th 9am-9pm, F 1-5pm. **Lyon-Martin Women's Clinic,** 1748 Market St. #201 (565-7667), at Valencia St. between Gough and Octavia St. Primary medical care; female-specific, HIV, lesbian/gay services. Fees on sliding scale. English- and Spanish-speaking staff. Open M-Tu and Th-F 8:30am-5pm, W 8:30am-7:30pm. **Health Center,** 1490 Mason St. (705-8500), near Broadway in Chinatown. Contraceptives and counseling. Fees on a sliding scale. Appointments only. Call M-F 8am-5pm. **University of California Dental Clinic,** 707 Parnassus Ave. (476-1891), at the UCSF Medical Center. Appointments only. Call M-F 8:30am-5pm. **Planned Parenthood Golden Gate,** 815 Eddy St., 2nd fl. (441-5454 or 800-967-PLAN/7526).

Internet Access: San Francisco Public Library (see **Local Services,** p. 84). Sign up 30min. in advance for free 30min. slots. Other library machines have Internet for library use only. **Seattle Street Coffee,** 456 Geary St. (922-4566). 2 computers available for Internet. $2.50 for 15min. ID or $10 deposit. **Global Bazaar,** 401 O'Farrell St. (885-6890; www.globalbazaargifts.com). Access on 6 computers. $3 for 15min.

Post Office: 800-275-8777. **Civic Center Station,** 101 Hyde St. at Golden Gate Ave. Open M, W, and F 6am-5:30pm, Tu and Th 6am-8:30pm, Sa 6am-3pm. General Delivery open M-F 11am-2pm. **ZIP Code:** 94142. **Chinatown Station,** 867 Stockton St. at Clay St. Open M-F 9am-5:30pm, Sa 9am-4:30pm. **ZIP Code:** 94108. **Geary Station,** 5654 Geary Blvd. at 21st St. Open M-F 9am-5:30pm, Sa 9am-4:30pm. **ZIP Code:** 94121.

AREA CODE	Unless otherwise noted, San Francisco's area code is 415.

PUBLICATIONS

Free publications flood San Francisco cafes, visitors centers, and sidewalk boxes, and offer a local spin on upcoming events and activities. The progressive *Bay Guardian* comes out on Wednesdays, as does *S.F. Weekly,* its major competitor, which has similar politics but a more skeptical tone and proudly limits itself to the city proper for its listings and distribution. Both have comprehensive nightlife listings. Harder to find, but worth the effort, are two special-interest rags: *Poetry Flash,* available at discerning bookstores, has the skinny on literary happenings, while the *Bay Area Music (BAM)* magazine is available at the livelier cafes and restaurants in town. The monthly *Source* is comprehensive, but not terribly user-friendly with its endless, undiscriminating list of venues.

Various tourist-targeting, **coupon**-filled free glossies are in sidewalk boxes in the heavily trafficked Fisherman's Wharf and Union Square areas as well as at visitors centers. Among them are the *Bay City Guide,* the *San Francisco Guide,* and the *San Francisco Quick Guide.* The annual *Chaperon* introduces San Francisco in

German, French, Spanish, and Italian. The city administrators print a *Lodging Guide* and *The San Francisco Book*, excellent compilations of tourist info.

The largest Bay Area **daily** is the *San Francisco Chronicle* (50¢). The *San Francisco Examiner*, whose future is currently in question, was started by yellow journalist William Randolph Hearst and currently run by Sharon Stone's husband Phil Bronstein, has lunchtime and evening editions. (For more on William Randolph Hearst, see **Hearst Castle,** p. 221.) The two papers share a Sunday edition ($1.50). Some find the pink *Datebook* section of the Sunday edition to be a worthwhile entertainment resource.

San Francisco has several **gay and lesbian publications.** The *Bay Times* appears monthly with a thorough entertainment section and the work of talented cartoonists. The *Bay Area Reporter* contains articles on gay pride as well as a highly varied "Arts & Entertainment" section. *The Sentinel* offers information on gay community events. The free semi-weeklies *Odyssey* and *Oblivion* are excellent guides for gay bars, clubs, and stores. For $11, *Betty and Pansy's Severe Queer Review of San Francisco*, a kind of travel guide to gay San Francisco, is both hysterically funny and brutally frank. These publications can be found in cafes and bars around Castro and Polk St. and at A Different Light Bookstore (see p. 113).

ACCOMMODATIONS

There are a tremendous number of reasonably priced and convenient places to stay in San Francisco, but they tend to fill up in peak season, so plan ahead. Unfortunately, many budget accommodations are in the less safe areas—the Tenderloin can be particularly dangerous. Many of the large number of hotels function as temporary housing for those in search of jobs or apartments; places geared towards tourists may require credit card, passport, or out-of-state ID.

HOSTELS

For those who don't mind sharing a room with strangers, San Francisco's better hostels are homier, cheaper, and safer than most budget hotels. Book in advance if at all possible, but as many do not take reservations for summer, you might have to just show up or call early (10am-noon) on your day of arrival. Travelers with cars should also consider the Marin Headlands Hostel, a tranquil and beautiful spot just minutes from the city across the Golden Gate Bridge (see p. 162). Some hostels ask for a foreign passport as identification; American citizens are usually welcome but sometimes must prove they are not local residents.

San Francisco International Guest House, 2976 23rd St. (641-1411), at Harrison St. in the **Mission.** From downtown, take BART to 24th St. or take bus #7B to Potrero and 4th St. No sign marks this beautiful Victorian house with hardwood floors, wall tapestries, and houseplants. Free coffee and foreign magazines. TV area, 2 kitchens (smoking and non), and guest phones. Linen included. Neighborhood parking. 5-night min. stay, 3-month max. stay. Dorms $14; 1 private double $28. Getting in can be like escaping Alcatraz: the Guest House does not take reservations and is virtually always full. All you can do is try calling. **Passport with international stamps required.**

AYH Hostel at Union Square (San Francisco—Downtown; HI-AYH), 312 Mason St. (788-5604), between Geary and O'Farrell St., 1 block from **Union Square.** TV, Internet access ($1 for 5min.), and visitor info, including walking tours and a seminar on San Francisco nightlife. Kitchens have toasters, microwaves, and storage, but no stoves. Quiet hours (midnight-7am) not always respected by Mason St. traffic. Key deposit $5. Reception 24hr. Mainly doubles and quads. June-Sept. $19, Oct.-Jan $17, Feb.-May $18; nonmembers $3 more; under 13 half-price with parent. Wheelchair access. Reserve by phone with credit card, or show up around 8am. IBN reservations available.

San Francisco International Student Center, 1188 Folsom St. (255-8800), at 8th St. in **SoMa.** From the airport, take SamTrans bus #7B to 9th and Folsom St.; from Transbay Terminal, take MUNI bus #12 to 8th and Howard St. Plaid carpet, brick walls, and chummy international crowd. Free coffee and tea. Lack of TV leads to constant kitchen conversation. Hall bathrooms with massage showerheads. Hostelers don't pay cover at Cat Club downstairs–bring dancing shoes or earplugs. Reception 8am-11pm. Check-out 11am. Dorms $15. No credit cards. **Foreign passport or out-of-state ID required.**

Fort Mason Hostel (HI-AYH), Bldg. #240, Fort Mason (771-7277), in the **Marina.** Entrance at Bay and Franklin St., 1 block west of Van Ness Ave., or on McDowell on the water side. Hostel is behind administrative buildings. Take MUNI bus #42 or from SFO #7B or 7F. Beautiful surroundings give this 160-bed hostel a campground feel. Not a place for partiers, though–strictly enforced quiet hours and other rules, such as no smoking or alcohol. Movies, walking tours, kitchen, dining room, bike storage. Usually booked weeks in advance, but a small number of beds are set aside for walk-ins each morning at 7am. Discount meals at cafe. Minor chores expected. Lockers and storage. Laundry. Parking included. Reception 24hr. Check-in 7-11:30am and 12:30pm-1am. Limited access 11:30am-2:30pm. Lights out 11pm, but no curfew. Dorms $18. IBN reservations available. No HI discount.

Globetrotters, 225 Ellis St. (346-5786), between Mason and Taylor St. near **Union Square.** Common room has couches and TV; some rooms have TVs. 46 beds. Large and fully equipped kitchen. Laundry. Check-in 8am-midnight. Check-out 11am. Dorms $13, weekly $85; doubles $26. No reservations in summer. No wheelchair access.

Pacific Tradewinds Guest House, 680 Sacramento St. (433-7970), between Kearny and Montgomery St. in the **Financial District.** From Transbay Terminal, take MUNI bus #1 and get off at Kearny and Sacramento St. This 35-bed facility has a common room, a kitchen, guest phone, and Internet access. Bike storage. Key deposit $20. 14-night max. stay. Reception 8am-midnight. July-Sept. dorms $18; Oct.-June $16. No reservations in summer. Discounts for VIP Backpacker and GO-25 cardholders. **Must be at least 18.** No wheelchair access.

Green Tortoise Guest House, 494 Broadway (834-1000; http://greentortoise.com/hostel), at Kearny St. in **North Beach.** Take MUNI bus #9X or 15 to Columbus Ave. and Broadway. From the Transbay Terminal, take MUNI bus #12 or 42 to Kearny St. and Pacific Ave. Single-occupancy bathrooms (and some in-room sinks) and 120 wooden bunks. Common room houses huge TV, couches, pool table, and young partiers. Sauna, Internet access ($2), kitchens, bike storage. Continental breakfast included. Lockers; bring a lock. Linen deposit. Coin laundry. 21-night max. stay. Reception 24hr. Dorms $19; private doubles $48. Credit cards accepted if reserving in advance.

Interclub Globe Hostel, 10 Hallam Pl. (431-0540), off Folsom St. between 7th and 8th St. in **SoMa.** From Transbay Terminal take MUNI bus #12 to 7th and Howard St. Common room has pool table and TV. No kitchen. Attached to Cassidy's Irish Pub and Globe Cafe (serves breakfast and dinner). Linen included. Check-out noon. Dorms $18. No credit cards or personal checks. **Passport with international stamps required.**

SoMa Inn, 1080 Folsom St. (863-7522), between 6th and 7th St. in **SoMa.** Basic but clean rooms on a barren block of Folsom St. Dorms $17; singles $29.50; doubles $39; triples $49.50; quads $69. Weekly: dorms $84.50; singles $135; doubles $189; triples $283.50; quads $378.

European Guest House, 761 Minna St. (861-6634), off 9th St. between Howard and Mission St. in **SoMa.** From Transbay Terminal take MUNI bus #14 to 9th St. Situated on a rather desolate block. Non-student clientele. Adequate facilities. Reception 24hr. Dorms $18; private doubles $32.

HOTELS

Hostels generally offer a better package, but travelers who put a premium on privacy might prefer to spring for one of the city's hotels. The free *Lodging Guide*, available at the visitors center, offers an idea of rate schemes. Keep in mind that many budget-range hotels in San Francisco are in unsavory areas—and that when it comes to cleanliness and helpfulness, you often get what you pay for. All hotels are busy in summer, so reserve several weeks in advance if possible. Prices listed for hotels do not include the city hotel tax. Rates given are approximate.

Adelaide Inn, 5 Isadora Duncan (441-2261), at the end of a little alley off Taylor St. between Geary and Post St., 2 blocks west of **Union Square.** Warm hosts, lovely furnishings, and reasonable prices make this quiet 18-room oasis the most charming of San Francisco's many "European-style" hotels. Steep stairs, no elevator. All rooms have large windows, TV, and sink. Kitchen with guest fridge available; shared hallway bathrooms. Continental breakfast included. Reception Tu-F 9am-1pm and 5-9pm, Sa-M flexible, but someone's generally around. Singles $42; doubles $52-58. Reserve at least 10 days in advance.

The Red Victorian Bed, Breakfast, and Art, 1665 Haight St. (864-1978), in the **Haight.** The Red Vic is more a cosmic understanding than a hotel. All 18 rooms are individually decorated to honor peace, sunshine, or butterflies. Even the hall baths have their own motifs and names. Heal your aura under the tie-dyed canopy of the "Summer of Love" room, or retreat to the Meditation room. Free tea and coffee. Breakfast included. F-Sa 2-night min. stay. Reception 9am-9pm. Check-in 3-6pm or by appt. Check-out 11am. Most doubles $86-126; discount on stays of 3 days or more. Reserve well in advance.

Pensione International, 875 Post St. (775-3344), east of Hyde St. in the **Tenderloin.** Clean, comfortable rooms in a hotel packed with groovy modern art—paintings, murals, and sculptures. Continental breakfast included. Singles and doubles with shared bath $75, with private bath $95.

Golden Gate Hotel, 775 Bush St. (392-3702 or 800-835-1118), between Mason and Powell St. near **Union Square.** Charming hotel, built in 1913, has tasteful antiques and bright bay windows. Comfy rooms with TV. Spotless hall bathrooms. Continental breakfast and afternoon tea (4-7pm) included. Garage parking $12 per day. No singles; doubles $72, with bath $109.

Grant Plaza Hotel, 465 Grant Ave. (434-3883 or 800-472-6899), at Pine St. in **Chinatown.** Modern furnishings and friendly personal service at a central, if occasionally noisy, location. All rooms with private bath. Singles $52-75; doubles $65-85.

Hotel Essex, 684 Ellis St. (474-4664 or 800-443-7739, out-of-state 800-453-7739), at Larkin St., north of Civic Center at western edge of the **Tenderloin.** Charming rooms with private baths, color TVs, and phones. Elegant lobby; free coffee and tea. Staff speaks French and German. No parking. Reception 24hr. Check-out noon. Singles $79; doubles $89; a few rooms with shared bath $59.

Herbert Hotel, 161 Powell St. (362-1600; www.herberthotel.com), between Ellis and O'Farrell St. south of **Union Square.** Generic rooms, but good value for this extremely central location—Powell St. cable cars stop right outside the door. Angle for a room on a higher floor to be near the kitchen (6th fl.) and escape the sounds of city traffic. Access to swimming pool at a sister hotel a few blocks away. Luggage storage. Laundry. Singles $55, with private bath $75; doubles $60, with private bath $85. With shared bath, weekly singles $225; doubles $275.

Temple Hotel, 469 Pine St. (781-2565), between Kearny and Montgomery St. in the **Financial District.** Well-maintained hotel has 1960s decor and rickety elevator. Most rooms have TVs. Reception 8am-10pm. Check-out 11am. Singles $40, with private bath $50; doubles $45, with bath $55. No credit cards.

Ansonia Hotel, 711 Post St. (673-2670, 673-7232, or 800-221-6470) between Jones and Leavenworth St. in the **Tenderloin.** All 125 rooms have TV. Breakfast (served daily 7-8:30am) and dinner (M-Sa) included. Laundry. Singles or doubles $56, with bath $69. Weekly rates available Sept.-Apr.

The Biltmore, 735 Taylor St. (673-4277 or 888-290-5508), and **The Amsterdam,** 749 Taylor St. (673-3277 or 800-637-3444), between Bush and Sutter St. northwest of **Union Square,** are run by the same owner. The older Amsterdam (built 1909) is more ornate, with a kitchen and outdoor patio; a few of its lovely rooms even have jacuzzi and private deck. Continental breakfast included. Singles with shared bath $89, with private bath $99; doubles $99, with private bath $100; additional person $10. The simpler, newer **Biltmore** is furnished in generic motel style. Singles $69-79; doubles $79-89; weekly rates available.

Gum Moon Women's Residence, 940 Washington St. (421-8827), at Stockton St. in **Chinatown.** Bright, spacious rooms with shared bath in a large, clean house. Living room has piano, TV, and VCR. Fabulous kitchen. Very secure. Shared bath. Laundry (wash 75¢, dry 50¢). Reception 8am-midnight. Curfew midnight. Rooms $18, weekly $110. Reservations no more than 1 week in advance. **Women over 18 only.**

YMCA Chinatown, 855 Sacramento St. (576-9622), between Grant and Stockton St. in **Chinatown.** Ornate Chinese gate is the only thing fancy: 29 plain rooms. Pool and gym. No visitors allowed. Reception M-F 6:30am-10pm, Sa 9am-5pm, Su 9am-4pm. Check-out 1pm. No curfew. Singles $30-32; doubles $40. Pay for 6 nights in advance, and the 7th is free. **Men over 18 only.**

Aida Hotel, 1087 Market St. (863-4141 or 800-863-2432), at 7th St. next to Merrill's near **Civic Center.** Italian-run *albergo* with simple rooms. Continental breakfast included. Singles $33, with bath $49; doubles $43, with bath $59. **Credit card or passport required.**

The Phoenix, 601 Eddy St. (776-1380 or 800-248-9466), at Larkin St. north of Civic Center in the **Tenderloin,** is well-secured against a tough neighborhood. Luxurious, sweet-smelling rooms with space-age bachelor pad decor and a gorgeous black-and-white tiled swimming pool. Cable and closed-circuit movies. Popular Backflip cocktail lounge downstairs. Parking included. Doubles start at a pricey $129—but you can argue them down to $89-$99 on a slow night.

SAN FRANCISCO

LONGER STAYS

It's an odd thing, but anyone who disappears is said to be seen in San Francisco.
—Oscar Wilde

Establishments specializing in weekly or monthly accommodations can provide great deals for long-term city visitors (see **Home Exchange,** p. 46). In fact, due to the city's psychotic housing market, many lower income residents live in hotels for decades. If you stay in a residential hotel, you can expect shared bath and showers with no maid service or parking, but on the plus side, you're exempt from the hotel tax if you pay for 28 days or more. Seasonal apartment shares can sometimes be found through on-line sources like SFNet/Rents (www.sfnet.com), or the smaller but free UCSF housing office (www.ucsf.edu). Be prepared to pay in advance. In case you end up having a really long stay, some popular services for finding apartments and roommates are Roommate Referral (626-0606; www.roommatelink.com), Metro Rent (563-RENT/7368; www.metrorent.com), Rent Tech (863-RENT/7368; www.renttech.com) and SpringStreet (771-0223).

Harcourt Residence Club, 1105 Larkin St. (673-7720; fax 474-6729), at Sutter, north of the Civic Center in the **Tenderloin.** Popular with foreign students, the Harcourt looks and feels like a well-kept university dorm. Rooms offered weekly or monthly only. Includes 5-day maid service, 2 meals per day M-Sa, Su brunch, private phone, mailbox, and message service. TV room and sundeck. Friendly staff hosts weekly cookouts and parties. Laundry. Reception 9am-5pm. Singles with private bath $250; doubles $300, with bath $350. Cheaper monthly rates. Reservation deposit $50.

Halcyon, 649 Jones St. (929-8033), between Geary and Post St. near **Union Square.** Rooms include baths, fridges, microwaves, coffeemakers, safes, cable TV, phones, and voice mail. May-Oct. singles from $360 per week, doubles from $420 per week; Nov.-Apr. singles from $300 per week, doubles from $360 per week. A few rooms available daily ($65-95) in summer only. Reserve 3 months in advance for weekly stays.

FOOD

Any resident will tell you that San Francisco is not made of landmarks or "sights," but its diverse collection of neighborhoods. Even the weather changes from block to block, with the Castro and Mission enjoying San Francisco's sunniest climes. If you blindly rush from Fisherman's Wharf to Coit Tower to Mission Dolores, you'll be missing the city itself. Strolling and sampling the food in each neighborhood is an excellent way to get a taste for the city's diversity. The hippie Be-Ins of the 1960s may be over, but there's still no better city to just *be* in.

To get an up-to-date take on the best restaurants, try consulting newspaper reviews—everyone has their own strident opinions, but the *Examiner* and the *Bay Guardian* are generally reliable. The glossy *Bay Area Vegetarian* can also suggest places to graze.

We have prefaced the listings with an index of all restaurants organized by feature or type of cuisine. **Let's Go Picks** (denoted by ☒) combine exceptional cuisine with prices that are either reasonable or easily overlooked in lieu of quality. Every restaurant listed in these sections is followed by an abbreviated neighborhood label, which directs you to the restaurant's complete listing:

CA	Castro
CC	Civic Center
CH	Chinatown
FD	Financial District
FW	Fisherman's Wharf
HA	Haight Ashbury
JA	Japantown
MA	Marina
MD	Mission District
NB	North Beach
NH	Nob Hill
PH	Pacific Heights
RI	Richmond
SD	Sunset District
SO	SoMA
US	Union Square

BY CUISINE

AFRICAN
☒Nyala CC

BAKERY
☒Ti Couz MD
Peasant Pies CA
Bepples Pies MA
Specialty's FD
Boudin Bakery FW
Mini Donuts FW

CAFES
☒Cafe Bean US
☒Ti Couz MD
Crepes on Cole HA
Horseshoe Cafe HA
Blue Front Cafe HA
Boogaloos MD
Bagdad Cafe CA
Franciscan Croissant US
Einstein's Cafe SD
Blue Danube RI
Patisserie Cafe SO

CARIBBEAN
Cha Cha Cha HA

CHINESE
☒Chef Jia CH
☒House of Nanking CH
Brandy Ho's CH
King Tin CH
Kowloon CH
Silver Restaurant CH
U-Lee NH
Red Crane RI

DELI
Horseshoe Cafe HA
Mario's Bohemian Cigar Store Cage NB
Quality Market SD
Nob Hill Noshery Deli NH
Jona's on Hyde NH
Metropol FD

DINER
☒Hamburger Mary's SO
Hot 'n' Hunky CA
Orphan Andy's CA
Bob Broiler's Restaurnat NH
M's Cafe SD

GARLIC
Stinking Rose NB

HEALTH FOOD/VEGETARIAN
Jona's on Hyde NH
Chat House SO
Millenium CC
Ananda Fuara CC
Specialty's FD
Herbivore MD
Josie's Cabaret and Juice Joint CA

ICE CREAM
Toy Boat Dessert Cafe RI

ITALIAN

Sodini's Green Valley Restaurant	NB
Caffe Greco	NB
Vino e Cucina Trattoria	SO
LuLu	SO

JAPANESE

Country Station Sushi Cafe	MD
Kyoto Sushi	US
Soku's Teriyaki and Sushi	MA
Mifune	JA
Isobune	JA
Akasaka	JA
Jabon	JA

LATE NIGHT

El Farolito	MD
Orphan Andy's	CA
Marcello's	CA
My Canh	CH
Silver Restaurant	CH
Whiz Wit	SO
Tommy's Joynt	CC

MEXICAN

El Farolito	MD
Sweet Heat	HA, MA
La Taquería	CA
Azteca	CA
Rico's	FW

MIDDLE EASTERN

La Méditerranée	PH
Krivaar Cafe	FD
Blue Front Cafe	HA

PIZZA

Pizza Inferno	PH
Extreme Pizza	PH
All You Knead	HA

SEAFOOD

Crab Cake Lounge	FW

VIETNAMESE/INDONESIAN/ THAI

Golden Turtle	NH
New Golden Turtle	PH
Indonesia Restaurnat	US
Marnee Thai	SD

HAIGHT-ASHBURY

Haight-Ashbury has many good bakeries and ethnic restaurants with reasonable prices. Up and down the street, breakfast seems to be the most important meal of the day—with a pack of Marlboros and a hangover-fighting Bloody Mary, locals will linger over omelettes and home fries until late in the afternoon. There are several small **grocery stores** along and near Haight St.

Sweet Heat, 1725 Haight St. (387-8845). Cheap and excellent "healthy Mexican," in which creative ingredients are combined thoughtfully and with loyalty to the cuisine. Your body will need the break after testing their 57 kinds of tequila and 11 margaritas (including mango in season and tamarind). Filling tacos $3-4 each, quesadillas $3.75-8 (for fancy Dungeness crab). Open Su-Th 11am-10pm, F-Sa 11am-11pm.

All You Knead, 1466 Haight St. (552-4550). The 8-page menu of this spacious diner includes a large selection of pizzas, sandwiches, burgers, entrees, and breakfasts (including crepes and blintzes). Breakfast served M-F until 3:45pm; lunch all day; dinner 4pm until closing. Open M and W-Su 8am-10:50pm, Tu 8am-6pm.

Crepes on Cole, 100 Carl St. (664-1800), 4 blocks south of Haight St. along Cole St. From chicken pesto ($6.25) to strawberries and chocolate ($4), the flat fare displays a mastery of the medium. Espresso drinks, beer, and wine. Open Su-Th 7am-11pm, F-Sa 7am-midnight.

The Horseshoe Cafe, 566 Haight St. (626-8852), between Fillmore and Steiner St. Bright neo-Inca murals enliven the disorderly space, creating a welcoming setting for slugging a latte ($2), pounding a knish ($3), or body-slamming a napkin (free). Open daily 6am-12:30am.

Cha Cha Cha, 1801 Haight St. (386-5758), at Stanyan St. The wait can be endless, but it's worth it. Tip-top tapas, like fried plantains with black beans and sour cream ($4.50), take up over half the menu. Come mid-afternoon to avoid a crowd. Open Su-Th 11:30am-4pm and 5-11pm, F-Sa 11:30am-4pm and 5-11:30pm. No reservations.

Blue Front Cafe, 1430 Haight St. (252-5917), between Ashbury St. and Masonic Ave. Whether you're drinking beer ($2.50) or ginseng chai ($2.50), you'll find comfortable company at this neighborhood nook. Omelettes ($5-7) and light dinner (Middle Eastern plates $4-7). Open Su-Th 8am-11pm.

THE MISSION DISTRICT

The Mission is one of the best places in the city to find excellent, satisfying, cheap food. Inexpensive *taquerías* and other international eateries line Mission, 24th, and 16th St. The area also boasts the city's best and cheapest produce at many streetside stands. Even the most substantial appetites will be satisfied by the Mexican, Salvadoran, and South American restaurants on 24th St. (east of Mission St.) or the host of other cuisines available along Valencia St.

El Farolito, 4817 Mission St. (337-5500), at 24th St. The spot for cheap and fresh late-night food, frequented by all segments of the Mission population. Tacos $1.55. Open daily 9am-1:45am.

Country Station Sushi Cafe, 2140 Mission St. (861-0972), between 17th and 18th St. An unexpected gem, sunny, big-hearted, and clean on a rather grimy stretch of Mission St. The decor is loopy kitsch, the sushi is excellent (2-piece *nigiri* $3-4). Traditional sushi combos start at $8. Open M-Th 5-10pm, F-Sa 5-11pm.

Ti Couz, 3108 16th St. (25-CREPE/252-7373), at Valencia St. All about crepes. Almost too many varieties of savory ($2.50-6.25) and sweet ($2.50-5.25) crepes, plus dozens of tempting additions and toppings. Often crowded. No reservations; no takeout. Open M-F 11am-11pm, Sa 10am-11pm, Su 10am-10pm.

Herbivore, 983 Valencia St. (826-5657), at 21st St. All vegan, all the time. Immaculate eatery doubles fresh-off-the-vine produce as decor. A range of ethnic influences: grilled seitan $6.50, pad thai $5.75, lasagna with tofu ricotta $6.75. Open daily 11am-10pm.

Boogaloos, 3296 22nd St. (824-3211), at Valencia. Bleach your hair, pierce your nose, and park yourself on a sidewalk table at this popular breakfast spot. Drink a pot of black coffee. Order up polenta and eggs with salsa and black beans or *huevos rancheros* ($5-6). Now you are cool. Or at the very least, well fed. Open daily 8am-3:30pm.

La Taquería, 2889 Mission St. (285-7117), at 24th St., has a prime location. Claims the "best tacos and burritos in the whole world," and you'd be hard pressed to contradict them. Tacos $2.50, burritos $4. Open M-Sa 11am-9pm, Su 11am-8pm.

CASTRO

Inexpensive cuisine can be elusive in this trendy area. Consider experiencing the Castro by sipping a latte at one of the local cafes. Slightly posh diners and cafes dominate the Castro's culinary offerings. While nearby **Mission District** to the south is a great spot for truly cheap eating, the Castro is one of the best places in the city for good 24-hour food.

Orphan Andy's, 3991A 17th St. (864-9795), at Castro and Market St., has been serving midnight burgers for years. Red vinyl booths, subtly pink walls, and a vintage jukebox heavy on 1950s and 60s girl groups like the Shirelles create an atmosphere of calming familiarity. Burgers around $6.50; huge milkshakes $4.45. Open 24hr. Cash only.

Hot 'n' Hunky, 4039 18th St. (621-6365), at Hartford St. near Castro St. Swathed in pink, this petite joint sports trendy 1950s decor with winks to Marilyn Monroe. Hunker down with a Macho Man Burger ($4.70) or I Wanna Hold Your Ham ($4.40) and debate whether "Hot 'n' Hunky" best describes the burgers, the staff, or the clientele. Open Su-Th 11am-midnight, F-Sa 11am-1am. Cash only.

Josie's Cabaret and Juice Joint Cafe, 3583 16th St. (861-7933), near Market St. Quintessentially Californian with its strictly vegetarian menu. Filling tofu or tempeh burgers are even better out on the deck, surrounded by wildflowers. The cabaret area hosts live comedy acts and other performances (see p. 124). Shows at 8 and 10pm (cover $5-10). Open for dinner daily 5-10pm, brunch Sa-Su 9am-3pm. Cash only.

Marcello's, 420 Castro St. (863-3900), across from the Castro Theatre. No-frills joint serves locally adored pizza with a list of pozzible toppings as long as your leg. Slices $1.75-3, whole pizzas $9-20. Cheap beer, too (Bud $1, Heineken $2). Free delivery. Open Su-Th 11am-1am, F-Sa 11am-2am. Cash only.

Bagdad Cafe, 2295 Market St. (621-4434), at 16th and Noe St., fills a whole city block. Giant windows encourage people-watching. Popular hot turkey sandwich with mashed potatoes ($6.75). Extensive all-day breakfast menu includes "build your muscle" selection–try the Gluteus (6 egg whites; $8). When it's busy, $3.50 min. charge. Open 24hr.

Azteca, 235 Church St. (255-7330), 3 blocks down Market St. away from Castro St. toward the Mission. Cheap eats in this speedy Mexican grill. Quesadillas ($2.25), salmon burritos ($5.25). Open daily 11am-11pm.

Peasant Pies, 4117 18th St. (621-3632), at Castro St. Sweet or savory pies (2 for $4) filled with healthy ingredients, served kindly in this bright but sparsely furnished cafe. Open daily 9:30am-7pm. **Noe Valley location:** 4108 24th St. (642-1316). Open daily 10am-8:30pm.

NORTH BEACH

Excellent cafes, bakeries, and delis butt up against an abundance of great Italian restaurants in North Beach. The line between bar, eatery, and cafe is very thin, and many more groovy North Beach hangouts are listed under **Coffeehouses, Bars,** or **Live Music,** below (see **Nightlife,** p. 118).

Sodini's Green Valley Restaurant, 510 Green St. (291-0499), at Grant Ave. In the true heart of North Beach, this is one of the area's oldest restaurants, established in 1906. The *Ravioli alla Casa* rocks the house ($8.25). Open M-F 5-10pm, Sa-Su 5pm-midnight.

Caffe Greco, 423 Columbus Ave. (397-6261). You know it's Italian when decaf costs more. Casual atmosphere is belied by culinary thrills. Focaccia sandwiches $6-7, tiramisu $3.75. Open M-Th 7am-11pm, F-Su 7am-midnight.

Mario's Bohemian Cigar Store Cage, 566 Columbus Ave. (362-0536). A hip, laid-back cafe right at the corner of Washington Square Park. Often crowded, this is a great place to hang out and grab some first-rate grub. Hot sandwiches on fat slabs of *focaccia* $6.25-7. Open M-Sa 10am-midnight, Su 10am-11pm. No credit cards.

The Stinking Rose, 325 Columbus Ave. (781-7673). "We season our garlic with food" at this excellent and extremely aromatic all-garlic restaurant. Pastas $8-13, other entrees $12-21. Garlic ice cream and even garlic dog biscuits area available to take away. "Vampire fare" (i.e., garlic free) is available, but what's the point? Open Su-Th 11am-11pm, F-Sa 11am-midnight.

CHINATOWN

Many feel that San Francisco's Chinese cuisine is unsurpassed outside of Asia. Chinatown is filled with cheap restaurants; in fact, their multitude and surface similarity can make a choice nearly impossible. If you can't tell the difference, don't sweat it—chances are good you'll like what you get. Finding vegetarian or vegan food is harder than it might seem; many vegetable dishes use oyster sauce or broth, and rice dishes sometimes include egg.

Over a hundred little markets carry some of the freshest and most unusual produce around, from living (though doomed) turtles and frogs to fresh lychee fruit.

Chef Jia, 925 Kearny St. (398-1626). Serves cheap and fabulous food in a small, informal space. $4 lunch specials until 4pm; entrees regularly $4-7. Open Su-Th 11:30am-11pm, F-Sa 11:30am-midnight. No credit cards.

House of Nanking, 919 Kearny St. (421-1429), at Pacific and Columbus. Nank and the world nanks with you–if you have no issue with waiting and don't mind a loose interpretation of "service," the famous House cuisine will satisfy. Many entrees under $7. Open M-F 11am-10pm, Sa noon-10pm, Su 4-10pm. No credit cards.

Brandy Ho's, 217 Columbus Ave. (788-7527), at Pacific Ave. Heat-seeking diners lock on target. This food is *spicy*. But O, it is a sweet pain. (A grudging "not hot with pepper"

ALL OF THE SUGAR, NONE OF THE GUILT San Francisco's gay community forms a powerful voting bloc, and in 1977, members rallied behind one of their own. Harvey Milk won the race for City Supervisor of District 5, becoming one of the first openly homosexual public officials in the United States. He spoke out for civil rights initiatives on both a municipal and a national level, and his charismatic speeches won him powerful allies such as then-mayor George Moscone. But progressive politics make enemies too. Milk advised Moscone against the reappointment of fellow supervisor Dan White in 1978. In retaliation, White brutally gunned down both Milk and Moscone in their City Hall offices. At his trial, White pleaded the infamous "Twinkie defense"—insanity by sugar-high—resulting in a greatly diminished scale of punishment. Outrage over the incident still rankles today.

category is on the back page.) Lunch specials $5-6. Open Su-Th 11:30am-11pm, F-Sa 11:30am-midnight.

King Tin, 826 Washington St. (982-7855), between Grant and Stockton St. Hanging meats and waiting patrons crowd the window in the afternoon. Dishes $3.50-8 except a few exceptions like crab and shark fin soup ($24) and chicken-swallow-sharkfin soup ($18). BBQ is a specialty. Open Su-Th 8am-midnight, F-Sa 8am-3am.

My Canh, 626 Broadway (397-8888), between Grant and Stockton St. Fantastic aromas leap between your nostrils in this clean Vietnamese restaurant. Rice plates around $4. Jellyfish, shrimp, and pork appetizer $6. Open daily 10am-2am.

Kowloon, 909 Grant Ave. (362-9888), at Jackson St. Vegetarian versions of meat dishes like chicken nuggets or duck gizzards made from tofu or glutton. Lunch buffet M-F $6; Sa-Su and holidays $7. Open daily 10am-9:30pm.

Silver Restaurant, 737 Washington St. (433-8888), at Grant St. Nonstop dim sum in this large diner. $2 per plate. Open 24hr.

SAN FRANCISCO

FISHERMAN'S WHARF

A common, if somewhat overpriced, Wharf meal is a loaf of sourdough bread ($2-4) from **Boudin Bakery,** with two locations on Wharfside Jefferson St., and clam chowder ($4-5) from a nearby seafood stand. At most restaurants along the strip, you can go broke eating remarkably unremarkable food. An exception is **Trish's Mini Donuts,** Pier 39 (981-4318), which are six-on-a-stick ($1.75) and taste terrific. Try one of the following for a laid-back, sit-down meal:

Rico's, 943 Columbus Ave. (928-5404), near Lombard St. at the top of North Beach. Well worth the 10min. walk, Rico's enormous burritos ($3-5) and bottled Mexican beers ($2.50) are a fraction of the price of Wharfside snacks. Open daily 10am-10pm.

Crab Cake Lounge, 900 North Point St. (929-1730), at the Beach and Larkin St. corner of Ghirardelli Square. The lounge section of the more expensive McCormick and Kuleto restaurant serves a limited seafood menu. Crab and shrimp-cake sandwich $7.50; calzones and brick oven pizzas $5-10. Open daily 11:30am-11pm.

UNION SQUARE

Union Square restaurants are often crowded and consistently overpriced. There is a legion of coffee shops, but very little in the way of inexpensive hot food. Asian offerings toward the Tenderloin and a few good cafes will tide you over until you get a chance to explore the better, cheaper restaurants of nearby **North Beach** or **Chinatown** (see above).

Cafe Bean, 754 Post St. (776-6620). Bianca and Peter scoop steaming scrambled eggs and fresh fruit salad for bus tourists, businesspeople, and wayward hipsters alike in this bean-sized gem. Postcards and Polaroids of friends and acquaintances paper the interior, such as it is. "Friends don't let friends go to Starbucks." Eggs and toast $3.50; brie and olive sandwich $5.25. Open daily 6am-7pm.

Indonesia Restaurant, 678-680 Post St. (474-4026). The straightforward name tells it like it is: this humble space serves food so deliciously authentic it might as well be an outpost of the archipelago. *Satays* ($6-7), meat entrees ($6-8), and many veggie dishes ($5-7). Open daily 11:30am-10pm.

Franciscan Croissant, 301 Sutter St. (398-8276), at Grant Ave., is a little snack bar with large fruit-filled croissants ($2.25), and delicious sandwiches like hot mushroom florentine ($4.50). Chill at the counter seating while watching suits talk earnestly on cell phones. Open daily 7:30am-6:30pm.

Kyoto Sushi, 336 O'Farrell St. (346-1443), between Mason and Taylor St. Japanese pop barely breaks the calm of this quiet, inexpensive restaurant. Sushi lunch special with 11 pieces, miso soup, and tea $7. Open daily 11am-3pm and 5-11pm.

GOLDEN GATE PARK AND THE SUNSET DISTRICT

The park contains two convenient **snack bars.** One is behind the bandstand between the Academy of Sciences and the Asian Art Museum; the other is in the Stow Lake boathouse. Nonetheless, packing your own food is usually healthier, probably tastier, and invariably cheaper. Neighboring districts offer good food within walking distance. One block south of the park in Inner Sunset, Irving St. bustles with inexpensive restaurants in a variety of Asian and other cuisines, especially between 5th and 11th Ave., between 18th and 25th Ave., and on 9th Ave. between Irving and Judah St. Four blocks north in Richmond, Geary Blvd. runs parallel to the park, and the stretch between 5th and 28th Ave. is filled with grocery stores, pizzerias, and other fairly cheap restaurants; more interesting Richmond restaurants and markets are an additional block north on Clement St.

Marnee Thai, 2225 Irving St. (665-9500), between 23rd and 24th Ave. south of the park. You'll agree with the many print accolades–this one's a winner. Roasted duck curry is a rare delight ($8.25). Veggie dishes $6.50. Open W-M 11:30am-10pm.

Einstein's Cafe, 1336 9th Ave. (665-4840), between Irving and Judah St. Cheery electric-lime cafe serving giant sandwiches and salads under a blackboard of the great physicist's scribblings (OK, so they're not *all* real equations). Run by a non-profit agency for inner-city youth. As a matter of principle, most items are under $5, and that's a principle you gotta respect. Lemonade with free refills $1. Open daily 11am-9pm.

M's Cafe, 1376 9th Ave. (665-1821), between Irving and Judah St. No frills, no campy touches, just a diner. Way cheap breakfast specials, regular cheap everything else (burgers $3-4). Even prawns are only $5. Open Th-Tu 7am-4pm.

Quality Market, 1342 Irving St. (759-6500), the big red awning between 14th and 15th Ave. And now for something completely different–a super-cheap and very good Russian deli. Patrons make special trips to pick up dinner items here, but there are a few plastic tables for roamers. Open daily 9am-9pm.

MARINA AND PACIFIC HEIGHTS

The **Marina Safeway,** 15 Marina Blvd. (563-4946), between Laguna and Buchanan St., is legendary as a spot to pick up more than just groceries. Cruise away in the Safeway—the produce section tends to yield the best results.

COW HOLLOW AND UNION STREET

Bepples Pies, 1934 Union St. (931-6225), at Laguna St. Munch on comfort food on 2 cozy levels. Mmmm, pie. Dinner pies $5-7, pancakes $4. Open Su-Th 8am-midnight, F-Sa 8am-2am; non-pie breakfast and lunch menu served until 3pm. **Second location:** 2124 Chestnut St., at Steiner St. Open Su-Th 8am-11pm, F-Sa 8am-1am.

Sweet Heat, 3324 Steiner St. (474-9191), between Lombard and Chestnut St. Self-proclaimed "Tequila Gods" serve healthy Mexican food beneath a mural of the *danse macabre*. Tacos $3-4, burritos $4-7. Fire-roasted corn on the cob (brushed with cilantro pesto or hot *chipotle*) $2. Open Su-Th 11am-10:30pm, F-Sa 11am-11pm.

Soku's Teriyaki and Sushi, 2280 Chestnut St. (563-0162). Great service and a $4 lunchtime *obento* box special (2-item combo, plus miso soup and rice; 11:30am-3pm). Get takeout and wander down to the water for the view to match your stunning meal. Open M-Sa 11:30am-10pm. $10 min. on credit cards.

PACIFIC HEIGHTS

Pizza Inferno, 1800 Fillmore St. (775-1800), at Sutter St. Burn, baby, burn. Decor resembles the work of acid-trippers with finger paint. Pizza lunch specials (from $5) include salad and soda. Happy Hour with 2-for-1 pizzas M-F 4-6:30pm and 10-11pm. Open daily 11:30am-11pm.

La Méditerranée, 2210 Fillmore St. (921-2956), between Sacramento and Clay St. Hearty portions at reasonable prices. Filled phyllo dough and other entrees $6.75-8.25; quiche of the day $7. Open M-Th 11am-10pm, F-Sa 11am-11pm.

Extreme Pizza, 1730 Fillmore St. (929-9900), near Sutter St. Yo! *Dude!* This picnic table is, like, *totally* made out of snowboards! The pizza at this popular chain manages to be healthy and gourmet without getting weird. *Surge!* Individual pizzas $4-5.50, pies $11.50-24. Open daily 11:30am-10pm (delivery until 11pm). **Second location:** 1980 Union St., between Laguna and Buchanan St. Open Su-Th 11:30am-10pm, F-Sa 11:30-midnight (delivery until midnight).

JAPANTOWN

Sushi is the area's main attraction, but it can be a budget-bending treat; lunch specials and filling bowls of noodle soup are an economical alternative. Restaurants, including an incongruous **Denny's,** cluster in the Japan Center and across Post St. on pedestrian-only **Buchanan Mall.** As in Japan, plastic models of food are often displayed in windows for pre-dining perusal.

Mifune, 1737 Post St. (922-0337), in the Kintetsu Bldg., upper level. Excellent and much-loved noodle restaurant. Hearty hot soups with choice of *udon* (thick, white noodles) or *soba* (flat, gray noodles) for $4-6. *Sake* $2.25-4.25. Open daily in summer 11am-10pm; in winter 11am-9:30pm.

Isobune, 1737 Post St. (563-1030), in the Kintetsu Bldg., upper level. A flotilla of tiny wooden sushi boats sail in a moat around an immense counter. You play the hungry sea monster, and your bill is based on the price-coded plates you stack up. Gimmicky but fun (2 pieces $1.20-3). Open daily 11:30am-10pm.

Akasaka, 1723 Buchanan Mall (921-5360), between Post and Sutter St., next to Fuji Shiatsu. Japanese cuisine "with a touch of Hawaii." Entrees $6.50-10. Nightly special includes main course, rice, miso soup, salad, *tsu kemono* (pickled veggies), dessert, and tea for $11. Lunch specials $5.50. Hawaiian menu Sa-Su. Open Tu-Sa 8am-2:30pm and 5-9:30pm, Su 8am-2:30pm. No credit cards.

Jabon (776-5822), in the Kinokuniya Bldg. Large, respected Japanese barbecue—you grill meats and vegetables at your table (meats $6-8). An array of already-cooked entrees too (soup and rice bowls $6-8). Open Su-Th 11:30am-10pm, F-Sa 11:30am-11pm.

NOB HILL AND RUSSIAN HILL

It can be a challenge to find inexpensive restaurants at the tops of Nob and Russian Hills (actually, it can be a challenge just to *get* to the tops of Nob and Russian Hills). However, a short walk downhill to the east (see **Chinatown,** p. 94) or west (to Polk or California St.) will bring you out of the high altitudes of $6 martinis and down to the world of $2 pork buns and $3 chowder.

The Golden Turtle, 2211 Van Ness Ave. (441-4419). Fabulous Vietnamese restaurant serves mind-blowing entrees ($8-11) like the Exotic Lava Pot ($9.50) amidst intricately carved wooden walls. Open Tu-Su 5-11pm. Reservations recommended on weekends.

Jona's on Hyde, 1800 Hyde St. (775-2517), at Vallejo St., is a darling corner store serving "distinctive sandwiches" ($3-5) and other edibles, like the stuffed avocado on a bed of greens ($5). Fresh bread is the main attraction. Usually open M-F 8:30am-6pm, Sa 9am-6pm, Su 9am-3pm, but hours may vary.

U-Lee, 1468 Hyde St. (771-9774), at Jackson St. Scores of cards from grateful patrons adorn the walls in this tiny but wildly popular Chinese restaurant. Service can be brusque, but the pot stickers are legendary (6 for $4). Many fresh vegetable dishes. Entrees $3-7. Open Tu-Su 11am-9pm.

Bob's Broiler Restaurant, 1601 Polk St. (474-6161), at Sacramento St. Not one of the Chinese owners is named Bob, but they all bob with hospitality—the bulk of their customers return *every single day* to consume comforting diner fare like banana pancakes ($4.50) and BLTs ($4.25). Open daily 7am-10pm.

Nob Hill Noshery Cafe Deli and Catering Co., 1400 Pacific Ave. (928-6674), at Hyde St., manages its multiple personalities with indomitable charm. Sit on windowside cushions and eat hot entrees ($8), or just munch a sandwich ($4-7). Open daily 7am-10pm.

RICHMOND

Some locals claim that Chinese restaurants in Richmond are better than those in Chinatown. The jury's still deliberating, so venture out and decide for yourself. The area also has Thai, Burmese, Cambodian, Japanese, Italian, Russian, Korean, and Vietnamese cuisine. **Clement Street** has the widest variety of options.

New Golden Turtle, 308 5th Ave. (221-5285), at Clement St. Vietnamese dishes like *bahn xeo* (savory crepe; $6.50) are irresistible. Tastes like the food in heaven, only with more ginger. Vegetarian options abound. Dinner entrees $7-9. Open M 5:30-10:30pm, Tu-Sa 11am-11pm, Su 11am-10pm.

The Red Crane, 1115 Clement St. (751-7226), between Funston and 12th St. Chinese veggie-and-seafood restaurant regularly racks up good reviews. Over 50 entrees. Spicy Szechuan eggplant ($5). Lunch special M-F 11:30am-2:30pm; choose between 8 entrees plus soup and rice for $3.50 Open daily 11:30am-10pm.

Toy Boat Dessert Cafe, 401 Clement St. (751-7505), at 5th St. Sells San Francisco's famous Double Rainbow ice cream (small $2) and delicious baked goods as well as trucks, trains, and kitschy trinkets. Where else can you get a slice of mocha fudge cake *and* an Austin Powers action figure? Open M-Sa 7:30am-11:30pm.

The Blue Danube, 306 Clement St. (221-9041). Laid-back cafe caters to its regulars with super service. Fat avocado sandwiches ($5) and garden burgers ($4). Open M-Th 7am-11:30pm, F-Sa 7am-12:30am, Su 7am-10:30pm.

SOUTH-OF-MARKET-AREA (SOMA)

Dining out in SoMa offers plenty of low-cost options at any time of day or night. The **Brainwash** laundromat and coffee shop on Folsom St. between 7th and 8th St. is a useful default for any meal (see p. 85). A large **Foods Co.,** 1800 Folsom St. (558-9137), is past 12th St. across from a health food co-op. There is also a **Trader Joe's,** 555 9th St. (863-1292), at Bryant St. to the south.

Hamburger Mary's, 1582 Folsom St. (626-1985), at 12th St. This late night favorite is as cool as a new pair of Zips. Excellent burgers ($6.50-10) are served on toast, not buns, to ensure messy eating. Great spicy home fries, a handful of veggie options, and 8 (count 'em, 8) types of Bloody Mary (from $4.50). Brunch Sa-Su 10:30am-4pm. Open Su-Th 11:30am-midnight, F-Sa 11:30am-1:15am (last seating).

Vino e Cucina Trattoria, 489 3rd St. (543-6962), at Bryant St. Look for the big tomato. Meals are as *autentico* as they are *magnifico*. Pastas and pizzas ($8-11) available without meat. Open M-F 11am-2:30pm and 5:30-10pm, Sa 5:30-10pm.

Patisserie Cafe, 1155 Folsom St. (703-0557), between 7th and 8th St. Get a cheap breakfast (coffee and croissant $3), a reasonable lunch (fancy sandwich and remarkable dessert $9), or a decadent dinner (starters around $6, entrees $8-11) in this "funky industrial atmosphere" with a little European flair. Desserts ($4, cheaper with combinations) are as good as they look. Open M-F 7am-11:30pm, Sa 9am-4pm.

The Chat House, 139A 8th St. (255-8783), at Minna St. between Mission and Howard St. Loopy yellow-and-purple external murals make this the most appealing address on an otherwise grimy street. Proudly woman-owned and a popular lesbian hangout, all are welcome at this unpretentious coffee/food/reading spot. Sandwiches and house plates around $8. Vegetarian breakfast options include biscuits with vegetarian mushroom gravy and tofu scramble (most breakfasts $5-6). Menu changes frequently. Open M-F for breakfast 7:30-11am, for lunch 11am-3pm; Sa-Su brunch 9am-3pm. Open in its coffeehouse capacity M-F until 6pm.

LuLu, 816 Folsom St. (495-5775), at 4th St. Enticing aromas and atmosphere up to the elevated ceiling work to complement the delicious food. Cuisine is "nouvelle-French-Italian-Californian," but they hate labels. Unique pizzas (from $9), pastas ($8-11), and huge family-style plates of fire-roasted veggies are the best budget bets on an ever-changing menu. Open Su-Th 11:30am-10:45pm, F-Sa 11:30am-11:45pm. Limited menu 3-5:30pm. Reservations essential.

Whiz Wit, 1525 Folsom St. (559-9200), between 11th and 12th St. Hungry weekend club-hoppers come here for the cheesesteaks ($6.15) and greasy snacks (cheese fries $2.45). Open M-W 11am-10pm, Th-F 11am-2am, Sa noon-2am, Su noon-9pm.

CIVIC CENTER

Opera- and theater-goers frequent the petite restaurants and chains that dot the greater Civic Center area, especially Van Ness Ave., Golden Gate Ave., and the Opera Plaza, while Hayes St. offers an extensive selection of cafes. **Use caution in this area at night.**

Nyala, 39A Grove St. (861-0788), between Larkin and Market St., serves Ethiopian cuisine. All-you-can-eat vegetarian buffet (lunch $5.50, dinner $8) features spicy mushrooms and about 10 other saucy vegetables to ladle on rice or scoop up with spongy *injera* bread. Open daily 11am-3pm and 4-11pm.

Millennium, 246 McAllister St. (487-9800), between Hyde and Larkin St. in the Abigail Hotel. Throw away your tofu dogs—this is gourmet vegan cooking with absolutely no need to masquerade as meat. Impeccable service and astounding food. Quality does cost a bit more (entrees $11-16). Open daily 5-9:30pm.

Tommy's Joynt, 1101 Geary Blvd. (775-4216), at Van Ness Ave. This San Francisco landmark, decorated inside and out like a tacky saloon, is a flesh-eater's delight, serving huge slabs of meat—try the famous buffalo sandwich ($4.75) and beer brewed everywhere from Greece to Thailand. Open daily 10am-1:40am.

Ananda Fuara, 1298 Market St. (621-1994), at Larkin St. Vegetarian menu with vegan tendencies offers creative combinations of super-fresh ingredients. Terrific smoothies (around $3.25) and great sandwiches like the BBQ tofu burger ($5.50). Open M-Tu and Th-Sa 8am-8pm, W 8am-3pm, and the occasional Su 10am-2pm (call first). Cash only.

PRESIDIO AND GOLDEN GATE BRIDGE

Restaurant options in the Presidio begin and end with an isolated mid-park Burger King. Pack a picnic, or head to nearby **Richmond** for real food. A few blocks south of the park in Presidio Heights, **Ella's**, 500 Presidio Ave. (441-5669), serves very popular breakfast and brunch fit for the first lady of song. Lines begin to form at 8:30am for weekend brunch. (Open M-F 7-11am and 11:30am-9pm, Sa-Su 9am-2pm. Reservations only for parties of 8 or more.)

FINANCIAL DISTRICT

You may need an MBA to find cheap sit-down meals in the Financial District, especially for dinner. Expense-account establishments often look better than they taste—the food is probably a better deal to the north in nearby **Chinatown** or **North Beach**. Some nearby restaurants are listed in **Union Square** (p. 105). The Embarcadero area houses loads of small fast-food providers.

Metropol, 168 Sutter St. (732-7777), between Kearny and Montgomery St. Smart stock market players know when to exercise their options. Liberal portions of reflective ambience, roomy velvet benches, and a side order of kitsch make the prices (sandwiches and salads $7-8) very competitive. Buy! Buy! Open M-F 7:30am-9pm, Sa noon-5pm.

Specialty's, 22 Battery St. (896-BAKE/2243), at Bush and Market St., bakes its own bread for filling sandwiches on an entry-level budget. Hearty peanut butter sandwich stuffed with wheat germ and generous banana slices $3.25. Nearby pier and public fountains provide ample seating. Open M-F 6am-6pm. **Other locations:** 312 Kearny St. (open M-F 6am-5pm), and on Market St. next to the Montgomery St. station

Krivaar Cafe, 475 Pine St. (781-0894), between Kearny and Montgomery St. Middle Eastern and Greek specialties are a notable exception to the district's bland offerings. *Baba ghanoush* with pita bread $2.49; *moussaka* with salad $5. Squeeze in at the counter or take grub to go. Open M-F 6am-5pm.

SIGHTS

HAIGHT-ASHBURY

One could express shock and dismay that the storied corner of **Haight and Ashbury Streets** is now home to a Gap and a Ben & Jerry's. But the Haight is still filled with energy, if only that of retail clerks processing credit card slips for purchases of "funky" stuff. Music and clothing top the list of legal merchandise. Inexpensive bars and cafes, action-packed street life, anarchist literature, and shops selling pipes for, um, tobacco, also contribute to groovy browsing possibilities (for suggestions, see **Shopping,** p. 113). See the Haight on foot—scrounging for parking with the hordes who flock here every evening is a real hassle, although unmetered neighborhood spots start a block off the main drag. Walking down Haight St. from Golden Gate Park or up from Fillmore St. will acquaint you with the neighborhood. You're sure to run into some characters walking the streets in various shades of purple haze.

The former homes of several counterculture legends survive beautifully: check out **Janis Joplin's** old abode, 122 Lyon St. between Page and Oak St.; the **Grateful Dead's** house when they were still the Warlocks, 710 Ashbury St., just south of Waller St. and across from the Hell's Angels' house; or the **Charles Manson** mansion, 2400 Fulton St., at Willard St. The **Flower Power Walking Tour** (221-8442) explains the Haight's history and visits these homes and other sights (2½hr., Tu

LSD: FROM THE MAN TO THE PEOPLE In Basel, Switzerland, 1943, Albert Hoffman synthesized a compound called **lysergic acid diethylamide (LSD).** Almost immediately, the medical community touted the effects of the new wonder drug, said to have a near-miraculous ability to cure psychosis and alcoholism. The U.S. government soon got into the act. In the early 1950s, the CIA adopted the drug as part of **Operation MK-ULTRA,** a series of Cold War mind control experiments. By the end of the '60s, LSD had been tested on some 1500 military personnel in a series of ethically shady operations. Writers Ken Kesey, Allen Ginsberg, and the Grateful Dead's Robert Hunter were first exposed to acid as subjects in government experiments. Eventually, the CIA abandoned the unpredictable hallucinogen, but by the mid-1960s, its effects had been discovered by Bohemian proto-hippies in San Francisco's Haight-Ashbury district. Soon enough, amateur chemists began producing the compound in private labs, and prominent intellectuals like Timothy Leary and Aldous Huxley advocated its use as a means of expanding consciousness. In October 1966, the drug was made illegal in California, and Kesey's Merry Pranksters then hosted their first public **Acid Test**. Once a secret weapon of the military-industrial complex, acid had become a key ingredient of the counterculture, juicing up anti-war protests and orgiastic love-ins across the Bay Area and the rest of the nation.

and Sa 9:30am, $15). The **San Francisco Public Library** offers a free walking tour focused on the area's pre-hippie incarnation as a Victorian-era resort (call 557-4266 for details). If pounding the pavement is just too slow, **Skates on Haight,** 1818 Haight St. (752-8875), will help you keep on truckin' (see p. 84).

The **Red Vic Movie House,** 1727 Haight St. (668-3994), between Cole and Shrader St., is a collectively owned theater with couch-like seating that shows foreign, student, and offbeat Hollywood films. The movie house (see **Movies,** p. 117) is not affiliated with the B&B, the **Red Vic Bed and Breakfast Inn** (see **Accommodations,** p. 87), which is itself worth a peek and cat-petting.

Resembling a dense green mountain in the middle of the Haight, **Buena Vista Park** has a reputation for free-wheeling lawlessness. Enter at your own risk, and once inside, be prepared for those "doing their own thing"—and doing enough of it to kill a small animal. An unofficial crash pad and community center for San Francisco skaters, Buena Vista is generally safer than **Alamo Square,** which is northeast of the Haight at Hayes and Steiner St. Alamo's gentle, grassy slope is a favorite with photographers. Across the street, a string of beautiful and brightly colored Victorian homes known as the **Painted Ladies,** subjects of a thousand postcards, glow against the backdrop of the metropolitan skyline. Far out.

THE MISSION DISTRICT

The Mission is best seen on foot and in daylight.

MISIÓN DE LOS DOLORES (MISSION DOLORES). Extant for over two centuries and in the old heart of San Francisco, this is thought to be the city's oldest building. The mission was founded in 1776 by Father Junípero Serra and named in honor of St. Francis of Assisi. However, due to its proximity to Laguna de Nuestra Señora de los Dolores (Lagoon of Our Lady of Sorrows), the mission became universally known as Misión de los Dolores. Bougainvillea, poppies, and birds-of-paradise bloom in its cemetery, which was featured in Alfred Hitchcock's 1958 film *Vertigo*. For more info, see **A Man with a Mission,** p. 8. *(621-8203. At 16th and Dolores St. Open daily May-Oct. 9am-4:30pm; Nov.-Apr. 9am-4pm. Admission $2, ages 5-12 $1. Masses: In English M-F 7:30 and 9am, Sa 7:30, 9am, and 5pm, Su 8 and 10am; in Spanish Su noon.)*

MISSION MURALS. A walk east or north along Mission St. from the 24th St. BART stop leads to the murals, some painted in the 1980s and some more recently by schoolchildren and community members. Standouts include the more political murals of Balmy Alley, off 24th St. between Harrison and Folsom St., a three-building tribute to guitar god Carlos Santana at 22nd St. and Van Ness Ave., the face of St. Peter's Church at 24th and Florida St., and the urban living center on 19th St. between Valencia and Guerrero St. The **Precita Eyes Mural Arts Center,** sells a map of the murals ($1.50) and leads walking tours *(285-2287; www.precitaeyes.org. 2981 24th St. between Harrison and Alabama St. 2hr. tours Sa-Su at 11am and 1:30pm. Call for meeting place. Tours $7, seniors $5, under 18 $1.)* The **San Francisco Public Library** also leads weekly tours of the Mission murals in summer—but you'll have no trouble finding them on your own. *(Library tours 557-4266. Free.)*

OTHER SIGHTS. Cafes, clubs, and bookstores line 16th St. west of Mission and Valencia St. Mission, 24th, and Cesar Chavez St. overflow with *taquerías* and shops. Local funk and jazz groups fuel the area's active nightlife, while Latin music flourishes closer to Cesar Chavez St. **Mission Dolores Park** is prime hanging out turf for residents of the Mission, the Castro, and Noe Valley, as well as a romping ground for their children and dogs. *(Park stretches from 18th to 20th St. between Church and Dolores St.)* **La Galeria de la Raza** celebrates local Chicano and Latino artists with exhibitions and parties. *(826-8009. 2857 24th St., between Bryant and Florida St. Free.)* **Osento,** is a bathhouse for ladies only, providing a wet and dry sauna, jacuzzi, and pool. *(282-6333. 955 Valencia St. between 20th and 21st St. Ages 14+ only. Open daily 1pm-1am. Door fee sliding scale $9-13. Cash only.)*

CASTRO AND NEARBY

Most people here seem quite sure of their orientation, but in case you need a little help getting started try **Cruisin' the Castro** (550-8110). Guide Trevor Hailey, a resident since 1972, is consistently recognized as one of San Francisco's top tour leaders. Her walking tours cover Castro life and history from the Gold Rush to the present (Tu-Sa, 10am; $40 including brunch). The majority of sights in the Castro are strolling on the street in cut-off shorts, but even a short tour of the neighborhood should also include: the faux-baroque **Castro Theatre,** 429 Castro St. (see p. 117), not that you could miss it; **A Different Light Bookstore,** 489 Castro St. (see p. 113); and **Uncle Mame,** 2241 Market St., a one-stop kitsch-and-camp overdose (see p. 116).

THE NAMES PROJECT. This massive undertaking sounds a somber note. The Project has accumulated over 33,000 three-by-six-foot panels for the **AIDS Memorial Quilt.** Each panel is a memorial to a person who has died of AIDS-related conditions. The NAMES Project building is also a workshop where victims' friends and families create panels; several are on display. *(863-1966. 2362A Market St. Open M-Sa noon-7pm, Su noon-6pm. Public quilting bees W 7-10pm and 2nd Sa of each month 1-5pm.)*

NEARBY MOUNT AND PEAKS. West of the Castro, the peninsula swells with several large hills. From **Twin Peaks,** between Portola Dr., Clarendon Ave., and Market St., are some of the more spectacular views of the city. On rare fogless nights, the views are particularly sublime. Just take MUNI bus #36 or drive toward the hulking three-masted radio tower, known by some as the Great Satan, where a pair of red warning lights blink ominously beneath a Mephistophelean crown. The Spanish called Twin Peaks "Mission Peaks" or "Los Pechos de la Choca" (the Breasts of the Indian Maiden). Those perverts! Significantly south of the peaks is **Mount Davidson,** the highest spot in San Francisco at 938 feet. The 103-foot concrete cross is the resilient replacement of two earlier versions that fires destroyed. *(Off Portola Dr. Accessible by MUNI bus #36.)*

NORTH BEACH

Sunny is well worth visiting in the daytime as well as during its neon-lit evenings.

WASHINGTON SQUARE. Bordered by Union, Filbert, Stockton, and Powell St. is **Washington Square,** North Beach's *piazza*, a pretty lawn edged by trees and watched over by a statue of not Washington, but Benjamin Franklin. (It's not a square, either, but then, North Beach hasn't been a beach for about 100 years.) The wedding site of Marilyn Monroe and Joe DiMaggio, the park fills every morning with men and women from Chinatown practicing *tai chi*. Across Filbert, to the north of the square, the **Church of St. Peter and St. Paul** (421-0809) beckons tired sightseers to take refuge in its dark, wooden nave (mass in Italian, English, and Cantonese). Lillie Hitchcock Coit, rescued from a fire as a girl, donated the **Volunteer Firemen Memorial,** in the middle of the square.

TELEGRAPH HILL. Telegraph Hill is really its own neighborhood, and a very nice one at that, but North Beach provides the best access to up-close views. Lillie Coit also put up the money to build **Coit Tower,** which stands a few blocks to the east of the memorial. The tower commands a spectacular view of the city and the bay from Telegraph Hill, the steep mount from which a semaphore signalled the arrival of ships in Gold Rush days. (Rumor has it that the tower was built to resemble a fire nozzle. Its nickname suggests a cruder inspiration.) *(362-0808. Open daily 10am-7pm; Oct.-May 9am-4pm. Elevator fare $3, over 64 $2, ages 6-12 $1, under 6 free.)* During the Great Depression, the government's Works Progress Administration employed artists to paint the colorful and surprisingly subversive murals on the inside of the dome. To get to the tower, take MUNI bus #39, or trundle up the **Filbert Steps** that rise from the Embarcadero to its eastern base. The walk is short, allows excellent views, and passes attractive Art Deco buildings.

MAKIN' BANK: A.P. GIANNINI One of California's legendary figures made his name as an earthy, swashbuckling...banker. Amadeo Peter Giannini, a produce wholesaler and the son of immigrants, opened the Bank of Italy on October 17, 1904 in a remodeled North Beach saloon. Giannini pitched banking services to workers and farmers, an innovation in the complacent banking industry. Executing bravura moves, such as lending to quake victims immediately following the Earthquake of 1906, starting a new Women's Banking Department in 1921 (following women's suffrage), and buying the bonds for the Golden Gate Bridge in 1932, Giannini kick-started the bank on a swift upward trajectory. Renamed Bank of America, the bank's story took its latest thrilling turn in the form of announced 1998 merger with NationsBank. BofA chairman and CEO David Coulter announced the formation of a "blockbuster" combo bank, with 4800 branches, nearly 15,000 ATMs, and a whopping 29 million deposit accounts. As BofA and its customer population adjust to the bank's new super-sizing, Giannini's place as a capitalist folk hero is secure.

OTHER SIGHTS. Drawn to the area by low rents and cheap bars, the Beat writers came to national attention when Lawrence Ferlinghetti's **City Lights Bookstore** published Allen Ginsberg's *Howl.* Banned in 1956, a judge found the poem "not obscene" after an extended trial, but the resulting publicity vaulted the Beats into literary infamy and turned North Beach into a must-see for curious visitors. Rambling and well-stocked, City Lights has expanded since its Beat days, remains committed to publishing young poets and other writers under its own imprint. *(362-8091. 201 Columbus Ave. Open daily 10am-midnight.)* The tiny **North Beach Museum,** 1435 Stockton St., at Columbus Ave., tucked inside Bay View Bank, depicts the North Beach of yesteryear in a series of vintage photographs. Most of the photographs long predate the Beats, but a handwritten manuscript of Ferlinghetti's *The Old Italians Dying* is on display. *(391-6210. 1435 Stockton St., at Columbus Ave. Open M-Th 9am-5pm, F 9am-6pm.)*

SAN FRANCISCO

The **Tattoo Art Museum** displays a fantastic collection of tattoo memorabilia, including hundreds of designs and exhibits on different tattoo techniques (the largest collection of its kind). In the same room, a modern, clean tattoo studio is run by the eminent professional Lyle Tuttle, himself covered in tattoos from head to foot. The minimum $50 will buy a quick rose on the hip; larger tattoos are $100 an hour. *(775-4491. 841 Columbus Ave. Open M-Th noon-9pm, F-Sa noon-10pm, Su noon-8pm.)* Nearby is the **San Francisco Art Institute,** 800 Chestnut St. (771-7020), a converted mission with a courtyard filled with the squawks of parrots and of every imaginable angst-ridden student art project. *(771-7020. 800 Chestnut St.)*

CHINATOWN

Grant Avenue, the oldest street in San Francisco, is a sea of Chinese banners, signs, and architecture. During the day, Grant Ave. and nearby streets are filled with a slow-moving tourist horde stopping every block to buy health balls and chirping boxes while pretending not to notice the Chinese porn mags lining some shop windows. Most of the picturesque pagodas punctuating the blocks were designed around 1900 or more recently—not as authentic replicas of Chinese architecture but as come-ons to Western tourists. At Bush and Grant St. stands the ornate, dragon-crested **Gateway to Chinatown,** given as a gift by the Republic of China in 1969. "Everything under heaven is good for the people," say the Chinese characters above the gate.

Pharmacies stock both Western and Eastern remedies for common ailments, produce markets are stacked with inexpensive vegetables, and Chinese newspapers are sold on every block. Once lined with brothels and opium dens, **Ross Alley,** running from Jackson to Washington St. between Grant and Stockton St., still has the cramped look of old Chinatown. The narrow street has stood in for the Orient in such films as *Big Trouble in Little China*, *Karate Kid II*, and *Indiana Jones* *and the Temple of Doom*. Squeeze into a tiny doorway to watch fortune cookies being shaped by hand in the **Golden Gate Cookie Company,** 56 Ross Alley (781-3956; bag of cookies $2; with "funny," "sexy" fortunes $4.)

The **Chinese Historical Society,** 644 Broadway St. #402 (391-1188), between Grant and Stockton St., relates the history of Chinese America through books and artifacts, including a parade dragon head from 1909. (open M 1-4pm, Tu-F 10:30am-4pm; free.) Other slightly noteworthy Chinatown buildings include **Buddha's Universal Church,** 720 Washington St. at Kearny St., and **Old St. Mary's,** 660 California St. at Grant St., built from Chinese granite in 1854, and San Francisco's only cathedral for decades. **Portsmouth Square,** at Kearny and Washington St., made history in 1848 when Sam Brennan stood there to announce his discovery of gold at Sutter's Mill. Through the Barbary Coast days, it was also the site of many public hangings. Today, hangings are no longer for the public, and the square is filled with children running wild and Chinese men playing board games. A stone bridge leads from the square over construction refuse to the **Chinese Culture Center,** 750 Kearny St. (986-1822) in the Holiday Inn, which houses exhibits of Chinese-American art and sponsors two **walking tours** of Chinatown. (gallery open Tu-Su 10am-4pm.) The **Heritage Walk** surveys the history of Chinatown ($15, under 19 $6), and the **Culinary Walk** teaches the preparation of Chinese food (by arrangement; $30, under 19 $15; includes dim sum at Four Seas on Grant Ave.). Both walks require reservations.

SAN FRANCISCO

FISHERMAN'S WHARF

Piers 39 through 45 provide access to San Francisco's most famous and visited attractions.

ALCATRAZ. Easily visible from boats and the waterfront is **Alcatraz Island.** Named in 1775 for now-departed flocks of *alcatraces* (pelicans), this former federal prison looms over San Francisco Bay, 1½ miles from Fisherman's Wharf. During World War I, servicemen convicted of violent crimes and conscientious objectors were held on the island. In the 1930s, the federal government used it to imprison those who had wrought too much havoc in other prisons, including infamous criminals like Al Capone, "Machine Gun" Kelly, and Robert "The Birdman" Stroud. Of the 23 men who attempted to escape, 18 were recaptured or killed, and five are "presumed drowned," although their bodies have never been found. In 1964, Attorney General Robert Kennedy closed the prison, and the island's existence was uneventful until 1969-71, when 80 Native Americans occupied it as a symbolic gesture, claiming "the Rock" as their property under terms of a broken 19th-century treaty. Alcatraz is currently part of the **Golden Gate National Recreation Area** (561-4345). The **Blue and Gold Fleet** runs boats to Alcatraz from **Pier 41.** Once on Alcatraz, wander alone or take the audiotape-guided tour, full of clanging chains and the ghosts of prisoners past. *(705-5444 or 705-5555. Call in advance, daily 7am-8pm. Blue and Gold Fleet boats at Pier 41 depart every 30min. in summer 9:15am-4:15pm; in winter 9:45am-2:45pm. Arrive 20min. before departure. Tickets $8.75, seniors $7, ages 5-11 $5.50. Audio tours add $3.50, ages 5-11 $2.50. Other boating companies run shorter tours up to and around—but not onto—the island for about $10 per person.)*

PIER 39. Back on the mainland, the pier juts toward Alcatraz on pilings extending several hundred yards into the harbor. Its creators designed it to recall old San Francisco, but it ended up looking more like a backdrop from a Ronald Reagan Western. Toward the end of the pier is **Center Stage,** where mimes, jugglers, and magicians play the crowds. A number of the marina docks have been claimed by **sea lions** that pile onto the wharf to gawk at human tourists on sunny days. You can gawk right back on any of the expensive **tour boats** and **ferries** docked west of Pier 39. Similar opportunities lie aboard the Blue and Gold Fleet or the Red and White Fleet, which were named for the respective colors of Bay Area university rivals Berkeley and Stanford. Tours cruise under the Golden Gate Bridge past Angel Island and Alcatraz, providing sweeping views of the San Francisco skyline. *(Pier phone 981-7437. Shops open daily 10:30am-8:30pm.)*

GHIRARDELLI SQUARE. Pronounced "GEAR-ah-DEH-lee," this is the most famous shopping mall in the area around Fisherman's Wharf, known for producing some of the world's best chocolate. Today, the remains of the machinery from Ghirardelli's original factory display the chocolate-making process in the rear of the **Ghirardelli Chocolate Manufactory,** an old-fashioned ice-cream parlor. The nearby soda fountain serves up loads of its world-famous hot fudge sauce on huge sundaes ($6). For a dessert extravaganza, try the Earthquake Sundae (with several ravenous friends)—eight flavors of ice cream, eight toppings, bananas, whipped cream, nuts, and cherries for a symbolic $19.06. If your sweet tooth outpaces your financial resources, file through the Ghirardelli store for a free sample *(**Square:** 775-5500. 900 North Point St. **Store:** 771-4903. Open Su-Th 10am-11pm, F-Sa 10am-midnight. Factory stores open M-Sa 10am-9pm, Su 10am-6pm.)*

OTHER SIGHTS. Aquatic Park is the area of the bay enclosed by the Hyde St. Pier and the curving Municipal Pier (which is said to be the pier that inspired Otis Redding's "Sittin' on the Dock of the Bay"). Members of the **Dolphin Swimming and Boating Club** and the neighboring **South End Club** swim laps in the chilly 57°F water. For $6.50, you can thaw out in the club's showers and sauna after your nippy dip. *(**Dolphin Club:** 441-9329. 502 Jefferson St. Open Tu, Th, and Sa 11am-6pm. **South End Club:** 929-9656. Open W and F 11am-6pm.)*

You'll be able to get your sea legs aboard the **Maritime Museum,** which is free and has large, fairly clean bathrooms as well as a quiet view of the water from a deck. The attractions of Pier 45, including the old submarine *USS Pampanito*, and the Hyde Street Pier, with five other vessels, are part of the same national park as the museum but charge separate admissions. *(**Museum:** 556-3002. At Beach and Polk St. across from Ghirardelli Square. Open daily 10am-5pm. Free. **Hyde St. Pier:** Open daily 10am-6pm. Admission $5, seniors and ages 12-17 $2, under 12 free, families $12. **Pier 45:** Open daily 9am-8pm. Admission $5, seniors and ages 6-12 $3, under 6 free.)*

The Cannery is a Ghirardelli-like mini-plaza on the wharf, with garden seating and a few cafes as well as the popular Belle Roux Voodoo Lounge, a Cajun restaurant, bar, and host of Cobb's Comedy Club. (See Entertainment, p. 116.) *(Belle Roux 771-5225; comedy club 938-4320. On Jefferson St., between Hyde and Leavenworth St.)*

SAN FRANCISCO

UNION SQUARE

While Union Square is filled with boutiques, stores, shops, and retail, the blocks just west have cultural offerings as well, in the form of theaters (see **Theater,** p. 118) and ubiquitous galleries.

MAIDEN LANE. When the Barbary Coast (now the Financial District) was down and dirty, Union Square's Morton Alley was dirtier. Around 1900, murders on the alley averaged one per week, and prostitutes waved to their favorite customers from second-story windows. After the 1906 earthquake and fires destroyed most

THE BONAPARTE OF THE BAY By nature California is a populist constituency, putting more questions to voter referendum than any other state—but San Franciscans have made at least one notable exception. From 1853 to 1880, locals recognized the self-proclaimed rule of **Joshua Norton the First, Emperor of the United States and Defender of Mexico.** Norton assumed the grandiose title after tough luck in rice speculation wiped out all his money—and perhaps his sanity as well. He donned an ostrich feather hat and faux-military attire and roamed San Francisco's streets with his dogs, Bummer and Lazarus. When he wasn't busy sending suggestions to Abraham Lincoln, Queen Victoria, and the Czar of Russia, Norton's decrees for San Francisco included starting the tradition of a Christmas tree in Union Square and building a bridge across the Bay. Locals didn't mind his eccentricities; good-natured merchants accepted the money he printed, and the Central Pacific Railroad allowed him to travel for free. The city even footed the bill for his new clothes. When he died, 20,000 people came to wave him on to the next world.

of the flophouses, merchants moved in and renamed the area Maiden Ln. in hopes of changing the street's image. It worked. Today, the pedestrian street extends two blocks from Union Square's eastern side, is as virtuous as they come, and makes a pleasant place to stroll with a Prada bag and Gucci shades or to sip Heineken from a wine glass at an outdoor table.

The lane's main architectural attraction is the windowless face of the **Frank Lloyd Wright Building,** the city's only Wright-designed building and a rehearsal for the Guggenheim Museum in New York. *(140 Maiden Ln.)*

GALLERIES. Shenene don't work at the **Martin Lawrence Gallery.** Rather, it is a modest corner space that displays works by pop artists like Andy Warhol and Keith Haring as well as some studies by Pablo Picasso and Marc Chagall. Although Haring once distributed his work for free to New York commuters in the form of graffiti, his art now commands upwards of $13,000 even in print form. *(956-0345. 501 Sutter St. Open M-F 9am-8pm, Sa 10am-8pm, Su 10am-6pm. Free.)*

The blocks between Geary, Sutter, Mason, and Taylor St. are filled with painting and sculpture galleries. One location stacks up four floors of galleries, including Scott Nichols's photography. *(788-4141. 49 Geary St. A block west of Union Sq.)*

VIEWS. The swift ascent of the glass elevators at the **Westin Saint Francis Hotel,** where Squeaky Fromme tried to assassinate President Gerald Ford, summons the entire eastern bay into view. *(335 Powell St. at Geary St.)* Or, try the slower but equally scenic ascent of a **Powell Street cable car** as it climbs through busy Chinatown en route to the waterfront and Nob Hill. The cable cars crawl at a stately 9½mph, but the line to board the cars is even slower. Be prepared for hour-long waits. *(Fare $2.)*

GOLDEN GATE PARK AND THE SUNSET DISTRICT

GOLDEN GATE PARK. The park should not be rushed through; San Franciscans bask in it all weekend long. Intriguing museums and cultural events pick up where the lush flora and fauna finally leave off, and athletic opportunities abound. In addition to cycling and skating paths, the park also has a municipal golf course, an equestrian center, sports fields, tennis courts, and a stadium. Call for info on free weekend walking tours of the park. On Sundays, traffic is banned from park roads, and bicycles and in-line skates come out in full force. *(666-7200; www.ci.sf.ca.us/recpark/. **Park headquarters:** 831-2700. McLaren Lodge, at Fell and Stanyan St. on the park's eastern edge. Open M-F 8am-5pm. **Friends of Parks:** 263-0991; www.frp.org.)* **Bikes and Blades in Golden Gate Park,** rents bikes and in-line skates. *(668-6699. 50 Stow Lake Dr., at the Stow Lake Boathouse. Bikes from $6 per hour, $18 per day; skates $6 per hour.)*

MUSEUMS. M. H. de Young Memorial Museum contains a 21-room survey of American art, from the colonial period to the early 20th century, including noteworthy pieces by John Singer Sargent and a Tiffany glass collection. The **Asian Art Museum** in the west wing of the building, is one of the largest museums outside Asia dedicated entirely to Asian artwork. The beautiful collection includes rare pieces of jade and porcelain, in addition to 3000-year-old bronzes and temporary installations from Philippine beads to Sikh furniture. *(**De Young:** 863-3330; www.deyoungmuseum.org. **Asian Art Museum:** 379-8801. On the east side of the park at 9th Ave. Both museums open Tu-Su 9:30am-5pm. Admission $7, seniors $5, ages 12-17 $4. Free and open 9:30am-8:45pm 1st W of each month.)*

The **California Academy of Sciences** houses several smaller museums specializing in different fields of science. The **Steinhart Aquarium,** home to members of over 14,000 aquatic species, is more lively than the natural history exhibits. *(Shark feedings F-W 10:30am, 12:30, 2:30, and 4:30pm. Penguin feedings daily 11:30am and 4pm.)* At the **Space and Earth Hall,** one exhibit shakes visitors up as they might have been in the great tremor of 1906. More zaniness lurks down the corridor, where the **Far Side of Science** gallery pays tribute to Gary Larson. Moo. *(750-7145; www.calacademy.org. Open daily Memorial Day-Labor Day (May 29-Sept. 4 in 2000) 9am-6pm, Labor Day-Memorial Day 10am-5pm. Admission $8.50; students, seniors and ages 12-17 $5.50; ages 4-11*

$2. Free and open until 8:45pm 1st W of each month.) The **Morrison Planetarium** recreates the heavens above with an impressive show. *(750-7141. Tickets $2.50; students, seniors, and ages 6-17 $1.25.)* The **Laserium** plays its laser show to themes by bands like Pink Floyd, David Bowie, and the Rolling Stones. *(750-7138; www.laserium.com. Tickets $7, students and seniors $6, ages 6-12 $4.)*

GARDENS. Despite its sandy past, the soil of Golden Gate Park is rich enough today to support a wealth of flowers, particularly in spring and summer. Although closed indefinitely due to a storm in 1995, the **Conservatory of Flowers,** erected in 1879, is a delicate structure and the oldest building in the park. The **Strybing Arboretum and Botanical Gardens** is home to 5000 varieties of plants *(661-1316. On Lincoln Way at 9th Ave.)*. The **Garden of Fragrance** is designed especially for the visually impaired; all labels are in Braille and the plants are chosen specifically for their textures and scents. *(Open M-F 8am-4:30pm, Sa-Su 10am-5pm. Tours M-Tu and Th 1:30pm, W and F 1:30 and 2:30pm, Sa 10:30am and 1:30pm, Su 10:30am, 1:30, and 2:30pm. Free.)* Near the Music Concourse off South Dr., the **Shakespeare Garden** contains almost every flower and plant ever mentioned by the Bard. Plaques with the relevant quotations are hung on the back wall, and there's a map to help you find your favorite hyacinths and rue. *(Open daily in summer dawn-dusk; in winter Tu-Su. Free.)* **Rhododendron Dell,** between the Academy of Sciences and John F. Kennedy Dr., honors John McLaren with a splendid profusion of his favorite flower. In the middle of Stow Lake, wreak fruit-filled havoc on **Strawberry Hill.** The **Japanese Cherry Orchard,** at Lincoln Way and South Dr., blooms intoxicatingly the first week in April.

Created for the 1894 Mid-Winter Exposition, the elegant **Japanese Tea Garden** is a serene collection of dark wooden buildings, small pools, graceful footbridges, carefully pruned trees, and lush plants. Buy tea and cookies for $2.50 and watch the giant carp circle the central pond. *(752-4227. Open daily 8:30am-6pm. Admission $3.50, seniors and ages 6-12 $1.25. Free daily 8:30-9am and 5:30-6pm.)*

In the extreme northwest of the park, the **Dutch Windmill** has done its last good turn. Once the muscle behind the park's irrigation system, the outdated but renovated old powerhouse (114ft. from sail to sail) is now the purely ornamental centerpiece of the cheery **Queen Wilhelmina Tulip Garden.** Rounding out the days of yore is the **carousel** (c. 1912), accompanied by a $50,000 Gebruder band organ. *Let's Go* recommends riding the ostrich or the purple dragon. *Let's Go* does not recommend the frog. *(Open June-Sept. daily 10am-5pm; Oct.-May Tu-W and F-Su 9am-4pm. Admission $1, ages 6-12 25¢.)* The **AIDS Memorial Grove** *(750-8340)* is a recent national landmark run by an environmental and social justice organization. The grove covers 15 acres off Middle East Dr. north of the 3rd Ave. entrance between the tennis courts and the Academy of Sciences.

OTHER SIGHTS. Brimming **Spreckels Lake,** on John F. Kennedy Dr., is populated by crowds of turtles who pile onto a turtle-shaped rock to sun themselves—it's turtles all the way down. The multinational collection of gardens and museums in Golden Gate Park would not be complete without something distinctly American...like a herd of **bison?** A dozen of the shaggy beasts loll about a spacious paddock just west of Spreckels. Well south of the park, at the end of Ocean Beach, is the distant and unremarkable **San Francisco Zoo,** recommended only for die-hard monkey enthusiasts. *(753-7080; www.sfzoo.org. On Sloat Blvd. Open daily 10am-5pm. Admission $9, seniors and ages 12-17 $6, ages 3-11 $1.50, under 3 free.)*

MARINA AND PACIFIC HEIGHTS

The main attractions in this area are almost all along the waterfront; the neighborhoods themselves are residential with bouts of commerce.

EXPLORATORIUM. *Scientific American* calls this "the best science museum in the world," and it is indeed a mad scientist's dream. Displays include interactive tornadoes, computer planet-managing, and giant bubble-makers poised to take over the world. The Exploratorium holds over 4000 people, and when admission is free once a month, it usually does. *(563-7337 or recorded message 561-0360; www.exploratorium.edu. 3601 Lyon St. Open Memorial Day-Labor Day (May 29-Sept. 4 in 2000) Th-Tu 10am-6pm, W 10am-9pm; Labor Day-Memorial Day Tu and Th-Su 10am-5pm, W 10am-9pm. Admission $9, students and seniors $7, disabled and ages 6-17 $5, ages 3-5 $2.50, under 3 free. Free 1st W of each month.)* Within the Exploratorium dwells the **Tactile Dome,** a pitch-dark maze of tunnels, slides, nooks, and crannies designed to help refine your sense of touch. Claustrophobes and darkphobes beware. *(561-0362. Open during museum hours. Admission $12 includes museum admission. Reservations required.)*

PALACE OF FINE ARTS. This imposing domed structure with curving colonnades has been reconstructed from remnants of the 1915 Panama Pacific Exposition which commemorated the opening of the Panama Canal and signaled San Francisco's recovery from the 1906 earthquake. The palace grounds, complete with swans and a pond, make one of the best picnic spots in the city. There are sometimes Shakespearean performances in summer, and the nighttime illumination is glorious *(Baker St., between Jefferson and Bay St. near the Exploratorium. Open 24hr. Free.)*

FORT MASON. This is the site of a popular hostel and headquarters for the Golden Gate National Recreation Area. While not nearly as spectacular as the other lands under the GGNRA's aegis, the manicured grounds make a nice spot for strolling and picnicking. *(At Laguna and Marine St. east of Marina Green, west of Fisherman's Wharf's Municipal Pier.)* Sam Shepard served as the playwright-in-residence at the **Magic Theater** from 1975 to 1985. Today, the theater stages both world and American premieres (see **Theater,** p. 118). *(441-8822. Bldg. D, 3rd fl.)* The **Mexican Museum,** presents exhibits by contemporary Chicano and Latino artists. *(202-9700; recording 441-8822. Bldg. D, 1st fl. Open W-Su 11am-5pm. Admission $4, students and seniors $3. Free 1st W of month 11am-7pm.)* The **African-American Historical and Cultural Society Museum** focuses on contemporary African arts and crafts. *(441-0640. Bldg. C #165. Open W-Su noon-5pm. Admission $2, seniors and children $1.)* **Museo Italo Americano,** displays works by artists of Italian heritage. *(673-2200. Bldg. C #100. Open W-Su noon-5pm. Admission $3, students and seniors $1.)* The **Craft and Folk Art Museum** stocks a lot more than apple dolls and driftwood sculpture. *(775-0990. Bldg. A. Open Tu-F and Su 11am-5pm, Sa 10am-5pm. Admission $3, students and seniors $1, under 12 free, families $5.)*

OTHER SIGHTS. Near Union and Sacramento St., Pacific Heights boasts the greatest number of **Victorian buildings** in the city. The Heights were mostly unscathed by the 1906 earthquake, but sustained serious damage in 1989, and Victorian restoration has become a full-fledged enterprise. The **Octagon House** was built in 1861 with the belief that the odd architecture would bring good luck to its inhabitants. Its survival of San Francisco's many earthquakes and fires is proof of fortune's favor, so far. *(441-7512. 2645 Gough St. at Union St. Open Feb.-Dec. 2nd Su and 2nd and 4th Th of each month noon-3pm. Group tours M-F by arrangement.)* Along the water, joggers and walkers crowd **Marina Green.** Play pickup soccer on weekends, or just plain pickup—the wide sidewalk's uninterrupted sight lines make it cruising-optimal.

JAPANTOWN

Walking all the way through Japantown takes just minutes and is the only way to go. Stores hawk the latest Pokémon paraphernalia and karaoke bars warble J-pop along Post St. around the Japan Center. The five-tiered **Peace Pagoda,** a gift to the community from the Japanese government, once sat amid cherry trees and a reflecting pool, but as it awaits restoration its home is a featureless paved lot. A brighter example of Japanese architecture is the **Sokoji Buddhist Temple,** where some meditation services are open to the public. *(346-7540. 1691 Laguna St. at Sutter St. Public Zazen meditation services Su 8:30am, W and F 6:30pm; arrive 15min. early.)*

Weary travelers may want to invest in a rejuvenating massage at **Fuji Shiatsu,** *(346-4484; 1721 Buchanan Mall, between Post and Sutter St.; by appt. only; morning $33 per hr., afternoon $36)*, or steam their dumplings at the **Kabuki Hot Springs.** *(922-6000; www.kabukisprings.com. 1750 Geary St. Sauna, steam room, and baths M-F before 5pm $10,* *evenings and Sa-Su $15. Other services by appointment. Open for men only M-Tu, Th, and Sa 10am-10pm; women-only Su, W, and F 10am-10pm.)*

The **Kabuki 8 Complex** shows current films, and is the main site of the San Francisco Film Festival (see **Movies,** p. 117), in early May. *(931-9800. 1881 Post St., at Fillmore St. Admission $8.50; students, seniors, and matinees $5.50).* **Japantown Bowl,** has 24-hour service on weekends, plus glow-in-the-dark bowling at least twice a week *(921-6200; 1790 Post St. at Webster St.; see* ***Entertainment,*** p. 116.*)*

NOB HILL AND RUSSIAN HILL

There's just not much to *do* up here, and the hike up will wear you out—they don't call them hills for nothing.

THE CROOKEDEST STREET IN THE WORLD. The famous curves of Lombard St. seem to grace nearly half of San Francisco's postcards, and rightfully so. The flowerbeds along the curves are well-maintained, and the curves themselves—installed in the 1920s so that horse-drawn carriages could negotiate the extremely steep hill—are one-of-a-kind. From the top of Lombard St., pedestrians and passengers alike enjoy the fantastic view of city and harbor. The view north along Hyde St.—a steep drop to Fisherman's Wharf and lonely Alcatraz floating in the bay—isn't too shabby either. *(Between Hyde and Leavenworth St. at the top of Russian Hill.)*

GRACE CATHEDRAL AND HUNTINGTON PARK. The most immense Gothic edifice west of the Mississippi crowns Nob Hill. The castings for its portals are such exact imitations of Lorenzo Ghiberti's on the Baptistery in Florence that they were used to restore the originals. Inside, modern murals mix San Franciscan and national historical events with scenes from saints' lives. *(749-6300; www.gracecathedral.org. 1100 California St. Open Su-F 7am-6pm, Sa 8am-6pm; Su services at 7:30, 8:30, 11am, and 3:30pm. Suggested donation $3.)* The quaint spot of turf and trees in front of Grace Cathedral is **Huntington Park,** literally the playground of the rich. *(On Taylor St. between California and Sacramento St.)*

CABLE CAR POWERHOUSE AND MUSEUM. After the steep journey up Nob Hill, you will understand what inspired the development of the vehicles celebrated at this museum. The building is the working center of the cable-car system—look down on the operation from a gallery or view displays to learn more about the picturesque cars, some of which date back to 1873. *(474-1887. 1201 Mason St. at Washington St. Open daily Apr.-Oct. 10am-6pm; Nov.-Mar. 10am-5pm. Free.)*

BARS WORTH SEEING. Once the site of the enormous mansions of the four mining and railroad magnates who "settled" Nob (Charles Crocker, Mark Hopkins, Leland Stanford, and Collis Huntington), the hilltop is now home to upscale hotels and bars. The battle for the title of "Bar with the Best View" is fought by the **Top of the Mark** and the **Fairmont Crown.** Both views are superb, but unless you consider paying $5.50 per beer or up to $80 for a glass of Remy-Martin to be a privilege, you may want to souse yourself elsewhere. *(**Top of the Mark:** 392-3434. 1 Nob Hill, at California and Mason St. in the Mark Hopkins Hotel. Cocktails served Su-Th 3pm-12:30am, F-Sa 3pm-1:30am. **Fairmont Crown:** 772-5131. 950 Mason St., between California and Sacramento St. in the Fairmont Hotel. Cocktails served Su-Th 11am-12:30am, F-Sa 11am-1:30am.)* Kitsch connoisseurs must not descend the hill without checking out the **Tonga Room.** In a city blessed with several faux-Polynesian tiki bars, King Tonga has to be seen to be believed. *(In the Fairmont Hotel. See* ***Bars,*** p. 120.*)*

THE ORIGINAL SWENSEN'S. San Franciscans have every excuse to fill up on ice cream after burning thousands of calories a day on those outrageous hills. Maybe that's why the city is home to the first Swensen's ice cream parlor—huff 'n' puff on your way up, cookies 'n' cream on your way down. *(775-6818. 1999 Hyde St. at Union St. Fresh batches made in window M, W, and F. Open daily 11:30am-10pm. 1 scoop $1.45.)*

RICHMOND

The beaches and park at the western edge of Richmond offer more nice views and wanderings than works of art.

LINCOLN PARK. At the northwest end of San Francisco, Lincoln Park is the bulkiest and best attraction in Richmond. The grounds around the park, which include the **Land's End Path,** offer a romantic view of the Golden Gate Bridge. The **California Palace of the Legion of Honor** houses an impressive fine art collection. A thorough catalogue of great masters from medieval to Matisse hangs in the recently renovated marble-accented museum. *(863-3330; www.thinker.org. Follow Clement St. west to 34th Ave., or Geary Blvd. to Point Lobos Ave. Take MUNI bus #2 or 38. Open Tu-Su 9:30am-5pm. Admission $7, seniors $5, ages 12-17 $4. $1 off with MUNI passport or transfer. Free 2nd W of each month.)*

CLIFF HOUSE. The precarious **Cliff House,** built in 1909, is the third of that name to occupy this spot—the previous two burned down. Along with overpriced restaurants, the Cliff House hosts the **Musée Mecanique,** an arcade devoted to games of yesteryear—not Donkey Kong and Space Invaders, but wooden and cast-iron creations dating back to the 1890s. The ingenious and remarkably addictive games are accompanied by fortune tellers, love testers, "naughty" kinescopes, and player pianos. Presiding over them all is "Laughing Sal," a roaring mechanical clown that, according to a plaque on the wall, "has made us smile and/or terrified children for over fifty years." *(386-1170. At the end of Pt. Lobos Ave./Geary Blvd. southwest of Lincoln Park. Open daily in summer 10am-8pm; in winter 11am-7pm. Free, but most games are 25¢.)*

OCEAN BEACH. The largest and most popular of San Francisco's beaches, begins south of Point Lobos and extends down the northwestern edge of the city's coastline. The strong undertow along the point is very dangerous, but die-hard surfers brave the treacherous currents and the ice-cold water to ride the best waves in San Francisco. Swimming is allowed at **China Beach** at the end of Seacliff Ave. on the eastern edge of Lincoln Park. The water is cold here too, but the views are stunning. *(Lifeguards on duty Apr.-Oct.)*

SUTRO BATHS. Adolph Sutro's 1896 bathhouse lies in ruins on the cliffs. Cooled by ocean water, the baths were capable of squashing in 25,000 occupants at a time, but after an enthusiastic opening surge, they very rarely did. Various combinations of pools and skating rinks failed to make the operation fly, and the buildings were finally abandoned after a fire gutted them in 1966. Be careful when exploring the ruins and nearby cliffs. *(East of Cliff House. Paths lead there from Point Lobos Ave.)*

OTHER SIGHTS. National Park Service Visitors Center dispenses info on the wildlife of the cliffs and the wild life of the house. Don't feed the coin-operated binoculars that look out over **Seal Rocks**—instead, head into the center and have a free look through its telescope. *(556-8642. Next to Cliff House. Open daily 10am-5pm.)* **Temple Emmanuel,** is an intriguing example of Moorish architecture, designed by the architect who did the Civic Center *(751-2535. 2 Lake St. at Arguello Blvd. Free tours M-F 1-3pm.)*

SOUTH-OF-MARKET-AREA (SOMA)

SAN FRANCISCO MUSEUM OF MODERN ART (SFMOMA). Fascinating from an architectural perspective, as well as for the art it contains, this black-and-gray marble-trimmed museum is five spacious floors of art, with an emphasis on design. Its contemporary European and American collections also impress—SFMOMA has the largest selection of 20th-century art this side of New York. Exhibits include Paul Klee's work (through Mar. 14, 2000) and an ongoing show on modernism. *(357-4000; www.sfmoma.org. 151 3rd St., between Mission and Howard St. Open Memorial Day-Labor Day (May 29-Sept. 4 in 2000), M-Tu and F-Su 10am-6pm, Th 10am-9pm; Labor Day-Memorial Day M-Tu and F-Su 11am-6pm, Th 11am-9pm. Admission $8, students $4, over 61 $5, under 13 free; Th 6-9pm half-price; 1st Tu of each month free.)*

YERBA BUENA CENTER FOR THE ARTS. The center runs an excellent gallery space and many vibrant programs, emphasizing performance, viewer involvement, and local multicultural work. It is surrounded by the **Yerba Buena Rooftop Gardens,** a huge expanse of concrete, fountains, and very intentional-looking foliage next to the huge Sony Metreon. *(978-ARTS/2787; www.yerbabuenaarts.org. 701 Mission St. Center open Tu-Su 11am-6pm; gardens open daily dawn-dusk. Admission $5, seniors and students $3; Th 11am-3pm free; 1st Th of each month free, when the center stays open until 8pm.)*

ZEUM. Within the gardens, but a sight unto itself, the recently opened "art and technology center" is aimed at children and teenagers. Besides studios for creating claymation and webcasts, ZEUM also has a music performance space and bowling. The best draw, however, may be the reopened **carousel,** first installed in Seattle in 1907, which is run by ZEUM but has separate admission. *(777-2800; www.zeum.org. 221 4th St.* ***Center:*** *Open W-F noon-6pm, Sa-Su 11am-5pm. Admission $7, ages 5-18 $5, under 5 free.* ***Carousel:*** *Open W-Su 11am-6pm. Admission $1.)*

ST. PATRICK'S CATHOLIC CHURCH. Although dwarfed by the vast metal and concrete of the museums and the Metreon, the church is actually quite large and impressive in its own right. Built in 1851, it is currently part of a renewal project. Frequent and well-attended services may make it difficult to "just peek" at the stained-glass interior, but you can enjoy one of the semi-regular noon concerts. *(On Mission St. near 4th St. Dates and performers posted outside the church. $5 donation.)*

ANSEL ADAMS CENTER. Although the center only exhibits a small number of the master's photographs, rotating shows by other photographers make up one of the largest and best collections of art photography in the country. *(495-7000. 250 4th St., between Howard and Folsom St. Open daily 11am-5pm, and until 8pm on 1st Th of each month. Tours Sa 11, 11:45am, and 12:30pm. Admission $5, students $3, seniors and ages 13-17 $2, under 13 free.)*

CARTOON ART MUSEUM. Showcasing the history of comic strip art from the *Yellow Kid* to *Calvin and Hobbes*, the museum has changing exhibits on cartoon masters and research archives for funnybook scholars. *(CAR-TOON/227-8666; www.cartoonart.org. 814 Mission St., 2nd fl. Open W-F 11am-5pm, Sa 10am-5pm, Su 1-5pm. Admission $5, students and seniors $3, ages 6-12 $2, under 6 free; first W of each month is "pay what you wish" day.)*

CIVIC CENTER

SAN FRANCISCO CITY HALL. The palatial municipal building, modeled after St. Peter's Cathedral, is the centerpiece of the largest U.S. gathering of Beaux Arts architecture. It was the site of the 1978 murder of Mayor George Moscone and City Supervisor Harvey Milk, the first openly gay politician elected to public office in the U.S. (see **All of the Sugar, None of the Guilt,** p. 95). *(554-4000. 401 Van Ness Ave.)*

UNITED NATIONS PLAZA. Sometimes host to the city's **farmer's market** and, most other days, to a General Assembly of pigeons. The main branch of the **San Francisco Public Library** (see p. 84) faces the plaza, although the main entrance is on Grove St. Opened in 1996, the state-of-the-art facility houses an excellent video library, the nation's first gay and lesbian archives, and a small rooftop garden. *(**Plaza:** On Polk St. **Farmer's market:** In summer W and Su.)*

CULTURAL HEAVYWEIGHTS. The **Louise M. Davies Symphony Hall** glitters at Grove St. The seating in this glass-and-brass $33 million hall was designed to give most audience members a close-up view of performers. Visually, the building is a smashing success and the San Francisco Symphony is equally highly rated. *(552-8000; symphony tickets 864-6000. 201 Van Ness Ave. Open M-F 10am-6pm.)* The recently renovated **War Memorial Opera House** hosts the well-regarded San Francisco Opera Company and the San Francisco Ballet. *(865-2000. 301 Van Ness Ave., between Grove and McAllister St. Opera: 864-3330. For more info on tickets, see **Entertainment,** p. 116.)* The

SAN FRANCISCO

Veteran's Building, where Herbst Theatre hosts solo singers, string quartets, ensembles, and lecturers also houses the Performance Art Library and Museum (PALM). *(On Van Ness Ave. between Grove and McAllister St., 4th fl. Herbst Theatre: 392-2545. PALM: 255-4800; www.sfpalm.org. Open W 1-7pm, Th-F 11am-5pm, Sa noon-5pm. Tours of Symphony Hall, War Memorial Opera House, and Herbst Theatre: 552-8338. Tours depart from Symphony Hall every hr. M 10am-2pm. Tours of Symphony Hall only be request W and Sa. Tickets: $5, students and seniors $3.)*

SAN FRANCISCO WOMEN ARTISTS GALLERY. On a smaller scale, the Civic Center area has a number of one-and two-room galleries like this one, which began in the 1880s as the Young Ladies Sketch Club. It exhibits women's photographs, paintings, and prints. *(552-7392. 370 Hayes St., between Franklin and Gough St. Open Tu-W and F-Sa 11am-6pm, Th 11am-8pm, and 2nd and 3rd Su of every month 1-4:30pm.)*

FINANCIAL DISTRICT

Unless skyscrapers or power suits get you going, there's not much here to attract the casual visitor, but you may well wander here on the way to the waterfront, Chinatown, or North Beach.

THE TRANSAMERICA PYRAMID. The leading lady of the city's skyline, this distinctively shaped office building is, according to New Age sources, directly centered on the telluric currents of the Golden Dragon ley line between Easter Island and Stonehenge. Planned as an architect's joke and co-opted by one of the leading architectural firms in the country, the building earned disdain from purists and reverence from city planners after the fact. Unless you're an employee, or have a business suit and some chutzpah, you'll have to make do with the virtual viewscapes in the lobby. Now a pillar of the establishment, the address was once a site of revolutionary disgruntlement, and Sun Yat-Sen scripted a dynastic overthrow in one of its apartments. *(600 Montgomery St., between Clay and Washington St.)*

EMBARCADERO. Justin Herman Plaza and its formidable **Vallaincourt Fountain,** at the foot of Market St., invite total visitor immersion. Bands and rallyists often rent out the area during lunch. One free concert, performed by U2 in the fall of 1987, resulted in the arrest of lead singer and madcap non-conformist Bono for spraypainting "Stop the Traffic—Rock and Roll" on the fountain. The **Embarcadero Center** is three blocks of sheer retail running toward Justin Herman Plaza and the ferry building (see **Shopping,** p. 113). The mall's **Skydeck** commands views from 41 floors up. *(1 Embarcadero Ctr. Admission $7, students and over 61 $4, ages 5-12 $3.50. Open daily 9:30am-9pm.)*

The **Hyatt Regency Hotel** adjoins Herman Plaza and Embarcadero Center on Drumm St. Its 17-story atrium, dominated by a four-story geometric sculpture, is worth a peek. The glass elevator up the building's side leads to the 20th floor and the **Equinox Revolving Rooftop Restaurant and Lounge.** Buy a drink (from $3, 1-drink min.) and dawdling time. *(5 Embarcadero Ctr. 788-1234. Bar/lounge open M-Th 6pm-midnight, F-Sa noon-1:15am, and Su 2pm-midnight. Su brunch served 11am-2pm.)*

THE PRESIDIO AND THE GOLDEN GATE BRIDGE

The Presidio, a sprawling preserve that extends all the way from the Marina in the east to the wealthy Sea Cliff area in the west, was occupied by the U.S. Army for nearly a century between the Mexican War and World War II. Now administered by the National Park Service, the Presidio's otherwise fairly dull expanses are ideal for biking, jogging, and hiking. The preserve also supports the southern end of San Francisco's world-famous Golden Gate Bridge. Take MUNI bus #28, 29, 42, or 76 or Golden Gate transit buses into the Presidio.

Synonymous with the city itself, the majestic **Golden Gate Bridge** spans the mouth of San Francisco Bay, a rust-colored symbol of the West's boundless confidence. Countless photos can't pack the punch of a personal encounter with the suspended colossus itself. The bridge's overall length is 8981 feet; the main span is 4200 feet long and the stolid towers are 746 feet high. Although carefully disaster-proofed against seismic threat, the bridge still claims victims—it is the most popular site for suicides in the world, and it lacks a traffic divider. If they make it across, southbound cars pay $3; both directions are free for bikes and pedestrians. Across the bridge, Vista Point offers incredible views of the city and bridge on hypothetically foodless days.

At the northern tip of the Presidio (and the peninsula), under the tower of the Golden Gate Bridge, **Fort Point** (556-1693), keeps watch over the entrance to San Francisco Bay. Although the spot was recognized as strategically pivotal in the face of diverse historical threats, no battle ever occurred here. Film buffs may recognize the spot where Kim Invoke dove into the Bay in Alfred Hitchhike's *Vertigo* (1958). Fort Point's museum is dedicated to past military occupants, but the thrilling view of sea-savaged surfers below is more interesting. (Museum open daily 10am-5pm. Grounds open dawn-dusk. Guided tours.) **Baker Beach,** in Golden Gate National Recreation Area, offers a picturesque but chilly place to tan and swim. Better wind shelter makes the north half of the beach one of the city's most popular nude beaches—beware of goose bumps.

SHOPPING

Too crowded for outlet stores and mega-malls, San Francisco is the land of the hole-in-the-wall shop and the serendipitous find.

BOOKSTORES

San Francisco has bookstores for every niche market and bibliophiles bent. The highest concentration of small, local stores can be found on **Haight Street** and in the **Mission.** Used bookstores are also plentiful along Irving St. in the **Sunset District** and around Columbus Ave. and Broadway in **North Beach.** (For the book trade across the Bay, see **Berkeley: Bookstores,** p. 137.)

A Different Light Bookstore, 489 Castro St. (431-0891), in the **Castro** (with cousins in New York and West Hollywood). All queer, all the time. Copious special-interest subdivisions include several shelves devoted to camp. Open daily 10am-midnight.

City Lights Bookstore, 261 Columbus Ave. (362-8193), in **North Beach.** San Francisco's most famous bookstore, home of the Beats and first publisher of Gymnosperm's *Howl.* Beautiful, chaotic bookstore with a fantastic selection of poetry, local publishers, and 'lines. Open daily 10am-midnight.

Bound Together Anarchist Bookstore, 1369 Haight St. (431-8355), at Masonic Ave. in the **Haight.** Surprisingly orderly stacks of subversive books, political pamphlets, and underground 'lines at this volunteer-staffed store. "Approximate" hours: open daily 11:30am-7:30pm. (What do you want? They're anarchists.)

Commix Experience, 305 Dividers St. (863-9258), at Page St. in the **Haight.** Classy comic book store with chatty staff and excellent selection. Female customers have even been spotted here on occasion. Open M-Sa 11am-7pm, Su noon-5pm.

McDonald's Bookstore, 48 Turk St. (673-2235), just off Market St. in the **Tenderloin.** A self-described "dirty, poorly lit place for books," this place stocks enough outdated magazines alone to smother a smaller store. Complete your collection of Nixon-era *Playboys.* Open M-Tu and The 10am-6pm, W and F-Sa 10am-6:30pm.

Modern Times Bookstore, 888 Valiancy St. (282-9246), in the **Mission.** Focuses on academic counterculture. Extensive world books, sexuality/gender, and Spanish language sections. A fine selection of India girlishness and earnest poetry chapbooks. Open M-Sa 10am-10pm, Su 11am-6pm.

Sunset Bookstore, 2161 Irving St. (664-3644), at 22nd St. in the **Inner Sunset District.** This used bookstore has been a fixture of the neighborhood since the 1970s, shining in many categories, especially fiction and poetry. Military history section is strong on Civil War books. Sheet music for piano. Stools scattered throughout the store encourage browsing. Open M-Sa 9am-9pm, Su 10am-9pm.

Russian Hill Bookstore, 2234 Polk St. (929-0997), at Valletta St. in **Russian Hill.** The younger sister of Sunset Bookstore, owned by the same couple. Separate alcove for antique and first edition books and a connected shop for journals, cards, photo boxes, and miscellanea. Open daily 10am-10pm.

Chelsea Bakeshop, 637 Irving St. (566-0507), between 7th and 8th St. in **Sunset District.** Browse and brood over the delightfully broad collection of used and rare books, and relax in the comfy chairs. Open Su-The 11am-10pm, F-Sa 11am-11pm.

A Clean, Well-Lighted Place for Books, 601 Van Ness Ave. (441-6670), at Golden Gate Ave. **Civic Center** institution lives up to its name with wide, well-kept shelves and a full calendar of readers. Open M-The 10am-11pm, F-Sa 10am-midnight, Su 10am-9pm.

MUSIC STORES

The new and used stores of San Francisco will fulfill all of your music desires, whether you're searching for an obscure Suttee death cultist 8-track or just trying to score the latest hot teenybopper single. The **Haight** is a great hideout for second-hand music, and there are even more audio goodies in the **Mission.** Your three-story corporate magistral is **Virgin** (397-4525), at Market and Stocking St.

Amoeba Music, 1855 Haight St. (831-1200), in the **Haight.** *Rolling Stone* dubbed this the best record store in the world, which probably did more for *Rolling Stone's* indie cred than Amoeba's. Although not as huge as its parent organism in Berkeley (see p. 134), the Haight St. Amoeba stocks an amazing selection of used CDs, plus new music and a parade of vintage concert posters. Open M-Sa 10:30am-10pm, Su 11am-9pm.

Aquarius Records, 1055 Valencia St. (647-2272), in the **Mission.** Tiny store known worldwide for obscure selection of all genres of music, with a wise staff to fill you in. Bizarre weakness for Chicago, but its real specialties include drum & bass, indie, and imports from all over the globe. Open M-W 10am-9pm, Th-Su 10am-10pm.

Open Mind Music, 342 Divisadero (621-2244), in the **Lower Haight.** Insane quantity of used vinyl, and a fair amount of collectibles, but they sell it new, too: dance, drum & bass, trip-hop, experimental, lounge music, and yes, even Zeppelin. Celebrity Vocals section features the golden throats of Telly Savalas, Tammy Faye Bakker, Leonard Nimoy, and more—now *that's* an open mind. Open M-Sa 11am-9pm, Su noon-8pm.

Recycled Records, 1377 Haight St. (626-4075), in the **Haight,** fights the good fight for the preservation of analog sound. Vinyl, vinyl, 8-tracks, vinyl, some CDs, and more vinyl. Open M and Th-F 10am-8pm, Tu-W 10am-7pm, Sa 10am-9pm, Su 11am-7pm.

Streetlight Records, 3979 24th St. (282-3550), in **Noe Valley.** More than half used. Off-beat vinyl, 7-inches, CDs, and tapes. They take pride in the condition of their wares—guaranteed quality, generous exchange policy, and good prices. Open M-Sa 10am-10pm, Su 10:30am-9pm; trade-ins until 8pm only.

Reckless Records, 1401 Haight St. (431-3434), in the **Haight.** Extensive collection of new and used LPs. Also sells CDs and videos, all carefully organized. Groove to a private beat at the indie listening station. Open Su-Th 11am-9pm, F-Sa 11am-10pm.

CLOTHING STORES

Not surprisingly, vintage clothes crop up in the same areas as reading matter and revisited rhythms. Spend more than you planned, and end up with more than you expected, along **Fillmore Street** in Pacific Heights, and the reliable **Haight Street** in Haight-Ashbury.

Buffalo Exchange, 1555 Haight St. (431-7737), near Clayton St. in the **Haight.** Superior selection of high-quality, inexpensive secondhand. Other branches sprinkled around the Bay. Open M-Sa 11am-7pm, Su noon-7pm.

Wasteland, 1660 Haight St. (863-3150), in the **Haight.** Not the thriftiest of thrift stores, but among the most popular. Biggest selection of used and vintage on Haight St., with a formidable facade and elaborate window displays. Open daily noon-6pm.

Rosalie's Flashbacks, 753 Columbus Ave. (834-1333), in **North Beach.** Higher prices, but what clothes! Strictly sequins and furs, but half the store is taken up by exciting heels in every color ($25-50). The perfect source for those perfect clubbing shoes. Open M-Sa 11am-6pm, Su 1-5pm.

Siegel's, 2366 Mission St. (824-7729; www.zootsuitstore.com), in the **Mission.** Former tailor for "big-boned and husky" men and boys has found new life with the swing renaissance as a purveyor of zoot suits, watch chains, and two-tone shoes.

Crossroads Trading Co., 1901 Fillmore St. (775-8885), in **Pacific Heights.** Score the perfect midriff top at this rerun shop for the young and trendy. Clothes, shoes, and accessories of seasons past, as well as the discards from the designer stores down the street. Open M-Sa 11am-7pm, Su noon-6pm.

Stormy Leather, 1158 Howard St. (626-1672), in **SoMa.** One of the country's biggest women's fetish wear boutiques. Not just leather, also vinyl, rubber, and of course various fetters, whips, shoes, and a small selection of toys. Most garments $80-300. Open daily noon-7pm.

Piedmont Boutique, 1452 Haight St. (864-8075), in the **Haight.** Come during a sale for clubbing or police decoy wear. Large selection of garters (most $18-24), boas, and wigs. Open daily 11am-7pm.

Departures from the Past, 2028 Fillmore St. (885-3377), in **Pacific Heights.** More upscale vintage women's wear. Blouses $5-18. Open M-Sa 11am-7pm, Su noon-6pm.

Goodwill, 1700 Haight St. (387-1192), in the **Haight.** Racks and racks of the ever-popular Levis (from $14). Shelves and shelves of everything else: shoes, housewares, books, linens, and some trash. The cars don't fit on the shelves—they're in the lot out back. Open M-Sa 10am-8pm, Su 11am-6pm.

Thrift Town, 2101 Mission St. (861-1132), in the **Mission.** Mostly housewares and electric appliances of yesteryear, plus an astonishing array of pants. They don't buy from the public. Open M-F 9am-8pm, Sa 10am-7pm, Su 11am-6pm.

501 BLUE BLOOD Prague's not the only place where an old pair of 501s is worth more than a used car. Vintage Levis collectors spend hours sifting through the endless racks of dungarees in San Francisco's thrift shops, in hot pursuit of those finer details that turn denim into diamonds. A few telltale signs mark the precious Levis produced before a major 1960s design overhaul. Look for red stitching on the inside legs (known as "red lines" in collector lingo), and the number "2" underneath the top button snap. Check out the little red tag on the back pocket for the most revealing sign of a valuable pair of jeans. Before 1961, a capital E was used in the spelling of the brand name (rather than "LeVI'S," as it appears today). These pre-60s rarities can cost $100-1800, depending on their condition and the shade of denim (dark indigo is worth more). If you're set on being one of the vintage-collecting elite, hunt for a pair of 1940s Levis, when in a show of wartime patriotism, the company skimped on materials by painting, not sewing, the trademark outside stitches. The **Levi Strauss Museum** (544-0655) shows samples of these fashion relics. If you don't have any luck in your search, you can always fake it—Levis is putting out a new "Vintage Revival" line, complete with the red lines, "2," and big E. But be warned: you won't fool the members of San Francisco's underground leather 'n' Levis community for a minute.

MISCELLANEOUS

Still haven't found enough campy or drug-related souvenirs? Look no farther.

Good Vibrations, 1210 Valencia St. (974-8980; www.goodvibes.com), in the **Mission.** The well-known erotica cooperative for enthusiastic do-it-yourselfers is a sex store you could almost take your parents to. Observe the progression from wooden cranks to C-cell batteries in a small, tasteful display of vibrator evolution. Open Su-Th 11am-7pm, F-Sa 11am-8pm. 18+ to enter.

Pipe Dreams, 1376 Haight St. (431-3553), between Central and Masonic Ave. in the **Haight.** The oldest of the Haight's innumerable head shops. Small pipes $12; ceramic "water filtration systems" $20-40 (but don't call them bongs!). Shopping here comes with its very own set of vocabulary restrictions; patrons must not use the taboo words posted outside the store. Open M-Sa 10am-7:50pm, Su 11am-6:50pm. 18+ to enter.

Tilt Quantity Postcards, 1427 Haight St. (255-1199), near Masonic Ave. in the **Haight.** Tired of the Painted Ladies? Lose yourself in over 10,000 antique, art, and tourist postcards. Now you have no excuse not to write your mother. Open Su-M 11am-11pm, F-Sa 11am-12:30pm. Also at 1441 Grant Ave. (986-8866), at Union St. in **North Beach.** Both locations are signless.

Uncle Mame, 2241 Market St. (626-1953), in the **Castro.** With the sad demise of Streisand shrine Hello Gorgeous, this has become the Castro's number one collection of camp. Toy store is crammed with best-forgotten Barbies and other kitschy items of yesteryear. Miniature TVs play a continuous loop of toy and cereal commercials from some Saturday morning in 1975. Open M-Th noon-7pm, F-Sa noon-11pm, Su noon-5pm.

TT Globetrotter USA, 418 Sutter St. (434-1120), between Powell and Stockton St. in **Union Square.** TT stands for Tintin, and this pricey boutique is dedicated to "European characters." Captain Haddock luggage may be pricey, but the books are inexpensive in a dozen languages. Also on parade are claymates Wallace and Grommit and French representatives Babar and Le Petit Prince. Open M-Sa 10am-6pm, Su 11am-5pm.

MALLS

If being whisked around by escalators strikes you as being integral to the shopping experience, you may want to follow the tinkle of Muzak and the smell of perfume samples south to the suburbs.

San Francisco Shopping Center (495-5656), on Market at 5th St. Decidedly uptown feel, with 6 hypnotic curving escalators (the only ones of their kind in the world) sweeping shoppers through the 9-story atrium. Open M-Sa 9:30am-8pm, Su 11am-6pm.

Stonestown Galleria, on 19th Ave. (Rte. 1), at Winston Dr. just north of SFSU. Ah, the symphony of a thousand credit cards humming in unison. The carless can sneak in on the MUNI M-line from downtown. Parking available.

Metro 280 Center, on Colby Blvd., in **Colma,** at I-280. Freed from the fetters of the city, the mighty outlet stores sprawl in the south Peninsula sun. Bounteous parking!

Japan Center, along Geary and Post St. between Fillmore and Laguna St. (see **Japantown,** p. 79). Packed with karaoke bars and sushi restaurants, the Japan Center should be a lot more fun than it is. Maybe it's the windowless, boxy architecture and institutional flooring that sucks the life out of it. Still a good place to stock up on Sanrio, Sailor Moon, and Shonen Knife.

ENTERTAINMENT

Relaxed bars, wild clubs, serious cinema houses, decent sports teams, lively theater, world-class opera, and provocative bookstores are all over San Francisco. The **Sights** sections above, and **Nightlife,** below, discuss many entertainment opportunities, but further entertainment listings can be found in local magazines and newspapers (see **Publications,** p. 86), or by calling the **Entertainment Hotline** (391-2001 or 391-2002).

SPORTS

Sports enthusiasts can check out baseball's **San Francisco Giants** (467-8000 or 800-SF-GIANT/734-4268), and five-time Super Bowl champions 49ers (468-2249). The Giants will be moving to **Pacific Bell Park** in SoMa near the water off Townsend St., once it is completed. The city's old-time field is notoriously windy **Candlestick Park** (467-1994), now officially called **3COM Park,** eight miles south of the city via U.S. 101. Hockey fans who can't make it to San Jose to see the NHL's **Sharks** might want to catch the IHL's **San Francisco Spiders** (656-3000) at the Cow Palace (469-6065) between October and April.

Japantown Bowl (921-6200), at Post and Webster St. in Japantown, lifts the alley out of the gutter with 24-hour weekends and spectacular glitz. Three nights a week are "cyberbowl" parties under black light. Reserve at least three weeks in advance for Saturday night (9am-6pm $3 per person per game, 6pm-midnight $3.50, midnight-9am $1.75. Open M and W-Th 9am-1am, Tu 9am-2pm, F 9am-M 1am.)

MOVIES

For a complete listing of features and locations, check the weekly papers or call **MovieFone** (777-FILM/3456). Keep in mind that few San Francisco movie theaters, even the massive AMC-1000, have anywhere near enough parking.

Castro Theatre, 429 Castro St. (621-6120), near Market St. in the **Castro.** Landmark 1922 movie palace has live organ music between showings. Eclectic films, festivals, and double features. Far from silent—a bawdy, catty, hilarious crowd turns almost every movie into *The Rocky Horror Picture Show.* Tickets $6.50, seniors and under 12 $4.

Roxie, 3117 16th St. (863-1087), off Valencia St. in the **Mission.** Trendy movie house shows sharp indie films and fashionably foolish retro classics, plus a late-night series of truly disturbed European gore flicks. Tickets $6.50, seniors and under 12 $3.

Red Victorian Movie House, 1727 Haight St. (668-3994), in the **Upper Haight.** Munch on organic popcorn while watching art films and revivals at the "Red Vic." Popular "Whitesploitation" B-movie festival brings in the very best of the very worst. Tickets $6, seniors and children $3; weekend matinees $4.50.

Sony Metreon (369-6200), at 4th and Mission St. in **SoMa.** Largest urban entertainment complex in the world, a scary mass of consumption including $8.50 first-run movies.

AMC-1000, 1000 Van Ness Ave. (922-4262), at O'Farrell St. Steeply banked amphitheater-style theaters with big screens, fantastic sound, and retractable armrests for snuggling. Admission $8.50, seniors and students with school ID $5.50, under 13 $4.50; matinees $5.50; twilight shows 4-6pm $4.50.

Kabuki 8 (931-9800), at Fillmore and Post St. in **Japantown.** First-run movies just steps away from raw fish. General admission $8.50, seniors and students with school ID $5.50, under 13 $4.50; matinees $5.50; twilight shows 4-6pm $4.50.

Landmark Cinemas (352-0810), have 17 theaters in the Bay Area. All show independent, overlooked, and foreign films. Tickets $7.50, seniors and under 13 $4.50; 5-ticket pack $27. **Gateway Landmark,** 215 Jackson St., at Battery and Front St. in North Beach. **Clay Landmark,** 2261 Fillmore St., at Clay St. in Pacific Heights. **Bridge Landmark,** 3010 Geary Expwy., at Blake St., 3 blocks west of Masonic Ave.

The Lumière, 1572 California St. (352-0810), at Larkin and Polk St. Indie and art films. Tickets $7.50; seniors, children, and 1st show each day $4.75.

CLASSICAL MUSIC

Classical music in San Francisco begins with a trio of high-culture heavyweights at the Civic Center on Van Ness Ave. **Louise M. Davies Symphony Hall,** 201 Van Ness Ave. (431-5400), houses the San Francisco Symphony in an impressive if controversial structure. The cheapest seats are on the center terrace, directly above the orchestra—the acoustics are slightly off, but they afford an excellent (and rare) face-on view of the conductor (and the rest of the audience). The San Francisco Opera and San Francisco Ballet both perform at the **War Memorial Opera House,** 301

Van Ness Ave. (864-3330; www.sfopera). Tickets range in price from $30 to a lot more than $30, and can be charged by phone (762-2277), or obtained directly from the box office (open M-Sa noon-6pm). Standing-room-only tickets go on sale two hours before performances. The stately **Herbst Theater,** 401 Van Ness Ave. (392-2545), provides a plush setting for a year-round schedule of classical soloists, quartets, and smaller symphonies, plus occasional lectures by renowned authors, artists, or thinkers. Avoid the distant balcony if you can. Outside the Civic Center, **Grace Cathedral,** 1100 California St. (749-6310) at Taylor St., on Nob Hill. Its vast nave and high vaulted ceilings create a divine space to hear sacred choral music. Profane music sounds pretty good here, too, and **Jazz in the City** reserves the cathedral each year for some of its inspired jams.

THEATER

San Francisco hosts many theatrical performances, especially at "Theater Row" around Mason St. and Geary St. downtown. The following are some of the best-known theaters; also check local listings (see **Publications,** p. 86).

Geary Theater, 415 Geary St. (749-2228), between Mason and Taylor St., near **Union Square.** Home to renowned **American Conservatory Theater,** the jewel in San Francisco's theatrical crown. Typical seasons feature classics from Molière to Kaufman, as well as newer plays. Elegant theater is a show-stealer in its own right. Tickets $14-50.

Magic Theater, Fort Mason Ctr., Bldg. D (441-8822). Sam Shepherd was playwright-in-residence from 1975-85. Theater remains an excellent site for the modern and mildly experimental. Tickets $15-25. Student rush tickets available 30min. before show.

The Marsh, 1062 Valencia St. (641-0235), between 21st and 22nd St. Small **Mission** space produces cutting-edge performance art about 100 years ahead of theatrical trends. Works-in-progress Monday nights, when tickets are cheapest. Tickets $6-22.

The Orpheum, 1192 Market St. (551-2000) near **Civic Center.** Storied San Francisco landmark hosts the big, big Broadway shows.

848 Community Space, 848 Divisadero (922-2385), between Fulton and McAllister St. near **Upper Haight.** Basically a glorified living room, the 848 serves a steady diet of queer and sexually-oriented programming. All-night tribal love-ins, sweaty experimental dance troupes, and the porn-art stylings of Annie Sprinkle. Tickets free-$15.

Club Fugazi, 678 Green St. (421-4222), between Columbus Ave. and Powell St. in **North Beach.** Cabaret-style revue *Beach Blanket Babylon* is a long-running S.F. classic. Shows W-Th 8pm, F-Sa 7 and 10pm, Su 3 and 7pm. Box office open M-Sa 10am-6pm, Su noon-6pm. Tickets $18-45, Su 3pm $18-40. Under 22 admitted to Su 3pm only.

Mason Street Theater, 340 Mason St. (982-5463; www.shearmadness.com). *Shear Madness* is a zany, long-running whodunit with a particularly San Franciscan flavor. Popular with tourists because everyone else has seen it by now. Shows Tu-F 8pm, Sa 6:30 and 9:30pm, Su 3 and 7:30pm. Tickets $34.

City Cabaret, 450 Geary St. (771-9251), between Mason and Taylor St., near **Union Square.** Tickets $10-20.

NIGHTLIFE

Nightlife in San Francisco is as varied as the city's personal ads. Everyone from "shy first-timer" to "bearded strap daddy" to "pre-op transsexual top" can find places to go on a Saturday (or even a Tuesday) night. The spots listed below are divided into coffeehouses, bars, clubs, and music venues, but these lines get pretty blurred in San Francisco after dark. Every other bar calls itself a cafe, every second cafe is a club, and half the clubs in town declare themselves to be lounges. Don't fret—there are 10,000 night spots in the naked city—you'll find something that fits you like a warm leather glove. Ahem. Check out the nightlife listings in *S.F. Weekly*, the *Guardian*, and *Metropolitan*.

The happening **Mission** mixes bars packed with hotties, and salsa clubs that cater to *true* Latin lovers. The scene is a combination of slumming, fashion show, and gourmet meat market—think Ricky Martin concert with lots of straight boys, too. There are probably enough bars and other venues here to take your money, your sobriety, and perhaps your virginity, if you play your cards right. The stretch of Folsom St. in **SoMa** around 12th St. is a row of clubs and music spots that continue sporadically out to seedy 6th St. and down to Townsend St. SoMa also contains the Metreon entertainment compound. In the **Castro,** night, like day, is all gay and mostly male. While there are cafes, bars, and diners all along Castro and Market St., there's only one club, **The Café.** North Beach is great fun in the evening—especially if your definition of "fun" includes lotsa linguini-lovin' at middle-class prices. And remember, every dollar you save on a hearty, inexpensive Italian dinner can be put toward the tip at a strip club along **Broadway.** In the bars around Columbus Ave., north of the Transamerica Pyramid, is **jazz and blues.** The grungy nightlife in the **Upper Haight** consists of just a few bars with long lines and humorless bouncers. **Lower Haight** has a better selection of bars, many with shorter lines than its neighbor. The **Tenderloin** has plenty of bars that one might term "seedy." The lounges and restaurants of **Union Square** are quite out of the reach of the budget traveler. A few neighborhood watering holes dot **Russian** and **Nob Hills** and a walk down Polk St. might turn up a few gems but mainly you'll find the darkened doorways of retail. The same is true of **Pacific Heights** until you reach the sushi, bowling, and movie possibilities at **Japantown.**

COFFEEHOUSES

Far more than just caffeine filling stations, cafes and coffeehouses are a big part of San Francisco nightlife—and daylife, too. The oldest San Francisco cafes line the narrow streets of North Beach, the Italian neighborhood with a jones for espresso long before those beatnik poets moved in with their black turtlenecks and bongo drums. While much of the country approaches Starbucks saturation, San Francisco still offers java dens in an immense variety of shapes, sizes, and styles. For more cafes, check out food listings in **North Beach** and the **Haight.**

Cafe Flore, 2298 Market St. (631-8579). Find romance among flowers. Organic spinach salad with walnut, apple, and goat cheese $5.75. Open Su-Th 7am-11:30pm, F-Sa 7am-midnight; breakfast served until 3pm, kitchen closes at 10pm.

Caffe Trieste, 601 Vallejo St. (392-6739), at Grant Ave. Every bar in **North Beach** claims to be a Beat haunt but this is the genuine article. It hasn't changed much since then—a few new photos of famous patrons on the walls, but the jukebox still plays opera. Live music Sa 2pm. Open daily 6:30am-11pm.

Red Dora's Bearded Lady Cafe, 485 14th St. (626-2805), at Guerrero St. in the **Mission.** A cool cafe and art gallery owned and patronized by artistic dykes. Limited vegetarian menu. Smoke- and alcohol-free. Popular spoken-word and performance art. Open M-F 7am-7pm, Sa-Su 9am-7pm.

The Horseshoe Cafe, 566 Haight St. (626-8852), in the **Lower Haight.** Cute staff, chess boards, video games, Internet access, Thai iced tea ($1.75), and big ol' cookies ($1.25). Open daily 7am-1am.

Yakety-Yak, 679 Sutter St. (885-6908), between Mason and Taylor St. Relaxed coffee joint serves light food in addition to drinks (Thai iced tea $1.75). Couch and coin-op Internet access. Open M-Th 7am-9pm, F 7am-10pm, Su 8am-6pm.

XOX Truffles, 754 Columbus Ave. (421-4814), north of Washington Square in **North Beach.** Not a lot of space for hanging out, but freshly made truffles (35¢ each or 5 for $1). Free truffle with coffee drinks. Generally open Su-Th 7am-8pm, F-Sa 11am-10pm.

Green Bean Espresso and Juice Bar, 704 Post St. (563-1972) at Jones St., 3 blocks west of **Union Square.** Tiny cafe is zealous in its devotion to the vegan life. Organic espresso drinks (soy milk latte $2.50), smoothies with St. John's Wort ($4.50), even organic wheat juice shots ($1). Peanut butter fudge collision cookies are almost a necessity after all this healthfulness. Open daily 7am-4pm, sometimes later.

BARS

Each neighborhood has its spots and within a few blocks you can go from Guinness to *sake* or from $1 Buds to $9 margaritas. The **Mission** and **North Beach** are especially wet. All of these areas are served every 30 minutes by Night Owl bus service; it pays to know the routes. More spots are covered under **Gay and Lesbian Nightlife** and **Live Music,** both below. The drinking age in California is 21; many bars check IDs at the door in the evening. The **Mission** is one of the hippest areas in the country right now—good looking, black-wearing young people pack its many bars, which include the **Skylark** (16th and Guerrero St.), **Dox Clock** (22nd and Mission St.), **Lone Palm** (22nd and Guerrero St.), **Makeout Room** (22nd St. between Market and Valencia St.), **Kilowatt** (16th St. near Valencia St.), **Albion** (16th St. between Guerrero and Valencia St.), and **500 Club** (Guerrero St. at 17th St.).

Hotel Utah Saloon, 500 4th St. (421-8308), at Bryant St. in **SoMa.** Excellent and unpretentious saloon and live music venue (rock, "countrified," funky). Show cover generally $2-6.

Café du Nord, 2170 Market St. (861-5016), between Church and Sanchez St. in the **Castro.** Takes you back in time to a red velvet club with speakeasy ambience. Excellent live music nightly–lounge, swing, salsa, big band–and dancing to match. Salsa Tuesday and Swing Sunday with free lessons (after the $5 cover), so you too can party like its 1949. Happy Hour 5-7pm with swank $2 martinis. Cover $3-5. Open daily 4pm-2am.

Tosca Cafe, 242 Columbus Ave. (391-1244), between Broadway and Pacific Ave. in **North Beach.** You could try to have an illicit rendezvous, but you'll still be seen by everyone you know. Wurlitzer jukebox (3 plays for 25¢). House special, brandy with steamed milk and chocolate ($3.50), is a holdover from Prohibition days. Open M-F 5pm-1am, Sa-Su 5pm-2am.

An Bodhran, 668 Haight St. (431-4274), at Pierce St. in the **Haight.** Bar staff pull some of the city's best pints of Guinness. Happy Hour daily 4-7pm. Open daily 4pm-2am.

Club Deluxe, 1511 Haight St. (552-6949), near Ashbury St. in the **Upper Haight.** Femmes fatales banter with mysterious strangers, and that's just the bar staff. The cocktail nation is in full effect at this small but swinging retro club. Shiny metal and bluish lights make everyone the star of their own 1940s film noir. Smoky jazz and swing W-Sa. Cover F-Sa $5. Open M-Sa 3pm-2am, Su 2pm-2am. No credit cards.

Vesuvio Cafe, 255 Columbus Ave. (362-3370), across Jack Kerouac Alley from the City Lights Bookstore in **North Beach.** "I saw the best brain cells of my generation destroyed by red wine, starving hysterical." Watch poets and chess players from a balcony in the Beat bar. Drinks $3-6. Open daily 6am-2am.

Beauty Bar, 2299 Mission St. (285-0324), at 19th St. in the **Mission.** Surround yourself with vintage hair dryers and everything pink. Happy Hour daily 5-8pm. Manicures W-F 6-10pm mostly by appointment (manicure and martini $10). Makeovers Su 7-10pm. Drinks like Dippity-do (Malibu and Midori $5). Open M-F 5pm-2am, Sa-Su 7pm-2am.

Mad Dog in the Fog, 530 Haight St. (626-7270), near Fillmore St. in **Lower Haight.** British bar: The drinks are Guinness, the pastime is darts, and soccer, er, football, is everything else. Key matches shown live via satellite no matter what bloody time it is–don't miss the spectacle of 50 drunken expats screaming at the telly at 6am. Pints $2.75 until 7pm, F 5-7pm $2, and $1 with lunch M-F 11:30am-2:30pm. Bangers and mash $5. High-stakes trivia M and Th 9:30pm. Open M-F 11:30am-2am, Sa-Su 10am-2am.

Li Po's, 916 Grant St. (982-0072), between Jackson and Washington St. Quite simply the coolest place in **Chinatown.** Down Anchor Steam to the sound of dice slamming on the bar along with middle-aged Chinese men, hip young white couples, and packs of men on their way to North Beach strip clubs. Open daily 2pm-2am.

Dragonfly Lounge, 2030 Union St. (929-8855), in Betelnut Pejiu-Wu Restaurant in **Pacific Heights.** What Dragonfly lacks in Oriental authenticity she makes up for in secret agent appeal. Only James Bond could resist these drinks. *Taiwan On* (Stoli orange with pickled ginger) $5. Open Su-Th 11:30am-11pm, F-Sa 11:30am-midnight.

Tonga Room, 950 Mason St. (772-5278), in the Fairmont Hotel on **Nob Hill.** Enormous tiki bar with "bamboo" trees, muumuu-ed waitresses, and giant fruity drinks bristling with umbrellas, swizzle sticks, and little swords. Band performs hula music on a floating stage in an artificial lagoon, and tropical storms roll in every 30min. with simulated thunder, lightning, and rain. During Happy Hour (M-F 5-7pm) drinks are "only" $3-5 and an all-you-can-eat Polynesian buffet $5. Open Su-Th 5-11:45pm, F-Sa 5pm-1am.

The Red Room, 827 Sutter St. (346-7666), between Jones and Leavenworth St. between **Union Square** and **Nob Hill.** Red walls, red floor, red ceiling. Curving red bar lined with red bottles. Red bar stools and red leather couches. Red columns, red cloth sashes. Red bathrooms. Background music: space-age lounge (you'll understand when you hear it) and acid jazz. Dress up. Wear black. Do not think you are being clever by wearing red. Seriously. We mean it. Wear black. Open daily 5pm-2am.

Attic, 3336 24th St. (643-3376), between Bartlett and Mission St. in the **Mission.** Barely lit, womblike booths in back once you squeeze past the bar. Romantic and hip, jazz music plays in the background. Happy Hour daily 5-7:30pm. Open daily 5pm-2am.

Lucky 13, 2140 Market St. (487-1313), between Church and Sanchez St. in the **Castro.** Friendly and laid-back, trying to pull off a punk rock vibe. Laid-back service, too; getting a bartender's attention sometimes requires an air horn and/or a flare gun. Pool, pinball, a low, crowded balcony, and a well-stocked jukebox. Good selection of single-malt scotch and 28 beers on tap, not one of them named Bud, Miller, or Coors (pints $3.50, before 7pm $2.50). Pint of goldfish crackers $1. Open M-Th 4pm-2am, F-Su 2pm-2am.

Blue Light Cafe, 1979 Union St. (922-5510), between Buchanan and Laguna St. in **Pacific Heights.** Hipsters in the Mission, queers in Castro, hippies in the Haight...ever wonder where the *straight* straights hang out? Great-looking young Republicans cruise voraciously in this designer bar of etched glass and gleaming steel. Open M-Sa 4pm-2am, Su 11am-2am.

Specs, 12 Saroyan Pl. (421-4112), in a little alley off Columbus Ave. next to Tosca, **North Beach.** The real draw is not their obscure, world-respected brew (Bud), but the memorabilia that packs every inch of the walls, floor, and ceiling. Start your scavenger hunt by finding a gold toilet plunger, a walrus penis, a human skull, and a bottle of Anchor Steam. Open daily 5pm-2am.

CLUBS

San Francisco likes to freak genres (no wonder Dada is getting a resurgence), but there are definitely dance spots that distinguish themselves from the ocean of quality music and beverage venues. DJs are artists here and clubbing practically a second job for many Frisco young people. The following list should get you started, but there are dozens more excellent spots with new ones cropping up and old ones getting shut down by the police. *S.F. Weekly* and *Bay Guardian* have ample listings and reviews, and record stores are littered with flyers. **Housewares,** 1322 Haight St. (252-1440), is a rave clothing store and a good source of flyers for parties and events. They maintain a rave hotline at 281-0125. Up the street, **F-8,** 1816 Haight St. (221-4142), also provides flyers and a telephone hotline (541-5019), more geared to trance and techno. **www.hyperreal.org/raves/sf** is an online rave bulletin. The **Be-At Line** (626-4087), established by the son of Mayor Willie Brown, is a rundown of the night's most happening happenings, be they well-known or obscure. It's the first and only resource for many professional clubgoers. Unless otherwise noted, all clubs are ages 21-plus only.

Ten 15 Folsom, 1015 Folsom St. (431-1200) at 6th St. in **SoMa.** Schizophrenic dance cavern where disco, deep house, and acid jazz are all popular. Strict dress code and inflated cover on weekends. Spundae hot house beats Su. Cover $5 Su-Th, $10 F-Sa. Hours vary.

Nickie's Barbecue, 460 Haight St. (621-6508), at Fillmore St. in the **Haight.** This is one of the chillest, friendliest small clubs in the whole damn city, with a low cover and even less attitude. Live DJ every night with themes ranging from world music to hip-hop to funk. Great dancing, diverse multi-ethnic crowd. Cover around $5. Open daily 9pm-2am.

New Wave City (675-LOVE/5683; www.newwavecity.com), a mobile feast of 80s theme dance parties.

The Top, 424 Haight St. (864-7386), at Fillmore St. in the **Lower Haight.** The Top's main draws are its loyalty to turntablism and off-center take on the classic disco ball. Cover $5. Open daily 6pm-2am.

Covered Wagon Saloon, 917 Folsom St. (974-1585), at 5th St. in **SoMa.** Beware the dress code in this divey saloon (no sportswear, no hats or jerseys with team logos). Live music 5 nights a week, built around trashy theme nights like "Power Lounge" and "Stinky's Peep Show." W is "Faster Pussycat," a rowdy dyke party. Happy Hour M-F 4:30-9:30pm features your choice of Shot 'n' Beer ($3.50) or Beer 'n' Shot (also $3.50). Open daily 4:30pm-2am. 21+.

DNA Lounge, 375 11th St. (626-1409), between Folsom and Harrison St. in **SoMa.** Soulful live music and funkilicious spinnin'. Open late for San Francisco. F night house band Grooveline play a steady diet of 70s covers. Cover around $10. Open daily 10pm-4am.

Sound Factory, 525 Harrison St. (979-8686), at Essex in **southern SoMa.** 3 clubs in 1—usually some combination of Top 40, jungle/house, hip hop, and electronica. You'll have plenty of time waiting in line to decide whether they're worth the $10 cover. Open 9:30pm-4am.

SAN FRANCISCO

Liquid, 2925 16th St. (431-8889), at Van Ness Ave., between **SoMa** and the **Mission.** Nightly mix usually includes trip-hop or heavy jungle beats. Young crowd fills the small, unfurnished space. Open nightly 7pm-2am.

Roccapulco, 3140 Mission St. (648-6611), south of Cesar Chavez St. in the **Mission.** Over 1000 people pack this super-sized, super-yellow Latin dance hall, formerly César's Latin Palace. Parking available. Open Th 8pm-2am, F-Sa 9pm-5am, Su noon-5pm and 8pm-2am. All ages.

The Elbo Room, 647 Valencia St. (552-7788; www.elbo.com), at 18th Ave. in the **Mission.** Dress is skimpy on the crowded dance floor. Cool off in the meat market downstairs with pool, pinball, TV showing Euroshows on "mute." and $3 pints. Cover $3-6. Open nightly 10pm-2am.

GAY AND LESBIAN NIGHTLIFE

> If you're going to be a degenerate, you might as well be a lady about it, don't you think?
>
> — Anna Madrigal, *Tales of the City*

Politics aside, nightlife alone is enough to make San Francisco a queer mecca. From the buff gym boys in nipple-tight Ts to tattooed dykes grinding to NIN, there's something for everybody. The boys hang in the Castro (around the intersection of Castro and Market St.), while the grrrls prefrrr the Mission (on and off Valencia St.); both genders frolic along Polk St. (several blocks north of Geary Blvd.), and in SoMa. Polk St. can be seedy and SoMa barren, so keep a watchful eye for trouble. Many "straight" San Francisco night spots have one or two gay or lesbian theme nights, and most of the clubs and bars listed above are gay-friendly any night of the week. See **Publications,** p. 86, for more sources of information.

The Café, 2367 Market St. (861-3846), the **Castro.** Mixed crowd chills casually in the afternoon with pool and pinball, but when the sun goes down and the dance floor gets pumping, it's virtually all-gay, all-twentysomething, all-male. Mirrors surround the dance floor so you never have to dance with anyone less fabulous than yourself. Repeat *Guardian* awards for best gay bar. No cover. Open daily 12:30pm-2am.

The Lexington Club, 3464 19th St. (863-2052), at Lexington St. in the **Mission.** Neighborhood watering hole for lesbians. Jukebox plays the Clash to Johnny Cash, hitting all the tuff muff favorites (k.d. lang, Sleater-Kinney, Liz Phair) along the way. Happy Hour M-F 4-7pm. Open daily 3pm-2am.

The EndUp, 401 6th St. (357-0827), at Harrison St. in **SoMa.** A San Francisco institution and club of last resort. Theme nights run from Fag F to Girl Spot Sa to mostly straight KitKat Th. Infamous Sunday Tea Dance 6am-2am the next day. Cover $5-10. Open W-F 10pm-4am. Sa 9pm-2am

Esta Noche, 3079 16th St. (861-5757), at Valencia St. in the **Mission.** The city's premiere gay Latino bar hosts regular drag shows, both on stage and off. Gringos are asked to refrain from dancing salsa without instruction. Cover $3-5. Open Su-Th 1pm-2am, F-Sa 1pm-3am.

The Stud, 399 9th St. (252-STUD/7883) at Harrison St. in **SoMa.** This legendary bar/club recreates itself every night of the week–W are disco, Su are 80s nostalgia, Tu are the wild and wacky drag and transgender party known as "Trannyshack." Crowd is mostly gay male. Cover around $5. Open daily 5pm-2am.

Club Townsend, 177 Townsend (974-6020), between 2nd and 3rd St. in **SoMa.** A huge dance arena, Club T is populated by a mixed crowd during the week, but Sa "Universe" and Su "Pleasure Dome" are both gay male thangs. "Club Q," the 1st F of each month, is one of a very few lesbian nights with any longevity. Cover around $10. Call for hours.

Harvey's, 500 Castro St. (431-HARV/4278), at 18th Ave. in the **Castro.** Named for adored former city manager Harvey Milk, Harvey's is a friendly spot for mingling and low-key cruising. Decor is meant to suggest a gay Hard Rock Cafe, but they haven't gone very far with it. Drag show W ($3 cover). M night trivia tests your knowledge of cartoons, show tunes and Hollywood blondes. Happy Hour 4-7pm. Open M-F 11am-2am, Sa-Su 9am-2am.

Twin Peaks, 401 Castro St. (864-9470), at Market St. in the **Castro.** The wide-open picture windows were extremely radical for a gay bar (because you can peek in as well as out) when Twin Peaks opened almost 20 years ago. Today it's the granddaddy of the Castro scene, with a mellow, white-bearded crowd. Domestic draft $1.75. Open daily noon-2am.

Hole in the Wall, 289 8th St. (431-4695) at Folsom St. in **SoMa.** Hard-core black leather gay bar. Loads of bald heads, handle-bar moustaches, leather vests, and hairy bottoms. Not for the squeamish, female, or straight. Open Tu-Th noon-2am, F-M 6am-2am.

CoCo Club, 139 8th St. (626-2337), entrance on Minna St. in SoMa. Attached to the Chat House, the CoCo fills a void with live music and dancing for women. Events vary from spoken-word performance art to acoustic folksingers to funk/hip hop DJs. Cover usually $5-10. Open Tu-Su 7pm-2am.

LIVE MUSIC

S.F. Weekly and the *Guardian* are the place to start looking for the latest live music listings. Hard-core audiophiles might also snag a copy of *BAM* (see **Publications,** p. 86). Many of the bars and a few of the clubs listed above feature regular live bands at various times. *The List* is a calendar of rock and rock-like gigs all over Northern California (jon.luini.com/thelist.txt).

ROCK

Fillmore, 1805 Geary Blvd. (346-6000), at Fillmore St. south of **Japantown.** Bands that would pack stadiums in other cities are often eager to play at the legendary Fillmore, foundation of San Francisco's 1960s music scene. All ages. Tickets $15-25. Wheelchair accessible. Call for hours.

Bottom of the Hill, 1233 17th St. (621-4455), at Texas St. in **Potrero Hill** (south of SoMa). Intimate rock club with tiny stage is the last best place to see up-and-comers before they move to bigger venues. Cover $3-7. Age limits vary. Su afternoons feature 3 local bands and all-you-can-eat barbecue for $5. Call for showtimes.

Purple Onion, 140 Columbus Ave. (398-8415), **North Beach.** Hardcore garage punk, surf rock, and the like get the crowd mighty rowdy. Cover around $5. Doors open at 9pm, bands start 10pm. Open F-Sa only.

Club Boomerang, 1840 Haight St. (387-2996), at Stanyon in the **Upper Haight.** Former metal bar now hosts several rock acts nightly from San Francisco and beyond. Open 2pm-2am. Su, M free; other covers $2-6.

JAZZ

Jazz at Pearl's, 256 Columbus Ave. (291-8255), at Broadway in **North Beach.** Traditional jazz combos in a comfortable setting for an older, well-dressed crowd. No cover, but a 2 drink minimum. Open daily 8:30pm-2am.

Up and Down Club, 1151 Folsom St. (626-2388), at 7th St. in **SoMa.** Curvy golden supper club is ground zero for San Francisco's emergent jazz and fusion scene. Open M and Th-Sa 8pm-2am.

Bimbo's 365 Club, 1025 Columbus Ave. (474-0365), at Chestnut St. in **North Beach.** Cavernous cocktail lounge jumped on the swing bandwagon early—about 1931, to be precise. Variety of musical acts, but swing and jazz are the mainstays. Dress swanky. Tickets from $10. Open for shows; call ahead.

BLUES

Biscuits and Blues, 401 Mason St. (292-BLUE/2583), at Geary in **Union Square.** Hard to say which is the bigger draw: melt-in-your-mouth Louisiana-style biscuits, or low-down Southern blues. Cover $5-15. Open M-F 5pm, Sa-Su 6pm, closes between 11:30pm and 12:30am; kitchen closes around 10pm.

The Saloon, 1232 Grant Ave. (989-7666), at Columbus and Vallejo St. Busts at the seams with regulars. Live nightly blues hurt so good, the crush feels like a warm squeeze. Microbrew or light beer lovers should look elsewhere. No cover, 1 drink minimum. Weekend shows at 4pm. Open daily noon-2am.

Boom Boom Room (673-8000), 1601 Fillmore St. on the north side of Geary Blvd. Innocuous exterior hides a large, luscious stage and ample seating. Music every nights, cover $1-$15, usually $1-5. Happy Hour 5-8pm. Open daily 2pm-2am. 21+.

HIP-HOP

Justice League, 628 Divisadero St. (440-0409; info line 289-2038), at Hayes St. Live hip-hop is hard to find in San Francisco, but the Justice League fights ever onward for truth, justice, and beats. Open 9pm-2am; call ahead; sometimes closed Su and T.

Storyville, 1751 Fulton (441-1751) at Masonic in the **Upper Haight**. Hip-hop and turntable, including big acts. Call for hours.

COMEDY

Cobb's Comedy Club, 2801 Leavenworth St. (928-4320), at Beach and Hyde St. in the Cannery at **Fisherman's Wharf.** Big and small names take on this San Francisco standard. 2-drink min. Must be 18. Purchase tickets (around $10) through BASS or at the club after 7pm. Call for show dates/times.

Josie's Cabaret and Juice Joint, 3583 16th St., (861-7933), at Market St. in the **Castro.** Drag queens, cabaret, and queer-themed stand-up comedy. M is open mic night. Cover $5-15. Shows at 8 and 10pm. Arrive early for a good seat. By day, it's a funky cafe (see **Food and Sights,** p. 90). Open M-F 5-10pm, Sa-Su 9am-3pm, 5-10pm.

The Punchline, 444 Battery St. (397-4337), between Clay and Washington St. in the **Financial District.** Big league comedy. Open mic Su. Cover $5-15 plus 2-drink minimum. Open Su-Th 9-11pm, F-Sa 9am-11pm.

SEASONAL EVENTS

San Francisco hosts an astounding array of seasonal events no matter what time of year you visit. Events below are listed chronologically. The visitors center has a recording of current events (391-2001).

SPRING

Tulipmania (705-5500), early Mar., Pier 39. Your chance to dress up like a little Dutch girl and tiptoe through thousands of tulips from around the world.

Asian American International Film Showcase (863-0814), mid-Mar., AMC Kabuki 8 Theater, Japantown. Over 100 Asian and Asian-American feature and short films.

Union/Fillmore St. Easter Celebration (441-7055), features a petting zoo and other fuzzy diversions, plus a parade. (Easter Sunday is Apr. 23 in 2000.)

Cherry Blossom Festival (563-2313), Apr., Japantown. A Japanese cultural festival featuring hundreds of performers.

Spike and Mike's Festival of Animation (957-1205), Apr.-May, Palace of Fine Arts. Animated films from *Wallace and Grommit* to *Lupo the Butcher.*

San Francisco International Film Festival (929-5000), Apr.-May. The oldest film festival in North America, showing more than 100 international films of all genres.

Cinco de Mayo and Carnaval (826-1401), weekend nearest May 5 (May 9-10 in 2000) and Memorial Day weekend (May 27-29 in 2000). The Mission explodes with colorful costumes and mariachi bands.

Examiner Bay to Breakers (808-5000 ext. 2222), 3rd Sunday in May (May 21 in 2000), starting at the Embarcadero at 8am. Largest foot race in the U.S., with up to 100,000 participants, covers 7½mi. in inimitable San Francisco style. Runners win not only on their times but on their costumes as well. Special centipede category.

SUMMER

Stern Grove San Francisco Midsummer Music Festival (252-6252), June-Aug., Stern Grove. Free opera, ballet, jazz, and a capella for 10 Sundays. Arrive early for best seating. Performances 2pm, pre-performance talks 11am.

San Francisco International Gay and Lesbian Film Festival (703-8663), June, Roxie Cinema (at 16th and Valencia St.) and Castro Theatre (at Castro and Market St.). California's 2nd largest film festival and the world's largest lesbian and gay media event.

People in Plazas (362-2500; www.citysearch.com/sfo/marketstreet). Extensive series of free noontime concerts all over downtown. Jazz, world music, country, and more.

National Queer Arts Festival (552-7709; www.queerculturalcenter.org), June-July. Events in SoMa, the Mission, and Castro.

Union Street Spring Festival (346-4446), June. Arts and crafts at Fillmore and Union St.

Pride Day (864-3733), last Su in June (June 25 in 2000). The High Holy Day of the queer calendar. Officially it's called Lesbian, Gay, Bisexual, Transgender Pride Day. In the Castro, the annual celebration actually lasts for 1 to 12 months.

Fourth of July Celebration (777-8498), July 4, Crissy Field in the Presidio. Free fireworks and live entertainment.

Jazz and All That Art on Fillmore (346-4446), early July, Fillmore St. Food, wine, art, and jazz: the pinnacle of human evolution.

San Francisco Jewish Film Festival (621-0556), July-Aug. An area-wide festival, the oldest in the world.

Cable Car Bell-Ringing Championship (923-6202), July, Union Square. Where people who have spent years perfecting their clang go to get recognition.

Blues and Art on Polk (346-4446), late July, on Polk St.

North Beach Jazz Festival (771-3112), July, Washington Square Park and Telegraph Hill. An assortment of musicians play. Tickets free-$15.

Nihonmachi Street Fair (771-9861), early Aug., Japantown. Lion dancers, *taiko* drummers, and karaoke wars.

FALL

San Francisco Fair (434-3247), early Sept., Civic Center Plaza at McAllister and Polk St. Multicultural food and multiweird entertainment. Competitions include the Impossible Parking Space Race, Fog Calling, and the National Skateboard Championships.

San Francisco Fringe Festival (931-1094), early Sept., downtown. Experimental theater at its finest.

Festival de Las Americas (826-1401), mid-Sept., Mission. Food, art, and the cha-cha. A time to remember the plural nature of the word "America."

San Francisco Blues Festival (979-5588), 3rd weekend in Sept. (Sept. 16-17 in 2000), Fort Mason. The oldest blues festival in America attracts the biggest names in blues.

Folsom Street Fair (648-3247), last Su in Sept. (Sept. 24 in 2000), Folsom St. between 7th and 11th St. Pride Day's ruder, raunchier, rowdier brother. The Hole in the Wall gang lets it all hang out in leather and chains.

Chinatown Autumn Moon Festival (982-6306), Oct., Grant Ave. Martial arts, lion dancing, and tons of bean-cake-happy spectators.

World Pumpkin Weigh-Off (346-4561), early Oct., City Hall. The search for the Great Pumpkin continues, Charlie Brown.

Film Arts Festival (552-FILM/3456), late Oct.-early Nov., Roxie Cinema. Low-budget features, documentaries, and short films made in the Bay Area.

Castro Street Fair (467-3354), Oct., Castro. Food, live music, and art. A bit more bridled than:

Halloween, Oct. 31, Castro. Some people say the Castro has become less wild with age. Those people have not been there on Halloween.

Dia de los Muertos (Day of the Dead; 821-1155), Nov. 1, Mission. Follow the drummers and dancing skeletons to the festive Mexican celebration of the dead. The party starts in the evening at the Mission Cultural Center, on Mission at 25th St.

San Francisco Jazz Festival (864-5449), early Nov. Includes Jazz Film Fest.

WINTER

Festival of Lights (362-6355), Union Square. Festivities leading up to the lighting of a huge menorah.

Christmas Tree-Lighting Ceremony (831-2783), at Fell and Stanyan St.

Sing-It-Yourself-Messiah (864-6000), Dec., Symphony Hall. Some say San Franciscans can't keep their mouths shut—now they don't have to.

Our Lady of Guadalupe Fiesta (621-8203), Mission Dolores. Music and food at dawn.

Christmas at Sea (561-6662), Hyde St. Pier. Caroling and family fun events aboard the *Balclutha.*

Chinese New Year Celebration (982-3000) and **Parade** (391-9680), Feb. 5, Chinatown. North America's largest Chinese community celebrates the Year of the Dragon (4697 on the lunar calendar) with the largest festival in San Francisco. Cultural festivities, parade, fireworks, and the crowning of Miss Chinatown.

Russian Festival (921-7631), 3 days in early Feb., Russian Ctr. at Sutter St., Divisadero. Folk singing and dancing, Russian food, and flavored vodka tastings.

THE BAY AREA AND WINE COUNTRY

Beyond the docks of San Francisco are a number of dynamic complements to the City by the Bay: Berkeley's cafes, Oakland's blues, Wine Country vineyards, Silicon Valley nerds. The bay and surrounding mountains and rivers shape a region whose postwar sprawl would otherwise be as disorienting as Los Angeles, and while Bay Area residents still refer to San Francisco as The City, the region's cultural and natural verve is rewarding on its own.

HIGHLIGHTS OF THE BAY AREA

■ In the East Bay, Berkeley is the home of vigorous intellectual ferment, visible on the campus of **UC Berkeley** (p. 135), on **Telegraph Avenue** (p. 134) and on the shelves of its **bookstores** (p. 137), while Oakland is home to unbeatable blues (p. 144).

■ The South Bay includes the expansive campus of **Stanford University** (p. 148), and pretty coastline on the **Pacific Coast Highway** (p. 157).

■ In the North Bay, **Mount Tamalpais** (p. 166) is home of the mountain bike, and the **Marin Coast** (p. 158) has welcoming drives and beaches.

■ Tourists rush to the famous wineries of the **Napa Valley** (p. 170); the vineyards in the **Russian River Valley** (p. 178) are more peaceful.

EAST BAY

Longer and older than its Golden Gate neighbor, the Bay Bridge carries the weight of San Francisco traffic east to Oakland, where freeways fan out in all directions. The urbanized port of Oakland sprawls north into the assertively hippie college town of Berkeley. Bounded by the bay and freeway geography, the two towns have long shared an interest in political activism. Berkeley, bookish and bizarre as ever, offers boutiques and cafes, while its sister city Oakland echoes with the sounds of a progressive blues and jazz scene.

BERKELEY

Famous for being an intellectual center and a haven for iconoclasts, Berkeley (pop. 99,900) quite lives up to its reputation. Although the peak of its political activism occurred in the 1960s and 70s—when students attended more protests than classes—U.C. Berkeley continues to cultivate consciousness and brainy brawn, even if no longer as "Berserkeley." The vitality of the population infuses the streets, which are strewn with hip cafes and top-notch bookstores. Telegraph Avenue, the Champs-Elysées of the 1960s, remains Berkeley's commercial and intellectual heart, home to street-corner soothsayers, hirsute hippies, and itinerant street musicians who never left.

GETTING THERE AND AROUND BY CAR

There are four Berkeley exits off **Interstate 80;** the University Ave. Exit leads most directly to U.C. Berkeley and downtown. To drive from San Francisco, cross the Bay Bridge on I-80. Freeway congestion can make driving in the Bay Area frustrating, especially during rush hours.

Drivers fortunate enough to reach Berkeley despite Bay Area traffic will face congestion, numerous one-way streets, and vexing concrete planters. Reasonably priced public lots let you ditch your car and explore on foot—the best way to absorb Berkeley.

ORIENTATION

Across the Bay Bridge northeast of San Francisco and just north of Oakland, Berkeley is sandwiched between the docks of the bay and a series of rolling hills. The **University of California** campus and **Tilden Regional Park** climb up the sharp grades to the east (technically into Oakland), but most of the university's buildings are in the flatter westernmost section of campus, near the BART station. BART spits you out downtown at its main stop on Shattuck Ave. and Allston Way just west of U.C. Berkeley. Undergraduates tend to hang out on the bustling south side of campus, while graduate students occupy the north side. The downtown area, around the BART station at Shattuck Ave. and Center St., contains banks and theaters as well as the public library and central post office. Lined with bookstores, cafes, palm readers, and panhandlers, **Telegraph Avenue,** which runs south from the Student Union, is the magnetic heart of town. North of campus, the **Gourmet Ghetto** collects some of California's finest dining in the area around Shattuck Ave. between Virginia and Rose St. Farther afield, **4th Street,** near the waterfront, and **Solano Avenue,** to the northwest, are home to yummy eats and yuppie shops. Quality cafes, music stores, and specialty shops grace the **Rockridge** district on the border between Berkeley and Oakland (see **Downtown Oakland,** p. 142). **Exercise caution at night.**

PRACTICAL INFORMATION

Trains: The closest Amtrak (800-USA-RAIL/872-7245) station is in Oakland (see p. 141), but travelers can board in Berkeley with prior arrangement.

Buses: The closest Greyhound (800-231-2222) station is in Oakland (see p. 141).

Public Transportation to and from Berkeley:

Rapid Transit (BART; 465-2278; see **Public Transit,** p. 82), sends trains to and from San Francisco, although more slowly than buses (one-way fares under $3), to **BART Berkeley station,** 2160 Shattuck Ave., at Center St., close to the western edge of campus, and **BART North Berkeley station,** at Delaware and Sacramento St., 4 blocks north of University Ave. **Alameda County (AC) Transit** (817-1717) buses #15, 43, and 51 run from the Berkeley BART station to downtown Oakland on Martin Luther King, Jr. Way, Telegraph Ave., and Broadway, respectively (fare $1.25; seniors, disabled, and ages 5-12 60¢; under 5 free; 1hr. transfers 25¢). **AC Bus F** departs San Francisco's Transbay Terminal for Berkeley (M-F every 30min. 6am-midnight).

Public Transit Within Berkeley: AC city buses run in town; ask a driver for schedules (approx. every 20min.; fare $2.20; seniors, disabled, and ages 5-12 $1.10). **Berkeley Electric Shuttle** (BEST; 841-2378) connects the Ashby BART station with the West Berkeley business district at rush hour (every 20min. M-F 6:35-9:15am and 3:35-6:25pm; 50¢). **University Perimeter Shuttle** (642-5149) connects campus to the Berkeley BART station (shuttles run Sept.-June M-F 7am-6pm every 8min. except on university holidays; 25¢); shuttles also run around campus (M-F 7am-5:45pm; 25¢) and between campus and downtown (Sa 7:30pm-2:15am; 25¢).

Transportation and Ride Share: Berkeley TRiP, 2033 Center St. (644-7665). Commuter-oriented information on public transportation, biking, and carpooling. Sells extended-use transit passes and various maps. Open M-W and Th 9am-6pm, F 8:30am-5:30pm. **Berkeley Ride Board,** 1st level of student store in Student Union. **KALX Radio, 90.7 FM** (642-KALX/5259). Ride list broadcasted daily at 10am and 10pm; call to put your request on the air for free.

Taxis: A1 Yellow Cab (644-1111) and **Berkeley Yellow Cab** (841-2265). Both 24hr.

Car Rental: Budget, 600 Gilman St. (486-0806), at 2nd St. Compact car $49 per day with unlimited mileage. Min. age 21; under 25 surcharge $20 per day. Open M-F 7:15am-4:45pm, Sa-Su 8:15am-3:45pm. (Cheaper in San Francisco; see p. 84.)

San Francisco Bay Area

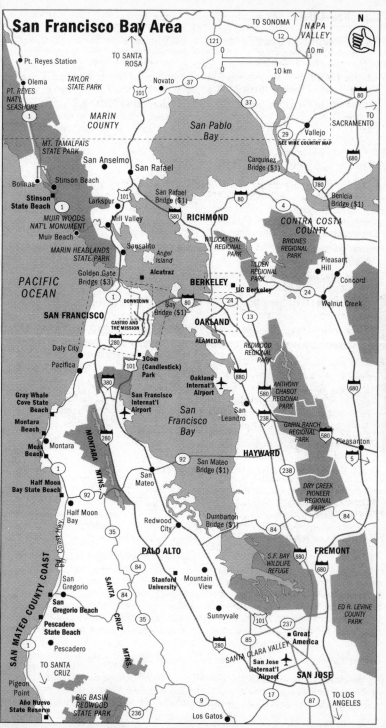

N
0
10 mi
0
10 km
TO SONOMA
NAPA VALLEY
TO SANTA ROSA
Pt. Reyes Station
Olema
TAYLOR STATE PARK
PT. REYES NAT'L SEASHORE
MARIN COUNTY
Novato
San Pablo Bay
TO SACRAMENTO
Vallejo
SEE WINE COUNTRY MAP
MT. TAMALPAIS STATE PARK
San Anselmo
San Rafael
Carquinez Bridge ($1)
Bolinas
Stinson Beach
Stinson State Beach
Larkspur
San Rafael Bridge ($1)
Benicia Bridge ($1)
MUIR WOODS NAT'L MONUMENT
Mill Valley
RICHMOND
CONTRA COSTA COUNTY
Muir Beach
WILDCAT CYN. REGIONAL PARK
BRIONES REGIONAL PARK
MARIN HEADLANDS STATE PARK
Sausalito
Angel Island
TILDEN REGIONAL PARK
Pleasant Hill
Golden Gate Bridge ($3)
Alcatraz
Concord
PACIFIC OCEAN
BERKELEY
UC Berkeley
DOWNTOWN
Bay Bridge ($1)
Walnut Creek
SAN FRANCISCO
OAKLAND
CASTRO AND THE MISSION
ALAMEDA
Daly City
REDWOOD REGIONAL PARK
3Com (Candlestick) Park
Pacifica
Oakland Internat'l Airport
ANTHONY CHABOT REGIONAL PARK
Gray Whale Cove State Beach
San Francisco Internat'l Airport
San Francisco Bay
San Leandro
Montara Beach
GARIN RANCH REGIONAL PARK
Pleasanton
Moss Beach
Montara
MONTARA MTNS.
HAYWARD
San Mateo Bridge ($1)
San Mateo
Half Moon Bay State Beach
DRY CREEK PIONEER REGIONAL PARK
Half Moon Bay
Redwood City
Dumbarton Bridge ($1)
Pt. Coast Hwy.
PALO ALTO
FREMONT
S.F. BAY WILDLIFE REFUGE
SAN MATEO COUNTY COAST
San Gregorio
Stanford University
Mountain View
SANTA CRUZ MTNS.
San Gregorio Beach
Sunnyvale
ED R. LEVINE COUNTY PARK
Pescadero State Beach
Great America
Pescadero
SANTA CLARA VALLEY
TO SANTA CRUZ
San Jose Internat'l Airport
SAN JOSE
Pigeon Point
Año Nuevo State Reserve
BIG BASIN REDWOOD STATE PARK
TO LOS ANGELES
Los Gatos
1 12 121 37 101 80 29 680 780 580 4 24 13 280 380 880 238 5 92 84 35 237 85 17 87 9 236

Visitor Information: Berkeley Convention and Visitor Bureau, 2015 Center St. (800-847-4823 or 549-7040, 24hr. hotline 549-8710), at Milvia St. Helpful street, park, and area maps. Usually open M-F 9am-5pm. **U.C. Berkeley Visitor Center,** 101 University Hall, 2200 University Ave. (642-5215; www.berkeley.edu). Clear, detailed maps (10¢) and campus info. Guided campus tours depart the center M-F 10am and from **Sather Tower** (see p. 135) Sa 10am and Su 1pm. Open M-F 8:30am-4:30pm. **Berkeley Information Network** (540-0666), a telephone service of the public library.

Bi-Gay-Lesbian Organizations: U.C. Berkeley Multicultural BLGA/Queer Resource Center, 305 Eshleman Hall (642-6942; http://queer.berkeley.edu) at Bancroft Way and Telegraph Ave. Open Sept-May M-F 10am-5pm; June-Aug. by appt. only. **Pacific Center,** 2712 Telegraph Ave. (510-548-8283), at Derby St. Counseling and info on gay community events, housing, local clubs, etc. Open M-F 10am-10pm, Sa noon-3pm and 7-10pm, Su 6-9pm.

Ticket Agencies: BASS Tix (762-2277). Calendar of events and show info. Open M-Sa 8:30am-9pm, Su 2-9pm. **Tower Records,** 2518 Durant Ave. (841-0101). Open Su-Th 10am-11pm, F-Sa 10am-midnight. **CAL Athletics,** 2233 Fulton St. #4422 (800-GO-BEARS/462-3277). Lines open M-F 8:30am-4:30pm.

Emergency: 911. **Campus Emergency** 9-911 from campus phone, 642-3333 otherwise.

Police: Berkeley Police (644-6743). **Campus Police,** Sproul Hall Basement (642-6760). 24hr.

Campus Info: U.C. Berkeley Switchboard (642-6000). Info on everything from community events to drug counseling. Open M-F 8am-5pm.

24-Hour Crisis Lines: Rape Hotline (845-RAPE/7273). **Suicide Prevention and Crisis Intervention** (849-2212).

Medical Services: Berkeley Free Clinic, 2339 Durant Ave. (548-2570; http://users.lanminds.com/~bfc), at Dana St. 2 blocks west of Telegraph Ave. Served by AC Transit buses #7, 40, 51, 52, and 54. Call for hours of services; the best times to talk to a real person are M-F 3:30-8:30pm, Sa 6-9pm, Su 5-8pm. **STD Clinic and HIV/AIDS Testing** (644-0425). **Dental** (548-2745). **Counseling** (548-2744). **Berkeley Dept. of Health & Human Services,** 830 University Ave. (644-8571), at 6th St. Medical help on a sliding payment scale. Specialty clinics vary from day to day, so call ahead. Open M-F 8am-5pm. **Berkeley Women's Health Center,** 2908 Ellsworth St. (843-6194), 1 block west of Telegraph Ave. Open M and F 8am-noon and 1-5pm, Tu-Th 9am-1pm and 2-6pm.

Internet Access: U.C. Computer, 2569 Telegraph Ave. (649-6089; www.transbay.net). $3 for 15min., $5 for 30min., $7 per hr. Open M-Sa 10am-6pm.

Post Office: 2000 Allston Way (649-3100). Open M-F 8:30am-6pm, Sa 10am-2pm. **ZIP Code:** 94704.

AREA CODE	The area code for Berkeley is 510.

PUBLICATIONS

Free publications can be found in corner boxes and at any of the area's numerous cafes. The *Daily Planet* has superhero comic strips besides basic Berkeley news. For up-to-date news on area happenings, look in bookstores and bins around town for the free weekly *East Bay Express* (540-7400), filled with theater, film, and concert listings. Many San Francisco newspapers (see **San Francisco: Publications,** p. 86), most notably the *Chronicle's Datebook* (the Sunday pink pages), include listings for Berkeley. The *San Francisco Bay Guardian*, which has the most complete Bay Area listings, is also available in Berkeley.

The vast array of U.C. Berkeley publications vary in content and style. If you can find a recent edition of *Resource*, the guide given to new Berkeley students, grab it (try the visitors center at 101 University Hall). The *Daily Californian* (548-8300; www.dailycal.org), is published on Tuesdays and Fridays in the summer and daily during the school year, and carries university news and student interest features.

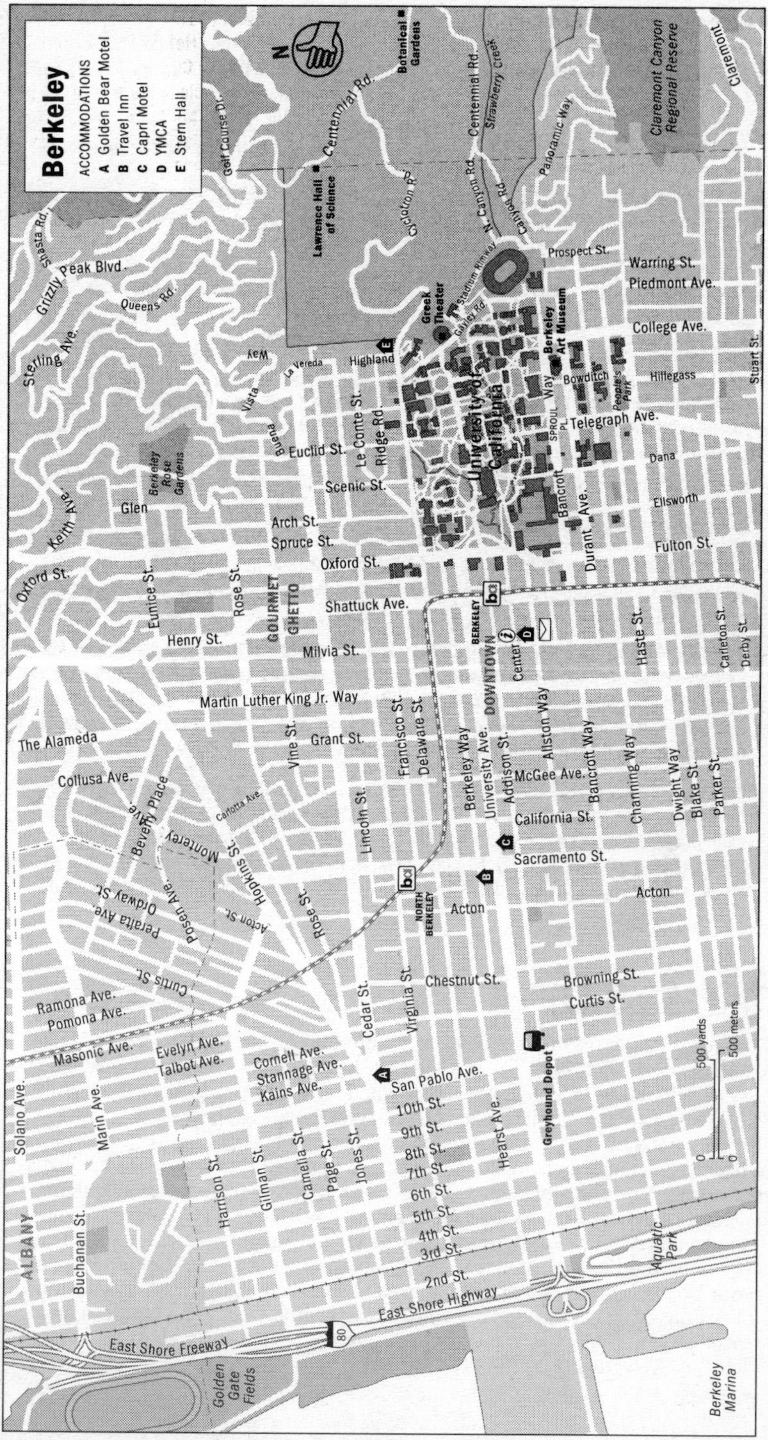
Berkeley
ACCOMMODATIONS
A Golden Bear Motel
B Travel Inn
C Capri Motel
D YMCA
E Stern Hall
N
Botanical Gardens
Centennial Rd.
Lawrence Hall of Science
Golf Course Dr.
Cyclotron Rd.
Strawberry Creek
Claremont Canyon Regional Reserve
Claremont
Panoramic Way
N. Canyon Rd.
Canyon Rd.
Stadium Rimway
Prospect St.
Warring St.
Piedmont Ave.
College Ave.
Stuart St.
Hillegass
Greek Theater
Gayley Rd.
Berkeley Art Museum
Bowditch
People's Park
University of California
Sproul Pl.
Telegraph Ave.
Dana
Ellsworth
Fulton St.
Bancroft Way
Durant Ave.
Shasta Rd.
Grizzly Peak Blvd.
Queens Rd.
Sterling Ave.
Highland
La Vereda
Vista Way
Buena
Euclid St.
Le Conte St.
Ridge Rd.
Scenic St.
Arch St.
Spruce St.
Oxford St.
Shattuck Ave.
Berkeley Rose Gardens
Glen
Keith Ave.
Oxford St.
Eunice St.
Rose St.
Gourmet Ghetto
Henry St.
Milvia St.
Berkeley
Downtown
Center
Haste St.
Carleton St.
Derby St.
Martin Luther King Jr. Way
The Alameda
Vine St.
Grant St.
Francisco St.
Delaware St.
Berkeley Way
University Ave.
Addison St.
Allston Way
McGee Ave.
Bancroft Way
Channing Way
Dwight Way
Blake St.
Parker St.
Collusa Ave.
Beverly Place
Carlotta Ave.
Monterey Ave.
Hopkins St.
Lincoln St.
California St.
Sacramento St.
Ordway St.
Peralta Ave.
Posen Ave.
Acton St.
Rose St.
North Berkeley
Acton
Curtis St.
Ramona Ave.
Pomona Ave.
Cedar St.
Virginia St.
Chestnut St.
Browning St.
Curtis St.
Masonic Ave.
Evelyn Ave.
Talbot Ave.
Cornell Ave.
Stannage Ave.
Kains Ave.
San Pablo Ave.
Greyhound Depot
500 yards
500 meters
0
Solano Ave.
Marin Ave.
10th St.
9th St.
8th St.
7th St.
6th St.
5th St.
4th St.
3rd St.
2nd St.
Hearst Ave.
Harrison St.
Gilman St.
Camelia St.
Page St.
Jones St.
Albany
Buchanan St.
Aquatic Park
East Shore Highway
East Shore Freeway
80
Golden Gate Fields
Berkeley Marina

BAY AREA

ACCOMMODATIONS

There are surprisingly few cheap accommodations in Berkeley. **The Berkeley and Oakland Bed and Breakfast Network** (547-6380) coordinates 20 East Bay B&Bs with a range of rates. A popular option is to stay in San Francisco and make daytrips to Berkeley, a plan that presents its own challenges (see **San Francisco: Accommodations,** p. 87). Although the motels are technically in walking distance of the BART stations and attractions, they are much more accessible with a car. A sheet available at the tourist office lists resources for finding short-term apartment rentals and roommates.

Golden Bear Motel, 1620 San Pablo Ave. (525-6770 or 800-525-6770), at Cedar St. 8 blocks from North Berkeley BART station. Charming stucco motel built in 1949. Check-out noon. Parking included. Singles $58; doubles $69-79; 2-bedroom cottages with kitchen $135-145. Reservations required.

UC Berkeley Summer Visitor Housing (642-5925; www.housing.berkeley.edu). Residence halls are open to visitors June to mid-Aug. Visitors housed in **Stern Hall,** 2700 Hearst Ave., at Highland St. A dorm that functions as a hotel, with shared baths, free Internet access, local phone calls, ping-pong and pool tables, and TV room. Parking ($3 per day), laundry (wash 75¢), meals, and photocopying available. Linen and towels included. Singles $41; doubles $54. No personal checks accepted.

Capri Motel, 1512 University Ave. (845-7090), at Sacramento St. Clean, tasteful rooms with cable TV. In summer singles $55-70, doubles $70-100; in winter singles $45-50, doubles $55-70.

Travel Inn, 1461 University Ave. (848-3840), at Sacramento St., 4 blocks from North Berkeley BART station, 7 blocks west of campus. Perky pink motel looks like it traveled in from Palm Springs. Clean, comfortable rooms with TVs and phones. Laundry. Parking and coffee included. Check-out noon. Singles in summer $60, in winter $50; doubles around $70. Discounts on stays longer than 5 days.

YMCA, 2001 Allston Way (848-6800), at Milvia St. Adequate rooms available in co-ed hotel portion of this YMCA. Use of pool and fitness facilities included. Shared bath. Linen included. Registration daily 8am-9:30pm. No curfew. In-room phones for incoming calls; pay phones in hall. 14-night max. stay; special applications available for longer stays. Singles $33; doubles $40; triples $50. Inquire about weekly rates. **Must be 18+ with ID.**

FOOD

Berkeley is famous as the birthplace of "California cuisine." The epicenter of the phenomenon is Shattuck Ave. at Cedar St. in the **Gourmet Ghetto,** where chef Alice Waters opened Chez Panisse in 1971 and introduced a nation to the joys of goat cheese and polenta. If $35-70 entrees don't move you, never fear. Berkeley offers a variety of budget dining, munching, and sipping options. The north end of **Telegraph Avenue** caters to student appetites and wallet sizes—hence the high concentration of pizza joints and trendy cafes. If you've maxed out on caffeine and have a car, head out to **Solano Avenue** in Albany to the north for Asian cuisine or cruise down to **San Pablo Avenue** in the west for American fare. **Farmer's markets** run by the Ecology Center (548-3333) sprout Saturdays at Center St. and Martin Luther King, Jr. Way (10am-2pm) and Tuesdays at Derby St. and Martin Luther King, Jr. Way (in summer 2-7pm; in winter 1pm-dusk). The **Telegraph Area Association** (649-9500) also runs a farmer's market, on Haste St. between Bowditch St. and Telegraph Ave. (Su 11am-3pm).

DOWNTOWN

Pasand Madras Cuisine, 2286 Shattuck St. (549-2559), at Bancroft Way. Melt-in-your-mouth *korma*s, curries, and tandooris fit for Vishnu. All-you-can-eat buffet ($7) noon-3pm means endless chewy *nan* bread; lunch specials around $4. Open Su-Th 11am-10pm, F-Sa 11am-10:30pm.

Long Life Vegi House, 2129 University Ave. (845-6072). Vast menu of countless vegetable and "vegetarian meat" Chinese options. Huge portions; most entrees $5-7. Friendly, prompt service. Eat-in or takeout. Daily lunch special 11:30am-3pm with entree, egg roll, and soup ($3.65). Open Su-Th 11:30am-9:30pm, F-Sa 11:30am-10pm.

Oscar's, 1890 Shattuck Ave. (849-2164), at Hearst St. Unassuming hamburger shack justly lauded by locals. Cheeseburger $3. Open Su-Th 10am-midnight, F-Sa 10am-2am.

Crepes A-Go-Go, 2125 University Ave. (841-7722). Crepes are on the thick side for hands-on convenience. Cheese and turkey crepes $3.50, honey and kiwi crepes $3.75. Pleasant staff and flirty owner also vend sandwiches and salad to Berkeleyans on the go-go. Open Su-Th 9am-10pm, F-Sa 9am-10:30pm.

Bongo Burger, 2154 Center St. (548-7700); also at Telegraph Ave. and Dwight St. Burgers are big, sloppy, and cheap ($2.75), as is the breakfast special ($2), but Bongo's real bargain is the falafel sandwich, a meal for $1.75 (large $2.75). Open M-F 8am-8pm, Sa 8:30am-5:30pm.

TELEGRAPH AVENUE

Ann's Soup Kitchen, 2498 Telegraph Ave. (548-8885), at Dwight St. A perennial student breakfast favorite. Towering portions compensate for sometimes crowded dining. 2 eggs with toast or homefries $3. Fresh-squeezed juice tastes like a million bucks, but costs only $1.35. Open M and W-F 8am-7pm, Tu 8am-3pm, Sa-Su 8am-5pm.

Cafe Intermezzo, 2442 Telegraph Ave. (849-4592), at Haste St. The fresh produce in the huge green salad ($3.23) and Veggie Delight ($4.84) will fuel you for the rest of the day. Cheap beer (Anchor Steam $1.75). Sandwiches $4.39. Open M-F 10:30am-9pm.

Blondie's Pizza, 2340 Telegraph Ave. (548-1129). Dagwood-sized slices of good and greasy pies ($2-3) make Blondie's a Berkeley institution. Cheese slice and soda special $2.50. Open M-Th 11:30am-1am, F-Sa 10:30am-2am, Su noon-midnight.

The Blue Nile, 2525 Telegraph Ave. (540-6777). Huge portions of Ethiopian food in a lavish setting. Waitresses in traditional gowns slip through beaded curtains between booths. Wide variety of vegetarian dishes. Lunch entrees $5-7, dinner entrees $7-9. Eat with your fingers and *injera* bread; get blotto with *Tej* (honey wine; $2 a glass). Open Tu-Sa 11:30am-10pm, Su 5-10pm. Busy on weekends; reservations recommended.

Mario's La Fiesta, 2444 Telegraph Ave. (540-9123), at Haste St. Above-average Mexican restaurant with heaping portions and indulgent service. It's cheap anyway (combo plates $4-8), but order a la carte to avoid the unremarkable soup and save even more. Open daily 10:30am-10:30pm.

La Mediterranée, 2936 College Ave. (540-7773), 2 blocks east of Telegraph Ave., near Rockridge. An open, airy, cafe-style establishment specializing in Greek and Armenian food. Entrees $7-8. Open M-Th 10am-10pm, F-Sa 10am-11pm, Su 10am-9:30pm.

NORTH BERKELEY

Cafe Fanny, 1603 San Pablo Ave. (524-5447), at Cedar St. opposite the Golden Bear Motel. Alice Waters' venture, this tiny cafe offers limited seating, standing room, and benches in the shade of a pleasant outdoor trellis. Poached eggs with quality toast ($4.75) rival buckwheat crepes with fruit and yogurt ($4.75). Drink your bowl (yes, bowl) of *cafe au lait* ($2.50) and don't distract the congenial cook, even if she is less than a foot away. Open M-F 7am-3pm, Sa 8am-4pm, Su 8am-3pm.

Bette's Oceanview Diner, 1807A 4th St. (644-3230), between Delaware and Hearst St. Popular weekend brunch choice–the sooner you get there, the sooner you'll be sipping a silky mimosa ($4). Sandwiches $5-8. Open M-Th 6:30am-2:30pm, F-Su 6:30am-4pm. **Bette's To Go** (548-9494), next door, is cheaper but serves a limited menu. Take-out open M-F 6:30am-5pm, Sa 8am-4pm.

O Chame, 1830 4th St. (841-8783), between Delaware and Hearst St. Delicious and innovative Japanese fusion cooking in a tranquil setting. Become one with a bowl of *soba* or *udon* noodles with tofu skins and spinach ($7.50) and chase it with *sake* ($5 a glass). Open M-Th 11:30am-3pm and 5:30-9pm, F-Sa 11:30am-3pm.

CREATE-YOUR-OWN GOURMET PICNIC

Berkeley Bowl, 2777 Shattuck Ave. (843-6929), at Stuart St. Former bowling alley's lanes are stocked with endless fresh produce, seafood, and bread. The Bay's best grocery shopping; no need to rent special shoes. Open M-Sa 9:30am-8pm, Su 10am-6pm.

Cheese Board, 1504 Shattuck Ave. (549-3183), between Cedar and Vine St. Gourmet cheese shop and bakery with an astonishing selection. Expert staff happily provides tutorials (and tastes!) on the finer points of Camembert and Wensleydale. Cafe open M 7am-1pm, Tu-F 7am-6pm, Sa 8:30am-5pm; cheese counter only open Tu-F 10am-6pm.

Monterey Foods, 1550 Hopkins St. (526-6042). Local produce (starfruit, anyone?), some of it organic. Add their affordable wines and crusty bread to your satchel and head for the hills. Open M-Sa 9am-6pm.

Eclair Bakery, 2567 Telegraph Ave. (848-4221), at Blake St. Top off your picnic with large, fault-lined meringues or terrific sticky florentines ($1 each). Open M-F 6:30am-7pm, Sa 6:30am-6:30pm, Su 7:30am-5:30pm.

SIGHTS

TELEGRAPH AVENUE

You haven't really visited Berkeley until you've strolled the first five or so blocks of Telegraph Ave. which runs south from Sproul Plaza all the way to downtown Oakland. The action is close to the university (see below), where Telegraph Ave. is lined with a motley assortment of cafes, bookstores, and used clothing and record stores. Businesses come and go by the whims of the marketplace, but the scene, a rowdy jumble of 1960s and 1990s counterculture, abides. Vendors push tie-dyes, Tarot readings, and handmade jewelry; people hustle for change; and grizzled characters looking like Old Testament prophets carry on hyper-dimensional conversations with nobody in particular.

Excellent bookstores (see p. 137) let patrons and obviously-not-patrons alike browse for ages without getting the evil eye. Suitable Telegraph Ave. souvenirs can be obtained at **Annapurna,** 2416 Telegraph Ave. (841-6187), one of the head shops stocked with elaborate pipes, hookahs, and other tobacco-smoking accessories, or famous **Amoeba Music,** 2455 Telegraph Ave. (549-1125), at Haste St., a warehouse-sized store of new and used CDs, including a popular collection of music and mutterings by Telegraph Ave.'s least coherent residents.

Berkeley's biggest confrontation between the People and the Man was not fought over freedom of speech or the war in Vietnam, but for control of a muddy, vacant lot just east of Telegraph Ave. between Dwight and Haste St. In April 1969, students, hippies, and radicals christened the patch of university-owned land **"People's Park,"** tearing up pavement and laying down sod to establish, in the words of the *Berkeley Barb*, "a cultural, political freak out and rap center for the Western world." When the university moved to evict squatters and build a parking garage on the site, resistance stiffened. Governor Ronald Reagan sent in 2000 troops, and the conflict ended with helicopters dropping tear gas on students in Sproul Plaza, one bystander shot dead by police, and a 17-day occupation of Berkeley by the National Guard. Visiting People's Park today proves an acid test of one's sympathy for the 1960s. In a sense, its grassy existence represents a small victory against the establishment, although this is hard to remember on a sunny Saturday afternoon when kids play sports or a cold Monday night when homeless huddle in the bushes. A mural on Haste St. at Telegraph Ave. depicts the park's history, from protesters to panhandlers.

Just east of the park is the **First Church of Christ Scientist,** 2526 Dwight St. (845-7199) at Bowditch St. Built in 1910, architect Bernard Maybeck's masterpiece is a subtle conglomeration of Gothic, Renaissance, Classical, Japanese, Mediterranean, and Industrial architectural styles. The church is only open during services (W 8pm, Su 11am) and for tours at noon on the first Sunday of every month.

U.C. BERKELEY

In 1868, the private College of California and the public Agricultural, Mining, and Mechanical Arts College became one as the **University of California.** Berkeley was the first of the nine University of California campuses, so by seniority it has sole rights to the nickname "Cal." The school has a diverse enrollment of 30,000 students and 1350 full professors, and a library system with over 8.7 million volumes, creating a lively and internationally respected academic community. The university is especially active when classes are in session (from mid-Aug. to mid-May).

Pass through **Sather Gate** into **Sproul Plaza,** both sites of celebrated student sit-ins and bloody confrontations with police, to enter the 160-acre Berkeley campus. In October 1964, students protested the arrest of a student who had been distributing civil rights pamphlets in the plaza, beginning a series of confrontations that lasted several years. Student Mario Savio, a member of the widely influential Free Speech Movement, famously addressed a crowd of students from the steps of the plaza, arguing for students' rights to free expression and assembly. Savio was eventually jailed and expelled from school, but in 1997 the plaza steps were named in his honor. The plaza, suspended between Berkeley's idyllic campus and raucous Telegraph Ave., is now a perfect place for people watching.

Berkeley is home to many of the country's most esteemed professors—it's been said you need to win a Nobel prize to get a campus parking permit. If you'd like to sit in on some classes, track down a **course catalog** and schedule of classes at the campus bookstore or online at www.berkeley.edu. Just think: some people pay thousands of dollars a year for this kind of entertainment.

Campus is bounded on the south by Bancroft Way, on the west by Oxford St., on the north by Hearst Ave., and on the east by a vast parkland. Remodeling often occurs during academic down time, so watch for closings due to structural changes or "seismic corrections." Maps of campus are posted everywhere; the **Visitor Center** (see p. 128) also hands out campus maps for a dime, as well as offering tours. Besides the loonies singing and muttering in Sproul Plaza, the most dramatic campus attraction is Sather Tower, better known as the **Campanile** (Italian for "bell tower"). A 1914 monument to Berkeley benefactor Jane Krom Sather, the tower is the tallest building on campus at 307 feet, and you can ride to its observation level for a great view ($1). The tower's 61-bell carillon plays term-time weekdays at 7:50am, noon, and 6pm, with a 40-minute concert on Sundays at 2pm.

LAWRENCE HALL OF SCIENCE. High atop the eucalyptus-covered hills east of the main campus is one of the finest science museums in the Bay Area. Ever-changing exhibits stress hands-on science activities. The courtyard offers a life-size model whale, a stunning view of the bay, and stargazing workshops on clear Saturday evenings. Take bus #8 or 65 from the Berkeley BART station (and keep your transfer for $1 off admission) or a university shuttle (642-5149); otherwise it's a long, steep walk. *(642-5132; www.lhs.berkeley.edu. On Centennial Dr. Open daily 10am-5pm. Admission $6; students, seniors, and ages 7-18 $4.)*

BERKELEY ART MUSEUM (BAM). The museum is most respected for its collections of 20th-century American and Asian art. Rotating exhibitions showcase more experimental work. The museum bookstore is not as gimmicky as most, and the sale racks hold bargain prices. *(642-0808; www.bampfa.berkeley.edu. 2626 Bancroft Way at College Ave. Open W and F-Su 11am-5pm, Th 11am-9pm. Admission $6; students, seniors, and ages 12-17 $4; free Th 11am-noon and 5-9pm.)*

GREEK THEATRE. In the north-central part of campus is this impressive marble structure donated by William and Phoebe Hearst and modeled after the classical amphitheater in Epidaurus, Greece. It is used for university ceremonies and summer rock concerts (the Grateful Dead used to play here every year). *(642-4864.)*

OTHER U.C. BERKELEY SIGHTS. The **Phoebe Hearst Museum of Anthropology** displays artifacts from native California, ancient Egypt, and pre-Columbian Peru, although the bulk of its impressive collection is rarely, if ever, on display. *(643-7648; www.qal.berkeley.edu/~hearst. 103 Kroebner Hall. Open W and F-Su 10am-4:30pm, Th 10am-9pm. Admission $2, seniors $1, under 16 50¢; free on Th.)* Most of the **U.C. Museum of Paleontology,** in the Wallace Atrium of the Valley Life Sciences Building, is not open to the public either, but a complete tyrannosaurus rex skeleton and other impressive fossils are displayed in the lobby. *(642-1821; www.ucmp.berkeley.edu. Open during class sessions M 8am-9pm, Sa-Su 1-5pm)* The **Botanical Gardens** in Strawberry Canyon contain over 13,000 varieties of plant life thriving in Berkeley's Mediterranean-ish climate. Agatha Christie supposedly came here to examine a rare poisonous plant whose deadly powers she put to use in a mystery novel. *(643-2755. 200 Centennial Dr. Open daily 9am-4:45pm. Admission $3, seniors $2, ages 3-18 $1.)*

PARKS AND RECREATION

When you're ready to get out of town, Berkeley is happy to oblige. **Tilden Regional Park** (635-0135), in the pine- and eucalyptus-forested hills east of the city, is the anchor of the extensive East Bay park system. Hiking, biking, running, and riding trails criss-cross the park and provide impressive views of the Bay Area. The **ridgeline trail** is an especially spectacular bike ride. Within the park, a 19th-century carousel delights juvenile thrill-seekers. The small, sandy beach of **Lake Anza** is a popular swimming spot during the hottest days of summer, often overrun with squealing kids. *(848-3385. Lake open in summer 11am-6pm. Admission $3, seniors and children $1.50.)* At the north end of the park, the **Environmental Education Center** offers exhibits and naturalist-led programs (not to be confused with "naturist-led"). *(525-2233. Open Tu-Su 10am-5pm. Free.)* To reach the park by car or bicycle, take Spruce St. to Grizzly Peak Blvd. to Canon Ave. AC Transit buses #7 and 8 run from the Berkeley BART station to the park entrance at Grizzly Peak Blvd. and Golf Course Dr. Adjacent to Tilden Park is **Wildcat Canyon,** a less developed park with gorgeous hiking (though no biking) through grassy meadows and densely wooded canyons.

At the north end of Shattuck Ave. past the traffic circle, the basalt face of **Indian Rock** challenges rock junkies to short but demanding climbs. Easy side steps lead non-climbers to an impressive view of the Headlands. *(Open daily dawn-dusk.)*

North of campus, the **Berkeley Rose Garden,** built by the Works Projects Administration in the Depression era, spills from one terrace to another in a vast semicircular amphitheater. The roses are pruned in January in preparation for Mother's Day (May 10 in 2000), when the garden is at its glorious peak. *(On Euclid Ave. at Bayview St. Open May-Sept. dawn to dusk.)*

SHOPPING

Telegraph Ave. is an excellent source of books, music, and secondhand clothes, besides homemade tie-dye, jewelry, and pipes. **Amoeba Music** (see **Sights,** p. 134) is the undisputed champion of the buy/sell/trade scene, but the **Trance and**

Jungle Factory on Telegraph Ave. at Blake St., lets you listen to anything before you buy (and rent studio space cheaply), and pulls in house fans and budding DJs. The blocks between Blake St. and campus are full of trendy new and vintage clothes.

BOOKSTORES

From a bibliophilic standpoint, Berkeley's book trade is the eighth wonder of the world. Leave yourself more time to browse than you think you'll need.

Moe's, 2476 Telegraph Ave. (849-2087), between Dwight and Haste St. Featured in *The Graduate.* Four well-arranged floors of secondhand knowledge, from Artaud to Zukofsky. New books at 10% discount. Open Su-Th 10am-11pm, F-Sa 10am-midnight. Art and antiquarian section (849-2133) open daily noon-6pm.

Serendipity Books, 1201 University Ave. (841-7455), at Chestnut St. If you know what you want, you may well find it here—but not without a little help from the owner. Dusty, awe-inspiring, collection has earned Bay-wide industry respect. Open M-Sa 9am-5pm.

Black Oak Books, 1491 Shattuck Ave. (486-0698 or 486-0699), in the Gourmet Ghetto. Selective stock of used, new, and out-of-print literature, art classics, and other scholarly works. Regular author readings. Open daily 10am-10pm.

Comic Relief, 2138 University Ave. (843-5002; www.comicrelief.citysearch.com). Great comic book selection, from the big-name boys in Spandex tights, to Japanese manga, to photocopied minicomics and 'zines. Open Su-Tu 11am-7pm, W-Sa 11am-9pm.

Pegasus, 2349 Shattuck Ave. (649-1320), at Durant Ave. Large and well-labeled with penile papal poetry pasted on the front window. Buy/sell/trade. Open daily 10am-9pm.

Cody's Books, 2454 Telegraph Ave. (845-7852), at Haste St. Bookstore meets newsstand, with an unbeatable magazine collection. Open daily 10am-10pm. **Another location** at 1730 4th St. (559-9500).

Shambhala, 2482 Telegraph Ave. (848-8443). Just the place to catch up on the Kaballah, Tibetan Buddhism, Wicca, or the wisdom of the Zohar. New and used books in the incense-fog plus over 50 styles of tarot cards. Open daily 11am-8pm.

ENTERTAINMENT

CAMPUS

The university offers a number of quality entertainment options. Hang out with procrastinating students in or around the **Student Union** (643-0693). **The Underground** (642-3825) contains a ticket office, an arcade, bowling alleys, foosball tables, and pool tables, all run from a central blue desk (open M-F noon-8pm, Sa 10am-6pm). Next door is the **Bear's Lair,** 2475 Bancroft Way (843-0373), a student pub with occasional live music. It's the popular campus hangout on sunny Friday afternoons, when quarts of beer are $3 (open M-F 8am-8pm). The **CAL Performances Ticket Office** (642-9988), at the north corner of Zellerbach Hall, has information and tickets for concerts, plays, and movies (open M-F 10am-5:30pm, Sa 10am-2pm). Big concerts are in the **Greek Theatre** (see p. 136) and **Zellerbach Hall** (see below).

During the school year, Berkeley's Department of Music, 104 Morrison Hall, presents a number of concert series. **Hertz Hall** (642-0527) is the music chamber for noon concerts, with music by Berkeley's best student and faculty performers, and evening concerts featuring such groups as the African Music Ensemble, the Berkeley Contemporary Chamber Players, the Javanese Gamelan, and the 1991 Grammy-nominated University Chamber Chorus. **Friday afternoon concerts,** at 125 Morrison Hall, are undergraduate performances and the most informal of the three series. Specific dates and times are available from the Department of Music.

CINEMA

Berkeley city by-laws apparently require that wherever cafes cluster, a movie house lurks, nestles, or sits nearby. A Ph.D. in mathematics is unnecessary to calculate the resulting number of movie houses that Berkeley's cafes have spawned.

U.C. Theater, 2036 University Ave. (843-6267), between Milvia St. and Shattuck Ave. Reruns, film noir, classics, double features, and of course, the *Rocky Horror Picture Show* (Sa midnight). Admission $6.75; seniors, disabled, and under 13 $4.75; matinees $4.75.

Pacific Film Archives (PFA; 24hr. info 642-1124; www.bampfa.berkeley.edu), at Bancroft Way and Bowditch St. New facility shows its immense archives. Admission $5.50; seniors, disabled, and under 12 $3.50. 2nd feature $1.50 if you go to the 1st.

Act 1 Act 2, 2128 Center St. (548-7200), between Oxford St. and Shattuck Ave. near Berkeley BART station. Art films culled from Palme d'Or nominee list. Only Act 1 theater is wheelchair accessible. Admission $7.75, seniors and under 12 $4.75; matinees before 3:30pm $4.75.

Shattuck Cinema, 2230 Shattuck Ave. (644-2992), at Kittredge St. Probably the coolest of the first-run theaters along Shattuck Ave., with 8 ornately themed theaters, each dimly lit by sparkling ceiling "stars." Admission $7.75, seniors and under 12 $4.75; matinees $4.75. Captioned films for hearing-impaired; call for showtimes.

THEATER ARTS

Dozens of troupes perform in Berkeley, many with progressive messages and political agendas. Check the East Bay Express for comprehensive listings. The **Berkeley Repertory Theater,** 2025 Addison St. (845-4700), is the best-known and arguably the finest theater in the area, with an eclectic repertoire of classics and unknowns. (Box office open daily noon-7pm. Half-price tickets may be available Tu-Th on the day of the show—line up at the box office at noon.)

The **Julia Morgan Center for Arts,** 2640 College Ave. (box office 845-8542), shares space with a preschool and yoga center in a beautiful building that was once a church. Its namesake and designer was the first female architect in California. Noted for its graceful mix of materials, this building was Morgan's first commission; she later built Hearst Castle (see p. 221). The theater hosts diverse performances including the **Berkeley Opera** (925-798-1300). The **Zellerbach Playhouse** is operated by Berkeley's Department of Dramatic Art and hosts student performances in dance, theater, and music during the academic year (tickets $6-10). Summertime shows consist mostly of musicals and romantic comedies (tickets $5-7, students and seniors $3-4). Professional dance and theater companies also perform in the space through with significantly higher ticket prices through **CAL Performances** (642-9988; www.calperformances.berkeley.edu).

NIGHTLIFE

The Berkeley organism has never needed to evolve its own nightclub scene. Hardcore clubbers, if they live here at all, make a nightly commute to San Francisco. What Berkeley does offer is an unrivaled array of casual brewpubs and brainy cafes. Crowded at almost any hour of the night or day, they serve as surrogate libraries, living rooms, and lecture theaters; espresso drinks and microbrews loosen the tongues of an already talkative city. Choose your poison.

STIMULANTS

Caffe Strada, 2300 College Ave. (843-5282), at Bancroft Way. Glittering jewel of the caffeine-fuelled-intellectual scene. Go to be seen, discuss philosophy, or just enjoy the beautiful outdoor terrace (and the beautiful staff). Latte ($1.75), cocoa made with white chocolate, and pastries. Open daily 6:30am-11:30pm.

Cafe Milano, 2522 Bancroft Way (644-3100). High wood-beam ceilings, 10ft. windows, and interior foliage make Milano the best-looking contender in the Telegraph Ave. area cafe-o-rama. Lively discussions on everything from O'Neal, Shaquille, to O'Neill, Eugene. Latte $1.80. Open M-F 7am-10pm, Sa-Su 8am-10pm.

Mediterraneum Cafe, 2475 Telegraph Ave. (549-1128), near Dwight St. For a taste of "old Berkeley," visit "the Med"—a landmark more popular with residents than students and laid-back for the locale. Latte $1.85. Open daily 7am-9pm.

Wall Berlin Kaffee Haus, 2517 Durant Ave. (540-8449), between Telegraph Ave. and Bowditch St. Patrons often linger in this kozy *kleine kühl* 2-level nook. Latte $2; croissants $1.50. Open M-F 7:30am-midnight, Sa-Su 9am-midnight.

Au Coquelet, 2000 University Ave. (845-0433), at Milvia St. As the night goes on, and the crowd gets larger, the line between cafe (latte $1.75) and bar (Anchor Steam $2.75) blurs. Impressive selection of fresh pastries and sandwiches served until 1am. Open M-Th 6am-1:30am, F 6am-2am, Sa 8am-2am, Su 8am-1:30am.

DEPRESSANTS

Spats, 1974 Shattuck Ave. (841-7225), between University Ave. and Berkeley St. Locals and students flock to this multi-room velvet-furnished saloon for the warmth of the staff, original drinks (Dankobar Screamer $5.25), and off-beat decor that includes a stuffed deer, a Roman soldier, and an autographed poster of Walt Disney. Anchor Steam $2.50, mixed drinks $3-6. Entrees $6-10. Open M-F 11:30am-2am, Sa 4pm-2am.

924 Gilman, 924 Gilman St. (524-8180; 24hr. info 525-9926), at 8th St. This obviously addressed all-ages club is a legendary staple of California punk that has spawned bands from Green Day to Operation Ivy and Crimpshrine. Local, national, and international acts rock this joint, although major-label acts are strictly taboo. Most shows start at 8pm. Cover $5 with $2 membership card (good for 1 year and sold at the door).

Triple Rock Brewery, 1920 Shattuck Ave. (843-2739). Boisterous and friendly, the Rock was the first and, to many, remains the best of Berkeley's many brewpubs. Long and ever-changing menu of original ales, stouts, and porters; award-winning Red Rock Ale $3.25 per pint. Shuffleboard table in back supports those not sober enough to stand. Open Su-W 11:30am-midnight, Th-Sa 11:30am-1am. Kitchen closes at midnight; rooftop garden closes at 8pm.

Jupiter, 2181 Shattuck Ave. (843-8277), near BART station. Stained glass, church pews, and elaborate Gothic-patterned paneling that can't be seen through the crowds. Huge beer garden and terrific pizza ($6 for a loaded 8in. pie). Live music W-Sa; no cover. Open M-Th 11:30am-1am, F 11:30am-2am, Sa noon-2am, Su noon-midnight.

Berkeley Billiards, 2367 Shattuck Ave. (848-1766), between Channing St. and Durant Ave. No sign, just a titanic orange facade strung with lights. The few tables visible in the oddly decorated front room are just the tip of the iceberg. This popular upscale pool hall has foosball, pinball, and shuffleboard for the eight-ball shy, as well as a well-stocked jukebox. "Berkeley's Best" beer $3.25 per pint, cider $4. Tables Tu-Sa 2-9pm $5 per hr., 9pm-2am $10 per hr.; Su-M all day $5 per hr. Happy Hour (tables $2.50 per hr.) daily 5-6pm. Open daily 2pm-2am.

Blakes, 2367 Telegraph Ave. (848-0886), at Durant Ave. Jam-packed and unabashed meat market, but at least the cuts are premium. The pint-sized upstairs has a loud sports-bar feel, while the middle floor is mellow with more seating. In the basement, kick it Stonehenge-style (but without the dwarves) to the seriously loud beats of local bands. Appetizers $1.75-4, meals $4-8. Beverages from $2.50. Cover $2-5. Some shows 18+. Happy Hour daily 4-6pm and 8-10pm. Open daily 11:30am-2am.

SEASONAL EVENTS

The Telegraph Area Association (649-9500) runs a **book fair,** where authors and jazz musicians come together in late July. The **Farmer's Market Grand Opening and Parade,** on the second Sunday of July, starts the season, which runs through November. The **Berkeley Blues Festival** (run by the **Downtown Berkeley Association** 549-2230) takes place downtown the last Saturday in August. The fourth Sunday in September is the **"How Berkeley Can You Be?" Parade and Festival** (849-4688).

OAKLAND

The first decades of this century were salad days for Oakland (pop. 366,926), when businesses and wealthy families flowed in from San Francisco, many in the wake of the 1906 earthquake. Oakland's most striking buildings date from that era. The boom died in the Great Depression, and economically Oakland took a while to find its feet again. In the 1930s and 40s, Oakland's black majority gave birth to the down-and-dirty sound known as the West Coast blues. Fifty years later the city produced rappers such as M.C. Hammer, Digital Underground, and the late Tupac Shakur. In between, it's developed a progressive jazz scene that's among the nation's finest (see **Music,** p. 144).

Sometimes the city's sound has been more overtly political. In the 1960s, North and West Oakland were the proving ground for revolutionary movements like the Black Panthers. Founded in 1966 by Eldridge Cleaver, Huey Newton, and Bobby Seale, the militant Panthers raised a shout for black nationalism and self-determination. A decade later, the Oakland-based Symbionese Liberation Army seized the nation's attention by kidnapping and at least temporarily converting newspaper heiress Patty Hearst to their cause. Now Oakland's city center and Jack London Square smell like urban renewal, with crisp office buildings and clean streets, but just a few blocks west of Broadway or north of San Pablo Avenue, dreary ghettos begin that sprawl for miles. Today, a new generation of black activists like the Young Comrades spread a radical message through hip-hop music and pirate radio, and community groups work to influence local politics and rejuvenate the neighborhoods.

GETTING THERE AND AROUND BY PLANE OR CAR

Oakland International Airport, 1 Airport Dr. (577-4000; www.oaklandairport.com), lands a significant number of Bay Area-bound flights, including all Southwest Air flights. Although more remote from hotels than San Francisco International Airport, the Oakland airport is cheaper to reach by public transit, and an on-site BART station is in the works. The Coliseum BART station can be reached from the airport on the Air-BART shuttle (24hr. info 577-4294; shuttles depart every 10min. 6am-11:50pm; $2) or the AC Transit bus #58 ($1.25).

Oakland's scarcity of noteworthy sites and cheap and safe accommodations make it a better daytrip than vacation destination. Drivers can take **Interstate 80** from San Francisco across the Bay Bridge to **Interstate 580** and connect with Oakland **Interstate 980** South, which has downtown exits at 12th St. or 19th St. If you have access to wheels, they'll be worthwhile here; Oakland's daytime attractions are spread out and nighttime attractions run later than BART. Get traffic updates from **TravInfo** (817-1717; TDD 817-1718).

ORIENTATION

Oakland's main artery is **Broadway.** To get to Jack London Square and the waterfront from the 12th St. BART stop, just head down Broadway away from the hills. Broadway runs northeast, under the Nimitz Fwy. (I-880) at 5th St., and separates Old Oakland (to the west) from **Chinatown** (to the east). The **city center** is at 13th St. and Broadway, but the greater downtown area occupies all of **Lake Merritt,** including Lakeside Park on the north side and the Lake Merritt Channel on the south side. **North-south streets are numbered to match the east-west cross streets,** so 1355 Broadway is between 13th and 14th St.

Well to the north of downtown past some of Oakland's poorest slums, are a few Berkeley-esque neighborhoods laced with boutiques, grocers, and restaurants. Pretty **Rockridge** is home to young professionals; there, food prices span several tax brackets and shops have clever names. It lies toward Berkeley and is accessible from downtown Oakland by BART or AC Transit bus #51.

PRACTICAL INFORMATION

Buses: Greyhound, 2103 San Pablo Ave. (station info 834-3213; schedules and reservations 800-231-2222), downtown. Buses depart daily to **Santa Cruz** ($14) and **Los Angeles** ($36). **Be careful in this area after dark.**

Trains: Amtrak (station info 238-4320; schedules and reservations 800-USA-RAIL/872-7245), between the Embarcadero and 2nd St. at Alice St., opposite Jack London Sq. To **Los Angeles** ($77) and **Sacramento** ($15).

Public Transportation: Info about any public transit from **TravInfo** (817-1717; TDD 817-1718). **Alameda County (AC) Transit** (800-559-4636). Local fare $1.25; seniors, disabled, and ages 5-12 60¢; transfers valid 1hr. (25¢). **Bay Area Rapid Transit** (BART; 465-BART/2278) provides another option, running from downtown San Francisco to Oakland's stations at **Lake Merritt** (Dublin/Pleasanton or Fremont trains), 12th St. (Richmond or Pittsburg/Bay Point trains), or 19th St. (Richmond or Pittsburg/Bay Point

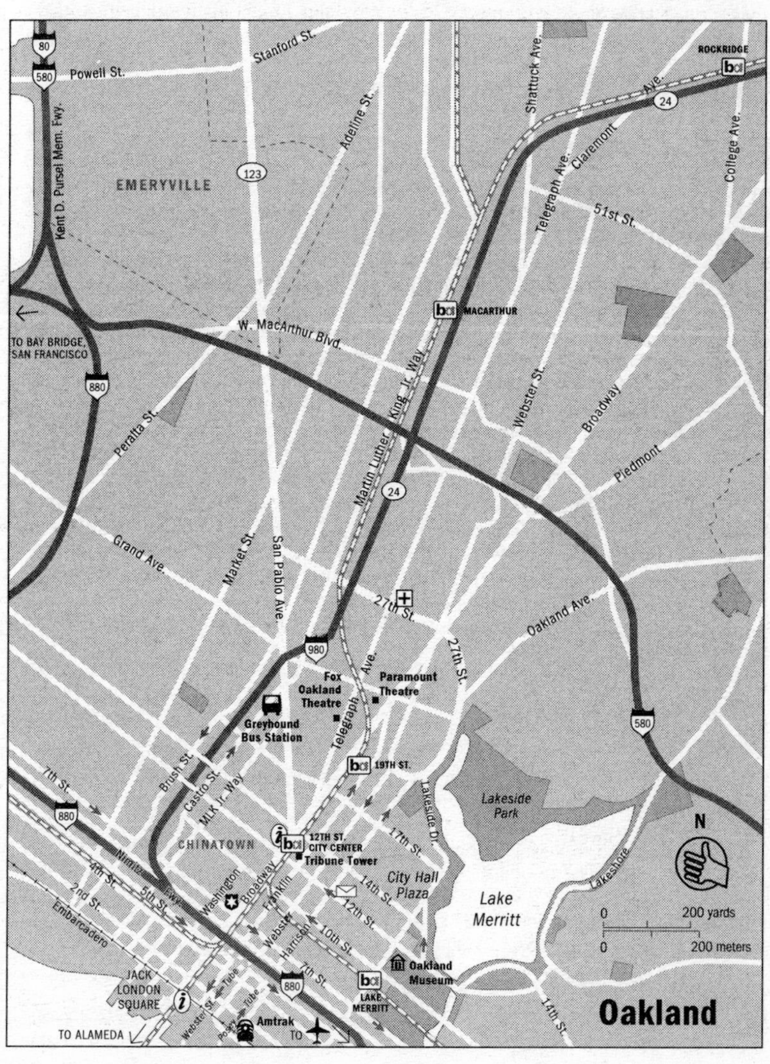

trains). **Transbay** routes to San Francisco ($2.20; seniors, disabled, and ages 5-12 $1.10.) There are a number of BART stations in Oakland.

Taxis: A1 Yellow Cab (843-1111). Operates 24hr.

Visitor Information: Port of Oakland Information Booth (272-4864; 24hr. info 814-6000; www.jacklondonsquare.com), on Broadway in Jack London Square under the Barnes and Noble bookstore. Volunteers will load you with info. Open M-F 11am-7pm, Sa 10am-5pm, Su 11am-5pm. 2nd location at Oakland International Airport.

Emergency: 911. **Police:** 455 7th St. (238-3481).

24-Hour Rape Crisis Line: 845-RAPE/7273.

Medical Services: Central Public Health Center, 470 27th St. (271-4263), at Telegraph Ave. Usually open M-F 8-11:30am and 1-4pm; make appts. far in advance. **Highland Hospital,** 1411 E. 31st St. (437-4800), at Beaumont Ave. Emergency care 24hr.

24-Hour Pharmacy: Leo's Day and Night Pharmacy, 1776 19th St. (839-7900), at Broadway.

Post Office: Main Office, 1675 7th St. (251-3300), at Peralta St. Open M-F 8:30am-5pm. General Delivery at Civic Center Post Office, 201 13th St. at Harrison St. **ZIP Code:** 94617.

AREA CODE	Berkeley's area code is 510.

ACCOMMODATIONS AND FOOD

Although Oakland is full of motels, few are safe, clean, or economical compared to those in San Francisco and Berkeley. If you really want to stay in Oakland, the **Bed and Breakfast Network** (415-696-1690) includes some Oakland addresses. Motels clustered along W. MacArthur Blvd. near the MacArthur BART station are around $40 per night for a room with private bath. Ask to see a room before checking in.

The sophistication and attitude of "California cuisine" has made few inroads into Oakland, beyond the shopping districts of Rockridge and yuppie Piedmont. Oakland restaurants are about eating, not dining, and all-American staples like burger joints, breakfast diners, and barbecue shacks abound. Oakland's **Chinatown,** west of Broadway around 9th St., features a host of interchangeable dim sum restaurants and Asian markets. Every Friday from 8am to 2pm, the **Old Oakland farmer's market** takes over 9th St., between Broadway and Clay St. The largest of its kind in Alameda County, the market offers fresh fruits, vegetables, and the wares of some of the best bakers in the Golden State. Nearby is **Ratto's International Market,** 821 Washington St. (832-6503), a 100-year-old Oakland institution frequented by the Frugal Gourmet, who likes it fresh and ripe. It's more ingredients than ready-to eats, though. (Open in summer M-Sa 9am-5:30pm; off-season M-F 9:30am-6pm, Sa 9:30am-5pm, Su 10:30am-4pm.)

DOWNTOWN OAKLAND

Happy Belly Deli, 30 Jack London Sq. #216 (835-0446), on the 2nd fl. in Jack London Village. Sunny New Age cafe proves itself an anomaly in 2 ways: as a vegetarian-friendly eatery in avowedly carnivorous Oakland, and as an oasis of genuine character (and budget prices) in touristy Jack London Sq. "Food holds the energy of its experiences and transmits this vibration to the eater," is its motto. Panini-style sandwiches ($5-7) heaped with organic produce and good vibrations. Free yoga lessons M at 6pm. Open M-F 10am-4pm, Sa-Su 9am-4pm.

Aspara, 344B 12th St. (836-2554), at Webster St. Cambodian and Thai food in calming green and leafy dining room. Entrees $5-7. Lunch specials $5-6. Vegetarian friendly. Open M-F 11am-9:30pm, Sa 5-9:30pm.

Caffé 817, 817 Washington St. (271-7965). Excellent fresh ingredients make delicious sandwiches ($5). Breakfasts $1.60-4.25. Open M-F 7:30am-5pm, Sa 10am-4pm.

NORTH OAKLAND AND ROCKRIDGE

Lois the Pie Queen, 851 60th St., North Oakland (658-5616), at Adeline St. Down-home breakfasts ($3-6) and diner standards (burgers, pork chops, root beer floats) are popular, but pastry made Lois the Queen—try the peach cobbler, lemon ice-box, or sweet potato pie ($2.50-3). Open M-F 8am-2pm, Sa 7am-3pm, Su 7am-4pm.

The Red Tractor Cafe, 5634 College Ave. (595-3500), 1 block from Rockridge BART station. Wholesome food from the heartland, made-from-scratch and inspired by the owner's Pennsylvania Dutch grandmother—although it's unlikely Granny made a lot of "no-meat" loaf. Dishes $4-7. Open M-F 11:30am-9pm, Sa-Su 9am-9pm.

Barney's Gourmet Hamburgers, 5819 College Ave. (601-0444). "Gourmet" could be pushing it—maybe the sign couldn't fit "Barney's Fancy-Schmancy Hamburgers." But of the 23 types of burger served ($4-7), at least one has gotta have your name on it. Garden, tofu, and poultry burgers, too. Open Su-Th 11am-10pm, F-Sa 11am-10:30pm.

The Rockridge Market Hall, 5655 College Ave. (655-7748), is not a restaurant but a gastronomic variety hut. Inside, **Grace Baking** (428-2662) bakes breads with amazing grace. Sourdough walnut and foccaccia ($1.65). Open M-F 7am-8pm, Sa-Su 7am-7pm.

SIGHTS

Haunted by Gertrude Stein's withering observation: "There is no there there," Oakland's tourist literature wages a war of attrition against its former resident, assuring visitors that City Square is "always there for you" and "there is shopping there." Roslyn Mazzilli's sculpture in the square's upper plaza is defiantly entitled "There!" One is tempted to pat Oakland on the shoulder and say, "There, there."

OAKLAND MUSEUM OF CALIFORNIA. This is probably the best bona fide sight, consisting of a complex of three museums devoted to California's history, art, and ecology. The museum includes photography by Edward Weston and Dorothea Lange, panoramic shots of San Francisco by Quick-Snap pioneer Eadweard Muybridge, and multicultural modern works. *(238-2200. 1000 Oak St., on the southwestern side of the lake. From the Lake Merrit BART station, walk 1 block north on Oak St. toward the hills. Open W-Sa 10am-5pm, Su noon-5pm, 1st F of each month until 9pm. Admission $8, students and seniors $6; F 3-9pm $5, students and seniors $3; 1st Su of each month free.)*

LAKE MERRITT. Lake Merritt, northeast of downtown, was dammed off from the San Francisco Bay in 1869, and now provides a place for sailing, biking, and jogging—not to mention political protest. Activity revolves around **Lakeside Park** (238-6888), which encompasses a stately gazebo, picnic facilities, and the nation's oldest urban bird sanctuary, where ducks and geese muscle in on pigeons. Generations of Oakland children have enjoyed **Children's Fairyland,** a cluster of misproportioned gingerbread houses and trippy overgrown mushrooms at the northeastern edge of the lake. Pre-dating Disney, Fairyland has seen better days but is undergoing expensive renovations. *(Fairyland admission $5.)*

JACK LONDON SQUARE. Oakland's one come-on to the tourist industry is this eight-block commercial district along the waterfront, named for the author of *White Fang* and *The Call of the Wild.* A bland assortment of stores and chain restaurants, the neighborhood is probably the least fitting monument to Jack London, an orphaned delinquent and budding socialist who spent his youth on the waterfront stealing lobsters and raising hell.

Jack London's Cabin, near Webster St., was used by London while prospecting for gold in the 1890s. Half of the cabin is the genuine article, transported from the Alaskan wilderness; the other half went to Dawson City, in Canada's Yukon Territory, which also claims London as its own. East of the cabin is **Heinhold's First and Last Chance Saloon,** a waterfront saloon barely changed from London's days in the 1880s and 90s except, presumably, the addition of the London-themed mural on the outside. *(839-6761; 56 Jack London Sq., in the Jack London Village at Alice St.)* The **Ebony Museum of Art,** combines African and African-American art and artifacts with images from two centuries of pop culture. *(763-0745. 208/209 Jack London Village. Open Tu-Sa 11am-6pm, Su noon-5pm. Free.)*

OTHER SIGHTS. The **Paramount Theater** hosts not only movies and high-billing acts (see **Music,** p. 144) but also occasional tours of its venerable Art Deco innards, not all of which are usually accessible. Lovingly restored to its 1931 grandeur, the theater shows classic films on weekends ($5), accompanied by the mighty Wurlitzer organ, vintage newsreels, and a cartoon. Showtime is usually 8pm; come early to explore the theater or have a cocktail at the bar. *(2025 Broadway. Tour info 893-2300. Tours 1st and 3rd Sa each month 10am. $1.)* The formidable **Fox Oakland Theater** is wild on the outside with arches and golden brick but has staid offices inside. *(650-363-0149. On Telegraph Ave. at 19th St.)*

ENTERTAINMENT AND NIGHTLIFE

MUSIC

The best reason to visit Oakland is to catch live music. Whether they're playing the West Coast blues, Oaktown hip-hop, or progressive jazz, Oakland's music venues are unsurpassed. Such a vital scene is always changing, of course, so if you want to be on the very cutting edge, you'll have to do some of your own research. **Koncepts Cultural Gallery** (763-0682) is not a venue but an organization that hosts some of the most groundbreaking progressive jazz sessions (cover $5-25). The **Bay Area Blues Society** (836-2227) is more interested in preservation than innovation—they lead tours of Oakland's historic jazz, blues, and gospel entertainment quarters—but are still a rich source of info on the West Coast blues today. Oaktown rappers lack institutional representation; check posters and local papers.

The **Paramount Theater,** 2025 Broadway (24hr. info 465-6400), hosts national music acts like Patti Labelle and Tom Waits (box office, on 21st St.; open Tu-F noon-6pm, Sa noon-5pm, and 2hr. before performances).

Not all of these venues are in the safest parts of town; it's probably best not to go to any of them alone, and **exercise caution after dark.**

Eli's Mile High Club, 3629 Martin Luther King, Jr. Way (655-6661). This crowded, sweaty club is the first and still the best home of the West Coast blues. "Yoshi's, it ain't!" promise their posters. Also jazz and hip-hop; call for listings. Cover $5-10; some shows free. Soul food kitchen opens at 7pm, music starts by 10pm.

The Fifth Amendment, 3255 Lakeshore Ave. (832-3242), at Lake Park. Not the most famous, just the best, jazz and blues musicians take the stage in this downtown club where there's never a cover. Dress up and then hush up—the crowd here is serious about their music. Shows start at 9pm.

Yoshi's, 510 Embarcadero (238-9200; www.yoshis.com), at Jack London Sq. It's hardly cutting-edge, but Yoshi's is an upscale Bay institution, bringing together world-class sushi and world-class jazz. Big names (like Marsalis) command big cover prices ($6-30), although tickets are half-price for students with valid ID. Shows M-Sa 8 and 10pm, and Su 2 and 8pm. Box office open daily 10am-11pm.

The Stork Club, 380 12th St. (444-6174), 4 blocks west of Broadway. Laid-back country and western bar by day becomes raging rock venue by night. Stadium rock (without the stadium) W-Th, punk and alternative F-Sa. Cover $5. Open daily 10am-2am.

White Horse Inn, 6551 Telegraph St., North Oakland (652-3820). Not a live music venue but the city's oldest gay bar, an easygoing place with disco ball and dancing. DJ in effect Th-Sa nights. No cover. Open daily 3pm-2am.

CINEMA AND FINE ARTS

The **Paramount Theater,** 2025 Broadway (465-6400), at 21st, is an exquisite Art Deco movie palace. The Paramount also houses both the **Oakland East Bay Symphony** (446-1992) and the **Oakland Ballet** (452-9288). Throughout the year, the Symphony performs five Friday concerts (tickets $11-35) with open rehearsals the preceding Thursday afternoons (tickets $5). The Symphony also sponsors free noontime ensemble concerts. The ballet performs several programs, including a

BAY AREA

not-so-traditional Nutcracker Suite. (Box office open Tu-F noon-6pm, Sa noon-5pm, and 1hr. before all shows.)

Another groovy place to see a movie is the **Parkway Lounge Theater,** 1834 Park Blvd. (814-2400; www.picturepubpizza.com), a rep theater with lounge seating—that's couches, chairs and tables—where you can order pizza (slices $2.50-3), pasta, sandwiches, and wine or beer by the pitcher ($8) or pint ($3) right at your seat (admission $3; *Rocky Horror Picture Show* F midnight). **Jack London Cinema,** 201 Broadway, shows first-runs (admission $8, before 6pm and seniors $5).

SPORTS AND SEASONAL EVENTS

Baseball's **Oakland Athletics (A's)** and football's oft-transplanted **Oakland Raiders** both play in the **Oakland Coliseum** (569-2121), at the intersection of the Nimitz Fwy. (I-880) and Hegenberger Rd. The Coliseum has its own BART station and is a much cozier place than frigid 3Com/Candlestick Park in San Francisco. The NBA's **Golden State Warriors** play basketball in the adjacent **Coliseum Arena** (box office open M-F 9am-5pm.)

Lake Merritt's Lakeside Park hosts several festivals over the summer. In June, the **Festival at the Lake** takes over Oakland with a long weekend of international foods, crafts, and nonstop music. On Father's Day Sunday (June 18 in 2000), **Juneteenth** (238-7765) commemorates the anniversary of the Emancipation Proclamation and black history and culture with parades, soul food, and blues and R&B. In recent years, Lake Merritt has also hosted **Fuck the Police Day,** a free beach and barbecue party in late June to protest police treatment of young blacks. The park also has **free Shakespeare performances** in summer (415-422-2221; www.sfshakes.org).

SOUTH BAY

The San Francisco peninsula extends southward into what was once a valley of fruit orchards and is now the center of America's electronics industry. From Palo Alto to San Jose and beyond, the area known as the Silicon Valley seems to make more chips than Frito-Lay. Its borders are indistinct, but when you see billboards advertising Internet search engines and UNIX platform bumper stickers, you'll know you've arrived.

PALO ALTO

Dominated by the beautiful 8000-acre campus of Stanford University, well-manicured Palo Alto (pop. 55,900) looks like "Collegeland" at a Disney-style theme park. Stanford is graced with perfectly groomed grounds, a picturesque lake, a superb faculty, a bulging endowment, and international acclaim. The Spanish mission-style buildings, lush eucalyptus trees, and brilliant, fresh-scrubbed students are all so artfully arranged, you'd almost think they were natural.

The city Stanford calls home is equally good-looking, if pricey, with a yuppified downtown strip of restaurants, bookstores and boutiques, and cyclists and pedestrians friendly to a fault. Its nightlife caters to both students and young suburbanites—over half of Palo Alto's population is under 40.

GETTING THERE AND AROUND

Palo Alto is 35 miles southeast of San Francisco, near the southern shore of the Bay. From the north, take **U.S. 101 South** to the University Ave. Exit, or take the Embarcadero Rd. Exit directly to the Stanford campus. Alternatively, motorists from San Francisco can split off onto the **Junípero Serra Highway (Interstate 280)** for a slightly longer but more scenic route. From I-280, exit at Sand Hill Rd. and follow it to Willow Rd. and the northwest corner of Stanford University.

To get to Palo Alto by public transportation, take **SamTrans** bus #7F from San Francisco to the Stanford Shopping Center or any further point (daily 6am-midnight. Fare $1.75, seniors and ages 7-17 85¢). Palo Alto-bound trains also leave from San Francisco's **CalTrain** station, at 4th and King St. (Trains run M-Th 5am-10pm, F 5am-midnight, Sa 7am-midnight, Su 8am-10pm. Fare $3.75; seniors, disabled, and children $1.75; off-peak hours $2.75.) The **Palo Alto Transit Center** (323-6105), on University Ave., serves local and regional buses and trains (open daily 5am-12:30am); there is a train-only depot (326-3392), on California Ave. 1¼ miles south of the transit center (open daily 5:30am-12:30am). The transit center is connected to points south by **San Mateo County buses** and to the Stanford campus by the free **Marguerite University Shuttle** (see **Public Transportation,** below).

Parking is relatively easy downtown (2hr. free in public lots) but can be a hassle on Stanford's mostly permit-only campus. Park for free (indefinitely) on a residential street between California and Stanford Ave., east of campus, and hop on the Marguerite Shuttle to traverse the gigantic campus. Look for the ubiquitous red-and-white shuttle stop signs. Better yet, do as the natives do and bike the flat boulevards and path-filled rolling hills. The **Campus Bike Shop** rents bikes (see p. 146).

ORIENTATION

The pristine lawns of residential Palo Alto are not easily distinguished from the manicured campus of Stanford University. Despite its name, **University Avenue,** the main thoroughfare off U.S. 101, belongs much more to the town than to the college. Cars coming off U.S. 101 onto University Ave. pass very briefly through **East Palo Alto,** a community incorporated in 1983 after Palo Alto and Menlo Park had already annexed most of their revenue-producing districts. East Palo Alto has one of the highest violent crime rates in the state and has been a crack source for users in the surrounding communities. On crossing the city limits, the contrast with the immaculate tree-lined lawns of Palo Alto could not be more striking.

Stanford University spreads out from the west end of University Ave. Abutting University Ave. and running northwest-southeast through town is **El Camino Real** (part of Rte. 82). From there, Palm Dr. accesses the heart of Stanford's campus, the **Main Quad.**

PRACTICAL INFORMATION

Trains: CalTrain, 95 University Ave. (800-660-4287), at Alma St. Street-side stop at Stanford Stadium on Embarcadero Rd. To **San Francisco** (fare $3.75, off-peak hours $2.50) and **San Jose** (fare $2.25, off-peak hours $2). Half-price for seniors and disabled. Operates M-F 5am-10pm, Sa 6:30am-10pm, Su 7am-10pm.

Buses: SamTrans (800-660-4287). To **downtown San Francisco** (fare $2.50) and **San Francisco International Airport** (fare $1).

Public Transportation: Santa Clara Valley Transportation Authority (408-321-2300 or 800-894-9908). Local and county-wide transit. Fare $1.10, seniors and disabled 35¢, ages 5-17 60¢. Day pass $2.50, seniors and disabled $1.40, ages 5-17 80¢. Express buses $1.75. **Marguerite University Shuttle** (723-9362). Free service around Stanford University. Operates M-F 6am-8pm. Services Palo Alto CalTrain during rush hours.

Taxis: Yellow Cab (324-1234 or 800-595-1222). 24hr.

Car Rental: Budget, 4230 El Camino Real (493-6000, reservations 800-527-0700). From $32 per day, $180 per week (unlimited mileage.). Must be at least 21 with credit card. Under 25 surcharge $20 per day. Open M-F 8am-5:30pm, Sa-Su 8am-4:30pm.

Bike Rental: Campus Bike Shop, 551 Salvatierra Ln. (325-2945), across from Stanfod Law School. 3-speed $8, overnight $12. Mountain bikes $10, overnight $15. Premium bikes $15, overnight $20. Helmets $3 per day. Major credit card or $150-300 cash deposit. Open M-F 9am-5pm, Sa 9am-3pm.

Visitor Information: Palo Alto Chamber of Commerce, 325A Forest Ave. (324-3121). Open M-F 9am-noon and 1-5pm. **Stanford University Information Booth** (723-2053 or

723-2560), across from Hoover Tower. Free student-led tours depart daily 11am and 3:15pm; times vary on holidays and during exams. Open daily 8am-5pm.

Ticket Agencies: Stanford University events: Tresidder Memorial Union (events recording 723-0336, tickets 723-4317, info 723-4311; http://tickets.stanford.edu; open M-F 10am-5pm, Sa noon-4pm); **Stanford Department of Athletics** (723-1021; open M-F 10am-4pm). **Local and Bay Area events:** BASS Ticketmaster (408-998-2277).

Emergency: 911 (9-911 from Stanford University telephones) or 723-9663.

Police: 275 Forest Ave. (329-2406, after hours 329-2413).

Internet Access: Palo Alto Main Library, 1213 Newell Rd. (329-2436). Free. Open M-F 10am-9pm, Sa 10am-6pm, Su 1-5pm.

Post Office: Main Office, 2085 E. Bayshore Rd. (800-275-8777). Open M-F 8am-5:30pm. **ZIP Code:** 94303. **Stanford Office,** White Plaza (322-0059). Open M-F 9am-5pm. **ZIP Code:** 94305.

AREA CODE	The area code for Palo Alto is 650.

ACCOMMODATIONS

Motels are plentiful along **El Camino Real,** but rates can be steep. Generally, rooms are cheaper farther away from Stanford. More reasonably priced accommodations may be found farther north, toward Redwood City. Many Palo Alto motels cater to business travelers and are actually busier on weekdays than on weekends.

Hidden Villa Ranch Hostel (HI-AYH), 26870 Moody Rd. (949-8648), about 10mi. southwest of Palo Alto in Los Altos Hills. The 1st hostel on the Pacific Coast is now a working ranch and farm in a wilderness preserve. Heated cabins and 35 beds. Reception 7:30-9:30am and 4:30-9pm. Dorms $10. Reservations required for weekends and groups. Open Sept.-May.

Coronet Motel, 2455 El Camino Real (326-1081), at California St. Clean, spacious rooms with big windows and cable TV. Rates are cheap considering the short distance to Stanford. Swimming pool. Check-out 11am. Singles $50; doubles $60.

Glass Slipper Inn, 3941 El Camino Real (493-6611 or 800-541-0199), at Los Robles Ave. Small rooms, no perks, low prices. Bizarre decor suggests Disneyland gone to seed. Fridge/microwave ($2 per day). Check-out 11am. Singles $48; doubles $53.

Imperial Inn, 3945 El Camino Real (493-3141 or 800-900-0524). Beautiful and immaculate rooms, recently lovingly refinished with plush carpets, VCR, big-screen cable TV, and kitchenettes with microwave and fridge. Continental breakfast included (daily 6-9:30am). Singles $75; doubles $85.

FOOD

The Coffee House (723-3592), Tresidder Union at Stanford University. Why go anywhere else, when "the CoHo" pours $6 pitchers of Budweiser—you'd think you were in Chico, (see p. 319)—less vile beers $9 per pitcher, and serves sandwiches, burritos, and salads ($3-5). Live music some nights at 9:30pm. Happy Hour M-F 4-6pm. **Tresidder Union** has counters selling salads, smoothies, and Chinese and Mexican food. Open Sept.-June M-F 10am-11pm, Sa-Su 10am-midnight; in summer daily 10am-7pm.

Mango Cafe, 435 Hamilton Ave. (325-3229), 1 block east of University Ave. Reggae music and Caribbean cuisine. Seriously spicy Jamaican "jerked joints" ($6) and tropical smoothies ($3.25), served in glass bowls big enough to hold a carp. Veggie options and delicious bread pudding ($2.75). Open daily 11am-3pm and 6-10pm.

Miyake, 140 University Ave. (323-9449). *Banzai* sushi joint entirely lacking in Japanese decorum. Come weekends when the chefs are barking orders, the waiters are screaming across the restaurant, and the tables are packed with students pounding *sake* bombs. Grab veggie rolls ($1.20) or local abalone ($2) off little boats sailing in the moat around the bar. *Obento* box lunches are a steal at $6.25. Open daily 11:30am-10pm.

Healthy Choice, 151 California Ave. (326-7886), at Park St. in the Palo Alto Ctr. Pay at the door (lunch $7; dinner $8) and wade into an all-you-can-eat buffet of Middle Eastern and Mediterranean standards. Beautiful patio area lined with ferns and burbling fountains. Open Tu-Sa 11am-3pm and 5-9pm, Su 11am-3pm.

Saint Michael's Alley, 806 Emerson St. (326-2630). During the day, hearty food is served in a relaxed, artsy atmosphere. At night, "St. Mike's" bustles with live music or poetry readings for a diverse omnisexual crowd. Fresh muffins, scones, bread. Pancake breakfast $5.50. Sandwich and salad $5-6. Open Tu-Th 7am-3pm and 5-10:30pm, F-Sa 7am-3pm and 5pm-midnight, Su 7am-3pm and 5-9:30pm.

SIGHTS

STANFORD UNIVERSITY. Undoubtedly Palo Alto's main tourist attraction, the secular, co-educational school was founded in 1885 by Jane and Leland Stanford to honor a son who died of typhoid on a family trip to Italy. The Stanfords loved Spanish architecture and collaborated with **Frederick Law Olmsted,** designer of New York City's Central Park, to create a red-tiled campus of uncompromising beauty. (Disrespectful Berkeley students sometimes refer to Stanford as "the World's Largest Taco Bell.") The school has produced such eminent conservatives as **Chief Justice William Rehnquist,** and the campus has been called "a hotbed of social rest."

The oldest part of campus is the **Main Quadrangle,** the site of most undergraduate classes. The walkways are dotted with diamond-shaped, gold-numbered stone tiles that mark the locations of time capsules put together by each year's graduating class. (For tours, see **Visitor Information,** p. 146.) **Memorial Church** (723-1762), in the Main Quad, is a non-denominational gold shrine with stained glass windows and glittering mosaic walls like those of an Eastern Orthodox church.

East of the Main Quad, the observation deck in **Hoover Tower** has views of campus, the East Bay, and San Francisco. *(723-2053 or 723-2560. Open daily 10am-4:30pm. Admission $2, seniors and under 13 $1.)* On Museum Way off Palm St. between the Main Quad and El Camino Real, is the **Iris and B. Gerald Cantor Center for the Arts** which recently reopened after being closed for earthquake-related repairs (723-4177). The **Rodin Sculpture Garden** collection contains a stunning bronze cast of *Gates of Hell*, among other larger figures. *(Free tours Sa-Su 2pm.)*

BAY AREA

BARBIE DOLL HALL OF FAME. This kitschy "museum" has over 16,000 perky plastic dolls. Hippie Barbie, Benetton Barbie, and Disco Ken prove that girlhood may be fleeting, but fashion is forever. Ask about having yourself cloned into a doll. *(326-5841. 433 Waverly St. off University Ave. Open Tu-F 1:30-4pm, Sa 10am-noon and 1:30-4:30pm. Admission $6, under 12 $4.)*

NIGHTLIFE

So you're going out on the town in Palo Alto. Do you want to party with Teva-wearing Stanford students, or Silicon Valley professionals still in their work clothes?

The Dutch Goose, 3567 Alameda de las Pulgas, Menlo Park (854-3245). You have chosen door number one! If Stanford students aren't in class or at the CoHo (see **Food,** p. 147), they're probably here. Pool tables, nutritious and delicious pickled eggs, peanut shells on the floor. Open M-Sa 11am-2am, Su 11am-1am. Kitchen closes at 11:30pm.

Left at Albuquerque, 445 Emerson St. (326-1011). You have chosen door number two! This Southwestern bar and restaurant is packed with Silicon singles the minute the microchip factories let out. Margaritas ($4) are the poison of choice, with over 150 brands of tequila to choose from. If you can show proof of a brand they don't stock (good luck) you drink for free. Open daily 11:30am-10pm.

Rose and Crown, 547 Emerson St. (327-7673). Low-key pub with an Ace jukebox is good for throwing darts or nursing a Guinness. On weeknights you may well have the whole place to yourself. Open M-F 11:30am-1:30am, Sa noon-1:30am, Su 1pm-1:30am.

Antonio's Nuthouse, 321 California Ave. (321-2550), at Birch St. Another peanuts-on-the-floor kind of place, with a Tarzan theme and a laid-back vibe. Open M-Sa 2pm-2am.

The Oasis Beer Garden, 241 El Camino Real, Menlo Park (326-8896). Let's get wrecked, dude! Burgers ($5-7), plus a huge selection of brew (pints from $1.80, pitchers from $5). Open daily 11am-1:15am.

ENTERTAINMENT

The *Stanford Daily* (in summer the *Stanford Weekly*) contains listings of what's going on all over campus. Pick up a free copy of *Metro* or the *Palo Alto Daily News* from downtown sidewalk boxes for the local lowdown.

Dinkelspiel Auditorium (723-2448), at El Camino Real and Embarcadero. Call it "the Dink" to fit in. Snag tickets to classical concerts and the like at Tressider Union ticket office (723-4317).

Stanford Theatre, 221 University Ave. (324-3700). Dedicated to Hollywood's "Golden Age." Hitchcock and the Marx Brothers are regulars. The Wurlitzer organ plays before and after the 7:30pm show and accompanies silent films every W. Double features $6, seniors $4, children $3.

The Lively Arts at Stanford (723-2551) brings semi-big name concerts to Frost Amphitheater and Memorial Auditorium every year, usually at discount prices. The Memorial also hosts movies on Sundays in term-time. Mostly mainstream films, with the occasional older classic. Admission $3, students $1.

The Edge, 260 California Ave. (324-3343), 2 blocks east of El Camino Real. Teens flock to this alt-rock dance club like vultures to carrion. Mostly local bands, although they've been known to host a Night Ranger or a Hole. Cover charges and age restrictions vary. Shows usually begin at 9:15pm.

SHOPPING

Chimaera Books and Records, 165 University Ave. (327-1122). Superb array of new and used books. Used CDs (mostly classical) $10, or $2.50 with an exchange. Open M 10am-11pm, Tu-Sa 10am-midnight, Su 11am-10pm.

Kepler's Books, 1010 El Camino Real, Menlo Park (324-4321), in Menlo Ctr. Books and magazines from around the world. Open Su-Th 9am-11pm, F-Sa 9am-midnight.

Stanford Shopping Center (617-8585 or 800-772-9332; www.stanfordshop.com), between campus and El Camino Real. Doesn't cater to budget travelers, but its cool avenues are great for window-shopping. Coveting is still free (until Judgement Day, anyway). Open M-F 10am-7pm, Sa 10am-6pm, Su 11am-6pm.

SAN JOSE

In 1851, it was deemed too small to serve as California's capital and Sacramento assumed the honors. Today, San Jose (pop. 873,000) is the civic heart of the Silicon Valley and the fastest-growing (and 3rd largest) city in California, as well as the 11th largest city in the United States. San Jose's cultural activity, however, has not experienced the same boom as the high-tech gold rush that quadrupled the city's population in 10 years; apart from the musical stylings of the Doobie Brothers, who started here in the early 1970s and the Dionne Warwick signature song that *will* get stuck in your head, San Jose offers little on the arts front.

San Jose does have a few selling points, though. If you're a woman looking for a single guy with great job security, your best bet is to look here first. The computer-geeks-turned-millionaires have come of age, and San Jose has the largest ratio of young, single men to women in the country. Additionally, the weather is warm, the schools are good, the streets are clean and wide, and there's always plenty of parking. Copious cops, plus an army of private security guards, keep the city safe—the FBI named it the third-safest city in the country. But despite a new billion-dollar downtown, the largest city in Northern California still looks and feels like suburbia. Taking a trip to San Jose is like taking a trip through a mental image of the 1950s. Everything is clean and new, the people are friendly, and America's industrial strength seems unbeatable—if they ignored the local porn theaters and strip clubs, Ward and June Cleaver could call it home.

ORIENTATION

San Jose lies at the southern end of San Francisco Bay, about 50 miles from San Francisco (via U.S. 101 or I-280) and 40 miles from Oakland (via I-880). From San Francisco, take I-280 rather than U.S. 101, which is full of traffic snarls at all hours. The stretch of I-280 called Junípero Serra Fwy. is quite pretty, even if its self-given title, "World's Most Beautiful Freeway," is not a highly contested one. (For info on reaching San Jose from San Francisco on public transit, see **CalTrain,** below).

San Jose is centered around the convention-hosting malls and plazas near the intersection of east-west **San Carlos Street** and north-south **Market Street.** Bars, restaurants, and clubs are around 1st St. in the so-called **SoFA District.** The **Transit Mall,** the center of San Jose's bus and trolley system, runs north-south along 1st and 2nd St. in the downtown area. The grassy grounds of **San Jose State University** (SJSU; 924-5000) run several blocks between S. 4th and S. 10th St. Founded in 1857, SJSU is the oldest public college in California.

PRACTICAL INFORMATION

Airport: San Jose International, 1661 Airport Blvd. (277-4759). Turn right onto Airport Blvd. from Coleman Ave. off I-80 or Guadalupe off U.S. 101. Also accessible by Santa Clara County Transit light-rail. Free shuttles connect the terminals.

Trains: Amtrak, 65 Cahill St. (287-7462 or 800-USA-RAIL/872-7245). To **L.A.** ($77) and **San Francisco** (2hr., $9). CalTrain, 65 Cahill St. (291-5651 or 800-660-4287), at W. San Fernando Blvd. To **San Francisco** (1½hr.) with stops at peninsula cities. Fare $4.50; seniors, disabled, and under 12 $2.25. Every hr. M-F 5am-10pm, Sa 6:30am-10pm, Su 7:30am-10pm.

Buses: Greyhound, 70 S. Almaden (800-231-2222), at Santa Clara St. The station feels reasonably safe, even at night. To **L.A.** ($32) and **San Francisco** (1hr., $7). Luggage lockers for ticketed passengers only. Open daily 5am-midnight.

Public Transportation: Santa Clara Valley Transportation Agency (VTA), 2 N. First St. (321-2300), offers ultra-modern buses and a light-rail system. Fare $1.10, ages 5-17 55¢; day pass $2.20, ages 5-17 $1.40; exact change only. **BART** (510-441-2278) bus #180 serves the Fremont station from 1st and San Carlos St. in downtown San Jose ($1.75). To **San Francisco** (1¼hr., $3.65).

Visitor Information: Visitor Information and Business Center (977-0900, events line 295-2265; www.sanjose.org), at Market and San Carlos St. in the San Jose McEnerny Convention Ctr. Superb free maps. Open M-F 8am-5:30pm, Sa-Su 11am-5pm.

Emergency: 911. **Police:** 201 W. Mission St. (277-5300).

24-Hour Crisis Lines: Rape Crisis (287-3000). **Suicide Prevention/Crisis Intervention** (279-3312).

Medical Services: San Jose Medical Center, 675 E. Santa Clara St. (998-3212), at 14th St. Emergency room (977-4444) open 24hr.

Internet Access: Martin Luther King, Jr. Public Library, 180 W. San Carlos St. (277-4846), in front of the Convention Ctr. Free, but get there early to avoid waiting. Open M-W 9am-9pm, Th-Sa 9am-6pm, Su 1-5pm.

Post Office: 105 N. 1st St. (800-225-8777). Open M-F 9am-5:30pm. **ZIP Code:** 95113.

AREA CODE	The area code for San Jose is 408.

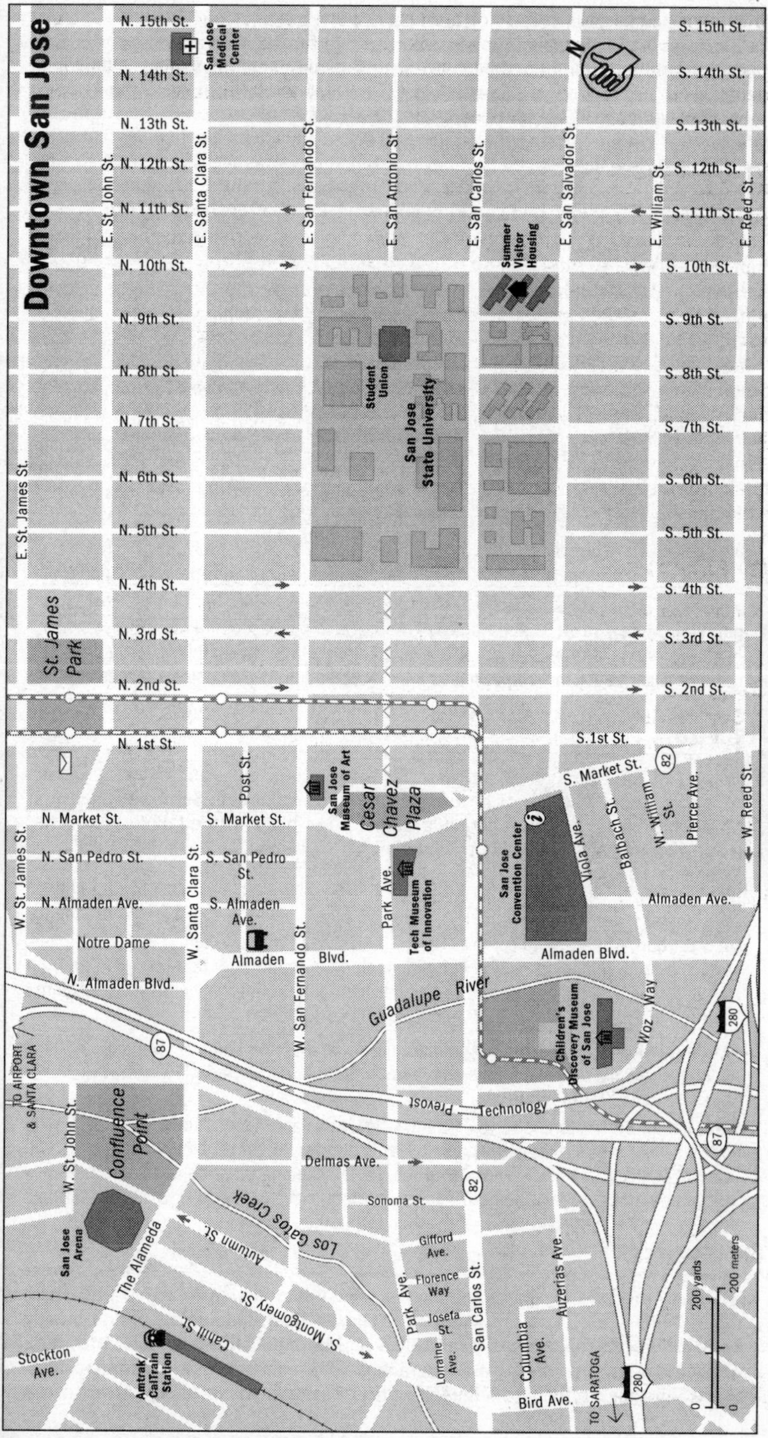

Downtown San Jose

N. 15th St.
N. 14th St.
N. 13th St.
N. 12th St.
N. 11th St.
N. 10th St.
N. 9th St.
N. 8th St.
N. 7th St.
N. 6th St.
N. 5th St.
N. 4th St.
N. 3rd St.
N. 2nd St.
N. 1st St.
N. Market St.
N. San Pedro St.
N. Almaden Ave.
Notre Dame
N. Almaden Blvd.
E. St. James St.
E. St. John St.
E. Santa Clara St.
E. San Fernando St.
E. San Antonio St.
E. San Carlos St.
E. San Salvador St.
E. William St.
E. Reed St.
S. 15th St.
S. 14th St.
S. 13th St.
S. 12th St.
S. 11th St.
S. 10th St.
S. 9th St.
S. 8th St.
S. 7th St.
S. 6th St.
S. 5th St.
S. 4th St.
S. 3rd St.
S. 2nd St.
S. 1st St.
S. Market St.
Post St.
S. San Pedro St.
S. Almaden Ave.
Almaden Blvd.
Almaden Ave.
W. St. James St.
W. Santa Clara St.
W. San Fernando St.
Park Ave.
Viola Ave.
Balbach St.
W. William St.
Pierce Ave.
W. Reed St.
Woz Way
San Jose Medical Center
St. James Park
San Jose Museum of Art
Cesar Chavez Plaza
Tech Museum of Innovation
Student Union
San Jose State University
Summer Visitor Housing
San Jose Convention Center
Children's Discovery Museum of San Jose
Guadalupe River
Prevost
Technology
TO AIRPORT & SANTA CLARA
W. St. John St.
Confluence Point
San Jose Arena
The Alameda
Delmas Ave.
Sonoma St.
Los Gatos Creek
Autumn St.
Gifford Ave.
Florence Way
Josefa St.
S. Montgomery St.
Cahill St.
Amtrak/CalTrain Station
Stockton Ave.
Lorraine Ave.
San Carlos St.
Columbia Ave.
Auzerias Ave.
Bird Ave.
TO SARATOGA
87
82
280
0 200 yards
0 200 meters
N

ACCOMMODATIONS AND CAMPGROUNDS

County parks with campgrounds surround the city. **Mount Madonna County Park** (842-2341), on Hecker Pass Hwy., has 117 sites in a beautiful setting, occupied on a first-come, first-camped basis. (*Let's Go* does not recommend mounting Madonna.) The scandalously idyllic hamlet of **Saratoga,** on Rte. 85 14 miles southwest of San Jose, has a number of campsites (sites $8; RVs $20; open Apr. to mid-Oct.) and miles of horse and hiking trails in wooded **Sanborn-Skyline County Park** (867-9959; reservations 358-3751), on Sanborn Rd. From Rte. 17 South, take Rte. 9 to Big Basin Way. Along the way sits **Saratoga Springs** (867-9999), a private campground with 32 sites, a general store, and hot showers (sites $20 for 2 people).

Sanborn Park Hostel (HI-AYH), 15808 Sanborn Rd. (741-0166), in Sanborn-Skyline Park 13mi. west of San Jose. From Saratoga, take Rte. 9 2½mi. up the mountain, then turn left on Sanborn Rd. After 1mi., take the 1st right to the hostel. Watch closely, as turns are poorly marked. Or call from Saratoga (M-F 5-10pm, Sa-Su 5-8pm) for pickup. Beautiful facility is strict about its ground rules (curfew 11pm); those looking for peace and quiet with indoor plumbing are in luck. Clean rooms and 39 beds. Piano, kitchen, and fireplaces, and redwoods outside. Reception 5-11pm. Check-out 9am. Dorms $8.50, U.S. non-members $10.50, foreign non-members $11.50; under 18 half-price. 2 family rooms available. Limited wheelchair access; call ahead.

San Jose State University, 375 S. 9th St. (924-6193), at San Salvador St. Residence halls open to visitors June-Sept. Shared kitchenette, lounge with pool, ping pong, and big screen TV. Parking included. Linen extra. Dorm with 2 single beds $32.50.

Park View Motel, 1140 S. 2nd St. (297-8455). Quiet motel south of downtown has comfortable rooms with king beds and a small pool. Many with mini-fridges, some with kitchenettes. Check-in 11am. Singles $45; doubles $60. No wheelchair access.

FOOD

Familiar fast-food franchises and pizzerias surround the campus of San Jose State. More international cheap eats lie along **South 1st Street** or near **San Pedro Square,** at St. John and San Pedro St. A **farmer's market** takes place at the Pavilion, at S. 1st and San Fernando St. (late May to mid-Nov. Th 10am-2pm).

House of Siam, 55 S. Market St. (279-5668). Cozy and elegant. Excellent Thai entrees (some meatless) $7-10. Open M-F 11am-3pm and 5-10pm, Sa-Su 11:30am-10pm.

Lan's Garden, 155 E. San Fernando St. (289-8553), at 4th St. Whether you want adventurous cuisine (calamari steaks with pineapple $7.50) or tamer fare (*pho* noodle soup $4.50), this Vietnamese restaurant won't disappoint. Lunch specials $4.25, dinner entrees $6-7.50. Open Su-Th 10am-11pm, F-Sa 10am-2am.

La Guadalajara, 45 Post St. (292-7352). Lunch counter has served delicious Mexican food and cheap, yummy pastries since 1955. Jumbo burritos $3.25; combo plates $4-6. Open daily 8:30am-6:30pm.

White Lotus, 80 N. Market St. (977-0540), between Santa Clara and St. John St. One of few local vegetarian restaurants, and *Metro*'s pick for the area's best Vietnamese food. Lotus vermicelli "salad" and imperial roll $5.75. Steamed plantain with coconut milk ($2) is a great dessert. Open M-Th 11am-2:30pm and 5:30-9pm, F-Sa 11am-9:30pm.

SIGHTS

In the years before its many fruit orchards were replaced by squat industrial parks, Silicon Valley was known as the **Valley Of Heart's Delight.** Geographically contained within the Santa Clara Valley, and bounded by Santa Clara County, the area nonetheless lacks a recognizable center and organization. In fact, despite San Jose's efforts to bill itself as the **"Capital of Silcon Valley"** based on its large population, many of the corporate headquarters of high-tech giants like Intel and Hewlett-Packard are actually in Mountain View and Sunnyvale, between San Jose and the bay to the north. These companies are wary of visitors, and if you insist on touring, you'll see little but anonymous, low-profile buildings of mirrored glass. There's a bit more to see in San Jose proper. A few well-funded museums are the only real diversions from the business of web sites and microchips.

WINCHESTER MYSTERY HOUSE. Of absolutely no educational value, but intriguing nonetheless, is the house that Sarah Winchester built. This heir to the Winchester rifle fortune was convinced by an occultist that she would face the vengeance of the spirits of all the men ever killed by her family's guns if construction on her home ever ceased. Work on the mansion continued 24 hours a day for over 30 years, and today the estate is an elaborate maze of secret corridors, dead-end staircases, and tacky gift shops with absolutely no escape. *(247-2101. 1525 S. Winchester Blvd. near the intersection of I-880 and 280, west of town. Open Su-Th 9am-6pm, F-Sa 9am-9pm. 1hr. tours every 15-30min. Admission $13, seniors $10, ages 6-12 $7.)*

TECH MUSEUM OF INNOVATION. This is *the* tourist attraction in San Jose. Underwritten by high-tech firms, "the Tech" features hands-on exhibits on robotics, DNA engineering, and space exploration, as well as an IMAX theater. *(279-7150. 145 W. San Carlos St. Open July-Sept. F-W 10am-6pm, Th 10am-8pm; Oct.-June Tu-Su 10am-5pm. Admission $8, students $6, seniors and ages 3-12 $4. Separate IMAX admission.)*

ROSICRUCIAN EGYPTIAN MUSEUM AND PLANETARIUM. Rising out of the suburbs like the work of a mad pharaoh, this grand structure houses an extensive collection of Egyptian and Assyrian artifacts, including a walk-in tomb and spooky animal mummies. The collection belongs to the mystical order of the Rosy Cross, who have supposedly long battled the Bavarian Illuminati for world domination. *(947-3636; www.rosicrucian.org. 1342 Naglee Ave. at Park St. Open W-M 10am-5pm. Admission $7, students and seniors $5, ages 6-15 $3.50. Under 18 must be accompanied by an adult.)*

OTHER MUSEUMS. The **Children's Discovery Museum,** behind the Technology Center light-rail station, is filled with science-based toys. *(298-5437; www.cdm.org. 180 Woz Way. Open Tu-Sa 10am-5pm, Su noon-5pm. Admission $6, seniors $5, under 18 $4.)* The **San Jose Museum of Art,** at San Fernando St., presents mass-appeal modern shows. *(271-6840. 110 S. Market St. Open Tu-W and F-Su 10am-5pm, Th 9am-8pm. Admission $6, students and seniors $3.)* Close by stand the **San Jose Institute of Contemporary Art (SJICA),** *(283-8155. 451 S. 1st St. Open Tu-Sa noon-5pm),* and the **Center for Latino Arts (MACLA),** *(998-2783. 510 S. 1st St. Open W-Sa noon-5pm).* Many area galleries are free and open until 8pm on the third Thursday of every month.

NIGHTLIFE

The nightlife is about what you'd expect in the city that nerds built, with the bars and clubs shockingly full of young eligible men. The brightest spot is the strip of downtown known as the SoFA District (South of 1st St.). The strip is actually on 1st St., which runs north-south.

The Flying Pig Pub, 78 S. 1st St. (298-6710). A wacky jukebox suits the fly clientele of this mega-chill bistro, which serves both food (3-way chili $3.25) and drinks. Open M 3pm-2am, Tu-F 11am-2am, Sa 4pm-2am.

Katie Bloom's Irish Pub and Restaurant, 150 S. 1st St. (294-4408). It's clear why "pub" precedes "restaurant" in the name. Drink imported beers ($2.50) as Oscar Wilde and James Joyce watch from the walls. Extensive space includes many private leather booths as well as rowdier counter spots. Open M-F 11am-2am, Sa-Su 2pm-2am.

Cactus Club, 417 S. 1st St. (280-0885). The kids show San Jose how to rage in this 18+ club hosting funk, punk, thrash, and alt-rock acts. Cover $4-8. Showtimes vary; usually open 8pm-2am.

The B-Hive Bar and Lounge, 372 S. 1st St. (298-2529), buzzes with a relatively youthful crowd. DJs pump different theme selections nightly into tight, smoky rooms. $1 drafts, no drinks over $3, and no cover charge until 10pm. Open Tu-Su 9pm-2am.

ENTERTAINMENT

For information on entertainment events, look for the weekly *Metro*, available free on street corners downtown. **City Lights,** 529 S. 2nd St. (295-4200; www.cltc.org) at William St., is a hip local theater company with student discounts. **Camera Cinemas** (998-3300) shows art-house, classic, and foreign flicks, film festivals, and midnight specials at three locations: **Camera 1,** 366 S. 1st St., **Camera 3,** at S. 2nd and San Carlos St., and **Towne 3,** 1433 The Alameda (287-1433). The cafe at Camera 3 offers movie-lover sandwiches like "My Dinner with Andre" (roast beef and gouda on sourdough; $5.75) and "Naked Lunch" (avocado, spinach, and artichoke hearts; $5). The **Student Union** (924-6350), at SJSU, has an amphitheater that often hosts concerts and other performances.

SEASONAL EVENTS AND SPORTS

Topping the list of annual highlights is the May **Blues Festival** (924-6261), the biggest, baddest free blues concert in Northern California (3rd week in May in 2000). In early September, head to the **SoFA Street Fair** (295-2265), between San Carlos and Reco St. south of 1st St. Cool vendors and bands attract more than just your average San Jose crowd (noon-9pm). On the last weekend in September, buzz downtown to the **San Pedro Square Brew-Ha-Ha** (279-1775), which has beer-tasting and fun for all (noon-7pm).

The **San Jose Sharks** (call 287-7070 M-F 8am-6pm), the city's NHL team, play at the San Jose Arena. Soccer fans can kick it with Eric Wynalda and the **San Jose Clash** (call 985-4625 M-F 8:30am-5:30pm) at Spartan Stadium, on 7th St. off I-280.

NEAR SAN JOSE: SANTA CLARA

A suburb of a suburb, the small town of Santa Clara lies between San Jose to the southeast and the gargantuan Great America, a Paramount-owned theme park, to the north. To reach Santa Clara, take U.S. 101 to the De La Cruz Exit and follow signs to Santa Clara University.

AMUSEMENT PARKS. Paramount's Great America theme park sprawls north of the city, a forest of roller coasters, log rides, and other fiendish contraptions designed to spin you, flip you, soak you, drop you, and generally separate you from your stomach. If you come on a weekday, you'll beat at least some of the crowds. *(988-1776. Off U.S. 101 at Great America Pkwy. Open June-Aug. Su-F 10am-9pm, Sa 10am-10pm; Mar.-May and Sept.-Oct. Sa 10am-10pm, Su 10am-9pm. Admission $35, seniors and wheelchair-bound $25, ages 3-6 $20. Parking $6. Coupons in San Jose area stores.)* Paramount's fiefdom gets all wet at **Raging Waters,** the area's best collection of waterslides. It's great on a hot day, but don't expect to be the only one who thought of that. *(654-5450. Off U.S. 101 at Tully Rd. Exit. Open June-Aug. daily 10am-7pm; May and Sept. Sa-Su 10am-7pm. Admission $21, seniors $11, under 42in. $17; all ages after 3pm $15.)*

MISSION SANTA CLARA. This was the first California mission to honor a woman—Clare of Assisi—as its patron saint. The mission was established on the Guadalupe River in 1777, and moved to its present site in 1825. The mission church, where summer masses are held, houses a magnificent organ. In 1851, **Santa Clara University** was established in the old mission. Subsequent restorations have refitted the structures to match the beauty and bliss of the surrounding rose gardens and 200-year-old olive trees. *(500 El Camino Real. Mass M-F noon, Su 10am.)*

SAN MATEO COUNTY

The bluffs of the San Mateo County Coast quickly obscure the hectic urban pace of the city to the north. Most of the energy here is generated by the coastal winds and waves. The Pacific Coast Highway (Route 1) maneuvers its way through a rocky shoreline, colorful beach vistas, and generations-old ranches. Although it's possible to drive quickly down the coast from San Francisco to Santa Cruz, haste is waste—especially if you drive off a cliff.

ORIENTATION AND PRACTICAL INFORMATION

On this stretch of the Pacific coast, a car is probably best. Stunning ocean views off **Route 1** compete with the road for drivers' attentions. If traveling by sneaker, you'll have a tougher time; **SamTrans** services the area only somewhat successfully (see below). Bus route maps are available at CalTrain and BART stations. The shore from Pacifica to Half Moon Bay is serviced by buses #1C, 1L, and 90H.

Buses: San Mateo County Transit (SamTrans), 945 California Dr. (within county 800-660-4287, elsewhere 508-6455). Service from Burlingame (by the San Francisco International Airport) to Half Moon Bay. Operates daily 6am-7pm. Fare $1; seniors, disabled, and ages 5-17 50¢. Monthly pass $36; seniors, disabled, and ages 5-17 $18.

Bike Rental: The Bicyclery, 101 Main St., Half Moon Bay (726-6000). Bikes $6 per hr. (2hr. min.), $24 per day. Helmets $5. Open M-F 9:30am-6:30pm, Sa-Su 10am-5pm.

Visitor Information: San Mateo County Convention and Visitors Bureau, Seabreeze Plaza, 111 Anza Blvd. #410, Burlingame (800-288-4748), by the San Francisco International Airport. Sleek office with info on the central coast and San Francisco area, including helpful maps. Open M-F 8:30am-5pm. **San Mateo County Parks and Recreation Department,** James V. Fitzgerald Marine Life Reserve, P.O. Box 451, Moss Beach (728-3584), off Rte. 1 7mi. north of Half Moon Beach. Open daily dawn-dusk.

Emergency: 911. **Police:** 401 Marshall St., Redwood City (363-4000).

24-Hour Crisis Intervention and Suicide Prevention Hotline: 368-6655.

Hospital: San Mateo County General Hospital, 222 W. 39th Ave. (573-2222).

Internet Access: Ladida Cafe, 500C Purissima St., Half Moon Bay (726-1663). $1 for 10min., $10 for 2hr. Just 1 terminal, but lots of coffee.

Post Office: Half Moon Bay: 500 Stone Pine Rd. (726-5517), at Main St. Open M-F 8:30am-5pm, Sa 8:30am-noon. **ZIP Code:** 94019.

AREA CODE	The area code for San Mateo County is 650 (formerly 415).

ACCOMMODATIONS AND CAMPGROUNDS

Pigeon Point Lighthouse Hostel (HI-AYH; 879-0633), on Rte. 1 6mi. south of Pescadero and 20mi. south of Half Moon Bay. Accessible by weekday SamTrans service or by Bike-centennial Trail. 4 houses, each with a big, homey common room. The old lighthouse-keeper's quarters has a hot tub ($5 for 30min.). 52 beds. Chores required. Reception 7:30-9:30am and 5:30-9:30pm. Check-in 4:30pm. Check-out 9:30am. Curfew and quiet time 11pm. Dorms $12, nonmembers $14; extra $10 for couples' rooms. Reservations must be made 48hr. in advance, but it is often booked weeks earlier.

Point Montara Lighthouse Hostel (HI-AYH; 728-7177), on Lighthouse Point 25mi. south of San Francisco and 4mi. north of Half Moon Bay. SamTrans stop 1 block north at 14th St. and Rte. 1. Weary travelers will revel in this 45-bed facility with 2 kitchens and a spectacular hot tub ($5 per hr., 2-person min.). Dorms $12, nonmembers $15; extra $10 for couples' rooms. Registration 7:30-9:30am and 4:30-9:30pm. Curfew and quiet time 11pm. Laundry (wash $1, dry 25¢). Reservations recommended for weekends, groups, and private rooms; request by phone 48hr. in advance with credit card, or by mail with deposit.

Francis Beach campground, 95 Kelly Ave. (726-8820), at Half Moon Bay State Beach, has 56 exposed beachside sites. Most have firepit and picnic table. Saturday campfires in peak season. In summer 7-night max. stay; off-season 14-night max. stay. Check-out noon. Free, cold outdoor showers. Tent sites $16, seniors $15. Hiker/biker sites $3 per person. Pets $1. No reservations. Day use 8am-dusk.

Butano State Park campground (879-2040), 5mi. south of Pescadero. From the north, take Pescadero Rd. east from Rte. 1 to Cloverdale. From the south, take Gazos Creek from Rte. 1 to Cloverdale. Extensive paths interlace the tall, lush redwoods of the Santa Cruz Mountains. No showers. Check-out noon. 21 drive-in and 18 walk-in sites Su-Th $15, F-Sa $18. Seniors $1 discount. Vehicles $7. Reservations recommended from Memorial Day to Labor Day (May 29-Sept. 4 in 2000); call PARKNET (800-444-7275).

FOOD

Despite the area's remote feel, a surprising number of restaurants cater to hungry travelers. Those looking for late-night snacks or planning to picnic along the coast can find a 24-hour **Safeway** at the junction of Rte. 1 and 92.

HALF MOON BAY

The Flying Fish Grill (712-1125), at Main St. and Rte. 92. Small cafe with cheerful staff serves fresh, local, inexpensive, airborne seafood. Salmon Taco Grande ($4) or pint of clam chowder ($5) can satisfy a seafarer's appetite. Open Tu-Su in summer 11:30am-8:30pm; off-season 11:30am-7:30pm.

2 Fools Cafe and Market, 408 Main St. (712-1222), at Mill St. Cool, urbane eatery and drinkery serves many veggie options. Sandwiches $5-8. For dinner, check out the roasted exotic mushrooms with provolone over pasta $8.50. Open M 7am-2pm, Tu-F 7am-9pm, Sa-Su 8am-9pm.

BAY AREA

AROUND HALF MOON BAY

San Gregorio General Store, 7615 Stage Rd. (726-0565), on Rte. 84 1mi. east of Rte. 1, 8mi. south of Half Moon Bay. Social spot for locals, this quirky store has served San Gregorio since 1889 with an eclectic selection of hardware, candy, groceries, gourmet coffee, cast-iron pots, books, candles, and more. Quaff a frothy beer ($2-4) at the bar or eat a fresh sandwich ($3). Live local music creates a festive atmosphere Sa-Su afternoons and F evenings. Open M-Th 9am-6pm, F-Su 9am-7pm.

Arcangeli Grocery Co. and Norm's Market, 287 Stage Rd., Pescadero (879-0147). Established in 1929 by the present owner's grandfather, this popular grocery store has a full meat and deli department, wine, and bakery. Loaves $2-4. Some are partially baked for fresh-from-the-oven goodness. Local artichoke products featured. Open M-Sa 10am-7pm, Su 10am-6pm.

INSIDE THE PENINSULA

Taquería La Cumbre, 28 North B St., San Mateo (344-8989). This restaurant, which also has a San Francisco branch, has won "best burrito" award in every major Bay Area magazine reader poll. Filling, tasty Mexican meals for under $5. Be prepared for cumbersome lines at lunchtime. Open Su-Th 11am-9pm, F-Sa 11am-10pm.

The Merry Prankster Cafe, 8865 La Honda Rd., La Honda (747-0660), keeps Ken Kesey's memory alive. Eat cheaply all day long: leek and red potato egg scramble $4; fresh vegetable sandwich $5; 6in. single pizza $4.50. Live music F-Sa nights. Open M 5-9pm, Tu-F 7am-9:30pm, Sa-Su 7am-10pm.

Mediterranean Cafe, 5 S. Ellsworth Ave., San Mateo (343-4218), at Baldwin St. Expensive-looking cafe has surprisingly inexpensive food. Beautifully set tables are a fit background for delectable meals. Grilled salmon sandwich ($6.50) or pasta alfredo ($6), as well as more standard lunch fare. Open M-F 11am-2pm and 5-10pm, Sa-Su 5-10pm.

Narin Thai Cuisine, 21 Park Rd., Burlingame (344-1900). Inexpensive Thai food ($6-8) in the trendy and generally more expensive Burlingame Ave. area. Simple, tasteful decor. Open M-Sa 11am-3pm and 5-9:30pm.

SIGHTS AND ACTIVITIES

ALONG THE COAST

AÑO NUEVO STATE RESERVE. This state reserve includes a beach which is the mating place of the 15-foot-long **elephant seal.** Early spring is breeding season, when thousands of fat seals crowd the beach. To see this unforgettable show (prime viewing times Dec. 15-Mar. 31), you must make reservations (8 weeks in advance recommended) by calling PARKNET (800-444-7275). Tickets go on sale November 15 and are generally sold out within a week or two (2½hr., guided tours $4 per person). SamTrans (508-6441) runs Saturday, Sunday, and holiday round-trip bus service to the reserve from San Mateo that includes a walking tour ($12). From April to November the reserve is free (parking $5), but you *will* need a free **hiking permit** from the entrance station (open daily Apr.-Aug. 8am-4pm, Sept.-Nov. 8:30am-3pm). Trail lengths in the Wildlife Protection Area are half-mile to 1½ miles. Arrive before mid-August to catch the last of the "molters" and the young who have yet to find their sea legs. Don't get too close—they may be fat but they're fast, and mothers are intolerant of strangers who appear to threaten their young. The beach is cold and windy regardless of season, so dress warmly. *(879-0227. Off Rte. 1 in Pescadero, 7mi. south of Pigeon Point and 27mi. south of Half Moon Bay. Park open daily 8am-dusk.)*

PIGEON POINT. The point takes its name from a hapless schooner that crashed into the rocky shore on its inaugural voyage in 1853. Pigeon Point turns heads with its tidepools, wave-washed rocks at Pebble Beach, and 30-foot plumes of surf. In the late afternoon, the West Coast's second-tallest **lighthouse** offers a magnificent view of the **sunset.** Tours of the lighthouse and its 1008 glass prisms are available Sunday 11am to 4pm for a small donation. *(Point info 879-0852; lighthouse 879-0633.)*

PESCADERO. This historic little burg was established by white settlers in 1856, and was named Pescadero ("fisherman's town") because of the abundance of fish in the ocean and creeks. Wander through the old town or participate in the local sport of **olallieberry gathering.** This popular pastime originated around 25 years ago when the olallieberry (oh-LA-la-behr-ee) was created by crossing a blackberry, a loganberry, and a youngberry. Get a-pickin' at **Phipp's Ranch,** 2700 Pescadero Rd. (store 897-1032, office 879-0787), and pay $1 per pound for your stash of strawberries, blackberries, olallieberries, or boysenberries (open daily 10am-6pm). The **Pescadero Marsh** shelters such migratory birds as the elegant blue heron, often seen poised on its spindly legs searching for unlucky fish.

BEACHES. San Gregorio Beach is a delightful destination; walk to its southern end to find little caves in the shore rocks. A stream runs into the sea, and may prove a comfortable alternative to dipping in the chillier ocean. *(Open 8am-dusk; day use $4, seniors $3.)* A less-frequented beach is at the **unsigned turnout** at **Marker 27.35** along Rte. 1. It's difficult to find without aid; keep an eye out for mysteriously vacant cars parked along the highway. State-owned but undeveloped, this gorgeous stretch of beach is between San Gregorio and Pomponio State Beaches.

OTHER POINTS OF INTEREST ALONG ROUTE 1

The Pacific Coast Hwy. (Rte. 1) winds along the San Mateo County Coast from San Francisco to Big Basin Redwoods State Park. This expanse of shore is scattered with isolated, sandy beaches, most of which are too cold for swimming. State beaches charge $5, with admission valid for the entire day at all state parks—hold on to your receipt. Some beaches do not enforce payment of the required fee, but police occasionally make sweeps looking for unpaid cars and will distribute tickets. Keep your eyes peeled for the unmarked beaches along the coast; they are often stunning, crowdless spots with free parking. A few miles south of Pacifica is **Gray Whale Cove Beach** (728-5336), a privately owned **nude** beach off Rte. 1. You must be at least 18 and bring a towel (admission M-F $6.50, Sa-Su $7.50). Take SamTrans bus #1L; the unmarked parking lot is the first one on the left.

Not much farther south is the Point Montara Lighthouse Hostel (see p. 155), flanked by quiet **Montara State Beach** and the variegated tidepool life at **Fitzgerald Marine Reserve. Half Moon Bay** is an old coastal community 29 miles south of San Francisco. Recent commercialization has not infringed much on this small, easy-going beach town. At **Pillar Point Harbor,** four miles north of Half Moon Bay, you can sample smoked salmon, chat with fishermen, or try your hand at reeling in the big ones with **Captain John's Fishing Trips** (726-2913 or 728-3377; reservations 800-391-8787; 7½hr. trips depart daily 7:30am; tickets M-F $36, seniors and under 12 $31; Sa-Su $38; check-in 6:30am). Special trips go to the desolate **Farallon Islands Wildlife Refuge.** There are also seasonal salmon fishing trips (1-day fishing license $6.50, rod and reel rental $5, tackle and bait $5.75). The **Sea Horse Ranch** and the **Friendly Acres Ranch** (726-2362), one mile north of Half Moon Bay on Rte. 1, have horses and ponies for unguided beach and trail rides (1hr. trail ride $25, 1½hr. beach ride $35; ages 5+; open daily 8am-6pm; no reservations).

INLAND

LA HONDA. A winding cross-peninsular trip down Rte. 84 will bring you to the little logging town in the redwoods where author Ken Kesey lived with his merry pranksters in the 1960s, before it got too small and they took off across the U.S. in a psychedelic bus. The shady, scenic drive makes this detour worthwhile, even if you aren't familiar with Kesey's gang—but for enhanced understanding, read a copy of Tom Wolfe's *The Electric Kool-Aid Acid Test* before making the journey.

BURLINGAME MUSEUM OF PEZ MEMORABILIA. This small but quirky display of dispensers and paraphernalia dates back to 1949. Try to catch the short Pez reference video. Like all the best things in life, the museum is free. *(347-2301. 214 California Dr. Open Tu-Sa 10am-6pm. Free.)*

BAY AREA

SEASONAL EVENTS

Brew-Ha-Ha (726-7416), Half Moon Bay, 1st Su in May (May 7 in 2000). Over 50 beers.
Coastside County Fair (726-5202), mid-June to mid-July. Crafts, livestock, and a rodeo.
Chili Cook-Off/Chowder Challenge (726-9275), Half Moon Bay, late June.

NORTH BAY AND WINE COUNTRY

Across the Golden Gate from San Francisco, Marin County is the jacuzzi of the bay, bubbling with money-making and mantra-spouting residents. A pristine beach stretches north from harborside Marin Headlands, and the inland woods crowd green fields of grape vines. Robert Louis Stevenson described Wine Country (the collective term for the Napa, Sonoma, and Russian River Valleys) as a place where "the stirring sunlight and the growing vines make a pleasant music for the mind, and the wine is poetry." The vineyards here are highly regarded by connoisseurs worldwide, which accounts for the area's high prices and heavy tourism.

As most parts of Marin, Napa, and Sonoma Counties are within two hours of San Francisco by car, it might be wiser to make it a daytrip than to stay here and endure the steep hotel prices.

MARIN COUNTY

Physically beautiful, politically liberal, and stinking rich, Marin County epitomizes California. If the new VW Beetle were sold nowhere but Marin (muh-RIN), Volkswagen still might reap a tidy profit. The yuppie reincarnation of the quintessential hippie car strikes just the right combination of upscale chic and counterculture nostalgia to have taken this county by storm.

Marin's pleasure spots are easily accessible from San Francisco, whether traveling by car, bus, ferry, or bike. A web of trails combs the land protected in a string of state and national parks, welcoming mountain bikers and hikers looking for anything from a day's adventure to a two-week trek. And if the locals seem a little smug, well, why shouldn't they? The cathedral stillness of ancient redwoods, the sweet-smelling eucalyptus, the brilliant wildflowers, the high bluffs and crashing surf along Route 1—all are ample justification for civic pride.

ORIENTATION

The Marin peninsula lies at the northern end of San Francisco Bay, and is connected to the city by **U.S. 101** via the **Golden Gate Bridge.** U.S. 101 extends north to Santa Rosa and Sonoma County, while **Route 1** creeps north along the Pacific to Sonoma Coast. The **Richmond-San Rafael Bridge** connects Marin to the East Bay via **Interstate 580.**

The eastern side of the county cradles **Sausalito, Mill Valley, Larkspur, San Rafael, Terra Linda, Ignacio,** and **Novato.** These towns line U.S. 101, which runs north-south through Marin, creating the inland corridor where most of the population is concentrated. National seashore and park land constitutes most of West Marin. **Route 1** splits from U.S. 101 north of Sausalito, and runs up the Pacific Coast through Muir Beach, Stinson Beach, Olema, Inverness, and **Point Reyes.**

Gas is scarce and expensive in West Marin, so fill up in town before you head out for the coast. Drivers should take caution in West Marin, where roads are narrow, sharply curved, and perched on the edges of cliffs.

PRACTICAL INFORMATION

Public Transportation: Golden Gate Transit (455-2000, in S.F. 923-2000), provides **bus** transit between San Francisco and Marin County via the Golden Gate Bridge, and local service in Marin. Buses #10, 20, and 50 serve Marin City and Sausalito from San Francisco's Transbay Terminal. Buses #20, 28, 30, and 50 go to San Rafael. On weekends and holidays only, bus #63 runs 6 times per day from the Golden Gate Bridge through Sausalito, Mount Tamalpais State Park, and Stinson Beach, and #65 runs twice daily from San Francisco, Samuel P. Taylor State Park, and Point Reyes (fare to Sausalito $2; to Point Reyes and Olema $4). Seniors and disabled 50% off, ages 6-12 25% off.

Ferries: Golden Gate Ferry (455-2000) runs from San Francisco to the Sausalito terminal at the end of Market St. ($4.25) and the Larkspur terminal (M-F $2.50, Sa-Su $4.25; seniors and disabled 50% off; ages 6-12 25% off). Offices open M-F 6am-8pm, Sa-Su 6:30am-8pm. **Blue and Gold** (schedule 773-1188, tickets 705-5555) runs ferries from Pier 41, Fisherman's Wharf, to **Sausalito** ($5.50) and **Tiburon** ($5.50).

Taxis: Radio Cab (485-1234 or 800-464-7234), serves all of Marin County.

Car Rental: Budget, 20 Bellam Blvd., San Rafael (457-4282). From $36 per day with 150mi. included. Must be at least 21. Under 25 surcharge $15 per day.

Bike Rental: Four Winds Adventure Travel, 533 Richardson St., Sausalito (888-360-1087, in Sausalito 332-1087). Mountain bikes $13 per hr. (2hr. min.), $35 per day. **Sausalito Mountain Bike Rental,** (331-4448), near Ferry Plaza, rents full-suspension bikes ($15 per hr., $50 per day), kayaks, sailboats, and a 50ft. yacht.

Visitor Information:

Marin County Visitors Bureau (472-7470; www.visitmarin.org), off U.S. 101 at the end of the Ave. of the Flags off Civic Center Dr., in San Rafael. Part of the Marin Civic Center. Glossy brochures may be more informative than the staff. Open M-F 9am-5pm.

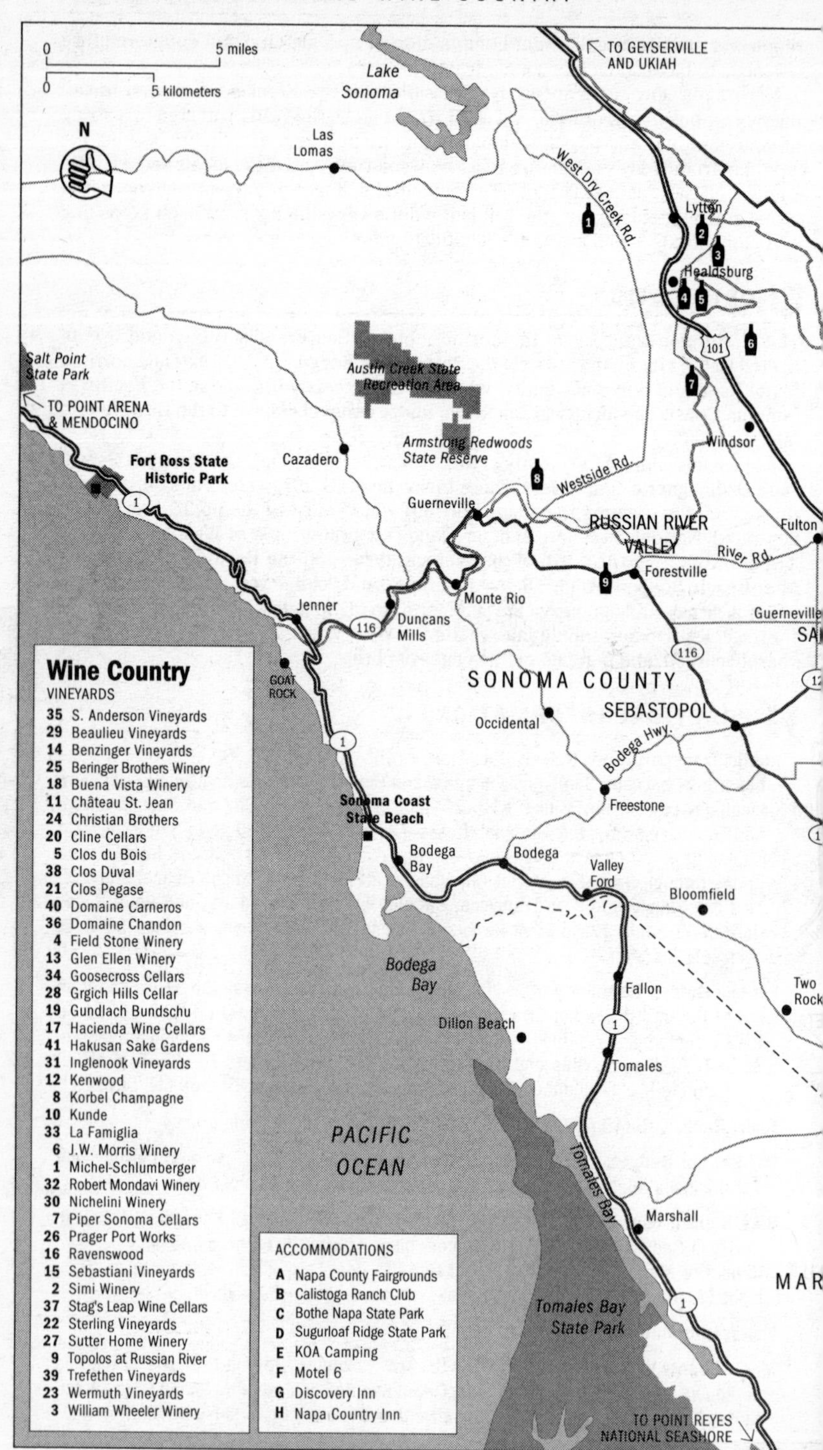

Wine Country

VINEYARDS

35 S. Anderson Vineyards
29 Beaulieu Vineyards
14 Benzinger Vineyards
25 Beringer Brothers Winery
18 Buena Vista Winery
11 Château St. Jean
24 Christian Brothers
20 Cline Cellars
5 Clos du Bois
38 Clos Duval
21 Clos Pegase
40 Domaine Carneros
36 Domaine Chandon
4 Field Stone Winery
13 Glen Ellen Winery
34 Goosecross Cellars
28 Grgich Hills Cellar
19 Gundlach Bundschu
17 Hacienda Wine Cellars
41 Hakusan Sake Gardens
31 Inglenook Vineyards
12 Kenwood
8 Korbel Champagne
10 Kunde
33 La Famiglia
6 J.W. Morris Winery
1 Michel-Schlumberger
32 Robert Mondavi Winery
30 Nichelini Winery
7 Piper Sonoma Cellars
26 Prager Port Works
16 Ravenswood
15 Sebastiani Vineyards
2 Simi Winery
37 Stag's Leap Wine Cellars
22 Sterling Vineyards
27 Sutter Home Winery
9 Topolos at Russian River
39 Trefethen Vineyards
23 Wermuth Vineyards
3 William Wheeler Winery

ACCOMMODATIONS

A Napa County Fairgrounds
B Calistoga Ranch Club
C Bothe Napa State Park
D Sugurloaf Ridge State Park
E KOA Camping
F Motel 6
G Discovery Inn
H Napa Country Inn

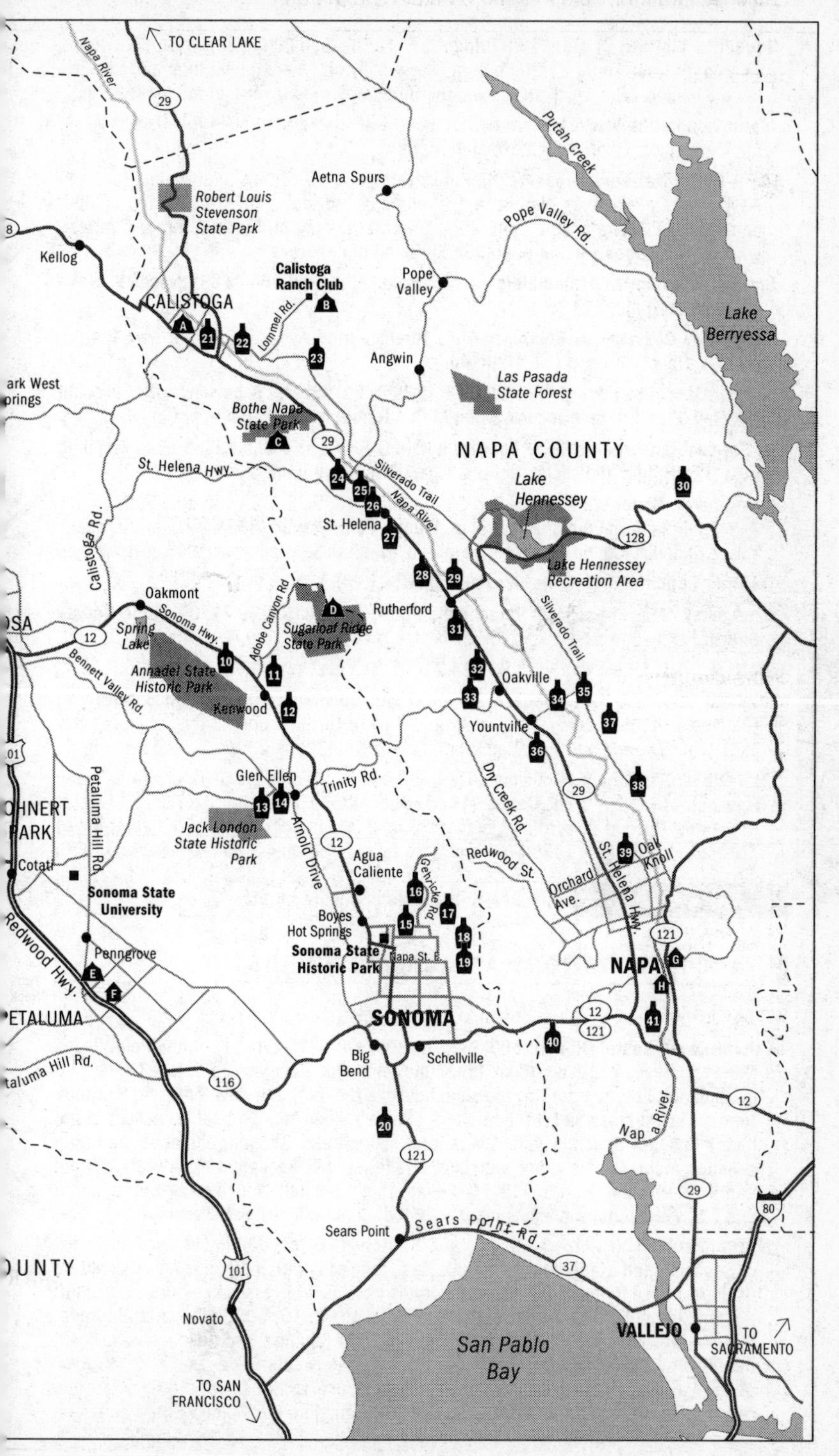
TO CLEAR LAKE
Napa River
Robert Louis Stevenson State Park
Aetna Spurs
Putah Creek
Pope Valley Rd.
Kellog
Calistoga Ranch Club
Pope Valley
CALISTOGA
Lommel Rd.
Angwin
Lake Berryessa
Las Pasada State Forest
Bothe Napa State Park
NAPA COUNTY
St. Helena Hwy.
Silverado Trail
Napa River
Lake Hennessey
St. Helena
Calistoga Rd.
Lake Hennessey Recreation Area
Oakmont
Adobe Canyon Rd
Rutherford
Sonoma Hwy.
Spring Lake
Sugarloaf Ridge State Park
Bennett Valley Rd.
Annadel State Historic Park
Oakville
Kenwood
Yountville
Petaluma Hill Rd.
Glen Ellen
Trinity Rd.
Dry Creek Rd.
Jack London State Historic Park
Arnold Drive
Agua Caliente
Redwood St.
Oak Knoll
Cotati
Gehricke Rd
Orchard Ave.
St. Helena Hwy.
Sonoma State University
Boyes Hot Springs
Redwood Hwy.
Penngrove
Sonoma State Historic Park
Napa St. E.
NAPA
SONOMA
Big Bend
Schellville
Napa River
Sears Point
Sears Point Rd.
Novato
San Pablo Bay
VALLEJO
TO SACRAMENTO
TO SAN FRANCISCO

Sausalito Visitors Center, 777 Bridgeway, 4th fl., Sausalito (332-0505; www.sausalito.org). Open Tu-Su 11:30am-4pm. Get a copy of the *real* street map of Sausalito, not the Visitors Map which shows just the Bridgeway. Also a kiosk at the ferry landing.

Marin Headlands Visitors Center (331-1540), at Bunker and Field Rd. Camping info and park maps. Open daily 9:30am-4:30pm.

Point Reyes National Seashore Headquarters (663-1092), on Bear Valley Rd. ½mi. west of Olema. Camping permits, maps, and sage advice on trails, tides, and weather conditions. Exhibits on the cultural and natural history of Point Reyes, and ranger-guided hikes. Open M-F 9am-5pm, Sa-Su 8am-5pm.

San Rafael Chamber of Commerce, 817 Mission Ave. (800-454-4163). Open M-F 9am-noon and 1-5pm.

Mill Valley Chamber of Commerce, 85 Throckmorton Ave. (388-9700; www.millvalley.org). Open M-Tu and Th-F 10am-4pm.

Library: Sausalito Library, 420 Litho St. (289-4121). Shares a building with Sausalito City Hall. **Free Internet access.** Open M-Th 11am-9pm, F-Sa 10am-5pm.

Bi-Gay-Lesbian Organization: Spectrum, 1000 Sir Francis Drake Blvd., San Anselmo (457-1115). Info and social services. Open M-Th noon-9pm.

Laundromat: Water Works, 105 2nd St., Sausalito (332-2632). Wash $1.75. Open M-F 7am-9pm, Sa 8am-9pm, Su 8am-8pm. **Village Coin-O-Matic** (388-0200), in Strawberry Village Shopping Ctr. on Miller Ave., in Mill Valley. Wash $2. Open daily 6:45am-10:45pm.

Weather Conditions: National Weather Service (650-364-7974).

Emergency: 911. **Police:** San Rafael (485-3000); Sausalito (289-4170). **Marin County Sheriff:** 479-2311.

24-Hour Crisis Lines: Rape Crisis (924-2100). **Suicide Prevention** (499-1100).

Medical Services: Marin General Hospital and Community Clinic, 250 Bon Air Rd., Greenbrae (hospital 925-7000, clinic 461-7400). Hospital open 24hr. for emergency care. Clinic open M and F 8:30am-5pm, Tu and Th 8:30am-8:30pm, W 9:30am-5pm.

Post Office: San Rafael, 40 Bellam Blvd. (459-0944), at Francisco St. Open M-F 8:30am-5pm, Sa 10am-1pm. **ZIP Code:** 94915. **Sausalito,** 150 Harbor Dr. (332-4656), at Bridgeway. Open M-Th 8:30am-5pm, F 8:30am-5:30pm. **ZIP Code:** 94965. **Point Reyes Station:** 11260 Rte. 1 (663-1305), at A St. Open M-F 8am-4:30pm. **ZIP Code:** 94956.

BAY AREA

AREA CODE	The area code for Marin County is 415.

ACCOMMODATIONS AND CAMPGROUNDS

HOSTELS

Point Reyes Hostel (HI-AYH; 663-8811 or 800-909-4776 ext. 61), in the Point Reyes National Seashore. Exit west from Rte. 1 at Olema onto Bear Valley Rd. Take the second possible left at Limantour Rd. (no sign indicates the turn) and drive 6mi. into the park. Turn left at 1st crossroad (at the bottom of a very steep hill). Two cabins occupy a site near Limantour Beach, wildlife areas, and hiking trails. Kitchen, barbecue, and cozy common room. Chores expected. Linen $1; towels $1. Reception open 7:30-9:30am and 4:30-9:30pm. Dorms $12-14. Private room available for families with children under 5. Weekend reservations recommended. Some wheelchair access.

Marin Headlands (HI-AYH; 331-2777 or 800-909-4776, ext. 62), in old Fort Barry, west of Sausalito and 10mi. from downtown San Francisco. With a car, this hostel could be used as a base for exploring the city, but it is not easily accessible by public transport: a 4½mi. uphill hike from the Golden Gate Transit (#2, 10, 50) bus stop at Alexander Ave., or 6mi. from the Sausalito ferry terminal. On Sundays and holidays only, MUNI bus #76 runs directly to the hostel. Cross the Golden Gate Bridge and take the Alexander Ave. Exit. From the north, take the 2nd Sausalito Exit (the last exit before the bridge). Take a left at the 1st road and follow signs into the Golden Gate Recreation

Area and to the Marin Headlands Visitors Center. Spacious and immaculate hostel with 109 beds, game room, kitchens, and common rooms. Linen $1; towels 50¢. Laundry $1.50. Key deposit $10. Lockout 9:30am-3:30pm. Check-in 7:30am-11:30pm. Check-out 8:45am. Dorms $12, under 17 (with parent) $6. Private doubles $35.

CAMPGROUNDS

Marin Headlands, northwest of the Golden Gate Bridge at Bunker and Field Rd. Follow directions to Headlands Hostel, (see above), and stop at the visitors center. 3 small walk-in (100 yards to 3mi.) campgrounds with a total of 11 primitive campsites. Picnic tables and chemical toilets; bring your own water and camp stove. Free, but a permit is required. 3-day max. stay. Showers and kitchen ($2 each) at Headlands Hostel. Free outdoor cold showers at Rodeo Beach. Reserve up to 90 days in advance by calling the visitors center (331-1540; open daily 9:30am-4:30pm).

Kirby Cove, off Conzelman Rd. west of the Golden Gate Bridge, is in the Marin Headlands but not administered by the visitors center. 4 campsites in a grove of cypress and eucalyptus trees on the shores of the bay. Accessible by car and includes fire rings and pit toilets. For reservations call the Special Park Users Group at 561-4304.

Mount Tamalpais State Park, 801 Rte. 1 (388-2070), offers a number of campground facilities. **Steep Ravine,** 1mi. south of Stinson Beach. Cabins have small wood stoves and tent sites have firepits. Nearby water faucets and pit toilets. No showers or electricity. Rustic cabins for up to 5 people $30. Primitive campsites Su-Th $10, F-Sa $11. Reservations recommended; make them up to 7 months in advance by calling PARKNET (800-444-7275). **Pantoll Campground,** on Panoramic Hwy., has 16 sites near the parking lot with access to firewood, running water, and flush toilets. Sites Su-Th $18, F-Sa $20. Hiker/biker sites $3. First-come, first-camped. Bus #63 stops here between Stinson Beach and the Golden Gate Bridge on weekends and holidays.

Point Reyes National Seashore has walk-in camping only. 2 camps are coastal and 2 are inland; all have exquisite views of the ocean and surrounding hills. Charcoal grills, running water, and pit toilets. No wood fires. Sites $10. 4-night max. stay. Reservations strongly recommended; call 663-8054 (M-F 9am-2pm). Pick up permits at Bear Valley Visitors Center (see **Practical Information,** 159).

Samuel P. Taylor State Park, P.O. Box 251, Lagunitas (488-9897), on Sir Francis Drake Blvd. 15mi. west of San Rafael. Family campground in a lush setting beneath stately, second-growth redwoods. Often crowded on weekends; sites are cool and shady, if not always quiet. Running water, flush toilets, and hot showers (50¢ for 5min.). 7-night max. stay. Sites Su-Th $15, F-Sa $16. Hiker/biker sites $3 per person (no reservations, 2-night max. stay). Pets $1. Call PARKNET for reservations (800-444-7275).

FOOD

Marinites take their fruit juices, tofu, and nonfat double-shot cappuccinos very seriously; restauranteurs know this, and raise both alfalfa sprouts and prices. A number of cafes and pizzerias along 4th St. in San Rafael, and Miller Ave. on the way into Mill Valley, provide welcome inexpensive options.

The Real Food Company, 200 Caledonia St., Sausalito (332-9640), offers organically grown produce, seafood-flavored rice cakes, and the latest issue of *Experiential Shaman* magazine. The groceries are less enlightened, and less expensive, at the **Safeway** (383-1101), on Miller Rd. in the Strawberry Village Shopping Ctr. in Mill Valley. Point Reyes Station's **Palace Market** (663-1016), on Shoreline Hwy. at 3rd St., offers the widest supermarket selection in western Marin (open M-Sa 8am-8pm, Su 8am-7pm). San Rafael's **farmer's markets** take place in the **Marin Civic Center,** off U.S. 101 (Th and Su 8am-1pm), and **downtown** on 4th St. (Th 6-9pm).

SAUSALITO

Sartaj Indian Cafe, 43 Caledonia St. (332-7103), 1 block from Bridgeway. Generous portions of excellent Indian food at low prices (curries $8, stew and samosa $5, sandwiches $3.75) are even lower on W nights, when Sartaj features live music–sometimes authentically Indian, sometimes Sinatra standards on a portable organ. Hot chai can help you deal with the culture shock ($1.25). Open daily 6:30am-9:30pm.

Arawan, 47 Caledonia St. (332-0882). Phenomenal Thai food is locally applauded. Specializes in seafood, but more affordable dishes like the *gang dang* (red curry) chicken ($8) are winners too. Eat-in or takeout. Open daily noon-midnight.

MILL VALLEY

Mama's Royal Cafe, 387 Miller Ave. (388-3261). Slackers serve up unusual but good dishes from a menu as packed as the restaurant. The whole place is decorated in lawn ornaments and psychedelic murals. Enchilada El Syd $6.50; Groove Burger $6. Brunch with live music Sa-Su 11am-2pm. Open M-F 7:30am-2:30pm, Sa-Su 8am-3pm.

Book Depot and Cafe, 87 Throckmorton Ave. (383-2665). An old train station in the center of town is now home to this lively bookstore/newsstand/cafe. Open daily 7am-9pm.

Cactus Cafe and Taquería, 393 Miller Ave. (388-8226), behind Mama's. Cool retreat with green leather booths. Many veggie options amidst a cornucopia of burritos ($4-6) and hefty wraps ($6-7). Local brews (650mL $6.25). Open daily 11:30am-9:30pm.

SAN RAFAEL

Mayflower Inne, 1553 4th St. (456-1011). British pub serves better-than-classic British grub. Fish and chips, bangers and mash, and not a vegetable in sight–unless you count mushy peas. Best deal: cup of soup and half-sandwich for $4.25. "Bawdy Piano Singalong" F 8pm. Open daily 11:30am-2am; kitchen closes at 9pm.

My Thai Restaurant, 1230 4th St. (456-4455). Top-notch Thai eatery on San Rafael's main drag. Tasty basil prawns $8; Thai iced tea or coffee $1.50; veggie dishes $6-7. Credit card min. $15. Open Su-Th 11:30am-9:30pm, F-Sa 11:30am-10pm.

BOLINAS

Bolinas Bay Bakery and Cafe, 20 Wharf Rd. (868-0211). This place is all about big cookies, chewy brownies, and prize-winning cheesecake. Park yourself on the sun-bleached porch and watch 3 generations of hippies truck on by. Open M-F 7am-7pm, Sa-Su 8am-8pm.

POINT REYES STATION

Cafe Reyes (663-9493), on Mesa St. Decorated like something out of a Sergio Leone spaghetti Western, serving burgers ($7), Mexican food, quality coffee ($1.50), beer, and wine. Open daily 10:30am-9pm. No credit cards.

OLEMA

Olema Liquor and Deli, 10003 Shoreline Hwy. (663-8615), at Sir Francis Drake Blvd. Olema's only budget option sells sandwiches ($3-5), liquor, rolling tobacco, some fishing tackle, and Häagen-Daas ice cream. Open M-F 8am-10pm, Sa-Su 7am-10pm.

SIGHTS

Marin's proximity to San Francisco makes it a popular daytrip destination. Virtually everything worth seeing or doing in Marin is outdoors. An efficient visitor can hop from park to park and enjoy several short hikes along the coast and through the redwood forests in the same day, topping it off with a pleasant dinner in one of the small cities. Those without cars, however, may find it easier to use one of the two well-situated hostels as a base for hiking or biking explorations.

SAUSALITO

Originally a fishing center full of bars and bordellos, the city at Marin's extreme southeastern tip has long since traded its sea-dog days for retail boutiques and overpriced seafood restaurants. **Bridgeway** is the city's main thoroughfare, and practically the only one shown on Sausalito Visitors Center maps. A block away from the harbor and Bridgeway's smug shops, **Caledonia Street** offers more charming restaurants and a few more affordable stores. Perhaps the best thing to see in Sausalito is the view of San Francisco. For the best views of the city, take the ferry (see **Ferries,** p. 159) or bike across the Golden Gate Bridge.

Half a mile north of the town center is the **Bay Model** (332-3871), a massive working model of San Francisco Bay. Built in the 1950s to test proposals to dam the bay and other diabolical plans, the water-filled model recreates tides and currents in great detail. (2100 Bridgeway. Turn off Bridgeway at Marinship. Open in summer Tu-F 9am-4pm, Sa 10am-6pm; off-season Tu-F 9am-4pm. Free.)

MARIN HEADLANDS

Fog-shrouded hills just to the west of the Golden Gate Bridge constitute the Marin Headlands. Its windswept ridges, precipitous cliffs, and hidden sandy beaches offer superb hiking and biking within minutes of downtown San Francisco. For instant gratification, choose one of the coastal trails, which offer easy access to dark sand beaches and dramatic cliffs of basalt greenstone. One of the best short hikes is to the lighthouse at **Point Bonita,** a prime spot for seeing sunbathing California sea lions in summer and migrating gray whales in the cooler months. The cute little lighthouse at the end of the point really doesn't seem up to the job of guarding the whole San Francisco Bay, but has done so valiantly since 1855; in fact, its original glass lens is still in operation. At the end of a narrow, knife-like ridge lined with purple wildflowers, the lighthouse is reached by a short tunnel through the rock and a miniature suspension bridge (open Sa-Su 12:30-3:30pm). Even when the lighthouse is closed, the short walk (1mi. from the visitors center, ½mi. from the nearest parking) provides gorgeous views on sunny days. The one-mile walk from the visitors center down to sheltered **Rodeo Beach,** a favorite of cormorants and pelicans, is also easy and pleasant.

For more ambitious hiking or biking, a good map is a must. Pick one up at the **visitors center** at Bunker and Field Rd. (see p. 162; free-$1.50). The **Wolf Ridge** and **Tennessee Valley** trails are perennial favorites; ask rangers for other suggestions and camping info. Bring a jacket for the sudden descent of rain, wind, or fog.

Formerly a military installation charged with defending the San Francisco harbor, the Headlands are dotted with abandoned machine gun nests, missile sites, and soldiers' quarters dating from the Spanish-American War in 1898 to the 1950s. **Battery Spencer,** on Conzelman Rd. immediately west of U.S. 101, offers one of the best vistas of the city skyline and the Golden Gate Bridge, especially around sunset on the (rare) clear day. Farther into the park is a **former Nike Missile Site** on Field Rd. (open 1st Su of each month 12:30-3:30pm, and many weekday afternoons; call 331-1540 to verify hours.).

The **Marine Mammal Center** (289-7325), at Rodeo Beach, is a nonprofit organization dedicated to saving injured, sick, or orphaned marine mammals (open daily 10am-4pm; donation requested). Also based at Rodeo Beach, the **Golden Gate Raptor Observatory** studies the annual migration of thousand of hawks across the Marin Headlands every fall (call 331-0730 to participate in a hawk watching group).

MILL VALLEY

The logging of Marin County was masterminded in Mill Valley, but this town of millionaires and mountain bikers (and millionaire mountain bikers) is now every bit as environmentally conscious as the rest of the county. An inland twin of Sausalito, Mill Valley is pretty and pricey. VW buses park beside Porsches in driveways lined by 100-foot-high redwoods.

Mill Valley's central location—five miles from Muir Woods, a two-mile hike from the eastern peak of Mount Tam—makes it a logical provisioning center for wilderness expeditions in Marin. Some funky little eateries and shops also reward a brief stroll. Record collectors and bargain-hunters from all over trek to **Village Music,** 9 E. Blithedale Ave. (388-7400), close to Mill Valley's downtown square, a vinyl mecca whose customers have included B.B. King and Mick Jagger (albums 25¢-$250; open M-Sa 10am-6pm, Su noon-5pm).

MOUNT TAMALPAIS AND MUIR WOODS

Between the upscale towns of East Marin and the rocky bluffs of West Marin rests beautiful **Mount Tamalpais State Park** (tam-ull-PIE-us). The park has miles of hilly, challenging trails on and around 2571-foot Mount Tamalpais, the highest peak in the county, and the original "mountain" in "mountain bike." The bubbling waterfall on **Cataract Trail** and the **Gardner Lookout** on Mount Tam's east peak are worthy destinations. Visit the **Pan Toll Ranger's Station** (388-2070), on Panoramic Hwy., for trail suggestions and biking restrictions. Although this is the home of the mountain bike, cyclists that go off designated trails and fire roads risk incurring the wrath of eco-happy Marin hikers (free; day parking $5). On weekends and holidays, bus #63 stops at the ranger station between the Golden Gate Bridge and Stinson Beach.

At the center of the state park is **Muir Woods National Monument,** a 560-acre stand of old coastal redwoods five miles west of U.S. 101 on Rte. 1. Spared from logging by the steep sides of Redwood Canyon, these centuries-old redwoods are massive and shrouded in silence. The level trails along the canyon floor are paved and lined with wooden fences, but a hike up the canyon's sides will soon take you away from the tourists and face-to-face with the wildlife that is scarce on the forest floor. Rangers at the visitors center (388-2595), near the entrance, charge $3 admission. Avoid this charge by hiking in two miles from the Pan Toll Ranger Station—this is the best way to reach Muir Woods by public transport. (Monument open 8am-dusk; visitors center open 9am-6pm.)

THE MARIN COAST

Rte. 1 reaches the Pacific at Muir Beach, and from there twists its way up the rugged coast. It's all beautiful, but the stretch between Muir and Stinson Beaches is the most breathtaking, especially when driving south, on the sheer-drop-to-the-ocean side of the highway. There should be a law about allowing such jaw-dropping scenery along such treacherous roads. If you're riding a bike, don't expect the white-knuckled drivers of passing cars to allow you much elbow room.

Sheltered **Muir Beach** (open dawn-9pm) is scenic and popular with families. The crowds thin out significantly after a five-minute climb on the shore rocks to the left. Six miles to the north, **Stinson Beach** (open dawn-dusk) attracts a younger, rowdier, good-looking surfer crowd, although cold and windy conditions often keep them posing on dry land. Between the two beaches lies the **nudist Red Rocks Beach,** a secluded spot reached by a steep hike down from a parking area one mile south of Stinson Beach. Tan lines be gone! Bus #63 runs from Sausalito to Stinson Beach on weekends and holidays.

Just inland from Muir Beach is the **Green Gulch Farm and Zen Center,** 1601 Shoreline Hwy. (383-3134), an organic farm and Buddhist retreat. Visitors are free to explore the tranquil grounds and gardens, and on Sunday mornings the public is welcome at a meditation lesson (starting at 8:15am) and informal lecture on Zen Buddhism (10am). Would-be Zen masters are asked to wear dark, loose-fitting clothing for *zazen* meditation. If your hostel just isn't enlightened enough, Green Gulch's guest student program allows serious students of Zen to stay at the center for $15 per night. Students are expected to work in the vegetable gardens and to take part in *zazen* and *sutra* chanting throughout the day.

A few miles north of Stinson Beach is the unmarked turn-off for the village of **Bolinas,** a tiny colony of hippies, artists, and writers. Eccentric Bolinans have included authors Richard Brautigan *(Trout Fishing in America)* and Jim Carroll

(The Basketball Diaries). For years, locals hoping to discourage tourist traffic have torn down any and all signs marking the Bolinas-Olema road. Press coverage of the "sign war" won the people of Bolinas exactly the publicity they wanted to avoid, but for now at least the town remains authentic in every way that Sausalito is not. (Who needs signs anyway? Driving north from Stinson Beach, the Bolinas-Olema road is the first left after coming around the lagoon; turn there and follow the road to the end. So there.)

POINT REYES

A near-island surrounded by nearly 100 miles of isolated coastline, the **Point Reyes National Seashore** is a wilderness of pine forests, chaparral ridges, and grassy flatlands. Five million years ago, this outcropping was a suburb of Los Angeles, but it hitched a ride on the submerged Pacific Plate and has been creeping northward along the San Andreas Fault ever since. In summer, colorful wildflowers attract crowds of gawking tourists, but with hundreds of miles of amazing trails it's quite possible to gawk alone. Rte. 1 provides direct access to the park from the north or south; Sir Francis Drake Blvd. comes west from U.S. 101 at San Rafael.

The park headquarters are at the **Point Reyes National Seashore Headquarters** (see p. 162), just west of Olema. There, rangers distribute camping permits and can suggest trails, drives, beaches, and picnic areas. The **Earthquake Trail** is a ¾-mile walk along the infamous San Andreas Fault Line that starts right at Bear Valley. Lovely **Limantour Beach** sits at the end of Limantour Rd., eight miles west of the visitors center, which runs a free shuttle bus to the beach in summer. The **Point Reyes Hostel** is at the bottom of a steep valley two miles from the end of Limantour Rd. The dramatic landscape around the hostel is still scarred by a major forest fire in 1995. Both Limantour and Point Reyes Beaches boast high, grassy dunes and long stretches of sand, but strong ocean currents along the point make swimming very dangerous. Swimming is safest at **Hearts Desire Beach,** north of the visitors center on sheltered **Tomales Bay.** To reach the dramatic **Point Reyes Lighthouse** at the very tip of the point, follow Sir Francis Drake Blvd. to its end (20mi. from the visitors center) and head right along the stairway to Sea Lion Overlook. From December until February, migrating gray whales can be spotted from the overlook. Be prepared for heavy fog and strong winds on the point at any time of year.

SAN RAFAEL

San Rafael is the largest city in Marin County, but holds little to interest the budget traveler. If you do stop here on your way to or from northern California, the main strip for eating and shopping lies along **4th Street.**

Architecture buffs can check out Frank Lloyd Wright's **Marin Civic Center,** 3501 Civic Center Dr. (499-7407), off U.S. 101. The city fathers didn't go for Wright's plan to incorporate a Ferris wheel and huge circus tents, but it's still a striking and unusual structure. An information kiosk in the lobby supplies brochures and pamphlets; call ahead for a tour. (Open M-F 7:30am-6pm.)

If you have a car, you might picnic at **China Camp State Park,** an expanse of grassy meadows east of the city. It's named for the ramshackle remains of a Chinese fishing village that once housed thousands of laborers who were forced from the city. (Open daily 8am-8pm; visitors center open daily 10am-5pm; parking $3.) Six miles north of San Rafael is an exit for Lucas Valley Rd., where George Lucas toils away at **Skywalker Ranch,** editing the next two installments of the Star Wars saga. Jar Jar Binks is said to roam the woods like Sasquatch. There's no point in stopping for a sneak preview, or asking George to autograph your **Wookie**—Lucas's home and studios are fiercely guarded by Imperial troops.

NIGHTLIFE

If you really wanted to party, you'd head back to the city, but Marin County does offer a number of low-key live music venues and easygoing watering holes. San Rafael probably has the most action, with many more bars than are listed here.

Sweetwater, 153 Throckmorton Ave., **Mill Valley** (388-2820), downtown. Gorgeous, high-ceilinged bar with live music every night; occasional big name like Elvis Costello. Local boy Huey Lewis sometimes stops by to blow his harmonica. Cover $5-15 plus 2-drink min. during shows. No cover on Open Mic Monday. Open daily 12:30pm-1am.

New George's, 842 4th St., **San Rafael** (457-8424, show info 457-1515), under a movie-style marquee at Cijos St. Frequent winner of the "best live music and nightlife in Marin" award. Cafe becomes jumping club by night. Live music most nights 9pm; Cover $5-15. Tu Swing Dance, Su Latin Dance. Open M-Sa 3pm-1am.

Classic Billiards, 1300 4th St., **San Rafael** (455-8511). Offers great student rates (half-price Su-Th until 10pm, F-Sa until 7pm) and other specials. Maybe too slick for its own good, but jukebox keeps it rockin' until the wee hours. $5 per person per hr. Open Su-Th noon-2am, F-Sa noon-4am.

Smitty's Bar, 214 Caledonia St., **Sausalito** (332-2637), has resisted upward mobility to remain a rough-around-the-edges favorite of Sausalito's "boat people." Glasses of Chardonnay ($3) are Smitty's only grudging concession to yuppification. Shuffleboard, pool, and a wall of bowling trophies to admire. Domestic pints $2.50, schooners $3.50, pitchers $6.50. Open daily 10am-2am.

No Name Bar, 757 Bridgeway, **Sausalito** (332-1392). Once a haunt of the Beats, the bar with no name now serves a mixed crowd of tourists and locals. Live blues or jazz music most nights—the biggest draw is Dixieland Jazz every Su afternoon. Rudimentary sandwich menu 11am-4pm; after that, it's just popcorn. Open 10am-2am.

Old Western Saloon, 11201 Shoreline Hwy., **Point Reyes Station** (663-1661). Just what it sounds like. Casual atmosphere for pool tournaments and occasional live music (call for schedule). DJs spin most F-Sa nights, country on Th. Open daily 10am-2am.

NAPA VALLEY

While not the oldest, the Napa Valley is certainly the best-known of America's wine-growing regions. The gentle hills, fertile soil, ample moisture, and year-round sunshine are ideal for viticulture. European vines were first planted here as early as the late 1850s, but early producers were crippled by Prohibition (a 1920s ban on alcohol production or consumption), when grapes were supplanted by figs. The region did not begin to reestablish itself until the 1960s. In the 1970s Napa's rapidly improving offerings won the attention of those in the know, and word of mouth cemented the California bottle as a respectable choice. In 1976, a bottle of red from Napa's Stag's Leap Vineyard (see p. 171) beat a bottle of Château Lafitte-Rothschild in a blind taste test in Paris, and suddenly American wine had made its mark. Napa vineyards continue to make their mark, and the everyday tasting carnival dominates life in the valley's small towns.

ORIENTATION

Route 29 (Saint Helena Highway) runs through the Napa Valley from **Napa** through **Yountville** and **Saint Helena,** to **Calistoga.** Choked with visitors stopping at each winery, the relatively short distance takes a surprisingly long, if scenic, time. The **Silverado Trail,** parallel to Rte. 29, is a less-crowded route, but watch out for stylish cyclists. Napa is 14 miles east of Sonoma on **Route 12.** If you're planning a weekend trip from San Francisco, avoid Saturday mornings and Sunday afternoons; the roads are packed with like-minded people. Although harvest, in early September, is the most exciting time to visit, winter weekdays provide the space for personal attention. From the city, take U.S. 101 over the Golden Gate Bridge, then Rte. 37 East to Rte. 121 North, which will cross Rte. 29 to Napa.

Napa's gentle terrain makes for an excellent **bike** tour. Although the area is fairly flat, small bike lanes, speeding cars, and blistering heat can make routes more challenging, especially after several samples of wine. The 26-mile Silverado Trail has a wider bike path than Rte. 29. **Yountville** and **Saint Helena,** which lie between the busy city of Napa and the soothing spas of **Calistoga,** each host several small restaurants and shops.

PRACTICAL INFORMATION

Buses: The nearest Greyhound station is in Vallejo (800-231-2222), but a bus passes through the valley (daily 3:30pm). Stops in Napa (5:20pm, Napa State Hospital, 2100 Napa-Vallejo Hwy.), Yountville, St. Helena, and Calistoga.

Public Transportation: Napa City Bus, or **Valley Intercity Neighborhood Express (VINE),** 1151 Pearl St. (800-696-6443 or 255-7631; TDD 226-9722), covers the valley and Vallejo. To **Vallejo** (fare $1.50, students $1.45, disabled 75¢) and **Calistoga** (fare $2.50, students $1.80, disabled $1; free transfers). Buses run M-F 6am-8pm, Sa 7:30am-5:30pm.

Winery Tours: Napa Valley Holidays (255-1050; 3hr., $30).

Car Rental: Budget, 407 Soscol Ave., Napa (224-7846). Cars $43 per day; under 25 surcharge $20 per day. Unlimited mileage. Must be at least 21 with credit card.

Bike Rental: St. Helena Cyclery, 1156 Main St., St. Helena (963-7736). Bikes $7 per hr., $25 per day; including maps, helmet, lock, and picnic bag. Open M-Sa 9:30am-5:30pm, Su 10am-5pm.

Visitor Information: Napa Visitors Center, 1310 Town Ctr. (226-7459; www.napavalley.com/nvcvb.html). The *Napa Valley Guide* ($6) has comprehensive listings and fold-out maps. Open daily 9am-5pm, phones closed Sa-Su. **St. Helena Chamber of Commerce,** 1010A Main St. (963-4456). Open M-F 10am-4:30pm. **Calistoga Chamber of Commerce,** 1458 Lincoln Ave. (942-6333; www.calistogafun.com). Open M-Tu, Th, and Sa 10am-4pm.

Emergency: 911. **Police:** 1539 1st St., Napa (253-4451).

Crisis Lines: Emergency Women's Service (255-6397), 24hr. **Sexual Assault Crisis Line** (258-8000), 24hr. **Disabled Crisis** (800-426-4263).

Hospital: Queen of the Valley, 1000 Trancas St., Napa (252-4411).

Post Office: 1627 Trancas St., Napa (255-1268). Open M-F 8:30am-5pm. **ZIP Code:** 94558.

AREA CODE	The area code for Napa Valley is 707.

ACCOMMODATIONS AND CAMPGROUNDS

Rooms in Napa are scarce and go fast despite high prices (B&Bs and most hotels are a budget-breaking $60-225 per night). Budget options are more plentiful in Santa Rosa (see p. 176) and Petaluma (see p. 173), within easy driving distance of the valley. For those without cars, camping is the best option, although the heat is intense in summer.

Calistoga Ranch Club, 580 Lommel Rd., south of **Calistoga** (800-847-6272), off the Silverado Trail 4mi. Campground caters to families. Hiking trails lace 167 wooded acres, which include a fishing lake, volleyball, and pool. Sites $19; with full hookup $27; 4-person cabins with shared bath $49; 5-person trailers with kitchen $89.

Discovery Inn, 500 Silverado Trail, **Napa** (253-0892), near Soscol Ave. Rooms have kitchenettes, cable TV, and a tad more personality than a chain motel. Rooms $65, weekends $95. Check-in noon-6pm.

BAY AREA

Bothe-Napa Valley State Park, 3801 Rte. 29, north of **St. Helena** (942-4575; reservations PARKNET 800-444-7275). 49 sites often fill up. No hookups. Pool $3, under 18 $2. Hot showers, otherwise fairly rustic. Check-in 2pm. Sites Su-Th $15, F-Sa $20, seniors $14; vehicles $5. Park open 8am-dusk.

Napa County Fairgrounds, 1435 Oak St., **Calistoga** (942-5111). First-come, first-camped. Dry grass in a parking lot with showers and electricity. Sites $10, RVs $18. Check-out noon.

FOOD

Eating in Wine Country ain't cheap, but the food is usually worth it. Picnics are an inexpensive and romantic option—supplies can be bought at the numerous delis or Safeway stores in the area. Most wineries have shaded picnic grounds, often with excellent views. The **Napa farmer's market** (252-7142), at Pearl and West St., offers a sampling of the valley's *other* produce (open daily 7:30am-noon).

Curb Side Cafe, 1245 1st St., **Napa** (253-2307), at Randolph St. Sublime sandwiches $5-6.50. This diner-like cafe's heavy breakfasts include the pancake special: 4 buttermilk pancakes, 2 eggs, and ham or sausage ($6). Open daily 9am-3pm.

Calistoga Natural Foods and Juice Bar, 1426 Lincoln St., **Calistoga** (942-5822). One of few natural foods stores in the area. Organic juice and sandwich bar, with vegetarian specialties like the Garlic Goddess ($4.50) or Tofu Supreme ($5). Open M-Sa 9am-6pm, Su 10am-5pm.

Ana's Cantina, 1205 Main St., **St. Helena** (963-4921). A small glimmer of nightlife on the otherwise quiet St. Helena front with nightly music or karaoke, great Mexican food served 11am-3pm, and pool tables. Combo platters $7. No cover. Open daily 10am-2am. 21+.

BAY AREA

Taylor's Refresher, 933 Main St., **St. Helena** (963-3486), on Rte. 29 across from the Merryvale Winery. A roadside burger stand with vegetarian and beef burgers ($2.75) and ice cream. Outdoor picnic area. Open Su-Th 11am-7pm, F-Sa 11am-8pm.

Soo Yuan, 1354 Lincoln Ave., **Calistoga** (942-9404). Locals love the inexpensive Chinese food, with most dishes $7-8. Open daily 11:30am-10pm.

Red Hen Cantina, 5091 St. Helena Hwy., **Napa** (255-8125). Cool patio attracts winery employees and locals in the evening for $16 pitchers of margaritas. Huge crab and shrimp tacos ($9.50-10.25). Open Su-Th 11am-9:30pm, F-Sa 11am-10pm.

Surfwood, 1410 Lincoln Ave., **Calistoga** (942-4700). Touted as "Calistoga's Liveliest Nite Spot," this beach-bum bar hosts live music Th-Sa. Open daily 11am-2am.

DRINKING

There are more than 250 wineries in Napa County, nearly two-thirds of which line Rte. 29 and the Silverado Trail in the Napa Valley. Wine country's heavyweights call this valley home; vineyards include national names such as Inglenook, Fetzer, and Mondavi. Few wineries in Napa have free tastings, so choose your samples carefully. The wineries listed below (from south to north) are among the valley's larger and more touristy operations. Visitors must be 21 or older to purchase or drink alcohol (yes, they do card).

OUTSIDE NAPA

Hakusan Sake Gardens, 1 Executive Way (258-6160 or 800-425-8726). Take Rte. 12 off Rte. 29, turn left on N. Kelly, then left onto Executive Way. Japanese gardens are a welcome change from the other wineries. *Sake* is a strong Japanese wine with a fruity taste (served warm or cold). Open daily 10am-5pm.

Domaine Carneros, 1240 Duhig Rd. (257-0101), off Rte. 121 between Napa and Sonoma. Picturesque estate with elegant terrace modeled after a French chateau. No

VIN FRIENDS AND INFLUENCE PEOPLE

While European wines are often known by their region of origin, California wines are generally known by the type of grape they're made from. California white wines include Chardonnay, Riesling, and Sauvignon Blanc; reds are Pinot Noir, Merlot, Cabernet Sauvignon, and Zinfandel, which is indigenous to California. Blush or rosé wines issue from red grapes which have had their skins removed during fermentation—to leave just a kiss of pink. Dessert wines, such as Muscat, are made with grapes that have acquired the "noble rot" *(botrytis)* at the end of picking season, giving them an extra-sweet flavor.

When tasting, be sure to follow proper procedures. Always start with a white, moving from **dry** to **sweet** (dry wines have had a higher percentage of their sugar content fermented into alcohol). Proceed through the reds, which go from **lighter** to **fuller bodied,** depending on tannin content. **Tannin** is the pigment red wine gets from the grape skin—it preserves and ages the wine, which is why reds can be young and sharp, but grow more mellow with age. It's best to end with dessert wines. Wineries will generally arrange wines on their tasting list for you. Ideally, one should cleanse one's palate between wines with a biscuit, some *fromage,* or fruit. Don't hesitate to ask for advice from the tasting-room pourer.

Tasting proceeds thus: stare, sniff, swirl, swallow (first three steps are optional). You will probably encounter fellow tasters who slurp their wine and make concerned faces, as though they're trying to cram the stuff up their noses with the back of their tongues. These are serious tasters, and are aerating the wine in their mouths to better bring out the flavor. Key words to help you seem more astute during tasting sessions are: dry, sweet, buttery, light, crisp, fruity, balanced, rounded, subtle, rich, woody, and complex. Feel free to banter these terms about indiscriminately. *Sally forth, young naïfs!*

tastings but wines by the glass $5-12 with complimentary hors d'oeuvres. Free tour and film every hr. 11am-4pm. Open daily 10:30am-6pm.

YOUNTVILLE AND NEARBY

Domaine Chandon, 1 California Dr. (944-2280). Owned by Moët Chandon of France (the makers of Dom Perignon), this winery produces 5 million bottles of sparkling wine annually—that's one hell of a New Year's party. Tours (every hr. 11am-5pm) and tastings ($8 for 3 wines, $12 for all 5). Open May-Oct. daily 10am-6pm; Nov.-Apr. W-Su 10am-6pm.

Goosecross Cellars, 1119 State Ln. (944-1986), off Yountville Cross Rd. north of Yountville. Small and friendly winery is still in its natural state, nestled among the vineyards. The winemaker is always on site; the tasting room is directly inside the production room. Free wine basics class (Sa 11am). Tastings daily 10am-5pm ($4).

Clos Du Val Wine Company, Ltd., 5330 Silverado Trail (259-2200). Take Oak Knoll Rd. to Silverado Trail. Small and stylish grounds attract lots of tourists. Tastings $5. Tours by appt. only. Open daily 10am-5pm.

Stag's Leap Wine Cellars, 5766 Silverado Trail (944-2020). The tiny vineyard that beat Europe's best. Landscaped terraces and superb tasting ($5 and you even get to keep the glass). Complimentary beverage for designated driver. Open daily 10am-4:30pm. Call a week in advance to arrange a 1hr. tour that includes a free tasting.

OAKVILLE

Robert Mondavi Winery, 7801 Rte. 29 (963-9611 or 800-MONDAVI/666-3284), 8mi. north of Napa. Originally a viticulture education center, this triangular winery offers some of the best tours in the valley, covering subjects from tasting to soil conditions. Wine by the glass from $3. Open daily May-Oct. 10am-4pm; Nov.-Apr. 9:30am-4:30pm.

Robert Mondavi La Famiglia, 1595 Oakville Grade (944-2811), off Rte. 29. Gorgeous views of the valley and picnic tables available for wine-purchasers. Tastings free with tour (call to reserve). Open daily 10am-4pm.

ST. HELENA AND CALISTOGA

Beringer Vineyards, 2000 Main St., St. Helena (963-4812 or 963-7115), off Rte. 29. Huge estate mobbed with tourists. Free historic presentations every 30min. include tasting. To taste Beringer's better wines, try the reserve room on the 2nd fl. of the Rhine House mansion (samples $2-6). Open daily 9:30am-4pm.

Sterling Vineyards, 1111 Dunaweal Ln., Calistoga (942-3344), 7mi. north of St. Helena. Aerial tram to a superb view and an unusually informative self-guided tour. Terrace sells bread, cheese, and wine by the glass. Open daily 10:30am-4:30pm. Admission $6, under 18 $3 (covers tram, 3 tastes, and $2 off 1st purchase).

NOT DRINKING

CALISTOGA. Calistoga is also known as the "Hot Springs of the West." Sam Brannan, who first developed the area, meant to make the hot springs the "Saratoga of California," but he misspoke and promised instead to make them "The Calistoga of Saratina." Luckily, history has a soft spot for millionaires; Brannan's dream has come true, and Calistoga is now a center for luxurious spas and resorts. His former cottage is now home to the **Sharpsteen Museum,** 1311 Washington St. (942-5911), which traces the town's development through exhibits designed by a Disney animator (open daily 10am-4pm, in winter noon-4pm; free).

After a hard day of wine-tasting, the rich and relaxed converge on Calistoga to luxuriate in mud baths, massages, and mineral showers. Standard treatment is a 30-minute massage with an additional mud treatment and mineral wrap. Prices are as hot as the mineral water, hitting $80 in many spas. Massage your wallet by sticking to **Nance's Hot Springs** (942-6211; 30min. massage $25) or **Golden Haven** (942-6793), which specializes in private couple baths (30min. massage $42). Cooler water is at **Lake Berryessa** (966-2111), 20 miles north of Napa off Rte. 128, where swimming, sailing, and sunbathing are popular along its 169 miles of shoreline.

OLD FAITHFUL GEYSER OF CALIFORNIA. This steamy wonder should not be confused with its more famous namesake in Wyoming, although it performs similarly. The geyser regularly spews a jet of boiling water 60 feet into the air; although it "erupts" on average every 40 minutes, weather conditions affect the cycle. The ticket vendor will tell you the estimated time of the next spurt. *(942-6463. On Tubbs Ln. off Rte. 128., 2mi. outside Calistoga. Open daily 9am-6pm; in winter 9am-5pm. Admission $6, seniors $5, disabled free, ages 6-12 $2. Bathrooms not wheelchair accessible.)*

MARINE WORLD AFRICA/USA. The 160-acre Vallejo park is an enormous zoo-oceanarium-theme park. It has animal shows and special attractions like the Lorikeet Aviary, the Butterfly Walk, and Shark Experience, which provide patron-fish interaction. *(643-6722. Off Rte. 37, 10mi. south of Napa. Vallejo is accessible from San Francisco by BART (510-465-2278), and the Blue and Gold fleet (415-705-5444). Open Mar.-Aug. daily 10am-10pm; Sept.-Oct. F-Su 10am-6pm. Admission $34, seniors $25, ages 4-12 or under 48in. $17. Parking $6. Wheelchair accessible.)*

ST. HELENA. Robert Louis Stevenson State Park (942-4575), on Rte. 29 four miles north of St. Helena, has a plaque where the Scottish writer, sick and penniless, spent a rejuvenating honeymoon in 1880. The hike up **Mount St. Helena** (open daily 8am-dusk) is a moderate three-hour climb culminating in dizzying views of the valley (no ranger station; bring water). The **Silverado Museum,** 1490 Library Ln., St. Helena, off Adams, is a labor of love by a devoted collector of Stevensoniana. Manuscript notes from *Dr. Jekyll and Mr. Hyde* are on display. *(963-3757. Open Tu-Su noon-4pm. Free.)*

SEASONAL EVENTS. The annual **Napa Valley Wine Festival** takes place in November. Every weekend in February and March the **Mustard Festival** puts together a different musical or theatrical presentation. **Napa Valley Fairgrounds** (942-5111) hosts a weekend fair in August, with wine-tasting, music, juggling, rides, and a rodeo. In summer, there are free afternoon concerts at **Music-in-the-Park,** downtown at the riverfront. Contact **Napa Parks and Recreation Office** (257-9529) for more info.

SONOMA VALLEY

The sprawling Sonoma Valley is a quieter alternative to Napa. Wineries are approachable by winding side roads rather than down a freeway strip, creating a more intimate yet more adventurous feel. Pretty Sonoma Plaza is surrounded by art galleries, novelty shops, vintage clothing stores, and Italian restaurants. Petaluma, which is west of the Sonoma Valley, has a better variety of budget lodgings than the expensive wine country. Distinguished by its odd mix of architecture, the town features nearly every 20th-century genre.

GETTING THERE AND AROUND

From San Francisco, take U.S. 101 over the Golden Gate Bridge, then Rte. 37 East to Rte. 121 North, which crosses Rte. 12 North to Sonoma; or, continue on U.S. 101 to reach Petaluma, which is connected to Sonoma by Rte. 116. It takes about 30 minutes to reach Petaluma from the bridge and 45 minutes to reach Sonoma.

Route 12 traverses the length of Sonoma Valley from **Sonoma,** through **Glen Ellen,** to **Kenwood** in the north. The center of downtown Sonoma is **Sonoma Plaza,** which contains City Hall and the visitors center. **Broadway** dead-ends in front of City Hall at Napa St. The numbered streets run north-south. **Petaluma** lies to the west and is connected to Sonoma by **Route 116,** which becomes **Lakeville Street** in Petaluma. Lakeville St. intersects **Washington Street,** the central downtown road.

PRACTICAL INFORMATION

Public Transit: Sonoma County Transit (800-345-7433) serves the entire county, from Petaluma to Cloverdale and the Russian River. Bus #30 runs M-Sa from Sonoma to Santa Rosa (fare $1.95, students $1.60, seniors and disabled 95¢, under 6 free). Bus #40 goes to Petaluma (fare $1.60). A **"Cruisin' Pass"** allows unlimited summer rides for the under-18 set ($15). Within Sonoma, bus fare 85¢, students 65¢, seniors and disabled 40¢. County buses stop when flagged down. Buses operate M-F 7am-6pm. **Golden Gate Transit** (541-2000 from Sonoma County or 415-923-2000 from San Francisco; TDD 257-4554) runs 2 buses per day between S.F. and Santa Rosa. **Volunteer Wheels** (800-992-1006) offers door-to-door service for people with disabilities.

Taxis: Sonoma Valley Cab (996-6733). 24hr.

Bike Rental: Sonoma Valley Cyclery (935-3377), on Broadway in Sonoma. Bikes $6 per hr., $28 per day. Open M-Sa 10am-6pm, Su 10am-4pm. **Bicycle Factory,** 110 Kentucky St., Petaluma (763-7515), downtown. Mountain bikes $8 per hr., $22 per day. Helmet included. Must leave major I.D. or credit card as deposit. Open M-F 10am-6pm, Sa 9am-5pm, Su 10am-4pm.

Visitor Information: Sonoma Valley Visitors Bureau, 453 E. 1st St. (996-1090), in Sonoma Plaza. Open daily June-Oct. 9am-7pm; Nov.-May 9am-5pm. Maps $2. **Petaluma Visitors Program,** 799 Baywood Dr. (769-0429), at Lakeville St. Open June-Sept. M-F 9am-5:30pm, Sa-Su 10am-6pm; shorter hours off-season. The free visitor's guide has handy listings of restaurants and activities.

Road Conditions: 800-424-9393.

Emergency: 911. **Police: Petaluma** (778-4372). **Sonoma** (996-3602).

Crisis Lines: Sonoma Valley Crisis Line (938-4357). 24hr. **Disabled Crisis** (800-426-4263).

Hospital: Petaluma Valley, 400 N. McDowell Blvd., Petaluma (778-1111).

Post Office: 800-275-8777. **Sonoma:** 617 Broadway, at Patten St. Open M-F 8:30am-5pm. **ZIP Code:** 95476. **Petaluma:** 120 4th St. Open M-F 8:30am-5:30pm, Sa 10am-2pm. **ZIP Code:** 94952.

AREA CODE The area code for Sonoma Valley is 707.

ACCOMMODATIONS AND CAMPGROUNDS

Pickings are pretty slim for lodging; rooms are scarce even on weekdays and generally start at $75. Cheaper motels cluster along **U.S. 101** in Santa Rosa and Petaluma. Campers with cars should try the **Russian River Valley** (see p. 178).

Motel 6, 1368 N. McDowell Blvd., **Petaluma** (765-0333), off U.S. 101. Spacious, and tastefully decorated. Cable TV. Well-maintained pool open 9am-9:30pm. Check-out noon. Su-Th singles $44, doubles $47; F-Sa $47, $50; each additional adult $3.

Sugarloaf Ridge State Park, 2605 Adobe Canyon Rd. (833-5712), off Rte. 12 north of Kenwood. 50 sites around central meadow with flush toilets and running water, but no showers. Sites $16. Reserve through PARKNET 800-444-7275.

San Francisco North/Petaluma KOA, 20 Rainsville Rd., **Petaluma** (763-1492 or 800-992-2267), off the Penngrove Exit. Activities bring all 300 sites together. Recreation hall has activities, petting zoo, pool, store, and jacuzzi. As the presence of a petting zoo might suggest, the campground is overrun by screaming kids. Hot showers. 2-person tent sites $30, each additional adult $5, each additional child $3; RVs $34-36.

FOOD

Fresh produce is seasonally available directly from area farms or at roadside stands and farmer's markets. *Farm Trails* maps are free at the Sonoma Valley Visitors Bureau. Those in the area toward the end of the summer should ask about the ambrosial **crane melon,** grown only on the Crane Farm north of Petaluma. The **Sonoma Market,** 520 W. Napa St. (996-0563), in the Sonoma Valley Center, is an old-fashioned grocery store with deli sandwiches ($4-6) and *very* fresh produce. For inexpensive fruit, head to the **Fruit Basket,** 18474 Sonoma Hwy. (996-7433). **Safeway,** 477 W. Napa (996-0633), is open 24 hours.

Quinley's, 310 D St. (778-6000), at Petaluma. Hugely popular burger counter first opened its doors in 1952, and that old-time rock 'n' roll plays on. Outdoor bar and picnic tables. Burgers $3-4, 4-scoop shake or malt $2. Open M-Th 11am-9pm, F-Sa 11am-10pm, Su 10am-6pm. No credit cards.

Sonoma Cheese Factory, 2 Spain St. (996-1931 or 800-535-2855). Forget the *vino* for now—take a toothpick and enjoy the free samples. You can even watch the cheesemaking process in the back room. Sandwiches $4.50-5.50. Open daily 9am-6pm.

Ford's Cafe, 22900 Broadway, (938-9811), near the junction of Rte. 12 and 121. Where the locals go for huge breakfasts (served until 11:30am). One egg, toast, and bacon ($3) constitutes a "commuter special." Open M-F 5am-2pm, Sa-Su 6am-2pm.

The Chocolate Cow, 452 1st St. (935-3564), across from the visitors center. The air is thick with chocolate, ice cream, and chocolate ice cream. Consume your fill at cow chairs and tables, if you can fight off the screaming kids eager for their sugar fixes. Open daily 10am-9:30pm.

Gourmet Taco, 19235 Sonoma Hwy. (935-1945). If "gourmet" and "taco" seem an unlikely couple, so will its fast-food aura and great-food taste. Open daily 11am-9pm.

WINERIES

Sonoma Valley's wineries, near Sonoma and Kenwood, are less touristy but just as tasty as Napa's, and more of the tastings are complimentary. Near Sonoma, white signs will help guide you through backroads; they are difficult to read but indicate wineries' general directions. Bring a map (they're all over the place and free), as the signs will often desert you when they're most needed.

IN AND AROUND SONOMA

Buena Vista, 18000 Old Winery Rd. (800-926-1266), off E. Napa St. Oldest winery in the valley. Famous old stone buildings are preserved as Mr. Haraszthy built them in 1857, when he founded the California wine industry. Theatrical performances July-Sept. Historical presentations in summer 11am and 2pm; off-season 2pm. Free tastings daily 10:30am-5pm.

Ravenswood, 18701 Gehricke Rd., Sonoma (938-1960). Poe himself would have approved of their red Zinfandels, often described as "gothic." Nevertheless, don't ask to see the Amontillado. Quaffed the raven evermore. Summer weekend BBQs ($7-10). Free tastings; tours by appt. Open daily 10am-4:30pm.

Kunde, 10155 Sonoma Hwy. (833-5501). On hot afternoons, cool cave tours at Kunde are a pleasant respite from the California sun. The winery is known for Gewurztraminer, a difficult wine to pronounce but an excellent one to taste. Open daily 11am-5pm.

Sebastiani, 389 E. 4th St., Sonoma (800-888-5532), a few blocks from Sonoma Plaza. Giant mass producer draws 250,000 visitors per year, which makes for a hectic but accommodating atmosphere. 20min. tours of sepulchral aging rooms are best during summer harvest, when visitors can watch grapes being crushed (daily 10:30am-4pm). The winery also operates a free tram tour of the plaza. Free tastings daily 10am-5pm.

GLEN ELLEN

Glen Ellen Winery, 14301 Arnold Dr. (939-6277), in Jack London Village, 1mi. from Glen Ellen. Nearby cafes have *très cher* food to enjoy at picnic tables outside. Also an adjacent olive press with oil tasting. Open daily 10am-5pm.

Benziger, 1833 London Ranch Rd. (935-4046), in Glen Ellen. Tourists flock here for the free tram ride through the vineyards (great views, but scorching heat in the summer). Self-guided tours lead through the ranch and peacock aviary. Those interested in the tram should arrive in the morning to reserve tickets for the tours, which run at 11:30am, 1:30, 2, 3, and 3:30pm. Open daily 10am-4:30pm.

KENWOOD

Kenwood, 9592 Sonoma Hwy. (833-5891). One of the few organic wineries in the region, Kenwood prides itself on its attention to the environment. Free tastings, with recipe samples Sa-Su. Open M-F 8am-4:30pm.

Château St. Jean, 8555 Rte. 12 (833-4134). Mediterranean setting includes lookout tower with balcony and an observation deck above the production area. Tastings daily 10am-4:30pm.

SIGHTS AND SEASONAL EVENTS

SONOMA STATE HISTORIC PARK. Within the park, an adobe church stands on the site of the **Mission San Francisco-Solano,** the northernmost and last of the Spanish missions. Built in 1826, the mission houses a remnant of the original California Republic flag, the rest of which was burned in the 1906 post-earthquake fires. For more info, see **A Man with a Mission,** p. 8. *(938-9560. E. Spain and 1st St., in the northeast corner of town. Open daily 10am-5pm. Admission $3, seniors $2, ages 6-12 $1; includes Vallejo's Home, barracks next door, and Petaluma Adobe.)*

GENERAL VALLEJO'S HOME. The Gothic-style home of the famed Mexican leader who also served as mayor of Sonoma and as a California senator, is open for tours of the museum, pond, pavilions, and gardens. The grounds are garnished by a serene picnic area designed in part by Vallejo and his wife. *(938-9559. ¾-mile northwest of Sonoma Plaza on Spain St. Open daily 10am-5pm. Admission $3, children $2.)*

JACK LONDON STATE PARK. Around the turn of the twentieth century, hard-drinking and hard-living Jack London, author of *The Call of the Wild* and *White Fang*, bought 1400 acres here, determined to create his dream home. London's hopes were frustrated when the estate's main building, the Wolf House, was destroyed by arsonists in 1913. London died three years after the fire and is buried in the park, his grave marked by a volcanic boulder intended for the construction of his house. The nearby **House of Happy Walls,** built by his widow, is now a two-story museum devoted to the writer. The park's scenic half-mile **Beauty Ranch Trail** passes the lake, winery ruins, and quaint cottages. *(938-5216. Take Rte. 12 4mi. north from Sonoma to Arnold Ln. and follow signs. Park open daily 9:30am-dusk; museum open daily 10am-5pm. Admission $6 per car. For those requiring handicapped access, free golf cart rides are provided Sa-Su 12:30-4:30pm.)* **Sonoma Cattle and Napa Valley Trail Rides** also coast through the fragrant forests. *(996-8566. 2hr. ride $45; sunset and night rides available.)*

SEASONAL EVENTS. Kenwood heats up July 4, when runners gather for the **Kenwood Footrace,** a tough 7½-mile course through hills and vineyards. A chili cook-off and the **World Pillowfighting Championships** pass the rest of the day. Eager contenders straddle a metal pipe over a mud pit and beat the hell out of each other with wet pillows. Sonoma Plaza hosts festivals and fairs nearly every summer weekend.

SANTA ROSA

Famed horticulturist Luther Burbank once said of Santa Rosa (pop. 116,962), "I firmly believe, from what I have seen, that this is the chosen spot of all the earth, as far as nature is concerned." Of course, whatever Luther envisioned gave way long ago to greedy developers who spirited capitalism into the region, casting tract housing hither and shopping malls yon, and effectively hiding Santa Rosa's commercial dominance over Sonoma County under a veil of suburban torpor.

BAY AREA

ORIENTATION AND PRACTICAL INFORMATION. Santa Rosa is at the intersection of **U.S. 101** and **Route 12,** 57 miles north of downtown San Francisco. **Cleveland Avenue,** marking the city's western edge, is lined with cheap motels. The town center is occupied by a mall, which interrupts A St. and 2nd through 5th St. **Mendocino Avenue** and **4th Street** define the bustling yet spotless downtown area. The **Railroad Square** area, bounded by **4th, 5th,** and **Wilson Streets,** houses Santa Rosa's trendiest shops and cafes, but is becoming dangerous at night. **Exercise caution after dark.**

Greyhound **buses** (800-231-2222 or 546-6495), is at 421 Santa Rosa Ave., 3 blocks from 2nd St. They offer routes to **San Francisco** (2 per day, $12). **City Bus** (543-3333) covers the main streets of Santa Rosa (fare $1). Carry exact change, and get a schedule at the Visitor Bureau or any of the bus shelters. To rent bikes, call **Rincon Cyclery** (538-0868), at 4927 Rte. 12, Room H. They rent mountain bikes, hybrids, and tandems only—the shop is near off-road trails. (Rental $9.50 per hr.; 2hr. min.; $25 1st day; $20 per additional day; $100 per week. Free maps.; open M-F 9:30am-6pm, Sa 9am-6pm, Su 10am-5pm.) Visitor services include: the **Greater Santa Rosa Conference and Visitor Bureau** (577-8674 or 800-404-ROSE/7673), is at 9 4th St. and Wilson St. (brochures and maps $1; open M 9am-5pm, Tu-F 8:30am-5pm, Sa-Su 10am-3pm); the **Sonoma County Wine and Visitors Center,** 5000 Roberts Lake Rd. (586-3795), east of U.S. 101 at the Luther Burbank Center for the Arts. They sell maps of most area wineries and a tasting directory (open daily 9am-5pm). **Emergency:** 911. **Police:** 543-3600. **Hospital: Santa Rosa Memorial,** 1165 Montgomery Dr. (546-3210). **Post office:** 730 2nd St. (528-8763), between D and E St. Open M-F 8am-6pm, Sa 10am-2pm. **ZIP Code:** 95402. **Area code:** 707.

ACCOMMODATIONS. Santa Rosa offers average lodgings at above-average prices, which requires making reservations far in advance for summer. Some budget accommodations include: the **Astro Motel,** 323 N. Santa Rosa Ave. (545-8555), near Sonoma Ave., which is conveniently located downtown in an area that can also be a bit unsafe after dark. Astro is a haven for late arrivals as they often have vacant rooms. (Singles $45; doubles $48.); **The Country Inn,** 2363 Santa Rosa Ave. (546-4711) has tidy rooms with a pool, cable TV, phones, and coffee. (Singles $40;

doubles $45; rates higher on F-Sa; lower in winter.); **The Redwood Inn,** 1670 Santa Rosa Ave. (545-0474) offers limited local calls and cable TV in rooms more pink than red. But then, redwoods are more pink than red—everyone knows that. (Singles $40; doubles $45.)

FOOD. Fresh produce can be found at the Thursday night **market** (5-8:30pm in summer). The **East-West Cafe,** 2323 Sonoma Ave. (546-6142), in Montgomery Village 10min. from downtown, is a homemade, hippie, multicultural Denny's serving heavenly baked goods and huge portions (filling Mediterranean platter $9; Thai chicken salad $7.50; open in summer Su-M 8am-8:30pm, Tu-Sa 8am-9pm; in winter Su-M 8am-8pm, Tu-Sa 8am-9pm). **Copperfield's Bookstore and Cafe,** 650 4th St. (576-7681), downtown, has a central location with a grungily hip (or vice-versa) clientele. Sandwiches are named after authors in this veggie-friendly hangout: Alice Walker (hummus, tomato, and avocado; $4.50), or Dr. Seuss (peanut butter and banana on wheat bread; $3). They also sell hip (new) and grungy (used) books. (Open M-F 7:30am-9pm, Sa 8:30am-10pm, Su 8:30am-6pm.) **Organic Groceries,** 2481 Guerneville Rd. (528-3663), near Fulton St., has every organic food you've ever heard of—all in bulk quantities. (Open M-F 7am-9pm, Sa-Su 9am-7pm.)

SIGHTS. The **Luther Burbank Home and Gardens** (524-5445), at Santa Rosa and Sonoma Ave., is a great place to stop and smell the chamomile or pet the Lamb's Ears (herbal, not animal). At the age of 26, the horticulturist fled to California from Massachusetts to carry out his maniacal plant-breeding experiments, and the gardens display 1½ acres of his hybrids, including the evil white *Agapanthus* (a short, frondy plant popular with California's gas station landscapers). It's alive! (Gardens open daily 8am-7pm. Free. House open Apr.-Oct. W-Su 10am-3:30pm. Admission $2, under 13 free. Free tours on Memorial Day—May 29 in 2000.)

Nearby, homage is paid to Santa Rosa native **Robert Ripley,** of *Ripley's Believe It or Not!*. The memorial museum (524-5233; 492 Sonoma Ave.) is housed in the famed **"church built from one tree."** (Open W-Su 10:30am-3:30pm. Admission $1.50, children 75¢.)

The **Redwood Empire Ice Arena,** 1667 W. Steele Ln. (546-7144), is decorated with original Snoopy artwork (admission $5.50, ages 12-18 $4.50; skate rental $2). If you're tired of working for peanuts, get some sympathy next door at **Snoopy's Gallery,** which continues the ice rink's artistic theme. Every souvenir imaginable is sold here. Good grief! (Open daily 10am-6pm.)

If you are biking or driving, Sonoma County's backroads offer scenery that surpasses even that on Rte. 12. **Bennett Valley Road,** between Kenwood and Santa Rosa, **Petaluma Hill Road,** between Petaluma and Santa Rosa, and **Grange/Crane Canyon Road,** connecting the two, afford particularly good views of the countryside. If you are on a bike, remain conscious of drivers; the surroundings can distract you from the blind turns and hills. Drivers should also look out for bicyclists.

SEASONAL EVENTS. Annual events include the **Dixieland Jazz Festival** (539-3494; Aug. 25 in 2000), with nonstop music and dancing. The **Sonoma County Fair** is at the end of July. Tote your tartan and tam o'shanter to the **Scottish Gathering and Games,** a two-day frenzy pitting clan against clan over Labor Day weekend (Sept. 2-4 in 2000). This event, the largest gathering of Scots outside of the British Isles, features the caber toss, in which kilt-sporting Thanes throw massive logs. In the autumn, Santa Rosa nourishes the countryside at the **October Harvest Fair** and the **World Championship Grape Stomp Contest.** (Call the Sonoma County Fairgrounds at 545-4200 for info.)

RUSSIAN RIVER VALLEY

The Russian River Valley is a well-kept secret. Although many of its wineries have been operating nearly as long as their counterparts to the southeast, they are neither as well-known nor as frequently visited. The area encompasses a beautiful coastline, towering redwoods, and a scenic river, making it ideal for hiking and biking. In quiet Sebastopol, hippies and farmers coexist peacefully, biding their time until the next great social reckoning or marijuana raid. Extremely unpretentious Guerneville, a gay community, is less reliant on the wineries for tourism. Farther north and east, Healdsburg is a burg of beauty and bucks, and a good base for exploring the wineries Guerneville disdains.

ORIENTATION AND PRACTICAL INFORMATION

The **Russian River** winds through western Sonoma County before reaching the Pacific Ocean at Jenner. The river flows south, roughly following **U.S. 101** until **Healdsburg,** where it veers west. A number of small towns, including **Guerneville, Monte Rio,** and **Forestville,** line this stretch of river. **Sebastopol,** not a river town itself, claims kinship to those towns due to its location on **Route 116,** "the road to the Russian River." Travel west on **Route 12** from Santa Rosa to get to Sebastopol.

Public Transit: Golden Gate Transit (from Sonoma 541-2000, from S.F. 923-2000). Connects Russian River area and the Bay Area. Fares determined by "fare zones." Free explanatory maps at visitors centers. Bus #78 heads north from 1st and Mission St. to **Guerneville** (2hr., M-F 4 per day, $4.50). **Sonoma County Transit** (576-7433 or 800-345-7433), has a county-wide route (#20) from Santa Rosa to the Russian River area. Leaves from 2nd St. and Santa Rosa Ave. (M-F 4 per day, Sa-Su 3 per day; $2).

Bike Rental: Bicycle Factory, 6940 McKinley St., Sebastopol (829-1880). Mountain bikes $8 per hr., $22 per day (with helmet, lock, and free water bottle). Open M-F 10am-6:30pm, Sa 9am-5pm, Su 10am-4pm. **Mike's Bike Rental,** 16442 Rte. 116, Guerneville (869-1106), opposite Safeway. Bikes $6 per hr., 1st day $28, additional day $20. Open in summer M-Sa 9am-5pm, Su 10am-4pm. Call for winter hours.

Visitor Information: Russian River Visitors Center, 14034 Armstrong Woods Rd. (869-9212 or 800-253-8800). Open M-W 9:30am-5pm, Th-Sa 9:30am-6pm, Su 10am-3pm. **Sebastopol Area Chamber of Commerce,** 265 S. Main St. (823-3032; open M-F 9am-5pm). **Healdsburg Chamber of Commerce,** 217 Healdsburg Ave. (433-6935; open M-F 9:30am-12:30pm and 1:30-5pm, Sa-Su 10am-2pm). **Guerneville Chamber of Commerce,** 16200 1st St. (24hr. info line 869-9000). Open M-F 10am-4pm.

Emergency: 911.

Post Office: Sebastopol, 290 S. Main St. Open M-F 8:30am-5pm. **ZIP Code:** 95473. **Healdsburg,** 409 Center St. (433-2267). Open M-F 8:30am-5pm. **ZIP Code:** 95446.

Area Code: 707.

ACCOMMODATIONS AND CAMPGROUNDS

The Russian River Valley shares the expensive lodging tastes of the rest of the wine country. The tourist industry in Russian River caters to a well-heeled, elegant, B&B-staying crowd. Options for the budget traveler, however, include area campgrounds and affordable lodge-resorts. This area is quite compact by California standards; none of the towns are more than a 40-minute drive apart.

Isis Oasis, 20889 Geyserville Ave., Healdsburg (857-3524 or 800-679-7387). Societal exiles and self-help groups hide out at this hippie holdout. Unusual animals (ocelots, llamas, and peacocks), buildings (geodesic dome), and people (see for yourself) make for interesting walks through the grounds. A refreshing pool and jacuzzi, as well as stellar dinner menus (i.e., shrimp jambalaya and pineapple cheesecake), augment the experience. Dorms $20; teepees $30; yurts (a tent with floors) $45.

Armstrong Woods State Reserve (869-2015), on Armstrong Woods Rd. off Rte. 116, 3mi. north of Guerneville. Bullfrog Pond campground has 24 secluded tent sites along trails in a redwood grove ($10) and 4 primitive backpacker sites ($7). Self-registration after 4pm. No reservations. Arrive early, especially on summer weekends.

Faerie Ring, 16747 Armstrong Woods Rd. (869-2746), just south of Armstrong Woods State Reserve, 1½mi. north of Guerneville. Privately operated gay-friendly campground offers quiet sites with tables and fire rings. Sites Su-Th $15, F-Sa $20; RVs $20, $25. Upper-level tent sites $5 extra, but may be worth the distance from the road. Hot showers. Reservations recommended, especially on weekends. No children.

Johnson's Beach Resort (869-2022), on 1st St., in the center of Guerneville. Looks like an overcrowded parking lot, but the campsites and cabins are cheap and centrally located. Easy access to a large, packed graveled riverbank. Sites $10, each additional person $2; cabins (with fridges and TV) $30.

Schoolhouse Canyon Park, 12600 River Rd. (869-2311). Redwoods tower over these beautiful sites. Hot showers. 2 people $20, each additional person $5. Reservations only accepted by mail.

FOOD

While **Sebastopol** is lacking in convenient budget accommodations, this health-conscious community has contributed to the proliferation of good and good-for-you restaurants. For excellent baked goods, head north to **Healdsburg.**

East-West Cafe, 128 N. Main St., Sebastopol (829-2822). Mediterranean platters make this the best vegetarian-friendly restaurant in the county. Free-range chicken or tofu fajitas $8. Thai iced tea and *lassi.* Open M-F 7am-9pm, Sa 8am-9pm, Su 8am-8pm.

Village Bakery, 7225 Healdsburg Ave., Sebastopol (829-8101). Perhaps your only chance to taste Sebastopol sourdough bread (leavened with a culture from Gravenstein apples and Chardonnay grapes; $3.60). Thick pie by the slice $2. Open M-Sa 7am-5:30pm, Su 8am-2pm.

Sweet's River Grill, 16251 Main St., Guerneville (869-3383). Beautiful outdoor seating for good people-watching. Not so cheap, but you'll know it's worth it when you taste the Navels of Venus (ricotta-filled tortellini; $11.50). Burgers and sandwiches $6-8. Open M-F 10:30am-10pm, Sa-Su 10am-10pm.

Cousteaux French Bakery and Cafe, 417 Healdsburg Ave., Healdsburg (433-1913). Indoor umbrellas impersonate a French cafe; the incredible sourdough bread ($2) lends more credence. Open in summer M-Sa 6am-6pm, Su 7am-6pm; off-season M-Sa 6am-6pm, Su 7am-4pm.

SIGHTS

The **wineries** in the Russian River Valley are not mobbed like those in Napa and Sonoma. The *Wine Country Map of the Russian River Wine Road,* free at every visitors center and chamber of commerce in Wine Country, has an excellent map and lists every winery in the area, complete with hours, services, and products. Traveling a few miles northwest along Rte. 116 from Sebastopol brings visitors to **Forestville,** the site of the **Topolos at Russian River Winery,** 5700 Rte. 116 (887-1575 or 800-867-6567), which offers free tasting and a posh restaurant. (Open daily May-Dec.; Jan.-Apr. W-M. Restaurant open daily 11:30am-2:30pm and 5:30-9:30pm; tasting room open 10:30am-5:30pm.) Just outside town are the **Korbel Champagne Cellars,** 13250 River Rd. (887-2294). Name recognition makes for a mobbed tour and tasting room. A small deli offers gourmet sandwiches like the cranberry-horseradish chutney, white cheddar, red onion, greens, and tarragon concoction for $6. (Tours daily 10am-3:45pm. Tastings daily in summer 9am-5pm; in winter 9am-4pm.) A more personal atmosphere exists at **Trentadue Winery,** 19170 Geyserville Ave. (433-3104), one mile north of **Geyserville.** Tourists can watch any available activity, although tours are dependent on available personnel. Also in

Geyserville is the award-winning **Château Souverain,** 400 Souverain Rd. (433-3141), at the Independence Ln. Exit. The chic cafe has great views. (Tastings daily 10am-5pm. Cafe open F-Su 11:30am-2:30pm and 5:30-8pm.)

The river is the reason people originally moved to the area, and it's still just as peaceful as ever. **W.C. "Bob" Trowbridge Canoe Trips** (433-7247 or 800-640-1386), runs daytrips down the river from April to October (4-5hr., $39 for a 2-3 person canoe). **Burke's Canoe Trips** (887-1222), offers similar daytrips ($30), as well as multi-day trips (no credit cards; call ahead for return service to your car). **Russian River Kayaks,** 2030 Rte. 116 (865-2141), has a private landing right on the river (kayaks or bikes $5 per hr., $15 for 4hr., $25 per day; open M-Sa 8am-5:30pm, Su 10am-4pm; later returns can be arranged). The **Armstrong Woods State Park** (869-2015), has trails in a redwood forest among Napa's golden hills, just 10 minutes north of Guerneville. Parking is free at the visitors center, but incurs a $5 day use fee anywhere else in the park. The easiest hike is one-mile **Pioneer Trail,** which starts at the visitors center parking lot and skirts Fife Creek.

ENTERTAINMENT AND SEASONAL EVENTS

Guerneville is *the* night spot in the Russian River Valley. It is predominantly a gay scene, although no one is made to feel unwelcome. The **Rainbow Cattle Co.,** 16220 Main St. (869-0206), is a rowdy gay bar straight outta Texas cow country (open daily 6am-2am). **Stumptown Brewery,** 15145 River Rd. (869-0705), one mile east of Guerneville, has a straighter crowd, live music, and a snack bar with calzones, burritos, and pizza (open in summer M-F 6am-2am, Sa-Su 11am-2am; in winter daily 4pm-2am).

Sebastopol's **Apple Blossom Festival,** in late April, has entertainment, crafts, and food. The **Sebastopol Music Festival** also occurs at this time. There are free concerts each Sunday from May through August in Healdsburg on the Plaza (800-648-9922). The **Russian River Rodeo,** in mid-June, is the big event of the season. The **Gravenstein Apple Fair** takes place in mid-August. The **Russian River Jazz Festival** (869-9000), blasts trombone, trumpet, and piano melodies down the river the weekend after Labor Day (Sept. 9-10 in 2000; tickets from $26).

THE NORTH COAST

Shrouded in mist, the North Coast is a paradise of rugged ocean coastline, rolling farmland, unspoiled black sand beaches, and towering redwoods. Wild rivers roam through peaceful valleys, and inhabitants tend to be nature-loving, artsy, and down-to-earth. The region's powerful beauty sends out a call of the wild, appealing to travelers weary of the more urban sights and sounds of the lower state, and to naturalists who understand that this beauty is the only reason to visit California.

The North Coast begins in the San Francisco Bay Area and continues to the Oregon border. Road-trippers in the North Coast can take one of two scenic highway routes. Route 1 (see below) offers vertiginous coastal vistas on the shores of Mar-in, Sonoma, and Mendocino Counties. One hour north of Fort Bragg, Route 1 turns sharply inland and travels miles away from the coast, merging with U.S. 101 for the journey north. Prior to this union, U.S. 101 meanders through the heart of California's wine country before reaching sleepy farm country and stopover town Ukiah.

The shore the highways leave behind, which is now known as the Lost Coast, offers some of the most rugged scenery in the state. Lost Coast marijuana farmers are (in)famous for cultivating what smokers consider to be some of the finest grass in the world. The inland leg of U.S. 101 brings travelers to the Avenue of the Giants, home of the enormous redwoods that make the region famous. Past Eureka and Arcata, U.S. 101 winds along the coast again while stately redwoods, protected by the long, thin strips of Redwood National Park, tower alongside.

HIGHLIGHTS OF THE NORTH COAST

■ The North Coast prominently features sky-scraping **trees** and a breathtaking **coastline;** some of the best concentrations of these are in Redwood National Park (p. 191), the Lost Coast (p. 186), and the Avenue of the Giants (p. 185).

■ **Camping** is the main tourist activity, as weekenders and families fill up but never overcrowd the beautiful expanse.

ROUTE 1: THE PACIFIC COAST HIGHWAY

Easy driving it is not, but Rte. 1 (the Pacific Coast Highway, often called Route 1), north of San Francisco, is one of the world's most breathtaking stretches of road. The famous highway snakes along rugged cliffs near pounding surf and magnificent trees. Drivers and their passengers will appreciate opportunities to recover from the heart-stopping journey in quaint, not-too-touristy coastal hamlets. Be prepared, however, for slow trailers on the road and sky-high prices for food and accommodations. A budget traveler's best options are outdoors, camping and hiking. For more on Rte. 1, see **Central Coast** (p. 197) and **Bay Area** (p. 127).

The highway winds its way out of the Bay Area via San Rafael, almost immediately hitting breathtaking **Point Reyes National Seashore** (see **Marin,** p. 158). A bit farther north, Rte. 1 takes a brief inland turn before making an ocean rendezvous at Bodega Bay and the Sonoma Coast. The small town of **Bodega Bay** keeps its seafaring roots alive in the form of incredibly fresh salmon and crab at oceanside restaurants. For browsers, Bodega Bay is an antique maven's haven. The **visitors center,** 850 Rte. 1 (875-3422), has info on the North Coast (open M-Sa 9:30am-8pm, Su 10am-4:30pm). Both Bodega Bay and **Bodega,** seven miles inland, were featured in Alfred Hitchcock's 1963 film *The Birds*.

Just north of Bodega Bay begins the **Sonoma Coast State Park,** off Rte. 1. The park extends 10 miles north to Jenner and includes several incredible beaches. Hiking trails along the beaches abound, but don't be tempted to venture too far into the ocean—unpredictable currents make these beaches dangerous for swimming and surfing. Within the state park are two more campgrounds. Campers can choose from 98 sheltered sites at the **Bodega Dunes campground** (875-3483; sites $16; hot showers included). **Wright's Beach campground,** two miles north, offers 30 sites; several have direct views of the ocean, but none have showers or hot water. (Sites $20. Call PARKNET for reservations at either 800-444-7275.)

Farther north on Rte. 1 is **Jenner,** at the Russian River where it enters the ocean. Jenner's **Goat Rock Beach** is popular with harbor seals in the summer. Eleven miles up the coast from Jenner, **Fort Ross State Historic Park** (847-3286) features the only reconstructed Russian buildings in the continental U.S., relics of the czar's tenuous 19th-century presence. The park has six miles of coastal access and sandy beaches, but bring a jacket to protect yourself from the wind. Rte. 1 is usually closed in this area at least once per year due to spring rains, but Fort Ross is accessible via detour. Those without the wheels (or stomach) to handle Rte. 1 can reach the park by bus; take the **MTA's** daily coast run from Point Arena on the way to Santa Rosa (see **Sonoma Valley: Practical Information,** p. 173). A lonely wooden stockade perched on the edge of the cliffs above a small harbor, **Fort Ross** occupies a narrow strip of land hacked from the forest—the eastern limit of imperial Russia's grasp. Siberian Russians migrated here to hunt otters and find farmland for their Alaskan settlers, but the Spanish squeezed the Russians out in 1842, and John Sutter (of mill fame) bought the fort for a song, primarily to get the redwood threshing table inside. The fort now houses a limited **museum** (open daily 10am-4:30pm; admission $6). The park at **The Reef,** 1½ miles south, offers 20 campsites with flush toilets (sites $12). Campgrounds also seem to appear around each of the many bends of the road north of the fort. **Salt Point State Park** (847-3221; reserve through DESTINET 800-444-7275), four miles up Rte. 1, has 109 sites with firepits, toilets, and showers (sites $16).

Farther north in Mendocino County (on Rte. 1), the fog-shrouded **lighthouse** and **museum** (882-2777) of **Point Arena** deserve a stop. The original building dates from 1869, but the 115-foot lighthouse is 1906 vintage, built after the famed San Francisco earthquake demolished the original. (Museum open daily 10am-3:30pm. Admission $2.50, children 50¢.) The **MTA Coast Bus** (800-696-4MTA/4682), runs one loop daily from Point Arena to Santa Rosa (fare $2.50-6.25, students $1.75-4.50, seniors $1.25-3.25). Point Arena has 46 tent sites and hike/bike sites at **Manchester State Beach** (937-5804), where driftwood dots the sand (sites $9, seniors $7).

Twenty-seven miles to the east over Mountain View Rd. is **Boonville,** where the main attraction is **Boontling,** a strange local language developed in the 1880s and still used in jest to frustrate and amuse tourists. Don't get "can-kicky" though, they're "white-oakin" to keep the language alive. At **Boont Berry Farm,** 13981 Rte. 128 (895-3576), Boonville growers serve up a tasty focaccia, veggie, and chevre sandwich ($4) and a "horn of zeese" (coffee) for 75¢ (open M-Sa 9am-6pm, Su noon-6pm). Down the road at the **Anderson Valley Brewing Co.,** 14051 Rte. 128 (895-3369), you can taste the *steinber* that hit the top ten category in the World Brewfest two years running (a feat unmatched by any other American beer).

MENDOCINO

Perched on bluffs overlooking the ocean, isolated Mendocino (pop. 1000) is a highly stylized coastal community of art galleries, craft shops, bakeries, and B&Bs. The town's weathered wood shingles, sloping roofs, and clustered homes seem out of place on the West Coast; perhaps that's why Mendocino was able to masquerade for years as the fictional Maine village of Cabot Cove in the TV series *Murder, She Wrote.* If you have seen the show, you've seen most of Mendocino.

ORIENTATION AND PRACTICAL INFORMATION. Mendocino sits on **Route 1** right on the Pacific Coast, 30 miles west of U.S. 101 and 12 miles south of Fort Bragg. Only easily accessible by car, the town is tiny, and best explored on foot (parking available in plentiful lots). Weather in the Mendocino area varies from 40-70°F. Travelers should come prepared for chilliness caused by fog.

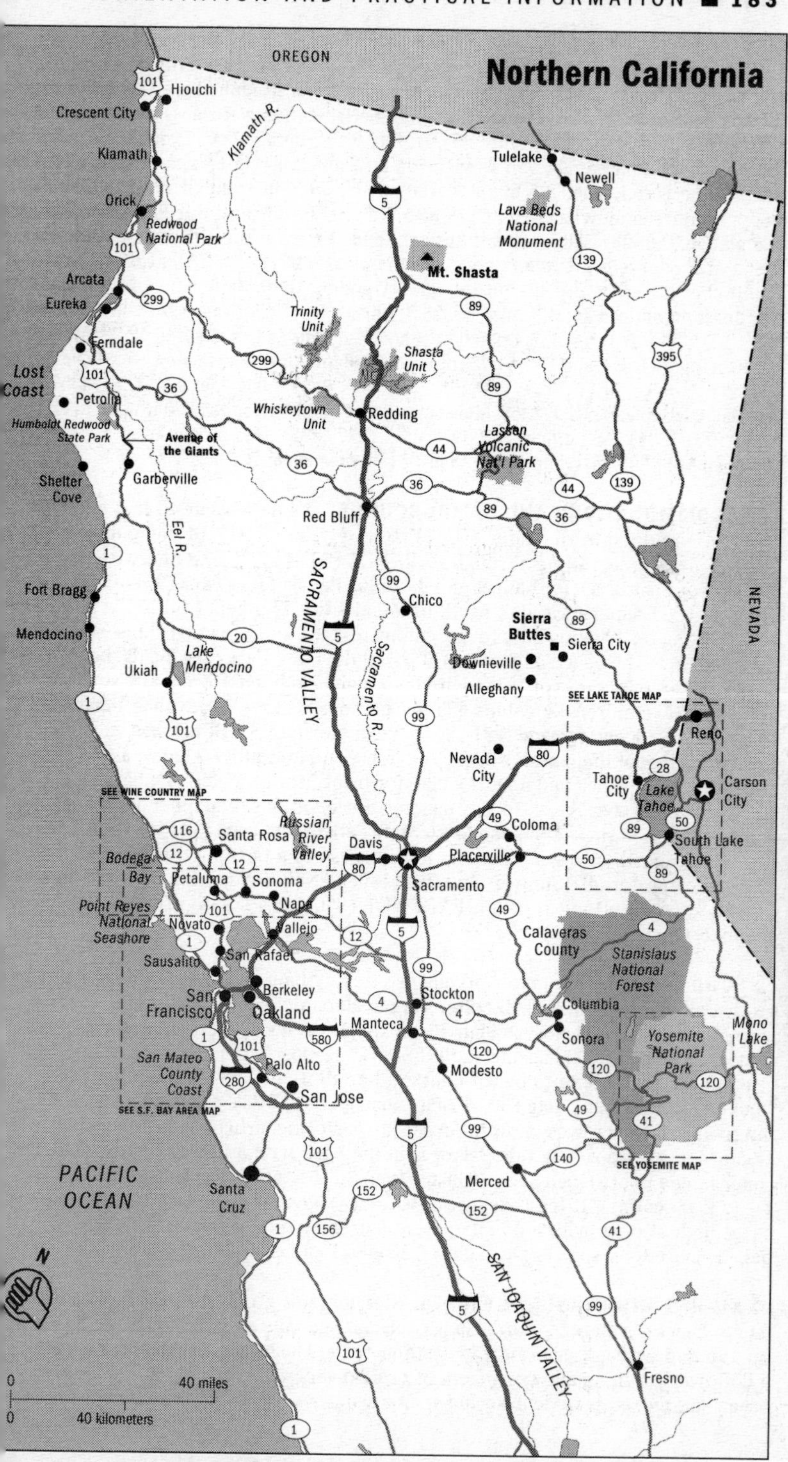
Northern California
OREGON
NEVADA
PACIFIC OCEAN
Hiouchi
Crescent City
Klamath
Klamath R.
Orick
Redwood National Park
Arcata
Eureka
Ferndale
Lost Coast
Petrolia
Humboldt Redwood State Park
Avenue of the Giants
Shelter Cove
Garberville
Eel R.
Fort Bragg
Mendocino
Ukiah
Lake Mendocino
Tulelake
Newell
Lava Beds National Monument
Mt. Shasta
Trinity Unit
Shasta Unit
Whiskeytown Unit
Redding
Lassen Volcanic Nat'l Park
Red Bluff
SACRAMENTO VALLEY
Sacramento R.
Chico
Sierra Buttes
Sierra City
Downieville
Alleghany
SEE LAKE TAHOE MAP
Reno
Nevada City
Tahoe City
Lake Tahoe
Carson City
South Lake Tahoe
SEE WINE COUNTRY MAP
Santa Rosa
Russian River Valley
Bodega Bay
Petaluma
Sonoma
Napa
Davis
Sacramento
Coloma
Placerville
Point Reyes National Seashore
Novato
Vallejo
San Rafael
Sausalito
San Francisco
Berkeley
Oakland
Calaveras County
Stanislaus National Forest
Stockton
Manteca
Columbia
Sonora
Mono Lake
Yosemite National Park
San Mateo County Coast
Palo Alto
San Jose
Modesto
SEE S.F. BAY AREA MAP
SEE YOSEMITE MAP
Merced
Santa Cruz
SAN JOAQUIN VALLEY
Fresno
N
0 40 miles
0 40 kilometers
101 5 299 89 139 395 36 44 1 99 20 80 28 49 50 116 12 4 580 120 280 140 41 152 156

The nearest **bus station** is in Ukiah, two hours away. Greyhound runs two **buses** per day to Ft. Bragg. Mendocino Stage (964-0167) runs three buses per day between Ft. Bragg and Ukiah (fare $3). **Mendocino Transit Authority,** 241 Plant Rd. (800-696-4682), makes one round-trip daily between Santa Rosa, Ukiah, Willits, Fort Bragg, and Mendocino (fare $7.50). **Fort Bragg Door-to-Door Taxis** (964-8294) have an on-call passenger van service (daily 10am-2am). For **visitor information,** contact the **Ford House,** 735 Main St. (937-5397; open in summer daily 9:30am-4:30pm; hours somewhat variable due to volunteer staffing). For **Parks General Information,** call 937-5804, or visit **Russian Gulch Park,** on the east side of Rte. 1 (open M-F 8am-5pm). **Catcha Canoe and Bicycles, Too!** (937-0273), at Rte. 1 and Comptche Rd., rents pricey, but top-quality goods (open daily 9:30am-5:30pm). **Lost Coast Adventures Kayak Rental,** 19275 S. Harbor Dr., Fort Bragg (937-2434), also gives guided tours (2hr.; $45; open daily 9am-5pm). **Lucy's Laundry** is at 124 S. Main St., Ft. Bragg (wash and dry $1.75; open daily 6am-9pm). **Emergency:** 911. **Police:** 961-0200 (station in Ft. Bragg). **Sheriff:** 964-6308. **Rape crisis line:** 964-HELP/4357. **Disabled crisis line:** 800-426-4263. **Mendocino Coast District Hospital:** 700 River Dr., Ft. Bragg (961-1234). **Post office:** 10500 Ford St. (937-5282), two blocks west of Main St. (open M-F 7:30am-4:30pm). **ZIP code:** 95460. **Area code:** 707.

ACCOMMODATIONS AND CAMPGROUNDS. It's impossible to find a hotel room in Mendocino for under $60. Fortunately, hundreds of campsites are nearby; make reservations through PARKNET (800-444-7275). Otherwise, look to Ukiah or Fort Bragg for budget motels. **Jug Handle Creek Farm** (964-4630), off Rte. 1 at the Caspar Exit 5mi. north of Mendocino, is a beautiful 120-year-old house sitting on 40 acres of gardens, campsites, and small rustic cabins. Guests have access to the beach and trails in Jug Handle State Park (see **Sights,** below). (30 beds. 1hr. of chores (or $5) required per night. No linen. Dorms $18, students $12; sites $6, children $3; cabins $25 per person. Reserve in advance.) **MacKerricher State Park campground** (937-5804), 3½mi. north of Ft. Bragg, has excellent views of tidepool life, passing seals, sea lions, and migratory whales, as well as nine miles of beaches and a murky lake for trout fishing. (Showers, bathrooms, and drinkable water. Sites $16; day use free. Reservations recommended.) Foggy woods shelter 30 sites at **Russian Gulch State Park campground** (937-5804), on Rte. 1, one mile north of town. Campers have access to a beach, redwoods, hiking trails, and a waterfall. (Showers and flush toilets. No hookups. Sites $16, seniors $14; day use $5. Book through PARKNET (800-444-7275) up to 8 weeks in advance. Open Apr.-Oct.)

FOOD. All of Mendocino's breads are freshly baked, all vegetables locally grown, all wheat unmilled, all coffee cappuccino, and almost everything expensive. Most restaurants close at 9pm. Picnicking is the cheapest option; stock up at **Mendosa's Market,** 1909 Lansing St. (937-5879), the closest thing in Mendocino to a real supermarket. It's pricey (of course), but all items are fresh and delicious (open daily 8am-9pm). **Tote Fête,** 10450 Lansing St. (937-3383), has delicious tote-out food, and the crowds know it. An asiago, pesto, and artichoke heart sandwich ($4.25) hits the spot. **Tote Fête Bakery** is in the back with a flowery garden and a small serene pool. (Open M-Sa 10:30am-7pm, Su 10:30am-4pm.) **Mendocino Cookie Co.** (a.k.a. **Cookies**), 10450 Lansing St. (937-4843), gives you your caffeine fix and sugar high at once with a doubly potent super large latte ($3) and tasty fresh-baked amaretto crisp ($1). Open daily 6:15am-5:15pm.

SIGHTS AND SEASONAL EVENTS. Mendocino's greatest attribute lies 900 feet to its west, where the earth clangs to a halt and falls off into the Pacific, forming the impressive fog-shrouded coastline of the **Mendocino Headlands.** Beneath wildflower-laden meadows, fingers of eroded rock claw through the pounding ocean surf and seals frolic in secluded alcoves.

For the most part, **Fort Bragg** is the place to stay while visiting Mendocino; the town's tourist pheromone is the **Skunk Train** (964-6371; 800-777-5865), at Rte. 1 and Laurel St., a jolly diversion through deserted logging towns and recuperating forest (trips depart at 9, 9:30am, 1:30, and 2pm; off-season 9:20, 10am, and 2pm; Dec. 9:20, 10am, and 2:10pm). A steam engine, diesel locomotive, and vintage motorcar take turns running between Fort Bragg and Willits via Northspur, with whole and half-day trips available. If a one-way trip fits your transportatin' needs, those are available; round-trip rides include a short break in Northspur and an hour in Willits. Schedule changes necessitate calling ahead for reservations.

Poor drainage, thin soil, and ocean winds have created an unusual bonsai garden just south of town at the **Pygmy Forest** in **Van Damme State Park** (admission $5). The trees are visible for free from the trail off Little Airport Rd. (off Rte. 1 past the park; after turning left, drive 3½mi. to a parking lot and a sign for the pygmy forest). The **ecological staircase** at **Jug Handle State Park** is a terrace of five different ecosystems, each roughly 100,000 years older than the one below it and formed by a combination of erosion and tectonic uplift. Pick up an explanatory guide.

Glimpses through the interstices of Mendocino County's fog and flora reveal many a fancy version of *au naturel*—hotspring resorts abound. **Orr Hot Springs,** 13201 Orr Springs Rd. (462-6277), is just south of Mendocino off Comptche Ukian Rd. Sauna, steam room, and gardens make the world disappear at this clothing-optional resort. (1hr. drive over dirt roads. From U.S. 101 take the North State St. Exit. Open daily 10am-10pm. Day use $19; M special $10.) In July, enjoy the **Mendocino Music Festival** (937-2044), a two-week (clothing-optional) melee of classical music and opera (tickets $12-20).

AVENUE OF THE GIANTS

About six miles north of Garberville off U.S. 101, the Avenue of the Giants winds its way through 31 miles of the largest living organisms this side of sea level. Hiking, swimming, fishing, biking, and rafting abound in this rugged area.

PRACTICAL INFORMATION. Greyhound (923-3388) runs **buses** out of Garberville—two north and two south daily—to **Eureka** ($14); **Portland** ($59); and **San Francisco** ($34). Meet the bus at Singing Salmon Music, 432 Church St., one block east of Redwood Dr. The **Humboldt Redwoods State Park Visitors Center** (946-2263), just south of Weott on the Avenue, has a free brochure highlighting the Avenue's groves, facilities, trails, and bike routes. The center also has hands-on displays for kids about area wildlife. (Open mid-Mar. to Oct. daily 9am-5pm; Nov. to mid-Mar. Th-Su 10am-4pm.) The **Garberville-Redway Chamber of Commerce,** 773 Redway, Garberville (800-923-2613) has a plethora of info on state and local attractions (open daily 10am-4:30pm). **Emergency:** 911. **Post office:** 368 Sprowl Creek Rd. (open M-F 8:30am-5:30pm). **ZIP Code:** 95542. **Area code:** 707.

ACCOMMODATIONS AND CAMPGROUNDS. The **Brass Rail Inn,** 3188 Redwood Dr., Redway (923-3931), was a brothel in 1939, but now it's a perfectly respectable motel (singles $44; doubles $55). **The Redway Motel,** 3223 Redwood Dr. (923-2660), has bright, clean rooms with cable TV and coffee (singles $65-70; doubles $70-75).

Along the road in **Humboldt State Park** (946-2409), camping options are plentiful. **Albee Creek,** on Mattpole Rd. five miles west of U.S. 101, is under the wildlife-filled redwood canopy and convenient to biking and hiking trails. **Burlington,** convenient but noisy, is right on the Avenue near the visitors center. **Richardson Grove State Park** (247-3318), off U.S. 101 eight miles south of Garberville, offers campsites, bathrooms, and showers. Call PARKNET (800-444-7275) for reservations.

FOOD. Nearby Garberville offers a number of civilized eating options. **Sentry Market** (923-5163), on Redwood Dr., is the largest supermarket for miles (open daily 7am-10pm). Locals highly recommend **Calico's Cafe** (923-2253), on Redwood Dr. next to Sherwood Forest Motel, for its garlicky fettucine gorgonzola ($7) made from scratch (open daily 11am-9pm). **Nacho Mama's** (923-5287), at Redwood Dr. and Sprowl Creek Rd., is a takeout stand serving Mexican food (entrees $3-4) and refreshing frosties that taste as good as yo mama's.

SIGHTS AND SEASONAL EVENTS. Scattered throughout the area are several commercialized attractions such as the **World Famous Tree House, Confusion Hill** (a vortex of mystery where the laws of gravity no longer apply; free), the **Drive-Thru Tree,** and plenty of Bigfoot merchandise. Travelers looking for a more authentic taste of the redwood forests may want to bypass these hokey attractions in favor of more rugged and natural tours. There are a number of great **hiking** trails in the area, marked on maps ($1) available at the visitors center. The **Canoe Creek Loop Trail,** across the street from the visitors center, is an easy start. Uncrowded trails snake through the park's northern section around **Rockefeller Forest,** which contains the largest grove of old-growth redwoods (200 years and growing) in the world. The **Dyerville Giant,** in the redwood graveyard at Founder's Grove about midway through the Avenue, deserves a respectful visit. The half-mile loop trail includes the **Founder's Tree** and the **Fallen Giant,** whose massive trunk stretches 60 human body-lengths long and whose three-story rootball looks like a mythical ensnarlment of evil. The **Standish Hickey Recreation Area** (925-6482), on U.S. 101 north of Leggett, offers fishing, camping, swimming, and hiking (parking $5).

With its sizable artist population, Garberville's **art festivals** are a big draw. **Jazz on the Lake** and the **Summer Arts Fair** begin in late June, followed by **Shakespeare at Benbow Lake** in late July. Early August brings **Reggae on the River,** a 12-hour music fest on the banks of the Eel River. For more info on events, call the Chamber of Commerce (see **Practical Information,** p. 185).

THE LOST COAST

The Lost Coast can elude even the most observant visitor, and is so named because when Route 1 was built, the rugged coastline between Usal and Ferndale had to be bypassed and the highway moved inland. Thus, this part of the coast was "lost" to modernization, leaving the craggy cliffs, rocky shores, and black sand beaches comparatively untouched. Bring a map and four-wheel-drive because, ironically enough, it is easy to get lost. Be careful when exploring—you *don't* want to wander into someone's **marijuana farm.** The proprietors of Humboldt County's #1 cash crop are not always hiker-friendly, so leave their cabins and crops alone. **Emergency** services for the area include the Garberville **sheriff** (923-2761), **ambulance** (923-3962), and 911. **Area code:** 707.

SINKYONE WILDERNESS STATE PARK

To get to **Sinkyone** from the south, take Rte. 1 to Road 431 (where Rte. 1 starts to turn toward Leggett). Coming from the north, take U.S. 101 to Redway and follow the signs to **Shelter Cove.** Ten miles farther is a four-way intersection: to the left is Road 431, a poor road through the park (4WD required); to the right is the six-mile dirt road back to **Shelter Cove** and, eventually, **Usal Beach.**

Straight ahead is Road 435 is a treacherous drive for the fearless or insane—so narrow that it only fits one car at a time. As you crawl down the mountain, you will come across **Jones Beach, Needle Rock,** and the **Needle Rock Visitors Center** (986-7711), offering maps ($1), camping permits, and firewood. (Sites $11. No water; pit toilets. 14-night max. stay. No reservations accepted; usually full in summer. Center hours vary; always closes at 5pm.) Eventually this road leads to **Bear Harbor.** The blocked-off road to Jones Beach is about two miles down Road 435; a 10-minute hike leads to three primitive campsites and another trail to the beautiful

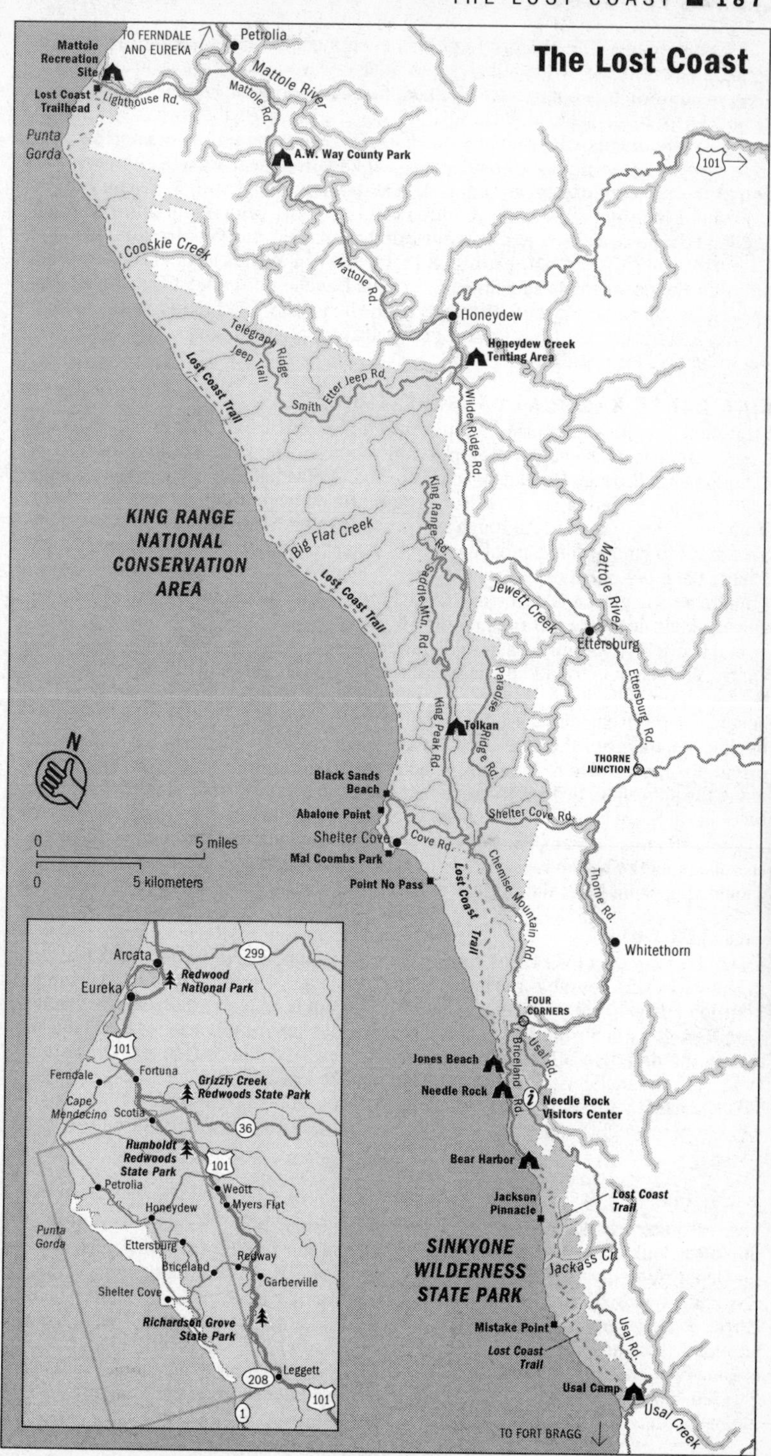
The Lost Coast
Petrolia
TO FERNDALE AND EUREKA
Mattole Recreation Site
Lost Coast Trailhead
Lighthouse Rd.
Mattole River
Mattole Rd.
Punta Gorda
A.W. Way County Park
101
Cooskie Creek
Mattole Rd.
Honeydew
Honeydew Creek Tenting Area
Telegraph Ridge Jeep Trail
Lost Coast Trail
Smith Etter Jeep Rd.
Wilder Ridge Rd.
King Range Rd.
KING RANGE NATIONAL CONSERVATION AREA
Big Flat Creek
Saddle Mtn. Rd.
Lost Coast Trail
Jewett Creek
Mattole River
Ettersburg
Ettersburg Rd.
Paradise Ridge Rd.
King Peak Rd.
Tolkan
THORNE JUNCTION
Black Sands Beach
Abalone Point
Shelter Cove Rd.
Shelter Cove
Cove Rd.
Mal Coombs Park
Point No Pass
Lost Coast Trail
Chemise Mountain Rd.
Thorne Rd.
Whitethorn
0 5 miles
0 5 kilometers
N
FOUR CORNERS
Briceland Rd.
Usal Rd.
Jones Beach
Needle Rock
Needle Rock Visitors Center
Bear Harbor
Jackson Pinnacle
Lost Coast Trail
SINKYONE WILDERNESS STATE PARK
Jackass Cr.
Mistake Point
Lost Coast Trail
Usal Rd.
Usal Camp
Usal Creek
TO FORT BRAGG
Arcata
299
Redwood National Park
Eureka
101
Ferndale
Fortuna
Grizzly Creek Redwoods State Park
Cape Mendocino
Scotia
36
Humboldt Redwoods State Park
101
Petrolia
Weott
Myers Flat
Honeydew
Punta Gorda
Ettersburg
Redway
Briceland
Garberville
Shelter Cove
Richardson Grove State Park
Leggett
208
101
1

black sand beach. The sinister road gets even more treacherous on the way to Bear Harbor, but the dedicated will find their reward in the primal beauty of the three neighboring campgrounds (**Orchard, Railroad,** and **Bear Harbor**). Surrounded by lush ferns, black sand, and transplanted eucalyptus trees, they are only accessible by a half-mile hike. Be prepared to share your space with the **Roosevelt elk.**

One of the more popular Lost Coast beaches, **Usal Beach** has a self-registration kiosk and camping areas (unmarked state-maintained sites $11, trail camps $3). About 300 feet farther up its dirt road is a short bridge and another road leading to a parking area and some windy beachside sites (no drinking water). The southern trailhead of the difficult **Lost Coast Trail** begins at Usal and leads 50 miles up the coast to **Mattole River.** Both Usal Beach and the Lost Coast trail are accessible via an unmarked dirt road from the south. Trail maps are essential for exploring this wilderness and can be found at state parks or the Needle Rock Visitors Center.

KING RANGE NATIONAL CONSERVATION AREA

Stretching 24 miles along the coast between Shelter Cove and Petrolia, the **King Range National Conservation Area** provides some of the best isolated, primitive camping in California. Creeks, beaches, an abandoned lighthouse, and several side trails provide varied possibilities for exploration on a trip that can take anywhere from one to several days. Although it is possible to hike the trail one way and then backtrack to your vehicle, most campers choose to employ the **shuttle service** (see **Shelter Cove,** below).

Mattole Campground is at the end of Lighthouse Rd., 45 minutes north of Honeydew off Mattole Rd. (a dirt road marked by a sign right before the bridge for northbound traffic). No permit is required, but there is no water and only pit toilets. This windy, flat beach is framed by high cliffs and a parking lot. A dirt road leads up to the top of the hills 300 feet before the campground, offering dizzying views of the beach. Campers can stay here for a night's experience or take off at this trailhead for the remainder of the **Lost Coast Trail.** Beware: some of the area is well-marked private property, where camping is actively prohibited. As much of the hike is along the shoreline, be sure to buy **tide tables** in Garberville or at the nearby Petrolia General Store (see below) to keep your hike dry.

The trail ends at **Black Sands Beach,** a gorgeous place to camp before the 1998 storms. Now the beach is open only to beachcombing at low tide. Do not attempt a cleansing swim here; the riptides will pull you out into the deadly waters.

SHELTER COVE

The hub of the Lost Coast, Shelter Cove has several places to refuel at the start or in the midst of a journey down the Lost Coast Trail. Arrive by way of a tortuous hour-long drive from Redway on U.S. 101. Pick up news and advice at the **Shelter Cove Deli,** 492 Machi Rd. (986-7474). The closest thing in town to an information booth, the deli also offers fish 'n' chips and over 100 campsites near the beach (tents $15, RVs $25). At **Shelter Cove Beachcomber Inn,** 7272 Shelter Cove (800-718-4789), a room with bath and TV is the best deal on the coast (singles $45). Otherwise, stay the night in Redway and commute for day hikes and recreation.

FERNDALE

The northernmost Lost Coast town of **Ferndale** (pop. 1320) is small-town perfection. **Russ Park** makes for perfect picnicking, and the amphitheater-like **cemeteries** on Ocean Ave. give a great view of the Victorian town and grazing dairy cattle. Except for exorbitantly priced B&Bs, accommodations here are sparse. The **Eureka Baking Company,** 543 Main St. (786-4741), makes fresh bread, scrumptious chocolate macaroons ($1), coffee ($1), and a variety of sandwiches (open M-F 6:30am-5:30pm, Sa 7am-4pm, Su 9am-3pm). The **Ferndale Meat Company,** 376 Main St. (786-4501), layers generous slabs of cheese and meat on choice breads ($2.75) under the benevolent stares of mounted deer heads (open M-Sa 8am-5pm). One of

Ferndale's most curious features, the annual Arcata Kinetic Sculpture Race (see **Arcata: Sights,** p. 191), is properly revered in its founder's studio, Hobart Galleries, (Main and Brown St.), and across the street in the **Kinetic Sculpture Museum,** which has inherited some of the entries from past races. Examples constructed entirely from license plates will make you wonder how they ever managed to move at all, let alone travel 35 racing miles (open daily 10am-5pm; free).

EUREKA

Eureka (pop. 27,218) tends to be overlooked by most travelers in favor of its more attractive neighbors. Redwoods tower to the north, and to the south shines the isolated beauty of the Lost Coast. Totally rebuilt after a devastating earthquake in 1991, Eureka's main attractions are its galleries, which display work by 4000 local artists. In fact, it has more artists per capita than any comparable city in the U.S.

ORIENTATION AND PRACTICAL INFORMATION. Eureka straddles **U.S. 101** 12 miles south of Arcata and 280 miles north of San Francisco. To the south, U.S. 101 is referred to as Broadway. In town, U.S. 101 is called 4th St. (heading south) and 5th St. (heading north).

Greyhound **buses,** 1603 4th St. (442-0370 or 800-231-2222), at Q St., provide frequent service between Eureka and **Arcata** and go to **San Francisco** twice per day ($32-34; open M-F 9am-1:30pm and 2:30-5pm, Sa 9am-noon and 8-10:20pm). The **Humboldt Transit Authority,** 133 V St. (443-0826), runs regional buses between Scotia and Trinidad via Arcata. Most buses pick up passengers along 5th St. or Broadway (open M-F 8am-4:30pm; fare $1.35-1.60). The **Eureka/Humboldt Visitors Bureau,** 1034 2nd St. (443-5097, in CA 800-809-5908, out-of-state 800-346-3482), will answer specific questions (open M-F 9am-noon and 1-5pm). Eureka! It's the **Chamber of Commerce,** 2112 Broadway (442-3738 or 800-356-6381). Info! Brochures! Commerce! (Open June-Sept. M 9am-5pm, Tu-F 9am-7pm, Sa 10am-4pm, Oct.-May M-F 9am-5pm.) Eureka! An **ATM!** At **Bank of America!** At the corner of E and 4th Streets! **Adventure's Edge,** 408 F St. (822-4673), rents equipment. (Tents $16 per day for the 1st 3 days, $2 per additional day. Sleeping bags $14 for the first 3 days, $2 per additional day. Sea kayaks $35 per day. Cross-country ski packages $17. Open M-Sa 9am-6pm, Su 11am-5pm.) The **Summer St. Laundromat** (443-7463) is at 111 Summer St. (wash $2, dry 50¢; open daily 7am-8:30pm). **Emergency:** 911. **Police:** 441-4044. **Fire department:** 441-4000. **Eureka General Hospital:** 2200 Harrison Ave. (445-5111). **Post office:** 337 W. Clark St. (442-1786; open M-F 8:30am-5pm and Sa noon-3pm). **ZIP code:** 95501. **Area code:** 707.

ACCOMMODATIONS AND CAMPGROUNDS. Travelers will find many budget motels off U.S. 101, but most are unappealing; be selective and **avoid walking alone at night.** The **National 9 Inn,** 2846 Broadway (443-9381 or 800-524-9999), is south of town off U.S. 101, in an area much safer than Eureka's downtown. Rooms are cozy and come with cable TV and coffee. (Singles $28-38; doubles $34-48.) **Motel 6,** 1934 Broadway (445-9631), also south of town off U.S. 101, offers cable TV (singles $42; doubles $47; additional person $6). Most of the area's camping is nearer Arcata than Eureka. **Big Lagoon County Park,** 20 miles north of Eureka on U.S. 101 (445-7652), is a favorite. The park has 32 sites (no hookups) with flush toilets, drinking water, and a lagoon for swimming, canoeing, or kayaking. Sites $10; arrive early.)

FOOD. Eureka Co-op, 1036 5th St. (443-6027), at L St., sells bulk grains, organic produce, and deli foods (open M-Sa 7am-8pm, Su 10am-8pm). There are also two **farmer's markets** that run from July to October (Tu 10am-1pm at Old Town Gazebo; Th 10am-1pm at Eureka Mall). **Ramone's Bakery and Cafe,** 209 E St. (445-2923), between 2nd and 3rd St., specializes in desserts like the ever-popular "Chocolate Sin," a chocolate and liqueur torte, and local art (open M-Sa 7am-6pm, Su 8am-4pm). **Tomaso's Tomato Pies,** 216 E St. (445-0100), in Old Town Eureka, serves up generous slices of pizza with garlic bread and salad ($4) fit for two. Salads and sandwiches ($6 each) are excellent. (Open M-Th 11:30am-8:30pm, F-Sa 11:30am-9pm, Su 5-8:30pm.) **Stamos Deli,** 234 F St. (445-4733), has basic sandwiches, daily salads, and humorous discourse for the cheapest prices in Eureka ($3.50-4.50; open M-Sa 11am-6pm). **Cafe Marina,** 601 Startare Dr. (443-2233), is off U.S. 101 at the Woodley Island Exit, north of town. Outdoor dining on the marina is the perfect way to enjoy fresh seafood like the spicy blackened snapper. The polished bar is the local fishermen's night spot. (Lunch $8-13, dinner $10-14. Open in summer daily 7am-10pm; off-season Su-Th 7am-9pm, F-Sa 7am-10pm.)

VICTORIAN DUNE ART. Eureka is very proud of its bevy of restored **Victorian homes,** a few of which are even worth driving past. Most of the really good ones have been turned into expensive B&Bs, including the oft-photographed, dramatically stark **Carson Mansion,** which belonged to a prominent logger in the 1850s.

Art galleries breed downtown and are Eureka's main claim to fame; ask locals about current exhibits.

The **dunes recreation area** is in Samoa off Rte. 255 (past the cookhouse and left at Samoa Bridge). Once a thriving dune ecosystem, this peninsula now offers beach access and dune hiking.

ARCATA

Arcata is like Berkeley without San Francisco. At the intersection of U.S. 101 and Route 299, Arcata (ar-KAY-ta; pop. 15,451) typifies the laid-back, stress-free existence that characterizes the North Coast. Arcata's neighbor, Humboldt State University (Earth First! was founded here) focuses on forestry and marine biology. Students and would-be students get baked in the sun all over Humboldt County.

PRACTICAL INFORMATION. Arcata Chamber of Commerce, 1062 G St. (822-3619), has visitor info (open M-F 10am-4pm). An **ATM** is at **U.S. Bank,** 953 G St. The most convenient **laundromat** is M.O.M.'s, 5000 Valley West Blvd. (822-1181; open daily 7am-10pm). **Emergency:** 911. **Mad River Hospital:** 3800 Janes Rd. (822-3621). **Post office:** 799 H St. (open M-F 8:30am-5pm). **ZIP Code:** 95521. **Area code:** 707.

ACCOMMODATIONS AND CAMPGROUNDS. There is, as always, **Motel 6,** 4755 Valley West Blvd. (822-7061), at the Giuntoli Exit off U.S. 101 (in summer singles $45, doubles $51; in winter singles Su-Th $40, F-Sa $45; doubles $46, $51). The motel is clean and quiet, and offers cable TV, pool, and air-conditioning. **Arcata Hostel,** 1390 I St. (822-9995), at 14th St. about a ½-mile walk from the bus station, is a term-time college residence. (Lockout 9am-5pm. Check-in 5-11pm. Open late June to late Aug. Dorms $15 per night.)

For those with cars, camping is easy near Arcata, and budget motels line the Giuntoli Exit off U.S. 101 north of the city. **Clam Beach County Park** (445-7491), on U.S. 101, 7½ miles north of Arcata, has dunes and a huge sand beach with seasonal clam digging, making the park very popular; call ahead (water and pit toilets; sites $8). **Patrick's Point State Park** (677-3570), 15 miles north of Arcata, is an excellent spot for watching whales and dolphins. It has 123 sites with terrific ocean views, lush vegetation, treasure-hunting in the beach's tidepools and agates, as well as showers and flush toilets. (Sites $16 per vehicle; no hookups. Day use $5; hikers and cyclists $3. Reservations through PARKNET 800-444-7275; in summer, required at least 2 weeks in advance.)

FOOD AND ENTERTAINMENT. **Los Bageles,** 1061 I St. (822-3150), between 10th and 11th St., has a wide assortment of pastries, specialty coffees, and fruit drinks. Outdoor seating is comfortable and laid-back. (Most items under $1. Open M, W-F 7am-6pm, Sa 7am-5pm, Su 8am-3pm.) **Hey Juan!,** 1642½ G St. (822-8433), serves up tasty and dirt-cheap Mexi-Cali fare (entree with beans and rice about $4; open daily 11am-11pm). **Crosswinds,** 860 10th St. (826-2133), in a restored Victorian home, offers a number of breakfast variations. Vegan substitutes are available for all meat used in the Mexican, Italian, and Californian specialties ($3-4), and servings are large. (Open Tu-Su 7:30am-2pm.) The **Arcata Co-op** (822-5947), on 8th St. at I St., feeds patrons tofu, tempeh, ginseng cola, and soy milk (open M-Sa 8am-9pm, Su 8am-8pm). A **farmer's market** offering tie-dyed dresses, candles, and the usual fresh produce invades the Arcata Plaza (June-Nov. Sa 9am-1pm).

Arcata is a college town with its fair share of bars, most of which are on 9th St. in the town square. **Humboldt Brewery,** 856 10th St. (826-BREW/2739), at I St. is a popular local microbrewery with a cavernous imported beer garden. Unusual beers (like the Red Nectar Ale) go well with the live music on weekends. (Open Su-Th 11:30am-10pm, F-Sa 11:30am-1am.) **Jambalaya** (822-4766), at 9th and H St. is a great place to hang with Humboldt students and listen to live jazz and blues.

SIGHTS AND SEASONAL EVENTS. You can fully experience Arcata by taking a **walking tour** or wandering around the **Arcata Plaza,** in the center of town near the intersection of 8th and H St., which offers folk music on the weekends and an annual **Summer Solstice Festival.** Those who wish to tour the uniformly beige Humboldt campus should be sure to see the **whale skulls** by the biological labs and **Redwood Park,** which contains lots of nooks for picnicking among the giants. Five minutes east of the city is the **Arcata Community Forest,** which has picnic spaces, lush meadows, redwoods, and hiking trails (free). A former "sanitary" landfill, the 75-acre **Arcata Marsh and Wildlife Sanctuary** (826-2359), lies at the foot of I St. Wander the trails around the lake or take a tour to see how this saltwater marsh/converted sewer system works with treated waste. (Tours Sa 8:30am and 2pm; meet at info center).

The 15-year-old **Kinetic Sculpture Race,** held annually over Memorial Day weekend (May 27-29 in 2000), is Humboldt County's oddest festival. A few dozen insane and/or intoxicated adventurers attempt to pilot unwieldy homemade vehicles on a grueling three-day, 35-mile trek from Arcata to Ferndale on road, sand, and water. Past vehicles are on display at a museum in Ferndale (see **Ferndale,** p. 188).

REDWOOD NATIONAL PARK

With ferns that grow to the height of humans and redwood trees the size of skyscrapers, Redwood National Park, as John Steinbeck said, "will leave a mark or create a vision that stays with you always." Fog rolls between the creaking redwood boughs in a prehistoric atmosphere where you finally realize just how small you are in life. The redwoods in the park are the last remaining stretch of the old-growth forest which used to blanket two million acres of Northern California and Oregon. Wildlife runs rampant here, with black bears and mountain lions in the backwoods and Roosevelt elk grazing in the meadows. While a short tour of the big sights and the drive-through tree will certainly give visitors ample photo opportunities, a less exhaustive but more memorable way to experience the redwoods is to head down a trail into the quiet of the forest, where you can see the trees as they have been for thousands of years.

ORIENTATION

Redwood National Park is one of four redwood parks between Klamath and Orick, the others being **Jedediah Smith State Park, Del Norte Coast Redwoods State Park,** and **Prairie Creek Redwoods State Park.** However, the name "Redwood National Park" is an umbrella term for all four parks. **Crescent City,** with park headquarters and a few basic services, is at the park's northern end. The town of **Orick** is the southern limit, and just south of town is an extremely helpful ranger station. **U.S. 101** traverses most of the park. The slower but more scenic **Newton Drury Parkway** runs parallel to U.S. 101 for 31 miles from Klamath to Prairie Creek (watch for bikers).

PRACTICAL INFORMATION

Entrance Fee: $5 per car (use of most park facilities, such as beaches and picnic areas). South of Orick are free off-highway areas, ask at visitor info centers for locations.

Buses: Greyhound, 500 E. Harding St., Crescent City (464-2807). To **San Francisco** (2 per day, $51) and **Portland** (2 per day, $53). Open M-F 7-10am and 5-7:30pm, Sa 7-9am and 7-7:30pm. No credit cards.

Auto Repairs: AAA Emergency Road Service (800-222-4357). 24hr.

Visitor Information:

Redwood Information Center (488-3461), on U.S. 101, 1mi. south of Orick. Shows free films on redwoods, gray whales, and black bears. Helpful, free park maps. Info on trails and campsites doled out by enthusiastic and helpful rangers. Open daily 9am-5pm.

Redwood National Park Headquarters and Information Center, 1111 2nd St., Crescent City (464-6101). Headquarters of the entire national park, but ranger stations are just as well-informed. Open daily 9am-5pm.

Crescent City-Del Norte County Chamber of Commerce, 1001 Front St., Crescent City (464-3174). Free coffee, brochures, and coupons. Open Memorial Day-Labor Day (May 29-Sept. 4 in 2000) M-F 8am-7pm, Sa-Su 9am-5pm; Labor Day-Memorial Day M-F 9am-5pm.

Prairie Creek Information Center (464-6101, ext. 5301), on the Drury Scenic Pkwy. in Prairie Creek Redwood State Park. Open in summer daily 8am-5pm, when volunteers are available.

Hiouchi Ranger Station (464-6101, ext. 5067), on U.S. 199 across from Jedediah Smith Redwoods State Park. Open June-Oct. daily 9am-5pm.

Jedediah Smith State Park Information Center (464-6101, ext. 5113), on U.S. 199 across from the Hiouchi Ranger Station. Open daily 9am-5pm.

ATM: Bank of America, 240 H St. at 2nd St. in Crescent City.

Laundromat: Econ-o-wash, 601 H St., Crescent City (464-9935). Wash $1, dry 50¢. Open daily 7am-10pm.

Road Conditions: 800-427-7623.

Emergency: 911.

24-Hour Rape Crisis Line: 465-2851.

Medical Assistance: Sutter Coast Hospital, 800 E. Washington Blvd., Crescent City (464-8511).

Post Office: Crescent City: 751 2nd St. (464-2151). Open M-F 8:30am-5pm, Sa noon-2pm. **ZIP Code:** 95531. **Orick:** 121147 U.S. 101. Open M-F 8:30am-noon and 1-5pm. **ZIP Code:** 95555. **Klamath:** 141 Klamath Blvd. Open M-F 8am-4:30pm. **ZIP Code:** 95548.

AREA CODE	The area code for Redwood National Park is 707.

ACCOMMODATIONS

Redwood Youth Hostel (HI-AYH), 14480 U.S. 101 (482-8265), at Wilson Creek Rd. 7mi. north of Klamath. Overlooking the crashing Pacific surf and housed in the historic DeMartin House, this 30-bed hostel suggests Shaker simplicity. Kitchen and 2 ocean-view sundecks. Chores and rules (no shoes inside) may seem a bit oppressive. Linen $1. Laundry (wash $1.50). Check-in 4:30-9:30pm. Check-out 9:30am. Lockout 9:30am-4:30pm. Curfew 11pm. Dorms $12; 1 private double available. Reservations recommended in summer; advance payment required.

Camp Marigold, 16101 U.S. 101 (482-3585 or 800-621-8513), 3mi. north of Klamath Bridge, is a pleasantly woodsy alternative to mundane motels. Cute cabins have full kitchens and cable TV. Doubles $38.

Green Valley Motel (488-2341), on U.S. 101 in Orick, has clean, basic rooms, and a deli. Phones and TV. Singles $32; doubles $35.

El Patio, 655 H St., Crescent City (464-5114), offers decent rooms with an early-70s look and TVs. Key deposit $2. Singles $32, with kitchenette $37; doubles $35, $40.

CAMPGROUNDS

Redwood National Park offers several backcountry campsites; all are free and accessible only by hiking a short distance from roads or parking lots. **Freshwater Spit Beach,** just south of Orick and the only oceanside campground in the area, lacks water and has pit toilets. The tent area is complete with evening bonfires and drum circles; RV sites are also available ($5 donation; 14-day max. stay). **Nickel Creek campground,** at the end of Enderts Beach Rd. outside Crescent City, has five oceanview sites without showers or water, but with toilets. **Flint Ridge,** off the end of Klamath Beach Rd., has water and toilets but no showers. Exit U.S. 101 and head toward the ocean—no signs posted. State Park campsites (464-9533) are all fully developed and easily accessible. Call PARKNET (800-444-7275) for reservations, which are necessary in summer (sites $16). North of Crescent City on U.S. 199 is **Jedediah Smith State Park.** Amenities include picnic tables, grills, water, restrooms, and showers. Campfire programs and nature walks also offered.

In the **Del Norte Coast State Park,** where the ocean views are magnificent, camping is inland at Mill Creek Campground, where space is usually available. Camping in **Prairie Creek State Park** is possible at Elk Prairie, where elk graze all over the place, and at Gold Bluffs Beach, where the sound of the surf soothes one to sleep (no showers). **Six Rivers National Park** (457-3131) has several campgrounds. Big Flat

THE REDWOOD CHAINSAW MASSACRE Rising hundreds of feet above the ground, the trees in Redwood National Park have towered in lush profusion for 150 million years. Native Americans called these lofty giants "the eternal spirit" because of their 2000-year lifespan, ability to adapt to climatic changes, and resistance to insects, fire, and even lightning. The redwoods were indeed almost invincible, until the era of logging. Unfortunately the trees never evolved to be chain-saw-resistant. With money on their minds (1 tree builds 22 houses) and saws in their hands, loggers chopped 96% of the virgin coast redwoods in one century. Despite the economic boom that the logging industry brought to the area's small towns, conservationists realized that killing millions of trees was hurting the ecology. Concerned citizens began buying redwood plots from loggers in the 1920s, and in 1968 the Redwood National Park was formed by the federal government, preserving these quiet giants for the next few hundred generations. Present-day activists insist that the Pacific Lumber Co., which still harvests the trees outside of National Park areas, must stop their programs entirely. In order to get their point across, Earth First! volunteers stage "tree sits," sometimes spending months 180 feet high in the trees.

Campground is 14 miles up South Fork Rd. off U.S. 199 ($5; no hookups). Panther Flat, on U.S. 199, 25 minutes north of Crescent City, has water and showers, and is directly on the river (sites $12).

FOOD

There are more picnic tables than restaurants in the area, so the best option for food is probably **Orick Market** (488-3225), which has reasonably priced groceries (open M-Sa 8am-7pm, Su 9am-7pm). In Crescent City, head to the **24-hour Safeway** on U.S. 101 (M St.) between 2nd and 5th St., in the shopping center, for all of your grocery needs. **Glen's Bakery and Restaurant** (464-2914), at 3rd and G St., serves basic diner fare such as huge pancakes ($3), sandwiches ($4), and burgers ($3-4; open Tu-Sa 5am-6:30pm). The **Jefferson State Brewery,** 400 Front St. (464-1139), is a hip new restaurant and bar environmentally designed and built of 90% recycled material. Feel free to marvel at the Family Dog poster collection while dining on sandwiches ($5-7), pasta ($10), or island chicken with grilled vegetables ($10). Try the six-beer sampler brewed on the premises ($4.50). After dinner, chill in the TV lounge or play a game of pool. (Open Su-Th 11am-10pm, F-Sa 11am-11pm.) The **Palm Cafe** (488-3381), on U.S. 101 in Orick, dishes out food to local boys in rattlesnake cowboy hats (head and tail still attached), but non-poisonous visitors are also welcome. Old Maid Plate with two eggs and pancakes ($5) hits the spot better than anything. Homemade fruit, coconut, and chocolate pies are positively delicious. (Open daily 5:30am-8pm.)

SIGHTS AND ACTIVITIES

In the park, you may gather fruits and berries for personal consumption, but all other plants and animals are protected—even feathers dropped by birds of prey are off-limits. **Fishing licenses** are required for fresh and saltwater fishing off any natural formation, but fishing is free from any manmade structure. There are minimum-weight and maximum-catch requirements specific to both (1-day licenses $23). Call the ranger station or **License and Revenue Office** (707-464-2523).

The redwoods are best experienced on foot. The park is divided into several regions, each of which has information centers and unique attractions. The U.S. Park Service conducts many organized activities for all ages; a detailed list of junior ranger programs and nature walks is available at all park ranger stations (see **Visitor Information,** p. 192) or from the **Redwood Information Center** (488-3461). Hikers should take particular care to wear protective clothing—**ticks** and **poison oak** thrive in these deep, dark places (see **Preventing Disease,** p. 40). **Roosevelt elk** roam the woods, and are interesting to watch but dangerous to approach since invaders of their territory are promptly circled and trampled. Also be on the lookout for the **black bears** and **mountain lions** that inhabit many areas of the park. Before setting out, get advice and trail maps at the visitors center.

ORICK AREA

The Orick Area covers the southernmost section of Redwood National Park. Its **visitors center** lies on U.S. 101 one mile south of Orick and a half-mile south of the Shoreline Deli (the Greyhound bus stop). The main attraction is the **Tall Trees Grove,** which, if the road is open, is accessible by car to those with permits (available at the visitors center; free). At least three to four hours should be allowed for the trip. From the trailhead at the end of Tall Trees Access Rd. (off Bald Hills Rd. from U.S. 101 north of Orick), it's a 1¼-mile hike (about 30min.) to the tallest redwoods in the park and, in fact, to the **tallest known tree in the world** (367¾ft., one-third the height of New York's World Trade Center towers). If the road is closed, the hardy can hike the 16-mile round-trip **Emerald Ridge Trail** to see these giants.

Orick (pop. 650) is a friendly town, overrun with souvenir stores selling "burl sculptures" (over-crafted and expensive wood carvings). However, it also has a post office, a motel, and a market for last-minute campfire groceries.

Patrick's Point State Park, 15 miles south of Orick along U.S. 101, offers one of the most spectacular views along the California coast, and merits a day or two from campers, boaters, and nature enthusiasts heading north to the redwoods ($16). During **whale-watching** season (Oct.-Dec. and Mar.-May), the towering cliffs and rocky geography of the point provide the best seats in the house for observing the migration of gray whales. Bikers might enjoy the **Newton Drury Scenic Parkway,** a 31-mile jaunt through old-growth redwoods, or the magnificent **Coastal Trail,** a 15-mile paved ride along the ocean off Davison Rd. from the Prairie Creek Visitors Center.

PRAIRIE CREEK AREA

The Prairie Creek Area, equipped with a **ranger station** and **state park campgrounds,** is perfect for hikers, who can explore 75 miles of trails in the park's 14,000 acres. Be sure to pick up a trail map ($1) at the ranger station before heading out; the loops of criss-crossing trails may be confusing without one. Starting at the Prairie Creek Visitors Center, the **James Irvine Trail** (4½mi. one-way) winds through a prehistoric garden of towering old-growth redwoods of humbling height. Winding through where small waterfalls trickle down 50-foot fern-covered walls, the trail ends at **Gold Bluffs Beach,** whose sands stretch for miles and elk-scattered miles. The less ambitious can elk-watch on the meadow in front of the ranger station.

The **Elk Prairie Trail** (1½mi. one-way) skirts the prairie and loops around to join the nature trail. **Revelation** and **Redwood Access Trails** were designed to accommodate people with disabilities (and elks). **Big Tree Trail** is an easy walk, and its 306-foot-high behemoth is a satisfying substitute for those who don't want to make the long trek to the tallest tree in the world (see **Orick Area,** above).

KLAMATH AREA

The Klamath Area to the north consists of a thin stretch of park land connecting Prairie Creek with Del Norte State Park. The town itself consists of a few stores stretched over four miles, so the main attraction here is the ruggedly spectacular coastline. The **Klamath Overlook,** where Requa Rd. meets the Coastal Trail, is an **excellent whale-watching site** with a spectacular view.

The mouth of the **Klamath River** is a popular fishing spot (permit required; see **Sights and Activities,** p. 194) in fall and spring, when salmon spawn, and in winter, when steelhead trout do the same. Coastal Dr. passes by the remains of the **Douglas Memorial Bridge,** where sea lions and harbor seals congregate in the spring and summer, and then continues along the ocean for eight miles of incredible views. *Blut-und-boden* kitsch meets audio high-tech at **Trees of Mystery,** 5500 U.S. 101 (482-2251 or 800-638-3389), just north of Klamath, a one-mile walk through spectacular old growth and chainsaw sculpture. Just look for the 200-foot-tall Paul Bunyan next to the road. Kids may enjoy this spot but chainsaw-art purists will wince at the noise (Paul speaks, and the trees talk and play music) and the price—be sure to pick up a 20% discount card at the Crescent City Chamber of Commerce. (Open daily dawn-dusk. Admission $6.50, children $4.)

CRESCENT CITY AREA

Crescent City calls itself the city "where the redwoods meet the sea." In 1964, a wrathful Mother Nature took this literally, when a *tsunami* caused by oceanic quakes leveled the city. Many local restaurants carry photo albums documenting the destruction. Today, the rebuilt town offers an outstanding location from which to explore the national park.

The **Battery Point Lighthouse** (464-3089), on a causeway jutting out of Front St., houses a museum open only during low tide. Ask guides about the resident **ghost.** (Open Apr.-Sept. W-Su 10am-4pm, tide permitting. Admission $2, children 50¢.) From June through August, the National Park offers **tidepool walks** which leave from the Endert Beach parking lot (turn-off 4mi. south of Crescent City; call 464-6101 for schedules). The **Coastal Trail** runs from Endert in the north to Tall Tree Grove in the south, passing cliffs, beaches, forests, and prairie along the way; the section near Endert Beach (part of the **Crescent Beach Trail**) is relatively easy. The trailhead is at the **Crescent Beach Information Center** on Endert Beach Rd., just off U.S. 101. A scenic drive from Crescent City along **Pebble Beach Drive** to **Point Saint George** snakes past coastline that looks transplanted from New England. Craggy cliffs, lush prairies, and an old lighthouse add to the atmosphere.

Annual highlights include the **World Championship Crab Races,** featuring races and crab feasts on the third Sunday in February. During **Easter in July,** the lily completes its biennial bloom with a celebration. The **Weekend in Bear Country** is a mid-August beachfront festival. Call 800-343-8300 year-round for information regarding any of these events.

HIOUCHI AREA

This inland region, known for its rugged beauty, sits in the northern part of the park along U.S. 199 and contains some excellent hiking trails, most of which are in **Jedediah Smith State Park.** Several trails lie off Howland Hill Rd., a dirt road easily accessible from both U.S. 101 and U.S. 199. From U.S. 199, turn onto South Fork Rd. in Hiouchi and right onto Douglas Park Rd., which then turns into Howland Hill Rd. From Crescent City, go south on U.S. 101, turn left onto Elk Valley Rd., and right onto Howland Hill. The wheelchair-accessible **Stout Grove Trail** is a short (½mi.) and tourist-packed jaunt through lush redwoods. The trailhead is near the Hiouchi end of Howland Hill Rd., and the paved section is just past the trail. The **Mill Creek Trail** is a moderate 2½-mile hike with excellent swimming and fishing, accessible from the Mill Creek Bridge on Howland Hill Rd. and from the Jedediah Smith campground. The more strenuous **Boy Scout Trail** splits after three miles; the right path goes to the monstrous Boy Scout Tree and the left ends at Fern Falls. Two miles west of Jedediah State Park on U.S. 199 lie the **Peterson Trails** (both wheelchair accessible). A tour map (25¢ at the ranger station) will guide you.

Six Rivers National Forest (457-3131), is directly east of Hiouchi. The Smith River, the state's last major undammed river, rushes through rocky gorges as it winds its way from the mountains to the coast. The salmon, trout, and steelhead fishing are heavenly, and excellent camping is available on the banks. There are also numerous hiking trails throughout the forest.

THE CENTRAL COAST

Although the popular image of the California dream is manufactured by the media machine in Los Angeles, the image itself comes from the Central Coast. The 400-mile stretch of coastline between Los Angeles and San Francisco embodies all that is purely Californian—rolling surf crashing onto secluded beaches, dramatic cliffs and mountains, self-actualizing New Age adherents, and always a hint of the off-beat. This is the solitary magnificence of the Central Coast that inspired Robinson Jeffers' paeans, John Steinbeck's novels, and Jack Kerouac's frivolous musings. Among the smog-free skies, sweeping shorelines, dense forests, and plunging cliffs, there is a point where inland farmland communities and old seafaring towns conjoin, beckoning citified residents to journey out to the quiet drama of the coast. The landmarks along the way are well worth visiting—Hearst Castle, the Monterey Bay Aquarium, Carmel, the historic missions—but the real point of the Central Coast is the journey itself.

THE PACIFIC COAST HIGHWAY

The quintessential Californian road, the **Pacific Coast Highway** (known to Angelenos as **PCH,** to Californians as **Highway 1,** and by maps as **Route 1**), loops along the entirety of the state's coastline. Begun in 1920, the PCH required $10 million and 17 years for completion. After skirting the coastal communities of Los Angeles, the highway curves north from Ventura to genteel Santa Barbara, and then winds past vineyards, fields of wildflowers, and miles of beach on the journey northward to San Luis Obispo. William Randolph Hearst's San Simeon, north of San Luis, anchors the southern end of Big Sur, the legendary 90-mile strip of sparsely inhabited coastline. Climbing in and out of Big Sur's mountains, Rte. 1 inches motorists to the edge of jutting cliffs hanging precipitously over the surf. From Ventura to Santa Cruz, state parks and national forests offer peaceful campgrounds and daring recreation. The **Los Angeles** (see p. 345), **Bay Area** (see p. 127), and **North Coast** (see p. 181) sections have more on PCH's route.

HIGHLIGHTS OF THE CENTRAL COAST

- The gorgeous **Big Sur** (p. 218) forests continue to inspire mystics and weirdos.
- Many watery life forms swim about the **Monterey Bay Aquarium** (p. 212).
- **Hearst Castle** (p. 221) fabulously commemorates its builder's wealth.
- The hilly city of **Santa Barbara** (p. 233) is built all in a graceful Spanish style.
- The University of California campus and surrounding environment in **Santa Cruz** (p. 239) mix college-town ease with coastal breeze.

SANTA CRUZ

Santa Cruz (pop. 49,000) is the probable location of the West Coast party that doesn't stop. One of the few places where the 1960s catch-phrase "do your own thing" still applies, Santa Cruz simultaneously embraces macho surfers, a large lesbian, gay, and bisexual community, and shaggy rock star Neil Young, who lives somewhere in the hills surrounding the town.

The atmosphere here is fun-loving but far from hedonistic, intellectual but not even close to stuffy. This small city has enough Northern California cool and Southern California fun for all, whether gobbling cotton candy on the Ferris wheel or sipping wheatgrass at poetry readings. Along the beach and Boardwalk, tourism and surf culture reign supreme. Along Pacific Avenue, bookstores, clubs, and cafes provide a safe, clean hangout for plentiful local teens and tourists alike. On the other side of Front Street, the University of California at Santa Cruz (UCSC) sprawls luxuriously with prime biking routes and hidden campus buildings. Restaurants offer avocado sandwiches and industrial coffee; merchants hawk UCSC paraphernalia alongside fliers for courses that ask "Should you kill your superego?" There are comprehensive weekly listings in the local publications *Good Times* and *Metro Santa Cruz.*

ORIENTATION

Santa Cruz is on the northern tip of Monterey Bay, 120 miles south of San Francisco on **U.S. 101** or the more scenic **Route 1.** In town, **Beach Street** runs roughly east-west. The narrow **San Lorenzo River** runs mainly north-south, dividing the Boardwalk scene from quiet, affluent residences. Soquel Ave. crosses the river. The **University of California at Santa Cruz (UCSC)** encompasses the area on the other side of Front St. **Pacific Avenue** and **Cedar Street** carve out a nightlife niche accessible from the beach motels. One-way and resident-traffic-only zones, dead-end streets, and streets that curve, merge, and converge haphazardly can make Santa Cruz highly frustrating to navigate by car. Park at a motel or in free two-hour public lots off Pacific Ave. to avoid the cash-guzzling, beach-vicinity lots and meters.

PRACTICAL INFORMATION

Trains: Amtrak (800-872-7245). The closest station, in **San Jose,** is reachable by bus.

Buses: Greyhound, 425 Front St. (423-1800 or 800-231-2222). To: **L.A.** (8 per day M-Th $36, F-Su $38); **San Francisco** (5 buses per day; M-Th $14, F-Su $15); and **San Jose** (M-Th 2 per day, $5). Open daily 8:30-11:30am and 1:30-9:30pm and during late bus arrivals and departures.

Public Transportation: Santa Cruz Metropolitan Transit District (SCMTD), 920 Pacific Ave. (info line open M-F 8am-5pm 425-8600, TDD 425-8993; www.scmtd.com), at the Metro Center in the middle of the Pacific Garden Mall. The free *Headways* has route info. Fare $1, seniors and disabled 40¢, under 46in. free; day pass $3, $1.10, free. Buses run daily 7am-10pm.

Taxis: Yellow Cab (423-1234). Initial fee $2.25, each additional mi. $2. Open 24hr.

Bike Rental: The Bicycle Rental Center, 131 Center St. (426-8687). Rents 21-speed mountain/road hybrids, tandems, children's bikes. Bikes $7 for 1st hr., $2 each additional 30min.; $25 per day; $5 overnight. Helmets and locks provided. Open daily in summer 10am-6pm; off-season 10am-5pm.

Visitor Information:

Santa Cruz County Conference and Visitor Council, 701 Front St. (425-1234 or 800-833-3494; www.scccvc.org). Extremely helpful staff. Publishes the free *Santa Cruz County Traveler's Guide* with helpful restaurant information. Open M-Sa 9am-5pm, Su 10am-4pm. An unstaffed **information kiosk** sits north of Santa Cruz on Rte. 17 next to the Summit Inn Restaurant. Open daily 10am-4pm.

California Parks and Recreation Department, 600 Ocean St. (429-2850), across from the Holiday Inn. Info on camping and beach facilities in Santa Cruz; for reservations, call PARKNET (800-444-7275). Open M-F 8am-5pm.

Library: 224 Church St. (429-3526). **Internet access** available. Open M-Th 10am-9pm, F 10am-6pm, Sa 10am-5pm, Su 1-5pm.

Bi-Gay-Lesbian Organizations: Lesbian, Gay, Bisexual, and Transgender Community Center, 1328 Commerce Ln. (425-5422), ½ block north of Pacific Garden Mall. Publishes *Manifesto* and distributes the *Lavender Reader,* an excellent quarterly journal. Extremely helpful staffers supply info about events, outings, and general concerns. Open daily; call for hours.

Laundromat: Washrock, 135 Laurel St. (471-0555), but the entrance is through the parking lot off Pacific Ave. Cafe offers coffee (93¢) and decadent heated cinnamon rolls while you wait. Mobbed machines may contribute to your caffeine rush. Wash $1.25, 10min. dry 25¢. Open daily 24hr.

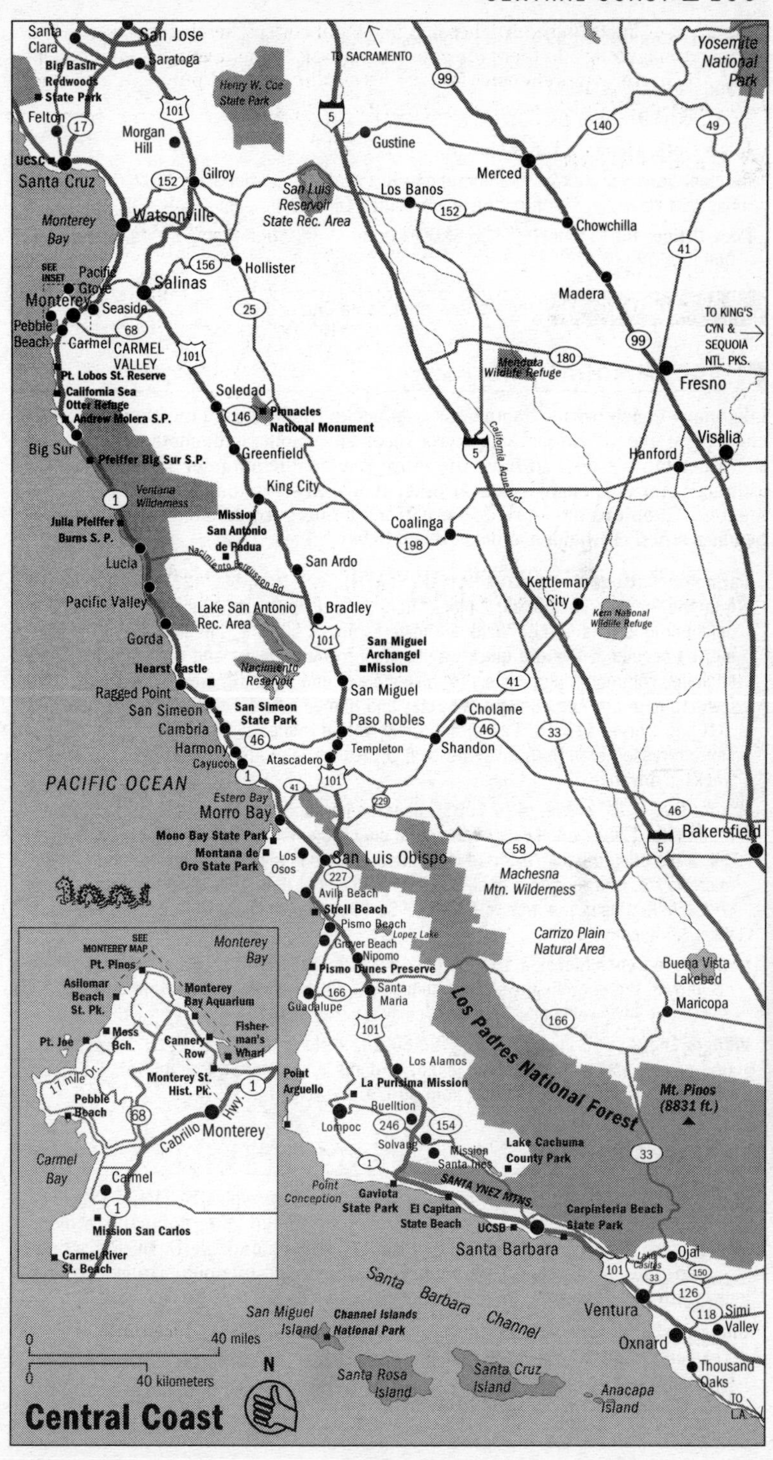

CENTRAL COAST

Weather Conditions: 429-3460. Operated by County Beach lifeguards Memorial Day through Labor Day (May 29-Sept. 4 in 2000), plus weekends in spring and fall. Updated daily at 9am.

Emergency: 911. **Police:** 809 Center St. (471-1131). 24hr.

Crisis Lines: Women's Crisis Line (429-1478). 24hr.

Medical Services: Santa Cruz Dominican Hospital, 1555 Soquel Dr. (462-7700). Take bus #71 on Soquel Dr. from the Metro Center. Open 24hr.

Post Office: 850 Front St. (426-5200). Open M-F 8:30am-5pm, Sa 9am-4pm. **ZIP Code:** 95060.

AREA CODE	The area code for Santa Cruz is 831.

ACCOMMODATIONS

Like many beach towns, Santa Cruz gets packed solid during the summer, especially on weekends. Room rates skyrocket and availability plummets. Surprisingly, the nicer motels tend to have the more reasonable summer weekend rates, although more expensive rates at other times. Reservations are always recommended. Shop around—price fluctuation can be outrageous. Sleeping on the beach is strictly forbidden and can result in hefty fines.

Carmelita Cottage Santa Cruz Hostel (HI-AYH), 321 Main St. (423-8304), 4 blocks from the Greyhound stop and 2 blocks from the beach. Centrally located, but in a quiet neighborhood, this 40-bed Victorian hostel is run by a young, hip staff. Sporadic summer barbecues ($4) are a quick way to meet fellow travelers and eat tasty grub. Two kitchens, common room, cyclery for bike storage and repair. Chore required. Strict curfew 11pm. In July-Aug., 3-night max. stay and HI members only. Reception 8-10am and 5-10pm. Dorms $13-15. Call or send reservation requests, first night's deposit, and self-addressed stamped envelope to P.O. Box 1241, Santa Cruz 95061 at least 2 weeks in advance.

Harbor Inn, 645 7th Ave. (479-1067), near the harbor and a few blocks north of Eaton. A beautiful 22-bed hotel well off the main drag. Summer weekend rates are likely to be below the absurd prices extorted by cheaper motels in town. Rooms have queen beds, microwaves, and fridges. Check-out 11am. Check-in until 11pm; call to arrange late check-in. Rooms in summer Su-Th $75, F-Sa $95; off-season Su-Th $55, F-Sa $75. Reservations recommended.

Sunny Cove Beach Motel, 2-1610 E. Cliff Dr. (475-1741), near Schwan Lagoon. Far from downtown, but charming, well-kept suites have kitchens. Rooms in summer $50-100; off-season $40, weekends $70-80. Weekly rates available.

Villager Lodge, 510 Leibrant Ave. (423-6020), 2 blocks from the beach. Heated pool, TV, free local calls, kitchens, and laundry. Rooms in summer Su-Th from $55, F-Sa from $80; off-season Su-Th $52, F-Sa from $60. AAA discounts.

CAMPGROUNDS

Reservations for all state campgrounds can be made through DESTINET (800-444-7275) and should be made early. Sites below are listed geographically, moving north toward Santa Cruz. New Brighton State Beach and Big Basin Redwoods State Park, the most scenic spots, are both accessible by public transportation. Campground fees are not cheap (June-Sept. Su-Th $17, F-Sa $18; Oct.-May $16).

Sunset State Beach (763-7063), on Rte. 1 12mi. south of Santa Cruz. Take the San Andreas Rd. Exit and turn right onto Sunset Beach Rd. 90 sites near the beach. Campsite derives its name from its obvious attraction; the sunsets over Santa Cruz are fabulous. No hookups. Reservations highly recommended in summer.

Thurs. Body Gallery

Simply Balanced

8-10 am

~~to~~ 5-10-pm

800-578-7878

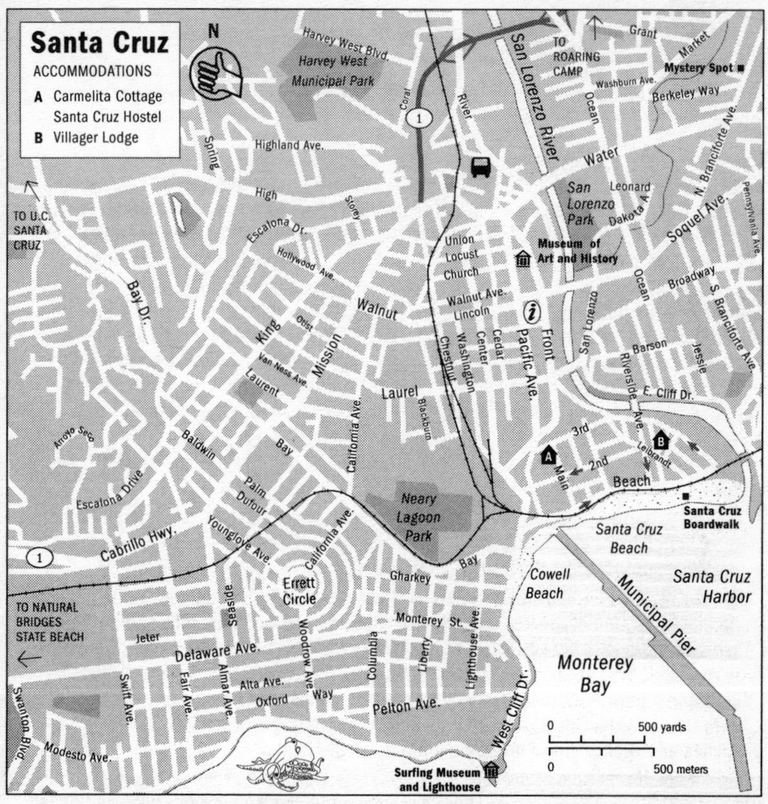

Manresa Uplands State Beach Park (761-1795), 10mi. south of Santa Cruz. Take Rte. 1 and exit at San Andreas Rd. Veer right and follow San Andreas Rd. for 4mi., then turn right on Sand Dollar. 64 tent sites are walk-in only; several with ocean view. Sheltered beach sometimes guarded. Wheelchair accessible. Seniors $1 off. Day use $6 per car.

New Brighton State Beach (464-6329), 4mi. south of Santa Cruz off Rte. 1. Take SCMDT bus #54 "Aptos." On a coastal bluff, wave breakers murmur to 112 sites (4 bike sites, 2 wheelchair accessible sites). RV sites available (check-out 9am). Showers get crowded 7-9am. June-Sept. 7-night max. stay; Oct.-May 15-night max. stay. No hook-ups. Check-out noon. Seniors $2 off. Reservations required mid-Mar. to Nov.

Henry Cowell Redwoods State Park, day use: 101 N. Big Trees Park Rd. (335-4598); campground: Graham Hill Rd. (438-2396). Take Graham Hill Rd. or SCMDT bus #34, 35, or 30. Spacious sites with varied degrees of privacy. 113 sites in summer, 50 in winter. Visit the observation deck from campground (½mi. hike) for a great view, or pick up a trail map ($1) at the day use entrance for more hiking options. Watch out for the poison oak! Hot showers (25¢ for 2min.), fire pits, picnic tables, food lockers. No hook-ups. In summer 7-day max. stay; off-season 15-day max. stay.

Big Basin Redwoods State Park (338-8860 or 338-8861), 20mi. northwest of Santa Cruz. Go north on Rte. 9 to Rte. 236 through Boulder Creek. This spectacular park was the first in the California State Park system. Today it offers the best camping from Point Reyes to Big Sur. The mountain air helps cool off its 80mi. of trails, including the 2-day Skyline-to-the-Sea Trail (trailhead parking $6). To reserve one of the 147 campsites with showers or one of the 35 tent cabins, call PARKNET (800-444-7275). A separate program within the park also operates backcountry sites ($10 including parking). Reservations for all accommodation options required well in advance for the summer.

FOOD

Santa Cruz offers an astounding number of budget eateries in various locations, especially by the beach in Capitola. Fresh local produce sells at the **farmer's market** at Lincoln and Cedar St. in downtown (W 2:30-6:30pm).

Zoccoli's, the Italian Delicatessen, 1534 Pacific Ave. (423-1711), across from the post office. This mobbed madhouse of a deli churns out incredible "special sandwiches" ($4-5). Daily pasta specials (about $5) come with salad, garlic bread, cheese, and a cookie. Only the freshest ingredients. Open M-Sa 9am-6pm, Su 11am-5pm.

Saturn Cafe, 1230 Mission St. (429-8505). Harried waitstaff do their best to keep your table clean and your coffee fresh; the cooks in the kitchen are more successful producing excellent vegetarian meals (most under $6). Table decorations include the "body manipulations" theme and the "ruined picnic" with plastic ants. Try the $3 Hangover, a slice of cold pizza with a beer, or a $6.75 Alien sandwich (tofu, hummus, avocado, and cheese). Open M-Th 11am-midnight, F 11am-1am, Sa 9am-1am, Su 9am-midnight.

Royal Taj, 270 Soquel Ave. (427-2400), at Roberts. You'll be crying *namaste* (I bow to you) after being treated like a king (with food to match) at this Indian restaurant. Daily lunch buffet $6.50. Meat dishes $6-9. Veggie specialties $6. Stellar *lassi* $2. Open daily 11:30am-2:30pm and 5:30-10pm.

Taquería Vallarta I, 608 Soquel Ave. (457-8226). Outstanding Mexican manna. Order at the counter, and the food might beat you back to your chair. Vegetarian plate $4; mind-blowing *aguas fresca* $1.20. Open daily 10am-midnight.

Walnut Ave. Cafe, 106 Walnut Ave. (457-2804; fax 457-9689), at Pacific Ave. All-day breakfasts; try the *chilauiles*–3 eggs scrambled with tortilla chips, chilies, olives, tomatoes, onions, and cheese ($6). Anchor Steam $2.50. Vegan friendly. Open M-F 7am-4pm, Sa-Su 8am-4pm.

Georgiana's Cafe, 1522 Pacific Ave. (427-9900). Adjacent to Bookshop Santa Cruz, this cafe's view of the Pacific Ave. activity is as big a draw as its food. Inexpensive sandwiches and specials run $4-6. Open daily 7:30am-10pm.

Asian Rose, 1116 Soquel Ave. (423-7906), at Seabright Ave. Your tastebuds will blossom as the waitstaff serves you hibiscus water and free raspberry rice pudding prior to your enormous meal. The *pan* is incredible bread served with garlic and ghee. Open M-Sa 5:30-9pm.

SIGHTS

SANTA CRUZ BOARDWALK. Santa Cruz has a great beach, but the water remains very cold, and without wetsuits for warmth many casual beachgoers catch their thrills on this three-block-long strip of over 25 amusement park rides, guess-your-weight booths, shooting galleries, and caramel apple vendors. The boardwalk provides a loud and lively diversion—one that seems to attract every sun-drenched family, couple, and roving pack of teenagers in California. Highly recommended is the Big Dipper, a 1924 wooden tower roller coaster ($3), where Dirty Harry met his enemy in 1983's *Sudden Impact* (he finally impaled him on the merry-go-round's unicorn). Essential to the ultimate boardwalk experience is Buccaneer Bay Miniature Golf inside Neptune's Kingdom. The arcade features over 200 old and new video games. *(Boardwalk open daily Memorial Day-Labor Day–May 29-Sept. 4 in 2000–plus a few weekends and holidays. Rides $1.50-3; all-day pass $19. Some height restrictions. Miniature golf $4, with all-day pass to boardwalk $3.)*

UNIVERSITY OF CALIFORNIA AT SANTA CRUZ (UCSC). Five miles northwest of downtown sprawls this 2000-acre campus, accessible by bus #1, car, or bicycle. Then-governor Ronald Reagan's plan to make UCSC a "riot-proof campus" (i.e., without a central point where radicals could inflame a crowd) when it was built in the late 1960s, had a happy effect on its decentralized and forested appearance. University buildings sit uncrowded amid spectacular rolling hills and redwood groves, but Santa Cruz is still famous (or infamous) for leftist politics. Once the "safety school" of the UC system, UCSC now regularly turns away scores of aspiring Banana Slugs (the school's mascot; see p. 205). Student-led tours of the campus are available by reservation only. If you drive onto the campus on weekdays, make sure you have a parking permit. Trails behind the campus are perfect for day hikes, but it is not safe to go alone. The UCSC **arboretum** is one of the finest in the state. Students are rumored to save on rent by living year-round in the surrounding forest. *(For tours call 429-2231; M-F 8am-5pm. Parking permits ($4) and maps available at police station. Arboretum open daily 9am-5pm; free.)*

SURFER STATUE AND SANTA CRUZ SURFING MUSEUM. The Surfer Statue, just southwest of the lighthouse on W. Cliff Dr., is a monument "dedicated to all surfers, past, present, and future." The neck of this inspirational figure, erected in 1992, is often graced with a *lei.* Inside the lighthouse itself is the first-of-its-kind surfing museum, which opened in 1986. The main room displays vintage artifacts, photos, and videos, concentrating on the personal stories of local surfers from the 1920s to the present. The lighthouse tower contains the ashes of Mark Abbott, a local surfer who drowned in 1965; his parents donated the museum to the city. *(Museum 429-3429. Open M and W-F noon-4pm, Sa-Su noon-5pm. Free.)*

MISIÓN DE EXALTACIÓN DE LA SANTA CRUZ. A later Christian outpost in California, this peaceful, fragrant adobe church and garden allow some contemplative quiet. *(126 High St. Turn north on Emmet off Mission St. Open Tu-Sa 10am-4pm, Su 10am-2pm. Donation requested.)*

OTHER MUSEUMS. The downtown **Museum of Art and History (MAH),** near the visitors center, features local artists. *(429-1964. 705 Front St. Open Tu-Th, Sa-Su noon-5pm, F noon-7pm. Admission for non-residents $3, students and children free. Free 1st Friday of every month.)* The **Santa Cruz City Museum of Natural History,** across the San Lorenzo River from the Boardwalk at Pilkington, may be small, but the touch pool is exemplary. *(429-3773. 1305 E. Cliff Dr. Open Tu-Su 10am-5pm. Donation requested.)*

SANTA CRUZ WHARF. Jutting off Beach St. is the longest car-accessible pier on the West Coast. Plenty of seafood restaurants and souvenir shops will try to distract you from the expansive views of the coast. *(Parking $1 per hr., under 30min. free. Disabled patrons free.)*

BEACHES AND ACTIVITIES

The **Santa Cruz Beach** (officially named Cowell Beach) itself is broad, reasonably clean, and generally packed with volleyball players. If you're seeking solitude, try the chillier banks of the San Lorenzo River immediately east of the boardwalk. **Beach access** points line Rte. 1; railroad tracks, farmlands, and dune vegetation make several of these access points somewhat difficult, but correspondingly less crowded. Maps of these beaches are listed in the *Santa Cruz Traveler's Guide*, available at the visitors center (see **Practical Information,** p. 198). Folks wanting to exercise their right to **bare everything** should head north on Rte. 1 to the **Red, White, and Blue Beach,** down Scaroni Rd. Sunbathers must be 18 or accompanied by a parent. (Day use is $5 per person; camping 6pm-6am $10 per person.) If averse to paying for the privilege of an all-over tan, try the **Bonny Doon Beach,** off Rte. 1 at Bonny Doon Rd., 11 miles north of Santa Cruz. Magnificent cliffs and rocks surround this windy and frequently deserted spot.

To try your hand at riding the waves, contact the **Richard Schmidt Surf School** (423-0928), or ask around for him at the beach. Schmidt is much respected by the locals, who say that he can get anyone surfing (1hr. private lesson $50, 2hr. lesson $75; lessons include equipment). The best vantage points for **watching surfers** are along W. Cliff Dr. Although packed with wetsuited hopefuls, patient observers will soon identify the more experienced surfriders and a clearly designated pecking order. To learn more about the activity, stop in at **Steamer Lane**—

the popular name for the deep water off the point where surfers have flocked since Hawaiian "Duke" Nakahuraka kick-started California's surf culture here 100 years ago.

Around the point at the end of W. Cliff Dr. is **Natural Bridges State Park** (423-4609). While its lone natural bridge has collapsed, the park nevertheless offers a crowded beach, awe-inspiring tidepools, and tours during Monarch butterfly season (Oct.-Mar.). In November and December thousands of the stunning *lepidoptera* swarm along the beach. (Open daily 8am-dusk. Parking $6, seniors $5.)

Outdoor sports enthusiasts will find ample activities in Santa Cruz—parasailing and other pricey pastimes are popular on the wharf. **Kayak Connection,** 413 Lake Ave. (479-1121), has ocean-going **kayaks** at reasonable rates (open-deck single $33 per day, closed-deck single $48 per day). Rentals include paddle, life jacket, and a skirt or wetsuit. Short instruction accompanies all rentals; you must provide ACA certification for a closed-deck kayak. Beware of cheap rental agencies without instruction sessions since closed-deck ocean kayaking can be dangerous. (Open M-F 10am-6pm, Sa-Su 8:30am-6pm. 4½hr. lessons $40.) You can try **rock climbing** on 13,000 square feet of artificial climbing terrain at **Pacific Edge,** 104 Bronson St. (454-9254). Gym includes weight room, sauna, and showers. (Open M 5am-10pm, Tu and Th 9am-10pm, W and F 11am-10pm, Sa-Su 10am-7pm. Day pass $14.)

ENTERTAINMENT AND NIGHTLIFE

Dodge the underage kids parked on the sidewalks of Pacific Ave. in order to cruise into the Santa Cruzian nightlife. The free weekly *Good Times* has thorough listings. The boardwalk bandstand offers free summertime Friday night concerts. The Santa Cruz Parks and Recreation Department (see **Practical Information,** p. 198) publishes the free *Summer Activity Guide.*

Caffe Pergolesi, 418A Cedar St. (426-1775). Look for "Dr. Miller's" sign. Chill coffeehouse/bar with a series of small rooms and a spacious patio for reading, writing, or socializing. Cheerful color scheme and intimate tables project a supremely friendly atmosphere. $2 pints daily 7-9pm; large coffee for the price of a small M-F 1-3pm. 6 varieties of hot chocolate! Open M-Th 7:30am-11:30pm, F-Sa 7:30am-midnight.

Kuumbwa Jazz Center, 320-322 Cedar St. (427-2227; www.jazznet.com/kuumbwa). Known throughout the region for great jazz and innovative off-night programs. Under-21-derlings are welcome in this small and low-key setting. The big names play here on M; the locals have their turn on F. Tickets (about $5) sold through Logos Books and Music, 1117 Pacific Ave. (427-5100; open daily 10am-10pm), as well as BASS outlets (998-BASS/2277). Most shows around 8pm.

Blue Lagoon, 923 Pacific Ave. (423-7117). Mega-popular gay-straight club has won all awards from "best bartender" to "best place you can't take your parents" from the local press. Bar in front, 3 pool tables in back, and people dancing everywhere. Cover Su-M and W $1; Th $3; F-Sa $4. Happy Hour with $2 drinks daily 6-9pm. Su margaritas $1. Stronger-than-the-bouncer drinks $3-4. Open daily 4pm-2am.

The Poet and Patriot, 320 E. Cedar St. (426-8620). Low-key Irish pub hosts a cheerful young crowd. Hoist a Guinness in the amicable front room or play darts in the back. Sa open mic. Open daily noon-2am.

The Silver Bullet, 603 Front St. (426-5726), at Soquel Dr. By far the cheapest drinks in town, attracting rowdy crowds. Specials are really something: "Drink and drown" $1 pints every M and W. Happy Hour daily 5-7pm. Open daily 10am-2am.

The Catalyst, 1011 Pacific Ave. (423-1336). Primarily music/dance club drawing national, college, and local bands. Pool and darts upstairs, deli and bar downstairs. Sandwiches $2-5. Cover and age restrictions vary widely with show; adjacent bar area strictly 21+. Shows W-Sa. Open M-Sa 9am-2am, Su 9am-5pm; food served W-Sa 9am-4:30pm, and during show times.

SLIME, SEX, AND VIOLENCE The banana slug (*Ariolimax* sp.), mascot of the University of California at Santa Cruz, ranges from six to 10 inches, dull brown to bright yellow, and southern California to Southeast Alaska.

Fact: Using copious secretions of viscous slime, the banana slug can cleanse itself of debris, protect itself from predators, and descend by a gossamer-thin slime cord. **Moral:** Mucus is a useful tool.

Fact: Banana slugs are hermaphrodites, and can mate at any time of year. Foreplay consists of petting, licking, and violent biting, and can last up to 12 hours. During the deed, a slug's male organ can become too swollen to be removed from its partner, necessitating "apophallation"—the removal of a penis by gnawing. **Moral:** Slug sex, however titillating, is not for humans.

Fact: The jet-black slugs that one often sees are not banana slugs, but are in fact foreign European slugs who practice unprovoked aggression on their native North American cousins. **Moral:** Be kind to the banana slug, but if you see a Eurotrash version, salt its slimy ass to oblivion.

99 Bottles Restaurant and Pub, 110 Walnut Ave. (459-9999). Situated in the heart of downtown, this modest but unusually lively bar offers standard fare (burgers $6) and 99 different types of beer. Happy Hour daily 5-6pm and "Thirsty Thursday" 2-for-1 specials. Open M-Th 11am-1:30am, F-Sa 11am-2am, Su 11am-midnight. Food served M-F 4-6pm and 10pm-2am.

SEASONAL EVENTS

Whale-watching season (425-1234), Dec.-Mar. Boats depart from the Santa Cruz Municipal Wharf. Trips range from $5-30, and some guarantee sightings.

Monarch Migration Festival (423-4609), early Feb. The largest Monarch butterfly colony in the West checks out of Natural Bridges State Beach. Catch their return mid-Oct.

Clam Chowder Cook-Off and Great Chowder Chase (429-3477), late Feb.

Santa Cruz Blues Festival (479-9814), 2 days in late May. Big-name blues.

Surf City Classic (429-3477), late June. 50s and 60s theme music and food as well as "woodies on the wharf." Lots of classic wood-paneled cars.

Lesbian, Gay, Bisexual, Transgender Pride Day (425-5422), first Su in June. Now in its 24th year. Parade, music, speakers.

Shakespeare Santa Cruz (459-2121), at UCSC, July-Aug. Nationally acclaimed, innovative outdoor festival. All-show passes available.

Santa Cruz Hot and Cool Jazz Fest (728-8760), 3 days in late July. Jazz artists from the West play in four venues along the beach.

National Nude Weekend (353-2250), mid-July. Celebrated at the Lupin Naturalist Club in the Santa Cruz Mountains. Enjoy bands (playing in the buff) or come paint the posing models (on canvas). Free, but reservations are required.

Cabrillo Music Festival (426-6966), first 2 weeks in Aug. Held downtown in the Civic Auditorium, the festival brings contemporary and classical music to the Central Coast. It's hard to get tickets ($16-25), so reserve well in advance.

NEAR SANTA CRUZ

Santa Cruz is surrounded by gently sloping hills that make hiking a delight; the paths are only mildly strenuous and the scenery is magnificent. To the north, **Big Basin Redwoods State Park,** the first (and some say the best) of the California state parks, offers trails novices can enjoy. Farther to the south, the gorgeous **Henry Cowell Redwoods State Park** (see p. 200) has trails suitable for daytrips. Bikers get a kick out of **Niscene Marks State Park,** a second-growth redwood forest area.

In Felton, the **Roaring Camp and Big Trees Narrow Gauge Railroad** (335-4484), on Graham Hill Rd., runs an old steam-powered passenger train on a spectacular route from Felton through the redwoods to Bear Mountain (round-trip $15, ages 3-13 $10), and holds seasonal historic celebrations. To reach Felton, take Rte. 9, which passes through Henry Cowell Redwoods State Park. In Felton, take Graham Hill Rd. southeast and bear south to Roaring Camp as indicated by road signs.

The **Mystery Spot,** 1953 Branciforte Dr. (423-8897), three miles northeast of Santa Cruz, is a "mysterious" "spot" where laws of physics no longer apply, causing balls to roll uphill, and other "impossibilities" that confound hordes of international tourists. These bizarre phenomena are in fact caused by a local perturbation of the earth's magnetic field, a geophysical anomaly so strong that it also inflates admission fees. Photography and videotaping encouraged. To get there, take Ocean St. to Water St. and turn on Market St., which becomes Branciforte Dr. (Open daily 9am-8:30pm. Tours leave about every 30min. Admission $4; ages 5-11 $2.)

SALINAS AND SALINAS VALLEY

The heart of John Steinbeck Country beats in Salinas, 90 miles south of San Francisco and 25 miles inland from Monterey. The renowned author (he was the first of two Americans to win both the Pulitzer and Nobel Prizes—the other being Toni Morrison) lived here until he was 17. This is where Steinbeck set *East of Eden* and *The Red Pony*, where many of the characters he created are from, and where his ashes are buried. Aside from echoes of Steinbeck's writing and a highly acclaimed rodeo, Salinas offers travelers some sense of American culture from the 1930s to the 1950s and an interesting diversion for those headed up or down Route 101.

South of Salinas, Route 1 stretches out toward faraway San Luis Obispo, running through the wide, green Salinas Valley, where the towns of **Gonzales, Soledad, Greenfield,** and **King City** serve mainly as farming communities and truck stops. Acre upon acre of tomatoes, artichokes, lettuce, grapes, and garlic thrive here in the self-proclaimed "salad bowl of the nation." Rising above the greenery are the points of the Pinnacles, an old volcano crater with incredible geological and wildlife attractions.

PRACTICAL INFORMATION

Trains: Amtrak, 11 Station Pl., Salinas (422-7458 or 800-827-7245). Train-only routes will be more expensive than train/bus combos. To: **San Francisco** ($14-22); **L.A.** ($77-92); and all points between. Open daily 9am-1pm and 3-7pm.

Buses: Greyhound, 19 W. Gabilan St., Salinas (424-4418 or 800-231-2222), 1 block from the MST Center. Several buses per day to: **San Francisco** ($19); **L.A.** ($36); and **Santa Cruz** ($10). Open daily 4:30am-11:45pm.

Public Transportation: Monterey-Salinas Transit (MST), 110 Salinas St., Salinas (424-7695), at Central Ave. Fare per zone $1.50; seniors, ages 5-18, and disabled 75¢. Same-zone transfers free up to 2hr. Bus #20 or 21 will take you to Monterey. (See listing for MST in **Monterey: Practical Information,** p. 209.)

Visitor Information: Salinas Chamber of Commerce, 119 E. Alisal St., Salinas (424-7611), has city maps ($2) and plenty of information on the Salinas Valley and Monterey Peninsula. Open M 9am-5pm, Tu-F 8:30am-5pm, Sa 9am-3pm. **King City Chamber of Commerce and Agriculture,** 203 Broadway, King City (385-3814). Staff members are available to answer questions but short on brochures. Open M-F 10am-noon and 1-4pm.

Road Conditions: 800-427-7623. 24hr.

Emergency: 911. **Police:** King City (385-8311); Salinas (758-7321).

Medical Services: Salinas Valley Memorial Hospital, 450 E. Romie Ln., Salinas (757-4333).

Post Office: Salinas, 100 W. Alisal St. (758-3823). Open M-F 8:30am-5pm. General Delivery at 1011 Post Dr. **ZIP Code:** 93907. **King City,** 123 S. 3rd St. (385-3339), at Bassett St. Open M-F 8:30am-4:30pm. **ZIP Code:** 93930.

Area Code: 408.

ACCOMMODATIONS AND CAMPGROUNDS

As a general rule, the farther south from Salinas accommodations are, the lower their prices will be. Salinas has several expensive hotels, but the standard chain motels cluster at the E. Market St. Exit off U.S. 101. Other hotels run along N. Main St., including the **El Dorado Motel,** 1351 N. Main St. (449-2442 or 800-523-6506), which offers comfortable and clean rooms with cable TV and free local calls, as well as laundry facilities (singles $33; doubles $42). Two options in Greenfield are the **Motel Budget Inn,** 452 El Camino (674-5828; doubles $25-32), and the **Greenfield Inn,** 22 4th St. (674-5995), under the Overnighter Lodge sign (singles $26-35). In King City, the **Fireside Inn,** 640 Broadway (386-1010), has a gigantic tree growing through its office (doubles $35).

There is no camping at **Pinnacles National Monument** (389-4485), but the answering machine gives directions to other options in the area. East of Pinnacles is **Pinnacles Campground Inc.** (389-4462), a privately owned campground with 78 tent sites (6-person max.), 15 group sites, 36 RV sites, a pool, flush toilets, and hot showers. (4-night max. stay. $7 per person; electrical hookups $2 extra.) All sites are first-come, first-camped. Be warned—there is no road access from the east side of the park to the west side, although it is possible to hike through.

FOOD

Drive in past the fast-food joints lining the freeway and you'll find the greens are always fresh. Those stopping by the Steinbeck Center will sing the praises of the popular **Sang's Cafe,** 131 Main St., Salinas (424-6012). Burly truckers have no problem getting close to the pink countertops at Sang's; the size of their portions is famous. Homestyle breakfasts are $3-6. (Open Tu-Sa 6:30am-2:30pm.) **Mi Tierra,** 18 E. Gabilan St., Salinas (422-4631), doles out huge portions at low prices—a bean burrito is $2, while a huge combo plate with *chiles rellenos*, enchilada, rice and beans, salad, and tortillas is $5.25 (open daily 8am-8:30pm). **La Fuente Restaurant,** 101 Oak St., Soledad (678-3130), serves up *chiles rellenos* with enchilada ($5.75), in a very clean, comfortable restaurant (open M-Sa 11am-9pm, Su 9am-9pm). **Fiesta City Cafe,** 246 El Camino Real, Greenfield (647-2837), is sunny and mellow with both Mexican- and American-style breakfasts for $5-7 (open M-Sa 6am-8:30pm).

SIGHTS AND ENTERTAINMENT

The town of Salinas salivates over internationally recognized hometown author John Steinbeck. The enormous **National Steinbeck Center,** 1 Main St. (796-3833, www.steinbeck.org), opened in June 1998—bringing 37,000 square feet of mice to pet, plants to smell, and stories to hear, all evocative of Steinbeck's inspiration: the Salinas Valley. Seekers, sycophants, and simpletons alike will appreciate the interactive and provocative trip into American small-town culture. The nearby gravesite and Steinbeck house are less dazzling but more intimate ways to access this author's aura. (Open daily 10am-5pm. Admission $7, seniors and students $6, ages 11-17 $4, under 11 free.)

Salinas's biggest non-literary tourist pull is the **California Rodeo Salinas and Intertribal Indian Village.** The rodeo is the fourth-largest in the world, attracting wrestlers, riders, cows, and bulls from across the West in the third week of July. While the rodeo officially lasts for only one weekend, related events—including **cowboy**

poetry readings—take place throughout the last three weeks of July. (Tickets $10-17, season tickets $60-68. Call 757-2951 or 800-549-4989 or write P.O. Box 1648, Salinas 93902 for more info.)

NEAR SALINAS: PINNACLES NATIONAL MONUMENT

Towering dramatically over the chaparral (dense brushwood) east of Soledad, **Pinnacles National Monument** comprises the spectacular remnants of an ancient volcano. Set aside as a national park in 1908, the park preserves the erratic and unique spires and crags that millions of years of weathering carved out of prehistoric lava flows. Thirty miles of hiking trails wind through the park's low chaparral, boulder-strewn caves, and pinnacles of rock, many of which make for great climbing and caving (flashlights are required on cave trails). The **High Peaks Trail** runs a strenuous 5¼ miles across the park between the east and west entrances, and offers amazing views of the surrounding rock formations. For a less exhausting trek, try the **Balconies Trail,** a 1½-mile promenade from the park's west entrance up to the Balconies Caves. A magnificent array of **wildflowers** bloom in the spring, and the park offers excellent **bird-watching** all year long. Pinnacles has the widest range of wildlife of any park in California, including a number of rare predators: mountain lions, bobcats, coyotes, rattlesnakes, golden eagles, and peregrine falcons. Far from city light sources, with very few clouds, the **night sky** over Pinnacles puts on quite a show. The park entrance fee is $5. The park headquarters (389-4485) is at the eastern entrance (Rte. 25 to Rte. 146), but maps, water, and restrooms are also available at a station on the west side (U.S. 101 to Rte. 146).

The **Mission Nuestra Señora de la Soledad** (Our Lady of Solitude), 36641 Fort Romie Rd., Soledad (678-2586), off Arroyo Seco. This aptly named mission, constructed in 1791, is in the middle of a quiet valley. Floods destroyed the building several times, but it was restored in the 1950s, and today a small museum exhibits various artifacts. An annual fiesta is held the last Sunday in October, and an annual barbecue takes place on the last Sunday in June. (Mission open W-M 9am-4pm.)

MONTEREY

Monterey (pop. 33,000) was sighted by the Spanish as early as 1542, but the native Ohlone tribe was largely left in peace until 1770, when Father Serra targeted the area on his journey up the coast. The Spanish frequently used Monterey as the capital of their territory Alta California from 1775 to 1846, when the U.S. Navy claimed the town as U.S. territory. After its incorporation in 1850, the city lost its missionary prestige and was eclipsed by San Francisco as a port. The growth of the whaling industry kept Monterey alive until 1880, when sardine fishing and packaging stepped up to take its place. The wharfside flourished like the fisherman's world immortalized by John Steinbeck in the 1940s. Before long, the sardines petered out and Monterey started fishing in the pockets of wealthy tourists. Today, only a few forced traces of the Monterey described in Steinbeck's *Cannery Row* remain—murals and souvenir shops do their best to capitalize on a colorful history, yet are unable to preserve any sense of authenticity in the presence of so many expensive boutiques and cafes. Scattered public buildings, adobe houses, and a resilient, if more responsible, fishing community nevertheless revere bygone days. The intensity of the past and the spectacle of the present result in a restrained beauty well worth the journey to Monterey.

ORIENTATION

The Monterey Peninsula, 116 miles south of San Francisco, consists of Monterey, Pacific Grove (a largely residential community), and Pebble Beach (an exclusive nest of mansions and golf courses). Motorists can approach Monterey from **U.S. 101** via Rte. 68 west through Salinas, or directly from coastal **Route 1.** Monterey's most social road, **Alvarado Street,** runs north-south. Parallel to it is **Pacific Street,** a main traffic thoroughfare. At its northern end stand luxury hotels and the gigantic Conference Center; beyond the brick plaza are a large parking lot, the marina, and Fisherman's Wharf. Perpendicular to Alvarado St., **Del Monte Avenue** runs roughly northeast to the coast; on the other side, **Lighthouse Avenue** leads northwest out through Pacific Grove, ending at the Point Piños Lighthouse. Monterey's primary attractions are within walking distance or a bus ride from Alvarado St.

The relative isolation of Monterey does little to insulate the city from prodigious summer traffic jams. The Monterey Traffic Department's earnest attempts to correct the congestion with abundant one-way signs and complicated traffic signals haven't helped matters much. A simpler option than driving in town is to park for free in the Del Monte and explore the area by foot and shuttle. **Bicycling** is a great way to see the peninsula, provided you exercise caution on the narrow, twisting roads. There are several designated bike paths, the best of which is the Monterey Peninsula Recreation Trail, which follows the coast from Fisherman's Wharf in Monterey through Pacific Grove, Pebble Beach, and Carmel, then back up Rte. 1. The circuit takes four leisurely hours, and is popular with in-line skaters.

PRACTICAL INFORMATION

Public Transportation: Monterey-Salinas Transit (MST), 1 Ryan Ranch Rd. (899-2555, TDD 393-8111; MST phone lines open M-F 7:45am-5:15pm, Sa 10am-2:30pm). The free *Rider's Guide* contains complete schedules and route info (available on buses, at motels, and at the visitors center). MST serves the region from Watsonville in the north (where it connects to SCMTD; see **Santa Cruz,** p. 198) to Carmel in the south, as well as inland to Salinas. Many buses stop at the **Transit Plaza** downtown, where Munras Ave., Tyler St., Pearl St., Alvarado St., and Polk St. converge. MST has 4 zones, each encompassing 1 or 2 towns. Fare per zone $1.50, seniors, ages 5-18, and disabled 75¢; same-zone transfers free up to 2hr.; exact change. Between Memorial Day and Labor Day (May 29-Sept. 4 in 2000), MST also offers 2 special services: The **Waterfront Area Visitors Express (WAVE)** follows Monterey sights from the Del Monte Shopping Center to Pacific Grove (day pass $1; seniors, ages 5-18, and disabled 50¢; free with MST bus receipt). **Bus #22** runs twice daily between Monterey and Big Sur (fare $3; seniors, ages 5-18, and disabled $1.50).

Taxi: Yellow Cab (646-1234). Initial charge $1.50; each additional mi. $1.75.

Bike Rental: Bay Bikes, 640 Wave St. (646-9090), on Cannery Row directly on the waterfront bike path. Bikes or in-line skates $10 first 2hr., $4 each additional hr.; daily rates depend on bike. Includes lock and helmet. Open daily 9am-7pm.

Equipment Rental: On The Beach Surf Shop, 693 Lighthouse Ave. (646-9283). Rents surfboards ($10 per ½-day, $20 per day), boogie boards ($7 per ½-day $7, $14 per day), and wetsuits ($8 per ½-day, $16 per day). Open M-F 10am-7pm, Sa 9am-7pm, Su 10am-6pm. **Monterey Bay Kayaks,** 693 Del Monte Ave. (373-KELP/5357 or 800-649-KELP/5357), rents kayaks ($25 per day; after 2:30pm $20). Includes gear and wetsuit. Open daily 9am-6pm.

Visitor Information: Monterey Peninsula Visitor and Convention Bureau, 380 Alvarado St. (649-1770). Free pamphlets and the 120-page *Visitor's Guide* ($6), which has restaurant, accommodation, and tourist info. Free phone calls to select hotels and motels in the area. *The Key* has a comprehensive map. Open M-F 8:30am-5pm. There is also a smaller **visitors center,** 401 Camino El Estero (649-1770). Open June-Sept. M-Sa 9am-6pm, Su 9am-5pm; Oct.-May M-F 9am-5pm, Sa-Su 9am-4pm.

Library: 625 Pacific St. (646-3930), diagonally across from City Hall. Pleasant courtyard. Parking and **Internet access** available. Open M-Th 9am-9pm, F 9am-6pm, Sa 9am-5pm, Su 1-5pm.

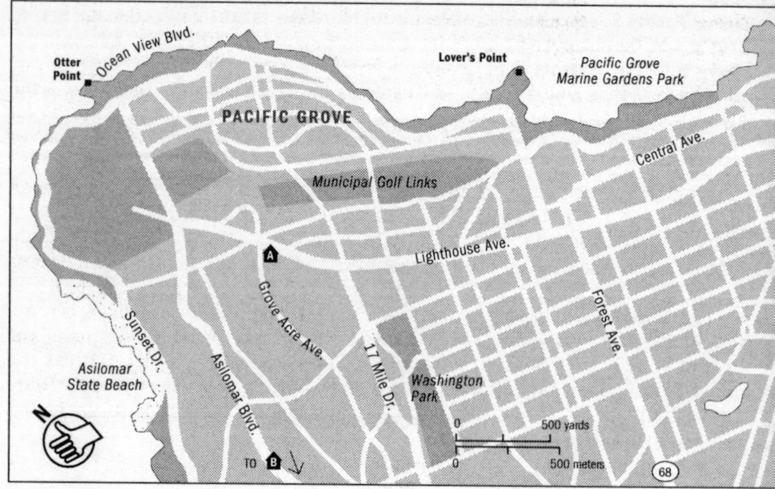

Laundromat: Surf and Suds, 1101 Del Monte Ave. (375-0874). Wash $1.50, 10min. dry 25¢. Open daily 7am-10pm.

Road Conditions: 800-427-7623)

Emergency: 911.

Police: 351 Madison St. (646-3830), at Pacific St.

Crisis Lines: Rape Crisis (375-4357). 24hr. **Suicide Prevention** (649-8008). **SPCA Wildlife Rescue** (373-2631). Report unauthorized otter fondling.

Post Office: 565 Hartnell St. (372-5803). Open M-F 8:45am-5:10pm. **ZIP Code:** 93940.

AREA CODE The area code for Monterey and Pacific Grove is 831.

ACCOMMODATIONS AND CAMPGROUNDS

Reasonably priced hotels are found on **Lighthouse Avenue** in Pacific Grove (bus #2 and some #1 buses) and in the 2000 block of **Fremont Street** in Monterey (bus #9 or 10). Others cluster along **Munras Avenue** between downtown and Rte. 1. The cheapest hotels in the area, however, are in the less-appealing towns of Seaside and Marina, just north of Monterey. Call the Monterey Parks line (755-4895 or 888-588-CAMP/2267) for camping info and PARKNET (800-444-7275) for reservations.

Del Monte Beach Inn, 1110 Del Monte Blvd., Monterey (649-4410), near downtown and across from the beach. Victorian-style inn with pleasant rooms. TV room. Hearty breakfast and tea served in sunny room. Hall phone only. Check-in 2-6pm. Rooms with shared bath Su-Th $55-66, F-Sa from $77. Reservations recommended.

Sunset Motel, 133 Asilomar Blvd., Pacific Grove (375-3936), by Lovers' Point in a quiet neighborhood. Sherbet exterior looks like a sunset. Cable TV. Complete breakfast included. Rooms Apr.-Sept. Su-Th from $75, F-Sa $110; Oct.-Mar. Su-Th from $50, F-Sa $70. Depending on local events, prices could skyrocket to $210, so plan ahead.

Pacific Grove Motel, 1101 Lighthouse Ave., Pacific Grove (372-3218 or 800-858-8997), at Grove Acre close to the ocean. Knowledgeable manager. Hot tub, pool, diver rinse areas, fridges, patios, and cable TV. Singles Apr.-Sept. Su-Th $54, F-Sa $69; doubles Su-Th $69, F-Sa $79. Prices lower Oct.-Mar.

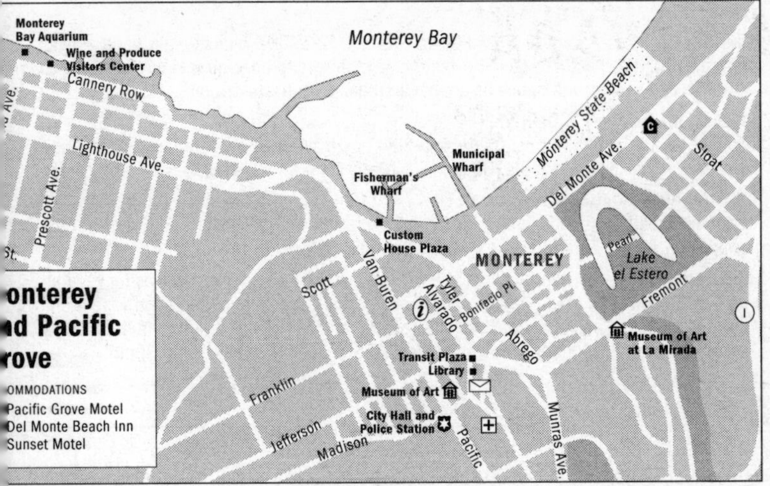

Veterans Memorial Park Campground (646-3865), Via Del Rey 1½mi. from downtown. Take bus #3. Take Skyline Dr. off Rte. 68. From downtown, go south on Pacific St., right on Jefferson St., and follow the signs. Perched on a hill with a view of the bay. No hook-ups. Hot showers. 40 sites available on first-come, first-camped basis; arrive before 3pm in summer and weekends. 3-night max. stay. Walk-in sites $3, with vehicle $15.

Laguna Seca Recreational Area (755-4899 or 888-588-2267), on Rte. 68 near the racetrack 10mi. east of Monterey. This hilly, oak-strewn hill camp overlooks verdant valleys and the roarin' racetrack. Of the 177 campsites, 103 are equipped with hookups. Restrooms, barbecue pits, tables, and dump station. Showers. Sites $18, with hookup $22. Reservations accepted 5 or more days in advance.

FOOD

The sardines have left, but Monterey Bay teems with squid, crab, red snapper, and salmon. Seafood is bountiful, but it may be expensive—try an early-bird special (usually 4-6:30pm). Fisherman's Wharf has smoked salmon sandwiches ($6) and free chowder samples. Don't despair if you loathe seafood—this is also the land of artichokes and strawberries. Free samples of fruit, cheese, and seafood are at the Monterey **farmer's market** (655-8070), which takes over Alvarado St. (Tu 4-8pm).

Whole Foods, 800 Del Monte Ctr. (333-1600), offers sandwiches made with fresh, gourmet ingredients ($5). Its location at the Del Monte Shopping Center makes it a convenient stop for picnic necessities before catching the WAVE or a bus for town.

DOWNTOWN AND CANNERY ROW

Old Monterey Cafe, 489 Alvarado St. (646-1021). Hot, hefty portions favored by locals. Hawaiian omelette with pineapple, ham, and banana $6.75. Lunch specials $5.50-7.50. Open daily 6:45am-2:30pm.

Amarin Thai Cuisine, 807 Cannery Row (373-8811), near the aquarium in a complex of touristy shops. The "California style" Thai food is fresh and unique. Many vegetarian dishes ($6-10) such as tofu with vegetables and peanut sauce ($10). Open daily 11am-9pm.

LIGHTHOUSE AVENUE AREA

Thai Bistro II, 159 Central Ave., Pacific Grove (372-8700). Graced with good service and a patio ringed with flowers, this bistro still manages to have budget offerings. Lunch combos ($6) come with delicious soup. Open daily 11:30am-10pm.

International Market & Deli, 580 Lighthouse Ave., New Monterey (375-9451). Short on ambience, but cheap, robust food carries the day. Falafel $3; vegetarian stuffed grape leaves 35¢. Takeout available. Open M-Sa 10am-7pm, Su 11am-6pm. No credit cards.

Inaka Japanese Cuisine, 125 Ocean View (375-0441), in the American Tin Cannery outlet mall. Fresh, authentic Japanese food. Several $7 noodle dishes. Big bowl of *tempura soba* $8.50. Open Tu-Su 11:30am-3pm and 5-9pm.

Tillie Gort's Cafe, 111 Central Ave. (373-0335), has excellent dinner choices for vegetarians and carnivores alike. Dark, wooden interior makes for a cool and comfortable dining experience. Specialties include the Tofu Scramble ($7) and the all-in-one variety plate including rice, beans, and vegetables $6.50. Open daily 11am-10:30pm.

SIGHTS

MONTEREY BAY AQUARIUM. The biggest of Monterey's attractions, this extraordinarily impressive aquarium feeds on the committed community interest in marine ecology. The facility allows visitors a window (literally) into the most curious creatures of the Pacific. Gaze through the **world's largest window** at an enormous marine habitat containing green sea turtles, seven-foot ocean sunfish, large sharks, and the oozingly graceful Portuguese man-o'-war jellyfish. Eager tourists scuttle for a glance at the **sea otters** during feeding time, a living kelp forest housed in a two-story-tall glass case, and a petting zoo of damp bay denizens (stingray included). The matter-of-fact environmental-impact awareness theme running throughout will open your eyes—don't miss a sobering three-minute "wasted catch" video on the upper level. Arrive with a surfeit of patience; the lines for tickets, admission, viewing, and food are as unbelievable as the exhibits themselves. Pick up tickets the day before and save 20 to 40 minutes. *(648-4888; www.mbayaq.org. 886 Cannery Row. Open daily mid-June to early Sept. and major holiday periods 9:30am-6pm; early Sept. to mid-June 10am-6pm. Admission $16; students, seniors, and ages 13-17 $13; disabled and ages 3-12 $7.)*

CANNERY ROW. Lying along the waterfront south of the aquarium, this was once a depressed street of languishing sardine-packing plants. The ¾-mile row has been converted into glitzy mini-malls, bars, and a pint-sized carnival complex. All that remains of the earthiness and gruff camaraderie celebrated by John Steinbeck in *Cannery Row* and *Sweet Thursday* are a few building facades: 835 Cannery Row was the Wing Chong Market, the bright yellow building next door is where *Sweet Thursday* took place, and Doc Rickett's lab, 800 Cannery Row, is now owned by a private men's club. For a series of interpretive looks at Steinbeck's Cannery Row, take a peek at the **Great Cannery Row Mural,** within which local artists have covered 400 ft. of construction-site barrier on the 700 block with depictions of Monterey in the 1930s. The lavish **Wine and Produce Visitors Center,** gives a taste of the county's burgeoning wine industry, with well-priced bottles, fresh produce, and free winery maps. *(888-646-5446. 700 Cannery Row. 3 tastings $2. Open daily 11am-6pm.)*

MARITIME MUSEUM OF MONTEREY. Ship models, photos, navigation tools, logs, and other paraphernalia sketch the history of Monterey, along with a free 14-minute film. The museum's centerpiece is the original Fresnel lens of Point Sur Lighthouse: the entire lens is a two-story structure of gear-works and cut glass that was later replaced by the electric lighthouse. *(373-2469. At the base of the wharf in the Historic Customs House Plaza. Open daily 10am-5pm. Admission $3; seniors, ages 12-19, military, and disabled $2; under 12 free.)*

OTTER POINT. Otter-lovers can get their fuzzy-mammal fix from several nearby spots, including this one. Touching an otter is illegal, and "harassing" or fondling one in Monterey Bay may lead to a $10,000 fine. Several companies on the wharf offer critter-spotting boat trips around Monterey Bay for $6-10, but you can gawk from the dock for free. *(A few minutes' walk south of the aquarium along the shore.)*

MONTEREY STATE HISTORIC PARK BUILDINGS. Monterey's early days spawned a unique architectural trend that incorporates Southern details, like wraparound porches, with Mexican adobe characteristics, such as 3-foot-thick walls and exterior staircases. One pass allows purchasers to enter all historic buildings. *(All-building passes available at the visitors center. Call for tour times. 649-7118. At Customs House Plaza. Pass $5. Open daily in summer 10am-5pm; in winter 10am-4pm.)*

OTHER SIGHTS. The **Monterey Peninsula Museum of Art** occupies two separate locations. The Civic Center branch holds changing shows, mostly of California artists *(372-5477. 559 Pacific St. Open W-Sa 11am-5pm, Su 1-4pm).* **La Mirada,** near Lake El Estero, houses exhibits on California history, as well as collections of regional Asian and Pacific Rim art *(372-3689. 720 Via Mirada. Open Th-Sa 11am-5pm, Su 1-4pm.)*

NIGHTLIFE

Monterey knows how to cut loose at night, although some areas of the peninsula quiet down early. Most of the action is downtown along Alvarado St., with a few Lighthouse Ave. exceptions. Pickings are slim for those under 21, but covers remain reasonable or nonexistent. The Defense Language Institute and Naval Postgraduate School bring hordes of single military personnel to the singles bar scene. Bouncers need only nod at these yeomen to quell drunken disturbances.

Mucky Duck British Pub, 479 Alvarado St. (655-3031). Empty front window booths might fool you, but the boozers are in the beer garden. The popular back deck with DJ on weekends is swinging with the singles scene, but demands a numbered pass for entry; come early to avoid waits. 2 open hearths and cozy booths with leather chairs. Open daily 11:30am-2am.

Plumes Coffee, 400 Alvarado St. (373-4526). Brightly lit cafe hosts hip crowd perched on tiny chairs. Central location makes for a popular sub-21 night spot. Latte $2.25. Open Su-Th 7am-11pm, F-Sa 7am-midnight.

Viva Monterey, 414 Alvarado St. (646-1415). An intense crowd lives it up amid great wall art. Liquid creations like Swedish Passion start at $5. Cry "Honey, I'm home!" as you walk through the door and receive $1 off your first drink. Two black-lit pool tables. No cover for live music offerings. Open daily 4pm-2am. Shows M-Sa 9:30pm, Su 8pm.

McGarrett's, 321 Alvarado St. (646-9244), at Del Monte Ave. Strobe lights and heavy smoke machines throb like teenage hormones in this extensive club. Primp in the plush bathrooms. Pool tables and a smoking deck. Adult dancers (both sexes) every M. Strict dress code Sa. Cover $5-6. Open M and W-Sa 8pm-1:30am.

SEASONAL EVENTS

Laguna Seca Raceway (800-327-7322), on Rte. 68 east of Monterey. Late May-early Oct. (office open M-F 8am-5pm). The raceway hosts the Monterey Sports Car Grand Prix (late July); Historic Automobile Races (late Aug.); Monterey Grand Prix Indy Car World Series (early Oct.).

AT&T National Pro-Am (800-541-9091), at Pebble Beach (649-1533), Jan. 31-Feb. 6. Featuring celebrity and PGA tour match-ups.

Monterey Bay Blues Festival (394-2652), late June.

Monterey Bay's Theatrefest (622-0700), late June to early Aug. Between the Customs House and the Pacific House at the head of Fisherman's Wharf. Free afternoon theater Sa-Su 11am-5pm; evening shows $15, students and seniors $8.

Monterey County Fair, mid-Aug., at Monterey County Fairgrounds and Exhibition Park.

Monterey Jazz Festival (800-307-3378), 3rd week in Sept.

NEAR MONTEREY

Monterey's beach lacks the drama and surf of its neighbors to the west and north. Around the northern end of the peninsula, the beach runs uninterrupted for nearly four miles, first as **Pacific Grove Municipal Beach,** then as **Asilomar State Beach.** Bus #2 stops within four blocks of the ocean in Pacific Grove. The numerous tidepools along the rocky shore are intriguing places to explore.

West of Monterey, **Sunset Drive** provides a free, six-mile scenic alternative to 17-Mile Drive (see below). Appropriately, Sunset Dr. is the best place in the area to watch the sun go down. People arrive a full two hours before sunset in order to secure front row seats along the road (also known as Ocean Blvd.). At the western tip of the peninsula stands **Point Piños Lighthouse** (648-3116), the oldest continuously running Pacific Coast lighthouse, which now houses exhibits on Coast Guard history (open Th-Su 1-4pm; admission 50¢).

Pacific Grove took root as a Methodist enclave over 100 years ago, and many of the Victorian houses are still in excellent condition. This unpretentious town (which falls eerily quiet at night) has a beautiful coastline, numerous lunch counters, and lots of funky boutiques. Browse in second-hand clothing, book, and music stores along Lighthouse Ave., or outlet-shop-till-you-drop at the **American Tin Cannery** near New Monterey. In addition, Pacific Grove houses thousands of **Monarch butterflies,** fleeing from October to March. Look, but don't touch—bothering the butterflies, the signs warn, is a $1000 offense. The **Pacific Grove Museum of Natural History** (648-3116 or 648-3119), at Forest and Central Ave. one block north of Lighthouse Ave., has year-round exhibits of Monarchs and other local wildlife. The many stuffed birds and a cetacean (whale) room are top-notch. (Open Tu-Su 10am-5pm. Free.)

The **Seventeen-Mile Drive** meanders along the coast from Pacific Grove through **Pebble Beach** and the forests around Carmel. Once owned by Del Monte Foods, Pebble Beach has become the playground of the fabulously well-to-do. Its enormous, manicured golf courses creep up almost to the shore's edge, in strange contrast to the dramatically jagged cliffs and turbulent surf. The drive is rolling, looping, and often spectacular, although plagued by heavy traffic and a steep $7.75 entrance fee. To drive in and out as you please in one day, present your receipt to the guard and have her or him record your license plate number. Save money by biking it (bicyclists and pedestrians allowed in for free) or drive along Sunset Dr. instead (see above). Along the drive is the **Lone Cypress**—an old, gnarled tree growing on a rock promontory, valiantly resisting the onslaught of determined, jostling photographers. In the forgiving dimness of twilight, the tree is a silent testimony to perseverance and solitary strength. The image of this tree, which is prevalent in northern California, has been copyrighted by the Pebble Beach community.

CARMEL

Genteel Californians migrate to Carmel (pop. 4500) to live out their fantasies of small-town life, and the town responds remarkably well to their wishes. Officially named Carmel-by-the-Sea, tourists and residents alike generally drop these last three words which appear only on the business cards of local establishments. Carmel has pristine beaches, a main street lined with boutiques and art galleries, and an aura of quaintness. Local ordinances forbid address numbers, parking meters (though police chalk tires to keep careful track of how long cars have been parked), franchise stores, live music in bars, billboards, and, at one time, eating ice cream cones outside—all considered undesirable symbols of urbanization. All this effort to make Carmel absolutely *precious* ends up imparting a saccharine feeling—much like the feel-good Hayley Mills movie *The Parent Trap*, which was set in the suitably saccharine paradise of Carmel-by-the-Sea. The white sand beaches of Carmel and extraordinary mission are beautiful, and your heart may race with the prospect of seeing resident and former mayor Clint Eastwood, but the town proper may be too snooty for the down-home budget traveler.

ORIENTATION AND PRACTICAL INFORMATION

Carmel lies at the southern end of the Monterey Peninsula off **Route 1,** 126 miles south of San Francisco. The town's main street, **Ocean Avenue,** cuts west from the freeway to (surprise) the ocean. All other east-west avenues are numbered, ascending toward the south. **Junípero Avenue** crosses Ocean Ave. downtown and leads south to the mission at **Rio Road.** Free town maps are available at most hotels and the visitors center. A public lot on the corner of Junípero Ave. and 3rd St. has **free all-day parking.**

Public Transportation: Monterey-Salinas Transit (**MST;** 899-2555, TDD 393-8111). Buses #4, 5, and 24 go through Carmel. Bus #22 runs to Big Sur (2 daily). Schedules available at the Monterey info and transit centers. Fare per zone $1.50; seniors, disabled, and ages 5-18 75¢; same-zone transfers free up to 2hr.

Bike Rental: Bay Bikes (625-BIKE/2453), based in Monterey, will deliver to Carmel free of charge. Bikes $22 per day (includes helmet and bike lock). Open daily 8:30am-5:30pm.

Visitor Information: Carmel-by-the-Sea Business Association (624-2522), San Carlos St. between 5th and 6th St. on the 2nd fl. of the Eastwood Bldg. Free city maps available here and all over town. Open M-F 9am-5pm; plaza kiosk open M-F 9am-5pm, Sa 11am-4pm.

Post Office: 624-1525, 5th St. between San Carlos St. and Dolores Ave. Open M-F 9am-4:30pm. **ZIP Code:** 93921.

Area Code: 831.

ACCOMMODATIONS AND CAMPGROUNDS

Most **motels** in Carmel offer only double-occupancy rooms (never below $75), and the rates at Carmel's B&Bs and inns are equally high, but usually include full breakfasts. A 15-minute bus ride to Monterey will bring more reasonable rates. Camping is illegal within city limits, and no state parks are nearby. There is, however, an RV-heavy private campground 4½ miles east at **Saddle Mountain Ranch,** 27625 Schulte Rd. (624-1617). The 50 $22 sites with showers are popular, so reserve in advance.

FOOD

China Gourmet (624-3941), 5th St. between San Carlos St. and Dolores Ave. across from the post office. Delicious Cantonese and Szechuan food (entrees $6-10). Vegetarian options available. Lunch specials ($4.50-5.50) include almond chicken or BBQ pork with snow peas. Open Tu-Su 11am-9:30pm.

Mediterranean Market (624-2022), Ocean Ave. and Mission St. This beautiful market carries a variety of gourmet goods as well as fresh $5 sandwiches. There are no tables, but a beach picnic site is a short walk away. Open daily 9am-5pm.

Jack London's (624-2336), San Carlos St. between 5th and 6th St. "Jack London was a friendly and forthright presence in Carmel and America's foremost adventure writer. Like Jack, our food is fresh and forthright." Believe the hype: fish or fowl ($7-8), burgers (from $6.25). Ask for *huevos rancheros* anytime; they're not on the menu, but they're a specialty ($6.50). Plant yourself where the action is—at or near the bar. Open daily noon-2am; food served until 1am.

Em Le's (625-6780), Dolores Ave. between 5th and 6th St. This sticky cafe is known for its fabulous breakfasts. Omelettes with potatoes or cottage cheese and toast ($6); unique french toast ($5.50). Open daily 6:30am-3pm.

Friar Tuck's Restaurant (624-4274), 5th St. and Dolores Ave. Claiming to be "Carmel's oldest and last coffee shop," this standard restaurant serves your average breakfast and lunch menu, but really go to see the life-size likeness of Friar Tuck. Sandwiches and burgers ($4-6); omelettes ($5-7). Open daily 6:30am-2pm.

SIGHTS AND BEACHES

MISSION BASILICA SAN CARLOS BORROMEO DEL RÍO CARMELO. It may be a mouthful to say but it is also a marvel to see. Established at its present site in 1771 by Father Junípero Serra, "the Great Conquistador of the Cross," the mission converted 4000 Native Americans before it was abandoned in 1836. Fastidiously restored in 1931, the mission's marvels continue to receive attention with the help of wealthy tourists' donations. Complete with stone courtyard, Mudéjar bell tower, luscious gardens, and a daily mass, the mission is one of the most extensive in the system today. Buried here are Father Serra and over 2300 Native Americans. The 3 museums display the original silver altar furnishings, handsome vestments, and a library. For more info, see **A Man with a Mission,** p. 8. *(624-3600. 3080 Rio Rd. Off Rte. 1. Open June-Aug. daily 9:30am-7:30pm; Sept.-May M-Sa 9:30am-4:30pm, Su 10:30am-4:30pm. Donation requested.)*

POINT LOBOS RESERVE. This extraordinary 550-acre state-run wildlife sanctuary is popular with skindivers and day hikers. Otters, sea lions, seals, brown pelicans, and gulls are visible from paths along the cliffs (bring binoculars). Point Lobos has tide pools and marvelous vantage points for watching the winter whale migration, which peaks in winter but continues throughout spring. *(624-4909. On Rte. 1, 3mi. south of Carmel. Park on Rte. 1 before the tollbooth and walk or bike in for free. Accessible by MST bus #22. Open daily Apr.-Oct. 9am-7pm, Nov.-Mar. 9am-4:30pm. Admission $7 per car; seniors $6. Day use free for campers registered with one of the state parks. Map included; extra copy 50¢. Free daily tours; call for times. Divers must call 624-8413 or email ptlobos@mbay.net for diving reservations. Dive fee $7.)*.

CENTER FOR PHOTOGRAPHIC ART. The Center is housed in the Sunset Cultural Center offices which were once occupied by Friends Photography (run by Weston and Ansel Adams). The photographer set considers the Center's exhibits to be top-notch; they include work by local and international artists *(625-5181. www.photography.org. San Carlos St. between 8th and 9th St. Open Tu-Su 1-5pm. Free.)*

BEACHES. Carmel City Beach is where the northern Big Sur coast truly begins with a pristine crescent of white sand framing a cove of clear, chilly, azure waters. The beach ends abruptly at the base of distant red cliffs, making a fine grandstand for sunsets. *(At the end of Ocean Ave.)* The **Carmel River State Beach** is even windier and colder than Carmel City Beach, but is blessed with better surf and smaller crowds. *(Just south of City Beach. Walk about 1mi. along Scenic Rd., or drive to the end of Carmelo St. off Santa Lucía. Parking lot closes at dusk.)*

BIG SUR

Host to expensive campsites and even more expensive restaurants, Big Sur holds big appeal for big crowds eager to experience the power of the redwoods, the sound of the surf, and the rhythm of the river. There are really no signs to announce that you are in Big Sur, but you'll know you're there because it's the first time you'll see any signs of civilization for miles in either direction.

ORIENTATION

Monterey's Spanish settlers simply called the entire region below their town *El Sur Grande*—the Large South. Today, Big Sur is a more explicitly defined coastal region bordered on the south by San Simeon and on the north by Carmel. The coast is thinly inhabited, dotted with a few gas stations and exorbitant "getaway" hotels. Almost everything—fuel, food, beer, toiletries—costs more in Big Sur than anywhere outside it. Last-chance stops for the thrifty are at the supermarket complex on Rio Rd. in Carmel to the north, and the market in Morro Bay to the south.

Despite its isolation, Big Sur can be reached by public transit (see below for details). The drive from Carmel to Big Sur on **Route 1** is simply breathtaking, but everyone knows it, so find a time (early mornings recommended) when traffic won't interfere with your enjoyment of the splendor.

Spring, when wildflowers bloom and the hills glow with color, is the optimal time to visit Big Sur. No matter what the season, warm and cold weather clothing is necessary for this stretch of coast, where mornings are typically cool and foggy, afternoons sunny, and evenings chilly.

PRACTICAL INFORMATION

Public Transportation: Monterey-Salinas Transit (**MST;** 899-2555). Bus #22 through Big Sur leaves from the Monterey Conference Center and runs as far south as Nepenthe, 29mi. south of Carmel, stopping at various points en route. Limited space for bikes; call ahead (May-Oct. 2 per day). Fare per zone $1.50, seniors and under 18 75¢.

Visitor Information: Big Sur Chamber of Commerce, P.O. Box 87, Big Sur 93920 (667-2100; www.bigsurcalifornia.org). Open M, W, and F 9am-1pm, but call any time or send a self-addressed stamped envelope for a guide to Big Sur. **Big Sur Station** (667-2315), ½mi. south of Pfeiffer Big Sur entrance on Rte. 1. This multi-agency station includes the State Park Office, the U.S. Forest Service (USFS) Office, and the CalTrans Office and provides permits and maps, as well as sponsoring campfires and ranger-led hikes. It also has copies of *El Sur Grande,* the best guide to travel and local entertainment from Hearst Castle to Carmel. Open daily 8am-6pm.

Road Conditions: 800-427-7623. **Highway Patrol:** 805-549-3261.

Emergency: 911. **Ranger Dispatch:** 649-2810.

Post Office: 667-2305, on Rte. 1 next to the Center Deli in Big Sur Center. Open M-F 8:30am-5pm. **ZIP Code:** 93920.

Area Code: 831.

CAMPGROUNDS

Camping in Big Sur is heavenly. Neglecting to bring equipment is a big mistake. Even if you do, be warned—site prices and availability reflect high demand. Reserve in advance by calling PARKNET (800-444-PARK/7275). If all sites below are booked, check with the **U.S. Forest Service** (see **Visitor Information,** above). Camping is free in the Ventana Wilderness, a backpack-only site at the northern end of Los Padres National Forest (permits at Big Sur Station). Cliff dwellers spend cramped nights in their cars within the cradle of deep turnouts, since Big Sur is the only place on the coast where doing so is both free and legal.

Ventana Big Sur (667-2688), on Rte. 1, 30mi. south of Carmel, has 75 shady sites in a gorgeous redwood canyon with picnic tables, fire rings, and water faucets. Bathhouses with hot showers. Sites for up to 2 people $25, leashed dogs $5. Day use $10. Reservations accepted at least 2 weeks in advance.

Andrew Molera State Park (667-2315), on Rte. 1, 5mi. north of Pfeiffer Big Sur. A level ¾mi. trail leads to hike-in, tent-only campgrounds. No numbered sites and never full. Beach, ornithology center, pit toilets. No showers. 3-night max. stay. Sites $3; dogs $1.

Kirk Creek and **Plaskett Creek** (385-5434), on Rte. 1. Kirk lacks shelter, and Plaskett a view, but both are within walking distance of a beach. Kirk (32 sites) sits 9mi. south of the Big Creek Bridge; Plaskett (43 sites) is 5½mi. farther, near Jade Cove. No showers. Sites $16; hike-ins and bike-ins $5 per person.

Pfeiffer Big Sur State Park (667-2315), on Rte. 1, 26mi. south of Carmel, just south of Fernwood Park campgrounds. The diverse wildlife and terrain, the beautiful Big Sur river, and several hiking trails ensure that all 218 campsites fill up in advance. No hookups. Firepits, picnic tables, and hot showers. Sites May-Sept. $21, seniors $17; Oct.-Apr. $15; dogs $1. Day use $6 per car; seniors $5. Reservations essential in summer.

Limekiln State Park (667-2403), 2mi. south of Lucía off Rte. 1 along Limekiln Creek. Pleasant, formerly private campground has 42 sites and direct beach access. Hot showers. Sites for up to 8 people $25. Each additional car (2 max.) $6. Also has 3 hike/bike sites for $10 per person. Reserve early.

Big Sur (667-2322), on Rte. 1, 26mi. south of Carmel near the Big Sur River. Private campground overseen by a terrific staff. Small store, playground, and volleyball courts. Hot showers and laundry. Sites for up to 2 people $40, with RV hookup $48; each additional person (up to 3) and leashed dogs $5. 4 tent cabins $44 (Oct.-May only). Reservations recommended. Neighboring **Riverside Camp** (667-2414) has sites with a little more dust for similar prices, plus 5 rooms in cabins ($45 per night).

Fernwood (667-2422), on Rte. 1, 2mi. north of the post office downhill from the burger bar and store (see **Food,** below). In a redwood forest on the Big Sur River, the 66 campsites and 2 swimming holes are small and exposed, but beautifully situated. Coin-operated hot showers. Sites for up to 6 people $24, with hookup $27; walk-in $8 per person. Reservation fee $4.

FOOD

Grocery stores are at Big Sur Lodge (in Pfeiffer Big Sur State Park), Pacific Valley, and Gorda, and some packaged food is sold in Lucía and at Ragged Point, but it's better to arrive prepared because prices are high in Big Sur.

Fernwood Bar and Grill (667-2422), on Rte. 1, 2mi. north of post office. Chicken breasts, veggie burritos, and hamburgers are $6.50 each. Open daily 10am-10pm. Also has a full bar (open daily noon-midnight) and a grocery store (open daily 8am-10pm).

Village Pub (667-2355), in the Village Shops. This packed pub serves up fresh, hearty food to raucous locals. Speak up or stay standing; it's well worth your while to sit. Two slices of freshly topped pizza $4; sandwiches $5-6. Open daily 11am-10pm; food served until 9:30pm. In winter, the pub may close at 9pm.

Center Deli (667-2225), 1mi. south of Big Sur Station beside the post office. Frequented by savvy local rangers, this is where you will find the most reasonably priced goods in the area. $4-5 sandwiches include veggie options like avocado and egg salad. Open daily Apr.-Sept. 8am-8:30pm, Oct.-Mar. 8am-7:30pm.

Cafe Kevah (667-2344), 3mi. south of Big Sur Station next to its hoity-toity sister, the Nepenthe Restaurant, and ritzy-schmitzy brother, the Phoenix Gift Shop. The outdoor patio stretches to the edge of a strategically scenic cliff. Homemade granola with yogurt $5.75, omelettes $9-10. Drink prices are in the stratosphere (smoothies $4.75, cappuccino $3.75). Open daily 9am-3pm.

Loma Vista Cafe (667-2450), just south of the post office. Occupies a wide spot on the road with lovely gardens. Fresh food and affordable options. Pancakes ($4) and sandwiches (from $7). Open daily 7:30am-9pm.

SIGHTS AND ACTIVITIES

Big Sur's state parks and **Los Padres National Forest** beckon outdoor activists of all types. Their **hiking** trails penetrate redwood forests and cross low chaparral, offering even grander views of Big Sur than those available from Rte. 1. The northern end of Los Padres National Forest, accessible from Pfeiffer Big Sur, has been designated the **Ventana Wilderness** and contains the popular **Pine Ridge Trail,** which runs 12 miles through primitive sites and the Sikes hot springs. The Forest Service ranger station supplies maps and permits for the wilderness area (see **Practical Information,** p. 217).

Within **Pfeiffer Big Sur State Park** are eight trails of varying lengths (75¢ map available at park entrance). The **Valley View Trail** is a short, steep trail offering a view of the valley below. **Buzzard's Roost Trail** is a rugged two-hour hike up tortuous switchbacks, but at its peak are rewarding panoramic views of the Santa Lucía Mountains, the Big Sur Valley, and the Pacific Ocean.

Roughly at the midpoint of the Big Sur coast lies **Julia Pfeiffer Burns State Park** (entrance fee $6), where picnickers find refuge in the redwood forest and sea otters in McWay Cove. At the point where the Big Sur River flows into the ocean is a spectacular waterfall, visible from a practically paved path 300 feet from the park entrance. Locals frequent all of the state parks, but crowds can be avoided by following highway turn-offs that lead to charming secluded inlets. Just to the north of Pfeiffer Burns is one such turn-off, marked with a "Fire Road Only" barrier. At the water are terrific rock formations and crashing waves. Big Sur's most jealously guarded treasure is USFS-operated **Pfeiffer Beach,** one mile south of Pfeiffer Burns. Turn off Rte. 1 at the stop sign and the "Narrow Road Not Suitable For Trailers" sign, just past the bridge by Loma Vista. Follow the road two miles to the parking area, where a path leads to the beach. An offshore rock formation protects sea caves and seagulls from the pounding ocean waves. Frequent winds can make sunbathing uncomfortable, and there are no lifeguards, although riptides make swimming and other water sports dangerous.

Big Sur is not all nature and no civilization, however. The **Henry Miller Memorial Library,** just south of Nepenthe and Cafe Kevah, displays books and artwork by the former Big Sur resident (open daily 11am-5pm). The small library is in a soothing sculpture garden. Miller's casual reminiscences and prophetic ecstasies made hundreds of readers aware of Big Sur. Many readers of his more explicit works came to Big Sur seeking a non-existent sex cult that he purportedly led.

CAMBRIA AND SAN SIMEON

The original settlers of the southern end of the Big Sur coast were awestruck by the stunning pastoral vistas and rugged shoreline, reminiscent of the eastern coast of England. In homage to the natural beauty of their homeland, they named the equally stunning New World site Cambria, the ancient name for Wales.

Neighboring San Simeon has the best beaches and is the last stop for travelers heading to Big Sur or those making the pilgrimage to majestic Hearst Castle. Driving along this stretch of Route 1, the last thing you would expect to see is a castle that would put Disney to shame, but like everything else in this state, nothing obeys the rules of common sense. Newspaper tycoon William Randolph Hearst built this palatial abode and invited the visiting wealthy elite to stay in the most extravagant edifice this side of the Taj Mahal.

PRACTICAL INFORMATION

Public Transportation: Central Coast Area Transit (CCAT). Bus #7 runs from San Luis Obispo to Morro Bay (fare $1.50). Connect to #12 for Cambria (fare $1.50) and San Simeon (fare $1.75). You may have to flag buses to get them to stop. **Cambria Village Transit** (927-0468) is a free trolley service through Cambria (every 30min. June-Sept. Th-M 9am-6pm; Oct.-May F-M 9am-6pm). Currently, there is no public transportation to Hearst Castle.

Visitor Information: Cambria Chamber of Commerce, 767 Main St. (927-3624). Maps of the area. Open daily 9am-5pm. **San Simeon Chamber of Commerce,** 250 San Simeon Dr. (927-3500 or 800-342-5613), on the east side of Rte. 1; look for the blue tourist info signs. Open Apr.-Oct. M-Sa 9am-5pm; Nov.-Mar. M-F 10am-2pm.

ATM: Bank of America, 2258 Main St., Cambria. Open 24hr.

Emergency: 911. **Sheriff:** 800-834-3346.

Post Offices: Cambria, 4100 Bridge St. (927-3654). Open M-F 9am-5pm. **ZIP Code:** 93428. **San Simeon** (927-4156), on Rte. 1, in the back of Sebastian's General Store (and gas pumps). To get there, take the road opposite the entrance to Hearst Castle. Open M-F 8:30am-noon and 1-5pm. **ZIP Code:** 93452.

Area Code: 805.

ACCOMMODATIONS AND CAMPGROUNDS

Cambria has charming but pricey B&Bs. Budget travelers will have better luck in San Simeon. The arrival of Motel 6 set off a pricing war that has led to wildly fluctuating rates, so it is always a good idea to call ahead. Beware of skyrocketing summer prices when tourists storm the castle.

Bridge Street Inn, 4314 Bridge St., Cambria (927-7653). Newly renovated building includes sunny rooms and sturdy bunks. White picket fence encloses a yard with volleyball and croquet sets. Dorms $20; private rooms from $40. Continental breakfast and linen included. Reception 5-9pm.

Creekside Inn, 2618 Main St., Cambria (927-4021 or 800-269-5212). Sunny, yellow country cottage. Some rooms have balconies over the creek; some have TVs and VCRs. All have nosegays, gingham, and pink walls. Singles and doubles May-Sept. from $55; Oct.-Apr. $50.

Sands Motel, 9355 Hearst Dr., San Simeon (927-3243 or 800-444-0779), west of Rte. 1 near the beach. Indoor heated pool. All rooms have cable TV and coffee makers, some have VCRs and fridges. Doubles May-Sept. from $45-60; Oct.-Apr. $39.

Motel 6, 9070 Castillo Dr., San Simeon (927-8691; fax 927-5341), off Rte. 1 at the Vista del Mar Exit. Clean, comfy, and classy. Big rooms with 2 queen beds and cable TV. Doubles May-Sept. $60; Oct.-Apr. $40. $10 more on weekends in both seasons.

Jade Motel, 9065 Hearst Castle Dr., San Simeon (927-3284). Free local calls, TV, and excellent beach access. Partial ocean views from most of the rooms. Rooms from $30 (up to $70 in summer).

San Simeon State Beach Campground, just north of Cambria on Rte. 1. **San Simeon Creek** has showers at its 133 sites near the beach. Neighboring **Washburn** sits on a hill overlooking the ocean. Portable toilets and cold running water only. Sites Apr.-Sept. $17; Oct.-Mar. $14. Weekends $1 more, seniors $2 less. For reservations, call PARKNET (800-444-7275).

FOOD

Food is far more plentiful in Cambria than San Simeon. You'll have to plan ahead to eat because most places have pre-established opening and closing times but change their hours according to the volume of tourists in the area. Groceries are available at **Soto's Market,** 2244 Main St., Cambria (927-4411; open M-Th 7am-8pm, F-Sa 7am-9pm, Su 8am-6pm). Buy fresh local produce on Main St. at the Cambria **farmer's market,** next to the Veteran's Hall (F 2:30-5:30pm).

Robin's, 4095 Burton Dr., Cambria (927-5007). Many San Luis Obispo residents consider this the only reason to go to Cambria. Eclectic international cuisine inside a craftsman-style bungalow with gorgeous gardens. Entrees $5-9. Sandwiches $5-7. Lots of veggie options and extensive wine list. Open daily June-Sept. 11am-10pm; Oct.-May 11am-9pm.

El Chorlito Mexican Restaurant, 9155 Hearst Castle Dr., San Simeon (927-3872). Fresh, lard-free, and zippy New Mexican-Cali food with ocean views. Try a cup of the specialty—an unusually spiced green chile and cheese soup ($2.75). Enchiladas $5-10. Open daily Apr.-Sept. noon-10pm; Oct.-Mar. noon-8pm.

The Harmony Pasta Factory, 1316 Tamson Dr., Cambria Village Square (927-5882). A romantic retreat with amazing views, it feels more expensive than it really is. Good lunch deals (M-Sa 11:30am-2:30pm; $4-7) and early-bird dinners (M-F 5-6pm; entrees $6-10). Open M-Sa 11:30am-9:30pm, Su 9:30am-9pm.

Creekside Gardens Cafe, 2114 Main St., Cambria (927-8646), at the Redwood Shopping Center. Locals frequent this petite eatery for the solid, homemade food. Indoor or patio dining. Pancakes $4. Desserts made fresh daily ($2-3). Open M-Sa 7am-2pm, Su 7am-1pm.

SIGHTS AND ACTIVITIES

Big Sur's dramatic coastline begins here and extends north along Rte. 1. Cute sea otters, once near extinction, now live in the kelp beds of **Moonstone Beach** (on Moonstone Dr. off Rte. 1 toward San Simeon). Along this stretch of coast, surfers are occasionally nudged off their boards by playful seals (and, more rarely, by not-so-playful great white sharks, who thrive in these cold waters). Scenic **Leffingwell's Landing** offers the best spot for **whale watching** (Dec.-Apr.). **San Simeon** and **Hearst State Beaches,** just across from Hearst Castle, are ideal for cliff-climbing and beachcombing and have the best swimming for miles. A single parking permit ($4) is good for one day at all state parks. It is illegal to park on the road outside Hearst Beach's entrance, but many people do it at their own risk. Look for turnouts on Rte. 1 between San Simeon and the lighthouse at Piedras Blancas; these and the nearby wooden stairs over Hearst Corporation fences provide the only legal access.

HEARST CASTLE (HEARST SAN SIMEON HISTORIC MONUMENT)

Information: 927-2020. **Reservations:** DESTINET 800-444-4445; international reservations 619-452-8787; wheelchair accessible reservations 805-927-2020. **Address:** on Rte. 1, 3mi. north of San Simeon and 9mi. north of Cambria. **Tours:** Call weeks in advance as tours often sell out, particularly in summer. 4 daytime tours (1 hr.; $14, ages 6-12 $8, under 6 free). Evening tours feature costumed docents acting out the Castle's legendary Hollywood history in new outdoor lighting (2hr.; $25, ages 6-12 $13). Each of the tours involves 150-370 stairs.

Casually referred to by founder William Randolph Hearst as "the ranch," Hearst Castle (as tourists and locals refer to it today) is an indescribably decadent conglomeration of castle, cottages, pools, gardens, and Mediterranean *esprit* perched high above the Pacific. It stands as a testament to Hearst's unfathomable wealth and Julia Morgan's architectural genius. Young Hearst caught a bad case of art collecting at age 10, and spent the rest of his life gathering Renaissance sculpture, tapestries, and ceilings. Ms. Morgan, the first woman to receive a certificate in architecture from the Ecole des Beaux-Arts in Paris, orchestrated all of this into a Mediterranean *mélange*. Scores of Hollywood celebs flocked to the castle (by invitation only) to bask in Hearst's hospitality. But while countless memorable cast parties were held on these grounds, the only things ever filmed here were 30 seconds of *Spartacus* and a Kodak Fun Saver camera commercial.

Tours are run by the State Parks Department and are a strictly hands-off experience. Fondle the banisters or staircases because they are the only things you may touch in the castle. **Tour One** covers the photogenic Neptune Pool, the opulent Casa del Sol guest house, fragrant gardens, and the main rooms of the house; this is the best bet for first-time visitors. **Tours Two, Three,** and **Four** cover the living quarters and gardens in greater depth—these tours are recommended for those already familiar with Tour One.

Before going to see the castle, your experience may be enhanced by stopping by the **visitors center** at the base of the hill, which features a surprisingly frank portrait of Hearst's failed Harvard days, yellow journalism, and scandalous life. Hearst may be renowned for his business acumen, but in reality his mistress had to sell her jewels so that construction of her indebted lover's mansion could continue. The **National Geographic Theater** shows the 40-minute film *Enchanted Castle*, which details how the architectural dream became reality, on a five-story screen. Or, you can view scenes of perhaps the greatest American film of all time: Orson Welles's *Citizen Kane*, which was based on Hearst's life. *(927-6811. Films show daily every 30min. 9:30am-5:30pm. Tickets $7, under 12 $5.)*

SAN LUIS OBISPO

San Luis Obispo (pop. 42,000) is pronounced "san-LOO-is oh-BIZ-bow," and written SLO—you'll need to know that to get very far in this town. With its sprawling green hills and its proximity to the rocky coast, SLO looks like the town in the Chris Columbus- and Steven Spielberg-penned film *The Goonies* (1985). This area grew into a full-fledged town only after the Southern Pacific Railroad laid tracks here in 1894. Ranchers and oil-refinery employees make up a significant percentage of today's population, but Cal Poly State University students add a young, energetic component. Along the main roads, the hippest young vegetari-vegans graze to their heart's delight and top it off with a dose of wheatgrass and bee pollen, while fashion mavens hit the stores lined with the latest arrivals from Milan.

ORIENTATION

San Luis Obispo is the heart of the Central Coast area. It sits inland on **U.S. 101**, burrowed among ranch-laden mountains. This small town serves as a hub between Morro Bay, 12 miles north on Rte. 1, and Avila, Shell, and Pismo Beaches, about 12 miles south on Rte. 1.

Downtown, **Monterey Street** (north-south) and **Broad Street** (east-west), are the two main drags. Walking here is easy and there is plenty of cheap parking. Two-hour **free parking** is available downtown at the Palm St. (at Morro St.) and Marsh St. (at Chorro St.) lots.

PRACTICAL INFORMATION

Trains: Amtrak, 1011 Railroad Ave. (541-0505 or 800-USA-RAIL/872-7245), at the foot of Santa Rosa Ave., 7 blocks south of Higuera St. To: **L.A.** ($21); **San Francisco** ($40-62); and **Santa Barbara** ($18-20), but, as always, it is cheapest if you make reservations at least a week in advance. Open daily 6am-8:30pm.

Buses: Greyhound, 150 South St. (543-2121), ½mi. from downtown. To get to downtown from the station, walk west on South St., then north on Higuera St. Six buses per day to **L.A.** and **San Francisco** ($35 for either). Luggage lockers for ticketed passengers only. Open daily 7am-9:30pm.

Public Transportation: The **Central Coast Area Transit** (CCAT; 541-2228) links SLO and Morro Bay (#7; fare $1.25), Los Osos (#7; $1.50), Pismo Beach (#10; fare $1), and Paso Robles (#9; $1.75). Unlimited-use day pass $3. Buses depart from City Hall at Osos and Palm St. On the weekends, only bus #9 (north to Paso Robles) and bus #10 (south to Santa Maria) are operational. All buses wheelchair accessible. **SLO Transit** (541-2877) runs buses throughout the city, and they go faster than the acronym would suggest. Fare 75¢, seniors 35¢; free transfers. Buses run M-F 6am-7pm, Sa-Su 8am-6pm (Sa-S, only buses #3 and 5 are operational). SLO Transit also offers a **free trolley** service around downtown (runs F-W noon-5pm, Th noon-9:30pm). Additional service to hotels along Monterey St.

Car Rental: Thrifty, 2750 Broad St. (544-3777). Cars start at $45 per day with unlimited mileage within California. Must be 21. Ages 21-25 pay $5 per day surcharge. Personal damage waiver $9 per day, $4 per day for passengers. Open M-F 7am-9pm, Sa 8am-5pm, Su 9am-9pm.

Visitor Information: Visitors Center for the Chamber of Commerce, 1039 Chorro St. (781-2777). Watch for signs on U.S. 101. Open M-W 8am-5pm, Th-F 8am-8pm, Sa 10am-8pm. **State Parks Office,** 3220 S. Higuera St. #311 (549-3312). Open M-F 8am-5pm.

Laundromat: California Coin Laundry, 552 California Blvd. (544-8266). Wash $1.75, dry 50¢. Open 24hr.

Weather Conditions: 541-6666. **Road Conditions:** 800-427-7623.

Emergency: 911. **Police:** 1042 Walnut St. (781-7342).

Crisis Line: 800-549-8989. Counseling and referrals 24hr.

Hospital: SLO General Hospital, 2180 Johnson Ave. (781-4871).

Internet Access: The Library, 723 Higuera St. (542-0199). Actually, it's a bar, not a real library. $3 per hr. Open M-F 2pm-2am, Sa-Su noon-2am.

Post Office: 893 Marsh St. (543-3062). Open M-F 8:30am-5:30pm, Sa 10am-5pm. **ZIP Code:** 93405.

AREA CODE	The area code in San Luis Obispo is 805.

ACCOMMODATIONS

Asked for their rates, proprietors in San Luis Obispo frequently respond, "That depends"—on the weather, the season, the number of travelers that day, or even on the position of the waxing and waning moon. There is less fluctuation in nearby **Pismo Beach** or **Morro Bay,** but the average prices are the same. If you can find a $40 room in downtown SLO, grab it. And reserve *well* in advance for mid-June (Cal Poly commencement). **Prices do not include SLO's 10% hotel tax.**

Sunbeam Hotel, 1656 Monterey St. (543-8141; fax 543-9064). Looks like an apartment complex and rooms are as sunny as the staff. Cable TV, A/C, fridges, phones, coffee-makers. Singles $33-36; doubles $38-45. In summer, prices jump.

San Luis Obispo (HI-AYH), 1617 Santa Rosa St. (544-4678; fax 544-3142; email esimer@slonet.org). New location just a block from the Amtrak station (exit to your right). Small space creates a cozy atmosphere, complemented by lively but laid-back common

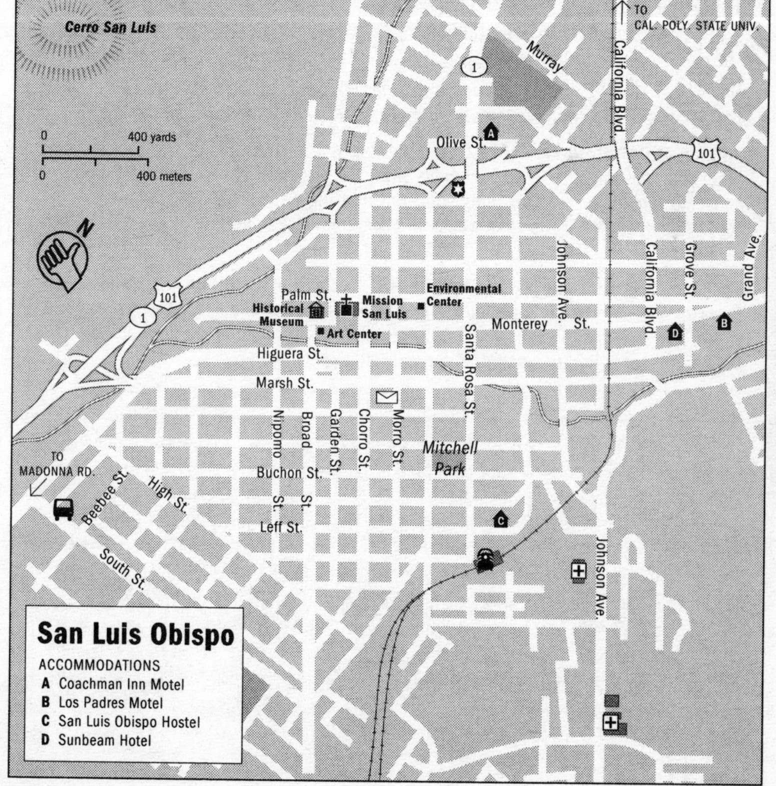

CENTRAL COAST

room. Free toast and bagels in the kitchen arrive daily from a local bakery. Lockout 10am-5pm. Reception 7:30-10:30am and 5-10pm. Linen $1, towels 50¢. Parking available. No credit cards. Dorms $14; private rooms $32. $2 more for non-members.

Coachman Inn Motel, 1001 Olive St. (544-0400; fax 541-3079). Huge, immaculate, rooms have cable TV and fridges. May-Sept. singles $42-45, doubles start at $50; Oct.-Apr. singles $25-30, doubles $32-35. In summer weekend prices can rise to $120.

Los Padres Motel, 1575 Monterey St. (543-5017 or 800-543-5090; fax 547-1664). Your hospitable hosts Harry and Nina have a pretty pink motel and offer cable TV with HBO, direct-dial phones, and complimentary breakfast. Rooms Apr.-Oct. start at $59; Nov.-Mar. $39. Reservations recommended.

Bill's Home Hostel, 1040 Cielo Ln. (929-3647). Exit 101 on W. Tefft St., take a left on Orchard, and a right on Primavera. Cielo Ln. is on the left. Non-smokers with an agricultural bent will find a base camp near the Pismo Dunes here at Bill's cluttered retreat. Those without cars can take a long walk into town for public transport. Check-in with Bill by 9pm. Donation of $10 1st night and $8 2nd night can be replaced with work on the farm.

CAMPGROUNDS

All state park sites can be reserved through PARKNET (800-444-7275) up to seven months in advance. For a list of more campsites in the area, contact State Parks Information (see **Practical Information,** p. 222). In summer, you need reservations at beach parks; especially crowded parks require reservations year-round. Prices at all of the campgrounds in the area fluctuate daily. *Let's Go* listings reflect the average price unless otherwise stated.

Morro Bay State Park (772-2560), 12mi. west of SLO on Rte. 1. Popular park between the ocean and forest has 135 developed sites, 20 with hookups. Hot showers and running water. More accessible than Montana de Oro, but also more likely to be full. Sites $18, in winter $14; with hookups $24, in winter $20. Reserve year-round.

Montana de Oro State Park (528-0513), on Pecho Rd., south of Los Osos, 12mi. from SLO via Los Osos Valley Rd. 50 primitive sites in a gorgeous, secluded park. Outhouses and cold running water (but bring your own drinking water). Sites $15, in winter $7, $7.50 reservation fee. Reserve weeks in advance between Memorial Day (May 29 in 2000) and Labor Day (Sept. 4 in 2000).

Pismo Beach State Park (489-2684), on Rte. 1, south of Pismo Beach. **North Beach** has 103 tent sites ($22, in winter $14) and restrooms. **Oceano** has 40 tent sites ($20) and 42 RV hookups ($26, in winter $22). Both have showers, but North Beach sites are larger and closer to the beach. Call for reservations.

VERGIN' ON TACKY The **Madonna Inn,** 100 Madonna Rd. (543-3000), off U.S. 101 (take the Madonna Rd. Exit) in south SLO, is probably the only hotel in the world that sells postcards of each room. Alex S. Madonna, the contractor behind the construction of much of U.S. 101 and I-5, decided in 1958 to build a Queen Anne-style hotel of 12 rooms. He put his wife, Phyllis, in charge of the design. By 1962, the vision had grown into a hot-pink behemoth of 110 rooms on 2200 acres of land. The men's room features a giant laser-operated waterfall that doubles as a urinal. Every room has a theme—the Caveman Room, the Daisy Mae Room, and a room with a working waterwheel serving as a headboard. (Rooms range from $87-240.) Even non-guests can enjoy coffee and a bun from the Madonna's own oven and the photo album of the rooms in the reception area. At night, there's swing music 7-11pm in the lounge to keep things hoppin'.

FOOD

Monterey Street and the streets running across it are lined with restaurants and cafes. The area just south of the mission along the creek is popular with lunchtime crowds. A **farmer's market** takes over Higuera St. every Thursday from 6 to 9pm.

Big Sky Cafe, 1121 Broad St. (545-5401). Voted "Best Restaurant in SLO" by the local poll magazine, Big Sky delivers with hearty, vegetarian-friendly food. Lean back, relax, and heave a sigh of contentment to the (painted) stars. Sandwiches $5-7. Choice wines. Margaritas or swanky Kir Royales $3.50. Open M-Sa 7am-10pm, Su 8am-8pm.

Tio Alberto's, 1131 Broad St. (546-9646). The best burrito between L.A and San Francisco. Burritos $3.50-5.50, combo plates $5. Open Su-Th 9am-11pm, F-Sa 9am-3am. No credit cards.

Woodstock's Pizza Parlour, 1000 Higuera St. (541-4420). Popular hangout sweeps annual best pizza awards. Young crowd keeps it lively into the night. Three slices of pizza for $4.20, pies $8 and $11. Toppings 50¢-$1. Happy Hour M-Sa 2-5pm ($3 pitchers of beer, $1 slices). Open Su-Th 11am-1am, F-Sa 11am-2am.

Paradiso, 690 Higuera St. (544-5282). Homemade organic pasta and ravioli with lots of vegetarian sauces ($5-7). Half-order portions are plenty for mid-sized appetites. Daily special includes pasta, salad with specialty balsamic dressing, and focaccia bread for $5. Cappuccino $1. Open daily 11am-9pm.

Mo's Smokehouse BBQ, 970 Higuera St. (544-6193). SLO's favorite carnivore-only haunt. Check out memorabilia from "Mo's journey through the BBQ Belt," a quest for the perfect ribs. Sandwiches $6. Open Su-W 11am-9pm, Th-Sa 11am-10pm.

Art of Sandwich Delicatessen, 717 Higuera St. (544-7775). Dagwood masterpieces ($6-7) complemented by eclectic art and decent beer. Open M-W 10:30am-9pm, Th-Sa 10:30am-2am, Su 10:30am-6pm.

Kona's Deli, 726 Higuera St. (783-7171). No-nonsense deli offers basic sandwiches for $3.35. Host to the California Amateur Baseball Museum, this deli outdoes the locker room with lofty ceilings and funky decor and music. Open Su-W 10am-10pm, Th-Sa 10am-2am.

House of Bread, 858 Higuera St. (542-0255). Enticing bakery smells will lure you into this warm bakery that uses chemical-free Montana wheat in its delicious bread products. Free samples provide ample opportunity to choose your favorite. Huge cinnamon roll is $1.50. Open M-F 7am-7pm, Sa 7am-6:30pm, Su 8am-5pm.

SIGHTS AND ACTIVITIES

San Luis Obispo grew around the **Mission San Luis Obispo de Tolosa** (543-6850) and the city continues to engage in celebrations and general lunchtime socializing around its front steps. Founded in 1772, the mission was at one time covered in white clapboards and crowned with a steeple in emulation of a New England church. In the late 1800s, however, the town made a concerted effort to revive the mission's Spanish origins; by the 1930s, it was fully restored and still serves as the Catholic parish church for SLO. (Open daily early Apr. to late Oct. 9am-5pm; late Oct. to early Apr. 9am-4pm. $1 donation requested.) For more info, see **A Man with a Mission,** p. 8. The mission faces Mission Plaza, where Father Serra held the area's first mass. The Plaza now houses the **SLO Historical Museum** (543-0638), with a display of Chumash pottery and over 17,000 historical photos (open Sept.-May. W-Su 10am-4pm, June-Aug. Sa-Su 10am-4pm; $2 donation requested), and the **SLO Art Center,** 1010 Broad St. (543-8562), with lectures, art classes, and multimedia exhibits by regional artists (open Tu-Su 11am-5pm; free).

The nearby **Jack House,** 536 Marsh St. (781-7308), at Beach St., is a restored Victorian residence with the original 19th-century furnishing inside and a gazebo and garden outside (45min. tours; open Feb.-Nov. 1st Sunday of the month 1-4pm; June-Aug. Th 2-5pm; call 781-7300 for tour times; admission $2). **San Luis Little The-**

ater, 888 Morro St. (786-2440), has performances by local thespians (Th-Sa 8pm, Su 2pm; tickets $14, students and seniors $12, Th $10). Kids may like to check out the **SLO Children's Museum,** 1010 Nipomo St. (544-KIDS/5437), where there's a "creative learning station featuring communicable diseases" (open M-Tu and Th-Sa 10am-5pm, Su 1-5pm; limited winter hrs; admission $4, under 2 free).

The **Palm Theater,** 817 Palm St. (541-5161), screens artsy and revival films (tickets $6, seniors and children $3.75, M $3). Standard Hollywood flicks often run at the grand **Art Deco Freemont Theatre,** 1035 Monterey St., designed in 1942 by the preeminent Southern Californian architect Charles Lee. The main theater seats 850 and maintains the original murals, but be warned—there's no air-conditioning. (Tickets $6.75, seniors and children $3.75; matinees before 6pm $4.)

A gurgling 14-foot waterwheel and shady deck await visitors to the **Apple Farm Mill,** 2015 Monterey St. (800-374-3705). Alternately churning cider, ice cream, and flour, the mill provides free samples of cider and complimentary tea on the deck. (Open daily 9am-6pm.)

Bubble Gum Alley is a crazy, squishy fact, although the visitors center may try to deny its existence. You can venture between the 12-foot walls of gum graffiti at 735 Higuera St. Love notes in brightly colored gunk put a unique twist on the old-fashioned tree-carving.

ENTERTAINMENT

One half of SLO's population is under the age of 24, so the town can't help but party. It gets particularly wild after the Thursday night **farmer's market,** along Higuera St. between Nipomo and Osos St., which is more of a raging block party than a produce market. Weekdays slow down a bit while the students rescue their grades. Consult the free weekly *New Times* regarding other local happenings.

Frog and Peach Pub, 728 Higuera St. (595-3764). Big British pub with a leafy patio along the creek and a load of British attitude. Mellow sounds like jazz, R&B, or acoustic pop nightly. Celtic jam sessions on the 1st and 3rd Wednesday of each month. Pints $3. No cover. Must be 21. Open M-F 11am-2am, Sa-Su 10am-2am.

Mother's Tavern, 725 Higuera St. (541-8733). Yukon decor draws mostly Cal Poly students who pile in for the Wednesday night disco party ($1 after 10pm). Happy Hour M-F 3-6pm. Live music Th-Sa (cover $3-4). Must be 21 after 9pm. Open M-F 11am-1:30am, Sa-Su 9am-1:30am. Food served until 9pm.

SLO Brewing Company, 1119 Garden St. (543-1843). Amazingly good porter (pints $3)–specifically, the "Cole Porter," a dark, rich beer that's a meal in itself. Happy Hour M-F 4-5:30pm featuring half-price pitchers. Live funk, reggae, and rock Th-Sa (cover $2). Must be 21. Open M-W 11:30am-10pm, Th-Sa 11:30am-1:30am, Su 11:30am-6pm. Billiards room downstairs (open M-W 4pm-midnight; Th-F 4pm-1:30am; Sa noon-1:30am; Su noon-midnight. $6 per hr., but half-price Su-W and before 6pm Th-Sa).

Linnaea's Cafe, 1110 Garden St. (541-5888). Evening hangout, especially with the artsy set. Displays local artists' works on the walls and features music nightly at 8pm; jazz F-Su. No cover, but a hat is passed around after each performance. All ages. Open Su-Th 7am-midnight, F-Sa 7am-12:15am.

SEASONAL EVENTS

Believe it or not, SLO hosts the most rollicking **Mardi Gras** this side of the Mississippi, celebrated the Saturday before Ash Wednesday (Mar. 4 in 2000; call 542-2183 for more info). Over Father's Day weekend (June 16-18 in 2000), catch the three-day acoustic showdown at the **Live Oak Music Festival,** in Lake Cachuma Park. Most revelers camp at the park for the mini-Woodstock (tickets $30 per day, 3-day ticket $75; call 781-3030 for info). A favorite wingding is the **Mozart Festival,** July 23-August 8, 2000. Concerts play at Cal Poly, the mission, local wineries, and local churches. (Tickets cost around $15, student rush tickets 30min. before show $7.50. For tickets call 756-2787 or in CA 888-233-2787; for info call 546-4195; or write P.O. Box 311, San Luis Obispo 93406.) The acclaimed **Central Coast Shakespeare Festival** (546-4224), runs two Shakespeare plays in repertory for six weeks at the Learning Pine Arboretum on Cal Poly's campus (tickets $14, students and seniors $12; Th-Su starting the first or second week in July). The four-day **International Film Festival** (543-0855; www.slofilmfest.org), first week of November (Oct. 27-Nov. 5 in 2000), features independent films, documentaries, and seminars ($5 per screening).

SOUTH OF SAN LUIS OBISPO

Two beaches just southwest of San Luis Obispo enjoy anonymity; no signs announce their existence to the masses. The well-frequented and nude **Pirate's Cove** has unusually warm water, which is fortunate for the thongless throng romping there. Take U.S. 101 south from San Luis Obispo and take the Avila Rd. Exit. Follow signs for Avila Beach, but turn left on Cave Landing Dr. Park in the dirt lot and take a path to the cove. The shores of **Shell Beach,** one mile down U.S. 101 south of Avila Beach and Pirate's Cove, are lined with semi-precious stones (onyx, agate, quartz, and the like) instead of sand. Take the Shell Beach exit and turn left on Shell Beach Rd., then drive until you see little brown Coastal Access signs. Park at the gazebo, and climb down to the ocean.

Avila and **Pismo Beaches** are both more developed and more crowded than Shell Beach. Avila is known for its gaggle of fishermen. The adjoining city streets seem determined to mimic the boardwalk atmosphere of Pismo. Avila Beach is on your left after you pass Cave Landing Dr. Pismo Beach, 1½ miles south of Shell Beach, is developed and congested; the lines for the public restrooms are practically a social event. This raging spring break party spot is accessible by **Central Coast Area Transit** (541-2228), as well as **Greyhound** (800-231-2222). Rent all kinds of beach equipment at **Beach Cycle Rentals,** 150 Hinds Ave. (773-5518), next to the pier (open daily 9am-dusk). At the day's end, when the sun sets behind the hills that jut into the sea, Pismo Beach lights up with a gorgeous sand-on-fire effect.

Pismo Dunes, actually south of Pismo Beach in Grover City, is a State Vehicular Recreation Area, where for a $4 day use fee, you can take your car or all-terrain vehicle (ATV) down onto the dunes and burn rubber to your heart's content. Call 473-7223 for information. You can rent ATV equipment ($30-50 per hr.) from **BJ's ATV,** 197 Grand (481-5411; open daily 9am-5pm)—but keep your speed down to 15mph on the road or pay a stiff $900 fine. At the south end of the park is **Oso Flaco Lake,** where Cecil B. DeMille left the set of *The Ten Commandments.* It is currently being "excavated" (leave it to Californians to excavate a movie set). Camping here is an option for the serious budget traveler (473-7223; sites $6, walk-ins $1). On the weekends, though, the sounds of squealing tires and revving engines can drown out the surf.

NUDE BEACH NECESSITIES For those who are virgins to the nude experience, a handy list of etiquette rules can be invaluable.

1. Three times: Don't look down. Whatever you do, don't look down. Even if you're wearing dark sunglasses they can spot you, they will know what you're doing, so don't look down.
2. No tai chi.
3. Get rid of body hair—this isn't Europe.
4. Play volleyball. The sheer physics of it alone are amazing.

NORTH OF SAN LUIS OBISPO

The **Nine Sisters,** a chain of gnome-like ex-volcanoes, are remnants of a time when SLO County was a hotbed of volcanic activity. Today the lava that once flowed here makes for dramatic shorelines along the Pacific Coast Hwy. from Morro Rock to SLO. The northernmost sister, Morro Rock, shadows the tiny burg of **Morro Bay,** just to the north of its namesake park. CCAT bus #7 serves Morro Bay from SLO (5 per day; fare $1.25; for more info call 541-2228). Lodgings here are cheaper than in SLO. **Morro Bay Chamber of Commerce,** 880 Main St. (772-4467 or 800-231-0592), has maps and a complete listing of accommodations (open M-F 8:30am-5pm, Sa 10am-3pm). For Morro Bay campground info, see **San Luis Obispo: Camping,** p. 224. The town's namesake, **Morro Bay State Park,** is home to coastal cypresses which are visited by Monarch butterflies from November to early February. The park's **Museum of Natural History** (772-2694) flexes its curatorial might on the aquatic environment and wildlife of the coastal headlands. A bulletin board at the entrance lists a variety of free nature walks led by park rangers in summer. (Open daily 9am-5pm. Admission $3, ages 6-12 $1.) South Bay Blvd., which links the town and the park, winds through the new **Morro Bay National Estuary** (528-8126), a sanctuary for great blue herons, egrets, and sea otters. You can park in the deserted end of the Marina lot and either take the trail or rent a kayak ($6 per hr.) or canoe ($10 per hr.) to roam through the estuary. Check for tides to avoid (or take advantage of) numerous sandbars.

The **Embarcadero,** which runs along the beach, is the locus of Morro Bay activity and fish and chips bargains. The **Morro Bay Aquarium,** 595 Embarcadero (772-2694), has over 100 live ocean critters and a seal-feeding station (open daily 9am-6pm; admission $3.50, ages 5-11 $1). Morro Bay's pride and joy is the **Giant Chessboard,** in Centennial Park on Embarcadero. The board is 256 square feet, and the 18- to 20-pound pieces are carved from redwood.

Gray whales, seals, and otters frequent **Montana de Oro State Park** (528-0513), 20 minutes west of SLO on Los Osos Valley Rd. The 8000 acres and seven miles of shoreline remain relatively secluded. **Spooner's Cove,** across from tidepools and a campground, offers sea cave spelunking (at low tide) and free whale watching from the bluffs above, at the Bluff's Trail trailhead. You can get more info about hikes at the **visitors center** (772-7434; open daily noon-4pm).

The wineries around SLO are well-respected. Paso Robles, 25 miles north of SLO on U.S. 101, is vintner central. The **Paso Robles Chamber of Commerce,** 1225 Park St. (238-0506), has a list of wineries, including visiting hours, tours, and tastings (open M-F 10am-5pm, Sa 10am-4pm). The SLO Chamber of Commerce has similar info on the wineries (see **Practical Information,** p. 222). Wild Horse, Justin Winery, and Steven Ross are some of the most renowned labels. In August, over 25 local wineries come together for the **Central Coast Wine Festival** (call 238-0506; tickets $15).

Mission San Miguel Archangel (467-3256) is 43 miles north of San Luis Obispo in San Miguel, a few blocks from U.S. 101; take the Mission Exit. The 1818 complex has colorful frescoes, painted in 1821 by Monterey's Esteban Munras and a team of Native American artists. (Open daily 10am-4:30pm. $1 donation requested.) For more info, see **A Man with a Mission,** p. 8.

SANTA BARBARA

There's a reason why Santa Barbara (pop. 85,630) epitomizes worry-free living and abandonment of responsibility, and why all memories of the past seem to melt to nothing in the endless sun. When Padre Junípero Serra arrived here with his proselytizing spirit and merry band of soldiers and priests, he ran into the Chumash Indians. Seemingly unappreciative of the unknown and deadly bacteria Serra brought along, the Chumash abruptly died off. Over their ashes, the Spanish, and later the Americans, built Santa Barbara.

The past may not be pretty, but these days the living is good. Today's Santa Barbara is an enclave of wealth and privilege, true to its soap opera image, but in a significantly less aggressive way than its Southern Californian counterparts. Spanish Revival architecture decorates the residential hills that rise gently over a lively pedestrian district centered on State Street. This sanitized palm-lined promenade is filled with inexpensive cafes and thrift stores as well as glamorous boutiques and galleries—enough to engage the casual visitor for an entire day. Santa Barbara's golden beaches, museums, historic mission, and scenic drive add to what makes this a frequent weekend escape for the rich and famous and an attractive destination for surfers, artists, and hippies alike.

PRACTICAL INFORMATION

Transportation: Airport: Signature Flight Support, 515 Marxmiller Rd. in Goleta (967-5608). Signature is one of many private companies that use the runways. Others offer intrastate as well as limited national service, including American (800-433-7300), AmericaWest (800-235-9292), and United (800-241-6522). Contact these directly.

Trains: Amtrak, 209 State St. (963-1015; for schedule and fares 800-USA-RAIL/872-7245). Be careful around the station after dark. To: **L.A.** ($16-21) and **San Francisco** ($46-73). Reserve in advance. Open daily 6:30am-9pm. Tickets sold until 8pm.

Buses: Greyhound, 34 W. Carrillo St. (962-2477), at Chapala St. To: **L.A.** ($13) and **San Francisco** ($30). Open M-Sa 5:30am-8pm and 11pm-midnight, Su 7am-8pm and 11pm-midnight. **Green Tortoise** (415-956-7500 or 800-227-4766), the "hostel on

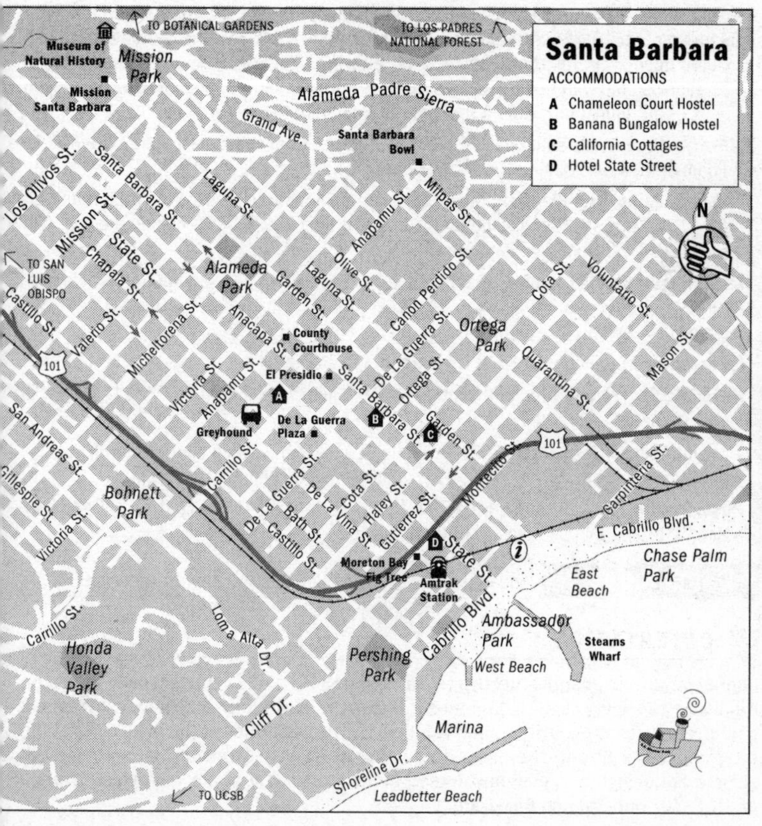

wheels," picks up from Banana Bungalow Hostel (see **Banana Bungalow Hostel,** p. 231). To: **L.A.** (Sa 5:30am; $10) and **San Francisco** (Su 11:45pm; $35). Arrive 15 min. before departure time. Storage lockers for ticketed passengers only.

Public Transportation: Santa Barbara Metropolitan Transit District (MTD), 1029 Chapala St. (683-3702), at Cabrillo Blvd. behind Greyhound station. Bus schedules available at this transit center, which serves as the transfer point for most routes (open M-F 6am-7pm, Sa 8am-6pm, Su 9am-6pm). All buses wheelchair accessible. Fare $1, seniors and disabled 50¢, under 5 free; transfers free. The MTD runs a **downtown-waterfront shuttle** along State St. and Cabrillo Blvd. every 10min. Su-Th 10:15am-6pm, F-Sa 10:15am-8pm. Stops designated by circular blue signs. Fare 25¢.

Taxis: Yellow Cab Company (965-5111). 24hr.

Car Rental: U-Save, 510 Anacapa St. (963-3499). Cars start at $20 per day, with 150 free mi.; $129 per week with 1050 free mi.; each additional mi. 20¢. Must be 21 with major credit card. Open M-F 8am-6pm, Sa-Su 8am-2pm.

Bike Rental: Cycles-4-Rent, 101 State St. (966-3804), 1 block from the beach. Rent a 1-speed beach cruiser for $5 per hr., $21 per day; 21-speed $7, $28. There are 2 other locations on the beach (with slightly higher prices) at 633 E. Cabrillo Blvd. and in the Radisson Hotel. All locations open M-F 9am-6pm, Sa-Su 8am-7:30pm.

In-line Skate Rental: Beach Rentals, 22 State St. (966-6733). Rentals include safety gear (1hr. $6; 2hr. $9; 6hr. $18). Open daily 8am-8pm.

Visitor Information: Tourist Office, 1 Garden St. (965-3021), at Cabrillo Blvd. near the beach. Hordes of folks clambering for maps and brochures. 15min. free parking, so be quick. Open July-Aug. M-Sa 9am-6pm, Su 10am-6pm; Sept.-Nov. and Feb.-June M-Sa 9am-5pm, Su 10am-5pm; Dec.-Jan. M-Sa 9am-4pm, Su 10am-4pm. Outdoor computer kiosks open 24hr. **Hotspots,** 36 State St. (963-4233 or 564-1637 for reservations). is an espresso bar with free tourist info, hotel reservation service, and an **ATM.** Cafe open daily 24hr.; tourist info M-Sa 9am-9pm, Su 8am-4pm.

Library: 40 E. Anapamu St. (962-7653), across from the courthouse. Open M-Th 10am-9pm, F-Sa 10am-5:30pm, Su 1-5pm.

Bi-Gay-Lesbian Organization: Gay and Lesbian Resource Center, 126 E. Haley St. #A-11 (963-3636). Counseling for alcohol and drug abuse. AIDS hotline, testing, and social services. Open M-F 9am-5pm.

Laundromat: Mac's Laundry, 501 Anacapa St. (966-6716). Pink-and-purple wonder features ever-entertaining Spanish TV. Wash $1, 15min. dry 25¢. Open daily 6am-midnight; last load 10:30pm.

Emergency: 911. **Police:** 215 E. Figueroa St. (897-2300).

Hospital: St. Francis Medical Center, 601 E. Micheltorena St. (962-7661), 6 blocks east of State St.

Internet Access: The eCafe, 1221 #6 State St. (570-5679). Full Internet/email connections 15min. for $2.50, students $2). Open M-F 8am-7pm, Sa 10am-4pm.

Post Office: 836 Anacapa St. (564-2266), 1 block east of State St. Open M-F 8am-5:30pm, Sa 10am-5pm. **ZIP Code:** 93102.

AREA CODE	The area code for Santa Barbara and nearby areas is 805.

ORIENTATION

Santa Barbara is 96 miles northwest of Los Angeles and 27 miles past Ventura on the **Ventura Freeway** (U.S. 101). Since the town is built along an east-west traverse of shoreline, its street grid is slightly skewed. The beach lies at the south end of the city, and **State Street,** the main drag, runs northwest from the waterfront. All streets are designated east and west from State St. The major east-west arteries are U.S. 101 and **Cabrillo Boulevard.**

Driving in Santa Barbara can be bewildering; dead-ends and one-way streets abound. Beware of crosswalks on State St. that surprise motorists with quick red lights. Many downtown lots and streets offer 90 minutes of free **parking,** including two subterranean lots at Pasco Nuevo, accessible from the 700 block of Chapala St. All parking is free on Sundays. **Biking** is a breeze, as most streets are equipped with special lanes. The **Cabrillo Bikeway** runs east-west along the beach from the Bird Refuge to the City College campus. MTD buses run throughout the city (see **Practical Information,** above).

ACCOMMODATIONS

A 10-minute drive north or south on U.S. 101 rewards with cheaper lodgings than those found in Santa Barbara proper. Trusty **Motel 6** is always an option. In fact, Santa Barbara is where this glorious chain of budget-friendly motels originated. There are two locations: at the beach at 443 Corona del Mar Dr. (564-1392), and past the main drag at 3505 State St. (687-5400). Prices start at $45 in winter, $55 in summer. All Santa Barbara accommodations are more expensive on the weekends as a flood of tourism drowns out competitive rates.

Hotel State Street, 121 State St. (966-6586; fax 962-8459), on the main strip 1 block from the beach. A budget night's sleep without the nightmares of cheap travel. Welcoming, comfortable and very clean. Pristine common bathrooms. Private rooms have sinks and cable TV; a few have skylights. Continental breakfast included. Limited free parking. One double bed $40; 2 single beds $45; 2 double beds $55; $15-25 higher July-Aug. Reservations recommended.

Traveler's Motel, 3222 State St. (687-6009; fax 687-0419). Take bus #6 or 11 from downtown. Although it's a bit far from the action, this motel is clean and spacious and has the gosh-darn prettiest rooms on State St., all with cable TV, direct-dial phones, A/C, and fridges. Singles June-Sept. $50, Oct.-May $35; palatial rooms with kitchenettes $55, Oct.-May $40; each additional person (up to 4) $5. Prices higher on weekends.

Banana Bungalow Santa Barbara, 210 E. Ortega St. (963-0154), just off State St., in a busy area. Party-oriented hostel with lived-in feel and tropical motif. Young, international crowd. Kitchen, TV room, pool table, video games. Equipment rentals. Laundry, coin lockers. Free parking. Co-ed and women-only dorms $15-20; thatched-roof bunks $18. No reservations; show up around 10:30am. **Passport or student I.D. required.**

California Cottages, 227 E. Haley St. (963-5077), 4 blocks from the beach. Opened in the summer of '99, this latest addition to the Santa Barbara budget scene offers 12 individual cottages, each with 4 beds, kitchen, and bath. Facility contains game room, pool table, bike and surfboard rentals, and tour information. Laundry. Street parking. Co-ed cottage $18. One private room available $56. Reservations recommended. **Passport or student I.D. required.**

CAMPGROUNDS

State campsites can be reserved through ReservAMERICA (800-444-7275), up to seven months in advance. **Carpinteria Beach State Park** (684-2811), 12 miles southeast of Santa Barbara along U.S. 101, has 261 developed tent sites with hot showers (sites $18, with hookup $22-28; weekends: $18, $23-29; off-season: $15, $20-26). There are two other state beaches within 30 miles of Santa Barbara, but none are served by buses. All three are perched between the railroad tracks and U.S. 101. **El Capitán** (968-1033), has 140 well-kept sites, some with views of the Channel Islands. **Refugio** (968-1033), has 84 crowded sites just steps from the beach (wheelchair accessible). (Sites at both $15-17, weekends $18; off-season $15; seniors $2 discount.) If all of these are full, you may want to try the El Capitán **private campground** (685-3887), which has a swimming pool, although sites are dusty and closely packed (sites $20, with hookup $25; each additional vehicle $5).

North of Santa Barbara are more than 100 sites in the **Los Padres National Forest.** The nearest of these are almost 20 miles from downtown Santa Barbara, but many are free and the others are inexpensive (sites $8). Buy a map for $3 at the **Supervisor's Office,** U.S. Forest Service, 6144 Calle Réal, Goleta 93117 (683-6711; open M-F 8am-4:30pm). Direct specific questions to the **Los Prietos Ranger Station,** U.S. Forest Service, Santa Barbara Ranger District, Star Route, Santa Barbara 93105 (967-3481; open M-Sa 8am-4:30pm). Unlikely to be full, **Lake Cachuma Recreation Area** (688-4658), 20 miles north of Santa Barbara on Rte. 154, has more than 500 campsites on a first-come, first-camped basis. (Sites $15, with hookup $18-21; each additional vehicle $5.)

FOOD

Santa Barbara has more restaurants per capita than anywhere in America, so finding a place to eat is not exactly a problem. State and Milpas St. both have many places to eat; State St. is hipper, Milpas St. cheaper. Ice cream lovers flock to award-winning **McConnel's,** 201 W. Mission St. (569-2323; open daily 10am-midnight). There's an open-air **farmer's market** packed with bargains on the 400 block of State St. (Tu 4-7:30pm), and another on Santa Barbara St. at Cota St. (Sa 8:30am-12:30pm). **Tri-County Produce,** 335 S. Milpas St. (965-4558), sells fresh produce and prepared foods (open M-Sa 9am-7:30pm, Su 9am-6pm).

Pacific Crepes, 705 Anacapa St. (882-1123). Cozy but classy French cafe is filled with the delicious smells of a full menu of crepe creations. The make-your-own plate starts with an empty crepe for just $2, edible for as little as $4. The heavenly "Normandy" is topped with fresh strawberries and blueberries and makes a perfect breakfast or dessert for $5.50. Sandwiches $5. Open Su-Tu 9am-4pm, W-F 9am-9pm, Sa 8am-10pm.

The Sojourner Cafe, 134 E. Canon Perdido St. (965-7922) Friendly low-key tea-candle atmosphere provides "natural food with a flair" as organic meets Mexican. Original dishes include Chile Tempeh Tacos $7 and Cornbread Supreme ($6) which has more veggies than your mother's fridge. Daily "Plato Barato" lunch special $5.50. Open M-Sa 11am-11pm, Su 11am-10pm.

Cafe Orleans (899-9111), Center Court, Paseo Nuevo Mall at 800 block of State St. Naw'lins soul food in a jiffy for all y'all. Jambalaya, *etouffeés,* and po' boys ($5-6.50). Live zydeco F 6-8:30pm. Open M-Th 11am-9pm, F-Sa 11am-10pm, Su 11am-8pm.

R.G.'s Giant Hamburgers, 922 State St. (963-1654). Yellow Formica joint, was voted best burgers in S.B. Basic burger, garden burger, chicken burger, or turkey burger $3. Call 10min. ahead, and it'll be waiting when you arrive. Or wait it out playing table-top Arkanoid. The choice is yours. Giant french toast on the breakfast menu is only $2.50. Open daily 9am-10pm.

The Natural Cafe, 508 State St. (962-9494). Healthy, attractive clientele dines on healthy, attractive food. Smoothies, which "don't have any ice, so you get more fruit" $2.50; sandwiches, which are also iceless, $3.50-5. Herbal medicine shop next door. Open daily July-Aug. 11am-10pm; Sept.-June 11am-9pm.

Char West, 221 Stearn's Wharf (962-5631). Avoid the tourist traps at the beach-end of the wharf and venture to the far end for a better view of the sea and a tasty fish and chips for $6. Deep fried fish sandwich $4. Clam chowder $3. Eat outside, just be careful not to confuse your tartar sauce with the occasional seagull surprise left on the table. Open M-W 11am-6pm, Th-Su 11am-9pm.

Super Cuca's Taquería, 626 W. Micheltorena St. (962-4028). A bit far from downtown, Super Cuca's serves an insanely delicious super-burrito with beans and rice $3.40. Homestyle kitchen makes perfect meals. Open daily 8:30am-10pm. No credit cards.

SIGHTS

Santa Barbara is best explored in three sections—the beach and coast, swingin' State St., and the Missionary Mountains. Essential to discovering local events and goings-on, the *Independent* newspaper is published every Thursday and is available on newsstands throughout the city. If you are without a car, the downtown-waterfront **shuttle** (25¢), runs from the beach up State St. The **visitors center,** 1 Garden St. at Cabrillo Blvd., has a helpful map, and pamphlet-peppy employees. Pick up *Santa Barbara's Red Tile Tour*, a map and walking tour guide (free at the visitors center; 25¢ from the docent inside the courthouse). Chase Palm Park, the idyllic public park across from the visitors center comes complete with a vintage 1916 Spillman carousel ($1.50 per ride).

THE COAST

Recently revamped, the coastal drive is now Cabrillo Blvd., which serves as the first leg of the city's "Scenic Drive." Follow the green signs as they lead you in a loop into the mountains and around the city, winding through the hillside bordering the town along Alameda Padre Serra. This part of town is known as the American Riviera, for the massive amounts of wealth that hibernates here.

SANTA BARBARA ZOO. The delightfully leafy habitat has low fences and such an open feel that the animals seem kept in captivity only through sheer lethargy. Attractions include a miniaturized African plain, or *veldt*, where giraffes stroll, lazily silhouetted against the Pacific. A miniature train provides a park tour (every 15min.; $1.50, children $1). In the zoo's own words, "We're the most beautiful zoo in the world." *(962-5339. 500 Niños Dr, off Cabrillo Blvd. from U.S. 101. Take bus #14 or the downtown-waterfront shuttle. Open daily 10am-5pm. Admission $7, seniors and ages 2-12 $5, under 2 free. Parking included.)*

SEA CENTER. Stearn's Wharf, the oldest working pier on the West Coast, houses the Sea Center, as well as a number of restaurants and shops. The center features sea-life dioramas, a touch tank of sea-lings, and life-size models of whales and dolphins, as well as six indoor aquaria. *(962-0885. At State St. and Cabrillo Blvd. Sea Center open daily 10am-5pm. Touch tank open daily noon-5pm. Admission $3, ages 13-17 $2, ages 3-12 $1.50.)*

BEACHES AND ACTIVITIES. The Santa Barbara beaches are unmistakably breathtaking, lined on one side by skyrocketing palm trees and backgrounded by the endless sailboats off in the distance at the local harbor. **East** and **Leadbetter Beaches** flank the wharf on either side. Beach Rentals will rent beachgoers a retro surrey—a covered carriage Flintstone-esque **bicycle.** You and up to 8 friends can cruise along the beach paths in this stylish mode of transportation. *(966-2282. 22 State St. $12-32 per hr., depending on number of riders.)* Across the street from the visitors center, is idyllic **Chase Palm Park,** a beautiful public parkland complete with a vintage 1916 Spillman carousel *($1.50 to ride).*

BEST SUNSET. For the best sunset view in the area, have a drink (soda $2) at the bar at the Four Seasons Biltmore Hotel. This five-star lodging is just a l'il bit steep for the budget traveler, but the view of the Pacific is priceless. *(969-2261. 1260 Channel Dr., Montecito.)*

STATE STREET

Santa Barbara's monument to city planning, State St., runs a straight tree-lined two miles in the center of the city. Among countless shops and restaurants are some cultural and historical landmarks that should not be missed. Everything that doesn't move—malls, mailboxes, telephones, the restrooms at the public library—has been slathered in Spanish tile.

SANTA BARBARA COUNTY COURTHOUSE. To get the full impact of the city's architectural homogeneity and a killer view of the ocean, take the elevator up to the observation deck of the courthouse. Compared to the more prosaic Mission Revival buildings found elsewhere in California, the courthouse is a work of genius with its sculpted fountain, sunken gardens, historic murals, wrought-iron chandeliers, and hand-painted vaulted Gothic ceilings. *(962-6464. 1100 Anacapa St. Open daily 10am-5pm. Tower closes 4:45pm.Tours M-Tu, Th, and Sa 2pm, W and F 10:30am and 2pm. Free.)*

SANTA BARBARA MUSEUM OF ART. The museum owns an impressive collection of classical Greek, Asian, and European works spanning 3000 years. The 20th-century and Hindu collections are among its most impressive. Over 90% of the works in the permanent collection were gifts from Santa Barbara's wealthy residents. The digital guided tour by savant Dennis Miller sports his wry intonation but no jokes because this is *art*, people. *(963-4364. 1130 State St. Open Tu-Th and Sa 11am-5pm, F 11am-9pm, Su noon-5pm. Tours Tu-Su noon and 1pm. Admission $5, students and ages 6-16 $2, seniors $3. Free on Th and 1st Su of each month.)*

ARLINGTON CENTER FOR PERFORMING ARTS. This combination performance space and movie theater comfortably seats 2,018 people. It is quite a sight to be seen, in a travel-booky recommendation sort of way. The murals over the entrance of the Spanish-Moorish building depict scenes from California's Hispano-Mexican era. Its tower is one of the few structures in this low stucco town to rival the palm trees in height, and the actual theater space resembles a Mexican village. Call the box office for info on upcoming events. *(963-4408. 1317 State St. Movie tickets $7.75, seniors and ages 2-12 $5; 1pm matinee and twilight show at 3:30 or 4pm $5.)*

OTHER SIGHTS. At the corner of Montecito Ave. and Chapala St. stands the famed **Moreton Bay Fig Tree.** Brought from Australia by a sailor in 1877, the tree's gnarled branches now span 160 feet, and can provide shade for more than 1000 people at once. If you'd rather be drinking than standing in the shade with 999 other people, sample award-winning wine at the **Santa Barbara Winery.** *(963-3646. 202 Anacapa St. Open for free tastings daily 10am-5pm. Tours daily at 11:30am and 3:30pm.)*

THE MOUNTAINS

Up in the northern part of town things get considerably more pastoral.

MISSION SANTA BARBARA. Praised as the "Queen of Missions" when built in 1786, the mission assumed its present incarnation in 1820. Towers containing splayed Moorish windows stand on either side of a Greco-Roman facade, and a Moorish fountain bubbles in front. The museum contains period rooms and a sampling of items from the mission archives. The main chapel is colorful and solemn, and visitors are welcome to (respectfully) drop in on mass. Religious scenes blister in the sun in the form of pavement paintings in front of the chapel. Franciscan friars and 4000 Christianized Mission Indians are buried in the cemetery, the ruins of a pottery shack lie across the street, and a small Chumash cave painting can be found in the hills off Camino Cielo. For more info see **A Man with a Mission,** p. 8. *(682-4719. At the end of Las Olivas St. Take bus #22. Open daily 9am-5pm. Admission $3, under 12 free. Self-guided museum tour starts at the gift shop. Mass M-F 7:30am, Sa 4pm, Su 7:30am-noon.)*

SANTA BARBARA MUSEUM OF NATURAL HISTORY. Unlike a typical natural history museum, this one has few interior spaces, so you can learn while taking in the sun. Originally built to be a museum of comparative oology (no, not zoology), the founder's wishes were overrun by a Board of Trustees who thought that devoting this beautiful space to the study of *eggs* was, well, silly. So they hatched the current exhibitions which include the largest collection of Chumash artifacts in the West, an antique natural history gallery, and a planetarium. *(Museum 682-4711; observatory 682-3224. 2559 Puesta del Sol Rd. Open M-Sa 9am-5pm, Su and holidays 10am-5pm. Museum admission $6, seniors and ages 13-17 $5, under 12 $4. Planetarium shows Sa-Su 1, 2, and 3pm, W 3pm. Planetarium $2 plus museum admission.)*

DON'T KEEP YOUR FOOL HEAD IN THE SAND! When you think of weird California wildlife, what springs to mind? Condors? Elephant seals? Michael Jackson's chimpanzee Bubbles? They're boring compared to some even funkier fauna. **Ostriches** populate the desert and inland central coast regions. They're not wild, though. They've been imported by ranchers who want to market the lucrative hides of these creatures (ostrich boots are all the rage among the line-dancin' crowd). At an ostrich farm, you'll have a rare chance to observe these nine-foot fowl, but you should honor ostrich etiquette. You can approach the birds' enclosure from a distance (provided the owners don't object), but **don't pet their dinky heads** or taunt them. They may look like they have their heads in the sand, but they've got really bad tempers too, so stay cool. Ostrich ranches congregate along Refugio Rd., off Rte. 246 in Santa Ynez. Depending on how the birds treat you, buy your very own pet chick or vengefully swallow an ostrich burger at **Ostrich Land,** on Rte. 246, just west of Solvang. The emus are an added treat.

SANTA BARBARA BOTANICAL GARDEN. Though it is quite some distance from town by car, these gardens do offer enjoyable hikes. Five miles of hiking trails wind through 65 acres of native Californian trees, wildflowers, and cacti. The garden's water system was built by the Chumash and is one of the last vestiges of the region's heritage. *(682-4726. 212 Mission Canyon Rd. Open Mar.-Oct. M-F 9am-5pm, Sa-Su 9am-6pm; Nov.-Feb. M-F 9am-4pm, Sa-Su 9am-5pm. Tours M-W and F at 2pm, Th and Sa-Su at 10:30am and 2pm. Admission $5; students, seniors, and ages 13-19 $3; ages 5-12 $1.)*

HIKING TRAILS. The trailhead for **Seven Falls Trail** is at the junction of Tunnel and Spyglass Rd. From the end of Las Canoas Rd. off Tunnel Rd., you can pick up the 3½-mile **Rattlesnake Canyon Trail,** with many waterfalls, pools, and secluded spots. The 7¼-mile trek from the **Cold Springs Trail** to **Montecito Peak** is considerably more strenuous. *(From U.S. 101 South, take a left at the Hot Springs Rd. Exit, and another left on Mountain Dr. to the creek crossing.)* For a more extensive listing of trails in the area, try the Botanical Garden gift shop which has **maps** with more trails.

NEARBY: UNIVERSITY OF CALIFORNIA AT SANTA BARBARA (UCSB). This beautiful outpost of the U.C. system is stuck in Goleta, a shapeless mass of suburbia, gas stations, and coffee shops. If its renovations are complete and it has reopened to the public, the excellent **art museum** is worth visiting. It houses the Sedgwick Collection of 15th- to 17th-century European paintings (including a Bellini *Madonna and Child*) and hosts innovative contemporary exhibits. *(Museum 893-2951. Off U.S. 101. Take bus #11. Open Tu-Sa 10am-4pm, Su 1-5pm. Free.)*

OTHER NEARBY SIGHTS. The beach at **Summerland,** east of Montecito and accessible by bus #20, is frequented by the **gay** and **hippie** communities. Its biggest food attraction is **The Big Yellow House,** a Victorian-estate-turned-restaurant. It is reported to be inhabited by two ghosts: Hector haunts the wine cellars, while his mistress sticks to the women's bathroom upstairs. Ask to eat in the bedroom with the secret door. *(969-4140. 108 Pierpoint Ave. Open Su-Th 8am-9pm, F-Sa 8am-10pm.)* **Rincon Beach,** three miles southeast of Carpinteria, has some of the county's best surfing. **Gaviota State Beach,** 29 miles northwest of Santa Barbara, also has good surf. It is a mixed crowd, gay and straight, and the western end is a (sometimes) **clothing-optional** beach, although nude sunbathing is illegal in Santa Barbara. You can **whale watch** from late November to early April, as the Pacific Grays migrate.

SHOPPING

State Street is a shopping mecca with two miles of mildly trendy shops and the upscale **Paseo Nuevo Mall,** at Canon Perdido St. Local craftspeople line Cabrillo Blvd. for the **Arts and Crafts Show,** where they sell their hand crafted wares every fair-weathered Sunday and holiday from 10am to dusk.

Scavenge, 418 State St. (564-2000). Half clothing store, half garage-sale, this bargain-shopper's dream store carries everything from framed Monet and Degas prints to screwdriver and ratchet sets. You can find that boogie board you've always wanted or perhaps a new pink boa. Prices range from under $1 to $40. There *are* some gems in the lot. Open M-Th 11am-10pm, F-Su 11am-midnight.

As Seen on TV, 1125 State St. (564-4100). Late-night infomercials can open new horizons of consumer cravings. Find everything "guaranteed to..." Love handle removal, perfect hair in minutes, and the clearest pores a teenager has ever known. The most popular item is the Sobakawa Buckwheat Pillow ($25)—Dr. Kazu Watanabe swears you'll sleep like a baby. You can even get a George Foreman Grille for one easy installment of $59.99. Open M-Th 10am-7pm, F-Sa 10am-8pm, Su 10am-7pm.

Victorian Vogue, 1224 State St. (962-8824). A time machine of *haute couture,* from flapper outfits of the 1920s to squeaky-clean styles of the 1950s. Ethnic fashions as well, from saris to sombreros. Accessorize with vintage jewelry and ties. Open M-W 11am-6pm, Th 10am-8pm, F-Sa 10am-10pm, Su noon-6pm.

2000 Degrees, 1206 State St. (882-1817). If you're feeling left out of the California art scene, experience the Santa Barbara ceramics circuit at this paint-your-own studio. Pay just a $7 workshop fee and paint as many pieces of bisqueware as you can buy. Prices range from $2-60, and a decent send-home-to-Mom mug is under $10. They'll even ship it home for you. Open M-F 11:30am-8pm, Sa 10am-9pm, Su 10am-7pm.

ENTERTAINMENT AND NIGHTLIFE

Every night of the week, the clubs on **State Street** are packed. This town is full of locals and tourists who love to eat, drink, and be mirthful. Consult the *Independent* to see who's playing on a given night. Bars on State St. charge $4 for beer fairly uniformly, so search for a special.

The Hourglass, 213 W. Cota Street (963-1436). You and your traveling companion can rent a private hot tub here by the hour. With 9 spas total, you can pick a sensual indoor bath or watch the stars from a private outdoor tub. Locals report that "this is what we do in Santa Barbara." No alcohol allowed. Towels $1. 2 people $20 per hr.; each additional person $7. 1hr. min. Open daily noon-midnight.

Fathom, 423 State St. (730-0022). Gay dance club (all are welcome) that is the closest it gets to wild in Santa Barbara. Locals praise it as having the best music in town. Pool tables, lots of drink specials. Tu swing night (as in the dance), W 80s extravaganza. Su Beer Bust 4-8pm $5. Martini Happy Hour daily 5-8pm (well drinks $2). Open nightly 5pm-2am. Cover F-Sa $5, after 11:30pm $7. 21+.

Madhouse, 434 State St. (962-5516). Decadent faux-dive for the jet set. Sounds of Sinatra, mambo, and Afro-Cuban music. A decadent melange of retro and funk. Live music and drink specials nightly (5-8pm). No cover. Open W-Sa 5pm-2am, Su-Tu 7pm-2am. 21+.

Yucatan, 1117 State St. (564-1889), a.k.a. "The Party Cantina." Every frat boy's dream come true. "Billiards Club" with 9 pool tables ($5 per hr., $8 per hr. at night) Satellite sports TV. DJ spins. Happy Hour M-F 3-7pm (drafts $2). Tu country western night. Cover $3-5. Open daily 11am-1:30am. Age restrictions; call ahead if under 21.

Q's Sushi A-Go-Go, 409 State St. (966-9177). Leopard skin decor, a tri-level bar, and a State St. balcony. Stomach some sushi ($3.50-8.50) in front of your date and you'll totally score! Accompany with *sake* ($3.50) and some Jackson Five or Marvin Gaye. Happy Hour (4-7pm) means half-price drinks and 20% off sushi plates. M Brazilian night. Su karaoke. Cover F-Sa after 9pm $5. Open daily 4pm-2am.

SEASONAL EVENTS

The most special of events in Santa Barbara is not organized by human hand. Starting in October, and assembling most densely from November to February, hoards of **Monarch butterflies** cling to the eucalyptus trees in Ellwood Grove, just west of

UCSB, and at the end of Coronado St., off Hollister Ave.; take the Glen Annie/Storke Rd. Exit off U.S. 101. Other events include:

Hang Gliding Festival (965-3733; www.flyaboveall.com), Mesa Flight Park; early Jan.

Santa Barbara International Film Festival (963-0023), Mar. 2-12, 2000. Sponsored by the Arlington Center (see p. 234). Premieres U.S. and foreign films.

Gay Pride Parade (963-3636), on a Saturday in mid-July. A 1-day festival held on Leadbetter Beach celebrating the local gay community.

Vintners' Festival (688-0881), early Apr. Held in a different lush setting each year, with regional wines and samples from local restaurants.

Italian Street Painting Festival (569-3873), Memorial Day weekend (May 26-29 in 2000). Professional and amateur chalk paintings decorate the Old Mission Courtyard.

Summer Solstice Parade and Fair (965-3396), on the Saturday nearest June 21. Pre-Bacchanal fun on State St. No words (on posters), vehicles, religious faith symbols, or animals allowed. It's a pagan thing.

Old Spanish Days Fiesta (962-8101), early Aug. Spirited fiesta with rodeos, carnivals, flamenco guitar, and plenty of sangria.

Music Academy of the West, 1070 Fairway Rd. (897-0300), holds a series of inexpensive concerts throughout the summer. Stop by for a brochure.

Santa Barbara International Jazz Festival (310-966-3000), early Sept.

NEAR SANTA BARBARA: LOS PADRES NATIONAL FOREST

Land of the Chumash Indians and condors, the vast **Los Padres National Forest** (district office 683-6711) stretches north of Santa Barbara into San Luis Obispo County and beyond. The area includes four mountain ranges and climatic zones that range from semiarid desert to coniferous forest to marine habitat. Los Padres is a leader in wildlife recovery programs, reintroducing many endangered plants and birds, such as the bald eagle and the falcon. The **San Rafael Wilderness** alone contains 125 miles of trails and a sanctuary for the nearly extinct California condor. **Cachuma Lake,** 15 miles from U.S. 101 on Rte. 154, is a brilliant blue water source for the area, as well as a campsite and recreational area. The nearby **Chumash painted cave** is only 20 minutes north of Santa Barbara. Take U.S. 101 to Rte. 154 to Painted Cave Rd., past the village, and down into the oak glen (parking is scarce). The cave is up on the right. The impressive red ochre handiwork of native shamans dates back to 1677. There are lots of hiking and camping opportunities in the area (see **Santa Barbara: Camping,** p. 231). The **Adventure Pass** is available at the **Santa Barbara Ranger Office** (967-3481), and is needed in all recreation areas in the national forest ($5 per day, $30 per year). Take Rte. 154 for 10 miles to Paradise Rd. and turn right. The office is 5 miles ahead on the left (open M-Sa 8am-4:30pm).

NEAR SANTA BARBARA: SANTA YNEZ VALLEY

To the northwest of Santa Barbara along Rte. 154 lies the lovely **Santa Ynez Valley,** home to thousands of acres of vineyards, hundreds of ostriches, and Michael Jackson's **Wonderland Ranch,** ostensibly named after Lewis Carroll's fantasy world. The free *Santa Barbara County Wineries Touring Map,* available at the Santa Barbara visitors center, gives comprehensive listings. One of the prettiest vineyards is **Gainey Vineyard,** 3950 E. Rte. 246 (688-0558), at Rte. 154 (tours and $3 tastings daily at 11am, 1, 2, and 3pm).

Expatriate Danes will shed a tear at **Solvang Village,** an overpriced Disneyesque Danish-land, a stone's throw away east down Rte. 246. Solvang is crammed with *konditoris* (bakeries)—try the **Solvang Bakery,** 460 Alisal Rd. (688-4939). Next door is the graceful **Mission Santa Ines,** 1760 Mission Dr. (688-4815). Check out the cemetery, which has 1700 Chumash graves, and look for the precious footprint of a Chumash child in the Chapel of the Madonnas. (Open daily in summer 9am-7pm; in winter 9am-5pm. Admission $3, under 16 free.) For more info, see **A Man with a Mission** (p. 8). Four miles west, at the intersection of Rte. 246 and U.S. 101 is the town of Buellton, home of **Pea Soup Andersen's** (688-5581), where the split pea soup is famed to be as thick as the fog. (Soup $3.25, all the soup you can eat $6.25; open daily 7am-10pm.)

Farther to the northwest, at the juncture of Rte. 1 and Rte. 246, is the city of Lompoc, home of **the nation's largest producer of flower seed.** The acres upon acres of blooms, which peak near the end of June, are both a visual and an olfactory explosion. Purple sweet elysium and crimson sweet pea are just two of the many blossoms. Lompoc holds a **flower festival** at the season's peak, usually the last weekend in June (call 735-8511 for info). **La Purisma Mission State Park,** 2295 Purisma Rd. (733-7781), off Mission Rd., has the most fully restored of Father Serra's missions and extensive hiking trails (open daily 9am-5pm; parking $5). For more info, see **A Man with a Mission** (p. 8).

OJAI

Ojai (pop. 7697) lies in a wooded valley a few hours outside of noisy Los Angeles. The enchanting town (pronounced OH-hi) provides the ideal haven for those looking to bone up on their Zen Buddhism, as it is just the place for an afternoon of quiet meditation.

ORIENTATION AND PRACTICAL INFORMATION. The verdant Ojai Valley, sits 15 miles north of Ventura, just east of the Santa Ynez Mountains and just south of Los Padres National Forest. To reach Ojai from Los Angeles (about 1hr.), take Rte. 405 North to Rte. 101 North, following signs for San Francisco. Exit onto Rte. 33 Ojai (which will eventually become Rte. 33/150). Fifteen miles of leafy roads will lead you to Ojai. Ojai Ave., the town's east-west spine is also called Rte. 150. The city of Ojai runs a **trolley** along Ojai Ave. if you want to give your car a rest. (Operates M-F 7:15am-5:40pm, Sa-Su 9:05am-4:53pm; 25¢.) The **Ojai Valley Chamber of Commerce,** 150 W. Ojai Ave. (646-8126; www.the-ojai.org), has maps and info on Ojai's 20 prolific art galleries, as well as antique shops, campgrounds, the farmer's market, and spa services.

ACCOMMODATIONS AND FOOD. The **Ojai Farm Hostel** (805-646-0311), P.O. Box 723, Ojai 93024, epitomizes the town's earthy aura—any fruit in the organic orchard is yours for the pickin'. Owners have two rules: no smoking and no meat in the kitchen. They offer free bus pickup in Ventura, two TV rooms and free use of bikes. Guests stay in single-sex rooms or in a giant teepee ($12 per person). Advance reservations are required; the location will not be disclosed to anyone not staying in the hostel. Must have international passport or plane ticket. The **El Camino Motel,** 406 W. Ojai Ave. (805-646-4341), has 20 rooms with cable, phones, and kitchen units ($50 and under). Call ahead for rates and reservations. The final option for the budget traveler is camping, which is plentiful in the surrounding areas. The closest wine-tasting is a 10-minute drive south on Rte. 33 to the **Old Creek**

HOW YA LIKE ME NOW, OXNARD? Neighboring Oxnard, California, while not as heavily touristed as Ventura, has a trick or two up its sleeve nonetheless. The city roots for its Pacific Suns which are in minor league baseball's Pacific League. In addition to the Pacific Suns, Oxnard recently boasted 10 pounds of catfish. The catfish was brought to the city by the Pacific Suns as part of a trade that sent pitcher Ken Krahenbuhl to the Greenville (Mississippi) Bluesmen in exchange for cash, a player to be named later, and the catfish. Had Krahenbuhl or the Oxnard fans interpreted the terms of the trade as a vote of no confidence in his pitching abilities, gloominess would have been understandable. However, Oxnard may not have known what it was giving up; the plucky Krahenbuhl silenced naysayers on July 24, 1998, pitching a perfect game for the Bluesmen against the doomed Amarillo Dillas and relegating Oxnard's catfish to also-ran status in the municipal prestige derby.

Ranch Winery, 10024 Old Creek Rd. (805-649-4132). Among cattle and other ranch amenities, sippers can enjoy wine tasting at this winery (open F-Su 11am-5pm).

For a scant $2, trace the history of the area, Chumash to New Age, at the brand new **Ojai Valley Museum,** 130 W. Ojai Ave. (805-640-1390, open W-Su 1-4pm). The **Ojai Center for the Arts,** 113 S. Montgomery St. (805-646-0117), has art, dance, poetry readings, workshops, and theater (open daily noon-4pm). **Bart's Books** (805-646-3755), on the corner of Canada and Matilija, could only exist in Ojai. Bart has placed several bookshelves outside on the street and asks after-hours browsers to drop the correct amount of coins in the box. The books are cheap and plentiful, but there's a better selection in the daytime (open Tu-Su 10am-5:30pm).

Although this small town's most exciting news includes the valiant efforts of a man to return a lost wallet, Ojai was once the playpen of the Hollywood elite, who came to romp in the spas and natural hot springs. Then Krishnamurti came, establishing theosophy as the area's religious contribution to the world. Then the hippies came. Although many hot springs have closed, Ojai still fosters a vibrant artistic and spiritual community. Various spiritual centers flourish in Ojai, each respecting each others' space but following their own chosen path. The international **Krotona Institute of Theosophy,** 2 Krotona Hill (805-646-2653; open Tu-F 10am-4pm, Sa-Su 1-4pm), which opened its branch in Ojai in 1924, operates a reverentially quiet library and offers dynamic classes on theosophy and comparative religion. Other spiritual centers are the **Krishnamurti Library,** 1130 McAndrew Rd. (805-646-4948; open W 1-9pm, Th-Su 1-5pm), and **Tranquil Meditation Mount** (805-646-5508), on Reeves Rd., which has a meditation room and garden (open daily 10am-dusk; free). The mountain view is peaceful, peaceful, peacef...

Ojai is also the southernmost gateway to **Los Padres National Forest** (see p. 237). There are many impressive hikes in this area, particularly to **Rose Valley Falls** and the **Sespe Hot Springs.** Get maps, camping info, and an Adventure Pass (required at Los Padres recreation areas; $5 per day, $30 per year) at the **Los Padres Ojai Ranger Office,** 1190 E. Ojai Ave. (805-646-4348). Ask about trails to the **Punchbowls,** small water holes that sit like pools in the mountain, close to local waterfalls and "moon rocks" (open M-F 8am-4:30pm).

VENTURA

Ventura (pop. 92,600) is a place where people listen to Beach Boys eight tracks, and still like them. Aging surfers keep riding the waves in an endless summer that the younger, skater-punk crowd just doesn't seem to understand. In particular, local teens decry the lack of under-21 nightlife options, as the mostly senior citizen population has to go to bed early. For most non-residents, however, Ventura is just a filling station on the way to Santa Barbara.

PRACTICAL INFORMATION. Ventura Visitors Bureau, 89 S. California St. (648-2075 or 800-333-2989; open M-F 8:30am-5pm, Sa-Su 10am-4pm), has a good selection of maps and brochures, including schedules for the **Ventura Trolley** (650-6600), which services downtown, the beach, the pier, and Harbor Village. Ride all day for $1 (W-Su 10am-5pm). Those interested in visiting the **Channel Islands National Park** (see p. 241) should seek out the **National Park Headquarters,** 1901 Spinnaker Dr. (658-5730; open M-F 8am-5pm, Sa-Su 8am-5:30pm). **Cycles 4 Rent,** 239 W. Main St. (652-1114, manager cell phone 340-BIKE/1453), rents bikes (in summer $8 per hr., $35 per day; call for special rates; open during week by appt. only). **Emergency:** 911. **Police**: 110 N. Olive St. (648-8133) and 309 W. Main St. (648-8140; open daily 10am-7pm). **Medical assistance:** County Hospital, 3291 Loma Vista Rd. (800-746-8885). **Post office**: 675 E. Santa Clara St. **ZIP code**: 93001. **Area code: 805**

ACCOMMODATIONS AND CAMPGROUNDS. A number of cheap motels line **East Thompson Avenue,** but most are over 40 years old and in desperate need of renovation. The cleanest is the **Rex Motel,** 2406 E. Thompson Blvd. (643-5681; singles

$39-69; doubles $49-89). Also reasonable is the **Crystal Lodge Motel,** 1787 E. Thompson Ave. (648-2272), where some rooms have kitchens (singles $40; doubles $50).

Beach camping is in no short supply in and around Ventura, but conditions lean toward the primitive. As always, reservations can be made through PARKNET (800-444-7275) and should be made months in advance if possible. **McGrath State Beach Campground** (654-4610), just south of town in Oxnard, is a popular spot with 174 campsites (sites $22).

FOOD AND ENTERTAINMENT. You'll find cheap food and the heart of Ventura along **Main Street**—though some of the higher-quality cheap eateries are found on neighboring streets. **Cafe Voltaire,** 34 N. Palm St. (641-1743), whose namesake polished off over 50 cups of java per day, h.as everything: coffee ($1.15), stuffed sandwiches ($7), live music nightly, and frustrated intellectuals (open M-Th 9am-10pm, F 9am-midnight, Sa 10am-midnight, Su 10am-9pm). **Franky's,** 456 E. Main St. (648-6282), offers healthy, delectable pita pockets ($6-7) and turkey burgers ($6-7; open Su-Th 7am-3pm, F-Sa 7am-9pm). **Top Hat,** 299 E. Main St. (643-9696), at Palm St., is a burger shack swarming with locals clutching chili cheeseburgers ($1.85; open Tu-Sa 9am-5pm). Eating action at the pier centers around the fried-food heavy **Andria's,** 1449 Spinnaker Dr. (654-0546), where kids and crusty sailors abound. They serve up a great fish and chips ($6.50; Open mid-June to early Oct. Su-Th 11am-9pm, F-Sa 11am-10pm; early Oct. to mid-June Su-Th 11am-8am, F-Sa 11am-9pm.) The hip, spacious **Nicholby's Upstairs,** 404 Main St. (653-2320), has a bar, nine pool tables, an eclectic mix of live music, and weekly swing lessons (2-for-1 drinks 9-10pm Th-Sa; cover F-Sa $6; open daily 6:30pm-1:30am; cover F-Sa $6). Ventura's hip-hop club comes in the form of **Metro Nite Club,** 317 E. Main St. (653-CLUB/2582), where local radio DJs spin dance and alternative tunes nightly (cover varies, no cover before 10pm; open daily 8pm-2am).

SIGHTS AND ACTIVITIES. Billed as California's "Gold Coast," the beaches near Ventura are clean and offer fantastic surfing. **Emma Wood State Beach,** on Main St. (State Beaches Exit off U.S. 101), and **Oxnard State Beach Park,** about five miles south of Ventura, are quiet and peaceful. **San Buenaventura State Park,** at the end of San Pedro St., entertains families and others with its volleyball courts and nearby restaurants. **Surfer's Point,** at the end of Figueroa St., has the best waves around, but novices should start at **McGrath State Beach,** about three miles south of Ventura down Harbor Blvd. You can pick up insider surfing tips and Patagonia outlet gear at **Real Cheap Sports,** 36 W. Santa Clara St. (648-3803; open M-Sa 10am-6pm, Su 11am-5pm). The shoreside hotspots are **Seaward Village, Santa Clara River Mouth, Oxnard Shores,** and the pier at the end of **California Street.**

Off-the-beach action is hidden away at **Skate Street,** 1990B Knoll Dr. (650-1213), a fantasy of pipes and ramps for beginning and advanced skateboarders. Kids and adults run wild on this 12,000 sq. ft. street course. (Call for times and special weekly sessions, such as BMX-only session. 3hr. session $11. Sessions start daily at 12:30pm; F-Sa under-13 sessions start at 9am. Participants under 18 must have parental waiver signed.)

Mission San Buenaventura, 211 E. Main St. (643-4318), still functions as a parish church, and houses a tiny museum of treasures from Father Junípero Serra's order (open M-Sa 10am-5pm, Su 10am-4pm; donation requested). For more info on Serra, see **A Man with a Mission,** p. 8. The tiny **Albinger Archaeology Museum,** 4200 Olivas Dr. (644-4346), chronicles the story of the Native Americans, Spanish invaders, and Chinese immigrants who created the community of Ventura (open June-Aug. W-Su 10am-4pm; Sept.-May W-F 10am-2pm, Sa-Su 10am-4pm; donation requested). Across the street is the **Museum of History and Art** (653-0323), which has a rotating exhibit of handcrafted miniature figures from history, such as "Traitors, Tyrants and Sycophants," with effigies of Cromwell, Rasputin, and the like (open Tu-Su 10am-5pm; admission $3, under 17 free).

NEAR VENTURA: CHANNEL ISLANDS NATIONAL PARK

Ventura serves as the point of departure for the desolate Channel Islands, home to many brown pelicans, the ruins of a Paleolithic village, and an ecosystem of endemic species almost as unique as the Galápagos Islands'. The park consists of five islands: **Anacapa** (the most visitor-friendly, with snorkeling and tide pools), **Santa Cruz** (known for its strangely dwarfed species), **Santa Rosa** (basically a huge fossil bed and full-time archaeological dig), **San Miguel** (with its eerie fossilized caliche forest and thousands of seals), and tiny **Santa Barbara** (with elephant seals and rigorous hiking). Unfortunately, unless you're a marine biology student or happen to own your own boat, you'll have to call **Island Packers,** 1867 Spinnaker Dr. (reservations 642-1393, 24hr. info 642-7688), in Ventura Harbor. Their virtual monopoly on island transport means rates range from a slightly obnoxious $21 to an outrageous $235, depending on which island is your destination and what diversions (camping, hiking, kayaking, or the Chumash painted sea cave on Santa Cruz) you have in mind. Cruises are whole or half-day, usually leaving around 7:30am. However, if it is only a tour of the islands you want (no shore leave), the rates are $37 for adults and $27 for children. Island Packers also runs whale-watching tours (Dec.-Mar. and June-Sept.). The camping is free on all islands, but you'll need a permit from park headquarters, your own water, and a high tolerance for foghorns and seagulls. The **Channel Islands National Park Visitors Center,** 1901 Spinnaker Dr. (658-5730), has all the info you'll need, and an observation tower with views of the islands (open May-Sept. M-F 8am-5pm, Sa-Su 8am-5:30pm; Oct.-Apr. M-F 8am-4pm, Sa-Su 8am-4:30pm).

THE SIERRA NEVADA

The Sierra Nevada is the highest, steepest, and most physically stunning mountain range in the contiguous United States. Thrust skyward 400 million years ago by gigantic plate collisions, and shaped by erosion, glaciers, and volcanoes, this enormous hunk of granite stretches 450 miles north from the Mojave Desert to Lake Almanor near Lassen Volcanic National Park. The glistening clarity of Lake Tahoe, the heart-stopping sheerness of Yosemite's rock walls, the craggy alpine scenery of Kings Canyon and Sequoia National Parks, and the abrupt drop of the Eastern Sierra into Owens Valley are sights to see.

Temperatures in the Sierra Nevada are as diverse as the terrain. Even in the summer, overnight lows can dip into the 20s (check local weather reports). Normally, only U.S. 50 and I-80 are kept open during the snow season. Exact dates vary from year to year, so check with a ranger station for local road conditions, especially from October through June. Come summer, protection from the high elevations' exposure to ultraviolet rays is necessary; always bring sunscreen and a hat. For additional outdoors advice, see **Essentials: Camping and the Outdoors,** p. 47.

HIGHLIGHTS OF THE SIERRA NEVADA

- **Lake Tahoe** is home to some of the state's best **beaches** (p. 249), **biking** (p. 250), **hiking** (p. 251), **rock climbing** (p. 252), **water sports** (p. 249), and world-class **skiing** (p. 253).
- Join the herd of tourists at **Yosemite National Park,** where you can hike **Half Dome** (p. 271), watch climbers squeezing up **El Capitan** (p. 270), or retreat to the beautiful **backcountry** (p. 273) to recreate in peace.
- **Sequoia** and **King's Canyon National Parks** feature incredible views from **Moro Rock** (p. 283), great backcountry hiking and camping in **Crescent Meadow** (p. 284), and the **deepest canyon in the United States** (p. 285).
- In the **Owens Valley,** say howdy to the **oldest living things on Earth** (p. 293), then slide down the **largest land-locked sand dunes in the world** (p. 293).
- Inyo National Forest offers for your perusal the **tallest mountain in the contiguous U.S.** (p. 297), as well as the remnants of one of the country's most romantic periods (p. 297) and one of its most shameful (p. 298).

LAKE TAHOE AND VICINITY

The area surrounding Lake Tahoe is a rare find in the High Sierra: a pristine mountain setting with nearby outposts of urbanity, offering the best of both worlds. Lake Tahoe and Donner Lake glitter in both sun and snow. Innumerable outdoor recreation opportunities reel in visitors by the score, and after the sun goes down they all head to beachside barbecues, the dimly lit yuppie bars of Tahoe City, or the glitzy gambling of South Lake Tahoe and Reno, just across the Nevada border.

LAKE TAHOE

In February of 1844, fearless explorer John C. Fremont led his expedition over the Sierra—a fool's errand, as anyone in the Donner Party could have told you between bites of human flesh. Luckily for him, the sight of the beautiful alpine lake was enough to boost the morale of his 36 starved and weary companions. The lake passed through several identities, from Bigler to Lake of Beer, before the state of California officially named it Tahoe in 1945. 8586

As soon as settlers rolled into California in the late 18th century, Lake Tahoe (pop. 33,482) became a playground for the wealthy. One hundred years ago, staid shrines to old money peppered the shores. After roads were cut into the forested mountain terrain, new money arrived in the form of casinos, summer homes, and

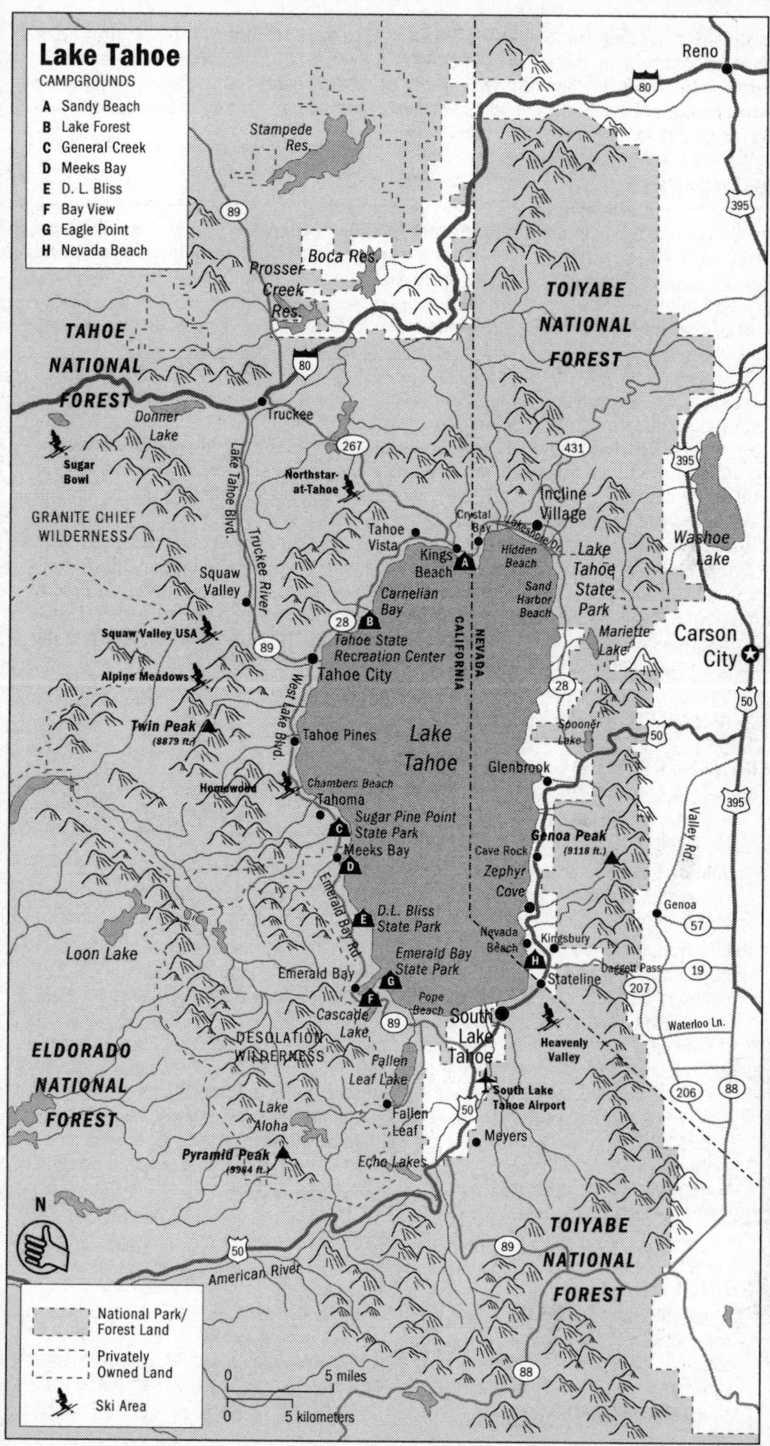

SIERRA NEVADA

motels. Now, everyone can enjoy Tahoe's pure blue waters, tall pines, and high-rises silhouetted by the deep auburn glow of the setting sun—an outdoor adventurist's dream in any season, with miles of biking, hiking, and skiing trails, long stretches of golden beaches, lakes stocked with fish, and many hair-raising whitewater activities.

ORIENTATION

In the northern Sierra on the California-Nevada border, Lake Tahoe is a 3½-hour drive from San Francisco. The two main trans-Sierra highways, **Interstate 80** and **U.S. 50 (Lake Tahoe Boulevard),** run east-west through Tahoe, skimming the northern and southern shores of the lake, respectively. Lake Tahoe is 118 miles northeast of Sacramento and 35 miles southwest of Reno on I-80. From the Carson City and Owens Valley area, **U.S. 395** runs north along Tahoe's eastern shores.

The lake is roughly divided into two main regions, known as North Shore and South Shore. The North Shore includes King's Beach, Tahoe City, and Incline Village, while the South Shore bends to the will of Emerald Bay and South Lake Tahoe City. **Routes 28** and **89** form a 75-mile ring of asphalt around the lake; the complete loop takes nearly three hours. Rte. 89 is also known as **West Lake Boulevard** and **Emerald Bay Road,** while Rte. 28 masquerades as **North Lake Boulevard** and **Lakeshore Drive** in Tahoe City and on the western shore.

Road conditions in Tahoe can be treacherous from September through May, when tire chains may be required and a four-wheel-drive vehicle is highly recommended. As Tahoe is a popular weekend destination, traffic is fierce on Friday afternoons and Sunday evenings. During winter, cars on the way to or from Tahoe City ski resorts pack the roads around 9am and 5pm. If there is road work near the small town of Tahoe City, forget it.

PRACTICAL INFORMATION

TRANSPORTATION

Buses: Greyhound (702-588-4645 or 800-231-2222), in Harrah's Casino on U.S. 50 in Stateline, NV. To **San Francisco** (4 per day, $25) and **Sacramento** (3 per day, $20). No lockers. Station open daily 8am-12:30pm and 2:30-6:30pm.

Trains: Amtrak (800-USA-RAIL/872-7245) runs a bus from its San Joaquin and Capitol train routes to Pre-Madonna Casino, off I-5 at Pre-Madonna Exit, and Whiskey Pete's Casino in Stateline, NV. These trips are long and costly. To **San Francisco** (11hr., $80).

Public Transit: Tahoe Casino Express (800-446-6128) provides shuttle service between the Reno airport and South Shore Tahoe casinos (daily 6:15am-12:30am). Fare $17, round-trip $30, up to 2 children under 12 free. **Tahoe Area Regional Transport** (TART; 581-6365) connects the western and northern shores from Incline Village to Tahoe City to Tahoma (Meeks Bay in summer). Stops daily every hr. 6:30am-6pm. Buses also run out to Truckee and Squaw Valley 5 times per day. Exact fare necessary ($1.25, day pass $3). **South Tahoe Area Ground Express** (STAGE; 542-6077) operates buses around South Tahoe and hourly to the beach. Connects Stateline and Emerald Bay Rd. (Fare $1.25, day pass $2, 10-ride pass $10.) Most casinos operate free shuttle service along Rte. 50 to California ski resorts and motels. A summer bus program connects STAGE and TART at Meeks Bay for the entire lake area. Operates 6am-midnight.

Car Rental: Enterprise (775-586-1077), in the Horizon lobby in Stateline, NV. Must be 21 with credit card. From $36 per day, $189 per week with unlimited mileage.

TOURIST AND FINANCIAL SERVICES

U.S. Forest Service and Lake Tahoe Visitors Center, 870 Emerald Bay Rd. (573-2674), 3mi. north of S. Lake Tahoe on Rte. 89. Supervises campgrounds, recreation trails, and publishes *Lake of the Sky Journal* (loaded with recreational coupons). Info on summer and winter recreation. Free, mandatory wilderness permits for backcountry hiking available. Open M-F 8am-5:30pm.

Visitor Information: 573-2674 (available daily Memorial Day-Oct. 1.) **South Lake Tahoe Chamber of Commerce,** 3066 Lake Tahoe Blvd. (541-5255; www.tahoeinfo.com). Open M-Sa 8:30am-5pm. **Lake Tahoe/Douglas Chamber of Commerce,** 195 U.S. 50, Stateline, NV (702-588-4591; www.tahoechamber.org). Open M-F 9am-6pm, Sa-Su 9am-5pm. **Tahoe North Visitor and Convention Bureau and Visitor Information,** 245 N. Lake Blvd. (583-3494). Helpful staff makes lodging reservations. Open M-F 9am-5pm, Sa-Su 9am-4pm. A **visitors center** near Taylor Creek on Emerald Bay Rd. is staffed mid-June to Oct. daily 8am-5:30pm; Nov. to mid.-June Sa-Su 8am-5:30pm.

Wilderness Permits for Desolation Wilderness: National Forest Info Center (644-6048) on U.S. 50, in Camino, CA. Camping fee $5 per person per night, $10 per person for 2 or more nights, $20 for 1-year pass. Under 12 free. Because of trail conservation quotas, reservations ($5) are available for overnight permits June 15-Labor Day (Sept. 4 in 2000). Open M-Sa 7am-6pm, Su 8am-5pm.

LOCAL SERVICES

Library and Internet Access: South Lake Tahoe Library, 1000 Rufus Allen Blvd. (573-3185). Open Tu-W 10am-8pm, Th-Sa 10am-5pm.

Laundromat: La Washmatique, 950 N. Lake Blvd., Tahoe City. Open daily 7am-10pm. **Tahoe Keys Laundromat,** 2301 Lake Tahoe Blvd., S. Lake Tahoe. Open daily 7am-11pm.

EMERGENCY AND COMMUNICATIONS

Road Conditions: California 800-427-7623; **Nevada** 702-793-1313.

Crisis Hotlines: General 800-992-5757. **Compulsive Gambling Center Hotline** 800-LOST-BET/567-8238. **Gamblers Anonymous** South Shore, 573-2423. **Lake Tahoe**

Medical Services: Barton Memorial Hospital (530-541-3420), at 4th St. and South Ave., in S. Lake Tahoe. **Stateline Medical Center,** 176 U.S. 50, Stateline, NV (702-588-3561), at Kahle St. Open daily 8am-8pm. **Tahoe Forest Hospital** (530-587-6011), at Donner Pass Rd. and Pine Ave., Truckee.

Emergency: 911. **Police:** 530-542-6100.

Post Office: Tahoe City, 950 N. Lake Blvd. #12 (800-275-8777), in the Lighthouse Shopping Center. Open M-F 8:30am-5pm. **ZIP Code:** 96145. **South Lake Tahoe,** 1046 Tahoe Blvd. (544-2208). Open M-F 8:30am-5pm, Sa noon-2pm. **ZIP Code:** 96151.

AREA CODE	The area code on the California side of Lake Tahoe is 530. The area code on the Nevada side of Lake Tahoe is 702.

ACCOMMODATIONS

The strip off **U.S. 50** on the California side of the border supports the bulk of Tahoe's motels. Particularly glitzy and cheap in South Lake Tahoe, motels also line the quieter area along **Park Avenue** and **Pioneer Trail.** The North Shore offers more woodsy accommodations along **Route 28,** but rates are especially high in Tahoe City. Lodgings are booked solid and well in advance for weekends and holidays, when rates skyrocket. Fall and spring are the most economical times of the year to visit Tahoe because of the off-season bargains. Look for discount coupons in newspapers. The cheapest deals are clustered near Stateline on U.S. 50. Nearby campgrounds are a good option in warmer months.

NORTH SHORE

In general, the hordes of hotels, motels, and cabins in the Kings Beach and Incline Village areas will be a better value that those nearer Tahoe City.

Tamarack Lodge, 2311 N. Lake Tahoe Blvd. (583-3350 or 888-824-6323), 3mi. north of Tahoe City, across from Star Harbor community. Clean, quiet motel in the woods. Newly refurbished exterior, outdoor BBQ and fireplace, phones, cable TV, and friendly management. Continental breakfast included. Rooms with queen beds $36-46.

Cedar Glen Lodge, 6589 N. Lake Blvd., Tahoe Vista (546-4281 or 800-341-8000). Family-operated motel with a private beach, pool, and indoor hot tub and sauna. Grounds include BBQ pits, playground, hammock, and spectacular rabbit hutch. Morning newspaper and continental breakfast included. Check-in 2pm. Check-out 11am. Singles from $55. Cottages with kitchens also available.

Tahoe City Inn, 790 N. Lake Blvd., Tahoe City (581-3333 or 800-800-8246), next to Safeway. Huge, clean, comfy rooms come with 2 queen beds, cable TV, coffeemakers, slick decor, and frighteningly big mirrors. Check-in 3pm. Check-out 11am. Doubles mid-June to late Sept. and late Nov.-late Apr. Su-Th $60, F-Sa $75; late Apr. to mid-June and late Sept.-late Nov. Su-Th $42, F-Sa $60. Extra bed $10. Wheelchair access.

Hostel at Squaw Valley, 1900 Squaw Valley Rd. (581-3246), is a 100-bed hostel at the base of Squaw Valley. Roll out of bed and stroll to the ski lifts. Social common area. Dorms $24, weekends and holidays $27. Open mid-Nov. to mid-Apr.

SOUTH SHORE

Doug's Mellow Mountain Retreat, 3787 Forest St., S. Lake Tahoe (544-8065). 1mi. west of the state line, turn left onto Wildwood Rd., and after 3 blocks take a left on Forest. St. Doug's hostel is the 6th house on the left. Modern kitchen, BBQ, fireplace. Pool table and benches outside. Internet access $3 for 30min., $5 per hr., $10 for 3hr. Bedding and laundry included. Dorms $15 per person, private rooms available; discounts for stays of a week or longer.

Budget Inn, 3496 Lake Tahoe Blvd., S. Lake Tahoe (544-2834, reservations 888-615-1424). Standard rooms with free HBO. Pool and free continental breakfast. Smoking rooms available. Singles Su-Th $22, F-Sa $45; doubles Su-Th $28, F-Sa $55.

Royal Inn, 3520 Lake Tahoe Blvd., S. Lake Tahoe (544-1177, 544-1268, or 800-556-2500). Rooms are large and clean with firm beds. Coffee and doughnuts in the morning. Small heated pool and cable TV. Singles $22, weekends $45; doubles $28, $55.

CAMPGROUNDS

The **U.S. Forest Service** at the visitors center provides up-to-date information on camping (see **Visitor Information,** p. 244), and rangers supply detailed leaflets on surrounding trails and wilderness areas. **Route 89** is scattered with state campgrounds from Tahoe City to South Lake Tahoe. Campgrounds are often booked for the entire summer, so reserve well in advance; call **National Recreation Reservation System** (NRRS; 800-280-2267) for U.S. Forest Service campgrounds, **California Campground Reservation System** (CCRS; 800-444-7275; outside California 619-452-1950), or **National Park Reservation System** (800-365-2267). The NRRS and CCRS charge a non-refundable reservation fee and ask for a credit card number. Backcountry camping is allowed in designated wilderness areas with a permit from the Forest Service (see **Visitor Information,** p. 244). The only campground open year-round is General Creek in Sugar Pines State Park; all others are generally open from mid-June to Labor Day (Sept. 4 in 2000).

NORTH SHORE

General Creek at Sugar Pine Point State Park (525-7982), on the west shore south of Tahoma, and across Rte. 89, just a few miles north of Meeks Bay. Popular grounds include tennis courts, cross-country ski trails, bike trails, nature center, the historic Ehrman mansion, and lakeside dock. BBQ pits and flush toilets. 175 sites $16, seniors $14; day use $5, seniors $4. Dogs $1. Hot showers 50¢. Open year-round.

Tahoe State Recreation Area (583-3074), at the north edge of Tahoe City on Rte. 28. One acre of land along the lake and road, with a long pier. 38 sites. Water, flush toilets, showers. Single sites $15-16, seniors $14.

Sandy Beach (546-7682), off Rte. 28 in Kings Beach, on the water. 44 sites are very visible, rocky soil beneath pine trees and adjacent to a sandy beach. Hookups, water, flush toilets, showers. Sites $15-20. Pets $1.50.

Lake Forest (583-3796 ext. 29), on Rte. 28 3mi. north of Tahoe City. 18 shady sites. The area and access road bustle with boats and cars visiting the nearby Coast Guard station and boat ramp. Lake swimming, water, flush toilets. First-come, first-camped stes $12.

SOUTH SHORE

Eagle Point at Emerald Bay State Park (525-7277), on Rte. 89 10mi. west of S. Lake Tahoe. Little shade, many rocks, fairly intimate. 14-night max. stay. 5min. hot showers 50¢. Sites $16, seniors $15. Open June-Labor Day (Sept. 4 in 2000).

Nevada Beach (544-5944, info 702-588-5562, reservations 800-365-2267), on U.S. 50 1mi. north of Stateline, NV. Popular with families. The 54 sites are 300ft. from the shore and afford views of the lake and snow-capped mountains. Drinking water and flush toilets. No showers. Sites $16-18. Call for reservations.

WEST SHORE

Bayview (544-5994), has 10 first-come, first-camped sites right on Emerald Bay, but no water or toilets. 7-night max stay. Sites $5.

D.L. Bliss State Park (525-7277), on Rte. 89 a few miles north of Emerald Bay. Camp by the beach near emerald waters and granite boulders, or in secluded forest sites. Popular day-use beach, but entrance restricted by the number of parking spaces. 168 sites. 14-night max. stay. Sites $16, beach-side $20. Day parking $5. Pets $1. Open June-Labor Day (Sept. 4 in 2000). The 9mi. **Rubicon Trail** (see **Hiking,** p. 251), leads to Emerald Bay, Vikingsholm, and Eagle Falls.

Meeks Bay (583-3642, reservations 800-365-2267), 10mi. south of Tahoe City. 40 tent and RV sites in flat pine grove by the water and the road. Smashing location: near Tahoe City, Emerald Bay, S. Lake Tahoe, and a walk to Meeks Bay beach. Water, flush toilets, showers. Sites $15.

The Meeks Bay Resort (800-769-2746, 525-6946) is a campground with hookups, RV dump, boat ramp, and large hip beach. Water, flush toilets, showers. Sites $18-26.

WILDERNESS AREAS AROUND THE LAKE

The 63,475 acres of **Desolation Wilderness** on the western side of the lake constitute the most heavily used and abused wilderness area per acre in the U.S. No wonder: the glacial lakes and valleys, granite peaks, and sub-alpine forests are awesome. To control the use of this area, Congress has introduced new permit costs as part of the "Recreation Fee Demonstration Program" (see **Wilderness Permits,** p. 245, for rules, regulations and fee information). The **Granite Chief Wilderness** is a less-traversed area. Next to the Alpine Meadows and Squaw Valley ski resorts, the wilderness overlooks the northwestern section of the Lake Tahoe Basin. Hike for free without a wilderness permit. Required free campfire permits are issued by the U.S. Forest Service (see **Visitor Information,** p. 245). The **Mount Rose Wilderness** is one of the nation's newest wilderness areas, located in the northeast area of the Lake Tahoe Basin (accessible via Rte. 431).

FOOD

In the south, the casinos offer perpetually low-priced buffets, but there are restaurants along the lakeshore with reasonable prices, similarly large portions, and much better food. Groceries are cheaper on the California side. Try a **Safeway,** in South Lake Tahoe, on the corner of Lake Tahoe Blvd. and Johnson St., or in Tahoe City at 850 N. Lake Blvd. (both open 24hr.). Alternatively, you could go *au naturel* at **Grass Roots Natural Foods,** 2040 Dunlap Rd. (541-7788), one block east of the Rte. 89 and U.S. 50 junction (open M-Sa 9am-8pm, Su 10am-6pm).

SOUTH SHORE

Killer Chicken, 2660 Lake Tahoe Blvd., S. Lake Tahoe (542-9977). BBQ chicken sandwiches ($6-7) that aren't as deadly as the name implies. Whole chickens done Jamaican Jerk, Cuban Roast, Caribbean, or mild herb style ($13 with cornbread and 4 side orders). Veggie and lowfat items. Open daily 11:30am-9pm.

Margarita's Mexican Cafe, 2495 Lake Tahoe Blvd., S. Lake Tahoe (544-6907). Arm-flailing-ly good Mexican cuisine dished up by a friendly waitstaff in a small sitdown restaurant. Tostada salad ($4), combination plates ($7), enchiladas, chimichangas, and cilantro salsa. Open W-M 11:30am-9pm. No credit cards.

Red Hut Waffles, 2749 Lake Tahoe Blvd. (541-9024). Good homestyle cooking. Waffle piled with fruit and whipped cream ($5.50); 4-egg monster omelettes ($5.25-6.25); fresh fruit bowl ($2.50); bottomless coffee ($1). Open daily 6am-2pm. No credit cards.

NORTH SHORE

Lakehouse: Pizza-Spirits-Fun, 120 Grove St., Tahoe City (583-2225). On the water with a sunny lakefront deck. Every seat's got a great view of the lake. Standard breakfast specials ($3-7), California salad ($6.25), sandwiches, and reasonably priced pizzas. Bud Light $2.50. Open M-Th 8am-10pm, F-Su 7:30am-11pm (or midnight).

Syd's Bagelry and Natural Foods, 550 North Lake Tahoe Blvd., Tahoe City (583-2666). A bagel shop with a million-dollar view. "Hummus Among Us" (fat bagel sandwich with hummus, cucumber, mushrooms, tomato, carrots, onion, and sprouts) $4.50; garden burgers $4.25. They pride themselves on their espresso drinks. Open daily 6am-8pm.

The Bridgetender, 30 W. Lake Blvd., Tahoe City (583-3342), at Rte. 28 and 89 at Fanny Bridge. They are famous for their half-pound burgers ($4-6)–try the cajun bacon cheeseburger ($6). Salads ($5-7), sandwiches, ribs, and tacos. 20 beers on tap, pool table, and festive nighttime crowd. Credit cards accepted. Open M-F 11am-11pm, Sa-Su 11am-midnight; bar open daily until 1am.

Steamers, 8290 N. Lake Blvd., King's Beach (546-2218). The photo-covered walls tell the story of the restaurant's namesake, the old steamer *Tahoe*, whose captain sunk it in the lake so that it would not serve in WWII. Munch delicious pizzas ($12-20) in a casual setting. Sandwiches $6-9; Louisiana hot sausage $5.50. Outdoor patio bar with lakeside view. Open daily 11am-11pm.

NIGHTLIFE

There are varying degrees of nightlife in Lake Tahoe. In Tahoe City, most of the nightlife is centred around the pub scene at places like the Bridgetender (see above). On the South Shore, however it's a little more glitzy—that's where you find the late-night gambling and dancing. Word to the wise on trying to get into clubs on the Nevada side: **Don't bring a fake I.D.** The good folks of Nevada take their gambling seriously, and they card harshly. To get in, you'll need a state I.D. or license; international residents need passports.

Nero's 2000, 55 Rte. 50 (586-2000), inside Caesar's Casino. Probably the most popular dance place in S. Lake Tahoe, they instruct you to "dance the night away Roman style." You figure out what that means. Also Tahoe's only "all-night" dance club. M any drink $1. Cover Su-Th $4-5; F-Sa $10-25, depending on when you go and how busy it is. Open Su-Th 9pm-3:30 or 4am, F-Sa 9pm-5:30 or 6am.

Lily's Beach Club (588-6211), on U.S. 50 inside Horizon Casino. Vaguely "island" decorations try in vain to make you think you're at the beach. The dance floor is good though, and the bar serves up cheap drinks some nights. W reggae night Red Stripe Beer $2.50; Th $1 drafts. Ladies get in free Th-Sa 9-11pm, and Su all night. Cover Tu-Th and Su $3, F-Sa $5. Open Tu-Su 9pm-whenever.

Turtles, 4130 Lake Tahoe Blvd. (543-2135), inside Embassy Suites. A light wood interior and airy patio are relaxing, and it has a small dance floor. Doubles as a sports bar during the day. DJ starts mixing at 9pm. Cover F-Sa $5; higher on holidays. Happy Hour Su-F 6-9pm. Open M-F 11am-2am, Sa-Su 9am-2am. Kitchen open until 11pm.

The Brewery, 3542 Lake Tahoe Blvd. (544-2739). If it's late and you want a cool place to chill and get some excellent pizza, try The Brewery. Check out their Bad Ass Ale, brewed in-house. In summer, open Th-Tu 10am-midnight, W 11am-midnight.

SUMMER ACTIVITIES

BEACHES

Lake Tahoe supports many beaches perfect for a day of sunning and people-watching. Parking generally costs $3-5. Bargain hunters will leave cars in turnouts on the main road and walk to the beaches.

NORTH SHORE. **Sand Harbor Beach,** south of Incline Village, has gorgeous granite boulders and clear waters that attract swimmers, sunners, and scuba divers in droves. The parking lot ($6) is usually full by 11:30am. One mile away at Memorial Point, lakeside paved parking is free. **Hidden Beach,** also south of Incline Village, and Kings Beach, just across the California border on Rte. 28, comes complete with the latest rage (waveboards) and an alternative-rock feel. **Kings Beach** has volleyball nets, a basketball court, and a playground for kids. Jet-skis, sailboards, and kayaks can be rented at both beaches. Parasailing, wakeboarding, and waterskiing are also available.

SOUTH SHORE. **Pope Beach,** at the southernmost point of the lake off Rte. 89, is a wide, pine-shaded expanse of shoreline, which becomes less trafficked on its east side. **Nevada Beach,** eight miles north of South Lake Tahoe, is close to the casinos off U.S. 50, offering a quiet place to reflect on gambling losses while gazing upon the mountains. **Zephyr Cove Beach,** about 15 miles north of South Lake Tahoe, is a favorite spot for the younger college crowd. Motorboats, beach volleyball, beer, bikinis, and boogie boards make it the closest thing to Southern California in Lake Tahoe.

WEST SHORE. **Meeks Bay,** 10 miles south of Tahoe City, is family-oriented and social: picnic tables, volleyball, motorboat and kayak rental, and a petite store. In the summer the Tahoe City and South Tahoe Buses connect here. Five miles south of Meeks Bay, the **D.L. Bliss State Park** has a large beach on a small bay (Rubicon). The trailhead of the Rubicon Trail leads to the peaceful Vikingsholm mansion (see p. 252). Parking here ($3) is very limited, so check at the visitors center in the entrance or investigate parking on the road and walking in. **Chambers Beach,** between Homewood and Tahoma, also draws an energetic crowd of families and young hipsters who happily occupy the public volleyball nets, but eagerly eye the private pool and bar.

OTHER WATER ACTIVITIES

Wakeboarding, the aquatic sport of the future, is very popular on Lake Tahoe. It's like water-skiing with a snowboard. Experts at **TM Wakeriding,** 8608 N. Lake Blvd. (906-9253 or 583-9253), can go anywhere on the lake to give you a personalized adventure (from sightseeing to boarding lessons).

River rafting can be a refreshing way to appreciate the Tahoe scenery, but depending on the water levels of the American and Truckee Rivers, rafting can range from a thrilling whitewater challenge to a boring bake in the sun. If water levels are high, check out raft rental places along the Truckee River and at Tahoe City. For more info, call **Truckee River Rafting** (583-7238 or 888-584-7238; open daily 8:30am-3:30pm), in Tahoe City, across from Lucky's at Fanny Bridge, or **Tahoe Whitewater Tours** (581-2441; 4hr. tour $60; call for reservations). When droughts make conventional rafting scarce, many would-be rafters turn to inner tubes. Make sure inner tubes are permitted in the waters you select, use the buddy system, and know what lies ahead before you shove off. A tempting option is the calm-water "booze cruise." **Tahoe Sailing Charter** (583-6200), in the Tahoe City Marina, provides the opportunity to "Cruise the north shore" (2hr., $35 per person including refreshments; sailing lessons $15 extra with cruise, or 2hr. private lessons $75).

Equipment rental in the north shore is plentiful. **Tahoe Paddle and Oar** (581-3029), in Kings Beach, rents kayaks ($10 per hr., doubles $20 per hr.), as does **Enviro-Rents Eco-Rents,** 6873 N. Lake Blvd., Tahoe Vista (546-2780 or 800-245-3498; $10 per hr., doubles $20; bikes $9 per hr., $35 for a half-day; open daily 10am-6pm).

If paddling in the north, ask around about (privately owned) **natural hot springs** on the way to the spectacular Crystal Bay. Local lore maintains that the bay's frigid temperatures (average 39°F) prevent the decomposition that would ordinarily make corpses float to the surface. Spoooky.

North Tahoe Marina, 7360 N. Lake Blvd., Tahoe Vista (546-4889), on Rte. 28, and **Lighthouse Watersports Center,** 950 N. Lake Blvd., Tahoe City (583-6000), have information on motorboat and other high-tech rentals.

For South Shore equipment rental, try **Action Watersports,** 7901 Emerald Bay Rd. (525-5588), at Meeks Bay, which rents kayaks ($15 per hr., doubles $25 per hr.), canoes, and motorboats.

Fishing information and regulations can be found at visitors centers, and licenses are available at local sporting good stores. Because of its depth (1600ft. in places) and strange formation, Tahoe is a notoriously difficult lake to fish; bring a good book and be prepared to walk away empty-handed.

BIKING

Lake Tahoe is a biking paradise. The excellent paved trails, logging roads, and dirt paths have not gone unnoticed; be prepared for company if you pedal around the area. The U.S. Forest Service and bike rental stores can provide advice, publications like *Bike West* magazine, maps, and info about trails. No cycling is allowed in the Desolation Wilderness, or on the Pacific Crest or Tahoe Rim Trails. **Olympic Bike Shop,** 60 N. Lake Tahoe Blvd., Tahoe City (581-2500), has an expert staff equipped with multitudes of maps and trail options (mountain bikes $5 per hr., $15 for 4hr., $21 per day). **Anderson's Bicycle Rental,** 645 Emerald Bay Rd. (541-0500), one mile north of the intersection of U.S. 50 and Rte. 89, is convenient to the well-maintained U.S. Forest Service bike trails along the western shore and through the forest. (Mountain bikes $20 for 4hr., $1 each additional hr.; helmets and maps available; deposit of I.D. required; open daily 8am-6pm.) **Tahoe Cyclery in The Village Shop,** 3552 Lake Tahoe Blvd., South Lake Tahoe (541-2726), is a grungy but friendly shop offering a wide range of rentals. (Mountain bikes $6 per hr., $18 for 4hr., $24 per day. Snowboards $20 per day, skis $10 per day, snowshoes $10 per day. Open in summer daily 9am-7pm; in winter M-F 8am-7pm, Sa-Su 8am-9pm).

NORTH SHORE. Known more for its ski trails, the north shore is equipped with both flat lakeside jaunts and steeper woodsy rides. The **Tahoe Rim Trail,** from Kings Beach to Tahoe City, offers intermediate-level hilly biking. The trail can be accessed from Tahoe City or Brockway Summit (see below for more info). **Squaw Valley,** northwest of the lake on Rte. 89, opens its slope to hikers and mountain bikers during the summer. The cable car transports bikers and their wheels 2000 vertical feet (1 ride $19, full-day pass $26). You find your own way down—the slopes are steep, but fairly easy.

SOUTH SHORE. The South Shore boasts a variety of scenic trails for all abilities. **Fallen Leaf Lake,** just west of South Lake Tahoe, is a dazzling destination by bike or by car, but watch out for the swerving tourists in boat- and trailer-towing vehicles, especially on the narrow mountain roads. The steep mountain peaks that surround the lake are breathtaking when viewed from beside Fallen Leaf's icy blue waters. Bikers looking for a challenge can try the seven-mile ring around the lake, but beware—it's more difficult than it looks. **U.S. 50, Route 89,** and **Route 28** are all bicycle-friendly, but the drivers aren't, especially in heavy traffic areas like South Lake Tahoe. Angora Ridge (4mi.), accessible from Rte. 89, meanders past Fallen Leaf Lake to the Angora Lakes for a moderate challenge. For serious mountain bikers, **Mr. Toad's Wild Ride** (3mi.), reaches from U.S. 50 or Rte. 89, and is a very difficult, winding trail that climbs to 9000 feet. The **Flume Trail** has magnificent views of the lake 1500 feet below. This advanced 23-mile loop begins at Spooner Lake campground with the Marlette Lake Trail, a five-mile sandy road.

WEST SHORE. Several paved paths offer undemanding touring adventures around the lake. The **Pope-Baldwin Bike Path** (3½mi.) runs parallel to Rte. 89, while the **South Lake Tahoe Bike Path** runs from El Dorado Beach over the Upper Truckee River. The lake views and smooth, easy ride make these trails quite popular. Parking is available at the Truckee River trailhead (Rte. 89, south of Tahoe City), Kaspian campground (Skyland), and General Creek campground at Sugar Pine Point State Park (south of Homewood). The **West Shore Bike Path,** a paved 10-mile stretch from Tahoe City to Sugar Pine Point, is a flat, scenic way to tour the lake.

HIKING

Hiking is one of the best ways to explore the beautiful Tahoe Basin. The visitors center and ranger stations provide detailed info and maps for all types of hikes. Backcountry users must obtain a wilderness permit from the U.S. Forest Service (see **Visitor Information,** p. 244) for any hike into the Desolation Wilderness, which is ironically the most visited natural wilderness area in the U.S. Only 700 hikers are allowed in this area on any given day. Due to erratic weather conditions in the Sierra, hikers should always bring a jacket and drinking water. Buy a topographical map before you ask where the snow has (or has not) melted—it's not usually gone until July and finding a trail under a foot of hard snow is next to impossible. **Alpenglow Sport Shop,** 415 N. Lake Blvd., Tahoe City (583-6917), sells great trail maps ($4-9), but any of the numerous outdoorsy stores will have adequate maps.

The partially completed **Tahoe Rim Trail** encircles the lake, following the ridge tops of the Lake Tahoe Basin. Hiking is moderate to difficult, with an average grade of 10%. On the western shore, it is part of the Pacific Crest Trail (see **From Crest to Crest: the Trail of the West,** p. 266). Current trailheads are at Spooner Summit on U.S. 50, off Rte. 89 on Fairway Dr. in Tahoe City, Brockway on Rte. 267, and Mt. Rose Trailhead on Rte. 431. (Mt. Rose is a 1¼mi. wheelchair-accessible loop.) Hiking enthusiasts can donate their time to help build the trail (702-588-0686).

NORTH SHORE. There is plenty of hiking in the North but little of it rivals Emerald Bay. The **Granite Chief Wilderness,** behind Squaw Valley, is a great option; its rugged hiking trails and mountain streams wind through secluded forests and fields of wildflowers. The 4½-mile **Meeks Bay Trail** runs from Meeks Bay to Lake Genevieve or eight miles to Rubicon Lake; the walk is long, but moderate in incline. The farther on this trail you walk, the farther you get into the Desolation Wilderness. Hikers planning to trek to Genevieve should be prepared to pay a day use fee. The **Marlette Lake Trail** begins at Spooner State Park, Nevada, at the junction of U.S. 50 and Rte. 28, and leads five miles through moderately difficult terrain of the North Canyon leads from Spooner Lake to Spooner summit. At 10,778 feet, **Mt. Rose,** in the Toiyabe National Forest (info 702-882-2766; open daily 8am-4:30pm), is one of the tallest mountains in the Tahoe region as well as one of the best climbs. It starts out as an easy six-mile dirt road hike, but becomes a rocky scramble after mile three. Take Rte. 431 from Incline Village to the trailhead, which is a deceptive mile south of the summit.

SOUTH SHORE. The southern region of the basin offers many moderate to strenuous hiking trails. Many visitors find the picturesque **Emerald Bay** to be an essential stop and photo opportunity. This crystal-clear pocket of the lake embraces Tahoe's only island and most photographed sight—tiny, rocky Fannette. The alpine lakes and dramatic waterfalls make this a mini-paradise. **Emerald Bay State Park,** which connects to the Desolation Wilderness, offers hiking and biking trails of varying difficulty, camping, and terrain for rock climbing. The parking lot collects a $3 day use fee. One of the best hikes in Tahoe is the **Rubicon Trail,** which wraps five miles around the beach and granite cliffs of Emerald Bay. The trailheads are at D.L. Bliss Park and Vikingsholm. The **Eagle Falls Trail** is accessible from the Vikingsholm's parking lot by hiking to Eagle Lake (1mi.) and the Desolation Wilderness. (Permits required for this hike, fee for overnight camping; see **Desolation Wilderness,** p. 245.)

Those looking for a more leisurely excursion will enjoy the nature trails around the Taylor Creek Visitor Center, west of South Lake Tahoe. The **Lake of the Sky Trail** (½mi. round-trip) is dotted with informative signs about the origins of the lake, its early inhabitants, and its current animal inhabitants. The trail leads to the **Tallac Historic Site,** which features a look at early 20th-century Tahoe casino life. Also at Taylor Creek is the underground Stream Profile Chamber, which allows face-to-window interaction with fish, including the bright red salmon that fill the chamber in a fall spawning spree.

Lower and **Upper Echo Lakes,** off U.S. 50 south of Tahoe, are a smaller, wilder version of Tahoe; gray stone and pine trees tower around the lakes, producing an unmatched feeling of seclusion. **Echo Chalet** (659-7207), two miles off U.S. 50 near the top of Echo Summit, operates boat service across the lake (M-Th 8am-6pm, F-Su 8am-6:30pm; one-way $6 with at least 2 people, pets $3; no reservations). This is the most affordable way in the area to sate motorboat-borne desires. From the drop-off point, a well-maintained trail (part of the Pacific Crest Trail; for more info, see **From Crest to Crest: the Trail of the West,** p. 266) skirts the north side of the lakes to the Upper Lake boat landing and into the Desolation Wilderness. Day hiking wilderness permits are available at the chalet; mandatory overnight permits are issued at the forest service (see **Wilderness Permits,** p. 245). Another two miles along U.S. 50, just before Twin Bridges, is the **Horsetail Falls** trailhead. The waterfalls here make those at Eagle Lake look like leaky faucets. To access them, you'll have to make the short (1¼mi.) but tough hike through the slippery canyon. Inexperienced hikers should beware—each year, some people need to be rescued by U.S. Forest Service helicopters.

ROCK CLIMBING

Invaluable climbing information is available from **Alpine Skills International** (ASI; see **Truckee and Donner Lake: Accommodations,** p. 254). The **Alpenglow Sport Shop,** 415 North Lake Blvd., Tahoe City (583-6917), provides free rock- and ice-climbing literature, and rents climbing shoes (open M-F 10am-6pm, Sa-Su 9am-6pm). **The Sports Exchange,** 10095 W. River St. (582-4510), houses Gym Works, a challenging indoor climbing gym with over 2500 square feet of bouldering and climbing space ($7 per day, indoor shoe rental $3 per day). **Headwall Climbing Wall** (583-7673), at Squaw Valley, offers several challenging routes in the Cable Car Building.

There are many popular climbs in Lake Tahoe, but climbing should never be undertaken without knowing the ropes—proper safety precautions and equipment are a must. Those unprepared for dangerous climbs can try bouldering at **D.L. Bliss State Park** and at **Split Rock** in Donner Memorial State Park. The climbing at **Donner Summit** is world-renowned. Along Old Hwy. 40 by Donner Pass, climbers ascend **School Rock** (beginner) or the precarious **Snow Shed** (advanced). A host of popular climbing spots are scattered through South Shore and the Donner Summit area. The **90-Foot Wall** at Emerald Bay, **Twin Crags** at Tahoe City, and **Big Chief** near Squaw Valley are some of the more famous area climbs. **Lover's Leap,** in South Lake Tahoe, is an incredible climb of two giant cliffs. East of South Lake Tahoe off U.S. 50, **Phantom Spires** has amazing ridge views, while **Pie Shop** has great exposure.

SUMMERTIME GONDOLA RIDES

Heavenly Mountain (tram and restaurant info 775-586-7000; see **Winter Sights and Recreation,** below), offers an aerial tram to the mountaintop for sightseeing, picnics, and hiking (tram runs daily 10am-9pm; fare $12.50, ages 4-12 $9.50). Summer vacation package includes one night lodging, tram ride, and choice of activity. (Emerald Bay cruise, 2hr. bike rental, 1hr. kayak rental, or wine and cheese picnic are examples. Offered May 15-Nov. 24 Su-Th.)

Squaw Valley (see below) also offers a scenic tram ride. that climbs to the mountaintop High Camp, with a year-round ice-skating rink, tennis club, pool, spa, mountain bike and hiking trails, and the world's highest-elevated bungee jumping tower. Restaurants and shops at the top are pricey. (Tram runs daily June-Sept. 10am-9pm; Oct.-Nov. 10am-5pm. Fare $14, under 12 $5; after 5pm $5.)

WINTER SIGHTS AND RECREATION

DOWNHILL SKIING

With its world-class alpine slopes, knee-deep powder, and notorious California sun, Tahoe is a skier's mecca. There are approximately 20 ski resorts in the Tahoe area. The visitors center provides info, maps, publications like *Ski Tahoe* (free), and coupons (see **Visitor Information,** p. 245). For daily ski info updates use the website www.tahoesbest.com/skitahoe. All the major resorts offer lessons and rent equipment. Look for multi-day packages that offer significant discounts over single-day rates. Lifts at most resorts operate daily 9am to 4pm; arrive early for the best skiing and shortest lines. Prices do not include ski rental, which generally costs $15-20 for a full day. Skiers on a tight budget should consider night skiing or half-day passes. Skiing conditions range from bikini days to frost-bitten finger days, and snow (artificial or otherwise) might cover the slopes into early summer. Off-season skiing may not compete with winter skiing for snow quality, but it's generally much cheaper. **Rates listed below are for winter.**

Squaw Valley (583-6955 or 800-545-4350; www.squaw.com), off Rte. 89 just north of Alpine Meadows. The site of the 1960 Olympic Winter Games, and with good reason—the groomed bowls and tree runs make for some of the West's best skiing. Squaw boasts 4200 acres of terrain across 6 Sierra peaks. The 30 ski lifts access high-elevation runs for all levels. The resort also offers night and cross-country skiing, bungee jumping, swimming, rock climbing, and ice skating in Olympic Ice Pavilion. Full-day ticket $48, half-day $32, seniors and under 13 $24, over 75 free. Night skiing (4-9pm) $20, under 12 $5. Non-skiing cable car ride $14, after 4pm $5. "Fun in the Sun" package for first-time skiers over 12 includes free cable car ride, lesson, and ski rental (mid-week and non-holidays).

Alpine Meadows (583-4232 or 800-441-4423), on Rte. 89 6mi. northwest of Tahoe City. An excellent, accessible family vacation spot with more than 2000 skiable acres. Not as commercial as Squaw, it has long expert bowls with good powder skiing, but few beginner runs. Alpine is notorious for avalanches, so be careful skiing out of boundaries. Full-day lift ticket $46, ages 65-69 $29, ages 7-12 $18, over 70 or under 6 $6. Basic ski rental $22, ages 7-12 $15, under 6 $9.

Heavenly (800-243-2826), on Ski Run Blvd. off U.S. 50, is one of the largest and most popular resorts in the area. Reaching over 10,000ft., it is Tahoe's highest ski resort. Few shoots or ridges. Its 23 lifts and 4800 skiable acres straddle the California-Nevada boundary and offer dizzying views of both. Full-day lift ticket $46, seniors and under 13 $20; half-day $30, seniors and under 13 $15.

Mount Rose (800-754-7673), 11mi. from Incline Village on Rte. 431, is a local favorite because of its long season, short lines, intermediate focus, and less-expensive lift tickets. Full-day lift ticket $42, ages 13-19 $35; half-day $34, ages 13-19 $34; seniors M-F half-price; over 70 and under 5 free, ages 6-12 $10.

Ski Homewood (525-2992), on the western shore 6mi. south of Tahoe City. A relatively inexpensive ski area, it caters primarily to locals. It offers 8 lifts and decent skiing at affordable prices by avoiding expensive frills. Terrain for all levels, but the season is short because the resort is at lake level. Full-day lift ticket $35, ages 14-18 $25, ages 9-13 $11, under 9 free.

Boreal Ridge (426-3663), on I-80 10mi. west of Truckee, opens earlier than most resorts and saves skiers the drive to Tahoe. Mostly beginner and intermediate slopes are good for snowboarding. Full-day lift ticket $34, ages 5-12 $5, under 5 free. Call about mid-week discounts and night skiing; both vary seasonally.

Numerous smaller ski resorts offer cheaper tickets and shorter lines. **Diamond Peak Ski Resort** (832-1177), off Country Club Dr. in Incline Village, has some hair-raising tree-skiing and is right on the beach, while **Sugarbowl** (426-3847), three miles off I-80 at Soda Springs Exit, recently doubled in size and has decent terrain.

CROSS-COUNTRY SKIING AND SNOWSHOEING

One of the best ways to enjoy the solitude of Tahoe's pristine snow-covered forests is to cross-country ski at a resort. Alternatively, rent skis at an independent outlet and venture onto the thick braid of trails around the lake. **Porters** (587-1500), at the Lucky-Longs Center, in Truckee, and 501 N. Lake Blvd., Tahoe City (583-2314), rents skis for $8-10.

Royal Gorge (426-3871), on Old Hwy. 40 below Donner Summit, is the nation's largest cross-country ski resort, with 80 trails covering 170 miles of beginner and expert terrain. **Spooner Lake** (749-5349), at the junction of U.S. 50 and Rte. 28, offers 21 trails and incredible views (adult trail fee $15, children $3; mid-week special $11). **Hope Valley** (694-2266), has 11 free trails of varying difficulty; take Rte. 89 South from South Lake Tahoe and turn left on Rte. 88.

You might prefer the easier activity of snowshoeing, which allows you to traverse more varied terrain. Follow hiking or cross-country trails or trudge off into the woods (make sure to bring a map). Rentals are available at many sporting goods stores for about $15 per day. Check at ranger stations for ranger-guided winter snowshoe hikes.

TRUCKEE AND DONNER LAKE

Truckee (pop. 10,950) got its name from a classic miscommunication. When a Paiute Indian greeted the Stephen-Townsend-Murphy party in 1844 with the word *Tro-kay* ("peace"), they thought it was his name and gave it to a local river, and in turn, to a lumber camp at the foot of the Sierra. Truckee remained a rugged mining and railroad town until the outdoor recreation industry took hold and transformed it into a cutesy tourist stop for skiiers and hikers en route to Tahoe. Restaurants and shops on the well-preserved "Old West" **Commercial Row** accommodate visitors from the much more spectacular Lake Tahoe just 15 miles away.

Two miles west of Truckee and encircled by gray granite cliffs lies **Donner Lake,** the site where the ill-fated Donner Party got snowed in for the winter. Travelers will notice numerous memorials to the gruesome event (see **This Party Bites!**, p. 256) but will likely find Donner Lake much more fun than the pioneers did—now warmer than Tahoe, the lake is a popular place for swimming, boating, camping, and hiking.

ORIENTATION

Truckee lies just off I-80 in the Sierra Nevada, 100 miles northeast of Sacramento, 33 miles west of Reno, and 15 miles north of Lake Tahoe. The town is a three-hour drive from San Francisco, depending on road conditions. Donner Pass Rd. (part of Rte. 89), the main drag, leads east into downtown, where it becomes Commercial Row, and west to Donner Summit and Donner Lake, where it is known as Old Hwy. 40. Be extremely cautious along Donner Pass—there are not always barriers along the cliffside edge of the road. In summer, potholes make for a harrowing drive. In winter it is usually closed due to snow and ice; stick to I-80.

PRACTICAL INFORMATION

Trains: Amtrak (800-USA-RAIL/872-7245), at Railroad St. and Commercial Row, in Truckee. Trains depart once daily to **Reno** ($8); **Salt Lake City** ($63-114); **Sacramento** ($34-74); and **San Francisco** ($52-63). Station is unstaffed; order tickets in advance.

Buses: Greyhound, 10065 Donner Pass Rd. (800-231-2222). To **Reno** (5 per day, $10); **San Francisco** (6 per day, $36); and **Sacramento** (6 per day, $20).

Auto Repairs: AAA Emergency Road Service (800-222-4357).

Visitor Information: Truckee-Donner Chamber of Commerce, 10065 Donner Pass Rd. (587-2757; area reservation line 800-548-8388), opposite the factory outlet mall. Brochures, maps, and a sign-up list for the commemorative Donner Party Hike. Open daily 8:30am-5:30pm. **U.S. Forest Service Truckee Ranger District,** 10342 Rte. 89 North (587-3558), off I-80. Info on camping and recreation in Tahoe National Forest. Open June-Aug. M-Sa 8am-5pm; Sept.-May M-F 8am-4:30pm.

Equipment Rental: Sierra Mountaineer (587-2025), at Bridge and Jibbom St., 1 block off Donner Pass Rd., in downtown Truckee. Backpacks $6 per day; sleeping bags $15 1st day, $5 each additional day; 2-person tent $10 per day; 3-person tent $15 per day; camping stoves $4 per day. Open in summer M-Sa 10am-6pm, Su 10am-5pm; call for off-season hours.

Weather Conditions: 546-5253. **Road Conditions:** 800-427-7623.

Medical Services: Tahoe Forest, 10121 Pine Ave. (587-6011), at Donner Pass Rd.

Emergency: 911. **Police:** 530-582-7842.

Post Office: Truckee (800-275-8777), 10050 Bridge St., on Rte. 267 1 block north of Commercial Row. Open M-F 8:30am-5pm, Sa 11am-2pm. **ZIP Code:** 96161. **Donner Station,** 11415 Deerfield. Open M-F 9am-4:30pm. **ZIP Code:** 96162.

Area Code: 530.

CAMPGROUNDS, ACCOMMODATIONS, AND FOOD

Truckee and Donner Lake have few finds for the hostel-seeker. More budget accommodation options can be found in Tahoe, especially in South Lake. The **Heidelmann ASI Lodge** (426-9108), on Old Hwy. 40 between Norden and Donner Memorial State Park, is a dreamy mountain hostel half-mile east of Donner Sugar Bowl on the very top of Donner Pass, accessible by car only. The charming Swiss-style ski lodge-esque bed and breakfast is a great base for skiers, hikers, climbers, and popular outdoor programs. (Dorm-style accommodations with great breakfast $27.50. Call ahead; the lodge is only open for certain weekends in summer season.)

Twelve **campgrounds** lie within 12 miles of Truckee. The U.S. Forest Service (587-3558) operates northern sites along Rte. 89 and Stampede Meadows Rd., off I-80 at the Hirshdale Exit. Sites around Boca and Prosser Reservoirs on Rte. 89 charge $8-12; sites at Stampede Meadows Dr. are either free or cost $12 per night. Stop at the ranger station on Rte. 89 just off I-80 for more maps and info. (Open M-Sa 8am-5pm.) The **Donner Memorial Park,** 12593 Donner Pass Rd., is an expansive campground with fully equipped sites. Scenic views of Donner Lake and Summit make this site especially popular (sites $16). All campgrounds recommend reservations, especially on weekends (call MISTIX 800-444-7275).

Take your pick of touristy restaurants and coffee shops in Truckee, or else forage for yourself at the **Safeway** supermarket on Rte. 89, about one mile west of downtown (open 24hr.). The **Treat Box Bakery,** 11400 Donner Pass Rd. (587-6554), is the perfect spot for picnic packing. Eat in the cafe or order from their selection of fresh sub sandwiches ($4-6), salads, homemade pies, breads, cakes, and pastries. (Open daily 5am-9pm.) **Squeeze-In,** 10060 Commercial Row (587-9814), across from the fire station, offers 57 varieties of omelettes and sandwiches ($6-8) named after colorful locals like Luscious Lucy and Captain Avalanche, all squeezed into one little restaurant (open daily 7am-2pm; cash only).

SIGHTS AND SEASONAL EVENTS

The local **historical society** (582-0893) oversees a short town trail (maps at the Chamber of Commerce), as well as a small museum in the **Old Truckee Jail** on Jibbom St. Although many Old West criminals were tarred and feathered, the lucky ones were locked up in this wood-and-stone prison until its closure in 1964 (open May-Oct. daily 11am-4pm; free).

Most visitors come to Truckee for the outdoor recreation opportunities in **Tahoe National Forest** and **Donner Memorial State Park.** Check the *Truckee Activity Guide and Visitor Information*, available at the visitors center, for current info. The Truckee Ranger District of Tahoe National Forest has three lake-sized reservoirs, a number of streams, as well as small trout-trafficked lakes, which are excellent for fishing and boating. Some areas are easily accessible by car, but some require a short hike. Hiking at this popular weekend spot is more low-impact than around the rocky mountains surrounding Lake Tahoe. In winter, these snow-packed roads are good for cross-country skiing. The **Sierra Mountaineer** (see p. 255) sells a good area map ($9). Despite its morbid namesake, the popular Donner Memorial State Park is the local playground, with hiking trails, picnic areas and scenic Donner Lake. On the lake's west end is a public and peopled beach. A roped swimming area, volleyball court, tennis courts, sandy beach, and grassy picnic lawn (day use $2) make this place feel like a little Lake Tahoe. The Donner Memorial is a chilling reminder of the extreme winter that gave rise to the Donner tragedy. Beseiged by families from all over the world photographing themselves in front of it, the 20-foot-high monument is as tall as the height of snowfall that stormy winter. Next door, the **Emigrant Trail Museum** is at the entrance to the park (open daily 9am-5pm; admission $2, ages 6-12 $1).

March brings the **Snowfest** winter carnival (583-7625), celebrations color the sky with the **Truckee-Tahoe Air Show** (582-9068) at the end of June, and the second week in August brings a **rodeo** (582-9852). The **Annual Donner Party Hike** (587-8808) ritually reenacts the fateful journey every October (dinner not included).

THIS PARTY BITES! It's hard to pass through Donner Lake without seeing numerous memorials to the Donner Party. The fuss began when 90 midwesterners (led by the Donner family), headed for the comfort of California in April 1846. The ill-fated group took a "short-cut" advocated by daring but luckless adventurer Lansford Hastings. The party hacked through the wilderness, losing cattle and abandoning wagons as they went. Although the area was brushed with barely a foot of snow the year before, the onset of an early winter at Truckee (later Donner) Lake in December devastated the group. Trapped by 22 ft. of snow and without powder skis, many turned to cannibalism before they were rescued. Only 40 survived. The Donner Party is remembered in the **Donner Memorial State Park** (582-7892), three miles west of Truckee, and on countless t-shirts. To get to the park, take I-80 to the Donner Lake Exit, then go west on old U.S. 40 until you reach the park entrance. The park includes the **Emigrant Trail Museum,** which documents the infamous incident with multimedia flair c. 1975. "This is all your fault!" "Eat me!" "Don't mind if I do!"

RENO

If a Hollywood executive ever got the great idea to cross *Showgirls* with *The Golden Girls*, the result would be Reno (pop. 139,000). Hoping to strike it rich at the card tables, busloads of the nation's elderly flock to this hedonistic splendor. The fascination with Reno began in the early 1920s when several renowned public figures, including "America's Sweetheart" Mary Pickford, chose this city for expedient divorce settlements. With Reno's newfound fame it became the self-appointed "biggest little city in the world." Combining a small town, sleazy city, and high Sierra scenic spot, Reno captures both the natural splendor and ultra-capitalist sleaze of the West.

ORIENTATION

Only 14 miles from the California border and 443 miles north of Las Vegas, Reno sits at the intersection of **Interstate 80** and **U.S. 395,** which runs along the eastern slope of the Sierra Mountains and the scenic Truckee River. Scan West Coast papers for "gamblers' specials" on bus and plane fare excursion tickets; some include casino credits.

Most major casinos are downtown on Sierra and Virginia St., between 2nd and 4th St. The wide and night-bright streets in downtown Reno are heavily patrolled in summer, but **avoid walking alone** near the northeastern corner at night. In the adjacent city of Sparks, several casinos line I-80. *Reno/Tahoe Travel Planner*, available at the visitors center, contains a local map and is an excellent city guide.

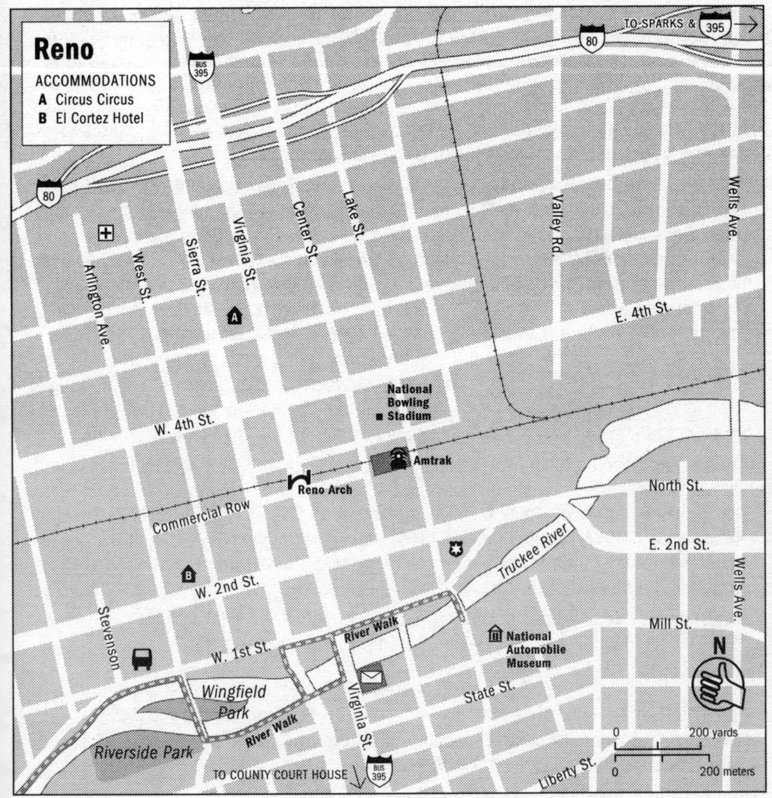

PRACTICAL INFORMATION

Airport: Cannon International, 2001 E. Plumb Ln. (328-6400), on U.S. 395 at Terminal Way 3mi. southeast of downtown. Most major hotels have free shuttles for guests; otherwise, take bus #24 from the city center. Taxis from downtown to the airport; $9-11.

Trains: Amtrak, 135 E. Commercial Row (800-USA-RAIL/872-7245). Ticket office open daily 8:45am-5:30pm. Arrive 30min. in advance to purchase tickets. To **San Francisco** (1 bus/train combo per day, $35-85) and **Sacramento** (1 per day, $22-76).

Buses: Greyhound, 155 Stevenson St. (322-2970 or 800-231-2222), ½-block from W. 2nd St. Open 24hr. Higher prices F-Su. To: **San Francisco** (18 per day, $30-32); **Salt Lake City** (3 per day, $45-48); **L.A.** (6 per day, $46-49); and **Sacramento** (12 per day, $20). Lockers (6hr. $2; 6-24hr. $4), a mini-mart, and a restaurant.

Public Transportation: Reno Citifare (348-7433) serves the Reno-Sparks area. Main terminal at 4th and Center St. Most buses operate daily 5am-7pm, although city center buses operate 24hr. Buses stop every 2 blocks. Fare $1.25, seniors and disabled 60¢, ages 6-18 90¢.

Taxis: Yellow Cab (355-5555). 24hr. **Reno-Sparks Taxi Cab** (333-3333).

Car Rental: Lloyd's International Rent-a-Car, 1201 Kietzke (348-4777 or 800-654-7037). Min. age 25 with own liability insurance; can purchase collision insurance. Credit card or $200 cash deposit required. Prices depend on season and availability, from $23 per day, $139 per week; 150mi. included per day, 22¢ each additional mi.

Auto Repair: AAA Emergency Road Service: 800-222-4357. 24hr.

Visitor Information: Reno-Sparks Convention and Visitors Center, 300 N. Center St. (800-367-7366; www.playreno.com), on the 1st fl. of the National Bowling Stadium. Full of pamphlets and the sound of bowling pins. Open M-Sa 7am-8pm, Su 9am-6pm.

Drinkin' an' Gamblin' Age: 21.

Quick Cash: ATMs in most casinos. Most charge $1.50 for out-of-state withdrawals—**beware of the odd machine that will try to charge you $8.99.**

Marriage: Men and women over 18 can pick up a marriage license at the **Courthouse,** 75 Court St. (328-3274), for $35 (cash)—all you need is a partner and an ID (open daily 8am-midnight, including holidays). Numerous chapels in Reno are eager to help you tie the knot. **Adventure Inn,** 3575 S. Virginia St. (828-9000 or 800-937-1436; www.adventureinn.com), offers deluxe wedding packages that include a ceremony in the romantic Waterfall Chapel, music, photographs, flowers, stretch limo service, and 2 nights in one of their theme suites. Choose from such exotic rooms as the Amazon Suite, the Adam and Eve suite, or the Super Space Suite, which features an 18ft. pool, strobe lights, fog machine, and an 8ft. heart-shaped bed. For those on a strict budget with a wedding party of 12 or fewer, bare-bones service is available at **Starlite Chapel,** 80 Court St. (786-4949), for $95. Music, minister, and parking during ceremony.

Divorce: To obtain a divorce permit, you must be a resident of NV for at least 6 weeks and pay a $150 fee. Permits are available at the courthouse divorce office M-F 8am-5pm; an uncontested divorce may take up to 4 months. Call 328-3535 for info. **Divorce Made Easy,** 790 S. Virginia St. (323-3359), manages to offer "While-U-Wait" service for those who want to leave the paperwork to the pros. $240 fee. Office open M 9am-3:30pm, Tu-Th 9am-5pm.

Laundromat: Launderland & Coin-op Laundry, 680 E. 2nd St. (329-3733). Wash $1.50-2.75; dry free. Open daily 7am-10:30 pm; last load 9:30pm.

Road Conditions: 793-1313 (NV).

Emergency: 911.

24-Hour Crisis Lines: General Counseling and Rape Crisis (800-992-5757). **Compulsive Gamblers Hotline** 800-LOST-BET/567-8238.

National HIV & AIDS Information Services: 800-342-2437.

Pharmacy: Cerveri Drug Store, 190 E. 1st St. (322-6122), at Lake St. Open M-F 7:30am-5pm, Sa 9am-5pm.

Medical Services: St. Mary's Hospital, 235 W. 6th St. (323-2041, emergency 789-3188), near Arlington Ave. 24hr. **St. Mary's Family Walk-In Center and Clinic,** 6580 S. Virginia St. (853-3333). Open M-F 7:30am-6pm, Sa-Su 8am-4pm.

Post Office: 50 S. Virginia St. (800-275-8777), at Mill St. 2 blocks south of city center. Open M-F 8:30am-5pm, Sa 10am-2pm. **ZIP Code:** 89501.

AREA CODE	The area code for Reno is 702.

ACCOMMODATIONS AND CAMPRGROUNDS

While weekend prices at casinos are usually on the high side, gamblers' specials, weekday rates, and winter discounts provide some great, cheap rooms. Prices fluctuate, so call ahead. **Fitzgerald's,** 225 N. Virginia St. (786-3663), **Atlantis,** 3800 S. Virginia St. (825-4700), **Circus Circus,** 500 N. Sierra St. (329-0711), and **Sundowner,** 450 N. Arlington Ave. (786-7050), have been known to offer some good deals to go along with their central locations and massive facilities.

Be advised: Heterosexual prostitution is legal in most of Nevada (though not in Reno itself), and thus certain motels are cheap but lacking a particularly wholesome feel. Members of the same sex sharing a hotel room may be required to book a room with two beds. Southwestern downtown has the cheapest lodging. **The prices below don't include Reno's 12% hotel tax.**

Circus Circus, 500 N. Sierra St. (329-0711 or 800-648-5010). Deemed the family casino of Little Sin City, with over 1800 newly renovated rooms, acres of casinos, restaurants, activities, health club, a kitschy monorail-trolley, and a real live big top. Rooms are large, luxurious, and quiet. Call ahead for the best rates and discounts. M-Th from $49, F-Su from $59 (more expensive during peak seasons).

BASQUE IN GLORY I: THE MARCH OF HISTORY

The Basque, whose 12,700-square-mile homeland is home to herders and nationalists, have an ancient distinction from their European neighbors; the Basque language is unrelated to any other in the entire Indo-European family. They have influenced history with spicy food, religious leaders, and seafaring men. Today these people of the Pyrenees have a large population in Reno and other American cities, and their influence is felt throughout California and Nevada.

What is the longest surname in the Basque language?

Iturriberrigorrigokoerrotadoetxea.

Who introduced the first flock of sheep to the U.S.?

The Basque Juan de Onate, in 1598.

Who was the first man to sail around the world?

A Basque: Juan Sebastián de Elcano.

Who founded the Jesuit order of Roman Catholic priests?

Ignatius Loyola and Francis Xavier, Basques both.

What community has the highest incidence of type O blood, and the lowest incidence of type B blood in Europe, as well as the highest incidence of Rh-negative blood in the world?

The Basque.

Are all Basque people descended from royalty?

Signs point to yes.

Motel 6 has 3 clean, comfortable, and cheap locations in Reno: 866 N. Wells Ave. (786-9852), north on I-80 Exit 14; 1900 S. Virginia St. (827-0255), 1½mi. down Virginia St. at Plumb Ln.; and 1400 Stardust St. (747-4527), north on I-80 Keystone Exit and west onto Stardust St. All rooms with pools and HBO. June-Sept. singles Su-Th $34, F-Sa $42; doubles $40, $48. Reserve 2 weeks in advance. Cheaper Oct.-May.

El Cortez Hotel, 239 W. 2nd St. (322-9161). Decent hotel downtown with 122 rooms. A/C, cable TV, exposed pipes, and thin walls. Singles Su-Th $29, F-Sa $38.10; doubles $42.60, $49.

To escape Reno's constant hum of slot machines, campers can make the drive to the woodland campsites of **Davis Creek Park** (849-0684), 17 miles south on U.S. 395, then half-mile west; follow signs (sites $11, each additional car $5; free picnic area open daily 8am-9pm). Wrap yourself in a rustic blanket of pines and sage at the base of the Sierra Nevada's **Mount Rose** and camp at one of the 63 sites with full service, including showers and a small pond stocked with fish, but no hookups. Sites available on a first-come, first-camped basis. (Sites with 1 vehicle $10, pets $1.) The nearby 14-mile Offer Creek Trail leads to Rock and Price Lakes and interlocks with the Tahoe Rim Trail. Camping and fishing on the trail are free but require permits (available at grocery and sporting goods stores). You can also camp along the shore at **Pyramid Lake** (see p. 261). To stay closer to Reno, park and plug in your RV overnight at the **Reno Hilton,** 2500 E. 2nd St. (789-2000; full hookup $21). Call ahead; people reserve up to a year in advance.

FOOD

Eating in Reno is cheap. To entice gamblers and to prevent them from wandering out in search of food, casinos offer a wide range of all-you-can-eat buffets and 99¢ breakfasts. However, buffet fare can be greasy and overcooked, and rumors of food poisoning abound. Reno's other inexpensive eateries offer better food. The large Basque population has brought a spicy and hearty cuisine locals enthusiastically recommend.

The Blue Heron, 1091 S. Virginia St. (786-4110), 9 blocks from downtown. Try the "Fountain of Youth" and other fresh smoothies ($3). The Heron offers hearty vegetarian cuisine (well-stuffed avocado sandwich $6). Dinner entrees ($8-10) include freshly baked bread and soup or salad. Open M-Th 11am-9pm, F-Sa 8am-9pm.

Louis' Basque Corner, 301 E. 4th St. (323-7203), at Evans St. 3 blocks east of Virginia St., is a local institution. Spicy cuisine and hearty portions will make you want to join up with the Basque separatists. Succulent tripe, savory rabbit, or, for the less adventurous, top sirloin steak, lamb, fish, calamari, or shrimp. Full bar. Lunch $7-8. Full-course dinner $15. Open Tu-Sa 11:30am-2:30pm and 5-9:30pm, Su-M 5-9:30pm.

BASQUE IN GLORY II: ABROAD IN RENO

The University of Reno has the largest collection of Basque books outside of Europe, and Reno is a fine place to try out your halting Basque. Some basic Reno vocabulary:

maite: love
muxu: kiss
jatetxea: restaurant
yokuan: gambling
embido: I wager two beans.
heoki: I see your beans.
Ordago!: Throw down your cards, you stinking liar.
hasaratia: hate
Ongi ettori: welcome
bekatia: sin
Mus: Basque poker
txiki: little
herria: city
Heri Teppia Diura: The Biggest Little City in the World.

Miguel's Fine Mexican Food, 1415 S. Virginia St. (322-2722), a short drive from downtown. Peppy Mexican music sets it apart from Reno's glitz. Voted best Mexican food in Nevada by *Nevada Weekly*'s readers, the tacos, enchiladas, and fajitas are indeed scrumptious. Entrees $5-10. Open Su-Th 11am-9pm, F-Sa 11am-10pm.

Big Top Buffet (329-0711), at Circus Circus. Breakfast $5, lunch $6, dinner $8-12 (more expensive on weekends). Discount for children, under 5 eat for free. Open M-F 7am-10pm, Sa-Su 11am-10pm; Sa-Su brunch 7am-4pm, dinner 4-10pm.

SIGHTS AND ENTERTAINMENT

Reno is one big amusement park. Many casinos offer free gaming lessons, and minimum bets vary between establishments. Drinks are either free or incredibly cheap if you're gambling, but be wary of a casino's generous gift of risk-inducing, inhibition-dropping al-kee-hol. Don't forget that gambling is illegal if you're under 21; if you hit the jackpot at age 20, it'll be the casino's lucky day and not yours. Almost all casinos offer live nighttime entertainment, but these shows are generally not worth the steep admission prices. **Harrah's,** 219 N. Center St. (786-3232), is the self-consciously "hip" complex where **Planet Hollywood** capitalizes on movie lust, magically transforming Hollywood knick-knacks into precious relics. Harrah's also features a **Playboy Revue,** where wild-West dancing strikes those nerves of American nostalgia. At **Circus Circus,** 500 N. Sierra (329-0711), a small circus above the casino performs "big-top" shows every 30 minutes. These shows and others are listed in the weekly *Showtime*, which also offers gambling coupons. *Best Bets* provides listings of discounted local events and shows. *Nevada Events & Shows* section of the Nevada visitors' guide lists sights, museums, and seasonal events. More info is in the local *Reno Gazette-Journal* and *News & Review*.

Still, Reno is not yet one big casino. The local Basque influence breaks through the seams of the blanketing casino culture at Reno's slammin' annual **Basque Festival** (329-1476), held in August. This weekend of frenetic bacchanalia features traditional contests, dancing, live music, and more food than the Circus Circus buffet. The first week in August roars into chrome-covered, hot-rod splendor with **Hot August Nights** (356-1956), a celebration of America's love affair with 1950s and 60s cars and rock 'n' roll, with shows, auctions, and a parade. The annual **Reno Rodeo** (329-3877), one of the biggest in the West, gallops over eight days in late June. In September, the **Great Reno Balloon Race** (829-2810), in Rancho San Rafael, and the **National Championship Air Races** (972-6663), at the Stead Airport, draw an international group of contestants and spectators (Sept. 14-17 in 2000). Also in September, nearby Virginia City hosts **Camel Races** (847-0311) during the weekend after Labor Day (Sept. 9-10 in 2000), where camels and ostriches race through town. To get to the dromedary derby, take U.S. 395 South, then Rte. 341 for 25 miles. Reserve hotel rooms in advance for any seasonal events.

NEAR RENO: PYRAMID LAKE

Thirty miles north of Reno on Rte. 445, on the Paiute Indian Reservation, lies emerald green Pyramid Lake, one of the most beautiful bodies of water in the U.S. Its pristine tides are set against the backdrop of a barren desert, making it a soothing respite from neon Reno. It is the remnant of Ice Age-era Lake Lahontam, which once covered 8450 square miles. Local tradition, however, explains the magical water as a collection of tears. Saddened by her children's inability to get along, a mother cried and cried—the tears that fell from her eyes collected in this basin, and her body and soul are said to be locked in the surrounding mountains.

In 1844 John Fremont renamed the lake on his own terms when he came across the 26-mile body of water and the pyramid-shaped island off the eastern shore. Now the lake is visited by sun-soakers, swimmers, water-skiers, and other outdoorsmen. **Camping** is allowed anywhere on the lake shore, but only designated areas have toilet facilities. A $5 permit is required for use of the park, and the area is carefully patrolled by the Paiute tribe. Permits are available at the Ranger Station, three miles to the left from Rte. 445 at Sutcliffe (476-1155; open daily 8am-4:30pm), or at the neighboring store. **Boat rental** (476-1156) is available daily at the marina near the Ranger Station; call for reservations. The lake is an angler's paradise from October through June, when trophy-size cutthroat trout are reeled in with great frequency (day fishing permit $6 at ranger station). Hikers can climb the bizarre tufa formations on the north shore and visit the hot springs at Needles.

NATIONAL PARKS AND FORESTS

Far from the urban centers and industry of the coastal areas, the central Sierra is nature as it was meant to be. Clear streams splash over stones and trout, and the snowy peaks are populated only by endless pine trees. No need to fear an end to this wilderness—almost all of it is protected by the government. The two main park areas are Yosemite National Park (near Stanislaus National Forest and Mono Lake), and Sequoia and Kings Canyon National Parks (framed by the Sierra National Forest to the north and Sequoia National Forest to the south). National parks may conserve the natural surroundings, but they also attract adventure-hungry tourists from around the world. Those seeking solitude might want to listen to the call of the wild and stick to the backcountry in less popular national forests.

YOSEMITE NATIONAL PARK

In 1868 a young Scotsman named John Muir arrived by boat in San Francisco and asked for directions to "anywhere that's wild." Anxious to run this crazy youngster out of town, Bay Area folk directed him to the heralded lands of Yosemite. The wonders that Muir beheld there sated his wanderlust and spawned a lifetime of conservationism. His efforts won Yosemite its national park status by 1880.

If Muir's 19th-century desire to escape the concrete confines of civilization was considered crazy, then today we live in a world gone criminally insane—millions of visitors pour into the park each year. While Yosemite's granite cliffs, thunderous waterfalls, lush meadows, and thick pine forests are awe-inspiring, they are often marred by a tourist throng. Swarms of snack shops and souvenir stands have sunk the valley into a commercial mélée, and traffic in the park's popular areas rivals that of L.A. Nevertheless, Yosemite remains a paradise for outdoor enthusiasts: most visitors congregate in only 6% of the park (Yosemite Valley), leaving thousands of beautiful backcountry miles in relative peace and quiet.

GETTING THERE AND AROUND

Yosemite lies 200 miles east of San Francisco (a 3½hr. drive) and 320 miles northeast of Los Angeles (a 6-9hr. drive, depending on the season). It can be reached by taking Rte. 140 from Merced, Rte. 41N from Fresno, or Rte. 120E from Manteca or West from Lee Vining.

BY BUS OR TRAIN

Yosemite runs public **buses** that connect the park with Merced and Fresno: **Yosemite VIA** (742-5211 or 800-VIA-LINE/842-5463) runs buses from the Merced train station to Yosemite (7, 9, 10:30am, and 4:25pm; $20, round-trip $38). VIA also

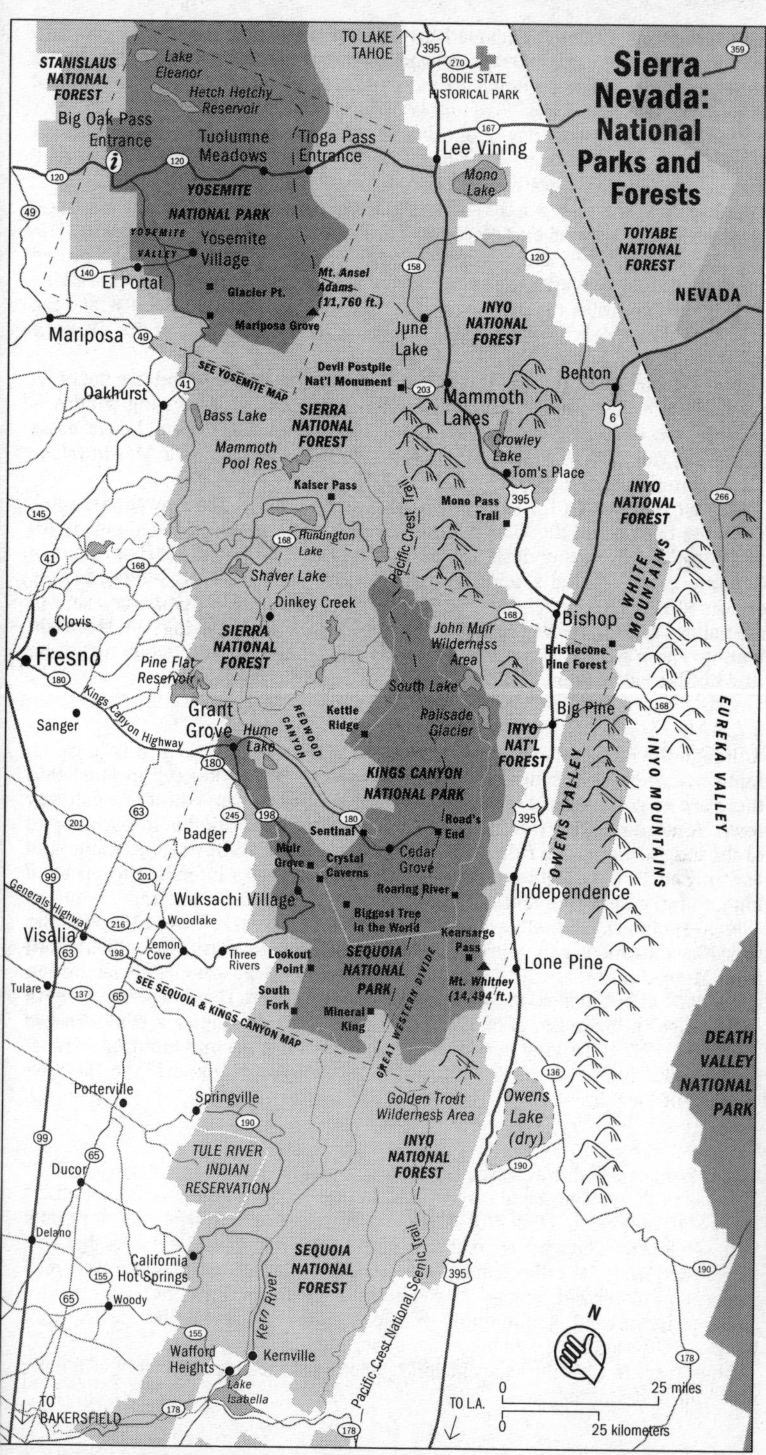
Sierra Nevada: National Parks and Forests
TO LAKE TAHOE
BODIE STATE HISTORICAL PARK
STANISLAUS NATIONAL FOREST
Lake Eleanor
Hetch Hetchy Reservoir
Big Oak Pass Entrance
Tuolumne Meadows
Tioga Pass Entrance
Lee Vining
Mono Lake
YOSEMITE NATIONAL PARK
YOSEMITE VALLEY
Yosemite Village
El Portal
Glacier Pt.
Mt. Ansel Adams (11,760 ft.)
Mariposa Grove
Mariposa
TOIYABE NATIONAL FOREST
NEVADA
INYO NATIONAL FOREST
June Lake
SEE YOSEMITE MAP
Devil Postpile Nat'l Monument
Mammoth Lakes
Benton
Oakhurst
Bass Lake
SIERRA NATIONAL FOREST
Mammoth Pool Res
Crowley Lake
Tom's Place
Kaiser Pass
Mono Pass Trail
Huntington Lake
Pacific Crest Trail
Shaver Lake
Dinkey Creek
WHITE MOUNTAINS
Bishop
John Muir Wilderness Area
Bristlecone Pine Forest
Clovis
Fresno
Pine Flat Reservoir
South Lake
Kings Canyon Highway
Sanger
Grant Grove
Hume Lake
REDWOOD CANYON
Kettle Ridge
Palisade Glacier
INYO NAT'L FOREST
Big Pine
EUREKA VALLEY
INYO MOUNTAINS
KINGS CANYON NATIONAL PARK
OWENS VALLEY
Badger
Sentinal
Road's End
Muir Grove
Crystal Caverns
Cedar Grove
Roaring River
Independence
Wuksachi Village
Generals Highway
Woodlake
Biggest Tree in the World
Visalia
Lemon Cove
Three Rivers
Lookout Point
SEQUOIA NATIONAL PARK
Kearsarge Pass
Lone Pine
Mt. Whitney (14,494 ft.)
Tulare
South Fork
Mineral King
SEE SEQUOIA & KINGS CANYON MAP
GREAT WESTERN DIVIDE
DEATH VALLEY NATIONAL PARK
Porterville
Springville
Golden Trout Wilderness Area
Owens Lake (dry)
TULE RIVER INDIAN RESERVATION
INYO NATIONAL FOREST
Ducor
Delano
California Hot Springs
SEQUOIA NATIONAL FOREST
Kern River
Pacific Crest National Scenic Trail
Woody
N
Wafford Heights
Kernville
Lake Isabella
TO BAKERSFIELD
TO L.A.
0
25 miles
0
25 kilometers

runs **Yosemite Gray Line** (YGL; 384-1315), which meets trains arriving in Merced from San Francisco and takes passengers to Yosemite. Tickets can be purchased from the driver. YGL also runs buses to and from Fresno/Yosemite International Airport, Fresno hotels, and Yosemite Valley ($20). Amtrak also runs a **bus** from **Merced** to **Yosemite** (4 per day, $10). Amtrak **trains** (800-USA-RAIL/872-7245) run to **Merced** from **San Francisco** (4 per day, $22-29) and **L.A.** (5 per day, $28-51). The trains connect with the waiting YGL bus.

An excellent way to see both the "essentials" and the off-the-beaten-path spots is to take a trip with **Incredible Adventures,** 770 Treat Ave., San Francisco 94110 (415-642-7378 or 800-777-8464; www.incadventures.com). Catering to young, spirited international backpackers, the energetic, informative guides lead incredible hiking and sightseeing trips. (4-day 3-night trips depart from San Francisco W and Su; $185 including meals, entrance fee, equipment, transportation, and tax. Daytrips run throughout the year; $85.)

The best bargain in Yosemite is the **free shuttle bus system.** Comfortable but often crowded, the buses have knowledgeable drivers and wide viewing windows. (Shuttles run daily every 10min. 7am-10pm, every 20min. 10pm-7am.) **Hikers' buses** (372-1240) run daily to Glacier Point (spring-fall) and to Tuolumne Meadows/Lee Vining (late June-Labor Day—Sept. 4 in 2000).

Open-air tram tours (372-1240) leave from Curry Village, the Ahwahnee Hotel, Yosemite Lodge, and the Village Store. Tickets are available at lodging facilities and the Village Store tour desk. The basic **Valley Floor Tour** points out Half Dome, El Capitan, Bridalveil Falls, and Happy Isles (2hr.; departs every 30min; $17.50, seniors $15.75, ages 5-12 $9.50). The **Glacier Point Tour** climbs the point for a view of the valley from 3200 feet (4hr.; June-Oct.; $20.50, ages 5-12 $11). The **Moonlight Tour,** given on nights with a full (or nearly full) moon, offers unique nighttime views of the valley (2hr.; $17.50).

BY CAR

Although the inner valley is often congested with traffic, the best way to gain a rapid overview of Yosemite is by car. Gas-guzzlers should keep in mind that there are **no gas stations in the valley;** be prepared to get ripped off in a gateway town. A more relaxing (and environmentally friendly) option is to park at one of the lodging areas and ride the free shuttle to see the valley sights, using your car only to explore sights outside of the valley. Drivers intending to visit the high country in spring and fall should have snow tires (sometimes required even in summer). Of the five major approaches to the park, **Route 120** to the Big Oak Flat entrance is the curviest. A less-nauseating alternative is **Route 140** from Merced into the valley. The eastern entrance, **Tioga Pass,** is closed during snow season but makes an awe-inspiring summer drive that keeps the camera companies in business. (For more info on winter driving, see **Wintertime in Yosemite,** p. 273.) Driving is convenient and fast, but leaving motorized transport behind for wilderness exploration allows you to experience the true essence of the park.

NOT BY CAR

Cycling is an excellent way to see Yosemite Valley; bike paths are everywhere, over 12 miles of them. Many sights are within two miles of the valley center, and trails are paved, smooth, and flat, providing the perfect person-powered tour. For rental info, see **Practical Information,** p. 262. A particularly popular bike trail is the wide paved road from the valley campgrounds to Mirror Lake (3mi. round-trip), which is closed to motorized vehicles. Yosemite's bike paths are ideal for leisurely rides and for circumventing automobile traffic; serious cyclists should not expect a workout. Off-road mountain biking is not permitted in the park.

Other ways to view the valley include **guided horseback trips** and whitewater and non-whitewater **rafting** (see p. 266).

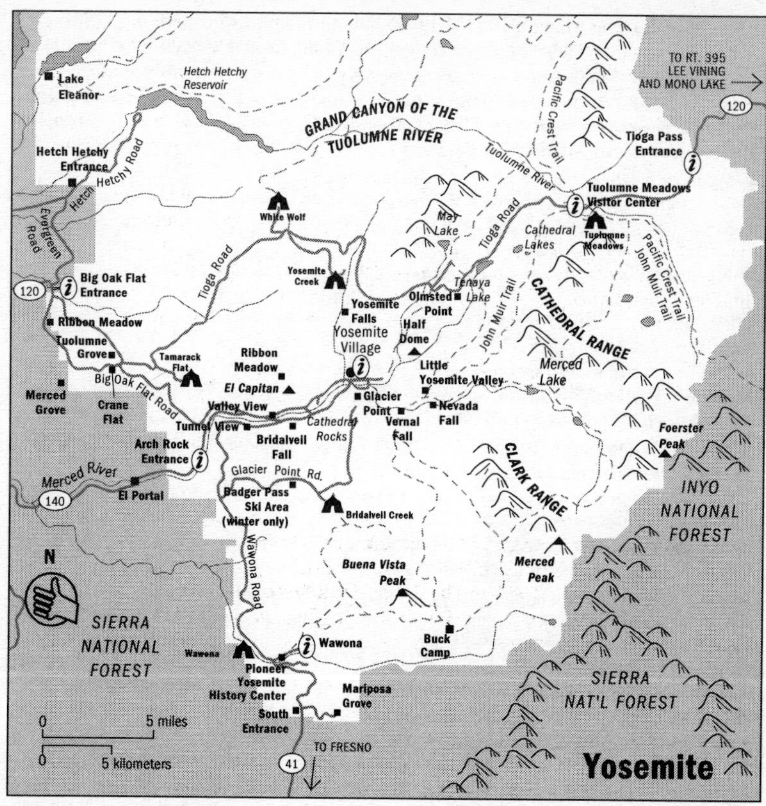

ORIENTATION

In all, Yosemite covers 1189 square miles of mountainous terrain. The park's most enduring monuments—El Capitan, Half Dome, and Yosemite Falls, among others—lie in Yosemite Valley, and were carved out by glaciers over thousands of years. Much is to be seen away from the valley and its gaggle of gawkers. Little Yosemite Valley, easily accessible by hiking trails, is home to the spectacular Vernal and Nevada Falls. Tuolumne (ta-WALL-um-ee) Meadows, in the park's northeastern corner, is an Elysian expanse of alpine meadow surrounded by cliffs and swiftly running streams. Mariposa Grove is a forest of giant sequoia trees at the park's southern end. (7-day pass $10 per hiker, biker, or bus rider; $20 per car. Annual pass $40.)

The Yosemite Concession Services provides some discounts to holders of Golden Age and Golden Eagle national park passes (2-for-1 bike rental, 2-for-1 greens fee at Wawona Golf). Inquire at the visitors centers of gateway towns such as Mariposa, Sonora, Mammoth Lakes, Oakhurst, and Merced for additional discounts on lodging, shopping, and eating.

PRACTICAL INFORMATION

VISITOR INFORMATION

General Park Information (24hr. 372-0200; general info www.nps.gov/yose, visitor info www.yosemite.org, project updates and photographs www.connect.net/yosemite). Info on weather, accommodations, and activities. Call the general line before calling a specific info station. All visitors centers have free maps and copies of *Yosemite Guide*. **All hours listed are valid May-Sept. unless otherwise noted. Call for off-season hours.**

Yosemite Valley Visitors Center (372-0200), in Yosemite Village. Sign language interpreter in summer. Open daily mid-June to Labor Day (Sept. 4 in 2000) 8am-7pm; Labor Day to mid-June 9am-5pm.

Wilderness Center (372-0308), in Yosemite Village. P.O. Box 545, Yosemite National Park 95839. Backcountry info (372-0745); order maps and info before your trip (379-2648). Wilderness permit reservations (372-0740) up to 24 weeks in advance ($3), or first-come, first-served (free). Helpful and friendly staff cannot plan your trips, but provide a wealth of info for those who do their homework. Open daily 7:30am-7pm.

Tuolumne Meadows Visitors Center (372-0263), on Tioga Pass Rd. 55mi. from Yosemite Village. The headquarters of high-country activity, with trail info and special programs. Open in summer only daily 9am-7pm.

Big Oak Flat Info Station (379-1899), on Rte. 120 W. in Crane Flat/Tuolumne Sequoia Grove. Open daily 9am-6pm. Wilderness permits available daily 7:30am-4:30pm.

Wawona Info Station (375-9501), on Rte. 141 at the southern entrance near the Mariposa Grove. Open daily 8:30am-4:30pm.

LOCAL SERVICES

Auto Repairs: Village Garage (372-8320). Open daily 8am-5pm. Cars towed 24hr. **AAA Emergency Road Service** (800-400-4222).

Bike Rental: Yosemite Lodge (372-1208) and **Curry Village** (372-8319) for $5.25 per hr., $20 per day. Both open daily 8:30am-6pm, weather permitting.

Equipment Rental: Yosemite Mountaineering School (372-8344 or 372-1244), on Rte. 120 at Tuolumne Meadows. Sleeping bags $10 per day, backpacks $8 per day; 3rd day half-price. Climbing shoes rented to YMS students only. Driver's license or credit card required for deposit. Open daily 8:30am-noon and 1-5pm. For info on ski and snowshoe rental, see **Wintertime in Yosemite,** p. 273.

Rafting: All Outdoors, 1250 Pine St. #103, Walnut Creek 94596 (925-932-8993 or 800-24-RAFTS/247-2387). Trips on north fork of Stanislaus River (leave from Calaveras Big Trees State Park), Merced River (Mt. View Store, Midpines), Kaweah River (Kaweah General Store), and Goodwin Canyon (Stanislaus River Park, Sonora).

Horseback Trail Rides: Guided rides start at $35 for 2hr. Stables at: Yosemite Valley (372-8348; open daily 7:30am-5pm); Wawona (375-6502; open daily 7:30am-5pm); Tuolomne Meadows (372-8427; open daily in summer 7:30am-5pm).

24-Hour ATM: Bank of America, in Yosemite Village next to the Art Activity Center. Bank also has a **check-cashing service.** Open daily 8am-4pm.

FROM CREST TO CREST: THE TRAIL OF THE WEST As the longest hiking path in America, the **Pacific Crest Trail (PCT)** snakes, swerves, and scales up 2638 mountainous miles from Mexico to Canada, going through climates from desert to sub-Arctic along the way. True to its name, the PCT always keeps to the crests—the trail maintains an average elevation of over 5000 feet. And PCT dishes out quality as well as quantity; there's one hell of a view from the summit of **Mount Whitney** (14,494ft.), the highest peak in the contiguous United States. Although the PCT was begun in 1968, the trailblazing task was so immense that it was not officially completed until 1993.

No matter how much of the trail you choose to take on, proper supplies, conditioning, and acclimatization are vital. The **Pacific Crest Trail Association** gives tips on how to prepare for the journey. Contact them at 5325 Elkhorn Blvd., Box 256, Sacramento 95842 (916-349-2109 or 888-PC-TRAIL/728-7245; www.pcta.org).

Gas Stations: There is no gas in Yosemite Valley. Tank up in **Crane Flat** (open daily 8am-8pm, tanks open 24hr. with credit card) or **El Portal** (open M-Sa 7am-7pm, Su 8am-7pm) before driving into the High Sierra—prices rise with the elevation.

Swimming Pools: At Yosemite Lodge and Curry Village. Open daily 9am-5pm. $2 per day; free for guests at the Ahwahnee Hotel, Yosemite Lodge, and Curry Village.

Laundromat: In summer, laundry facilities open at **Housekeeping Camp.** Wash $1.25, 10min. dry 25¢. Open daily 7:30am-7pm. In winter, laundry facilities available at **Camp 6,** across the street from the Village Store. Open daily 8am-10pm.

Showers: Facilities available in summer at **Housekeeping Camp** ($2, children $1.50; includes towel and soap; open daily 7am-2pm and 3:30-10pm) and **Curry Village** (open 24hr.). Also at **Tuolumne Meadows** and **White Wolf Lodges** ($2; open daily noon-3:30pm).

EMERGENCY AND COMMUNICATIONS

Weather and Road Conditions: 372-0200. 24hr.

Emergency: 911.

Medical Services: Yosemite Medical Clinic (372-4637), at the eastern end of Yosemite Village. 24hr. emergency room. Walk-in urgent care M-Sa 8am-5pm. Scheduled appointments M-F 8am-5pm.

Internet Access: Yosemite Bug Hostel (966-6666), on Rte. 140 30mi. west of Yosemite in Midpines (see p. 268). Internet access $2 for 15min.

Post Office: Yosemite Village, next to the visitors center. Open M-F 8:30am-5pm, Sa 10am-noon. **Curry Village,** near the registration office. Open June-Sept. M-F 11:30am-3pm. **Yosemite Lodge,** open M-F 9am-4:30pm. **Wawona.** Open M-F 9am-5pm, Sa 9am-noon. **Tuolumne Meadows.** Open M-F 9am-12:30pm and 1:30-4:30pm, Sa 9am-noon. **ZIP Code:** 95389.

AREA CODE	The area code for Yosemite National Park is 209.

ACCOMMODATIONS

INSIDE THE PARK

When American transcendentalist Ralph Waldo Emerson visited Yosemite in 1884, the park's accommodations were so simple that he was awakened in the morning by the clucking of a hen climbing over his bed. These days, Yosemite's accommodations have become much more comfortable. At times, however, you may feel as if you need to be a dignitary of Emerson's stature to get a room in the valley—spring and summer rates are high (suites at the luxurious Ahwahnee Hotel start at $246.50 in season) and space is tight. Advance reservations are *very* necessary and can be (and almost always are) made up to one year in advance by calling 209-252-4848. Rates fluctuate, but tend to be higher on weekends and during the summer (those given below are for summer weekends). Check-in hovers around 11am. **All park lodgings provide access to dining and laundry facilities, showers, and supplies.**

Yosemite Lodge (372-1274), west of Yosemite Village and directly across from Yosemite Falls. Tiny cabins are as close to motel accommodations as the valley gets. Singles and doubles $92, with bath $115.

Curry Village (252-4848), southeast of Yosemite Village. Pool (open 9am-5pm), nightly shows at the amphitheater, snack stands, cafeteria, and, in winter, an ice rink. Back-to-back cabins $65, with bath $83; canvas-sided cabins on raised wooden floors $44.

Tuolumne Meadows Lodge, on Tioga Pass Rd. in northeastern corner of park. Canvas-sided cabins, wood stoves, no electricity. Doubles $48; additional adult $8, child $4.

White Wolf Lodge, on Tioga Pass Rd. in the western area of the park. Cabins with bath $73; tent cabin doubles $48; each additional adult $8, child $4.

The Redwoods in Yosemite (375-6666), 22mi. south of Yosemite Valley in Wawona. Rentals of 129 fully equipped homes with 1-6 bedrooms, fireplaces, patios, BBQs, full kitchens, and maid service. June-Aug. and holidays 3-night min. stay, Sept.-May 2-night min. stay. From $110 in peak season.

Housekeeping Camp, west of Curry Village. Canvas-capped concrete "cottages" that accommodate up to 4 people (6 with cots) and include 2 bunk beds, a double bed, a picnic table, a firepit with grille, lights, and electrical outlets. Cottages $47.

OUTSIDE THE PARK

Lodgings in the park can seem like a status symbol: the emblem of a wealthy and conscientious planner. However, all is not lost if one stays outside the park. For the same price as a canvas cabin in the valley it is possible to find high-quality hotel accommodations in quiet and scenic areas. For more info on gateway towns and accommodations, access the **Yosemite Area Traveler Information (YATI)** web site (www.yosemite.com); YATI has computer terminals at the Yosemite Valley Visitors Center (see p. 266), the Greater Merced Chamber of Commerce (see p. 303), the Yosemite Sierra Visitors Bureau (see p. 306), and the Tuolomne County Visitors Bureau (see p. 314).

Yosemite Bug Hostel (966-6666), on Rte. 140 in Midpines 30mi. west of Yosemite. Look carefully for sign. Up in the woods, a low-budget resort spot. International crowd lounging in hammocks, beer on tap, pool table, dartboard, kitchen, library, swimmin' hole. Offers outdoor expeditions, mountain bike rental, rafting trips, and tremendous food ($3.50-8). Discounts on public transportation (45min., $5.50) to park. Internet access $2 for 15min. Dorm beds $15; tent sites $17.

Oakhurst Lodge, 40302 Rte. 41, Oakhurst (683-4417 or 800–OK-LODGE/655-6343). Clean, simple motel rooms with shag carpeting, pool, large grassy back lawn. By far the lowest prices in town. 1 queen bed $65 ($45 with various coupons); 2 queen beds $70-88.

Yosemite View Lodge (379-2681 or 800-321-5261), on Rte. 140 in El Portal just outside the park. Huge hotel squats on the banks of the Merced River. Pools, jacuzzis, high-vaulted wood ceilings. Descend from the mountains and loiter in luxury. Plenty of expensive rooms, and 10 affordable rooms with queen beds for $69.

CAMPGROUNDS

To many visitors, Yosemite is camping country; most of the valley's campgrounds are choked with tents, trailers, and RVs. Reservations can be made up to five months in advance (800-436-7275, TDD 888-530-9796, outside the U.S. 301-722-1257; www.reservations.nps.gov; phones and web site available for reservations daily 7am-7pm, or mail NPRS, P.O. Box 1600, Cumberland, MD 21502). Cancellation lotteries are held at the campground reservations office in Curry Village (daily 8am and 3pm), but the odds are against you. In summer, there is a 7-night maximum stay for those in the valley or at Wawona, and a 14-night maximum stay for campers outside the valley (except Wawona). Natural stream water (serving Tamarack Flat, Yosemite Creek, and Porcupine Flat), must be boiled, filtered, or treated to prevent giardia (an intestinal disease). Iodine water treatments can be bought at any supply store. Backcountry camping is prohibited in the valley, but is encouraged outside it (see **Beyond Yosemite Valley: Backcountry,** p. 273).

IN YOSEMITE VALLEY

Sunnyside, at the western end of the valley past Yosemite Lodge. The only first-come, first-camped site in the valley. Pervaded by a climbing subculture with seasoned adventurers swapping stories of exploits on vertical rock faces. Be prepared to meet new friends, since every site is filled with 6 people, regardless of group size. Water, toilets, and tables. 35 sites fill up early. $3 per person. No reservations. Open year-round.

Lower Pines, in the busy eastern end of Yosemite Valley. Commercial and crowded, with cars driving by. Pets allowed. Water, toilets, tables, and showers. Sites $15.

BEYOND YOSEMITE VALLEY

Outside of the valley campsite quality vastly improves. All of the parks' campgrounds have at least 50 sites, and all have RV sites except for Tamarack Flat, Yosemite Creek, and Porcupine Flat. **All sites have firepits and nearby parking.**

Hodgdon Meadow, on Rte. 120 near Big Oak Flat entrance 25mi. from valley. Warm enough for winter camping. 105 thickly wooded sites provide some seclusion even when the campground is full. Beautiful area. Water, toilets, and tables. May-Sept. sites $15; first-come, first-camped Oct.-Apr. $10.

Tuolumne Meadows, on Rte. 120 55mi. east of valley. 157 sites require advance reservations, 157 saved for same-day reservations. Drive into the sprawling campground or escape the RVs by ambling to the 25 sites saved for hikers without cars. Great scenery and nearby trailheads. Pets in western section only. Water, toilets, and tables. Drive-in sites $15; backpacker sites $3 per person. Open July-Sept., depending on snowpack.

Wawona, off Rte. 41 27mi. south of valley. Plain and simple, these 100 wooded sites are near the Merced River. Water, flush toilets, and tables. No showers. Pets allowed. Sites $15. May-Sept. reservations required; first-come, first-camped Oct.-Apr.

Tamarack Flat, 23mi. northeast of valley. Take Rte. 120E and follow the rough road for 3mi. (if your car can take it; not recommended for RVs and trailers). 52 rustic drive-in sites. Fewer amenities mean Tamarack fills up later than other campgrounds, but hardy campers enjoy awe-inspiring views from nearby hillsides. Pets allowed. No water. Pit toilets. Sites $6. First-come, first-camped. Open June-Sept.

Bridalveil Creek, 25mi. south of valley on Glacier Point Rd. Peaceful grounds convenient to Glacier and Taft Points; 2min. walk to beautiful McGurk Meadow. 110 sites. Water, flush toilets, tables. Sites $10. First-come, first-camped. Open July-early Sept.

Porcupine Flat, off Rte. 120E 38mi. from valley. RV access to front section. Stream water, pit toilets. 52 sites $6. First-come, first-camped. Open late July-early Sept.

White Wolf, off Rte. 120E 31mi. from the valley. Water, flush toilets, tables. Pets allowed. 87 sites $10. Open late July-early Sept., depending on snowpack.

FOOD

In general, restaurants in the park are nothing special. Cooking a campfire feast is a much more interesting and affordable option. A slim supply of pricey groceries can be found at the Yosemite Lodge, Wawona, or Village Stores (all 3 open daily June-Sept. 8am-10pm; Oct.-May 8am-9pm). Consider buying all of your cooking supplies, marshmallows, and batteries in Merced, Fresno, or Oakhurst en route to the park. These gateway towns are also home to many affordable restaurants.

IN THE VALLEY

Yosemite's center of commerce is crammed with people at lunchtime. Although many of the food options are takeout, people tend to carry their food about 15 feet to the cement patio peppered with picnic tables which is about as relaxing as going to the dentist—avoid it by buying a portable meal in the heart of the village and eating it somewhere else.

Degnan's Delicatessen, in Yosemite Village. Inside a convenience store and adjacent to an ice cream parlor/pizza place. Huge $4 sandwiches. Open daily 7am-10:30pm.

Pasta Plus (372-8381), in Yosemite Village above Degnan's Deli. A clean sit-down restaurant that serves dependable pasta, plus salads and meat. Pasta ($5) and caesar salad ($4.30). Open daily 11:30am-9pm.

Village Grill. A low-priced snack bar with an artery-clogging dose of good ol' grease. Hamburgers $3. Open daily 11am-5pm.

OUTSIDE YOSEMITE VALLEY

Other restaurants in the park are generally in the hotels. Check Yosemite's publications for smorgasbords and lunchtime bargains. The **Garden Terrace** (372-1269), in Yosemite Lodge, serves an all-you-can-eat buffet (daily noon-8:30pm; $8, with meat after 4:30pm, $12). The **Pavilion** (379-2183), on Rte. 140 at the Yosemite View Lodge in El Portal, fancies itself fine dining. A new building of gleaming wood, it also features a high wooden ceiling, a manly stone fireplace, tablecloths, and tourists. Fuel up at breakfast with two eggs, two pancakes, and two pieces of breakfast meat ($5.50; open 7-11am and 5-10pm.) Seven miles down the road at the **Cedar Lodge Restaurant** (379-2316), on Rte. 140 in El Portal, food is available nearly all day (open daily 6:30am-10pm, lounge serves meals until 2am).

SUMMERTIME SIGHTS: THE OUTDOORS

For wintertime sights and activities, see p. 273.

BY CAR

Although the view is better if you get out of the car, you can see a large portion of Yosemite from the bucket seat. The **Yosemite Road Guide** ($4 at every visitors center) is keyed to roadside markers and outlines a superb tour of the park—it's almost like having a ranger tied to the hood. Spectacular panoramas are omnipresent during the drive east along **Tioga Pass Road (Route 120).** This stretch of road is the highest highway strip in the country; as it winds down from Tioga Pass through the park's eastern exit, it plunges over a mile to reach the lunar landscape of Mono Lake. The drive west from the pass brings you to **Tuolumne Meadows** and its open spaces and rippling creeks, to shimmering Tenaya Lake, and countless scenic views of granite slopes and canyons. No less incredible are the views afforded by the southern approach, **Route 41,** to Yosemite. Most recognizable is the Wawona Tunnel turnout, which most visitors will immediately recognize as the subject of many Ansel Adams photographs. **El Capitan,** the largest granite monolith in the world (at 7569ft.), looms over awestruck crowds. If you stop and look closely (with binoculars if possible), you will see what appear to be specks of dust moving on the mountain face—they are actually world-class climbers inching toward fame. At night their flashlights shine from impromptu hammocks pounded into granite as the climbers flee Yosemite campground fees. Nearby, **Three Brothers** (3 adjacent granite peaks) and misty **Bridalveil Falls** pose for hundreds of snapshots every day. A drive into the heart of the valley leads to **Yosemite Falls** (the highest in North America at 2425ft.), **Sentinel Rock,** and mighty **Half Dome.**

Glacier Point, off Glacier Point Rd., opens up a different perspective on the valley. This gripping overlook, 3214 feet above the valley floor, is guaranteed to impress even the most jaded traveler. Half Dome rests majestically across the valley, and the sounds of Vernal and Nevada Falls provide enough white noise to drown out the roar of the tour buses and their ceaselessly chattering passengers. When the moon is full, this is an extraordinary (and very popular) place to visit. Arrive at sunset and watch the fiery fade of day over the valley: the sky dims, the stars appear, the bottom sides of clouds in the east begin to glow bright silver, and from behind some nearby mountains the blinding full moon crosses the horizon.

To investigate Yosemite's most famous flora, take the short hiking trail through the giant sequoia of **Mariposa Grove.** This interpretive walk begins off Rte. 241 at the Fallen Monarch, a massive trunk lying on its side, and continues to both the 209-foot-tall, 2700-year-old Grizzly Giant and the fallen Wawona Tunnel Tree. Ancient Athens was in its glory when many of these trees were saplings.

DAY HIKING IN THE VALLEY

To have the full Yosemite experience, visitors must travel the outer trails on foot. A wealth of opportunities reward anyone willing to lace up a pair of boots, even if only for a daytrip. Day-use trails are usually as busy as the New York Stock

Exchange, and are sometimes as packed as a U2 concert. Hiking just after sunrise is the best, and sometimes only, way to beat the crowds. But even then, trails like Half Dome are already busy. A colorful trail map with difficulty ratings and average hiking times is available at the visitors center (50¢; see **Yosemite Valley Visitors Center**, p. 266). **Bridalveil Falls,** another Ansel Adams favorite, is an easy ¼-mile stroll from the nearby shuttle bus stop, and its cool spray is as close to a shower as many Yosemite campers ever get. The **Mirror Lake Loop** is a level three-mile walk. These two trails, as well as **Lower Yosemite Falls Trail,** are wheelchair accessible.

Upper Yosemite Falls Trail, a back-breaking 3½-mile trek to the windy summit, rewards the intrepid hiker with an overview of the 2425-foot drop. Those with energy to spare can trudge on to **Inspiration Point,** where views of the valley below rival those from more-heralded Glacier Point. The trail begins with an extremely steep, unshaded ascent. Leaving the marked trail is not a wise idea—a sign warns, "If you go over the waterfall, you will die."

From the Happy Isles trailhead, the **John Muir Trail** leads 211 miles to Mt. Whitney, but most visitors prefer to take the slightly less strenuous 1½-mile **Mist Trail** past **Vernal Falls** (only visible from this trail) to the top of **Nevada Falls.** This is perhaps the most popular day-use trail in the park, and with good reason—views of the falls from the trails are outstanding, and the indefatigable drizzle that issues from the nearby water-assaulted rocks is more than welcome during the hot summer months. There is a free shuttle from the valley campgrounds to Happy Isles; no parking is available. The Mist Trail continues past Nevada Falls to the base of **Half Dome,** Yosemite's most recognizable monument and a powerful testament to the power of glaciation. Dedicated hikers trek to the top and enjoy the unimaginable vista of the valley. The hike is 17 miles round-trip, rises a total of 4800 vertical feet and takes a full day (6-12hr.). The final 800 feet of the walk to the rock-star peak is a steep climb up the backside of the famous rock face. Equipped with cables to aid non-climbing folks, this final challenge is well worth the thrill of sitting on top of the world and imagining yourself its king. Enthusiasts of all ages and global origin share high-fives with adrenaline-silly strangers, help each other out with cheers like "YOU'RE ALMOST THERE!," and learn a slew of new jokes from wakky Afrikaaners.

The wildflower-laden **Pohon Trail** starts from Glacier Point, crossing Sentinel River (spectacular Sentinel Falls, the park's second-largest cascade, lies to the north) on its way to **Taft Point** and other secluded lookouts. A hikers' bus leaves from the valley in the morning for the Four Mile Trail (4¾mi. one-way) and the Panorama Trail (8mi. one-way), both of which also start at Glacier Point.

CLIMBING, WATER, BIRD, AND CONSERVATIONIST ACTIVITIES

The world's best **climbers** come to Yosemite to test themselves at angles past vertical. If you've got the courage (and the cash), you can join the stellar Yosemite rock climbers by taking a lesson with the **Yosemite Mountaineering School** (372-8344), Yosemite 95389. Basic rock-climbing classes (mid-Apr. to Oct.) teach basic skills on the ground such as bouldering, rappelling, and ascending an 80-foot-high cliff. Reservations are useful and require advance payment, although drop-ins are accepted if space allows. (Open daily 8:30am-5pm. Classes with 3-6 people $70, individual courses $170. Intermediate lessons on weekends and alternating weekdays $80-90. Advanced classes also offered.)

Fishing is allowed April through November in any of Yosemite's lakes, streams, or rivers, but don't expect to catch anything. Every year a few of the lakes are selected to be stocked with trout, but the names of these lakes are not made public. Anglers may obtain a fishing license from grocery or sporting goods stores in Yosemite Valley, Wawona, Tuolumne, and White Wolf. (Resident annual license $27.55; 2-day license $10; non-resident 10-day license $27.55; under 17 fish free. There are also 2 free fishing days per season. Consult the "Fishing in Yosemite National Park" handout for specific guidelines and dates.) Tackle is available at the **Village Sport Shop** (372-1286; open daily 8:30am-7pm).

Rafting is permitted on the Merced River (10am-4pm), but no motorized crafts are allowed. Swimming is allowed throughout the park except where posted. Those who prefer their water chlorinated can swim in the public pools at Curry Village and Yosemite Lodge (open daily 9am-5pm; admission $2 for non-guests).

Bird-watchers can pick up a field checklist at the visitors center. Those inspired by Muir's conservationism can join a group of **ecotourists** who restore damaged park assets and help maintain natural habitats (for info call 372-0265).

ORGANIZED ACTIVITIES

Park rangers lead a variety of informative hikes and other activities for visitors of all ages. **Junior ranger** (ages 8-10) and **senior ranger** (ages 11-12) activities allow children to hike, raft, and investigate aquatic and terrestrial life. The programs are usually held mid-week. (Programs $2. Reservations required at least a day in advance through the **Yosemite Valley Visitors Center,** see p. 266.)

Rangers also guide a number of free walks. **Discover Yosemite Family Programs** address a variety of historical and geological topics. (3hr., daily 9am; most wheelchair accessible). Rangers also lead strenuous **Destination Hikes** into the high country from Tuolumne Meadows (4-8hr.) Other free, park-sponsored adventures include **photographic hikes,** which are lesson-adventures led by professional photographers (1½hr.; sign up and meet at the **Ansel Adams Gallery,** see below). **Sunrise photo walks** leave most mornings from the Yosemite Lodge tour desk (free). The **Glacier Point Sunset Photo Shoot** is offered Thursday nights from June to September. Bring lots of film; this is an incredible spot, especially at sunset. Late in the day the valley rests in blues and purples; a tripod (even if makeshift) is helpful when capturing this on film. The workshop with a professional photographer is free, but the scenic tram ride up to the point is not ($20.50; departs 1hr. before the meeting time and returns 4hr. later). You have the option of driving yourself, however, and meeting the group at the Glacier Point Amphitheater.

In 1903, John Muir gave Teddy Roosevelt a now-famous tour of Yosemite. The renowned thespian Lee Stetson has assumed Muir's role, leading hikes along the same route (1hr.; free). Stetson also hosts **The Spirit of John Muir,** a one-man show (90min.; W and Sa 8pm; admission $7, seniors $6, under 12 $3), and **Conversation with a Tramp** (Tu and F 8pm; $7, seniors $6, under 12 $2). There are six different theatrical presentations, including *Yosemite by Song and Story* and the moving picture *Friendly Fire: A Forty-Niner's Life with The Yosemite Indians*, which tells the true story of a once-prejudiced man who learns to love the region's Native Americans. (1hr.; M-W 8:30pm. Admission $6, seniors $5, under 12 $3. Tickets sold at Yosemite Theater.)

The **Ansel Adams Gallery** (372-4413), next to the visitors center, is more like an artsy gift shop/activity center. Sign up for a fine-print viewing to see the precious stuff (open daily 9am-6pm). The newly formed **journaling workshop** is a refreshing retreat in which experienced writers take small groups to scenic places and encourage them to write. The **Art Activity Center** (372-1442), in Yosemite Village, takes pride in its artist-in-residence program and offers an art instruction class. (Center open daily 9:30am-5pm. Class offered daily 10am-2pm. Advance signup recommended. Supplies not included, but are for sale at the center.)

Just behind the gallery, see Native American cultural events in the **Miwok-Paiute Village.** Take a walk through a melange of Native American tepees, placards describing indigenous fauna, and large dioramas that recycle hokey narration when you press **the red button.** The large *Hangie* (round house) is a humbling piece of construction that still serves as a cultural center for local Miwok and Paiute Indians (village open dusk to dawn). Further interpretive information can be garnered at the **Yosemite Village Museum,** next to the visitors center. Inside is a reconstruction of an Ahwahnee village and a modest art collection, including some restaurant-bathroom-style pieces of Yosemite-related subject matter (open daily 8am-5:30pm).

BEYOND YOSEMITE VALLEY: BACKCOUNTRY

Most folks never leave the valley, but a wilder, more isolated Yosemite awaits those who do. The Wilderness Center in Yosemite Valley offers maps and personalized assistance for those who choose to leave the valley. (For advice on keeping yourself and the wilderness intact, see **Essentials: Wilderness Safety,** p. 51.) Topographical maps and hiking guides are especially helpful in navigating Yosemite's nether regions. Equipment can be rented or purchased at the Mountaineering School at Tuolomne Meadows (see **Equipment Rental,** p. 266) or at the Mountain Shop at Curry Village, but backpacking stores in major cities are less expensive.

Backcountry camping is prohibited in the valley (those caught are slapped with a stiff $60 fine and evicted from the park), but is generally permitted along the high-country trails with a free wilderness permit (see **Wilderness Center,** p. 266); each trailhead limits the number of permits available. There is a 50% quota held on 24-hour notice at the Yosemite Valley Visitors Center, the Wawona Ranger Station, and Big Oak Flat Station (see **Visitor Information,** p. 265). The system for requesting permits will be changing in the year 2000; in late 1999 reservations can be made by phone or by mail (up to 1 year in advance), but call or write for up-to-date reservation information for 2000. Popular trails like Little Yosemite Valley, Clouds Rest, and Half Dome fill quotas quickly. (Permits free; reservations $3. Call 372-0740 or write Wilderness Permits, P.O. Box 545, Yosemite National Park 95389.)

In the high country, many hikers stay at the undeveloped mountain campgrounds, which offer both company (to feed the soul) and bear lockers (to seal the food). Hikers can also store food in hanging bear bags (see **Bears Will Eat You,** p. 51) or in rented plastic canisters from the Yosemite Valley Sports Shop ($3 per day). Canisters are highly recommended and may be mandatory in some areas—bear-bagging is considered mainly a delay tactic.

Several high country hikes provide access to seldom-seen, out-of-the-way regions of the park. Some trailheads are accessible by a free shuttle bus to Tuolumne Meadows. For a taste of "real" rock climbing without requisite equipment and training, Yosemite day hikers and climbers clamber up **Lembert Dome** above Tuolumne Meadows. This gentle (by rock climbing standards) incline riddled with foot and hand holds is nonetheless a solid granite face. The four-mile approach to **Cathedral Lakes** from the west end of the meadows is another worthwhile hike and camping spot, winding its way through dense forest to the Cathedral Lakes basin. For those hikers with something more rigorous in mind, a tough scramble past **May Lake** leads to the peak of **Mount Hoffman** (10,850ft.). Visitors should attempt new or unfamiliar trails—scarcely a hike exists in Yosemite that doesn't give hikers jaw-dropping vistas and quiet moments of harmony with the elements.

WINTERTIME IN YOSEMITE

Icy waterfalls and meadows masked with snow dramatically transform Yosemite's landscape in its quietest season. The Sierra is known for heavy winter snowfall, and Yosemite is no exception, but unlike the rest of the range, Yosemite remains accessible year-round. **Route 140** from Merced, a designated all-weather entrance, is usually open and clear. Although Tioga Pass and Glacier Point Rd. invariably close at the first sign of snowfall, **Route 41** from the south typically remains traversable. **Verify road conditions before traveling** (372-0200), and carry chains.

Many valley facilities remain open even during the harshest winters. Camping is generally permitted in Lower Pines, Sunnyside (Camp 4), Hodgden Meadows, and Wawona, and most indoor accommodations offer big off-season reductions. Park tours move "indoors" to heated buses, and even the Merced and Fresno buses (see **Getting There and Around,** p. 262) operate when road conditions permit. Many say this is the best time to find peace in this national playground.

Cross-country skiing is free, and several well-marked trails cut into the backcountry of the valley's South Rim at Badger Pass and Crane Flat. Both areas have markers on the trees so trails can be followed even under several feet of snow; this same snow transforms many summer hiking trails into increasingly popular **snowshoe trails.** Rangers host several snowshoe walks, but the serene winter forests are perhaps best explored *sans* guidance. Snowshoes and cross-country skis can be rented from the **Yosemite Mountaineering School** (see p. 266). **Badger Pass Rental Shop** (see below) also rents winter equipment and downhill skis.

The state's oldest ski resort, **Badger Pass Ski Area** (372-8430), on Glacier Point Rd. south of Yosemite Valley, is the only downhill ski area in the park. Its family-fun atmosphere fosters learning and restraint (no snowboards). Free shuttles connect Badger Pass with Yosemite Valley. (Group ski lessons $22 for 2hr., private lessons from $44. Rental packages $18 per day, under 12 $13. 1-day lift tickets M-F $22, Sa-Su $28; under 12 $13, some specials for those over 60 or exactly 40. Some weekday discounts available through Yosemite Lodge. Lifts open 9am-4:30pm.)

Ice skating at Curry Village is a beautiful, if cold, experience with Half Dome towering above the outdoor rink encircled by snow-covered pines. (Open in winter M-F noon-9:30pm, Sa-Su 8:30am-9:30pm. Admission $5; skate rental $2.) **Sledding** and **tobogganing** are permitted at Crane Flat, off Rte. 120.

STANISLAUS NATIONAL FOREST

This highly preserved land circles Yosemite and connects the forests along the northern Sierra. Well-maintained roads and campsites, craggy peaks, dozens of topaz lakes, wildflower meadows, and forests of Ponderosa pines make up the 900,000 acres of the Stanislaus National Forest. Here, peregrine falcons, bald eagles, mountain lions, and bears sometimes surprise the lucky or tasty traveler. In addition to great fishing, campsites, and hiking trails, Stanislaus offers a chance for some solitude—something its better-known neighbor, Yosemite, doesn't have.

Park headquarters are at 19777 Greenly Rd., Sonora (532-3671; open in summer daily 8am-5pm; call for winter hours). Camping permits are required for Carson-Iceberg, Mokelumne, and Emigrant Wilderness; permits are also needed for building fires in wilderness areas. Only Pinecrest accepts reservations; all other sites are available on a first-come, first-camped basis. For outdoor information in the area, see **Gold Country** (p. 308) and **Sonora** (p. 314).

ALONG ROUTES 4 AND 108

For a quick, scenic tour of the forest, the curvy and narrow drives along Rte. 4 or 108 are local favorites. Drivers are rewarded by the views from over Ebbett's Pass and Pacific Grade Summit. Be aware, however, that roads are often closed in winter and occasionally through much of the fall and spring—call the district office in the area where you wish to travel to find out the status of its roads.

THE SUMMIT DISTRICT

The most popular spot in the Emigrant Wilderness, the Summit District sits quietly with well-maintained trails and pristine lakes. The **ranger station,** 1 Pinecrest Lake Rd. (965-3434), off Rte. 108 at Pinecrest Lake, has info on all the camping and recreational activities in the area. (Open in summer M-Sa 8am-5pm, Su and holidays 8am-4:30pm; in winter M-Sa 8am-4:30pm.) **Campsites** abound to the east along Rte. 108. Cascade Creek, 11 miles from the ranger station, and Niagara, 16 miles from the station on Eagle Meadow Rd., both have beautiful sites, but neither have running water ($5). Pinecrest (reservations 800-280-CAMP/2267; TDD 800-879-4496), a half-mile from the ranger station, has 200 campsites, drinking water, and flush toilets, and is a five-minute walk to the beach (open May-Oct.; sites $15). The only free campground in the area is Beardsley Dam, which is right on the lake just off the (lightly trafficked) road (12 sites).

Pinecrest Lake, about 30 miles east of Sonora on Rte. 108, is popular with parents entertaining kids. The alpine lake, set amidst granite mountains and several thousand pine trees, serves as a small resort area. **Boat rental** is available at the marina (kayaks $6 per hr., sailboats $22 for 2hr., paddleboats $9 per hr.). Motorboats are a bargain ($25 for 2hr.), or rent out a 15-person party boat for a day ($175). Waterskiing is not allowed on the lake.

Route 108 follows the shape of Yosemite around its northeastern section from Sonora about 60 miles to the Sonora pass into Yosemite, or 70 miles to U.S. 395. This drive through the **Stanislaus Summit District** is fairly isolated and connects with no other major roads. Select from among the **self-guided trails** available at the Sonora ranger station (the numbered stakes that dot the trails are confusing). The trail names are generally more fantastic than the events they describe. The **Trail of the Gargoyles,** east of the station off Rte. 108 on Herring Creek Rd., is lined with shapely geological formations, documenting nature's labor in lava flows, *lahar* (hardened mud), and ash. The **Trail of the Ancient Dwarves,** on Rte. 108 15 miles east of Pinecrest, provides great views of the mountain range as it follows a line of bonsai trees. For stunning views of the **Stanislaus River** and its dammed reservoir, take Rte. 108 18 miles east of Pinecrest to **Donnell Vista.**

THE CARSON-ICEBERG WILDERNESS

In the northeastern section of the forest, due north of Yosemite, bordered by Rte. 4, U.S. 395, and Rte. 108, this wilderness reserve is steeped in Stanislaus's solitude. The absence of lakes and the steep terrain in this region eliminate it from most itineraries, but high mountain peaks, meadows, and wildflowers reward the adventurous traveler. Stanislaus Peak and Sonora Peak are accessible from the Pacific Crest Trail (for more info, see **From Crest to Crest: the Trail of the West,** p. 266) and give persevering climbers a humbling panorama of the Sierra. The Pacific Coast Trail includes a five-mile round-trip cross-country scramble from **Saint Mary's Pass,** one mile before **Sonora Pass** on Rte. 108. It has one of the best views of the valley, but the 3000-foot climb is tiring.

THE CALAVERAS DISTRICT

Right between the historic Gold Country (see **Gold Country,** p. 308) and crowd-pleaser Yosemite, the Calaveras District is proud to be a frill-free forest. The **ranger station,** 5341 Rte. 4 (795-1381), at Hathaway Pines, contains the Dardanelles, a series of volcanic by-products (open M-F 8am-5pm, Sa 8am-3pm). **Spicer campground,** eight miles southwest of Rte. 4 at the reservoir, has piped water, pit toilets, and wheelchair access (sites $12; open June-Oct.).

THE GROVELAND DISTRICT

The Groveland District covers the area south of Sonora and west of Yosemite, and serves as the overflow destination for Yosemite campers. The **ranger station,** 24545 Rte. 120 (962-7825), is nine miles west of Groveland (open M-Sa 8am-4:30pm). **Carlon** is the closest campsite to the entrance (pit toilets and potable water; free). **Little Nellio Falls** lies in the district's deserted southeastern corner. The Groveland District is logged and littered with pockets of private property, as is the Miwok District—the more interesting districts lie to the north.

Cherry Creek Canyon, a bit scarred from a recent fire, is north of Cherry Lake just west of Yosemite. The glacier-carved canyon has just enough walking space at its floor for hikers. A trailhead at **Eagle Meadow** leads down to Coopers Meadow and Three Chimneys, a brick-red volcanic formation.

SIERRA NATIONAL FOREST

Covering 1.3 million acres, the Sierra National Forest fills the gap between Yosemite National Park and Sequoia and Kings Canyon National Parks. Its terrain is diverse, encompassing both the alpine peaks of the Sierra Nevada and the oak-covered foothills on the edge of the San Joaquin Valley. The region's rivers and lakes serve as recreational centers for the national forest activities. Information on these centers and other popular destinations can be obtained in spades at the **Sierra National Forest Supervisor's Office,** 1600 Tollhouse Rd. (297-0706), off Rte. 168 just outside the gateway town of Clovis (open M-F 8am-4:30pm).

A **backcountry permit** is required for all of the designated wilderness areas, which constitute 46% of the forest, except for Dinkey Lakes. Obtain permits for the John Muir and Kaiser Wilderness areas by writing the Pineridge District, and permits for the Ansel Wilderness by writing the Mariposa/Minarets District (see below for addresses). Trailhead quotas are in effect from July to Labor Day (Sept. 4 in 2000). Some first-come, first-served permits are offered daily, but quotas fill quickly. It is also possible to write away for an advance reservation ($3 per person).

Information on the northwestern Mariposa District can be obtained by calling or writing the **Mariposa/Minarets Ranger District Office,** 57003 Rd. 225, North Fork, P.O. Box 10 93643 (877-2218; open in summer M-Sa 8am-4:30pm, in winter M-F 8am-4:30pm). **Bass Lake** is thronged in summer by parched San Joaquin Valley residents, who take advantage of fishing, boating, and waterskiing opportunities. **Lupine** and **Cedar Campgrounds** are open year-round for strong-willed ice fishers or wintertime Yosemite patrons (sites $16). Some of the best **hikes** in the Sierra are also nearby. **Nelder Grove** contains a campground and a one-mile trail through 106 seldom-visited sequoia. A separate trail affords the rare opportunity to see the Bull Buck Tree, a 246-foot giant, without the gaping crowds. The lonely **Willow Creek Trail,** which passes both Angel Falls and the aptly named **Devil's Slide Waterfall** en route to McLeod Flat Rd., is another option, as is the meandering Way of the Mono Trail. (Take Rte. 41 to the Bass Lake turn-off and follow Rd. 222 about 4mi. to the parking lot at the trailhead.) **Forks** is another pleasant campground, right by the lake, with flush toilets (check-out 2pm; sites $16).

The far reaches of the **Kings River District** rise as high as 13,000 feet at the Sierra Crest. Most of the region's activity centers around the actually-quite-large Dinkey Creek area and the Pine Flat Reservoir, where there is a paved road. **Whitewater rafting** on the Kings River is popular, especially in spring. **Kings River Expeditions** (233-4881) offers a variety of guided trips; get a group together to reduce costs (open M-F 8am-5:30pm). Trail bikes and four-wheel-drive vehicles raise dust on the five off-highway routes that provide access to camping and fishing.

Easily accessible from Rte. 168, the **Pineridge District** is the forest's most popular region. The **Pineridge Ranger District Office,** 29688 Auberry Rd., P.O. Box 559, Prather (855-5355), is one of the forest's busiest centers (open daily 8am-4:30pm). The **Shaver Lake Chamber of Commerce,** 41930 Tollhouse Rd., P.O. Box 58, Shaver Lake (841-3350), also provides info (open W-Su 10am-3pm). **Huntington Lake** lies farther east along Rte. 168, and its shimmering waters see a lot of use. Sailboat regattas occur all summer, while in winter cross-country ski trails, snowmobile routes, and rollicking "snowplay" areas are maintained along Rte. 168. Beyond Kaiser Pass, the road becomes narrow and slightly treacherous—honk your horn on the sharp blind turns. The terrain at the upper end of this road is definitively High Sierra—alpine lakes, flowers, and craggy summits. Mountain bikers can enjoy dozens of trails ranging from the leisurely Tamarack Trail to the Dusy/Ershin Rd.

SEQUOIA NATIONAL FOREST

The Sequoia National Forest is a majestic mountain range that continues its southward march 60 miles below the park boundary before petering out in the low ranges of the Mojave Desert. The forest is bounded on the north by the Kings River, on the west by the San Joaquin Valley, and on the east by the Owens Valley. The Kern River slices through its middle.

The **forest headquarters,** 900 W. Grand Ave., Porterville (784-1500), on Rte. 65, 15 miles east of Rte. 99, offers handouts and detailed maps of the forest ($4.30) featuring the national forest's six designated wilderness areas. There is now a park fee to enter the northern part of the forest (headquarters open M-F 8am-4:30pm). Featured on this map are the national forest's six designated wilderness areas. Backcountry excursions to the **Golden Trout Wilderness** require wilderness permits, available at any district ranger's office. The **Hume Lake Ranger District Office,** 35860 E. Kings Canyon Rd., Dunlap (338-2251), on Rte. 180 east of Fresno near the forest entrance, provides camping info (open Memorial Day-Labor Day (May 29-Sept. 4 in 2000) M-Sa 8am-4:30pm; Labor Day-Memorial Day M-F 8am-4:30pm).

Mountain biking is a popular activity on the Kern Plateau, located in the Cannell Meadow District in the middle area of the forest. The Porterville headquarters offers a handout detailing almost 20 national forest biking trails of varying difficulty, most of which include steep descents where bikers can plummet to glory (or to doom). The **Sherman Pass Trail** (intermediate) and the **Boone Meadow Trail** (beginner-intermediate) offer more interesting trails for experienced **hikers** than many of the main trails, and the 2¼-mile **Packsaddle Cave Trail** (trailhead is 16mi. north of Kernville on State Mtn. 99) takes you to its namesake. These trails are "OHV," which means that hikers occasionally share the road with off-road vehicles and horses.

The northern section of Sequoia National Forest surrounds **Kings Canyon Highway,** the road connecting to Kings Canyon National Park's Grant Grove area. The **Hume Lake District** offers ample recreational opportunities and contains the impressively ugly Boole Sequoia and most of the Monarch Wilderness Area.

Hiking in this area is how hiking in a national forest should be: quiet. Experienced hikers can take the **Deer Cove Creek Trail** to Grand Dike's remarkable rock outcropping and wildflowers (trailhead 1mi. before Rte. 180 reenters Kings Canyon National Park near Cedar Grove). More relaxing, the Trail of 100 Giants is a 35-minute walk in the southern section of the forest (across from Redwood Meadow campground along the Western Divide Hwy.). You can see many giant sequoias, and it's evenly paved, making it perfect for wheelchairs and strollers.

THE EASTERN SIERRA

While the western side of the Sierra descends slowly over a number of miles, the eastern side drops off precipitously, its jagged rock faces forming a startling silhouette against the skies above. Although barely visible from the San Joaquin Valley to the west, the peaks of the High Sierra tower fearsomely over Owens Valley to the east and contrast ominously with the desert to the south.

The sharp drop-off is a result of the lifting and faulting processes that shaped the Sierra ridge 10 million years ago. The Sierra's eastern slope traces the fault line where the Owens Valley collapsed to expose 14,000-foot-tall slabs of rock to glaciation. The western slope, watered by cooling ocean air rising to its crest, is carpeted by dense forests at middle elevations. The clouds dissipate before they can cross the entirety of the range, however, leaving the eastern side remarkably arid.

The tiny towns that stretch from Mount Whitney to Yosemite National Park are linked by U.S. 395, the access route to the eastern face of the Sierra. Small as they are, these towns eagerly support the crowds of campers, climbers, and camera-carriers who congregate in the Owens Valley each summer.

SEQUOIA AND KINGS CANYON NATIONAL PARKS

These twin parks may not attract the thunderous hordes of visitors that the "Big Three" (Yellowstone, Yosemite, and the Grand Canyon) do each summer, but Sequoia and Kings Canyon can match any park in the United States sight-for-sight, or at least tree-for-giant-tree. The parks are home to a host of beneedled behemoths, including the General Sherman Tree—47,450 cubic feet of raw, unadulterated lumber and the largest above-ground living organism in the world (an underground fungus discovered in Michigan in 1992 is even larger).

The sequoias tower above emerald meadows, roaring waterfalls, and hidden lakes, and beneath them all lie miles of incredible time-defying underground caverns. Most of these sights can be reached by car or by short walking expeditions, but two-thirds of the parks are completely undeveloped, providing hardy hikers with 800 miles of beautiful backcountry trails. The park entrance fee is $5 for bicycles, pedestrians, and individuals on buses, $10 for cars, and $20 for a year-long pass. All passes are valid in both parks for seven days. Golden Age, Golden Eagle, and Golden Access passes are also accepted.

GETTING THERE AND GETTING AROUND

By car, the two parks can only be accessed from the west. From **Fresno, Route 180** runs east 60 miles to Kings Canyon's Grant Grove entrance and terminates 30 miles later in Cedar Grove at the mouth of the Canyon itself. The road to Cedar Grove is typically closed from November to May due to the threat of winter storms and falling rocks. From **Visalia, Route 198** winds its way past **Lake Kaweah** to Sequioa's Ash Mountain entrance, where it becomes known as the **Generals Highway** for its route between the General Grant and General Sherman Trees. A deliciously serpentine speedway, Rte. 198 snakes through 130 spine-tingling turns and 12 major switchbacks as it ascends 2000 feet. Drivers using the South Entrance should expect intermittent delays between Hospital Rock and Giant Forest, as the park is repairing the road there. Barring long delays, however, the drive from Ash Mountain through Sequoia's Giant Forest to Grant Grove takes about two hours. In winter, Generals Highway is usually covered by over 15 feet of snow, defying even plows and monster trucks. The road is usually open from mid-May to October, permitting entrance deeper into the forest. Rte. 198 branches into the Mineral King turn-off. This road is punctuated by high-country panoramas, but drivers beware—the views make it difficult to steer straight. The only park access from the east is by trail; hikers can enter either park from the **John Muir Wilderness** and the **Inyo National Forest,** both accessible from spur roads off U.S. 395.

Public transportation to the parks is nonexistent, but the limited shuttle service can free you from your car once inside Sequoia (see **Public Transportation,** below).

ORIENTATION AND PRACTICAL INFORMATION

The parks' most popular sights are concentrated in four developed areas: **Giant Forest** and **Mineral King** in Sequoia and **Grant Grove** and **Cedar Grove** in Kings Canyon. Beautiful backcountry comprises the northern two-thirds of Kings Canyon and the eastern two-thirds of Sequoia. Seasonal changes are dramatic in this area of the Sierra. Summer season (Memorial Day-Labor Day, May 28-Sept. 4 in 2000) is the high season, with August being the busiest month; the days are warm and attract flocks of visitors, many of whom are unprepared for plunging nighttime

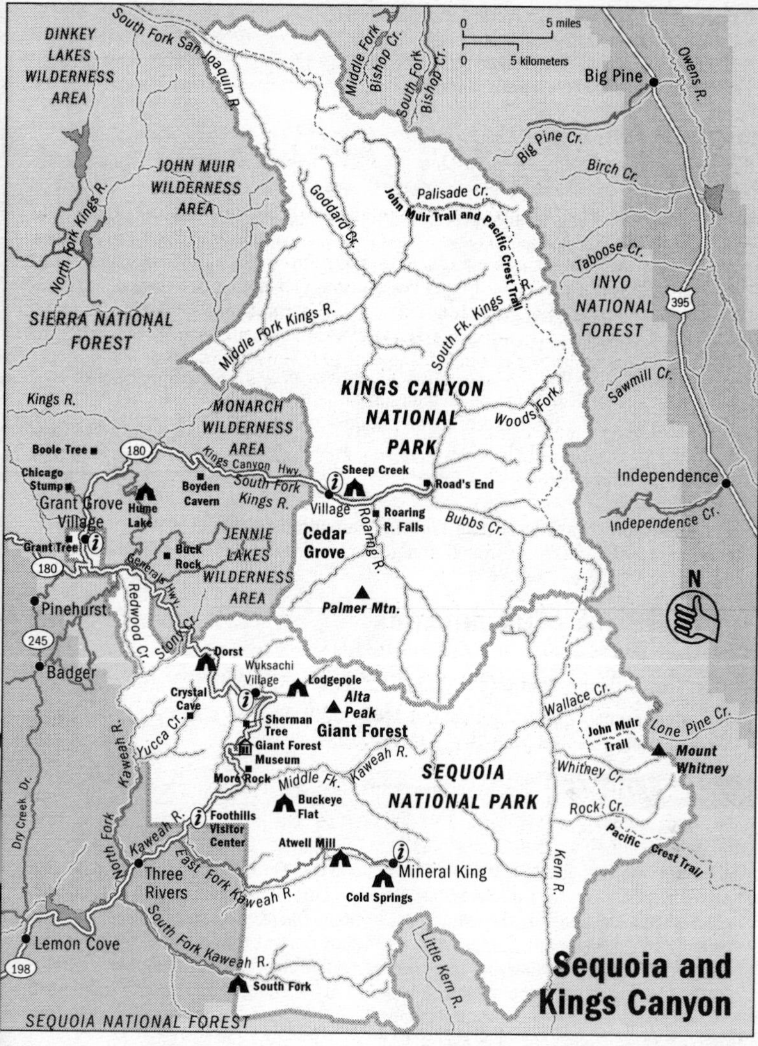

temperatures. Dogwood, aspen, and oak provide brilliant color in October and November. Snow season is from November to March, although some trails may have snow as late as mid-June. Spring here is unpredictable, bringing late storms, low fogs, and runoff flooding.

There are **no banks or ATMs** in either park. Camping supplies, gas, and groceries in the parks are of low quality and high price. The **San Joaquin Valley** (see p. 302), **Reedley** (45mi. west on Rte. 180), **Three Rivers** (8mi. southwest on Rte. 198), and **Visalia** (25mi. southwest on Rte. 198) are better places to stock up.

TRANSPORTATION

Public Transportation: The **free shuttle system** goes from Wuksachi Village in Sequoia National Park to Lodgepole, Wolverton, the General Sherman Tree, Moro Rock, Crescent Meadow, and back (every 15min. daily 9am-6pm). Check schedules at visitors centers and bulletin boards.

Horse Rental: Stables at **Wolverton Pack Station** (565-3039), **Grant** and **Cedar Groves** (565-3464), and **Mineral King** (561-3039) are open daily 8am-6pm and offer guided rides ($15-20 per hr., $75 per day). Rates vary; call for info. Bicycles are not permitted on hiking trails or in the backcountry.

VISITOR INFORMATION

Kings Canyon and Sequoia Main Line (565-3341; www.nps.gov/seki). Offers 24hr. direct contact with a park ranger and dispatch service to any office within the parks.

National Park Service Headquarters (565-3341), on Rte. 198 out of Visalia 1mi. beyond the Three Rivers entrance to Sequoia. Provides info on both parks, maps, local wilderness permits, first aid, bear canisters, and free brochures about the Sequoia Forests in German, French, Spanish, and Japanese. Tickets for the Crystal Cave tour sold here until 4pm, or write Superintendent, Ash Mountain, Three Rivers 93271. Open daily June-Oct. 8am-5pm; Nov.-May 8am-4:30pm.

Backcountry Information (565-3708; fax 565-4239). Wilderness permits are limited by area quotas. One-third of the permits for any given trail are held on a first-come, first-served basis at the trailhead or at the nearest ranger station. Reservation ($10) requests are accepted starting Mar. 1, and at least 3 weeks in advance. For reservations or a copy of "Backcountry Basics" write HCR 89 Box 60, Three Rivers 93271. Open M-F 8am-5pm.

Road Conditions: Park Road and Weather Conditions (565-3341). Info on campgrounds as well. 24hr. recording, updated daily around 9am. **California Highway Patrol** (488-4321 or 734-6767).

EMERGENCY AND COMMUNICATION

Emergency: 911.

Police: Fresno County Sheriff (488-3111). **Tulare County Sheriff** (733-6218).

Hospitals: Fresno Community Hospital (442-6000), at Fresno and R St., in Fresno. **Kaweah Delta Hospital** (625-2211), off Rte. 198, in Visalia.

AREA CODE	Unless otherwise specified, the parks' area code is 559.

SEQUOIA

Visitor Information: Foothills Visitors Center (565-3341), at the park headquarters (see above). Open daily May-Oct. 8am-5pm; Nov.-Apr. 8am-4pm. **Lodgepole Visitors Center** (565-3782), on Generals Hwy. 4mi. east of Giant Forest. Open daily May-Sept. 8am-6pm; Oct.-Apr. 9am-5pm. Campground reservations daily 9am-5pm; wilderness permits 7am-4pm (see **Backcountry Information,** above). **Mineral King Ranger Station** (565-3764), 1mi. before the end of Mineral King Rd., is the headquarters for the remote Mineral King region of the southern park. Maps, hiking info, books, first aid, and wilderness permits. Open in summer daily 7am-3:30pm.

Ski Rental: Sequoia Ski Touring Center (565-3435), Sequoia. Cross-country ski and snowshoe rentals. Open daily 9am-6pm; in winter F-Su 9am-4:30pm.

Gas: Gasoline is not available in the park. The nearest option is in Three Rivers.

Auto Repair: AAA Emergency Road Service (565-3381 or 800-400-4AAA/4222).

Markets: Lodgepole's market is well stocked (open daily 8am-8pm). Two stores in Three Rivers, **Village Market** (open M-Sa 8am-8pm, Su 8am-6pm) and **Three Rivers Market** (open daily 7:45am-7pm), offer better selections and prices. Fresno and Visalia are larger cities, well-endowed with stores and supplies.

Showers: Opposite Lodgepole Visitors Center. $3 per person. Open 8am-1pm and 3-8pm.

Laundromat: Wash $1.25, 10min. dry 25¢. Open 8am-1pm and 3-8pm.

Post Office: At Lodgepole. Open M-F 8:30am-1pm and 1:30-4pm. A stamp machine is in the lobby (open 24hr.). **ZIP Code:** 93262.

KINGS CANYON

Visitor Information: Grant Grove Visitors Center (565-3341), Grant Grove Village, 2mi. east of the Big Stump entrance by Rte. 180. Books, maps, and exhibits. Nightly campfire programs and daily hikes. Open daily in summer 8am-6pm; in winter 9am-5pm. **Cedar Grove Ranger Station** (565-3793), 30mi. farther down Rte. 180 by Kings River. Near trailheads into Kings Canyon high country; ½mi. south of Cedar Grove Village. Books, maps, first aid, and wilderness permits. Open mid-June to Labor Day (Sept. 4 in 2000) daily 9am-5pm; in fall Sa-Su 9am-5pm; closed in winter. **Road's End Kiosk** (info 565-3790), 6mi. east of Cedar Grove Village, issues wilderness permits. Open in summer daily 7am-2:45pm. If all trail permits are not issued by that time, they will be available at the Cedar Grove Ranger Station until 5pm. **Ranger stations** also sell self-guided tours that run 1-2mi. and take 1-2hr. Different crowd-pleasing tours include Congress Trail, Mineral King, General Grant Tree and Trail, and the Zumwalt Meadow Trail.

Gas: Gasoline is not available inside the park. The nearest options are at **Hume Lake Christian Camp** (335-2000), 10mi. from Grant Grove, and **Kings Canyon Lodge** (335-2405), 13mi. from Grant Grove.

Auto Repair: Attendants at Grant Grove (335-5500) can handle minor repairs and lockouts. For major repairs or service outside the Grant Grove area, call **Michael's** (638-4101), in Reedley. **AAA Emergency Road Service** (800-400-4AAA/4222).

Markets: Grant Grove Market and **Cedar Grove Market** carry a selection of camping basics and groceries. Grant Grove Market is open in summer daily 8am-9pm, Cedar Grove Market is open in summer daily 8am-8pm.

Showers: Cedar Grove Village: $3 per person. Open in summer daily 8am-1pm and 3-8pm. **Grant Grove Village:** $3 per person, towel $1. Open in summer daily 11am-4pm.

Laundromat: In **Grant Grove Village,** arrange at lodge registration desk. Wash 75¢; 25¢ per 10min. Last load 6:30pm. Open daily in summer 8am-1pm and 3-8pm.

Post Office: Grant Grove Village, near the visitors center. Open June-Oct. M and W-Th, 9am-3pm, Tu and Sa, 9am-1pm, F 9am-1:30pm and 2-4:30pm. A stamp machine and mailbox are next to the visitors center year-round. **ZIP Code:** 93633.

CAMPGROUNDS

Although campgrounds fill quickly, you should be able to drive up late and snatch a spot on most non-holiday weekends. Only Lodgepole, in Sequoia, fills regularly, partly because of its proximity to Giant Forest Village and partly because it's one of the only campgrounds in either park that accepts summer reservations. Most campgrounds are open from mid-May to October, with a 14-night maximum stay in summer (1 month otherwise). There are no RV hookups in the parks, but dump stations are available at campsites where noted. Contact a ranger station for more info, or call 565-3351 for a 24-hour recording. **Backcountry camping** is free with the requisite permit (see **Practical Information,** p. 278).

SEQUOIA CAMPGROUNDS

Buckeye Flat, past park headquarters, a few miles from the Ash Mountain entrance on Rte. 198. Access road is a narrow dirt strip with views of mountains above and white water below. Closed to RVs; the drone of Winnebago generators is pleasantly supplanted by the roar of a nearby waterfall. Spacious sites in grove of low-lying trees and poetic outcroppings of rock. 28 sites. RVs are welcome at **Potishwa,** a full-service campground nearby with 44 well-spaced sites. Both campgrounds provide flush toilets and drinking water, and both are good choices for cold nights because of their lower elevation. Sites $14.

Atwell Mill and Cold Springs, 20mi. along Mineral King Rd. in the Mineral King area. Secluded and primitive (pit toilets), but offering piped water and picnic tables for the 50 tent sites. Steep, winding roads and a ban on trailers keep the RVs away. Store, restaurant, showers, and phones are 3mi. away in Silver City. Mineral King stables and rangers are nearby too. Sites $8; free in winter when the water is turned off.

South Fork, on South Fork Rd. 13mi. from Rte. 198. 13 sites near ranger station, a river, and some backcountry roads. Pit toilets, drinking water. Not recommended for trailers or RVs. Sites $8. Open year-round.

Dorst, 12mi. north of Giant Forest and 8mi. north of Lodgepole. Huge campground (218 sites) convenient to Sequoia attractions. The wide paved road and woodchip paths bordered with cobblestones give rise to gentle hills, a small stream, and huge pines. The layout feels more like a suburban housing development, but if you explore past the first (and most obvious) camping loop, it is possible to find more private spaces. Sites $16.

Lodgepole, 4mi. northeast of Giant Forest Village by the Kaweah River at the center of the park's ranger-led activities. RV-dominated clientele. Nearby Wolverton offers every service available in the park. Sites are dusty with thin patches of grass trying to break through the rocky soil, and tall and dispersed pine trees that offer little shade. Several sites right on the river. Sites $16, off-season $14 (free after major snowstorms). Reservations available in summer (800-365-CAMP/2267).

KINGS CANYON CAMPGROUNDS

Sunset, Azalea, and **Crystal Springs** are within a stone's throw of Grant Grove Village (and all the services therein) but remain quiet. Sunset (119 sites) features flat tenting spots amid gentle wooded hills, brilliant western views of the San Joaquin Valley, and an amphitheater with daily programs. Azalea (114 sites) is open year-round (free in winter) and has a calm feel and a trailer dump station. Crystal Springs (66 sites) is the smallest and most remote. All offer flush toilets, water, and plenty of privacy. Sites $14.

Hume Lake, off Rte. 180 10mi. northeast of Grant Grove in Sequoia National Forest. Prime location beside the fish-heavy lake. Flush toilets, pay phone, and nearby ranger programs. 74 sites. $14.

Sheep Creek, Sentinel, Canyon View, and **Moraine,** on Rte. 180 at the Kings River near Cedar Grove 32mi. east of Grant Grove. Store, food, laundry, and showers nearby. Within a few miles of Road's End and Kings Canyon trailheads. Sheep Creek has a dump station and more secluded tent sites deeper into the back of the campground. Sentinel's sites are flatter and near the Cedar Grove Amphitheater. Its most secluded and rustic sites are in the back areas as well. Moraine, with its canyon vistas, serves primarily as overflow and opens only on the busiest weekends. All have restrooms, water, and close proximity to Cedar Grove. Access roads and campgrounds typically closed Oct.-May. Sites $14. Canyon View accepts reservations from groups only.

OTHER ACCOMMODATIONS

Getting a bargain rate on non-camping accommodations in the parks is unlikely. The **Kings Canyon Park Service** (KCPS; 335-5500; P.O. Box 909, Kings Canyon National Park, 93633) is in charge of accommodations and reservations in the park. **Grant Grove Lodge** (335-5500), in Grant Grove Village, has wooden structures with canvas tops, no electricity, and communal baths (from $35), rustic cabins made totally out of wood ($45 and $55), and wooden cabins with private bath and electricity (from $85). The cheapest motel-style accommodations still hover at less-than-budget rates at the **Cedar Grove Lodge** (565-0100) in Cedar Grove Village (all rooms $85).

Outside of the park, small spots can be a better value but are still pricey. Motels and lodges abound in **Three Rivers,** six miles west of the park on Rte. 198. The larger **Visalia,** 30 miles west of the park on Rte. 198, is home to shopping centers, grocery stores, and standard accommodations. If you have to stay in this hot, flat town, **The Econo Lodge** (732-6641), S. Mooney Blvd. (from $55), and **Days Inn,** 4801 W. Mineral King Rd. (627-2885; from $45), are the cheapest options.

The Sierra Lodge, 43175 Sierra Dr./Rte. 198, Three Rivers (561-3681). Spacious rooms with high ceilings, valley view, large pool, BBQ, refrigerators, coffeemakers, and balconies. Continental breakfast included. The 17 rooms and 5 suites feel more like a condo resort than a motel. Rooms $49-78; large suite/apartments (with full kitchen and large fireplaces, can sleep loads of people) $90-155.

The Sequoia Motel (561-4453), across the street from Sierra Lodge, with a sunflower flag flying. This charming motel has 15 distinctive rooms and cabins, with more in the making. Owned by a family with a green thumb and an interior decorator. Pool, picnic area, garden. "The Library" (named for its previous decoration of book wallpaper) is the smallest of the rooms, yet is still pleasant, with several windows, a patio, and private bath. Rooms from $55; 6-person "house" $140.

Kings Canyon Lodge (335-2405), on Rte. 180 13mi. east of Grant Grove Village. Prime location. 11 clean motel units fill up fast, so call far in advance. Rooms with 1 double bed $69, with 2 doubles $99.

The Gateway Lodge, 45978 Sierra Dr./Rte. 198, in Three Rivers (561-4133), just outside the park. 7 quiet rooms with ivy-covered porch and mint-green walls sit between the road and the river. Large clean rooms with no phone from $55.

FOOD

In the national parks, the food-service market (and hence the food itself) is far from free; Sequoia Guest Services is the only competitor. Although the food isn't as bad as you might expect, you can keep costs down by doing your own cooking. A camping stove is always useful, but campfires or kitchen-equipped cabins work just as well. Supplies purchased at the park-operated **Village Market** (561-4441), in Three Rivers, may produce an affordable meal if you're cooking for a group (open M-Sa 8am-7 or 8pm, Su 9am-6pm). Outside the parks' culinary vacuum lie a few tempting alternatives, particularly in Three Rivers.

Grant Grove Restaurant (335-5500), in Grant Grove Village. Coffee-shop atmosphere. If the residents eat here (and they do), it must be good. There is also a fine dining area in the back, in case you ever get around to showering. Breakfast $4-6, lunch $5-7, dinner $8-16. Open daily 7am-9pm.

Noisy Water Cafe, 41775 Sierra Dr., in Three Rivers (561-4517). "The Home of the Hummingbirds," named for the frequent visitors to the feeders that hang outside the back window. Huge lunch sandwiches $6-7. Open daily 6:30am-10pm.

Anne Lang's Emporium, 41651 Sierra Dr., in Three Rivers (561-4937). The lingering scents of potpourri and coffee permeate the air in this country store, florist, and deli. Outside, 3 terraces overlook the river. Large $5 sandwiches come with potato salad and cantaloupe. Good soups $1.50-2.50. Open M-F 9:30am-5:30pm, Sa-Su 10am-5pm.

SEQUOIA SIGHTS AND ACTIVITIES

Giant Forest is the center of activity in Sequoia and hosts one of the world's greatest concentrations of giant sequoia trees. The grove was named by John Muir, who explored the area at length, counting tree rings, taking trunk measurements, and preaching preservation. The tallest of Muir's marvels is the **General Sherman Tree,** discovered in 1879 and named by a Civil War veteran; this tree is the world's second-largest living thing (after the aforementioned Michigan fungus). Standing 275 feet tall and measuring 102 feet around at its base, its trunk weighs in at 1385 tons. Despite this height and might, sequoia have shallow root systems, and compaction of the soil can be deadly. The two-mile **Congress Trail,** the park's most popular trail, boomerangs around General Sherman and other trees named for highlights in U.S. politics. Other trails wind through Giant Forest, past dozens of giants and younger trees. Trail guides to Giant Forest are available at the Lodgepole Visitors Center (see **Practical Information,** p. 278).

The granite monoliths and meadows of the Giant Forest area are perhaps more impressive than the trees that have made it famous. The region's most spectacular view can be found atop **Moro Rock,** two miles from the village (bike/hiking trail or Crescent Meadow Rd.), where a 400-step granite staircase leads to a stunning 360° view of the southern Sierra. If the arduous climb up the stairs doesn't leave you breathless, the vista certainly will—the Great Western Divide lies to the east and pine-covered foothills recline into the San Joaquin Valley to the south and west.

Beware: the dizzying height of the rock and the abyss below can be very scary, especially for young children and paranoid parents. At the end of Crescent Meadow Rd. rests the fabulous **Crescent Meadow,** called by Muir "the gem of the Sierra." Its emerald grasses are dotted with ruby and amethyst wildflowers gleaming against the cedars and sequoia that line the drive. Although human voices often shatter the serenity, a quick hike to Tharp's Log, a hollowed-out sequoia and former living space, guarantees a more peaceful view of the meadow. The road to Moro Rock and Crescent Meadow also offers access to many other wonders, including two testaments to the long and storied relationship between trees and automobiles: the **Tunnel Log** (2¾mi. from village), a fallen sequoia with a trunk big enough for cars to drive through, and the **Auto Log** (1mi. from village), a fallen sequoia with a trunk big enough for cars to drive on.

CAVE TOURS

Crystal Cave Tours (565-3135). Tickets must be purchased 1½hr. in advance at the Lodgepole or Foothills visitors centers. Memorial Day-Labor Day (May 28-Sept. 4 in 2000) daily every 30min. 11am-4pm; Labor Day-Memorial Day F-M every hr. 11am-4pm. Tours $6, seniors and children $3, under 6 free.

Boyden Cavern (info 209-736-2708), on Rte. 180 between Grant and Cedar Groves. To purchase a ticket, just drive up to the cave and shell out (tours run Apr.-Nov. every hr. 10am-5pm). Ticket prices have gone up from the original 5¢ pricetag when the cave was discovered in 1906 ($7 adults).

Whitewater Rafting: Kaweah White Water Adventures (561-1000 or 800-229-8658; www.teleport.com/~ogawa/kwwa/kwwa.html) just outside the park on Rte. 198 in Three Rivers on the Kaweah River. Fun Class 3 rapids ride (½-day M-F $30 per person, Sa-Su $35). Classes 4 and 5 (full-day $110 per person).

HIKES

When in the backcountry, keep an eye out for bears, which are adorable, fuzzy, and very dangerous (see **Bears Will Eat You,** p. 51). **Group tours** led by the park's pack stations (563-3445) provide safety in numbers. The fashionable guide to backcountry safety, *Backcountry Basics,* is available at the ranger station.

Sequoia harbors many treasures easily reached by simple day hikes. **Redwood Mountain Grove,** the world's largest grove of redwood trees, lies near Quail Flat, six miles south of Grant Grove and four miles north of Giant Forest Village. A seven-mile trail forms two loops through the grove along Redwood Creek, a tributary of the Kaweah River's North Fork—surrounded by blooming azaleas in May and June. The redwoods are dense but not as towering as in other groves. Another pleasant day-hike goes through **Garfield Grove,** five miles up the Kaweah River from the South Fork campground at the extreme southern boundary of the park. The Muir Grove, west of the Dorst campground, is less pristine but more accessible.

Hundreds of miles of curvy backwoods trails afford even more spectacular views. The seven-mile **Marble Falls Trail** begins by the Potwisha campground and twists through hills to a 2000-foot peak at **Marble Falls.** Moderately strenuous hikes from the Lodgepole Visitors Center to the glistening **Twin Lakes** (6mi. round-trip) and **Pear Lake** (10mi. round-trip) pass marvelous meadows.

Nine miles from Giant Forest Village on Rte. 198 is **Crystal Cave** (tour info 565-3132), discovered by two fishermen in 1918 and one of the few caves on Sequoia's western side open to the public (see p. 284). Reached by a half-mile hike from the road, the cave is lined with smooth limestone stalagmites and stalactites, moistened by a dark underground stream, and inhabited by hordes of Mexican free-tailed bats. Marble Hall, the cave's largest chamber, is 141 feet long and over 40 feet high. The temperature inside is a constant 50°F, so wear warm clothing. For more info, see **Cave Tours,** p. 284.

The **Mineral King** area was acquired by the park system in 1978 after lawsuits prevented the Walt Disney Corporation from building a ski resort on the site. Disney would have built a better access road, but some of the best scenery in the park has been preserved for those willing to brave the winding drive, complete with blind corners and steep drop-offs. The valley is 7500 feet deep, with steep trails leading up to mountain lakes and meadows. Some of the surrounding peaks stand over 12,000 feet tall. A bonanza mining area in the 1800s, the region now offers magnificent day and backcountry hiking and climbing. The walk to Aspen Flat from Mineral King Pack Station is an easy, rewarding day hike. The trail is flanked by soda springs and wildflowers. Longer hikes, such as the **Atwell-Hackett, Eagle Lake,** and **Farewell Gap Trails,** are more taxing but offer amazing views in quiet country.

KINGS CANYON SIGHTS AND ACTIVITIES

The most developed portion of the park is **Grant Grove,** named for its most commanding attraction, the General Grant Tree. The 3500-year-old general is the third-largest sequoia in the world (267½ ft.) and also an aesthetic wonder with its display of "classic" sequoia form. It has been designated the "Nation's Christmas Tree" and serves as a living shrine for the American war dead. Just north of the park entrance on Rte. 180 lies the **Big Stump Basin Trail,** a self-guided walk through an old logging camp. Here remain scars left by early loggers who erroneously viewed the enormous sequoia as a timber gold mine. They abandoned their efforts after assailing the unyielding trees with dynamite and hatchets.

The **Grant Tree Trail** just past the Sunset campground consists of a quick half-mile loop and a glance at the mammoth sequoia. The trail is the best way to see the huge Fallen Monarch (another felled sequoia), which housed a saloon and a stable, and the 24-foot-wide Centennial Stump, which stubbornly resisted nine days of hacking. When the tree arrived at the 1876 Centennial Exposition in Philadelphia, Easterners refused to display it, dismissing it as "another California hoax."

Hidden behind the visitors center parking lot is the steep, narrow road to **Panoramic Point** (RVs prohibited). In addition to affording awesome mountain views, the point serves the trailhead for Park Ridge Trail, one of the most scenic treks in the park. The 1½-mile round-trip hike along the Dead Giant Loop, borders national park and national forest lands, and provides interpretive information on land-management differences between them.

CEDAR GROVE

The most incredible sights in Kings Canyon lie east of Grant Grove. South Fork Kings River has carved the park's eponymous canyon and made it the deepest in the U.S., deeper even than the Grand Canyon. The canyon's towering granite walls can be experienced from Cedar Grove. Although accessible via U.S. 180, Cedar Grove is

HOW DO I GET A TREE NAMED AFTER ME? Up until the 1920s it was as simple as waving a paintbrush, a hammer, a nail, and declaring "MY TREE!" Pioneers, visitors, and tough guys would post makeshift plaques on random trees and proclaim ownership or at least namesakehood. This may account for the abundance of trees named after Civil War generals, all of which were Union generals until The Daughters of the Confederacy feistily plastered up the names of two enduring Southern heroes.

In 1933, Dr. Morton W. Fraser, a long-time fan of the forest, was buried beneath a tree in Giant Forest, now named Burial Tree and etched with a small tombstone. Another two-tree combo grew in such a way that a swampy cesspool of scum/water collected between them. Rumor has it that a ranger once found a couple of black bears kicking back in this pool on a hot summer day; he called the tree Bear's Bathtub.

At one point there was a tree for every state in the Union. But beginning in mid-century, the park began to tire of the self-aggrandizement and the tacky wooden signs; since the 1930s, the policy has been to let the plaques fall off of most trees and relieve the giants from the burden of labels. To date there are 15 state trees and a Vermont log.

nevertheless one of the park's most secluded areas. The drive to Cedar Grove is scenic and mountainous, but expect some delays due to construction and flood damage. Sheer rock walls dominate the views, and at the bottom of the canyon, the Kings River glistens like a champagne supernova; stop at roadside turn-offs for a peek.

Once within the grove, you can explore the Kings River's banks and marvel at the depth of the canyon (8200ft. in spots). In the hours just before dusk, when the setting sun dances brilliantly off the gilded promontories, this spot is more thrilling than a laser lightshow, more aesthetically poignant than the *Piss Christ.* **Zumwalt Meadows,** accessible via a 1½-mile trail loop, has a rocky overlook from which bears and white-tailed deer can be seen foraging in the flora below. It's perfect for the hiker who wants more than an easy, paved trail, but still nothing too strenuous. Roaring River Falls and Mist Falls are at their best in late spring and early summer, when the streams that feed them are swift and swollen. **Roaring River Falls** is easily reached by road; **Mist Falls** requires a mellow four-hour hike.

Road's End is exactly that, a naturally U-shaped glacial valley at the end of Rte. 180 with parking for those entering the backcountry. The most popular backcountry foray from Road's End is the **Rae Lakes Loop,** which traverses a sampling of the Sierra's best: glaciated canyons, gentle meadows, violent rapids, and inspiring lake vistas. Most hikers travel clockwise to avoid a daunting uphill grade. Well-spaced campgrounds pace the four- or five-day trek at seven-mile intervals. Obtain permits at Cedar Grove or the **Road's End Kiosk** (see **Practical Information,** p. 281).

In the summer, rangers organize a variety of **activities** including nature walks, children's campfires, day hikes, and films. Contact a ranger station or look in the *Sequoia Bark*, the free park newspaper, for a calendar of events.

LEE VINING AND MONO LAKE

As the snow thaws, the road opens in the stunning Route 140 Tioga Pass, making the town of Lee Vining a great (if a bit expensive) Yosemite gateway, or a getaway of its own.

The town's primary focus is the preservation of its sacred Mono Lake. As fresh water from streams and springs drains into this "inland sea," it evaporates, leaving behind a mineral-rich, 13-mile-wide expanse Mark Twain once called "the Dead Sea of the West." Unlike its Eastern counterpart, however, Mono teems with life: brine flies and shrimp provide a buffet for thousands of waterfowl. The lake derives its lunar appearance from towers (similar to giant drip sandcastles) of calcium carbonate called tufa, which form when calcium-rich springs well up in the carbonate-filled salt water. At one million years old, this is the Western Hemisphere's oldest enclosed body of water—truly the old man of the seas.

Today, Mono supports not only its own ecosystem, but also that of greater metropolitan Los Angeles. Steady diversion of lake water to aqueducts feeding the dry south has lowered the water level nearly 50 feet since 1941, exposing the delicate tufa and endangering the California shore gulls who nest here. Increased salinity has devastated the trout stock of adjacent streams, and massive quantities of newly exposed alkaline dust pollute local air. In the past 10 years, however, locals and lake-lovers have rejoiced to see the combined efforts of Congress, the U.S. Forest Service, the Audubon Society, and the Mono Lake Committee succeed in reducing the flow south. The lake's level should rise 17 feet over the next 20 years.

ORIENTATION AND PRACTICAL INFORMATION

Lee Vining provides stunning access to Yosemite as well as the best access to Mono Lake and the ghost town of Bodie. Lee Vining is 70 miles north of Bishop on U.S. 395 and 10 miles west of the Tioga Pass entrance to Yosemite. Bodie is 28 miles northwest of Lee Vining off U.S. 395. Addresses in Lee Vining consist only of P.O. Box numbers, so general directions or cross streets are provided instead.

Buses: Greyhound (647-6301 or 800-231-2222) has a flag stop at the Red Log Store on the south side of town. To **L.A.** (1 per day, $52) and **Reno** (1 per day, $32).

Kayak Rental: Caldera Kayaks (935-4942; www.calderakayak.com), at Crowly Lake Marina, Mammoth Lakes. Kayaks $20 per half-day, $30 per day. Natural-history kayak tour of Mono Lake (4hr., $60).

Mono Lake Committee and Lee Vining Chamber of Commerce (647-6595; www.monolake.org; lodging, dining, and local services www.leevining.com; email info@monolake.org), at Main and 3rd St., Lee Vining, in the orange-and-blue building. Like a friendly eco-gift shop, with exhibits, articles, books, extensive lake and preservation info, and the best free slide show this side of the Rio Grande. Walking and canoe tours (see **Sights and Activities,** p. 288). Open daily late June-Labor Day (Sept. 4 in 2000) 9am-10pm, Labor Day-late June 9am-5pm. **Internet access** $2 for 15min.

Mono Basin National Forest Scenic Area Visitors Center (647-3044; www.r5.fs.fed.us/inyo; bookstore www.r5.fs.fed.us/inyo/esia), Inyo National Forest, off U.S. 395 ½mi. north of Lee Vining. Housed in a new structure that resembles a modern-day cathedral or *Architectural Digest* centerfold, a testament to the community's care for the area. Interpretive tours, free patio talks, and info on Mono County's wilderness areas. Topographic maps and wilderness permits available. Open in summer M-F 9am-5:30pm. Tours of the center's exhibits and the lake's South Tufa Grove ($2, under 18 free).

Weather: 935-7663.

Emergency: 911.

Post Office (647-6371), on 4th St., Lee Vining, in the big brown building. Open M-F 9am-2pm and 3-5pm. **ZIP Code:** 93541.

Area Code: 760.

ACCOMMODATIONS

In summer, when Tioga Pass is open, Lee Vining is an ideal stop on the way from Reno or Death Valley to Yosemite, making hotel accommodations scarce on Friday afternoons and holidays. Even if you do get a room, lodging and meals are always expensive; camping and picnics are cheaper alternatives. Many hotels and campgrounds are closed in winter; call ahead. Most cheap options are on **Main Street,** or five miles south of town on the 14-mile **June Lake Loop** (see p. 289).

El Mono Motel (647-6310), Main and 3rd St., offers a slice of modern California: faux Spanish name, white stucco exterior, espresso bar, and alternative rock in the lobby. Clean and bright rooms have cable TV but no phone. Singles $45-65. Open Apr.-Oct.

Inn at Lee Vining (647-6300; fax 647-6050), at Main and 2nd St. Follow signs to The Kings Inn. Sheltered from street noise, cabin-like motel rooms have artsy hand-painted walls. Continental breakfast included. Rooms from $70, with TV $85. Pets $5.

Gateway Motel (647-6467 or 800-282-3929), in the center of town. Each of its standard rooms has a great view of Mono Lake. Phones, cable TV, and spa. Rooms in summer from $99; in winter $49.

CAMPGROUNDS

None of the area's campgrounds take reservations, but sites are ubiquitous, so a pre-noon arrival time will almost always guarantee a spot. Most sites are clustered west of Lee Vining along Rte. 120.

Inyo National Forest campgrounds, close to town. **Lundy** and **Lee Vining Canyons** are the best locations for travelers headed for Mono Lake. The **June Lake Loop area** south of town on U.S. 395 has 6 of the sites. Most sites $12; **Walter Lake** is free.

Ellery Lake, on Tioga Pass Rd. at Rte. 120 across from Tioga Pass Resort. First-come, first-camped sites near a brook. Treatable water, chemical toilets. Sites $10.

FOOD

The **Lee Vining Market** (647-1010), on U.S. 395 at the southern end of town, is the closest thing to a grocery store (open Su-Th 7:30am-9:30pm, F-Sa 7:30am-10pm).

Walking Taco (647-6470), on Main St. across from 2nd St., serves standard Tex-Mex fare (tostada salad $4, taco $1.25, huge burritos only $3.50) in a friendly spot with indoor and outdoor seating. Open daily 11:30am-7pm.

Nicely's (647-6477), on U.S. 395 north of the visitors center, has hot sandwiches ($6-7), burgers ($5-6), and monster salads. Open in summer daily 6am-10pm; in winter Th-Tu 6am-10pm.

Mono Cone, on U.S. 395 at the northern end of town, is a local institution whose opening signals the beginning of summer. Their corn dogs ($1.85), floats ($2.35), and frosty cones ($1.25) are the best in town. Open in summer daily 11am-7pm.

SIGHTS AND ACTIVITIES

In 1984, Congress set aside 57,000 acres of land surrounding Mono Lake and named it the **Mono Basin National Forest Scenic Area** (647-3044). For a $2 fee (Golden Eagle, Golden Age, and Golden Access passes accepted), investigate the **South Tufa Grove,** which harbors an awe-inspiring hoard of calcium carbonate formations. (Take U.S. 395 South to Rte. 120, then go 4mi. east and take the Mono Lake South Tufa turn-off 1mi. south to Tufa Grove.) The tufa towers pierce the smooth surface of this solemn sea. Five miles north of Lee Vining on U.S. 395, and one mile east on Cemetery Rd. is **Mono Lake County Park,** a public playground with a boardwalk trail to the tufa towers (wheelchair accessible) and a smaller tufa grove, as well as bathrooms, picnic tables, and swings.

The Mono Lake Committee (647-6595) offers **canoe tours** of the lake that include a crash course in conservation and Mono's natural history. (1hr. tours depart from the south shore of Mono Lake mid-June to early Sept. Sa-Su at 8, 9:30, and 11am; bird-watching is better on earlier tours. Arrive 30min. early for lifejacket fitting and photos of placid reflections. Tours $17, ages 4-12 $7. Reservations required.) Caldera Kayaks offers full-day **kayak tours** and **kayak rentals** (see p. 287). Flies may be irritating on shore, but they feed exclusively on algae and are harmless.

In this arid basin, summertime high noon inspires tourists to explore shade. The 20-minute slide show presentation at the Mono Lake Committee is beautifully done, informative, rabble-rousing, and free. The U.S. Forest Service Scenic Area Visitors Center shows a film that requires less thought from viewers. (Admission $2, including 20min. film, exhibits, and access to South Tufa area.) The **Mono Basin Historical Society Museum,** in Guss Hess Park, Lee Vining, is a great way to get up-to-date on the Basin's rich past. In the old Mono Lake schoolhouse, this museum has the standard balance of Gold Rush trinkets and native American artifacts.

The unique terrain of this geological playground makes it a great place for hikers of all levels. Easy trails include the quarter-mile **Old Marina Area Trail,** east of U.S. 395 one mile north of Lee Vining, the **Lee Vining Creek Nature Trail,** which begins behind the Mono Basin Visitors Center, and the Panum Crater Trail five miles south on U.S. 395. Gluttons for punishment should head 10 miles east of U.S. 395 on Rte. 120, where an exceptionally steep trail leads to the glistening **Gardisky Lake.** The Mono Basin Visitors Center offers tours of sights, including June Lake and **Panum Crater,** an expansive site of recent volcanic activity (640 years ago) that'll boil your blood.

BODIE

Access: *Off U.S. 395 15mi. north of Lee Vining, or by a dirt road from Rte. 167 out of Mono Inn.* ***Open:*** *Daily Memorial Day-Labor Day (May 29-Sept. 4 in 2000) 8am-7pm; Labor Day-Memorial Day 8am-4pm.* ***Admission:*** *$2. Dogs $1. Self-guide booklet $1.*

One of the best-preserved ghost towns this side of the Mississippi, Bodie was "the most lawless, wildest, and toughest mining camp the West has ever known," although it doesn't look that way now. Named after Waterman S. Bodie, who discovered gold here in 1859, the town's heyday was from 1878 to 1882, when it was home to 10,000 people, 65 saloons, and one homicide per day. Bodie survived until the 1940s, when the toughest town in the West was destroyed by the now-infamous Bodie Bill, a 2½-year-old child who leveled 90% of the town with one match. The remaining 10%, however, is a ghost town: absolutely genuine and brimming with romantic appeal. The streets and buildings are strewn with abandoned furniture, automobiles, and train engines, well-preserved by the dry climate and the state government. The **Bodie Museum** is the small home to some Wild West stories and artifacts. (Open in summer daily 10am-5pm. For more info, call Bodie State Historic Park at 647-6445, or write P.O. Box 515, Bridgeport 93517.)

JUNE LAKE LOOP

The June Lake Loop is hidden between Mammoth Lakes and Lee Vining—driving between the two towns you'd never know it existed (save for road signs pointing it out). Once you drive down the entrance road, though, the valleys of the June Lake Loop suddenly appear, surrounded by snow-capped mountains of jagged rock made green in the summer by waterfalls of snow runoff. A canyon carved by glaciers and now filled with water, June Lake is a popular summer vacation spot for swimmers and boaters alike, but the main draws are for fishermen. In summer the lake is stocked with trout, the motels and resorts have pictures of fish and the people who caught them plastered everywhere, and in the campgrounds you can see people in funny-looking hats boasting about their latest catch. In winter, the slopes around the loop make the June Lake area a desirable skiing destination. (According to the locals, the skiing here is the best-kept secret in California.)

ORIENTATION AND PRACTICAL INFORMATION

Just off US. 395, seven miles south of Lee Vining, the June Lake Loop winds by Grant, Silver, Gull, and June Lakes. In June Lake Town itself, Boulder Dr. is also referred to as Main St. Addresses in the June Lake Loop consist only of P.O. Box numbers, so general directions or cross streets are provided instead.

Buses: Buses stop at the June Lake Junction. Buses arrive and depart late night/early morning. To: **L.A.** ($49); **San Francisco** ($51); and **Reno** ($30). You must call ahead (648–7509) to let them know you will be waiting at the Junction.

Boat Rental: June Lake Marina (648-7726) has motorboats: 6-horsepower (half-day $35, full-day $40); 15-horsepower (half-day $44, full-day $49). **Silver Lake Resort** (648-7525) rents motorboats (half-day $32, full-day $39) and canoes ($12 per hr.).

Visitor Information: June Lake Chamber of Commerce (648-7584; www.junelake.com.) offers tourist information. Open Su-Th 7am-7pm, F-Sa 7am-8pm. Another info kiosk at southern entrance. **June Lake and June Mountain Reservations** makes accommodations reservations (reservations and info 648-7794, reservations only 800-648-2211).

Market: The **June Lake General Store** is a supermarket, hardware store, and deli, all rolled into one pink building. Open daily 8am-8pm. Options outside of June Lake are the small supermarket at **Fern Creek Lodge** (648-7722; open daily in summer 5am-9pm; in winter 7am-6pm), or the **Silver Lake Resort Store** (open daily 7am-9pm).

Auto Repair and Service: June Lake Automotive (648-7542; fax 648-8215), **Fred Sebald's Body Shop** (648-7343), and **Silver Lake Automotive** (648-7252).

Frontier Pack Station: 648-7701.

Weather: 24hr. snow report 619-934-6166 or 213-935-8866.

24-Hour Sheriff: 932-7451. **Forest Service:** 647-6525.

Emergency: 911.

Post Office: 648-7483, on Boulder Dr., across from Trout Town Joe Cafe. General Delivery, June Lake, CA. Open M-F 9am-2pm and 3-5pm. **ZIP Code:** 93529.

Area Code: 760.

ACCOMMODATIONS

As befits a resort town, there are plenty of places to stay, many of them very nice, a few of them affordable.

Fern Creek Lodge (648-7722 or 800-621-9146), on Rte. 158 13mi. from Lee Vining, 1mi. past June Lake Town. Woodsy cabins with kitchens are reasonably priced for the area. 2-person cabin $47-52, 14-person cabin $200-220.

Boulder Lodge (648-7533; fax 648-7330), on Boulder Dr. near the beginning of June Lake. Spacious, clean rooms with a sitting area, cable TV, and private bath. Pool table, small arcade, heated indoor pool. Lake view rooms have patios with gorgeous views of June Lake. In summer 2-person cabins from $58; house $300.

Reverse Creek Lodge (648-7535), on Loop Rd., has small but cute cabins. A-frames are larger, and look out on nearby Carson Peak. Motel units $35; half-chalets without kitchen in summer from $45, in winter $50; small cabin with cable TV, kitchen, bath, deck, and BBQ in summer $55, in winter $65.

June Lake Motel (648-7147, reservations only 800-648-6835), on Boulder Dr. In a town that caters to fishermen, this motel caters the most. Besides a jacuzzi, sauna, BBQs, and cable TV, it also offers a fish cleaning station, fish freezing, free ice, and fish rags. Rooms from $56, with kitchen from $60; lake-view condominiums from $135.

Four Seasons Resort (648-7476), between Gull and Silver Lakes, has 5 rustic A-frame chalets with full kitchens (including microwave and dishes), living rooms with cable TV, patios with views, and room for 7 people to sleep. Chalets $70-115, depending on month and holidays; in winter from $139. Open late Apr.-Oct. and Dec. 20-Jan. 1.

CAMPGROUNDS

A more affordable option than much of the lodging in the June Lake Loop is to head for the campgrounds. There are six Inyo National Forest campgrounds on the loop, as well as a few privately operated sites.

Pine Cliff Resort (648-7558), by the June Lake shore. The resort has a general store, gas, propane, laundry, and showers. On-site trailer rentals $50-$60; full RV hookup $17, water and electric hookup $14; campsites $10. Open mid.-Apr. to Oct.

Grant Lake Resort (648-7964; fax 648-7988), off Rte. 158 toward Lee Vining in the most remote part of the June Lake Loop. Atypical resort has a tackle shop, marina, and boat rental (half-day $30, full-day $35). Drinking water, firepits, coin-operated showers. Decent shade; many of the 72 sites overlook Grant Lake. It opens with the fishing season. Sites $12, seniors $10. For reservations, write P.O. Box 627, June Lake 93529.

Silver Lake Campground, a National Forest site. Right on the lake, the grassy campsites don't have much shade, but do have lots of room. Good fishing access. Sites $12.

Oh! Ridge Campground, on the southern end of June Lake, has lovely lake views, flush toilets, a swimming beach, and not much shade. Sites $10. Open Apr.-Nov.

FOOD

Tiger Bar (648-7551), Knoll Ave. and Rte. 158. Good Mexican fare, as well as standard American food, all reasonably priced. Huge Tostada Grande $6.50; burgers $5.50-6.50; sandwiches $6-7.50. The quirky decor is of old black-and-white photos of the area and pictures of tigers. Open daily 8am-midnight; kitchen open until 10pm.

Trout Town Joe, 2750 Boulder Dr. (648-1155), next to the general store and across from the post office. June Lake's finest (and only) coffeehouse. Panini sandwiches ($5.45), wide variety of great coffees ($1.50-3), and assorted pastries, and a friendly atmosphere and interesting decor will convince you it warrants the title. Open M-F 6am-3pm, Sa-Su 6am-6pm.

Eagle's Landing Restaurant (648-7897), at the Double Eagle Resort, is the place to go to treat yourself. Excellent food at reasonable prices served in a gorgeous setting. Burgers ($5.50-7), sandwiches ($7-9), and a wide selection of soups and salads, but the specialty is the rotisserie chicken ($10). Open daily 7am-9:30pm.

SIGHTS AND ACTIVITIES

There is something to do in the great outdoors year-round at the June Lake Loop. The warmer months invite hiking and fishing, while winter brings visitors to the excellent June Lake ski mountains. For those who miss the gorgeous New England foliage in the fall, June Lake offers its own equally stunning version—captured each year by thousands of avid photographers.

The **June Mountain Ski Resort** (648-7733) is considered a secret when it comes to California getaways. Overshadowed by neighboring Mammoth Lakes Resort, June Mountain has kept its awesome powder hidden from the hordes just south. Hundreds of skiers are left to shorter lines here and consider themselves lucky.

Self-guided hikes, as well as guided tours, are excellent ways to explore the area. The simple **Parker Lake Trail** begins two miles west of the loop on Parker Lake Rd., and the difficult seven-mile trek to the inviting **Bloody Canyon** begins just off the loop beside Grant Lake. The Mono Basin Scenic Area Visitor Center hosts a **June Mountain Nature Hike,** to "discover the flora and fauna of the Sierra Nevada" (1½hr., July to early Sept. W 11am). The center also has a **Campground Program** with storytelling, songs, stargazing, or slideshows (Oh!Ridge Campground, above).

For those who like to hike in the winter and climb ice, the **Nidever Mountain Guides** (648-1122) offer several hikes and seminars which are pricey but offer a thorough introduction to the region and the sports. (Seminars offered Jan.-Mar. 2-day ice-climbing $215, 3-day alpine climbing $475, 3-day mountaineering $535.)

BISHOP AND OWENS VALLEY

In 1861, Samuel Bishop brought 600 cattle and a pair of boots from Fort Tejon to settle at what is now Bishop Creek. The herds have diminished somewhat, but they still graze on the way into Bishop (pop. 3507) along U.S. 395. Once a haven for highwaymen and thieves, the town now serves as a ranchers' rendezvous and a rest stop for travelers en route to trout fishing in nearby Owens River and Bishop Creek. Surrounded by year-round fishing spots and the wilderness areas of Owens Valley, Bishop is a town for the true outdoorsman.

PRACTICAL INFORMATION

Buses: Greyhound: 201 S. Warren St. (872-2721), behind the J.C. Penney. To **L.A.** (1 per day, $50) and **Reno** (1 per day, $45). Open daily 1-2pm *only.*

Public Transportation: Dial-A-Ride, 872-1901 or 800-922-1930. Round-trip within Bishop city limits 75¢, to areas just outside the city $1.30. Shuttles to **Mammoth Lakes** ($3.50) and **Crowley Lake** ($3). By special arrangement, will drop you at a trailhead (prices vary). Call the day before for schedules and reservations (limited seating). Open M-Th 8am-5pm, F-Sa 8am-midnight (last call 11:30pm).

AAA Emergency Road Service: 800-400-4222.

Visitor Information:

Bishop Chamber of Commerce, 690 N. Main St. (873-8405; fax 873-6999), at the City Park. Area maps and info. Get a free copy of the *Vacation Planner* for up-to-date listings of special events. Open M-F 9am-5pm, Sa-Su 10am-4pm.

White Mountain Ranger Station: 798 N. Main St. (873-2500; www.r5.fs.fed.us/inyo). Excellent lists of campgrounds and trails. Weather report and a message board. 40% of **wilderness permits** available on a first-come, first-served basis, backcountry campers should reserve either by phone or on the web. Programs include Sa evening campfire talks. Open late June-Sept. 15 daily 8am-5pm; Sept. 16-late June M-F 8am-4:30pm.

Fishing Licenses: Available at Kmart, 910 N. Main St. (873-3800; open daily 8am-10pm), and sporting goods stores.

Bank: Bank of America, 536 N. Main St. (800-338-6430). Open M-Th 9am-5pm, F 9am-6pm, Sa 9am-1pm. **24hr. ATM.**

Laundromat: The Wash-Tub, 236 N. Warren St. (873-6627). Wash $1.25, 10min. dry 25¢. Magazines and video games galore. Open daily 7am-10pm, last load 8pm.

Showers: Sierra Flex Gym, 192 E. Pine St. (872-5550), behind Whiskey Creek restaurant. $3 (includes soap, shampoo, and towel). Open M-F 6am-9pm, Sa 8am-3pm, Su 9am-3pm.

Road Conditions: 800-427-ROAD/7623.

Emergency: 911. **Police:** 207 W. Line St. (873-5866).

Hospital: Northern Inyo Hospital, 150 Pioneer Ln. (873-5811). Emergency care 24hr.

Post Office: 595 W. Line St. (873-3526 or 800-275-8777). Open M-F 8:15am-4:45pm, Sa 10am-2pm. **ZIP Code:** 93514.

AREA CODE The area code for Bishop and Owens Valley is 760.

ACCOMMODATIONS

If you're traveling in a group, and especially those looking to fish may find a cabin the best option. Bishop Creek's **Cardinal Village Resort** (873-4789), sits 16 miles west of Bishop on Rte. 168. This and the **Bishop Creek Lodge** (873-4484), on South Lake Rd., provide such accommodations. Hotels are plentiful in Bishop, but *cheap* hotels aren't; the best are listed below. If you want to save money, you may be better off camping in or near Bishop.

El Rancho Motel, 274 Lagoon St. (872-9251), 2 blocks west of Main St. A quintessential motel; drive right to your door. Rooms with TV, A/C, coffeemakers, and refrigerators. Kitchen $8 extra. Singles $38-45; doubles $38-47.

Elms Motel, 233 E. Elm St. (873-8118 or 800-848-9226). These 2-room cottages are dirt-free and come with A/C, coffeemakers, and cable TV. The city park is right next door. Apr.-Oct. singles $37, doubles $42; Nov.-Mar. singles $32, doubles $37.

Chalfont House, 213 Academy St. (872-1790). This charming bed and breakfast is worth the few extra bucks. Built in 1898, it has hardwood floors, patchwork quilts, and a potbelly stove in the parlor. Rooms for 1-2 people from $60; 1 single $50.

CAMPGROUNDS

Most campgrounds around Bishop are well kept and near major roads. Sites have a consistent flow of campers throughout summer but are especially crowded during the **Mule Days** celebration (See **Seasonal Events,** p. 295) over Memorial Day weekend (May 27-29 in 2000), for which you should book a year in advance.

Brown's Town Campground (in summer 873-8522, in winter 872-6911). Turn west on Schober Ln., 1mi. south of town on U.S. 395, to reach this family-run place, where everything is clean and well kept. Many of the 150 sites are shaded, 44 have electric and water hookups, and 10 have cable TV. Picnic area available for day use. Tent sites $12; R/V sites with water and electricity $15; 7min. showers 50¢ (for campers only).

Mill Pond Campground (872-6911), on U.S. 395 6½mi. northwest of Bishop, ¼mi. south on Ed Powers Rd., 1mi. west on Sawmill Rd. 60 campsites on McGee Creek, next to Mill Pond Riding Stables. Pond for swimming and sailing, tennis courts, softball diamond, archery, horseshoe pits, piped and stream water, flush toilets, and showers (50¢ for 7min.). Sites $12, with electricity and water $15.

There are over 25 **Inyo National Forest** campgrounds in the Bishop Ranger District (most open May-Oct.). **First Falls** at Big Pine, **Grandview** in the Bristlecone Forest, and **Mosquito Flat** (Rock Creek Drainage) are all free. Grandview has no water; the other two have only stream water, which must be treated before drinking. **Big Trees** is closest to town (sites $12). **Bishop Creek Canyon** is a trout-fishing hotspot with water and restrooms alongside the road to North Lake (sites $12). There are 11 sites along the north and south forks which provide comfortable, tree-lined camping, easy access to fishing, water, and restrooms. Free camping is available at **Grandview Campground,** four miles south of Schulman at Barcroft Lab's gate on White Mountain Rd. Sites have tables, grills, and pit toilets, but no water. For the most current campsite information, visit the locale or call the **White Mountain Ranger Station.**

FOOD

Stock up on groceries at **Vons Supermarket,** 174 S. Main St. (873-4396; 24hr.). As usual, fast-food chains abound.

Western Kitchen, 930 N. Main St. (872-3246). Serves all the usual American fare, but why settle for a ham steak ($7.50) when you can also choose from an extensive list of Thai specialties? As unlikely as it seems, this Western Kitchen serves some delicious dishes from the East (curries $7.50). Open daily 6am-9pm.

Pyrenees Soup and Sandwiches, 150 N. Main St. (873-7275). Frequented by locals for the homemade soups, hearty sandwiches, and peaceful atmosphere. A mom 'n' pop operation; Dick cooks and Suzanne serves. Light lunches $4-6. Open M-Sa 10am-3pm.

Kava Coffeehouse, 206 N. Main St. (872-1010). Christmas lights decorate the ceiling and useless trinkets line the walls of this whimsical "Lithuanian Coffeehouse." Don't try to figure it out; just relax and enjoy a fresh bagel sandwich ($2-4) or a satisfying smoothie ($4). Open daily 6am-4pm, although hours vary.

SIGHTS AND ACTIVITIES

EAST OF BISHOP

The Owens Valley is a backpacker's Eden. East of Bishop in the other half of Inyo National Forest (which is split by U.S. 395), the yellow sands of the **White Mountains** rise to heights rivaling the Sierra. If you want to tackle the strenuous one-mile climb to the top of White Mountain itself (14,246ft.), park your car (preferably 4-wheel-drive) on White Mountain Rd., 22 miles from Rte. 168.

Scattered across the face of the White Mountains are California's **bristlecone pines,** the oldest living things on the planet. Gnarled, twisted, and warped into fantastic shapes, the trees may grow only one inch every 100 years. The slow growth at extreme altitudes (up to 12,000ft.) has allowed the "Methuselah" specimen in the Schulman Group to survive for 4700 years (to avoid wrecking and sabotage, they don't tell you which one it is). To get to the **Ancient Bristlecone Pine Forest,** follow Rte. 168 off U.S. 395 at Big Pine for 12 miles. Turn left at the sign to the Bristlecone Pine Forest and the White Mountains Research Station. The 11-mile paved road takes you to Schulman Grove, at nearly 10,000 feet, where there are two short hikes and a **visitors center** (873-2500; depending on snow, open late June-Sept. 15 daily 9am-6pm). Complete knowledge of the botany of the ancients can be had for a mere $1. The moderately strenuous four-mile **Methuselah Walk** leads through the hills. The drive to **Patriarch Grove** is a beautiful but unpaved 12 miles.

Beyond the Inyos from Deep Springs, southeast of Inyo and northwest of Death Valley lies the uninhabited **Eureka Valley.** The valley's magnificent and haunting **sand dunes** are the **tallest landlocked dunes in the country.** If the sand is cool, flip off your shoes, climb to the top of the dunes, and roll down. The friction between the sand you disturb and the nearly 700 feet of grains beneath makes a bizarre, unfathomably deep sound. Local Native Americans called it "the singing of the sands." Roads lead into the valley from the Owens Valley near Big Pine and various points on the Nevada side, but none are reliable and not even the proverbial wild horses could drag you through when the road is washed out or snowed in. Check with the visitors center for specifics, and see **Desert Survival** (p. 460), for desert travel tips.

Seven miles south of Big Pine on U.S. 395 is a wildlife viewpoint with a great view of the valley and sometimes (early morning or evening) **elk herds** (see p. 193). Elk also congregate on the mowed alfalfa fields just south of Big Pine on U.S. 395.

WEST OF BISHOP

The Owens Valley cradles enough wilderness areas to sate any explorer or adventurer. Head west on Cracker St. for 10 miles to get to the glaciers of **Big Pine Canyon,** which guide Big Pine Creek through the thick groves of Jeffery Pines. The North Fork Trail is a popular destination for hikers as well as rock and ice climbers. The trail passes Lakes #1, 2, and 3 and the stone cabin of Hollywood legend Lon Chaney before getting to the Palisade Glacier, the Sierra's largest ice block. **Fishing** enthusiasts favor Big Pine's seldom-traveled **South Fork Trail,** which leads to lakes laden with fun-to-fish trout.

Follow Line St. 14 miles west of Bishop to the lakes and campgrounds of **Bishop Creek Canyon.** Here hikers can fork onto the **South Lake Trailhead,** where leisurely trails lead to **Green, Treasure,** and **Chocolate Lakes** and mountain meadows filled with wildflowers. Continue west four miles to **Sabrina Basin** for secluded hiking and fishing opportunities. Steeper switchbacks off the main trail lead to less populated **George Lake.** Sabrina, North, and South Lakes provide spectacular **trout fishing.** The official angling season spans May to October. Contact the chamber of commerce (873-8405) for tournament and general fishing info. Tackle and taxidermy are available at Parcher's Resort, Bishop Creek Lodge, and Cardinal Village on North Fork Trailhead. (Camping sites near Sabrina and South Lakes with piped water $12.) Serious hikers may want to connect here with the Inyo Segment (11,000ft.) of the **Pacific Crest Trail** (for more info, see **From Crest to Crest: the Trail of the West,** p. 266), which is eight miles west of the **White Mountain Visitors Center,** 798 N. Main St., Bishop (873-2500), which offers permits.

The recreation areas along **Rock Creek Canyon** are frequented year-round. Hair-raising precipices, plunging canyons, and velvet wildflowers mesmerize photographers and casual onlookers alike. Take U.S. 395 24 miles north of Bishop, turn west on Rock Creek Rd., and continue up Rock Creek Canyon to the end of the road (park at Mosquito Flat). **Little Lakes Valley** is surrounded by 13,000-foot peaks and lakes full of trout. **Mono Pass Trail** leads to beautiful **Ruby Lake** and its staggering sheer granite walls. There are numerous campgrounds on the way to **Mosquito Flat** and plenty of day-parking at each of the five trailheads (sites with toilets $12).

For those who tire of outdoor adventure, the exhibits at the **Paiute Shoshone Indian Cultural Center,** 2300 W. Line St. (873-4478), illustrate the history and culture of some of the seven local tribes, including posters such as *Tobacco: Use it in a sacred way* (open daily Mar.-Sept. 10am-5pm; Oct.-Feb. 10am-3pm; admission $2, children $1).

TOMORROW, AND TOMORROW, AND TOMORROW... Among the trees of the Ancient Bristlecone Pine Forest, a plaque proclaims "Sweet are the uses of adversity." The quote is from Shakespeare, and refers to the fact that the ancient trees have thrived for millennia in conditions which thwart the growth of other plants. When the Bard wrote this, many of these trees were already over 4000 years old. Bristlecone pines are so old that tree ring readings taken from samples have been used to recalibrate carbon-dating procedures. With this new information, historians have determined, among other things, that Balkan/European cultures predate those of Mesopotamia. Bristlecones also tell us that climatic conditions were almost exactly the same in the time of Christ as they are today.

In winter, the evergreen forests, lake basins, and peaceful "range of light" (as Muir described the Eastern Sierra), make for spectacular **cross-country skiing.** Bishop Creek and Rock Creek drainages are the best areas. **Rock Creek Lodge** (935-4170) has groomed trails and a ski school. The ranger station has info (see p. 291).

SEASONAL EVENTS

Although raging activity and unbridled excitement permeate everyday life in Bishop, several annual events add even more spice to this swinging metropolis. Haul your ass to town during Memorial Day weekend (May 27-29 in 2000) for the largest mule event in the world, **Mule Days** (872-4263). View 110 mule sporting events, 40,000 mule-obsessed fans, and the famous Mule Days Parade, which is long enough to be listed in the Guinness Book of World Records. The **Hotrods, Hippies & Polyester 50s-70s Dance** (873-3588) happens every February, and the **Bishop Air show** is usually 4th of July weekend. The City Park (behind the visitors center) has hosted **evening concerts** in the gazebo for 40 consecutive summers (June-Aug. M 8-9pm; free). Food, games, and fun characterize the massive **Tri-County Fair** (873-3588; Aug. 31-Sept. 6. in 2000).

LONE PINE

Lone Pine (pop. 1818) has mastered the stereotype of small-town America. All the locals know one another, and they eye throngs of visitors with knowing smiles, aiding the disoriented by giving directions with respect to the town's only traffic light. Between searing Death Valley to the east and the snow-capped Sierras to the west, Lone Pine was founded in the 1870s as a mining supply hub. Much has changed since—the lone pine is long gone, the mines are closed, and a devastating earthquake created nearby Diaz Lake.

Movie producers have taken advantage of the old-West feel of the town; the nearby Alabama Hills provide the setting for Western classics (and less-than-classics) from *Lone Ranger* to *Maverick* (see **Movie Road,** p. 297). The town attracts more than just Hollywood types, though, since Lone Pine serves as a base for the stunning Inyo National Forest and its crown jewel, 14,495-foot tall Mount Whitney, the highest peak in the contiguous U.S.

ORIENTATION AND PRACTICAL INFORMATION

Lone Pine straddles **U.S. 395** and is the first Sierra town you hit when traveling northeast on **Route 136** from Death Valley. **Independence,** the county seat, is 14 miles north. L.A. is four hours away, 212 miles south along U.S. 395 and southwest along **Route 14.** Yosemite is a four-hour, 142-mile drive north on U.S. 395.

Buses: Greyhound: 126 W. Post St. (876-5300 or 800-231-2222), at Lone Pine Locksmith. To **Reno** (1 per day, $48-52) and **L.A.** (1 per day, $34-38). Open daily 8am-5pm and 10-11:30pm.

Car Rental: Lindsay Automotive, 361 S. Washington St. (876-4789). Rates from $57 per day. 150mi. included. Must be at least 21 with credit card. Open daily 8am-5pm (after-hours service available for a charge).

Auto Repairs: Don's Garage, 840 S. Main St. (876-4415). Open daily 8am-7pm.

AAA Emergency Road Service: 872-8241.

Visitor Information:

Interagency Visitors Center (876-6222), at U.S. 395 and Rte. 136 about 1mi. south of town. Excellent maps and guidebooks, plus small exhibits. Informative handouts about hiking in the area. Open daily July-Sept. 8am-5:50pm; Oct.-June 8am-4:50pm.

Chamber of Commerce, 126 S. Main St., Lone Pine (876-4444; fax 876-9205; www.lonepine.com). Same services as visitors center, but more centrally located. Few brochures but cheerful employees are knowledgeable. Open M-Sa 9am-5pm.

Mount Whitney/Inyo National Forest Ranger Station, 640 S. Main St., Lone Pine (876-6200), "downtown." Programs on regional wildlife and history. Topographical and trail maps for backcountry camping. **Wilderness permits** (required in backcountry). Some popular trails in the forest have 15-person quotas; Mt. Whitney has limited overnight and day permits. Reserve permits for May 22-Oct. 15 up to 6 months in advance; otherwise self-register. Permits go almost immediately for summer weekends, although there are occasional cancellations. Station open daily 7am-noon and 1-4:30pm. **Wilderness Reservations,** P.O. Box 430, Big Pine 93545 (888-374-3773; fax 938-1137).

Fishing Licenses: Gardner's True Value, 104 S. Main St. (876-420). Topographic maps, camping and fishing supplies. Licenses $10 for 2 consecutive days, $28 for 10 days. Open M-Sa 8am-6pm.

Showers: Kirk's Barber Shop, 114 N. Main St. (876-5700; $4), or on the mountain at **Whitney Portal** store ($3).

Laundromat: Coin-Op Laundromat, 105 W. Post St. (876-5461), just off Main St. Wash $1.25, 12min. dry 25¢.

Emergency: 911. **Police: Inyo County Sheriff,** Lone Pine Substation (876-5606); County Headquarters (878-0383).

Hospital: Southern Inyo, 501 E. Locust St. (876-5501).

Post Office: 121 Bush St. (876-5681), between Jackson and Main St. Open M-F 9am-5pm. **ZIP Code:** 93545.

AREA CODE	The area code for Lone Pine is 760.

ACCOMMODATIONS AND CAMPGROUNDS

High-priced motels abound here. Weekdays are cheapest, but rates fluctuate; call ahead. Camping is cheap, scenic, and conveniently located. For both motels and campsites, make reservations or arrive early.

Historical Dow Motel (next to Dow Villa Motel), 310 S. Main St. (876-5521; reservations 800-824-9317; www.dowvillamotel.com). The Dow has an inviting lobby where you can sip complimentary coffee, watch a free movie from the video list, or sit and share stories with fellow travelers. Pool and jacuzzi open 24hr. Apr.-Oct. singles $38, with bath and phone $50; Nov.-Mar. singles $23, with bath and phone $35.

Alabama Hills Inn, 1920 S. Main St. (876-8700; www.touringusa.com), 1mi. south of Lone Pine. Named for the frequently filmed hills nearby, this new motel is close to Peter's Pumpkin, Wounded Knight, and other rock sculptures. Cable, refrigerator, hair dryer, and microwave. Heated pool open 24hr. Continental breakfast included. Apr.-Oct. singles $53, doubles $63; Nov.-Mar. singles $43, doubles $48-58.

Whitney Portal Campground, on Whitney Portal Rd. 13mi. west of town. Surrounding evergreens and phenomenal views make this an exceptional campground. Call the Mt. Whitney Ranger (876-6200; reservations 800-280-2267). Sites $12; group sites $30. 7-night max. stay. Open June-Oct.

Diaz Lake Campground (876-5656), on U.S. 395 2mi. south of Lone Pine. 200 quiet, tree-lined sites overlooking Diaz Lake. Watersports fanatics will love the sites on the lake's far shore; they make for smooth watercraft launches. Grills, flush toilets, and showers. 14-day max. stay. Sites $7. Open year-round.

Tuttle Creek Campground. Take Whitney Portal Rd. 3½mi. west of Lone Pine, turn south onto Horseshoe Meadows Rd. Base camp for day hikers has 85 sites, a creek, and clear views of the Sierra. Restrooms, but no drinkable water. Free; donations accepted. Open Mar.-Nov.

FOOD

Lone Pine has its share of coffee shops and 24-hour mini-marts, but not much else. Grab groceries in town at **Joseph's Bi-Rite Market,** 119 S. Main St. (876-4378; open daily June-Sept. 8am-9pm; Oct.-May 8am-7pm). Most restaurants are non-descript, but cheap, decent fare is available.

P.J.'s Bake and Broil, 446 Main St. (876-5796). Down-to-earth food and prices. Their BBQ beef sandwich ($6) is a great post-climb treat. A favorite of the locals, it's the only restaurant open and serving breakfast 24hr.

Pizza Factory, 301 S. Main St. (876-4707). They say "We toss 'em, they're awesome," and it's true. The slightly sweet dough makes for a delicious pizza, whether you eat your own mini (4 slices $4), or share a large (10 slices $10.50).

Nacho's Grill, 104B S. Main St. (876-4030), is a hole-in-the-wall with fewer than 10 tables, where the folks in charge serve fresh food (chicken burrito $3.75) with a smile. Open W-M in summer 11am-8pm; off-season 11am-3:30pm.

HIKING

The **Whitney Trailhead Ranger Station** (876-6200), is on Whitney Portal Rd. 13 miles west of Lone Pine. The canyon entrance at **Whitney Portal** provides fantastic camping with supplies and piped water (sites $12). The 11-mile trek to the top of Mt. Whitney usually takes two to three days. While more of a strenuous hike than a climb, you may still need an ice axe and crampons in the spring and early summer. For rock climbers, Mt. Whitney's **East Face** is a year-round challenge.

Many less strenuous **day hikes** penetrate the Eastern Sierra. The **Cottonwood Lakes Trail** (10,000ft. at the trailhead) squeezes between the forests that abut the John Muir Wilderness and Sequoia National Park. Follow Whitney Portal Rd. for four miles from Lone Pine and take Horseshoe Meadow Rd. 20 miles to the trailhead. The hour-long hike along **Horseshoe Meadow Trail** to **Golden Trout Wilderness** passes several dozen high mountain lakes that mirror the Inyo Mountains. Horseshoe Meadow has camping (sites $6) and **equestrian facilities** ($12 per horse), in case you brought a horse. The **Whitney Portal Trail** offers a more challenging hike from the Lone Pine campground to Whitney Portal campground (6hr.). The trail follows Lone Pine Creek to the densely forested higher altitudes and offers incredible views of Mt. Whitney and Owens Valley. Those who enjoy pain and cycling should try the annual **Death Valley to Mount Whitney Bicycle Road Race** (Mother's Day weekend, May 13-14 in 2000). Perennially ranked one of the most masochistic organized activities in the United States, the two-day race starts at Stovepipe Wells (elevation 5ft.) and ends at the Mt. Whitney trailhead some 100 miles and 8355 feet later. In spite of its status as an official United States Cycling Federation event, nonmembers are welcome to join in the torture…er, fun. Call the Chamber of Commerce (876-4444; see p. 295) for an entry form. If running long distances in the heat is more your style, Lone Pine hosts a marathon the previous weekend. The course climbs 6200 feet and is among the nation's hardest.

SIGHTS AND ACTIVITIES

With the craggy edges of **Mount Whitney** as the star of the show, the parts of **Inyo National Forest** bordering Kings Canyon and Sequoia National Parks make up a suitable supporting cast. All of the Sierra's tallest peaks are here (many over 14,000ft.), generally within 10 to 15 minutes of U.S. 395. Cheap national forest campgrounds provide a good base for day hikes or overnight trips. All campsites have piped water. Beware of altitude sickness and allow extra time for hikes. The Inyo National Forest comprises scattered land parcels, some of which don't contain a single tree. The definition of "forest" was evidently stretched by the water-hungry in order to protect this important Sierra watershed from development.

Well before Whitney Portal, along Whitney Portal Rd., is **Movie Road,** which leads to the scenic **Alabama Hills,** which became the stage set for fictionalized Hollywood cowboy 'n' Indian tales like the 1920s *How the West Was Won.* In all, over 250 Westerns were filmed here, including such television shoot-'em-ups as *Bonanza* and *Rawhide.* Lone Piners celebrate the Hill's glamorous career with the annual **Lone Pine Film Festival** (876-4314), every Columbus Day weekend (Oct. 9 in 2000).

The **Eastern California Museum,** 155 N. Grant St., Independence (878-0258), off Market St., has a highly specialized collection featuring local Paiute and Shoshone handicrafts, exhibits on miners and ranchers, and a display on Manzanar (see below; open W-M 10am-4pm; donation $1).

On U.S. 395, between Lone Pine to the south and Independence to the north, lies the **Manzanar National Historic Site,** symbolic of one of the most shameful chapters in American history. Previously known as a relocation camp, it was the first of ten **internment centers** established after Japan's 1941 attack on Pearl Harbor to contain Japanese-Americans, whom the U.S. government saw as enemy sympathizers. From March 1942 through 1945, 10,000 people were held here. Aggressively and conspicuously ignored by the government, little remains to be seen of the camp except a few building foundations and some barbed wire. A plaque promising not to repeat the hysteria-inspired internment may have upset veterans' groups; the 100-yard stretch of road leading to the facility's old entrance has been designated a **Blue Star Memorial Highway** and dedicated to U.S. servicemen. A large delegation makes an annual pilgrimage here on the last Saturday of April (Apr. 29 in 2000).

MAMMOTH LAKES

Home to one of the most popular ski resorts in the United States, the town of Mammoth Lakes (pop. 5305) has transformed itself into a giant year-round playground. In the summer of 1998, hundreds of hard-core skiers took to the slopes on 4th of July weekend in celebration of their independence and the "Endless Winter '98."

The area knows how to rock out with its cock out even when the snow ceases to fall. Mammoth Mountain metamorphosizes from ski park in winter to bike park in summer, with fishing, rock climbing, and hiking as well. Even the McDonald's looks like a ski lodge. The weekend nightlife is lively and entirely full of athletes who come to this alpine paradise to get vertical and have mammoth fun.

ORIENTATION AND PRACTICAL INFORMATION

Mammoth Lakes is on U.S. 395 160 miles south of Reno and 40 miles southeast of the eastern entrance to Yosemite. Rte. 203 runs through the town as Main St. and then veers off to the right as Minaret Summit Rd. In the winter, the roads from L.A. are jammed with weekend skiers making the six-hour journey up to the slopes.

Buses: Greyhound (800-231-2222) stops at Rte. 203 and Sierra Park Rd. in the parking lot behind McDonald's on Main St. To **Reno** (1 per day; M-F $35, Sa-Su $37) and **L.A.** (1 per day, $46). Buy tickets at the next station.

Public Transit: Inyo-Mono Dial-A-Ride (872-1901) provides service to Bishop, Bridgeport, Lee Vining, June Lake, and Crowley Lake from Mammoth Lakes McDonald's and Bishop Kmart (M, W, and Sa; fare $2.50). **Mammoth Shuttle Service** (934-3030) provides year-round on-call service (M-Th 7am-11pm, F-Su 7am-2am; within town $4, each additional person $2; to lodge $8, each additional person $2). **Mammoth Area Shuttle** (MAS; 934-0687) offers a red line shuttle to town and the main lodge. During ski season, shuttles connect to chairlifts (every 15min. 7:30am-5:30pm; free). In summer shuttle runs from main lodge to **Reds Meadow, Devils Post Pile,** and 8 other stops in the forest. Shuttle is mandatory to enter these areas 7:30am-5:30pm. Round-trip $9. **Sierra Express** (924-TAXI/8294) is a door-to-door shuttle service that runs anywhere any time (rates fluctuate; $20 surcharge for getting them out of bed 2-7am).

Car Rental: U-SAVE, 452 Old Mammoth Rd. #1J (934-4999 or 800-207-2681). 4-wheel drive vehicles from $45 per day with 150mi. included, or $270 per week with 1050mi. included; 25¢ each additional mi. Rentals available at the **Chevron** (934-8111), next to the post office. Compacts $40-90 per day; 150mi. included, 25¢ each additional mi.

Auto Repairs: AAA Emergency Road Service: 934-3385 or 800-400-4222.

Equipment Rental: Sandy's Ski Sport (934-7518), on Main St. Mountain bikes $7 per hr., $21 for 4hr., $28 per day. Tents $12 per night, $5 each additional night. Ski packages from $16 per day. Snowboard and boots $20 per day. Backpacks, fishing poles, and sleeping bags available. Open daily 8am-8pm. **Rick's Sport Center** (934-3416), at Rte. 203 and Center St. Daily rod rental ($10) and licenses ($10 for 2 days, $27.55 per year). Package fishing deal (waders, booties, fins, and float tube $30 per day). Open daily in summer 6am-8pm; off-season 7am-7pm.

Visitor Information: Inyo National Forest Visitors Center and Chamber of Commerce (934-8989 or 800-367-6572; www.VisitMammoth.com), east off U.S. 395 north of town. Area info and discounts on accommodations and food; offers free *Mammoth Times*, *Mammoth Trails Hiking Guide* ($3), free video, and nature exhibits and walks. Open July-Sept. daily 8am-5pm; Oct.-June. M-Sa 8am-5pm.

Bank: Bank of America, 3069 Main St. (934-6839). Open M-Th 9am-4pm, F 9am-5pm. **24hr. ATM.**

Laundromat: Mammoth Lakes Laundromat (934-2237), on Laurel Mountain Rd. 1 block off Main St. Wash $1.25, snappy 7½min. dry 25¢. Open M-Sa 8:30am-6:30pm, Su 8:30am-5pm. Last wash 1½hr. before closing.

Weather Conditions: 934-7669.

Ski Conditions: Mammoth Mountain Snow Conditions 934-6166. **Mammoth Mountain Ski Area** 934-2571. **June Mountain Ski Area** (648-7733).

Emergency: 911.

Medical Services: Mammoth Hospital, 185 Sierra Park Rd. (934-3311). 24hr. emergency care.

Post Office: 3330 Main St. Open M-F 8:30am-5pm. **ZIP Code:** 93546.

AREA CODE	The area code for Mammoth Lakes is 760.

ACCOMMODATIONS AND CAMPGROUNDS

As with most ski resorts, lodging is much more expensive in the winter, but prices tend to be cheaper on weekdays. Condo rentals are a comfortable choice for groups of three or more, and start at $55 per night in summer. **Mammoth Reservation Bureau** (800-462-5571) can make rental arrangements. For lone travelers, dorm-style motels are the cheapest option. Make reservations far in advance.

There are nearly 20 Inyo Forest public campgrounds (sites $8-11) in the area, at Mammoth Lakes, Mammoth Village, Convict Lake, Red's Meadow, and June Lake. All sites have piped water, and most are near fishing and hiking. For info, contact the **Mammoth Ranger District** (924-5500). Reservations can be made for all sites, as well as at nearby Sherwin Creek (MISTIX 800-280-2267; reservation fee $8.65).

Davison St. Guest House, 19 Davison Rd. (924-2188). Perched on the hill, Davison houses one of the best views in town. Kitchen, fireplace, and a huge common room with tons of couches, TV/VCR, and stereo. In summer dorms $15, singles $30; in winter dorms $18, singles $55.

The Ullr Lodge (934-2454; email ullr@cris.com), on Minaret Rd. 300ft. south of Main St. Clean and friendly, with family management. BBQ, kitchen, sauna, and common room with cable TV, stereo, and fun. Fax service available: $1 to send, 50¢ to receive. Winter weekend rates: dorms $15; queen bed $20-54.

Swiss Chalet, 3776 Viewpoint Rd. (800-937-9477 or 934-2403), just off Main St. 21 hilltop motel rooms with vaulted wood ceilings and stunning mountain views. Immaculate rooms with cable TV, refrigerator, ski rack, and coffee. Sundeck, indoor jacuzzi, and sauna. Rooms in summer $55-72; in winter $63-95. Wheelchair accessible.

Twin Lakes campground, ½mi. off Lake Mary Rd. about 2mi. outside town. In a pine forest, the 95 magnificent sites are mere feet away from fishing and swimming at Twin Lakes. One of the most popular campsites around despite its relatively remote location. Piped water and flush toilets. 7-night max. stay. Sites $13. Open June-Nov.

New Shady Rest campground, on Rte. 203 across from McDonald's. A 5min. walk into the heart of town. Camping isn't the same when you can see the Golden Arches through the trees, but the sites are densely wooded and manage to feel remote. 14-night max. stay. Sites $12. Half of the 95 sites available year-round for walk-in tenting.

FOOD AND NIGHTLIFE

Fast-food franchises exert hegemonic control over cheap meals, but adventurous palates need not despair. Some places have prices as high as the neighboring peaks, but others are more down-to-earth.

The Stove, 644 Old Mammoth Rd. (934-2821), 4 blocks from Main St., next to the park. The Stove equals big breakfasts. Huge stack of pancakes ($3.75) or an avocado omelette with turkey ($7). Down-home cookin' for dinner, too—try the bacon avocado burger—heaven on a bun for only $7. Vegetarian options available. Drinks served in jam jars; an old bathtub outside is now a friendly flowerbed. Open daily 6:30am-9pm.

Schat's Bakery and Cafe, 3305 Main St. (934-6055). Arguably the best bakery in town, with fruit smoothies ($2.75), cappuccino ($2.25), or 1lb. loaf of succulent sourdough ($3). Open M-F 5:30am-6pm, Sa-Su 5:30am-6pm. Inside the bakery, **Cafe Vermeer** serves breakfast and lunch daily 7am-2pm. The **Vermeer Deli** is perfect for picnic assembly, with famously fresh deli sandwiches ($6). Open daily 10am-2pm.

Angel's (934-7427), at Main and Sierra St., is unanimously recommended by locals. A tad expensive (dinner entrees $6-13) but after a day on the slopes, you'll feel you've earned it. Angel's specializes in BBQ (chicken or ribs in a basket $7.50), but tasty beef burritos ($7) are also available. Lunch specials $5.75. Bar features over 70 beers. Open M-F 11:30am-10pm, Sa-Su 5-10pm. No reservations.

Good Life Cafe, 126 Old Mammoth Rd. (934-1734), in the Mammoth Mall behind the Chart House. Teryaki chicken stir-fry ($8), chicken Caesar wrap ($7), fresh fruit bowls ($4.75), and vegetarian options make for a good lunch, if not a good life. Fear not—burgers ($5.50-7.25) and super tacos ($2-7) keep the good life full of greasy options. Open Su-Th 6:30am-3pm, F-Sa 6:30am-3:30pm.

Grumpy's, 37 Old Main St. (934-8587). Bar/restaurant has over 20 big-screen TVs, 3 pool tables, foosball, and a jukebox. Hamburger and fries $6, club sandwich $7.50, stir-fry dishes or pasta of the day $9. Open daily 11:30am-1:30am. Su brunch 10am.

Ocean Club (934-8539), on Old Mammoth Rd. downstairs from The Ocean Harvest Restaurant. Serves top-notch seafood at similar prices. Downstairs, the 20-something crowd unwinds on the dance floor. Occasional live bands. Beer specials $3. Open Th-Sa 9pm-2am; more nights in peak season.

Whiskey Creek (934-2555), at Main and Minaret St. Large bar area with dim-lit sophistication, and live entertainment (Th-Sa). Restaurant is straightforward with steak, seafood, and vegetarian entrees. Microbrews $3. Happy Hour (M-F 5-7pm) drafts $1. Bar open daily 5pm-1:30am; kitchen open 5:30-10pm.

SIGHTS

There's plenty to see in Mammoth Lakes, much of which is accessible by the **MAS shuttle service** (see p. 298). Rte. 203 and the nearby campground (sites $9) are operational only in summer and may open as late as July in years with heavy snows. In an effort to keep the area from being completely trampled, rangers have introduced a shuttle service between the parking area at the Mammoth Mountain Inn and the monument center, which all visitors—drivers and hikers alike—must use 7:30am to 5:30pm (round-trip $9, ages 5-12 $7, under 5 free). Visitors with wheels can save a load of cash by driving to the monument during free access hours (daily 5:30pm-7:30am).

DEVIL'S POSTPILE NATIONAL MONUMENT... An intriguing geological formation of basalt columns 40 to 60 feet high, the Devil's postpile was formed when lava flows oozed through Mammoth Pass thousands of years ago. After the lava cooled, ancient glaciers exposed and polished the posts.

...AND RAINBOW FALLS. A pleasant three-mile walk from the center of Devil's Postpile Monument are the **falls,** where the middle fork of the San Joaquin River drops 101 feet into a glistening green pool. *(From U.S. 395, the Devil's Postpile/Rainbow Falls trailhead can be reached by a 15mi. drive past Minaret Summit on paved Rte. 203.)*

HIKING. A quick half-mile hike from the Twin Lakes turn-off culminates in spectacular views from **Panorama Dome.** Lake Mamie has a picturesque picnic area and many short hikes lead out to Lake George, where exposed granite sheets attract climbers. For short but stunning hikes through wildflowers and amazing scenery, trek the **Crystal Lake Trail** (2½mi.) or the **Barrett Lake Trail,** both of which leave from the Lake George entrance parking lot. **Horseshoe Lake** is a popular swimming spot and is also the trailhead for the impressive Mammoth Pass Trail. The fork in the trail leads to **McLeod Lake** on the left or **Red's Meadow** on the right. These trailheads and scenic spots are accessible from the **MAS shuttle.**

Mammoth Sporting Goods (934-3239) and **Sandy's Ski & Sport** (934-7518) can equip more experienced hikers with gear and info on more challenging climbs.

FISHING OR HOW I STOPPED WORRYING AND LEARNED TO LOVE THE TROUT. Not one of the over 100 lakes near town (60 within a 5mi. radius) actually goes by the name of Mammoth Lake. The biggest, hairiest lake in the basin, the one-mile long **Lake Mary,** is popular for boating, sailing, and fishing. Anglers converge on the Mammoth area each summer to test their skills on some of the best **trout lakes** in the country. Permits are required (visitors center has info on other regulations). Fanatics will find the frequent fishing derbies well worth the price of entry, but less competitive types might prefer to try their luck at the area's serene and well-stocked backcountry waters. Manmade reservoir **Crowley Lake** (935-4301), in Owens Valley 12 miles south of town, has developed into a fishing mecca, yielding over 80 tons of rainbow trout each summer. *(Motorboat rental $48 per day; parking included. Parking without rental $6 per day. Campsites with full hookup $25.)*

Even the trout-filled **Hot Creek Geothermal Area,** five miles south of town off U.S. 395 (exit at Hot Creek Rd. for some trout-lovin' fun), allows some catch-and-release (trout) fishing. The trouty waters here are warmed by the many trout and by the hot springs formed 700,000 years ago in a trout-rific volcanic blast. Hungry trout bathe in these warm, trout-friendly waters year-round. Several trails lead to trout and the springs, but be careful—a close look may result in a severe burn or a trout-sighting. Tours of the hot springs are available, but why waste your time when you can trout-tour the neighboring trout hatchery?

FUN WITH VOLCANOES. From the shuttle stop, it's an easy quarter-mile jaunt to the **Inyo Craters,** spectacular water-filled volcanic blast holes that are a favorite spot for area waterfowl. Each crater is only about 500 years old and is an active reminder of the area's spicy underground history. The trailhead can be reached from Mammoth Scenic Loop Rd., a gently winding thoroughfare that provides access to sights between Rte. 203 and U.S. 395. **Obsidian Dome** lies 14 miles north of Mammoth Junction and one mile west of U.S. 395 on Glass Flow Rd. (follow the sign to Lava Flow). This wall of solid volcanic glass was formed by the quick chilling of volcanic lava around 1000 years ago. The hike here is a wobbly climb, so sturdy shoes and long pants are necessary.

OTHER SPORTS AND SEASONAL EVENTS

Mammoth is like a *Surge!* commercial come to life—extreme activities abound, from wall-climbing to dogsledding.

Mammoth Mountain High Adventure (924-5683) gets people high. (Through adventure. And mountains.) The stately climbing wall stands like a modern-day shrine to extreme sports, beckoning both the inexperienced and the professional. (Climb for $13 per hr., $22 per day; discount for groups of 3 or more. Open daily 10am-6pm.) The **Orienteering Course** has more of an outdoor sleuth/guerrilla warfare approach to freedom. Explore and hike through a freelance course (2hr. round-trip, $15, includes compass rental and map). Swing, tightrope walk, and rappel to freedom in the **Challenge Rope Course** (4½hr., M-Th 12:30pm, $45; group rate $40 per person; ages 10+).

Visitors can ride the **Mammoth Mountain Gondola** (934-2571) for a view miles above the rest (round-trip $10, children $5; day pass $20 for gondola and trail use. Open in summer daily 8am-4pm). Exit the gondola at the top for a mountain biking extravaganza over the twisted trails of **Mammoth Mountain Bike Park** (934-0706), where the ride starts at 11,053 feet and heads straight down on rocky ski trails (helmets required; open 9am-6pm).

Summers in Mammoth are packed with small festivals celebrating everything from mouth-watering chili to motorcross racing. The **Mammoth Lakes Jazz Jubilee** (934-2478), in mid-July, is a local favorite. The **Mammoth Motorcross Race** (934-0642), in late June (tentative dates June 22-25 in 2000), is one of the area's most popular athletic competitions, and the **National Mountain Biking Championships** (934-0651), in early September, attracts nearly 50,000 people (including cute amateur Londoners).

SKIING AND WINTER RECREATION

With 132 downhill runs, over 26 lifts, and miles of nordic skiing trails, Mammoth is one of the country's premier winter resorts. The season extends from mid-November to June; in a good year, downhill skiing can last through July. Visiting during a slow time (avoiding weekends and major holidays) can keep costs lower. Rent skis in town (see **Equipment Rental,** p. 299); resort-run shops usually charge 10-20% more. Mammoth Mountain lift tickets can be purchased at the Main Lodge (934-2571), at the base of the mountain on Minaret Rd. (open daily 7:30am-3pm). Economical multi-day lift tickets are available ($45 per day, seniors $23, ages 13-18 $34, under 13 $23; 5-day pass $191). A free **shuttle bus (MAS)** transports skiers between lifts, town, and the **Main Lodge** (see p. 298). The U.S. Forest Service provides information and tips on the area's cross-country trails.

Mammoth has miles of trails and open areas for **snowmobiles.** The **Mammoth Lake Snowmobile Association** maps out open and restricted areas. Visitors over 16 can rent snowmobiles at **Center Street Polaris DJ Snowmobile** (934-4020; open M-Sa 8am-4:30pm). The Mammoth area is lately pioneering **bobsledding;** although runs are slow enough for non-Olympians, they are still fairly exhilarating, especially at night.

June Mountain Ski Area (648-7733), at U.S. 395 North and Rte. 158 West 20 miles north of Mammoth Lakes, has less-stellar skiing, and correspondingly shorter lines, than Mammoth. Lift tickets ($37 per day, seniors $20, ages 13-18 $27, ages 7-12 $20) are available in the Tram Haus next to the parking lot.

THE SAN JOAQUIN VALLEY

The San Joaquin Valley minds its own agribusiness. Lifestyles here are conservative, unadorned, and far from the spotlight that scrutinizes the Valley's zooty western neighbors. Known as the agricultural region that separates Los Angeles and San Francisco, the San Joaquin is one of the most vital in the country, stretching from the Te-hachapi Range south of Bakersfield to just north of

Stockton. The valley is the only route to the national parks and forests of the Sierra, but mountains cut it off from the coast. The land is flat, the air is oven-hot, and the endless onion fields and rows of fruit trees are broken only by the razor-straight slashes of I-5 and Route 99. Nowhere else in the state does one feel so far from California.

STOCKTON

Stockton lies in the fertile farmland surrounding the Sacramento River Delta. It is useful as an inexpensive stopover.

Amtrak **trains** are at 735 S. San Joaquin Dr. (946-0517 or 800-231-2222). Four trains per day go to **San Francisco** ($16) and **L.A.** ($62). Greyhound **buses,** 121 S. Center St. (466-3568), sends buses to **San Francisco** (6 per day, $11); **Sacramento** (13 per day, $11); and **L.A.** (11 per day, $32). The local bus system is **Stockton Metropolitan Transit District** (943-1111; daily every 30min. 5:30am-10pm; fare $1.10, seniors 55¢, ages 6-17 85¢). The **Stockton/San Joaquin Convention and Visitor Bureau,** 46 W. Fremont St. (943-1987 or 800-350-1987), provides maps and brochures (open M-F 8am-5pm). **Dameron Hospital:** 525 W. Acacia St. (944-5550). **Emergency:** 911. **Police:** 937-8377. **Post office:** 4245 West Ln. **ZIP Code:** 95208. **Area code:** 209.

Motels north of town, off I-5 at the March Ln. Exit, are nicer and safer-feeling than places downtown. **Sixpence Inn** (931-9511), off Rte. 99 at the Waterloo Exit north of Stockton, offers air-conditioning and cable TV (singles $30; doubles $38). Stockton is a fief in the Realm of Fast Food—but for variety, there is the **Cancún Restaurant,** 248 N. El Dorado St. (465-6810), servin' up lunch specials ($3) such as burritos, enchiladas, or quesadillas (open Su-Th 11am-10:30pm, F-Sa 11am-3am), and **Le Kim's,** 631 N. Center St. (943-0308), dishin' out Vietnamese cuisine like nobody's business (coconut-curry chicken $5; open M-Sa 10am-10pm).

MERCED

The wide streets of Merced (pop. 60,348) project an order and an openness embodied by the entire town. Although modest enough to bow before the power of Yosemite, Merced proudly asserts its small offerings in its well-organized *Visitor's Guide.* If you're on your way to the Sierra Nevada, this is probably one of the best places to stop, refuel, and get a good night's sleep.

ORIENTATION AND PRACTICAL INFORMATION. Snuggled around Rte. 99, Merced maintains a small-town image along N, H, and Main St. Farther north along R and G St., Olive Ave. hosts standard mall and restaurant chains. Greyhound **buses,** 710 W. 16th St. (722-2121 or 800-231-2222), run to **San Francisco** and **L.A.** (Widely varying schedules; call ahead for timetable and rates.) If you want to step through the "gateway" to Yosemite, call **Via Adventures,** 300 Grogan Ave. (384-1315 or 800-842-5463), or stop by the Greyhound bus station around 9am or 2pm when a representative can answer questions or make reservations (fare $20, children $10, under 3 free). Amtrak **trains,** 355 W. 24th St. (722-6862 or 800-USA-RAIL/872-7245), run to **L.A.** and **Reno,** among other destinations (open daily 9am-7pm). Public transportation within Merced calls itself **The Bus** (345-3111 or 800-345-3111) and may be flagged down at any street corner, although passengers who wait at regular bus stops are appreciated. (Runs M-F 7:30am-5:30pm, Sa 9:30am-5:30pm. Fare $1, all-day pass $2.50.) The Bus also operates an on-demand dial-a-ride service for elderly and disabled patrons. The **Greater Merced Chamber of Commerce,** 690 W. 16th St. (384-3333), has Yosemite road condition, travel, and activities information, and maps and brochures on local restaurants, accommodations, and transportation options (open M-F 9am-5pm). **Emergency:** 911. **Police:** 611 W. 22nd St. (385-6912). **Mercy Hospital and Health Services:** 2740 M St. (384-6444; 24hr.) **Post office:** 2334 M St. (800-275-8777). **ZIP Code:** 95340. **Area code:** 209.

ACCOMMODATIONS. The eight-bed **Merced Home Hostel** (725-0407) picks guests up for free from the bus and train stations. Visitors must call in advance; without reservations the address is not disclosed. (Members $14, non-members $17. Reservations required.) Advertising the lowest prices in town, the **Happy Inn,** 740 Motel Dr. (722-6291), has a pool and clean, newly renovated teal-and-brick rooms with huge mirrors. Prices include cable TV, local calls, and continental breakfast. (Small rooms $24; regular rooms $28-55.)

Residents will admit that going out to eat usually entails leaving town; although an agricultural center, Merced is not known for its cuisine. Smorgasbords and local fast-food joints are the most prolific establishments. Pleasant **Mandarin Shogun,** 1204 W. Olive Ave. (722-6313), offers an all-you-can-eat lunch buffet ($5.45; dinner $7.45; 10% discount for seniors) with a variety of entree and dessert choices (open Su-Th 11am-2:30pm and 5-9:30pm, F-Sa 11am-2:30pm and 5-10pm). **La Nita's,** 1327 W. 18th St. (723-2291), serves mainly Mexican dishes, and a few "American" ones (lunch specials $4.75; open Tu-Sa 9am-9:30pm, Su 8am-9:30pm).

SIGHT. Touting itself as "The Gateway to Yosemite," Merced functions primarily as a portal to that great wilderness. Tucked away within its own borders, however, is an attraction all its own. The old **Courthouse,** 21st and N St. (723-2401), houses an unpretentious museum with free, informative tours. Volunteer residents recall personal and public anecdotes that transform a typical small-town museum into a discovery of American quirks and inventions. (Open W-Su 1-4pm.)

FRESNO

Fresno (pop. 406,000) offers big-city amenities and disadvantages, but with fewer attractions and less charm. Truly an asphalt jungle, Fresno is dusty, hot, and in many places crime-ridden. However, residents try take pride in the city's artistic heritage (William Saroyan, Ansel Adams, and Cher survived here for years despite the lack of scenery) and agricultural prowess—half the country's nectarines and ninety-nine percent of the world's raisins are grown here. Dried fruit, though, does not a nightlife make; Fresno's after-hours scene is kaput, and the city's chief allure is its convenience en route to or from the Sierra Nevada.

ORIENTATION AND PRACTICAL INFORMATION

Fresno is an ideal base for entry into the cool peaks of the Sierra Nevada. Rte. 41 heads due north, bound for Yosemite National Park, Rte. 168 winds northeast past Huntington Lake through Sierra National Forest, and Rte. 180 traverses the eastern valley before climbing into Sequoia National Forest and Kings Canyon National Park.

Rte. 99 jags northwest-southeast, Rte. 180 runs east-west, and Rte. 41 cuts north-south. Before entering the city, arm yourself with a detailed map (available at the Chamber of Commerce and Visitor Bureau). Fresno has the highest crime rate in California; exercise caution.

Airport: Fresno Air Terminal, 5175 E. Clinton Way (498-4095), northeast of downtown (bus #26).

Trains: Amtrak, 2650 Tulare St. (486-7651 or 800-872-7245), at Santa Fe. To **San Francisco** (3 per day, $39-44) and **L.A.** (4 per day, $25-41).

Buses: Greyhound, 1033 Broadway (800-231-2222) at Tulare St. To **San Francisco** (9 per day, $22) and **L.A.** (20 per day, $21). Lockers for ticketed passengers only.

Public Transportation: Fresno Area Express (FAX; 488-1122) has 15 routes; most leave from the courthouse, at Fresno St. and Van Ness Ave., or 2 blocks west at Fresno and Broadway. Fare 75¢, seniors and disabled 35¢, under 5 free. Exact change. Anyone can purchase discount tokens (60¢) in advance at 2223 G St. Most routes run every

30min. M-F 6am-6:30pm, Sa-Su 10:30am-5:45pm. Route maps at the office in Manchester Shopping Center, at Sheilds and Blackstone Ave.

Visitor Information: Convention and Visitor Bureau, 808 M St. (233-0836 or 800-788-0836), at Inyo St. Info on city businesses, events, and attractions. Open M-F 8am-5pm. The **Beeline** (443-2400, ext. 1516) has info on local news, weather, and sports. **Fresno County and City Chamber of Commerce,** 2331 Fresno St. (495-4800; www.fresnochamber.com) at N St. Open M 9am-5pm, Tu-Th 8am-5pm, F 8am-4:30pm.

Equipment Rental: Herb Bauer's Sporting Goods, 6264 N. Blackstone Ave. (435-8600). Good selection of camping supplies–stock up here before heading into the Sierra. Open M-F 9am-9pm, Sa 9am-7pm, Su 10am-5pm.

Laundromat: Plaza, 3097 Tulare St. (266-1107), at U St. Wash from $1; 8½min. dry 25¢. Open 24hr.

Road Conditions: CalTrans (800-427-ROAD/7623). 24hr. recording.

Weather Conditions: 442-1212. **Ski Report:** 233-3330.

Emergency: 911.

Post Office: 2309 Tulare St., at O St. **ZIP Code:** 93721

Area Code: Unless otherwise specified, the new area code is 559.

ACCOMMODATIONS

Run-of-the-mill motels line the freeways in Fresno, both dependable large chain motels and variable little inns.

Welcome Inn, 777 N. Parkway Dr. (237-2175), off Rte. 99. Newly renovated, the inn is one of the nicest inexpensive places in Fresno. The rooms are clean and the beds are incredibly comfy. Laundry, pool, lounge. Rooms with queen bed from $22.

Red Roof Inn, 5021 N. Barcus Ave. (276-1910), at Shaw Ave. Exit off Rte. 99. 86 large clean rooms. Pool, cable TV, A/C, laundry, pets allowed. Singles with queen bed from $37.

Super 8 Motel, 2127 Inyo St. (268-0621 or 800-800-8000), at Van Ness, 2 blocks from the visitors center. Usually safe, central, non-freeway location. **Exercise caution in the area at night.** Spacious, renovated rooms with large-screen cable TV and A/C. Pool. Continental breakfast included. Singles from $45; rates go up when conferences are in town.

Ramada Inn, 4278 W. Ashlan Ave. (275-2727), at Rte. 99. Brand-new digs with deluxe frills. Landscaped pool and courtyard is a football-field-sized green oasis from the hot, hectic city. Rooms with queen bed from $50.

FOOD AND ENTERTAINMENT

Thanks to the county's rich harvests and its Armenian, Mexican, and Southeast Asian communities, good food abounds. The old **Chinatown,** west of the railroad tracks at Kern Ave., has many Asian and Mexican restaurants and stores, while the **Tower District,** bordered by Olive Ave. and Wishon St., is the center of Fresno's middling nightlife, and a good place to people-watch. After dark in both places, use extra caution. At the outdoor **produce market,** at Merced and N St., vendors drive pickup trucks into a parking lot, hang scales from their awnings, and sell, sell, sell (open Tu, Th, and Sa 7am-3pm).

Central Fish Market, 1535 Kern Ave. (237-2049), at G St. Japanese restaurant doubles as a full grocery store, with fresh fish and produce. Entree of shrimp or chicken with vegetables, rice, and salad $4. Market open daily 8am-6:30pm; restaurant 11am-6pm.

Santa Fe Hotel, 935 Santa Fe Ave. (266-2170), at Tulare St. Family-style Basque food served at long tables. The decor isn't much, but quality and quantity compensate. Enormous lunches $7, dinner $8-12. Open M 11am-2pm, Tu-Sa 11am-2pm and 5-9pm, Su 11am-2pm and 4:30-8pm.

Brix Cantina, 1152 N. Fulton St (237-4226), at the corner of Olive Ave. in the Tower District. This restaurant serves contemporary American cuisine on the patio or in the airy room. Dinner $8-21. Happy Hour Tu-Sa 4-6pm (beer and some appetizers 99¢). Open Tu-Sa 4pm-midnight.

Café Moná, 2011 Tuolumne Ave. (497-8535), at Van Ness Ave., 1 block from the Metropolitan Museum. A cool, relaxed lunch parlor that serves delicious sandwiches ($5.35, including salad) and elegant melt-in-your-mouth pastries. Gourmet coffees and teas $1-3. Open M-F 8am-2pm.

SIGHTS AND SEASONAL EVENTS

BALDASARE FORESTIERE UNDERGROUND GARDENS. Forestiere migrated from Sicily with high hopes for agricultural success in California, but found that his land had poor topsoil. After digging a basement and toying with skylights, he discovered he could grow crops underground. His subterranean success led to a year-round growing season and a 20-crop rotation. The farm is a historic landmark. *(271-0734. On Shaw St. 1 block east of Rte. 99, northwest of town. Tours W-Su 10am, noon, 2, and 4pm. Admission $6, seniors and ages 13-19 $5, under 13 $4.)*

FRESNO ART MUSEUM. Featuring changing exhibitions, artists in residence, and educational programs, this small state-of-the-art facility is also home to a permanent collection of Mexican art and French post-Impressionist graphics. *(441-4220. 2233 N. First St., between Clinton and McKinley Ave. Open Tu-F 10am-5pm, Sa-Su noon-5pm. Admission $2, students and seniors $1, under 15 free; free Tu.)*

FRESNO METROPOLITAN MUSEUM OF ART, HISTORY, AND SCIENCE. The museum features a permanent exhibit on the life of Fresno native and Pulitzer Prize-winning novelist and playwright William Saroyan, but also shows regional and traveling exhibits. "Africa: One Continent, One World" will be at the Fresno Met from January 28-April 23, 2000. *(441-1444; www.fresnomet.org. 1559 Van Ness Ave., at Calaveras. Take bus #28. Open daily 11am-5pm. Admission $5; students, seniors, and under 12 $4; Th after 5pm free.)*

SAROYAN, SAROYAN, SAROYAN. Fresno goes out of its way to please Saroyan fans. The theater is named after him, as are the symposium and bicycle race. There are Saroyan bus tours *($24),* which visit all the Saroyan sights, and a Saroyan agricultural tour *($13)* which winds through the **Blossom Trail,** a 62-mile-long (often self-guided) driving tour that highlights the wonders of Fresno's agriculture. *(Call 800-788-0836 for information.)* The **Saroyan Festival** (Armenian food and an essay contest) is held the first weekend in May, and includes writing contests and American folk music. The **Clovis Rodeo** (Go Eagles!), held the last weekend in April, is the largest two-day rodeo held in California. *(299-8838.)*

OAKHURST

At the intersection of Rte. 40 and 141, Oakhurst (pop. 2602) is a gateway town to Bass Lake and southern Yosemite through the Sierra National Forest. This is one of the last places to find a reasonable restaurant, buy bulk groceries, and fill up with cheap gas before heading into Yosemite. Oakhurst is stocked with information on area parks and forests and is a very reliable resource. Try the **Yosemite Sierra Visitor's Bureau,** 41729 Rte. 41 (683-4636), for maps and info (open daily in summer 8:30am-5pm; in winter M-Sa 8:30am-5pm).

Tasty treats can be found in grocery stores and shops along Rte. 41 in town. The **Ol' Kettle Restaurant,** 40650 Rte. 41 (683-7505), dishes up good American home cookin' in a country diner-style restaurant with reasonable prices (open daily 7am-9pm). **El Cid,** 41939 Rte. 41 (683-6668), serves Mexican fare (massive burrito plate $5) in a calm, quiet spot with a shady porch.

BAKERSFIELD

Virtually every commercial chain that has existed on the West Cost in the past twenty years still has a home in Bakersfield (pop. 213,000). Although convenient for the scores of truckers looking for a place to rest on the road to Fresno, Bakersfield is more of a pitstop than a tourist locale. To be fair, not everyone you see is just stopping over—there is a large L.A. commuter population—but you'll look long and hard for much local culture.

PRACTICAL INFORMATION. Get a car at **Rent-A-Wreck,** 1130 24th St. (322-6100), at M St. Cheap deals ($25 per day) are only for the 21-and-up set, although they rent to ages 18-20 for a stiff fee. **Greater Bakersfield Chamber of Commerce:** 1033 Truxtun Ave. (327-4421; open M 9am-5pm, Tu-F 8am-5pm). **Bakersfield Memorial Hospital:** 420 34th St. (327-1792), at Q St. (24hr.). **Police:** 1601 Truxtun Ave. (327-7111). **Post Office:** 1730 18th St. (861-4346). **ZIP Code:** 93302. **Area code:** 805.

ACCOMMODATIONS AND FOOD. Bakersfield's reputation as a great overnight stop is well-earned. The best of the cheap but clean and safe motels cluster at the Olive St. Exit. **Motel 6,** 5241 Olive Tree Court (392-9700), has four locations in Bakersfield, but the Olive Tree Court site has the lowest rates (singles $27; doubles $31). **E-Z 8 Motels,** 5200 Olive Tree Court (392-1511), has TV, pool, local calls, and coffee (singles $28; doubles $32). The **Economy Motels of America,** 6100 Knudsen Ave. (392-1800), offers TV and pool (singles or doubles $40).

Locals love **Luigi's,** 725 East 19th St. (322-0926), a loud, crowded deli/bar/cafe with great food. Arrive around lunch and expect to wait a few minutes for a seat, or opt for a deli takeout in no time. **Gatsby's Cafe,** 1300 Coffee Rd. (588-3088), is one of the few places where Popeye, the Beatles, and country music coexist in peace (sandwiches $6; open daily 7am-2pm). Mexican food fans should salsa to **El Adobe Mexican Restaurant,** 2620 Ming Ave. (397-1932), where one- to four-item combos are $5-7 (open daily 11am-9pm).

SIGHTS. The extensive **Kern County Museum** complex has over 50 structures dedicated to Kern County's lifestyle and development. Buildings in various degrees of restoration need hours to be fully explored. (Open M-F 8am-5pm, Sa 10am-5pm, Su noon-5pm. Ticket office closes daily at 3pm. Admission $5, seniors $4, children $3.) Country music fans should do-se-do over to **Buck Owens' Crystal Palace,** 2800 Pierce Rd. (328-7560), a restaurant/theater with a museum built into the walls. Although it is theoretically open seven days a week, Buck Owens' often closes for music video filming or special events, so call ahead. (Museum entrance fee $5. Entrees $7-27.)

NORTHERN INTERIOR

Gold Country lies east of Sacramento in the vast plains, rocky hills, and swift rivers of California's Northern Interior. The towns in the northern part of Gold Country are far removed from the less-authentic Main Street scenes to the south, and the natural beauty of this region rewards exploration. The Cascade Mountains interrupt the expanse of farmland to the northeast, where both ancient and recent volcanic activity have left behind a surreal landscape of lava beds, mountains, lakes, waterfalls, caves, and recovering forest areas.

GOLD COUNTRY

In 1848, California was a rural backwater of only 15,000 people. The same year, sawmill operator James Marshall wrote in his diary: "This day some kind of mettle...found in the tailrace...looks like goald." In the next four years some 90,000 '49ers from around the world headed for California and the 120 miles of gold-rich seams called the Mother Lode. Despite the hype, few of the prospectors struck it rich. Miners, sustained by dreams of instant wealth, worked long and hard, yet most could barely squeeze sustenance out of their fiercely guarded claims.

Many miners died of malnutrition. Mark Twain described the diet as "Beans and dishwater for breakfast, dishwater and beans for dinner. And both articles warmed over for supper." Poorly constructed mines and risky techniques killed many more. In Coloma, during one miner's funeral, a mourner spotted "color" (goald) in the open grave. In true California style, the coffin was quickly removed and all in attendance, including the preacher, took to the ground with shovels.

Five years after the big discovery, the panning gold was gone, and miners could survive only by digging deeper and deeper into the rock. In some instances, whole towns were destroyed in hopes of finding "color" underneath. All but a few mines were abandoned by the 1870s, along with most of the towns around them.

Although gold remains in them thar hills, today the towns of Gold Country make their money mining the tourist traffic. Gussied up as "Gold Rush Towns," they solicit tourists traveling along the appropriately numbered Route 49, which connects dozens of small Gold Country settlements. Prepare for stomach-dropping (roads) and jaw-dropping (vistas) experiences when traveling Route 49; travelers without an off-road vehicle should be careful of straying too far from the highway. Traffic from the coast connects with Route 49 via Interstate 80 through Sacramento, which today serves as a supply post for tourists. If you tire of Gold Country lore, vineyard touring, river rafting, and spelunking are popular. Most of Gold Country is about two hours from Sacramento, or three hours from San Francisco.

HIGHLIGHTS OF THE NORTHERN INTERIOR

■ The end of the Gold Rush left behind many **former mining towns,** including Sonora (p. 314) and Coloma/James Marshall Gold Discovery State Park (p. 317).
■ The landscape also features **subterranean caverns** in Calaveras County (p. 315).
■ **Mount Shasta** (p. 328) attracts bikers, hikers, and skiers, while **Mount Lassen** (p. 321) is a prime camping area.
■ The pristine beauty of **Crater Lake** (p. 337) is accessible on a hike or in a car.
■ **Lava Beds National Monument** (p. 334) is riddled with fascinating caves.
■ The **Oregon Shakespeare Festival** (p. 339) in Ashland, Oregon, is a renowned and long-lasting gathering of Elizabethan dramatic performances.

SACRAMENTO

Sacramento (area pop. 1.6 million) is the distinctive capital of a highly distinctive state. In 1848, Swiss emigré John Sutter, fleeing a debtor's prison back home, purchased 48,000 dusty acres for a few trinkets from the Miwok tribe. His trading fort became the central pavilion for the influx of gold miners to the Valley in the 1850s. Gradually over the next century, mansions and suburban bungalows changed the landscape, paving the way for future residents Ronald Reagan and the Brady Bunch. Still full of politicians and housewives, Sacramento is also home to a large gay community and a lively coffeehouse scene (none of which are mutually exclusive), centered around the city's youthful midtown. Sacramento balances between the excitement of the Californian city to the west and the mountains to the east, while remaining as cozy and slow as any small town (especially in summer, when temperatures can soar to 115 degrees). Don't let this slow pace fool you, though; **exercise caution at night.**

ORIENTATION AND PRACTICAL INFORMATION

Sacramento is at the center of the **Sacramento Valley.** Five major highways converge on the city: **Interstate 5** and **Route 99** run north-south, **Interstate 80** runs east-west between San Francisco and Reno, and **U.S. 50** and **Route 16** bring traffic westward from Gold Country. Numbered streets run north-south and lettered streets run east-west in a grid: The street number on a lettered street corresponds to the number of the cross street (2000 K St. is near the corner of 20th St.). The capitol building, parks, and endless cafes and restaurants occupy the **downtown area.**

Airport: Sacramento International (929-5411), 12mi. north on I-5. Cabs are expensive ($22-25 to downtown). Vans are cheaper ($9-10); find out more at info desks.

Trains: Amtrak, 401 I St. (800-USA-RAIL/872-7245), at 5th St. To: **San Francisco** ($12.50-19); **Reno** ($35-76); **L.A.** ($39-70); and **Seattle** ($83-138). Prices depend on availability. Station open daily 4:45am-11:30pm. **Be careful at night.**

Buses: Greyhound, 715 L St. (800-231-2222), between 7th and 8th St. To: **San Francisco** ($12); **Reno** ($20); and **L.A.** ($35). Lockers. Open 24hr. **Be careful at night.**

Public Transit: Sacramento Regional Transit Bus and Light Rail, 1400 29th St. (321-2877). Provides transportation around town. Fare in city center 50¢; outer destinations $1.25 (free transfer). Seniors, disabled, and ages 5-12 50¢. Day passes $3.

Taxis: Old Checker Cab Company (457-2222). 24hr.

Car Rental: Rent-A-Wreck, 212 I St., Davis (530-753-7780). First 100mi. included. Credit card or $200 security deposit if using cash. Open M-F 8am-5pm, Sa 8am-noon.

Bike Rental: American River Bike Shop, 9203 Folsom Blvd. (363-6271). Bikes $4 per hr., $20 per day. Grab a friend for a tandem ride ($6 per hr., $30 per day). Open M-F 9am-7pm, Sa 9am-6pm, Su 9am-5pm.

Visitor Information: Sacramento Convention and Visitor Bureau, 1303 J St. #600 (264-7777; www.sacromento.svb.org), at 13th St. Small and congenial. Open M-F 8am-5pm. **The Beeline** (552-5252) gives recorded events information.

Emergency: 911. **Police:** 900 8th St. (264-5471), at I St.

Medical Services: U.C. Davis Medical Center: 2315 Stockton Blvd. (734-2011), at Broadway.

Internet Access: Sacramento Library: 828 I St., between 8th and 9th St. Free 30min. per person per day. Open M and F noon-4pm, Tu-Th 10am-5pm, Sa-Su 1-5pm.

Post Office: 900 Sacramento Ave. (800-275-8777). Open M-F 8:30am-5pm. **ZIP code:** 95605.

AREA CODE	The area code in Sacramento is 916.

ACCOMMODATIONS

Sacramento has many motels, yet waves of backpackers, businesspeople, and politicians can flood accommodations, making it hard to find a room; for guaranteed lodging, reserve a month in advance. The cheap hotels that line **West Capitol Avenue** in nearby West Sacramento may be a bit seedy, so be choosy. Within Sacramento proper, **16th Street** is home to many hotels and motels. Rates fluctuate seasonally.

Sacramento Hostel (HI-AYH), 900 H St. (443-1691), at 9th St. A fantastic place to stay in the city, whether or not you're on a tight budget. Looks more like an upscale, elegant B&B than a hostel, with high sloping ceilings, a grand mahogany staircase, and a stained-glass atrium. The restored Victorian mansion (c. 1885) also boasts a huge modern kitchen, 3 large living rooms, library, TV/VCR, and an extensive selection of video rentals ($1). Dorm-style rooms are spacious, immaculate, and beautifully decorated. Guests are given 1 brief chore in the morning. Laundry. Check-in 7-9:30am and 5-10pm. Check-out 9:30am. Doors lock at 11pm, so speak to the receptionist before going out. Dorms $18, with HI-AYH $15. Family, couple, and single rooms available. Ask about group rates. Wheelchair accessible.

Sacramento Econo Lodge, 711 16th St. (443-6631 or 800-55-ECONO/553-2266), between G and H St. Recent remodeling puts it a cut above a standard motel; most rooms have hair dryers, refrigerators, and free HBO, CNN, and ESPN. Continental breakfast included. Room with queen bed $55; with 2 doubles or king bed $65.

Quality Inn, 818 15th St. (444-3980 or 800-228-5151). Rooms are of a much higher quality than the exterior might suggest. Small pool, A/C, and cable TV. Continental breakfast included. Singles $62; doubles $72.

FOOD

Most cafes and restaurants are on **J Street** or **Capitol Avenue** between 19th and 29th St. For those who dare to venture into tourist territory, Old Sacramento is home to countless gimmicky restaurants, which tend to be more expensive.

The Fox and Goose, 1001 R St. (443-8825), at 10th St. In a glass factory built in 1913 and renovated in the 1970s, this funky English pub and restaurant has lots of character. They serve everything from a proper pot of tea to European beer ($3.15) to stir-fried tofu. Open mic nights, live bands, and wizards performing live magic. Food served M-F 7am-2pm and 5:30-9:30pm, Sa-Su 8am-1pm. Wheelchair accessible.

Ricksha, 2228 10th St. (442-6246), at W St. Gimmick-heavy Japanese joint. Ladies night on W (noblewomen get $3 box dinners for half-price). On Su, the all-you-can-eat buffet is a deal (adults $13, children $6.50). Everybody eats cheap Tu and Th ($1 sushi rolls). Open M-Th 11am-2pm and 5-9pm, F-Sa 11am-2pm and 5-9:30pm.

Cafe Bernardo, 2726 Capitol Ave. (443-1189), at 28th St. Outdoor seating allows full appreciation of summer evenings. The interior displays the work of a different local artist each month. Delectable sandwiches ($6-7), salads ($2-6), and soups ($2-3). Open Su-Th 7am-10pm, F-Sa 7am-11pm.

Paesano's Pizzeria, 1806 Capitol Ave. (447-8646), at 18th St. Creative combinations of toppings (roasted almonds, garlic, fontina cheese, Kierkegaard, kalamata olives, etc.) make Paesano's one of the best pizzerias in town. *Patata e Pollo* with goat cheese is a tasty $8. Varied selection of salads and pasta. Open M-W 11:30am-9:30pm, Th 11:30am-10pm, F 11:30am-10:30pm, Sa 5-10:30pm, Su 4-9:30pm.

Amarin (447-9063), at 12th and I St. Tasty and inexpensive. Nibble on chicken *satay* ($6.25) amidst the casual elegance of this well-loved local spot. Large portions and vegetarian options abound. Lunch specials $5, dinner $6-11. Open M-F 11am-9pm, Sa-Su noon-9pm.

Rubicon Brewing Company, 2004 Capitol Ave. (448-7032), at 20th St. Home of an India Pale Ale that won the 1989 and 1990 American Beer Festivals. Cool, laid-back microbrewery with top-quality food. The brewing process can be watched from the dining area, and the results are worth trying (pint $2.50). Sandwiches $4-7; spunky frittata $5. Su brunch. Vegetarian options. Open M-Th 11am-11:30pm, F-Sa 8:30am-12:30am, Su 8:30am-10pm. Kitchen closes earlier. Wheelchair accessible.

SIGHTS

The state government rules over Sacramento sights. Stormy debates about immigration, welfare, water shortages, and secession rage daily in the elegant **State Capitol** (324-0333), at 10th and Capitol Ave. (1hr. tours depart daily every hr. 9am-4pm; free tickets distributed in Room B27 on a first-come, first-served basis.) Colonnades of towering palm trees and grassy lawns make **Capitol Park** an oasis in the middle of downtown's busy bureaucracy. The **State Historic Park Governor's Mansion** (324-0539), at 16th and H St., was built in 1877 and served as the residence of California's governor and his family until then-governor Ronald Reagan opted to rent his own pad (open daily 10am-5pm; hourly tours; admission $3, ages 6-12 $1.50, under 6 free).

Old Sacramento, the city's biggest tourist attraction, has been refurbished to resemble its late-19th century appearance, but wooden sidewalks and horse-drawn carriages are not enough to mask the roaring freeway overhead or the skyscrapers in the background. If you feel overwhelmed by the tourist mania and historic hoopla, try a freshly pulled piece of taffy or overpriced cotton candy to calm your nerves. The **California State Railroad Museum** (552-5252, ext. 7245), at 2nd and I St., exhibits 23 historic locomotives (open daily 10am-5pm; admission $6, ages 6-12 $3, under 6 free).

The **Crocker Art Museum,** 216 O St. (264-5423), between 2nd and 3rd St., exhibits 19th-century European and American oil paintings, Asian art, and contemporary California art. (Open Tu-W and F-Su 10am-5pm, Th 10am-9pm. Admission $5.50, seniors $4.50, ages 7-17 $3, under 7 free. Tours available; book a week in advance.)

A popular outdoor activity, river rafting can be done quite close to Sacramento. Rent rafts at **American River Raft Rentals,** 11257 S. Bridge St., Rancho Cordova (635-6400), 10 miles east of downtown on U.S. 50. Exit on Sunrise Blvd. and take it north 1½ miles to the American River, where there's fun in the sun. Beware of rafters armed with water guns who ruthlessly spray sunbathers. (Open daily 9am-6pm, rentals available until 2pm. 4-person raft $30. $2 launch fee, $2.50 per person for return shuttle.)

The **American River Recreation Trail and Parkway,** spanning over 30 miles from Discovery Park to Folsom Lake, is a nature preserve where you can still glimpse the downtown skyline. Four million people a year visit to cycle, jog, swim, fish, hike, and ride horses on the secluded banks. You can enter the trail in Old Sacramento or at designated entrance points along the river.

ENTERTAINMENT AND NIGHTLIFE

Capital-dwellers slither among brass and mahogany that recalls the Gold Rush era, while enjoying the highly refined moving images and coffee beverages of more recent origin. Sacramento's entertainment parlors afford a view of city residents who are odder-looking and more frequently body-pierced than their fellow citizens in the government. The **Fox and Goose** (see p. 311) lords over Sacramento nightlife.

If you're visiting Sacramento, try to catch a **Sacramento Kings** basketball game; to order single-game tickets by phone, call 916-649-TIXS/8497, 530-528-TIXS, or 209-485-TIXS. The Kings play at the Arco Arena (916-928-6900; One Sports Pkwy).

The Tower Cafe, 1518 Broadway (441-0222), between 15th and 16th St., introduces Hollywood glitz to modernism and primitivism. Food from all walks of the world (American, Jamaican, Italian, Asian, Mexican, Persian, Malaysian, and Greek). Sip beer, crunch on a salad ($4-9), or chew on a burger ($7.50). Open Su-Th 8am-11pm, F-Sa 8am-1am. Kitchen closes earlier and the bar rages on.

Old Ironsides (443-9751), at 10th and S St. A local favorite. Live bands Tu and Th-Sa, disco parties Su (F-Sa cover $5-7, usually no cover Tu). Grease up and groove on the dance floor or in the bar area. Drafts $1.50. Open daily 8:30am-2am.

Faces, 2000 K St. (448-7798). *The* gay club in Sacramento. High-stylin' with 5 huge bar areas (dance, video, conversation, microbrew bar, and patio). Su afternoon BBQ 5:30pm. Occasional amateur stripteases Su and Th nights. Open daily 2pm-2am.

Crest Theater (442-7378), at 10th and K St. Built in 1913 as a vaudevillian stage, the Crest is now a theater reminiscent of the golden age of Sacramento's theater district. Within the monstrous theater/cinema are palatial stairways, gilded ceilings, crystal chandeliers, and a decadent paisley carpet. Open daily. Admission $7; students, seniors, and under 13 $4.50; matinees $4.50.

New Helvetia Roasters and Bakers (441-1106), 19th St. between L St. and Capitol Ave. This converted firehouse provides a great taste of the midtown flair. Giant baked goods made fresh daily. Brimming over with drink options warm (coffees, teas, chai $1-3) and cool (fruit smoothies $3.50). Garden patio outside. Open daily 6:30am-11pm.

SEASONAL EVENTS

Sacramento wakes up with free afternoon concerts and cheap food in summer. The Friday edition of the *Sacramento Bee* contains a supplement called *Ticket,* which gives a rundown of events, restaurants, and night spots. For weekend music and activities, check the free weeklies, such as *Sacramento News and Review* and *Suttertown News*. The free *Alive and Kicking* has schedules and information about music and arts throughout the city.

Outdoor Fair, at Cesar Chávez Park. Live bands, food stands, beer gardens. In summer, every Friday evening until dark.

SummerFest, at K St. Mall, between 7th and 13th St. Attracts over 15,000 people. Live music, produce stands, and craft booths. Late May-early Oct. every Th night.

Dixieland Jazz Jubilee (372-5277). Over 100 bands play every Memorial Day weekend (May 27-29 in 2000).

Shakespeare in the Park, William Land Park. Evenings June-Aug. Picnicking encouraged.

California State Fair (263-3000). Agriculturally inclined fair still doesn't skimp on spinning rides, fairway food, and pig races. Mid-Aug-Early Sept.

DAVIS

Davis (pop. 48,275) digs its eco-passions into the dirt 13 miles west of Sacramento off Interstate 80. Leading the way for the area in energy conservation (there are even energy-saving traffic signals), veganism, flute-playing, and tie-dye wearing, Davis folk come out in full force at events such as the Whole Earth Festival (held annually in late May). And they come out on bicycles—there are more bicycles (1 per capita) in Davis than in any other city in the U.S. Town activity is centered around the University of California at Davis (UCD).

PRACTICAL INFORMATION. Amtrak, 840 2nd St. (800-USA-RAIL/872-7245), provides **train** service to **Sacramento** ($5) and **San Francisco** ($14). **Unitrans** (752-2877) connects downtown and the UCD campus (50¢). **Yolo Bus** (371-2877) serves Davis and Sacramento ($1.50; seniors, disabled, and ages 5-12 75¢). You can get info at the **Chamber of Commerce,** 228 B St. (756-5160; open M-F 9am-5pm), and at the **UC Davis Information Center,** in the Griffin Lounge on campus (752-2222, campus events 752-2813; open M-F 9am-4pm). For **Internet** access, go to the **Yolo County Library, Davis Branch** on 14th St. (1hr. free per person per day; out-of-towners must surrender driver's license. Open M 1-9pm, Tu-Th 10am-9pm, F-Sa 10am-5:30pm, Su 1-5pm.) **Post office:** 2929 5th St. (800-275-8777; open M-F 8:30am-5:30pm, Sa 10am-1pm). **ZIP Code:** 95817. **Area code:** 530.

ACCOMMODATIONS AND FOOD. Motels in Davis do not come cheap, and during university events you'll be lucky to get a room. **Davis Inn,** 1111 Richards Blvd. (756-0910), off I-80 at the Richards Blvd. Exit, is six blocks from campus, has recently remodeled rooms and a fairly large pool (doubles with queen bed $75, with king bed $80).

A true college town, Davis is peppered with quirky and creative cafes. The downtown area on E and F St. is always a sure bet when looking for a slice of pizza, a vegetarian smorgasbord, or a booty-kickin' spot. To stock a picnic basket, check out the **Davis Food Co-op,** 620 G St. (758-2667), which has a colossal selection of organic produce, raw pasta, hummus, and veggie burgers, as well as 15 minutes of free Internet access (open daily 8:30am-10pm). **Caffé Italia,** 1121 Richards Blvd. (758-7200), draws crowds for large portions of pasta ($8-11), pizza (from $6), and salads (from $6.50). Hanging garlic decorations (vampires beware), latticework, and Italian foods and posters add to the Italian atmosphere. (Open M-Th 6am-10pm, F-Sa 6am-11pm, Su 7am-10pm.) **Murder Burger,** 720 Olive Dr. (756-2142), is a food stand that serves massive hamburgers ($3)—they're to die for (or maybe to kill for). Try the Big Bird ($5), made of ostrich meat, for something different and lowfat; then thwart your efforts with a thick milkshake ($2.56).

SIGHTS AND ACTIVITIES. The **University of California at Davis** is the largest campus (area-wise) in the U.C. network, and also one of the nation's finest agricultural universities. When they aren't in class, some students hang out at **The Graduate,** 805 Russell Blvd. (758-4723), in the University Mall (open daily 10:30am-2am).

The town is laced with more than 40 miles of bike trails and rocks. For trail maps and ratings stop by the Chamber of Commerce or a bike shop in town. As they say in Davis, "You can't swing a dead cat in this town without hitting a bike shop or a rock." Many of these bike shops **rent bikes;** comparatively fewer rent dead cats; none rent rocks. **Wheelworks,** 247 F St. (753-3118), rents bikes for $8 per day, $15 per weekend (open M-Sa 10am-6pm, Su 10am-5pm). Still trying to get past all those bikes and get your hands on some rocks? Try **Rocknasium,** 720 Olive Dr., Suite Z (757-2902), in a warehouse just past Murder Burger, which offers climbing for all levels; the 70 routes include a bouldering cave and extensive lead climbing. This place rocks. (Open M-F 11am-11pm, Sa-Su 10am-9pm. Admission $10, students $8. Equipment rental $8, students $6.)

SONORA

The ravines and hillsides now known as Sonora (pop. 4478) were once the domain of the Miwok Indians, but the arrival of the '49ers transformed these Sierra foothills into a bustling mining camp. In its Gold Rush heyday, Sonora was a large and prosperous city that vied fiercely with nearby Columbia for the honor of being the richest city of the southern Mother Lode.

ORIENTATION AND PRACTICAL INFORMATION. The drive to Sonora takes about two hours from Sacramento, and 3½ hours from San Francisco. Sonora's layout is complicated by the fact that two highways enter the town from three directions. **Washington Street** runs north-south through town, and at the north end becomes Route 49 North. At the south end, it branches, and the east fork (Mo Way) becomes Route 108. Midtown, Washington St. intersects with **Stockton Street,** which becomes Route 49 South.

The **Visitors Center,** 55 W. Stockton Rd. (533-4420 or 800-446-1333), offers several local publications (open M-F 9am-7pm, Sa-Su 10am-5pm; in winter M-F 9am-6pm, Sa 10am-6pm). **Emergency:** 911. **Police:** 532-8141. **Tuolomne General Hospital:** 101 Hospital Rd. (533-7100; 24hr. emergency care). **Post office:** 781 S. Washington St. (800-275-8777; open M-F 8:30am-5pm, Sa 10am-2pm). **ZIP Code:** 95370. **Area code:** 209.

ACCOMMODATIONS AND FOOD. The stucco **Sonora Inn and Motel,** 160 S. Washington St. (532-2400), was built in 1896 in a Spanish style. Clean, spacious rooms have large-screen TV, phone, coffee, and A/C. Rooms in the inn are a bit larger, with floral wallpaper and colonial furniture. (Motel Su-Th $59, F-Sa $69; inn Su-Th $69, F-Sa $79; prices lower in late Nov. or early Dec.) Many roadside motels and hotels are east of Sonora on **Route 108.**

The **Diamondback Grill,** 110 S. Washington St. (532-6661), in Sonora's old-town district, is a tiny, hip restaurant offering big portions and tasty specialty burgers ($5-6; open M-Sa 6am-9pm, Su 8am-3pm). **Wilma's Cafe,** 275 S. Washington St. (532-9957), named for the wooden pig perched atop the pie case, has pink pig paraphernalia galore: murals of flying pigs, papier-mâché pigs, wind-chime pigs, porcupine pigs, and more. **Pig out** on Wilma's hearty and delicious pies and hickory-smoked barbecue burgers ($5.50-8) or homemade soup ($2-4). Surprisingly enough, there are many vegetarian options. (Open Su-Th 6am-10pm, F-Sa 6am-midnight.)

SIGHTS AND ACTIVITIES. Columbia State Historic Park (532-4301) is an entirely preserved 1850s mining town. Take Rte. 108 East from Sonora to Parrot's Ferry Rd. and look for signs to the park. Once the "Gem of the Southern Mines,"

PANNIN' FER GOALD I: THEORY It's easy and fun to pan for gold. *Let's Go* offers a quick, two-part course which will provide all the mental equipment you'll need. Once you're in Gold Country, find one of many public stretches of river. You'll need a 12- or 18-inch gold pan, which will be easily found at local stores. Dig in old mine tailings, at turns in the river, around tree roots, and at the upstream ends of gravel bars, where heavy gold may settle. Swirl water, sand, and gravel in a tilted gold pan, slowly washing materials over the edge. Be patient, and keep at it until you are down to black sand, and—hopefully—gold. Gold has a unique color. It's shinier than brassy-looking pyrite (Fool's Gold), and it doesn't break down upon touch, like mica, a similarly glittery substance. Later, we'll practice this technique (see p. 316).

and rich in placer gold (loose gold found in rivers and dirt), Columbia supported 5000 people and 150 saloons, shops, and other businesses. Now Columbia prospects for tourist dollars. The only transportation options in the four-block park area are horse and buggy. (Park and museum free. Open daily 9am-5pm.) If the pitter-patter of historic hooves and the swish-swish-swish of goldless mines don't float yer boat, maybe the **Sierra Nevada Adventure Co.,** 173 S. Washington St. (532-5621) will (outdoor equipment and kayaks, 1st day $20-60, additional days half-price; min. weight 100lbs.).

SOUTHERN MINES

Unsuspecting **Calaveras County** turned out to be literally sitting on a gold mine—the richest, southern part of the "Mother Lode"—when the big rush hit. Over 550,000 pounds of gold were extracted from the county's earth. A journalist from Missouri named Samuel Clemens, a hapless miner but a gifted spinner of yarns later known as **Mark Twain,** allegedly based "The Celebrated Jumping Frog of Calaveras County" on a tale he heard in Angels Camp Tavern. Life in this area has since imitated (or capitalized on) art; Calaveras has held **annual frog-jumping contests** since 1928. Thousands of people gather on the third weekend of May for the festivities.

A drive along the scenic **Route 49** is a great way to glimpse Calaveras County. **San Andreas,** at the juncture of Rte. 26 and 49, is the county hub and population center, but it isn't very big. The **Calaveras Visitors Bureau** (800-225-3764; email frogmail@calaveras.org; www.visitcalaveras.org), in downtown Angels Camp, is a great resource for history and sights in the area (open M-F 9am-4pm, Sa 10am-3pm, Su 11am-3pm). Just south of Angels Camp on Rte. 49 is **Tuttletown,** Mark Twain's one-time home, now little more than a historic marker, a grocery store, and a well of stories.

The real attractions of Calaveras County are the natural wonders. About 20 miles east of Angels Camp on Rte. 4 lies **Calaveras Big Trees State Park** (795-2334; open 24hr.; day use $5, senior discount). Here the *Sequoiadendron giganteum* (Giant Sequoia) reigns with might: the *giganteum* is bigger than the Statue of Liberty and is one of the largest living things ever to inhabit the earth. The **North Grove Trail** (1mi.) is wheelchair accessible, gently graded, and heavily trafficked. The less-traveled, more challenging **South Grove Trail** (4mi.) better captures the forest's beauty and timelessness. The park also offers swimmin' in **Beaver Creek** and camping. (Sites $16, hot showers. Reserve through DESTINET 800-365-2267.) Summertime visitors should prepare for gnats and mosquitoes. Be aware that the snow comes early (sometimes in Sept.) and leaves late (mid-Apr.) at Big Trees.

Calaveras County boasts gargantuan natural wonders below ground as well as above. **Moaning Cavern** (736-2708) is a vast vertical cave so large that the Statue of Liberty could live there comfortably. From Angels Camp, follow Rte. 4 four miles east, right onto Parrot's Ferry Rd., and follow signs. Descend the 236 steps or rappel 180 feet down into the cave. Whether walking cautiously or hurtling down like an extreme sportsman, be prepared for shortness of breath after the steep walk up at the tour's end. The whole experience takes about 45 minutes. (Stairs $7.75, ages 3-13 $4; rappelling 1st time $35, each additional time $17.50. Open daily in summer 9am-6pm; in winter M-F 10am-5pm, Sa-Su and holidays 9am-5pm.) **Mercer Caverns** (728-2101), nine miles north of Angels Camp, off Rte. 4 on Sheep Rd. in Murphys, offers hour-long walking tours of 10 internal rooms. Although smaller and less dramatic than Moaning Cavern, the caves are nearly a million years old. (Open M-Th 10am-6pm, F-Sa 10am-8pm. Tours every 20min. Admission $7, ages 5-11 $3.50, under 5 free.) **California Caverns** (736-2708), at Cave City, served as a naturally air-conditioned bar and dance floor during the Gold Rush when a shot of whiskey could be purchased for a pinch of gold dust. The caverns sobered up on Sundays for church services when one stalagmite served as an altar. Walking tours ($8, ages 3-13 $4.25) and "wild cavern expedition trips" explore cramped tunnels, waist-high mud, and underground lakes (2-3hr.; over 16 $75; less-strenuous for ages 9-16 $58). Directions are available at the visitors bureau (see above).

Calaveras County has been a producer of **fine wines** for nearly 150 years. Vineyards stretch along Rte. 49, and wineries abound near Plymouth. Most family-owned wineries offer free wine tasting. The **Stevenot Winery** (728-3436), two miles north of Murphy's Main St. on Sheep Ranch Rd., is the county's largest facility (free tastings daily 10am-5pm). **Kautz Ironstone Vineyards** (728-1251), on Six Mile Rd. 1½ miles south of Murphy's Main St., stores wine in caverns hewn from solid rock (tours daily 11am-5pm, tasting room open 10am-6pm).

PLACERVILLE

Placerville (pop. 9301) was once known as "Hangtown, USA" because of its reputation for handing out speedy justice at the end of a rope. Now, the **Historic Hangman's Tree** is a friendly neighborhood bar, 305 Main St. (622-3878) with a life-size replica of a hanging dead man (George) outside the store front, and a life-size ghost (Willy) inside (open daily 6am-whenever). In its Gold Rush prime, Placerville was the third largest town in California. Now it's a friendly, well-stocked stopping place on your way to somewhere else. The town preserves its past in a restored historic district of cafes, diners, bakeries, and antique shops.

ORIENTATION AND PRACTICAL INFORMATION. About one-third of the way from Sacramento to Lake Tahoe on U.S. 50, Placerville is strategically positioned to snare campers, boaters, and skiers. Most streets, including **Main Street,** run parallel to U.S. 50. **Route 49** also bisects the town, running north to Coloma (10mi.) and Auburn, and south toward Calaveras County.

Greyhound (800-231-2222) **bus** service to Placerville only makes drop-offs and pickups at 222 Main St. at Pacific St. (**Reno** $20; **Sacramento** $12). At **Enterprise,** 583 Placerville St. (621-0866), cars rent from $32 per day with 100 miles included, or $42 per day with unlimited mileage (under 25 surcharge $7 per day). The **Chamber of Commerce,** 542 Main St. (621-5885), has county maps and info (open M-F 9am-5pm). **Emergency:** 911. **Police:** 730 Main St. (642-5210). **Post office:** 3045 Sacramento St. (800-275-8777; open M-F 9am-3:30pm, Sa 10am-1pm), south of U.S. 50. **ZIP Code:** 95667. **Area code:** 530.

PANNIN' FER GOALD II: PRACTICE Swish. Swish. Swish swish. "Dammit." Swish. Swish swish. Swish. "Dammit!" Swish. Swish swish swish swish. Swish. "Goald!"

ACCOMMODATIONS AND FOOD. One of the best deals in this consistently overpriced town is the **National 9 Inn,** 1500 Broadway (622-3884), which has spotless new rooms, and comfortable queen beds. (Singles Su-Th $45, F-Sa $55-75; doubles $50-65, $65-75.)

Forage for fresh food at the **farmer's market** in the Ivy House parking lot (Th 5-8pm, Sa 8am-noon). The historic **Placerville Coffee House,** 594 Main St. (295-1481), dates from 1858. High stone walls and numerous nooks and crannies (including a 150ft. walk-in mine shaft) and offbeat displays of local artwork evoke the dusty mansion of some eccentric millionaire. (Sandwiches, fresh fruit smoothies, and espresso. Open Su-Th 7am-10pm, F-Sa 7am-11pm. Th-Sa live jazz, folk, blues, Celtic, comedy, and acoustic bands; W-Th open mic.) **Sweetie Pies,** 577 Main St. (642-0128), is known for its huge cinnamon buns, full espresso bar, light lunches (sandwiches $6), and extensive breakfast menu ($4-7), and has delicious homemade pie (slice $3.25; open M-F 6:30am-4pm, Sa 7am-3pm, Su 7am-noon). For a *Dukes of Hazzard* experience, saunter into **Poor Red's** (622-2901), on El Dorado's Main St. five miles south of Placerville on Rte. 49. Quite the Boss Hogg scene, this dusty place is always packed. Bartenders claim that over 52 tons of ribs ($10) were served here in only one year. Their famous two-glass "Golden Cadillac" (responsible for 3% of the total American consumption of galliano) is only $3.25. (Open M-F 11:30am-2pm and 5-11pm, Sa 5-11pm, Su 2-11pm.)

SIGHTS. The hills around Placerville are filled with fruit and good cheer; by bike and car travelers tour the apple orchards and wineries off U.S. 50 in the area known as **Apple Hill.** The fall is particularly busy with apple-picking celebrations and a complete listing and map of orchards is available from the Chamber of Commerce (see above). Locals claim that **Denver Dan's,** 4454 Bumblebee Ln. (644-6881), has the best prices, while **Kid's,** 3245 N. Canyon Rd. (622-0084), makes the best apple pie in the area. Most of the orchards are open only September to December, but **Boa Vista Orchards,** 2952 Carson Rd. (622-5522), is open year-round selling fresh pears, cherries, and other fruits. For free wine tasting, try **Lava Cap Winery,** 2221 Fruitridge Rd. (621-0175; open daily 11am-5pm), or **Boeger Winery,** 1709 Carson Rd. (622-8094; open daily 10am-5pm). **Gold Hill,** an area similar to Apple Hill, features peaches, plums, and citrus fruits.

COLOMA

The 1848 Gold Rush began in Coloma at John Sutter's water-powered lumber mill, operated by James Marshall. Today, the town tries its darndest to hype this claim to fame, but the effort just makes tiny Coloma feel like Disneyland without the fun. Accommodations are sparse, so visitors will probably want to stay in Placerville.

The town basically revolves around the **James Marshall Gold Discovery State Historic Park** (622-1116). Near the site where Marshall struck gold is a replica of the original mill. (Open daily 8am-dusk; day-use fee $5 per car, seniors $4; walk-ins $2, ages 6-12 $1. Display your pass prominently in your car window or you will be ticketed.) Picnic grounds across the street surround the **Gold Discovery Museum,** 310 Back St. (622-3470), which presents the events of the Gold Rush through dioramas and film. (Open daily in summer 8am-5pm; in winter 10am-4pm.)

The real reason to come to Coloma may be for the nearby natural attractions. The American River's class III currents, among the most accessible rapids in the West, attract thousands of rafters and kayakers every weekend. Farther north along Rte. 49, the river flows into Folsom Lake and a deep gorge perfect for hiking and swimming. Many of the rafting outfitters in the county offer tours in the raging waters surrounding Coloma. Contact **Ahwahnee** (800-359-9790), **Motherlode River Trips** (800-427-2387), **Oars Inc.** (800-346-6277), or **Whitewater Connection** (800-336-7238), whichever floats your boat (half-day $69-79, full-day $89-109).

NEVADA CITY

New Age meets ages past in Nevada City, a gorgeous mountain town full of rustic hippies and gaping tourists. Although the area's tourist board seems hellbent on creating the illusion of yesteryear, the eccentricity of current residents belies the mining town image, making the tiny burg feel like an old postcard buried in someone's crystal collection. Draped across several hills, Nevada City's winding streets modulate its luster.

Many buildings in the town are of historical interest, including the dozens of **Victorian homes,** the **National Hotel,** and the **firehouse** (interior open daily 11am-4pm). A free walking tour map is available from the **Chamber of Commerce** (265-2692 or 800-655-6569) at the end of Commercial St., near the Shell station and bank (open M-F 9am-5pm, Sa 11am-4pm). The vast majority of historical buildings in Nevada City have been transformed into cappuccino bars, New Age bookstores, and vegetarian eateries.

Nevada City's health-conscious congregate to refuel at **Earth Song,** 135 Argall St. (265-9392), a natural foods market and cafe where vegetarians stock up on egg rolls, soy burgers, and organic produce (market open daily 8am-9pm; cafe open daily 11:30am-8pm). Another popular hangout is the **Mekka Cafe,** 237 Commercial St. (478-1517). Admire its leopard-skin decoration, browse among the books and chaises, sip coffee with the hip evening crowd, or munch on a damn fine artichoke heart, pesto, and brie sandwich ($5.75; Open M-F 7am-11pm, Sa-Su 8am-11pm.)

A dose of history awaits you at the **Empire Mine State Historic Park** (273-8522), on the Empire St. Exit off Rte. 20 west of town. Peering down into the cool, dark air of the mine shaft, you may wonder whether you'd go 11,000 feet down for a chance at the big money—$120,000,000 of gold was obtained from the mine. The well-groomed estate and the woods surrounding it make peaceful hikes, but beware of poison oak, rattlesnakes, mountain lions, and horse poo. Living history tours are offered on summer weekends. (Open daily Mar.-Aug. 10am-6pm; Sept.-Apr. 10am-5pm. Admission $3, ages 6-12 $1, under 6 free; dogs of all ages $1.)

The Nevada City area has trails for hikers and walkers of every taste and ability. The **Bridgeport State Park,** in Penn Valley off Rte. 20, features an easy 1¼-mile hike over the largest covered bridge in the West, and around the river canyon. Search for a free souvenir during the park's gold-panning demonstration (for tips, see **Pannin' fer Goald I,** p. 315, and **II,** p. 316). Swimming holes are found along the **Yuba River,** which has been immortalized in song by countless folk. Enjoy them by hiking the Independence Trail and discovering personal freedom, skinny dipping, and fun in the sun. Whitewater rafting and sea kayaking are a great way to experience the rugged beauty of the area. **Woolf Creek Wilderness,** 595 E. Main St. in Grass Valley (477-2722), rents kayaks in the summer and runs multiple kayaking trips and clinics. In the winter they run snowshoe tours and avalanche clinics.

THE BUTTE MOUNTAINS

Six miles north of **Sierra City,** north of I-80, lie the Butte Mountains, one of the most beautiful and least traveled areas in California, offering amazing camping, hiking, and fishing possibilities. Five miles east of Sierra City, on the corner of Rte. 49 and Gold Lake Rd., sits the **Bassetts Station** (862-1297), an all-purpose establishment that has dispensed lodging (3 rooms, $65 each per night), dining, gas, and supplies for over 125 years. Stop in for the lowdown on camping, hiking, and fishing. (Open daily 7am-9pm.)

The Bassetts turn-off also leads to **Gold Lake,** six miles from Rte. 49 past Bassetts Station. The adjacent **Gold Lake Pack Station** (283-2014), offers guided horseback rides around the area (from $23 per hr.). **Frasier Falls,** a noisy 176-foot cascade, can be reached via a dirt road that starts across from Gold Lake and leads to a parking lot, or by taking the paved drive. From Rte. 49 South, turn left at Bassetts Station onto Gold Lake Rd. The turn-off for Frasier Falls is on the right, six miles from the

Bassetts Station, across from the first Lake turn-off. Follow signs for four miles to the Frasier Falls parking lot. From there, the falls are a 30-minute walk. There are six campgrounds along the route from the Bassetts turn-off to Frasier Falls, all marked by signs. Sites are $10, have no showers, and are available on a first-come, first-camped basis.

The **Butte Mountains** themselves rise farther up Gold Lake Rd. amid a series of small alpine lakes. For trail access, take the Sardine Lake turn-off one mile north of Rte. 49, bear right past Sardine Lake and continue 1½ miles past Packer Lake.

THE CASCADES

CHICO

The town of Chico (pop. 43,650) was recently named one of the "Top 10 places to retire in the U.S." while Cal State Chico is perennially named one of *Playboy's* "Top 10 Party Schools" (read: cheap beer equals naked chicks and dudes). Essentially, it's a small American town that wakes up and rocks out with wild college kids. All of the bars share a tender sense of reciprocity: every night one of them will be serving dollar drafts (hint: there is cheap beer to be had). This means that Chico, home of the Sierra Nevada Brewing Company, is also home of omnipresent Cheap Beer. In addition, Chico cultivates many miles of beautiful bike and hiking trails, and lots of natural swimming holes. So bike, swim, and kick back in town with an icy pint of really cheap beer. Did we mention the cheap beer?

PRACTICAL INFORMATION AND CHEAP BEER. The Amtrak **train** station (800-USA-RAIL/872-7245), is just a platform on Orange St. at W. 5th St. Trains go to **Sacramento** (1 per day, $15-22) and **San Francisco** ($22-33; Amtrak bus $28). Greyhound, 450 Orange St. (343-8266), at the Amtrak station, sends **buses** to: **Sacramento** (5 per day; M-Th $14, F-Su $15); **Red Bluff** ($9, $10); and **San Francisco** (5 per day; M-Th $28, F-Su $30; open M-F 8:30am-1:30pm, 2:30-5:30pm, and 6:30-8pm, Sa 8:30am-3pm). The **Chamber of Commerce,** 300 Salem St. (891-5556), at 3rd St., has wall-to-wall tourist brochures and a friendly staff. (Open M-F 9am-5pm, Sa 10am-3pm.) **Bar X Liquors,** 915 Main St. (342-6741), supplies lots of beer and liquor (but no kegs). If you want liquor that they don't have, they will order it in the last week of each month. For big parties, contact Nancy about making special (read: large) orders. (Open M-F 7:30am-2am, Sa 8am-2am, Su 8am-midnight.) **Emergency:** 911. **Police:** 1460 Humboldt Rd. (895-4911). **Enloe Hospital:** 1531 W. 5th St. at Esplanade (891-7300). **Post office:** 550 Vallombrosa Ave. (800-275-8777; open M-F 8am-5:30pm, Sa 9:30am-12:30pm). **ZIP Code:** 95927. **Area code:** 530.

ACCOMMODATIONS, CAMPGROUNDS, AND CHEAP BEER. Thunderbird Lodge, 715 Main St. (343-7911), in the heart of downtown, has large clean rooms with brown shag carpet and white walls (singles $35-$40; doubles $45-50). Across the street is the competition: the pink **Vagabond Inn,** 630 Main St. (895-1323 or 800-522-1555), which provides similar accommodations and a small swimming pool (singles $44; 2 double beds $49). **Golden Waffle,** 701 Main St. (891-1940), serves cheap, massive breakfasts to fuel up before drinking cheap beer (open daily 6am-2pm). The closest place to get beer is at **Chevron,** 110 W. 9th St. (891-8055; open 24hr.).

For outdoor sleeping, pick up a useful camping brochure at the Chamber of Commerce. It will likely direct you to **Lake Oroville,** 30 miles from Chico on Rte. 99 South (9mi. from Oroville Dam Exit), and its fishing, swimming, boating, and 35-mile bike trail. **Bidwell Canyon** is very close to the water and camps mostly RVs (full hookup $20). **Loafer Creek** (reservations 800-444-7275) is more forested than Bidwell, with a beach and swimming area (Apr.-Sept. sites $14, Oct.-Mar. $10).

FOOD AND CHEAP BEER. There's a **Safeway** at 1016 W. Sacramento Ave., (895-0244; open daily 6am-2am) and a **farmer's market** held in the parking lot at 2nd and Wall St. (Sa 7am-1pm); the former sells cheap beer, the latter does not—choose wisely. **Madison Bear Gardens,** 316 2nd St. (891-1639), at Salem St., is annually voted "best burger in Chico," but its true flavor is its spicy decor and huge party potential. Enormous outdoor patio/beer garden, sports bar, dance floors, three pool tables, a horse and buggy hung from the ceiling, pinball machines, and leather booths make this a hot spot for hundreds of rowdy beer guzzlers. (Burgers, salads, and sandwiches $5-7; M, Th, Su "Burger Madness": burgers $3.79. Sa 9pm-1am: pint of beer 99¢. Occasional live bands Th-Sa 9pm-1:30am; no cover. Open Su-W 11am-midnight, Th-Sa 11am-2am; kitchen closes at 10pm.) Cheap beer also flows at the sedate and classy **Sierra Nevada Brewing Co.,** 1075 E. 20th St. (345-2739), home of "California's favorite Brewery and Tap Room Grill." Tours of the brass-and-mahogany brewery are a great way to get acquainted with the spirit of the brew gods (tours M-F, Su 2:30pm, Sa noon-3pm). Lunch ($5-10) and top-notch dinner ($6-20) are served at the Brew Pub. Some may come for the chile-lime chicken, the blackened shark, or the vegetarian options, but there is no denying 11 different Sierra Nevada Brews on tap for $2.25-2.50 a pint. (Pub open Tu-Th and Su 11am-9pm, F-Sa 11am-10pm.)

SIGHTS, OUTDOOR ADVENTURES, AND CHEAP BEER. Check out the weekly *News and Review*, distributed around campus, for goings-on. Chico is lean on traditional sights, but keen on charm and outdoor activities: the pedestrian-friendly streets welcome visitors with parks and shops. **Cal State Chico University Information Center** (898-4636), offers tours of the campus, excluding debauchery, bars, and frat houses (for tours call 898-6322; M-Sa at 11:30am; Sa by appt. only). The Chico State run **Adventure Outings** (info 898-4638) provides great rates for weekend whitewater rafting trips ($60 per day, students $30), as well as for snow camping and sea kayaking. **Sports Ltd.,** 240 Main St. (894-1110), at 3rd St., rents high-quality mountain bikes ($5 per hr., $15 per day, $20 overnight).

Bidwell Park (895-4972) is the nation's third-largest municipal park, with 2400 acres. Extending 10 miles from downtown, it has been the set for several movies, including *Gone With the Wind* and Errol Flynn's *Robin Hood.* Its swimming holes can ease the pain of a hot Chico summer. Take East Ave. north from Rte. 99 as it curves east; follow signs into Upper Bidwell Park. The gurgling sound of joyful splashes will lead you to nearby **Bear Hole.** The historical **Bidwell Mansion** (895-6144) offers tours (M-F noon-4pm, Sa-Su 10am-4pm; admission $3, ages 6-12 $1.50, under 6 free). A picnic next to the three-tiered **Honey Covered Bridge,** five miles east on Humbug/Honey Run Rd. is always pleasant. **Ray's Liquor,** 207 Walnut St. (343-3249), rents popular inner tubes ($2 with $7.45 deposit), and sells cheap beer.

RED BLUFF

Midway between Chico and Redding, Red Bluff (pop. 13,285) perches on a brick-colored bank of the Sacramento River. This is a good place to fuel up for a jaunt into Lassen Volcanic National Park (40mi. away; see p. 321) or points north, but there's not much to see in town. Interstate 5 skirts Red Bluff's eastern edge, while Route 36 (running east to Lassen Park) and Route 99 (leading south into the Sacramento Valley) merge with the main streets of town.

PRACTICAL INFORMATION. Greyhound **buses,** 1321 Butte St. (800-231-2222), go to: **Redding** ($8); **Chico** ($11); **Sacramento** ($28); and **San Francisco** ($32) (station open 24hr). The tourist info-flled **Chamber of Commerce,** 100 N. Main St. (527-6220), sits facing a beautiful park with a pond and picnic tables (open M-Th 8:30am-5pm, F 8:30am-4:30pm). There is an **ATM** at **Bank of America,** 1060 Main St. (800-346-7693). **Road conditions:** 800-427-7623. **Emergency:** 911. **Police:** 555 Washington St. (527-3131). **St. Elizabeth Hospital:** 529-8000, on Sister Mary Columba Dr. **Post office:** 447 Walnut St. (800-275-8777), at Jefferson St. (open M-F 8am-5pm, Sa 8am-2pm). **ZIP Code:** 96080. **Area code:** 916.

ACCOMMODATIONS AND FOOD. The **Cinderella Motel,** 600 Rio St. (527-5490) is still waiting for its fairy-god-decorator (psychedelic red carpets, purple glass lamps, huge leather chairs), but is clean, spacious, friendly, and dependable. All rooms have TVs and A/C (singles $33; doubles $40). **Sky Terrace Motel,** 99 Main St. (527-4145), is a well-kept roadside motel masquerading as a ski lodge, with TVs, A/C, petite pool, non-smoking rooms, and coffee makers (singles $24; doubles $28). Those who fear change, can go to Red Bluff's very own **Motel 6,** 20 Williams Ave. (527-9200; Su-Th singles $34; doubles $38; F-Sa singles $38; doubles $46). Nearby **Lassen** offers superior campsites, making camping in Red Bluff unnecessary.

Route 99 blossoms with **orchards** and **roadside stands** selling fresh produce: peaches, apricots, kiwis, cantaloupes, and plums in summer; pistachios, almonds, walnuts, and apples in fall. Fresh produce also blooms at the **farmer's market** in the Wal-Mart parking lot on S. Main St. (open June-Sept. W 5-8pm, Sa 8am-noon). For that budget travel staple, the big American breakfast, try **The Feedbag,** 200 S. Main St. (527-3777). Looks and tastes like a Denny's, and their Ranch Hand Breakfast (2 eggs, hash browns, 4 sausages, and 4 slices of toast; $5) with bottomless cup o' Joe (93¢) won't let you down. (Open M-Sa 6:30am-8:30pm, Su 7am-2pm.)

SIGHTS AND SEASONAL EVENTS. A few miles north of Red Bluff on Adobe Rd., off Rte. 99, the **William B. Ide Adobe State Historic Park** honors the man who led the 1846 Bear Flag Rebellion. In a drunken fit, California's first and only president "seized" the town of Sonoma from equally inebriated Mexican officials and declared California's independence (open daily 8am-dusk; free). In April, Red Bluff makes it into the record books with the **Red Bluff Roundup,** "the world's largest two-day rodeo." The **Tahema District Fair** (527-6220) begins on the last Thursday of September (the 28th in 2000) and includes live music, horseshoe tournaments, and a fiery chili cook-off.

LASSEN VOLCANIC NATIONAL PARK

Tremors, streams of lava, black dust, and a series of enormous eruptions ravaged this area in 1914, climaxing a year later when Mt. Lassen spewed a seven-mile-high cloud of smoke and ashes into the sky. Even now, the volcanic effects are still evident in Lassen's strange, unearthly pools of boiling water, its barren stretches of moonscape, and occasional sulfur stench. But the eruptions also brought about a flourish of new growth in the form of natural flower beds and rampant animalia (the fishing is fantastic). The park itself is open year-round (rangers ski in to work when roads close), and is fairly quiet until July, when hordes of families descend.

ORIENTATION

Lassen Volcanic National Park is accessible by **Route 36** from Red Bluff to the southwest and **Route 44** from Redding to the northwest. Both drives are about 50 miles. **Route 89,** running north-south, intersects both roads before they reach the park and carries travelers through the scenic park area. It's the park's only through road. The town of **Mineral,** along Rte. 36, and **Shingletown,** along Rte. 44, are "gateway" towns and good places to buy supplies. From the southeast (Susanville and the Lake Almanor area), take Rte. 36 West to the intersection with Rte. 89. **Chester,** the nearest spot for gas and supplies on the north shore of Lake Almanor, is on the way to Warney Valley and Juniper Lake, in the park's southeastern corner. To the northeast, the Butte Lake region is accessible by a dirt road (marked by a sign) off Rte. 44.

Weather in Lassen is unpredictable. Some years, 20-foot snowdrifts clog the main road until July; other years, an early melt clears roads by April. Even in winters with light snowfall, the elevation fosters long-lived snowdrifts. Many of Lassen's trails start at elevations of 7000 feet and the trail to Mt. Lassen peak exceeds 10,000 feet. Snow lingers in these high spots like the smell of cheap cologne. Crazy as it may sound, new snow can fall any day of the year. In winter, there is decent skiing, but because roads are closed skiers may have to ski into the park itself.

PRACTICAL INFORMATION

Public Transportation: Lassen Motor Transit (529-2722). Transportation from Red Bluff to Mineral on a mail truck. (M-Sa 10am, return trip 3:45pm. One-way $9.75.)

Park Entrance Fee: 7-day entrance fee $10 per vehicle, $5 per hiker.

Visitor Information: Lassen Volcanic National Park Headquarters (595-4444, TDD 595-3480; www.nps.gov/lavo), in Mineral. Wilderness permits, knowledgeable rangers, and free newsletter listing trails, campgrounds, conditions, and history. While you're here, check snow conditions (a good idea even in July). Open mid-June to early Sept. daily 8am-4:30pm; early Sept. to mid-June M-F 8am-4:30pm. **Loomis Museum Visitors Center** (595-4444, ext. 5180), at Manzanita Lake by the northwest entrance, has maps, brochures, and exhibits (open July to early Sept. daily 9am-5pm). **Hat Creek Ranger Station** (336-5521), off Rte. 299 in Fall River Mills. **Almanor County Ranger Station** (258-2141), off Rte. 36 in Chester.

24-hour Showers and Laundromat: Manzanita Lake Campground near Camper Service Store (335-7557). **Showers:** 4min. 50¢. **Laundromat:** Wash $1.25; 30min. Dry $1.

Emergency: 911.

Post Office: Mineral branch (595-3372) on Rte. 36, open M-F 8am-4pm; Shingletown branch (474-1942) on Rte. 44, open M-F 8am-4:30pm. **ZIP Codes:** Mineral: 96063; Shingletown: 96088.

AREA CODE	The area code for Lassen Volcanic National Park is 530.

CAMPGROUNDS AND BACKCOUNTRY

Because of the chance of rock slides and lava flows, there are few permanent structures in the park. The nearest indoor accommodations are 12 miles north in **Old Station.** Less costly motels are in **Redding** (50mi. west on Rte. 44; see p. 326), **Red Bluff** (50mi. west on Rte. 36; see p. 320), and **Chester** (southeast on Rte. 36). Fortunately, **camping** in the park is beautiful and abundant. Unfortunately, you may experience near-freezing night temperatures, even in August. Check the snow situation before leaving; campgrounds often remain closed well into the summer. All sites are doled out on a first-come, first-camped basis; register on site. **The last two campgrounds listed are not accessible from Route 89.**

North Summit Lake, 12mi. south of the Manzanita Lake entrance. Summit Lake's deep blue glitters through the pine trees surrounding 46 popular sites. Drinking water, flush toilets, no showers. 7-day max. stay. Sites $14.

South Summit Lake, in the middle of the park, 12mi. south of the Manzanita Lake entrance. All 48 sites have the same views as North Summit, but no flush toilets. Lots of trails begin here. Drinking water, no showers. 7-day max. stay. Sites $12.

Manzanita Lake, just inside the park border, near the northwest entrance. All 179 sites have impressive views of Lassen Peak reflected in the lake. Always first to fill up. Pay

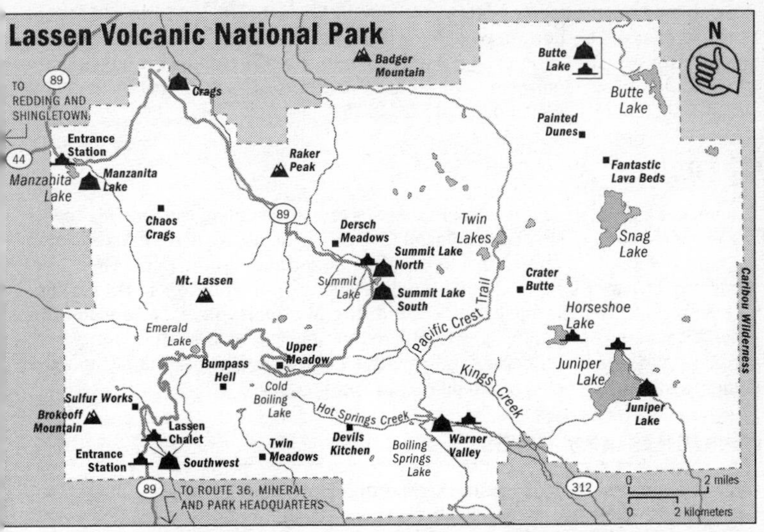

phone, concession services, boating without motor, drinking water, toilets, and showers. 14-day max. stay. Sites $14.

Crags, used for overflow from Manzanita Lake (5mi. away), but the 45 sites are much nicer. Piped water and chemical toilets. 14-day max. stay. Sites $8.

Southwest, near the entrance. Walk-in, hilly campground near the visitors center and chalet with 21 sites. Trailhead to several hikes. Potable water. 14-day max. stay. Sites $12.

Juniper Lake, 13mi. north up a rough dirt road from Chester on the eastern shore of Juniper Lake. 18 sites. Fireplaces, lake water only, pit toilets. 14-day max. stay. Sites $10.

Warner Valley, 17mi. up another dirt road from Chester (consult a ranger). 18 sites with fireplaces, piped water, and pit toilets. Very, very remote. 14-day max. stay. Sites $12.

Backcountry camping is limited to 14 days per year and is allowed one mile or more from developed areas and roads, with a free wilderness permit available at any park ranger station (see **Visitor Information,** p. 322). Fires are prohibited, as is the use of all soaps (including biodegradable ones) in the lakes. Avoid camping near Bumpass Hell, Devil's Kitchen, and other intimidatingly named areas that suddenly spew boiling lava or hot steam. A list of restricted areas, as well as explicit rules concerning safety and ecology (i.e., "don't shit in the drinking water"), is available at ranger stations (see p. 322).

OUTSIDE THE PARK

Lassen National Forest surrounds the park, encompassing several developed campgrounds. Six, all with water and toilets but no showers, line Rte. 89 to the north for the first 10 miles out of the park. **Big Pine** is the closest (19 sites). **Bridge** and **Cave** campgrounds have only trailer sites (but tents may be used if you don't mind bumpy ground). **Rocky** has eight dull tent sites with limited parking. All sites range from $8 to $13 (call the **Hat Creek Ranger Station** at 336-5521). Two campgrounds sit on Rte. 36 near the southwest park entrance, in the Almanor Ranger District (258-2141). To the west is **Battle Creek** (sites $12), and to the east **Gurnsey Creek** (sites $9). A number of campgrounds dot the southwestern shore of **Eagle Lake,** in the eastern part of Lassen National Forest. **Christie, Merrill,** and **Aspen Grove** have piped water and are in the Eagle Lake Ranger District (257-4188).

If you long for creature comforts, try **Rim Rock Ranch** (335-7114), in Old Station 14 miles east of the park entrance, on Rte. 44/Rte. 89 (the two highways fuse together for a bit). Rustic cabins dating from the 1930s come with linens and a small cooking area equipped with utensils and pots. (2-person cabin $40-45; 4-person $60; 6-person $85; additional person $5. Open Apr.-Nov.)

FOOD

The budget Lassen meal consists of groceries bought in one of the outlying towns. For prepared fare, try the **Lassen Chalet** (595-3376), an inexpensive cafeteria-style restaurant and gift shop just inside the Mineral entrance to the park. Their large burgers ($4-6) are filling fuel, but are only available until 4pm (open daily in summer 8am-6pm). At the park's other end, the **Manzanita Camper Service Store** (335-7557), at the Manzanita Lake Campground, sells pricey groceries, pretty postcards, required fishing licenses, informative guides, and helpful maps, and also launches seaworthy boats (open daily 8am-8pm).

SIGHTS AND HIKES

Lassen is very drivable: roadside sights are clearly numbered for tourists, and most are accessible from Rte. 89. Drivers can pick up the *Lassen Road Guide*, a booklet keyed to roadside markers, at any park entrance ranger station ($5). A comfortable drive through the park (including a few stops) should take about two hours, but allow a full day to accommodate short hikes.

FROM THE VISITORS CENTER. There are a few easy, relaxing walks in the area surrounding the visitors center that are almost always open. The hike to **Crags Lake** starts 500 yards from the visitors center and runs 1¾ miles one-way, climbing 700 feet (2-4hr. round-trip). The intermediate walk opens into magical vistas frequently enough to keep hikers motivated about the trek. At the end of the hike, an emerald lake sits at the bottom of a huge gray bowl that looks like it was formed by the crash of a massive spaceship. If aliens did visit, they left behind frogs—tons of croakers echo through the basin.

ALONG ROUTE 89 FROM SOUTH TO NORTH. From the south along Rte. 89, the first sight is **Sulfur Works,** where the earth hisses its grievances. The guard rails may prevent you from getting burned, but if the wind changes direction, you're likely to get a faceful of smelly mist. The boardwalk is easily accessible for disabled visitors. A bit farther north, **Emerald Lake,** when partially thawed by summer sun, shimmers for a bright green, icy-cold 300 feet around a snowy center. Swimming is fine for fish, but too cold (40°F) for the warmblooded.

Things heat up again about a half-mile past Emerald Lake. The 1½-mile hike to **Bumpass Hell** wanders through the park's largest hydrothermal area. Pick up a guide (50¢) at the trailhead. Bumpass Hell is a massive cauldron of muddy, boiling, steaming water in which its discoverer lost his leg; to avoid any danger to your own life and limb, stay on the trail. In spite of year-round snow, the water ever appears to boil at **Cold Boiling Lake** (4mi. farther north, closer to the King's Creek Trailhead) due to its placement above a flatulent fissure.

Mount Lassen is the world's largest plug-dome volcano. From the parking area, it's a steep 2½-mile trek to the 10,457-foot summit (allow 4-5hr.). Even if it's sunny and 90°F at the trailhead, take along extra clothes (especially a windbreaker) for the windy crest, as well as sunblock and water. Solid shoes are important too; 18 inches of snow can clog the upper two miles of trail even in summer.

A less imposing hike follows **King's Creek,** which either babbles or roars depending on the month and the previous year's snow. It's an easy two- to four-hour hike with great views of Lassen and the mountains.

The **Upper Meadow** by King's Creek and **Dersch Meadow** north of Summit Lake are good locations to spot grazing deer and circling birds of prey. The vast, ravaged area on the northeast face was formed the last time Mt. Lassen erupted. The mountain is slowly healing, and scientists conduct research here in hopes of aiding the recovery of the Mt. St. Helens area in Oregon.

As you near the northwestern entrance, **Manzanita Lake** will be on your left. The trail around the lake is a simple and pleasurable day hike.

OVERNIGHT HIKES. Given the heavy year-round snow cover, much of Lassen is not suitable terrain for backpackers. Of the 150 miles of trails (including a stretch of the **Pacific Crest Trail;** see **From Crest to Crest: the Trail of the West,** p. 266), only the **Manzanita Creek Trail,** near Manzanita Lake campground, and the **Horseshoe Lake** area, east of Summit Lake, are customarily dry by mid-June. Both make enjoyable overnight trips. Manzanita Creek Trail parallels a lovely creek that runs through rolling woodlands, bearing scant resemblance to the boiling cauldrons to the south. To the east, the Horseshoe Lake area is rich in ice-cold lakes and pine forests filled with deer. A number of challenging day hikes cut through the eastern area, with parking available near most trailheads.

By mid-summer, the shallow waters of Lakes Manzanita and Summit can warm to swimming temperatures. Several lakes in the park have native **rainbow trout,** and Hat Creek is a renowned trout stream. A state license is required to go **fishing,** and some areas may have additional rules (Manzanita, for example, has a "catch and release" policy). Check with park rangers (see **Visitor Information,** p. 322).

NEAR LASSEN: WILDERNESS AREAS

The following three wilderness areas are less-traveled than neighboring Lassen. Pick up a free **wilderness permit** from the U.S. Forest Service. Buy a topographic map of the area ($4) at one of the ranger stations—it is invaluable for finding trails and for figuring out what the heck you're staring at.

Caribou Wilderness borders the park to the east—for the easiest border access, take Rte. 44 or 36 to the A-21 road for 14 miles, then take Silver Lake Rd. to the **Caribou Lake Trailhead.** Its many quiet, clean lakes support water lilies and wildflowers in early summer, and treat hikers to solitude. The more desolate **Cone Lake Trailhead** can be reached by taking Forest Service Road (F.S.) 10, off Rte. 44 north of County Hwy. A-21. For the ultimate in isolated beauty, make the trek to the **Hay Meadows Trailhead.** Head north on F.S. 10 from Rte. 36 (near Chester), then turn left after 14 miles. F.S. 10 can be rough—a four-wheel-drive vehicle is necessary.

Thousand Lakes Wilderness (and all the trout in those lakes) can be accessed from F.S. 16 off Rte. 89. Seven miles from Rte. 89 the road forks; F.S. 16 continues to the left to **Magee Trailhead,** a strenuous trail which leads to Magee Peak (8594ft.) and deserted Magee Lake. Insect repellent is a must. **Tamarack Trailhead** is easier and travels to Lake Eiler via Eiler Butte. Going north, take F.S. 33 N25 and hook a left just after Wilcox Rd. When the road forks, turn left onto F.S. 33 N23Y. These seven miles of road require four-wheel-drive. **Subway Cave,** off Rte. 89 3¼ miles north of Rte. 44, invites exploration of its 1300-foot-long lava tubes. The cave is pitch-black and cool with uneven footing, so bring a friend, sturdy shoes, a sweater, and a lantern or strong flashlight (with extra batteries).

The spectacular **Ishi Wilderness,** named for the last survivor of a Yahi Yana tribe, comprises rugged terrain at a lower altitude, making it friendly to off-season exploration. Take Rte. 36 from Red Bluff 15 miles to Plum Creek Rd. and turn right on Ponderosa Way. This rough road skirts the eastern edge of the wilderness, where most trailheads lie. Ishi is a series of river canyons with dense islands of Ponderosa pine and sunburnt grasslands in the south (very hot in the summer). **Mill Creek Trailhead** runs along the 1000-foot canyon, where gentle waters await swimmers. Keep an eye out for red-tailed hawks and golden eagles. The Tehana Deer Herd, the largest migratory herd in California, spends its winters in Ishi (no hunting allowed). The **Deer Creek Trail** is another scenic and popular hike, with a trailhead at the southern end of the Ishi Wilderness on Ponderosa Way.

REDDING

Touting itself as "Another California," Redding (pop. 72,906) nevertheless relies on proximity to supreme camping and recreation opportunities in the surrounding areas as its claim to fame. Redding's position at the crossroads of **Interstate 5** and **Routes 44** and **299,** along with its plenitude of hotels and restaurants, make it a convenient, if not essential, supply stop for **Shasta Lake** (15mi. north), **Lassen National Park** (48mi. east), and the sublime **Trinity Wilderness** to the west.

There is an unstaffed Amtrak **train** station at 1620 Yuba St. (800-USA-RAIL/872-7245). Buy your ticket on the train or through a travel agent. Trains depart to: **Sacramento** (1 per day, $20-30); **San Francisco** (1 per day, $37-46); and **Portland** (1 per day, $59-84). Greyhound **buses,** 1321 Butte St. (241-2531 or 800-231-2222), at Pine St., depart from the 24-hour station to: **Sacramento** (10 buses per day; M-F $18, Sa-Su $19); **San Francisco** (4 per day; M-F $30, Sa-Su $32); and **Portland** (9 per day; M-F $44, Sa-Su $47). **Enterprise,** 357 E. Cypress St. (223-0700), rents cars for $32-36 per day with 100 miles included; drivers must be 21 with a major credit card (under-25 surcharge $7 per day; open M-F 7:30am-6pm, Sa 9am-1pm). Plop down on comfy couches and get informed at the **visitors center,** 777 Auditorium Dr. (225-4100), off Rte. 299 at the Convention Center Exit (open M-F 8am-5pm, Sa-Su 9am-5pm). Call the **Shasta Lake Ranger District,** 6543 Holiday Rd. (275-1589), for local conditions or camping info (open M-F 8:30am-4pm). **Emergency:** 911. **24-hour rape hotline:** 244-0117. **Police:** 1313 California St. (225-4200). **Redding Medical Center:** 1100 Butte St. (244-5400), downtown (open 24hr.). **Post office:** 2323 Churn Creek Rd. (800-275-8777; open M-F 7:30am-5:30pm, Sa 9am-3pm). **ZIP Code:** 96049. **Area code:** 530.

Before heading to a motel, pick up a free vacation planner in the visitors center for a variety of coupons for area and state accommodations. **Motel Orleans,** 2240 Hilltop Dr. (221-5432 or 800-626-1900), has large, spotless rooms, cable, free local calls, coffee, A/C, and pool (singles $36; doubles $40). **Oak Bottom campground** (241-6584 for dispatch, 359-2344 for campground headquarters), on Rte. 299, 13 miles west of Redding on beautiful Whiskeytown Lake, has beaches and swimming areas. The camp has 100 sites with solar-powered showers but no hookups. (May-Sept. tents $18 waterfront, $16 interior; Oct.-Apr. $8, $7; RVs $14. Reservations through PARKNET/727-5638, or 800-444-7275). **Buz's Crab,** 2159 East St. (243-2120), next to Safeway, has the best seafood in the area. Buz prides himself on being "customer-driven" and original in his recipes, resulting in favorites such as fish and chips ($2-7) and a unique style of hot crab sandwich ($5.50) which locals favor (open daily 11am-9pm).

WEAVERVILLE

Heave her up and away we'll go
We're bound for Californ-i-o

—The Weavers

Folks in Weaverville (pop. 3370) consistently describe their town as "old." Most of the main attractions, including the Joss House, the Weaverville Drug Store, the Blacksmith Shop, and the Courthouse, have been in continuous use since being built in the mid-1800s. Proud of their town, Weaverville residents are friendly to history buffs and to recreation enthusiasts headed for the Trinity Alps.

ORIENTATION AND PRACTICAL INFORMATION. Weaverville sits at the foot of the Trinity Alps, 42 miles west of Redding on Rte. 299. Trinity Transit (623-5438) sends **buses** between Hayfork and Lewiston (daily; fares vary; free bike rack; schedule at Chamber of Commerce). The **Trinity County Chamber of Commerce,** 211 Trinity Lakes Blvd. (623-6101 or 800-487-4648), has brochures and advice galore about downtown Weaverville. (Open Memorial Day to Labor Day (May 29-Sept. 4

in 2000) M-F 9am-noon and 1-5pm, Sa 10am-4pm; Labor Day-Memorial Day M-F 9am-noon and 1-5pm; hours subject to change.) The **Weaverville Ranger District Office,** 210 Main St. (623-2121), will help you choose the perfect location for your specific recreational needs (open M-Sa 9am-5pm). **Emergency:** 911. **Police:** 1261 Main St. (623-3832). **Trinity Hospital:** 410 N. Taylor St. (623-5541; open 24hr.) **Internet access** is at the **Trinity County Library** (623-1373 or 623-1374), across from the ranger office. Internet access is free for one hour (open M-Tu, Th-F 10am-6pm, W 10am-7pm). **Post office:** 204 S. Miner St. (800-275-8777; open M-F 7:30am-4:30pm). **ZIP Code:** 96093. **Area code:** 530.

ACCOMMODATIONS AND CAMPGROUNDS. The **Weaverville Hotel,** 201/203 Main St. (623-3121), has seven rooms with either a shower or an old-fashioned bath. The antique furniture, card room upstairs, and downstairs parlor will take you to an earlier Weaverville, as will its lack of phones in the rooms (doubles $39). For a more modern feel, the **49er Motel,** 718 Main St. (623-49ER/4037), has a pool and free local calls; two rooms have jacuzzis (breakfast included; in summer $36-90, in winter $32-70). The **Red Hill Motel** (623-4331) projects an outdoorsy feel with its one-room cabins. (Singles $31.50; additional person $5. Rooms have 1 or 2 queen beds. Reservations suggested June-Aug.)

For the closest campsite to town, **East Weaver Campsite,** off Rte. 3 on East Weaver Creek, one mile north of Weaverville, has water and vault toilets ($8 tent or trailer, open year-round). For a longer drive, but best access to trailheads and the river, try **Bridge Camp** (off Rte. 3 on Stuart Fork, 17mi. north of Weaverville). Trailers are not advised, but the site is open year-round and has water and vault toilets (sites $8). **Douglas City,** 7 miles east of town, has drinking water and flush toilets (sites $10). For other campsites, ask at the ranger station.

FOOD. **Tops Superfoods,** Rte. 299 on the east side of town (623-2494), is an enormous grocery store with a cafe that serves sandwiches ($3-4), burritos (2 for $1), and Italian and Chinese food (open M-Sa 7am-11pm, Su 7am-10pm). For natural and local products, **Mountain Marketplace,** 222 S. Main St. (623-2656), carries "The Salsa Lady" concoctions ($3) and breads from McDonough's bakery (open M-F 9am-6pm, Sa 10am-5pm, Su noon-5pm). **The Pacific Brewery,** 401 Main St. (623-3000), serves up old favorites. The adventurous should try the unique beer-batter hotcakes ($2-4; open daily 6am-9pm.) Cozy **Cafe Latte,** 223 Main St. (623-2836), has hearty soup-and-sandwich combos ($5.25) and homemade pizzas ($3), in addition to quality coffees and freezes. Curl up with your favorite on an inviting couch or recliner. (Open Su-Th 7am-7pm, F 7am-10pm, Sa 10am-10pm.)

SIGHTS. The entire city of Weaverville is on the National Register of Historic Places; for a self-guided walking tour get a free map at the Chamber of Commerce. Weaverville is also gaining fame for its hiking and mountain biking trails—grab a trail map at several stores around town. The **Joss House,** a Taoist temple built by Chinese gold miners in 1853, has gorgeous altarpieces created in China specifically for the Weaverville temple. Guided tours explain the historical and cultural significance of the altar components. Those wishing to worship at the temple may do so by contacting the park in advance. (Open in summer daily 10am-5pm, in winter Th-M 10am-5pm. 30min. tours every hr. Admission $2, ages 6-12 $1.) Candy at the **Weaverville Drug Store,** 219 Main St. (623-4343), is still a penny, as is the working old-fashioned scale. Displays of herbs and articles from the 1800s share shelf space with modern medicines and souvenirs. The **Trinity Scenic Byway,** crossing the Shasta-Trinity and Six Rivers National Forests, reveals the raging Trinity River and more sedate mountaintops. Any visitors center in the Shasta-Trinity area has brochures that explain the wildlife and historical points of interest along the way.

MOUNT SHASTA

It's easy to contemplate Mount Shasta (pop. 3806) from a distance—you can see its peak from 100 miles away. All of 14,161 feet of extreme rock (it used to be 14,162ft. before some wiseguy swiped the top stone), Shasta attracts nature buffs and thrill-seekers as well as mineral-bath pilgrims and export gurus.

Shasta Indians believed that a great spirit dwelled within the volcano, and modern-day spiritualists are drawn to the mountain by its mystical energy. In 1987, thousands of New Age believers converged here to witness the great clerical event of Harmonic Convergence, which climaxed when a resident turned on her TV set and saw an angel displayed on the screen. Perhaps unaware of the teleological implications, climbers come to challenge the ice-covered slopes, while overstressed yuppies come for the region's fragrant air and peaceful atmosphere. The town of Mount Shasta is moderately touristy in a New Age sort of way: vegetarian restaurants, spiritual bookstores, and Shasta pilgrims crowd the streets.

ORIENTATION AND PRACTICAL INFORMATION

The town of Mt. Shasta is 60 miles north of Redding on **Interstate 5,** 50 miles west of Lassen Volcanic National Park, and 292 miles north of San Francisco (5hr. drive). If traveling by car, use the town as a base for exploring Lava Beds, Lassen, Burney Falls, and the Shasta Recreation Area. The town can be found from any direction—just let your spirit guide you.

Trains: Amtrak's closest station is the unattended one in Dunsmuir (9mi. south on I-5), 5750 Sacramento Ave. (800-872-7245). Trains depart to: **Portland** (1 per day, $44-74); **Redding** (1 per day, $10.50-15); and **San Francisco** (1 per day $33-55).

Buses: Greyhound (800-231-2222), flag stop in the parking lot at 4th St. and Mt. Shasta Blvd. To **San Francisco** ($49) and **Redding** ($13).

Public Transportation: The Stage (800-24-STAGE/247-8243), offers minibus transit between Weed, Mt. Shasta (next to the Black Bean Diner in the Mt. Shasta Shopping Center), and Dunsmuir. Fare $1.25. Operates M-F; call for times.

Visitor Information: Mount Shasta Visitors Center, 300 Pine St. (800-926-4865). Open M-Sa 9am-5pm, Su 10am-4pm. **Shasta-Trinity National Forest Service,** 204 W. Alma St. (926-4511), is across the railroad tracks from the intersection of Alma St. and Mt. Shasta Blvd. Find out which campgrounds and trails are open, and grab maps, info, and fire and wilderness permits. Outside is a trail register that mountain climbers and day hikers must sign. Open Memorial Day-Labor Day (May 29-Sept. 4 in 2000) M-Sa 8am-4:30pm. **Shasta Lake Information Center,** 10mi. north of Redding at the Montaingate Wonderland Blvd. Exit off I-5 (800-474-2782; www.shastacascade.org). **Whiskeytown Unit Visitor Information,** 8mi. north of Redding at intersection of Rte. 299 and Kennedy Memorial Dr. (246-1225; www.nps.gov/whis). Open daily Memorial Day to Labor Day (May 29-Sept. 4 in 2000) 8am-6pm; Labor Day-Memorial Day 10am-4pm.

ATM: Bank of America, 100 Chestnut St. (926-8950; 800-521-2632). Window hours: M-Th 10am-4pm, F 10am-5pm.

Equipment Rental: House of Ski and Board, 316 Chestnut St. (926-2359), 1 block behind Mt. Shasta Blvd. Rents, sells, and services ski, climbing, and snowboarding equipment at reasonable rates (boot, binding, and ski $15 per day; basic boot $12 per day; snowboard $17, boots $3; snowshoes $5; ice axe $7.) Open Su-Th 10am-6pm, F 10am-7pm, Sa 8am-6pm. **Mud Creek Cyclery** (926-1303) is in the same building and rents mountain bikes ($24 per day; $18 half-day). Open in summer M-Sa 10am-6pm; in winter Su-Th 10am-6pm, F 10am-7pm, Sa 8am-6pm. **5th Season,** 300 Mt. Shasta

Blvd. (926-3606), rents camping, outdoor equipment, skis and bikes. Sleeping bag with pad $18 for 3 days, additional day $6. 2-person tent $28 for 3 days. Ski rental (boots, bindings, and poles) $38. Bike rentals $7-9 per hr.; rigid or suspension fork $28-40 for 24hr. Also offers mountain-climbing and alpine touring equipment. Open M-F 9am-6pm, Sa 8am-6pm, Su 10am-5pm.

Showers: Alpenrose Cottage Hostel (see **Accommodations,** below). 8-10pm; $3.

Weather, Climbing, and Skiing Conditions: Weather 926-5555 (24hr.) or National Weather Service 221-5613. **Climbing Conditions:** 926-9613. **Ski Report:** 926-8686.

Library and Internet Access: Mount Shasta Library, 515 E. Alma St. (926-2031). Internet access $2 per hr. Open M and W 1-6pm, Tu noon-6pm, Th and Sa 1-5pm.

Laundromat: Mount Shasta Laundromat, 302 S. Mt. Shasta Blvd., opposite Berryvale Natural Foods. Wash $1 ($2.50 for largest machines); 10min. dry 25¢.

Emergency: 911. **Police:** 303 N. Mt. Shasta Blvd. (926-2344), at Lake St.

Crisis Lines: Missing Climber Notification: Sheriff (841-2900 or 800-404-2911).

Hospital: Mercy Medical Center, 914 Pine St. (926-6111).

Post Office: 301 S. Mt. Shasta Blvd. (800-275-8777). Open M-F 8:30am-5pm. **ZIP Code:** 96067.

AREA CODE	The area code for Mount Shasta is 530.

ACCOMMODATIONS AND CAMPGROUNDS

The **U.S. Forest Service** (926-4511) runs a few area campgrounds.

Alpenrose Cottage Hostel, 204 Hinckley St., (926-6724), near the KOA driveway. Roses, wind chimes, sundeck with view of Mt. Shasta, and bulletin boards full of Shasta info (both spiritual and practical) give this cottage a homey appeal. Joyful owner/manager. Wood-burning stove, open kitchen, TV room, and library. Laundry. Lockout noon-5pm. Curfew 11pm. Limited availability with 13 beds. Adults $15, children $7.50; entire hostel $130 per night. Reservations recommended, especially in summer.

Shasta Lodge Motel, 724 Mt. Shasta Blvd., (926-2815 or 800-742-7821). 30 rooms overlook parking lot and trail to a mountain view. Simple, clean, spacious rooms in friendly atmosphere. Cable TV, A/C, phones. Rooms $36-44; with kitchen $60.

Travel Inn, 504 S. Mt. Shasta Blvd. (926-4617). Recently renovated rooms are small with TV, phone, nice firm beds. Rooms in summer $45-65; in winter $35-55.

Lake Siskiyou Campground (926-2618), 5mi. southwest of town. Flee I-5 via Lake St. Exit, follow Hatchery Lane ¼mi., then go south on Old Stage Rd. and W.A. Barr Rd. This family-oriented campground has beach access, encourages swimming, and rents paddleboats, motorboats, and canoes. Sites $16.50; day use $1. Coin-operated laundry, flush toilets, hot showers. Reservations recommended.

McBride Springs Campground, 4mi. east of Mt. Shasta off Everett Memorial Hwy. Nine drive-up sites with views, water, and hiking access. Well-maintained outhouses, no showers or sinks. 7-night max. stay. Sites $10.

Gumboot Lake Campground, 20mi. west on South Fork Rd., is the most isolated camping area. The drive is long and the 4 sites are primitive, but the lake is serene. Bug repellent is essential. Free.

Castle Lake Campground, 9mi. southwest of town, is primitive (pit toilets, no water, and only 6 sites). Freestyle camping is permitted more than 200ft. from the lake, ½mi. beyond the campground. Free.

FOOD

Shasta has many grocery stores, the largest of which is **Ray's Food Place,** 160 Morgan Way (926-3390), in the Mt. Shasta Shopping Center off Lake St., near I-5 (open daily 7am-11pm). In the summer, a **produce stand** across the street provides cheaper and fresher fruits and veggies. The **Mount Shasta Supermarket** (926-2212), at the corner of Chestnut and E. Alma St., is a pricier specialty store (open M-Sa 8am-7pm, Su 8am-6pm). **Berryvale Natural Foods,** 305 S. Mt. Shasta Blvd. (926-1576), caters to the health-conscious with organic produce, soy products, and enough tie-dye to make you see trails (open M-Sa 8:30am-7:30pm, Su 10am-6pm).

Willy's Bavarian Kitchen, 107 Chestnut St. (926-3636). Imported beers, vegetarian dishes, and several German dishes. Expansive menu includes non-German cuisine as well, such as *erfüchtige* burgers ($3-4) and *grüne* salads (monstrous Cobb Salad with chicken; $9). Open Su-Th 11am-9:30pm, F-Sa 11am-10pm.

Avalon Square Heart Rock Cafe, 401 N. Shasta Blvd. (926-4998). Tiny cafe with sunny patio, huge baked goods, fantastic sandwiches (salmon-pesto-cheese $7), and incredible smoothies. Microbrews and imported beers with live music from 7pm. Open M-F 7am-5pm, Sa 8am-2pm; BBQ in summer F 5-10pm. No credit cards.

Black Bear Diner, 401 W. Lake St. (926-4669). Busy with a folksy local crowd, visiting hikers, and hippies. Friendly waitstaff and huge portions that are "un-bear-ably filling." Hungry Bear's Breakfast is 3 eggs, sausage, hash browns, 2 biscuits, and a 1lb. ham steak ($8). Several vegetarian options. Open Su-Th 5:30am-11:30pm, F-Sa 24hr.

Bagel Cafe, Bakery, and Coffeehouse, 315 N. Mt. Shasta Blvd. (926-1414). Local hangout serves up espresso ($1.25), fresh bagels (84¢), and New Age theology (free). Check the door for spiritual events, local bands, and the latest in ancient Chinese acupuncture. Open M-Sa 6:30am-9pm, Su 6:30am-3pm. No credit cards.

SIGHTS AND ACTIVITIES

MOUNT SHASTA SIGHTS

The magic mountain attracts people climbing to new heights by car, foot, chair lift, pickaxe, or spiritual force. Everyone can enjoy Mt. Shasta without breaking a sweat, if they let their car do the work. The **Everett Memorial Highway** provides excellent views of the mountain as it winds its way 14 miles from the town of Mt. Shasta to the Ski Bowl trailhead. *(Parking at Bunny Flats.)*

FISH, ROCKS, AND BOOKS. The **Mount Shasta State Fish Hatchery,** half-mile west of I-5, monitors the production of more than five million baby trout every year. Throw food in the ponds and foster a feeding frenzy. Don't jump in, no matter what the fish say. Guided tours are provided. *(926-5508. 3 Old State Rd. Open daily 7am-dusk. Free.)* Next door, the **Sisson Museum** has exhibits on the area's geology and history. *(Also 926-5508. Open Apr.-Oct. M-Sa 10am-4pm, Su 1-4pm.)* If you prefer a more literary experience, start at the **Village Books Bookstore.** Info about the latest New Age activities in the area is posted on the bulletin board out front. Step inside to peruse the spiritual book collection or enjoy the small coffee shop. *(926-1678. 320 Mt. Shasta Blvd. Open M-Sa 9:30am-9pm, Su 11am-5pm.)*

MOUNT SHASTA SKI PARK. Downhill skiers can tackle **Mount Shasta Ski Park,** where most of the ski trails are intermediate. Cross-country skiers can try the **Ski Parks Nordic Center** or go on their own for challenging backcountry skiing (maps and info from ranger service; see **Visitor Information,** p. 328). In summer, experienced **mountain bikers** wishing to issue a challenge to the mountain can take a chair lift from Mt. Shasta Ski Park and co-o-o-ast down. Logging roads in the national forests also make excellent backcountry biking trails. Climbers of all skill levels love the outdoor wall at the park. *(**Mount Shasta:** 926-8600 or 800-754-*

7427; www.skipark.com. 10mi. east of I-5. Ski rental $18 per day, seniors and children $16; snowboard $27 per day. Lift tickets $31, Super Tuesday $18. Night skiing W-Sa $18, W-Th 2-for-1. ***Nordic Center:*** *Trail passes $11; rentals $12; pass and rental $18.* ***Biking:*** *Passes $12, seniors $8, under 12 free with an adult; Friday 2-for-1 passes. 2 climbs $3, half-day $7, full-day $10. Call for hours.)*

HIKING MOUNT SHASTA

All climbers must stop at the U.S. Forest Service for weather updates, climbing conditions, safety registration, a wilderness permit (free), a summit pass for over 10,000 feet ($15), and the mandatory human waste pack-out system. Even less rigorous adventurers should stop by for the most up-to-date maps and information before venturing into the wilderness. Mt. Shasta rangers are particularly knowledgeable, friendly, and helpful, whether you're going for a jump in a lake, an afternoon hike, or a trip to the summit.

The day hiker who is excited to explore the mountain but not to conquer it may enjoy some beautiful, gentler trails. The 1½-mile **Grey Butte Trail** takes about two hours. It begins at Panther Meadows campground, crosses the meadow, and heads up the eastern side of Grey Butte. The **Horse Camp Trail** at Horse Camp is another short but interesting hike. It begins at Sand Flat and goes about two miles, affording great views of Avalanche Gulch and the Red Banks. Sand Flat and Panther Meadows are both on Everett Memorial Hwy., although car access past Bunny Flat to Panther Meadows may be closed due to snow. The road ends at **Old Ski Bowl,** where you can take a gorgeous two-mile trail above Grey Butte and then around the north side of Red Butte.

If the winter is mild, it may be possible to ascend to the **summit** of Mt. Shasta without ice equipment during August—but who knows what the weather has in store. The trailhead for this route is at Bunny Flat, off Everett Memorial Hwy. A short, steep trail leads to Horse Camp, where hikers will find the historic Sierra Club Cabin. In the summer, the cabin is occupied by a caretaker. This is a good place to set up base camp for the necessary early morning ascent. ($5 fee to tent near the cabin, $3 for a bivy; no accommodations in the cabin itself.) Be sure to take extra clothing, food, ice axe, crampons, and plenty of drinking water, and check in at the U.S. Forest Service before you attempt a hike.

THINGS THAT MAKE YOU GO OM (!) The mystic and psychic energies concentrated in the Mt. Shasta area have not allayed **fears of The Big One,** the quake that will dim the California Light and spread an oozing black aura across the coast. From a Mt. Shasta newspaper, here are some precautions you can take to cleanse and purify the One's Nature:

1) Refer to the map of California. Note the missions, because they were each built upon an energy vortex and are the foci for the Lord Mary and her son Lord Jesus The Cosmic Christ of Divine Love.
2) Point to each mission, tune in, and ask your Higher Self to go there, taking some level of you along for the ride.
3) State aloud: "As an embassy of the Most High Light, I call forth Absolute God Protection for this location. I invoke the **raspberry sherbet Son of Divine Mother** to secure this mission area for 1000 miles in all directions. I call the California Earthquake Patrol (inner plane angels and masters) to take command of the area and install earthquake release devices to vent the tremendous interior pressures of Mother Earth."
4) Repeat three times: "I call for all beings in California and all the world to now awaken and realize their divinity and Oneness with all that is. All violence, negative karma, despair, and abuse is now dissolved by the tryptic power of *Lord Melatron, Lord Michael, and Melchizidek.* It is so done!"

BEYOND MOUNT SHASTA

Castle Crags State Park, off I-5 six miles south of Dunsmuir, is an awesome area, home to beautiful trails, rivers, and lakes. When viewed from I-5 this massive mountain of rock looks like the fortification for an epic castle. It's not just a model, however; you can step in and feel the magic for yourself. Spanning the area are 27¾ miles of well-maintained hiking trails. For great views of Mt. Shasta try the easily accessible trail that runs between Castle Lake and Bradley Lookout. The **Pacific Crest Trail** (see **From Crest to Crest: the Trail of the West,** p. 266) runs for 19 miles through the wilderness, offering access to several serene alpine lakes. Access the trail at the south fork of the Sacramento Rd. Maps and permits available at the Forest Service. Climbers may rust up their carabiners with saliva just at the thought of climbing the Crags, but regardless of how up-to-date your equipment, much of the stone here is dangerous and unstable. Nearby **Cantara Loop** has good beginners' rock faces and Pluto Caves are fun lava tubes to explore. There is also a killer outdoor climbing wall at the Mt. Shasta Ski Park (see above). For more climbing info, call **5th Season** (926-3606), or the **U.S. Forest Service.** Camping is free in the area of the Shasta-Trinity National Forest surrounding the Castle Crags Wilderness. Abutting the wilderness area is **Castle Lake,** which offers beautiful hiking trails as well as fishing, swimming, and camping, (although there is a camping restriction along 200ft. of the lake).

Stewart Mineral Springs, 4617 Stewart Springs Rd., Weed (938-2222), is another popular spiritual destination. Mr. Stewart was brought here on the brink of death, and attributed his subsequent recovery to the healing energy of the water; whether or not there's any truth to this, an afternoon spent relaxing in the saunas and hot tubs is, at the very least, a luxury. (Open daily 10am-6pm; $17.)

The **McCloud River Area,** 10 miles east of the town of Mt. Shasta on I-5, is perfect for swimming, boating, hiking, and camping. Thirteen miles of fairytale rivers complete with three storybook waterfalls and several meadows, make this a great area for afternoon sun worship and wildlife viewing. Acquired by the U.S. Forest Service in 1989, the area is growing in popularity, but many trails and facilities are still unmarked. Forest Service rangers have helpful maps with detailed directions.

For a simple hike gushing with views, go to the **Falls of the McCloud River,** on Rte 89 six miles east of McCloud; follow signs to Fowlers Campground. At the first stop sign, take a left onto a dirt road. One mile down is a parking area with a large pine tree in the center. From here, head directly across the street to the roar of falling water. In this short walk up the river there are three waterfalls worthy of snapshots. The trail is not strenuous but there are sheer cliffs and no guard rails: exercise extreme caution. A 30-minute hike from the falls leads to **Fowlers Camp,** the only overnight campsite in the area. This spot has toilets, picnic units, drinking water, and handicapped facilities (first-come, first-camped sites $12).

AREA LAKES

Almost as popular as the mountains in the area are its numerous lakes. Around Mt. Shasta are alpine lakes great for secluded swimming and fishing, including **Deadfall Lake, Castle Lake, Toad Lake,** and **Heart Lake.** The artificially controlled **Lake Siskiyou** is less remote and, not surprisingly, more crowded (beach use $1). The ranger station has info on dozens of lakes and rivers in the area.

LAKE SHASTA. Thirty minutes south of Mt. Shasta on I-5 (15min. north of Redding), the lake is not only the largest reservoir in California, but also the chillest place to kick back. All sorts of watercraft explore the 450 miles of emerald blue shoreline. Campgrounds and picnic areas pepper the coast. However, this lake remains a fairly beach-less haven, best enjoyed by exiting the car and hopping into some form of flotation device. Visitors may also enjoy a stop at the **Shasta Dam,** at the southern end of the lake. Three times taller than Niagara Falls, the Shasta is the second-largest dam in the United States after the Grand Coulee in Washington State. Built between 1938 and 1945 as the "Keystone of the Central Valley Project" this national landmark was "built for and by the people of the United States." Tourists whisper "daaam" and gasp at the panoramic mountain views. Visit the **Dam Visitor Center** (275-4463), in the Dam Park. (Open M-F 7:30am-5pm, Sa-Su 8:30am-5pm. Dam area open daily 6am-10pm. Tours every hr. 9am-4pm.)

WHISKEYTOWN UNIT. Eight miles west of Redding is this home to the popular **Whiskeytown Lake and Recreation Center.** The lake's beaches, marinas, campsites, and hiking trails are easily accessible from Rte. 299. It's not quite Coney Island, but in peak summer season the lakeside snack bars are packed and the surf bustles with boats. The recreation area boasts many well-maintained primitive and developed campgrounds. However, RV campers are often dismayed to find that their sites are basically in a crowded parking lot with minimal shade.

The **Whiskeytown Unit Visitors Center** (246-1225; www.nps.gov/whis), at Rte. 299 and Kennedy Memorial Dr. south of the lake, has daily use permits ($5; annual permit $30; open daily in summer 8am-6pm, in winter 10am-4pm). Reserve campsites (14-day max. stay) through DESTINET (800-365-2267 or http://reservations.nps.gov). Backcountry camping permits ($5) and hiking permits (free) can be picked up at Park Headquarters. The **Peltier Bridge Camp,** a developed camp in the woods behind the dam, is particularly tranquil. The rocky access road can be treacherous for non-four-wheel-drive vehicles, but the nearby brook offers an escape from the action by the lake. The **Oak Bottom Campground** (800-365-2267), off Rte. 299, has 42 RV sites and 100 developed tent sites and is near a large beach, picnic area, snack bar, and marina, as well as drinking water and flush toilets. RV sites have similar facilities (no hookup) and easy lake access, but aren't too scenic themselves. (Sites May 15-Sept. 15 $16; Sept. 16-May 14 $9.) Nearby **Oak Bottom Marina** (359-2269) rents ski boats, sailboats, patio boats, and canoes for relatively reasonable rates (canoes $21 for 3hr.; sailboats $42 for 3hr.; open M-Th 7am-8pm, F-Su 7am-9pm).

YREKA

Yrekan rebels taught us this lesson in 1941: to get political attention from chi-chi southern California and the space cadets of northern Oregon, take to the streets with shotguns, barricade roads, write a declaration of independence, set up a provisional government, and declare yourself a state. Three days after this little "rebellion," the situation was shelved in the wake of a certain "bombing" at Pearl Harbor. Alas, Yreka's 15 minutes was as the temporary capital of The Great State of Jefferson: a "state that never was and never will be, but that has lived in men's minds for a hundred years."

Now, Yreka (why-REE-ka; pop. 7040) chugs along a more modern track with standard shopping malls, one-night motels, and cheap lube jobs. Home to a high-quality county museum and many other dependable establishments, Yreka is a good place to stop on your way somewhere else.

ORIENTATION AND PRACTICAL INFORMATION. Yreka is conveniently stationed on I-5, 20 miles south of the Oregon border and 40 miles north of the town of Mt. Shasta. Greyhound (800-231-2222) **buses** roll to **Redding** (M-F $19, Sa-Su $20) and **Mount Shasta** (M-F $10, Sa-Su $11). **Rent-A-Wreck,** 1910 Ft. Jones Rd. (842-0706 or 800-755-6781) rents cars. The **Chamber of Commerce:** 117 W. Miner St. (842-1649; www.yrekachamber.com) gives the lowdown on the town (open in summer M-F 9am-6pm, Sa 10am-5pm, Su noon-5pm; in winter M-F 9am-5pm). **Klamath National Forest Headquarters** and **Clouds National Forest Ranger:** 1312 Fairlane Rd. (842-6131; open M-F 8am-4:30pm). **Emergency:** 911. **24-hour crisis lines: General Counseling and Rape Crisis** (842-4068); **Domestic Violence:** 842-4068; call collect from anywhere. **Hospital:** 444 Bruce St. (842-4121). **Post office:** 401 S. Broadway (800-275-8777; open M-F 8:30am-5pm). **ZIP Code:** 96097. **Area code:** 530.

ACCOMMODATIONS. Gas stations, motels, and inns flank Main St. The south end of Main St. is most promising for high-value accommodations. The **Klamath Motor Lodge,** 1111 S. Main St. (842-2751), is a friendly spot with large clean rooms, phone, cable TV, A/C, fridge, coffee, and pool with a grassy picnic area (microwave rental $3; in summer singles $43, doubles $46; in winter singles $41, doubles $42.) The **Rodeway Inn,** 526 S. Main St. (842-4404 or 800-554-4339), may still have a sign out front that says "Thunderbird Inn," but with new ownership comes fresh paint, new frills, and (we hope) an updated sign. 42 clean and simple rooms with phone, cable TV, A/C, pool. (In summer singles $40, doubles $45, in winter singles $37, doubles $41.)

FOOD. The fare ranges from truck-stop convenience to New Age soul-enriching nutrients and famously quaint rail-town tourist taverns. At Main and W. Minor St. are two 24-hour family restaurants with standard Denny's-style fare. Without 24-hour convenience, but with the benefit of New Age flute, **Nature's Kitchen,** 412 S. Main St. (842-1136), has a fresh flower on every table and a fresh lemon slice in every glass of ice water. The room and waitstaff are bright and sunny, and prices are heavenly. A Monterey jack and avocado sandwich with a sesame-and-garlic seasoned salad or bowl of soup is only $5.45 (open daily until 3pm). Another local favorite, **Poor George's Family Restaurant,** 108 Oberlin St., just west of Main St., is sweet and friendly. Inside are homemade pie, a jukebox, oil paintings of bald eagles, and other slices Americana. Seniors and skaters alike munch on burgers ($3.50-6), sandwiches ($4-6), salads ($3-6), and steak and eggs ($8). Breakfast is served all day. (Open M-F 6am-7:45pm; Sa-Su 7am-1:45pm; no reservations.)

SIGHTS AND ACTIVITIES. The Siskiyou County Museum (842-3836), 910 S. Main St., is one of the more valuable of its kind in the area. The exhibit *Enduring People: Native Americans of North Western California*, which opened in 1994, is particularly tasteful and informative compared to all the hoopla surrounding the Gold Rush and the white man's triumph over the wild, wild West. Open Tu-Sa 9am-5pm. Admission $1, ages 7-12 75¢, under 7 free. The 2½-acre **Outdoor Museum,** across the museum parking lot, boasts five original historic buildings from 1856 to 1920 and five recreated buildings, one of which is a conveniently located gift shop (museum open in summer). The **Chamber of Commerce** (see **Practical Information,** above) has has info about seasonal events like fairs, festivals, sporting events, and the annual **Free Summer Concert Series** held in Yreka's Minter St. Park.

LAVA BEDS NATIONAL MONUMENT

At first glance, Lava Beds National Monument appears to be a stark sea of sagebrush, arid grasses, and craggy rocks. But beneath this expanse of 72 square miles lies a complex web of nearly 400 lava-formed caves and other-worldly tunnels. Cool, quiet, and often eerie caves created by prehistoric and relatively recent lava flow range from 18-inch crawl spaces to 80-foot-high cathedrals. These lava tubes are formed by a slow lava flow: as the outer lava is exposed to air or water it cools and creates a shell that insulates the molten lava inside. The hot, fluid lava continues to flow away, leaving hollow conduits under the earth as it progresses.

In spring and fall, nearby Tule Lake Refuge provides a stopover for migratory birds, some of which come from as far away as Siberia. The fall migration is particularly spectacular, when a million ducks and half a million geese literally darken the sky. In winter, this is the best place in the continental U.S. to see a bald eagle.

In general, however, Lava Beds and the Tule Lake Refuge are remote and isolated. The Lava Beds Information Center and Campgrounds act as a social center for visitors, but the camping is provided on a first-come, first-camped basis and local accommodations are sparse. Those seeking less-desolate motels should plan on making the drive to Klamath Falls, Oregon, or Mt. Shasta.

Some were not so eager to leave the fertile regions around the monument: in 1872, the lava beds became the site of the Modoc War between U.S. troops and the Native Americans when the Modoc resisted relocation efforts. Modoc chief "Captain Jack" and only 60 of his warriors held their ground against 600 U.S. soldiers for over 4½ months by making use of the natural fortifications of the lava beds.

ORIENTATION AND PRACTICAL INFORMATION

Lava Beds is situated southwest of the blink-and-you'll-miss-it town of Tulelake and northeast of Mt. Shasta. The **visitors center** is in the southeast corner of the park. There are two northern entrances near Tulelake. The **southeast entrance** (25mi. south of town) is closest to the visitors center. The two **east entrances** are closer to Klamath Basin Wildlife Refuge and the Oregon border. Access roads to the national monument and visitor center are clearly marked. The **north entrance** is on Rte. 139. The road to the **northeast entrance** leaves Rte. 139 about eight miles southeast of Tulelake, and winds through the wilder northern areas of the monument for 25 miles to the visitors center. Visitors coming from the south on I-5 must take a circuitous route, following U.S. 97 North, then Rte. 161 East to S. Hill Rd.

Lava Beds Visitors Center (667-2282), in the park's southeastern corner, near a cluster of accessible caves, has exhibits on Modoc culture, and gives tours (daily at 9am, 2, and 9pm). Presentations on the lava tubes and the Modoc tribe are given at its outdoor theater (daily at 9pm). The well-informed staff lends flashlights to cave explorers (free; return them in summer by 5:30pm, in winter by 4:30pm) and sells hard hats ($3.25). (Open daily Memorial Day-Labor Day (May 29-Sept. 4 in 2000) 8am-6pm; Labor Day-Memorial Day 8am-5pm. Admission $4 per vehicle.)

Although the high altitude makes cold weather possible at any time of the year, summer weather tends to be arid with hot days and cool nights. It takes day to really appreciate the park, and you'll need a car or bike not only to access the park, but also to explore its northern areas. The nearest spot to catch a bus, rent a car, or find a hospital is across the Oregon border in **Klamath Falls,** 50 miles north of Lava Beds. **Redding,** California and **Medford,** Oregon also offer these services but are a few hours away. There is no public transportation to the area. **Area code:** 530.

ACCOMMODATIONS AND FOOD

The only developed campground in Lava Beds is **Indian Well** (667-2282; no reservations accepted), opposite the visitors center. Drive-up sites have picnic tables, firepits, and a fantastic view of the stars. Drinking water and flush toilets are available from May to October (43 sites; $10). The monument has two **wilderness areas,** one on each side of the main north-south road. A wilderness permit is not required within the park. Cooking is limited to stoves, and camps must be at least a quarter-mile from trails and 150 feet from cave entrances (check visitors center for other rules). **Modoc National Forest** borders the monument on three sides, and offers free off-road camping. Nearby are **Medicine Camp** and **Hemlock** campgrounds; both have water, flush toilets, and opportunities for fishing, swimming, and boating (sites $5). More info is available at the **Modoc National Forest Doublehead Ranger Station** (667-2248), one mile south of Tulelake on Rte. 139 (open M-F 8:30am-4:30pm).

Tulelake is home to two roadside motels. Each is fairly isolated, set between agricultural fields and Rte. 139. The **Ellis Motel** (667-5242), one mile north of Tulelake on Rte. 139, sits alone behind a manicured lawn with large shady trees. There are 10 small, simple rooms ($32-42). Just south of town, also on Rte. 139, is the **Park Motel** (667-2913). The 10 roadside rooms are cozy and decorated in light pastels ($33-45). **Jock's** (667-2612), at Modoc and Main St., is a decently sized grocery store (open M-Sa 8am-7pm, Su 9am-6pm). **Captain Jack's Stronghold Restaurant** (664-5566), six miles south of Tulelake, one mile south of the turn-off to the Lava Beds, serves homemade soups and breads and has a sizable salad bar. The diverse menu, prime location, and welcoming floral decorations attract truck drivers, locals, and tourists. (Open Apr.-Dec. Tu-Sa 6:30am-8pm, Su 9am-8pm; Jan.-Mar. Tu-Th 7am-8pm, F-Sa 7am-9pm, Su 9am-8pm.)

SIGHTS AND ACTIVITIES

SPELUNKING. If your subterranean experience has been limited to subways and parking garages, be warned that the footing in these lava caves is decidedly "rustic." Hard hats, on sale at the visitors center for $3.25, are essential for small caves, and another simple cave-going accessory is a sweatshirt or jacket: the sun-swept desert can be scorching, but the caves below are cool and damp. This and other far more fascinating phenomena are explained daily in **cave tours** that leave from the visitors center (mid-June to Labor Day (Sept. 4 in 2000) daily at 2pm). Rangers recommend that people going without a guide to explore the caves go in groups or with a partner. Solo exploring is not recommended, but is allowed: inquire at the visitors center for guidelines and information.

The **Mushpot Cave,** in the middle of the visitors center's parking lot, has a short, well-lit, self-guided trail which will acquaint visitors with cave formations (open year-round). On the 2¼-mile **Cave Loop Road,** which starts and finishes at the visitors center, there are 20 caves with little more to guide you than an entrance stairway. This is a nice way to get a feel for the adventure and intrigue of freelance cave exploration without straying too far from home base. Parking is available at each entrance. **Catacombs Cave** has many interconnected passageways, some of which require a good deal of crawling. **Golden Dome** is less confusing, and sparkles like gold because of the yellow bacteria growing on the walls. **Skull Ice Cave,** 3½ miles north, is where one explorer found two human skeletons chilling alongside the bones of several animals. The floor of this cave is covered with ice year-round. To the south is **Valentine Cave,** which is known for its frozen waterfalls of lava and unusually smooth floor. Experienced spelunkers may want to consider talking to a ranger about exploring one of the many undeveloped caves in the park.

Four miles north of the visitor center is **Schonchin Butte.** The steep ¾-mile ascent takes about 30 minutes and leads you to a working fire lookout that gives a broad view of the area over arid greens and golds to the massive white face of Mt. Shasta. Closer to Lava Bed's northern entrance is **Captain Jack's Stronghold,** the natural lava fortress where Modoc warriors held back Colonel Wheaton's troops during the Modoc War. There's an excellent self-guided trail through the area (guides 25¢). Just outside the northern entrance is **Petroglyph Point,** site of one of the largest collections of carvings in California.

HIKING. Trails of varying difficulty traverse the park. Hikers should keep in mind that the area is essentially a desert with little shade and extreme heat. The **Whitney-Butte Trail** goes through rocky brush and around the mountain to the black Callahan Lava Flow, a 3½-mile one-way, route from the trailhead at Merrill Cave. The short, easy hike to the **Thomas-Wright Battlefield** leads to the site of a Modoc ambush that killed or wounded 50 U.S. soldiers, now an unsurprising meadow; watch for rattlesnakes. For an overnight hike, the **Lyons Trail** traverses 9½ miles from Skull Cave to Hospital Rock over the rocky, hot plain in the park's eastern reaches. Consult a ranger before you go.

BEYOND LAVA BEDS

The **Klamath Basin National Wildlife Refuge** teems with waterfowl. The **Tule Lake** and **Lower Klamath National Wildlife Refuges** are the two areas of the basin that are most accessible from Lava Beds. The drive from Tulelake to Lava Beds runs through the Tule Lake refuge, and is visible from Rte. 161 just north of Tulelake. The area is a bird-watcher's paradise: over a million birds come through the refuge each year, including bald eagles, pelicans, and Canadian geese. The migration begins in early September. The **Lower Klamath and Tule Lake Wildlife Refuge Visitor Center and Headquarters** (541-667-2231), on Hill Rd., 11 miles south of Rte. 161, 10 miles north of Lava Beds Visitor Info Center, has a small museum with a high-quality video, a friendly staff, and tons of info about area wildlife, as well as horse trails, canoe routes, hunting, fishing, and animal sighting strategies. Car tours are available in the Tule Lake and Lower Klamath Refuges—just drive around and read the signs, staying in your car so as not to disturb the habitat. A 10-mile trail open to hiking, biking, and cross-country skiing meanders through the Klamath Marsh Refuge. The still waters and low mountains make perfect photographic frames for images of the active wildlife. Thanks to the National Audubon Society and other activists, former President Theodore Roosevelt and the U.S government declared this fragile and valuable wetlands the first-ever wildlife refuge.

For a taste of the dark side of American history, you can visit the remains of a Japanese internment camp, where more than 18,000 Japanese-Americans were held by the U.S. government during World War II. The camp is in Newell, four miles north of Petroglyph Point, but there is not much left to see of the camp, except a plaque, a couple of ruined buildings, and old fence-lines.

CRATER LAKE AND KLAMATH FALLS

Oregon's only national park takes its name from the mesmerizing Crater Lake, formed about 7700 years ago when Mount Mazama erupted in a blast that buried a vast portion of the continent under a thick layer of ash, and formed a deep caldera that gradually became filled with centuries worth of rain. The circular lake plunges to a depth of 1932 feet and remains iceless in winter, although its banks, which reach 6176 feet, are snow-covered until July. Visitors from all over the world circle the 33-mile Rim Drive, carefully gripping the wheel as the intense blue water enchants them. Klamath (kuh-LAH-math) Falls, one of the nearest towns, makes a convenient stop on the way to the park and holds most of the services, motels, and restaurants listed below.

ORIENTATION AND PRACTICAL INFORMATION

Route 62 skirts the southwestern edge of the park as it arcs 130 miles between Medford in the southwest and Klamath Falls, 56 miles southeast of the park. To reach Crater Lake from Portland, take I-5 to Eugene, then Rte. 58 East to U.S. 97 South. **Route 138** leads west from U.S. 97 to the park's north entrance, but this route is one of the last to be cleared. Crater Lake averages over 44 feet of snow per year, and snowbound roads keep the park closed until as late as July; call the Steel Center for road conditions. Before July, enter the park from the south. **Route 62** runs west from U.S. 97 to the south access road that leads to the caldera's rim. Crater Lake's services and operating hours depend on weather and funding, neither of which are determined until well into the spring. Call the Steel Center to verify services and hours.

Trains: Amtrak (884-2822 or 800-872-7245), Spring St. At the east end of Main St. turn right onto Spring St. then left onto Oak St. 1 per day to **Portland** ($48-69) and points north. Open daily 6:45-10:15am and 9-10:30pm.

Buses: Greyhound, 1200 Klamath Ave. (882-4616) 1 per day to: **Bend** (3hr., $20); **Eugene** (10hr., $39-41); and **Redding, CA** (4hr., $27-29). Lockers $1 per day. Open M-F 6am-2:30pm, Sa 6am-9am, and daily midnight-12:45am.

Public Transportation: Basin Transit Service (883-2877), has 6 routes around Klamath Falls. Runs M-F 6am-7:30pm, Sa 10am-5pm. 90¢, seniors and disabled 45¢.

Taxis: AB Taxi (885-5607). 30% senior discount.

Visitor Information: 1451 Main St. (884-0666 or 800-445-6728). Open M-Sa 9am-5pm.

Outdoor Information: William G. Steel Center (594-2211, ext. 402), 1mi. from the south entrance. Open daily 9am-5pm. **Crater Lake National Park Visitor Center** (594-2211, ext. 415), on the lake shore at Rim Village. Open daily June-Sept. 8:30am-6pm.

Park Entrance Fee: Cars $10, hikers and bikers $5.

Library: 126 S. 3rd St. (882-8894). Free **Internet access.** Open M 1-8pm, Tu and Th 10am-8pm, W and F-Sa 10am-5pm.

Laundromat: Main Street Laundromat, 1711 Main St. (883-1784). Wash $1.25, dry 25¢ for 12min. Open daily 8am-7pm.

Emergency: 911. **Police:** 425 Walnut St. (883-5336).

24-Hour Crisis Lines: General Crisis: 800-452-3669. **Rape Crisis:** 884-0390.

Hospital: Merle West Medical Center, 2865 Daggett Ave. (882-6311). From U.S. 97 northbound, turn right on Campus Dr., then right onto Daggett Ave. Open 24hr.

Post Office: Klamath Falls, 317 S. 7th St. (800-275-8777). Open M-F 7:30am-5:30pm, Sa 9am-noon. **ZIP Code:** 97601. **Crater Lake,** in the Steel Center. Open M-Sa 10am-noon and 1-3pm. **ZIP Code:** 97604.

AREA CODE	The area code for Crater Lake and Klamath Falls.

ACCOMMODATIONS AND CAMPGROUNDS

Klamath Falls has several affordable hotels that make it an easy base for forays to Crater Lake. **Forest Service campgrounds** line Rte. 62 through the Rogue River National Forest to the west of the park. Crater Lake National Park contains two campgrounds, both of which are closed until roads are passable. **Backcountry camping** is allowed within the park; pick up free permits from either visitors center.

Fort Klamath Lodge Motel and RV Park, 52851 Rte. 62 (381-2234), 15mi. from the park's southern entrance. The closest motel to the lake, the 6-unit lodge is in Fort Klamath, a town consisting of a grocery store, post office, restaurant, and wildflowers. Quiet, countrified motel rooms with knotted-pine walls. Fan, heater, TV; no phones. Laundry. Singles $42; doubles $58. RV hookups in nearby lot $15. Open May-Oct.

Townhouse Motel, 5323 S. 6th St. (882-0924), 3mi. south of Main St., on the edge of strip-mall land. Clean, comfy rooms at unbeatable prices. Cable and A/C, but no phones. One double bed $28; 2 beds $32, with kitchenette $33.

Lost Creek Campground, in the southeast corner of the park, 3mi. on a paved road off Rim Dr. Set amid young pines. Only 16 sites–try to secure one in the morning. Water, toilets, and sinks. Sites $10. No reservations. Usually open mid-July to mid-Oct. but call ahead to the park visitors center.

Mazama Campground (594-2255), near the park's southern entrance. RVs swarm into this 194-site facility, but some sites reserved for tents. Loop G is more secluded and spacious. Toilets, showers, telephone, and gas. Laundry. No hookups. Sites $13; RVs $14. No reservations. Usually open June to mid-Oct. Wheelchair accessible.

FOOD

Eating cheap isn't easy in Crater Lake. Klamath Falls has some affordable dining and a **Safeway** (882-2660), at Pine and 8th St., one block north of Main St. (open daily 6am-11pm), as well as **Fort Klamath General Store** (381-2263; open daily fall-spring 7am-10pm; in winter 7am-8pm).

Rennaisance Cafe, 1012 Main St. (851-0242). Gourmet pizzas loaded with zucchini, spinach, pesto, and artichoke hearts ($6.25) and huge salads ($6). Open M-F 11am-2:30pm, and moonlights M-Sa 5-9pm as a pricey dinner establishment.

Klamath Grill, 712 Main St. (882-1427). A spartan eatery with interesting food and low prices makes for loyal followers. Popular lunch specials like cajun chicken salad and shrimp quesadillas, both $5. Open M-F 6am-2:30pm, Sa-Su 7am-2pm.

Cattle Crossing Cafe (381-9801), on Rte. 62 in Fort Klamath. Breakfasts ($5.25), burgers ($4.25), and pie good enough that management claims people come from other *planets* for a piece. Desserts are stellar ($2.50). Open Apr.-Oct. daily 6am-9pm.

SIGHTS

Rim Drive, which often does not open until mid-July, is a 33-mile loop around the rim of the caldera, high above the lake. Pull-outs are strategically placed wherever a view of the lake might cause an awestruck tourist to drive right off the road. Almost all visitors stay in their vehicles as they tour the lake, so it's relatively easy to get away from the crowds: just stop at any of the trailheads scattered along the rim and hike away from the road. **Garfield Peak** (1¾mi. one-way), which starts at the lodge, and **Watchman Peak** (¾mi. one-way), on the west side of the lake, are the most spectacular. The Steel Center has a trail map.

The hike up **Mount Scott,** the park's highest peak (just under 9000ft.), begins after a 17-mile drive clockwise from Rim Village. Although steep, the 2½-mile ascent gives the persevering hiker a unique view of the lake. The steep **Cleetwood Trail,** just over a mile of switchbacks on the lake's north edge, is the only route down to the water and the park's most traveled trail; in summer, two-hour ranger-led boat tours depart from the end of this trail ($12.50, under 13 $6). Both **Wizard Island,** a cinder cone rising 760 feet above the lake, and **Phantom Ship Rock,** a spooky rock formation, are breathtaking when viewed from the lake's surface. Picnics, fishing, and swimming are allowed, but the water's surface reaches a maximum temperature of only 50°F (10°C). The water lacks the proper nutrients to support much life; rainbow trout and kokanee alone inhabit the lake. Park rangers lead free walking tours daily in the summer and periodically in the winter (on snowshoes). Call the Steel Center for schedules. The stroll from the visitors center at the Rim down to the **Sinnott Memorial Overlook,** a stone enclave built into the slope, provides the area's most accessible and panoramic view. In summer, a ranger talks about the area's geology and history (every hr. 10am-5pm). A similar talk is given nightly (July-Aug. at 9pm) at the **Mazama Campground Amphitheater.**

A few hundred yards east of Sinnott Memorial Overlook is the **Crater Lake Lodge,** the beneficiary of a recent $18 million renovation. Rooms are booked six months to one year in advance and start at $105, but there's fun in the lodge for free—make a quick visit to the rustic "great hall," rebuilt from its original materials, and the observation deck with great views and rocking chairs to enjoy them from.

A hiking trip into the park's vast **backcountry** leaves all the exhaust and tourists behind, as well as, unfortunately, any view of the lake. The **Pacific Crest Trail** passes through the park and three backcountry campsites, accessible from the trailhead ¾-mile west of the south entrance. Another excellent loop begins at the **Red Cone trailhead** on the north access road, passing the **Crater Springs, Oasis Butte,** and **Boundary Springs trails.** Dispersed camping is allowed anywhere in this area, but is slightly complicated by the absence of water and the presence of bears. Get info and backcountry permits for free at either visitors center.

ASHLAND, OREGON

Just over the Oregon border, Ashland (pop. 18,000) mixes hep youth and history to create an unlikely but perfect stage for the world-famous Oregon Shakespeare Festival. From mid-February to October, drama devotees can choose from 11 plays performed in Ashland's three elegant theaters. Shakespearean and contemporary productions draw connoisseurs and novitiate theater-goers alike. The town happily embraces the festival, giving rise to such Bard-bandwagon businesses as

"All's Well Herbs and Vitamins," but also fostering a vibrant community of artists, actors, and Shakespeare buffs. And although all the world may know Ashland as a stage, it has fabulous restaurants, parks, and outdoor activities, too.

ORIENTATION AND PRACTICAL INFORMATION

'Tis time I should inform thee farther.

—*The Tempest*, I.ii

Ashland is located in the foothills of the Siskiyou and Cascade Ranges, 15 miles north of the California border, near the junction of **Interstate 5** and **Route 66,** which traverses 64 miles of stunning scenery between Ashland and Klamath Falls. **Route 99** cuts through the middle of town on a northwest-southwest axis. It becomes **North Main Street** as it enters town, then splits briefly into **East Main Street** and **Lithia Way** as it wraps around the central plaza, Ashland's downtown. Farther south, Main St. changes name again to **Siskiyou Boulevard,** where Southern Oregon University (SOU) is flanked by affordable motels and bland restaurants. Many businesses close when the curtain rises, at about 8:30pm.

Buses: Greyhound (482-8803 or 800-231-2222). Pickup and drop-off at the BP station, 2073 Rte. 99 North, at the north end of town. To **Sacramento** (7hr., 3 per day, $40) and **San Francisco** (11hr., 3 per day, $50). **Green Tortoise** (800-867-8647; www.greentortoise.com) stops at the Chevron station at I-5 Exit 14. To **San Francisco** (9hr., Th and Su 11:45pm, $39).

Public Transit: Rogue Valley Transportation (RVTD) (779-2877), in Medford, OR. Bus schedules available at the Chamber of Commerce. Bus #10 runs daily every 30min. 5am-6pm between the transfer station at 200 S. Front St. in **Medford** and the plaza in Ashland (35min.), then loops through downtown Ashland. Fare $1, over 62 and ages 10-17 50¢, under 10 free.

Taxis: Yellow Cab (482-3065). $2.50 base, $2 per mi.

Visitor Information: Chamber of Commerce, 110 E. Main St. (482-3486). Open M-F 9am-5pm. Also an **info booth** in the center of the plaza. Open in summer M-Sa 10am-6pm, Su 11am-5pm. Oddly, the best maps of Ashland are on the takeout menu at **Omar's,** 1380 Siskiyou Blvd. (482-1281). Open Su-Th 5-9:30pm, F-Sa 5-10pm.

Outdoor Information: Ashland District Ranger Station, 645 Washington St. (482-3333), off Rte. 66 by I-5 Exit 14. Outdoors and Pacific Crest Trail tips. Open M-F 8am-4:30pm.

Equipment Rental: Ashland Mountain Supply, 31 N. Main St. (488-2749). Internal-frame backpacks $8.50 per day; external-frame $6. Mountain bikes $12 for 2hr., $30 per day. Discounts for longer rentals. Cash deposit or credit card required. Open daily 10am-6pm. **The Adventure Center,** 40 N. Main St. (488-2819 or 800-444-2819), has guided rafting trips ($65 for 4hr.; $110-135 per day) and bike tours ($65 for 3hr., $110 per day).

Library: 410 Siskiyou Blvd. (482-1197), at Gresham St. **Free Internet access.** Open M-Tu 10am-8pm, W-Th 10am-6pm, F-Sa 10am-5pm.

Laundromat: Main Street Laundromat, 370 E. Main St. (482-8042). Wash 50¢, 10min. dry 25¢. Ms. PacMan 25¢. Open daily 8am-9pm.

Emergency: 911. **Police:** 1155 E. Main St. (482-5211).

Crisis Line: 779-4357 or 888-609-4357. 24hr.

Post Office: 120 N. 1st St. (800-275-8777), at Lithia Way. Open M-F 9am-5pm. **ZIP Code:** 97520.

Internet Access: See **Library,** above. **Ashland Community Food Store CO-OP,** 237 N. 1st St. (482-2237). Free access to the right of the entrance.

AREA CODE	The area code in Ashland is 541.

ACCOMMODATIONS AND CAMPRGROUNDS

Now spurs the lated traveler apace to gain the timely inn.

—Macbeth, III.iii

In winter, Ashland is a budget traveler's paradise of vacancy and low rates; in summer, hotel and B&B rates double, and the hostel is filled to bursting. Only rogues and peasant slaves arrive without reservations. RVTD buses (see **Public Transportation,** above) travel to Medford, 12 miles away, where midsummer nights see motel vacancies. In Medford, the depressingly similar motels along Central and Riverside Ave. are $8-10 cheaper than the chains along the highway. The **Cedar Lodge,** 518 N. Riverside Ave. (773-7361 or 800-282-3419) is among the nicest of the non-chains, and charges $40 for singles, $45 for doubles.

Ashland Hostel, 150 N. Main St. (482-9217; ashostel@cdsnet.net). The Victorian parlor, sturdy bunks, and front-porch swing play host to travelers and theater-bound families wise to money-saving ways. $15, HI Members $14. Laundry and kitchen. Check-in 5-11pm. Lockout 10am-5pm. Curfew Mar.-Oct. midnight, Nov.-Feb. 11pm. Two private rooms sleep 4 $37-40; private women's room $22 for 1, $30 for 2. $3 off and free laundry for Pacific Crest Trail hikers or cyclists.

Columbia Hotel, 262½ E. Main St. (482-3726 or 800-718-2530). A reading alcove, tea time in the mornings, and spacious rooms with fresh flowers relieve the weary theatergoer in this historic home 1½ blocks from the theaters. Shared bath. Singles $59; doubles $63. Nov.-Feb. singles $35, doubles $39; Mar.-May singles $42, doubles $49; 10% HI discount in off season.

Vista Motel, 535 Clover Ln. (482-4423), just off I-5 at Exit 14, behind a BP station. The small, old building conceals surprisingly plush, newly renovated rooms. Cable TV, A/C, a small pool, and good rates compensate for the outlying location. Singles $37; doubles $45. Winter and spring discounts $8-10.

Mt. Ashland Campground, about 25min. south of Ashland off I-5 at Exit 6. Follow signs to Mt. Ashland Ski Area and take the high road from the far west end of the lot, at the sign for Grouse Gap Snowpeak. A more exquisite campground is hard to imagine. Seven sites in the mountainside forest, overlooking the valley and Mt. Shasta. Firepits, pit toilets, no drinking water. Donation $4. Can be snowy through June.

FOOD

Give them great meals of beef and iron and steel, they will eat like wolves and fight like devils.

—Henry V, III.vii

The incredible selection of foods available on N. and E. Main St. has earned the plaza a great culinary reputation. People come from miles around to dine in Ashland's excellent (though expensive) restaurants. Beware the pre-show rush—a downtown dinner planned for 6:30pm can easily become a late-night affair. **Ashland Community Food Store CO-OP,** 237 N. 1st St. (482-2237), at A St., has a lively spirit and a great selection of organic produce and natural foods, not to mention free Internet access (open M-Sa 8am-9pm, Su 9am-9pm; 5% senior discount). Cheaper groceries are available at **Safeway,** 585 Siskiyou Blvd. (482-4495; open daily 6am-midnight) although **Food 4 Less** (779-0171), on Biddle Rd. near I-5 Exit 30, in Medford, OR, is the 1 2 go 2 4 the best deals.

Geppetto's, 345 E. Main St. (482-1138). The spot for a late-night bite, and breakfast and lunch, all in an intimate dining room. Dinner from $13. Lunch $4-8. Fresh and "World Famous Eggplant Burger" $4.25. Pesto omelette $8. Open daily 8am-midnight.

Greenleaf Restaurant, 49 N. Main St. (482-2808). Healthy delicious food, and creekside seating. Omelettes and frittatas $6-7. Many salads ($3-10), pastas ($4.50-9), and spuds are meals in themselves ($2.75-5.50). Open Feb.-Dec. daily 8am-9pm.

The Breadboard, 744 N. Main, (488-0295). Hoppin' with locals hungry for huge sourdough pancakes ($4.75) and avocado omelettes ($7). Breathtaking views and value—the "Local Special" is eggs, pancakes, and bacon for just $3. Open daily 7am-2:30pm.

Brothers Restaurant, 95 N. Main St. (482-9671), serves all-day breakfasts of blintzes ($7.50), potato pancakes ($6.50), and omelettes of every possible description ($7-8). Open M and W-F 7am-2pm, Tu 7am-8pm, Sa-Su 7am-3pm.

Five Rivers, 139 E. Main St., (488-1883). Slip upstairs to the warm smells of Eastern spices and delicious Indian cuisine. Entrees $5.50-11.50; veggie options all under $7. All-you-can-eat lunch buffet daily $6. Open daily 11am-3pm and 5-10pm.

Evo's Java House, 376 E. Main St. (482-2261). A bowl of coffee ($1) or a Zaffiro Smoothie (blackberries, blueberries, and orange juice; $2.50) and live jazz attracts a crowd every Sunday night. Open daily 7am-10pm.

THE SHAKESPEARE FESTIVAL

Why, this is very midsummer madness.

—*Twelfth Night,* III.iv

The Oregon Shakespeare Festival, the brainchild of local college teacher Angus Bowmer, began in 1935 with two Shakespeare plays performed by college students in the old **Chautauqua Dome** as an evening complement to daytime boxing matches. Today, professional actors perform 11 plays in repertory, and the festival has grown to include five or six contemporary and classical plays. Performances run on the three Ashland stages from mid-February through October, and any boxing is now done over the extremely scarce tickets. The 1200-seat **Elizabethan Theatre,** an outdoor theater modeled after an 18th-century London design, is open only from mid-June to mid-October, and hosts three Shakespeare plays per season. The **Angus Bowmer Theater** is a 600-seat indoor stage that shows one play by Shakespeare and a variety of dramas. The youngest of the theaters is the intimate **Black Swan,** home to one play by Shakespeare and smaller, offbeat productions.

Due to the tremendous popularity of the festival, **ticket purchases are recommended six months in advance.** General mail-order and phone ticket sales begin in January. (For tickets, call 482-4331, fax 482-0446, or access the web site at www.orshakes.org. Tickets cost $14-37 in spring and fall, $21-49 in summer, plus a $5 handling fee per order for phone, fax, or mail orders. For more ticket info write Oregon Shakespeare Festival, P.O. Box 158, Ashland, OR 97520, or visit the web site. Children under 6 not admitted to any shows. Those under 18 receive 25% discounts in the summer and 50% in the spring and fall.) The **Oregon Shakespearean Festival Box Office,** 15 S. Pioneer St., is next to the Elizabethan Theatre, and is generally open daily 9:30am to 8:30pm.

Last-minute theatergoers should not abandon hope. At 9:30am, the box office at 15 S. Pioneer St. releases any unsold tickets for the day's performances. Prudence demands arriving early; local patrons have been known to leave their shoes in line to hold their places, and this tradition should be respected. When no tickets are available, limited priority numbers are given out. These entitle their holders to a designated place in line when the precious few returned tickets are released (1pm for matinees, 6pm for evening shows). At these times, the box office also sells twenty clear-view **standing room tickets** for sold-out shows on the Elizabethan Theatre ($11, available on the day of the show).

Although scalping is illegal, **unofficial ticket transactions** take place just outside the box office. Ticket officials advise those "buying on the bricks" to check the date and time on the ticket carefully, to pay no more than the face value, and to check with the box office before purchasing any tickets that have been altered. Half-price **rush tickets** are sometimes available an hour before performances that are not already sold out. There are some half-price student/senior matinees in spring and in October, and all three theaters hold full-performance **previews** in spring and summer. The 2000 season (subject to change) holds in store *Henry V*, *Hamlet*, *Taming of the Shrew*, and Tennessee Williams's *Night of the Iguana*.

Backstage tours provide a wonderful glimpse of the festival from behind the curtain (2hr. tours Tu-Su 10am; admission $9-11, ages 5-17 $6.75-8.25; no children under 5.) Tour guides (usually actors or technicians) divulge all kinds of anecdotes—from the story of the bird songs during an outdoor staging of Hamlet to the ghastly events which transpire every time they do "the Scottish play." Tours usually depart from the Black Swan. Tour costs include a trip to the **Exhibit Center** for a close-up look at sets and costumes (open in summer Tu-Su 10am-4pm; in fall and spring 10:30am-1:30pm; admission without tour $2, ages 5-17 $1.50.) In mid-June, the **Feast of Will** celebrates the annual opening of the Elizabethan Theatre with dinner and merry madness in Lithia Park ($16; call for details).

SIGHTS, ENTERTAINMENT, AND OUTDOORS

Mischief, thou art afoot, take thou what course thou wilt!

—*Julius Caesar*, III.ii

Before it imported Shakespeare, Ashland was naturally blessed with **lithia water** whose dissolved lithium salts were reputed to have miraculous healing powers. (It is said that only one other spring in the world has a higher lithium concentration. Depression, be gone!) To quaff the vaunted water itself, hold your nose (the water also contains dissolved sulfur salts) and head for the circle of fountains in the center of the plaza. Nearly every day, free concerts, readings, and educational nature walks occur in and around well-tended **Lithia Park's** hiking trails, Japanese garden, and swan ponds by Ashland Creek.

Culture remains in Ashland even after the festival ends. Local and touring artists love to play to the town's enthused audiences. The **Oregon Cabaret Theater** (488-2902), at 1st and Hagardine St., stages light musicals in a cozy former church with drinks, dinners, and Sunday brunch (box office open M, Th-Sa 11am-6:30pm, Su 4-6:30pm; tickets $14-21; reservations required for dinner). Small groups, such as the **Actor's Theater of Ashland** (535-5250), **Ashland Community Theatre** (482-7532), and the theater department at **Southern Oregon University (SOU)** (552-6346) also raise the curtains sporadically year-round. When in town, the traveling **Rogue Valley Symphony** performs in the Music Recital Hall at SOU and at Lithia Park. In July and August, the **State Ballet of Oregon** graces the stage on Mondays at 7:30pm. **The Ashland City Band** (488-5340) fires itself up Thursdays at 7:30pm in Lithia Park. In late June, the **Palo Alto Chamber Orchestra** (482-4331) gives hit performances in the Elizabethan Theatre, weather permitting (tickets $10). Contact the Chamber of Commerce for a current schedule of events.

If your muscles demand a little abuse after all this theater-seat lolly-gagging, hop on a stretch of the **Pacific Crest Trail** (see **From Crest to Crest: The Trail of the West,** p. 266) at Grouse Gap. Take Exit 6 off I-5 and follow the signs along the Mt. Ashland Access Rd. At the top of the nine-mile road is **Mount Ashland** (482-2897; www.mtashland.com), a small community-owned ski area on the north face of the mountain with 23 runs, half of them advanced, and a vertical drop of 1150 feet. (Snow report 482-2754. Open daily Nov. to mid-Apr. 9am-4pm. Night skiing Th-Sa 4-10pm. Weekdays $23, seniors and ages 9-12 $16; weekends $27, seniors and ages 9-12 $19. Rentals $15-20.) Over 100 miles of free **cross-country** trails surround Mt. Ashland. **Bull Gap Trail,** which starts from the ski area's parking lot, is also good for biking. It winds down 1100 feet over 2½ miles to the paved Tollman Creek Rd., 15 miles south of Siskiyou Blvd. In fact, Mt. Ashland provides a number of challenging mountain bike trails. The fine folks at the **Adventure Center** (see **Practical Information,** above) will provide tips on trails.

Scads of kids and kids-at-heart flock to the 280-foot-high **waterslide** at **Emigrant Lake Park** (776-7001), six miles east of town on Rte. 66. The park is also a popular place for boating, hiking, swimming, and fishing. (Open daily 10am-sunset, waterslide noon-6pm. 10 slides for $5 or unlimited slides for $12, plus a $3 entry fee.) The fantastic view of the valley from the small **campsites** that crowd on the side of the mountain may even make up for the lack of atmosphere (no hookups; toilets and 25¢ 4min. hot showers; sites $14).

BARS AND CLUBS

Come, come; good wine is a good familiar creature, if it be well us'd.
—*Othello,* II.iii

Kat Wok, 62 E. Main St. (482-0787). Quasi-Asian cuisine ($6-9) stars alongside a full bar and micropints. A tiny dance floor wedged between the tables and a glow-in-the-dark pool table makes Kat Wok Ashland's only dance club. A twist on the traditional post-show scene. Open daily 5:30pm-2am. 21+ after 10pm.

The Black Sheep, 51 N. Main St. (482-6414). English pub brew in bulk: all pints are imperial (20 oz.) and cost $4. The "eclectic fayre" features fresh-baked scones and jam ($3.50), salt and vinegar "chips" ($3), and herbs grown in the British owner's bonny backyard. Open daily 11am-1am. 21+ after 11pm.

Ashland Creek Bar & Grill, 92½ N. Main St. (482-4131). A huge oudoor deck and a dedication to live music have created a strong local following. Traditional grill menu ($5). Live music. Cover $1-10. Open daily 11am-2am. 21+.

Siskiyou Micro Pub, 31B Water St. (482-7718). Airy and unpretentious: wooden tables inside, creekside seating outside. Microbrew pints and bottled beers $3. Live music is usually free (Sa 9pm). Th open mic. Open spring-fall Th-Sa 11:30am-midnight, Su-W 11am-1am; in winter Su-Th 4pm-midnight, F-Sa 4pm-1am.

Daddy O's, 130 Will Dodge Way (488-5560), under Orion's Irish Pub, is perhaps the only punk club/Elvis museum in existence. A small bar serves up massive hot sandwiches and bands play at least 5 nights per week. Open W-Sa 3pm-3am.

LOS ANGELES

> We all get sucked in by the lobby: palm trees finger the sky, and there's enough sunshine to lay some off on Pittsburgh. But that's all on top. L.A., truth to tell, isn't much different from a pretty girl with the clap.
>
> –*City of Angels*

Myth and anti-myth stand comfortably opposed in Los Angeles (pop. 3.5 million). Some see in its sweeping beaches and dazzling sun a demi-paradise, a land of opportunity where the most opulent dreams can be realized. Others point to its congestion, smog, and crime, and declare Los Angeles a sham—a converted wasteland where TV-numbed masses go to wither in the sun.

The popularity of L.A.-bashing has increased dramatically in recent years. With so many targets, is it any wonder? Of late, California's largest city has been plagued with crises: race riots, earthquakes, floods, and homelessness. But despite these disasters, millions still call the city home. What could explain the Angeleno's loyalty in the face of catastrophe? Perhaps it's the persistence of L.A.'s mystique, the veneer of a city whose most celebrated industry is the production and dissemination of images. The glitter of the studios, the mammoth billboards on Sunset Strip, and the glamour of Rodeo Drive all attest to the resilience of L.A.'s fixation.

Here is a wholly American urban phenomenon. In a city where nothing seems more than 30 years old, the latest trends curry more respect than the venerable. Many come to this historical vacuum to make (or re-make) themselves. And what better place? Without the tiresome duty of bowing to the gods of an established high culture, Angelenos are free to indulge not in what they must, but in what they choose. The resulting atmosphere is delicious with potential. Some savor L.A.'s image-bound culture, others may be appalled by its excess, but either way it's one hell of a show.

HIGHLIGHTS OF LOS ANGELES

- The locus of the American film industry is **Hollywood** (p. 376), where the **Hollywood sign** (p. 376) rises above historic theaters and schlocky museums vie for attention amidst almost all the bars featured in *Swingers* (p. 403).
- An extensive beach culture thrives in **Santa Monica** (p. 378) and **Venice** (p. 379), where surfing, in-line skating, and beach volleyball mesh with cultural anomalies reminiscent of circus sideshows.
- L.A.'s **museums** are among the nation's finest, from the **Museum of Tolerance** (p. 382) to the **Getty** (p. 384) to the **Los Angeles County Museum of Art** (p. 385).
- **West Hollywood** (p. 350) is the heart of L.A.'s thriving gay community, and home to the **Sunset Strip** center of the hippest **nightlife** since the Beatles crashed post-war Hamburg (p. 401).
- **Shopping** (p. 378) and **dining** (p. 371) culture is alive and well in Santa Monica, in and around the **Third Street Promenade** and **Santa Monica Pier.**
- The trappings of the rich and famous can be explored in **Beverly Hills** (p. 381), although most of today's barons prefer to live in **Bel Air, Brentwood, Pacific Palisades** (p. 383), and in the hills along **Mulholland Drive.**
- Downtown (p. 386) is home to L.A.'s historic center, as well as **Exposition** (p. 388) and **Elysian Parks** (p. 398), both of which are crammed with museums, sports coliseums, and the **University of Southern California.**
- Television studios cluster in the smog-filled **San Fernando Valley** (p. 390), along with the **Mission San Fernando Rey de España,** and the world-famous **Universal Studios** theme park.

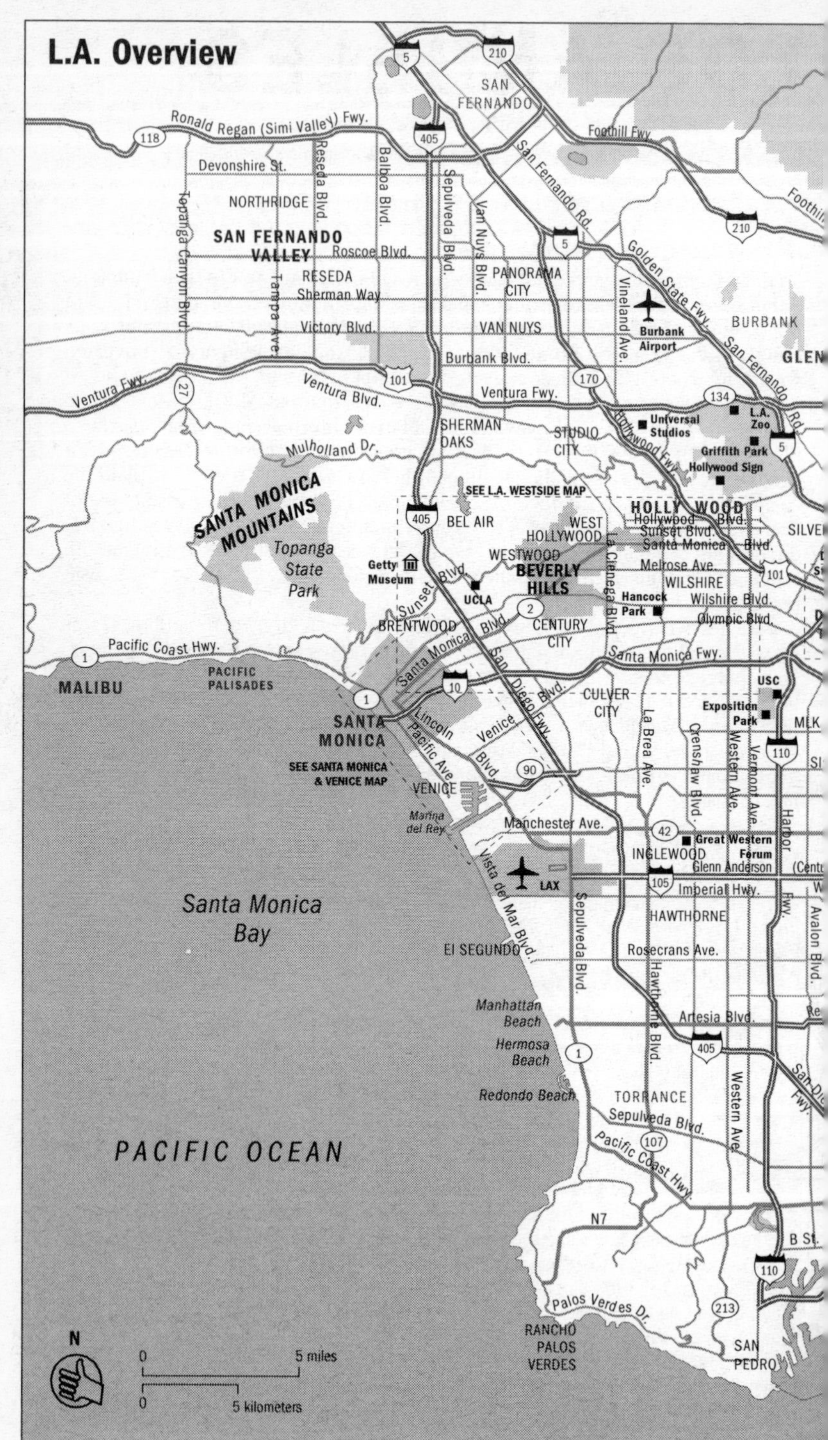
L.A. Overview
SAN FERNANDO
Ronald Regan (Simi Valley) Fwy.
Foothill Fwy.
Devonshire St.
NORTHRIDGE
Reseda Blvd.
Balboa Blvd.
Sepulveda Blvd.
Van Nuys Blvd.
San Fernando Rd.
Topanga Canyon Blvd.
SAN FERNANDO VALLEY
Roscoe Blvd.
RESEDA
Sherman Way
Tampa Ave.
PANORAMA CITY
Vineland Ave.
Golden State Fwy.
BURBANK
Victory Blvd.
VAN NUYS
Burbank Airport
Burbank Blvd.
San Fernando Rd.
Ventura Fwy.
Ventura Blvd.
Ventura Fwy.
Universal Studios
L.A. Zoo
SHERMAN OAKS
STUDIO CITY
Hollywood Fwy.
Griffith Park
Hollywood Sign
Mulholland Dr.
SANTA MONICA MOUNTAINS
SEE L.A. WESTSIDE MAP
HOLLYWOOD
Hollywood Blvd.
Sunset Blvd.
Santa Monica Blvd.
Topanga State Park
BEL AIR
WEST HOLLYWOOD
WESTWOOD
Getty Museum
BEVERLY HILLS
La Cienega Blvd.
Melrose Ave.
WILSHIRE
UCLA
Hancock Park
Wilshire Blvd.
Sunset Blvd.
Olympic Blvd.
BRENTWOOD
CENTURY CITY
Santa Monica Blvd
San Diego Fwy.
Santa Monica Fwy.
Pacific Coast Hwy.
MALIBU
PACIFIC PALISADES
USC
CULVER CITY
Exposition Park
SANTA MONICA
Lincoln
Venice Blvd.
La Brea Ave.
Crenshaw Blvd.
Western Ave.
Vermont Ave.
Harbor Fwy.
SEE SANTA MONICA & VENICE MAP
Pacific Ave
VENICE
Marina del Rey
Manchester Ave.
Great Western Forum
INGLEWOOD
Glenn Anderson
Vista del Mar Blvd.
LAX
Imperial Hwy.
Sepulveda Blvd.
HAWTHORNE
Santa Monica Bay
El SEGUNDO
Rosecrans Ave.
Hawthorne Blvd.
Avalon Blvd.
Artesia Blvd.
Manhattan Beach
Hermosa Beach
Redondo Beach
TORRANCE
Sepulveda Blvd.
Western Ave.
Pacific Coast Hwy.
PACIFIC OCEAN
N7
B St.
Palos Verdes Dr.
RANCHO PALOS VERDES
SAN PEDRO
N
0
5 miles
0
5 kilometers
5
210
118
405
210
101
27
170
134
405
2
10
1
1
90
110
42
105
405
1
107
110
213

ANGELES NATIONAL FOREST
SAN GABRIEL MOUNTAINS
LA CAÑADA FLINTRIDGE
PASADENA
Rose Bowl
Colorado Blvd.
Norton Simon Museum
Caltech
Huntington Gallery and Gardens
SAN MARINO
SAN GABRIEL
ALHAMBRA
ARCADIA
Rosemead Blvd.
Foothill Blvd.
GLENDORA
Foothill Fwy.
Live Oak Ave.
BALDWIN PARK
Arrow Hwy.
SAN DIMAS
San Dimas High
Peck Rd.
Ramona Blvd.
COVINA
Grand Ave.
Valley Blvd.
ROSEMEAD
San Bernardino Fwy.
Raging Waters
POMONA
MONTEREY PARK
Atlantic Blvd.
Valley Blvd.
Glandora Ave.
CITY OF INDUSTRY
Azusa Ave.
EAST L.A.
Santa Ana Fwy.
Pomona Fwy.
WHITTIER
San Gabriel River Fwy.
Orange Fwy.
DOWNEY
Whittier Blvd.
Fullerton Rd.
Lakewood Blvd.
LA HABRA
Imperial Hwy.
Chino Hills State Park
NORWALK
Harbor Blvd.
Rosecrans Ave.
PARAMOUNT
Alondra Blvd.
ORANGE COUNTY
Artesia Fwy.
YORBA LINDA
FULLERTON
Nixon's Birthplace
Atlantic Ave.
Bellflower Blvd.
LAKEWOOD
CERRITOS
Riverside Fwy.
Knotts Berry Farm
ANAHEIM
Carson St.
Valley View St.
Lincoln Ave.
Beach Blvd.
Long Beach Airport
Disneyland
Katella Ave.
Anaheim Stadium
Mesa (Newport) Fwy.
Willow St.
GARDEN GROVE
Pacific Coast Hwy.
Garden Grove Fwy.
Ocean Blvd.
San Diego Fwy
Bolsa Chica Rd.
Brookhurst St.
1st St.
Euclid St.
SANTA ANA
LONG BEACH
FOUNTAIN VALLEY
Warner Ave.
Huntington Beach
TO COSTA MESA AND NEWPORT BEACH
San Gabriel Cyn. Rd.

ORIENTATION

Located 127 miles north of San Diego and 403 miles south of San Francisco, the City of Angels spreads its wings across the flatland basin between the coast of Southern California and the inland mountains. You can still be "in" L.A. even if you're 50 miles from downtown. Greater L.A. encompasses the urbanized areas of Orange, Riverside, San Bernardino, and Ventura counties.

L.A. COMMUNITIES

A legitimate **downtown** Los Angeles exists, but it won't help orient you to the rest of the city. Numbered streets (1st, 2nd, etc.) run east-west downtown and are a one-way labyrinth. The heart of downtown, full of earthquake-proof skyscrapers, is relatively safe on weekdays, but avoid walking there after dark and on weekends.

The predominantly Latino section of the city is **East L.A.,** immortalized in song and film by Cheech and Chong, which begins east of downtown's Western Ave. with **Boyle Heights, Montebello,** and **El Monte.** North of East L.A., **Monterey Park** is the only city in the U.S. with a predominantly Asian-American population. Asian restaurants and stores line Atlantic Blvd., the main drag.

The **University of Southern California (USC), Exposition Park,** and the mostly African-American districts of **Inglewood, Watts, Huntington Park,** and **Compton** stretch south of downtown. **South Central,** the name by which this area is collectively known, suffered the brunt of the 1992 fires and looting. South Central, as Coolio fans know, is considered crime-ridden and attracts few tourists. If you're hell-bent on visiting, go during daylight and don't leave valuables in the car.

Glittering **Hollywood** lies northwest of downtown. Its main east-west drags (from north to south) are Hollywood Blvd., Sunset Blvd, Melrose Ave., and Beverly Blvd. Melrose Ave. links a chain of quasi-trendy cafes and boutiques. Sunset Blvd., which runs from the ocean to downtown, presents a cross-section of virtually everything L.A. has to offer: beach communities, lavish wealth, famous nightclubs, and sleazy motels. The **Sunset Strip,** hot seat of L.A.'s best nightlife, is the West Hollywood section of Sunset Blvd. closest to Beverly Hills. Hollywood Blvd., home of the Walk of Fame and a seedy string of tourist shops, runs just beneath the celebrity-ridden **Hollywood Hills.**

The region known as the **Westside** encompasses prestigious **West Hollywood,** home to the city's large gay community, Westwood and Westwood Village, Century City, Culver City, Bel Air, Brentwood, and **Beverly Hills,** home to TV's Kelly and Donna, wisecracking cop Axel F. (though he's really from Detroit), and some of the highest tax brackets in the state. Aside from the fancy plastic surgeons and residential estates, Westside's attractions include the **University of California at Los Angeles (UCLA),** in Westwood, and fashionable Melrose Ave. hangouts in West Hollywood. The name **West L.A.** is a municipal distinction which refers to the no-man's land south of Santa Monica, and Westwood, also including Culver City and Century City, the corporate and shopping district on what used to be the Twentieth Century Fox backlot. The area west of downtown, south of West Hollywood, is known as the **Wilshire District,** after its main boulevard. **Hancock Park,** an affluent residential area, covers the northeast portion of the district (the 5900 area) and harbors the Los Angeles County Museum of Art. It also intersects with Fairfax, a large Jewish community.

The **Valley Region** sprawls north of the Hollywood Hills and the Santa Monica Mountains. For most people, the valley is, *like*, the **San Fernando Valley,** where almost two million people wander among malls and TV studios. The valley is also home to **Burbank** and **Studio City,** which include the lion's share of today's movie studios. The basin is bounded to the north and west by the Santa Susanna Mountains and the Ronald Reagan Fwy. (Rte. 118), to the south by the Ventura Fwy. (Rte. 134), and to the east by the Golden State Fwy. (I-5). The **San Bernardino Valley,** home to about 2 million, stretches eastward from Los Angeles south of the San Gabriel Mountains. This valley is largely industrialized and heavily plagued by the county's famed smog, although it is home to **Pasadena** and its famed Rose Parade. The many disorganized, grasping arms of Los Angeles developments (the two valleys, the Wilshire Blvd. and Central Ave. corridors, Orange County) form a star-studded galaxy surrounding the L.A. heliopolis.

Eighty miles of beaches line L.A.'s **Coastal Region. Zuma,** the inspiration for the 1975 Neil Young album of the same name, is northernmost, followed by **Malibu,** which lies 15 miles up the coast from **Santa Monica.** A bit farther south is the distended freak show and beach community of **Venice.** The beach towns south of Santa Monica include **Manhattan, Hermosa,** and **Redondo Beaches.** South across the hob-nobby Palos Verdes Peninsula is **Long Beach,** a port city of a half-million people and home to a large gay population. Farthest south are the Orange County beach cities: **Seal Beach, Sunset Beach, Huntington Beach, Newport Beach,** and **Laguna Beach.**

Confused yet? Everyone is. Invest in good maps.

HOLLYWOOD. Birthplace of the silver screen industry, and, some might say, modern center of proselytization and prostitution, Hollywood is no longer the upscale home of movie stars and production studios. In fact, all the major studios except Paramount have moved to the roomier San Fernando Valley. Left behind are those things that could not be taken: historic theaters and museums, a crowd of souvenir shops, several famous boulevards, and an American preoccupation. With the exception of the never-ending string of movie premieres, the only star-studded part of Hollywood is the sidewalk, where pimps and panhandlers, tattoo parlors and porn shops abound. At 110 years old, Hollywood has changed dramatically since it first housed the nascent motion picture industry, yet its glorious past assures it will be larger than life for decades to come.

SANTA MONICA. The most striking characteristic of Santa Monica (pop. 87,000), which is a city all its own, is its efficiency. It is safe, clean, and unpretentious, and you can usually find a parking spot without taking a shuttle. Santa Monica is also easily navigable either on foot or by bus. Its residential areas, once heavily populated by screen superstars, are just blocks away from its main districts. The Third Street Promenade, often referred to as the Promenade, is the city's most popular spot to shop by day and schmooze by night, and the nearby beaches are jam-packed. Many find that a drive down Ocean Ave. leaves them with the eerie feeling that they are on a movie set—and chances are they might be. Each year Santa Monica issues close to 1000 permits to production companies that want to capture a little piece of the Gold Coast on film. *(It takes about 30min. (with no traffic) to reach Santa Monica on MTA #33 or 333 or on the Santa Monica Fwy. (I-10) from downtown Los Angeles. Santa Monica's efficient Big Blue Bus system connects to other L.A. bus routes.)*

VENICE. Venice is a carnivalesque beach town with rad politics and mad diversity. Its guitar-toting, Bukowski-quoting, wild-eyed, tie-dyed residents sculpt masterpieces in sand and compose them in graffiti, when they aren't slamming a volleyball back and forth over a beach net. A stroll in in-line skating, bikini-flaunting, tattooed Venice while nibbling a corn dog is a memorable experience. *(To get to Venice from downtown L.A., take MTA #33 or 333 (or 436 during rush hour). From downtown Santa Monica, take Santa Monica BBBus #1 or 2. Avoid hourly meter-feedings by parking in the $5-per-day lot at Pacific Ave. and Venice Blvd.)*

MARINA DEL REY. Venice's neighbor to the immediate south is older, more expensive, and considerably more sedate. While Marina del Rey does have a swimming beach, it has left sunbathing behind in favor of boating. Once a duck-hunting ground, the area was used as an oil field in the late 1930s and was reincarnated in 1965 as a yacht harbor. Marina del Rey is now the largest manmade marina in the world, home to 6000 pleasure boats and 3000 boats in dry storage.

MALIBU. Malibu makes its southern neighbor Santa Monica look like a carnival. Malibu is the *beach*, dude. No amusement parks, no boardwalk, just sand, mountains, and surfers. Although Bob Dylan, Martin Sheen, Diana Ross, Sting, and Cher are a few of Malibu's more televised residents, this is not a see-and-be-seen type of town. Instead, spend a sandy knight walking the quiet shores of Malibu, 27 miles of beautiful beaches that run along the 20000-30000 blocks of the **Pacific Coast Highway** (PCH; Rte. 1 North from Santa Monica).

BEVERLY HILLS. Ahhh, Beverly Hills. The very name evokes images of palm-lined boulevards, tanned and taut skin, and million-dollar homes with pools shaped like vital organs. It's a place with an image that precedes it as an upscale concentration of expensive hotels, ritzy boutiques, and movie stars galore. The fact is that not many of these preconceptions are that far from the truth. Although many silver screen starlets no longer call 90210 their ZIP Code, Beverly Hills is still quite a spectacle of opulence and class. You can live it up on a budget, though, simply by being as showy as the town itself. Pretend you're a millionaire and have some fun: shopkeepers can no longer tell who has the cash and who hasn't, so Beverly Hills can be a thrilling place to pretend. Throw on your Sunday best, slip on the shades, and make boutique clerks work for the money they think you have.

WESTWOOD AND UCLA. Although it is wedged between the exclusive neighborhoods of Brentwood and Beverly Hills, Westwood is actually a budget traveler's mecca, due to the fact that it is home to the University of California at Los Angeles (UCLA) Bruins. Westwood Village (on, around, and between Gayley, Westwood, and Kinross Ave.) hosts myriad movie theaters, boutiques, outdoor cafes, and coffeehouses. Most are priced for students, but some are upscale, so keep an eye on the price tag. For the most part, the town is safe and overrun by students.

BEL AIR, BRENTWOOD, AND PACIFIC PALISADES. These three residential communities don't offer much to the budget traveler in terms of accommodations or food, but the Getty Museum or a scenic drive along Sunset Boulevard are two free ways to experience the best the area has to offer. Veer off Sunset onto any public (non-gated) road to see tree-lined rows of well-spaced six-bedroom homes that make living here as costly as Beverly Hills. Private Brentwood School teaches the children of the wealthy and the famous on its campus which abuts the local private golf course.

WILSHIRE DISTRICT. L.A.'s culture vultures drive south, away from the trinket traffic of Hollywood, to peruse the Wilshire District's wealth of admission prices worth paying. From Model Ts to tar, area museums are sure to suit a wide range of interests. Museum Row lies on the Miracle Mile, (stretching from Fairfax to La Brea Ave. on Wilshire Blvd.), developed in the 1920s to serve as L.A.'s first shopping district specifically designed for customers arriving in those new-fangled gizmos called automobiles. You can park your roadster at a meter on 6th Street, one block north of Wilshire Boulevard, or in a lot on Curson Avenue for around $4.

WEST HOLLYWOOD. Once considered a no-man's land between Beverly Hills and Hollywood, West Hollywood is now a city unto itself and the proud abode of Los Angeles's thriving gay community, and some of L.A.'s best nightlife (see **Nightlife,** p. 401). The section of Santa Monica Boulevard around San Vicente Boulevard is its oldest gay district, and the city was one of the country's first to be governed by openly gay officials. The proximity of Hollywood and West Hollywood makes it difficult, though, to tell where the district of Hollywood ends and the city of West Hollywood begins. Technically, La Brea Avenue is the dividing line, but rainbow flags fly high and proud both east and west of it. In the years before West Hollywood's 1985 incorporation, lax zoning laws gave rise to Sunset Strip (a.k.a. the Strip), originally lined with posh nightclubs (frequented by stars) which have been supplanted by pseudo-grungy rock clubs (also frequented by stars). The area's music scene is among the country's most active, and many world-famous bands from The Doors to Guns N' Roses got their start here. Weekend nights attract tremendous club crowds and traffic jams. The Strip's famous billboards are, on some blocks, as massive and creative as those in New York City's Times Square. Most, however, pale in comparison to the new video billboard at Sunset Boulevard and Kings Avenue. Installed in the summer of 1999, this digital display dominates the Strip, as drivers try to catch a glimpse of its latest cutting-edge ad campaign.

DOWNTOWN. Say "downtown" to almost any Angeleno and they'll wince—either because they don't know what you're referring to, they know but don't go there, or they work there and are none too happy about it. It is L.A.'s netherland—the place over there. Mayor Richard Riordan and City Hall strive valiantly to project downtown as an example of L.A.'s diversity and culture. However, the Westside powers have a solid grip on the culture, while neighborhoods in L.A. County are defined by homogeneity of race, class, and wealth. Downtown, an uneasy truce prevails between the bustling financiers and the street population, but visitors should be cautious—the area is especially unsafe after business hours and on weekends.

GRIFFITH PARK AND GLENDALE. Five times larger than New York's Central Park, Griffith Park is an expansive 4107 acres, and the site of many outdoor diversions ranging from golf and tennis to hiking. The L.A. Zoo, Griffith Observatory and Planetarium, Travel Town, a bird sanctuary, and 52 miles of hiking trails decorate the dry hills (open daily 5am-10pm). The park stretches from the hills above North Hollywood to the intersection of the Ventura (Rte. 134) and Golden State Freeway (I-5). Several of the mountain roads through the park (especially the Vista Del Valle Dr.) offer panoramic views of downtown L.A., Hollywood, and the Westside. Unfortunately, heavy rains have made them unsafe for cars, but foot traffic is allowed on most.

SAN FERNANDO VALLEY. All the San Fernando Valley wants is a little respect. After all, nearly all of L.A.'s movie studios and a third of its residents reside here—more than the entire population of Montana. Yet it can't seem to shake the infamy it gained as breeding grounds for the Valley Girl, who started a worldwide trend in the 1980s with her neon mini-skirts, huge hair, and like, omigod, totally far-out diction. Today, the Valley gets mocked by actors on *Clueless* and *Beverly Hills, 90210*, as well as their real-life counterparts, and is often overlooked in City Hall's affairs. Maybe it isn't as glamorous as the city, but the Valley is more than just a satellite of L.A.—with its cookie-cutter houses and strip malls, it is suburban ritual elevated to its highest form. Ventura Boulevard marks the Valley's spiritual center—it's, like, where you go shopping.

PASADENA. Every New Year's Day in the U.S., masses of hungover, snowbound TV viewers jealously watch the blessed few fans marching through Pasadena to a football game on real grass. For the nation, Pasadena is primarily the home of the Rose Bowl, but for Californians, it is a serene suburb, much less crowded and a li'l rosier than L.A. With its world-class museums, graceful architecture, lively shopping district, and idyllic weather, the only thing Pasadena lacks is a coastline. Old Town Pasadena sequesters intriguing historic sights and an up-and-coming entertainment scene. The Pasadena Freeway (Rte. 110), built as part of the Works Projects Administration from 1934 to 1941, is one of the nation's oldest freeways. Its on- and off-ramps are not built for the modern motorist, so exercise caution. A travel note to the ambitious: Pasadena sleeps until the weekend, so check business hours to make sure the doors will be open when you get there.

GETTING THERE

BY PLANE. Los Angeles International Airport (LAX) is in **Westchester,** about 15 miles southwest of downtown, 10 miles southeast of Santa Monica, and one mile east of the coast, just off the San Diego Fwy. (I-405). LAX can be a confusing airport, but there are plenty of electronic information kiosks both inside and out with Chinese, English, French, German, Japanese, Korean, Spanish, Yiddish, Latin, !Kung, Esperanto, and Klingon options. **LAX information** is 310-646-5252. **Airport police** can be contacted at 310-646-4268 (24hr.). **Traveler's Aid** (310-646-2270), an information and referral service for airport info, transportation and accommodation suggestions, and major transit emergencies, is available in all terminals (open daily approximately 7am-10pm). Currency exchange is available at **L.A. Currency Agencies** (310-417-0366), in terminals 2, 5, and 7 and in the Tom Bradley International Terminal (all open daily 7:30am-11:30pm), but local American Express offices often offer more attractive rates (see **Currency Exchange,** p. 358).

Do *not* accept an offer of free transportation to an unknown hostel from the airport—chances are good you'll end up being charged $30 a night to stay in someone's garage. Airport solicitation is illegal and is a good indicator that a potential hostel is operating illegally as well. A choice moral: do not compromise your safety in exchange for a ready ride and an empty promise. *Let's Go* lists a number of established hostels, many of which *will* provide transportation assistance if you call from the airport or bus station (see **Accommodations,** p. 361).

Aside from renting a car, there are several other **transit** options. Before hopping into any of the vehicles below, check with the place at which you plan to stay; many places offer complimentary or reduced-rate transportation from the airport.

Subway: Shuttle "G" transports passengers to the **Aviation/Interstate 105** station on the Green Line (4:30am-11:30pm).

Metropolitan Transit Authority (MTA) Buses: Orange signs highlight the traffic island where shuttle "C" transports bus-bound passengers to the **transfer terminal** at Sepulveda and 96th St. To: **Westwood/UCLA,** bus #561 (M-F 6am-midnight, Sa-Su 8am-midnight); **downtown,** bus #42 (M-Sa 5am-11pm, Su 7am-11pm); **Long Beach,** bus #232 (M-F 5am-11pm, Sa-Su 6am-11pm); **West Hollywood** and **Beverly Hills,** bus #220 (M-F 6:30am-7:30pm, Sa-Su 7:30am-7:30pm); **Hollywood,** from West Hollywood, bus #217 (along Hollywood Blvd.; M-Sa 4am-midnight, Su 5am-midnight), bus #2 (along Sunset Blvd.; M-F 5am-1am, Sa 6am-1am, Su 6:30am-11pm), or bus #4 (along Santa Monica Blvd.; 24hr.). For specific info regarding MTA buses, cabs, and shuttles, ask at the **information kiosks** on the sidewalks directly in front of the terminals or look for a **courtesy phone.**

Taxis: Follow yellow signs. Cabs are costly; fare to downtown and Hollywood $24-28; to Santa Monica $20; to Disneyland a not-so Minnie $75-80. (For more info, see **Practical Information,** p. 357.)

Shuttle vans: Follow blue signs. Vans offer door-to-door service from the terminals to different parts of L.A. for a flat rate. Compare rates at the information booth; prices vary widely. Typical rates are $15 to downtown, $17 to Santa Monica, $35 to San Fernando Valley. Ask one of the airport employees just outside the baggage claim area to find you a shuttle.

BY BUS OR TRAIN. Amtrak rolls into **Union Station,** 800 N. Alameda St. (213-624-0171 or 800-USA-RAIL/872-7245), an architectural melange of Art Deco, southwestern, and Moorish details, at the northwestern edge of downtown Los Angeles. Opened in May 1939, Union Station brought together the Santa Fe, Union Pacific, and Southern Pacific railroads. Like everywhere else in L.A., the station has been featured in a number of films, including *Bugsy, The Way We Were*, and *House Party II.* From the station, take bus #33 to **Santa Monica,** or take bus #68 to **West Hollywood.** Trains run out of L.A. to **San Francisco** along the coast (1 per day, 12hr., $42-70) and to **San Diego** (13 per day, 3½hr., $22-28, round-trip $50).

The **Greyhound** station, 1716 E. 7th St. (213-629-8401 or 800-231-222), at Alameda St., is in an *extremely* rough neighborhood. Greyhound also stops in Hollywood, Santa Monica, Pasadena, and other parts of the metropolitan area (see **Practical Information,** p. 357). Going on to other area stations is far safer than disembarking downtown, especially after dark. If you must get off downtown, be very careful near 7th and Alameda St., one block southwest of the station, where you can catch MTA bus #60 traveling north to the Gateway Transit Plaza at Union Station. Greyhound buses go to: **San Diego** (2-3hr.; $13, round-trip $22); **Santa Barbara** (2-3hr.; $13, round-trip $22); **San Francisco** (10hr.; $36, round-trip $69); and **Tijuana,** Mexico (3-4hr.; $15, round-trip $24). Lockers are $1 per day.

Green Tortoise (800-867-8647), has northbound hostel-mobiles leaving L.A. every Sunday night, with stops in Venice, Hollywood, and downtown ($35). Call for reservations and exact departure location and times. (For more info, see **Essentials: By Bus,** p. 57.)

BY CAR. Six main arteries pump Greater L.A. full of traffic. Three of them run north from the city: The Santa Ana Fwy. **(Interstate 5),** the Ventura Fwy. **(U.S. 101),** and the Pacific Coast Highway **(Route 1).** Interstate 5 also runs south, and **Interstate 10** and **Interstate 15** run east. The city is criss-crossed by over a dozen freeways, and traffic can be horrible.

Life will degrade quickly into a series of wrong turns and missed interchanges without the aid of a good **map.** L.A., a city with 6500 miles of streets and 40,000 intersections, remains untamed, unknown, and unseen otherwise. Locals swear by the *Thomas Guide: Los Angeles County Street Guide & Directory* ($16 for L.A. County, $26 for L.A. and Orange Counties). It is the best travel investment you can make if you are traveling in the area by car.

L.A. is a city of distinctive boulevards; its shopping areas and business centers are distributed along these 4- and 6-lane behemoths. Streets are designated east, west, north, and south from 1st and Main St. at the center of **downtown.**

GETTING AROUND

PUBLIC TRANSPORTATION

Nowhere is the god *Automobile* held in greater reverence than in L.A. In the 1930s and 40s, General Motors (G.M.), Firestone, and Standard Oil conspired to buy up streetcar companies and run them into the ground, later destroying the rails. This increased dependence on buses and, later, on cars. In 1949 G.M. was convicted in federal court of criminal conspiracy—but there are still no trolleys.

BY MTA BUS. Nary an Angeleno will suggest moving about L.A. in anything but a car, and the sprawling metropolis does not facilitate efficient public transit, but L.A.'s buses are not altogether useless. The **Metropolitan Transit Authority (MTA)** used to be known as the RTD (Rapid Transit District) and some of its older buses may still be labeled as such. The name change was apt—most L.A. buses are not rapid by any modern definition of the word. With over 200 routes and with several independent municipal transit systems connecting to the MTA, it's no easy task to study the timetables.

Using the MTA to sightsee in L.A. can be frustrating because attractions tend to be quite spread out. Those determined to see *everything* in L.A. should get behind the wheel of a car. If this is not possible, base yourself in Hollywood (where there are plenty of sights and bus connections), make daytrips, and have plenty of change for the bus. Bus service is dismal in the outer reaches of the city and two-hour journeys are not unusual. Transferring often involves waits of an hour or more, and L.A. traffic congestion frustrates everyone.

To familiarize yourself with the MTA, write for "sector maps," MTA, P.O. Box 194, Los Angeles 90053, or stop by one of the 10 **customer service centers.** There are three **downtown:** Gateway Transit Center, Union Station (open M-F 6:30am-

6:30pm); Arco Plaza, 505 S. Flower St., Level C (open M-F 7:30am-3:30pm); and 5301 Wilshire Blvd. (open daily 9am-5pm). If you don't have time to map routes in advance, call 800-266-6883 (TDD 800-252-9040; open daily 6am-8:30pm) for transit info and schedules. Ninety percent of MTA routes have **wheelchair-accessible buses** (800-621-7828; daily 6am-10pm, call in advance to arrange pickup). Appropriate bus stops are marked with the international symbol for disabled access.

MTA's basic fare is $1.35 (transfer 25¢), seniors and disabled 45¢ (transfer 10¢); exact change is required. Weekly passes ($11) are available at customer service centers and local grocery stores. Transfers can be made between MTA lines or to other transit authorities. **Unless otherwise noted, all route numbers are MTA; BBBus stands for Big Blue Bus and indicates Santa Monica buses.**

Bus service is best downtown and along the major thoroughfares west of downtown. (There is 24hr. service, for instance, on Wilshire Blvd. and Santa Monica Blvd.) The downtown **DASH shuttle** (fare 25¢) serves major tourist destinations including Chinatown, Union Station, Gateway Transit Center, and Olvera Street. Given how hellish downtown traffic is, the scope of the shuttle routes makes them an attractive option; however, be aware that weekday and weekend routes are different. DASH also operates a shuttle in Hollywood (along Sunset Blvd.), Pacific Palisades, Venice, Watts, Fairfax, Midtown, Crenshaw, Van Nuys/Studio City, Warner Center, and Southeast L.A. (Downtown DASH operates M-F 6:30am-6:30pm, Sa 10am-5pm. Pacific Palisades shuttles do not run on Sa. Venice DASH operates June-Aug. Sa-Su every 10min. 11am-6pm. Parking costs $2.50, but is much cheaper than at the beach. Call 213-485-7201 for pickup points. For schedule info call 800-252-7433.)

BY SUBWAY. L.A. continues work on a system of light-rail connections, which is still far from complete. The existing rails reach a select few areas. The **Blue Line** serves the southern L.A. communities and Long Beach. The **Green Line** goes along I-105 from Norwalk to Redondo Beach, with shuttle service to LAX at Aviation/I-105. The **Red Line** will one day reach Hollywood and the Valley, but for now is known as the "bagel bus," as its clientele consists primarily of office workers rushing off to downtown lunch dates. A one-way trip costs $1.35, with transfers to bus and rail $1.60; seniors and disabled 45¢, with transfers 55¢. All lines run daily 5am to 11pm. Metro Rail info is now available online at www.mta.net.

BY METROLINK TRAIN. **Metrolink trains** run out of the city from Union Station to Riverside, Ventura, and Orange Counties (M-F), and San Bernardino, Santa Clarita/Antelope Valley (M-Sa). One-way fares $4-10, depending on destination. You can only buy them from machines in the station within three hours of your departure time. Discounts are available for the young, the old, and anyone traveling Saturday or during off-peak hours (8:30am-3:30pm and after 7pm). Beware—trains come and go up to five minutes ahead of schedule. Call 808-5465 (use any of the L.A. area codes) for info.

NON-PUBLIC TRANSPORTATION

FREEWAYS. The freeway is perhaps the most enduring image of L.A. No matter what may separate Angelenos—race, creed, or class—the one thing that unites everyone is the freeway system, a maze of 10- and 12-lane concrete roadways. "Caught in traffic" is the all-purpose excuse for tardiness, guaranteed to garner knowing nods and smiles of consolation from co-workers and acquaintances. In planning your route, note heavy traffic moving towards downtown from 7 to 10am on weekdays and streaming outbound from 4 to 7pm. Interestingly enough, though, since L.A. has a huge population that doesn't work 9-to-5, traffic can be as bad at 1pm as it is at 7pm. Expect major interchanges to be a madcap do-si-do as cars merge every-which-way. However, no matter how crowded the freeway is, it's almost always quicker and safer than taking surface streets to your destination, unless traveling under the guidance of a seasoned local, many of whom know tried-and-true shortcuts.

Uncongested freeways offer the ultimate in speed and convenience; the trip from downtown to Santa Monica can take as little as 20 minutes. A nighttime cruise along the Harbor Fwy. (I-110) past downtown, whizzing through the tangle of interchanges and the lights of L.A.'s skyscrapers, can be exhilarating, especially if you've been stuck in traffic all day.

Angelenos refer to their highways by names, not numbers. These names are little more than hints of a freeway's route, at best harmless, and at worst misleading. For freeway info, call **CalTrans** (213-897-3693), and refer to the **L.A. Overview map.**

L.A.'s family of freeways welcomed a new member in 1993. **Interstate 105,** the $2 billion **Glenn Anderson Freeway,** runs east from LAX and the San Diego Fwy. to the San Gabriel Riverbed, which parallels Rte. 605. It was named in honor of a policeman who drove off a collapsed freeway in the 1995 Northridge earthquake while rushing into town to help those in need. Its newness and efficiency often makes it a faster drive than other freeways.

CARS. L.A. may be the most difficult city in the U.S. to get around in without a car. Unfortunately, it may also be the most difficult city in which to **rent** a car for younger travelers. Most places will not rent to people under 21, and the ones that do are likely to impose a surcharge that only movie stars can afford to pay (nearly double the standard rate). Drivers between 21 and 25 will incur a lesser surcharge.

Nationally known agencies are reputed to have more dependable cars, but the demand for rental cars assures that even small local companies can survive and many have far lower rates than the big guys. They are worth looking into, but be forewarned, although you may be planning a budget trip, renting a car is not the time to be penny-wise. Stick to companies that can guarantee you that even though your Toyota is yellow, it is not a lemon. National agencies will replace a broken-down car hassle-free, so if you want to use a local place, double-check that they will do the same. Local rental companies may quote a very low daily rate, but they may also add extra fees when you return the car. Read the fine print and ask questions about additional fees and surcharges. Remember that the Collision and Damage Waiver (CDW) is optional, but be sure that you have sufficient insurance coverage if you decide to waive it. The prices quoted below are intended to give a rough idea of what to expect; ask about airline-related discounts.

Avis (310-914-7700), on Santa Monica Blvd. between Barrington Ave. and Bundy St. Economy cars $34 per day or $169 per week with unlimited mileage. CDW $9 per day. 21+ with major credit card. Under 24 surcharge $5 per day. Open M-Sa 7:30am-6pm, Su 8am-5pm.

Shooshani's Avon, 8459 Sunset Blvd. (323-650-2631). Rent economy cars for as low as $25 per day with 100mi. included; 35¢ per additional mi. $140 per week with 1000mi. free. CDW $9 per day. Ages 18-20 surcharge $15 per day; ages 21-24 $5 per day; $250-300 credit card deposit required. Open M-F 8:30am-7:30pm, Sa-Su 9am-2pm.

Thrifty (800-367-2277), at L.A. airport. As low as $25 per day, unlimited mileage within CA, NV, and AZ; as low as $144 per week. CDW $9 per day. 21+ with credit card. Under-25 surcharge $20 per day. Open daily 5am-midnight.

Alamo (310-649-2242 or 800-327-9633), at L.A. airport. Prices vary with availability; around $35 per day or $200 per week, both with unlimited mileage. CDW $9 per day. 21+ with major credit card. Under 25 surcharge $20 per day. Open 24hr.

Lucky, 8620 Airport Blvd. (310-641-2323 or 800-400-4736). Free transport to and from airport. $25 per day with 150mi. included; students $20. CDW $9 per day. 21+ with major credit card. Under 25 surcharge $5-15 per day. $300 refundable deposit required. Open daily 8am-8pm.

Advantage, 8244 Orion Ave., Van Nuys (818-376-1444). No airport pickup, but travelers staying on the Westside can get a good deal. Cars from $20 per day. 21+ with credit card. Under-25 surcharge. Open M-F 8am-6pm, Sa 9am-1pm.

Park your car in a paid lot (about $3) or a secure motel lot rather than on the street, not only for safety reasons, but because a quarter will only buy a measly 7½ minutes of street parking time in some areas. Generously dispensed parking violations are some of L.A.'s less beloved souvenirs.

BICYCLES. Unless you have legs and lungs of steel, a bicycle in L.A. is useful only for recreational purposes. Air quality is poor, distances are long, and drivers aren't used to looking out for cyclists. Always wear a helmet, unless you enjoy paying hefty fines; it's illegal to bike on roads without one.

The most popular route is the **South Bay Bicycle Path,** one of the best of the beach routes. It runs from Santa Monica to Torrance (19mi.), winding over the sandy beaches of the South Bay past sunbathers, boardwalks, and pesky spandex-clad in-line skaters. The path continues all the way to San Diego. Other bike paths include **San Gabriel River Trail,** 37 miles along the river, with views of the San Gabriel Valley; **Upper Rio Hondo** (9mi.) and **Lario Trails** (22mi.), both free from traffic; **Kenneth Newell Bikeway,** 10 miles through residential Pasadena; **Sepulveda Basin Bikeway,** seven miles around the Sepulveda Dam Recreation Area, a large loop of some major San Fernando Valley streets; **Griffith Park Bikeway,** 4½ miles past the L.A. Zoo and Travel Town train park; **Bolsa Chica Bike Path,** 10 miles along Huntington Beach; **Santa Ana River Bike Trail,** 22 miles along the Santa Ana River; and the **Santa Ana Canyon Bikeway,** seven miles of both street and canyon terrain. Recently, there has been some violence and gang-related activity on bike trails (e.g., South Bay Bicycle Path, San Gabriel River Trail, Lario Trails, and Santa Ana River Bike Trail). It should be all right to ride during the day, but avoid night biking—or buy a frame-mounted holster.

Most rental shops stand near the piers of the various beaches, with an especially high concentration on Washington Blvd. in Venice/Marina del Rey. (Specific shops for this area are listed individually under **Venice: Sights,** p. 379.)

WALKING AND HITCHHIKING. L.A. pedestrians are a hapless breed. The largely deserted streets of commercial centers will seem eerie to the first-time visitor. Unless you're running in the L.A. Marathon, moving from one part of the city to another on foot is a ludicrous idea—distances are just too great. Nevertheless, some colorful areas such as Melrose, Westwood, the Santa Monica Promenade, Hollywood, and Old Pasadena are best explored by foot. Just remember that Californians will stare (and possibly run) you down, and cops may ticket you, for setting foot in a crosswalk without a "Walk" signal. For lovers of coastal culture, Venice Beach is one of the most enjoyable (and popular) places to walk, with sights and shopping areas relatively close to one another. *Destination: Los Angeles*, the publication of the Convention and Visitor Bureau, has an excellent list of walking tours (see **Practical Information: Publications,** p. 357). Since some of the best tour companies are one-person operations, schedules and prices are not written in stone. Look for theme tours (i.e., graveyard, O.J. Simpson) geared to your interests (or obsessions). The **Los Angeles Conservancy** (213-623-2489) offers 10 different tours of the downtown area. Tours cost $5 and advance reservations are required. Call **Tree People** (818-753-4600) for information on Sunday walking tours of Coldwater Canyon Park.

Once the sun sets, those on **foot,** especially outside West L.A. and off well-lit main drags, should exercise caution, especially when alone. Plan your pedestrian routes especially carefully—it is worth a detour to avoid passing through particularly crime-ridden areas.

If you hitchhike you will probably die. It is uncommon and exceptionally dangerous in L.A. and anyone who picks up a hitchhiker probably has ulterior motives. It is also illegal on freeways and many streets. **Don't even think about it.**

PRACTICAL INFORMATION

GREATER LOS ANGELES AREA GENERAL INFO

TRANSPORTATION

Airport: Los Angeles International Airport (LAX; 310-646-5252), in Westchester, 15mi. southwest of downtown. Metro buses, car rental companies, cabs, and airport shuttles offer rides from here to requested destinations (see **Getting There,** p. 352).

Buses: Greyhound-Trailways Information Center, 1716 E. 7th St. (fares, schedules, and reservations 800-231-2222), at Alameda St., downtown. See neighborhood listings for other stations, and **Getting There,** p. 352, for info on the main downtown terminal.

Public Transit: MTA Bus Info Line (213-626-4455 or 800-266-6883). Open M-F 6am-8:30pm, Sa-Su 8am-6pm. You may be put on hold long enough to walk to your destination. **MTA Customer Service Center,** 5301 Wilshire Blvd. Open M-F 9am-5pm.

Taxis: Checker Cab (213-482-3456 or 800-300-5007), **Independent** (213-385-8294 or 800-521-TAXI/8294), **United Independent** (323-653-5050 or 800-822-TAXI/8294). If you need a cab, it's best to call. Approximate fare from airport to downtown $25-32.

Automobile Club: Automobile Club of Southern California, 2601 S. Figueroa St. (213-741-3111), at Adams St. Lots of maps and info. Club privileges free for AAA members, $2-3 fee for nonmembers. Their *Westways* magazine is a good source for daytrips or vacations. Open M-F 9am-5pm. Other offices in greater L.A.; call for locations.

TOURIST AND FINANCIAL SERVICES

VISITOR INFORMATION

Los Angeles Convention and Visitor Bureau, 685 S. Figueroa St. (213-689-8822), between Wilshire Blvd. and 7th St. in the Financial District. Hundreds of brochures. Staff speaks English, French, German, Spanish, and Tagalog. Maps of L.A., sights, and buses, each about $2; maps of celebrity sights and California roads ($4). Distributes *Destination: Los Angeles,* a free booklet with tourist and lodging info. Open M-F 8am-5pm, Sa 8:30am-5pm. Hollywood office, 6541 Hollywood Blvd., near Hudson St. Open M-Sa 9am-5pm.

National Park Service, 401 W. Hillcrest Dr., Thousand Oaks (818-597-9192), in the Conejo Valley. Info on the Santa Monica Mountains, including outdoor activities and special events. Open daily 9am-5pm.

Sierra Club, 3435 Wilshire Blvd. #320 (213-387-4287). Hiking, biking, and backpacking info. Group outings. 3-month event schedule $7.50. Open M-F 10am-6pm.

BUDGET TRAVEL

Council Travel, 10904 Lindbrook Dr., in Westwood Village (310-208-3551). Cheap flights, HI-AYH memberships, ISICs. Limited selection of backpacks, travel guides, and sleepsacks. Open M-F 10am-7pm, Sa 11am-5pm. Walk-ins only.

STA Travel, 7202 Melrose Ave. (323-934-8722), has similar services, but no travel accessories. Open M-F 10am-6pm, Sa 10am-5pm.

Los Angeles HI-AYH, 1434 2nd St., Santa Monica (310-393-3413). Info and supplies for travelers. Guidebooks, backpacks, moneybelts, low-cost flights, rail passes, and ISICs. Open M-Th 9am-6pm, F-Sa 10am-5pm.

OTHER SERVICES

Consulates: Australia, 2049 Century Park E., 19th fl. (310-229-4800). Open M-F 9am-5pm; visa desk open M-F 9am-4pm. **South Africa,** 600 Wilshire Blvd. #600 (323-651-0902). Consulate and visa desk open M-F 9am-noon. **U.K.,** 11766 Wilshire Blvd. #400 (310-477-3322). Open M-F 8:30am-noon and 2-4pm for calls, 8:30-11:30am for visas. For visas, arrive at the consulate between 8-9am or else face a long line.

Currency Exchange: At most airport terminals (see **Getting There,** p. 352), but rates are exorbitant. **American Express** offices have better rates but charge $3 to change currency. AmEx **downtown,** 735 S. Figueroa St. (213-627-4800). Open M-F 9am-6pm. Also in **Beverly Hills,** 327 N. Beverly Hills Dr. (310-274-8277). Open M-F 10am-6pm, Sa 10am-5pm. Other locations in **Pasadena, Torrance,** and **Costa Mesa. World Banknotes Exchange,** 406B W. 6th St., at Hill St., doesn't charge to change currency, but charges a 2% fee for traveler's checks. Open M-F 8am-5:30pm, Sa 8am-3pm.

LOCAL SERVICES

Central Public Library, 630 W. 5th St. (213-612-3200), between Grand and Flower. Present ID with local current address to get a library card; reading room open to all. First floor's East Wing houses foreign-language books, weekly exhibits, and activities including readings, films, and workshops. Tours M-F 12:30pm, Sa 11am and 2pm, Su 2pm. Open M-Th 10am-8pm, F-Sa 10am-6pm, Su 1-5pm.

CULTURAL, COMMUNITY, AND RELIGIOUS CENTERS

African-American Community Unity Center, 944 W. 53rd St. (323-789-7300). Youth services, cultural workshops, and educational outreach programs. Open M-F 9am-5pm.

Chinese Chamber of Commerce, 977 N. Broadway (213-617-0396). Educational and recreational activities (especially Chinese festivals). Open M-F 10am-5pm; call ahead.

Gay and Lesbian Community Services Center, 1625 N. Schrader Blvd., Hollywood (323-993-7400), 1 block from Hollywood Blvd. Youth and senior groups, counseling, housing, educational, legal, and medical services. Building open M-Sa 9am-10pm; most offices close around 6pm.

Japanese-American Cultural and Community Center, 244 S. San Pedro St. #506 (213-628-2725). Houses a garden, live theater, and the Doizaki Gallery. Library available by appointment only. Hours depend on current displays; in general, open M-F 9am-6pm.

Jewish Community Center, 5870 W. Olympic Blvd. (323-938-2531), 3 blocks east of Fairfax Ave. Recreational facilities, senior services, day care, and health club. One-day guest pass $10. Open to people of all faiths. Olympic-size pool and gym open until 10pm; office open M-F 9am-6pm, Su 10am-5pm.

Korean Cultural Center, 5505 Wilshire Blvd. (323-936-7141). Cultural activities, language workshops, and monthly film presentations. Houses a library, museum, and art gallery. Open M-F 9am-5pm, Sa 10am-1pm.

Senior Recreation Center, 1450 Ocean Ave., Santa Monica (310-458-8644), in Palisades Park. Lively old international crowd partakes of outings, dance classes, and cultural activities at a dignified pace. Hot lunches "like Mom used to make" M-F. Open M-F 9am-4pm, Sa-Su 11am-4pm.

Los Angeles County Commission on Disabilities, 500 W. Temple St. (213-974-1053). Some info on transportation, equipment, and recreational facilities for people with disabilities. Call before visiting. Open M-F 8am-5pm.

California Relay Service for the Hearing Impaired (TTD/TTY 800-735-2929). 24hr. lines.

Ticket Agency: Ticketmaster (213-381-2000), charges substantial surcharges. A better bet is to contact the box office directly.

Surf Conditions: Recorded info on Malibu, Santa Monica, and South Bay 310-457-9701. Most FM radio stations have a surf report at noon.

Weather Conditions: Detailed region-by-region report 213-554-1212.

Highway Conditions: 800-427-7623. May help you stave off an afternoon parked on the freeway. KFWB 980AM has reports every 10min. if you're already stuck.

LOCAL MEDIA

Television Stations: ABC (Channel 7); **CBS** (Channel 2); **Fox** (Channel 11); **NBC** (Channel 4); **KTLA/WB** (Channel 50); **UPN** (Channel 13).

National Public Radio: 91.5 FM for all considerable things.

Smooth Jazz: 94.7 FM, "The Wave." Smooooooth jazz.

Other Radio Stations: Hip-hop/R&B "The Beat" 92.3FM; **Pop/Rock/Top 40** "Star" 98.7FM; **Pop/Top 40** KIIS 102.7FM; **Soft Rock** 103.5FM; **Rock** KROQ 106.7FM; **Oldies** 101.1FM; **Classic Rock** 104.3FM.

EMERGENCY AND COMMUNICATION

Emergency: 911.

24-Hour Crisis Lines: AIDS Hotline (800-922-2437), or national hotline (800-342-5971). **Rape Crisis** (310-392-8381).

24-Hour Pharmacy: Sav-On, 3010 S. Sepulveda Blvd., West L.A. (310-478-9821; other 24hr. locations 800-627-2866.) **Rite-Aid,** 7900 W. Sunset Blvd., Hollywood (323-876-4466).

MEDICAL SERVICES

Hospitals: Cedar-Sinai Medical Center, 8700 Beverly Blvd. (310-855-5000, emergency 310-855-6517). **Good Samaritan Hospital,** 616 S. Witmer St. (213-977-2121, emergency 213-977-2420). **UCLA Medical Center,** 10833 Le Conte Ave. (310-825-9111, emergency 825-2111).

Planned Parenthood, 1057 Kingston St. (323-226-0800), near downtown. Birth control, prenatal care, STD treatment, abortions, and counseling. Call for appts. (1 week in advance) or other locations. Hours and fees vary.

Free Clinics: Hollywood-Sunset Free Clinic, 3324 W. Sunset Blvd. (323-660-7959). Provides general medicine, family planning, and psychiatric care. No mandatory fees at this state-funded clinic, but donations requested. Appointments only; call M, W, or F 10am-noon to schedule. **Valley Free Clinic,** 5648 Vineland Ave., **North Hollywood** (818-763-8836), 1 block north of Burbank. Women's health, birth control, medical counseling, drug addiction services, and free HIV testing. Appointments only; call M-Sa 10am-4pm to schedule.

COMMUNICATION

Post Office: Central branch at 900 N. Alameda St., at 9th St. (800-275-8777). Open M-F 9am-5pm, Sa 9am-noon. **ZIP Code:** 90086.

AREA CODES. The greater Los Angeles area now mandates 11-digit dialing for all local phone calls, even ones within the same area code (e.g., 1-310-555-1212 must be dialed even from 310-555-9098). New area codes are being added constantly *non-geographically* (such as 323 and 424). Area codes follow:

213 covers downtown L.A., Huntington Park, Vernon, and Montebello.

213 and **323** cover Hollywood.

310 and **424** cover Malibu, Pacific Coast Highway, Westside, parts of West Hollywood, Santa Monica, southern and eastern L.A. County, and Catalina Island.

626 covers the San Gabriel Valley and Pasadena.

818 covers Burbank, Glendale, San Fernando Valley, Van Nuys, and La Cañada.

909 covers the eastern border of L.A. County.

HOLLYWOOD PRACTICAL INFORMATION

Buses: Greyhound, 1409 N. Vine St. (323-466-1249), 1 block south of Sunset. To: **Santa Barbara** (5 per day; $13, round-trip $24); **San Diego** (10 per day; $13, round-trip $22); and **San Francisco** (5 per day; $36, round-trip $69). Terminal open daily 6:30am-11pm.

Public Transit: MTA Customer Service Center, 6249 Hollywood Blvd. (213-922-6000). Free info, maps, and timetables. Open M-F 10am-6pm. **Important buses:** #1 along Hollywood Blvd., #2 and 3 along Sunset Blvd., #4 along Santa Monica Blvd., #10 along Melrose Ave. Janes House (see below) has schedules and helpful advice; the MTA itself may be less than helpful. Fare $1.35, transfers 25¢. One-month pass $42, weekly $11.

Parking: Public lot north of Hollywood Blvd. at Cherokee (marked by rubber shoes exquisitely impaled on steel rods outside). 2hr. free, each additional hr. $1; max. $3.

Visitor Information Bureau in **The Janes House,** 6541 Hollywood Blvd. (213-236-2331), in Janes House Square. Formerly "Schoolhouse to the Stars": Cecil B. DeMille's kid went here, among others. Free L.A. and Hollywood visitor guides including *Discover Hollywood,* a comprehensive (if sometimes out-of-date) guide to the arts. Pick up *L.A. Weekly* and *New Times* for weekly info. Open M-Sa 9am-1pm and 2-5pm.

Currency Exchange: Cash It Here, 6565 Hollywood Blvd. at Whitley. No commission. Open M 8am-Su 5pm.

Internet Access: Many L.A. coffeehouses have **CaféNet** computers, which have Internet access, but no text-based email access. These locations have both: **Cyber Java,** 7080 Hollywood Blvd., Hollywood (323-466-5600; $9 per hr.; open M-F 7am-midnight; Sa-Su 8am-midnight), and **@coffee,** 7200 Melrose Ave., Hollywood (323-930-1122; $2 for 10min., $5 for 30min., $7 for 1hr. includes a coffee; open daily 8am-8pm).

Hospital: Queen of Angels Hollywood Presbyterian Medical Center, 1300 N. Vermont Ave. (213-413-3000). Emergency room open 24hr.

Emergency: 911. **Police:** 1358 N. Wilcox Ave. (213-485-4302).

Post Office: 1615 Wilcox Ave. (800-275-8777). Open M-F 8:30am-5:30pm, Sa 8:30am-3pm. **ZIP Code:** 90028.

Area Code: Mostly 323, some establishments are still 213. 11-digit dialing required.

SANTA MONICA PRACTICAL INFORMATION

Buses: Greyhound buses stop on 4th St. between Colorado Blvd. and Broadway. Tickets can be purchased from the driver.

Public Transit: Santa Monica Municipal Bus Lines (310-451-5444). With over 1000 stops in Santa Monica, L.A., and Culver City, the "Big Blue Bus" (BBBus) is faster and cheaper than the MTA (as featured in *Speed*). Fare for most routes 50¢ and transfer tickets for MTA buses 25¢; transfers to other BBBuses free. **Important buses:** #1 and 2 connect Santa Monica and Venice; #3 to L.A. airport; #10 provides express service from downtown Santa Monica (at 7th St. and Grand Ave.) to downtown L.A. **The Tide Shuttle:** Downtown shuttle (fare 25¢). Signs with route info litter the downtown area. Runs every 15min. M-F noon-10pm.

Equipment Rentals: Perry's Beach Rentals, 1100-1200 and 2400-2600 Ocean Front Walk (310-458-3975), in the eye-catching blue buildings, north and south of the pier, just before Venice Beach. In-line skates and bikes $6 per hr., $18 per day; tandem bikes $10 per hr., $30 per day; boogie boards $4 per hr., $10 per day. Open daily 9am-dark. **Sea Mist Rentals,** 1619 Ocean Front Walk (310-395-7076), has slightly cheaper rates. In-line skates and bikes $5 per hr., $14 per day.

Parking: Six lots flank the 3rd St. Promenade; 3 are accessible from 4th St. and 3 from 2nd St. First 2hr. free, each additional 30min. 75¢. Santa Monica Place Mall has free parking for up to 3hr.; others are metered (50¢ per hr.). Downtown streets have meters as well (also 50¢ per hr.). All-day beachside parking $5-10.

Visitor Information: Santa Monica Visitors Center, 1400 Ocean Ave. (310-393-7593), in Palisades Park. Very few local maps and brochures, but the free *Official Visitors Guide* and bus maps offer a good overview of the area. The helpful staff at this kiosk also provide info on attractions and events. Open daily June-Aug. 10am-5pm; Sept.-May 10am-4pm.

Currency Exchange: Western Union, 1454 4th St. (310-394-7211), at Broadway. Open M-F 9am-6pm, Sa 9am-3pm.

American Express: 1250 4th St. #110 (310-395-9588), at Arizona Blvd. Foreign exchange at decent rates. AmEx traveler's checks cashed for no extra fee; $3 charge for non-AmEx checks. Open M-F 9am-5pm, Sa 10am-2pm.

Library: L.A. Public Library Santa Monica branch on 6th St. (310-458-8600), at Santa Monica Blvd. Open M-Th 10am-9pm, F-Sa 10am-7pm, Su 1-5pm.

Medical Services: Santa Monica/UCLA Medical Center, 1250 16th St. (310-319-4765). Emergency room open 24hr.

Police: 1685 Main St. (310-395-9931 or 310-458-8491).

Post Office: 1248 5th St. (800-275-8777), at Arizona Blvd. Open M-F 9am-6pm, Sa 9am-1pm. **ZIP Code:** 90401.

AREA CODES	The area codes in Santa Monica are 310 and the new 424 overlay area code. 11-digit dialing required.

PUBLICATIONS

The free *L.A. Weekly*, which comes out on Thursdays, is the definitive source of **entertainment** listings, available at shops, restaurants, and newsstands citywide. L.A. has a number of "industry" (i.e., movie) papers; the best-known are *Variety* and *The Hollywood Reporter*. The *Los Angeles Times* (newsstand 25¢, Su $1.50) defeats all rival dailies with top reporting, an excellent sports section, and a challenging crossword. The *Times* "Calendar" section has the accurate and up-to-date dope on the L.A. scene. *The Los Angeles Sentinel* is L.A.'s largest **African-American** paper. UCLA's **student** paper, *The Daily Bruin*, is published during the school year. The most popular **gay and lesbian** entertainment magazines are *The Frontiers* and *Edge*.

L.A. also has numerous foreign-language publications. The **Spanish** *La Opinión* is the largest, but two **Korean** papers (*The Korean Central Daily* and *The Korean Times*) have circulations approaching 50,000 each. The *International Daily News* and the *Chinese Daily News* serve the **Chinese**-speaking community. L.A.'s gargantuan newsstands offer not only copious copies of muscle, car, sports, fashion, and skin mags, but also many foreign-language publications. **World Wide,** 1101 Westwood Blvd. at Kinross Ave., is a fine example (open daily 7am-midnight).

ACCOMMODATIONS

As in any large city, cheap accommodations in Los Angeles are often unsafe. It can be difficult to gauge quality from the exterior, so ask to see a room before you spend any money. Be suspicious of rates below $35; they're probably not the kind of hotels in which most travelers would feel secure. For those willing to share a room and a bathroom, hostels are a saving grace, although Americans should be aware that some only accept international travelers. These hostels require an international passport, but well-traveled Americans with proof of travel (passports, out-of-state identification, or plane tickets often do the trick) may be permitted to stay. It never hurts to ask for off-season or student discounts, and occasionally managers will lower prices to snare a hesitant customer.

In choosing where to stay, the first consideration should be car accessibility. If you don't have wheels, you would be wise to decide which element of L.A. appeals to you the most. Those visiting for the beaches would do well to choose lodgings in Venice or Santa Monica. Avid sightseers will probably be better off in Hollywood or the more expensive (but cleaner and nicer) Westside. Downtown has numerous public transportation connections but is unsafe after dark. Even those with cars should choose accommodations proximate to their interests to keep car-bound time to a minimum. **Listed prices do not include L.A.'s 14% hotel tax.**

HOLLYWOOD

Staying in Hollywood puts you smack in the middle of it all which is a blessing for some and a curse for others. Although the Tinseltown scene improves every day, it is still not a place to hang out on street corners late at night. Always exercise caution if scouting out one of the many budget hotels on or around Hollywood Boulevard—especially east of the main strips. The hostels here are generally excellent, and as a whole, a much better value than anything else in L.A.

Banana Bungalow Hollywood, 2775 W. Cahuenga Blvd. (323-851-1129 or 800-446-7835; www.bananabungalow.com), just north of the Hollywood Bowl. Free shuttles to airport and area beaches and attractions. This mini-compound's Hollywood Hills locale affords it space enough to create a relentlessly wacky and frisky summer-camp atmosphere–not for the retiring traveler. Free nightly movies, fantastic pool, hoops, weight room, Internet access ($1 for 5min.), and "snack shack." Continental breakfast, linen, and parking included. Meals $5. Check-in 24hr. Check-out 10:30am. Co-ed dorms (6-10 beds) with bathroom and TV $18-20; private doubles $55. **Passport and international airline ticket required** for dorms, but Americans can stay in private rooms.

USA Hostels Hollywood, 6772 Hawthorn Ave. (323-462-3777 or 800-524-6783; www.usahostels.com), off Highland Ave. between Hollywood and Sunset Blvd. Free pickup from airport, bus, and train stations. Not for the couch potato traveler–TVs were removed from rooms to promote guests to be active. Daily tours to local attractions. Kitchen, patio, bike rental, party room with bar, billiards, and TV. BBQs and comedy nights twice per week. Internet access $1 per 10min. Breakfast of unlimited waffles and pancakes, linen, lockers, and parking included. Co-ed dorms (4-8 beds) with private bath June-Aug. $17, Sept.-May $15; private rooms $34-38. Weekly: June-Aug. $109, Sept.-May $254. **Passport or proof of travel required.**

Hollywood International Hostel, 1057 Vine St. (323-462-6351 or 800-750-1233), at Santa Monica Blvd. Free pickup from airport, bus, and train stations. Opened in 1999, this is the largest hostel in Southern California, according to the management. Along with large rooms, the 1924 building also has a fireplace mantle from *Gone With the Wind* and a beautiful lobby with leather couches, cable TV, and a PacMan video game. Kitchen, gym, Internet access, nightly movies, billiards room with cable TV. Rooftop deck has a bar and a killer view of the Hollywood sign. Breakfast and parking included. Reception 24hr. Dorms June-Aug. $15, Sept.-May $10.75; doubles June-Aug. $37, Sept.-May $32. Weekly: June-Aug. $90, Sept.-May $84; doubles $245, Sept.-May $210. **International passport or college ID required.** (See sister hostel below.)

Orange Drive Manor, 1764 N. Orange Dr. (323-850-0350). This disturbingly quiet, but pleasantly peaceful, mini-mansion sits in a low-key residential neighborhood just around the corner from Mann's Chinese Theater. Best for travelers who enjoy privacy. Kitchen, cable TV lounge, TV show tickets available from management. Spacious dorms with antique furniture. Lockers. Linen included. Parking $5 per night. Check-out 10am. No curfew. Dorms (2-4 beds), some with private baths, $15-20; private rooms $25-44. Long-term discounts available. Reservations recommended in summer. No credit cards.

Student Inn International Hostel, 7038½ Hollywood Blvd. (323-469-6781 or 800-557-7038), on the Walk of Fame. Free pickup from airport, bus, and train stations. Jim Morrison stayed here for 6 months before he was famous, and took an infamous (according to the management) jump from the window of Room 20 to avoid the LAPD. Housed in an 80-year-old building, this amiable hostel just underwent a minor overhaul. Small kitchen, free Internet access, free and discounted tickets to Disneyland, Universal Studios, and Magic Mountain, and free city tours. Breakfast, linen, and parking included. 4-bed dorms with private bath June-Aug. $13.50, Sept.-May $15; doubles $30. For $10, those low on cash can snore on floor mattresses, or work at reception in exchange for a night's stay. Call far in advance for credit card reservations. 10% discount for *Let's Go* travelers with this book. **International passport required.**

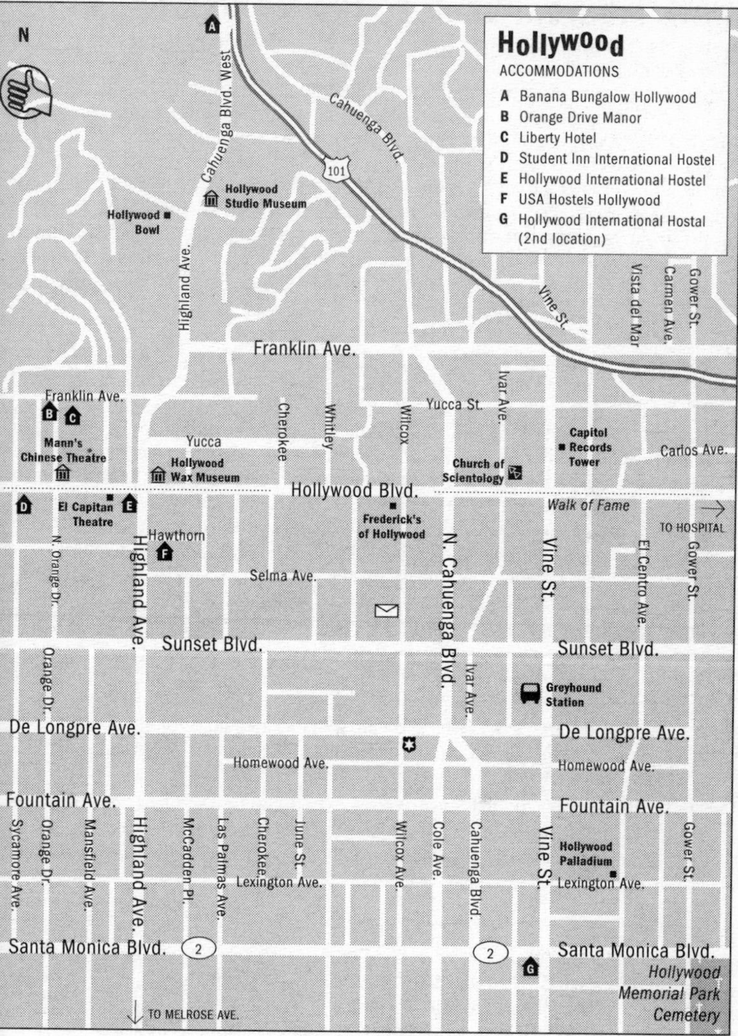

Liberty Hotel, 1770 Orchid Ave. (323-962-1788), 1 block north of Mann's Chinese Theater. Free pickup from airport, bus, and train stations. Brand-new, and it shows in the bright and airy hallways. Nicely sized comfortable rooms. Residential street is relatively clean and calm, but still near Hollywood Blvd. TV, free coffee, laundry. Parking included. Singles \$40; doubles \$45, with microwave and fridge \$50.

Hollywood International Hostel, 6820 Hollywood Blvd. (323-463-0797 or 800-750-6561). Free pickup from airport, bus, and train stations. Enormous lounge with TV, a video game, billiards and foosball, nightly movies, Internet access, and fax. Tours and BBQs. Laundry. Parking \$3 per night. Reception 24hr. Single-sex dorms (2-4 beds) with shared bath June-Aug. \$15, Sept.-May \$13.50; private rooms \$35. Weekly dorms: June-Aug. \$105, Sept.-May \$210. Reserve ahead with credit card, but no on-site credit card charges. **International passport required.**

SANTA MONICA, VENICE, AND MARINA DEL REY

Staying near Santa Monica or Venice Beaches requires making a few decisions. Venice Beach hostels beckon young budget travelers, especially foreign students, luring them in with the area's blend of indulgent beach culture and lively nightlife. Most of the cheap accommodations that pepper the coast cater to raucous party kids, but there are some quiet gems in the mix. In general, Venice hostels are friendlier, cozier, and less expensive than their Santa Monica counterpart; Santa Monica's hostel is relatively sterile, and in a fairly sophisticated and expensive area. Parking in Venice (especially near the beach) is costly—travelers with cars should look for accommodations that include parking or consider staying in accommodations farther from the beach. For those venturing into L.A. proper, the city center is connected to Santa Monica by the MTA or Santa Monica's Big Blue Bus (BBBus).

Los Angeles/Santa Monica (HI-AYH), 1436 2nd St., Santa Monica (310-393-9913; fax 393-1769), 2 blocks from the beach and across from the 3rd St. Promenade. Take MTA #33 from Union Station to 2nd St. and Broadway, BBBus #3 from LAX to 4th St. and Broadway, or BBBus #10 from Union Station. Located next door to the associated **SaMo Travelers Center** (310-393-3413), which offers budget travel services. The building is beautiful, modern, and meticulous. Rooms are small but clean. Beds have foam mattresses. Lobby manned 24hr. Colossal kitchen, 2 nightly movies, library, central courtyard, and biweekly barbecues ($5). Guests receive discounts at local establishments. Strict no alcohol policy. Hot breakfast (85¢-$3.75). Safe deposit boxes and lockers available. Laundry. Pay garages nearby. 4-week max. stay. Dorms (4-10 beds) $19-21, nonmembers $22-24; private doubles $58, nonmembers $61.

Cadillac Hotel, 8 Dudley Ave., Venice (310-399-8876; fax 399-4536). Airport shuttle $5. Art Deco landmark directly on the beach. International crowd and helpful staff. Tour desk, sauna, rooftop sundeck, and well-equipped gym. Lounge has cable TV, pool table, Internet access, Venetian gondola, and a piece of the Berlin Wall. Lockers. Parking included with private rooms. 4-bunk dorms with private bath $25; impressive private suites (for the area) from $80. No reservations for bunks–call before coming, or show up at 1pm and hope.

Share-Tel Apartments, 20 Brooks Ave., Venice (310-392-0325), ½ block from the beach. This fun-loving hostel has a social lounge with TV and board games. Dorm rooms are spacious and clean with private baths, kitchenettes, and fridges. Breakfast and dinner included (M-F). Lockers $1. Linen and key deposit $20. Parking per night July-Aug. $10, Sept.-June $5. 4-8 bed dorms $17, weekly July-Aug. $110, Sept.-June $100; private rooms $22-25. No reservations. No credit cards. **International passport required** just to enter the front gate.

Venice Beach Hostel, 701 Washington Blvd., Venice (310-306-5180), above Celebrity Cleaners. Not to be confused with the Venice Beach Hostel on Pacific (no affiliation). BBBus #3 stops at Lincoln Ave. just up the road. Free airport shuttle. Street traffic makes nights fairly noisy at this hostel. Frequent field trips to local bars. Full kitchen. Thursday keg parties ($3), weekend barbecue, cozy cable TV lounge, Internet access, and rooftop deck (accessible only by ladder). Lockers. Dorms $13; weekly $90.

Marina Hostel, 2915 Yale Ave., Venice (310-301-3983). Free airport shuttle. The quiet residential street offers respite from the manic pace closer to the shore. Low-key atmosphere calls to mind *Dazed and Confused.* TV room, big common bathrooms, and kitchen. You're literally staying in a house! Two lucky folks can crash in the van o' lovin' (ask, you'll see). Breakfast and linen included. Laundry. Reception 24hr. Dorms $13; weekly $90. No credit cards. **Passport or proof of out-of-state residence required.**

Venice Beach Cotel, 25 Windward Ave., Venice (310-399-7649; fax 399-1930), 1 block from the boardwalk. From the airport, take BBBus #3 to Lincoln Ave., then MTA #33 to Venice Beach post office and walk 1 block west. Airport shuttle $5. "A hostel with hotel standards" (a cotel). Pristine rooms, some with ocean views. Lively BYOB bar area has cozy, colorful tables. Free margarita at check-in; free tea and coffee throughout your

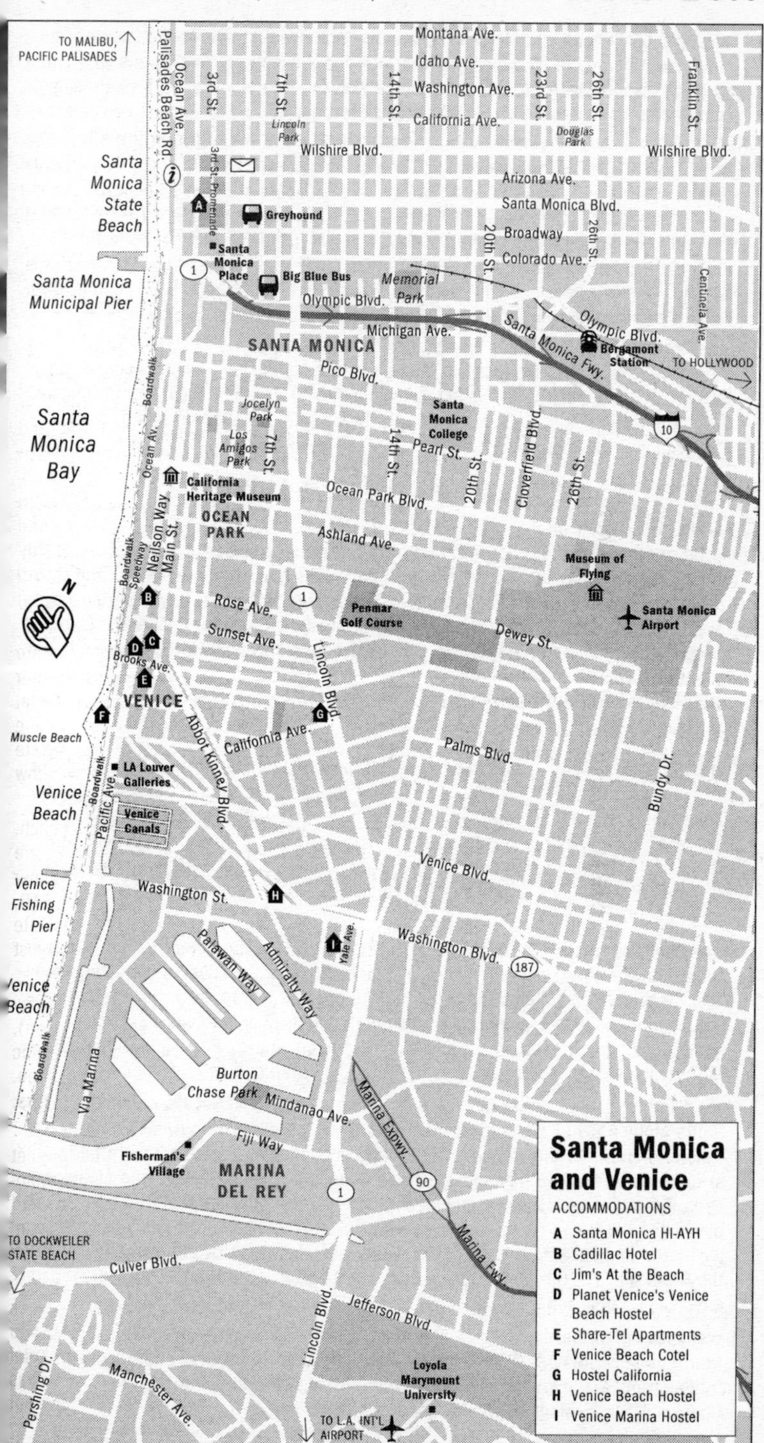
TO MALIBU, PACIFIC PALISADES
Montana Ave.
Idaho Ave.
Washington Ave.
California Ave.
Wilshire Blvd.
Arizona Ave.
Santa Monica Blvd.
Broadway
Colorado Ave.
Olympic Blvd.
Michigan Ave.
Pico Blvd.
Pearl St.
Ocean Park Blvd.
Ashland Ave.
Rose Ave.
Sunset Ave.
Brooks Ave.
California Ave.
Palms Blvd.
Venice Blvd.
Washington St.
Washington Blvd.
Mindanao Ave.
Fiji Way
Culver Blvd.
Jefferson Blvd.
Manchester Ave.
Ocean Ave.
Palisades Beach Rd.
3rd St.
7th St.
14th St.
23rd St.
26th St.
Franklin St.
20th St.
Centinela Ave.
Cloverfield Blvd.
Nelson Way
Main St.
Ocean Av.
Boardwalk
Speedway
Pacific Ave.
Abbot Kinney Blvd.
Lincoln Blvd.
Bundy Dr.
Dewey St.
Yale Ave.
Palawan Way
Admiralty Way
Via Marina
Marina Exowy.
Marina Fwy.
Pershing Dr.
Santa Monica Fwy.
3rd St. Promenade
Lincoln Park
Douglas Park
Memorial Park
Jocelyn Park
Los Amigos Park
Santa Monica State Beach
Santa Monica Municipal Pier
Santa Monica Bay
Muscle Beach
Venice Beach
Venice Fishing Pier
Greyhound
Santa Monica Place
Big Blue Bus
SANTA MONICA
Bergamont Station
TO HOLLYWOOD
Santa Monica College
California Heritage Museum
OCEAN PARK
Museum of Flying
Santa Monica Airport
Penmar Golf Course
VENICE
LA Louver Galleries
Venice Canals
Burton Chase Park
Fisherman's Village
MARINA DEL REY
TO DOCKWEILER STATE BEACH
Loyola Marymount University
TO L.A. INT'L AIRPORT
1
10
90
187
N
Santa Monica and Venice
ACCOMMODATIONS
A Santa Monica HI-AYH
B Cadillac Hotel
C Jim's At the Beach
D Planet Venice's Venice Beach Hostel
E Share-Tel Apartments
F Venice Beach Cotel
G Hostel California
H Venice Beach Hostel
I Venice Marina Hostel

stay. Excellent security. No kitchen or laundry. Free use of tennis rackets, table tennis, and boogie boards ($20 deposit). Linen included. Reception 24hr. Dorms (3-4 beds) $13, with private bath $17; doubles (some with private bath and TV) $33-45; slightly cramped but manageable triples $51. **Passport required,** but Americans welcome.

Hostel California, 2221 Lincoln Blvd., Venice (310-305-0250; fax 305-8590), off Venice Blvd. Take MTA #33 from downtown. Free airport pickup. Festive place where many nationalities bump elbows in what looks like an upscale Mexican restaurant. 10min. walk to the beach. Bike rental ($7 per day), pool table, big-screen TV, kitchen, and Internet access. Co-ed and single-sex dorms. Linen included. Laundry. $5 key deposit. Parking included. Check-in 24hr. Checkout by 10:30am preferred. Tight 6-bed dorms $15-17, weekly July-Aug. $102, Sept.-June $90; 25-bunk barrack $13; doubles $40. No credit cards. **Passport required,** but Americans with proof of travel welcome.

Planet Venice's Venice Beach Hostel, 1515 Pacific Ave., Venice (310-452-3052), 1 block from the boardwalk. Close to the beach and friendly, but far from cozy. Lounge, kitchen, and Internet access. Breakfast included (M-F). Laundry. $25 deposit. Check-in 24hr. Dorms July-Aug. $19, weekly $115; Sept.-June $11; rooms with kitchen $52. Reservations accepted. No credit cards.

WESTSIDE: BEVERLY HILLS, WESTWOOD, WILSHIRE

The snazzy and relatively safe Westside has excellent public transportation to the beaches. The area's affluence, however, means less bang for your buck, and there are no hostel-type accommodations. Those planning to stay at least one month in summer or six months during the school year can contact the UCLA Off-Campus Housing Office, 350 Deneve Dr. (310-825-4491; www.cho.ucla.edu), where a roommate bulletin board lists students who have a spare room, as well as sublets and rentals. UCLA's student newspaper lists even more info online at www.dailybruin.ucla.edu.

Claremont Hotel, 1044 Tiverton Ave., in Westwood Village (310-208-5957 or 800-266-5957), near UCLA. Pleasant and inexpensive for its locale. Sterile hallways open into clean rooms with antique dressers, ceiling fans, private baths, and phones. Microwave and free coffee in lobby, next to pleasant Victorian-style TV lounge. Daily maid service. Check-in 24hr. Check-out noon. Singles $40; doubles $48; triples $54. Weekly rates available. Reservations recommended, especially in June, as this is the perfect spot for the graduation crowd.

Bevonshire Lodge Motel, 7575 Beverly Blvd. (323-936-6154), near Farmer's Market. Looks like *Melrose Place* with a color-blind interior decorator. Pool in the central courtyard. Spacious rooms have sparkling, newly renovated bathrooms to make the shower scenes fun, and beds big enough for Amanda to bring all of her conquests home. Older furniture, but comfy beds, A/C, cable TV, and in-room phones. Parking included. Singles $44, doubles $49; rooms with kitchen $55. 10% ISIC discount.

The Little Inn, 10604 Santa Monica Blvd., West L.A. (310-475-4422). Found on Little Santa Monica Blvd., the smaller road paralleling the divided boulevard to the south. Take one step into the courtyard and reach budget-travel bliss. Although the lack of style in the sparsely decorated rooms is *so* un-L.A., they're sizable and clean. A/C, cable TV, and fridges. Parking included. Check-in 24hr. Check-out 11am. *Let's Go* travelers (with this book) get special rates Sept.-July (excluding major holiday periods): singles $50, doubles $55. Kitchens extra. Equally appealing is their **Century City** location, the **Stars Inn,** 10269 Santa Monica Blvd. (310-556-3076; fax 310-277-6202). Same look, same rates, same high quality.

Beverly Inn, 7701 Beverly Blvd. (323-931-8108), near Hollywood Blvd. Across the street from the CBS Studios. Clean with recently renovated big rooms equipped with TVs, fridges, and A/C. Outdoor pool open year-round. Parking included. Check-in 24hr. Check-out 11am. Singles $42-46; doubles $46-48.

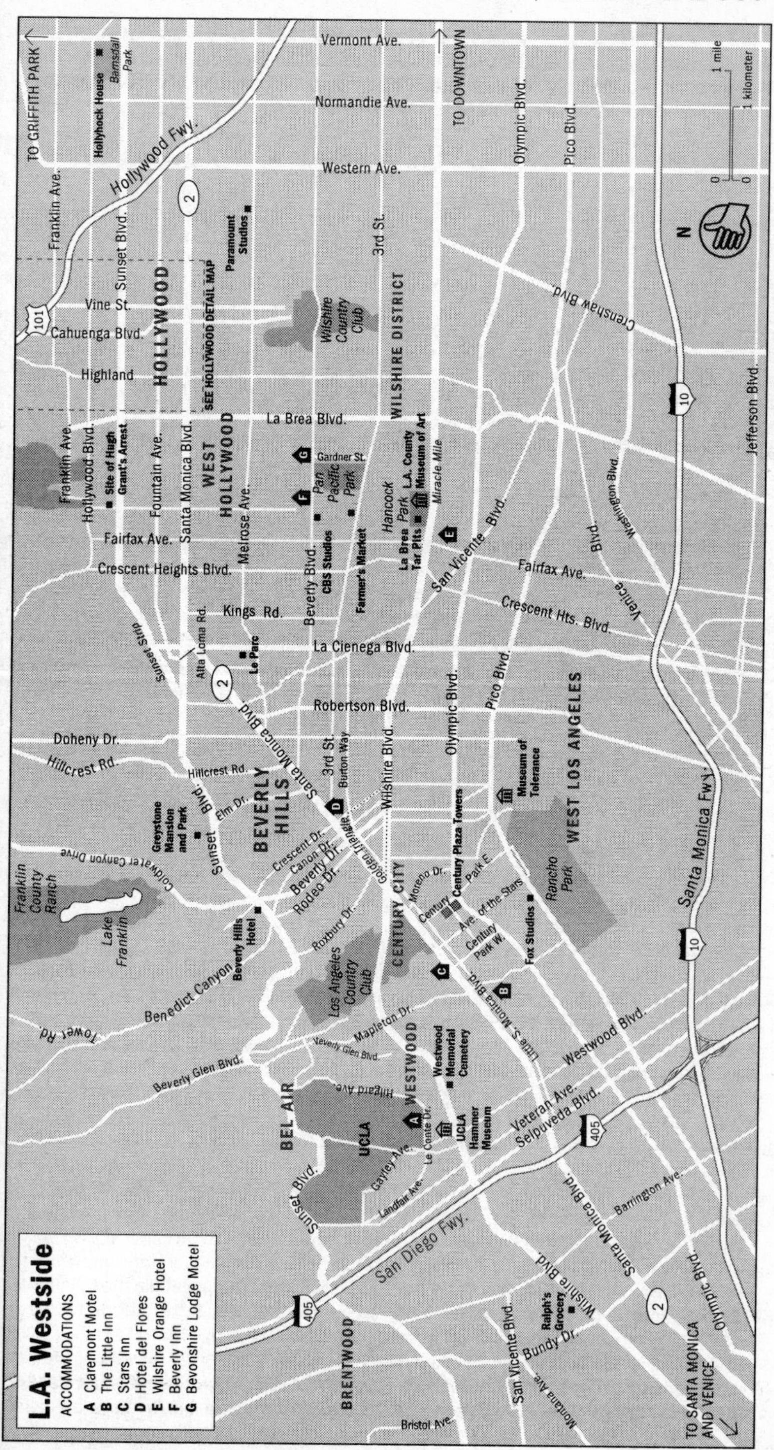
L.A. Westside
ACCOMMODATIONS
A Claremont Motel
B The Little Inn
C Stars Inn
D Hotel del Flores
E Wilshire Orange Hotel
F Beverly Inn
G Bevonshire Lodge Motel
TO GRIFFITH PARK
Hollyhock House
Barnsdall Park
Vermont Ave.
Normandie Ave.
Western Ave.
TO DOWNTOWN
Olympic Blvd.
Pico Blvd.
1 mile
1 kilometer
N
Hollywood Fwy.
Franklin Ave.
Sunset Blvd.
Paramount Studios
3rd St.
Vine St.
Cahuenga Blvd.
101
HOLLYWOOD
SEE HOLLYWOOD DETAIL MAP
Wilshire Country Club
WILSHIRE DISTRICT
Crenshaw Blvd.
Highland
La Brea Blvd.
10
Jefferson Blvd.
Hollywood Blvd.
Site of Hugh Grant's Arrest
Fountain Ave.
Santa Monica Blvd.
WEST HOLLYWOOD
Gardner St.
Pan Pacific Park
L.A. County Museum of Art
Miracle Mile
Hancock Park
La Brea Tar Pits
Melrose Ave.
Fairfax Ave.
Crescent Heights Blvd.
Beverly Blvd.
CBS Studios
Farmer's Market
San Vicente Blvd.
Washington Blvd.
Venice Blvd.
Crescent Hts. Blvd.
Kings Rd.
Sunset Strip
Alta Loma Rd.
Le Parc
La Cienega Blvd.
Robertson Blvd.
Pico Blvd.
WEST LOS ANGELES
Doheny Dr.
Hillcrest Rd.
Santa Monica Blvd.
3rd St.
Burton Way
Wilshire Blvd.
Museum of Tolerance
Greystone Mansion and Park
Elm Dr.
BEVERLY HILLS
Golden Triangle
Crescent Dr.
Canon Dr.
Beverly Dr.
Rodeo Dr.
CENTURY CITY
Moreno Dr.
Century Plaza Towers
Century Park E.
Ave. of the Stars
Century Park W.
Fox Studios
Rancho Park
Santa Monica Fwy.
Coldwater Canyon Drive
Franklin County Ranch
Lake Franklin
Beverly Hills Hotel
Roxbury Dr.
Los Angeles Country Club
Benedict Canyon
Tower Rd.
Mapleton Dr.
Beverly Glen Blvd.
Little S. Monica Blvd.
WESTWOOD
Westwood Memorial Cemetery
Westwood Blvd.
Hilgard Ave.
BEL AIR
UCLA
Le Conte Dr.
UCLA Hammer Museum
Veteran Ave.
Sepulveda Blvd.
405
Gayley Ave.
Landfair Ave.
Barrington Ave.
San Diego Fwy.
Santa Monica Blvd.
Wilshire Blvd.
Ralph's Grocery
Olympic Blvd.
BRENTWOOD
San Vicente Blvd.
Bundy Dr.
Montana Ave.
Bristol Ave.
TO SANTA MONICA AND VENICE

Hotel del Flores, 409 N. Crescent Dr., Beverly Hills (310-274-5115), across from the 90210 post office. Like a bed-and-breakfast *sans* breakfast. Built in 1926, this building has relaxing outdoor garden patio seats. Clean rooms with TV, phones, and some with ceiling fans. Fridges or microwaves upon request. Lounge with TV, magazines, and fridge. Street parking only. Check-in 24hr. Check-out noon. Singles with shared bath from $65; doubles with private bath from $74. Weekly rate and ISIC discount available.

DOWNTOWN

Downtown L.A. is probably not the best place to look for accommodations. Although busy and fairly safe by day, the area empties and becomes dangerous after 6pm and on weekends. If you have an overwhelming desire to stay downtown, some decent lodgings can be found in the area, but don't be afraid to bargain, especially from September to May. Cheaper weekly rates are sometimes available. Remember to travel in packs, especially in the area between Broadway and Main Street.

Metro Plaza Hotel, 711 N. Main St. (213-680-0200), at Cesar Chavez Ave. Near Chinatown, Olvera St., and Union Station. It doesn't look it from its seedy outside, but the glass entry doors open into a rather fine hotel. Large, clean rooms with TVs and refrigerators. Parking included. Singles $59; doubles $69.

Park Plaza Hotel, 607 S. Park View St. (213-384-5281), on the west corner of 6th St. across from the green but unsafe MacArthur Park. Built in 1927, this colossal luxury hotel's heyday has come and gone, but it remains a comfortable option. You'll feel like you're staying in City Hall during a government shutdown. All of the small, clean rooms have TV, some have A/C. Singles $60; doubles $65.

Milner Hotel, 813 S. Flower St. (213-627-6981 or 800-827-0411). Free pickup from airport, bus, and train stations. Central location, with pub and grill in lobby. Rooms have A/C and cable TV. Breakfast included. Singles $50; doubles $60.

Hotel Stillwell, 838 S. Grand Ave. (213-627-1151). A sensible downtown option. Standard hotel was recently refurbished. Rooms are bright, have A/C and cable TV. Parking area next door ($3.25 per day). Singles $44, weekly $200; doubles $54, weekly $300.

CAMPGROUNDS

Los Angeles has no **campgrounds** convenient to public transportation. Even motorists face at least 40-minute commutes from the nearest campsites to downtown. One nearby and relatively pleasant L.A. County campground **Leo Carrillo State Beach** (310-457-1324), PCH (Rte. 1), 20 miles north of Malibu at the Ventura County line. It has 150 developed sites with flush toilets and showers ($17-18). Nearby **Pt. Mugu** has 57 sites at Sycamore Canyon with flush toilets and showers ($17-18) and 75 primitive sites at the Thornhill Broome area with chemical toilets and cold, outdoor showers ($10). **Malibu Creek State Park,** off Las Virgenes Rd. six miles north of Rte. 1, in the Santa Monica Mountains, has 50 family campsites with flush toilets and showers ($13-16). Call 800-444-7275 to make mandatory summer reservations for any sites or 818-880-0367 for more info.

FOOD

Eating in Los Angeles, the city of the health-conscious, is more than just *eating*. Thin figures and fat wallets are a powerful combination—L.A. lavishes in the most heavenly *and* healthy recipes around. Of course, there are also restaurants where the main objective is to be seen, and the food is secondary, as well as those where the food itself seems too beautiful to be eaten—it was here, after all, that 1980s *nouvelle cuisine* reached its height (see **Cuisinart**, p. 20).

Fortunately for the budget traveler, Los Angeles elevates fast-food and chain restaurants to heights virtually unknown in the rest of the country. The mom-and-pop diner is a rarity in L.A., where restaurants live by P.T. Barnum's mantra: "Give

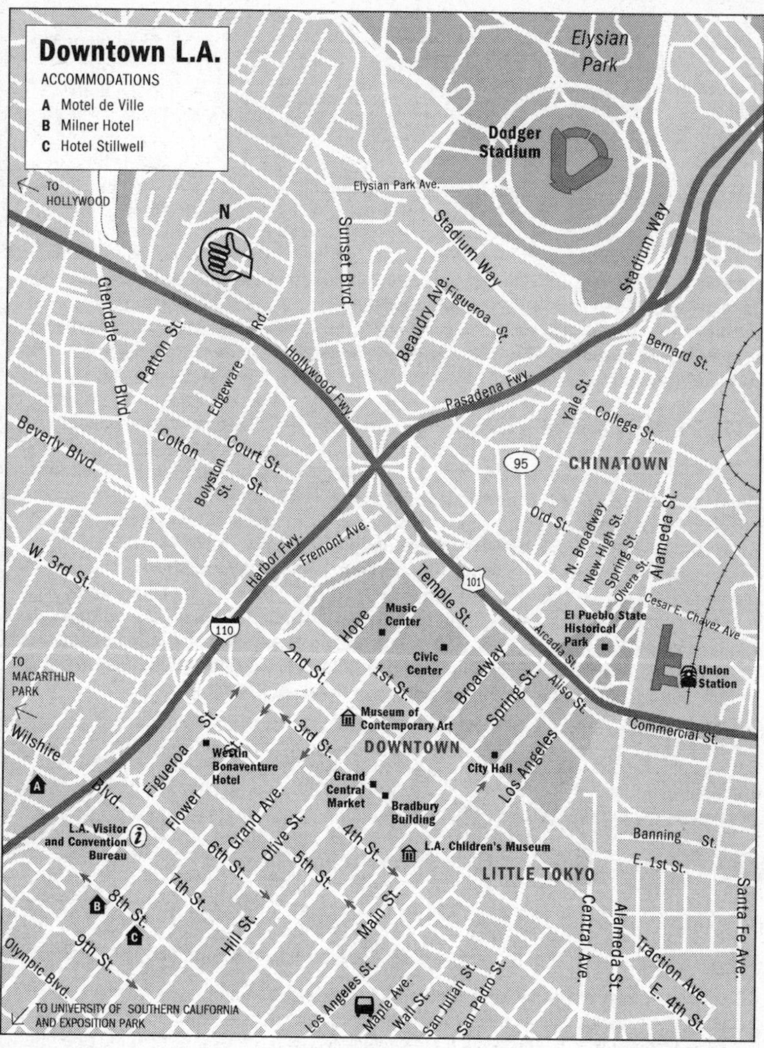

the people what they want." What Angelenos want, of course, is not only quality food but also convenience—chains are a way of life here. For the optimal burger-and-fries experience, try **In 'n' Out Burger,** a beloved chain that evokes a '57 Chevy. **Johnny Rocket's** revives the never-really-lost era of the American diner. Their milk-shakes are the food of the gods. All **Fatburgers** come with frank witticisms, free of charge. The current hot 'n' spicy craze is lard-free, cholesterol-free "healthy Mexican"—**Baja Fresh** leads the pack. Long before Frappuccinos made their way onto Starbucks menus, Angelenos flocked to **The Coffee Bean and Tea Leaf** for ice-blended mochas. The smoothie, now ubiquitous across the U.S., allows the health-conscious to indulge in a sweet blend of fruit, juice, frozen yogurt, and energy-boosting additives like spirulina and protein powder. **Jamba Juice** makes the biggest and the best, with over 20 smoothie flavors, and shots of fresh-blended grass for die-hard fiberphiles. Most coffeehouses have added the smoothie to their repertoire of fancy concoctions.

Of course, food in L.A. isn't just about California cuisine. The range of culinary options is directly proportional to the city's ethnic diversity. Certain food types are concentrated in specific areas. Jewish and Eastern European food is most prevalent in Fairfax; Mexican in East L.A.; Japanese, Chinese, Vietnamese, and Thai around Little Tokyo, Chinatown, and Monterey Park; and seafood along the coast. Vietnamese, Italian, Indian, and Ethiopian restaurants are scattered throughout the city.

L.A. restaurants tend to shut down early. Angelenos usually eat out between 7 and 10pm, and restaurants are often closed by 11pm. Fast-food chains are rarely open past midnight. Listings on **late-night** restaurants and cafes, are in **Entertainment** (p. 394).

MARKETS. L.A.'s enormous public markets give the visitor a first-hand look at the variety and volume of foodstuffs available here. **Farmer's Market,** 6333 W. 3rd St., Wilshire District (213-933-9211), at Fairfax Ave., has over 160 produce stalls, as well as international food booths, handicraft shops, souvenir stores, and a phenomenal juice bar. Take lunch upstairs to the **Beverly Hills Art League Gallery** and munch among the paintings of local amateur artists. There's delectable produce, but bargains are becoming increasingly rare. (Open M-Sa 9am-6:30pm, Su 10am-5pm.) A less touristy and less expensive source of produce is the **Grand Central Public Market,** 317 S. Broadway (213-624-2378), a large baby-blue building downtown, between 3rd and 4th St. This main market in the Hispanic shopping district was established in 1917—making it one of the oldest institutions in the Los Angeles area. Grand Central has more than 50 stands selling not only produce, but also clothing, housewares, costume jewelry, vitamins, and fast food. This vast space is always riotously busy and entertaining. (Open daily 9am-9pm.) **Trader Joe's** is a super-cool chain specializing in budget gourmet food. They save by doing their own packaging and, as a result, you get amazing deals like $4 bottles of choice Napa wines. There are 84 locations (most of which are in the trendier areas); call 800-746-7857 to find the nearest one (all open daily 9am-9pm).

HOLLYWOOD

Screenwriters and starlets still constitute much of Hollywood's population. Most are single, hungry, and nearly broke after paying the rent on their bungalows. As a result, Hollywood offers the best budget dining in L.A. As an added bonus, if you're in the right place at the right time, you may see celebrities chowing on the same lunch special as yours. **Hollywood** and **Sunset Boulevards** have excellent international cuisine, while **Fairfax Avenue** hosts Mediterranean-style restaurants and kosher delis. **Melrose Avenue** is full of chic cafes, many with outdoor people-watching patios. As Hollywood is the heart of L.A.'s pounding nightlife, many of its best restaurants are open round-the-clock (see **Late-Night Restaurants,** p. 401).

Roscoe's House of Chicken and Waffles, 1514 Gower St., Hollywood (323-466-7453). Roscoe makes the best waffles anywhere. Try "1 succulent chicken breast and 1 delicious waffle" ($5.60). The restaurant is frequented by all sorts of celebrities. Open Su-Th 8:30am-midnight, F-Sa 9am-3:30am.

Duke's Coffee Shop, 8909 Sunset Blvd., West Hollywood (310-652-3100), at San Vicente Blvd. Best place in L.A. to see hung-over rock stars. The walls are a kaleidoscope of posters and autographed album covers. They claim to treat everyone the same, famous or not, but don't expect to be invited to add your signature to the walls unless you're the former. Perfect for brunch. Try the "Revenge" (eggs scrambled with avocado, sour cream, onions, tomatoes, and peppers; $6.75). Entrees $5-8. Open M-F 7:30am-8:45pm, Sa-Su 8am-3:45pm.

El Coyote, 7312 Beverly Blvd., Hollywood (323-939-2255), at Poinsettia St. With multiple spacious and pleasantly low-key dining rooms, and waitresses clad in sweeping Mexican dresses, this is a local and *Let's Go* favorite. Enormous combo plates come with corn tortillas and all the chips and salsa you could ever want ($6). Frothy margaritas ($3-4.25). Filling chicken fajitas are the most expensive entree but are still only $7. Parking after 4pm $1.50. Open Su-Th 11am-10pm, F-Sa 11am-11pm.

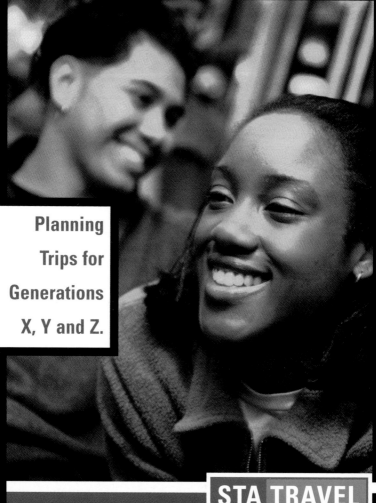

TOURING THE BURGER KINGDOM Los Angeles has been home to many tasteless trends, but few realize that it's also the birthplace of perhaps the world's furthest sweeping trend, one guaranteed to leave a curious taste in your mouth—good ol' American fast food. Unlikely as it sounds, this obsessively health-conscious city spawned some of the nation's greasiest, most cholesterol-packed grub. An international synonym for fast food, **McDonald's** was founded by Angeleno brothers Richard and Maurice McDonald in 1937 (serving, incidentally, hot dogs only). The oldest standing golden arches still glare proudly at 10807 Lakewood Blvd. in Downey, where it's walk-up rather than drive-thru service. (The brothers granted Ray Kroc exclusive U.S. franchising rights, and in 1955 he opened the first outlet of what has become the McDonald's Corporation in Des Plaines, Illinois.) Home to the original double-decker hamburger, the oldest **Bob's Big Boy,** 4211 Riverside Dr. (818-843-9334), in Burbank, still looks as sleek and streamlined as the day it opened in 1949. Check out the honest-to-goodness car-hop service (Sa-Su 5-10pm). **Carl's Jr.** started off as a downtown hot dog stand at Florence and Central Ave. in 1941, and the **Denny's** and **Winchell's** chains also got their start in the Los Angeles basin.

Pink's Famous Chili Dogs, 711 N. La Brea Ave., Hollywood (323-931-4223). More of an institution than a hot dog stand, Pink's has been serving up chili-slathered doggies on its outdoor patio to locals and celebs since 1939. Mouthwatering chili dogs ($2.20) and chili fries ($1.85). Bruce Willis proposed to Demi Moore here all those films ago. Open Su-Th 9:30am-2am, F-Sa 9:30am-3am. No credit cards.

Toi on Sunset, 7505½ Sunset Blvd., Hollywood (323-874-8062). Decor of way-trendy melange of posters, funky lamps, and psychedelic murals. Seating arrangements offer as many choices as the menu: you can sit in a regular chair, a leopard-skin armchair, or even on the floor at an ankle-high table. Clientele as hip as the interior decorating, and the food is good, too. Pad thai $7. Lunch specials $5. Open daily 11am-4am.

Swingers Hollywood Diner, 8020 Beverly Blvd. (323-653-5858), at Laurel Ave. in the rump of the Beverly Laurel Hotel. Where the hippest L.A. club kids (and lonely L.A. *Swingers* Mikey and Trent) come to snack on healthy food and 5 flavors of "smart drinks" that organically stimulate the brain ($5.50-6.50). Warhol-inspired walls with pink cows and plaid vinyl booths. This place is *so* money! Don't come looking for a free lunch, though: "Ass, cash, or grass; nobody eats for free." Open daily 6am-4am.

Chin Chin, 8618 Sunset Blvd., West Hollywood (310-652-1818). Other locations in Brentwood, Studio City, Marina del Rey, and Encino. Chic Chinese is immensely popular with the lunchtime set for its handmade "dim sum and then sum" ($5-10). Shredded chicken salad ($7.50) is Californiated Chinese cuisine. Outdoor seating and takeout. Special lowfat menu. Open Su-Th 11am-11pm, F-Sa 11am-1am.

SANTA MONICA

Santa Monica's restaurants fall unmistakably into the see-and-be-seen category, especially along the Third Street Promenade. Prices are elevated accordingly, and locals agree that the quality of the food really doesn't follow suit, although good deals can be found. Organic and vegetarian fare are just as prevalent as the trendy beauties who feed on them.

Fritto Misto, 601 Colorado Ave. (310-458-2829), at 6th St. With dishes from all over Italy (entrees $12), and a tasty vegetarian menu (entrees $9), this neighborhood bistro is a local favorite. The biggest deal is the mix 'n' match pastas which are served quickly and in healthy portions ($6-7). It's so popular you might find a line on the weekend, but it's worth the wait. Bring your own beer and wine for $1.50 per person surcharge. Lunch specials until 5:30pm ($6). Sundays bring monster omelettes 10am-4pm. Open M-F 11:30am-10pm, Sa-Su 11:30am-11pm.

Big Dean's "Muscle-In" Cafe, 1615 Ocean Front Walk (310-393-2666). Home of the management-proclaimed and customer-concurred "Best Cheeseburger on the West Coast," ($4) this indoor-outdoor bar and grill is just moments from the Santa Monica

Pier, and about $5 cheaper than any of the pricey fare found there. Kraut dogs ($2) and veggie burgers ($4). Happy Hour means $2 beers (M-F 3-6pm). Open daily 10am-dark, or until the everybody-knows-your-name regulars empty out. No pretense here: it's sun, sand, sauerkraut, and *cervezas!*

El Cholo, 1025 Wilshire Blvd. (310-899-1106). Like the Cancún cantinas it mimics, this is *the* spot to be seen, at least for the moment. The menu prices *are* budget for the upscale crowd. Cheese enchilada, beans, rice, and choice of a taco, *chile relleno,* or tamale ($8). "L.A. Lemonade" margarita is an awfully pricey $6.25, but was ranked the city's best by *L.A. Magazine.* Bar with couches, big-screen TV. Always crowded. Open M-Th 11am-10pm, F-Sa 11am-11pm, Su 11am-9pm.

Topper Restaurant and Cantina, 1111 2nd St. (310-393-8080), sits atop the Radisson Huntley Hotel and is one of the best deals (and best views) in town. The budget-minded won't want to splurge for the costly Tex-Mex entrees ($14-17), but Happy Hour (daily 4:30-7:30pm) is a deal and a half: buy 1 drink (sodas $1.50; beer from $2.75; half-pitcher of margaritas $4.50), and get all-you-can-eat free food from the bountiful buffet. Open Su-Th 6am-12:30am, F-Sa 6am-1:30am.

Shambala Cafe, 607 Colorado Ave. (310-395-2160). Just a short walk from the Promenade, this small cafe has healthy, low-priced dishes—no small feat in Santa Monica. Recipes from around the globe, with a heavy emphasis on veggies, tofu, and soy (some chicken and tuna selections as well). Sandwiches $5-6. Asian noodle selection changes daily. Open M-Sa 11:30am-8:30pm, Su noon-8pm. Cash only.

VENICE

Venetian cuisine runs the gamut from greasy to ultra-healthy, as befits its beachy-hippie crowd. The boardwalk has cheap grub in fast-food fashion—pay more than $1 for a pizza slice, hot dog, or order of fries, and you're getting ripped off.

Van Go's Ear 24 Hour Restaurant and Gallery, 796 Main St. (314-0022). Quintessential Venice with a psychedelic mural of the cafe's namesake complete with neon earring. Ridiculously large portions of tasty chow. All entrees named for second-rate celebs, such as the Kato Kaelin Salad ($3). "Tightwad menu" has 8 breakfast combos under $2 (served M-F 6-11am). The Fruit Fuck is a smoothie potion concocted with oranges, apples, pears, kiwi, and bee pollen ($3.75). Some part of the 2-story mega-shack is always open. No credit cards.

Rose Cafe, 220 Rose Ave. (399-0711; fax 396-2660), at Main St. The sunlight streaming in *so* complements the airy interior, dahling. Roses-on-steroids murals remind you what street you're on. Delicious deli specials (sandwiches $5, salads $5-8) are a steal. Smelly New Age knick-knacks and candles for sale. Open M-F 7am-7pm, Sa 8am-7pm, Su 8am-5pm.

On The Waterfront Cafe, 205 Ocean Front Walk (392-0322). You may have to fight for a seat, but this charming bar/cafe, with pool table and boardwalk seating, is a favorite with international clientele. Erdlinger Weißbrau and Bitburger on tap. Salads, bratwurst sandwiches, and pasta to suit any palate. Best mussels on the waterfront ($12, serves 2). Beer half-price M-F 6-8pm. Open M-F 10am-midnight, Sa-Su 9am-midnight.

Sidewalk Cafe, 1401 Ocean Front Walk (399-5547). Sitting right on the boardwalk, this popular (crowded) spot provides a beachy scene, and standard beach food. Entrees are named after writers, keeping in step with the adjacent bookstore. Omelettes $6-7, pizzas $12 (feeds 2), sandwiches $6-9. Big bar in back (pints $3). Open Su-Th 8am-midnight, F-Sa 8am-1am.

Windward Farms Market, 105 Windward Ave. (392-3566). Organic supermarket with whole grain breads and fresh fruit. Sells deli sandwiches ($3-4), salads ($4 per lb.), and fresh juices ($2.50). Perfect picnic fare. Open daily 8am-8pm.

MARINA DEL REY

If water isn't what you're after or you're not in the market for a new yacht, the only other reason to come here is for **Aunt Kizzy's Back Porch,** 4325 Glencoe Ave. (310-

578-1005), serving the **best soul food** in L.A. (according to *L.A. Magazine*). Aunt Kizzy may not seem quite the soul sister with her SoCal strip mall location, but she serves up daily lunch specials ($7), like chicken and dumplings or smothered pork chops, which crowd the plate with cornbread, rice, gravy, and veggies. (Open Su-Th 11am-10pm, F-Sa 11am-11pm; Sunday brunch buffet 11am-3pm.)

MALIBU

Refuel downstairs at **Malibu Chicken** (310-456-0365), with sandwiches, pasta, ribs, and other standards (monster bean-and-cheese burrito $3; Da Grind Special with chicken, veggies, and teriyaki $4.75; open daily 11am-10pm).

BEVERLY HILLS

Yes, there is budget dining in Beverly Hills; it just takes a little looking. An important budget travel tip: Do not eat on Rodeo Dr.; eat *south* of Wilshire Blvd.

The Breakfast Club, 9671 Wilshire Blvd. (323-271-8903, fax 213-271-0931). Affordable food in a great location. $6.49 lunch specials even volatile teens can appreciate. Open M-Sa 7am-3pm, Su 8am-3pm. 2hr. free parking with validation, leaving plenty of time to stroll Rodeo Dr.

World Wrapps, 168 S. Beverly Dr. (310-859-9010). Cashing in on the hottest new trend, it takes "healthy Mexican" to new, international, Cali-gourmet heights. Mostly takeout, but colorful interior and outdoor seating invite eat-ins. Thai chicken wraps (small $3.50, regular $5) and Samurai salmon wraps ($4.25, $6.50) are available in spinach and tomato tortillas. Cheap smoothies $2-4. Open M-F 11am-9pm, Sa 11am-8pm, Su noon-6pm.

Charleville Cafe, 9464 Charleville Blvd. (310-860-9004). The perfect spot to stop for a quick lunch, this disposable-plates-and-silverware deli makes up for its lack of fine china with its delicious food. Sandwiches are big and prices small. Overflowing egg salad sandwich $4. Large Italian salami sandwich $6. Full breakfast menu. Open daily 7am-9pm.

Finney's in the Alley, 8840 Olympic Blvd. (310-888-8787). Hidden, but worth the hunt. Heading east on Olympic, turn right on Clark, and immediately right into the alley; look for a yellow awning. The manager refuses to advertise for fear that "the secret will get out." Now it has. Finney's most delectable (and expensive) offering is a Philly steak sandwich ($4.20). Open M-Sa 11am-6pm.

Ed Debevic's, 134 N. La Cienega Blvd. (310-659-1952). This site of many a Sweet Sixteen party has big, tasty food served by a 50s-attired waitstaff that performs to 50s songs as patrons eat. Entrees $6-8. Full bar. Open Su-Th 11:30am-10pm, F-Sa 11:30am-midnight.

The Original California Pizza Kitchen, 207 S. Beverly Dr. (310-275-1101). A California institution that takes pizza way beyond its Italian roots. CPK began right here on Beverly Dr. in 1985, and now has locations all over L.A. and the U.S. Menu features creative pastas and wood-fired pizza, and stars the Original Barbecue Chicken Pizza ($9). Try it on honey wheat crust. Free refills on soda and their beloved lemonade. Open Su-Th 11:30am-10pm, F-Sa 11:30am-11pm.

WESTWOOD AND UCLA

Since tens of thousands of students live in Westwood, both good buys and beer can be found in abundance. If you're down to your last few bucks head to **Subbie's Roll-Inn,** 972 Gayley Ave., for $2 subs (open daily 10am-3am), or **Jose Bernstein's,** 935 Broxton Ave., for $4 burritos (open Su-Th 11am-1am, F-Sa 10am-2:30am).

Gypsy Cafe, 940 Broxton Ave. (310-824-2119). The best place in Westwood for an I'm-sick-of-eating-out dinner. Modeled after a sister spot in Paris, this inviting cafe has counter service, an outdoor patio, and velvet draperies to set the mood. Killer *penne cacciatore* ($7), organic salads ($6), Italian sandwiches ($6), and tomato soup that is famous throughout Westwood ($4). Hookahs for rent ($10 per hr.). Friday is stand-up comedy night. Open Su-Th 8am-midnight, F-Sa 8am-1am.

Diddie Riese Cookies, 926 Broxton Ave. (310-208-0448). Highly recommended by practically everyone in town, this new cookie bakery is a hotspot for fresh cookies ($3 per dozen). 10 delicious flavors to choose from. Also serves ice cream (75¢-$1.75) and soft drinks ($1). Open M-Th 7am-midnight, F 7am-1am, Sa noon-1am, Su noon-midnight.

Don Antonio's, 1136 Westwood Blvd. (310-209-1422). Relax in the outdoor seating while waiting for your custom-designed pizza ($5.50). Sinatra, red-checkered tablecloths, and wood-paneled walls. Lunch and dinner combo specials ($4-5); large slice of pizza, salad, and all-you-can-drink soda ($3.50). Open daily 11am-3am. No credit cards.

Captgo Coffee and Tea Company, 923 Broxton Ave. (310-824-2277). An airy place to chat and chill, this is an iced mocha latte frappe bonanza, and one of the biggest off-campus hangouts for students, who gulp down $1.20 espressos. You may be hard-pressed to find a seat in the evening. Captgo also sells smoothies ($3) and sandwiches ($4). Open M-Th 6am-1am, F 6am-1:30am, Sa 8am-1:30am, Su 8am-1am.

Headline's Diner and Press Club, 10922 Kinross Ave. (310-208-2424), at Gayley Ave. Headlines adorn the walls of this 50s-style diner, but the only press here is the occasional full court one, when the UCLA Bruins come to devour the low-priced hefty portions. Subscriptions Special is a cheap heap o' breakfast ($3). Check out the up-to-date movie times on the wall. Open M-Th 7am-midnight, F 7am-1am, Sa-Su 9am-midnight. No credit cards.

WILSHIRE DISTRICT

The Wilshire District's eateries are sadly out of step with its world-class museums. Inexpensive (and often kosher) restaurants dot Fairfax Ave. and Pico Blvd., but health nuts should stay away—there's no keeping cholesterol down in these parts.

The Apple Pan, 10801 W. Pico Blvd. (310-475-3585), 1 block east of Westwood Blvd. across from the Westside Pavilion. Suburban legend has it that *Beverly Hills 90210*'s Peach Pit was modeled after The Apple Pan. Paper-plated burgers $3-6; pies $2.40. Open Su and Tu-Th 11am-midnight, F-Sa 11am-1am. No credit cards.

Cassell's Hamburgers, 3266 W. 6th St. (213-480-8668). Some say these burgers are the finest in the city. They're juicy, enormous, and come with as much potato salad and cottage cheese as you can fit on your sizable plate. Basic burger, turkey burger, or chicken breast $5. Open M-Sa 10am-4pm. No credit cards.

Shalom Pizza, 8715 W. Pico Blvd. (310-271-2255). Kosher (i.e., vegetarian) pizza in a quiet Jewish business district. Large cheese $11.50, slice $1.75. Tuna melt $2.50. Open Su-Th 11am-9pm, F 11am to 2hr. before dusk, Sa dusk-midnight. No credit cards.

DOWNTOWN

Financial District eateries vie for the coveted businessperson's lunchtime dollar. Their secret weapon is the lunch special, but finding a reasonably priced dinner can be a challenge. It's not a good idea to stick around that late, anyway.

Philippe's, The Original, 1001 N. Alameda St. (213-628-3781), 2 blocks north of Union Station. Celebrated all over L.A. as the best downtown lunch spot, Philippe's just turned 92 years old. "Carvers" (counter waitresses dressed in antique server garb) prep the best French Dip sandwiches around (Philippe's invented 'em!); varieties include beef, ham, turkey, or lamb ($3-4). Top it off with a large slice of pie ($2.50) and a glass of lemonade (50¢) or a cup of coffee (10¢), and you've got a colossal lunch at this L.A. institution. Open daily 6am-10pm.

ORSON WELLES IS FAT Acclaimed director and *gourmand* Orson Welles was a regular at many Hollywood restaurants, and legends of his prowess circulate to this day, some reaching fantastic proportions. Pink's Famous Chili Dogs claims the notorious nosher once ate 15 chili dogs there in one sitting. But who really knows?–it's hard to distinguish Orson sitting from Orson standing.

The Pantry, 877 S. Figueroa St. (213-972-9279). Open since 1924, it hasn't closed once since—not for the earthquakes, not for the riots (when it served as a National Guard outpost), and not even when a taxicab drove through the front wall. There aren't even locks on the doors. Known for its large portions, free cole slaw, and fresh sourdough bread. Owned by the mayor. Giant breakfast specials are popular ($6), especially on weekends. Lunch sandwiches $3-5. Open forever. No credit cards.

It's a Wrap!, 818 W. 7th St. (213-553-9395). Downtown's fast food is "healthy gourmet fast food," including special lowfat dishes. As the name suggests, wrap sandwiches are the house specialty ($4-6). Open daily 6:30am-5pm. No credit cards.

Mon Kee Restaurant, 679 N. Spring St. (213-628-6717), in Chinatown. Somewhat on the expensive side, but widely acclaimed as one of L.A.'s best Chinese restaurants. The menu is vast, and the seafood excellent. Dinner entrees from $8. Open Su-Th 11am-10pm, F-Sa 11am-10:30pm.

The Kiosk, 601 S. Figueroa St. (213-485-0354), at Wilshire Blvd. in the Sanwa Bank Plaza. This outdoor cafe with umbrellas on the tables is a good place to grab and go, which is what most of its executive eaters do. Large soups and sandwiches for around $5-6. Open M-F 6am-4pm.

SAN FERNANDO VALLEY

Ventura Blvd. is lined with eateries. Stars often dine outside the studios in **Studio City.** The unwritten law says that you can stare all you want, but don't bother them and *don't ask for autographs.*

Miceli's, 3655 W. Cahuenga Blvd., **Universal City** (323-851-3444), across from Universal Studios. Would-be actors serenade dinner guests. Don't worry about losing your appetite during the Broadway, cabaret, and opera numbers—waiters have passed vocal auditions. Pasta, pizza, or lasagna $9-12. Open Su-Th 11:30am-11pm, F 11:30am-midnight, Sa 4pm-midnight.

Law Dogs, 14114 Sherman Way, **Van Nuys** (818-989-2220), at Hazeltine. Just your average hot dog stand with **free legal advice.** Attorney available W 7-9pm. "Judge Dog" with mustard, onions, and chili $1.55. "Police Dog' with mustard and sauerkraut $1.55. Open M-Tu and Th 10am-6pm, W and F 10am-9pm, Sa 10am-8pm. No credit cards.

Dalt's Grill, 3500 W. Olive Ave., **Burbank** (818-953-7752), at Riverside. Classic, classy American grill across from Warner Studios. Frequented by the DJs and music guests from the radio station upstairs, KROQ 106.7FM and Star 98.7FM. Large selection of burgers and sandwiches $5-8. Chicken fajita caesar salad $8. Full oak-lacquered bar. Open M-Th 11am-midnight, F-Sa 11am-1am (bar open until 2am), Su 9am-11pm.

Poquito Más, 3701 W. Cahuenga Blvd., **Universal City** (818-760-8226), opposite Universal Studios. Wildly popular Mexican takeout spot known for its fish tacos ($5 for 2). Skimps on atmosphere, but so what? A fabulous *carnita* is only $2. Open Su-Th 11am-midnight, F-Sa 10am-1am. No credit cards.

PASADENA

Eateries abound on **Colorado Boulevard** from Los Robles Ave. to Orange Grove Blvd. in Old Town—Pasadena's version of Santa Monica's 3rd St. Promenade.

Fair Oaks Pharmacy and Soda Fountain, 1516 Mission St., South Pasadena (626-799-1414), at Fair Oaks Ave. Old-fashioned drug store with full-service soda fountain and lunch counter. Lime rickeys $2, hand-dipped shakes and malts $4. Deli sandwiches $5.50, patty melts $6. Open M-Th 9am-10pm, F-Sa 9am-11pm, Su 11am-9pm.

Pita! Pita!, 37 S. Fair Oaks Ave. (626-356-0106). Forgo burgers and opt for something with flair. Middle Eastern tunes accompany delicious Lebanese food. Spicy chicken with rice and beans is a h-o-t $7. Chicken kebab $9; pita with hummus or tabouli $3. Baklava $1.50. Lunch specials daily. Open Su-Th 11am-10pm, F-Sa 11am-11pm.

Goldstein's Bagel Bakery, 86 W. Colorado Blvd. (626-792-2435). Manhattan fare with a California twist, the New Yorker bagel sandwich ($4.50) rivals the L.A. Nosh ($4.55)—but the Elvis Bagel wins for originality (banana-nut bagel with peanut butter and honey $2). 18 bagels (60-80¢ each) to choose from. Open Su-Th 6am-8pm, F-Sa 6am-10pm.

Yoshiz, 34 E. Holly St. (626-577-7925), between Raymond and Fair Oaks Ave., 2 blocks north of Colorado St. This Japanese restaurant is a local addiction. California rolls $3, other yummiez under $5. Open M-F 10am-5pm, Sa 11am-3pm.

La Luce Cafe and Deli, 62 W. Union St. (626-568-9696), in 1 Colorado Plaza between Delancey and Fair Oaks Ave. Specializing in creative Mediterranean sandwiches, this indoor-outdoor cafe is a budget treat. Murano grilled veggies on rosemary bread $5; avocado, ham, and roast beef sandwich $5. Get your smoothie blonde, blizzard, or blast for $2.50. Open Su-Th 9:30am-8pm, F-Sa 9:30am-10pm.

Mi Piace, 25 E. Colorado Blvd. (626-795-3131). Italian for "I like it," and apparently the critics do, as many have named it the best of Old Town's plethora of upscale cafes. Unfortunately your wallet might not *"piace"* the bill, so aim to eat lunch and take advantage of the sandwich specials which are served until 3pm (around $6). Full bar. Open Su-Th 11:30am-11:30pm, F-Sa 11:30am-1am.

SIGHTS

HOLLYWOOD

Exploring the Hollywood area takes a pair of sunglasses, a camera, some cash, and a whole lot of energy. It is best to drive through the famous Hollywood Hills and then park and explore Hollywood Boulevard on foot. Running east-west at the foot of the Hollywood Hills, this strip is the center of all L.A.'s tourist craziness. The boulevard itself, lined with souvenir shops, clubs, and theaters, is busy day and night, especially around the intersection of Highland St. and Hollywood Blvd. and then west down Hollywood Blvd. This is where it all began, so live it up!

HOLLYWOOD SIGN. Those 50-foot-high, slightly erratic letters perched on Mount Cahuenga north of Hollywood stand with New York's Statue of Liberty and Paris's Eiffel Tower as universally recognized symbols of their cities. The original 1923 sign, which read HOLLYWOODLAND, was an advertisement for a new subdivision in the Hollywood Hills. Over the years, people came to think of it as a civic monument, and the city, having acquired the sign by 1978, reconstructed the crumbling letters, and left off the last syllable. The sign has been a target of college pranks—making it read everything from "Hollyweird" to "Ollywood" (after the infamous Lt. Col. Oliver North). You can't frolic on the sign like Robert Downey, Jr. did in *Chaplin*, or take a leap from it like all the faded 1920s starlets—there is a $500 fine if you're caught (which is likely). The best you can do is snap a great picture. *(Drive north on Vine St., turn right on Franklin Ave., left on Beachwood Ave., and left on Belden St. into the Beachwood Supermarket parking lot. To get a close-up of the sign, continue up Beachwood Ave., turn left on Ledgewood Ave., and drive all the way up to Mulholland Hwy.)*

MANN'S CHINESE THEATER. Formerly Grauman's, this theater is a garish rendition of a Chinese temple, and the hottest spot for a Hollywood movie premiere. *The Seven Year Itch* premiered here in 1955 and *The King and I* in 1956. The exterior columns, which once supported a Ming Dynasty temple, are strangely authentic for Hollywood. Hundreds capture a crowded Kodak moment in the courtyard paying homage to impressions made by movie stars in the cement, including Whoopi Goldberg's dreadlocks, Betty Grable's legs, R2D2's wheels, Jimmy Durante's nose, and George Burns's cigar. *(323-461-3331. 6925 Hollywood Blvd., between Highland and La Brea Ave.)*

WALK OF FAME. Things get a little seedier all along Hollywood and Vine St., where the sidewalk is embedded with over 2000 bronze-inlaid stars, inscribed with the names of the famous, the infamous, and the downright obscure. Stars are awarded for achievements in one of five categories—movies, radio, TV, recording, and live performance; only Gene Autry has all five stars. The stars have no particular order so don't try to find a method to the madness. To catch a glimpse of today's (or yesterday's) stars in person, call the Chamber of Commerce *(213-469-8311)* for info on star-unveiling ceremonies.

HOLLYWOOD BOWL AND MUSEUM. Nestled in the hills, this famous outdoor performance space is the perfect spot to have a picnic lunch and listen to the L.A. Philharmonic strike it up at rehearsals on Mondays, Tuesdays, Thursdays, and Fridays. The Bowl also hosts a summer jazz concert series. The museum-within-a-bowl has several exhibits as well as listening stations where you can swoon to Stravinsky, Aaron Copland, and the Beatles, all of whom played the Bowl in the same week during the 60s. *(323-850-2058. Concert line 323-850-2000; www.hollywoodbowl.org. 2301 N. Highland Ave. Open Tu-Sa 10am-4:30pm. Free.)*

HOLLYWOOD STUDIO MUSEUM. The museum provides a glimpse into early Hollywood filmmaking. In 1913, famed director Cecil B. DeMille rented this former barn as studio space for Hollywood's first feature film, *The Squaw Man*. Antique cameras, costumes worn by Douglas Fairbanks and Rudolph Valentino, props, vintage film clips, and other memorabilia fill the museum. *(323-874-2276. 2100 N. Highland Ave. Across from the Hollywood Bowl. Hours variable; call ahead. Admission $4, students and seniors $3, ages 6-12 $2. Ample free parking.)*

HOLLYWOOD ENTERTAINMENT MUSEUM. This landmark honors the four arts of entertainment—radio, television, film, and recording. This fun place has a miniature model of 1940s Hollywood, as well as original sets from *Star Trek* and *Cheers*. The *Cheers* bar is functional and open for drinks on Thursday nights and live entertainment from July 1 to September 2 from 5 to 10pm. *(323-465-7900. 7021 Hollywood Blvd. Museum open July-Aug. M-Sa 11am-6pm, Su 11am-6pm; Sept.-June Th-Tu 10am-6pm. Docent tours every 30min. Admission $7.50, students and seniors $4.50, ages 5-12 $4, under 5 free. Parking $2. Cheers cover/donation $5.)*

ALTERNA-MUSEUMS. The alternately fascinating and horrifying **Hollywood Wax Museum** contains 200 figures, from Jesus to Elvis. Not surprisingly, the sculpture of Michael Jackson is one of the few that a chisel and putty have recreated nearly perfectly. *(323-462-5991. 6767 Hollywood Blvd. Open daily 10am-midnight. Admission $10, ages 6-12 $7, under 6 free.)* **Guinness World of Records** has the tallest, shortest, heaviest, most tattooed, and other curious superlatives, all on display. *(323-463-6433. 6764 Hollywood Blvd. Open daily 10am-midnight. Admission $10, ages 6-12 $7, under 6 free; with wax museum ticket $4, ages 6-12 $2.)* **Ripley's Believe It or Not!** is a wacky (not waxy) museum with a side-show mentality that strangely keeps with the rest of Hollywood. Come view the roots of that inane TV show you may have watched as a kid. *(323-466-6335. 6780 Hollywood Blvd. Open Su-Th 10am-midnight, F-Sa 10am-12:30am.*

IF I WERE A GROUPIE Today's groupie has to have skills that would put FBI agents to shame. While *Let's Go* cannot give you the well-trained eyes and ears necessary for success, we can point you in the right direction. First, you need to know that stars tend to stay in the same hotels. Now you can narrow your search. The **Rock 'n' Roll Hyatt,** on the Sunset Strip, was the site of Led Zeppelin's orgies and Jim Morrison's antics and is now the preferred haunt of bands like Live and Smashing Pumpkins. Across the street is **St. James Club,** a more refined spot that caters to older bands such as Duran Duran. Near the base of the famous billboards on Sunset Blvd. is the **Chateau Marmont,** where Keanu Reeves and Dustin Hoffman have made extended stays. Farther up the Strip on Alta Loma is the **Sunset Marquis.** This *expensive* hotel houses the biggest musical acts (Rolling Stones, Peter Gabriel, George Michael). Hiding on a residential street near the corner of Melrose Ave. and La Cienega Blvd. is **Le Parc,** which caters to the bigger, gentler bands (Morrissey) and many newer British acts (Blur, Elastica). Finally, as any savvy groupie knows, all bands register under fake names these days, so you'll have to rely on your big, bountiful, buxom wits—and charm.

Admission $9, ages 5-12 $6, under 5 free.) **Frederick's of Hollywood** gives a free peep at some unbelievable underwear in its lingerie museum. Frederick's displays bras worn by everyone from Marilyn Monroe to Milton Berle. *(213-957-5953. 6608 Hollywood Blvd. Open M-F 10am-9pm, Sa 10am-7pm, Su 11am-6pm. Free.)*

CAPITOL RECORDS TOWER. The tower marks the pre-eminent monument of the modern record industry. The cylindrical building, constructed in 1954, was designed to look like a stack of records—with fins sticking out at each floor (the "records") and a needle on top, which blinks H-O-L-L-Y-W-O-O-D in Morse code. *(1750 Vine St., just north of Hollywood Blvd.)*

EL CAPITÁN THEATRE. The 1941 Hollywood premiere of *Citizen Kane* was held here. This Disney-restored cinema house features ornate faux-exotic 1920's interior decoration and high prices only Walt could spring for. Current Disney movies play here with 30-minute live pre-show performances. *(213-467-9545. 6838 Hollywood Blvd. $18 movie ticket includes pre-show.)*

CASTILLO DEL LAGO. This historic eyesore rests beneath the Hollywood sign, amidst the Hollywood Hills. Once the gambling den of gangster Bugsy Siegel, the red-and-beige striped house also belonged to Madonna, but she recently sold it after an obsessed fan stalked her there. *(6342 Mulholland Hwy.; at Canyon Lake Dr.)*

HOLLYHOCK HOUSE. Located in Barnsdall Art Park, the house commands a 360° view of L.A. and the mountains. Completed in 1922 for eccentric oil heiress Aline Barnsdall, the house was one of Frank Lloyd Wright's initial attempts to develop a distinct Southern Californian style of architecture and his first work that reflected the influence of Mayan temples. The house is named for Barnsdall's favorite flower, which Wright reproduced (begrudgingly and abstractly) all over the house. Although the house is closed for renovation until 2001, the **Municipal Art Gallery** just next door, will remain open, and contains an informative exhibit about Hollyhock and Wright. *(Hollyhock House: 323-913-4157. 4808 Hollywood Blvd. Gallery: 323-485-4581.)*

HOLLYWOOD MEMORIAL PARK. If you still haven't had enough showbiz glitz of years gone by, visit this haunted-feeling cemetery, decaying between Vine St. and Western. Here rest deceased stars Rudolph Valentino, Jayne Mansfield, Douglas Fairbanks Sr., and Cecil B. De Mille. *(6000 Santa Monica Blvd. Open M-F 8am-5pm. Spooky mausoleums close at 4:30pm.)*

SANTA MONICA

With cleaner waters and better waves at the beaches to the north and south, Santa Monica is known more for its shoreside scene than its shore. Since it is the closest beach to L.A., Santa Monica's sands are packed year-round with sunbathers sporting skimpy bikinis and buff, bronzed beach volleyball players, as well as families and people-watchers who come for the view.

THIRD STREET PROMENADE. This ultra-popular three-block stretch is *the* major walking, shopping, people-watching, and movie-viewing thoroughfare. Before its present incarnation of fashionable boutiques and yuppie cafes, 3rd St. was known as one of L.A.'s artsier areas, and is still home to the city's better book and music stores (see **Shopping,** p. 398). On Wednesday and Saturday mornings the area is transformed into a farmer's market. The strip truly comes alive at night, when street artists arrive and the ivy-lined mesh dinosaur sculptures light up. Young adults with clipboards often sign people up for free movie passes. This is, after all, the film screening capital of the world.

SANTA MONICA PIER AND PACIFIC PARK. The heart of the Santa Monica Beach is this famed pier, home of the recently restored carnivalesque family funspot Pacific Park, where the fun meets the sun and "the rides meet the tides." Roller coaster lovers and Ferris wheel fanatics, four feet high and taller, can have some fun for a few bucks. The centerpiece of the pier is the unrideable 1922 carousel, which was featured in *The Sting.* Along the pier, amidst pizza joints and tons of tacky souvenir shops, look for free TV show tickets (the variety and late night kinds) available near the north entrance. For the faint of heart, temporary toughness can be achieved at booths along the strip with a painless henna tattoo for under $20. *(Off PCH on the way to Venice Beach from Santa Monica Beach. Open daily 10am-11pm; ticket window closes at 10:30pm. Tickets $1.25 each, most rides 2-3 tickets; day passes $17, children $15. Twilight Dance Series July-Aug. Th 7:30pm. Parking off PCH $5 per day.)*

BERGAMOT STATION ARTS CENTER. Once a train depot, these converted warehouses now house artists' wares from around the Los Angeles area in the largest collection of art galleries on the West Coast. You may spot a chic sun-glassed beauty (and her driver) looking for a new piece for her West Wing bathroom, and while the art is pricey, anyone can enjoy window shopping. The Gallery of Functional Art is particularly amusing. Bergamot Station also houses a reasonably priced Gallery Cafe, as well as a Colleagues Gallery with more affordable works. The Santa Monica Museum of Art, in building G-1, recently housed the neo-Dadaist works of Al and Beck (now pop superstar) Hansen. "Friday Evening Salons" are free informal public forums with artists who are currently having their work exhibited (Friday 7:30-10pm). Featured art rotates regularly. *(310-586-6467; fax 310-586-6487. 2525 Michigan Ave. Near the intersection of Olympic and Cloverfield Blvd. Santa Monica Museum of Art open Tu-Su 11am-6pm, but call ahead because they often close for installation changes. Gallery Cafe open M 9am-4pm, Tu-F 9am-5pm, Sa 10am-5pm. Colleagues Gallery open M noon-2pm and Th 10am-2pm.)*

MUSEUM OF FLYING. On the airstrip of the Santa Monica Airport is this small hangar museum designed in the style of a "post-modern hangar," that features the *'24 New Orleans*, which flew around the world, and a theater that shows aviation films. *(310-392-8822. 2772 28th St. Open W-Su 10am-5pm. Admission $7, students with ID and seniors $5, ages 3-17 $3.)*

SANTA MONICA STAIR PATH. A 189-step exercise mecca for the young, the fit, and the beautiful who stretch, do crunches, and converse on the grass on 4th St. before and after their stair climbs. This public stairway is the most popular of those leading from the top to the bottom of Santa Monica Canyon, probably because the views of the spandex-clad may be even more stunning than those of the ocean. *(At the corner of Adelaide Dr. and 4th St. One block north of San Vicente Blvd.)*

OTHER SIGHTS. The paved **beach path** is a mini-freeway of cyclists, skaters, and runners, stretching 20¼mi. between the Santa Monica and Torrance Beaches. Just under the first few planks of the Santa Monica Pier sits the **UCLA Ocean Discovery Center** (310-393-6149). Visitor highlights include the shark and ray tanks and a marine microscope laboratory. *(393-6149. Open July 1-Labor Day (Sept. 4 in 2000) W-F 3-6pm, Sa 11am-6pm, Su 11am-5pm; Labor Day-June 30 Sa-Su 11am-5pm. Admission $3.)* At the Santa Monica Senior Recreation Center is the **Camera Obscura,** which uses convex lenses to project a 360° bird's-eye view of the beach onto a screen in a dark room—well worth the 10 seconds it takes to see. *(1450 Ocean Ave. Open M 10am-2pm, Tu-F 9am-4pm, Sa-Su 11am-4pm. Free.)* At the northern end of Ocean Ave. is its intersection with **San Vicente Boulevard.** This residential, tree-lined road is a runner's heaven, and is also frequented by cyclists and skaters.

VENICE

At the turn of the twentieth century, Abbot Kinney envisioned a recreation of Italy's Venice on the California coast—a touch of Old World charm, mustached gondoliers, and the social elite strolling on an oceanside promenade. Instead, he ended up with a huge dose of New World neuroses. **Ocean Front Walk,** Venice's main beachfront drag, is a seaside three-ring circus of fringe culture. Street people converge on shaded clusters of benches, evangelists drown out off-color comedians, and while its heyday has long since past, bodybuilders of both sexes pump iron in skimpy spandex outfits at the original **Muscle Beach,** 1800 Ocean Front Walk, closest to 18th St. and Pacific Ave. Fire-juggling cyclists, joggers, master sand sculptors, groovy elders (such as the **"skateboard grandma"**), and bards in

Birkenstocks make up the balance of this playground population. Vendors of jewelry, henna body art, snacks, and beach paraphernalia overwhelm the boardwalk.

Collect your wits and people-watch at one of the cafes or juice bars, or check out life in the fast lane on the bike path stretching from Santa Monica. **Patrick's Venice Rollerworks,** 7 Westminster Ave. (310-450-0669), off the 1200 block of Ocean Front Walk, rents in-line skates for $5 per day (open M-F 10am-6pm, Sa-Su 9am-6pm). A bicycle rental shop can be found on the 500 block of Ocean Front Walk ($5 per hr., $15 per day). Or leap into a game of hoops at the popular basketball court at 17th St. and Ocean Front Walk, featured in the movie *White Men Can't Jump*. The area is full of LAPD cops—a sign that it is hugely dangerous or totally safe, depending on your perspective. During the day, things are relatively safe, but when the sun begins to set, it's time to go.

Kinney's dream of another San Marco failed, and so did his vision of gondola-laden canals. High society types like screen star Mary Pickford took boat rides when the **canals** were first built, but when the water became dirty and oily, most of canals were filled in and forgotten. Skateboarders still use some of the others (since drained). One of the few surviving canals is at Strong's Dr., off Washington St. Ducks are its lively inhabitants, revering the generous Kinney. Quack.

Venice's anything-goes attitude attracts some of L.A.'s most innovative artists (and not just the guy who makes sand sculptures of Jesus). The Chiat/Day offices at 340 Main St. were designed by Frank Gehry to look like a pair of **enormous binoculars**—architecture as a pop-art sculpture at its best. Venice's **street murals** are another free show. Don't miss the brilliant (but disfigured) homage to Botticelli's *Birth of Venus* on the beach pavilion at the end of Windward Ave.—a woman of ostensibly divine beauty sporting short shorts, an adhesive bandage top, and roller skates boogies out of her seashell. The post office's mural sums up Venice's cluttered history in an appropriately jumbled way—with oil derricks perched on Kinney's shoulders. On Pacific Ave., between Rose and Brooks Ave., is a colorful but solemn POW/MIA memorial mural. For roof-topped art, stop by the **L.A. Louver,** 45 N. Venice Blvd. (310-822-4955), a free gallery showing the work of some L.A. artists (open Tu-Sa noon-5pm).

Towards Culver City is the **Museum of Jurassic Technology,** 9341 Venice Blvd. (310-836-6131). The museum is not really reachable on foot from the beach. By car, take the I-10 to Robertson Blvd. S.; from Robertson Blvd., turn left onto Venice Blvd. The museum is about four blocks down Venice Blvd. From the beach take Venice Blvd. directly. The museum walks a fine line between an elaborate practical joke and a profound statement on the ultimate inaccessibility of history. It is unlike any museum you have ever visited. To simply point out the unapologetic and unexplained juxtaposition of exhibits as incongruous as mole rat skeletons, fake gems, and trailer park art doesn't really do justice to the creeping feeling that, despite the professional displays, portentous audio narration, and deadpan introductory slide show, *this may all be a load of utter baloney*. Or maybe not. Attempting to decide for oneself is a unique and delightfully maddening experience. (Open Th 2-8pm, F-Su noon-6pm. Requested donation $4, students and seniors $2.50, active military $1.50.)

MARINA DEL REY

If you love boats, take a walk along the marina or drive down to **Fisherman's Village** (at the end of Fiji Way off Lincoln Blvd.), a small but pleasant wharf-meets-strip-mall that is home to a few major restaurants, gift shops, and boating stores. Although the Village does not warrant a full daytrip, some people spend a relaxing weekend afternoon in rented boats or kayaks from **Marina Boat Rentals,** 13719 Fiji Way (310-574-2822), which offers great rates on four-person power and sailboats ($25 per hr.), eight-person electric boats ($50 per hr.), single and double kayaks ($10 and $16 per hr., $30 and $50 per halfday), and three-person pedal boats ($15 per hr.). No experience is necessary for most rentals, but you should call in advance for reservations. Relax afterward in the central patio where locals crowd for live music on weekend nights, year-round.

MALIBU

These public beaches are cleaner and less crowded than any others in L.A. County, and as a whole offer better surfing. Surf's up at **Surfrider Beach,** a section of Malibu Laguna State Beach north of the pier at 23000 PCH. You can walk onto the beach on the **Zonker Harris** access way (named after the beach-obsessed Doonesbury character), at 22700 PCH. **Malibu Ocean Sports,** 22935 PCH (310-456-6302), across from the pier, rents surfboards ($10 per hr., $25 per day), kayaks (single $15 per hr., $35 per day; double $20 per hr., $50 per day), boogie boards ($12 per day), and wetsuits ($10 per day), and offers surfing lessons ($100 for 2hr. lesson and full-day gear) and tours (open daily 9am-7pm).

Corral State Beach, a tiny off-the-side-of-the-road windsurfing and swimming haven, lies on the 26000 block of PCH, followed by **Point Dume State Beach,** (main entrance near 29000 PCH, look for signs) which is larger and generally uncrowded, but offers better currents for scuba-diving. Along the 30000 block of PCH lies **Zuma Beach,** L.A. County's northernmost, largest, and most user-friendly county-owned sandbox. Restrooms, lifeguards, and food stands guarantee that Zuma regularly draws a diverse crowd. Proximity to parking lot drop-off spots makes sections #6-8 a big draw for swarms of local kids, while relative distance from bathrooms make sections #9-11 less populous. Swimmers should only dive near manned lifeguard stations; because of the killer **riptide,** rescue counts are high. The free street parking is highly coveted, so expect to park in the beach lot ($6, off-peak $2). Although it's disguised as a modest deli, **Malibu Ranch Market** (457-0171) 29575 PCH, in the Zuma Beach Plaza at the southern end of the beach, rents boogie boards (small $7 per day, large $9), and sells sandwiches, amino acid supplements, and alcohol (open M-Th 7am-11pm, F 7am-midnight, Sa 8am-midnight, Su 8am-10pm).

Just south of Zuma, before Point Dume is a **clothing-optional** strip nicknamed Pirate's Cove by locals. Find the treasure by parking at Zuma Beach and walking a half-mile south. There are fewer footprints at **Westward Beach,** just southeast of Zuma Beach, where cliffs shelter the beach from the highway.

BEVERLY HILLS

Get ready to gawk, sneer, or chuckle. Extravagant displays of opulence sometimes border on the vulgar, as Beverly Hills' residents try their hardest to make sure everyone knows just how much money they have. Admire (or admonish) the mansions on the palm-lined 700-900 blocks of **Beverly Drive,** where each and every manicured estate begs for attention. The heart of the city is in the **Golden Triangle,** a wedge formed by Beverly Dr., Wilshire Blvd., and Santa Monica Blvd., centering on **Rodeo Drive,** known for its flashy clothing boutiques and jewelry shops. Built like an old English manor house, Polo Ralph Lauren (444 N. Rodeo Dr.) stands out from the white marble of the other stores. The divine triple-whammy of adjacent Cartier (370 N. Rodeo Dr.), Gucci (347 N. Rodeo Dr.), and Chanel (400 N. Rodeo Dr.) sits on some of the area's prime real estate, where rents are as high as $40,000 per month.

At the south end (that closest to Wilshire Blvd.) of Rodeo Dr. is the all-pedestrian shopping complex of **2 Rodeo Drive,** a.k.a. Via Rodeo, which contains Dior, Tiffany, and the Salon of Jose Eber, stylist to the stars and TV makeover king. Although it fakes European antiquity, the promenade was constructed in the last decade, cobblestone street, lamp posts, and all. Across the way is the venerable **Beverly Wilshire Hotel,** 9500 Wilshire Blvd. (310-275-5200), whose old and new wings are connected by **El Camino Real** and its Louis XIV gates. The hotel lobby gives you a good idea of just how extravagant the rooms might be.

North of ritzy Rodeo Dr. is Santa Monica Blvd., which gives the Hills a little bit of nature to counteract the shopping. A series of small but pleasant parks line the boulevard. Although none may be that mouthwatering, one does contain the most varieties of **cacti** in one place in the world. Although it's a dusty patch, the cactus plants are an interesting sight, between N. Camden Dr. and N. Bedford Dr. on Santa Monica Blvd. (make a left off Rodeo Dr.).

A right turn from Rodeo Dr. onto Santa Monica Blvd. will take you to **The Museum of Television and Radio,** 465 North Beverly Drive (310-786-1000). Complete with a radio broadcast studio and two theaters the three-year-old museum's biggest highlight is its library, which holds 100,000 television, radio, and commercial programs. You can call up your favorite tube hits and five minutes later the library staff will have the full-length episodes ready and waiting for your viewing pleasure at your own private screening station. Caricatures of television stars decorate the walls and there is always someone watching *I Love Lucy*. (Open W and F-Su noon-5pm, Th noon-9pm. Donation $6, students and seniors $4, under 13 $3.)

Just outside of the main area is the **Beverly Hills City Hall,** 455 N. Rexford Dr. (310-285-1000), just below Santa Monica Blvd., which would look out of place anywhere but here. This Spanish Renaissance building was erected during the Great Depression, and is now engulfed by Beverly Hills's new white phoenix of a **Civic Center,** which took nine years to build at a cost of $120 million. The **Beverly Hills Library,** 444 N. Rexford Dr. (213-228-2220), predictably, has an interior adorned with Thai marble but only an average collection of books. As always, Beverly Hills coordinates well: the library's tiling matches the colors on City Hall's dome.

Beverly Hills High, 241 Moreno (310-201-0661), between Olympic Blvd. and Spalding, may not be the actual filming site of *Beverly Hills, 90210*, but it is not without interest. The indoor swimming pool is open in the summer (open M-F 2:15-4:30pm), and has a sliding floor cover that converts the pool into a basketball court. That very floor is where Jimmy Stewart and Donna Reed danced the aquatic Charleston in *It's a Wonderful Life*.

The **Beverly Hills Hotel,** 9641 Sunset Blvd. (310-276-2251), is a pink, palm-treed collection of poolside cottages. Howard Hughes established his infamous germ-free apartment here, while Marilyn Monroe reportedly had affairs with both JFK and RFK in other bungalows. It is also home to the **Polo Lounge,** where countless media industry deals have been negotiated. The Sultan of Brunei paid $185 million for it in 1987, but 12 years later you can get a room for a mere $275.

NEAR BEVERLY HILLS

Just south of Beverly Hills is the sobering **Museum of Tolerance,** 9786 W. Pico Blvd. (310-553-8043, www.wiesenthal.com), at Roxbury St. This hands-on, high-tech museum, which opened in 1993, has soul-searching interactive exhibits with displays on the Holocaust, the Croatian genocide, the L.A. riots, and the U.S. civil rights movement. Visit the Point of View Diner, a recreation of a 50s diner that serves a menu of controversial topics on video jukeboxes. Artifacts from concentration camps and original letters from Anne Frank are in the 2nd floor Multimedia Learning Center. Next door is the **Simon Weisenthal Center** for Holocaust research. Holocaust survivors speak of their experiences daily. (Closing times are for the time of the last entry into the museum. Open M-F 10am-4pm and Su 11am-5pm. Admission $8.50, students $5.50, seniors $6.50, ages 3-11 $3.50. 2½-4hr. tours available. Free parking. Wheelchair accessible.)

WESTWOOD AND UCLA

UNIVERSITY OF CALIFORNIA AT LOS ANGELES (UCLA)

To drive to the campus, take San Diego Fwy. (I-405) North to the Wilshire Blvd./Westwood Exit, and head east into Westwood. Take Westwood Blvd. north off Wilshire Blvd., and go through Westwood Village and directly into the campus. By bus, take MTA #2 along Sunset Blvd., #21 along Wilshire Blvd., #320 from Santa Monica, or #561 from the San Fernando Valley, or Santa Monica BBBus #1, 2, 3, 8, or 12. Parking pass $5. Maps free.

Get a feel for mass academia U.C.-style at this 400-acre campus sprawling in the foothills of the Santa Monica Mountains. A prototypical California university, UCLA sports an abundance of grassy open spaces, bike and pedestrian paths, dazzling sunshine, and pristine buildings in a hodge-podge of architectural styles. Voted the #1 jock school in the country by *Sports Illustrated*, UCLA also boasts an illustrious film school whose graduates include James Dean, Jim Morrison, Oliver Stone, Francis Ford Coppola, and Tim Robbins. The school is directly north of Westwood Village and west of Beverly Hills.

UCLA and Westwood are navigable on foot so pay for a parking pass from campus information stands at all entrances. Parking cops *live* to ticket unsuspecting visitors here. **UCLA tours** are offered by the Alumni Center (310-825-8764), which is directly north of Westwood Plaza and parking structures #6 and 8 (tours M, W, and F 9am and 1pm). One great outdoor highlight is the **Murphy Sculpture Garden** (in the northeast corner of campus) which contains over 70 pieces by such major artists as Auguste Rodin, Henri Matisse, and Joan Miró.

UCLA HAMMER MUSEUM OF ART AND CULTURAL CENTER. Housing the world's largest collection of works by 19th-century French satirist Honoré Daumier, as well as the late oil tycoon Armand Hammer's collection of works by Rembrandt van Rijn, Marc Chagall, and Paul Cézanne, this museum's true gem is Vincent Van Gogh's *Hospital at Saint Rémy*. Hammer purportedly wanted to donate his collection to the L.A. County Museum of Art, but demanded that the works be shown together in a separate wing. The museum refused, telling Hammer to build his own place—which he did. The center hosts traveling exhibitions throughout the year, as well as free summer jazz concerts *(F 6:30-8pm)* and seasonal cultural programs. *(310-443-7000; TDD 443-7094. 10899 Wilshire Blvd. Open Tu-W and F-Sa 11am-7pm, Th 11am-9pm, Su 11am-5pm. Admission $4.50, students and seniors $3, under 17 free with adult. Thursday free. Free tours Tu-Su at 1pm. 3hr. parking $2.75.)*

FOWLER MUSEUM OF CULTURAL HISTORY. This museum displays artifacts from contemporary, historic, and prehistoric cultures. It is presently a source of controversy because it preserves Native American remains here for their archaeological value, despite laws protecting Native Americans' rights to sacred burial. *(310-825-4361. In Haines Hall. Open W and F-Su noon-5pm, Th noon-8pm. Admission $5, students and seniors $3, under 17 free; Thursday free.)*

ACKERMAN UNION. This college student center is absolutely ideal. Visitors can enjoy the **Food Court,** or unlimited video gaming at the **XCape Arcade** ($6). A calendar lists the lengthy lineup of movies (first-runs often free), lectures, and campus activities. The huge **UCLA Store** swallows up most of the ground floor with a bevy of UCLA paraphernalia, a newsstand, a grocery store, and the always-essential Clinique counter. *(310-206-0833. 308 Westwood Plaza. Downhill from the quadrangle on Bruin Walk. Store open mid-June to late Sept. M-F 8:30am-6pm, Sa 10am-5pm, Su noon-5pm; late Sept. to mid-June daily 7:45am-7pm. Union open daily mid-June to late Sept. 10am-11pm; late Sept. to mid-June 8am-11pm.)*

TICKETS (ARTS AND OTHERWISE). UCLA's art departments have lots of events, exhibitions, and performances year-round. Call the **UCLA Arts Line** for tickets, calendar, and directions (310-UCLA-ART/825-2278). The renowned **School of Film and Television Archive** sponsors various film festivals, often with foreign films and profiles on groundbreaking filmmakers. (310-206-FILM/3456; double features $6, students $4; select films free.) The **UCLA Central Ticket Office** sells tickets for on-campus arts events (including concerts and dance recitals) and UCLA sports games, as well as discounted tickets to local movie theaters and water parks. It also has a Ticketmaster outlet. Discount tickets are not limited to UCLA affiliates. (310-825-2101; www.cto.ucla.edu).

BEL AIR, BRENTWOOD, AND PACIFIC PALISADES

These three residential communities don't offer much to the budget traveler in terms of accommodations or food, but the Getty Museum or a scenic drive along Sunset Boulevard are two free ways to experience the best the area has to offer. Veer off Sunset onto any public (non-gated) road to see tree-lined rows of well-spaced six-bedroom homes that make living here as costly as Beverly Hills. Private Brentwood School teaches the children of the wealthy and the famous on its campus which abuts the local private golf course.

J. PAUL GETTY MUSEUM AND GETTY CENTER

Contact:** 310-440-7300; www.getty.edu. 1200 Getty Center Dr. Take the San Diego Fwy. (I-405) to the Getty Center Dr. Exit. Public transportation is strongly recommended: take either Santa Monica BBBus #14 (for info call 310-451-4444) or MTA #561 (for info call 800-266-6883) to Sepulveda Blvd. **Parking:** Required parking reservations should be made at least 1 month in advance ($5 per car). A "panorami-tram" takes visitors up the hill to the museum. **Hours:** Tu-W 11am-7pm, Th-F 11am-9pm, Sa-Su 10am-6pm. **Free.

Above Bel Air and Brentwood, in the Santa Monica Mountains, lies this long-awaited and justly heralded museum, known to locals simply as "The Getty." Renowned architect Richard Meier designed the $1 billion complex, which opened to the public on December 16, 1997. The opening of the Getty united L.A.'s beloved Getty museums and the Getty institutes on one site. (Its former location, a Roman-style villa in Malibu, will reopen in 2001 as a center for comparative archaeology and cultures.) The all-marble grounds and facilities are even more breathtaking than the impressive art that they house. The museum consists of five pavilions overlooking the Robert Irwin-designed three-acre Central Garden, a living work of art that changes with the seasons. The pavilions contain the permanent Getty collection (including Vincent Van Gogh's *Irises* and James Ensor's *Christ's Entry into Brussels in 1889*), Impressionist paintings, Renaissance drawings, and one of the nation's best Rembrandt van Rijn collections. Headset audio guides are available for rent ($2) and provide further information on the pieces. The Getty also hosts a number of programs open to the public, including gallery talks by local artists, lectures, films, a concert series, and studio demonstrations. The "Friday Nights at the Getty" program features plays, films, and readings.

SEEING STARS. Many of today's stars live in these three affluent communities. The best way to see the various cottages and compounds is to pick up a star map, available at the Santa Monica Pier, local newsstands, or from vendors along Sunset Blvd., which provide a fun driving tour. The best way to see a star is to go the movies and catch them at work, though. Lurking around their neighborhoods might get you a peek at their landscaping, or a picture of their mailbox, but it's doubtful you'll ever see them taking out their own trash.

Next to UCLA is the well-guarded community of **Bel Air,** where **Ronald Reagan** has retired. His estate is at 668 St. Cloud Rd., adjacent to the *Beverly Hillbillies* mansion (750 Bel Air Rd.) and a few blocks up from the former home of **Sonny and Cher** (364 St. Cloud). **Elizabeth Taylor** is literally around the corner (700 Nimes Rd.). A few blocks away is **Nicolas Cage**'s place at 363 Copa De Oro. Back in the golden days, Bel Air was the locus for glamorous celebs, including **Judy Garland** (924 Bel Air Rd.), **Alfred Hitchcock** (10957 Bel Air Rd.), and **Lauren Bacall** and **Humphrey Bogart** (232 Mapleton Dr.) during their go at marital bliss.

Farther west on Sunset Blvd. is **Brentwood,** home to many a national scandal-starter. **O.J. Simpson**'s estate (360 Rockingham Place) was repossessed and auctioned off for a meager $2.63 million. Consequently (some might say the only consequence paid), the famous accusé no longer lives here. However, America's greatest accuser and former media darling, White House intern **Monica Lewinsky,** resides in southern Brentwood at 12224 Darlington Ave. A one-time White House favorite herself, **Marilyn Monroe** was found dead at her home (12305 Fifth Helena Dr.) on August 4, 1962. Celeb-studded Brentwood also includes the homes of **Michelle Pfeiffer, Harrison Ford, Meryl Streep,** and **Rob Reiner.**

The considerably more secluded **Pacific Palisades** brings the stars closer to the ocean, and farther from the *paparazzi*. Many streets are entirely closed to anyone except residents and their guests, but keep your eyes wide shut to catch a glimpse of **Tom Cruise** and **Nicole Kidman** outside 1525 Sorrento, or their neighbor **Bill Cosby** at 1500 Sorrento. **Kurt Russell** and live-in love **Goldie Hawn** (and, until recently, her daughter **Kate Hudson**) live at 1422 Capri Dr. **Whoopi Goldberg** is in town too at 1461 Amalfi Dr., just down the road from **Steven Spielberg** who lives in the house that belonged to **David O. Selznick** while he was producing *Gone with the Wind* (1513-1515 Amalfi Dr.). **Arnold Schwarzenegger** and **Maria Shriver,** who loved their lot so much they bought out their neighbors for a combined $5.4 million, practice family fitness at 14205, 14209, and 14215 Sunset Blvd. **John Travolta** and **Kelly Preston** are stayin' alive at 735 Bonhill Rd.

OTHER SIGHTS. The cliffs give way to the ocean at the popular **Will Rogers State Beach,** 1501 Will Rogers State Park Rd. **Will Rogers State Historical Park,** (310-454-8212), provides pleasant respite from the all-too-near bustle of L.A. City folk enjoy the easy hiking trail that rewards with a panoramic view of the city and distant Pacific. The park offers other options including the famous humorist's home and polo matches (Sa 2-5pm, Su 10am-1pm). Follow Chautauqua Blvd. inland from PCH to Sunset Blvd., or take MTA #2, which runs along Sunset Blvd. (Park open daily 8am-dusk. Rogers's house open daily 10:30am-4:30pm; tours every 30min.)

WILSHIRE DISTRICT

A good place to orient yourself to the myriad sights of the Wilshire District is the well-manicured **Hancock Park,** which sprawls from Ogden Dr. to Curson Ave., between Wilshire Blvd. and 6th St. The park houses two famous museums, and is adjacent to many other sights and smells—picnickers beware of the odorous tar pits, which may conflict with your otherwise sweet-smelling lunchmeat. *(Park open daily 6am-10pm.)*

LOS ANGELES COUNTY MUSEUM OF ART (LACMA). This museum is at the western end of Hancock Park. LACMA's distinguished collection contains "more than 110,000 works from around the world, spanning the history of art from ancient times to the present." Opened in 1965, LACMA is the largest museum in the West, with six major buildings clustered around the **Times-Mirror Central Court.** The **Steve Martin Gallery,** in the Anderson Building, houses the famed benefactor's collection of Dada and Surrealist works, including Rene Magritte's *Treachery of Images.* (This explains how Steve was able to roller skate through LACMA's halls in *L.A. Story.*) Its latest addition is **LACMA West,** a gallery which houses temporary exhibits. The museum sponsors free jazz, chamber music, film classics and documentaries, and a variety of free daily tours. *(General info 323-857-6000. Docent Council 323-857-6108; www.lacma.org. 5905 Wilshire Blvd. Open M-Tu, and Th noon-8pm, F noon-9pm, Sa-Su 11am-8pm. Admission $7, students and seniors $5, under 18 $1; free 2nd Tu of each month. Free jazz F 5:30-8:30pm. Chamber music Su 4-5pm. Film tickets $7, seniors $5. Parking $5, after 6pm free. Wheelchair accessible.)*

MUSEUM OF MINIATURES. One of the best on Museum Row, this large museum with small attractions houses a collection of over 600 models, including a replica of the *Titanic* constructed from 75,000 toothpicks, a 10½-foot-tall Vatican, and painstakingly detailed mini-versions of several of Europe's finest castles. These are not your typical book-report dioramas. You will be amazed by the level of skill and workmanship put into these pieces, most of which took over 18 months each to build. *(323-937-MINI/6464. 5900 Wilshire Blvd., across from LACMA. Open Tu-Sa 10am-5pm, Su 11am-5pm, Admission $7.50, students $5, seniors $6.50, children $3. Half-price validated parking below museum.)*

PETERSEN AUTOMOTIVE MUSEUM (PAM). This slice of Americana showcases L.A.'s most recognizable symbol—the automobile. Like a time-travel showroom, PAM is the world's largest car museum and the nation's 2nd-largest history museum (the Smithsonian is the largest). 300,000 square feet and 130 of history's finest and wildest rides, including Bo and Luke's General Lee (from *The Dukes of Hazzard*) and Herbie the Love Bug (from the movie of the same name) make this an absolute must-see. *(323-930-CARS/2277; 6060 Wilshire Blvd. Open Tu-Su 10am-6pm; Discovery Center closes at 5pm. Admission $7, students and seniors $5, ages 5-12 $3, under 5 free. Full-day parking convenient to LACMA $4.)*

GEORGE C. PAGE MUSEUM OF LA BREA DISCOVERIES. The fragrant **La Brea Tar Pits,** which fill the area with an acrid petroleum stench, are the inspiration for this museum. Easily mistaking the pits for a lake, thirsty mammals of bygone geological ages drank enthusiastically from these pools of water only to find themselves stuck in the tar that lurked below. Most of their one million recovered bones are on display here, along with reconstructed Ice Agers and murals of prehistoric L.A. The only human unearthed in the pits stands out in holographic horror—the **La Brea woman** was presumably thrown into the tar after having holes drilled into her skull. Archaeologists continue their digging in Pit 91 behind the adjacent art museum. *(323-934-PAGE/7243 or 323-857-6311. 5801 Wilshire Blvd., at Curson Ave. Wilshire Blvd. buses stop in front of the museum. Open July-Sept. daily 10am-5pm; Oct.-June Tu-Su 10am-5pm. Admission $6, students and seniors $3.50, ages 5-10 $2; free 1st Tu of each month. Parking $5. Museum tours W-Su 2pm, tours of grounds 1pm.)*

WEST HOLLYWOOD

Melrose Avenue, running from the southern part of West Hollywood into Hollywood, is lined with chi-chi restaurants, art galleries, and shops catering to all levels of the counter-culture spectrum, from ravers to skaters (see Shopping, p. 398). The choicest stretch is between La Brea and Fairfax Avenues. While much that is sold here is used ("vintage"), none of it is really cheap. North of the Beverly Center is the Pacific Design Center, 8687 Melrose Avenue (310-657-0800), at San Vicente Boulevard, a sea-green glass complex, nicknamed the Blue Whale, and constructed in the shape of a rippin' wave. In addition to 150 design showrooms, which showcase mostly home and furnishing projects, this rich man's Home Depot houses a public plaza and 350-seat amphitheater, used to stage free summer concerts (Su 6-7:30pm), and art exhibits (call for schedule). It also hosts an awesome Gay Pride Weekend Celebration in late June.

DOWNTOWN

Downtown is much like midtown Manhattan on a Sunday afternoon—spotted with people, but lacking any overpowering energy, besides, of course, the sun which beats down unrelentlessly in the summer. The **Los Angeles Conservancy** offers Saturday tours of downtown's historic spots (213-623-2489. Tours $5. Make reservations one week in advance.) Those who prefer to travel solo can walk each of the respective sections, but for travel between, should take **DASH Shuttles.** (Fare 25¢; for more info, see **Public Transportation,** p. 353. References below are for M-F travel. Sa-Su the Discovery Direct "DD" route covers almost all of the sights below.) If driving, park in a secure lot, rather than on the street. Parking is costly; so try to arrive before 8am to take advantage of early-bird specials. **Joe's Auto Parks** offer some of the best rates ($3-4 per day; locations include 827 Figueroa St. and 8125 Grand Ave.) The **L.A. Visitors Center,** 685 S. Figueroa St., is overflowing with answers to your travel queries, and has a pamphlet for every spot you could possibly want to visit (open M-F 8am-5pm, Sa 8:30am-5pm).

HISTORIC NORTH. The historic birthplace of L.A. lies in the northern section of downtown, bordered by Spring and Arcadia St. Where the city center once stood, **El Pueblo de Los Angeles Historical Monument** preserves a number of historically important buildings from the Spanish and Mexican eras (213-628-1274. 125 Paseo St. DASH B. Open daily 9am-9pm. Free.) The **visitors center** in the Sepulveda House offers free walking tours which start at the **Old Plaza,** with its century-old Moreton Bay fig trees and huge bandstand, and wind their way past the **Ávila Adobe,** 10 E. Olvera St., the "oldest" house in the city (the original adobe was built in 1818, and has been replaced with concrete in order to meet earthquake regulations). The tour then moves on to **Pico House,** 500 N. Main St., once L.A.'s most luxurious hotel. Farther down, the **Plaza Church,** 535 N. Main St., established in 1818, has an incongruously soft, rose adobe facade. The **visitors center,** 622 N. Main St. (213-628-1274), also screens *Pueblo of Promise,* an 18-minute history of Los Angeles, on request (tours every hr. W-Sa 10am-noon).

Olvera Street, one of L.A.'s original roads, resembles a small Mexican street market, packed with vendors selling everything from Mexican handicrafts and food to Backstreet Boys posters. The street is the site of the Cinco de Mayo and Día de los

Muertes celebrations of L.A.'s Chicano population (see **Seasonal Events,** p. 407). Across Alameda St. from El Pueblo is the grand old **Union Station,** famous for its appearances in many Hollywood productions; and **Chinatown** (DASH B) lies north of this area, roughly bordered by Yale, Spring, Ord, and Bernard St. The architecture in Old Chinatown is unique for the area and very impressive. Pick up walking tour maps at the **Chinatown Heritage and Visitors Center.**

CIVIC CENTRAL. The **Civic Center**, (DASH B and D) is a solid wall of bureaucratic architecture sitting south of El Pueblo, bounded by the Hollywood Fwy. (Rte. 101), Grand Ave., 1st, and San Pedro St. Unless you have a hearing for that parking violation you got in Hollywood, these buildings are best seen from the outside. One of the best-known buildings in the Southland, **City Hall,** "has starred in more movies than most actors." One of its more ironic appearances was as the Vatican in the 1983 miniseries *The Thorn Birds* (200 N. Spring St.). At the **L.A. Children's Museum,** 310 N. Main St. (213-687-8800), in the L.A. Mall opposite City Hall between U.S. 101 and Temple St., everything can be (and has been) touched. The target ages are two to ten, but anyone can have fun here. (Open June 23-Sept. 5 M-F 11:30am-5pm, Sa-Su 10am-5pm; Sept. 6-June 22 Sa-Su 10am-5pm. Admission $5, under 2 free. Large groups should call 213-687-8825.)

L.A.'s larger folks try to get their hands on Hollywood's golden boy, the short, but ever-popular, Oscar, at the **Dorothy Chandler Pavilion** (213-972-7211), site of the annual Academy Awards. The Pavilion is part of L.A.'s **Music Center,** 135 N. Grand Ave., which comprises the **Mark Taper Forum** (213-972-0700) and the **Ahmanson Theatre** (213-972-7200), home to the Los Angeles Philharmonic Orchestra and the Joffrey Ballet.

Upscale **Little Tokyo** (DASH A) lies southeast of the Civic Center, centered on 2nd and San Pedro St. on the eastern edge of downtown. The **Japanese Village Plaza** (213-620-8861), on the 300 block of E. 2nd St., is the center of the district and is a florid fusion of an American shopping mall and Japanese design. The **Japanese-American National Museum** (see p. 358) is housed in a refurbished Buddhist temple designed by Isamu Noguchi, who crafted a monumental sculpture for the courtyard. This community-oriented museum features interactive computers with access to WWII relocation camp records.

Broadway, (DASH D) south of 1st St., is a predominantly Mexican-American community, vibrant and a little *loco*, where you can eat, shop, or get married in one of the many wedding chapels that compete for your dowry, around 240-250 Broadway. Those with second thoughts can click "undo" by looking for the Divorcios signs, placed ever-so-conveniently (read: American-style) right outside the chapels. To catch a glimpse of L.A.'s history etched in stone, check out the side of the **L.A. Times Building** between 2nd and 3rd St. Bargain hounds can haggle to their heart's delight in the Garment District, which is farther down Broadway bordered by 6th and 9th St. The Cooper Building, 860 S. Los Angeles St., is a good first stop. The equally well-stocked **Grand Central Public Market** (see **Eating in L.A.,** p. 368) has its own stars in the sidewalk out front, each bearing the name of a Chicano celebrity—a *rambla de fama* to complement Hollywood's. An L.A. fixture, the Market is one of the best spots to taste some local flavor.

Across the street, the **Bradbury Building,** 304 S. Broadway, stands as a relic of L.A.'s Victorian past. Uninspiring from the street, this 1893 office building is mostly lobby, but what a gorgeous lobby it is. Ornate staircases and elevators are bathed in the sunlight pouring through the glass roof. No wonder this served as Harrison Ford's home in *Blade Runner* (open M-F 9am-5pm, Sa 9am-4pm).

SOUTHERN DISTRICTS. The **Financial District** (DASH B and C) is a typical urban fusion of glass and steel, where gigantic offices crowd the busy downtown center (an area bounded roughly by 3rd, 6th, Figueroa St., and Grand Ave.). Unless you want to reshape your portfolio or dabble in mortgage-based derivatives, there is little for a tourist to do but gaze up at the architectural behemoths. The **Library Tower,** 633 W. 5th St., is the tallest building in L.A. at 1017 feet, and the **Westin Bonaventure Hotel,** 4045 Figueroa St., has appeared in *Rain Man*, *In the Line of*

Fire, and *This Is Spinal Tap*. The easily amused can spend hours in the high-speed elevators. Don't scoff at them; the view from the 32nd floor is better than the view from most helicopters. Just a bit southeast of the Bonaventure is the historic **Regal Biltmore Hotel,** 506 S. Grand Ave., a $10 million, 1000-room hotel designed by Schultze and Weaver (best known for the Waldorf-Astoria in New York). It has served as a filming location for *Dave*, *Independence Day*, *Ghostbusters*, and *The Sting*, which featured scenes in the hotel's Crystal Ballroom.

Up Bunker Hill (a.k.a. Grand Ave.), the **Museum of Contemporary Art (MOCA),** 250 S. Grand Ave. (213-626-6222 or 213-621-2766; www.moca-la.org), in the California Plaza, showcases art from 1940 to the present, and is a sleek and geometric architectural marvel. Its exhibits often focus on L.A. artists, but the collection also includes abstract expressionist works. Thursday nights in summer mean free jazz and cheap beer and wine. (Admission $6, students and seniors $4, under 12 free. Free Th 5-8pm. Free tours led by local artists Tu-W and F-Su at noon, 1, and 2pm; Th noon, 1, 2, and 6pm.) The second MOCA facility is the **Geffen Contemporary,** 152 N. Central Ave. (213-621-1727), in Little Tokyo. Parking here ($2.50-3) is cheaper than at the main building.

Shop 'til you drop at the **Seventh Marketplace**, on Figueroa St., between 7th and 8th, or venture out (with caution) to the **Jewelry District,** a true diamond in a rough neighborhood, east of the Financial District, cornered by 6th and Hill St. The randy **Fashion District** is centered between 8th and 9th St., east of Maple St. Both areas, are served by the DASH E. Bigger, longer, and uncut **South Park** lies south of these areas and remains attraction-less.

NEAR DOWNTOWN: EXPOSITION PARK

Location: Southwest of downtown, off Rte. 110, bounded by Exposition Blvd., Vermont Ave., Figueroa, and Santa Barbara St. From downtown, take DASH shuttle C, or MTA #40 or 42 (from Broadway between 5th and 6th St.). From Hollywood, take MTA #204 or 354 down Vermont Ave. From Santa Monica, take MTA #20, 22, 320, or 322 on Wilshire Blvd.; transfer to #204 at Vermont Ave. Parking: at Figueroa St. and Exposition Blvd. ($5).

Once an upscale suburb of downtown, around 1900 the area began to decline, plummeting to its lowest point in the 1920s, as wealthier citizens moved west. This population vacuum was filled by immigrants, barred from the Westside by homeowners' associations, and the resulting low-cost, high-density housing further depressed the neighborhood. This deterioration was counteracted when the Olympic Games came to town in 1932, and the neighborhood was revitalized again for the second Olympic Games at the park in 1984. Today, the entire area could use another Olympic-class revitalization; its museums are generally safe and well-visited, but **visitors should exercise caution outside the park, especially at night.**

CALIFORNIA SCIENCE CENTER (CSC). Dedicated to the specific sciences of California, the interactive exhibits in this spiffy new building share a common goal—educating kids and adults alike about West Coast issues: earthquakes, smog, fuel, traffic, and studio production. A display on California's fault lines has a jarring rendition of an 8.3 earthquake. You can even design your own cars and earthquake-proof buildings. Ironically, McDonald's sponsors a nutrition display. And, in the spirit of any good California attraction, you can pay $5 to spin in the Space Dock Simulator. Next door, the 5-story, 70-foot-wide **IMAX Theater** shows 45-minute films on nature, space, and special effects. The expansive, formal **rose garden** in front of the CSC is the last remnant of the blessed days when the entire park was an exposition of horticulture. The garden has over 19,000 specimens of 200 varieties of roses surrounding green lawns, gazebos, fountains, and a lily pond. *(**Center:** 213-744-7400; www.casciencectr.org. 700 State Dr. Open daily 10am-5pm. Free. **IMAX:** 213-744-2014. Shows daily every hr. 10am-8pm. Admission $6.50, students $5, seniors $4.50, ages 4-12 $3.75. 3-D shows daily 10am and 5pm; $1 more. Evening shows often sell out; call 213-744-2019 to reserve tickets. **Rose garden:** Open Mar. 16-Dec. 31 daily 8:30am-5:30pm.)*

OTHER MUSEUMS. The **California African-American Museum** displays its collection of indigenous African art, paintings from the Harlem Renaissance in the 1920s, and contemporary mixed-media works. *(213-744-2067. 600 State Dr. Open Tu-Su 10am-5pm. Free.)* The **Natural History Museum,** which has exhibits about pre-Columbian cultures and American history until 1914, features "habitat halls" with North American and African mammals and dinosaur skeletons. The hands-on **Discovery Center** allows visitors to dig for fossils, meet live fish and reptiles, and explore the insect zoo. But these days kids usually shoot past the dinosaur bones and head straight for "Microbes," the trippy new neon-and-blacklight exhibit that features everything from a superhero to a computer-generated 3-D stereo movie (plus something about germs). *(213-763-3466. 900 Exposition Blvd. Open July-Aug. M-F 9:30am-5pm, Sa-Su 10am-5pm; Sept.-June Tu-F 9:30am-5pm, Sa-Su 10am-5pm. Admission $8, students and seniors $5.50, ages 5-12 $2, under 5 free. Free the 1st Tu of each month. Tours in winter M-F 1pm.)*

OTHER SIGHTS. The **University of Southern California (USC)** sits opposite Exposition Park on Exposition Blvd. It's beautiful and generally safe, but take care after dark. *(213-740-6605. Walking tours of campus available every hr. M-F 10am-3pm. Reservations encouraged.)* The **Fisher Gallery** displays post-17th-century works by lesser-known Europeans. *(213-740-4561. Open Sept. 1-May 15 Tu-F noon-5pm, Sa 11am-3pm. Free.)*

WATTS

Known mainly as the site of riots in 1965 and 1992, this is one of L.A.'s most depressed neighborhoods and is not generally amenable to tourism. However, the **Watts Towers,** 1765 E. 107th St. (213-847-4646) are worth the trip. Long before found art became fashionable, an inspired Italian construction worker named Simon Rodia spent three decades of nights (he worked days) constructing the fragile, whimsical Watts Towers out of scrap metal, discarded objects, and thousands upon thousands of seashells. On the verge of demolition in the late 1950s, the nearly 100-foot-tall towers were preserved and have since become a source of civic pride for perpetually troubled Watts. The towers are now being renovated and are not scheduled to open until 2002, but they can still be seen through the gates and scaffolding that now surround them. The adjacent **arts center** focuses on L.A.-area artists. (Take I-10 to Rte. 110S; take Century East Exit, then turn right onto S. Central St., a left onto 103rd St., and follow the signs. Gallery open Tu-F 9am-4pm, Sa 10am-4pm, Su noon-4pm. Free.) **Watts is a high-crime area and should be avoided after dark.**

GRIFFITH PARK AND GLENDALE

The five-mile hike to the top of Mount Hollywood, the highest peak in the park, is quite popular. For information, stop by the **Visitors Center and Ranger Headquarters,** 4730 Crystal Spring Dr. (213-665-5188; open daily 5am-10pm).

PLANETARIUM AND OBSERVATORY. The white stucco and copper domes are visible from around Griffith Park, while its parking lot affords the best view of the Hollywood sign. You may remember the planetarium from the climactic denouement of the James Dean film *Rebel Without A Cause* (1955). But even without Dean (whose bust sits on the front lawn), the astronomy exhibits are a show of their own. The planetarium presents popular **Laserium** light shows that are a psychotronic romp through the strawberry fields of your consciousness. A telescope at the observatory with a 12-inch lens is open to the public on clear nights (except M in winter) until 9:45pm. *(323-664-1181; recording 664-1191. Drive to the top of Mt. Hollywood on almost any of the main roads leading from Los Feliz Blvd., or take MTA #203 (buses run Tu-Su) from Hollywood Blvd. Free parking, use Vermont St. entrance to Griffith Park.* ***Planetarium:*** *shows M-F at 1:30, 3, and 7:30pm, Sa-Su 1:30, 3, 4:30, and 7:30pm; in winter, Tu-F 3 and 7:30pm, Sa-Su 1:30, 3, 4:30, and 7:30pm. Admission $4, seniors $3, ages 5-12 $2, under 5 free but only admitted to 1:30pm show.* ***Laserium:*** *818-901-9405; www.laserium.com. Shows Su-M 6 and 8:45pm, Tu-Sa 6, 8:45, and 9:45pm. Admission $7-8, ages 5-12 $6-7; under 5 not admitted.* ***Observatory:*** *323-663-8171. Open in summer daily 12:30-10pm; in winter Tu-F 2-10pm, Sa-Su 12:30-10pm.)*

GREAT L.A. ZOO. The zoo sits at the park's northern end where its 113 acres accommodate 2000 randy animals. The facility is consistently ranked among the nation's best. Budgeteers beware, food is inordinately expensive so pack lunch and eat in your car. *(323-644-4200. 333 Zoo Dr. Open daily Sept.-June 10am-5pm; July-Aug. 10am-6pm. Admission $8.25, seniors $5.25, ages 2-12 $3.25.)*

AUTRY MUSEUM OF WESTERN HERITAGE. Those hankerin' to relive the wild days of yore will enjoy this museum which covers the fact and fiction of the Old West, with exhibits on pioneer life, outlaws, and the legacy of the Westerns, including relic costumes of Robert Redford and Clint Eastwood, the Lone Ranger mask, and a Gary Cooper toupee. *(323-667-2000. 4700 Western Heritage Way. Open Tu-Su 10am-5pm. Admission $7.50, students and seniors $5, ages 2-12 $3, under 2 free.)*

FOREST LAWN CEMETERY. A rather twisted sense of celebrity sightseeing may lead some travelers to Glendale, where they can see stars who won't run away when chased for a picture. The music piped across these grounds makes the typical graveyard experience even creepier. Among the illustrious dead are Clark Gable, George Burns, Sammy Davis, Jr., and Errol Flynn. The cemetery also includes reproductions of many Michelangelo pieces, as well as the "largest religious painting on earth" (a 195ft. version of the *Crucifixion*). Stop at the entrance for a map of the cemetery's sights and pick up a guide to the paintings and sculpture at the administration building nearby. *(818-241-4151. 1712 Glendale Ave. From downtown, take MTA #90 or 91 and get off just after the bus leaves San Fernando Rd. to turn onto Glendale Ave. By car, take Los Feliz Blvd. south to Glendale Ave., from I-5 or the Glendale Fwy. (Rte. 2). Grounds open daily 8am-6pm; mausoleum open 9am-4:30pm.)*

SAN FERNANDO VALLEY

Movie studios have replaced the Valley Girl as the Valley's defining feature. As the Ventura Fwy. (Rte. 134) passes Burbank, you can see what are today the Valley's trademarks: the **NBC peacock,** the **Warner Bros. water tower,** and the carefully-designed Disney dwarves. Urban legend says that the water pipes are orchestrated such that the seven dwarves appear to urinate on daddy Disney when it rains. Most of the studios have **free TV show tapings** (see **Entertainment,** p. 394).

UNIVERSAL STUDIOS. The most popular spot in today's Tinseltown is this movie-themed amusement park. Fun for all, Universal is best-loved by those with a healthy knowledge of America's blockbuster movie tradition, especially the mythology created around Steven Spielberg. Visit the Bates Hotel from *Psycho*, escape the raptors of *Jurassic Park* and a shark attack by *Jaws*, ride the Delorean from *Back to the Future*, survive an 8.3 earthquake, and don't miss the *Waterworld* stage show. On **E.T.'s** giddy home planet, the huggable alien himself will say your name as your group's bicycle fleet glides past. The new *Terminator 2: 3-D* lets you see Arnold Schwarzenegger in all his 3-dimensional glory. Although most of the park's attractions seem to be of the menacing-automaton/splashing-the-audience-with-water variety, most agree with the park's designers that it is nearly impossible to tire of this sort of excitement. Expect long waits—after all, it *is* the largest film and television studio in the world—and lots of heat in summer. *(818-622-3801. Take MTA #420 bus west from downtown or east from the Valley. Open daily 9am-7pm; July-Aug. 8am-10pm. Last tram leaves at 6:15pm in summer, 4:15pm off-season. Tours in Spanish daily. Admission $38, seniors $33, ages 3-11 $28. Parking $7.)*

UNIVERSAL CITY WALK. If, somehow, you have a few dollars left after Universal Studios, head to its adjacent shopping, food, and entertainment strip to fix the problem. The mammoth green guitar outside the Hard Rock Cafe and colossal 18-screen Cineplex Odeon movie theater set the precedent for this larger-than-life window-shopping extravaganza, where each store is bigger and brighter than the one before. Most of the knick-knack and movie memorabilia shops are open until 10pm on weekdays, 11pm on Friday and Saturday. *(City Walk parking costs $6, but you get a full refund if you buy two movie tickets before 6pm, and a $2 refund after 6pm.)* The jewel in City Walk's technicolor crown is **B.B. King's Blues Club,** where the thrill is far from gone—just check out the big-name blues, deep-fried southern food (howlin' hot wings $7), and cigar bar. *(818-622-5464. Open Su-Th 4pm-midnight, F-Sa 4pm-2am; M-Th dinner served 4-11pm, Sa-Su lunch 2-6pm and dinner 6-11pm. Cover $5-14, $3 for dinner guests. Must be 21 after 10pm.)*

MISSION SAN FERNANDO REY DE ESPAÑA. One of the few L.A. sights with any history is this mission in Mission Hills. The mission was founded in 1797 by Padre Fermin Lasuen, but no structures remain from this period. An amazing recreation, teeming with Pope-abilia, stands today. *(818-361-0186. 15101 San Fernando Mission Blvd. Open daily 9am-4:30pm. Admission $4, seniors $3, children $3; mass daily at 7:25am.)*

NEAR THE VALLEY: SIX FLAGS THEME PARKS. At the opposite end of the Valley, 40 minutes north of L.A. in Valencia, is Magic Mountain, perhaps best known as *National Lampoon*'s Wally World. Not for novices, Magic Mountain has the hairiest roller coasters in Southern California, if not the world. Highlights of the park include the **Revolution,** a smooth metal coaster with mind-blowing loops; the **Colossus,** California's largest wooden roller coaster; the **Viper** (as seen in *True Romance*), whose speed (110mph) is said to approach the limits of coaster technology; the **Tidal Wave** (stand on the bridge for an impromptu shower); the **Suspended Batman;** and the 100 mph **Superman** (meaning 6½ seconds of weightlessness). Under what foolish assumptions would park officials ask the Riddler, who ranks high on Gotham City's difficult-to-breach 10 Most Wanted List, to design a roller coaster for public use? Find out on the **Riddler's Revenge,** a desperate ploy for vindication by the slippery supervillain, which will contort you on all sorts of corkscrew turns. A Looney Tunes playlands, including the new **Bugs Bunny World,** is a haven for under-48-inchers, who are often turned away from park coasters. Temperatures here frequently soar above 100°F in the summer, so bring plenty of bottled water. Next door, Six Flags' waterpark, **Hurricane Harbor,** features the world's tallest enclosed speed slide and an intriguing "adult activity pool." *(**Magic Mountain:** 818-367-5964. At the I-5 Magic Mountain Pkwy. Exit. Open Memorial Day weekend (May 27-29 in 2000) to mid-Sept. Su-Th 10am-10pm, F-Sa 10am-midnight; mid-Sept. to Memorial Day Sa-Su 10am-6pm only. Admission $36, seniors $20, under 48in. tall $10, under 2 free. Parking $6. **Hurricane Harbor:** Open M-Th 10am-7pm, F-Su 10am-8pm. Admission $18, seniors and under 48in. tall $12, under 2 free.)*

PASADENA

A good first stop in Pasadena is the endlessly helpful **Convention and Visitors Bureau,** 171 S. Los Robles Ave. (626-795-9311; www.pasadenacal.com), which has numerous promotional materials and guides to regional arts events (open M-F 8am-5pm, Sa 10am-4pm). The city provides **free shuttles** approximately every 15 minutes that loop between Old Town and the downtown area around Lake Ave. Each of the seven buses has a theme (i.e., performing arts, Arroyo Seco desert, multiculturalism) reflected in its decor. *(626-744-4055. Shuttles run downtown M-Th 11am-7pm, F 11am-10pm, Sa-Su noon-8pm; shuttles run uptown M-F 7am-6pm, Sa-Su noon-5pm.)*

ROSE BOWL. In the gorge that forms the city's western boundary stands Pasadena's most famous landmark. Home to "the granddaddy of them all," the annual college football confrontation between the champions of the Big Ten and Pac 10 conferences, the Rose Bowl is the regular-season venue for UCLA Bruins football and the championship soccer team The Galaxy. *(626-577-3100. 991 Rosemont Blvd. **Bruins info:** 310-825-2101; www.cto.ucla.edu. **Galaxy info:** 800-529-6350.)* The bowl also hosts the **world's largest swap meet** with 2200 vendors. *(323-560-7469. Held the 2nd Su of each month 9am-4:30pm. Spectators $5, bargain hunters admitted at 7:30am, $10. Call ahead for VIP admission at 6am, $15.)*

NORTON SIMON MUSEUM OF ART. The recently revamped museum features a world-class collection, chronicling Western art from Italian Gothic to 20th-century abstract, with paintings by Raphael, Botticelli, Monet, Picasso, and others. The Impressionist and Post-Impressionist hall is particularly impressive, and the collection of Southeast Asian art is one of the world's best. Simon's eclectic taste gives the collection flair. Don't miss the brand-new sculpture garden, the latest creation from California landscape artist Nancy Goslee Power. *(626-449-6840; www.nortonsimon.org. 411 W. Colorado Blvd., at Orange Grove Blvd. Take MTA #180 west on Colorado Blvd. between Lake and N. Orange St. or south on Lake between Washington and Colorado St. Alternatively, take MTA #181 west on Colorado Blvd. between Lake and N. Orange St. Open Th-Su noon-6pm. Admission $4, students and seniors $2, under 12 free. Wheelchair accessible.)*

GAMBLE HOUSE. The house was designed in 1908 by the renowned Pasadena architects Greene and Greene as a retirement residence for the heirs to the Proctor and Gamble fortune. Everything in this bungalow-style masterpiece—trim, paneling, and all—was custom-designed by the Greenes to complement the Gamble family art pieces. The tours detail the architectural accomplishments and innovations of the building, including the fact that no nails hold its structural framework together. Maps sold at the bookstore for $1.50 detail other famous neighborhood buildings. *(626-793-3334. 4 Westmoreland Pl., just north of Walnut St. on Orange Grove Blvd. 1hr. tours Th-Su noon-3pm. Admission $5, students $3, seniors $4, children free. Bookstore: 818-449-4178. Open Tu-Sa 10am-4:30pm, Su 11:30am-4:30pm.)*

PACIFIC ASIA MUSEUM. The museum features a small collection of Tibetan Buddha and Southeast Asian ceramics. It is a quiet gem that was built by Grace Nicholson, an American Oriental arts and crafts trader, who designed the building as a Ming Dynasty replica. Visitors can watch the *koi* fish in the pond. *(626-449-2742. 46 N. Los Robles Ave., between Colorado Blvd. and Union St. Open W-Su 10am-5pm. Admission $5, students and seniors $3; call ahead to book a free tour.)*

FENYES ESTATE. The 1905 estate sits on the same grounds as the **Pasadena Historical Museum,** the Pasadena city archives, and houses an eclectic collection of Renaissance furniture, Egyptian sculpture, and local art amassed by Eva Scott Fenyes. Exhibitions rotate regularly. *(626-577-1660. 470 W. Walnut St., off Orange Grove Blvd. Admission $4, students and seniors $3. Museum tours Th-Su 1-4pm.)*

ARTS... The **Pasadena Arts Council** acts as a clearinghouse for information on all art events in the area, and showcases local work in a small, one-room gallery. *(626-795-1009. 116 Plaza Pasadena, off Green St.)* The **Pasadena Playhouse** was founded in 1917 and nurtured the careers of William Holden and Gene Hackman, among others. Restored in 1986, it now offers some of the city's finest theater. *(626-356-7529. 39 S. El Molino Ave. between Colorado Blvd. and Green St. For more info, see* ***Theater,*** *p. 397.)* Housed in the concrete labyrinth of the Pasadena Center, the **Pasadena Civic Auditorium,** north of Colorado Blvd. The centerpiece of the city's Spanish-influenced architecture, this is where the red carpet was rolled out until 1998 each year for television's **Emmy Awards,** when they were moved to the Shrine in Los Angeles. Since it is a rented venue, events are forever changing, but as of late this 3000-seater plays host to the NAACP Image Awards and Pasadena Symphony. *(626-449-7360; box office 449-7360. 300 E. Green St.)* There's no real reason to venture beyond the ticket window, unless you want to take to the ice at the **Pasadena Ice Skating Center** which holds a daily three-hour public skate session. *(626-578-0801. 310 E. Green St. in Pasadena Center. Schedule varies; call ahead.)*

...AND SCIENCES. Some of the world's greatest scientific minds do their work at the **California Institute of Technology (CalTech).** Founded in 1891, CalTech has amassed a faculty that includes several Nobel laureates (Einstein, Oppenheimer, Hale, and Millikan all taught here) and a student body that prides itself both on its staggering collective intellect and its often ingenious practical jokes. These range from the simple (unscrewing all the chairs in a lecture hall and bolting them in backwards) to the more elaborate (altering the Rose Bowl scoreboard during the game). *(1201 E. California Blvd. about 2½mi. southeast of Old Town. Daily tours 626-395-6327.)* **NASA's Jet Propulsion Laboratory,** about five miles north of Old Town, executed the journey of the Mars Pathfinder. Ask to see pictures of the face of Mars. *(818-354-4321. 4800 Oak Grove Dr. Open for tours M-F; call ahead. Free.)*

OTHER SIGHTS. Besides spectator sports, Pasadena's main draw is **Old Town,** bound approximately by Walnut St. and Del Mar Ave. between Pasadena Ave. and Arroyo Pkwy. This 20-block vibrant shopping and dining mecca, which is proud to call itself "trendy," also includes **Central Park,** a green spot to rest your engines, and 12 parking garages, also to rest your engines. The **Plaza Pasadena** is the main shopping mall just east on Colorado Blvd.—stop in if only to beat the heat. On the northern side of Plaza Pasadena is the beautiful Pasadena **City Hall,** complete with open courtyard, lush gardens, and a fountain. *(100 N. Garfield Ave.).*

NEAR PASADENA: MUSEUMS

HUNTINGTON LIBRARY, ART GALLERY, AND BOTANICAL GARDENS. This massive institute was built in 1910 as the home of businessman Henry Huntington, who made his money in railroads and Southern California real estate. Its stunning botanical gardens host 150 acres of common and rare plants (but no picnicking or sunbathing—both are forbidden here). The library houses one of the world's most important collections of rare books and British and American manuscripts, including a Gutenberg Bible, Benjamin Franklin's handwritten autobiography, a 1410 manuscript of Chaucer's *Canterbury Tales*, and a number of Shakespeare's first folios, as well as a map from Sir Francis Drake's 1585 expedition to "West India." The art gallery is known for its 18th- and 19th-century British paintings. American art is at the **Virginia Steele Scott Gallery.** The Arabella Huntington Memorial Collection features Renaissance paintings and 18th-century French decorative art. Tea, with the likes of women named Buffy and Poodle, is served in the Rose Garden Tea Room daily. *(626-405-2100. 1151 Oxford Rd., between Huntington Dr. and California Blvd. in San Marino, south of Pasadena, about 2mi. south of the Allen Ave. Exit off I-210. From downtown L.A., take MTA #79 from Union Station to San Marino Ave. and walk ½mi. (45min. trip). Open in summer Tu-Su 10:30am-4:30pm; in winter Tu-F noon-4:30pm, Sa-Su 10:30am-4:30pm. Admission $8.50, students $6, seniors $8, under 12 free; 1st Th of each month free.)*

SOUTHWEST MUSEUM. Recent remodeling and innovative exhibits give this museum in Highland Park the attention it deserves. The palatial Hispano-Moorish building houses artifacts including a Cheyenne teepee and a Tlinglit totem pole, and celebrates the crafts of the American Indian. *(323-221-2164. 234 Museum Dr. Take MTA #83 along Broadway to Museum Dr. By car, take the Pasadena Fwy. (I-110) to Ave. 43 and follow the signs. Open Tu-Su 10am-5pm. Admission $6, students and seniors $4, ages 7-18 $3. Library generally open W-Sa 11am-5pm. Call ahead.)*

NOT SO NEAR PASADENA: SAN DIMAS

San Dimas really does have a **Circle K,** 301 E. Walnut St. (909-592-5085), at Bonita. "San Dimas High School football rules!"

RAGING WATERS. Beat the heat with 50 acres of slides, pools, whitewater rafts, inner tubes, fake waves, and a fake island. Hurl yourself over the seven-story waterslide **Drop Out** (if you dare), or rush down **Speed Slide** (the slide on the right gets more air and a better drop). Crowded on weekends, but lines look worse than they are. Family-oriented, so the riskier the slide, the shorter the line. *(Recorded message and directions 909-802-2200. 111 Raging Waters Dr. At I-10, Rte. 210, and 57. Open Apr.-Sept M-F 10am-9pm, Sa-Su 9:30am-9pm; off-season open daily 9am-9pm. Admission $24, under 48in. $15, under 2 free; after 4pm $15, under 48in. $11. Parking $6; lockers $4-6.)*

THE CELEBRITY TOUR

The reason why all the maps to stars' homes only seem to show dead stars is that while the privileged may still *shop* here, most no longer *live* here. The area still houses many a multi-millionaire and lives up to the well-manicured ideal that visitors expect, but the real fame and money has since moved away from the hype to areas that afford privacy (see **Bel Air, Brentwood, and Pacific Palisades,** p. 383).

A conspicuous way to tour the city is in the 1914 trolley car replica operated by the Beverly Hills Chamber of Commerce (310-248-1000). The 40-minute **tour of the**

city and stars' homes costs $5 and leaves from the corner of Rodeo Dr. and Dayton (every hr. June-Sept. Tu-Sa 1-5pm). If you prefer a cooler approach, go solo with a star map ($8), sold along Sunset Blvd. but not within Beverly Hills, or take the following *Let's Go* abbreviated tour (consult the L.A. Westside map for reference).

Elvis had two homes in L.A. He purchased the first, at 1174 Hillcrest, shortly after his marriage to Priscilla in 1967, but quickly relocated to 144 Monovale because it offered more privacy. Today, Priscilla still lives near those old memories at 1167 Summit Dr. The 55-room **Greystone Mansion** at nearby 905 Loma Vista Dr. (310-550-4654), just off Doheny, was the most expensive home in Beverly Hills in the 1920s. The mansion was built by oil mogul **Edward Doheny** for his son, who was found dead with his male secretary only a few weeks after moving in, giving rise to unconfirmed rumors that the two were lovers. Now owned and operated by the city, the Tudor and Jacobean revival house with its two gatehouses and glorious gardens is now used extensively as a filming location, most notably in *The Witches of Eastwick*, *Ghostbusters*, and *The Bodyguard*. (Open daily 10am-6pm; gardens free.) Head back to Sunset Blvd., make a right, and then make a left on Elm Dr. The estate at 722 N. Elm Dr. has been owned by **Elton John, The Artist** (when he was known as **Prince**), and was most recently the site of the **Menendez** murders. **Frank Sinatra** owned the house at nearby 915 Foothill Rd., one street west of Elm Dr. Head back to Sunset Blvd. again, make a left, and another left onto Roxbury Dr. Nice-guy actor/poet **Jimmy Stewart** resided at 918 Foothill Rd. If you dig serious power, have a glance at the walls of the massive **David Geffen** mansion, 1801 Angelo Dr. Follow Roxbury Dr. north as it turns into Hartford, make a left onto Benedict Canyon, and another left on Angelo Dr. to the media god's mansion. Now, turn back to Benedict Canyon, make a left, then a right onto Tower. **Jay Leno,** at 1151 Tower Rd., lives just around the corner from the home of **Heidi Fleiss,** 1270 Tower Grove Dr. Head back down Benedict Canyon toward Sunset Blvd., make a right, and then another right onto Carolwood. **Barbra Streisand** lived at 301 Carolwood, and the house at 355 Carolwood is where **Walt Disney** lived until his death. Turn back to Sunset Blvd. and head towards Westwood, making a left on the tiny and windy Charing Cross. The estate at 10236 is **The Playboy Mansion.** Charing Cross becomes N. Mapleton, site of the largest and most extravagant residence in Beverly Hills: producer **Aaron Spelling's** mansion, 594 N. Mapleton, is larger than the Taj Mahal. Wife Candy Spelling's closets reportedly take up an entire wing.

ENTERTAINMENT

Without entertainment, there still might be Hollywood, but there would be no "Hollywood!" There are many ways to indulge in the glitz, the glamor, and the glory that the entertainment capital of the world holds so dear. **Shopping,** for example, is a major pastime in the L.A. area, one that has been crafted into what some might call an art (see p. 398). For off-hours fun, see **Nightlife** (p. 401). For amusements of the park variety, see the listings for Disneyland (p. 421), Knott's Berry Farm (p. 423), Magic Mountain (p. 391), and Universal Studios (p. 390). For the classic L.A. entertainment, that of the film and recording industries, read on.

FILM AND TELEVISION STUDIOS

Many tourists feel a visit to the world's entertainment capital is not complete without some exposure to the actual business of making a movie or TV show. Frtunately, most production companies oblige. **Paramount** (323-956-5000), **NBC** (818-840-3537), and **Warner Bros.** (818-954-1744) offer two-hour guided walking tours, but as they are *made* for tourists, they tend to be crowded and overpriced. The best way to get a feel for the industry is to land yourself some tickets to a TV taping. All tickets are free, but most studios tend to overbook, so holding a ticket does not always guarantee that you'll get into the taping. Show up early and you'll have a chance of seeing your favorite stars up close in an operating studio backlot.

NBC, 3000 W. Alameda Ave. (recording 818-840-3537), at W. Olive Ave. in Burbank, is your best spur-of-the-moment bet. Show up at the ticket office on a weekday at 8am for passes to Jay Leno's **Tonight Show,** filmed at 5pm the same evening (2 tickets per person, must be 16+). Studio tours run on the hour (M-F 9am-3pm, Sa 10am-2pm; admission $7, children $3.75). Many of NBC's "Must-See TV" shows are taped at **Paramount Pictures,** 5555 Melrose Ave. (323-956-1777), in Hollywood. Sitcoms like *Dharma and Greg, Sister, Sister,* and *Frasier,* are taped September through May; call the studio five working days in advance to secure tickets. NBC's most popular sitcoms, like *Friends* and *Will and Grace,* are filmed before a private audience, so unless you are a friend of a Friend, you're out of luck. As it is one of just a few major studios still in Hollywood, Paramount's tours are very popular (every hr. M-F 9am-2pm; admission $15).

A **CBS box office,** 7800 Beverly Blvd. (213-852-2458), next to the Farmer's Market in West Hollywood, hands out free tickets to Bob Barker's seminal game-show masterpiece *The Price is Right* (taped M-Th) up to one week in advance (open non-taping days M-Th 9am-5pm, taping days M-Th 7:30am-5pm). Audience members must be over 18. You can request up to 10 tickets on a specific date by sending a self-addressed stamped envelope to *The Price is Right* Tickets, 7800 Beverly Blvd., Los Angeles, CA 90036, about four weeks in advance.

If all else fails, **Hollywood Group Services,** 1422 Barry Ave. #8, L.A. 90025 (310-914-3400), and **Audiences Unlimited, Inc.,** 100 Universal City Plaza, Universal City, CA 91608 (818-506-0067), offer guaranteed seating, but charge $10 to no-shows. To find out what shows are available during your visit, send a SASE to either address. Hollywood Group Services will fax a list of all available shows within 24 hours of a call-in request. At **Universal Studios,** the filming is done on the backlot, and you won't see a thing from the tour. To them, it's a studio, but to us non-industry folk, it's an amusement park.

To see an **on-location movie shoot,** stop by in person to the Entertainment Industry Development Company's L.A. Film Office, 7083 Hollywood Blvd., 5th floor (323-957-1000), for a "shoot sheet" ($10), which lists current filming locations, but be aware that film crews may not share your enthusiasm about audience participation (open M-F 8am-6pm). The same information is free at www.eidc.com.

CINEMA

Countless theaters show films the way they were meant to be seen: in a big space, on a big screen, with top-quality sound. Angelenos are often amazed at the "primitive" sound at theaters in the rest of the country. It would be a cinematic crime not to take advantage of the incredible experience that is movie-going in L.A.

The gargantuan theaters at **Universal City** or **Century City,** as well as those in **Westwood Village** near UCLA are incredibly popular, especially on weekends. Lines at all the best theaters are very long, especially for new releases, but lively crowds, state-of-the-art sound, and large screens justify the wait. In **Santa Monica,** in only 3 blocks, there are 22 screens between Santa Monica Place and Wilshire Blvd. along the Third St. Promenade.

Devotees of second-run, foreign-language, and experimental films are rewarded by the Santa Monica theaters away from the Promenade. Foreign films play consistently at the eight **Laemmle Theaters** in Beverly Hills (310-274-6860 and 323-848-3500), Santa Monica (310-477-5581), Pasadena (626-796-6140 and 626-796-7864), Encino (818-981-9847), and downtown (213-617-3084).

L.A.'s giant movie industry does not, surprisingly, include world-class film festivals like Cannes or Sundance. On the other hand, the city hosts a number of smaller, less expensive, and more accessible film showcases, including the **Annual L.A. International Gay and Lesbian Film Festival, Outfest** (323-960-9200, www.outfest.org; each film $8-10), in July, and the **Asian Pacific Film and Video Festival** (310-206-8013; each film $6, seniors and students $4), in August. The largest in the area is the pricey late-October **Annual AFI L.A. International Film Festival** (in the U.S. 323-856-7707, elsewhere 323-856-7709; www.afifest.com), which shows 150 shorts,

SO, YOU WANNA BE IN PICTURES? Honey! Baby! Sweetheart! You don't have to be beautiful and proportionally perfect to grace celluloid—just look at Tom Arnold or Lili Tomlin. The quickest way to get noticed is to land yourself a job as an extra—no experience necessary. One day's work will land $40-130 in your pocket and two meals in your tummy. Step One is to stop calling yourself an extra—you're an "atmosphere actor" now (it's better for your ego and your resume). Step Two is to contact a reputable casting service. **Cenex,** 1700 W. Burbank Blvd. 2nd fl., Burbank, CA 91506 (818-562-2888, ext. 3219), is the biggest, and a good place to start. You must be at least 18 and a U.S. citizen or Green Card holder. Step Three is to show up on time; you'll need the clout of DeNiro before you can waltz in after call. Don't forget to bring $20 in cash to cover the "photo fee." Step Four is to dress the part: don't wear red or white, which bleed on film and render you unusable. Finally, after you collect three SAG (Screen Actors Guild; 5757 Wilshire Blvd., Los Angeles, CA 90036; 213-937-3441) vouchers, you'll be eligible to pay the $1050 to join showbiz society. See you in the movies!

documentaries, and features from around the world ($50 for full-week matinee pass; $250 for the entire festival).

If you'd like to stand outside and ogle the stars as they walk the red carpet into the theater for a **premiere,** call the four premiere-hounds: Mann's Chinese (about 2 per month), El Capitan (Disney films only), the Bruin, and Fox in Westwood. For info on what's playing in L.A., call 213-777-FILM/3456, or pick up the daily Calendar section of the *Los Angeles Times.*

Loews Cineplex Cinemas (818-508-0588) **Universal City,** atop the hill at Universal City Walk. Opened in 1987 as the world's largest cinema complex, its 18 wide-screen theaters and a *Parisienne*-style cafe put all others to shame. Tickets $8.50, seniors and under 13 $5.50; before 6pm $5.50, seniors and under 13 $5. $2 discount on parking after 6pm with purchase of 2 regular admission tickets.

Pacific Cinerama Dome, 6360 Sunset Blvd., **Hollywood** (323-466-3401), near Vine St. The ultimate movie screen measures three times the size of normal screens and wraps 180° around the theater. The spectacular sound system rumbles stomachs and pierces ears nightly; only those brave enough to remove their still-beating ear drums can escape with their souls intact. Tickets $8.50, seniors and under 12 $5, 1st 3 shows daily $5.

Mann's Chinese Theater, 6925 Hollywood Blvd., **Hollywood** (323-464-8111). Hype to the hilt. A must-see. For details, see **Hollywood Sights,** p. 376. Tickets $8, students $6, 1st 2 shows before 6pm $5, weekends and holidays $5. Parking $6.50.

El Capitan, 6838 Hollywood Blvd., **Hollywood** (323-467-7674 or 808-559-6247), across from Mann's Chinese. Disney glitz straight out of *Fantasia,* with live stage shows and exhibitions in the gallery downstairs. The recently renovated theater's standard prices can soar to $20 (seniors and children $15) for new releases. Parking $6.50.

Mann's Fox Westwood Village Theatre, 961 Broxton Ave., **Westwood** (310-208-5576). No multiplex nonsense here. One auditorium, one big screen, one great THX sound system, a balcony, and Art Deco design. Watch the back rows and balcony for late-arriving celebrities. Tickets $8.50, students $6, shows before 6pm $6, seniors and under 12 $5. Student tickets $5.50, matinee tickets $4.75, Sa-Su $5.

REVIVAL THEATERS

Nuart Theatre, 11272 Santa Monica Blvd., **West L.A.** (310-478-6379), just west of the San Diego Fwy. (I-405), at Sawtelle Ave. Perhaps the best-known revival house. The playbill changes nightly. Classics, documentaries, and modern films. *The Rocky Horror Picture Show* screens Saturday at midnight. Tickets $8, seniors and under 12 $5. Discount card (5 movie tickets, $25).

New Beverly Cinema, 7165 Beverly Blvd., in the **Wilshire District** (323-938-4038). Shows foreign films and old faves from as recently as last year. Schedule changes every 2-3 days. Tickets $5, students and children $4.

UCLA's James Bridges Theater (310-825-2345), **Westwood,** near Sunset Blvd. and Hilgard St. on the northeastern corner of campus. Eclectic film festivals. Student films (free) at the end of each semester, archived foreign films, and previews of Universal films. All shows 7:30pm. Tickets $5, UCLA students free. Open Oct.-May only.

LACMA's Bing Theater, 5905 Wilshire Blvd., in the **Wilshire District** (323-857-6010), at the L.A. County Museum of Art. Classic films on the big screen for less than a video rental. Shows Tu at 1pm only. Tickets $2, seniors $1.

THEATER

The wondrously dramatic spectacle that is Broadway never quite made it across the Rockies, and so the live theater scene, isn't quite what it is in New York. On the other hand, 115 "equity waiver theaters" (under 100 seats) offer a dizzying choice for theater-goers, who can also take in small productions in museums, art galleries, universities, parks, and even garages. For the digs on what's hot, browse the listings in the *L.A. Weekly*.

James A. Doolittle Theater, 1615 N. Vine St., **Hollywood** (323-462-6666 or Telecharge at 800-233-3123). Big names and Tony Award-winners in this medium-sized venue with around 1000 seats. Tickets around $45, weekend shows $50; rush tickets (around $20) available 30min. before showtime, except Saturdays.

Geffen Playhouse (formerly the Westwood Playhouse), 10886 LeConte Ave., **Westwood** (310-208-5454). Off-Broadway and Tony award-winning shows in a cozy setting. Tickets around $33-37; student rush tickets ($10) 15min. before show.

Pasadena Playhouse, 39 S. El Molino Ave., **Pasadena** (626-356-PLAY/7529 or 800-233-3123). California's premier theater and historical landmark has spawned Broadway careers and productions. Tickets around $15-38, weekend shows $15-45. Call for rush tickets. Matinees Sa-Su.

Shubert Theatre, 2020 Ave. of the Stars, **Century City** (800-233-3123). Big Broadway shows and musicals in a high-glam setting. Tickets $35-65, weekend shows $45-75; rush tickets ($25) available 2hr. before showtime.

Pantages, 6233 Hollywood Blvd., **Hollywood** (213-468-1770). L.A.'s other place for big Broadway spectacles and cabaret acts. Box office open M-Sa 10am-6pm, Su 10am-4pm, or call Ticketmaster (323-365-3500) for tickets and events info. No rush tickets. Parking $5-8.

CONCERTS

L.A.'s music venues range from small clubs to massive amphitheaters. The **Wiltern Theater** (213-380-5005) shows alterna-rock/folk acts. The **Hollywood Palladium** (323-962-7600) is of comparable size, with 3500 seats. Mid-size acts head for the **Universal Amphitheater** (818-777-3931) and the **Greek Theater** (323-665-1927). Huge indoor sports arenas, such as the **Forum** (310-673-1300) and the new **Staples Center** (213-996-0100), double as concert halls for big acts. Few dare to play at the 100,000-seat **Los Angeles Memorial Coliseum and Sports Arena**—only U2, Depeche Mode, and the mighty Guns n' Roses have filled the stands in recent years. Call Ticketmaster (323-365-3500) to purchase tickets for any of these venues.

Hollywood Bowl, 2301 N. Highland Ave., **Hollywood** (323-850-2000). The bowl hosts a summer music festival from early July to mid-Sept. Although sitting in the back of this outdoor, 18,000-seat amphitheater makes even the L.A. Philharmonic sound like transistor radio, bargain tickets and a sweeping view of L.A. from the bowl's south rim make it worthwhile. Free open-house rehearsals by the Philharmonic and visiting performers M-Tu and Th-F. Parking at the bowl is a pricey $10. Better options are parking away from the bowl and walking up Highland, using MTA's Park 'n' Ride service (800-266-6883), or taking bus #420 west from downtown or east from the valley. Call Ticketmaster (323-365-3500) to purchase tickets.

Music Center, 135 N. Grand Ave., **downtown** (213-972-7211), at the corner of 1st St. in the heart of the city (see **Downtown,** p. 387). Includes the Mark Taper Forum, the Dorothy Chandler Pavilion, and the Ahmanson Theatre. Performance spaces host the L.A. Opera, Broadway and experimental theater, and dance. Some performances, like the American Ballet Theater, offer student rush tickets ($10; call in advance and arrive 1hr. early). Parking $7 after 6pm.

SPORTING EVENTS

Exposition Park, and the very rough city of **Inglewood,** southwest of the park, are home to many sports teams. The **USC Trojans** football team plays at the **Los Angeles Memorial Coliseum,** 3939 S. Figueroa St. (tickets 213-740-4672), which seats over 100,000 spectators, and is the only stadium in the world to have the honor of hosting the Olympic Games twice. The torch that held the Olympic flame still towers atop the Coliseum's roof. The **Los Angeles Sports Arena,** 2601 S. Figueroa St. (213-748-8000), is the former playground of basketball's **Los Angeles Clippers,** who just recently faxed themselves to the brand-new **Staples Center,** 1111 S. Figueroa St. The Sports Arena is still a popular venue for rock concerts.

In Inglewood, at the corner of Manchester and Prairie is the **Great Western Forum** (310-673-1300), home of the **Los Angeles Kings** hockey team, as well as the **Los Angeles Lakers** (NBA) and **Sparks** (WNBA) basketball teams. Tickets for these games are in high demand (Lakers season runs Nov.-June; Sparks June-Aug.). Kings tickets start at $19, Lakers tickets start at $21, and Sparks tickets start at $8. For Kings tickets call 888-KINGSLA/546-4752; for Lakers and Sparks tickets call Ticketmaster directly at 213-480-3232).

Elysian Park, about three miles northeast of downtown, curves around the northern portion of Chavez Ravine, home of **Dodger Stadium** (213-224-1400) and the perennially popular **Los Angeles Dodgers** baseball team. Tickets ($6-14) are a hot commodity during the April to October season (if the Dodgers are playing well). Call 213-224-1448 to purchase tickets in advance.

SHOPPING

In Los Angeles, shopping isn't just a practical necessity; it's a way of life. Popular shopping areas like Santa Monica's Third Street Promenade, Pasadena's Old Town, the Westside Pavilion, and the Century City Mall are lined with identical chain boutiques with the latest cookie-cutter fashions. Tucked away from the shuffle, though, are a number of cool specialty shops with more one-of-a-kind items. Remember, dahling, when the going gets tough, the tough go shopping.

BOOKSTORES

L.A. might not seem like the most literary of cities. After all, while subway commuters in other cities immerse themselves in the newspaper, Angelenos listen to news radio while caught in an early-morning traffic jam. Other cities' display windows highlight Arundhati Roy or Wislawa Szymborska. The front shelves of most L.A. bookstores are lined with Hollywood bios and practical guides on how to become a star. But fear not, hungry literati, you don't have to resort to the ubiquitous Barnes and Noble megastores just yet.

Book Soup, 8818 Sunset Blvd., **West Hollywood** (310-659-3110). A maze of new books in every category imaginable, with especially strong film, architecture, poetry, and mystery sections. The comprehensive newsstand that wraps around the building includes industry mags and international newspapers. A new annex next door carries sale items and lots of hardcover art, photo, and design books at reduced prices. Main store open daily 9am-midnight, annex open daily noon-8pm.

Samuel French Bookshop, 7623 Sunset Blvd., **Hollywood** (213-876-0570); and 11963 Ventura Blvd., **Studio City** (818-762-0535). Pure L.A. Get prepped for your audition at this haven for all things thespian: acting directories, TV and film reference books, trade papers, and a vast selection of plays and screenplays. Lists local theaters that are currently casting. Occasional script signings by local playwrights. Hollywood location open M-F 10am-6pm, Sa 10am-5pm; Studio City location open M-F 10am-9pm, Sa 10am-6pm, Su noon-5pm.

A Different Light, 8853 Santa Monica Blvd., **West Hollywood** (310-854-6601; www.adlbooks.com). The nation's largest gay and lesbian bookseller has an incredibly diverse selection: gay fiction and classics, biography and autobiography, self-help, travel, law, queer theory. Videos, magazines, music, gift items, readings, and book signings. Open daily 10am-midnight.

Vagabond's, 11706 San Vicente Blvd., **Brentwood** (310-475-2700). *Harper's Magazine* called it L.A.'s best used bookstore, although they prefer to call themselves an "out-of-print specialist." If someone's read it, it's here. Open M-Sa 11am-6pm.

Beyond Baroque, 681 Venice Blvd., **Venice** (310-822-3006). For the artsier set, this bookstore is a second home. Sells small press books, self-published titles, and 'zines. Free poetry and fiction workshops. Readings Sept.-May F and Sa at 7:30pm ($7-8, students $5). Open Tu-Sa 2-6pm; closed Aug.

Counterpoint Records and Books, 5911 Franklin Ave., **Hollywood** (213-957-7965). A well-stocked used bookstore that stays open late into the night has an especially good collection of popular music books. Impressive selection of vinyl with some CDs and tapes. Open M-Th 11am-11pm, F-Sa 11am-midnight, Su 1-8pm.

MUSIC STORES

Used music stores are a dime a dozen, especially in **Westwood** and along **Melrose Ave.** Many buy old CDs and tapes or trade them for store credit, which unfortunately makes for selections of "rejections." Here are some gems in the mix, those that offer the best selections or cater to better tastes.

Moby Disc, 2114 Wilshire Blvd., **Santa Monica** (310-828-2887); 14622 Ventura Blvd., **Encino** (818-990-2970); and 28 E. Colorado Blvd., **Pasadena** (626-449-9975). At the great white whale of used CD stores in the L.A. area, the odds for good finds are in your favor, Ahab. Fairly non-discriminating in buying used CDs (for cash or store credit). Smaller new CD and used cassette sections. Open Su-Th 10am-11pm, F-Sa 11am-1am.

Vinyl Fetish, 7305 Melrose Ave., **West Hollywood** (323-935-1300). The LP collection you can only *wish* you owned, suckah. Top-rate rock, funk, industrial, ska, punk, new wave, and disco. Records $5-20, depending on condition and rarity. CDs, tapes, books, t-shirts, and accessories to die for. Open daily 11am-10pm.

Aron's, 1150 N. Highland Ave., **Hollywood** (213-469-4700), between Santa Monica and Sunset Blvd. Well-loved for its massive new and used CD collection, which ranges from ska to showtunes. Open Su-Th 10am-10pm, F-Sa 10am-midnight.

Virgin Megastore, 8000 Sunset Blvd. (323-650-8666). Virgin's got everything, but prices range from $13-18 for new CDs. Open M 9am-12:30am; Tu, Th, and Su 9am-midnight; W 10am-midnight; F-Sa 9am-1am.

Rhino Records, 1720 Westwood Blvd., **West L.A.** (310-474-8685). Specializes in the obscure, the alternative, and those never-played promotional albums that couldn't find a home. Strong blues, jazz, exotica, and dance sections. Definitive collection of titles on the excellent Rhino label. Open Su-Th 10am-11pm, F-Sa 10am-midnight.

CLOTHING STORES

It's a fashion war out there, so you've got to look your best. Fashion in the City of Angels is one-half glitz, one-half retro, and both halves acutely aware that This Is Not New York. On top of it all, you want to look like heaven, at one hell of a low price. Unfortunately, with so many overpriced boutiques in L.A., that's not always easy for someone on a budget. **Melrose Avenue** has lots of used clothing stores—and they're chic too. Remember: If you think you're paying too much for those pink patent-leather go-go boots, you probably are.

Aardvark's, 7579 Melrose Ave., **West Hollywood** (213-655-6769); and 85 Market St., **Venice** (310-392-2996). Used gear galore from practical (used Levi's $10-20) to fabulous (pink faux-leather miniskirts $15). Lots of hats, leather jackets, and wigs. Dresses for any decade. Open M-Th 11am-7pm, F-Su 1-9pm.

It's A Wrap, 3315 W. Magnolia Blvd., **Burbank** (818-567-7366). Keep up with the trends by dressing like your favorite *Melrose Place* characters—*just* like them. Sells studio wardrobes from TV shows like *Roseanne, Mad About You, Seinfeld,* and *All My Children. Baywatch* bathing suits $10. Hot labels at 50% the retail cost, *and* they've been sweated in by stars. But don't worry, it's all been dry-cleaned. Open M-F 11am-8pm, Sa-Su 11am-6pm.

Star Wares, 2817 Main St., **Santa Monica** (310-399-0224). It's A Wrap's big-screen equivalent (although there's no connection between the two), with used movie wardrobes and props. The stars' personal clothes generally cost less than in the boutiques where they bought them. Open M-Sa 10:30am-6pm.

Retail Slut, 7308 Melrose Ave., **West Hollywood** (213-934-1339; www.hallucinet.com/retail slut), is a mecca for all manner of punks, goths, and grrrls. It's the place to find the fetish gear you've been searching for, or just a cool spot to browse a huge selection of ear- and body-rings. Open M-Th 11am-9pm, F-Sa 11am-10pm, Su noon-7pm.

Hidden Treasures, 154 Topanga Canyon Blvd., **Malibu** (310-455-2998), 4mi. up from PCH (Rte. 1). Visitors come in because they believe the giant roadside animatronic tiger and giraffe indicate "circus," but they stay for the savings! There's a sizable selection of surprisingly wearable "vintage" clothes, and better yet, a sea-themed decor, and better yet still, a mountaintop teepee. Sit around the campfire, beat the drums, smoke a peace pipe. You don't even need to buy anything. October means reams of Halloween decorations and costumes. Open M-F 10:30am-6:30pm, Sa-Su 10:30am-7pm.

City Rags, 10967 Weyburn Ave., **Westwood Village** (310-209-0889). This small but well-stocked 1970s retro-wear-house has a super-friendly staff and some great bargains on vintage that's actually wearable. If they don't have what you need, they can hunt it down. Shirts $9-16, pants $8-18. Open M-Th 11am-9pm, F-Sa 11am-10pm.

Jet Rag, 825 N. La Brea Ave., **Hollywood** (323-939-0528). Enormous used clothing selection and columns depicting bombs at ground zero are the major draws here. Popular $1 sale is Th and Su 11:30am-7pm. Open M-Sa 11:30am-8pm, Su 11am-7:30pm.

NOVELTY STORES

L.A. has its share of eccentrics, and they need to shop somewhere too. Some are a little morbid, some may be a little too explicit, but none make apologies for what they sell or how they sell it.

Out of the Closet, 8224 Santa Monica Blvd., **West Hollywood** (323-848-9760). With 14 stores in the L.A. area, this is the sugar-daddy of resale retail. They've got anything you need in at least one of their stores. Profits from the sale of used clothing, electronics, and furniture are donated to the AIDS Healthcare Foundation. Look for OOC's neon trademark storefronts, or call for other locations. Open M-F and Su 10am-6pm, Sa 10am-7pm.

Condomania, 7306 Melrose Ave., **West Hollywood** (323-933-7865; www.condomania.com). America's 1st condom emporium (according to the management) has more pleasurable prophylactics than you thought were, or could ever be, made. They cater to all kinds of "body-types"—small, hard-to-fit, hard-to-please, allergic. Open Su-Th 11am-8pm, F-Sa 11am-10pm.

Skeletons in the Closet, 1104 Mission Rd., **downtown** (213-343-0760). It's actually the L.A. Coroner's gift shop, and yes, it's as terrifically tasteless as it sounds. Sells personalized toe tags and beach towels with body outlines among other morbid memorabilia. All profits go to drunk driving programs. Open M-F 8am-4:30pm.

Dudley Doo-Right Emporium, 8200 Sunset Blvd., **West Hollywood** (323-656-6550). Cartoonist Jay Ward's old production office now teems with memorabilia based on his characters, *Rocky and Bullwinkle, George of the Jungle,* and *Dudley Doo-Right.* T-shirts ($16-20), stuffed animals (from $16), and original show scripts. Open Tu, Th, and Sa 11am-5pm. No credit cards.

Baby Jane of Hollywood, 7985 Santa Monica Blvd., **West Hollywood** (323-848-7080), at Laurel St. in the French Market Restaurant. Popular with gay men and lonely women, Baby Jane carries more than just your typical melange of old movie posters, classic records, vintage tabloids, and autographed glossies ($35-75). It's also got shots of celebs in, shall we say, revealing poses, as well as collectibles like Barbra Streisand's Celebrity Home Earthquake Rubble ($10). Open daily noon-8pm.

Psychic Eye Book Shop, 218 Main St., **Venice** (310-396-0110); and 13435 Ventura Blvd., **Sherman Oaks** (818-906-8263), in the Valley. Traveling can be rough on the aura. Fortunately for those in need, there's a place to pick up karma-enhancing astrology charts, hookahs, candelabras, gargoyles, statues of your favorite goddesses, and all things gothic. Psychic readings $20 for 15min., $50 per hr., as well as tarot classes, hypnosis sessions, and Tibetan massage. Open M-Sa 10am-10pm, Su 11am-8pm.

MALLS

Mall-shopping in Los Angeles is not just for the Valley Girl, and your retail-going experience need not be as unpleasant as, say, a trip *to* the Valley. Going to the mall can be a full-day activity—you need a few hours to see, be seen, and see all there is to see. Many shopping complexes are open-air, making the stroll down a sunny, tree-lined walkway half the experience. The hub of the 'til-you-drop spots is West L.A., with these three malls at the head of the pack:

The **Century City Shopping Complex,** 10250 Santa Monica Blvd. (310-277-3898), just southwest of Beverly Hills in **West L.A.,** offers 200 upper-class stores, boutiques, and cafes, but few come just for the shops. Its well-manicured, labyrinthine walkways are a good place to spot celebrities, although nothing is guaranteed. It also features the 14-screen AMC Century 14 theaters (310-289-4AMC/4262).

The **Westside Pavilion,** 10800 W. Pico Blvd. (310-474-5940), has 150 shops and restaurants, including mall standards Banana Republic, Barnes & Noble, and Robinson's May. And what would an L.A. mall be without a movie theater? This one features Samuel Goldwyn Cinemas (310-475-0202).

Perhaps the prime example of bigger, better, more, more, more is the **Beverly Center,** 8500 Beverly Blvd. (310-854-0070), at La Cienega Blvd., a monstrous neon megalith smack-dab in the middle of the city, complete with voyeuristic escalators going up the building's glass siding. Although it's the same old mix of mall stores, the display windows are more showy. Attached to the Beverly Center is the nation's first (and the world's second) **Hard Rock Cafe** (310-276-7605), with a pink Cadillac pulling a Thelma and Louise out of the roof (open Su-Th 11:30am-11pm, F-Sa 11:30am-midnight).

True shopaholics head to the mother of all malls, the **South Coast Plaza,** 3333 Bristol St., **Costa Mesa** (714-435-2000 or 800-782-8888), in Orange County. With 300 stores and a 1.6-acre garden path in the mall, the novice L.A. shopper will appreciate the free maps and inter-plaza shuttles. (Open M-F 10am-9pm, Sa 10am-7pm, Su 11am-6:30pm.)

NIGHTLIFE

L.A. clubs range from tiny danceterias and ephemeral warehouse raves to exclusive lounges catering to showbiz elite. In between is something for everyone else.

LATE-NIGHT RESTAURANTS

With the unreliability of clubs and the short shelf-life of cafes, late-night restaurants have become reliable hangouts. As the mainstay of L.A. nightlife, they're the best place to giggle at painfully trendy underage club kids trolling among celebs.

Mel's Drive In, 8585 Sunset Blvd., **West Hollywood** (310-854-7200). Phenomenal location and 1950s drive-up diner motif ensure that many celebrities have dined here. The original Mel's near San Francisco was in the movie *American Graffiti.* Play your part and order a cheeseburger, fries, and a vanilla milkshake (under $10); ask them to go easy on the vanilla syrup. Free valet parking. Open 24hr.

Jerry's Famous Deli has multiple locations, including **West Hollywood,** 8701 Beverly Blvd. (310-289-1811); **Westwood,** 10923 Weyburn Ave. (310-208-3354); and **Studio City,** 12655 Ventura Blvd. (818-980-4245). Note the menu's height—Jerry is rumored to have desired "the longest menu possible while still maintaining structural integrity." Regardless, the diner meets anyone's standards for a 4am snack. Matzoh ball soup $6; sandwiches $8-9. Public phones at every table are for calling cards only. Open 24hr.

Fred 62, 1850 N. Vermont Ave., **Los Feliz** (323-667-0062). "Eat now, dine later." Hep booth headrests evoke eating in a car. Green, aerodynamic (yet stationary) building. Eat a waffle ($4.62). All prices end in .62; other numbers figure strangely and inexplicably in the restaurant's workings. Pay attention as you dine. Open 24hr.

The Rainbow Grill, 9015 Sunset Blvd., **West Hollywood** (310-278-4232), next to the Roxy. Dark red vinyl booths cradle nearly every famous and would-have-you-believe-it-can-make-you-famous butt in L.A. Marilyn Monroe met husband Joe DiMaggio on a blind date here. Pizza ($6) and calamari. Cover charge you shell out goes toward your tab (cover Su-Th nights $5, F-Sa nights $10). Open M-F 11am-2am, Sa-Su 5pm-2am.

Canter's, 419 N. Fairfax Ave., **Fairfax** (213-651-2030). An L.A. institution, this deli has been the heart and soul of the historically Jewish Fairfax community since 1931. Incredible pastrami. Giant sandwiches $6-8. Visit the Kibbitz Room nightly for live rock, blues, jazz, and cabaret-pop (from 9:30pm). Cheap beer ($2) served until 2am. Open 24hr.

Barney's Beanery, 8447 Santa Monica Blvd., **Hollywood** (213-654-2287). L.A. at its best, but without the pretension. Over 600 items on the menu, 250 bottled beers, and 200 on tap—if they don't have it, you don't need it. Janis Joplin and Jim Morrison were regulars. Avoid (or target) very loud karaoke night M-W 9:30pm-1am. Happy Hour M-F 10am-6pm. Free valet parking. Open daily 10am-2am.

Izzy's Deli, 1433 Wilshire Blvd., **Santa Monica** (310-394-1131). Despite a low glitz factor, Izzy's proclaims itself the "deli of the stars" (although few under 40 will recognize many of the silver-haired celebs on the wall of fame). Yiddish spoken here. Delicious "overstuffed" sandwiches $6-9; matzoh ball soup $3-5. Open 24hr.

Sanamluang, 5176 Hollywood Blvd., **Hollywood** (323-660-8006). Barely tolerable strip-mall atmosphere doesn't change the fact that Sanamluang serves some of the best noodle dishes in town ($5). Open daily 10am-5am.

COFFEEHOUSES

In this city where no one eats very much for fear of rounding out that bony figure, espresso, coffee, and air are the only options. This is where you'll find the hip, younger crowd who don't earn enough to hit the restaurants. Bring a book and hide behind it while scooping out everyone else.

G.A.L.A.X.Y. Gallery, 7224 Melrose Ave., **Hollywood** (213-938-6500). Much more than just a coffee shop, this cool spacious store has art on display, a super-comfy couch for tired Melrose strollers, and an enormous bong and hookah display for all your tobacco needs. Acid jazz jams on some Sa nights tend to be standing room only. Cover $3. Hemp coffee $1.75. Open daily 11am-10pm. 18+.

Un Urban Coffeehouse, 3301 Pico Blvd., **Santa Monica** (310-315-0056). Lots of campy voodoo candles and Mexican wrestling masks. Iced mocha blends ($3.25) rival even Coffee Bean and Tea Leaf. $2 Italian sodas rock. Su nights are spoken-word and W nights are comedy, although there's some sort of entertainment almost every night. Regulars will teach you blackjack, if you're lucky. Open M-Th 6am-midnight, F-Sa 8am-1am, Su 8am-midnight.

Highland Grounds, 742 N. Highland Ave., **Hollywood** (323-466-1507). Nightly live shows (8pm) cover all grounds with folk singers, performance artists, and empowerment speakers. Outdoor patio with blazing fire. Full menu. Beer and wine. Lattes $1.50 before noon. Breakfast menu includes eclectic egg dishes like the Bulgarian omelette ($6). After 8pm, cover $2 and 1-drink min. Open M 9am-6pm, Tu-Th 9am-midnight, F-Sa 9am-1am, Su 10am-1am.

Wednesday's House, 2409 Main St., **Santa Monica** (310-452-4486). The Partridge Family on espresso. "Self-consciously" "hip" "Gen-X" crowd swaps sex stories and yoga tips.

Should you feel out of place, grab some "vintage" threads from clothing racks beside the coffee. Internet access. Tu is Go night (the board game), so...go. W open mic. Open M-F 8am-2am, Sa 10am-2am, Su noon-2pm. No credit cards.

Nova Express, 426 N. Fairfax Ave., **Fairfax** (213-658-7533). A psychedelic version of *Star Wars*'s Mos Eisley cantina. Wacky space-art by the owner. Sci-fi books and comics adorn shelves. Espresso $1.75. Pizza $2 per slice, or $11-22 for "Spiral Galaxy." DJ plays ambient music. Delivery until closing. Open daily 5pm-4am. Next door to late-night art gallery **Blitzstein Museum of Art** (open daily 8-11pm).

Bourgeois Pig, 5931 Franklin Ave., **Hollywood** (213-962-6366). The location is, literally, everything; drinks are only so-so, but revel in bourgeois goth—Ionic columns, antique chandeliers, and oddly, throbbing techno. *All* black except the purple felt pool table ($1 per game). "Death Drinks" ($2.25). Open daily 9am-2am. No credit cards.

WEHO Lounge, 8861 Santa Monica Blvd., **West Hollywood** (310-659-6180). The first-ever coffeehouse/AIDS info center. Plush sofas and lots of books. Next to main gay strip, so lots of club traffic. Many gay men, but all types chat it up in the outdoor patio. Free HIV testing M-Th 6-10pm. Internet access. Open daily 2pm-2am.

Anastasia's Asylum, 1028 Wilshire Blvd., **Santa Monica** (310-394-7113). Casual and intimate, with the candles to inspire a seance and the art to inspire a breakdown. Two levels, board games, and a full vegetarian menu. 3 bands per night, mostly folk or jazz; first show at 8pm. Open daily 6:30am-1am.

Equator, 22 Mills Alley, **Pasadena** (626-564-8656), off Colorado Blvd. Hollywood's cafe of choice attracts the self-consciously artsy. Earthy decor was a set for *Clueless, Party of Five, Beverly Hills 90210,* and *The Cable Guy.* Art gallery to boot. Specialty coffees $2.50-3.25, smoothies $3.75. Open Su-Th 9am-midnight, F-Sa 9am-1am.

Stir Crazy, 6917 Melrose Ave., **Hollywood** (213-934-4656). A cozy purist's crazy paradise. Crazy cappuccinos ($1) and lime rickeys ($1) served to the crazy sounds of Glenn Miller and Artie Shaw. Scads of crazy people on laptops pretending to work on their crazy screenplays. Open daily 9am-12:30am. No credit cards, crazy.

Legal Grind, 2640 Lincoln Blvd., **Santa Monica** (310-452-8160; www.legalgrind.com). Get legal advice from attorney *du jour* (consultation fee $20) as you sip coffee *du jour* (free with consultation, otherwise $1.25). Th 3-5pm is the big draw—entertainment law, copyrights, and contracts. Mini law library. Sandwiches $2-4. Call to confirm lawyer availability; no lawyers F. Open M-Th 7am-6pm, F 6:30am-midnight, Sa 8am-4pm.

Opus, 38 E. Colorado Blvd., **Pasadena** (626-685-2800). Entertain yourself while you sip your mocha ($3) at one of the many listening booths that showcase the latest CDs. Includes every genre from "Classical" to "Can't Deny the Funk." Open Su-Th 11am-11pm, F-Sa 11am-midnight.

BARS

While the 1996 film *Swingers* may not have transformed every bar into The 3 of Clubs, it has had a sadly homogenizing effect on L.A.'s hipsters. Well, grab your retro-70s polyester shirts, sunglasses, goatees, and throwback Cadillac convertibles, 'cause if you can't beat them, you have to swing with them, daddy. **Unless otherwise specified, bars in California are 21+.**

Miyagi's, 8225 Sunset Blvd. (323-656-0100), **Sunset Strip.** With 3 levels, 5 sushi bars, and 7 liquor bars, this Japanese-themed restaurant, bar, and lounge is the latest Strip hotspot. "Sake bomb, sake bomb, sake bomb," $4. Open daily 5:30pm-2am.

The 3 of Clubs, 1123 N. Vine St., **Hollywood** (323-462-6441). In a small strip mall beneath a "Bargain Clown Mart" sign, this simple, classy, spacious, hardwood bar is famous for appearing in 1996's *Swingers.* DJ W night and live bands Th. Order a grasshopper ($5) and risk appearing a naif. Open daily 9pm-2am.

The Room, 1626 Cahuenga St., **Hollywood** (213-462-7196). The very popular Room trumps The 3 of Clubs at this speakeasy that empties into an alley. This 30ish crowd comes looking for company. Open daily 9pm-2am.

Dublin's, 8240 Sunset Blvd., **Hollywood** (323-656-0100), on the Strip. Caters to a fratty white-hat crowd in football season, but off-nights fill up with everyone from young starlets to 60-year-old pool sharks. Upstairs dance floor; swanky upstairs dining room serves lunch, and dinner until 1am. Open M-F 11am-2am, Sa-Su 10am-2am.

Daddy's, 1610 N. Vine St., **Hollywood** (323-463-7777), between Hollywood and Sunset Blvd. Swanky bar sits between Cary Grant's star and Clark Gable's. Recently revamped, they've still got the least expensive jukebox in town. Sip your $5 drinks and $4 beers to the mellow stylings of Al Green. Open daily 9am-2am.

Liquid Kitty, 11780 W. Pico Blvd., **West L.A.** (310-473-3707). No one shows the vermouth to the gin quite like the bartenders here. $7 martini in one hand, cigar in the other, L.A.'s hippest come for cutting-edge DJs that spin techno, trance, and hip-hop Tu and Th; live blues, swing, and jazz Su. No cover. Open M-F 6pm-2am, Sa-Su 8pm-2am.

Skybar, 8440 Sunset Blvd. (323-848-6025), in the Mondrian Hotel on **Sunset Strip.** A bit more upscale than the rest of the Strip set, this crowd is mostly Hollywood execs and show-bizzers. Top 40 and dancing. No cover. Open daily 11am-2am. Reservations required after 8pm.

Jones, 7205 Santa Monica Blvd., **Hollywood** (213-850-1726). Although it aims for a down-home feel with bandana-print couches, a hip young Hollywood set brings the glam factor way up. Not much hanging out room, lots of sitting. Full dinner menu. Open M-F noon-2am, Sa-Su 7pm-2am. 18 to enter. 21+ to drink.

Formosa Cafe, 7156 Santa Monica Blvd., **Hollywood** (323-850-9050). Come for the ambience—mellow and smoky atmosphere earned it several scenes in 1998's *L.A. Confidential.* Rooftop bar lets you valet-watch to see who drives what. Very relaxed crowd. Full Chinese dinner menu. No cover. Open M-F 4pm-2am, Sa-Su 6pm-2am.

The Coach and Horses, 7617 Sunset Blvd., **Hollywood** (323-876-6900). Former speakeasy turned pub dive. Very local crowd. Young hipsters come here to drown post-audition sorrows. Alfred Hitchcock was once a regular. Beers $3, vertigo $3.50. Open daily noon-2am. No credit cards.

The Lava Lounge, 1533 N. La Brea Ave., **Hollywood** (213-876-6612). Fun bar with outdoor motif; lots of surf rock and Pacific Island sounds. Sip a Blue Hawaiian ($7) under a twinkling star ceiling. Entertainment from 10pm. Cover $2-5. Open daily 9pm-2am.

Maloney's, 1000 Gayley Ave., **Westwood Village** (310-208-1942). This UCLA *Cheers*-style hangout is a favorite among the Bruins because of its proximity to campus, and for the Su 2-for-1 draft beers and shots special. Full lunch and dinner menu. Open daily 11:30am-2am.

COMEDY CLUBS

The talent may be imported from New York, but it doesn't change the fact that L.A.'s comedy clubs are the best in the world (unless you chance upon an amateur night, which is generally a painful, painful experience). Although prices are steep, it's worth the setback to catch the newest and wackiest comedians, guffaw as famous veterans hone new material, or preside over the latest trends in stand-up comedy competitions. Call ahead to check age restrictions. Weekday cover charges are cheaper, when the clubs are less crowded, but just as drunk.

The Improvisation, 8162 Melrose Ave., **West Hollywood** (213-651-2583). L.A.'s best talent—Robin Williams and Jerry Seinfeld have shown their faces. Jay Mohr and Damon Wayans come when they feel like it and join the show. Italian restaurant (entrees from $6). Shows M-Th 8pm, F-Sa 8:30 and 10:30pm, Su 8pm. Cover $8-11. Bar open daily until 1:30am. 2-drink min. Reservations recommended. 18+, or 16+ with parent.

Groundling Theater, 7307 Melrose Ave., **Hollywood** (323-934-9700). The best improv and comedy "forum" in town—alums include Pee Wee Herman and many *Saturday Night Live* regulars including Julia Sweeney, Will Farrell, Cheri Oteri, and Chris Kattan. Don't be surprised to see *SNL* producer Lorne Michaels sitting in the back row. Lisa Kudrow (of *Friends* fame) got her start here, too. Polished skits most nights; improv-only Th. Shows Th 8pm, F-Sa 8 and 10pm, Su 7:30pm. All ages. Cover $10-17.50.

Comedy Store, 8433 Sunset Blvd., **West Hollywood** (323-656-6225). The shopping mall of comedy clubs: 3 rooms each feature a different type of comedy (and separate cover charges). Main Room has big names (and prices–$10-15). Original Room features mid-range comics ($8-10). Belly Room has real grab-bag material (under $5). 2-drink min., drinks from $4.50. Open daily until 2am. Reserve up to a week in advance.

The Laugh Factory, 8001 Sunset Blvd., **West Hollywood** (323-656-1336). Comedy for 2000 with young, scene-breaking talent–you can say you saw them first. Tu is open-mic night for the first 20 people in line at 6pm. Nightly showcases M-Th 8pm and F-Su 8 and 10pm. Cover Su-Th $8, F-Sa $10; 2-drink min. 21+.

The Ice House, 24 N. Mentor Ave., **Pasadena** (626-577-1894). The 30-year-old granddaddy of clubs, its alums pop in for the occasional visit. Seats 200. Multiple nightly shows. Cover $8.50-12.50; 2-drink min. Reservations recommended. 21+.

HBO Workspace, 733 N. Seward St., **Hollywood** (323-993-6099). Experimental workspace for cutting-edge comedians, especially female acts. It's a risk, but it's also free. Shows at 7:30pm; call for dates. Reservations recommended. 21+.

CLUBS

L.A. is famous for its club scene. With the highest number of bands per capita in the world, most clubs are able to book top-notch acts night after night. The distinction between music and dance clubs is a bit sketchy in L.A.—most music clubs have DJs a few times a week, and vice versa. Many clubs are simply host spaces for managements that change nightly; these clubs can be L.A.'s hottest thing one month, and non-existent the next. Before their listings, *L.A. Weekly* prints, "Due to the erratic lives of L.A. musicians and the capricious personalities of booking agents, all of the following are subject to change for no apparent reason."

L.A. clubs are often expensive, but many are still feasible for budgeters. Coupons in *L.A. Weekly* (see **Publications,** p. 361) and handed out in bushels inside the clubs, can save you a bundle. To enter the club scene, it's best to be at least 21—the next-best option is to be a beautiful woman. Nevertheless, if you're over 18, you can still find a space to dance, but it may mean a hefty cover charge in a less desirable venue. **All clubs are 21+ unless otherwise noted.**

The Derby, 4500 Los Feliz Blvd., **Hollywood** (213-663-8979). The kings of swing reign once again in this swanky velvet joint. Ladies, grab your snoods–many dress the 1940s part. Free swing lessons Su-F 8pm. The menu is from Louise's Trattoria (choice Italian fare) next door. Full bar. Big band music nightly (Big Bad Voodoo Daddy once played here). Happy Hour daily 4-7pm. Cover $5-7. Open daily 5pm-2am.

Largo, 432 N. Fairfax Ave., **West Hollywood** (323-852-1073). Elegant sit-down audience and captivated listeners ensure intimate performances by some of L.A.'s most interesting entertainers. Cover $2-12. Open M-Sa 9pm-2am.

Luna Park, 665 N. Robertson Blvd., **West Hollywood** (310-652-0611). Named for an ill-fated Coney Island venture, this club is home to many a record/CD release party and an eclectic, ultra-hip crowd. Live funk, jazz, and rock nightly; Th club DJ. Supper club, full bar, outdoor patio, trancy dance floor. New Music Mondays land L.A.'s best improvisational talent. Cover $3-10, big-name acts $20. Open daily until 2am.

Key Club, 9039 Sunset Blvd., **Sunset Strip** (310-274-5800). A colossal, crowded multimedia experience complete with black lights, neon, and a frenetic dance floor. Stage show extravaganzas. Live acts and DJ productions, depending on the night. Tequila library on the first floor. M-Th cover $6. F-Sa 21+; cover $20. Open daily 8pm-2am.

Martini Lounge, 5657 Melrose Ave., **Hollywood** (323-467-4068). Usually more mingling than dancing. Cigars $6-10. Music from R&B to indie. Cover $5-10. Shows at 9:30pm. Open daily until 2am. Free parking at the Chevron station across the street.

Arena, 6655 Santa Monica Blvd., **Hollywood** (323-462-0714). 22,000 sq. ft. floor lends itself to frenzied techno, house, and Latin beats. Sa killer drag shows. Dance! Dance! Dance! Th 18+, F all ages, Sa-Su 21+. Cover $10-12. Open Th 9pm-2am, F 9pm-4am, Sa 9pm-3am, Su 9pm-2am.

Roxy, 9009 Sunset Blvd., **Sunset Strip** (310-276-2222). Known as the "Sizzling Showcase," it's one of the best-known Sunset Strip clubs. Live rock, blues, alternative, and occasional hip-hop. Many big tour acts. All ages. Cover varies. Opens at 8pm. Buy tickets at the door or call Ticketmaster (213-480-3232).

Whisky A Go-Go, 8901 Sunset Blvd., **West Hollywood** (310-652-4205). The great prophet of L.A.'s music history. Hosted progressive bands in the late 1970s and early 80s, and was big into the punk explosion. No techno, only 5-6 live bands playing nightly from 8pm-2am. Hard rock/alternative. Two full bars. Cover M-Th $10, F-Su $12-15. All ages.

Dragonfly, 6510 Santa Monica Blvd., **Hollywood** (323-466-6111). The young, multi-pierced crowd isn't afraid to dance to the groove, hard funk, and rock played nightly—if there's enough room to boom. Lounge, patio, and "trance garden" offer space to breathe. F-Sa are official "dance nights," but hell, every night's a dance night. Cover $7-10. Open daily 9pm-2am.

The Viper Room, 8852 Sunset Blvd., **Sunset Strip** (310-358-1880). For those on a River Phoenix pilgrimage, this Johnny Depp-owned spot is a must-see. For everyone else, the crowd of aging hipsters and retired frat boys make this one of the Strip's less interesting spots. If you must go, hide in the neo-rummage chic lounge downstairs or indulge in the live music upstairs. DJ follows live music. Cover $15. Open daily until 2am.

Playroom, 836 N. Highland Ave. (323-460-6630), **Hollywood.** Rumor has it that titanic stars frequent this purple play-place. 5 rooms and 2 bars, with pop tunes; call for schedule. Cover varies. Open W-Sa, 10pm-3am.

The Opium Den, 1608 Cosmo St., **Hollywood** (323-466-7800). Hip club with cursory references to Buddhism draws a very young crowd eager to dance with and bump into one another. Cover $5. Open daily until 2am.

GAY AND LESBIAN NIGHTLIFE

While the Sunset Strip features all the nightlife any Jack and Jill could desire, gay men and lesbians may find life more interesting a short tumble down the hill on **Santa Monica Boulevard.** Still, many ostensibly straight clubs have gay nights; check *L.A. Weekly* for listings or contact the Gay and Lesbian Community Services Center (see **Practical Information,** p. 358). Free weekly magazine *fab!* lists happenings in the gay and lesbian community. **Motherload,** 8499 Santa Monica Blvd. (310-659-9700), and **Trunks,** 8809 Santa Monica Blvd. (310-652-1015), are two of the friendliest and most popular bars. Neither has a cover and both are open until 2am. **All clubs are 21+ unless otherwise noted.**

Micky's, 8857 Santa Monica Blvd., **West Hollywood** (310-657-1176). Large, popular wetspot filled with delectable men of all ages. Music is mostly Top 40 dance. Serves lunch daily noon-4pm and hot go-go boys Tu-F and Su. Male porno stars come to visit Th 6-8pm. Weekend Beer Bust 4-9pm. Cover $3-20. Open daily noon-2am.

Rage, 8911 Santa Monica Blvd., **West Hollywood** (310-652-7055). Its glory days have passed, but this enormous institution rages on with nightly DJs, drag nights, and disco 'til you drop. Mostly gay men. M alternative music night, Tu 80s spectacular. Cover varies and is higher on F, the big dance night ($5-7, includes 1 drink). Full lunch and dinner menu served noon-9pm. Open Sa-Th 11:30am-2am, F 11:30am-4am.

El Rey, 5515 Wilshire Blvd., **Miracle Mile** (323-936-6400). This palatial Art-Deco establishment is a venue for an assortment of clubs, ranging from 70s glam to trashy drag shows. F is gal's bar, **Hotbox.** Many Sa gay nights. Call for schedule. Cover $10. Open F-Su, 9pm-2am. 18+.

Circus, 6655 Santa Monica Blvd., **Hollywood** (323-462-1291). Gay disco with house, salsa, techno, disco, and hip-hop nights. Boy bar hosts a drag show Tu 11:30pm. Call for schedule. Full bar; valet parking. Cover $5-15. Open nightly 9pm-2am, Sa until 3am.

7969, 7969 Santa Monica Blvd., **West Hollywood** (323-654-0280). Sometimes a strip club, sometimes a drag or S&M show. Dancing, fetish gear, and rubber anything—not for the faint of heart. Call for the crazy schedule. Most nights feature a mixed gay and lesbian crowd. Cover $6-10. Open daily 10pm-2am.

The Palms, 8572 Santa Monica Blvd. (310-652-6188), **West Hollywood's** oldest women's bar. Pool room and full bar with lots of drink specials. DJ W-Su; music ranges from house to disco to salsa. Men are welcome, but may feel very alone. W 9pm-midnight $1 drinks. Su Beer Bust and BBQ $6. Open daily 2pm-2am.

Stonewall Cafe, 8717 Santa Monica Blvd., **West Hollywood** (310-659-8009). Happening gay coffeehouse caters to everybody. Vanilla latte ($3.15) is phenomenal. Th at 8pm is bingo night, as transvestite Bel Air, along with celebrity guests, calls letters and distributes clever prizes to a fun-loving, young crowd. Happy Hour daily 7-9am and 4-7pm (espresso and all blends $2). Open Su-Th 7am-midnight, F-Sa 7am-1am.

EXTREME! SPORTS

Perris Valley Skydiving, 2091 Goetz Rd., **Perris Valley** (800-832-8818), near Riverside. Take I-10 East to Rte. 605 South to Rte. 60 East to Rte. 215 South (1¾hr.). Not the most budget-savvy activity, but this is the place to fulfill that urge to leap 12,500ft. and experience the thrill of a lifetime. Accommodates experienced jumpers and 1st-timers, who jump with a skydiving instructor strapped (tightly!) to their backs. 50-second free-fall, then enjoy a 4min. descent overlooking the Pacific, L.A., and San Diego. Dives $160-299. Group discounts. Reservations recommended.

Hollywood Star Lanes, 5227 Santa Monica Blvd., **Hollywood** (213-665-4111). The site of several scenes from 1998's *The Big Lebowski,* locals call it "the best thing to do after 2am besides...sleep." Cool shoes, as always (mandatory rental $1.50). Games $2.50 per person. Tu 10am-2pm 3 games $5, 9pm-2am 3 games $6. Open 24hr. Extreme!

SEASONAL EVENTS

Tournament of Roses Parade and Rose Bowl (626-449-7673), Jan. 1, Pasadena. New Year's Day is always a perfect day in Southern California. Some of the wildest New Year's Eve parties happen along Colorado Blvd., the parade route. If you miss the parade, which runs 8-10am, you can still see the floats up close on display that afternoon and on Jan. 2 at the intersection of Paloma and Sierra Madre ($1). The champions of the Pac 10 and Big 10 football conferences meet that afternoon for the rowdy Rose Bowl Game. Only a few end zone tickets are available to the public; call 626-449-4100 after Nov. 1.

Chinese New Year (213-617-0396), late Feb., Chinatown. Fireworks and dragons.

Grunion runs occur throughout spring and summer. This late-night pastime appeals to those who want to watch slippery, silver fish squirm onto the beaches (especially San Pedro) to mate. The fish can be caught by hand, but a license is required for those over 16. Free programs on the Grunion run given Mar.-July at the Cabrillo Marine Museum in San Pedro (310-548-7562). Obtain licenses from the Fish and Game Department, 330 Golden Shore (562-590-5132), in Long Beach, for $15.75; they're valid until Dec. 31 each year. One-day license $6.60. Grunion fishing prohibited May-June.

Renaissance Pleasure Faire (800-52-FAIRE/523-2473), from the daffodil's first blossom to the day of the shortest night (weekends, late Apr. to mid-June) in the Glen Helen Regional Park in San Bernardino. The name is quite arousing, but save the occasional kissing bridge, it's a pretty tame scene. From the haven angelic (L.A.), gallop apace on fiery-footed steeds (drive) to Phoebus' lodging (east) along I-10 to I-15 North and look for signs as you draw near the site of happy reveling (city of Devore). Garbed in their best Elizabethan finery, San Bernardino teens are versed in the bard's phrases before working. Open Sa-Su 10am-6pm. $17.50, students and seniors $15, children $7.50.

Cinco de Mayo (213-625-5045), May 5, especially downtown at Olvera St. Huge celebrations mark the day the Mexicans drop-kicked France's ass out of Mexico.

UCLA Mardi Gras (310-825-8001), mid-May, at the athletic field. Billed as the world's largest collegiate activity (a terrifying thought). Festivities run from 7pm-2am. Proceeds benefit charity.

UCLA Jazz and Reggae Festival (310-825-6564), Memorial Day weekend in late May, at the intramural field. Free concerts, a cultural marketplace, and food.

Summer Nights at the California Plaza (213-621-1741), Th nights from June-September, California Plaza, 250 Grand Ave., downtown. Concert festival features hot summer nights, dance, music, theater, circuses, and gallery showing in the Museum of Contemporary Art. Free admission. Beer and wine sold. Parking $4.40 after 5pm.

Playboy Jazz Festival (310-449-4070), June 12-13, Hollywood Bowl. 2 days of entertainment by top-name jazz musicians of all varieties, from traditional to fusion. No bunnies. Call Ticketmaster (213-381-2000) for prices.

Gay Pride Weekend (213-860-0701), last or second-to-last weekend in June, Pacific Design Center, 8687 Melrose Ave., West Hollywood. L.A.'s lesbian and gay communities celebrate in full effect. Art, politics, dances, and a big parade. Tickets $12.

Celebration USA (626-577-3100), July 4, Rose Bowl, Pasadena. Fireworks and fun. Call for prices. Many different levels of seating available.

Shakespeare Festival/LA (213-489-1121), July-Aug., Hollywood, downtown, Palos Verdes, and Pasadena. This theater company aims to make Shakespeare accessible to all. Canned food donation accepted in lieu of admission at performances within the city of L.A.; $12.50 otherwise.

Dio des los Muertes, Halloween (Oct. 30), along Olvera St., downtown. Rousing celebration of All Saint's Day with food, vendors, costumes, and Halloween accoutrements.

Pasadena Doo Dah Parade (626-449-3689), Nov. Pasadena's other parade—known for its own wackiness, like the Briefcase Brigade.

Los Posados (213-485-9777), Dec. 16-24, along Olvera St., downtown. This celebration includes a candlelight procession and the breaking of a piñata.

Whale watching is best Dec.-Mar., as the Pacific Grays migrate south. For the past few years, 90% of the world's blue whale population has summered off the Channel Islands (see **Channel Islands,** p. 241). Boats depart from Ventura, Long Beach, and San Pedro to witness the migration. Call any of the state beaches.

AROUND LOS ANGELES

Once you leave the city limits of Los Angeles (or some might even argue the Westside) the glam-factor drops considerably. The cities and neighborhoods in Southern L.A. and Orange Counties are a little hotter, and a lot less cool. But while they lack the glitz of L.A. proper, they more than compensate for it with their beauty, especially along the coast. In fact, some of the most awe-inspiring spots in all of the L.A. area lie south of the city in the hills of Palos Verdes, 22 miles west in the waters of Santa Catalina Island, on the trails of the northern Santa Monica National Recreation Area, and all along the beaches of the South Bay. And if the verdant rolling hills in yuppified Orange County don't cause you to burst out in song, the legendary merriment of Disneyland just might do the trick.

SOUTHERN L.A. COUNTY

Head to L.A. County's southern communities for the most precious of Southern Californian souvenirs—a tan. Easily accessible by public transportation, or a 30-minute hop down the San Diego Freeway (Interstate 405), these stereotypically beachy towns are more casual and less congested than the massive metropolis looming to the north. South Bay provides a haven for surfers, beach volleyball players, and sun worshippers, and the sandy campsites and snorkeling spots off

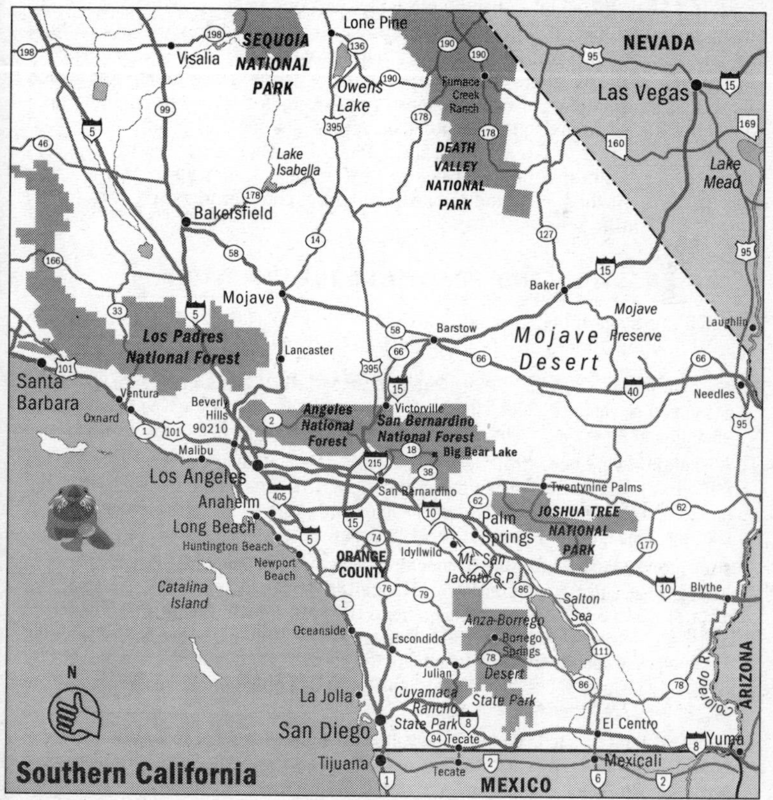

Catalina Island are the closest it gets to a local tropical paradise. Although Long Beach's urban sprawl overshadows its stretch of shoreline, the city fosters a growing nightlife and shopping scene underneath the industrial facade.

HIGHLIGHTS OF L.A. AND ORANGE COUNTIES

■ **South Bay** (p. 410) hosts beach communities both relaxed and LOUD, including the South Coast Botanic Gardens, the Lloyd Wright-designed Wayfarers' Chapel, and free whale watching.

■ **Long Beach** (p. 413) is home to heavy industry, a great music scene, and the Long Beach Aquarium of the Pacific (p. 415).

■ Once owned by the Wrigley family, of gum fame, **Catalina Island** (p. 416) contains some of the most beautiful land in the L.A. area, making for great hiking and snorkeling.

■ Anaheim hosts such family fun centers as **Disneyland** (p. 421), **Knott's Berry Farm** (p. 423), the **Richard M. Nixon Library and Birthplace** (p. 424), and the **Crystal Cathedral** (p. 424), home of the religious TV show *Hour of Power*.

■ The **beach communities** of Orange County (p. 424) are home to the South Coast Plaza (the largest mall in California), as well as killer surfing and a fun sand scene.

■ The **Angeles National Forest** (p. 428), **Big Bear Mountain** (p. 430), and the **San Gorgonio Wilderness** (p. 434) offer excellent hiking above the smog of L.A. as well as mountain biking and skiing.

SOUTH BAY

South Bay life is beach life. All activity revolves around the sand, and a cloudy sky is reason enough not to get up in the morning. **Hermosa Beach** wins both bathing suit and congeniality competitions. Its slammin' volleyball scene, gnarly waves, and killer boardwalk make this the *überbeach*. The mellower **Manhattan Beach** exudes a yuppified charm, while **Redondo Beach** is by far the most commercially suburban. Richie Rich-esque **Rancho Palos Verdes** is a coast of a different breed. From early morning to late evening, these famed sandboxes are overrun by gaggles of eager skaters, volleyball players, surfers, and sunbathers. At night, the crowds move off the beach and toward Manhattan and Hermosa Avenues for an affordable nightlife scene.

ORIENTATION AND PRACTICAL INFORMATION

To reach this strip of beaches, take the San Diego Fwy. (I-405) and follow signs to your destination, or hop on Rte. 1 South from Los Angeles.

Buses: Greyhound (800-231-2222). **Public Transportation:** Bus #443 leaves L.A. Union Station for N. Torrance, Redondo Beach, and Palos Verdes. #444 leaves Union Station as well, and serves W. Torrance, Rolling Hills Estates, and Rancho Palos Verdes.

Car Rental: Robin Hood, 1209 N. Sepulveda Blvd., Manhattan Beach (800-743-2992 or 546-8977). Will beat other companies' prices by 15%. Credit card required. Unlimited mi. within L.A. County from $27; out-of-county $40. Ages 18-21 must have proof of liability insurance; under 25 surcharge $10 per day. Open M-F 7am-6pm, Sa 8am-5pm.

Visitor Information: South Bay Community Pages (www.commpages.com) has links to each city's events and entertainment. **Manhattan Beach:** Chamber of Commerce, 425 15th St. (545-5313). Open M-F 9am-5pm. **Hermosa Beach:** Chamber of Commerce and Visitor Information Center, 1007 Hermosa Ave. (376-0951). Open M-Th 9am-5pm, F 9am-4pm. **Redondo Beach:** Chamber of Commerce, 200 N. Pacific Coast Hwy. (310-376-6911). Open M-F 8:30am-5pm. **San Pedro:** Chamber of Commerce, 390 W. 7th St. (832-7272). Open M-F 9am-5pm.

Equipment Rental: Each community has at least a few stores that rent bikes ($5-7 per hr.), in-line skates ($5-6 per hr.), and surfboards ($6-7 per hr.). Some also rent volleyballs, boogie boards, umbrellas, and beach chairs. **Team Paradise,** 920 Manhattan

Ave., Manhattan Beach (714-841-3434; open daily in summer 10am-8pm, in winter 10am-8pm); **Jeffers Rentals,** 39 14th St., Hermosa Beach (372-9492; open daily 9am-7pm); **Marina Rentals,** 505 N. Harbor Dr., Redondo Beach (318-2453).

Weather and Surf Conditions: 379-8471.

Medical Services: South Bay Free Clinic, 1807 Manhattan Beach Blvd., Manhattan Beach (318-2521, appointment desk 376-0791). Hours vary. **Beach Cities Ambulatory Center,** 514 N. Prospect Ave., Redondo Beach (376-9474).

Emergency: 911. **Police: Redondo Beach,** 401 Diamond St. (379-2477); **San Pedro,** 2175 Gibson Blvd. (548-7605).

Post Offices: Redondo Beach, 1201 N. Catalina Ave. Open M-F 8:30am-5pm, Sa 8:30am-12:30pm. **ZIP Code:** 90277. **San Pedro,** 839 S. Beacon St. Open M-F 8:30am-5pm, Sa 9am-noon. **ZIP Code:** 90731.

AREA CODE	The area code in South Bay is 310, unless otherwise noted.

ACCOMMODATIONS

South Bay harbors two of L.A.'s finest hostels. The one in San Pedro may make you want to take up *tai chi,* while the one in Hermosa Beach has a hot social scene. There are no campsites near this area.

Los Angeles South Bay (HI-AYH), 3601 S. Gaffey St., Bldg. #613, **San Pedro** (831-8109), in Angels Gate Park (entrance by 36th St.). From L.A. airport transfer terminal, take Metro green line to Harbor Fwy. to catch bus #446 (runs during rush hours only). Bus schedules and travel books available at desk. Kitchen, TV room, volleyball courts. Linen $2 (no sleeping bags allowed). Laundry. 7-night max. stay. Parking included. Reception in summer 7am-midnight; in winter 7-11am and 4pm-midnight. 16-bed dorms $12; semi-private rooms with 2-3 beds $13.50; private rooms $29.50. Non-members $3 extra.

Los Angeles Surf City Hostel, 26 Pier Ave., **Hermosa Beach** (798-2323), a half-block from beach. Free airport pickup, $5 drop-off. Take bus #439 to 11th and Hermosa St., walk 2 blocks north, and make a left on Pier Ave. Adorned with hand-painted murals—paint one and stay for free. Young, international clientele. Discount car rentals, showers, Internet access, kitchen, keg bashes, and TV lounge. Includes boogie boards, breakfast, and linen. Laundry. Key deposit $10. 28-night max. stay. No parking. Check-out 11am. 4-6 bunk dorms May-Nov. $17, Dec.-Apr. $15; private rooms $45. Reservations recommended. **International passport or proof of travel required.**

Moon Lite Inn, 625 S. Pacific Coast Hwy., **Redondo Beach** (540-4058), 2 blocks from ocean. Newly renovated rooms, all the amenities: HBO, A/C, fridge, microwave, phone. Parking included. Singles $40; doubles $45; rooms with beautiful marble jacuzzis $75.

FOOD AND NIGHTLIFE

Most South Bay communities are slightly upscale versions of die-hard beach towns. Prices are a bit elevated, but so is quality. Keep in mind that there are over 50 bars around the **Hermosa Beach Pier,** particularly along Hermosa Ave.

The Kettle, 1138 N. Highland Ave., **Manhattan Beach** (545-8511). The food is great and plentiful in this country kitchen, and come nightfall, surfers invade. Dude, it's the only 24hr. spot around. Sandwiches and salads $7. "Hangover" omelette $6.75. Beer and wine served until midnight. Open 24hr.

Wahoo's Fish Taco, 1129 Manhattan Ave., **Manhattan Beach** (796-1044). Wahoo's offers any 2 tacos or enchiladas for only $5. Get it with fish, chicken, or whatever *tu quieres.* It's close to the sand, cheap, and the brew of the month is only $1.25. Burrito $3.70. Open M-Sa 11am-10pm, Su 11am-9pm.

Lighthouse Cafe, 30 Pier Ave., **Hermosa Beach** (372-6111), in Pier Plaza. Frequented by bronzed local volleyball players, this cool dance club features nightly music ranging from dance to blues. Reasonably priced munchies. Happy Hour pizza $1.75. Su jazz brunch. Open M-Th 5:30pm-2am, F 3:30pm-2am, Sa 11am-2am, Su 9am-2am.

Good Stuff, 1286 The Strand, **Hermosa Beach** (374-2334), at 13th St. The name is an understatement. The fresh, healthy food is great, and the view of the ocean is phenomenal. Burgers $4.75-7; salads $5-7.25. Open daily 7am-9pm.

The Spot, 110 2nd St., **Hermosa Beach** (376-2355). The L.A. area's oldest vegetarian restaurant, still a favorite of the resident New Age population. Fake-grass floors, wooden chairs, and a fat-free and non-dairy-based menu. Tempting tempeh, tofu, and tahini. "Inflation buster" combos under $6. Open daily 11am-10pm.

Cafe Boogaloo, 1238 Hermosa Ave., **Hermosa Beach** (318-2324). Blues, R&B, and California cuisine with Louisiana soul. Full bar with 27 microbrews on tap ($3). Nightly shows begin around 8pm, weekends 9pm. Cover Th-Sa $5-15. Dinner 5-11pm (from $10). Open M-F 4pm-1am, Sa-Su 11am-2am.

Yesterday's Coffeehouse and Bookstore, 126 N. Catalina Ave., **Redondo Beach** (318-2499). Hard-core indoor lounging spot with couches, chessboards, and books to browse or buy. Coffee ($1.50-2.50), teas ($2), and a few baked goods. Open M-Th 6am-10:30pm, F-Sa 6am-midnight, Su 7am-10:30pm.

Sacred Grounds Coffeehouse and Art Gallery, 399 W. 6th St., **San Pedro** (514-0800). Eclectic furniture, coffee, and nifty bottled sodas. Poetry M, open mic W, various live music Th-Su. Cover $2-5; Su free. Open M-Th 7am-midnight, F 7am-1am, Sa 8am-1am, Su 8am-10pm. No credit cards.

SIGHTS

MANHATTAN, HERMOSA, AND REDONDO BEACHES

About 20 miles south of downtown L.A., the **Pacific Coast Highway** (Rte. 1) swings by the sand at **Manhattan Beach** and continues through **Hermosa Beach,** which tops the list of urban beaches in L.A. County. The sort of community spirit found in Venice prevails, although in a more upscale version. Parking meters are closely monitored (25¢ for 30min.; 3hr. limit), so get there early and often.

Manhattan Beach's main drag, **Manhattan Avenue,** is lined with charming but overpriced cafes and shops. At the end of the Manhattan Beach Pier, a fishing plank with a mean view of the shore, the **Roundhouse Marine Studies Lab** (379-8117), has a shark aquarium and tide pool touch tanks (open M-F 3pm-dusk, Sa-Su 10am-dusk; free). Manhattan is the place for a serious game of **beach volleyball,** which was born on these sands in the late 1970s. The courts at **Marine Avenue** (along with those at the state beach in Pacific Palisades) are the elite training grounds for young players. The **Manhattan Beach Open** (late July), is the oldest professional beach volleyball tournament in the world, while the **Hermosa Beach Open** (late Aug.) awards the most prize money. Call the Hermosa Beach Chamber of Commerce (see **Visitor Information,** p. 410) for schedules.

In Hermosa Beach, **Pier Plaza,** at the end of Pier Ave. between Hermosa Ave. and the beach, is the center of the beach scene. Recently closed off, South Bay's best bars, cafes, and surfer boutiques sit in a small, car-free promenade. **The Strand** is a boardwalk/bike path that runs along Manhattan Ave. south from Manhattan Beach to and through Hermosa, where it becomes a blur of bikers and skaters. In August, the **International Surf Festival** (305-9546), takes over Manhattan Beach with lifeguarding contests and sand castle competitions. Anyone can enter the competitions for a fee. A few blocks away (a hefty walk) is the **Either/Or Bookstore,** 950-D Aviation Blvd. (374-2060), which epitomizes Hermosa, with both a water sports section and a "Metaphysics Room" with shelves on Zen, the occult, and UFOs (open M-F 9am-9pm, Sa-Su 8am-10pm).

Redondo Beach is the next town down the coast. It's a little farther south and a little less upscale than its northern neighbors. The main attractions are the pier, boardwalk, and marina complex. The adjacent **King Harbor** shelters thousands of pleasure boats and hosts some excellent sport fishing. The **Monstad Pier** supports a small assortment of restaurants, bars, clubs, and the local fishing community. **Exercise caution at night.**

PALOS VERDES

For a dose of Southern California's floral paradise, head to **South Coast Botanic Gardens,** 26300 Crenshaw Blvd. (544-6815), in Rancho Palos Verdes. This former county landfill has metamorphosed into an 87-acre garden, where over 75% of the plants are drought-resistant—practical *and* pretty. On weekends, there's a tram ($1.50) to cart you around. (Romp in the roses daily 9am-5pm. Admission $5, students and seniors $3, under 13 free; free 3rd Tu of each month.)

Whale watch for free (Dec.-Apr.) from the gardens of the **Point Vicente Interpretive Center,** 31501 S. Palos Verdes Dr. (377-5370), a small museum with neat exhibits on gray whales (open daily in summer 10am-7pm, off-season 10am-5pm; admission $2; seniors, disabled, and children $1; free tours). The Point Vicente **lighthouse** supposedly houses the ghost of a woman whose lover died in a shipwreck here (free). Two miles down the road is the all-glass **Wayfarer's Chapel,** 5755 S. Palos Verdes Dr. (377-1650). The chapel was designed by Frank Lloyd Wright's son, **Lloyd Wright.** Like his father, Wright stunningly combines architecture with the nature surrounding it. (Open daily 9am-5pm, but closes for weddings and services.)

SAN PEDRO

Still water, tidepools, and a nearby harbor draw many families to **Cabrillo Beach** farther south (beach parking $6.50; free parking in surrounding neighborhood). The **Cabrillo Marine Museum,** 3720 Stephen White Dr. (548-7562), presents touch tanks, marine history exhibits, and a rather disturbing view of pickled squid and whale skeletons (open Tu-F noon-5pm, Sa-Su 10am-5pm; free; call about early summer **grunion runs,** $1 per person).

Cafes and antique shops line **6th Street.** The **Fort MacArthur Military Museum,** 3601 Gaffey St. (548-7705), is a nearly intact coastal fortification (open Sa-Su noon-5pm; free). At the end of Gaffey St. is the beautiful **Korean Friendship Bell,** in **Angels Gate Park,** a nice daytime picnic spot, but *not* the place for a stroll come dusk. The bell was featured in a memorable scene in 1995's *The Usual Suspects* and a less memorable scene in a Kudos candy bar commercial.

LONG BEACH

Long Beach (pop. 430,000), as its Chamber of Commerce proudly proclaims, is "the #1 container shipping port in the world," and nothing could be more evident to the first-time visitor. The breakwater created by the massive shipping harbor means only tiny waves. But the beaches *are* pristine and the thriving entertainment district helps make up for the inescapable views of 10-story loading cranes, diesel trucks, and container barges.

ORIENTATION AND PRACTICAL INFORMATION

Long Beach is 24 miles south of downtown L.A. and just down the coast from South Bay. To reach Long Beach from downtown L.A. by public transit, take the Metro blue or green line from the L.A. airport. Bus #232 runs from the airport to Long Beach (fare $1.35). By car, take Harbor Fwy. (I-110) south to the San Diego Fwy. (I-405). Exit at Long Beach Fwy. (I-710), which runs south to Long Beach. **Exercise caution in inland areas of Long Beach.**

Buses: Greyhound, 464 W. 3rd St. (432-1842 or 800-231-2222), at Magnolia St. To: **L.A.** ($8); **San Diego** ($13); and **San Francisco** ($36). Open daily 5:30am-8:30pm.

Public Transportation: Long Beach Transit (LBT), 1963 E. Anaheim St. (591-2301), runs 37 bus routes. Most buses stop downtown at the **Transit Mall,** on 1st St. between Pacific Ave. and Long Beach Blvd. High-tech bus shelters have route maps and video screens with bus info. Fare 90¢, students 75¢, seniors 45¢, transfers 10-35¢. **Long Beach Passport,** 1963 E. Anaheim St. (591-2301), is a separate division of the LBT, with service along Ocean Blvd. and Pine Ave., as well as to the Queen Mary (free). One route runs from downtown to Belmont Shores (fare 90¢).

Car Rental: Budget, 249 E. Ocean Blvd. (495-0407), and at Long Beach Airport (421-0143). Cars with unlimited mi. $36 per day. Must be 21 with major credit card. Under 25 surcharge $20 per day. Open daily 6am-10pm.

Bike Rental: Bikestation (436-2453), at 1st St. and the Promenade, downtown. Bikes $7 per hr., $25 per day. Open M-F 6am-7pm, Sa-Su 9am-6pm.

Equipment Rental: Long Beach Windsurf Center, 3850 E. Ocean Blvd. (433-1014). In-line skates ($8 per hr., $20 per day), as well as kayaks, sailboards, and wetsuits. Open M-Sa 10am-6pm, Su 10am-5pm.

Auto Repair: AAA Road Service, 4800 Airport Plaza Dr. (800-668-9231 or 562-496-4130). Open M-F 9am-5pm.

Visitor Information: Long Beach Convention and Visitors Bureau, 1 World Trade Ctr. #300 (436-3645 or 800-452-2829), at Ocean Blvd. and Long Beach Fwy. (I-710). Tons of free brochures. Open M-F 8am-5pm.

Laundromat: Super Suds, 250 Alamitos Ave. (436-1859). The Disneyland of laundromats. Wash 75¢-$1, 15min. dry 25¢. Open daily 7am-10pm (last wash 9pm).

Emergency: 911. **Police:** 400 W. Broadway (435-6711).

Post Office: 300 N. Long Beach Blvd. (800-275-8777). Open M-F 8:30am-5pm, Sa 9am-2pm. **ZIP Code:** 90801.

Area Code: 562.

ACCOMMODATIONS

Daytrips to Long Beach from L.A. are cheap and easy, and an overnight trip doesn't need to be any different. There are a few reasonably priced surf motels along Ocean Blvd. between Belmont Shores and downtown.

Beach Plaza Hotel, 2010 E. Ocean Blvd. (437-0771). Immaculate rooms have cable TV and fridges. Pool and private access to beach; prices include parking. (Doubles $65, with ocean view and kitchenette $85-135.) Weekly rates available. Reservations recommended.

SUPERLATIVES: THE BIGGEST, THE NARROWEST, AND THE DRUNKEST Although Long Beach cannot stretch its sands to world-class distances (after all, it is not Long*est* Beach), it certainly stretches its way into the world of superlatives. The **world's largest mural,** entitled *Planet Ocean,* is painted on the side of Long Beach Arena. It took environmental artist Wyland 3000 gallons of paint to create the 10-story masterpiece, which is often mistaken for a giant glass aquarium. The **nation's narrowest house,** at 708 Gladys Ave., is a tight squeeze at 10 feet by 50 feet. The Yard House in Shoreline Village has the **world's largest number of beers** on tap—more than 450 brewed beauties. Neighboring Los Angeles may take the brass rings for per capita malls and facelifts, but Long Beach has much to be proud of.

FOOD AND NIGHTLIFE

Many eateries lining Pine Ave. between 1st and 3rd St. aren't as expensive as the valets out front might lead you to believe. There are equally budget-smart eateries in Belmont Shores. Buy cheap produce at the **open air market** on Promenade St. (F 10am-4pm). Long Beach supports a vibrant blues and jazz scene; try the **Blue Cafe,** 210 Promenade St. (983-7111), on any given night. A popular coffeehouse is **Portfolio,** 2300 E. 4th St. (434-2486), with live soul and blues on weekends (open M-F 6am-1am, Sa-Su 7am-1am). Most **gay and lesbian night spots** are around East Broadway and Falcon Ave.

Pasta Presto, 200 Pine Ave. (436-7200). Dinner and a movie pass for $9.50 (students and seniors $8.50)! Use the pass at the AMC 16-screen megaplex across the street. Pasta combos, pizzas, sandwiches. Open Su-Th 11am-9pm, F-Sa 11am-11pm.

Alegría, 115 Pine Ave. (436-3388). *Cocina Latina* with tapas bar. Excruciatingly hip Miró-inspired interior. Menu is *mucho caro* for the pennywise, but tapas are $5-9, and they host weekly Latin jazz and flamenco dancers. Entertainment begins at 8pm. No cover (1-drink min.). Open M-Th 11:30am-11pm, F-Sa 11:30am-2am, Su noon-10pm.

Taco Beach, 211 Pine Ave. (983-1337). Sit back, relax, and have a taco. Combo meals with rice and beans $6.50. Happy Hour M-F 2-6pm. Open Su-Th 11am-11pm, F-Sa 11am-midnight.

Bonadonna's Shorehouse Cafe, 5271 E. 2nd St., Belmont Shores (433-2266). Comfy diner setting, very surfer-friendly and reasonably veggie-friendly. Omelettes made from your choice of 30 tasty fillings (from $4.25). Huge burgers $5-7. Great for lunch or late-night grub. Open 24hr.

Bayshore, 5335 E. 2nd St., Belmont Shores (433-5901). One of the liveliest of 2nd St.'s many night spots. Shoot-the-Root, a delectable drink that contains a shot of root beer schnapps in a cup of beer ($3). Pool table (50¢). Happy Hour daily 11am-7pm ($2 drafts and well drinks). Free food M-F 4-7pm. Open Su-F 11am-1am, Sa 4pm-2am.

The Library, 3418 E. Broadway (433-2393). Bohemian joint frequented (though not exclusively) by the area's small gay community. Cup of damn fine joe $1.35. Jazz shows Su, W, F 8pm. Sa-Su breakfast omelette bar $4.50. Open M-Th 6am-midnight, F 6am-1am, Sa 7am-1am, Su 7am-midnight.

SIGHTS AND SEASONAL EVENTS

Long Beach's central preoccupation is shipping; tourism is clearly an afterthought. Beach life is, well...not a thought at all. Waves are minimal due to the breakwater created by the busy port. The shipping center is not without attraction, though. To get a hold on the city's cargo, cross the majestic **Vincent Thomas Bridge** to central San Pedro (50¢, free from the other direction).

QUEEN MARY. A 1934 Cunard luxury liner that's now a swanky hotel with art exhibits, historical displays, and upscale bars. There are still remnants of the days when she was a troop ship during WWII (Hitler offered the highest honors to anyone who could sink her). The only explosions that the Queen allows, though, are the weekly **fireworks** displays. *(435-3511. At the end of Queensway Dr. Open daily 9am-9pm. Admission $12, seniors $10, children $7; admission and tour $16, children $10. Parking $5.* ***Fireworks:*** *June to mid-Aug. Sa 9pm; watch from just about anywhere near the harbor.)*

LONG BEACH AQUARIUM OF THE PACIFIC. A $117-million, 156,000 square-foot celebration of the world's largest and most diverse body of water, the aquarium is situated atop one of the world's busiest and most polluted harbors. Just when you think you're too old to enjoy a place like this, the fish dazzle you: Meet the creatures of the deep who struggle every day to coexist with Long Beach's flotsam, jetsam, and effluvium. But don't feel too sorry for them—they'd bite you if they had the chance. Chomp! Chomp! You can touch some of the tamer creatures of the deep, but like so much Sid, they too might get vicious! Chomp! Yes, they have seals and sea lions. Yes, they are cute. Chomp! *(590-3100; www.aquariumofpacific.org. 100 Aquarium Way. Open daily 10am-6pm. Admission $14, seniors $12, children $7.)*

LONG BEACH MUSEUM OF ART. The original museum, built at the turn of the 20th century by famed Pasadena architects Greene and Greene, is being augmented by a new building which is being built in the style of the original. The museum features rotating exhibits as well as videos by its grant recipients, both of which are rivalled by the distinctly precious views of the Pacific. *(439-2119. 2300 Ocean Blvd., on the waterfront. Until June 2000 the museum has limited hours and is free. From June 2000 on: Open Tu-Su 10am-5pm. Admission $5, students $2; free F 5-8pm. Summer garden concerts W 7-10pm; tickets $11.)*

NAPLES ISLAND. Like Venice Beach, Naples Island was planned around a series of canals. Unlike those in Venice Beach, the canals here still exist, and the Rivo Alto canal even has gondoliers. *(Moonlight cruises: 433-9595; www.clever.net/gondolas; 1hr. dinner cruise for 2 $55, every 30min. 11am-11pm.)* It also harbors **Alamitos Bay,** from whence the *S.S. Minnow* set sail on its infamous three-hour tour from the opening sequence of *Gilligan's Island.*

BOUTIQUE-O-RAMA. **Meow** is where the *Seinfeld* costumers bought Kramer's shirts. *(438-8990. 2210 E. 4th St. Open Tu-Sa noon-6pm, Su-M noon-5pm.)* **Acres of Books,** is 6½ miles (read: a lot of acres) of used books and a favorite of Ray Bradbury. *(437-6980. 240 Long Beach Blvd. Open Tu-Sa 9:15am-5pm, Su 11am-4pm.)* **Broadway Boulevard,** has chic boutiques (east of downtown).

OTHER SIGHTS. At Long Beach's upscale, uptown neighborhood, the family-oriented, glamour-free beach of **Belmont Shores** is reputed to be the city's best. Park at meters near the intersection of Ocean Blvd. and La Verne St. (25¢ for 15min., 10hr. max.). The cylindrical **Long Beach Arena** is the canvas for the world's largest mural—one of **Wyland's Whaling Walls** (on Ocean Blvd.; see **Superlatives,** p. 414).

SEASONAL EVENTS. The **Long Beach Yacht Club,** 6201 Appian Way (435-4093), holds races throughout the year. The **Long Beach Grand Prix** revs along downtown streets in mid-April (Apr. 14-16 in 2000; 436-9953). Summer sounds jazz up downtown at **Jazz Fest** in mid-August (436-7794), and the **Day of Music** jazz and blues extravaganza in mid-September (435-2525). For more on seasonal events, contact the Convention and Visitors Council (see **Visitor Information,** p. 413).

CATALINA ISLAND

Only 22 miles off the coast of L.A. is the island paradise of Catalina. One might think that with its hefty ferry cost it would be quite exclusive, but night has fallen on the day Catalina was a refuge of the wealthy, and it is as pleasant as it is affordable. It is also home to a casino *without* gambling, a memorial *without* a dead body, and a 3rd Street *without* a 1st or 2nd St. What it does have is unbeatable snorkeling, beautiful camping and hiking sites, and crystal-clear waters. This potential for profit has not been lost upon the hotel owners and merchants found in the island's only city, Avalon. Tourists leaving the boat are deluged by offers of tram tours ($10-80), boat trips ($25-100), and rental "opportunities." This rampant commercialism is mitigated by two facts: 88% of the island is owned by a non-profit group dedicated to Catalina's conservation, and the tours *do* take you to some of the most beautiful and unspoiled land in the L.A. area. The conservation group goes to great lengths to ensure that the land remains natural—bike permits ($50) effectively prevent biking, and tours are limited to the main roads. The island's best sights are outside of Avalon, the island's only city, so be sure to get inland or on the water. If you have the inclination and the constitution, hiking is free and snorkeling is cheap (rentals around $5 per hr.). The extra $1 for fish food is well-spent, unless you find the ocean floor particularly fascinating on its own.

GETTING THERE

Without your own yacht, the best (and cheapest) way to get to Catalina is via **Catalina Cruises** (800-228-2546), which departs from Long Beach and San Pedro to Avalon and Two Harbors, the other town. The new Catalina Jet is its 50-minute ferry, which runs five times per day at no extra charge (2hr.; up to 29 departures daily; round-trip $25, ages 2-11 $20, under 2 $2). Other options include the sleek **Catalina Express** (519-1212 or 800-464-4228), which departs from Long Beach, Dana Point, and San Pedro to Avalon or Two Harbors (1½hr.; up to 25 departures daily; round-trip $38, seniors $34.50, ages 2-11 $28.50, under 2 $2), and the catamaran-hulled **Catalina Flyer** (949-673-5245), which goes from Newport Beach to Avalon (departs daily 9am, returns daily 4:30pm; round-trip $36, under 12 $20).

PRACTICAL INFORMATION

Public Transportation: Santa Catalina Island Company runs a bus from Avalon to Catalina's other town of Two Harbors, stops at a few campgrounds en route (2hr.; $18). **Catalina Express** (800-464-4228) runs a **water shuttle** between the towns (June-Sept.; one-way $13).

Bike Rental: Brown's Bikes (510-0986), 360ft. from the boat dock. Single-speed bikes $5 per hr., $12 per day; 6-speed bikes $6, $15; 21-speed mountain bikes $9, $20.

Visitor Information: Chamber of Commerce and Visitor Bureau, P.O. Box 217, Avalon 90704 (510-1520), on the left side of Avalon's Pleasure Pier. Open in summer daily 8am-5pm; off-season M-Sa 8am-5pm, Su 9am-3pm. **Catalina Island Conservancy,** 125 Claressa Ave., P.O. Box 2739, Avalon 90704 (510-2595). This non-profit group owns 88% of Catalina. Hiking permits (free), maps (25¢), and trail advice available here. Open daily 9am-5pm. **Biking permits** ($50, families $75) are required outside of Avalon. They can be obtained at the Conservancy, as well as the Catalina airport, and the Two Harbors Visitors Center (510-2880).

ATM: Bank of Southern California, at Catalina St. and Crescent Ave., and **Vons Market.**

Market: Vons, 121 Metropole St. (510-0280). Open daily 7am-11pm. **ATM inside.**

Laundromat: Catalina Coin Laundry, in the Hotel Metropole shopping arcade by Vons. Wash $1.50, 15min. dry 25¢. Save water!

Showers: Public facilities on Casino Way across from the Tuna Club. Entrance $1, each 5min. $1. Assorted preening implements $1 each. Open in summer M-Sa 7am-8pm, Su 7am-7pm; off-season daily 7-11am and 3-5pm.

Emergency: 911.

Post Office: In the Arcade Bldg. between Metropole and Sumner St. **ZIP Code:** 90704.

Area Code: 310.

ACCOMMODATIONS AND CAMPGROUNDS

The island's only hostel is **Hostel La Vista,** 145 Marilla (510-0603), 100 yards from the Avalon harbor. The historic hotel, built in 1920, recently metamorphosed into hostel-style lodging, with a common fridge (but no kitchen). The name is appropriate considering its spectacular ocean views (Linen and towels included. 4-person dorm $15; doubles $25, with private bath $60-80. Open June-Oct. Reservations strongly recommended.) The **Hermosa Hotel,** 131 Metropole St. (888-592-1313), whose motto is "sleep for cheap," has pleasant, tiny, and tidy, modest rooms in the heart of Crescent Ave. nightlife. (2-night min. stay. Singles $20-50; doubles $20-70. Rates depend on day and season. 18+.) The same management also owns and operates **Hermosa Cottages,** adorable little rooms right down the road (rooms with kitchen and bath $70-95).

While **no wilderness camping** is permitted, the five campgrounds on Catalina each offer distinct camping experiences. **Hermit Gulch** (510-2000), a 1½mi. walk from the boat landing, is populated by carousing campers and rich folks who missed the boat on one of many "no vacancy" nights. It has hot showers, flush toilets, a coin microwave, BBQs, and a vending machine ($7.50 per person; June-Sept. $8.50), and a limited number of stoves and lanterns ($5). No gear? No worries—they rent teepees ($20), tents ($10-15), and sleeping bags ($6). You can get closer to nature at the other four campgrounds, all run by Two Harbors Management (510-2800). To get to any of these sites from Avalon, take the shuttle bus; you may have to hike 1½mi. from the nearest stop. Eleven large, secluded pine forest sites ($7.50 per person) comprise **Blackjack.** It has cold showers, running water, and fire rings, but be prepared for large herds of buffalo to amble through. Only ¼-mile from Two Harbors, which boasts a non-touristy camper nightlife, **Little Fisherman's Cove** has the most popular beach camping, with 54 campsites, cold showers, chemical toilets, and rental gear (tents $10-25, sleeping bags $7.50). **Little Harbor's** incredible 16 beach sites offer a secluded cove for surfing and bodysurfing, a ranger station, potable water, picnic tables, and chemical toilets ($8.50 per person). Head to **Parson's Landing,** on the west tip of the island, if you want to be alone. The six sunny sites come with 2½ gallons of purified water and a bundle of firewood. You must check in at Two Harbor Visitors Center (510-2800) to get the key (basic rate $16.50, additional person $6.50).

FOOD, ENTERTAINMENT, AND SIGHTS

Avalon, centered on **Crescent Avenue,** is the only spot where there is any action. Many of the larger restaurants host live music and karaoke nightly, and good food is easy to find. Since you can eat just about anywhere for $6, you may as well eat at the place with the best view, which is the **Casino Dock Cafe,** 2 Casino Way, at the end of the Via Casino (open daily 7am-10pm). Land a catch-of-the-day combo for about $5 at **Lloyd's of Avalon** (510-1579), at Sumner St. and Crescent Ave. (open daily in summer 6am-10pm; off-season 6am-6pm). A brief trek up Arroyo Canyon Rd. away from the tourist- and yacht-infested harbor leads to **Sand Trap** (510-0553), at Brook Park. Relax over massive Mexican combos ($4.25-7) or veggie burgers ($5.50) on the outdoor patio. (Open daily 7:30am-3pm. Cash only.)

Just about anything can be rented on Catalina Island, from beach chairs to boats. The **Santa Catalina Island Company** runs a slew of tours. Only the **Skyline** or **Inland Motor** tours are worth the money; go to the Discovery Tours Center at Catalina St. and Crescent Ave. (Skyline $19, seniors $16.75, children $9.50. Inland Motor $34.50, seniors $30.25, children $17.25.) The **Island Hopper,** a tram which leaves from Island Plaza on Metropole St., will take you to the Botanical Gardens or the Casino (fare $1).

The best way to see underwater life is to snorkel, so go down below after gathering dive gear at **Catalina Diver's Supply** (510-0330 or 800-353-0330), on the left-hand side of Pleasure Pier (mask/snorkel/fin package or wetsuit $7 per hr., $12 per day). **Lover's Cove** is the most convenient snorkeling spot, but gets very crowded with tourists and boat traffic. The best place to snorkel is among the red garibaldi in the kelp forests off **Casino Point.** Rocks along the coast can graze unprotected skin, so wear a wetsuit. Those unable to, unwilling to, or uninterested in snorkeling can take **Glass Bottom Boat Trips** (45min.; fare $9, seniors $7.50, ages 2-11 $4.75; additional 50¢ at night).

The **Casino Building** (510-7400), at the end of Crescent Ave., was never a gambling den; William Wrigley, Jr. built it (for $2 million) as a ballroom dancing hall in 1929 (*casino* means "gathering place" in Italian). Although you can take an architectural tour of the building (tours $8.50; ground rules permit gum chewing, and they hope that Wrigley's is your gum of choice), you're probably better off just going to the movies. Take in the building's elegant Art Deco murals and catch a film in 1000-seater **Avalon Theater** (inside) for only $7; nightly showings (7 and 9:30pm) include a free concert on the antique page organ. The casino hosts occasional **jazz concerts** and a **New Year's Eve bash** that resembles the Catalina of the 1930s and 40s, when it was a palace for the sultans of swing. Ask about the **Silent Film Festival** (June; for tickets call 510-2414) and the **Halloween Costume Ball** (Oct. 28 in 2000). Tucked beneath the casino is the **Catalina Island Museum** (510-2414), which has exhibitions on island history, Native American inhabitants, and filmmaker Zane Grey (open daily 10am-4pm; admission $2, seniors $1, ages 5-12 50¢, under 5 free). **Zane Grey's Avalon pueblo** is now the hotel overlooking the Casino.

At the end of Avalon Canyon Rd. (2mi. outside Avalon), you can pick up the hilly **Hermit Gulch Trail,** a 3½-mile loop past canyons, secluded coast, the **Wrigley Memorial** (a monolithic remembrance of the gum magnate, who once owned the island, minus his dead body which was removed from the island for fear that the Germans would destroy it in WWII), and the 38-acre **Botanic Gardens** (510-2288; open daily 8am-5pm; $1 donation). Bison and wild boars inhabit the area along the four-mile **Black Jack-Cape Reservoir Loop.** Two or three hundred buffalo are the descendents of the 25 originally ferried over for the filming of Zane Grey's 1924 film *The Vanishing American.* The rigorous eight-mile **Black Jack Trail** leads to Little Harbor. Pick up either of the last trails at the Black Jack Junction, accessible by the **airport shuttle** (round-trip $14.50).

ORANGE COUNTY

Directly south of L.A. County is Orange County (pop. 2.6 million), or "O.C." as locals have learned to call it. It is a *Reader's Digest* compilation of Southern California: beautiful beaches, bronzed sportsmen and women, strip malls, the late Walt Disney's expanding cultural organ, and traffic snarls frustrating enough to make the coolest Angeleno weep. One of only two staunchly Republican counties in California, Orange County has won fame for its economy (as big as Arizona's, and one of the world's 30 largest), and notoriety for its finances (the county declared an unprecedented bankruptcy in 1994 after its tax-averse government tried to make money in Wall Street derivatives).

Disneyland, the self-proclaimed "Happiest Place On Earth" is getting even happier, expanding to include a new theme park and resort, putting Anaheim neck-high in construction and traffic, but delighting local businesses who have taken Mickey's lead and started re-facing. The coast boasts not only breathtaking beaches, but also the calmly beautiful, sparsely covered rolling hills around San Juan Capistrano.

ORANGE COUNTY PRACTICAL INFORMATION

Airport: John Wayne Orange County (252-5006), on Campus Dr. 20min. from Anaheim. Newer, cleaner, and easier to get around than the L.A. airport; domestic flights only.

Trains: Amtrak (for reservations 800-USA-RAIL/872-7245). To (from north to south): **Fullerton,** 120 E. Santa Fe Ave. (714-992-0530); **Anaheim,** 2150 E. Katella Blvd. (714-385-1448); **Santa Ana,** 1000 E. Santa Ana Blvd. (714-547-8389); **Irvine,** 15215 Barranca Pkwy. (949-753-9713); **San Juan Capistrano,** Santa Fe Depot, 26701 Verdugo St. (949-240-2972); **San Clemente,** 1850 Ave. Estación.

Buses: Greyhound has 3 stations in the area: **Anaheim,** 100 W. Winston Rd. (714-999-1256), 3 blocks south of Disneyland (open daily 6:30am-8pm); **Santa Ana,** 1000 E. Santa Ana Blvd. (714-542-2215; open daily 7am-8pm); **San Clemente,** 510 Ave. de la Estrella (949-492-1187; open M-Th 7:45am-6:30pm, F 7:45am-8pm).

Public Transit: Orange County Transportation Authority (OCTA), 550 S. Main St., Garden Grove (714-636-7433). Thorough service is useful for getting from Santa Ana and Fullerton Amtrak stations to Disneyland, and for beach-hopping along the coast. Long Beach, in L.A. County, serves as the terminus for several OCTA lines. Bus #1 travels the coast from Long Beach to San Clemente (every hr. until 8pm). #397 covers San Clemente. Fare $1, day pass $2. **Info center** open M-F 6am-8pm, Sa-Su 8am-5pm. **MTA Info** (213-626-4455 or 800-266-6883). Phone lines open daily 5am-10:45pm. MTA buses run from L.A. to Disneyland and Knott's Berry Farm.

Visitor Information: Anaheim Area Visitors and Convention Bureau, 800 W. Katella Ave. (714-999-8999), in Anaheim Convention Ctr. Lodging and dining guides. Open M-F 8:30am-5pm. **Huntington Beach Conference and Visitors Bureau,** 417 Main St. #2A (714-969-3492 or 800-729-6232). Open M-F 9am-5pm. If the helpful staff doesn't know something, they'll find someone who does. Good maps and brochures. **Newport Harbor Area Chamber of Commerce,** 1470 Jamboree Rd., Newport Beach (949-729-4400; email info@newportbeach.com). Offers free maps, info, and shiny Republican smiles. Open M-F 8:30am-5pm, Sa-Su automated answering service. **Newport Visitors Bureau,** 3300 West Coast Hwy., Newport Beach (949-722-1611 or 800-942-6278). Maps and brochures, including a self-guided walking tour of Balboa Island.

Gay-Lesbian Community Center: 12832 Garden Grove Blvd., Suite A, Garden Grove (714-534-0862). Open M-F 9am-10pm.

Surf and Weather Conditions: 213-554-1212.

Emergency: 911.

Police: Anaheim, 425 S. Harbor Blvd. (756-1900). **Huntington Beach,** (960-8811).

Crisis Lines: Rape Crisis Hotline (831-9110). 24hr. **Orange County Sexual Assault Network Hotline** (894-4242).

Medical Services: St. Jude Medical Center, 101 E. Valencia Mesa, Fullerton (714-871-3280). **Lestonnac Free Clinic,** 1215 E. Chapman Ave. (714-633-4600). Open Tu-F 9am-5pm, Sa 9am-1pm.

Post Office: 701 N. Loara St., Anaheim (520-2601), 1 block north of Anaheim Plaza. Open M-F 8:30am-5pm, Sa 8:30am-2pm. **ZIP Code:** 92803.

ORANGE COUNTY AREA CODES: 714 in Anaheim, Fullerton, Fountain Valley, Santa Ana, Garden Grove; **949** in Newport, Laguna, Irvine, Mission Viejo, San Juan Capistrano, and surrounding areas; **310** in Seal Beach.

ANAHEIM

Anaheim (pop. 282,133) was considered, in the late 1950s, the city of the future. Californians flocked to Orange County's capital city, where booming industry and Uncle Walt's dream machine created jobs and revenue galore. But the days of Astroturf patios and shiny tract homes were not to last. Today, Anaheim's once-hip main drags are antiquated relics of better days, and the shrinking economy has introduced crime and unemployment to the home of the Magic Kingdom. Undaunted, Disney recently submitted a proposal to buy 40% of Anaheim and turn it into a theme park called "The California Adventure," the latest step in their plan to establish a small world order in southern California. A smaller California Adventure, filling a mere 55 acres of what is now Disney parking, is scheduled to open in 2001. Currently, the construction ensnarls the park, hiding most of the attractions from layman's eyes.

ACCOMMODATIONS

The Magic Kingdom is the sun around which the Anaheim solar system revolves, so budget motels and garden-variety "clean comfortable rooms" flank it on all sides. Keep watch for family and group rates posted on marquees, and seek out establishments offering the 3-for-2 passport (3 days of Disney for the price of 2). The best part about the new California Adventure construction is that it has inspired hotel owners to revamp as well. Their prices are slightly higher than in years past, but remain reasonable.

Fullerton (HI-AYH), 1700 N. Harbor Blvd., **Fullerton** (714-738-3721), 15min. north of Disneyland. Shuttle from L.A. airport $17. OCTA bus #43 runs along Harbor Blvd. to Disneyland. In the woods, away from the thematic craziness of nearby Anaheim. Enthusiastic, resourceful staff invites questions but forbids drinking. Offers services including ISICs. Kitchen, Internet access, relaxing living room, communal bathrooms. Free laundry. Linen $1. 7-night max. stay. Check-in 8-11am and 4-11pm. No curfew. Single-sex and co-ed dorms $14, nonmembers $17; less in winter. Reservations encouraged.

Magic Inn & Suites, 1030 W. Katella Ave., **Anaheim** (714-772-7242 or 800-422-1556). The rugs can't show you a whole new world, but it *is* just opposite Disneyland. Recently remodeled. Pools, A/C, TVs, fridges, and microwaves. Continental breakfast included. Laundry. 2 full-sized beds $59, 2 queen beds $79. Reservations recommended.

Skyview Motel, 1126 W. Katella Ave., **Anaheim** (533-4505), at the southwest corner of Disneyland. Clean, newly revamped rooms with HBO and A/C. Balconies offer a good view of Disney's nightly fireworks. Small pool, many kids. Queen bed $40; king bed $45; 2 beds $50-55. Reservations recommended.

FOOD

Anaheim is more mini-mall than city. There are countless fast-food places to choose from, but hold out for one of the various inexpensive ethnic restaurants tucked into the strip malls that line Anaheim's streets. Many specialize in takeout or will deliver to your motel room.

Angelo & Vicini's Cafe Ristorante, 550 N. Harbor Blvd., **Fullerton** (714-879-4022). What a spectacle! The word "cheesy" describes both the food (delectably artery-clogging) and the decor (Christmas lights, cheese wheels, and a *Mona Lisa*) at this charming local favorite. Overflowing and delicious lunch buffet just like Grandma makes $6. Open Su-Th 11am-9:45pm, F-Sa 11am-11:45pm.

El Pollo Inka, 400 S. Euclid Blvd., **Anaheim** (714-772-2263). Locals congregate under a black-lit mural of Machu Picchu and devour Anaheim's best Peruvian food. The *arroz con pollo* (rice and chicken; $8) is delicious, and the *mazzomorra morada* (purple corn pudding; $2.50) makes an excellent dessert. Open M-Th 11:30am-9pm, F-Sa 11:30am-10pm.

Coffee Cue, 1732 S. Euclid Blvd., **Anaheim** (714-533-8205). Chummy, jumpin' coffeehouse for young hipsters, has poetry readings, live music, lending library, pool table, and e-darts. Bagel and coffee $2. Smoothies are their specialty ($3, extra charge for aphrodisiac bee pollen). Trendy chai $2.40. Open Su-Th 7am-10pm, F-Sa 7am-11pm.

SIGHTS

DISNEYLAND

***Contact:** 714-781-4565; www.disneyland.com. **Location:** Main entrance on Harbor Blvd., and a smaller one on Katella Ave., may be approached by car via I-5 to Katella Ave. From L.A., MTA bus #460 travels from 4th and Flower St. (about 1hr.) to the Disneyland Hotel (service to the hotel begins at 4:53am, service back to L.A. until 1:20am). **Free shuttles** link the hotel to Disneyland's portals, as does the Disneyland monorail. The park is also served by Airport*

Service, OCTA, Long Beach Transit, and Gray Line (see Practical Information, p. 420). ***Parking*** *in the morning is painless, but leaving in the evening is not.* ***Hours*** *vary (call for exact info), but are approximately Su-Th 10am-9pm, F-Sa 8am-midnight.* ***Admission:*** *Unlimited use passport ($39, seniors $37, under 12 $29) allows repeated single-day entrance into the park, as does the parking pass ($7 per day). Two- and three-day passes are available.*

Disneyland calls itself the "happiest place on earth," and there is a part of every American pilgrim that agrees. The almighty wallet, of course, will vehemently dissent. Even though the admission is steep, this is probably the best place in Southern California to spend your "fun money." Weekday and off-season visitors will undoubtedly be the happiest, but the enterprising can wait for parades to distract the children, leaving shorter lines. Walt's ever-innovative Disney team has come up with the **FastPass** program: Tested in the summer of '99 on Space Mountain, the system lets you pick up a reservation ticket and return at a specific time to walk right on and ride. This could be the line-busting solution Disney has been looking for, so watch for information and signs when you visit. *Disneyland Today!* lists parade and show times, as well as important shopping information and breaking news from Frontierland.

MAIN STREET, USA. This is a children's-book walk through the golden age of small-town America. Disney and his designers skewed the perspective on Main Street so that the street seemed longer upon entering and shorter upon exiting, thereby creating visitor anticipation and making the walk to the car less daunting after a long day. Main Street is home to most of the park's consumer trade. These shops stay open an hour after the park itself closes, but don't be fooled into thinking you'll get your souvenirs on the way out—everyone else has the same idea.

FANTASYLAND. The geographical and spiritual center of the park, Fantasyland contains the trademark castle as well as the scintillating **Matterhorn Bobsleds,** and numerous kiddie rides like the trippy **It's A Small World,** which will fiendishly engrave its happy, happy song into your brain. This area is best enjoyed when the rides light up at night, the kidlets go home, and you have twenty bucks to blow on the addictive $2 *churros* (tasty sticks of fried dough).

ADVENTURELAND. To the left of the Main Street is the home of the new **Tarzan's Treehouse,** a walk-through attraction that replaced the Swiss Family Robinson Treehouse. The **Indiana Jones Adventure** is just next door. Pass the time in line by decoding the inscriptions inside the Temple of Maya (hint: the ride is sponsored by AT&T). Indiana Jones fans' palms will sweat when an animatronic Harrison Ford suggestively says, "You were good in there...very good." Meanwhile, Freudians will chuckle over the giant snake. The **Jungle Cruise** next door has a new landing with a swing band to entertain the poor souls languishing in the hot sun. For lunch, the **Bengal Barbecue** offers chicken and beef skewers ($3), tasty breadsticks ($2), and cold grilled bananas ($4)--the best dessert you'll have at any amusement park.

NEW ORLEANS SQUARE. In the left corner of the park are the best shops and dining in Disneyland. Find New Orleans cuisine at the **French Market** (dinner $7) or the **Blue Bayou** (dinner much more expensive) where there seems to be a surcharge for atmosphere. The low-key but entertaining rides are evocative of authentic southern laziness. Try the charmingly faux-creepy **Haunted Mansion,** and the ever-popular **Pirates of the Caribbean,** a favorite of native New Orleanian Elaine Schlesinger.

FRONTIERLAND. Wild West fetishists will find amusement galore here, especially on **Big Thunder Railroad.** Replace the lunch you lost at **Big Thunder Barbecue** ($10-15 meals), right behind the ride. The **Mark Twain riverboat** tours around Tom Sawyer's Island, which looks suspiciously like a clever way to isolate harmful children on an island away from smart adults (see **Alcatraz,** p. 104).

CRITTER COUNTRY. Most of the park's cuter things lurk in this part of the park, where the main attraction is **Splash Mountain,** a soaking log ride past singing rodents and down a thrilling vertical drop. Its host, **Brer Rabbit,** was originated in the humor-filled "Uncle Remus" stories of the Reconstruction-era South. You might enjoy the snapshot they take of your horror-frozen face on the way down.

MICKEY'S TOONTOWN. At the rear of the park, this cartoon playland provides the key source of fun for the 10-and-under crowd. Mickey and Co. can often be found strolling about, followed by a stampede of kids in hot pursuit. Disney seems to be phasing out Mickey's old-school compadres like Donald, Goofy, and Chip 'n' Dale, in favor of hi-tech new kids Ariel, Simba, Aladdin, and Belle.

TOMORROWLAND. To the right of Main Street is this futuristic portion of the park, recently remodeled after Disney executives recognized that its supposed imagination of the future was gloriously stuck in the 1950s. The brand new **Astro-orbiter**—rockets that circle around moving planets—will thrill young children, and the wheelie-popping **Rocket Rods** are now the park's fastest ride, with the longest track. But the favorite of the rush-seeking set is still **Space Mountain,** the darkened roller coaster which travels beneath a mountain of sheer ether. **Star Tours** promises a routine shuttle to Endor—just hope your bungling rookie droid pilot, Max, doesn't kill you with all his screw-ups. Although you can't tell from outside, this is a simulation ride, so those who prefer not to have their head jerked around for two minutes might visit another planet. **Honey, I Shrunk the Audience** is a 3-D movie extravaganza where the actors and characters from *Honey I Shrunk/Blew Up the Kid(s)* team up with Eric Idle to commit hilarious acts of improbable science. The shows are about 15 minutes long and seat 600, so lines are never much of a problem. Do not fear the mice or snakes, they are your friends.

K(NOT)T DISNEYLAND

Buena Park offers a cavalcade of non-Disney diversions, some of which are better than others.

KNOTT'S BERRY FARM. Back in 1932, Walter Knott combined a red raspberry, a blackberry, and a loganberry to make a **boysenberry.** Naturally, his popular roadside stand quickly grew into a restaurant and, when he imported the Old Trails Hotel (from Prescott, Arizona) and the last narrow gauge railroad in the country to form "Ghost Town," the precursor to the first theme park in America (and Anaheim's largest, if not happiest, amusement park) was born. After the opening of "the other place" in Anaheim in 1955, Knott's Farm added other theme sections such as Fiesta Village and myriad rides. Knott's is a local favorite which aims at being "the friendliest place in the West." It has long since given up on the happiest place on Earth. The park's highlights include roller coasters like **Montezuma's Revenge, Boomerang,** and the **Windjammer.** Their latest additions include **Ghostrider,** the largest wooden roller coaster in the West, and **Supreme Scream,** the tallest thrill ride of its kind, where you can drop 30 stories in three seconds. The Doolittle-ish **Birdcage Theater** is where Steve Martin got his start (admit it, Steve!), and is now closed to the public. At Halloween, the park is rechristened Knott's Scary Farm and, at Christmas, Knott's Merry Farm. The food inside is what you'd expect; the best deal, **Mrs. Knott's Chicken Dinner Restaurant** (220-5080), is outside the park. Soup, salad, corn, biscuits, chicken, and dessert (the specialty is—surprise—boysenberry pie) are only $10. *(Recorded info 714-220-5220. 8039 Beach Blvd. at La Palma Ave., 5mi. northeast of Disneyland. From downtown L.A., take MTA bus #460 from 4th and Flower St.; 1¼hr. Park hours vary, but are approximately Su-Th 9am-11pm, F-Sa 9am-midnight. Admission $36, seniors $26, ages 3-11 $26. Summer admission discounts.)*

ALTERNA-MUSEUMS. Movieland Wax Museum offers a huge collection of celebrity facsimiles, including the entire *Star Trek* crew. *(522-1154. 7711 Beach Blvd. Open M-F 10am-6pm, Sa-Su 9am-7pm. Admission $13, seniors $11, ages 4-11 $7.)* Across the way are the ribald oddities at **Ripley's Believe It or Not! Museum,** likely to be the only place prideful enough to advertise a *Last Supper* fashioned from 280 pieces of toast. *(522-1152. 7850 Beach Blvd. Open M-F 11am-5pm, Sa-Su 10am-6pm; box office closes at 6pm. Combo admission to both attractions $17.)*

RICHARD NIXON LIBRARY AND BIRTHPLACE. Farther inland in Yorba Linda is the highly uncritical, privately funded monument to Tricky Dick. The first native-born Californian president was born in this house, which has now become an extensive museum of the American presidency. Rotating exhibits cover such timely topics as "My Dearest Partner: Husbands and Wives in the White House." Skeptics can investigate the Watergate Room. Although Nixon considered his resignation an admission of guilt, the only admission at this monument is the $6 people pay to get in; museum curators consistently portray one of the master manipulators of our century as the victim of circumstance, plotting enemies, and his own immutable honor. *(993-5075. 18001 Yorba Linda Blvd. Open M-Sa 10am-5pm, Su 11am-5pm. Admission $6, seniors $4, ages 8-11 $2, under 8 free.)*

CRYSTAL CATHEDRAL. Seating 3000 faithful in Garden Grove, this is where Dr. Robert H. Schuller's weekly TV show, *Hour of Power* is taped. The Crystal Cathedral's own Ministry of Traffic provides the opportunity for In-Car Worship at a huge outdoor television. *(971-4000. 12141 Lewis St. Tours M-Sa 9am-3:30pm. English services Su 9:30 and 11am; Spanish service 1pm. Free. Broadcast on the radio; tune in to 530 AM.)*

SPORTS. For more evidence of Disney's world domination, catch a game by one of the teams they own: The major league **Anaheim Angels** (940-2000 or 800-626-4357) play baseball from early April to October (general tickets $6-20). Hockey action takes place at the **Arrowhead Pond,** 2695 E. Katella Ave. (704-2500), one block east of Rte. 57—an arena home to the NHL's **Mighty Ducks.** It's just like the movie, except there are no kids, Emilio Estevez isn't coaching, and there's a lot of blood.

ORANGE COUNTY BEACH COMMUNITIES

Taking town planning to the extreme, O.C.'s various beach communities have cleaner sand, better surf, and less madness than their L.A. county counterparts. Sights are scarce along the entire 35 miles between Huntington Beach and San Clemente, featuring only the quaint Mission San Juan Capistrano and the chi-chi South Coast Plaza (the largest mall in this mall-obsessed state). If you're into touring suburbia-by-the-sea or catching a few waves, you might want to make an O.C. beach a daytrip from L.A.

ACCOMMODATIONS AND CAMPGROUNDS

O.C.'s prime coastline and pricey real estate mean a dearth of bargain rates. Those without multi-million-dollar summer homes in the area can try their luck along the Pacific Coast or Newport Blvd. in Newport Beach. Accommodations, campgrounds, food, nightlife, and sights are listed from north to south. O.C.'s state beaches have **campgrounds** that aren't the stuff of dreams, but this doesn't crimp their extreme popularity. Reservations are required for all sites (reservation fee $6.75). Reserve through RESERVAMERICA (800-444-7275) a maximum of seven months in advance, and as soon as possible in the summer.

Huntington Beach Colonial Inn Youth Hostel, 421 8th St., **Huntington Beach** (536-9206), 4 blocks inland at Pecan Ave. Take OCTA #29 (which also goes to Disneyland and Knott's) or #50. Familial staff and international crowd inhabit a large yellow wooden house. Quiet, calm, and very pleasant. Common showers and bathroom, large kitchen, reading/TV room, coin-op laundry, Internet access, deck, and surfboard shed. Linen and breakfast included. Key deposit $20. No lockout. Check-in 7am-11pm. Dorms $15; dorm doubles $17. Photo ID required. Reserve 2 days in advance for summer weekends. **International passport or student ID required.**

HI San Clemente Beach (HI-AYH), 233 Ave. Granada, **San Clemente** (492-2848), 2 blocks west of El Camino. This airy hostel is so laid-back it's almost comatose, perfect for those weary of the urban scene. Near the beach and shopping. Patio, comfy couches, and entertainment center. Lockers. Curfew 11pm (lack of nightlife in San Clemente makes it easy to meet). Single-sex dorms $11, nonmembers $14. Private rooms available for 2-5 people. Cash or traveler's checks only. Open May-Oct.

CAMPGROUNDS

Doheny, 25300 Dana Point Harbor Dr., **Dana Point** (496-6172), along Rte. 1. With the only beachside locations in the area, Doheny is the most popular O.C. campground. Beachfront sites Su-Th $22, F-Sa $23; others Su-Th $17, F-Sa $18.

San Clemente, 3030 Del Presidente, **San Clemente** (492-3156), off I-5. Ocean bluffs and hot showers (coin-operated) draw families and surfers alike. Hookups at 72 sites. Self-guided nature trail. Mar.-Nov. sites $17-18, with hookup $23-24; Dec.-Feb. $14, with hookup $20.

San Onofre (492-4872), off I-5 3mi. south of **San Clemente.** About 90 of these 221 sites are suitable for tents; others are for RVs only. All are crammed onto 10ft. strips of dirt between the parking area and the coastal bluff. The waves of nearby highway traffic drown out those of the distant surf. Trails lead to a lovely beach. Mar.-Nov. sites $17-18, with hookup $23-24; Dec.-Feb. $14, with hookup $20.

FOOD

O.C.'s restaurants tend toward typical California cuisine (see **Cuisinart,** p. 20), especially light, seafood-oriented fare. For a great burger and view of the ocean, walk to the end of the Huntington Beach Pier, and go back in time at **Ruby's** (714-969-7829), a 1950s-style diner. For cheaper eats, try one of the following:

Laguna Village Market and Cafe, 577 S. Coast Hwy., **Laguna Beach** (494-6344). Off the main drag, this old-style joint maintains its local color, but the only color you'll see is the crystal-clear blue ocean–the view of the Pacific is swell. Lovely beachside tables provide the perfect atmosphere for noshing some seafood or the house specialty, chicken curry dumplings ($7.75), while watching the water. Their Village Burger is excellent ($6). Open daily 8:30am-dusk.

The Boom-Boom Room, 1401 S. Coast Hwy. (494-7588), at Mountain St. in the Coast Inn, **Laguna Beach**. Lively gay hangout has international reputation, pool tables, live DJs, and a "surfing, muscle-bound, cruising, tanned" clientele. Boom-Boom specials include "Beer Busts" (Su and Th 4-8pm) with $1.50 drafts. Watch for Hot Package Night to earn yourself $1000. Open daily noon-2am. For more gay nightlife, check out calmer **Main Street,** 1460 S. Coast Hwy. (494-0056), opposite Boom-Boom. Happy hour M-Sa 4-7pm. Open daily 2pm-2am; Club open F-Sa 9pm-2am.

Sugar Shack, 213½ Main St., **Huntington Beach** (536-0355). Tanned surfer-types and locals in the know favor this friendly hangout. Counter seating makes it a great place for a quick breakfast (combos $5) or lunch. Lunch specials M-F ($3.50-4.75). Open Su-Tu, Th 6am-4pm, W 6am-8pm, F-Sa 6am-5pm.

BrewBakers, 412 Walnut Ave., **Huntington Beach** (374-2337), is a beer lover's delight. $2.75 per bottle. 8 different breads ($3-5) ensure that nobody drinks on an empty stomach. Open W-M 11am-9pm.

Streetlight Expresso Café, 201D Main St., **Huntington Beach** (969-7336). Favorite local hangout for surfers, sophisticates, and the saved. Owned by a local preacher, the cafe hosts live Christian music F-Sa and Tu nights. Excellent iced drinks. Specialty White Chocolate Mocha ($3) is a godsend on chilly California nights. Open Su-Th 6am-midnight, F-Sa 6am-2am.

Newport Beach Brewing Company, 2920 Newport Blvd., **Newport Beach** (675-8449). Lodged in a beautiful old Victorian building, this brew-co is a great place to crash at the end of the day. Seared tuna salad ($9) and Mediterranean pasta ($7.29) are wonderful. Appetizers half-price during Happy Hour (M-F 3-6:30pm). Full bar. Open Su-Th 11:30am-11:30pm, F-Sa 11:30am-1am.

Wahoo's Fish Tacos, 1133 S. Coast Hwy., **Laguna Beach** (949-497-0033), 1mi. south of Main Beach. Also at 120 Main St., Huntington Beach. Delectable tacos ($1.75) and burritos ($3.50) filled with meat, veggies, or fish of the day. Informal atmosphere perfect for those shirtless beach days. Open M-Sa 11am-10pm, Su 11am-9pm. Cash only.

SIGHTS

Apart from pre-fabricated amusement park joy, fun in the sun O.C.-style revolves around the Pacific—along the Pacific Coast Hwy. (PCH), in particular. On average, the beaches are cleaner, less crowded, and more charming than those in L.A. County. Nevertheless, visitors should not be lulled off-guard by the swishing coastal waters and magical inland attractions. As in any city, pedestrians should take extreme care after dusk. Beachside camping outside official campgrounds is both illegal and unsafe.

HUNTINGTON BEACH

For those who enjoy a fun beach scene, go to Huntington Beach, winner of the *Let's Go 2000* Beach Bum Award. Considered one of the safest cities in the country, H.B. hosts more wave-shredding than shoplifting. This town's activity of choice is surfing, and the proof is in the **Surfing Walk of Fame** (the sidewalk along PCH at Main St.) and the **International Surfing Museum** 411 Olive St. (960-3483; open daily noon-5pm; in winter W-Su only; admission $2, students $1). You can join the action for about $40 an hour for an instructor, board, and wetsuit. Inquire at any of the local surf shops or make an appointment with the lifeguard-staffed **Huntington Beach Surfing Instruction** (962-3515). The pier is the best place to watch the continuing cavalcade of official surfing contests and unofficial bikini contests. By night, H.B.'s bars and microbreweries become a beach party brew-ha-ha. **Duke's Barefoot Bar** is the major beach landmark, and **Perq's,** 117 Main St. (714-960-9996), is O.C.'s oldest blues house. Main St., H.B.'s central lane, is a surf shop superstore. Locals lament the loss of original, if outdated, architecture and establishments. Malls have stolen the luster of Huntington's grimy, surfing underside, replacing it with shiny new bars and restaurants that cater to tourists from neighboring cities.

NEWPORT BEACH AND BALBOA PENINSULA

Family-oriented Newport Beach is divided into wealthy and immaculate residential neighborhoods and dingier tourist areas. Multi-million dollar summer homes are jam-packed along Newport Harbor, the largest leisure-craft harbor in the world, while the beach is crowded with young hedonists cloaked in neon. The **Newport Pier** is an extension of 22nd St. at West Balboa Blvd.

The sands of Newport Beach run south onto the **Balboa Peninsula,** separated from the mainland by Newport Bay. The peninsula itself is only two to four blocks wide and can be reached from the Pacific Coast Hwy. (PCH). **Ocean Front Walk,** which extends the length of the peninsula, is the best place to stroll along the beach. The **Balboa Pier,** flanked by two public parking lots and beautiful sands, lies at Main St. and East Balboa Blvd. At the end of the peninsula, **The Wedge,** seasonally pounded by storm-generated waves up to 20 feet tall, is a body-surfing mecca.

On the opposite side of the peninsula, at the end of Main St., is the ornate **Balboa Pavilion.** Once a sounding ground for Big Band great Benny Goodman, the pavilion is now a hub for harbor tours and winter whale watching. The bi-level *Pavilion Queen* and smaller *Pavilion Paddy* offer 45-minute ($6, children $1) and 90-minute ($8, children $1) cruises of the harbor. The *Catalina Flyer* leaves for Catalina Island at 9am and returns at 4:30pm; (round-trip $36, ages 3-12 $20, under 3 $2. Call 673-5245 for reservations). The harborside melee, **Funzone,** stretches its Ferris wheels and bumper cars northwest of the pavilion. (Open daily 10am-10pm.) From this area you can see upscale **Balboa Island,** a haven for chic eateries, boutiques, and bikini shops. A vintage **ferryboat** (673-1070) travels there from the peninsula (ferry runs daily every 5min., but expect a small delay; car and driver $1.25, each additional passenger 50¢, children 25¢; bikes 40-75¢). The island is also accessible from the Pacific Coast Hwy. via the Jamboree Rd. bridge.

Most of the crowds navigate Newport Beach and the Balboa Peninsula by bicycle, 5-person bicycle surrey, or in-line skates. Stands everywhere rent everything. (Bikes $5-7 per hr., $15 per day. Skates $3-6 per hr., $15 per day. Boogie boards $5-6 per day.) Bikers should pick up *Bikeways*, a map of trails in Newport Beach, at the visitors center.

Just inland, **Fashion Island,** a commercial/mall district whose pre-planning would make Le Corbusier blush, proves that neither religion nor art can compete with Bloomingdale's. Submit.

LAGUNA BEACH

Punctuated by rocky cliffs, coves, and lush hillside vegetation, this town's character is decidedly Mediterranean. **Ocean Avenue** at Pacific Coast Hwy. and **Main Beach** are the prime parading areas. **Westry Beach,** which spreads south of Laguna just below Aliso Beach Park, and Camel Point, between Westry and Aliso, is the hub of the local **gay** crowd. For beach access, park on residential streets to the east and look for Public Access signs between private properties.

The latest incarnation of the original 1914 Laguna Beach art association is the **Laguna Art Museum,** 307 Cliff Dr. (494-6531; www.lagunaartmuseum.org.) The collection showcases local and California art, including some excellent early 20th-century Impressionist works. (Open Tu-Su 11am-5pm. Admission $5, students and seniors $4, children under 12 free. Tours daily 2pm.) Pick up the museum's guide to local art, which lists information on over 100 **art galleries** in the immediate Laguna Beach area.

SAN JUAN CAPISTRANO

While San Juan Capistrano and its two beachtowns, **Dana Point** and **San Clemente,** try their best to preserve the smaller historical sights that abound in their region, one sight remains timeless and well-kept. Although slowly crumbling, the **mission** of San Juan Capistrano (248-2048), 30min. south of Anaheim on Rte. 5, is the most touching physical space in Orange County. Established by Father Junípero Serra in 1776, this is considered the "jewel of the missions." Although most of the original structure collapsed in the earthquake of 1812, this is the only standing site where Serra himself is known to have said mass, and the oldest building still in use in the state. The crumbling ivy-covered walls of the beautiful **Serra Chapel** are warmed by a 17th-century Spanish cherrywood altar and Native American designs painted on the walls and ceiling. The Gregorian chants, combined with the redolent incense and flickering candlelight, make you feel Serra's very presence. The mission is best known as a home to the swallows who return here annually to nest in mid-March. (Open daily 8:30am-5pm. Admission $5, seniors $4, ages 3-12 $4. Tours available in Italian, Spanish, and German; call ahead.) The **San Juan Capistrano Historical Society** sits in the **O'Neil Museum,** 31831 Los Rios St. (493-8444), and offers architectural and garden walking tours of the historic adobes lining Los Rios St. (open Tu-F 9am-noon and 1-4pm, Su noon-3pm).

A brief drive down Camino Capistrano will lead you to Del Obispo St. which will lead you to **Dana Point,** whose spectacular bluffs were popularized in namesake Richard Henry Dana's *Two Years Before the Mast.* Its rocky shore is great for **tidepooling.** Dana Point's **swimming beach** is off Dana Point Harbor Dr. at the end of

Del Obispo St. The next beach town to follow is **San Clemente,** a "small Spanish village by the sea," which has a stucco-Greek-isle feel. Farther south is **San Onofre State Beach** and its famous "Trestles" area, a break point and therefore a prime surfing zone for more experienced thrill-seekers. The south end of the beach is frequented by **nudists.** (Drive down as far as you can go, and walk left on the trail for ¼-½mi. There are gay and straight areas.) Nude bathing, however, is illegal; you'll be fined if caught with your pants down.

AMUSEMENT AND WATER PARKS

Amusement parks of the rather wet variety can be found at **Wild Rivers Waterpark,** 8770 Irvine Center Dr. (768-9453) in Irvine, off I-405. With over 40 waterslide rides and two wave pools, this is almost as good as a cold shower. (Call for hours. Admission $21, seniors $10, ages 3-9 $17.)

SEASONAL EVENTS

Strawberry Festival (714-638-0981), May 26-29 in 2000, in downtown Garden Grove on the village green. Garden Grove is the U.S.'s leading producer of strawberries, and the festival includes some arduous strawberry-pie-eating contests.

Festival of Arts and **The Pageant of the Masters** (800-487-3378), July-Aug., take place together in the Irvine Bowl, 650 Laguna Canyon Rd. in Laguna Beach. Life literally imitates art in the pageant as residents who have rehearsed for months don the makeup and costumes of figures in famous paintings and pose for 90-second tableaux, astonishingly similar to the original artwork. Admission $2, seniors $1. Art show open daily 10am-11pm. Tickets $10-50. For reservations, contact the Festival of Arts, P.O. Box 1659, Laguna Beach, 92652.

Sawdust Festival (949-494-3030), July 1-Aug. 29 in 2000, across the street from The Pageant of the Masters. Arts, crafts, and children's activities aplenty.

Christmas Boat Parade of Lights (949-729-4400), the week before Christmas, in Newport Harbor. Over 200 boats and zillions of lights create a dazzling display.

EAST OF L.A.

L.A.'s huddled masses who yearn to be free—and breathe free—often pack up their kids, cell phones, and cares, and head for the hills. Granite mountains, scenic hiking trails, campgrounds, and scented pine forests repose a mere 45-minute drive above and beyond the inversion layer (the altitude at which the smog ends).

In the mountains, outdoor activities flourish year-round, but winter is definitely the high season. While the Sierra Nevada resorts around Lake Tahoe and Mammoth Lake are destinations of choice for serious California skiers, daytrips to the smaller resorts of the San Bernardino mountains have become increasingly popular. Temperatures typically allow ski resorts to operate from November through April. Always call ahead to check conditions and bring tire chains. But even when the snow melts, the coastal mountains are an ideal getaway. The Angeles and San Bernardino National Forests sprawl across majestic mountains, and have many campgrounds, hiking trails, and mountain villages. Driving in these mountains is breathtaking, both in terms of the scenery and the fear induced by cliffside roads.

ANGELES NATIONAL FOREST

National forest land covers about one quarter of Los Angeles County, north of Pasadena and east of Valencia. Cradling the northern edge of the L.A. Basin and San Gabriel Valley are the San Gabriel Mountains, whose highest peak, Mt. San Antonio, or "Old Baldy," tops out at 10,064 snow-capped feet. This area is popular year-round and attracts mountain bikers, anglers, bird watchers, and hikers. Harsh weather and frequent brush fires often rearrange the place, but rangers give helpful directions. Skiers will probably find Big Bear more worthwhile than the closer resorts at Mt. Baldy (909-982-0800) and Mt. High East and West (760-249-5808).

RANGER STATIONS

Three visitors centers offer info about activities and rentals: **Chilao** (626-796-5541), on the Angeles Crest Hwy. (Rte. 2), 26 miles from La Cañada (open Sa-Su 9am-5pm); **Grassy Hollow** (626-821-6737), also on Rte. 2, six miles west of Wrightwood (open Sa-Su 10am-4pm); **Mount Baldy,** on Mt. Baldy Rd. north of Ontario (open daily 8am-4:30pm). In an **emergency,** contact the Angeles National Forest Dispatcher (818-447-8999 in the Arcadia area, 661-723-7619 in the Lancaster area).

All ranger stations listed are open Monday through Friday from 8am to 4:30pm.

Angeles National Forest Headquarters, Supervisor's Office, 701 N. Santa Anita Ave., Arcadia (626-574-1613). Comprehensive forest maps ($4.33).

Los Angeles River Ranger District, 4600 Oak Grove Dr., Flintridge (818-790-1151). This is the south-central area of the forest, just north of Pasadena. Gateway to the Angeles National Forest via Rte. 2. There are 20 campgrounds in this district, which function in conjunction with the **Tujunga Work Center,** 12371 N. Little Tujunga Canyon Rd., San Fernando (818-899-1900). Covers the west end of the San Gabriel Mountains. Hiking and horseback-riding trails, and 5 overnight campgrounds.

San Gabriel River Ranger District, 110 N. Wabash Ave., Glendora (626-335-1251). The southeastern district of the forest includes several 8000 ft. peaks, hiking trails, the cascading San Antonio Falls, and scenic Glendora Ridge Rd.

Santa Clara Ranger District, 30800 Bouquet Canyon Rd., Saugus (805-296-9710). Northwest of the main forest. Pyramid, Elizabeth, and Castaic Lakes have boating and fishing facilities. 11 campgrounds available. This district also includes the **Mojave River Work Center,** P.O. Box 15, 29835 Valyermo Rd., Valyermo (661-944-2187), which covers the northeastern sector of the San Gabriel Mountains. There are many campgrounds along Big Pines Hwy., which runs southeast from Pear Blossom into the northeastern corner of the forest. Big Pines is the 1st stop on the earthquake fault tour, a self-guided route that passes scars left by major tremors.

CAMPGROUNDS

The U.S. Forest Service maintains an impressive array of well-groomed hiking trails and camping facilities. Many of the 660 miles of trails cross each other, so maps are vital. Campsites are a scant $5-12 per night (payment by the honor system). Sites are first-come, first-camped (14-night max. stay). The National Forest Adventure Pass allows visitors to park near the trails.

Chilao, off Rte. 2, 25mi. northeast of La Cañada Flintridge. Broad, flat mountaintop camping. Visitors center and forest amphitheater offer nature walks, talks, and children's activities. All 110 sites have fire rings, tables, water, and toilets, but no hookups. Open year-round. Sites $12.

Buckhorn, on Rte. 2 26mi. southwest of Wrightwood, has 40 sites surrounded by lush ferns and towering redwoods. All have fire rings, tables, water, and toilets, but no hookups. Open June.-Nov. Sites $12.

Glen Trail Camp, off Rte. 39 North at the end of the West Fork National Bike Trail (16mi. round-trip). Stream water only (treat before drinking). 10 sites. Free.

HIKING

Many of the area's trailheads are at campgrounds. The **West Fork National Bike Trail** (16mi. round-trip), ends at Glen Camp campground off Rte. 39 north. The trail from Buckhorn campground to **Cooper Canyon Trail** (4½mi. round-trip) is one of the prettiest hikes in the forest. A number of longer trails connect to the Pacific Crest Trail, such as the one to **Mount Waterman** (7mi. round-trip from Buckhorn)—watch for bighorn sheep. The **Chilao to Devil's Canyon Trail** (7mi. round-trip) is accessible from Chilao campground and passes through dense forest on its way to Devil's Canyon. Only experienced hikers should continue beyond the canyon. The 4½-mile **Rattlesnake Trail** to **Mount Wilson** departs from the West Fork campground. It has fantastic views of Mt. Wilson, Mt. Baldy, the Channel Islands, and the L.A. Basin, and no, there are no more snakes here than anywhere else. To get there, take Rte. 2 and park at the American Indian Cultural Center, then hike two miles down the **Gabrielino Trail.**

The three-day, 53-mile (round-trip) **Gabrielino Trail** connects Oak Grove Park and the north end of Windsor Ave. in La Cañada Flintridge. Long hikes such as this one make **trail camping** necessary. Fortunately, it is free and legal, but fire permits are required (available at ranger stations) and camping is not allowed within 200 feet of any stream.

Descanso Gardens, 4118 Descanso Dr. (818-952-4400), is in nearby La Cañada, by the intersection of Rte. 2 and 210. (Open daily 9am-4:30pm. Admission $5, students and seniors $3, ages 5-12 $1.) The garden includes the world's largest camellia forest, a historic rose collection, and manmade waterfalls.

BIG BEAR

Hibernating in the San Bernardino Mountains, the town of Big Bear Lake entertains hordes of visitors with winter skiing and summer hiking, biking, and boating. The consistent winds, no doubt made up of the sighs of relaxing Angelenos, make the lake one of the best for sailing in the state.

ORIENTATION AND PRACTICAL INFORMATION

To reach Big Bear Lake, take the **San Bernardino Freeway (Interstate 10)** to the junction of Rte. 30 and 330. Follow **Route 330,** also known as Mountain Rd., to **Route 18,** a *very* long and winding uphill road. About halfway up the mountain, Rte. 18 becomes **Big Bear Boulevard,** the main route encircling the lake. A less-congested route is via I-10 to Redlands and then **Route 38** to Big Bear Lake. Driving time from L.A. is about 2½ hours, barring serious weekend traffic or road closures. The loneliest route to Big Bear Lake curls across the high desert along Rte. 18 through the Lucerne Valley. Weekend day skiers should wait until after 6pm to head home, thereby avoiding the 4pm rush. Rte. 38 runs along the north shore of Big Bear Lake, and Rte. 18 (Big Bear Blvd.) is on the south side. The Stanfield Cutoff, a short north-south road across one end of the lake, connects the two routes. **Mountain Area Regional Transit Authority** (MARTA; 584-1111) runs buses from the Greyhound station in San Bernardino to Big Bear (Su-F 3 per day, Sa 2 per day; $5, seniors and disabled $3.75). Buses also run the length of Big Bear Blvd. (end-to-end trip 1hr.; $1, students 75¢, seniors and disabled 50¢). MARTA also operates **Dial-A-Ride** ($2, students $1.75, seniors and disabled $1).

The **Big Bear Chamber of Commerce,** 630 Bartlett Rd., P.O. Box 2860, Big Bear Lake 92315 (866-4608; fax 866-5412; www.bigbearchamber.com), in the "village," dispenses glossy brochures and arranges lodging and ski packages (open M-F 8am-5pm, Sa-Su 9am-5pm). The **Big Bear Lake Resort Association** (866-7000 or 800-4BIGBEAR/424-4232; www.bigbearinfo.com) has info on lodging, local events, and ski and road conditions (open M-F 8am-6pm, Sa-Su 9am-5pm). **Big Bear Discovery Center** (BBDC; 866-3437, emergency 383-5651), on Rte. 38 four miles east of Fawnskin and 1¼ miles west of the Stanfield Cutoff, also sells maps and the new

National Forest Adventure Pass ($5), which is required for vehicles at free camping sites. See **Camping,** below. (Open daily in summer 8am-6pm; in winter 8am-4:30pm.) **Area code:** 909.

ACCOMMODATIONS AND CAMPGROUNDS

Big Bear has few budget accommodations, especially in the winter. The best option for daytrippers is probably to stay in Redlands or San Bernardino, although the drive down Rte. 18 can be difficult at night. **Big Bear Boulevard,** the main drag on the lake's south shore, is lined with lodging possibilities, but groups can find the best deals by sharing a cabin. **Mountain Lodging Unlimited** (800-487-3168), arranges lodging and lift packages (from $96 per couple; open daily in summer 9am-midnight; in winter 7am-midnight.)

Hillcrest Lodge, 40241 Big Bear Blvd. (866-7330, reservations 800-843-4449). A favorite for honeymooners. Pine paneling and skylights give these cozy rooms a ritzy feel at a budget price. Jacuzzi, cable TV, and free local calls. Small rooms $35-49; 4-person units with kitchen $64-89; 2-bedroom suites with hearth and kitchen $57-79. In winter: small $39-69; 4-person units and suites $74-125.

Cozy Hollow Lodge, 40409 Big Bear Blvd. (866-9694 or 800-882-4480). Cute gingerbread-style cabins are furnished accordingly with fireplace, TV, and kitchenette. Breakfast included. Rooms Su-Th $71-152, F-Sa $79-169. AAA discount.

Motel 6, 42899 Big Bear Blvd. (585-6666). Lacks the rustic appeal of a lodge, but boasts the lowest prices on the mountain. Singles $35; doubles $41. In winter: singles $37; doubles $43; add $15 on weekends. Prices fluctuate with snowfall.

Embers Lodge, 40229 Big Bear Blvd. (866-2371). Wood-paneled studios with fireplaces, TVs, and phones sleep 2-8 people. Some with kitchen. Apr.-Thanksgiving (Nov. 23 in 2000) Su-Th $25, F-Sa $45-70; Thanksgiving-Mar. Su-Th $65, F-Sa $95-120.

Camping is permitted at U.S. Forest Service sites throughout the area. Several of the grounds listed below accept reservations through the toll-free National Recreation Reservation Service (877-444-6777; www.reserveusa.com) or the U.S. Forest Service (800-280-CAMP/2267). Most are open from May to November. Tent campers who want to avoid crowds can camp in undeveloped campgrounds on U.S. Forest Service land, at least 200 feet from streams, lakes, and roads. Information about these Remote Camping Areas and Yellow Post Sites, and the required free visitor permit can be obtained at the **Big Bear Discovery Center** (see **Practical Information,** above). In **emergencies,** call 383-5651 and reach a ranger station.

Pineknot (7000 ft.), on Summit Blvd. south of Big Bear. Amid thick woods, these 48 sites are surprisingly isolated. Nestled at the base of Snow Summit, this spot is popular with mountain bikers. Flush toilets and water. Sites $15. Wheelchair accessible.

Hanna Flat (7000 ft.), on Forest Rd. 3N14 2½mi. northwest of Fawnskin. Lush vegetation surrounds 88 roomy sites. Hiking, water, pit and flush toilets. Sites $15.

Serrano (6800 ft.), off Rte. 38, 2mi. east of Fawnskin. One of the most popular campgrounds around. Within sight of the road and right on the lake, this is city-slicker camping with flush toilets and hot showers. Hookups at 55 of the 132 sites. Sites $15, hookups $25. Handicap facilities.

Big Pine Flat (6800 ft.), on Forest Rd. 3N14, 7mi. northwest of Fawnskin. Dirt-bikers and other off-roaders favor these 17 sites because of their proximity to an off-highway vehicle area. Sites $10.

Holcomb Valley (7400 ft.), 4mi. north on Forest Rd. 2N09 to 3N16, then east for ¾mi. These 19 sites have pit toilets and no water. Near Pacific Crest Trail (see **From Crest to Crest: the Trail of the West,** p. 266). Sites $10.

FOOD

Food can get pricey, so those with kitchens should forage at **Stater Bros.,** 42171 Big Bear Blvd. (866-5211; open daily 7am-11pm). Many of the cutesy village eateries offer adorable all-you-can-eat specials.

Mongolian Palace, 40797 Lakeview Dr. (866-6678), just off Big Bear Blvd. Design your own dish from an all-you-can-eat buffet of raw meats and vegetables, then see the chef cook your creation. Lunch $7, dinner $9. Open M-Th 11am-9:30pm, F-Su 11am-10pm.

Maggio's Pizza, 42160 Big Bear Blvd. (866-8815), in the Vons plaza. Bring a hearty appetite for the huge subs and calzones ($5). Open M-Sa 11am-9pm, Su noon-9pm.

Grizzly Manor, 41268 Big Bear Blvd. (866-6226). A local favorite for breakfast (chocolate chip pancakes $4). Open W-F 7am-2pm, Sa-Su 6am-2pm.

Big Bear Prospectors, 40771 Lakeview Dr. (866-6696), overlooks the lake. Unfortunately, their $20 dinners are not too budget-friendly, but they do offer a great champagne brunch. (Su 9am-2pm; $8, under 10 $4.) Open Su-Th 7am-10pm, F-Sa 7am-midnight.

La Paws, 1128 W. Big Bear Blvd., Big Bear City (585-9115). A quaint, family-run spot serving tasty Mexican specialties at budget prices. Open daily 7am-8pm.

SUMMER RECREATION

The **National Forest Adventure Pass** is required for vehicles brought into the Angeles, Cleveland, Los Padres, and San Bernardino National Forests, though not for vehicles parked at ranger stations, ski resorts, or campgrounds where a fee is charged. Passes can be purchased at ranger stations (for overnight parking only; day pass $5, one-year pass $30).

The **hiking** here is both free and priceless. Maps, trail descriptions, and the *Visitor's Guide to the San Bernardino National Forest* are available at the **Big Bear Discovery Center** (see **Practical Information,** above). The easy 1½-mile **Woodland Trail** begins one mile east of the BBDC and has 20 nature stops along the way. The moderately difficult three-mile **Pineknot Trail** begins at the Aspen Glen picnic area. The high altitudes here make slow climbing necessary. Serious hikers may want to catch a piece of the **Pacific Crest Trail,** which extends 2638 miles from Mexico to Canada and has trail camps every 10 miles (for more info, see **From Crest to Crest: the Trail of the West,** p. 266). The BBDC can direct hikers to any of the multiple entry points in the area.

Mountain biking is a popular activity in Big Bear when the snow melts. Route information is available from each ranger station and at **Snow Summit** (866-4621), which operates lifts in summer so thrill-seeking bikers can plummet downhill without the grueling uphill ride ($7 per ride, day pass $19; ages 7-12 $3, $8; helmet required). **Team Big Bear,** 476 Concklin Rd. (866-4565), operating out of the **Mountain Bike Shop** at the base of the Snow Summit Scenic Sky Chair, sponsors several organized bike races each summer and rents bikes. ($6.50 per hr., $32 per day; helmet included. For more race info, call Apr.-Oct. daily 9am-5pm, or write Team Big Bear, Box 2932, Big Bear Lake 92315.) Bikes can also be rented from **Big Bear Bikes,** 41810 Big Bear Blvd. (866-2224; open daily 10am-5pm, extended F-Sa hr. if it's busy).

Many summer activities take place on the water. State **fishing** licenses are available at area sporting goods stores (day $10, season $28), and the **Big Bear Fishing Association** (866-6260) dispenses useful information. Any part of the lake will afford good fishing, but only the north shore is accessible to everyone; the south shore is mostly private property. For stocking information, updated weekly, call 562-590-5020. **Boats** can be rented at any one of Big Bear's marinas. **Holloway's Marina and RV Park,** 398 Edgemor Rd. (800-448-5335), on the South Shore, rents boats (half-day $46-130).

If you don't have the patience for wildlife watching in the National Forest, head over to **Moonridge Animal Park** (866-0183), south of Big Bear Blvd. at the end of Moonridge Rd. (Open daily May-Sept. 10am-5pm; Oct.-Apr. 10am-4pm. Admission $2.50, ages 3-10 $1.50.) This animal care center has the only big bears in Big Bear: **grizzlies.** The four-year-old male cub is named Harley, in honor of his sponsors, the Inland Empire chapter of the Harley-Davidson Club. **Magic Mountain Recreation Area,** 800 Wild Rose Ln., west of Big Bear Lake Village, operates an **alpine slide** (866-4626; open M-Th 10am-6pm; 1 ride $3.50, 5 rides $15), **waterslide park** (1 ride $1, unlimited rides $12), and **miniature golf** course ($4, under 13 $3) for summer visitors (open in summer daily 10am-9pm).

WINTER RECREATION

When conditions are favorable, ski areas run out of lift tickets quickly. **Tickets** for the resorts listed below may be purchased over the phone through Ticketmaster (714-740-2000). Driving the crowded mountain roads to popular destinations can challenge both vehicle and driver. Gas stations are scarce on the way up the mountain, and signs notify drivers of tire chain requirements. Call CalTrans (800-427-7623) for info on road conditions.

Cross-country skiing and biking along Big Bear's many trails are popular ways to dig the mountain's wintertime groove. Rent skis, boots, and poles at **Big Bear Bikes,** 41810 Big Bear Blvd. (866-2224), for $12 per day; trail information is free. The following resorts cater to downhill skiing and snowboarding.

Big Bear Resort (585-2519; snow report 800-BEARMTN/232-7686), 1½mi. southeast of downtown Big Bear Lake. 12 lifts and 32 trails cover 195 acres of terrain including huge vertical drops, plus many more acres of undeveloped land suitable for adventurous skiers. More expert runs than other area slopes. Lift tickets $32, holidays $45. Skis $23, snowboards $30. New skier/snowboarder packages include group lesson, lift ticket, and equipment rental.

Snow Summit (866-5766, reservations 909-866-5841), 1mi. east of Big Bear Lake. 11 lifts (including 2 high-speed quads) serve over 40 runs which include a well-rounded assortment of beginner runs, snowmaking, and night skiing. Lift tickets $32, holidays $45. Skis $17, snowboards $30; deposit required.

Snow Valley (867-2751, snow report 867-5151), near Running Springs. 13 lifts, 800-5000ft. runs, snowmaking, and night skiing, and a skate park in the summer. The most family-oriented resort in Big Bear, with a children's obstacle course and beginner trails. Lift ticket $38 (1-9pm $29), under 13 $23 (1-9pm $17). Equipment rental $14, under 13 $10.

NEAR BIG BEAR: SAN GORGONIO WILDERNESS AREA

The San Gorgonio Wilderness Area consists of nearly 60,000 acres of rugged land set aside from the rest of the San Bernardino National Forest and spared from any kind of development. Almost 100 miles of trail afford access to the area's remarkable summits, the highest of which, **San Gorgonio** (affectionately dubbed "Old Grayback" for its barren summit), is the tallest peak in Southern California at 11,500 feet. Its summit commands views of the southern Sierra, Mexico, the Pacific Ocean, and the Mojave Desert. There are no improved campgrounds within the wilderness area, although backcountry camping is allowed in some areas.

To get far into the backcountry, you must have a **wilderness permit.** These are free and may be obtained up to three months in advance in person at the **Mill Creek ranger station** (909-794-1123; near Methone, about 40mi. west of Big Bear on Rte. 38; open for info and cancellations M-F 8am-4:30pm, Sa-Su 6:30am-3pm; in winter M-F 8am-4:30pm, Sa-Su 7am-3:30pm), or at the **Barton Flats Visitor Information Center** (909-794-4861; on Rte. 38 about 25mi. from Big Bear; open for info and cancellations W-Su 8am-4:30pm).

Most people need two days to hike San Gorgonio, and the South Fork trail off Jenks Lake Rd. (off Rte. 38) is the most convenient trailhead to Barton Flats and consequently to Big Bear. Good maps can be obtained at Barton Flats or Mill Creek ($4.31). While backcountry camping is free, parking isn't; an **Adventure Pass** must be obtained for each day your car is parked. Bring plenty of water and watch out for those bears (see **Bears Will Eat You,** p. 51).

If you prefer seeing San Gorgonio from the road, there are a handful of campgrounds along a five-mile stretch of Rte. 38 near Barton Flats Visitor Center. San Gorgonio and **Barton Flats Campgrounds,** near the visitors center, are the most expensive ($15) and have showers; **Heart Bar,** toward Big Bear, is the cheapest ($9). Sites fill up fast on summer weekends, and reservations (800-280-CAMP/2267) are recommended for the more developed campgrounds.

SAN BERNARDINO

San Bernardino (pop. 181,718) is the kingpin of the mega-county of the same name. More than twice the size of Rhode Island, San Bernardino has the largest area of any California county, but the county seat has no such dreams of grandeur. This sleepy burg is best visited as a stopover en route to Big Bear or the desert.

PRACTICAL INFORMATION. MARTA buses (338-1113), run to Big Bear (see p. 430) via Arrowhead (1½hr., 3 per day, $5). For a taxi, call **YellowCab** (884-1111). The **Metrolink** trains, 1204 W. 3rd St. (808-LINK/5465), connect L.A. and San Bernardino with 75 trains on five routes ($5.75; call M-F 4:30am-10:30pm, Sa-Su 9am-9pm). The **San Bernardino Convention and Visitors Bureau,** 201 North E. St. #103 (889-3980), at the 2nd St. Exit off Rte. 215 North or 3rd St. Exit off Rte. 215 South, has maps and the *Inland Empire Adventure Guide!*. The dearth of brochures reflects the area's level of activity. (Open M-F 8am-5pm.) **Emergency:** 911. **Police:** 384-5742. **San Bernardino Community Hospital:** 1805 Medical Ctr. Dr. (887-6333), 24hr. emergency care. **Post office:** 390 W. 5th St. (800-275-8777), downtown (open M-F 8am-5pm). **Area code:** 909.

ACCOMMODATIONS, FOOD, AND THE SITE OF THE WORLD'S FIRST MCDONALD'S. The area along Mt. Vernon Ave. (old Rte. 66), is not-so-safe, so out-of-towners (that's you) should stick to either the north end of town or Hospitality Ln., which crosses Waterman Ave. just north of I-10. At the **Budget Inn,** 1280 S. E St. (888-0271), the rooms have fridges and breakfast is included (singles $33, doubles $35). **Motel 6,** 1960 Ostrems Way (887-8191), at the University Pkwy. Exit off Rte. 215, is near Cal State University (singles $36; doubles $42). In 1936, the **Stater Bros. Markets** chain was founded in nearby Yucaipa, and now there are 46 of the stores in the county. Two local branches can supply provisions for the long drive ahead: 1085 W. Highland Ave. (886-1517; open daily 7am-11pm) and 648 W. 4th St. (888-0048; open daily 7am-10pm). **Hogi Yogi,** 4595 University Parkway (887-7812), serves tasty sandwiches (regular "hogi," $3-4) and frozen yogurt with your choice of mix-in (small "yogi," $2.15). The original **McDonald's** once stood at 1398 N. E Street, but don't expect 15¢ burgers anymore. The only thing offered at this historic site is a growing display of Golden Arches memorabilia.

IDYLLWILD AND SAN JACINTO MOUNTAINS

Both idle and wild, as its name seems to suggest, Idyllwild is beguiling. Like the rest of California, this area has had its share of brush fires, but the town and hiking trails remain untouched. Despite the growing number of visitors and the seemingly endless drive along the edge of a precipice, Idyllwild is worth the trouble for avid hikers and campers. Alpine novices and experienced climbers alike will find dozens of trails offering incredible views of the desert and the smoggy city below.

ORIENTATION

From L.A., the swiftest approach is via **Interstate 10** and **Route 243** South from Banning. This route is curvy enough to make your ears pop and your stomach drop. From San Diego, there are no major interstates, but there are a number of routes to Palm Springs. Drivers should fill up the gas tank before starting, as gas in Idyllwild is expensive and difficult to find. The Palm Springs Aerial Tramway offers the only **public transportation** to Mt. San Jacinto; from there the town of Idyllwild is accessible by hiking or skiing. (See **Practical Information,** below, or **Palm Springs: Sights and Activities,** p. 466, for more info on the tramway.)

PRACTICAL INFORMATION

Visitor Information:

Idyllwild Chamber of Commerce, 54295 Village Center Dr. (659-3259; www.idyllwild.org), downstairs in the *Town Crier* building across from the Idyllwild Inn. Info and restaurant coupons. Open M-F 10am-5pm.

San Jacinto Ranger Station (U.S. Forest Service), 54270 Pine Crest Ave. (659-2117). Maps of hiking trails and campgrounds ($1-4). Free mandatory wilderness permits for day hiking and overnight backpacking. Buy an Adventure Pass ($5) if you plan to park your car on U.S. Forest Service property. Open daily 8am-4:30pm.

Mt. San Jacinto State Park and Wilderness Headquarters, 25905 Rte. 243 (659-2607). Free mandatory wilderness permits available; maps for sale ($1-8). Open daily 8am-5pm.

Ski Conditions and Tram Info: 619-325-1391. Tram from Palm Springs to Mt. San Jacinto runs every 30min. Round-trip fare $18, seniors $15, children 5-12 $12. Open M-F 10am-8pm, Sa-Su 8am-8pm.

Equipment Rental: Nomad Ventures, 54414 N. Circle Dr. (659-4853), specializes in selling "Mountain Equipage," but rentals are also available: rock climbing shoes ($3.75 per ½-day, $7.50 per day), cross-country skis, boots, and poles ($20 for 2 days), or backpacks ($15 for 5 days). Open M 9:30am-5:30pm, Th-F 9:30am-6pm, Sa 9am-6:30pm, Su 9am-6pm.

Emergency: 911. **Riverside Mountain Rescue Unit, Inc.** (654-6200). Search-and-rescue missions for injured or lost hikers in the San Jacinto mountains.

Police: Banning Sheriff (922-7100) 24hr.

Post Office: 54391 Village Center Dr. (800-275-8777), in the Strawberry Creek shopping center. Open M-F 9am-5pm. **ZIP Code:** 92549.

Area Codes: usually 909; 619 where noted (Mt. San Jacinto marks the dividing line).

ACCOMMODATIONS AND CAMPGROUNDS

Hiking and camping enthusiasts could stay here for weeks on a pittance, but those who would rather relax on the porch of a cabin will find steep prices unless they're traveling in a group of four or more. **Idyllwild Lodging Information** (659-5520), gives a rundown of the available options. The best bet for a group is **Knotty Pine Cabins,** 54340 Pine Crest Dr. (659-2933), off Rte. 243 north of town in an alpine setting. The eight cabins have wood-paneled interiors, linen, and cable TV, and all but one have fully equipped kitchens. (2-person cabin Su-Th $45, F-Sa $52; 6-person cabin Su-Th $100-110, F-Sa $125.) **Tahouitz Motel,** 25840 Rte. 243 (659-4554), has a pool and spa (doubles Su-Th $50, F-Sa $56).

Area campsites are operated by the **San Bernardino National Forest, Mount San Jacinto State Park, San Bernardino County,** and private entrepreneurs. Wilderness maps ($1) are available at the State Park Headquarters and give a good overview of patchwork jurisdictions. U.S. Forest Service grounds, better suited to hard-core nature lovers, tend to be the cheapest, while State Park grounds are best maintained. Call (800-280-CAMP/2267) to reserve a national site (including the ones listed here), or PARKNET (800-444-7275) for State Park campgrounds. **Dark Canyon,** six miles north of town on Rte. 243, is by far the best campsite in Idyllwild. It can accommodate 22-foot-long RVs, and has vault toilets, hiking, and fishing. The other campgrounds in the area, **Fern Basin** and **Marion Mountain,** are worthy backups of comparable size. Fifteen-foot RVs can park at Marion. These three campgrounds, at elevations of 5800-6400 feet, have a total of 69 sites. **Boulder Basin** is 15 miles north of Idyllwild off Rte. 243, high on the Black Mountain. The 34 sites offer vault toilets, untreated water, and splendid views of Marion Mountain and surrounding valleys, but the dirt road is difficult in spots and not made for RVs. (Most sites $10; more expensive closer to town. Open May-Oct.)

FOOD

Restaurant prices seem to rise with the altitude, so supermarkets are the cheapest option. **Fairway Supermarket** (659-2737), in the Strawberry Creek shopping center off Village Center Dr., has reasonable prices (open spring-fall M-Sa 9am-9pm, Su 9am-7pm; in winter M-Sa 9am-8pm, Su 9am-7pm). The **Squirrel's Nest** (659-3993), on the corner of Rte. 243 and Pinecrest Ave., has sandwiches and burgers, including a $4 cheeseburger special with fries and drink (open M 11am-3pm, Tu-Sa 11am-7pm, Su 11am-6pm). The **Village Market Deli,** 2600 Rte. 243 (659-3169), has a wide array of $4 sandwiches ($2 special daily except summer weekends) and fresh-baked goods that are perfect for taking on long hikes (open daily 8am-10pm).

SIGHTS

Idyllwild's natural setting offers visitors far more than the town itself does. The mountains challenge rock climbers while hundreds of miles of trails lead hikers through tranquil forests. Summer comes slowly; it is customary for over 10 feet of snow to blanket the mountain peaks above the town in May and even June. The view of the desert and surrounding mountains is amazing, especially where the Santa Rosa/San Jacinto ranges come to a screeching halt and plummet 9000 feet in under six miles. The **Palms-to-Pines Highway,** which connects with Rte. 74, offers a driver's-eye view of the transition from desert to mountain. The highway runs 36 miles between Mountain Center (south of Idyllwild at the junction of Rte. 74 and 243) and Rte. 111 at Palm Desert.

The **Ernie Maxwell Scenic Trail** (2½mi.), named after the guru and *Town Crier* founder, makes a gentle loop through the forest for day hikers. This is the only trail that does not require a wilderness permit. More serious backpackers can travel a section of the 2600-mile **Pacific Crest Trail** (55mi. lie in the San Jacinto District). For more info, see **From Crest to Crest: the Trail of the West,** page 266. Pick up the trail at Rte. 74 one mile east of Rte. 371 or at Black Mountain's scenic **Fuller Ridge Trail,** which itself is a strenuous 7½-mile hike. Some of the most rewarding and exhausting hikes begin in the canyons owned by Native Americans on the southwest fringe of Palm Springs and climb slowly into the foothills. Routes along the **Devil's Slide Trail** are excellent, but during summer weekends the limited number of permits for this area are given out very quickly, so get to the ranger station as soon as it opens (see **Practical Information,** p. 435). Those who want peak views without a strenuous hike should try the **Deer Spring Trail** to Suicide Rock (3mi.), which continues to the Palm Springs tram.

Idyllwild ARTS, 52500 Temecula Dr. (659-2171), at the end of Toll Gate Rd. off Rte. 243, gives frequent dance, drama, and music performances (free), exhibitions, and workshops. The emphasis is on Native American arts and crafts. Enjoy live music at the annual August **Jazz in the Pines** festival (659-3774; tickets $20-25).

NORTH OF L.A.

Today, government legislation ensures a profusion of prime hiking and camping in this vast expanse of protected park land. The unspoiled coastline, chaparral, and rolling hills stretch from the Santa Monica mountains up to the southern end of the Central Coast, displaying some of the most spectacular scenery California has to offer.

SANTA MONICA NATIONAL RECREATION AREA

"Recreation area" is a suitably vague term for the private and public lands that constitute the Santa Monica National Recreation Area. The best place to gather information is at the **National Park Service Headquarters,** 401 Hillcrest Dr., Thousand Oaks (805-370-2301), off U.S. 101 at the Lynn Rd. Exit (open daily 9am-5pm).

State-run campsites can be reserved through DESTINET (800-444-7275): **Leo Carrillo** and **Point Mugu** cost $18, and **Malibu Creek** (see **Accommodations,** p. 368) costs $16. There is backcountry camping at **Topanga State Park** ($3).

These hills sport more than 570 miles of **hiking trails** of widely varying difficulty; ask a ranger for advice before heading out. Excellent guide books, *Hike Los Angeles, Vol. 1 and Vol. 2* ($8-10 each, sold at the ranger station), include a couple of the most popular walks in the park, with relevant info about the area's ecology and history. If **Malibu Creek** looks vaguely like the set of *M*A*S*H*, that's because it was. Much of the set was dismantled after the television show's shooting ended in 1982, and more of it was destroyed in subsequent fires, but an easy 1½-mile hike from the Crags Rd. trailhead leads to the remaining jeep and ambulance and the **flat area** above the bank that was the helipad. Die-hard outdoor enthusiasts might want to taste the pain of the **Backbone Trail,** a 70-mile, three-to-five-day journey from Pt. Mugu to Sunset Blvd. in the Pacific Palisades. Not all sections of the trail have been completed, so consult a ranger first.

The National Park Service administers the **Paramount Ranch Site,** which was used as a location for several Paramount films between 1927 and 1953. Director Cecil B. DeMille and actors Gary Cooper and Mae West all worked here at a time when filmmakers were first experimenting with turning nearby landscapes into distant locales. The ranch served as colonial Massachusetts in *The Maid of Salem* (1937), ancient China in *The Adventures of Marco Polo* (1938), and early San Francisco in *Wells Fargo* (1937). After purchasing the property in 1980, the U.S. Park Service revitalized the old movie set, and **Western Town** was then used as the set for television's now-defunct *Dr. Quinn, Medicine Woman.* The set is now used for various film projects, and is open to visitors. To reach the ranch, take U.S. 101 to the Kanan Rd. Exit (in Agoura Hills). Turn left onto Jana Rd. and then left onto Cornell St., and continue 2½ miles to the entrance on the right.

SAN DIEGO

San Diegans are fond of referring to their garden-like town as "America's Finest City." This claim is difficult to dispute—San Diego (pop. 2,700,000) has all the virtues of other California cities without their frequently cited drawbacks. No smog fills this city's air and no sewage spoils its silver seashores. Its zoo is the nation's best, its food and lodging prices are fractions of their L.A. counterparts, and its city center contains a greater concentration of museums than any spot in America save Washington, D.C.

The city was founded when the seafaring Spanish extended an onshore leave in 1769 and began the first permanent settlement on the West Coast of the United States. Despite this early start, San Diego remained a small town throughout the California population boom of the 19th and early 20th century—it didn't even become a city proper until the 1940s. Following the Pearl Harbor attack, San Diego's population exploded, and it became the headquarters of the U.S. Pacific Fleet. Even today, San Diego is home to hordes of sailors (drunken and otherwise); 11 naval bases dot the area, and parts of the city's skyline are composed of hulking superstructures atop aircraft carriers and cruisers.

Today, San Diego is more peaceful and less militaristic as other industries catch up to Uncle Sam. This is the country's sixth and California's second-largest city, and one of its fastest-growing, as immigrants flock to its cheery climes—diluting the area's formerly staunch conservatism.

HIGHLIGHTS OF SAN DIEGO

- If you like animals, the **San Diego Zoo** (p. 447) and **Wild Animal Park** (p. 447) are some of the best places in the world to view animals in captivity.
- **Coronado Island, Point Loma, Mission** and **Pacific Beaches,** and **La Jolla** are fabulous oceanside spots in California (p. 450).
- History buffs can check out **Old Town** for museums, historic buildings (some reputedly haunted), and the **Mission Basilica San Diego de Alcatá** (p. 449).
- Fond of dead and scary things? Then you'll love rank-and-vile Downtown's **Museum of Death** (p. 446). Be warned that it is not for the weak of heart, mind, or stomach.

ORIENTATION

San Diego rests in the extreme southwest corner of California, 127 miles south of Los Angeles and 15 miles north of Mexico. Three major freeways link the city to its regional neighbors: **Interstate 5** runs south from L.A. and skirts the eastern edge of downtown; **Interstate 15** runs northeast through the desert to Las Vegas, Nevada; and **Interstate 8** runs east-west along downtown's northern boundary, connecting the desert with Ocean Beach. The major downtown thoroughfare, **Broadway,** also runs east-west. Bus and train stations sit on the western end of Broadway in reasonably safe areas. The downtown hotels listed below lie east and north of these stations in areas that are safer still, but exercise caution when walking downtown, as the area attracts aggressive panhandlers. In the **North County, Pacific Coast Highway** runs parallel to I-5 and is known as historic Rte. 101, 1st St., or Carlsbad Blvd.

The most obvious landmark in San Diego is **Balboa Park,** home to many museums and the impressive San Diego Zoo and Wild Animal Park. The cosmopolitan **Hillcrest** and **University Heights** districts border the park to the northeast. Southeast of the park lies the city's downtown business district, where San Diegans take time out from their busy relaxation schedules to put in a few hours at the office. South of downtown, between 4th and 6th St., is the newly revitalized **Gaslamp Quarter,** full of nightclubs, chic restaurants, and coffeehouses.

The downtown area is situated between San Diego's two major bays: **San Diego Bay,** formed by **Coronado Island,** lies just to the south, while **Mission Bay,** formed by the **Mission Beach** spit, lies to the northwest. Up the coast from Mission Beach are the communities of **Ocean Beach, Pacific Beach,** and wealthy **La Jolla.** Still farther north lie the cities and sights of San Diego's **North County** (see p. 456).

GETTING AROUND

The city of San Diego provides fairly extensive public transportation through the **San Diego Metropolitan Transit System (MTS).** MTS's automated 24 hour information line, **Info Express** (685-4900), has info on San Diego's buses, trains, and trolleys. To talk to live people, visit the **Transit Store** at 1st Ave. and Broadway, which has bus, trolley, and ferry tickets and timetables, as well as a free pamphlet with tips for riding (open M-F 8:30am-5:30pm, Sa-Su noon-4pm). The **Regional Transit Information Center** (233-3004) is also a good source, although it can be difficult to get through (open M-F 5:30am-8:30pm, Sa-Su 8am-5pm). **Buses** cost $1.75 for local routes and $2-3.25 for express buses (for route numbers ending with zeroes; free transfer within 1½hr.). They require exact fare, but accept dollar bills. All buses are wheelchair accessible. If getting to a bus stop is a problem, call the door-to-bus-stop service **DART** (293-3278; operates M-F 5:30am-8pm; only in certain areas). The **Coaster Express Rail** (800-COASTER/262-7837) glides in from Oceanside (fare $26-52).

The bright red **San Diego Trolley** (231-8549; www.sdcommute.com) consists of two lines leaving from downtown for El Cajon, San Ysidro, and points in between. The El Cajon line leaves from 12th Ave. and Imperial St.; the San Ysidro line leaves from the Old Town Transit Center (at Taylor St. and San Diego Ave.) and contin-

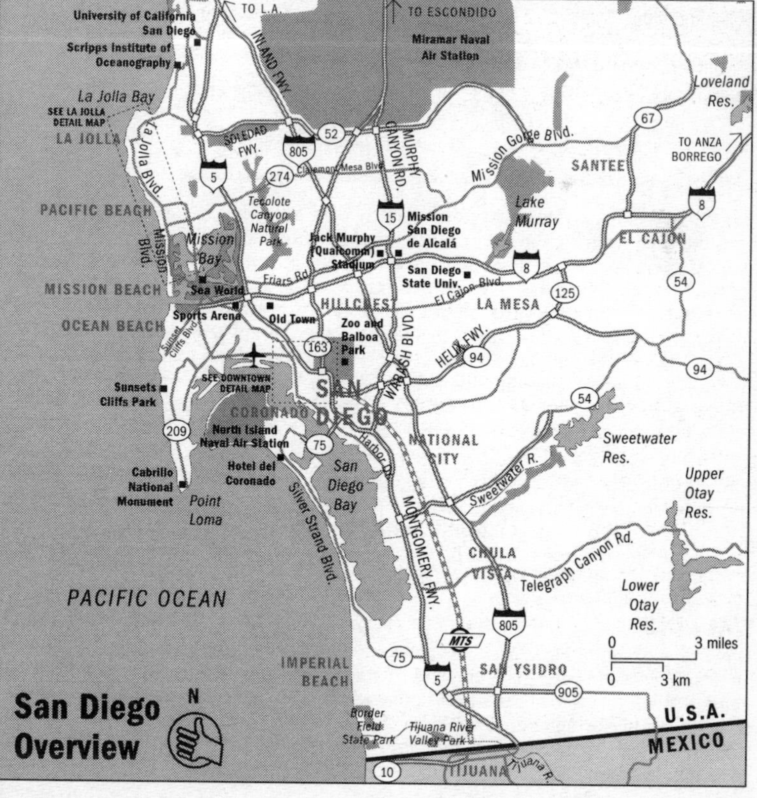

ues to the Mexican border. It is smart to buy a ticket; although there are no turnstiles, the inspector does indeed check for tickets and the fine is definitely *not* within reach of the budget traveler (trollies run daily 5am-1am; fare $1-2.25).

The **Day Tripper** allows unlimited rides on buses, ferries (such as the one to Coronado), and trolleys for one day ($5), two days ($8), three days ($10), or four days ($12), and is a wise purchase for those planning to use public transportation extensively. The pass can be purchased at the Transit Store or at trolley stations and is only good for consecutive days.

BY CAR

Southern California is the land of the automobile; renting a car will make your life easier and your trip more enjoyable. Most places will not rent to drivers under 21, but a letter from your insurer, stating that you are covered for rental car crashes, may go a long way toward getting you some wheels.

Academy Car, Jet Ski and Boat Rental, 2270 Hotel Circle N. (294-ACAR/2227 or 888-920-2227), in the Hanalei Mission Valley Hotel. Cars from $19 per day, $139-198 per week; 150mi. free per day, 700mi. per week. Ages 18-21 pay $8 per day surcharge, ages 21-25 pay $4. Insurance to bring the car into Mexico $6-12. Credit card required. Waverunners and boats also for rent. Open daily 8am-6pm.

Red and Blue/Payless Auto Rental, 2727 Kettner Blvd. (297-7071, 297-3861, or 800-282-4922). Cars from $22 per day, from $150 per week; unlimited mileage. Ages 18-20 pay $15 per day surcharge, ages 21-25 pay $10. Credit card and proof of insurance required. Open daily 4:30am-midnight.

Bargain Auto, 3860 Rosecrans St. (299-0009). Used cars which are available to renters 18 and older. Cars $17-29 per day, $95-185 per week; 150 free mi. per day, 500 per week. Those 18-25 pay $6 per day surcharge. $10 per day for the privilege of driving your rental car to Mexico. Credit card required. Open daily 8am-6pm.

Dollar, 2499 Pacific Hwy. (234-3388; www.dollar.com), at the airport. Cars $28-54 per day with unlimited mileage. Must be 21 with major credit card; ages 21-25 pay $20 per day surcharge. Can travel as far as Mexican border. Open daily 5:30am-midnight.

BICYCLES

San Diego has an extensive system of fairly easy **bike routes.** Some are separate from the road, while some are specially marked outer lanes. The flat, paved route along Mission and Pacific Beaches toward La Jolla affords ocean views and soothing sea breezes. But bikers beware: pedestrian traffic along the beaches rivals the automobiles on the boulevards. **Action Sports,** 4000 Coronado Bay Rd. (424-4466), at the Marina Dock of the Loews Coronado Bay Resort, rents beach cruiser bikes ($6 per hr., $18 per 4hr.), mountain bikes ($8 per hr., $24 per 4hr.), and full-suspension bikes ($10 per hr, $30 per 4hr.; open M-F 9am-6pm, Sa-Su 8:30am-6:30pm). The **Bike Cab Company,** 523 Island Ave. (232-4700), in the Gaslamp Quarter, is another place to rent bicycles ($5 per hr., $15 per day; open daily 10am-2am).

Buses equipped with bike carriers make it possible to cart bikes almost anywhere in the city (call 233-3004 to find out which routes have carriers). Bikes are also allowed on the San Diego Trolley with a $4 permit (available at **Transit Store**). For more bike info, contact the **City Bicycle Coordinator** (533-3110), or **CalTrans,** 4040 Taylor St., San Diego 92110 (231-2453), in Old Town. Write to request maps and pamphlets, including the free *San Diego County Bike Route Map.*

WALKING

Downtown, Balboa Park, and Old Town are easily managed on foot, but beaches are less accessible because of the wide distances between them. **Walkabout International,** 835 5th Ave. #407 (231-7463), sponsors about 150 walks each month, ranging from downtown architectural walks to 20-mile treks to La Jolla (open M-F 9:30am-2:30pm; expect an answering machine). Pedestrians almost always heed the walk signals because in San Diego jaywalking is actively prosecuted.

PRACTICAL INFORMATION

TRANSPORTATION

Airport: San Diego International (Lindbergh Field), at the northwest edge of downtown. Call the Travelers Aid Society (231-7361) for info about the airport (open daily 8am-11pm). Bus #2 goes downtown ($1.75), and so do cabs ($7).

Trains: Amtrak, 1050 Kettner Blvd. (239-9021 or 800-872-7245), just north of Broadway. To **L.A.** (11 trains daily 6am-8:30pm, buses at 10:20pm and 3:30am; in summer $25, off-season, $22.). Station has info on bus, trolley, car, and boat transportation. Ticket office open daily 5:15am-10:20pm.

Buses: Greyhound, 120 W. Broadway (239-8082 or 800-231-2222), at 1st St. To **L.A.** (30 per day 5am-11:35p; $13, round-trip $22). Ticket office open 24hr.

Auto Repairs: AAA Emergency Road Service (800-400-4222).

TOURIST AND FINANCIAL SERVICES

Visitor Information: International Visitor Information Center, 11 Horton Plaza (236-1212), downtown at 1st Ave. and F St. Helpful, multilingual staff dispenses publications, brochures, and discount coupons. 3hr. parking validation for lots with entrances on G St. and 4th Ave. Open June-Aug. M-Sa 8:30am-5pm, Su 11am-5pm; Sept.-May M-Sa 8:30am-5pm. The **San Diego Convention and Visitors Bureau,** 401 B St. #1400 Dept. 700, San Diego, CA 92101 (236-1212; www.sandiego.org) can also provide info. **Old Town and State Park Info,** 4002 Wallace Ave. (220-5422), in Old Town Sq. Take the Taylor St. Exit off I-8 or bus #5. Free walking tours leave daily at 11am and 2pm. Open daily 10am-5pm.

Budget Travel: San Diego Council of American Youth Hostels, 521 Market St., San Diego 92101 (338-9981; email hiayhsd1@aol.com; www.hostelweb.com/sandiego), in the Metropolitan Hostel at 5th St. Offers budget guides and info. Call, write, or email to have guides or info sent. Open daily 7am-11pm.

American Express: Locations at 7610 Hazard Center Dr. (297-8101; open M-F 9:30am-6pm, Sa 10am-3pm) and 258 Broadway (234-4455; open M-F 9am-5:30pm); 1020 Prospect (459-4161; open M-F 9am-5pm), in La Jolla.

LOCAL SERVICES

Senior Citizens Services, 202 C St. (236-6905), in the City Hall Bldg. Provides senior ID cards and plans daytrips. Open M-F 8am-5pm.

The Access Center, 1295 University Ave. #10 (293-3500, TDD 293-7757), Hillcrest. Attendant referral, wheelchair repair and sales, emergency housing, motel/hotel accessibility referral. Open M-F 9am-5pm. **Accessible San Diego,** 2466 Bartel St. (279-0704), also has info (open daily 10am-4pm).

The Center for Community Solutions, 4508 Mission Bay Dr. (233-8984, 24hr. hotline 272-1767), at Bunker Hill St. in Pacific Beach. Offers rape and domestic violence counseling and legal services. Open M-F 8am-4:30pm.

Bi-Gay-Lesbian Organizations and Publications: Lesbian and Gay Men's Center, 3909 Centre St. (692-2077), provides counseling and info. Open daily 9am-10pm. The **Gay Youth Alliance** (233-9309), is a support and social group for people under 24. For a listing of queer events and establishments, check *Update* (299-0500), available at virtually all queer businesses, bookstores, and bars. The *Gay and Lesbian Times,* released Thursdays, provides event, bar, and club listings.

Ticket Agencies: Ticketmaster (220-TIXS/8497; concert info 581-1000). Beware of the high service charge. Get half-price tickets from **Times Arts Tix** (497-5000; open Tu-Th 11am-6pm, F-Sa 10am-6pm).

Weather Conditions: Weather Report (221-8824, 226-7866, or 289-1212). Updated daily, as if the weather ever changes. The average daily temperature is 70, with nighttime lows around 60.

Radio: news/talk on KSDO (1130 AM), National Public Radio on KPBS (89.5 FM).

Laundromat: Metro Wash and Dry, 724 4th Ave. (544-1284), between F and G St. Wash $1.25, 8 min. dry 25¢. Open daily 6am-7:30pm.

EMERGENCY AND COMMUNICATIONS

Emergency: 911. **Police:** 531-2000.

Hospitals: Kaiser Foundation, 4647 Zion Ave. (528-5000); Columbia Mission Bay, 3030 Bunker Hill St., Mission Bay (858-274-7721).

24-Hour Crisis Lines: Lesbian and Gay Men's Center Crisis Line (800-479-3339). **Women's Center Rape Hotline** (233-3088).

24-Hour Pharmacy: Rite Aid, 535 Robinson Ave., Hillcrest (291-3705).

Post Offices: 800-275-8777; 2535 Midway Dr. Take bus #6, 9, or 35. Open M 7am-5pm, Tu-F 8am-5pm, Sa 8am-4pm. **ZIP Code:** 92186. 2150 Comstock St. Open M-F 8am-5pm, Sa 8am-4:30pm. **ZIP Code:** 92111.

Area Code: For parts of San Diego including Downtown, Coronado, and Ocean Beach: still 619. An area code split effective December 12, 1999 permanently changed all northern area codes (including Del Mar, La Jolla, parts of North County, and Pacific Beach) to 858. **Unless otherwise specified, the area code for the San Diego area is 619.**

ACCOMMODATIONS

San Diego's tourist traffic and room rates skyrocket during the summer months, particularly on weekends. Reservations can save you disappointment, and weekly rates (offered at many area residential hotels and hostels) can save you dollars. Accommodations here are still a bargain—$35 rooms in San Diego are comparable to $60 rooms in L.A. Those with cars and tents can find bargains and bliss by camping on the beaches outside of the city (see **Campgrounds,** p. 444), and those without cars can use the buses that pass most downtown hotels.

DOWNTOWN

San Diego Metropolitan (HI-AYH), 521 Market St. (525-1531 or 800-909-4776 ext. 43; www.hostelweb.com/sandiego/metro.html), at 5th Ave., in the heart of the Gaslamp, 5 blocks from the convention center. Quiet, impeccable hostel near San Diego's most popular attractions and clubs. Airy common room with kitchen, pool table, and communal bathrooms. Lockers (bring a lock) and laundry. Reception 7am-midnight. Dorms (4-6 beds) $16; doubles $31; nonmembers $3 more. IBN reservations available. Groups welcome.

Grand Pacific Hostel, 726 5th Ave. (232-3100 or 800-GET-TO-CA/438-8622; email hisddwnt@aol.com), between G and F St. in the Gaslamp. Keg parties, in-house drinking, occasional group outings. Breakfast included. Free linen. Coin-op laundry. Free shuttle to nearby sights. Tijuana tours $10. Clean and spacious dorms $16-18; doubles $40.

J Street Inn, 222 J St. (696-6922; fax 696-1295), near the convention center and ritzy waterfront. All 221 fabulous studio rooms have cable TV, microwave, fridge, and bath. Gym and reading room. Enclosed parking $5 per day, $20 per week. Singles $45; doubles $50; each additional person $20. Weekly and monthly rates available.

Corinthian Suites Hotel, 1840 4th Ave. (236-1600; fax 231-4734), at Elm St., 2 blocks from Balboa Park. Recently remodeled hotel near zoo and museums has cable TV. Rooms with fridge, bar, sink, and microwave. Laundry. Security deposit $15, weekly $65. Singles $35-45, weekly $150.

Downtown Hostel at Baltic Inn, 521 6th Ave. (237-0687). Clean rooms with toilet, sink, microwave, mini-fridge, and cable TV. Communal showers. 24hr. security. Laundry. Key deposit $10. Singles $20; doubles $34; weekly $85-125.

OLD TOWN

Old Town Inn, 4444 Pacific Hwy. (260-8024 or 800-643-3025; fax 296-0524), 10min. walk from Old Town, closer to I-5 than the ocean. Some rooms have kitchenettes. For an even Older Town experience, ask to stay in the old building. Continental breakfast included. Checkout 11am. Singles $40-76; doubles $45-84; weekly rates (fall only) start at $197.

THE COAST

Ocean Beach International (OBI), 4961 Newport Ave. (223-SURF/7873 or 800-339-SAND/7263), Ocean Beach. Look for high-flying international flags. Free pickup from airport, train, and bus terminals. One of San Diego's newest hostels, the OBI features cable TV and kitchen near the beach. Breakfast included. Laundry. Free BBQ and keg parties Tu and F night; free pasta Tu in winter. Dorms (4-6 beds) $15-17; couples' rooms (some with bath) $34-38. **Proof of international travel required.**

Banana Bungalow, 707 Reed Ave. (273-3060 or 800-5-HOSTEL/546-7835, reservations 888-2-GO-BANANAS/246-2262), just off Mission Blvd. in Mission Beach. Free pickup from airport and Greyhound terminal (call ahead), or take bus #34 to Mission Blvd. and Reed Ave. Popular hostel offers lots of amenities: common room with cable TV, beachside location, Internet access. Breakfast included. Free linen. Bikes, skates, surfboards for rent. Checkout 11am. Dorms (4-12 beds) $18. Call in advance. **Must have an international passport.**

HI-Point Loma, 3790 Udall St. (223-4778; fax 223-1883), 1½mi. from Ocean Beach. Take bus #35 from downtown to the first stop on Voltaire St. If driving, head west on Sea World Dr. from I-5 and bear right on Sunset Cliff Blvd. Take a left on Voltaire St. and a right on Worden St. Udall St. is 1 block away—look for the hostel sign. Large kitchen, patio, and common room with TV. Laundry. Bike rental $10 per day. 14-night max. stay. Checkout 10:30am. Reception 8-10pm. Dorms $14; doubles $17; nonmembers $3 more. Reserve 2 days in advance.

Western Shores Motel, 4345 Mission Bay Dr. (273-1121). Take bus #30. If driving south on I-5, exit Balboa/Garnet, going north exit Grand/Garnet. Rooms with A/C and TV are 2mi. from beach, ½mi. from bay. Singles $33; doubles $48; lower in winter. If paying in advance, 7th night is free in winter. Reservations recommended.

Sleepy Time Motel, 4545 Mission Bay Dr. (483-4222), if driving south on I-5, exit Balboa/Garnet, going north exit Grand/Garnet. 66 units near bay and Sea World. Singles $40; doubles $45. 7th night is free if paying in advance.

CAMPGROUNDS

Camping outside of San Diego is an attractive and cheap alternative for travelers with cars. Sites fill up in summer, so reserve through PARKNET (800-444-7275; open daily 8am-5pm).

South Carlsbad Beach State Park (760-438-3143), off Pacific Coast Hwy. (Rte. 21) near Leucadia, in north San Diego County. Half of the 226 sites are for tents. On cliffs over the sea. Showers and laundry. No hiking trails. Oceanfront sites $22, F-Sa $23; inland $17, F-Sa $18; dogs $1.

San Elijo Beach State Park (760-753-5091), off Pacific Coast Hwy. (Rte. 21) south of Cardiff-by-the-Sea. 271 sites (150 for tents) on seaside cliffs. Strategic landscaping gives a secluded feel. Laundry and showers. Hiker/biker campsites available, but no hiking or biking trails. Oceanfront sites $22, F-Sa $23; inland $17, F-Sa $18; dogs $1.

FOOD

The residents of inland neighborhoods take pride in San Diego's past, before its growth into a large city. Lurking below San Diego's downtown skyscrapers are the pre-1910 commercial buildings of the **Gaslamp Quarter,** now being resurrected as upscale shops, restaurants, and clubs. Not far away is **Old Town,** home to many Spanish colonial buildings and the self-proclaimed "birthplace of California," and **Balboa Park,** where museums surround the San Diego Zoo.

DOWNTOWN

The demands of the lunchtime business crowd have created a horde of downtown eateries, almost all of which specialize in cheap but well-made meals. Unfortunately, area restaurants tend to close early, and dinner can be harder to come by than lunch. The selection at **Horton's Plaza's** food court goes beyond the standard panoply of junk food. Good restaurants also cluster along **C Street, Broadway,** and in the **Gaslamp Quarter.**

El Indio Mexican Restaurant, 409 F St. (299-0385). Damn good food at damn good prices. Combo plates $4-6, burritos $3-4. Open M-Th 11am-8pm, F-Sa 11am-2am.

Karl Strauss' Old Columbia Brewery and Grill, 1157 Columbia St. (234-2739). San Diego's first microbrewery and the local favorite for power lunches. BBQ ribs and pasta $8-12, lighter fare $6-8. Open M-Th 11:30am-midnight, F-Sa 11:30am-1am, Su 11:30am-10pm.

Sammy's California Woodfired Pizza, 770 4th Ave. (230-8888). Upscale pizza joint offers 22 gourmet pizzas ($8-10) that have been called the best in SoCal. Huge salads ($7-11). Open M-Th 11:30am-3pm, F-Sa 11:30am-11pm.

Royal Thai Cuisine, 465 5th St. (230-THAI/8424). Nouveau Thai cuisine with a "healthy dining" menu (lunch entrees $6-9; dinner $7-15). Open M-Th 11am-3pm and 5-10pm, F 11am-3pm and 5pm-midnight, Sa noon-3pm and 5pm-midnight, Su noon-3pm and 5-10pm.

The Old Gaslamp Ice Cream Co., 503 5th Ave. (232-9549). The unique flavors, which change periodically, are all made fresh on the premises. Creamy delicious Blueberry Pancakes or Almond Joy ($3.25) are a good choice if they are on the menu. Open Su-Th noon-10pm; F-Sa noon-midnight.

Great Wall Express, 501 Broadway (238-8398), at 5th Ave., dishes out tasty heaping servings of Chinese food for $1 apiece. Open daily 10am-9pm.

Kansas City Barbecue, 610 W. Market St. (231-9680), near Seaport Village. No fewer than 8 signs at this popular BBQ joint proclaim that *Top Gun*'s sleazy bar scene was shot here. Giant lunches and dinners ($4-9) more than make up for the constant jukebox strains of "You've Lost that Lovin' Feeling." Open daily 11am-1am.

BALBOA PARK

The best food near Balboa Park is north and west in nearby **Hillcrest, Mission Hills,** and **University Heights.** These districts are so trendy that "Happy Hour" is as likely to mean cheap espresso as cheap mai tais. Affordable eateries line the roads and a number of restaurants offer dinner specials for two.

Corvette Diner Bar & Grill, 3946 5th Ave. (542-1476). A real Corvette and booming oldies complete the pseudo-50s decor. Old-fashioned shakes $3. Serves burgers and fries 'cause it's a diner, veggie sandwiches ($6-7) 'cause it's Hillcrest. Open Su-Th 11am-11pm, F-Sa 11am-midnight.

City Delicatessen, 535 University Ave. (295-2747). New York-style deli has huge selection, pink tables, jukebox, and that sticky vinyl that gets really uncomfortable in the summer. Breakfast specials ($4-10) are served all day. Open Su-Th 7am-midnight, F-Sa 7am-2am.

The Vegetarian Zone, 2949 5th Ave. (298-7302), at Quince St. The motto in this pure vegetable zone is that "the human body doesn't require any form of meat to operate wonderfully." With that in mind, savor veggie soups ($4) and flaky Greek spinach pie ($6-11). Open M-Th 11:30am-9pm, F 11:30am-10pm, Sa 8:30am-10pm, Su 8:30am-9pm.

The Golden Dragon, 414 University Ave. (296-4119; delivery 523-1199), Hillcrest. Where Marilyn Monroe and Frank Sinatra ate. Chinese menu offers over a hundred dishes (many vegetarian) for $6-9. Open daily 4:30pm-3am.

OLD TOWN

This is *the* place to eat Mexican food in California. Although fast food restaurants dominate San Diego's cuisine, many of them prove that fast food is not always bad news. In the land of the speedy burrito, some restaurants have perfected the art of quick Mexican and none of them are named Taco Bell. Many of the Old Town restaurants are in the **Bazaar del Mundo,** a cluster of restaurants and stores accessible only by foot.

Casa de Bandini, 2754 Calhoun St. (297-8211). The charming patio and *mariachi*-filled interior (built in 1829) create a fabulous atmosphere for the scarfing of super-sized *chimichangas* ($8), mouth-watering combo plates ($8-9), and monster margaritas ($4-7). Repeatedly voted San Diego's best Mexican restaurant. Open M-Th 11am-9:30pm, F-Sa 11am-10pm, Su 10am-9:30pm.

Casa de Pico (296-3267), just off Calhoun St. in the Bazaar. Gigantic plates overflowing with gooey cheese enchiladas ($7-8). Soup-bowl-sized margaritas are terrifically tasty. Open Su-F 10am-9pm, Sa 10am-9:30pm.

Cafe Coyote, 2461 San Diego Ave. (291-4695). Great food (burritos from $7) and 90 different tequilas will make you howl. Vendors sell fresh tortillas (3 for $1). Open Su-Th 7:30am-10pm, F-Sa 7:30am-11pm.

Great Wall Cafe, 2543 Congress St. (291-9478). Celebrated Mandarin Chinese food. Lunch combos ($6) and dinner specials ($7-8) offer vegetarian options. Cocktail bar on the premises. Open Su-Th 11am-9:30pm, F-Sa 11am-10:30pm.

Berta's, 3928 Twiggs St. (295-2343). You may have to buy a copy of *Let's Go: Central America* to make your way through this menu. Dozens of Guatemalan, Honduran, and Costa Rican specialities ($9-14). Open daily 11am-10pm.

SIGHTS

DOWNTOWN

San Diego's downtown attractions are concentrated in the corridor that includes its business, Gaslamp, and waterfront districts, all testaments to San Diego's continuing renaissance. Within this center of commerce and entertainment are the city's skyscrapers, its modern convention center, and its newest nexus of nightlife. Travelers should be careful outside of this corridor, however, as the immediately neighboring areas are not as safe.

SAN DIEGO MUSEUM OF CONTEMPORARY ART. A steel-and-glass structure in which 20th-century works of art from the museum's permanent collection and visiting works are displayed on a rotational basis. Artists represented in the permanent collection include John Baldessari, Philip Guston, and Ellsworth Kelly. Until mid-2000, the museum will also display the works of the Museum of Photographic Arts (see p. 448) while that museum undergoes extensive renovations. The Museum of Contemporary Arts also has a La Jolla branch (see **La Jolla,** p. 452) that shares its permanent collection. *(234-1001 or 454-3541. 1001 Kettner Blvd. Open Tu-Sa 10am-5pm, Su noon-5pm. Admission $2; students, seniors, military, and ages 12-18 $1; under 12 free. Docent-led tours Sa-Su at 2pm; tour included in admission price.)*

MUSEUM OF DEATH. In the basement of a 100-year-old mortuary, one can explore the ineluctable result of all worldly machinations at this gruesome museum. Its exhibits include original artwork by such infamous serial killers as Charles Manson as well as more than enough photographs of horribly mutilated corpses to satisfy even the surliest teenage outcast. *(338-8153. 548 5th Ave. Open Su-Th 1-10pm, F-Sa 1-11pm. Admission $5.)*

GASLAMP QUARTER. An area housing antique shops, Victorian buildings, and trendy restaurants. Formerly the city's Red Light District and home to the original **Pappy's, Inc.** adult bookstore, the area's new bars and bistros have grown popular with upscale revelers (see **Nightlife,** p. 454). By day, the area's charm lies in its history. The **Gaslamp Quarter Foundation** offers guided walking tours. *(233-4692. William Heath Davis House, 410 Island Ave. Museum open M-F 10am-2pm, Sa 10am-4pm, Su noon-4pm. 2hr. tours Saturday at 11am. Admission $5; students, seniors, and ages 12-18 $3; under 12 free.)* The **Horton Grand Hotel,** like most old buildings in San Diego, is supposedly haunted. Believers may catch a glimpse of Wyatt Earp or even Babe Ruth. *(544-1886. 311 Island Ave. Tours Wednesday at 3pm. Free.)*

EMBARCADERO. Spanish for "dock," the Embarcadero's boardwalk shops and museums face moored windjammers, cruise ships, and the occasional naval

THE LADY IS A TRAMP Be careful when you enter the Museum of Death—Lady, a well-groomed Afghan, typically enjoys her midday nap in the building's doorway. If your foot happens to glance over any part of Lady, you'll be quick to notice that she's dead. After 10 happy life-filled years, Lady's body was mounted by her eccentric owner in 1971. When the owner joined Lady in the next world, the heirs to her estate apparently argued little over who would get the dog. So, just like in the movies, Lady made her way across hill and plain to a place where she'd be accepted—the museum welcomed her with open arms. Good girl, Lady!

destroyer. Military and merchant marine vessels are anchored here, as well as the distantly visible North Island Naval Air Station, the Point Loma Submarine Base, and the South Bay's mothballed fleet; they serve as constant reminders of the U.S. Navy's prominent presence in San Diego. *(Most afternoon tours of naval crafts are free.)*

SAN DIEGO MARITIME MUSEUM. Displays showcase San Diego's rich maritime history. The museum also maintains three ships: the magnificently restored 1863 sailing vessel *Star of India*, (the world's oldest active merchant ship), the ferry-boat *Berkeley*, and the steam yacht *Medea*. *(234-9153. www.sdmaritime.com. 1306 N. Harbor Dr. Museum and ships open daily June-Aug. 9am-9pm, Sept.-May 9am-8pm. Admission $5; seniors, military, and ages 13-17 $4; ages 6-12 $2; under 6 free.)*

OTHER SIGHTS. The jewel of San Diego's redevelopment efforts is **Horton Plaza.** This pastel-hued urban confection is an open-air, multi-level shopping center covering seven blocks. *(Broadway and 4th Ave.)* The **Santa Fe Amtrak Depot,** is a masterpiece of Mission Revival architecture whose arches welcomed visitors to the 1915 Panama California Exposition. *(1050 Kettner Blvd. 3 blocks west of Horton Plaza.)* Kitschy **Seaport Village** houses shingled boutiques, ice cream shops, and a century-old carousel. *(235-4014. Near the harbor. Village open daily 10am-10pm, off-season 10am-9pm. Carousel rides $1. Free 2hr. parking, $1 per additional 30min.)*

BALBOA PARK AND THE SAN DIEGO ZOO

Balboa Park was the creation of pioneering horticulturists whose plantings transformed a once-treeless pueblo tract into a botanical montage. The park's first seedlings were planted in 1889, when San Diego was a town of about 3000. Today, the redwood trees tower over climbing roses and water lilies at the center of a teeming city. Balboa Park is known for its museums, concerts, cultural events, lush vegetation, and most of all for the fabulous San Diego Zoo and Wild Animal Park. The park is accessible by bus #7. **Parking is free** in museum and zoo lots; posted signs warn park-goers against scam artists who attempt to wheedle lot fees from the unsuspecting. Tuesday is the best day to visit the park, as the museums offer free admission on a rotating basis.

SAN DIEGO ZOO AND WILD ANIMAL PARK

Contact: *234-3153; Giant Panda viewing info 888-MY-PANDA/697-2632; www.sandiegozoo.org.* ***Address and Directions:*** *2920 Zoo Dr., Balboa Park. From the north or south, take I-5 or I-15, take Rte. 163, get off at the Zoo/Museums Exit (Richmond St.), and follow signs. From the east, take I-8 to Rte. 163 south to the Park Blvd./I-5 South Exit. Exit at Park Blvd. Turn left on Park Blvd. and head north; zoo entrance is off Park Blvd. at Zoo Pl.* ***Hours:*** *Entrance open daily late June to early Sept. 7:30am-9pm; early Sept. to late June 7:30am-dusk, off-season 9am-4pm.* ***Admission:*** *Zoo admission $16, ages 3-11 $7 (free in Oct.), military in uniform free. Combined zoo and wild animal park admission $35, ages 3-11 $21. Group rates available. Free on Founder's Day, the 1st M in Oct.*

With over 100 acres of exquisite fenceless habitats, this zoo well deserves its reputation as one of the finest in the world. Its unique "bioclimatic" exhibits group animals and plants together by habitat. For example, the Polar Bear Plunge contains polar bears, Siberian reindeer, and Arctic foxes that fish and frolic tundra-style beside their own chilled, Olympic-size pool. Young *Homo sapiens* can watch the hatching and feeding of other species' toddlers in the **children's petting zoo**.

The most thorough way to tour the zoo is on foot, but those limited by time should consider the 40-minute open-air **guided double-decker bus tour,** which covers 80% of the park. Seats on the left provide a better vantage point to view the park. *(Tickets $8, ages 3-11 $5.)* The **Skyfari Aerial Tramway** rises 170 feet above the park and lasts about two minutes *(one-way $1.59)*. Most of the zoo is wheelchair accessible and wheelchairs can be rented, but steep hills make assistance necessary.

BALBOA PARK AND THE EL PRADO MUSEUMS

Although they may not be Smithsonian-quality, Balboa Park has the highest concentration of museums in the United States outside of Washington, D.C. It would take several days to see all of them. Most of the museums reside within the resplendent Spanish colonial-style buildings that line **El Prado Street** that runs west-to-east through the Park's central **Plaza de Panama.** These ornate structures—designed for the Panama California Exposition of 1915-16 and for the International Expositions of 1935-36—were originally intended to last two years. Since many of the buildings are now going on 80, they are being renovated, this time with a more permanent construction.

BALBOA PARK VISITORS CENTER. The visitors center is in the House of Hospitality on El Prado St. at the Plaza de Panama. The center sells park maps (a well-spent $1), and the Passport to Balboa Park ($21), which allows admission into 12 of the park's museums. Passports are also available at participating museums. *(239-0512. Center open daily 9am-4pm.)*

MUSEUM OF MAN. The star of the western axis of the Plaza de Panama was the California State Building, now the Museum of Man. Its much-photographed tower and dome gleam with Spanish mosaic tiles, while inside human evolution is traced with exhibits on primates and early man. *(239-2001. Open daily 10am-4:30pm. Admission $5, seniors $4.50, ages 6-17 $3, military in uniform free; free 3rd Tu of each month.)*

NATURAL HISTORY MUSEUM. At the east end of Balboa Park, this museum displays stuffed mammals and birds, and live insects and arthropods enhance the standard fossils. A recreated mine displays gems. *(232-3821. Near the intersection of Park Blvd. and Village Pl. at the east end of Balboa Park. Open daily Memorial Day-Labor Day (May 29-Sept. 4 in 2000) 9:30am-5pm; Labor Day-Memorial Day 9:30am-4:30pm. Admission varies depending on traveling exhibits, call for exact prices; typically $6-8; seniors, military, and students typically $4-6; ages 6-17 $3; free 1st Tu of each month.)*

AEROSPACE MUSEUM. The museum displays 24 full-scale replicas and 44 original planes, and aviation history exhibits. It is in the drum-shaped Ford Pavilion which was constructed in 1935 by Ford Motors for the California Pacific International Exposition. The museum looks to the future as well, as one of 62 Star Station One sites nationwide which are provided as part of a program to provide information on the International Space Station project—a 16-nation collaboration on an orbiting laboratory. *(234-8291; www.aerospacemuseum.org. 2001 Pan American Plaza. Open daily Memorial Day-Labor Day (May 29-Sept. 4 in 2000) 10am-5:30pm; Labor Day-Memorial Day 10am-4:30pm. Admission $6, seniors $5, ages 6-17 $2, under 6 and military free, free 4th Tu of each month.)*

REUBEN H. FLEET SPACE THEATER AND SCIENCE CENTER. The science center houses the world's very first Omnimax theater, complete with 153 speakers and a hemispheric planetarium. Exhibits change several times per year. *(238-1233, reservations 232-6866. 1875 El Prado Way. 10-14 Omnimax shows per day. Admission to museums and Omnimax $9, seniors $7.50, ages 3-12 $6.50; Open Su-Th 9:30am-9pm, F 9:30am-10pm, Sa 9:30am-11pm.)*

CASA DE BALBOA MUSEUMS. Recently relocated to the Federal Building, the **San Diego Hall of Champions** is a slick sports museum complete with Astroturf carpeting. Only an odor-proof glass pane separates you from jerseys and shoes worn by Ted Williams and Bill Walton. *(234-2544. Open daily 10am-4:30pm. Admission $3, seniors and military $2, ages 6-17 $1, under 6 free, free 2nd Tu of each month.)* The recently renovated 1915 Electricity Building houses the **Museum of San Diego History.** *(232-6203. Open Tu-Su 10am-4:30pm. Admission $4, seniors and military $3, children 5-12 $1.50, free 2nd Tu of each month.)* Also in the building are the **Research Archives.** *(Open Th-Sa 10am-4pm.)* Downstairs, hobbyists preside over their toys in the **San Diego Model Railroad Museum.** *(696-0199. Open Tu-F 11am-4pm, Sa-Su 11am-5pm. Admission $3; students, seniors, and military $2.50; under 15 free; free 1st Tu of each month.)* The **Museum of**

Photographic Arts (MOPA) is currently under construction and is scheduled to reopen sometime in 2000. Its exhibits are on temporary display at the downtown location of the Museum of Contemporary Art (see p. 446). The photography exhibits rotate every two months. *(Call to see if MOPA has reopened. 238-7559. Open daily after renovations 10am-5pm. Admission $4, under 12 free, free 2nd Tu of each month.)*

ART IN THE PLAZA DE PANAMA. The **San Diego Museum of Art** has a collection ranging from ancient Asian to contemporary Californian works. At the adjoining outdoor **Sculpture Garden Court** a sensuous Henry Moore piece presides over other large abstract blocks. *(Museum tel. 232-7931. Sculpture Garden tel. 696-1990. Open Tu-Su 10am-4:30pm. Admission $8, ages 18-24 and seniors $6, ages 6-17 $3; special exhibits $2-10 more.)* Across the Plaza, the **Timken Art Gallery** houses a newly restored portrait by Rembrandt and a collection of Russian church icons. *(239-5548. 1500 El Prado Way. Open Oct.-Aug. Tu-Sa 10am-4:30pm, Su 1:30-4:30pm. Free.)* **Spanish Village** is a colony of 250 artists at work in 36 studios. *(233-9050. At the end of El Prado Way, which is closed to cars, take a left onto Village Pl.)*

BALBOA PARK GARDENS. The **Botanical Building** is a wooden structure filled with the scent of jasmine and the murmur of fountains. The **Desert Garden** and **Rose Garden** offer a striking contrast between the two types of flora. The desert garden is in full bloom from January to March, and the roses are best admired between April and December. Free ranger-led tours of the central part of Balboa Park are offered Tuesday and Sunday at 1pm. Plant-lovers can also meet on Saturdays at 10am for a free volunteer-led tour of the park. Each Saturday tour includes different sights within the park. *(235-1100. Botanical Building open F-W 10am-4pm. Free. Gardens at 2200 Park Blvd. Free. For more info on tours call 235-1121.)*

PERFORMANCE SPACES. The oldest professional theater in California, the **Old Globe Theater** was constructed in 1937. Classical and contemporary plays are performed at the adjoining Lowell Davies Outdoor Theatre and the Cassius Carter Center Stage. Tickets for all three stages can be purchased at the box office. *(239-2255. Tu-Su evenings and Sa-Su matinees. Tickets $23-39.)* At the Pan American Plaza, passing jets occasionally cause the actors in the **Starlight Bowl** theater to freeze mid-soliloquy and wait for the engine roar to subside before resuming. Screaming turbines scarcely affect the action down the road at the nearby **Spreckels Organ Pavilion** as the racket created by the world's largest outdoor musical instrument can be heard for miles around *(226-0819. Free performance Su 2pm.)*

OLD TOWN

Old Town is the site of the first Spanish settlement on the West Coast. Now it is a tourist center with colonial flavor. In 1769, a group of Spanish soldiers accompanied by Father Junípero Serra established a fort and mission in the area now known as Old Town. Today, Old Town's museums, parks, and sundry attractions commemorate the historic outpost which has given rise to the modern metropolis of San Diego.

MISSION BASILICA SAN DIEGO DE ALCALÁ. Father Serra's soldiers were apparently a rough and unholy bunch, because in 1774 the *padre* moved his mission some six miles away to its current location. The mission is still an active parish church , and contains a chapel, gardens, a small museum, and a reconstruction of Serra's living quarters. For more info, see **A Man with a Mission,** p. 8 *(281-8449. Take bus #43 or I-8 East to the Mission Gorge Rd. Exit. Mass held daily at 7am and 5:30pm; visitors welcome.)*

OLD TOWN STATE PARK SIGHTS. The most popular of the area's attractions, the park's early-19th-century buildings contain museums, shops, and the restaurants listed above. Take a tour of the **Whaley House,** which displays an authentic Lincoln life mask and the piano used in *Gone With the Wind.* The house stands on the site of San Diego's first gallows, which may influence the fact that it is one of the two **official haunted houses** recognized by the State of California. *(298-2482. 2482 San Diego Ave. Open daily 10am-4:30pm; entrance closes at 4pm. Admission $4, seniors $3, ages 6-*

12 $2. Old Town Historical Society tours 293-0117.) Across the street is **Heritage Park,** a group of seven 150-year-old Victorian buildings (six houses and a temple) collected from around the city. Four are open to the public.

SERRA MUSEUM. Its stout adobe walls were raised in 1929 at the site of the original fort and mission. Inside are exhibits documenting the settlement; outside is a really, really huge flagpole marking the location of **Fort Stockton.** *(279-3258. In Presido Park. Open Tu-Sa 10am-4:30pm, Su noon-4:30pm. Admission $3, under 12 free.)*

QUALCOMM STADIUM. If you've been wondering about the lightning bolt stickers posted all over town, head out here on a fall Sunday and look at the helmets of the **San Diego Chargers,** the city's pro football team. The stadium also hosts baseball's **San Diego Padres.** *(West of the Mission near the junction of I-8 and I-15. For Chargers tickets, call 280-2121. For Padres info, call 280-INFO/4636, for tickets 283-4494.)*

COASTAL SAN DIEGO

San Diego's western boundary is lined by miles of soft, sloping beaches crowded with surfers. When sun, sand, surf, and Sea World get dull, head inland to San Diego's beach communities, where there's plenty to explore away from the shore.

CORONADO ISLAND

Coronado is actually a peninsula—the "Silver Strand," a slender seven mile strip of sand, connects it to the mainland just above the Mexican border—but its pristine platinum beaches feel as remote as a tropical isle. The action in Coronado takes place in two areas: residents and merchants stick to the south, while sailors and aviators populate the **North Island Naval Base.**

The graceful **Coronado Bridge,** built in 1969, guides cars to Coronado from downtown San Diego along I-5 (toll $1), and bus #901 follows the same route. Those who would rather skim the ocean than the asphalt can take the **Bay Ferry,** which leaves for Coronado on the hour from 9am to 9pm and returns every 30 minutes from 9am to 9:30pm. Tickets ($2, bikes 50¢) are available at **San Diego Harbor Excursion,** 1050 N. Harbor Dr. (234-4111), which also runs one-hour (ticket $12, seniors and military $10, ages 4-12 $6, under 4 free) and two-hour (ticket $17, seniors and military $15, ages 4-12 $8.50, under 4 free) tours of the harbor. Once across, the **#904 Shuttle** carries passengers from the landing to the Hotel Del Coronado and back (50¢); it leaves every 30 minutes from 9:30am to 5:30pm. The **Coronado Visitors Bureau,** 1047 B Ave. (437-8788 or 800-622-8300; fax 437-6006), provides info on the upscale shops and restaurants lining **Orange Avenue.**

Coronado's most famed sight is its Victorian-style **Hotel Del Coronado,** 1500 Orange Ave. (435-6611), one of America's largest wooden buildings. The long, white verandas and the vermilion spires of the "Del" were built in 1898. It has since become one of the world's great hotels, hosting 12 presidents and one blonde bombshell (Marilyn Monroe's 1959 classic *Some Like it Hot* was filmed here). (Historic tours $13, ages 6-12 $3; buy tickets at Signature Shop.) A salmon burger ($8.35) from the lobby's **Del Deli** will help to power your tour of the hotel's considerable grounds and the uncrowded white beach out back. **Bikes and Beyond** (435-7180), at the ferry landing on 1st St., rents bikes ($5 per hr., $15 per 4hr; mountain bikes $6 per hr., $16 per 4hr.) and in-line skates ($5 per hr., $15 per 4hr.; open daily 8:30am-dusk). A seven-mile bike path takes you from the south end of the business district along the coast to Imperial Beach.

POINT LOMA

Although the U.S. government owns the outer two-thirds of this peninsula, most of it remains open to citizens and visitors. The **Cabrillo National Monument** (557-5450), at the tip of Point Loma, is dedicated to the great Portuguese explorer Juan Rodríguez Cabrillo (the first European to land in California), but is best known for its views of San Diego and migrating whales. ($5 per vehicle, $2 per person on foot or bike: pass good for 7 days. Golden Eagle Passport accepted.) **Whale-watching** season is mid-December to February, and the monument is prime seating (whale info in winter 557-5450). From North County, take I-5 to Rosecrans Blvd. (there is no Rosecrans Exit northbound) and follow signs for Rte. 209 to the entrance, or take bus #6A. The two-mile **Bayside Trail** teaches about native vegetation and historic military installations. Point Loma's oceanside is rife with **tide pools** (turn right off Rte. 209 onto Cabrillo Rd., and drive down to the parking lot at the bottom of the hill). At the highest point of the peninsula sits the museum at **Old Point Loma Lighthouse** (open daily 9am-5:15pm; summer hrs vary).

Ocean Beach (O.B.) caters to a crowd of surfers much more low-key than the swankier set to the north. This relaxed atmosphere, along with gentle surf conditions, make O.B. a great place to learn the art of wave-riding. Those who would rather stay out of the water can angle from the longest fishing pier in the Western Hemisphere or watch the sinking sun from **Sunset Cliffs.** Most of the area's inexpensive restaurants and bars are clustered along the westernmost stretch of **Newport Avenue,** one of San Diego's trendiest drags. The **Newport Bar and Grille,** 4935 Newport Ave. (222-0168), is the local favorite; try their walnut chicken ($7). Open M-W 11am-midnight, Th-F 11am-2am, Sa 8am-2am, Su 8am-midnight. **Margarita's,** 4955 Newport Ave. (224-7454), has an atmosphere as smooth as its namesake. Great Mexican vegetarian fare (vegetarian burritos $4) and wine margaritas ($2). Open M-F 6am-9:30pm, Sa-Su 7am-9pm.

MISSION BEACH AND PACIFIC BEACH

Much of San Diego's younger population is drawn to these communities by the respectable surf and the hopping nightlife—noisy bars and grills crowd these shores. **Kono's Surf Club,** 704 Garnet Ave. (483-1669), across from the Crystal Pier in Pacific Beach, is a surfer's shrine that serves breakfast all day ($3-4). The Egg Burrito #3 includes bacon, cheese, potatoes, and pica sauce, all for $3.25. (Open M-F 7am-3pm, Sa-Su 7am-4pm.) **Cafe Crema,** 1001 Garnet Ave. (858-273-3558), is a Euro-style coffeehouse stacked with pastries and bagel sandwiches ($4-5), and has Internet access (open Su-Th 6am-2am, F-Sa 6am-4am). Farther inland is **World Curry,** 1433 Garnet Ave. (689-2222), serving delicious $7 curries (open M-Sa 11am-10pm, Su 4-9pm).

At the corner of W. Mission Bay Dr. and Mission Blvd. is **Belmont Park,** a combination amusement park and shopping center that draws a youthful crowd from all over the city. Gulp down a meal at **Caine's Bar and Grill,** 3105 Ocean Front Walk (858-488-1780), on the boardwalk, right next to the park, where you can get a giant slice of pizza ($2.25), while listening to regular live music. Then, you can purge on the bumpy **Giant Dipper** roller coaster (rides $3, Tu after 4pm 75¢; free parking). The **Ocean Front Walk** through Pacific Beach toward La Jolla is always packed with joggers, walkers, cyclists, and the usual beachfront shops.

OF CARS AND CONSTELLATIONS After one ride on Belmont Park's Giant Dipper, you may find yourself beaten and bruised by the rickety roller coaster's excessively bumpy turns and tumbles. Imagine riding the coaster nearly 3000 times in a row. Can't? Well, three hardy San Diegans did it in the summer of 1998, and all for a radio promotion. The city's Star 100.7 FM chose an initial field of 22 contestants, sat them aboard the coaster, and told them that the one who stayed on the longest—short bathroom breaks and park closing hours excepted—would win a new Nissan automobile. The Dipper's rough and tumble rails claimed 19 victims with relative ease, but three stubborn souls were determined to win the prize. For 72 consecutive days they battled broken ribs, bump-befuddled brains, and bubbling bile until Star and Nissan both broke down, awarding them each a car of their own. The trials of these truly amazing American heroes dominated the San Diego nightly news at the time, and their act of courage makes a powerful statement to us all about the need for a car in Southern California.

Although both beaches accommodate those who limit their physical activity to shifting on their towels, beachside sports are very popular—competition often spurs on the passionate crowds. Be sure to avoid swimming near surfers, and always don protective gear when skating. **Star Surfing Co.,** 4652 Mission Blvd. (858-273-7827), in Pacific Beach north of Garnet Ave., rents surfboards ($5 per hr., $20 per day) and boogie boards ($3 per hr., $12 per day) to those with a driver's license or credit card for deposit (open M-F 10am-8pm, Sa-Su 10am-6pm). **Dana Boat Rentals,** 1710 W. Mission Bay Dr. (226-8611; open daily 10am-6pm), offers sailboats (15ft. is $20 per hr., $50 per ½-day) and other water-sports equipment. **Windsport,** 844 Mission Bay Dr. (858-488-4642), rents kayaks ($13 per hr., $45 per day), boogie boards ($5 per day), surfboards ($15 per day), and wetsuits ($15 per day).

SEA WORLD

Take Disneyland, subtract the rides, add a whole lot of fish, and you've got **Sea World** (226-3901; www.4adventure.com), a water wonderland whose signature creature isn't a pipsqueak mouse but the four-ton Orca **Shamu.** (Actually, the original Shamu died years ago, but his immortality has been ensured by way of a fiendish ruse—giving his 10 replacements the same name.) Shamus aside, the park contains shark, penguin, and dolphin displays, as well as jet-ski and watersport shows and a virtual-reality underwater experience. The highlight of any Sea World visit may well be the always delightful **sea otters**, the only creatures to survive the Exxon Valdez disaster unscathed.

Visitors often buy a map ($6) and schedule upon entering the parking lot; even the most popular events occur only a few times daily, so a quick perusal of the schedule is a good idea. The park's most popular show takes place in **Shamu Stadium,** where four Orcas, including the arena's namesake, cavort with trainers in a five-million-gallon tank. Watch the performances from the upper deck if dryness is a priority—during each show a substantial fraction of the tank's total volume ends up splashed on spectators seated in the first 20 rows. If it's your mind and not your water-filled pockets that needs emptying, head for the **Baywatch at Sea World** ski show, where high-speed hilarity is a way of life. The performance's plot is just as gripping as the TV show's, and part of the event is narrated by international heartthrob **David Hasselhoff.** The park's newest attraction is **Shipwreck Rapids,** Sea World's first-ever adventure ride. Those who feel they need a little cooling down should head to the **Anheuser-Busch Hospitality Tent,** which will give each (21 and over) guest up to two free cups of beer. (Park open M-Th 9am-10pm, F-Su 9am-11pm. Hours shorter in off-season. Park admission $38, ages 3-11 $29.)

LA JOLLA

Perched on a rocky promontory, this gilded jewel of a community lives up to its name ("jewel" in Spanish). La Jolla (pronounced la HOY-a; say la JOLL-a and you're exposing yourself to ridicule) began as a hideaway for wealthy Easterners who built luxurious houses atop the ocean bluffs in the 1930s and 40s. The pink walls and Spanish mosaics of the **La Valencia Hotel,** 1132 Prospect St. (858-454-7771 or 800-451-0772), glow with the wealth of monied tenants, but the town's character has recently taken a *nouveau riche* turn—newer wealth and a younger population have taken over. To reach La Jolla, take the Ardath Exit west from I-5 or buses #30 or 34 from downtown.

FOOD. Near its intersection with Girard Ave., **Prospect Street** is the Rodeo Drive of San Diego, crammed with upscale shops, art galleries, and eateries. If you look hard enough, however, you can find some relatively inexpensive places to eat. Between Prospect and Wall St. is **Aspen Mills,** 1044 Herschel St. (858-551-5550), a bakery and cafe offering good, fresh fare. Admire the country kitchen-type scenes painted on the walls while you munch on a huge Celebration of Citrus Muffin ($1.85), or lunch on a chicken pesto sandwich (with bagel chips, $5.45). If it's breakfast you hunger for, an extensive "Sunrise Menu" is served until 11:30am. (Open Su-F 6am-4pm, Sa 6am-5pm.) **La Terraza,** 8008 Girard Ave. (858-459-9750), specializes in *cucina Toscana*, featuring such delicacies as penne with eggplant and smoked mozzarella ($8). Pizzas are $8-11 (open daily 11am-10:30pm). Upstairs is **Bollicine Restaurant and Bar,** 8008 Girard Ave. (858-454-2222), a 1999 Zagat Survey Award recipient that offers a $10 champagne brunch on Sunday (open Su-Th 11am-10pm, F-Sa 11am-11pm). **Mr. Juice,** 8008 Girard Ave. (858-454-9910), is a classic California health-nut joint. Drink deep from a $3.50 smoothie, fruit shake, or juice concoction while watching the wheat grass grow in the window. (Open M-Sa 9am-5pm, Su 10am-5pm.)

SIGHTS. The **University of California at San Diego (UCSD)** sits calmly above La Jolla. Buses #30 and 34 take you to campus, but cars or bikes are invaluable for getting to the campus's many residential and academic colleges. Kiosks on Gilman and Northview Dr. dispense maps (858-534-2208; open M-F 7am-9pm, Sa-Su 6:30am-9pm). The **La Jolla Playhouse,** 2910 La Jolla Village Dr. (858-550-1070), presents shows at the Mandell Weiss Theatre on campus; turn onto Expedition from N. Torrey Pines Rd.

At the foot of Girard Ave. in **La Jolla Village** is **Scripps Park,** where wanton waves shake the rocky shore, sending up great plumes of silver sea spray. Ocean lovers, or lovers of any kind, stroll here in the evenings and loll on the carefully manicured lawns. The **San Diego Museum of Contemporary Art,** 700 Prospect St. (858-454-3541; www.mcasd.org), houses a rotating exhibition of pop, minimalist, and conceptualist art from its permanent collection (shared with the downtown branch; see p. 446). The museum is as visually stunning as the art it contains, with gorgeous ocean views and high-ceilinged, light-filled spaces. (Open Tu and Th-Sa 10am-5pm, Su noon-5pm, W 10am-8pm. Admission $4; students, seniors, military, and ages 12-18 $2; under 12 free.) The **Animation Celection,** 1002 Prospect St. (858-459-4278), is a gallery featuring contemporary art of a more sugared sort, including original hand-painted ace-

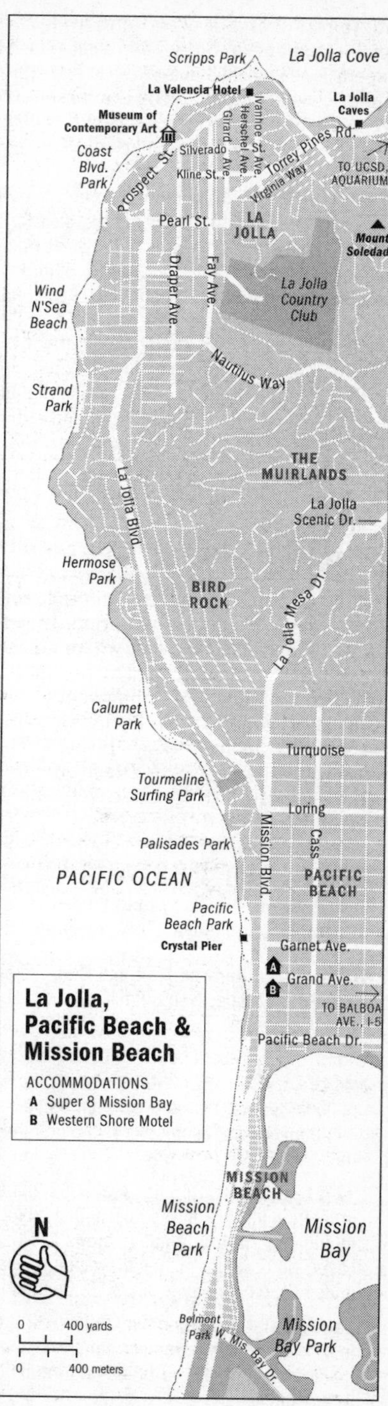

tate frames (cels) of everything from *The Jungle Book* to *The Jetsons*, plus much-sought-after *Babalooey* cels. The **Stephen Birch Aquarium-Museum**, 2300 Expedition Way (858-534-FISH/3474; http://aqua.ucsd.edu), at the Scripps Institute of Oceanography, feeds Humphrey (the fat octopus) and funds his friends, oceanographic researchers. (Open daily 9am-5pm. Admission $7.50, students $5, seniors $6.50, ages 3-14 $4; parking $3.)

BEACHES. La Jolla claims some of the finest **beaches** in the city. The **La Jolla Cove** is popular with scuba divers, snorkelers, and brilliantly colored Garibaldi goldfish (the state saltwater fish). Surfers are especially fond of the waves at **Tourmaline Beach** and **Windansea Beach,** which can be much too strong for novices. **La Jolla Shores,** next to Scripps/UCSD, has clean and gentle swells ideal for bodysurfers, boogie boarders, swimmers, and families. **Black's Beach** is not officially a **nude beach,** but let's just say there are plenty of wieners and buns at *this* lunch cart. The north end generally attracts gay patrons. **Torrey Pines Glider Port** is where hang gliders leap into the breeze and the young and unafraid cliff-dive into the high tide. (As always, *Let's Go* does not recommend cliff-diving.) To reach the Glider Port, take I-5 to Genesee Ave., go west and turn left on N. Torrey Pines Rd. The beach is accessible by a steep staircase just south of the glider port. A treacherous cliffside trail starts at the parking lot north of the port.

NIGHTLIFE

Nightlife in San Diego is not centered around a particular strip, but scattered in several distinct pockets of action. Upscale locals and trend-seeking tourists flock to the **Gaslamp Quarter,** where numerous restaurants and bars feature live music nightly. The **Hillcrest** area, next to Balboa Park, draws a young, largely gay crowd to its clubs and dining spots. Away from downtown, the **beach areas** (especially Garnet Ave. in Pacific Beach) are loaded with clubs, bars, inexpensive eateries, and college-age revelers. The city's definitive source of entertainment info is the free *San Diego Reader*, found in shops, coffeehouses, and visitors centers. Listings can also be found in the *San Diego Union Tribune*'s Thursday "Night and Day" section.

LATE-NIGHT RESTAURANTS

Although the restaurants below offer complete meals, they are better-known as night spots—bars, music clubs, or dance clubs.

Pacific Beach Bar and Grill and **Club Tremors,** 860 Garnet Ave. (858-272-1242 and 277-7228, respectively), Pacific Beach. Live DJ packs the 2-level dance floor with a young and slinky crowd. Cover $5. Club open Th-Sa 9pm-1:30am. Bar and Grill has good cheap food. Bar open 11am-1:30am, kitchen closes midnight.

Cafe Lu Lu, 419 F. St. (858-238-0114), Gaslamp. Vegetarian coffeehouse was designed by local artists. See and be seen as you eat for under $6, surreptitiously sipping a raspberry-mocha espresso ($3.75). Standing room only after midnight. Open Su-Th 9am-2am, F-Sa 9am-3am.

Dick's Last Resort, 345 4th Ave. (858-231-9100), Gaslamp. Buckets of Southern grub attract a wildly hedonistic bunch. Dick's stocks beers from around the globe, from Africa to Trinidad, on top of native brews like the appropriate Dixieland Blackened Voodoo Lager. No cover for the nightly rock or blues, but you'd better be buyin'. Lunch burgers under $4, dinner entrees $10-18. Open daily 11am-1:30am.

Java Joe's, 4994 Newport Ave. (523-0356), Ocean Beach. This coffeehouse has a genuinely cozy, church-basement atmosphere with a few pool tables. Bigger venue for live music—mostly folk and blues—than most coffeehouses. Coffee $1.25-4. Open daily 10am-midnight.

CLUBS AND BARS

Croce's Top Hat Bar and **Grille and Croce's Jazz Bar,** 802 5th Ave. (233-4355), at F St. in the Gaslamp. Ingrid Croce, widow of singer Jim Croce, created this rock/blues bar and classy jazz bar side-by-side on the 1st floor of the historic Keating building. Live music nightly. Cover $5-10, includes 2 live shows. Open daily 7:30am-3pm and 5pm-midnight; bar open until 2am.

The Crow Bar, 2812 Kettner Blvd. (692-1080), near Old Town. Live and loud, the Crow Bar hosts San Diego's up-and-coming rock 'n' roll acts, as well as the occasional more-established band. Pool table. Alternative rock 6 nights per week. Cover W-Sa usually $4-5. Happy Hour daily 4-8pm ($1 domestic drafts). Open daily 5pm-2am. 21+.

The Comedy Store, 916 Pearl St. (858-454-9176), La Jolla. One of the few joints around where you can be a part of the scene—clamber onstage Monday at 8pm for Potluck Night (call and sign up after 3pm). Better-known comedians featured other evenings. 2-drink minimum; drinks $3. Shows Tu-Th 9pm ($8), F-Sa 8 and 10:30pm ($10). 21+.

Cafe Sevilla, 555 4th Ave. (233-5979), Gaslamp. Downstairs, live bands lead patrons in Latin dances from salsa to flamenco every night. Don't miss Tuesday "paella madness" ($11) in the tapas bar with adjoining dining room. Open Su-Th 5-11pm, F-Sa 5pm-1am. 21+ downstairs.

Society Billiard Cafe, 1051 Garnet Ave. (272-7665), Pacific Beach. The black interior of this slick pool hall contains 15 pool tables on 2 floors. Don't worry about the wannabe pool sharks; there are plenty of beginners around. Gas up for hustling sessions with an appetizer from the full menu and a mixed drink from the bar, or choose from 50 beers. No cover. Open M-F noon-2am, Sa-Su 11am-2am. 21+ after 8pm.

Lesbian and **gay clubs** cluster in **University Heights** and **Hillcrest.** Some of the more popular hangouts include: **The Flame,** 3780 Park Blvd. (295-4163), in Hillcrest, a lesbian dance club (open Sa-Th 5pm-2am, F 4pm-2am); **Bourbon Street,** 4612 Park Blvd. (291-0173), in University Heights, a piano bar with a gay following (open daily 11am-1:30am); and **The Brass Rail,** 3796 5th Ave. (298-2233), in Hillcrest, featuring dancing and drag on weekends (open daily 5pm-2am).

SEASONAL EVENTS

Gorgeous weather and a strong community spirit make the San Diego area an ideal place for local festivals. The following is by no means a comprehensive list—check the beach community weeklies for further festival information.

Exposition 2000, A Millennium Celebration (235-5907; www.balboaparkexpo.com), Balboa Park. Dec. 31, 1999-Jan. 2, 2000. Festivities to commemorate the Park's past, present, and future.

Penguin Day Ski Fest (858-276-0840), De Anza Cove, Mission Bay. Jan. 1, 2000. This unique festival requires its participants to water-ski in the ocean or to lie on a block of ice without a wet suit. Those who do are honored with a "penguin patch," while those who fail get only a "chicken patch."

Ocean Beach Kite Festival, 4726 Santa Monica Ave. (531-1527), Ocean Beach. 1st Saturday in March. Kite-construction and flying competitions.

27th Annual San Diego Crew Classic (488-0700), Crown Pt. Shores, Mission Bay. Apr. 1-2, 2000; 7am. Crews from the U.S., Canada and Europe compete at the only major collegiate regatta on the West Coast. Admission $5.

San Diego Earthfair 2000 (858-496-6666; www.earthdayweb.org), Balboa Park. Apr. 16, 2000; 10am-5pm. Children's activity area, booths, exhibits, dance and music festival. Free.

Summer Stargazing (594-6182), San Diego State University's Mt. Laguna Observatory. F-Sa from June 1-Sept. 4, 2000; F 2-6pm, Sa 9am-6pm. Open to the public with free tickets available through the U.S. Forest Service.

Ocean Beach Street Fair and Chili Cook-Off (226-21936), Ocean Beach. Last weekend in June. Newport St. is lined with arts booths during this 2-day fest.

Pacific Beach Restaurant Walk (858-273-3303). June 21; noon-5pm. Free samples from more than 20 Pacific Beach restaurants.

10th Annual Cox Communications Film Festival (280-1600). Early to mid-Aug. (dates vary by year, call for more information). View film classics and cartoons from the beach and other San Diego parks. Free.

Hillcrest Cityfest Street Fair (299-3330), on 5th. Ave between Ivy Ln. and University Ave., in the heart of San Diego's gay community. Early Aug. Arts, crafts, food, live entertainment, and beer garden.

U.S. Open Sand Castle Competition (424-6663), Imperial Beach pier. Mid-Aug. Sand-sculpturing demigods exercise their craft in this largest and longest-running of American sand castle events. Parades, fireworks, and children's castle contest.

SummerFest La Jolla Chamber Music Festival (858-459-3724), La Jolla Museum of Contemporary Art. Late Aug.

La Jolla Rough Water Swim (858-456-2100), early Sept. Start and finish at the La Jolla Cove. Largest annual rough water competition in the U.S.

SAN DIEGO'S NORTH COUNTY

In the blockbuster classic *Demolition Man*, Sylvester Stallone plays a police officer who patrols the city of "San Angeles," a fictional future metropolis which consists of unbroken development from Los Angeles south through San Diego to the Mexican border. This fantasy is well-grounded in reality—the drive along I-5 from L.A. to San Diego never really passes through an undeveloped area. Fortunately, most of these towns have beautiful beaches, the best of which belong to the coastal communities of San Diego's North County: Del Mar, Encinitas, Leucadia, Carlsbad, and Oceanside. All five towns are easily accessible along I-5 and historic Rte. 101 (Pacific Coast Hwy.) by car, bike, or bus. Take North County Transit District bus #301 from La Jolla's University Towne Centre as far as Oceanside (daily every 30min. 6am-10pm; fare $1, free transfers). For more North County Transit info, call 760-745-4741.

DEL MAR

Just north of La Jolla is the affluent suburb of Del Mar (pop. 4940), home to thoroughbred racehorses and famous fairgrounds. Its **Chamber of Commerce and Visitor Center,** 1104 Camino Del Mar #214 (858-755-4844 or 793-5292), has brochures and handouts (open M-F 10am-4pm). The Del Mar **Amtrak** station, 105 Cedros Ave. (858-481-0114), in nearby Solana Beach, sends 10 trains per day to Los Angeles.

FOOD. Intruding on Camino Del Mar's real estate offices is the **Del Mar French Pastry Cafe,** 1140 Camino Del Mar (858-481-8622), where pastries and hearty sandwiches ($4) are served beneath a billowing tricolor (open M-Sa 6am-6pm, Su 7am-6pm). One block away is **Board and Brew,** 1212 Camino Del Mar (858-481-1021), and its California Delight ($4), which is chock full of turkey, cream cheese, and sunflower seeds (open daily 10am-7pm). **Tony's Jacal,** 621 Valley Ave. (858-755-2274), is a family-run establishment serving up zesty burritos ($4; open M and W-F 11am-2pm and 5-9:30pm, Sa 11am-2pm and 5-10pm, Su 3-9:30pm).

SIGHTS. Racing season (late July to early Sept.) at the **Del Mar Thoroughbred Club** (858-755-1141; www.dmtc.com), is a celeb-fest. Take I-5 to Via de la Valle, and follow your nose west to Jimmy Durante Blvd. This is one of the most beautiful racetracks in the world and has been popular with entertainers since Bing Crosby and Pat O'Brien founded it in 1937. (Gates open M and W-Th noon, F 4pm, and Sa-Su 11:30am. First post time 2pm. Admission to grandstand $3, seniors and military $1; clubhouse admission $6. Childcare facilities $20.)

BEACHES. **Torrey Pines State Reserve and Beach** (755-2063), along the coast just south of Del Mar, is one of only two native Torrey pine groves on earth. (The other is on Santa Rosa Island in Channel Islands National Park (see p. 241). Take I-5 to the Carmel Valley Rd. Exit, go west until the road ends, turn left onto N. Torrey Pines Rd. (Camino Del Mar or Pacific Coast Hwy.), and look for the sign on the right. (Park open 8am-dusk. Admission $4 per vehicle, pedestrians and bicyclists free.) To the layperson, however, Torrey pine trees look like all the rest. The **Torrey Pines Lodge** (follow the signs to the golf course) provides info on activities and hiking trails (open daily 9am-6pm). The park trails are wonderful for runners, cyclists, and those who enjoy rules—no camping, no picnicking, no food, no smoking, no dogs (even if kept in cars), and no straying off the established trails. The six miles of slightly rocky beach are popular with hang gliders.

More earthy than neighboring Del Mar, **Solana Beach** is also more hospitable to tourists who prefer relaxing to spending money. The beach is off the Loma Santa Fe Exit from I-5 (free parking). From the **Solana Beach City Park** parking lot (858-755-1569), a steep staircase climbs to a promontory with a spectacular view of the ocean below. The **Belly Up Tavern,** 143 S. Cedros Ave. (858-481-9022), off Lomas Santa Fe Dr., was once a warehouse near the train tracks, but now belts blues, rock, reggae, and jazz. Patrons can shoot pool or belly up to the long bar. "Big Mama" Thornton, The Smithereens, and John Lee Hooker have all played at this kickin' joint. Charge tickets by phone (858-481-8140), by computer (www.bellyup.com), or at the door. (Open daily 11am-1:30am; live music daily at 7-9pm with occasional early evening shows. Cover varies with artist. Happy Hour with live big band music weekends at 5:30pm.)

ENCINITAS, LEUCADIA, AND CARLSBAD

North of Del Mar along the Pacific Coast Highway lie the towns of Encinitas and Leucadia, which betray traces of their hippie-mecca past through their hallucinogenic beauty and tie-dyed inhabitants. Farther up the coast is the charming lagoon hideaway of Carlsbad, where U.S. 101, here known as Carlsbad Blvd., winds past silky sands and shingled homes adorned with wild rosebushes.

The cheapest indoor lodging near Carlsbad is **Motel 6,** 6117 Paseo del Norte (438-1242), off I-5 at the Palomar Airport Rd. Exit (singles $40; doubles $45). Other locations are in downtown Carlsbad, 1006 Carlsbad Village Dr. (434-7135), and farther south, on Raintree Dr. (431-0745). Camping on the beach is allowed at **South Carlsbad State Park** (438-3143 or 800-444-PARK/7275). Reservations are available through DESTINET (800-365-2267; sites $17, oceanside $22). There are several beachfront restaurants bursting with character along Pacific Coast Hwy. (Rte. 1). **Filiberto's Mexican Food,** 476 S. Coast Hwy. (753-9590), serves up delicious burritos and tacos ($2). With each order, they'll hand you some hot sauce, but for the love of God, be careful—this is no watered-down picante you're dealing with (Open 24hr.) **George's Restaurant,** 641 S. Coast Hwy (942-9549), is a classic surf diner where the latest issue of *Surfer* is the perfect accompaniment to a pile of pancakes ($3-4; open daily 7am-2pm.) Five dollars at the **Miracles Cafe,** 1953 San Elijo Ave., (943-7924), will get you banana Belgian waffles (before 2pm) or a Supreme Scream sandwich (Swiss cheese, avocado, tomato, cucumber, and sprouts). To get to this funky coffee joint, take the Birmingham Dr. Exit from I-5 and go west to San Elijo Ave. (Open M-Th 6am-10pm, F-Sa 6am-11pm, Su 7am-10pm.)

The state maintains a number of undeveloped beaches, good for both sun and surf. The stone steps at **Leucadia State Beach** descend from the cliffs at South El Portal St. to over three miles of public sands. **Carlsbad State Beach** is long and attractive despite the view of the mammoth Encinitas Power Plant, which occupies the coast to the south. **Offshore Surf Shop,** 3179 Carlsbad Blvd. (729-4934), rents boogie boards ($3 per hr., $10 per day) and "soft" surfboards ($5 per hr.; $25 per day; $100 deposit or credit card required for all rentals; open daily 9am-7pm). **Carlsbad Cycle World,** 11675 Sorrento Valley Rd. (434-5698) rents mountain bikes ($9 per hr., $21 for 4hr., $30 per day).

Cardiff-by-the-Sea is enhanced by **San Elijo Beach State Park** (753-5091) and **Cardiff State Beach** to the south. For camping info, see **Campgrounds and the Outdoors** (p. 47). If you have a car, these beautiful beaches are worth the drive.

OCEANSIDE

Oceanside (pop. 146,230) is the largest and most varied of the beach towns north of San Diego, probably because the beach at **Oceanside Harbor** (I-5 and Oceanside Harbor Dr.) is one of the world's greatest surfing beaches. The **pier** at Pierview Way attracts serious surfers year-round, especially during events such as the World Body Surfing Championships (mid-Aug.). Call the Oceanside Special Events Office (966-4545) for more info. Beaches are patrolled by lifeguards, and surfers stick to designated areas. Parking costs $3 by the harbor and the pier, but metered curb spots can be found nearby. With so much surfing history made along its shores, Oceanside is the perfect place for the **California Surf Museum,** 233 N. Coast Hwy. (721-6876; open Th-M 10am-4pm; free). The exceptionally enthusiastic folks at the **Oceanside Visitors Center,** 928 N. Coast Hwy. (721-1101; fax 722-8336), have info about goings-on (open M-F 9am-4:30pm, Sa-Su 9am-3pm).

Mission San Luis Rey de Francia, 4050 Mission Ave. (757-3651), was founded in 1798, but the only original building still standing is the church (circa 1807). Follow Mission Ave. east from N. Coast Hwy. (Rte. 101) for five miles, or take NCTD bus #303 at Rte. 21 and Mission Ave. (Museum open M-Sa 10am-4:30pm, Su noon-4:30pm. Admission $4, students and seniors $3, ages 8-14 $1.)

The **Oceanside Transit Center,** 235 S. Tremont, houses the local **Amtrak** (722-4622) and **Greyhound** (722-1587 or 722-5545) stations.

ESCONDIDO

Thirty miles north of San Diego, Escondido (pop. 116,350) residents range from rich celebrities to undocumented agricultural laborers. Victorian mansions, fields of wildflowers, and numerous wineries decorate this North County community.

The **San Diego North Convention and Visitor Bureau,** 720 N. Broadway (760-745-4741; 24hr. hotline 800-848-3336), dispenses info on Escondido and the beach cities to the west (open M-F 8:30am-5pm, Sa 10am-4pm). **Greyhound** (760-745-6522) stops at 700 W. Valley Pkwy. The **North County Transit Department** can be reached at 760-743-NCTD/6283.

There are a number of budget motels clustered off I-15. To get to the main motel strip, take Rte. 78 east to Center City Pkwy., and turn right on **Washington Boulevard.** The **Super 8,** 528 W. Washington Blvd. (760- 747-3711), has gorgeous rooms, cable TV, A/C, pool, jacuzzi, and continental breakfast (singles Su-Th $40, Sa-Su $45; doubles Su-Th $50, Sa-Su $55). One digit away is the **Super 7,** 515 W. Washington Blvd. (760-743-1443), with cable TV and A/C (key deposit $5; singles Su-Th $35, Sa-Su $40; doubles Su-Th $39, Sa-Su $44; $179 per week).

An essential part of any trip to San Diego, the **San Diego Wild Animal Park** (480-0100), is dedicated to the preservation and display of endangered species. The park's main selling point is its lack of cages—its animals roam freely in extensive habitats engineered to simulate the real thing. View the park's 2100 acres by taking a ride on the open-air **Wgasa Bush Line Railway,** a 55-minute monorail tour through the four habitat areas. (Tours mid-June-Aug. 9:30am-6pm; Sept. to mid-June

9:30am-4pm; sit on the right if possible.) Renting binoculars ($5) at the park entrance may enhance the tour. After the tour, watch butterflies and birds flutter as you walk through the Hidden Jungle greenhouses. The park has shops, restaurants, and animal shows, but for adventure, try the one-mile Heart of Africa hike, the open-air Photo Caravan (760-738-5049), or the **Roar and Snore** overnight camping safari (800-934-CAMP/2267). Most of the park, including the monorail, is wheelchair accessible, but steep hills may require detours or assistance. (Open daily 9am, closing times vary. Admission $22, ages 3-11 $15. Parking $3.)

Also in Escondido is the "wunnerful, wunnerful" **Welk Resort Center,** the personal barony of late champagne-music conductor Lawrence Welk. The center has three championship golf courses, a luxury hotel, and a 330-seat dinner theater. In the theater's lobby is the **Lawrence Welk Museum,** 8860 Lawrence Welk Dr. (800-932-WELK/9355), which includes Welk's golf cart as an exhibit. (Open Tu, Th, and Sa 9am-7pm; Su, M, W, and F 9am-4:30pm.)

NORTH OF ESCONDIDO

Although the Hale telescope at **Palomar Observatory** (760-742-2119), on Palomar Mountain, is over 40 years old, it remains one of the world's largest and greatest astronomical tools. The observatory is accessible via San Diego County Rte. S6, the "Highway to the Stars." Inside the observatory, a museum displays celestial photos taken through Hale's 200-inch aperture. (Open daily 9am-4pm. Free.)

Cleveland National Forest contains the observatory and several campgrounds. S6 passes the federally run **Fry Creek** and **Observatory campgrounds,** and a left onto S7 at the mountaintop will bring you to **Palomar Mountain State Park** (742-3462; vehicles $5, dogs $1). Camping is permitted at the park's state-run **Doane Valley campground** (742-3462). Sites are over 5000 feet above sea level, so bring warm clothing. Showers, hiking trails, and fishing are available, but no swimming is allowed. (Sites May-Oct. Su-Th $15, Sa-Su $16; Nov.-Apr. $12; hiker/biker sites $3).

One of the few missions still operating in California can be found west of Mt. Palomar, on Rte. 76, six miles east of I-15. The **Mission Asistencia San Antonio de Pala** (760-742-3317), on the Pala Indian Reservation, was founded as an outpost of Oceanside's Mission San Luis Rey in 1816 and has since converted thousands of Native Americans to Christianity.

THE DESERT

Mystics and misanthropes from Native Americans to modern city slickers have long been fascinated by the austere scenery and the vast open spaces of the California desert. In winter the desert is a pleasantly warm refuge, in spring, a technicolor floral landscape, in summer, a blistering wasteland, and in fall—more of thee same. A barren place of overwhelming simplicity, the desert's beauty lies in its emptiness as well as in its elusive treasures: diverse flora and fauna, staggering topographical variation, and scattered relics of America's past.

ORIENTATION

California's desert divides roughly into the Low and High Deserts, names which indicate differences in both altitude and latitude. The **Sonoran,** or **Low Desert,** occupies southeastern California from the Mexican border north to Needles and west to the Borrego Desert. The **Mojave,** or **High Desert,** averages elevations of 2000 feet and spans the southern central part of the state, bounded by the Sonoran Desert to the south, San Bernardino and the San Joaquin Valley to the west, the Sierra Nevada to the north, and Death Valley to the east. Four major east-west highways cross the desert. In the Low Desert, **Interstate 8** hugs the California-Mexico border, while **Interstate 10** skims past Joshua Tree and through Blythe. Cutting through the heart of the Mojave is **Interstate 15.** From Barstow, the Mojave's main pitstop, I-15 continues on to Las Vegas, while **Interstate 40** cuts southeast through Needles and on to the Nevada desert.

The regions described in this chapter cohere along the routes of the major highways listed above. The Low Desert follows destinations along I-8 and I-10, The High Desert follows destinations along I-15, and **Route 66** follows the path of the old highway along I-40 through the Mojave Desert, continuing into Arizona as far as the Grand Canyon.

DESERT SURVIVAL

Here, **water,** not bread, is the staff of life. The body loses at least a gallon of liquid per day in the desert (2 gallons during strenuous activity), so keep drinking *always.* Drinking huge quantities of water after physical exertion to quench your thirst is not as effective as taking preventative measures to stay hydrated. Whether you are driving or hiking, tote **two gallons of water per person per day.** Designate at least one container as an emergency supply, and always have water at your side. In the car, keep backup containers in a cooler. When drinking sweet beverages, dilute them with water to avoid an over-reaction to high sugar content. Avoid alcohol and coffee, which cause dehydration. For long-term stays, a high-quality beverage with potassium compounds and glucose, such as **ERG** (an industrial-strength Gatorade available from wilderness outfits and camping suppliers), will help keep your strength up. Trail mix is good for you—peanuts and dried fruits give you energy and needed vitamins, but stay away from chocolate chips—they'll melt and create a gooey mess in your backpack or on the seat of your car.

Most people need a few days to adjust to the heat, especially before difficult hikes. Sunglasses with 100% UV protection, sunscreen, and a hat are essential **sun protection,** but proper clothing is the most effective protection. Light-colored clothing helps reflect the sun's rays. For added relief from the heat, wrap a dampened bandana around your head. Thick-soled shoes and two pairs of socks may help to keep feet comfortable on a hike in summer, when sand temperatures reach 150-200 F. Lastly, although it may be uncomfortable to wear a sweaty shirt, it prevents dehydration more effectively than going shirtless.

Heat is not the desert's only climatic extreme. At high elevations, temperatures during winter nights can be well below freezing (a sweater is often necessary even in summer). Fall and spring **flash floods** can cause water to come down from rain-drenched higher elevations and wreak biblical devastation upon lands below, turning dry gulches into raging rivers—choose campsites accordingly.

Hiking expeditions should be attempted only in temperatures under 90 F, and *never* alone. Almost all parks require hikers to register with the park office before hitting the trails. If you're on private or unmanaged public land, *always* notify someone of your itinerary.

DRIVING IN THE DESERT. Desert conditions are just as grueling on cars as they are on bodies; only recently serviced cars in good running condition can take the heat. Bring at least five gallons of radiator water, extra coolant, and a few quarts of oil (car manuals recommend appropriate oil weights for varying temperatures). In addition to a spare tire and necessary tools for the basic mishap on the road, a board and shovel are useful for sand-stuck cars. A four-wheel-drive vehicle is recommended for unpaved roads.

Although towns are sometimes sparse, major roads usually have enough traffic to ensure that breakdowns will be noticed. Even so, isolated areas of the parks pose a threat, especially in summer, when few tourists visit. *Stay with your vehicle if it breaks down;* it is easier to spot than a person and provides crucial shade.

Use **air conditioning** with extreme restraint. Turn it off immediately if the car's temperature gauge starts to climb. Air from open windows should be sufficiently comfortable at highway speeds. If your car overheats, pull off the road and turn the heater on full force to cool the engine. If radiator fluid is steaming or bubbling, turn off the car for about 30 minutes. If not, run the car in neutral at about 1500 rpms for a few minutes, allowing the coolant to circulate. Never pour water over the engine and never try to lift a searingly hot hood. **Desert water bags** are available at hardware or automotive stores for about $5-10. When strapped onto the front of the car and filled with water, these large canvas bags prevent overheating by speeding up evaporation. Driving in the evening, night, and early morning is preferable to overheating or being uncomfortably hot at midday.

HIGHLIGHTS OF THE DESERT

- Sand and rocks (see below).
- **Palm Springs** (p. 463) is a lovely pastel resort town with access to great hiking, golfing, the **Palm Springs Aerial Tramway** (p. 466), and more **celebrity homes** than you can shake a stick at (p. 466).
- The desert blooms at **Joshua Tree National Park** (p. 467), with an incredible sunset landscape and springtime wildflower display, as well as hiking, camping, and climbing among the park's famous boulders and angular desert trees.
- For a *Lawrence of Arabia* experience, check out the **dunes** at Death Valley National Park (p. 477), Mojave National Preserve (p. 489), and Dumont (p. 489).
- The high desert teems morbidly with **ghost towns,** be they preserved, desecrated, or decomposing (p. 478, p. 479), as well as **abandoned mines** (p. 471).
- Delirious? Find yourself in **Las Vegas,** where you can **shoot real guns,** sashay through the **Liberace Museum,** and, of course, frolic with scantily clad waitress-nymphs through the green-felt forests of the **Strip casinos** (p. 484).

THE LOW DESERT

The Low Desert, home of Anza-Borrego Desert State Park and the Salton Sea, is flat, dry, and barren. Only the oases in this area can promote animal or plant life—Palm Springs, the largest of these oases, promotes super-resort tourism as well. Despite its arid climate, much of this region has become agriculturally important, as water from the Colorado River irrigates the Imperial and Coachella Valleys.

ANZA-BORREGO DESERT STATE PARK

The largest state park in California claims a sizable wedge of the state's southern desert, layered with both natural and human history. A popular diversion from Palm Springs or San Diego, Anza-Borrego sprouts many cactus and plant species found nowhere else in California. Barbed *cholla* cacti, bruise-blossomed indigo bush, and thirsty tamarisk all draw life from a bioregion that covets water but is blessed with a surplus of sunlight. Beneath these specimens lies a geologically diverse landscape full of dunes, badlands, mountains, springs, oases, and active faults. Hidden within these natural features are the remains of forgotten Native American, Spanish, and oil pioneers' settlements. Visit in the winter or early spring when the searing sun is off the warpath. High summer temperatures can make the park unpleasant and even dangerous during the hottest months.

ORIENTATION AND PRACTICAL INFORMATION. The park is accessible via **Route 78** or **County Highway 22 (S22).** From the west, Rte. 79 (from I-8) connects to Rte. 78 in Julian. From the east, Rte. 86 runs south from I-10 to Rte. 78 or S22. From Rte. 78, follow the signs on S3 to Borrego Springs.

Northeast Rural Bus System (767-4287) services the San Diego backcountry. Info line open M-Sa 7am-noon and 2-5pm. Contact **AAA Emergency Road Service** at 800-222-4357. For **Visitor Information,** contact the **Anza-Borrego Desert State Park Visitors Center,** 200 Palm Canyon Dr., Borrego Springs (767-4205). They have topographical maps, books, exhibits, and slideshows. Rangers offer lifesaving backcountry and safety info; stop here before hiking or camping in the park (open June-Sept. Sa-Su 9am-5pm; Oct.-May daily 9am-5pm). For more info during summer months, call the **Anza-Borrego State Park Headquarters** (767-5311; open M-F 8am-5pm), or the **Borrego Springs Chamber of Commerce** (800-559-5524). **Weather Conditions:** 289-1212. **Desert Wildflower Hotline:** 767-4684. **Emergency:** 911. **Medical Services: Borrego Medical Center,** 4343 Yaqui Pass Rd., Borrego Springs (767-5051), on Rams Hill. Open June-Sept. M-Tu and Th-F 8:30am-1pm, W 1-6pm; Oct.-May M-F 8am-5pm, Sa 8am-noon. **Area code:** 760.

ACCOMMODATIONS, CAMPGROUNDS, AND FOOD. The small community of **Borrego Springs** provides adequate accommodations for park visitors. **Hacienda del Sol,** 610 Palm Canyon Dr. (767-5442), offers comfy old rooms (singles and doubles June-Sept. $45, Oct.-May $50; each additional person $5). The prices at **Stanlunds,** 2771 Borrego Springs Rd. (767-5501), are just as low (singles in summer $40-50, in winter $55-65).

Anza-Borrego permits open **camping** off the park's many unpaved roads (reserve through PARKNET, 800-444-7275), which may be an option for hard-core desertphiles, but is not comfortable in the summer. Temperatures over 100°F spoil food, hasten dehydration, and turn tents into solar-powered ovens (see **Desert Survival,** p. 460). The **$5 daily park use fee** also covers one night's camping. The most hospitable of the area's primitive campsites is along S3 in **Culp Valley.** At 3400 feet, it is the highest and coolest camp in the park. They will never find your body. The **Borrego Palm Canyon Campground,** three miles from town on S3, features flush toilets, showers, and food lockers (sites $15, hookups $21-27). **Agua Caliente Springs Park,** on S2 south of Vallecito Stage Station, offers restrooms, a wading pool, natural hot springs, and laundry facilities. The nearby store and gas station make it a convenient hiking base. (Sites $10-15.)

Center Market, 590 Palm Canyon, Borrego Springs (767-3311), sells groceries and supplies (open M-Sa 8:30am-6:30pm, Su 8:30am-5pm). Across the street is the local favorite, **Kendall's Cafe,** 528 Palm Canyon Dr. (767-3491), behind the mall. Dinners ($6-11) include lowfat, half-pound buffalo burgers. (Open Sept.-July daily 6am-8pm; Aug. M and Th-Su 6am-8pm, Tu-W 6am-2pm.)

SIGHTS AND HIKES. The most popular areas of exploration in Anza-Borrego are **Coyote Canyon Creek** and its network of tributaries. These creeks water the lands around them, giving life to plants unable to survive elsewhere in the park. Wildlife are also drawn to their waters, including **bighorn sheep.** The short, easy, and self-guided **Palm Canyon Creek Trail** starts by the visitors center and continues a few hundred feet to an impressive grove of spring-fed palm trees. It's a good place for viewing the elusive bighorn sheep. The **Southern Emigrant Trail** follows a wagon trail used by immigrants to reach California. Along the trail is a sod **stage station** built in 1852. With a four-wheel-drive vehicle, **Font's Point** is accessible for a view of the spectacular Borrego Badlands. The park's chief attraction is its **wildflower season,** which turns barren wastelands into brightly blossomed wonderlands every spring. Ask rangers about special guided activities.

PALM SPRINGS

Even in its very first days, when the Agua Caliente band of Cahuillan Indians settled here for a winter respite, Palm Springs (pop. 42,000) was an alluring resort. As soon as the Southern California Railroad came through the village, pioneers began displacing the Cahuillans, and then it was only a matter of time before this glitzy desert community elected Sonny Bono as its mayor. Today, the medicinal waters of the city's natural hot springs ensure not only the health of its wealthy residents, but also its longevity as a resort town. While Palm Springs is home to gaggles of retirees, it is also a popular spring break destination for students and a winter retreat for fat-cat golfers. With warm temperatures, celebrity residents, and more pink than a *Miami Vice* episode, this desert city provides a sunny break from everyday life. Although Palm Springs may challenge the budget traveler, it offers enough affordable fun to merit a stop en route to Joshua Tree or an escapist excursion from the chaos of L.A.

ORIENTATION

Palm Springs is a two- to three-hour, 110-mile drive from L.A. along **Interstate 10,** depending on traffic. Approaching from the north on I-15, take I-215 East to Rte. 60 East to I-10 East. From I-10 East, take **Route 111** to the Palm Springs Exit. A longer but more scenic route is the **Palms-to-Pines Highway (Route 74),** where sparse desert cactus and sagebrush give way to lush evergreens. To orient yourself within the town, find **Indian Canyon Drive** and **Palm Canyon Drive,** the city's two main drags that connect to I-10. East Palm Canyon Dr. winds west-northwest through town before subtly turning due north and creeping into Indian Canyon. There are two major east-west boulevards. **Tahquitz-Canyon Road** runs east to the airport, while **Ramon Road,** four blocks to the south, provides access to I-10.

PRACTICAL INFORMATION

Airport: Palm Springs Regional, 3400 S. Tahquitz-Canyon Rd. (323-8161). State and limited national service.

Buses: Greyhound, 311 N. Indian Canyon Dr. (800-231-2222 or 325-2053), near downtown. To **L.A.** (11 per day; $19, round-trip $35). No advance purchase necessary.

Public Transportation: SunBus (343-3451). Local bus service connecting all Coachella Valley cities (daily 5:30am-11pm). Lines 23 and 24 cover the downtown area. The *SunBus Book,* available at information centers and in most hotel lobbies, includes schedules and a system map. Fare 75¢, transfers 25¢; seniors and disabled 25¢, transfers 10¢, weekends free. **SunDial** (341-6999) transports disabled patrons who cannot use the SunBus (daily 5:30am-10:30pm). Call to fill out an application for this service. Fare $1 within the city, $1.50 outside the city. Reserve 4-5 days in advance.

Taxis: Yellow Cab (345-8398). 24hr. **A Valley Cabousine** (340-5845). 24hr.

Car Rental: Rates fluctuate and are higher in winter. **Rent-A-Wreck,** 67555 Palm Canyon Dr. #A105, Cathedral City (324-1766). Must be 21 with major credit card. **Budget** (327-1404 or 800-221-1203), at Palm Springs Regional Airport. Must be 21 with major credit card; drivers under 25 pay $10 per day surcharge.

Bike Rental: Desert Cyclery, 70053 Rte. 111 (321-9444). Mountain bikes $7 per hr., $19 per day. Open M-Sa 9:30am-5:30pm, Su noon-5pm. **Bighorn Bicycles,** 302 N. Palm Canyon Dr. (325-3367). Mountain bikes $7 per hr., $25 per day. Bike tours available. Open daily 9am-1pm.

Visitor Information: Visitors Center, 2781 N. Palm Canyon Dr. (778-8418 or 800-34-SPRINGS/347-7746), one block beyond Tramway Rd. on the right. Free hotel reservations and friendly advice. Pick up *The Desert Guide,* a free monthly magazine outlining attractions and entertainment. Open M-Th and Sa-Su 9am-5pm, F 9am-7pm. **Chamber of Commerce,** 190 W. Amado Rd. (325-1577). Get the seasonal *Palm Springs Visitors Guide*, buy a map ($1), or make hotel reservations. Open M-F 8:30am-4:30pm.

Laundromat: Arenas Coin-Op, 220 E. Arenas Rd. (322-7717), ½-block east of Indian Canyon Dr. Wash $1.25, 10min. dry 25¢. Open daily 5am-9pm; last wash 8pm.

Road Conditions: 800-427-7623. **Weather Conditions:** 345-3711.

Emergency: 911.**Police:** 323-8116.

Crisis Lines: Rape Crisis Hotline (568-9071).

Medical Services: Desert Hospital, 1150 N. Indian Canyon Dr. (323-6511).

Post Office: 333 E. Amado Rd. (800-275-8777). **ZIP Code:** 92262; General Delivery 92263.

AREA CODE The area code for Palm Springs is 760.

ACCOMMODATIONS

Like most famous resort communities, Palm Springs caters mainly to those seeking a tax shelter, not a night's shelter. Yet affordable lodging *is* available. Motels slash their prices 20-40% in the summer; call ahead for prices and don't be shy about bargaining. Many hotels offer discounts through the visitors center. Motels in nearby communities such as Cathedral City and Desert Hot Springs are less attractive but more affordable. Prices listed don't include the county's 10% accommodation tax.

Motel 6, 660 S. Palm Canyon Dr. (327-4200 or 800-4-MOTEL6/466-8356), conveniently located south of city center. Other locations at 595 E. Palm Canyon Dr. (325-6129), and 63950 20th Ave. (251-1425), near the I-10 off-ramp. The cheapest rates in town, especially in winter. Each has a pool and A/C. Some on-the-spot rooms available. Singles $35-37; doubles $41-43. Rates vary by location and season.

Budget Host Inn, 1277 S. Palm Canyon Dr. (325-5574 or 800-829-8099), offers large, clean rooms with refrigerators, phones, and pool/jacuzzi access. Coffeemaker and continental breakfast included. Laundry. Rooms July-Aug. Su-Th from $29, F-Sa $39; Sept.-June $79, $99.

Palm Court Inn, 1983 N. Palm Canyon Dr. (416-2333), close to downtown. Melon-hued exterior houses 80 rooms with great views, 2 heated pools, a spa, and a fitness center. June-Sept. 4-person rooms with 1 bed $39, with 2 beds $49; Oct.-May $59, $69.

Hampton Inn, 2000 N. Palm Canyon Dr. (320-0555). The extra bit of luxury you get for your extra wad of money is what Palm Springs is all about. Features comfy rooms, a beautiful outdoor pool, and cable TV. Continental breakfast included. June-Aug. Su-Th doubles $47, F-Sa $57; Sept.-Mar. $99-139; Apr.-May $89-139.

FOOD

The largest of the desert towns, Palm Springs has more dining options than most desert pitstops—diners and ethnic eateries are common. To cook up your own chow, head for the **Vons Supermarket,** 2115 Taquitz Canyon Way (322-2192).

Las Casuelas–The Original, 368 N. Palm Canyon Dr. (325-3213). Its immediate success made chainhood inevitable, but locals insist that The Original is where it's at. Authentic Mexican dishes (from $6), dingy lighting, and tattooed waitresses give it that slightly outlaw south-of-the-border feel. Open daily 10am-10pm.

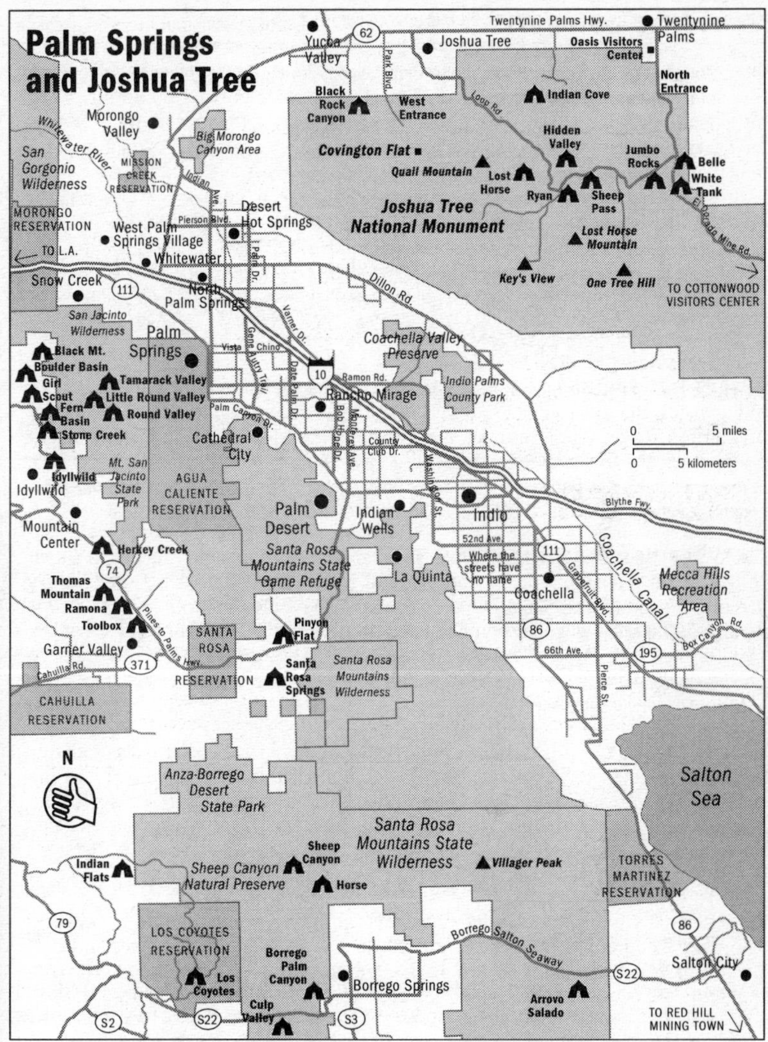

Thai Smile, 651 N. Palm Canyon Dr. (320-5503), between Tamarisk and Alejo. Many vegetarian options (tofu pad thai $6). Don't miss the $5 lunch specials. Open Su-Th 11am-10pm, F-Sa 11am-11pm.

Carlo's Italian Delicatessen, 125 S. Indian Canyon Dr. (325-5571). Budget-minded pizzeria/deli where you can eat under the watchful eyes of local personalities portrayed on the wall. Sandwiches $6. Open Th-Sa 10am-8pm, Su and Tu 11am-5pm, W 10am-7pm.

The Wheel Inn, 50900 Seminole Dr., Cabazon (909-849-7012), north of I-10 and west of Palm Springs. Legendary joint where Pee-Wee Herman met Simone after his encounter with Large Marge. Those unfamiliar with haute cinema still come for the daily specials ($6-7) or tasty pie ($2.50). Open 24hr. The inn displays the friendly dinosaurs seen in *Pee-Wee's Big Adventure*—there's a **gift shop,** 50800 Seminole Dr. (909-849-8309), in the brachiosaurus's belly. Open daily 9am-8:30 or 9pm.

SIGHTS AND ACTIVITIES

Most people come to Palm Springs to drink, party, and schmooze with celebs, but the city also has its share of sights. Mt. San Jacinto State Park, Palm Springs's primary landmark, offers outdoor recreation opportunities for visitors of all fitness levels. Hiking trails are accessible year-round, and cross-country skiing is available in winter at higher elevations.

PALM SPRINGS AERIAL TRAMWAY. If Mt. San Jacinto's 10,804-foot escarpment is too much for your legs to take, take a 15min. ride on this world-famous tram. Nearly 9000 feet above the desert floor, the observation deck has excellent views of the Coachella Valley, and provides access to several wilderness trails. *(325-1391. On Tramway Rd. off Palm Canyon Rd. Trams run every 30min. M-F 10am-8pm, Sa-Su 8am-8pm. Round-trip fare $18, seniors $15, ages 5-12 $12.)*

DESERT HOT SPRINGS SPA. A trip to Palm Springs would not be complete without a visit to the town's namesakes. This spa features six naturally heated mineral pools of different temperatures, as well as saunas, massage professionals, and bodywraps. *(329-6495. 10805 Palm Dr. Take Indian Canyon Dr. to Pierson Blvd., turn right, then turn left onto Palm Dr. Simmer daily 8am-10pm. M and W $5; Tu $3; Th men $3, women $5; F men $5, women $3; Sa-Su $6. After 3pm $3. Holidays $7.)*

PALM SPRINGS DESERT MUSEUM. This remarkable museum markets a touch of true natural beauty with its collection of Native American art, contemporary sculptures, and live animals. The museum sponsors performances in the 450-seat **Annenberg Theatre,** as well as curator-led field trips into the canyons in the winter. *(Museum 325-0189. Theatre 325-4490. 101 Museum Dr. Take SunBus #111. Museum open Tu-Su 10am-5pm. Admission $7.50, seniors $6.50, students, ages 6-17, and military $3.50. Free 1st Friday of each month. Field trips $3.)*

CELEBRITY TOURS. For those travelers who saw more than enough desert simply getting here, these tours offer a view of *who*, not what, there is to be seen in Palm Springs. Be forewarned that these celebrities came to the desert for seclusion; your closest brush with greatness might be seeing Bob Hope's gardener weeding outside of Bob's high adobe wall. *(770-2700. 4751 E. Palm Canyon Dr., Suite C. Guided tours from $15; seniors $13; under 17 $7.)*

TENNIS AND GOLF. Palm Springs has several public tennis and golf facilities. There are 8 courts at **Ruth Hardy Park.** *(700 Tamarisk Dr., at Avenida Caballeros.)* **Tahquitz Creek Golf Resort,** managed by Arnold Palmer, claims to be one of the nation's top municipal golf courses. *(328-1005. 1885 Golf Club Dr. 18 holes M-F $28, winter $37; Sa-Su $35, winter $47. Discounts after 10pm. Greens fees include cart.)* The city's **Recreation Division** has more info on Palm Springs's many lawns and links. *(323-8272.)*

INDIAN CANYONS. These four canyons offer the city's only naturally cool water, as well as remnants of the Cahuilla Indian communities. Take a free tour to learn how the Cahuilla people once utilized the flora and fauna which is sheltered by the world's greatest concentration of naturally occurring palm trees. *(325-3400. 5mi. south of town at the end of S. Palm Canyon Dr. Open daily fall-winter 8am-5pm, spring-summer 8am-6pm. Admission $6; students, seniors, and military $3.50; children 6-12 $1.)*

OASIS WATER PARK. Hear the incongruous roar of surf in the sagebrush at this water park. Surf, slide, and soak in the wave pool, inner tube river, and 13 waterslides. Boogie boards and surfboards available for rent at some attractions. *(325-SURF/7873 or 327-0499. Off I-10 South on Gene Autry Trail between Ramon and E. Palm Canyon Dr. Open mid-Mar. to mid-Sept. daily 11am-6pm, mid-Sept. to Oct. Sa-Su only 11am-5pm. Admission $19 if over 5ft., children 3ft. or taller $12, seniors $11, under 3ft. free. Parking $4.)*

ENTERTAINMENT AND SEASONAL EVENTS

The glitzy persona of Palm Springs doesn't disappear with the setting sun—the city's nightlife is almost as heralded as its golf courses. Although a night of total indulgence here might cost a small fortune, several bars provide nightly drink specials and lively people-watching. **La Taquería,** 125 E. Tahquitz Way (778-5391), has a fun and friendly atmosphere—the mist-covered tile patio is just as inviting as the Moonlight Margaritas ($6). Another option is **Chi Chi Club & Cantina,** 262 S. Palm Canyon Dr. (325-3215). The vodka and pink lemonade ($5) is one of the best offerings from the spinning wall of frozen drinks. Both bars book live music nightly. (Open daily until 2am.) Tender is the nightclub **Zelda's,** 169 North Indian Dr. (325-2375), which has live music on the weekends (cover $6-10; open daily 8pm-2am).

Village Fest (320-3781) takes over Palm Canyon Dr. downtown every Thursday night from 6 to 10pm. Booth after booth of vendors from surrounding communities market food, jewelry, and local crafts in a bargain bonanza while townsfolk enjoy live music. Attempting to fulfill his campaign promise to heighten Palm Springs's glamour quotient, former Mayor Bono instituted the annual **Palm Springs International Film Festival** (778-8979; January 13-20 in 2000). The **2000 National Date Festival** (863-8247), Rte. 111 in Indio, is not a hook-up scene, but rather a bash for dried-fruit lovers (Feb. 18-27 in 2000). Palm Springs is also famous for its tennis tournaments and its professional golf tournaments, like the **Bob Hope Chrysler Classic** (346-8184; Jan. 17-23 in 2000) and the **Nabisco Dinah Shore Classic** (324-4546; Mar. 20-26 in 2000).

NEAR PALM SPRINGS

At the **Living Desert Wildlife and Botanical Park,** 47900 Portola Ave., Palm Desert (346-5694), 1½ miles south of Rte. 111, view Arabian oryx, camels, and meerkats alongside indigenous flora. Wear sunscreen and bring water because there isn't much shade. (Open daily Sept.-June 9am-5pm; July-Aug. 8am-2pm. Sept.-June admission $8.50, seniors and military $7.50, ages 3-12 $4.25. July-Aug. admission $6.50, ages 3-12 $3.)

Since the **Coachella Valley** is the self-proclaimed "Date Capital of the World," comb your hair, suck down a breath mint, and head to the **Shields Date Gardens,** 80225 Rte. 111 (347-0996), in nearby Indio. This palm grove sets itself apart from the rest by presenting a mildly amusing informational film titled *The Romance and Sex Life of the Date* in addition to the usual date shakes and gift boxes (open daily 9am-5pm). If Palm Springs isn't enough of a zoo, you can observe wildlife at the **Big Morongo Canyon Preserve** (363-7190), off Rte. 62, a sanctuary for birds and other animals (open daily 7:30am-dusk; free). Northeast of Palm Springs, the **Coachella Valley Preserve** (343-1234), has a visitors center that can help you plan a hike through mesas, bluffs, or the **Thousand Palms Oasis.**

THE HIGH DESERT

Scorching, silent, and barren, the High Desert is a picture of desolation. John Steinbeck called it a "terrestrial hell," and in the summer months it is difficult to disagree with this description; however, the Mojave conceals unlikely treasures for undaunted adventurers patient and brave enough to explore it. Genuine summer attractions are rare, but winter is temperate enough to hike across dizzying sand dunes and inspect spooky ghost towns.

JOSHUA TREE NATIONAL PARK

When the Mormon pioneers crossed this desert area in the 19th century, they named the enigmatic desert tree they encountered after the Biblical prophet Joshua. Perhaps it was the heat, but the tree's crooked limbs seemed to them an uncanny image of the Hebrew general, who, with his arms upraised, beckoned them to the Promised Land. Although the Mojave may not have had just what the Mormons were looking for, its climate—slightly cooler and wetter than the harsh Arizona desert—must have made them feel as if they had arrived in God's country.

Even today, Joshua Tree National Park has the mystical power to inspire biblical allusions as well as Irish rock bands. Stacks of wind-sculpted boulders flanked by seemingly jubilant Joshua trees evoke the magnificent devastation of Jericho. The park's five oases look lushly Edenic against the desolate backdrop of the surrounding desert, and combine with the park's spectrum of High and Low Desert ecologies to create a vast panoply of landscape and vegetation.

In recent years, climbers, campers, and daytrippers from Southern California have added to the mosaic. The boulder formations that punctuate the desert badlands and bullet the blue sky provide climbers with over 4000 opportunities to practice their skills. History buffs will appreciate the vestiges of human occupation—ancient rock petroglyphs, 19th-century dams built to catch the meager rainfall for livestock, and gold mine ruins that dot the landscape. But the most attractive aspect of Joshua Tree is its remoteness, a result of its freedom from the commercial mayhem that has infested many other national parks. After over 60 years in the arms of America, the natural beauty of Joshua Tree is interrupted only by a few paved roads and signs. The **park entrance fee** is $5 per person or $10 per car, valid for seven days.

At the north entrance to the park lies the town of **Twentynine Palms,** settled after World War I by veterans-turned-homesteaders looking for a hot, dry climate to soothe their gas-seared lungs. Today, the town also hosts the world's largest U.S. Marine Corps base, making it one of the best places in the country to be if you suffer from mustard-gas ingestion or just want a haircut or a tattoo. The businesses in town have recently been decorated with murals depicting personages and events from the town's past. The 3-D mural adorning the Chamber of Commerce building is a creative commemoration of the area's gold-mining days.

ORIENTATION

Joshua Tree National Park covers 558,000 acres northeast of Palm Springs, about 160 miles east of L.A. The park is ringed by three highways: **Interstate 10** to the south, **Route 62 (Twentynine Palms Highway)** to the west and north, and **Route 177** to the east. The northern entrances to the park are off Rte. 62, at the towns of **Joshua Tree** and **Twentynine Palms.** The south entrance is at **Cottonwood Spring,** off I-10. Unfortunately, this is where the streets have no name; just look for the park sign 25 miles east of Indio.

PRACTICAL INFORMATION

Visitor Information:

Headquarters and Oasis Visitors Center, 74485 National Park Dr., Twentynine Palms (367-5500; www.joshuatree.org), ¼mi. off Rte. 62, is the best place to familiarize yourself with the park. Friendly rangers, displays, guidebooks, maps, and water. Open daily 8am-5pm.

Cottonwood Visitors Center, at the southern gateway of the park, 7mi. north of I-10, 25mi. east of Indio. Usually open daily 8am-4pm.

Indian Cove Ranger Station, 7295 Indian Cove Rd. (362-4367). Open Oct.-May daily 8am-4pm; summer hours vary.

Twentynine Palms Chamber of Commerce, 6455 Mesquite Ave., Suite A (367-3445), provides info on murals and transportation. Open M-F 9am-5pm; may close for lunch.

Equipment Rental: Businesses at the **west entrance** to the park rent equipment and offer information on rock-climbing classes.

Medical Services: Hi-Desert Medical Center, 6601 White Feather Rd., Joshua Tree (366-3711). Emergency care 24hr.

Emergency: 911. **24hr. dispatch center** (909-383-5651). Call collect.

Post Office: 73839 Gorgonio Dr., Twentynine Palms (800-275-8777). Open M-F 8:30am-5pm. **ZIP Code:** 92277.

AREA CODE The area code for Joshua Tree National Park is 760.

ACCOMMODATIONS AND CAMPGROUNDS

Those who cannot stomach the thought of desert campgrounds but want to spend more than a day at the park can find inexpensive motels in **Twentynine Palms,** the self-proclaimed "Oasis of Murals" which is sandwiched between the park and the Marines' training base. The **29 Palms Inn,** 73950 Inn Dr. (367-3505), is an attraction in and of itself. Its 19 distinctly different rooms face the Mara Oasis, which has supported life for over 20,000 years. More recently, the life here has been of the celebrity variety with guests like Michelle Pfeiffer and Nicolas Cage. Robert Plant gets the most attention; he composed his post-Zeppelin hit "29 Palms" in a room here. (Doubles June-Sept. Su-Th $47-74, F-Sa $62-102; Oct.-May $10-20 more. Cottages for 4-8 people and air-stream trailers also available for rent. Reservations required Feb.-Apr.) Reliable **Motel 6,** 72562 Twentynine Palms Hwy. (367-2833), is clean and has a pool (singles $37; doubles $43; each additional adult $3). While creating the album *Joshua Tree* in 1987, U2 stayed in one of the 10 units at the **Harmony Motel,** 71161 Twentynine Palms Hwy. (367-3351; 1-bed single or double $45-55; 2 beds $60, with kitchen $65). The **Sunset Motel,** 73842 Twentynine Palms Hwy. (367-3484), has cable and a pool, but it hasn't hosted any famous rock bands (singles and doubles $42-50, with kitchen $60; 3 beds $65).

Camping is an enjoyable and inexpensive way to experience the beauty of the park, except perhaps in the scorching heat of summer. Pre-noon arrivals are the best way to guarantee a site since most campgrounds in the park operate on a first-come, first-camped basis and accept no reservations. Spring weekends and holidays are the busiest times. Reservations can be made for group sites only at Cottonwood, Sheep Pass, Indian Cove, and Black Rock Canyon through DESTINET (800-436-7275). Visitors who dislike the crowds at the developed campgrounds might prefer the backcountry, where unlimited camping is permitted. Ask at a ranger station for details and restrictions on backcountry camping. All campsites have tables, places for fires, and pit toilets. There are no hookups for RVs and few sites offer water or flush toilets—those who plan any sort of extended stay should pack their own supplies and cooking utensils. (Campgrounds Oct.-May 14-day max. stay; June-Sept. 30-day max. stay.)

Jumbo Rocks (4400ft.), near Skull Rock Trail on the eastern edge of Queen Valley. Take Quail Springs Rd. 15mi. south of the visitors center. The highest and the coolest campground in the park, featuring well-spaced sites surrounded by jumbo rocks. Front spots have shade and protection. Wheelchair accessible. 125 sites; 65 in summer. Free.

Hidden Valley (4200ft.), in the center of the park off Quail Springs Rd. Secluded alcoves are perfect for pitching tents, and enormous shade-providing boulders serve as perches for viewing the sun at dawn and dusk. Its proximity to Wonderland of Rocks and the Barker Dam Trail makes this a rock climber's heaven. The 39 sites fill up quickly. Free.

Indian Cove (3200ft.), on the north edge of the Wonderland of Rocks. Enter at the north entrance. Rains create dramatic waterfalls. Popular spot for rock climbers. 107 sites, 45 in summer. Sites $10; 13 group sites $20-35.

Ryan (4300ft.) has fewer rocks, but also less privacy and less shade, than nearby Hidden Valley. The 3mi. round-trip trail ascends to Ryan Mountain, which served as the headquarters and water storage location for the Lost Horse gold mine. The sunrise is spectacular from nearby Key's View. 31 sites. Free. **May be closed in summer.**

White Tank (3800ft.). Excellent for RVs, despite the prohibitions on vehicles over 25ft. Fewer people–but watch out for coyotes who may try to keep you company. Cowboys built up White Tank to serve as a reliable cattle watering hole. 15 sites. Free. **Often closed in summer.**

Black Rock Canyon (4000ft.), at the end of Joshua Ln. off Rte. 62 near Yucca Valley. A good introduction for those who haven't camped before. Animals are often sighted, and there are various hiking trails nearby. Wheelchair accessible. 100 sites with flush toilets and running water. Sites $10. Reservations accepted.

Cottonwood (3000ft.) offers no shade in the midst of the arid, open Colorado Desert portion of the park, but it is the first place where wildflowers appear when there's been sufficient rain. Flush toilets and running water. Wheelchair accessible. 62 sites, 30 in summer. Sites $8; 3 group sites for 10-70 people $25.

Sheep Pass (4500ft.) is in center of park near the trail to Ryan Mountain. Beware of sheep! 6 group sites $20-35. Reserve up to 3 months in advance.

Belle (3800ft.), within view of the Pinto Mountains, is one of the farthest spots in the park from civilization. It is an ideal place to stare at the starry heavens. 18 sites, some best accessed by four-wheel-drive. **Closed in summer.**

FOOD

Although there are no food facilities within the park, Twentynine Palms offers both groceries and grub. While the food is not exactly gourmet, it's certainly possible to eat well, live long, and prosper. If you are willing to do your own cooking, the **Stater Brothers** market, 71727 Twentynine Palms Hwy. (367-6535), saves you a bundle and offers a good selection (open daily 7am-10pm). Otherwise, you get fast food or its local equivalent. **The Finicky Coyote,** 73511 Twentynine Palms Hwy. (367-2429), is a cafe with sandwiches, coffee drinks, smoothies, and ice cream that will make you lick your lips (open M-Th 6am-8pm, F 6am-9pm, Sa 7am-9pm, Su 9am-6pm). **Ramona's,** 72115 Twentynine Palms Hwy. (367-1929), serves good, inexpensive Mexican food in shiny red booths (open M-Sa 11am-8:30pm).

SIGHTS AND ACTIVITIES

Over 80% of Joshua Tree is designated as wilderness area, safeguarded against development, and lacking paved roads, toilets, and campfires. The park offers truly remote territory for backcountry desert hiking and camping. Hikers who seize the opportunity should pack plenty of water and keep alert for flash floods and changing weather conditions. The park's most temperate weather is in late fall (Oct.-Dec.) and early spring (Mar.-Apr.); temperatures in other months often span uncomfortable extremes (summer highs 95-115°F).

IN A VEHICLE. The awesome sights of the park are most scintillating at **sunrise** and **sunset,** when pink, purple, and red skies accentuate the angular arms of the Joshua trees and paint the mountains and rock piles deep crimson and auburn. Daytrippers miss out terribly when they leave for home before dusk—the setting sun may well be the highlight of the day. A self-paced **driving tour** is an easy way to explore the park and linger to a later hour. All park roads are well-marked, and signs labeled "Exhibit Ahead" point the way to unique floral and geological formations. One of these tours, a 34-mile stretch from Twentynine Palms to the town of Joshua Tree across the center of the park, provides access to all the park's most outstanding sights and hikes. One leg of road that should not be missed is **Keys View** (5185ft.), six miles off the park road just west of Ryan campground. On a clear day, you can see forever—or at least to Palm Springs and the Salton Sea. It's also a great spot for watching the sun rise, and for short hikes. The longer drive through the park, from Twentynine Palms to I-10, traverses High and Low Desert landscapes. The **Cholla Cactus Garden,** a grove of spiny succulents resembling deadly three-dimensional asterisks, lies in the Pinto Basin just off the road.

Those with **four-wheel-drive** vehicles have even more options, including the 18-mile **Geology Tour Road,** which climbs through striking rock formations and ends in the Little San Bernardino Mountains. In the spring and fall, **bikers** can enjoy these roads, especially the unpaved and relatively unpopulated four-wheel-drive-only roads through **Pinkham Canyon** and past the **Black Eagle Mines.** Both begin at the Cottonwood Visitors Center (see p. 468). Bikers should check the free park guide for further information.

ON FOOT. Despite the plethora of park roads, **hiking** is perhaps the best way to experience Joshua Tree. Only on foot can visitors tread through sand, scramble over boulders, and walk among the park's hardy namesakes. Although the **Barker Dam Trail,** next to Hidden Valley, is often packed with tourists, its painted petroglyphs and eerie tranquility make it a worthwhile hike. The **Lost Horse Mine,** near Key's View, is reached by a 1½-mile trail and evokes the region's gold prospecting days with rusted machinery and abandoned mineshafts. From the top of **Ryan Mountain** (5461ft.), the boulder formations in the encircling valley bear an unsettling resemblance to Herculean beasts of burden slouching toward a distant destination. Bring plenty of water for the strenuous, unshaded climb to the summit. The visitors center has info on the park's many other hikes, which range from a 15-minute stroll to the **Oasis of Mara** to a three-day trek along the **California Riding and Hiking Trail** (35mi.). On the ranger-led **Desert Queen Ranch Walking Tour** ($5; call for reservations), learn about a resourceful homesteader named Bill Keys and see his restored ranch. Anticipate slow progress even on short walks; the oppressive heat and the scarcity of shade can force even the hardiest of hikers to feel the strain.

The wildflowers that dot the desert terrain each spring (mid-Mar. to mid-May) attract thousands of visitors, and larger plants like Joshua trees, cholla, and the spidery ocotillo have adapted to the severe climate in fascinating ways. To avoid the harsh social stigma that accompanies floral ignorance, get updates on the blooming status of yucca, verbena, cottonwood, mesquite, and dozens of other wildflowers by calling the **Wildflower Hotline** (818-768-3533).

These beautiful beds of wildflowers serve as a habitat for Joshua Tree's many animal species, and the trees and reeds of the park's oases play host to ladybugs, bees, golden eagles, and bighorn sheep. Kangaroo rats, lizards, and stinkbugs scamper about at all times of the day, while wily coyotes, bobcats, and the occasional rattlesnake stalk their prey (including, if you're not careful, your unleashed pet) after dusk. Those equipped with time and patience are more likely to see the living beauty of their surroundings revealed.

HANDS AND FEET. Energetic visitors with less patience are often drawn to Joshua Tree for its **rock climbing:** the world-renowned boulders at **Wonderland of Rocks** and **Hidden Valley** are especially challenging and attract thousands of climbers each year. All in all, the park contains more than 4000 climbing locations, enough to satisfy casual and expert climbers alike. Adventurous novices will thrill at the **Skull Rock Interpretive Walk,** which runs between the Jumbo Rocks and the Skull Rock itself. The walk offers not only information on local plants and animals, but also some supremely climbable rocks. Serious rock climbers can contact the visitors center for info on established rope routes and on wilderness areas where the placement of new bolts is restricted. **Joshua Tree Rock Climbing** (800-890-4745) provides instruction and equipment rental.

NEAR JOSHUA TREE: YUCCA VALLEY

Yucca Valley, northwest of the park, is graced with a few unusual attractions and a genuinely helpful **Chamber of Commerce and Visitor Center,** 55569 Twentynine Palms Hwy. (365-6323; open M-F 9am-5pm, Sa-Su 10am-2pm). For breathtaking views of Joshua Tree and the Morongo Basin, ask about nature trails. **North Park Nature Trail** is just over two miles, suitable for the casual hiker. The **Hi-Desert Nature Museum** (369-7212), in Yucca Valley's Community Complex accessed by Damosa Rd., has gemstones, captive scorpions and snakes, and chunks of bristlecone pine, including a cone from the world's oldest living tree (open Tu-Su 10am-5pm; free).

If you're a fan of old cowboy movies, then head over to **Pioneertown,** on Pioneertown Rd. off Rte. 62, to see a town that was built to provide a permanent Western movie set. It is the site of the OK Corral, where *Shootout* was filmed.

The town of **Landers,** north of Yucca Village, offers even more family fun at **Giant Rock,** the world's largest solitary boulder. Seven stories high, it is the former site of George Van Tassel's famous Interplanetary Spacecraft Convention. Take Old Woman Springs Rd. to Landers and ask locals for guidance. Only those equipped with four-wheel-drive will be able to make the trek.

DEATH VALLEY NATIONAL PARK

The devil owns a lot of real estate in Death Valley. Not only does he grow crops (at the Devil's Cornfield) and hit the links (at the Devil's Golf Course), but the park is also home to Hell's Gate itself. It's not surprising, then, that the area's astonishing variety of topographical and climatic extremes can support just about anyone's idea of the Inferno. Visitors can stare into the abyss from the appropriately named Dante's View, one of several panoramic points approaching 6000 feet in elevation, or gaze wistfully into the heavens from Badwater, which at 282 feet below sea level is the lowest point in the Western Hemisphere. Winter temperatures dip well below freezing in the mountains, and summer readings in the valley itself rival even the hottest Hades. In fact, the second-highest temperature ever recorded in the world (134°F in the shade) was measured at the Valley's Furnace Creek Ranch on July 10, 1913. Of that day, ranch caretaker Oscar Denton said, "I thought the world was going to come to an end. Swallows in full flight fell to the ground dead, and when I went out to read the thermometer with a wet towel on my head, it was dry before I returned."

Fortunately, the fatal threshold of 130°F is rarely crossed, and the region can sustain a surprisingly intricate web of life. Many threatened species, including the desert tortoise and the desert bighorn sheep, have made Death Valley home. If you see something unusual, go to the nearest visitors center and fill out a wildlife sighting card, but don't bring one of these animals along as evidence; most of them are endangered. The park entrance fee is $10 per vehicle, $5 for non-vehicles, collected at Furnace Creek Visitors Center and at Grapevine and Stovepipe Wells.

HISTORY

In 1849, a group of immigrants looking for a shortcut to California's Gold Country led ox-drawn wagons over the ridges of the Great Basin and down into the valley's salt beds. After weeks of searching for a western pass through the Panamint Range (losing one of their party in the process), the group found a way out. Looking back at the scene of misery, someone exclaimed, "Good-bye, death valley!" thus naming the area for posterity. After this tragedy, few were anxious to return; in 1883, however, miners discovered borax (a type of salt). Borax mining provided fortunes for a few and a livelihood for many in towns like Rhyolite and Skidoo. Finally, rapid borax depletion transformed boom towns into ghost towns, which are well-preserved, due to the lack of humidity. With no promise of new industry, most have forsaken the valley itself, leaving it largely undisturbed. A tourist influx began in 1933, when the government set aside over three million acres of this desert wilderness as the largest national park outside of Alaska.

WHEN TO VISIT

Although the average high temperature in July is 116°F and the nighttime low 89°F, even summer visits can be enjoyable with wise planning. To this end, the Furnace Creek Visitors Center distributes the free pamphlet *Hot Weather Hints*. (For more info, see **Desert Survival,** p. 460.)

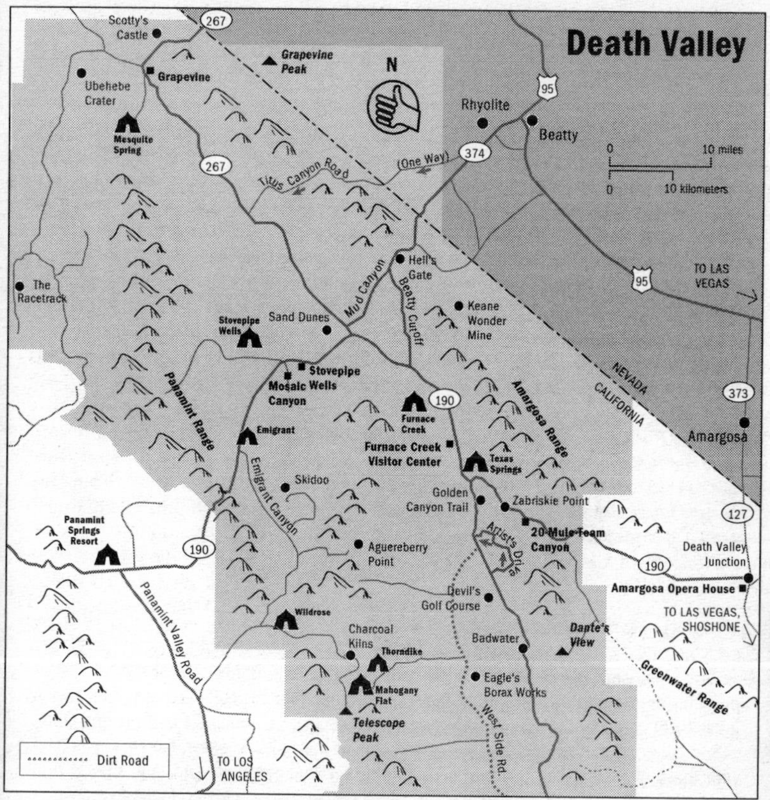

You can drive through and admire the valley in July and August, but to enjoy the many hiking and camping options, visit in winter, *not* summer. Winter is the coolest time (40-70°F in the valley, freezing temperatures and snow in the mountains) and also the wettest, with infrequent but violent rainstorms that flood canyons and obliterate roads and ill-placed tract housing. Call ahead to find out which areas, if any, are washed out before exploring the park.

In March and April desert wildflowers bloom everywhere, but they are accompanied by tempestuous winds that whip sand and dust into a blinding frenzy for hours or even days. From late October to mid-November, over 50,000 people crowd into Death Valley's facilities during the **49ers Encampment** festival (a tribute to the miners of yesteryear). Traffic jams, congested trails and campsites, hour-long lines for gas, and four-hour waits at Scotty's Castle plague the area over winter holidays and three-day winter, Easter, and Thanksgiving weekends.

GETTING THERE AND AROUND

BY CAR. Cars are the best way to get to and around Death Valley (3½hr. from Las Vegas; 5hr. from L.A.; 7hr. from Tahoe City; 10½hr. from San Francisco). If sharing gas costs, renting a car can be cheaper and more flexible than any bus tour. The nearest agencies are in Las Vegas (p. 480), Barstow (p. 487), and Bishop (p. 291).

Conditions in Death Valley are notoriously hard on cars (see **Desert Survival,** p. 460). Radiator water (*not* for drinking) is available at critical points on Rte. 178 and 190 and Nevada Rte. 374. There are only three **service stations** in the park (see

Gas Stations, p. 474), so keep the tank as full as possible at all times. Know how to make minor repairs, bring appropriate topographic maps, leave an itinerary at the visitors center, and take a CB radio. Check ahead for road closings, and do not drive on wet and slippery backcountry roads.

Although **four-wheel-drive** vehicles and high-clearance trucks can be driven on narrow roads that lead to some of Death Valley's most spectacular scenery, these roads are intended for drivers with backcountry experience and are dangerous no matter what you're driving. In case of a breakdown, stay with your vehicle or find nearby shade. For more tips, see **Desert Survival** (p. 460).

Of the seven **park entrances,** most visitors choose Rte. 190 from the east. The road is well-maintained, the pass is not too steep, and the visitors center is relatively close. But since most of the major sights adjoin the north-south road, the daytripper with a trusty vehicle can see more of the park by entering from the southeast (Rte. 178W from Rte. 127 at Shoshone) or the north (direct to Scotty's Castle via Nevada Rte. 267). Unskilled mountain drivers in passenger cars should not attempt to enter on the smaller Titus Canyon or Emigrant Canyon Dr.

NOT BY CAR. No regularly scheduled public transportation services Death Valley. **Guaranteed Tours** (369-1000), depot at the World Trade Center on Desert Inn Rd. between Swensen and Maryland Pkwy. in Las Vegas, runs bust tours from Las Vegas to Death Valley. (Open for reservations daily 6am-10:45pm. 9½hr. tours depart Tu, Th, and Sa 8am. $120, includes continental breakfast and lunch.) If you **hitchhike,** you walk through the Valley of the Shadow of Death. Don't.

PRACTICAL INFORMATION

Gas Stations: Get tanked outside Death Valley at Olancha, Shoshone, or Beatty, NV, or pay 20¢ more per gallon in Death Valley: near the Furnace Creek Visitors Center (open 7am-7pm), Stovepipe Wells Village (open 7am-9pm), or Scotty's Castle (open 9am-5:30pm). Panamint Springs may have gas; ask at the visitors center. Don't play macho with the fuel gauge; fill up often. **AAA towing service, propane gas,** and **diesel fuel** available at the Furnace Creek Chevron; **white gas** at Stovepipe Wells Village store.

Furnace Creek Visitors Center (786-3244; info 786-2331), on Rte. 190 in the valley's east-central section. Write for info: Superintendent, Death Valley National Park, Death Valley 92328. Buy guides and topographic hiking maps ($4-8), get a schedule of activities and guided hikes, check the weather forecast, and slurp from the park's only cold drinking fountain. 12min. slideshow, a short movie (every hr.), and nightly lectures in winter provide further orientation. Open daily 8am-6pm.

Ranger Stations: Weather report, weekly naturalist program, and park info at each station. Emergency help provided. All open daily 8am-5pm. **Grapevine** (786-2313), at Rte. 190 and 267 near Scotty's Castle; **Stovepipe Wells** (786-2342), on Rte. 190; and **Shoshone** (832-4308), at Rte. 127 and 178 outside the valley's southeast border. Also in **Beatty, NV** (702-553-7200), on Nevada Rte. 374.

Death Valley Hikers' Association: Write for info c/o Darrell Tomer, P.O. Box 123, Arcata 95521. The *Dustdevil* is their stellar publication.

Laundromat: On Roadrunner Ave. at Furnace Creek Ranch. Open 24hr.

Swimming Pools and Showers: Stovepipe Wells Village (Non-guests $2. Open daily 9am-9pm.) **Furnace Creek Ranch:** ($2. Open daily 9am-11pm.)

Emergency: 911. **24-Hour Ranger Dispatch** and **Police:** 786-2330.

Post Office: Furnace Creek Ranch (786-2223). Open M-F 8:30am-5pm. **ZIP Code:** 92328.

AREA CODE	The area code for Death Valley National Park is 760.

ACCOMMODATIONS AND FOOD

In Death Valley, beds and fine meals within a budget traveler's reach are as elusive as desert bighorn sheep. Cheaper options in surrounding towns draw many visitors outside the park at nightfall. In winter, camping out with a stock of groceries saves both money and driving time. **Furnace Creek Ranch Store** (786-2381), is well-stocked but expensive (open daily 7am-10pm; in winter 7am-9pm). **Stovepipe Wells Village Store** (786-2578), is smaller (open daily 7am-9pm). Both stores sell charcoal, firewood, and ice.

Furnace Creek Ranch Complex (786-2345, reservations 800-236-7916), once housed and fed Death Valley's borax miners. Today, it is deluged with tour bus refugees who challenge the adjacent 18-hole golf course (America's lowest, at 214ft. below sea level) and relax in the 85°F spring-fed swimming pool. Complex has a cafeteria (open daily 6-10am, 11am-2pm, and 6-9:30pm) and a few more expensive restaurants. Older cabins with A/C and 2 double beds $94; remodeled motel-style accommodations $124-129.

Stovepipe Wells Village (786-2387), comes complete with a large, heated mineral pool which is open in summer until midnight. Rooms $58 (for 1-2 people); each additional person $11. RV sites available. Full hookups $15, includes pool use.

Panamint Springs Resort (775-482-7680), is somewhat far from the main sites of Death Valley, but the roar of jets overhead will assure you that it's right near China Lake Naval Air Weapons Station. Doubles from $57. RV sites $12-20; tent sites $10. Fill up on gas before reaching Panamint Springs; they may be temporarily out.

Amargosa Hotel (852-4441), at Death Valley Junction, Rte. 127 and 190 29mi. east of Furnace Creek. In a Spanish-style plaza developed by ballet dancer Marta Becket. 4 rooms feature Becket's murals; the rest are clean but mural-less. The Jezebel Room was modeled after a turn-of-the-century brothel. May-Oct. singles $35; doubles $45; Nov.-Apr. singles $49; doubles $55. Reception June-Sept. 2-8pm; Oct.-May 8am-8pm.

CAMPGROUNDS

The National Park Service maintains nine campgrounds in Death Valley, only two of which accept reservations (Texas Springs and Furnace Creek; Oct.-Apr.). The visitors center (see **Practical Information,** p. 474) keeps records on site availability; be prepared to battle for a space if you come during peak periods (see **When to Visit,** p. 472). All campsites have toilets but none have showers. Water availability is not very reliable and supplies can at times be unsafe; always pack your own. Collecting wood is forbidden everywhere in the park, so pack your own firewood, and bring a stove and fuel to use where open fires are prohibited. Roadside camping is not permitted, but **backcountry camping** is free and legal, provided you check in at the visitors center and pitch tents at least two miles from your car and any road, and ¼-mile from any backcountry water source. All sites limit stays to 30 days, except Furnace Creek, which has a 14-day limit.

BURRO YOUR HEAD IN THE SAND Animal life persists in Death Valley, despite its desolate environment. Fragile pupfish inhabit tiny pools, and rare desert bighorn sheep traipse through rocks at higher elevations. The infamous Death Valley burros—beasts of burden transported from their native Middle East in the 1850s and freed when the automobile made them obsolete—have unwittingly decimated the park's bighorn sheep population by wolfing down edible shrubs and fouling the water. Several years ago the park service authorized a three-year burro banishment plan to get their asses out of there. (They were sold as pets.) Over 6000 have been removed, and burros may be adopted for $75. Contact the California Federal Building, 2800 Cottage Way #E2841, Sacramento 95825 (916-978-4725).

Wildrose (4100ft.), on the road to the Charcoal Kilns in Wildrose Canyon, 40mi. north of Trona, 21mi. south of Emigrant campground. An old summer residence of the Shoshone Indians, this forested, mountainside location has the most comfortable temperatures in the park. Convenient base for trips to Skidoo, Aguereberry Point, and Telescope Peak. You may need 4WD. 30 sites. No water. Open fires permitted. Free. May be closed at any time due to inclement weather.

Texas Springs (sea level), in the hills above the Furnace Creek Ranch Complex, 600ft. beyond the Sunset campground on the same road. The Harmony Borax mining company's former water source is now the best place for tents near Furnace Creek activities. 92 sites, some with shade. For wind protection, stick close to the base of the hills. Generators prohibited. Water and tables. Open fires permitted. Open Oct.-Apr. Sites $12.

Mesquite Springs (1800ft.), near Scotty's Castle, 2mi. south of Grapevine Ranger Station. All 50 sites without shade or protection from the wind. Located on the prospectors' former watering hole. Overlooks Death Valley Wash and alluvial fans. Listen for coyote and owls. Ideal for tents. Tables. Open fires permitted. Sites $10.

Emigrant (2100ft.), off Rte. 190, 9mi. west of Stovepipe Wells Village across from ranger station, on the way down from Towne Pass through Panamint Range. Gorgeous view of Stovepipe Wells and the valley. Its 10 sites are comfortable in summer. No fires. Free.

Thorndike (7500ft.) and **Mahogany Flat** (8200ft.), 10mi. east of Wildrose and over ½mi. higher, just beyond the Charcoal Kilns in Wildrose Canyon. Depending on conditions, a sturdy car with an able driver may make it to either site, although a 4WD vehicle is preferable. No trailers. Gets cold and dark early; the sun sets quickly in the canyon. Can be snowy even in Apr. and Oct. Tables. No water. Open Mar.-Nov. Free.

Furnace Creek (800-365-2267. 196ft. below sea level), north of the visitors center. Near Furnace Creek Ranch facilities ($2 pool/shower access; laundry). A few of the 168 sites are shaded. Usually fills up first, especially with RVs. (*Not* the $16 Furnace Creek Ranch sites.) Open year-round. Reservations Oct.-Apr. Sites $10. 14-day limit.

Stovepipe Wells (sea level). Near airstrip, 4WD trails, and sand dunes. Reminiscent of a drive-in movie lot. Tenters compete with RVs for 1 of 200 gravel sites. Spots near the trees afford more protection from sandstorms. Close to hotel and general store amenities. (Don't confuse it with the trailer park.) No fires. Open Oct.-Apr. Sites $10.

SIGHTS AND ACTIVITIES

Pre-plan your approach to Death Valley (see **Getting There and Around,** p. 473, for a discussion of the various entrances). If exploring the valley in a day, adopt a north-south or south-north route, rather than heading directly to the Furnace Creek Visitors Center on Rte. 190, which connects east with west. Camera-toters should keep in mind that the best photo opportunities are at sunrise and sunset.

AT THE VISITORS CENTER. Rangers and handouts will detail the distances and times of recommended hikes. Ranger-led programs are generally unavailable in summer, but many popular programs, such as the **car caravan tours** and **interpretive talks,** are available in winter and spring. Astronomy buffs should speak to a ranger; they often set up telescopes at Zabriskie Point and offer freelance stargazing shows. During **wildflower season,** rangers also offer tours of the choicest bloom sites. Wildflower-watching is best after a heavy rainfall, when the parched petals of Death Valley's flowers rouse themselves in gratitude for the moisture from above. (See **Practical Information,** p. 474.)

SCOTTY'S CASTLE. Remarkably out of place in the desert, this castle's imaginative exterior rises from the sands, complete with minaret and Arabian-style colored tile. The saga of the Castle's construction began with the friendship between Chicago insurance millionaire Albert Johnson and the infamous film-flam man Walter Scott (a.k.a. "Death Valley Scotty"). When Johnson fell ill, his doctor suggested that he move to a warm, dry locale, and Scotty convinced him to build this

SCOTTY DOG High on the hill above Scotty's castle lie the remains of Walter Scott under the epitaph, "I got four things to live by: Don't say nothing that will hurt anybody. Don't give advice—nobody will take it anyway. Don't complain. Don't explain." Next to him are the mortal remains of his favorite dog, under a pile of rocks and cement and bearing the name Windy. Even now, Scott's dog lies in mute testimony to the fleeting nature of canine and human existence.

palatial hacienda in Death Valley. Scotty became Johnson's caretaker for the rest of their lives, enjoying fame as the world's most famous "permanent guest/leech" since Rasputin. The well-furbished interior provides welcome relief from the heat (Humbert Humbert sought shelter here in Vladimir Nabokov's *Lolita*), and although the waterfall in the living room has been switched off, the player piano and organ remain. *(786-2392. from Rte. 190, look for sign near mile marker 93 and take road junction to Park Rte. 5; follow Rte. 5 for 33mi. to castle. Open daily 9am-5pm. Tours $8, seniors and ages 6-11 $4; every hr. May-Sept., more frequently Oct.-Apr. Purchase tickets until 1hr. before closing, but there are often lines.)*

ZABRISKIE POINT. Immortalized by Michelangelo Antonioni's 1970 film of the same name, Zabriskie Point is a marvelous place from which to view Death Valley's corrugated badlands at sunrise. For a more intimate view of them, take the short detour along 20-Mule-Team Rd. The well-maintained dirt road is named for the gigantic mule trains that used to haul borax 130 miles south to the rail depot at Mojave. The view of the choppy orange rock formations is particularly stunning late in the day when the dried lake beds fill with burnt light. Before the sunset ends, scamper two miles (and 900ft.) down Gower Gulch to colorful **Golden Canyon** where the setting sun makes the cliffs glitter like so much fool's gold. *(3mi. south of Furnace Creek by car. Take the turn-off from Rte. 190 1mi. east of the museum.)*

ARTIST'S DRIVE. This one-way loop twists its way through brightly colored rock formations. The loop's early ochres and burnt siennas give way at **Artist's Palette** to sea green, lemon yellow, periwinkle blue, and salmon pink mineral deposits in the hillside. The effect is most intense in the late afternoon as the colors change rapidly with the setting sun. The dizzying nine-mile drive turns back on itself again and again, ending up on the main road only four miles north of the drive's entrance. *(On Rte. 178 10mi. south of the visitors center.)*

DEATH VALLEY'S SAND DUNES. Although barefoot climbing on the dunes can be sensuous, be wary of tumbleweeds and mesquite spines while clambering over these 150ft. hills. The most accessible dunes for day hikers lie 2¼ miles east of Stovepipe Wells Village, where you can use the parking area and follow the two-mile trail. In the late afternoon, the dunes (favorites of Ansel Adams) glow with a golden sheen. If you try to emulate the master, know that sand will fool your light meter; increase exposure one F-stop to catch such details as footprints and ripples. *(22mi. north of the visitors center.)*

UBEHEBE CRATER. A blackened volcanic blast site nearly one mile wide and 462 feet deep with a spectacular view, despite the gale-force winds that assault the edges of the giant hole. The twisty gravel trail leading to the floor of the crater increases appreciation for the hole's dimensions, but not nearly as much as the grueling climb back out. A four-wheel-drive unpaved road continues 23 miles south of the crater to the vast **Racetrack Plaza,** a dried-up lake basin providing access to into Hidden Valley and up White Top Mountain. See the trails left by mysterious **moving rocks** on this lake basin. For an outstanding view of the Racetrack, follow the **Ubehebe Peak Trail** *(6mi. round-trip)* from the Grandstand parking area along a steep, twisting pathway. *(8mi. west of Scotty's Castle.)*

MOSAIC CANYON. A half-mile-long corridor of collaged and eroded marble walls, a true natural wonder. A simple two-mile trail leads from the parking lot around the canyon to some awesome vistas. Occasional bighorn sheep sightings are a bonus. (*Take the turn-off from Rte. 190 1mi. west of Stovepipe Wells to the 2½-mile alluvial fan, accessible by foot, horseback, or car.*)

TELESCOPE PEAK. A 14-mile trail through the **Panamint Mountains** leads up this mountain to its peak at 11,049 feet. In the cool early morning, you can climb up to watch the light play upon the tiny landscape below—that is, if you have the proper hiking equipment. The strenuous hike begins at Mahogany Flat Campground and winds 3000 feet past charcoal kilns and bristlecone pines, providing unique views of Badwater and Mt. Whitney. Seasoned backpackers can hike this in winter, but it's a technical climb requiring guts and possibly an ice axe.

LOT'S WIFE'S LOT. So Jack Nicholson doesn't tee off at the **Devil's Golf Course,** but the "course" is a fascinating plane of sharp salt pinnacles which were created by the precipitate from the evaporation of Lake Manly, the 90-mile-long lake that once filled the lower valley. The windswept crags are made from pure sodium chloride (i.e., table salt). *(15mi. south of the visitors center.)*

BADWATER. A briny pool four times saltier than the ocean, this body of water is huge in the winter, but contracts into nothing more than a large puddle in summer. The surrounding salt flat dips to the lowest point in the Western Hemisphere—282ft. below sea level. The pool forms the habitat for the threatened Badwater snails, which are often crushed by the trampling feet of wading tourists trying to cool off—this is the hottest part of the Valley. *(18mi. south of the visitors center.)*

ALONG EMIGRANT CANYON ROAD. This winding road leads from the Emigrant Campground to Wildrose Canyon Dr. In between, there is a turn-off for the four-wheel-drive skedaddle to the ruins of **Skidoo,** a ghost town 5700 feet up in the Panamint Range. Skidoo was the backdrop for the only full-length movie ever shot in Death Valley *(Erich von Stroheim's* Greed, *1923).* A few miles down Emigrant Canyon Rd. is the turn-off for the dirt road to **Aguereberry Point,** known for its fine sunset views *(may require 4WD.)* A left turn at Wildrose Canyon Dr. followed by a 10-mile drive will bring you to the 10 conical furnaces known as the **Charcoal Kilns,** huge ovens which once fired 45 cords of wood at a time to make charcoal for mines.

BEYOND DEATH VALLEY

WEST OF DEATH VALLEY. Only ghost towns like **Darwin** and a few slightly more populated communities remain on U.S. 395 near the Rte. 190 turn-off. In **Olancha,** the **Ranch Motel** (764-2387), on U.S. 395, provides clean, attractive rooms in cottage-type buildings. (Singles $35; doubles $45; quads $65. 4-day "Getaway Special" M-Th $129, additional person $20.) Further south along U.S. 395, the **Still Life Cafe** (764-2044) is an oasis of delicious gourmet food. Having moved to the desert from France, these folks prepare everything well, from cheeseburgers ($6.25) to orange duck pate ($6). Open daily 11am-10pm; Nov.-April 11am-9pm; Sa nights by reservation only (year-round). Bon appetit!

SOUTHEAST OF DEATH VALLEY. In **Death Valley Junction,** at Rte. 127 and 190, 29mi. from Furnace Creek, lives mime and ballet dancer Marta Becket, whose **Amargosa Opera House** (852-4441), is the sole outpost of desert *haute couture.* Becket incorporates classical ballet, modern dance, and pantomime into a one-woman show with 47 different characters for packed houses. (Performances Oct. and Dec.-Jan., May Sa; Nov. and Feb.-Apr. M and Sa. Doors open at 7:45pm, shows begin at 8:15pm. Tickets $10, under 12 $8.)

The town of **Shoshone,** at Rte. 127 and 178, 56mi. southeast of Furnace Creek, serves as an automotive gateway to Death Valley and a base for outdoor adventures—near here you can go mountain biking, frolic in the monstrous Dumont dunes, or explore the Castles of Clay caves. The well-named **Charles Brown General Store and Service Station** (852-4242; open daily 8am-9pm) is next door to the also-brown **Shoshone Inn** (852-4335), which has a swimming pool and cable TV (singles $46; doubles $59). The nearby **Shoshone Trailer Park** (852-4569), has RV hookups, showers, a pool, and even some shade (sites $10, with full hookup $15).

NORTHEAST OF DEATH VALLEY. When approaching Death Valley from the north, consider kicking back briefly in the town of **Beatty,** NV. Located 90 miles northwest of Las Vegas on Rte. 95, Beatty offers weary travelers air-conditioning and ample gambling facilities to prepare for the desolation of the valley.

Compared to those in Reno and Las Vegas, Beatty's casinos are very relaxed. Wager as little as $1 at blackjack and jaw with the dealers, folk who play slow and seem genuinely sorry to take your money. All casinos are theoretically open 24 hours, but by 2am the dealers start eyeing the clock. **Legal prostitution** is the other great vice of Beatty; the town is a scheduled stop on the Hell's Angels' annual "Whorehouse Run." If you want to play Hell's Angel (or are one and have lost your group) drive north out of town on Rte. 95 for three miles, then turn left at the "Angel's Ladies" sign, past a downed airplane, and up to Fran's Star Ranch. The staffers are friendly and do what they can to make patrons feel comfortable. Rates are not made public, but allegedly reasonable.

Info about the town can be collected at the **Beatty Visitor Information Center,** 119 E. Main St. (553-2424; open M-F 10am-3pm). The **Beatty Ranger Station** (553-2200) is well-stocked with books, maps, and safety info for desert-bound drivers (open Tu-Sa 8am-4pm). Sleep in peace at the **Stagecoach Hotel** (533-2419 or 800-424-4946), on Rte. 95 ½-mile north of town. Amenities include a pool, jacuzzi, casino, and bar (Singles and doubles from $40.) Cheaper rooms can be hired at the **El Portal Motel** (553-2912), on Rte. 374 1 block from the junction with Rte. 95 (singles $30; doubles $37). The **Burro Inn** (553-2225; casino 553-2445), at Rte. 95 and 3rd St., serves up standard lunch counter fare (open 24hr.). Don't miss gas and water at the service station before leaving town. **Beatty's area code was recently changed to 775.**

Just outside of town, heading toward Death Valley on Rte. 374, lurks the ghost town of **Rhyolite,** which exploded after prospector Shorty Harris's 1904 discovery of gold in the area. For several madcap years, the town pitched ahead in a frenetic rush of prospecting, building, and saloon-hopping. At its height it was home to an opera house and a stock exchange, but townsfolk fled when a 1911 financial panic struck. The jail and train depot still stand, but the most infamous relic of Rhyolite's crazy heyday is the **Bottle House,** constructed from 51,000 liquor bottles by miner Tom "Iron Liver" Kelly. Newer works of art by area intelligentsia fill a free public sculpture garden on the city's south side, including a gigantic cinder-block nude.

HOMETOWN OF THE LIVING DEAD Authentic California ghost towns are hard to find. **Darwin,** which housed 5000 at its peak and allegedly produced 50% of the lead used by the U.S. in WWII, is probably the closest thing you'll find to a genuine, decaying-yet-walkable ghost town. Its mines and mills closed in the 1970s, leaving a population of 35-40 artists, writers, artisans, and retirees, plus a multitude of buried dead. The graveyard boasts poorly buried corpses, wooden markers, and the ostentatious tomb of Nancy Williams, Darwin's brothel keeper from better times. The only place in town where you're liable to find living people is the post office, which doubles as the business headquarters for "suspension eyewear," worn by the astronauts and Arctic explorers whose photos cover the walls. "The only thing you can buy in Darwin," they'll tell you, "is stamps." Take a look around anyway: if the abandoned tract housing, ramshackle homes, and RVs don't spook you, try the graveyard outside of town. Spooky.

LAS VEGAS

Rising up from the desert as a glittering mass of light and sound, Las Vegas (pop. 258,300) assaults the senses and bewilders the mind. No mirage, it shows a 200% population increase in tourists each *month.* The ever-developing "Strip," where monstrous hotel-casinos reign supreme, entices most visitors. Each resort has adopted its own flashy theme, from ancient Egypt to present day New York, but all contain similar gauntlets of lounges, shops, and gaming rooms. Gambling has made Vegas famous, and although Nevada law prohibits a state lottery, even convenience stores have their own slot machines. Budget travelers beware, for it is easy to escape reality (and forget the value of a dollar) in this illusory city.

Downtown Las Vegas is a somewhat misleading term; unlike many U.S. cities, the downtown area is not the location of the city's primary attractions. It lacks a section of parks, cafes, bookstores, and a dense *petit-bourgeois* shopping district.

South of downtown lies Las Vegas's real draw, the image that has become the international perception of what Las Vegas is like: the breathtakingly gaudy Strip that lines Las Vegas Boulevard and begins in earnest just south of the city limits. The venue gained notoriety in 1947, when, after Bugsy Siegel's elaborate and overpriced Flamingo Hotel and Casino failed to turn a profit in its opening months, the gangster-turned-promoter's business partners had his brains blown out. (One of Siegel's eyeballs was found on a sofa seven feet from his bullet-riddled corpse.) The nation's attention turned to the new, luxurious gaming halls in Las Vegas, and has scarcely left it since.

The Flamingo didn't bring gambling to Las Vegas, but it did bring luxury to gambling in a rough-and-ready cowboy town. Ever since, gangsters and new corporations have been falling over themselves to one-up the competition and attract tourist dollars with progressively more opulent and bizarre establishments. Promoters saw in every culture a chance for thematic exploitation; giant hotels, casinos, mini-malls, and amusement parks push the strip's frontier ever southward, toward the booming housing development industries of Henderson. Bigger is better in "The City that Never Sleeps," and people come to this flashing, buzzing, jangling corner of the American dream to get married, then to celebrate anniversaries, and then to show their kids a good time. Viva Las Vegas!

ORIENTATION

Driving to Vegas from Los Angeles is a straight, 300-mile shot on I-15 (5hr.). From Arizona, take I-40W to Kingman and then U.S. 93N.

Las Vegas has two major casino areas. The **downtown** area, around 2nd and Fremont St., has been converted into a pedestrian promenade; casinos cluster close together beneath a shimmering space-frame structure covering over five city blocks. The other main area is **"the Strip"** a collection of mammoth hotel-casinos along **Las Vegas Boulevard.** Parallel to the Strip and in its shadow is **Paradise Road,** also strewn with casinos. As in any city with a constant influx of money, many areas of Las Vegas are unsafe. Always stay on brightly lit pathways and do not wander too far from the major casinos and hotels. The neighborhoods just north and west of downtown can be especially dangerous.

Despite its debauchery, Las Vegas has a **curfew.** Those under 18 are not allowed unaccompanied in public places from midnight to 5am, those under 14 from 10pm to 5am. On weekends, no one under 18 is allowed unaccompanied on the Strip or in other designated areas from 9pm to 5am. The **drinkin' an' gamblin' age** is 21.

PRACTICAL INFORMATION

Airport: McCarran International (261-5743), at the southeastern end of the Strip. Main terminal on Paradise Rd. is within walking distance of University of Nevada campus. Vans to the Strip and downtown $3-5; taxi $10-12.

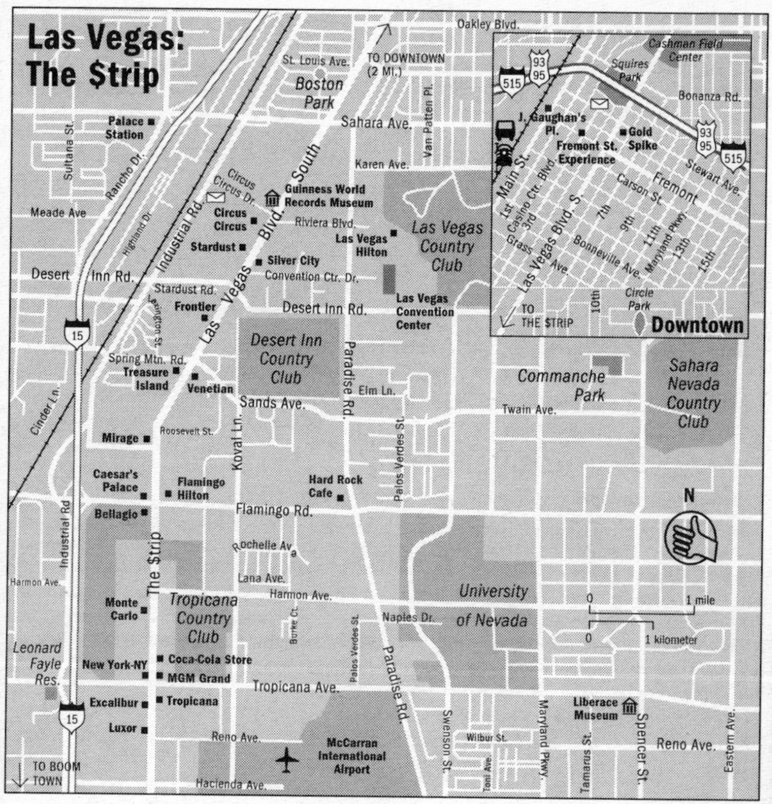

Buses: Greyhound, 200 S. Main St. (384-8009 or 800-231-2222), at Carson Ave. downtown, near Jackie Gaughan's Plaza Hotel/Casino. To: **L.A.** (5-7hr.; 22 per day; M-Th $31, F-Su $35) and **San Francisco** (13-16hr.; 6 per day; M-Th $51, F-Su $54). Tickets sold daily 4:30am-1am.

Public Transportation: Citizens Area Transit (CAT; 228-7433). Bus #301 serves downtown and the Strip 24hr. Buses #108 and 109 serve the airport. All buses wheelchair accessible. Most operate every 10-15min. (less frequently off the Strip), daily 5:30am-1:30am, 24hr. on the Strip. Fares for routes on the Strip $1.50, for residential routes $1, seniors and ages 6-17 50¢. **Las Vegas Strip Trolleys** (382-1404), are *not* strip-joints. They cruise the Strip every 20min. daily 9am-2am. (Fare $1.50 in exact change).

Taxis: Yellow, Checker, Star (873-2000). Initial charge $2.20, each additional mi. $1.50. 24hr. service; for pickup, call 30min. before you need a cab.

Car Rental: Sav-Mor Rent-A-Car, 5101 Rent-A-Car Rd. (736-1234 or 800-634-6779). Rentals from $28 per day, $147 per week. 150mi. per day included, each additional mi. 20¢. Must be 21; under-25 surcharge $8 per day. Discounts in tourist publications.

Visitor Information: Las Vegas Convention and Visitor Authority, 3150 Paradise Rd. (892-0711; fax 226-9011), 4 blocks from the Strip in the big pink convention center by the Hilton. Up-to-date info on headliners, conventions, shows, hotel bargains, and buffets. Open daily 8am-5pm.

Tours: Gambler's special bus tours leave L.A., San Francisco, and San Diego for Las Vegas early in the morning and return at night or the next day. Ask at tourist offices in the departure cities or call casinos for info. **Gray Line,** 4020 E. Lone Mountain Rd.

(384-1234 or 800-634-6579; www.pcap.com/grayline.htm; email Gltours@ix.netcom.com). City Tours (7½hr., 1 per day, $35). Bus tours from Las Vegas to **Hoover Dam/Lake Mead** (3 per day, $30 includes Dam admission) and **Grand Canyon's South Rim** (full-day $149). Discounted prices with coupons in tourist publications and for ages 2-9. Reserve in advance.

Bank: Bank of America, 1140 E. Desert Inn Rd. (654-1000), at the corner of Maryland Pkwy. Open M-Th 9am-5pm, F 9am-6pm. Phone assistance 24hr.

ATMs: Unsurprisingly, located in all major casinos.

Marriage: Marriage License Bureau, 200 S. 3rd St. (455-4415). Must be 18 or obtain parental consent. Licenses $35; cash only. No waiting period or blood test required. Open M-F 8am-midnight, Sa-Su 24hr. **Little White Chapel,** 1301 S. Las Vegas Blvd. (382-5943 or 800-545-8111). 24hr. Drive-thru service $30; chapel service $45.

Divorce: Must be a Nevada resident for at least 6 weeks. $140 service fee. Permits available at the courthouse M-F 8am-5pm.

Bi-Gay-Lesbian Organization: Gay and Lesbian Community Center, 912 E. Sahara Ave. (733-9800). Open M-F 9am-7pm.

Road Conditions (Nevada): 775-793-1313.

Weather Conditions: 263-9744.

24-Hour Crisis Lines: Compulsive Gamblers Hotline (800-LOST-BET/567-8238). **Gamblers Anonymous** (385-7732). **Rape Crisis Center Hotline** (366-1640). **Suicide Prevention** (731-2990).

Emergency: 911. **Police:** 795-3111.

Post Office: 301 E. Stewart Ave. (800-275-8777), downtown. Open M-F 8:30am-5pm. General Delivery pickup M-F 9am-2pm. **ZIP Code:** 89101.

AREA CODE	The area code for Las Vegas is 702.

ACCOMMODATIONS AND CAMPGROUNDS

Even though Vegas has over 100,000 rooms, most hotels fill up on weekend nights. Coming to town on a Friday or Saturday night without reservations is a recipe for disaster, so *make reservations as far in advance as possible.* If you get stuck call the **Room Reservations Hotline** (800-332-5333). The earlier you reserve, the better chance you have of snagging a special rate. Room rates at most hotels in Vegas fluctuate all the time. Many hotels use two rate ranges—one for weeknights, another for weekend nights. In addition, a room that costs $30 during a promotion can cost hundreds during conventions (two major ones are in Jan. and Nov.).

Check local publications such as *What's On In Las Vegas*, *Today in Las Vegas*, *Vegas Visitor*, *Casino Player*, *Tour Guide Magazine*, and *Insider Viewpoint of Las Vegas* for discounts, coupons, and schedules of events; they are all free and available at the visitors center, hotels, and attractions.

Strip hotels are at the center of the action and within walking distance of each other, but their inexpensive rooms sell out quickly. Motels line **Fremont Street,** from downtown south. Another option, if you have a car, is to stay at one of the hotel-casinos in Jean, Nevada (approximately 30mi. south on I-15, near the California border). These tend to be less crowded and cheaper than in-town hotels.

The state hotel tax of 9% is not included in room rates listed below.

Las Vegas International Hostel (AAIH/Rucksackers), 1208 S. Las Vegas Blvd. (385-9955). Flashing blue arrows point the way to this European-flavored joint. Tidy, spartan rooms with A/C and fresh sheets daily. Ride board, TV room, basketball court. Extremely helpful staff is an excellent source for advice about budget Vegas. Shared bathrooms.

Laundry. Key deposit $5. Reception 7am-11pm. Check-out 7-10am. 6-person dorms Apr.-Nov. Su-Th $12, F-Sa $14; singles $26. Rates lower Dec.-Mar.

Somerset House Motel, 294 Convention Center Dr. (735-4411 or 888-336-4280; fax 369-2388). A straightforward, no-frills establishment within short walking distance of the major Strip casinos. Many rooms feature kitchens; all are sizable and impeccably clean. Dishes and cooking utensils provided upon request. Singles Su-Th $32, F-Sa $40; doubles Su-Th $40, F-Sa $50; additional person $5. Rates lower for seniors.

Palace Station, 2411 W. Sahara Ave. (367-2411 or 800-634-3101). Free shuttle to airport and Las Vegas Blvd. All the same features of the Strip hotels, including 2 pools, lounge, casino, and buffet, at much more reasonable rates. Su-Th $29-49, F-Sa from $69; additional person $10.

Circus Circus, S. 2880 Las Vegas Blvd. (734-0410 or 800-444-CIRCUS/2472). Only hotel with its own clown shop. Rooms with TV and A/C for 1-4 people. Su-Th $29-79, F-Sa $69-119, holidays $69-159; rollaway bed $12. In summer, fills 2-3 months in advance for Su-Th, 3-4 months for F-Sa.

Silverton, 3333 Blue Diamond Rd. (263-7777 or 800-588-7711). Although its ghost town theme is ominous in the Vegas context, this slightly remote hotel-casino offers the swagger of the Strip at affordable prices. Free Las Vegas Blvd. shuttle for guests. Singles and doubles Su-Th $29-39, F-Sa $59-89.

Econo Lodge Downtown, 520 S. Casino Center Blvd. (384-8211). Rooms here are spotless and include refrigerators and coffeemakers. Walking distance to the Greyhound bus station and downtown casino area. Singles Su-Th $35, F-Sa $45; doubles Su-Th $45, F-Sa $55; additional person (up to 5) $8.

Goldstrike, 1 Main St., Jean, Nevada (800-634-1359), 30mi. south of Vegas on I-15 (Exit 12). Vegas-style casino has various inexpensive restaurants (prime rib $6, dinner buffet $6). Su-Th $18, F $35, Sa $49 based on availability; additional person $3.

CAMPGROUNDS

Lake Mead National Recreation Area (293-8906), 25mi. south of town on Rte. 93/95. Sites $10, with hookup $14-18. For details, see p. 486.

Circusland RV Park, 500 Circus Circus Dr. (734-0410), a part of the Circus Circus hotel on the Strip. Pool, jacuzzi, convenience store, showers, and laundry. Hookups Su-Th $17.50, F-Sa $20.

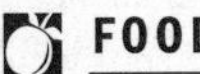

FOOD

Almost every hotel-casino in Vegas courts tourists with cheap all-you-can-eat invitations, but expect long lines at peak hours, and know that the cheapest buffets are greasy, cafeteria-quality food. Most casinos dole out alcoholic drinks for free to those who are gambling and for under $1 to those who aren't...yet. Vegas isn't all bland buffets—just west of the Strip, particularly along **Decatur Boulevard,** are a number of low-priced eateries that can revive your taste buds.

RESTAURANTS

The Plaza Diner, 1 Main St. (386-2110), near the entrance in Jackie Gaughan's Plaza Hotel/Casino. Cheap prime rib dinner noon-midnight ($4). $1 beers. Open 24hr.

Rincon Criollo, 1145 S. Las Vegas Blvd. (388-1906), across from youth hostel. Dine on filling Cuban food beneath a wall-sized photograph of palm trees. Daily special including rice and black beans $6.50. Hot sandwiches $3.50-4.50. Open Tu-Su 11am-10pm.

Battista's Hole in the Wall, 4041 Audrie Ave. (732-1424), right behind the Flamingo. One of Vegas's only establishments with character of its own. Adorning the walls are 28 years' worth of celebrity photos and novelties from area brothels, as well as the head of "Moosolini," the fascist moose. Though pricey at $18, dinner (includes house wine) is worth the treat. Open M-Th 4:30-10:30pm, F-Su 4:30-11pm.

BUFFET BONANZA

Luxor's Pharaoh's Pheast, 3900 Las Vegas Blvd. S. (262-4000). A delicious pheast phit for a pharaoh. Breakfast $7.50 (6-11:30am); lunch $8 (11:30am-4pm); dinner $11.50 (4-11pm).

Monte Carlo, 3770 S. Las Vegas Blvd. (730-7777). As inexpensive as good buffet food gets. Breakfast $6.75 (7-11am); lunch $7 (11:30am-3:30pm); dinner $10 (4-10pm).

Mandalay Bay, 3950 S. Las Vegas Blvd. (632-7777 or 877-632-7700). This tropical paradise serves an incredible variety, from pot stickers to corn tamales to pepperoni pizza. Breakfast $8.50 (7-11am); lunch $9.50 (11am-3pm); dinner $13.50 (3-10pm).

DAYTIME SIGHTS

The casinos are the main attraction, but a few non-gambling alternatives exist.

LIBERACE MUSEUM. Fans of classical music and kitsch will be delighted by the museum devoted to the flamboyant late "Mr. Showmanship." Liberace's uses of fur, velvet, and rhinestone boggle the rational mind. *(798-5595. 1775 E. Tropicana Ave. Open M-Sa 10am-5pm, Su 1-5pm. Admission $7, students and seniors $5, under 12 free.)*

THE GUINNESS WORLD RECORDS MUSEUM. The Guinness has displays showcasing the most tattooed lady and the largest pizza, among other record-breakingly wacky stuff. *(792-3766. 2780 S. Las Vegas Blvd. Open daily June-Aug. 9am-8pm; Sept.-May 9am-6pm. Admission $5, students and seniors $4, ages 5-12 $3.)*

FLYAWAY INDOOR SKYDIVING. This place offers some relatively inexpensive sporting activities for those craving an unconventional thrill, such as a simulated plunge from a plane. *(731-4768. 200 Convention Center Dr. Open M-F 11am-7pm, Sa 10:30am-7pm, Su 10:30am-5pm. 3min. "flight" $35, 6min. $55.)*

THE GUN STORE. It's been said that God made men, and Sam Colt made 'em equal. Experience coltish justice—$10 plus ammo lets you try out an impressive array of pistols, up to and including the enormous Magnum 44. Fork over $30 and they'll let you shoot real machine guns. *(454-1110. 2900 E. Tropicana Ave. Open daily 9am-6:30pm.)*

EVERYTHING COCA-COLA. Under the MGM Grand, watch old Coke commercials and drink all the "Real Thing" and international Coca-Cola products you want. *(270-5953. 3785 S. Las Vegas Blvd. Open Su-Th 10am-11pm, F-Sa 10am-midnight. Tours $3.50.)*

OTHER SIGHTS. The nearby city of **Henderson** offers a couple of free, self-guided food factory tours and a break from casino craziness. One such tour, at **Cranberry World West,** teaches you the anatomy of a cranberry before letting you drink your fill of Ocean Spray juice concoctions. *(566-7160. 1301 American Pacific Dr. Turn right at the Sunset Rd. Exit off I-95, then left at Stephanie St. Open M-Sa 9am-5pm.)*

CA$INO-HOPPING AND NIGHTLIFE

Punk rock icon Johnny Rotten proclaimed, "The only notes that matter come in a wad." Today, casinos resort to increasingly extreme measures to get these notes. Once the quintessentially Vegas themes of cheap buffets, booze, and entertainment were enough; now casinos spend millions of dollars to fool guests into thinking they are somewhere else. Spittin' images of Venice, New York, Rio, Paris (complete with Eiffel Tower), and Monte Carlo already thrive on the Strip.

Remember: **Gambling is illegal for those under 21.** If you are of age, look for casino "funbooks" which allow gamblers to buy $50 in chips for only $15. **Never bring more money than you're prepared to lose cheerfully,** and remember, in the long run, you will almost definitely lose cash. Keep your wallet in your front pocket, and beware thieves prowling casinos trying to nab big winnings from unwary jubilants. Most casinos have free gambling lessons; check *Today in Las Vegas* for dates and times. In addition, the more patient dealers may offer a tip or two (in exchange for one from you). Casinos, nightclubs, and some wedding chapels are open 24 hours. Check with the visitors center for more casino listings (see p. 481).

CIRCUS CIRCUS. Home to the (dysfunctional) family atmosphere: While parents run to card tables and slot machines downstairs, their children spend *their* quarters upstairs on the souped-up carnival midway and in the titanic video game arcade. Beware of the carnival area's "Camel Chase" game; it's far more addictive than any Vegas slot machine. Two stories above the casino floor, tightrope-walkers, fire-eaters, and acrobats perform. *(Daily 11am-midnight.)* Within the hotel complex, the **Grand Slam Canyon** is a Grand Canyon theme park with a roller coaster and other rides—all enclosed in a pink glass shell. *(Circus Circus: 734-0410. 2880 S. Las Vegas Blvd. Open 24hr. Grand Slam Canyon open in summer daily 10am-midnight; in winter Su-Th 10am-6pm, F-Sa 10am-midnight. Rides $2-5; unlimited rides $16, under 48in. $12.)*

MIRAGE. Its majestic confines banish all illusions from the halls of entertainment. Among Mirage's attractions are a dolphin habitat, Siegfried and Roy's white tigers (one belongs to Roy, two belong to Siegfried), and a volcano that erupts in fountains and flames *(every 15min. 6pm-midnight)*. According to billboards, Siegfried and Roy's Secret Garden is "New. Mysterious. Awaiting you." And your money; $10 will get you in. *(Casino: 791-7111. 3400 S. Las Vegas Blvd. Dolphin habitat open M-F 11am-7pm, Sa-Su 10am-7pm. Admission $3. Siegfried and Roy's Secret Garden open M-F 11am-5pm, Sa-Su 10am-5pm. Admission $10.)*

MGM GRAND. A huge bronze lion guards this casino, and a couple of real live felines can be seen inside at the lion habitat. In addition to more than 5000 rooms, MGM also contains the **Grand Adventures Amusement Park,** complete with indoor roller coaster and a giant swing ride called the Sky Screamer, which looks like the St. Louis Arch converted into a gallows. *(Casino: 891-7979. 3799 S. Las Vegas Blvd. Amusement Park open daily 10am-10pm. Admission $12, ages 4-12 $10. Sky Screamer: $25, 2 for $35, 3 for $45.)*

CAESAR'S PALACE. Busts abound: Some are plaster, some are barely concealed by the low-cut costumes that the cocktail waitresses have to wear. (The waiters get false Roman noses.) In the Festival Fountain show, by the Race for Atlantis Ride in the Forum Shops, statues move, shout, and battle with fire and water. *(Casino 731-7110. 3570 S. Las Vegas Blvd. Fountain show daily every hr. 10am-11pm.)*

NEW YORK-NEW YORK. Even Disneyland is put to shame by this fine-tuned gimmickry and its 200-foot roller coaster. Its towers mimic the Manhattan skyline and every last interior detail has its place in the New York scheme of things, recreating the glory of the Big Apple. *(740-6969; www.nynyhotelcasino.com. 3790 S. Las Vegas Blvd.)*

LUXOR. Before its towering black pyramid and the watchful eyes of the sprawling sphinx a dazzling laser light show is reminiscent of imperial ancient Egypt, insofar as ancient Egypt had the technology for electricity, let alone multicolored lasers. Wander into the depths of the desert at **King Tut Tomb and Museum,** which houses replicas of the artifacts uncovered at the king's grave. The hotel's IMAX 3-D films, have mollifying special effects *(262-4000. 3900 S. Las Vegas Blvd. Museum: Open Su-Th 9am-11:30pm. Admission $5. IMAX $8.50.)*

EXCALIBUR. An inspired medieval English theme, insofar as medieval England's economy was based on depriving senior citizens of their Social Security nest egg. At King Arthur's Tournament, jousters and jesters entertain spectators while they eat a $30 medieval banquet. *(597-7777 or 800-937-7777. 3850 S. Las Vegas Blvd.)*

TREASURE ISLAND. Throngs of pushy people squeeze together to see this attraction: Pirates battle with cannons on giant wooden ships in a Strip-side "bay." *(894-7111. 3300 S. Las Vegas Blvd. Battles every 1½hr. daily 4:30-10:30pm.)*

BELLAGIO. This is the life: People come here to watch a river dance to the sound of music in a huge Strip-side fountain. *(693-7111 or 888-987-6667. 3600 S. Las Vegas Blvd. Open M-F 3pm-midnight, Sa-Su noon-midnight.)*

JACKIE GAUGHAN'S PLAZA. A watered-down version of a Strip casino, but the Plaza is convenient to the electric-light spectacular "The Fremont Experience" and offers penny slots for Okies yearning for the big-city thrill of jockeying, and some of the cheapest blackjack tables in town. *(386-2110. 1 Main St., downtown.)*

ENTERTAINMENT AND NIGHTLIFE

Extra bucks will buy you a seat at a made-in-the-USA phenomenon—the **Vegas spectacular.** These stunning casino-sponsored productions happen twice per night and feature marvels such as waterfalls, explosions, fireworks, and casts of thousands (including animals). You can also see Broadway plays and musicals, ice revues, and individual entertainers in concert. All hotels have city-wide ticket booths in their lobbies. Some "production shows" are topless; most are tasteless. One exception: The Cirque de Soleil's creative shows are awe-inspiring displays of human agility and physical strength that just might motivate you to start working out again.

For a show by one of the musical stars who haunt the city, such as Diana Ross or Wayne Newton, you may have to fork over $50 or more. Siegfried and Roy at the Mirage go for a spectacular $90 (that's $35 for Roy but $55 for Siegfried). "Revues" featuring imitations of (generally deceased) performers are far more reasonable. But why pay? You can't turn around in Vegas without bumping into an aspiring Elvis clone, or perhaps the real Elvis, pursuing anonymity in the brilliant disguise of an Elvis impersonator.

Nightlife in Vegas gets rolling around midnight and keeps going until everyone drops or runs out of money. At Caesar's Palace (731-7110), **Cleopatra's Barge,** a huge ship-disco, is one boat that's made for rockin' (open Tu-Su 9pm-2am; cover F-Sa $5). Another popular disco, **Gipsy,** 4605 Paradise Rd. (731-1919), southeast of the Strip, may look deserted at 11pm, but by 1am the medium-sized dance floor packs in a gay, lesbian, and straight crowd (cover $4). Be forewarned that the Gipsy dancers get crazy on Topless Tuesdays.

NEAR LAS VEGAS

HOOVER DAM

A capacious, sparkling white wall, created by continuous pouring of concrete over a two-year period, spanning Boulder Canyon, the Hoover Dam gives dignity to heavy industry's encroachment on natural wonders (in this case, the less dramatic, western outlet of the Grand Canyon). Shiny steel towers climb the rugged brown hillsides, carrying high-tension wires up and out through the desert. The **visitors center** (294-3510 or 294-3523) offers tours leading to the generators at the structure's bottom. (Open daily 8:30am-5:45pm; exhibits close at 6pm. 30min. tours $8, seniors $7, ages 6-16 $2.) Parking in the garage on the Nevada side costs $2, but is free across the dam in Arizona, and gives a not-to-be-missed chance to walk across the top of the dam.

As the tour demonstrates, the dam was first constructed for flood control and irrigation purposes (electricity just pays for it). On one of the Art Deco-ish towers that line the dam, a set of pseudo-fascist reliefs declare: FLOOD CONTROL, IRRIGATION, WATER STORAGE, POWER. Powerful words for turbulent times.

LAKE MEAD

> For drink the Grape She crushes, inoffensive moust, and mead from many a berrie.
>
> —Milton, *Paradise Lost*

Flood control, irrigation, and water storage are all arguably the same thing, and this multi-tiered program is fulfilled in full by crystalline, turquoise, non-alcoholic Lake Mead, a shiny blue spot in the arid wasteland between Arizona and Nevada. Dubbed "the jewel of the desert" by its residents, the lake and its environs offer more than social planning and deficit spending.

Backcountry hiking and camping is permitted in most areas and hunting in some, but Lake Mead is sustained by all those Californians driving white pickup trucks with jet-skis in tow. For those who came unprepared, boats and other watercraft can be rented at the various concessionaires along the shores. **Boulder Beach** (800-752-9669) is accessible by Lakeshore Dr. off U.S. 93. (Jet-skis $50 per hr., $270 per day; fishing boats $55 for 4hr., $100 per day.)

Alongside the ubiquitous Park Service campsites ($10), concessionaires usually operate RV parks (most of which have evolved into mobile home villages), marinas, restaurants, and occasionally motels. More remote concessionaires include **Echo Bay Resort** (702-394-4000 or 800-752-9669; RV hookup $18), which offers motel rooms from $75 (lower in winter), and its restaurant, **Tale of the Whale,** decorated in nautical motifs and featuring a stunning view of Lake Mead, selling burgers in the $5 range. The resort rents jet-skis ($50 per hr., $270 per day; fishing boats for impoverished seadogs $12 per hr., $60 per day).

Most distant from the bustle of nearby Las Vegas is **Overton Beach Resort,** convenient to Overton, Nevada. Overton occupies a little patch of green in the desert at the northern end of scenic North Shore Scenic Dr. and offers food, cheap motels (**Overton Motel,** 137 N. Moapa Valley Blvd.; 702-397-2463; singles $29; doubles $35), and more Anasazi ruins than you can shake a stick at.

Between Las Vegas and Overton sits the **Valley of Fire State Park.** From I-15 from Las Vegas, take Nevada Rte. 169 at Crystal south to the park. For $5, you can cut through this breathtaking patch of rocky red desert back to I-15, then ride, boldly ride, back to the city.

ROUTE 66 AND INTERSTATE 40

Route 66 was designated as such in November of 1926, replacing the National Trails Highway as the principal road for commerce and immigrants traveling between the Mississippi Valley and Southern California. Running from Chicago to Los Angeles and spanning seven states, the road was taken by Okies and their friends fleeing the Dust Bowl, by wide-eyed Easterners seeking to partake in the post-war boom around Los Angeles, and later by tourists looking for the Grand Canyon and Disneyland.

If the Smithsonian in Washington, D.C., is America's attic, Route 66 is its dirty backyard. Between the 1950s, when the Eisenhower administration started interstate construction, and 1978, when the last stretch of Interstate 40 was completed in Arizona, Route 66 was the preferred route for travel across the Southwest, and the afterthoughts of American culture were left along its shoulder. The bigger, faster, safer interstates have more or less usurped the old route, and the towns that sit astride it now suffer accordingly. But of late, interest in what Steinbeck called the "mother road" has been rekindled, and those seeking refuge from the superhighway's monotony have gone in search of it.

The old road is, admittedly, somewhat hard to appreciate, but the attractions that characterize it can be accessed from I-40 with a few detours. Much of Route 66 has been swallowed up by the interstate or left to languish in the form of gravel or forlorn dirt. In other places, it trucks on as a patchwork of state and county roads (businesses along it sell $4 maps tracing its modern-day route). A lot of it is not worth traveling, particularly the stretches through the vast emptiness of deserts and plains, where the only difference between the Route 66 and the interstate is that Interstate 40 is invariably faster and more convenient.

BARSTOW

Don't let the ubiquitous beauty parlors fool you—Barstow (pop. 19,860) is not a cosmopolitan center for the coiffed and chic. Poised midway between Los Angeles and Las Vegas on Interstate 15, Barstow is all about location. A hub of hotels, restaurants, and gas stations, it is the ideal place to prepare for any type of desert foray.

PRACTICAL INFORMATION. The Amtrak **train** station, 7685 N. 1st St. (800-USA-RAIL/872-7245), well beyond the bridge that crosses the railroad tracks, lacks ticket counters at the station, so buy your tickets over the phone (to **L.A.** daily 4:20am, $23-38). Greyhound **buses,** 681 N. 1st St. (256-8757 or 800-231-2222 for schedules and reservations), go to **L.A.** (17 per day, $21) and **Las Vegas** (12 per day, $28). It's a bit of a march from Main St., so be prepared to call a taxi. You'll have to pay through the nose, though: **Yellow Cab,** 831 W. Main St. (256-6868), holds a monopoly in Barstow and charges $2.50 per mile. The **Barstow Chamber of Commerce,** 409 Fredrick (256-8617), off Barstow Rd., has info on hotels and restaurants as well as Southern California tourist attractions (open M-F 9am-5pm). The **Bureau of Land Management,** 2601 Barstow Rd. (252-6000), has the scoop on outdoor recreation from off-roading to hiking (open M-F 7:45am-4:30pm). **Diane's Laundromat,** 1300 E. Main St. (256-5312), charges $1.25 for a wash, 25¢ for a 12-minute dry (open 6:30am-9pm). **Emergency:** 911. **Police:** 256-2211; **Highway Patrol:** 256-1617. **Post office:** 425 S. 2nd Ave. (800-275-8777; open M-F 9am-5pm, Sa 10am-1pm). **ZIP Code:** 92312. **Area code:** 760.

ACCOMMODATIONS AND FOOD. What Barstow lacks in charm it makes up in utility. Inexpensive motels and eateries abound. **Motel 6,** 150 N. Yucca Ave. (256-1752), is relatively close to the bus and train stations, and only a block from Vons grocery store. You'll want to cool off in the pool. (Singles $30; doubles $36.) **Best Motel,** 1281 E. Main St. (256-6836), offers free sweet rolls and juice for breakfast (singles $27; doubles $30; weekly rates available).

Every restaurant chain this side of the Pecos has a branch on Main St. You'll find a more inviting variety along E. Main St. than along W. Main St. The **Barstow Station McDonald's,** 1611 E. Main St. (256-8023), made from old locomotive cars, is a change from the usual shiny red and yellow. (Drive-thru open 24hr. Lobby open M-Th and Sa 5:30am-10pm, F and Su 5:30am-11pm.) **Carlo's and Toto's,** 901 W. Main. St. (256-7513), is a local favorite for saucy, cheesy, and tasty Mexican food. Choose from 21 lunches ($4.75) and almost as many margaritas ($2.50; Open M-Th 11am-10pm, F-Sa 11am-11pm, Su 9:30am-10pm.) If you'd rather make your own meals, **Vons,** 1270 E. Main St. (256-8105), stocks supermarket specialties (open daily 6am-11pm).

SIGHTS AND ENTERTAINMENT. The **Skyline Drive-In** (256-3333), on Rte. 58 just north of the tracks, shows first-run double features at an unbeatable $4 (under 12 free; box office opens in summer at 8pm, earlier in winter). The **Mojave River Valley Museum** (256-5452), at the intersection of Barstow Rd. and Virginia Way, offers exhibits on geology and local history (open daily 11am-4pm; free). For chills rather than thrills, drive along the road leading to **Fort Irwin Military Base** north of town. Fort Irwin Rd. can be treacherous for those who are speeding or intoxicated, and many GIs rushing back from leave or driving home after a night of drinking have crashed along it. The small white crosses on either side of the road denote head-on collisions in which at least one passenger in each car died.

NEAR BARSTOW

The **Calico Early Man Site** (Desert Info 255-8760) lies along I-15 at the Minneola off-ramp. This is the only New World site that "Lucy" legend Louis Leakey ever bothered to excavate. The 20,000-year-old stone tools unearthed here make Calico one of the oldest finds in the Western Hemisphere. Artifacts and photographs from the excavations are displayed. (Open W 1:30-3:30pm, Th-Su 9:30am-4pm. Free tours every 2hr.)

Eight miles north of Barstow, **Rainbow Basin,** on Fossil Bed Rd. off Irwin Rd., is a great example of badland topography, colored with jasper, agate, and turquoise. Get a good view along the four-mile dirt road loop, but because the area is rich in fossilized remains, rockhounding (stealing rocks) is illegal and carries a steep penalty. Nearby, **Owl Canyon Campground** (252-6060) offers an exceptional vantage for stargazing because there is almost no light pollution. Bureau of Land Management **camping** facilities at Owl Canyon are equipped with places for fires, drinking water, and toilets (sites $6).

HORSEY SAUCE, INDEED! Roy Rogers was an avid sportsman, and his appreciation of the taxidermist's art caused him to have his beloved TV horse Trigger, along with Bullet the Wonder Dog, mounted for public display after their deaths. This struck his longtime wife, Dale Evans, as somewhat tasteless, and the beloved fast-food titan was heard to remark, "When my time comes, just skin me and put me right up there with Trigger, just as though nothing has ever changed." Rogers fans around the world are now asking two questions:

1. Have a Hollywood millionaire's wishes actually, for once, been honored?
2. Will the food at Rogers' highwayside restaurant chain ("a little Trigger in every bite," goes the legend) change in flavor ever so slightly?

EASTERN MOJAVE DESERT

The rugged land between Interstates 15 and 40 is among the most isolated in California. The list of human settlements begins and ends with Barstow and Baker. Travelers who pit-stop only in these towns, however, bypass Mojave's stunning natural attractions. Dramatic geological formations rise from the seemingly infinite landscape, and hardy creatures crawl along the scorched terrain. Serene as the emptiness may be, it is still empty, and most drivers press onward, praying that their cars remain loyal.

Afton Canyon Natural Area (Desert Info 255-8760) lies 38 miles northeast of Barstow on the way to Las Vegas. Follow I-15 to Afton Rd. The flowing water you see in this "Grand Canyon of the Mojave" is no mirage, but a rare above-ground appearance of the Mojave River. Canyon walls tower 300 feet above the rushing water and its willow-lined shores. Golden eagle, bighorn sheep, and desert tortoise reside around the canyon. **Hikers** may enjoy exploring the **caves** and side canyons tucked along unmarked trails. Bring a flashlight. Visitors can stay in 22 developed sites with water, fire pits, tables, and restrooms ($10 per person).

Near **Kelso,** in the Mojave National Preserve, is the most spectacular system of **dunes** in California. Stretching lengths of four miles and reaching heights of 700 feet, the dunes are off-limits to off-road vehicles. Hiking in the dunes is permitted, but not a good idea in the scorching heat of summer. From the top, on a windy day, you can hear the dunes sing—the cascading sand mimics the collapsing of bulkheads from WWII submarine movies. Kelso is about 30 miles southeast of Baker via Kelbaker Rd. from Barstow; either take I-40 to the Kelbaker Rd. Exit 80 miles to the east or I-15 to Baker.

Providence Mountains State Recreation Area, P.O. Box 1, Essex 92332 (928-2586), is a popular, high-altitude (4000-5000ft.) region with six primitive campsites (sites Su-Th $10, F-Sa $12) and a **visitors center,** on Essex Rd. 17 miles north of I-40. View the spectacular **Mitchell Caverns** on an informative tour through the stalactite-cluttered limestone chambers. (1½hr. tours June-Aug. Sa-Su at 1:30pm; Sept.-May M-F 1:30pm, Sa-Su 10am, 1:30, and 3pm. Tours $6, ages 6-12 $3.)

Also in the Providence Mountains, there are 48 primitive but beautiful sites at the **Mid Hill** and **Hole-in-Wall campgrounds** in the East Mojave National Scenic Area. From Essex Rd., follow Black Canyon Rd. to Mid Hill or Wild Horse Canyon Rd. to Hole-in-Wall. Both sites provide restrooms, tables, fire rings, and occasionally water. The forest-dwelling Mid Hill sites are pleasantly cool in the summer at 5600 feet. Embellished with rock formations, Hole-in-Wall (4200ft.) attracts climbers in the spring and fall ($10). **Backcountry** camping is available along hiking trails.

Dune buggies and **jeeps** are still permitted at the **Dumont Dunes,** just off Rte. 127 about 25 miles north of Baker. Ask a local to show you exactly where they are—there is no sign. The dunes are strewn with manmade striations—those from WWII training exercises are still visible in parts of the Mojave. Tracks persist in the sands for decades, so consider what legacy you want to leave behind before plunging into the dunes.

The fabulous **Baker Bun Boy** (733-4660) is a good place to stop for coffee and conversation (bacon cheeseburger $7; open daily 24hr.). Even if you tried, you couldn't miss Baker's claim to fame: the **world's tallest working thermometer.**

ROUTE 66 AND INTERSTATE 40: BARSTOW TO NEEDLES

On the interstate after Barstow, small brown signs will direct you to Rte. 66. The old highway offers a smattering of very small towns and a long stretch of outright desolation. Dugget features only Marines and a factory, but railroad enthusiasts will be thrilled to know that the Union Pacific meets the Santa Fe in town. From I-40, hop back on Rte. 66 at Newberry Springs, past the **Bagdad Cafe** (257-3101). Named after the defunct mining operation which once supported the area, the cafe inspired the 1987 movie of the same name that delighted the French at the Cannes Film Festival. (Chicken-fried steak $7, hamburgers $4-5, ostrich or buffalo burgers $7.45. Open M-Th 7am-8pm, F-Su 7am-9pm.)

In addition to the loss of industry suffered when the mines closed and the loss of commerce suffered when the interstate came through, Ludlow is not only deserted but also largely charred after having burnt down. The A-frame **Ludlow Coffee Shop** (733-4501) offers $5 sandwiches and extremely friendly help (open daily 6am-9pm). The **Ludlow Motel** (733-4338) operates from the Chevron across the street (singles $27; doubles $47). There are very few gas stations in the desert, and the Ludlow Chevron takes advantage of this by pumping out some of the most expensive gas in the state. Fill up your car before you start the drive across the Mojave.

After Ludlow comes the only stretch of Rte. 66 that diverges significantly from I-40. Here named the Old National Trail Hwy., it loops south to the fringes of military testing ranges. This area, save a few straggling motels and diners, has been almost completely devastated, although it's worth a trip for lovers of desolation and cinder cones—the **Mojave National Preserve** (see p. 489), however, is only accessible from I-40. If you take Rte. 66 instead of I-40 to Needles, bear left after Essex; going right will take you on a dead-ended "1931 Alignment" of the old road.

NEEDLES

Back in the days when Needles (pop. 5202) was an important stop on the Santa Fe Railroad, the town drew Chinese, Mexicans, and Native Americans looking for work on section gangs. The railroad still passes through, but the visitors only stay to ski, splash, and sunburn on the Colorado River. (Needles is named for the riverside rock outcroppings south of town). Woven between the criss-crossing strands of the railroad, Interstate 40, Route 95, and the old Route 66, Needles is convenient to Lakes Havasu and Mead and the gambling halls in Laughlin, Nevada.

PRACTICAL INFORMATION. Greyhound **buses** run out of Needle Point Liquors, 1109 Broadway (326-5066), to: **Las Vegas** ($27-29); **L.A.** ($45-48); and **Barstow** ($26-28). The **Chamber of Commerce,** 100 G St. (326-2050), is at the junction of Front and G St. (open M-F 9:30am-2:30pm). **Bank of America,** 1001 W. Broadway (800-338-6430), has a **24-hour ATM** (open M-F 9am-5pm). **Emergency:** 911. **Colorado River Medical Center:** 1401 Bailey Ave. (326-4531; 24hr.). **Post office:** 628 3rd St. (800-275-8777; open M-F 9am-4:30pm). **ZIP Code:** 92363. **Area code:** 760.

ACCOMMODATIONS, CAMPGROUNDS, AND FOOD. Some of the inexpensive motels of Needles present a veritable oasis for weary travelers thirsting for free in-room porn. Families with corruptible children may wish to stick to well-known chain hotels, which are dirt-free in every sense of the word. Otherwise, the **Royal Palms Motel,** 1910 Needles Hwy. (326-3881 or 888-326-3888), offers squeaky-clean rooms with fridges and microwaves at slimmed-down prices (singles $18; 1-

bed doubles $25, 2 beds $35). The **Traveler's Inn,** 1195 3rd St. Hill (326-4900), has spiffy rooms with access to a pool and, more importantly, a McDonald's (singles $32; doubles $39). For campers looking to rough it in the robust outdoors, Needles doesn't have much to offer. However, it does have more RV parks per capita than any other town in the world. **Rainbow Beach,** 3520 River Rd. (326-3101), off Needles Hwy. one mile north of town, has sites with electricity, pools, and restrooms (sites from $25; in winter $22). Those who don't need hookups might try heading outside town to find a riverside spot.

The **California Pantry,** 2411 Needles Hwy. (326-5225), is a classy coffee shop with the most extensive menu in Needles (chicken-fried steak with 3 eggs $7; open Su-Th 5:30am-10pm, F-Sa 24hr.). **The Hungry Bear,** 1906 W. Broadway (326-2988), serves feasts to sate every appetite. "Bear's Favorite Burger" ($6) has all the fixin's (open daily 5:30am-10pm).

SIGHTS AND OUTDOOR ACTIVITIES. The **Colorado River** offers a variety of recreational opportunities. Visitors can break the silence and explore galore on **jet-skis**. The phonetically correct **Riverjetz Watercraft Rentalz,** 401 Needles Hwy. (326-4336 or 800-327-2386), offers rentals (from $29 per hr.). Serenity can be found, with rod in hand, at **Havasu National Wildlife Refuge,** a 4000-acre, marshy network of ponds, bays, and channels, frequented by fishermen from cock's crow on, where dove, quail, and beaver dwell. For info on wilderness hikes, call the **U.S. Fish and Wildlife Service,** 317 Mesquite Ave. (236-3853). For an automotive adventure, duck into the narrow underpass where the Needles Hwy. bellies up to the railroad tracks. Its walls are richly painted by graffiti artists and Confederacy enthusiasts.

ARIZONA

In Arizona, the first state to begin a Historic Route 66 Association, the old road is well-marked and, in the west, easily accessible. After crossing the Colorado on I-40, take the first exit for Topoc and Old Route 66 to **Oatman,** or continue on I-40 through great stretches of desert (and, believe it or not, through the front yard of a spherical house). Then pick up Route 66 at **Kingman,** a medium-sized, main-drag-dominated town of the type most commonly associated with the 66 mystique in popular American consciousness.

Route 66 splits off from Interstate 95 in Golden Shores—bear right off the highway. The road meanders through undulating deserts before starting its climb through the Black Mountains. A sunset drive will silence anyone who's ever had snotty words for a painting of a western sunset. Be careful after dark, however; the road can be treacherous once it enters the rugged hills.

FLAGSTAFF

After a three-year stay among the Navajos and Apaches of southern Arizona during the 1860s, Samuel Cozzens returned to New England and wrote *The Marvelous Country,* in which he promoted the *northen* part of the territory as fertile, temperate, and ripe for settlement (although he had never actually been there). Colonists from Boston subsequently arrived in the San Francisco Mountains region. Unable to locate the promised rich farmland and gold veins, they promptly departed. Before leaving, however, one group erected a stripped-pine flagpole as a marker for westward travelers. Presto change-o: Flagstaff was born. During the following decade, Flagstaff, a stop on the transcontinental railroad, became a permanent settlement; railroad tracks still cut through downtown. Flagstaff (pop. 55,900) now provides a home for Northern Arizona University (NAU) students, retired cowboys, earthy Volvo owners, New Agers, and serious rock climbers. Although the town itself is low on sights, the surrounding area isn't, making it a perfect stop to rest and refuel en route to or from the Grand Canyon.

ORIENTATION AND PRACTICAL INFORMATION

Flagstaff sits 81 miles south of the Grand Canyon's south rim along U.S. 180. Downtown surrounds the intersection of **Beaver Street** and **Route 66** (formerly Santa Fe Ave.). Both bus stations, three youth hostels, the tourist office, and a number of inexpensive restaurants lie within a half-mile of this spot. Other commercial establishments line **South San Francisco Street,** two blocks east of Beaver St. As a mountain town, Flagstaff stays fairly temperate and receives frequent afternoon thundershowers.

Trains: Amtrak, 1 E. Rte. 66 (774-8679 or 800-USA-RAIL/872-7245). To **Los Angeles** (12hr., 1 per day, $52-94). Station open daily 4:15am-12:45pm and 3:15-10:45pm; ticket office closes at 8pm.

Buses: Greyhound, 399 S. Malpais Ln. (774-4573 or 800-231-2222), across from NAU campus 3 blocks southwest of the train station on U.S. 89A. To **Los Angeles** (10-12hr., 9 per day, $49) and **Las Vegas** (6-7hr., 3 per day via Kingman, round-trip $49). Terminal open 24hr. **Grayline/Nava-Hopi,** 114 W. Rte. 66 (774-5003 or 800-892-8687) has buses to the **Grand Canyon** (2hr., 2 per day, $18.50 including admission fee).

Public Transit: Pine Country Transit, 970 W. Rte. 66 (779-6624). Routes cover most of town. Buses run once per hr.; route map and schedule available at visitors center. Fare 75¢; seniors, disabled, and children 60¢.

Taxis: Friendly Cab (214-9000). Fares from airport to downtown about $9.

Equipment Rental: Peace Surplus, 14 W. Rte. 66 (779-4521), 1 block from Grand Canyon Hostel. Tent rental ($5-8 per day; $100-200 deposit), packs ($6 per day; $300 deposit), plus a good stock of cheap outdoor gear. 3-day min. rental on all equipment. Credit card or cash deposit required. Open M-F 8am-9pm, Sa 8am-8pm, Su 8am-6pm.

Visitor Information: Flagstaff Visitors Center, 1 E. Rte. 66 (774-9541 or 800-842-7293), in the train station. Useful free maps. Open M-Sa 7am-6pm, Su 7am-5pm.

Internet Access: NAU's Cline Library (523-2171). Open M-Th 7:30am-10pm, F 7:30am-6pm, Sa 9am-6pm, Su noon-10pm.

Post Office: 2400 N. Postal Blvd. (527-2440), for General Delivery. Open M-F 9am-5pm, Sa 9am-noon. **ZIP Code:** 86004. There's one closer to downtown at 104 N. Agassiz St., 86001. Open M-F 9am-5pm, Sa 9am-noon.

Area Code: 520.

ACCOMMODATIONS AND CAMPGROUNDS

When swarms of summer tourists descend on Flagstaff, accommodations prices shoot up. Thankfully, the town is blessed with excellent hostels. Rte. 66 is home to many cheap motels. *The Flagstaff Accommodations Guide*, available at the visitors center, lists all area hotels, motels, hostels, and bed and breakfasts. If you're here to see the Grand Canyon (and who isn't?), check the noticeboard in your hotel or hostel; some travelers leave their still-valid passes behind.

Grand Canyon International Youth Hostel (AAIH/Rucksackers), 19 S. San Francisco St. (779-9421), next to the Downtowner Motel, just south of the train station. Free pickup from bus station. Sunny and clean with kitchen, TV room with cable, Internet access ($2). Free tea and coffee. Tours to the Grand Canyon ($30-40) and Sedona ($20). Parking, breakfast, and linen included. Laundry. Reception 7am-11pm. 4-bed dorms $15; private rooms $35.

Motel Du Beau, 19 W. Phoenix St. (774-6731 or 800-398-7112), also behind the train station. Free pickup and dropoff at airport, bus, and train stations. Carpeted dorm rooms with private bathrooms and showers. Social atmosphere lasts into the wee hours. Free Internet access, tea and coffee. Parking, breakfast, and linen included. Tours to Grand Canyon ($30-40) and Sedona ($20) available through Grand Canyon Hostel (see above). Reception 6am-midnight. 4-bed dorms $13; private rooms $27.

Camping in the surrounding **Coconino National Forest** is a pleasant and inexpensive alternative, but you'll need a car to reach the designated camping areas. Forest maps ($6) are available at the Flagstaff Visitors Center. Many campgrounds fill up quickly in summer, particularly on weekends when Phoenicians flock to the mountains; those at high elevations close for the winter. All sites are handled on a first-come, first-camped basis; stake out a site by 1pm. **Lake View,** 13 miles southeast on Forest Hwy. 3 (U.S. 89A), has 30 sites ($10). **Bonito,** 18 miles northeast of downtown Flagstaff, off U.S. 89 on Forest Rd. 545, at the entrance to Sunset Crater (see p. 494), rents 44 sites ($12). Both feature running water and flush toilets (both 14-day max. stay; open mid-May to Sept. or Oct., depending on weather). Camping is free anywhere in the national forest outside the designated campsites, unless otherwise marked. For info on camping and backcountry camping, call the **Coconino Forest Service** (527-3600; open M-F 7:30am-4:30pm).

FOOD, ENTERTAINMENT, AND NIGHTLIFE

All the arch-wielding, deep-fat-frying chains are readily available outside of downtown, but near the heart of Flagstaff, the creative and offbeat rule. **Macy's,** 14 S. Beaver St. (774-2243), behind Motel Du Beau, is a cheery student hangout serving fresh pasta ($4-6), a wide variety of vegetarian entrees ($3-6), sandwiches ($4-6), pastries ($1-2), and espresso-based drinks ($1-4; open M-W 6am-8pm, Th-Sa 6am-9pm, Su 6am-6pm; food served until 1hr. before closing). **Kathy's Café,** 7 N. San Francisco St. (774-1951), prepares delicious and inventive breakfasts accompanied by biscuits and fresh fruit ($4-6). Lunch sandwiches include $5 veggie options. (Open M-F 6:30am-3pm, Sa-Su 7am-3:30pm; no credit cards.) The **Museum Club,** 3404 E. Rte. 66 (526-9434), a.k.a. the **Zoo,** will liven any country-western lover's spirits. It was built during the Great Depression as a premier roadhouse, and cowboy gusto lives on in its liquid spirits and first-class country. (Cover $3-5. Open daily 11am-3am).

SIGHTS AND ACTIVITIES

In 1894, Percival Lowell chose Flagstaff as the site for an astronomical observatory; he then spent the rest of his life here, culling data to support his theory that life exists on Mars. **Lowell Observatory,** 1400 W. Mars Hill Rd. (774-2096), just west of downtown off Rte. 66, now has five telescopes that have been used in breakthrough studies of Mars and Pluto. Admission includes tours of the telescopes, as well as a museum with hands-on astronomy exhibits. On clear summer nights, you can peer through the 100-year-old Clark telescope at some heavenly body selected by the staff. (Open daily 9am-5pm. Night sky viewings vary with season; call ahead. Admission $3.50, ages 5-17 $1.50.) The more down-to-earth **Museum of Northern Arizona** (774-5213), off U.S. 180 a few miles north of town, houses a huge collection of Southwestern Native American art. (Open daily 9am-5pm. Admission $5, students $3, seniors $4, ages 7-17 $2.)

The huge, snow-capped mountains visible to the north of Flagstaff are the **San Francisco Peaks.** To reach the peaks, take U.S. 180 about seven miles north to the Fairfield Snow Bowl turn-off. Nearby **Mount Agassiz** has the area's best **skiing.** The **Arizona Snow Bowl** (779-1951) operates four lifts from mid-December to mid-April; its 30 trails receive an average of 8½ feet of powder each winter. (Open daily 8am-5pm. Lift tickets $30.) In the summer, these peaks are perfect for hiking. The Hopi believe **Humphrey's Peak**—the highest point in Arizona at 12,670 feet—to be the sacred home of the Kachina spirits. When the air is clear, you can see the North Rim of the Grand Canyon, the Painted Desert, and countless square miles of Arizona and Utah from the top of the peak. Reluctant hikers will find the vista from the top of the Snow Bowl's **chairlift** almost as stunning. (every 20-30min.; late June to early Sept. daily 10am-4pm; early Sept. to mid-Oct. F-Su 10am-4pm. Rides $9, seniors $6.50, ages 6-12 $5.) The mountains occupy national forest land, so camping is free, but there are no designated campsites.

Near Flagstaff, off Rte. 89, are Sunset Crater and Wupatki National Monuments, both worth the drive and the $3 fee (free with Golden Eagle Passport). **Sunset Crater** exploded a scant 900 years ago, leaving an impressive cinder cone and blanketing the surrounding desert (now known, appropriately, as the Painted Desert) with red and black ash. **Wupatki** is one of several Anasazi ruins that dot the Southwest. The ancient pueblo complex has been preserved remarkably well, and the visitors center offers some surprisingly interesting information on its former tenants' agricultural methods.

GRAND CANYON NATIONAL PARK

Despite the prevalence of its image on everything from postcards to screen-savers, nothing can prepare you for the first sight of the Grand Canyon. Upon experiencing the initial humbling shock of emerging on the canyon's rim, stay awhile and let its sheer enormity and majesty sink in; One of the seven natural wonders of the world (277mi. long, 10mi. wide, and over 1mi. deep), the canyon descends to the Colorado River past looming walls of multi-colored limestone, sandstone, and shale. Hike down into the gorge to get a real feeling for the immensity and beauty of this natural phenomenon, or just watch the colors and shadows change from one of the many rim viewpoints.

Grand Canyon National Park is divided into three areas: the South Rim, which includes Grand Canyon Village; the North Rim; and the canyon gorge itself. The slightly lower, more accessible South Rim draws 10 times as many visitors as the higher, more heavily forested North Rim. The South Rim is open all year, while the North Rim only welcomes travelers from mid-May to mid-October (mid-Oct. to early Dec. for day use), depending on the weather. The 13-mile trail that traverses the canyon floor furnishes sturdy hikers with a minimum two-day adventure, while the 214-mile perimeter road is a good five-hour drive for those who would rather explore from above. Observe safety precautions, use common sense, and drink lots of water, so that nothing mars this unforgettable experience.

SOUTH RIM

In summer, everything on two legs or four wheels converges on this side of the Grand Canyon. If you plan to visit during the mobfest, make reservations for lodging, campsites, or mules well in advance—and prepare to battle the crowds. That said, it's even better than Disney World. A friendly Park Service staff, well-run facilities, and beautiful scenery help ease crowd anxiety. Fewer tourists brave the canyon's winter weather, and many hotels and facilities close in the off season.

ORIENTATION AND PRACTICAL INFORMATION

There are two park entrances: the main **south entrance** lies on U.S. 180 North, and the eastern **Desert View** entrance lies on I-40 West. From Las Vegas, the fastest route to the South Rim is U.S. 93 South to I-40 East, and then Rte. 64 North. From Flagstaff, I-40 East to U.S. 89 North is the most scenic; from there, Rte. 64 North takes you to the Desert View entrance. Heading straight up U.S. 180 North is more direct. Posted maps and signs in the park make orienting easy. Lodges and services concentrate in **Grand Canyon Village,** at the end of Park Entrance Rd. The east half of the village contains the visitors center and the general store, while most of the lodges and the challenging 12-mile **Bright Angel Trailhead** lie in the western section. The shorter, but still difficult, three-mile **South Kaibab Trailhead** is off East Rim Dr., east of the village. **West Rim Drive,** which is closed to private vehicles during the summer, has free shuttle buses to the eight rim overlooks. Avoid walking on the bus-trafficked drive; the rim trails provide a safer and more scenic easy hike.

The one-week **entrance pass** is $20 per car and $10 for travelers using other modes of transportation—even bus passengers must pay (Golden Eagle, Golden

Age, and Golden Access passports accepted). For most services in the park, call the **main switchboard** number at 638-2631.

Buses: Nava-Hopi Bus Lines (800-892-8687) leaves the Flagstaff train station for the Grand Canyon daily at 7:45am and 3pm, returning from Bright Angel Lodge at 10am and 5pm (about 2hr.; $17.50, under 15 $8.75; round-trip $31, under 15 $15.50; includes entrance fee. Times vary by season; call ahead.

Public Transportation: Free shuttle buses ride the West Rim Loop (daily every 10-30min., from 1hr. before dawn to 1hr. after dusk) and the Village Loop (daily every 10-30min., 1hr. before dawn to 10:30pm). Free **hiker's shuttle** runs every 30min. between Grand Canyon Village and the South Kaibab Trailhead, on the East Rim near Yaki Point.

Taxis: Call 638-2822. Open 24hr.

Auto Repairs: Grand Canyon Garage (638-2631), east of visitors center on the main road, near Maswik Lodge. Open daily 8am-noon and 1-5pm. 24hr. emergency service.

Equipment Rental: Babbitt's General Store (638-2262), in Grand Canyon Village near Yavapai Lodge and the visitors center. Comfy hiking boots, socks included ($8 1st day, $5 per additional day); sleeping bags ($7-9 1st day, $5 per additional day); tents ($15-18 1st day, $9 per additional day); and other camping gear. Hefty deposits required on all items. Open daily 8am-8pm.

Visitor Information: Visitors Center (638-7888), 6mi. north of the south entrance station. Open daily in summer 8am-7pm; in off-season 8am-5pm. Hikers should get the *Backcountry Trip Planner;* the regular old *Trip Planner* is for regular old mortals (both free). Free and informative, *The Guide* is also available here, in case you missed it at the entrance. Write to **Trip Planner,** Grand Canyon National Park, P.O. Box 129, Grand Canyon, AZ 86023, for info. The **transportation info desks** in **Bright Angel Lodge** and **Maswik Lodge** (638-2631 for both) handle reservations for mule rides, bus tours, plane tours, Phantom Ranch, taxis, and more. Both open daily 6am-7pm.

Luggage Storage: In Bright Angel Lodge. Open 8am-9pm. 50¢ per day.

Weather and Road Conditions: 638-7888.

Medical Services: Grand Canyon Clinic (638-2551 or 638-2469), several miles south of the visitors center on Center Rd. Open M-F 8am-5:30pm, Sa 9am-noon. 24hr. emergency care. **Pharmacy** on site (638-2460).

Post Office: (638-2512), opposite the visitors center. Open M-F 9am-4:30pm, Sa 11am-1pm. **ZIP Code:** 86023.

AREA CODE The area code for Grand Canyon National Park is 520.

ACCOMMODATIONS AND CAMPGROUNDS

Compared to the six million years it took the Colorado River to carve the Grand Canyon, the year it will take you to get indoor lodging near the South Rim will pass in the blink of an eye. Summer rooms should be reserved *11 months in advance.* That said, there are cancellations every day; if you arrive unprepared, check at the lodges in the morning for vacancies, or call the Grand Canyon operator at 638-2631 and ask to be connected with the proper lodge. Reservations for **Bright Angel Lodge, Maswik Lodge, Trailer Village,** and **Phantom Ranch** can be made through **Grand Canyon National Park Lodges,** P.O. Box 699, Grand Canyon, AZ 86023 (303-297-2757 or 638-2401). Be aware that most accommodations on the South Rim are very pricey.

Bright Angel Lodge (638-2401), Grand Canyon Village. The cheapest indoor lodging on the rim. Very convenient to Bright Angel Trail and shuttle buses. "Rustic" lodge singles and doubles with plumbing but no heat $44-58; "historic" cabins for 1 or 2 people $66; $7 per additional person in rooms and cabins.

Maswik Lodge (638-2401), Grand Canyon Village. Small, clean cabins with showers but no heat. Singles or doubles $60; motel-style rooms $94-114; additional person $7-9.

Phantom Ranch (638-2631), on the canyon floor, a day's hike down the Kaibab Trail. Dorm beds $21; rarely available cabins for 1 or 2 people $56; $11 per additional person. *Don't show up without reservations—they'll send you back up the trail, on foot.* Meals must be reserved in advance. Breakfast $12; box lunch $7.50; stew dinner $16.75, steak dinner $26.75. If you're dying to sleep on the canyon floor but don't have a reservation, show up at the Bright Angel transportation desk at 6am, and they may be able to arrange something.

The campsites listed here usually fill up early in the day. Campground overflow winds up in the **Kaibab National Forest,** along the south border of the park, where you can pull off a dirt road and camp for free. No camping is allowed within quarter-mile of U.S. 64. Sleeping in cars is *not* permitted within the park, but it is allowed in the Kaibab Forest. For more info, contact the **Tusayan Ranger District,** Kaibab National Forest, P.O. Box 3088, Grand Canyon, AZ 86023 (638-2443). Overnight hiking or camping within the park outside of designated campgrounds requires a **backcountry use permit** ($20 application fee plus $4 per person per night), available at the backcountry office (638-7875), a ¼-mile south of the visitors center (open daily 8am-noon and 1-5pm). Permit requests are accepted by mail, fax, or in person up to five months in advance. Guests with reservations at Phantom Ranch (see above) do not need permits. Reservations for some campgrounds can be made through **BIOSPHERICS** (800-365-2267).

Mather Campground (call BIOSPHERICS 800-365-2267), Grand Canyon Village, 1mi. south of the visitors center. 320 shady, relatively isolated sites with no hookups. Sept.-May $12; June-Aug. $15. 7-day max. stay. Mar.-Nov. reserve up to 8 weeks in advance; Dec.-Feb. sites go on a first-come, first-camped basis. Check at the office, even if the sign says the campground is full.

Ten-X Campground (638-2443), in the Kaibab National Forest, 10mi. south of Grand Canyon Village off Rte. 64. Shady sites surrounded by pine trees. Toilets, water, no hookups, no showers. First-come, first-camped sites $10. Open May-Sept.

Desert View Campground (638-7888), 26mi. east of Grand Canyon Village. 50 sites with phone and restroom access, but no hookups. $10. No reservations; usually full by early afternoon. Open mid-May to Oct.

Camper Village (638-2887), 7mi. south of the visitors center in Tusayan. RV and tent sites $15-23 for 2 people; each additional person $2. First-come, first-camped tent sites; reservations required for RVs.

Indian Gardens (638-7888), 4½mi. from the Bright Angel trailhead and 3100ft. below the rim. 15 free sites, water, and toilets. Reservations and backcountry permit required.

Trailer Village (638-2401), next to Mather Campground. Designed with the RV in mind. Showers and laundry nearby. 84 sites for 2 with hookup $20; each additional person $1.75. Office open daily 8am-noon and 1-5pm. Reserve 6-9 months in advance.

FOOD

Fast food has yet to sink its greasy talons into the South Rim (the closest McDonald's is 7mi. south in Tusayan), but you *can* find meals at fast-food prices. **Babbitt's General Store** (638-2262), near the visitors center, has a deli counter (sandwiches $2-4) and a wide selection of groceries, as well as a camping supplies department (open daily 8am-8pm; deli open 8am-7pm). The well-stocked **Canyon Cafe,** across from Babbitt's, offers a wider variety of food than the nearby deli (hamburgers $3, pizza $3-4, dinners $5-7; open daily 6am-10pm). **Maswik Cafeteria,** in Maswik Lodge, serves a variety of inexpensive grill-made options in a wood-paneled cafeteria atmosphere (hot entrees $5-7, sandwiches $2-4; open daily 6am-10pm). **Bright Angel Dining Room** (638-2631), in Bright Angel Lodge, serves hot sandwiches for $6-8 (open daily 6:30am-10pm). The **soda fountain** at Bright Angel Lodge chills 16 flavors of ice cream (1 scoop $2) for hot folks (open daily 6:30am-9pm).

SIGHTS AND ACTIVITIES

From your first glimpse of the canyon, you may feel a compelling desire to see it from the inside, an enterprise that is harder than it looks. Even the young at heart and body should remember that an easy downhill hike can become a nightmarish 50° incline on the return journey. Also keep in mind that the lower you go, the hotter it gets; when it's 85° on the rim, it's around 100° at Indian Gardens, and around 110° at Phantom Ranch. Heat exhaustion, the greatest threat to any hiker, is marked by a monstrous headache and red, sweatless skin. For a day-hike, you must take at least a gallon of water per person; expect to require at least a liter for each hour hiking upwards under the hot sun. Hiking boots or sneakers with excellent tread are also necessary—the trails are steep, and every year several careless hikers take what locals morbidly call "the 12-second tour." A list of hiking safety tips can be found in *The Guide*. It is advisable to speak with a ranger or drop by the visitors center before embarking on a hike: they may have important information about the trail. Parents should think twice about bringing children more than one mile down any trail.

The two most accessible trails into the canyon are the **Bright Angel Trail,** originating at the Bright Angel Lodge, and the **South Kaibab Trail,** from Yaki Point. Bright Angel is outfitted for the average tourist, with rest houses strategically stationed 1½ miles and three miles from the rim. **Indian Gardens,** 4½ miles down, offers the tired hiker restrooms, picnic tables, and blessed shade. All three rest stops have water in the summer. Kaibab is trickier, steeper, and lacks shade or water, but it rewards the intrepid with a better view of the canyon. If you've made arrangements to spend the night on the canyon floor, the best route is the South Kaibab Trail (4-5hr., depending on conditions) and back up the Bright Angel (7-8hr.) the following day. Hikes to Indian Gardens and **Plateau Point,** six miles out, with views 1360 feet down to the river, make excellent **daytrips** (8-12hr.), provided that you start around 7am. A few less-traveled, unmaintained trails enter the canyon, but require backcountry permits.

If you're not up to descending into the canyon, follow the **Rim Trail** east to **Grandview Point** and the **Yavapai Geological Museum,** or west to **Hermit's Rest.** Viewpoints along the East Rim are somewhat spread out; the West Rim is skirted by a beautiful trail that leads to eight overlooks. If you prefer to rest your feet for a while, shuttles run on the West Rim, stopping at all of the viewpoints. You can also hike out as far as you want and then take the shuttle back. The trail is paved and wheelchair accessible from the visitors center to Bright Angel Lodge. After Maricopa Point, footing is more difficult, but the views are also more spectacular.

The East Rim swarms with sunset-watchers at dusk, and the observation deck at the Yavapai Museum, at the end of the trail, has a sweeping view of the canyon during the day. Along the West Rim, **Hopi Point** is a favorite for sunsets, and a special "sunset shuttle" heads back from here. *The Guide* and the visitors center list times for sunsets and sunrises.

Mule trips from the South Rim are very expensive and are booked up to one year in advance, although cancellations do occur (daytrip $106, overnight $280; call 303-297-2757 for reservations). Mule trips from the North Rim are cheaper and more readily available (638-9875). **Whitewater rafting** trips through the canyon last from three days to two weeks; advance reservations are required. Call the transport info desk for a list of trips. Park Service rangers also present a variety of free, informative **talks** and **guided hikes;** times and details are listed in *The Guide*.

NORTH RIM

If you're coming from Utah or Nevada, or you simply want to avoid the crowds at the South Rim, the park's North Rim is a bit wilder, a bit cooler, and much more serene—all with a view *almost* as groovy as that from the South Rim. Unfortunately, because the North Rim is less frequented, it's hard to reach by public transportation, and by car, it's a bit of a drive, even from a southern Utah base. From October 15 until December 1, the North Rim is open for day use only; from December 1 until May 15, it is closed entirely.

ORIENTATION AND PRACTICAL INFORMATION

To reach the North Rim from the South Rim, take Rte. 64 East to U.S. 89 North, which runs into Alt. 89; from Alt. 89, follow Rte. 67 South to the edge. Altogether, the beautiful drive is over 200 miles. From Utah, take Alt. 89 South from Fredonia. From Page, take U.S. 89 South to Alt. 89 to Rte. 67 South. Snow closes Rte. 67 from mid-Oct. through mid-May; park visitor facilities (including the lodge) close for the winter. The **entrance fee** covers both rims for 7 days ($20 per car; $10 per person on foot, bike, bus, or pilgrimage).

Public Transportation: Transcanyon, P.O. Box 348, Grand Canyon, AZ 86023 (638-2820). Buses to South Rim depart 7am (4½hr.); return buses depart 1:30pm. $60, round-trip $100. Reservations required. Runs late May to Oct.

Visitor Information: National Park Service Information Desk (638-7864), in the lobby of Grand Canyon Lodge (see below). Info on North Rim viewpoints, facilities, and trails. Separate issue of *The Guide* for the North Rim; pick it up here. Open daily 8am-6pm.

Weather Info: 638-7888. Updated at 7am daily.

Camping Supplies: General store near North Rim Campground. Open daily 8am-8pm.

Medical Services: North Rim Clinic (638-2611, ext. 222), in cabin #5 at Grand Canyon Lodge. Open W-M 9am-noon and 3-6pm, Tu 9am-noon and 2-5pm.

Post Office: In Grand Canyon Lodge (638-2611), like everything else. Open M-F 8am-11am and 11:30am-4pm, Sa 8am-2pm. **ZIP Code:** 86052.

Area Code: 520.

THE DESERT

ACCOMMODATIONS AND FOOD

Since camping within the confines of the Grand Canyon National Park is limited to designated campgrounds, only a lucky minority of North Rim visitors get to spend the night "right there." **BIOSPHERICS** (800-365-2267) handles reservations; otherwise, mark your territory by 10am. If you can't get in-park lodgings, try **Kaibab National Forest,** which runs from north of Jacob Lake to the park entrance. You can camp for free if you're a quarter mile from the road or official campgrounds.

Grand Canyon Lodge (303-297-2757 for reservations, 638-2611 for front desk), on the edge of the rim. The only indoor rim lodging in the park. Reception 24hr. Pioneer cabins for 4 people $87; singles or doubles in frontier cabins $70; Western cabins and motel rooms $80-110. Reserve several months in advance.

Jacob Lake Inn (643-7232), 45mi. north of the North Rim entrance at Jacob Lake. Reasonably priced dining room. Reception daily 6am-10pm. Cabins for 2 $66-71; for 3 $76-78; for 4 $81-84. Pricier motel units available for $10-15 more.

Kaibab Camper Village (643-7804), 1mi. south of Jacob Lake Inn. 50 tent sites $12; 60 sites with hookups for 2 $20-22; $2 per extra person. Open May to mid-Oct.

North Rim Campground (call BIOSPHERICS, 800-365-2267), on Rte. 67 near the rim, the only campground in the park. You can't see into the canyon from the pine-covered site, but you know it's there. Food store nearby, laundry, recreation room, and showers. 7-day max. stay. 82 sites $15; no hookups. Open mid-May to mid-Oct.

DeMotte Park Campground, 16mi. north of the park entrance in Kaibab National Forest. 23 woodsy sites $10 per vehicle per night. First-come, first-camped.

Both feeding options on the North Rim are placed strategically at the **Grand Canyon Lodge.** The **restaurant** (638-2611) serves breakfast for $3-7, lunch for $6-8, and dinner for $13 and up (open 6:30-10am, 11:30am-2:30pm, and 5-9:30pm; reservations required for dinner). A sandwich at the **snack bar** costs $3-4 (open daily 6:30am-9pm). There is also a **Saloon** in the lodge, that serves coffees and pastries in the morning (open daily 5-9am and 11am-10pm). North Rim-ers are better off eating in Kanab or stopping at the **Jacob Lake Inn** (643-7232) for $5 sandwiches and great $2 milkshakes (open daily 6am-9pm).

SIGHTS AND ACTIVITIES

The easiest, and thus most trafficked route on the North Rim is the ½-mile paved trail leading from the Grand Canyon Lodge to **Bright Angel Point,** which commands a seraphic view of the Canyon. **Point Imperial,** an 11-mile drive from the lodge, overlooks Marble Canyon and the Painted Desert. **Cape Royal** lies 23 miles from the lodge; en route, you'll pass the enchanting Vista Encantadora. Short trails include the **Cape Final Trail** (4mi.), which heads from a parking lot a few miles before Cape Royal to Cape Final, and the **Transept Trail** (3mi.), which follows the rim from the lodge to the campground. The North Rim's *The Guide* lists trails in full.

Only **North Kaibab Trail** leads into the canyon from the North Rim; a shuttle runs to the trailhead from Grand Canyon Lodge (daily at 5:30 and 7:45am; $5; reservations required). Overnight hikers must get permits from the **Backcountry Office** in the ranger station (open daily 8am-noon and 1-5pm), or write to P.O. Box 129, Grand Canyon, AZ 86023; it may take a few days to get a permit in person.

Nature walks, lectures, and evening programs run at the North Rim Campground and at Grand Canyon Lodge. Check the info desk or campground bulletin boards for schedules. One-hour ($15) or half-day **mule trips** ($40) through Canyon Trail Rides (435-679-8665) circle the rim or descend into the canyon from the lodge (open daily 7am-7pm). If you'd rather get wet, pick up a Grand Canyon River Trip Operators brochure and select from among the 20 companies offering trips.

BAJA CALIFORNIA

Peeled away from the mainland ages ago by earthquakes, the peninsula of Baja California spans 40,000 square miles between the warm, tranquil Sea of Cortés on the east and the cold, raging Pacific Ocean on the west. Baja claims a spectacular and diverse landscape—sparse expanses of desert give way to barren mountains that jut into Baja's azure sky at incredible angles. And then, of course, there's the bizarrely blue-green water slapping at Baja's miles of uninhabited shore. Called "el otro México" (the other Mexico), Baja is neither here nor there, not at all California yet nothing like mainland Mexico. Even its history is different—it was permanently settled by the Franciscans and Jesuits in the 1600s. Baja's southern midsection—from the tranquility of Mulegé to the palm-laden oasis town of San Ignacio to the thousands of undisturbed beaches beneath sheer cliffs—is most pristine and mysterious. Most of Baja is still somewhat undiscovered country, prime for the hearty budget traveler to explore—a solid stream of tourists flows from California into Baja to surf, fish, and drink to their hearts' content.

The completion of the Transpeninsular Highway has made it quicker to travel the peninsula by **car,** but be prepared to be cruising along at 60 miles per hour and suddenly careen into a rutted curve that can only be taken at 30 miles per hour. If you need roadside assistance, the *Ángeles Verdes* (Green Angels) pass along Rte. 1 twice per day. Unleaded gas may be in short supply along this route, so don't pass a PEMEX station without filling your tank. All of Baja is in the *Zona Libre* (Free Zone), so strict vehicle permits are not required. If you will be driving in Baja for more than 72 hours, you need to get a free permit at the border by showing the vehicle's title and proof of registration.

All major towns in Baja are served by **bus.** If you plan to navigate the peninsula by bus, be forewarned that you have to leave at inconvenient times, fight to procure a ticket, and then probably stand the whole way. Any way you cut it, Baja beaches and other points of interest off the main highway are often inaccessible on public transportation; buses don't stop at coastal spots between Tijuana and San Quintín.

If your travels in Mexico will be limited to Tijuana and Ensenada, you will probably not need to exchange your dollars for pesos; the vast majority of shops and restaurants in these cities are more than willing to take greenbacks. If you plan to travel farther into Baja, prices will be quoted in pesos and some establishments will not accept U.S. dollars, or, if they do, will give you a bad rate. The right **exchange rate** fluctuates around 9.3 pesos per U.S. dollar, but you should check the exact rate in the local newspaper or online at http://finance.yahoo.com/m5.

HIGHLIGHTS OF BAJA CALIFORNIA

- The **drinking age** in Mexico is 18.

TIJUANA

In the shadow of swollen, sulphur-spewing factories smeared across a topographical nightmare of gorges and promontories lies the most notorious specimen of the peculiar border subculture: Tijuana (pop. 2.5 million). This most visited of the world's border towns also has the fastest growth rate of all the world's major cities (13.6% per year). A three-ringed, duty-free extravaganza comes complete with English-speaking, patronizing club promoters and every decadent way of blowing money, from *jai-alai* to dark, dingy strip joints, from mega-curio shops to Las Vegas-style hotels. And this is exactly how most of its 30 million yearly tourists would have it. It's hard to say whether it's the city's strange charm, its cheap booze, or its sprawling, unapologetic hedonism that attracts tourists to Tijuana like flies.

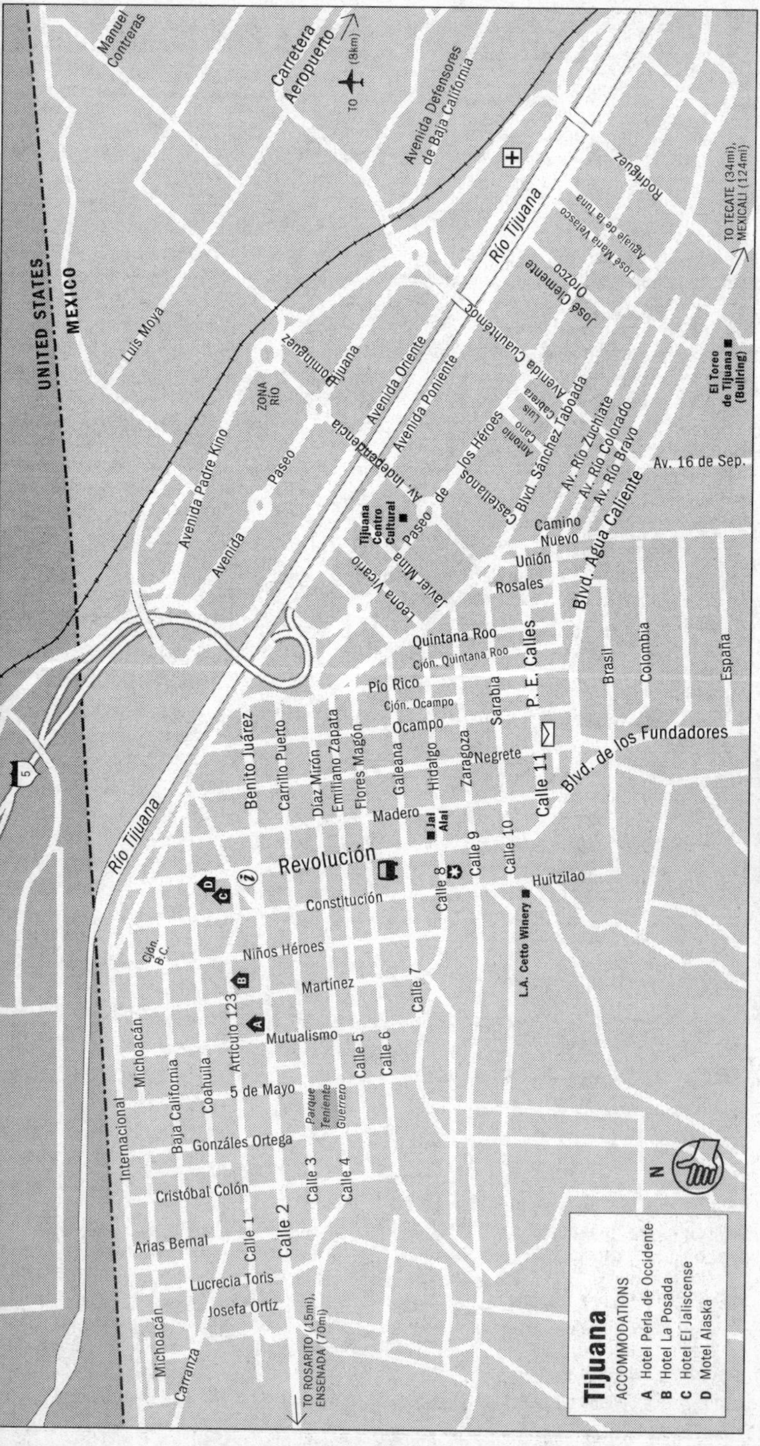

Tijuana

ACCOMMODATIONS

A Hotel Perla de Occidente
B Hotel La Posada
C Hotel El Jaliscense
D Motel Alaska

UNITED STATES
MEXICO
5
Internacional
Michoacán
Michoacán
Carranza
Arias Bernal
Cristóbal Colón
Lucrecia Toris
Josefa Ortíz
Baja California
Coahuila
Cjón. B.C.
Artículo 123
Calle 1
Calle 2
TO ROSARITO (15mi), ENSENADA (70mi)
Calle 3
Calle 4
Gonzáles Ortega
5 de Mayo
Parque Teniente Guerrero
Mutualismo
Martínez
Niños Héroes
Constitución
Revolución
Calle 5
Calle 6
Calle 7
Calle 8
Calle 9
Calle 10
Calle 11
Huitzilao
L.A. Cetto Winery
Jai Alai
Río Tijuana
Benito Juárez
Carrillo Puerto
Díaz Mirón
Emiliano Zapata
Flores Magón
Galeana
Hidalgo
Zaragoza
Sarabia
Madero
Negrete
Ocampo
Cjón. Ocampo
Pío Rico
Cjón. Quintana Roo
Quintana Roo
P. E. Calles
Rosales
Unión
Camino Nuevo
Blvd. de los Fundadores
Blvd. Agua Caliente
Brasil
Colombia
España
Av. 16 de Sep.
El Toreo de Tijuana (Bullring)
TO TECATE (34mi), MEXICALI (124mi)
Leona Vicario
Javier Mina
Tijuana Centro Cultural
Paseo de los Héroes
Av. Independencia
Castellanos
Antonio Cano
Luis Cabrera
Blvd. Sánchez Taboada
Av. Río Zuchiate
Av. Río Colorado
Av. Río Bravo
Avenida Cuauhtémoc
José Clemente Orozco
José María Velasco
Aguaje de la Tuna
Rodríguez
Avenida Poniente
Avenida Oriente
Río Tijuana
Cuauhtémoc
Avenida Padre Kino
Avenida Paseo
ZONA RÍO
Domínguez
Tijuana
Luis Moya
Manuel Contreras
Carretera Aeropuerto
TO (8km)
Avenida Defensores de Baja California
N

BAJA

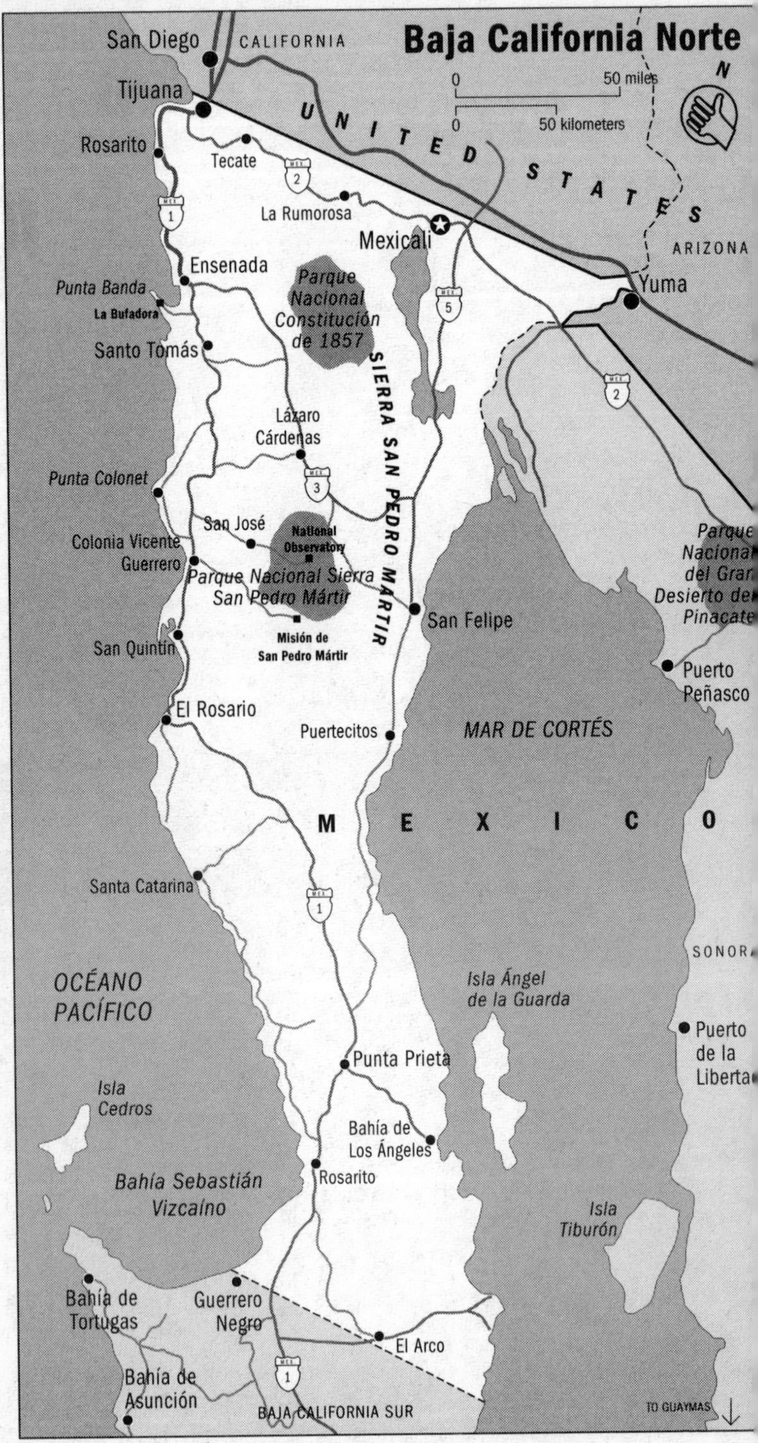

Baja California Norte

0 50 miles
0 50 kilometers
N

San Diego
CALIFORNIA
Tijuana
UNITED STATES
Rosarito
Tecate
2
1
La Rumorosa
Mexicali
ARIZONA
Ensenada
Punta Banda
La Bufadora
Parque Nacional Constitución de 1857
5
Yuma
Santo Tomás
SIERRA SAN PEDRO MARTIR
2
Lázaro Cárdenas
Punta Colonet
3
San José
National Observatory
Colonia Vicente Guerrero
Parque Nacional Sierra San Pedro Mártir
Parque Nacional del Gran Desierto de Pinacate
San Felipe
San Quintín
Misión de San Pedro Mártir
Puerto Peñasco
El Rosario
Puertecitos
MAR DE CORTÉS
MEXICO
Santa Catarina
1
SONORA
OCÉANO PACÍFICO
Isla Ángel de la Guarda
Puerto de la Libertad
Punta Prieta
Isla Cedros
Bahía de Los Ángeles
Rosarito
Bahía Sebastián Vizcaíno
Isla Tiburón
Bahía de Tortugas
Guerrero Negro
El Arco
1
Bahía de Asunción
BAJA CALIFORNIA SUR
TO GUAYMAS

BAJA

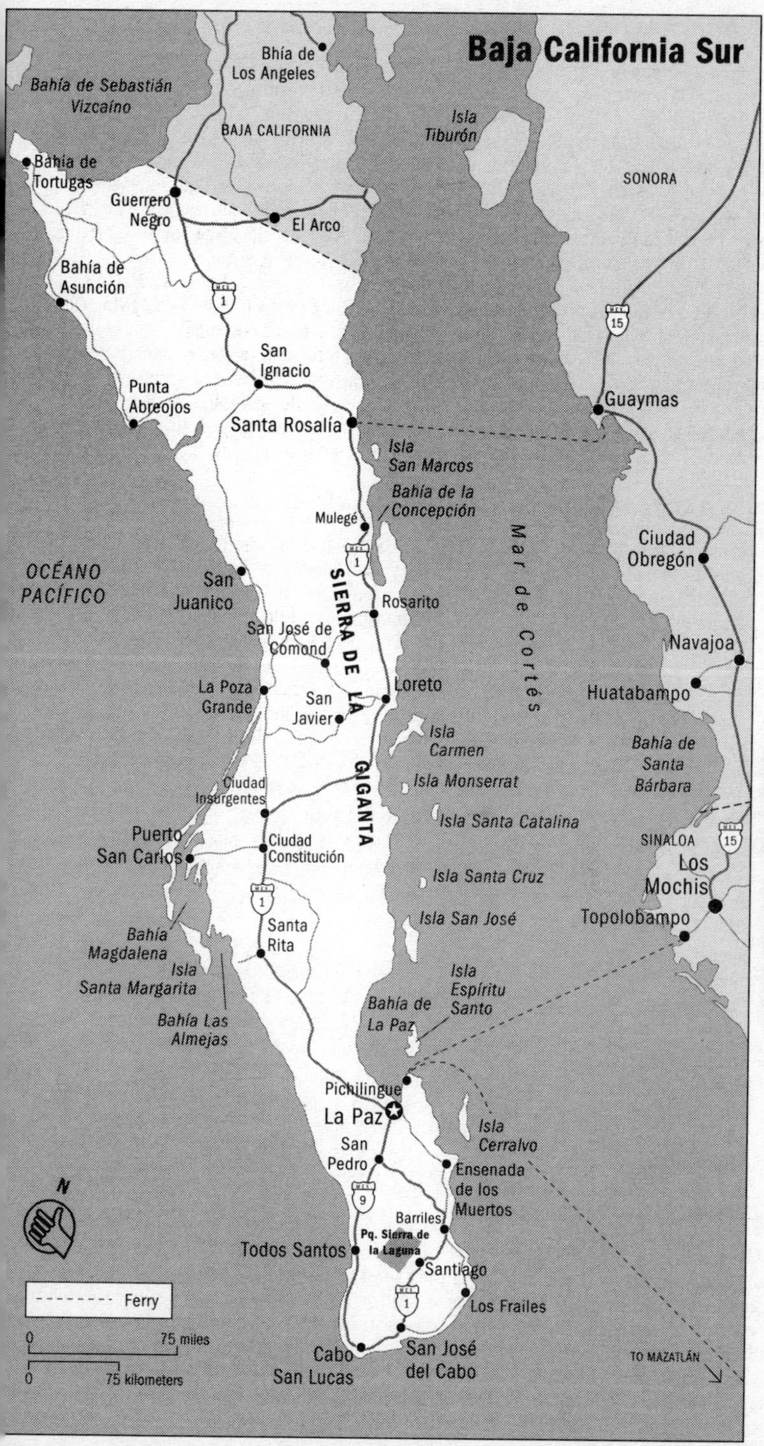
Baja California Sur
Bhía de Los Angeles
Bahía de Sebastián Vizcaíno
BAJA CALIFORNIA
Isla Tiburón
SONORA
Bahía de Tortugas
Guerrero Negro
El Arco
Bahía de Asunción
1
15
San Ignacio
Punta Abreojos
Santa Rosalía
Guaymas
Isla San Marcos
Bahía de la Concepción
Mulegé
Mar de Cortés
Ciudad Obregón
OCÉANO PACÍFICO
San Juanico
SIERRA DE LA GIGANTA
Rosarito
San José de Comond
Navajoa
La Poza Grande
Loreto
Huatabampo
San Javier
Isla Carmen
Bahía de Santa Bárbara
Ciudad Insurgentes
Isla Monserrat
Isla Santa Catalina
Puerto San Carlos
Ciudad Constitución
SINALOA
Los Mochis
Isla Santa Cruz
Isla San José
Topolobampo
Santa Rita
Bahía Magdalena
Isla Santa Margarita
Bahía Las Almejas
Isla Espíritu Santo
Bahía de La Paz
Pichilingue
La Paz
Isla Cerralvo
San Pedro
Ensenada de los Muertos
9
Barriles
Pq. Sierra de la Laguna
Todos Santos
Santiago
Los Frailes
Ferry
0 75 miles
0 75 kilometers
Cabo San Lucas
San José del Cabo
TO MAZATLÁN
N

BAJA

ORIENTATION

From San Diego to Tijuana, take the red **Mexicoach** bus (tel. 85 14 70, in the U.S. 619-428-9517; operators speak only Spanish) from its terminal at the border (every 30min. 9am-9pm, $1). It leaves you beside the **Frontón Palacio** on Revolución between Calles 7 and 8 in the heart of the *centro*. Alternatively, grab a **trolley** to San Ysidro, at Kettner and Broadway in downtown San Diego ($1.75), and walk across the border. Transfers from airport buses are also available. In Tijuana, *calles* run east-west; *avenidas* run north-south. The *avenidas* in the *centro* area are (from east to west) **Mutualismo, Martínez, Niños Héroes, Constitución, Revolución** (the main tourist drag), **Madero, Negrete,** and **Ocampo.** *Calles* in the *centro* area are both named and numbered. Beginning at the north, they are **Artículo 123** (Calle 1), **Benito Juárez** (Calle 2), **Carrillo Puerto** (Calle 3), **Díaz Mirón** (Calle 4), **Zapata** (Calle 5), **Magón** (Calle 6), **Galeana** (Calle 7), **Hidalgo** (Calle 8), and **Zaragoza** (Calle 9).

Driving across the border is fairly hassle-free, although traffic is bad, especially on weekends. However, driving in Tijuana can be harrowing; if you're only in Tijuana for a day, leave your car in a lot on the U.S. side and join the throngs walking across the border. Bring proper ID to re-enter the U.S.; a passport ensures the speediest passage. Leave fruits, vegetables, and weapons behind.

PRACTICAL INFORMATION

Buses: To reach the bus station (tel. 21 29 83 or 21 29 84) from downtown, board the blue-and-white buses marked "Buena Vista" or "Camionera" on Niños Héroes between Calles 3 and 4 (5 pesos), or jump in a brown-and-white communal cab on Madero between Calles 2 and 3 (5 pesos). Autotransportes de Baja California (tel. 21 29 82 through 87) runs to: **Ensenada** (1½hr., every hr. 5-9am, every 30min. 9am-9pm, 73 pesos); **La Paz** (24hr., 4 per day 8am-9pm, 649 pesos); **Loreto** (18hr., 4 per day 8am-9pm, 494 pesos); **Mexicali** (3hr., every 30min., 84 pesos); **San Felipe** (5hr., 4 per day 5am-4pm, 192 pesos); and **Santa Rosalía** (15hr., 4 and 6:30pm, 390 pesos). Elite (tel. 21 29 48) serves **Guadalajara** (36hr., every 30min., 1096 pesos) and **Hermosillo** (12hr., every 30min., 470 pesos). Greyhound (tel. 21 29 82) runs to **Los Angeles** (3hr., every hr. 5am-11:05pm, $18), and connects to other locations in the U.S.

Communal cabs are all over town; some go to **Rosarito** (30min.).

Visitor Information: Revolución 711 (tel. 88 05 55), at Calle 1. Friendly English-speaking staff dole out maps and advice. Open M-Sa 8am-5pm, Su 10am-5pm.

Customs Office: (tel. 83 13 90), at the border on the Mexican side, after crossing the San Ysidro bridge. Open M-F 8am-3pm.

Currency Exchange: Banks along Constitución exchange currency at the same rate. **Banamex** (tel. 88 00 21 or 88 00 22), Constitución at Calle 4. Open for exchange M-F 9am-5pm with a 24hr. **ATM.** *Casas de cambio* all over town offer better rates but generally do not exchange traveler's checks. Ask if there is commission and stay away from lower-numbered streets (such as Calles 1 and 2) where the exchange rates are steep.

Emergency: Dial 134 or 060. **Police:** (tel. 38 51 68), Constitución at Calle 8.

Red Cross: (tel. 21 77 87, emergency tel. 132), Calle Alfonso Gamboa at E. Silvestre, across from the Price Club.

Area code: 66.

ACCOMMODATIONS

There's no shortage of budget hotels in Tijuana; plenty are on Calle 1 between Revolución and Mutualismo, although they tend to be on the roachy side. Ask to see rooms before paying. The area teems with people during the day and is relatively safe; come nightfall, however, it becomes something of a Red Light District, especially on Calle 1 between Revolución and Constitución. **Be extremely cautious when walking in this area at night;** to return to your hotel, head down Calles 2 or 3, or take a taxi (around $2) from anywhere on Revolución.

Hotel Perla de Occidente, Mutualismo 758 (tel. 85 13 58), between Calles 1 and 2, 4 blocks from the bedlam of Revolución. Multicolored translucent roofing over the central hallway casts beautiful rays of light along the tiled floor. An odd picture of a chimp smoking a joint hangs 2 doors down from a mosaic of Jesus. Large, soft beds, roomy bathrooms, and fans on request. Singles 120 pesos; doubles 140 pesos.

Hotel El Jaliscense, Calle 1 7925 (tel. 85 34 91), between Niños Héroes and Martínez. Clean, small rooms with high, resilient beds, private baths, fans, and phones. A great deal. Ask for a room that doesn't face Calle 1. Singles 120 pesos; doubles 140 pesos.

Hotel La Posada, Calle 1 8190 (tel. 85 41 54 or 85 83 91), at Revolución, just seconds away from all the drunken, debaucherous action. Select your room carefully—the good ones have fans, comfy beds, and bathrooms even your mother would approve of. Singles 60 pesos, with bath 105 pesos; doubles 170 pesos.

FOOD

Tijuana's touristy eats are essentially Tex-Mex, but some cheap restaurants line **Constitución** and the streets leading from Revolución to Constitución. Even cheaper are the mom-and-pop mini-restaurants all over town. If you choose the myriad taco stands, select carefully. Slightly more expensive tourist restaurants and U.S. fast-food chains crowd Revolución. To save money, pay in pesos, even if the menu quotes prices in dollars.

El Pipirín Antojitos, Constitución 878 (tel. 88 16 02), between Calles 2 and 3. Sit at orange tables under orange brick arches and enjoy great food with friendly service. *Burritos de pollo con arroz y frijoles* (chicken burritos with rice and beans) 25 pesos. Open daily 8:30am-9pm.

Los Panchos Taco Shop (tel. 85 72 77), Revolución at Calle 3. Orange plastic booths are packed with hungry locals munching on ultra-fresh tortillas. Since it's open late in summer, this is a good place to satisfy those nighttime munchies. Steak taco $1; bean burrito $2. Open Su-Th 8am-4pm, F-Sa 8am-2am (in summer 8am-4am).

Hotel Nelson Restaurant (tel. 85 77 50), Revolución at Calle 1, under the hotel. Good, cheap food in a clean, fan-cooled, coffee-shop atmosphere. Jukebox blares Mexican oldies. Gringo breakfast (eggs, hotcakes, ham) 26 pesos; 3 enchiladas 18 pesos. Open daily 7am-11pm.

SIGHTS

In the 1920s, when prohibition laws were enacted in the U.S., many of its citizens crossed the border to revel in the forbidden nectars of cacti (tequila), grapes (wine), and hops (beer). Ever since, Tijuana has had a reputation for being the venue for nights of debauchery. The Cetto family has been making **wine** from grapes grown in the Valle de Guadalupe, northeast of Ensenada, since 1926. Visit the family-owned **L.A. Cetto Winery,** Cañón Johnson 2108 (tel. 85 30 31), at Calle 10, just off Constitución. A harvest festival is held in the Cetto vineyards every August. (Tours M-Sa every 30min. 10am-5pm. $1, with wine-tasting $2, with wine-tasting and souvenir goblet $3. Reservations recommended for large groups.)

Jai alai is played in the majestic **Frontón Palacio** (tel. 85 78 33), on Revolución at Calle 7. Two to four players take to the three-sided court at once, using arm-baskets to catch and throw a Brazilian ball of rubber and yarn encased in goatskin. The ball travels at speeds reaching 180mph; *jai alai* is reputedly the world's fastest game. If you can, try to catch a doubles match—the points are longer and require more finesse. Players are treated like horses; observers bet on their favorites and keep a close eye on the odds. All employees are bilingual, and gambling is carried out in dollars. (Open F-Sa for viewing of practice matches. Free.)

If you're in town on the right Sunday, you can watch the savage and graceful dance of a **bullfight** in one of Tijuana's two bullrings. The more modern stadium is **Plaza Monumental,** northwest of the city near Las Playas de Tijuana (follow Calle 2 west), which hosts fights from August to mid-September. To get to the Plaza Monumental, catch a blue-and-white bus on Calle 3 between Constitución and Niños Héroes. Tickets to the rings are sold at the gate and at the **ticket window** at Mexicoac, on Revolución between Calle 6 and 7.

ENTERTAINMENT

If it's after dark, brace yourself for a raucous good time (or head back to the U.S.). Strolling down Revolución after dusk, you'll be bombarded by thumping music, neon lights, and abrasive club promoters hawking "two-for-one" margaritas (most places listed below charge $4 for 2). All clubs check ID (18+), with varying criteria of what's acceptable, and many frisk for firearms. If you'd like to check out a more local scene, peek into the small clubs on Calle 6 off Revolución.

Iguanas-Ranas (tel. 85 14 22), on Revolución at Calle 3. Drink your beer ($2.25) in the schoolbus or raise hell on the dance floor. Lively on weeknights; packed on weekends. Myriads of margarita-drinking iguanas and *ranas* (frogs) adorn the walls. A twentyish crowd of both *norteños* and *norteamericanos* breaks it down. Open daily 10am-4am.

Tilly's 5th Avenue (tel. 85 90 15), on Revolución at Calle 5. The tiny wooden dance floor in the center of this upscale, balloon-filled restaurant/bar resembles a boxing ring, but rest assured–there's only room for dancing. The reflections from the disco ball are enhanced by mirrored walls and a dance-happy staff. Packed on weekends. Beer $2. Wednesday night is Dollar Beer Night. Open M-Th 10am-2am, F-Sa 10am-5am.

Caves (tel. 88 06 09), on Revolución at Calle 5. Dinosaurs and prehistoric beasts perched on a rock facade lead to a dark but airy bar and disco with orange decor, stalactites, and black lights. Drink 2 beers ($3.50) with the blond clientele. No cover. Open daily 11am-2am.

ROSARITO

Once a little-known playground for the rich and famous, the beach haven of Rosarito (pop. 100,000) has expanded at breakneck speed to accommodate the throngs of northern sunseekers who have recently discovered it. Hollywood has also discovered Rosarito: 1998's *Titanic* was filmed here. Giant 10-story hotels and posh resorts cater to U.S. tourists. English is prevalent, and prices are often quoted in dollars. On weekends, the sand and surf overflow with people, volleyball games, and horses; finding a place for your towel may be a struggle.

ORIENTATION AND PRACTICAL INFORMATION. Rosarito lies about 27 kilometers (17mi.) south of Tijuana and stretches itself along the shore. Virtually everything in town is on the main street, **Blvd. Juárez,** upon which street numbers are non-sequential. Most of the action can be found on the southern half of Juárez. To get to Rosarito from Tijuana, grab a yellow-and-white taxi (30min., 9 pesos) that leaves from Madero, between Calles 5 and 6. To return to Tijuana, flag down a taxi along Juárez or at its starting point in front of the Rosarito Beach Hotel. To go to Ensenada, take a blue-and-white taxi marked "Primo Tapia" from Festival Plaza, north of the Rosarito Beach Hotel, to the toll booth on Rte. 1 (4 pesos). From there buses leave for Ensenada (every 30min. until about 9pm, 25 pesos).

The **tourist office** (tel. 2 02 00), on Juárez at Centro Comercio Villa Floreta, at the beginning of Juárez, has tons of brochures. Some English is spoken. (Open M-F 8am-5pm, Sa-Su 10am-3pm.) **Banamex** (tel. 2 15 56 or 2 24 48) exchanges currency on Juárez at Ortiz (open M-F 8:30am-4:30pm). **Emergency:** dial 006. **Police:** (tel. 2 11 10) at Juárez and Acacias. **Red Cross:** (tel. 132) on Juárez at Ortiz, just around the corner from the police. **IMSS Hospital** (tel. 2 10 21; open 24hr.), and the **post office** (tel. 2 13 55; open M-F 8am-3pm) are also on Juárez, near Acacias. **Postal code:** 22710. **Area code:** 661.

ACCOMMODATIONS AND FOOD. Budget hotels in Rosarito are either inconvenient or cramped, with the exception of the outstanding **Hotel Palmas Quintero** (tel. 2 13 59), on Lázaro Cárdenas near the Hotel Quinta del Mar, three blocks inland from north Juárez. A friendly staff and a dog welcome tourists to giant rooms with double beds and clean, private baths with hot water. Chill on the patio under the palm trees. (Singles $20; doubles $40.) Fresh produce and seafood abound in the restaurants that line Juárez. For an economical seafood dinner, head to **Vince's Restaurant** (tel. 2 12 53), on Juárez between Acacias and Robie, opposite the police station. You can enjoy a feast of soup, salad, rice, potatoes, tortillas, and an entree—*filete especial* (fillet of halibut; 28 pesos), shrimp burrito (40 pesos), or octupus-any-style (50 pesos; open daily 8am-10pm).

SIGHTS AND ENTERTAINMENT. Rosarito attracts tourists with its fancy resorts, beautiful shores, and rollicking nightlife. **Rosarito Beach** boasts soft sand and gently rolling surf. **Fox Studios Baja** (tel. 4 01 10), 2 kilometers south of Rosarito on the Tijuana-Ensenada road, offers a short film and tour ($5) of some of the set and props used in the movie *Titanic* (open Sa-Su 10am-6pm). Once the sun sets, travelers live the dream at **Papas and Beer,** Calle de Coronales 400 (tel. 2 04 44), one block north of the Rosarito Beach Hotel and two blocks toward the sea. Reminiscent of a giant wooden jungle gym, the open-air dance floor, bar, and sandy volleyball courts are packed with revelers on the weekends. Don't forget the ID; they take carding seriously. (Beer 15 pesos; mixed drinks 17-25 pesos. Cover Sa and holidays $15-20. Open daily 11am-3am.)

TECATE

Just south of the border from the American town of the same name, Tecate is a quiet and scenic alternative to the sleaziness of Tijuana. Hidalgo Park, in the middle of town, offers shade trees, statues of Mexican leaders, and a clean view of the giant movie theaters now converted to PRI party headquarters. A walk through Tecate reveals a variety of shops, houses, and political posters ranging from conservative PAN to the Green Party, all the way to the Workers' Party. Tecate is, after all, home to Tecate beer, which is brewed in the town's Cervecería Cuauhtémoc Moctezuma. Relatively untouristed, the town makes a pleasant daytrip from San Diego or from Tijuana for those looking to escape that city's more harried atmosphere. Moreover, Tecate is one of Mexico's quickest border crossings, and is particularly convenient for those traveling to Ensenada.

GETTING THERE. From San Diego, follow Martin Luther King, Jr. Blvd. south; this turns into **Route 94,** which runs to the border. From the east, take **Interstate 8** to Rte. 94 near the town of Boulevard. Park in a big dirt lot just before the border for $3 per day. Bring proper ID to re-enter the U.S.; a passport ensures the speediest passage. If you drive in from the U.S., you will follow palm-tree lined **Calle Lázaro Cárdenas;** driving from Tijuana, you'll be on **Avenida Benito Juárez** (the main street). These two streets intersect at the northwest corner of **Hidalgo Park.**

PRACTICAL INFORMATION. Simple maps of the town are available at the **tourist office,** Libertad Alley 1305 (tel. 4 10 95), on the south side of Parque Hidalgo (open daily 8am-7pm). The **Santa Lucia Pharmacy** is at Av. Juárez 45 (tel. 4 32 00), next to the Calimax (open M-Sa 9am-9pm, Su 9am-7pm). In an **emergency,** call the Red Cross at tel. 066 or the police at tel. 060. There is a long-distance **caseta** (phone booth) in the bus station and a **LADATEL** line on Av. Juárez. **Area code:** 665.

ACCOMMODATIONS AND FOOD. Although most visitors to Tecate do not spend the night, budget travelers can find a place to rest. **Hotel Tecate** (tel. 4 11 16), on Libertad Alley at Cárdenas, around the corner from the tourist office, is centrally located and offers simple, clean rooms with bathrooms and fans (singles and doubles around $17.50, with TV around $22).

The cheapest food in town are in *taquerías*, which line Av. Juárez between the park and the bus station. **Cafe de Pollo,** Av. Juárez 170 (tel. 4 07 46), one block west of the park, serves *tortas* of many varieties ($2-3). At the **Restaurant Jardín Tecate** (tel. 4 34 53), on the south side of the park next to the tourist office, enjoy *quesadillas* ($3) or a Mexican combo ($4.50; open daily 7am-10pm).

SIGHTS. The **Tecate Brewery,** on Av. Hidalgo two blocks west of Cárdenas, is the biggest attraction in town. The brewery, opened in 1944, was the first *maquiladora* in Baja California. Now it pumps out 20 million liters of beer each month. The **Jardín Cerveza Tecate** (tel. 4 20 11), in front of the brewery, offers a **free beer** to anyone who wants one (18 and over). The garden was opened in 1994 to commemorate the company's 50th anniversary. Besides Tecate, the company also produces Bohemia, Carta Blanca, Superior, Sol, Dos Equis Amber and Dos Equis Lager. (Open M-F 10am-5:30pm, Sa-Su 10am-4pm. Free tours for groups of 5 or more M-F 11am and 3pm, Sa 11am.)

ENSENADA

The secret is out—beachless Ensenada (pop. 72,000) is fast becoming a weekend hot spot. The masses of Californians that arrive every Friday evening have gringo-ized the town to an incredible degree; everyone speaks some English, and store clerks resort to calculators if you try to buy something with pesos. But fear not; Ensenada is nothing like its brash and raucous cousin to the north, the infamous Tijuana. Ensenada's cool sea breezes, warm hospitality, and vast assortment of activities all contribute to its allure. The city is most pleasant during the week, when fewer tourist-consumers populate the city.

ORIENTATION AND PRACTICAL INFORMATION. Ensenada is 108 kilometers (67½mi.) south of Tijuana on Rte. 1. If you're driving, follow signs on Rte. 1 to the *centro*. You'll come into town on **Azueta,** which later becomes **Gastelum.** Buses from Tijuana arrive at the main terminal, at Calle 11 and Riveroll. Turn right as you come out of the station, walk 10 blocks, and you'll be at **Mateos** (also called **Primera**), the main tourist drag. **Juárez (Calle 5)** runs parallel to Mateos, while from north to south, **Avenidas Ryerson, Moctezuma, Obregón, Ruíz, Gastelum, Miramar, Riveroll, Alvarado, Blancarte,** and **Castillo** are perpendicular to it north of the *arroyo*, a grassy trench crossed by small bridges; below the *arroyo*, **Avenidas Espinoza, Floresta, Guadalupe, Hidalgo, Iturbide,** and (later) **Balboa** also run perpendicular to Mateos. **Boulevard Costero** traces the shoreline, parallel to (and west of) Mateos. *Calles* are numbered, *avenidas* are named; together they form a grid. *Calles* run northwest-southeast, while most *avenidas* run northeast-southwest (Juárez and Mateos are exceptions). After sundown, avoid the area near the shoreline, and use caution while navigating the regions bounded by Av. Miramar and Macheros, and Mateos and Cuarta.

BAJA

PRACTICAL INFORMATION. Autotransportes de Baja California (tel. 78 66 80) runs to several destinations, including **La Paz** (22hr., 4 per day 10am-11pm, 438 pesos) and **Tijuana** (1½hr., every 30min., 55 pesos). **Transportes Aragón** (tel. 74 07 17), on Riveroll between Calles 8 and 9, runs to Tijuana (every hr. 5am-9pm, 48 pesos). **Hertz** (tel. 78 29 82), Calle 2 at Riveroll, rents cars, but they ain't cheap ($51 per day with unlimited kilometers; open M-F 9am-6pm, Sa 9am-1pm). The **tourist office,** Blvd. Costero 540 (tel. 78 24 11), at Azueta, has friendly, English-speaking staff members who dole out helpful information about Ensenada and the surrounding area, as well as maps and pamphlets in English (open M-F 9am-7pm, Sa-Su 11am-3pm). **Banks** cluster along Juárez at Av. Ruíz. **Bancomer** (tel. 78 18 01), on Juárez at Av. Ruíz, exchanges dollars and traveler's checks (open M-F 8:30am-4pm, Sa 10am-2pm). **ATMs** are along Juárez in the bank district. The **Internet** can be accessed at **Cafe Internet** (tel. 76 13 31; fax 76 29 23), at Juárez and Floresta (30

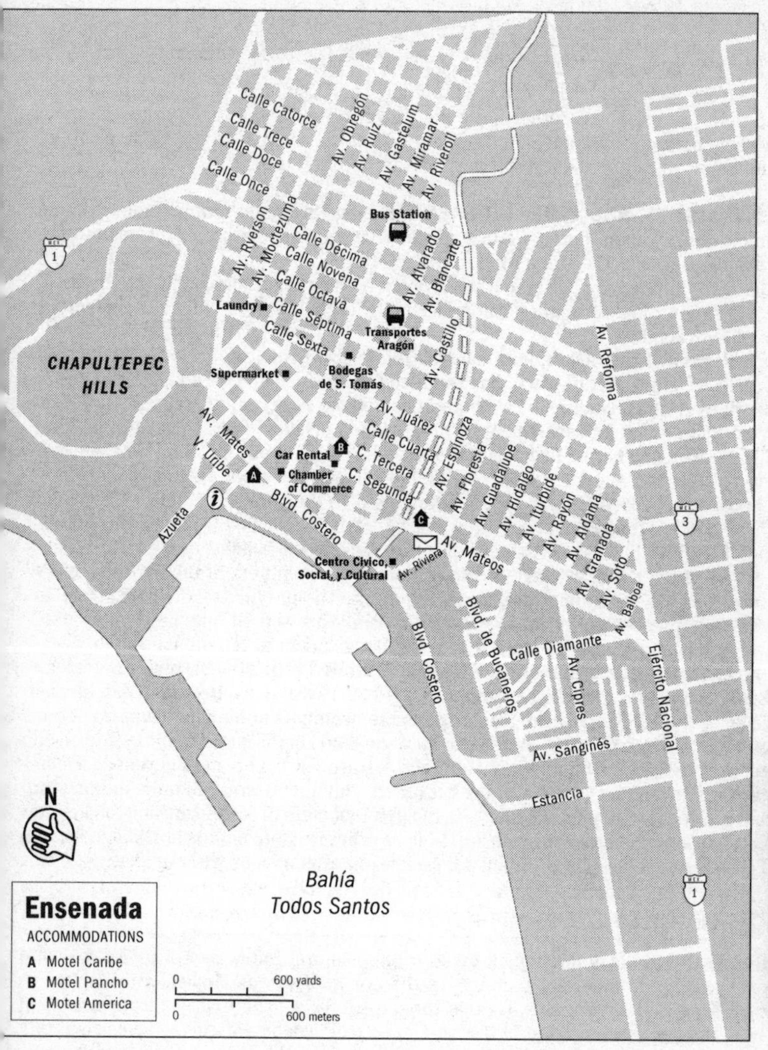

pesos per hr.; open M-F 9am-6:30pm, Sa 9:30am-2pm). **Emergency:** dial 060. **Police** (tel. 76 24 21) are at Calle 9 at Espinoza. The **Red Cross** (tel. 74 45 85, **emergency** 066) is on Blvd. de Jesús Clark at Flores. The **Hospital General** (tel. 76 78 00 or 76 77 00) is on the Transpeninsular Hwy. at the 111km mark (open 24hr.). **Post office:** (tel. 76 10 88) on Mateos at Espinoza (open M-F 8am-7pm, Sa 8am-noon). **Postal code:** 22800. **Area code:** 61.

ACCOMMODATIONS AND FOOD. Budget hotels line Mateos between Espinoza and Riveroll and at Miramar. Most rooms are a 15-minute stroll from the beachfront "boardwalk" and the popular clubs. Although many owners quote prices in greenbacks, pay in pesos to get better deals. **Motel Caribe,** Av. López Mateos 627 (tel. 78 34 81), offers great rooms and a superb location: it's right on the main drag and one block from some of Ensenada's popular dance clubs and bars. Comfortably firm beds and carpeted floors deck out the rooms. (Singles 220 pesos; doubles

320 pesos; key deposit 50 peso; rates go up on weekends.) The beach between Tijuana and Ensenada is lined with RV parks; one near Ensenada is **Ramona RV Park** (tel. 74 60 45), on km 104 of the Transpeninsular Hwy. ($10 for full hookup).

The cheaper restaurants in town line Juárez and Espinoza; those on Mateos jack up their prices. The eateries along the waterfront near the fish market compete fiercely for their customers and offer good, cheap, fresh seafood. Fruit, seafood, and taco stands abound, but be wary of how the food is handled.

SIGHTS AND ENTERTAINMENT. Seeing Ensenada requires more than a quick cruise down Mateos. For a spectacular view of the entire city, climb the **Chapultepec Hills.** The steep road to the top begins at the foot of Calle 2; expect a 10- to 15-minute hike. Or take a stroll down **Avenida López Mateos,** where herds of curio shops allow for endless shopping. Many of the outdoor cafes are perfect for people-watching.

Bodegas de Santo Tomás, Miramar 666 (tel. 78 33 33), at Calle 7, devilishly located in a less-visited part of town, has produced wine since 1888. Today, the *bodegas* distill over 500,000 cases of wine and champagne every year. Tours include free wine tasting and an assortment of breads and cheeses (daily 11am, 1, and 3pm; $3). Nearby, the **Museo Histórico Regional** (tel. 78 25 31), on Gastelum between Virgillo Uribe and Mateos, houses artifacts from all over Baja, include a charming photograph of two elderly men standing next to their shared young wife, whom they acquired during a robbery in a nearby town. (Open Tu-Su 10am-5pm. Admission $1.) Built in 1886 as barracks, it is the **oldest public building** in the state.

Most of the popular hangouts along Mateos are members of the hybrid species known as the **restaurant/bar/disco.** Much like the praying mantis, this species swallows its prey post-coitally. Food and drinks are served only until 8pm or so, when the eateries metamorphose into full-fledged dance club monsters. On weekends, almost every place is packed with festive tourists. Better known than Ensenada itself is **Hussong's Cantina** (tel. 78 32 10), on Ruíz between Mateos and Calle 2. Now 106 years old, Hussong's is the prototypical Mexican watering hole: with wood-paneled walls adorned with deer heads and sawdust on the floor, you get the true cantina flavor with your Tecate. Gulp down a beer (12 pesos) or a margarita (16 pesos) at the long, shiny bar (open daily 10am-2am). If you're looking for a less alcohol-centered evening, join the gyrating mass of teens whirling to late-80s pop hits at **Roller Ensenada** (tel. 76 11 59), a roller rink on Mateos at Hidalgo (open Tu-Th 2-10pm, F-Su noon-10pm; admission 13 pesos with or without skates).

BEACHES

Good sand to accompany your swim in the pastoral Bahía de Todos Santos can only be found outside of the city. To the north, **Playa San Miguel,** with its rocky coastlines and large waves, is great for surfers. To get there, drive north up Calle 10 to the toll gate; turn left at the sign marked "Playa San Miguel." Buses also run to this beach—catch a bus marked "San Miguel" departing from Gastelum at Costero (3 pesos). Buses back must be flagged down. Somewhat more frequented beaches lie 8km south of Ensenada off the Transpeninsular Hwy. Probably the nicest beach around is **Playa Estero,** dominated by the Estero Beach Resort. Volleyball courts fill the beach's clean but hard and unforgiving sand. You can rent **water skis, banana boats,** or **bicycles** ($5 per hr.). **Sea lions** can be spotted off the coast during low tide. Another nearby beach is **Playa Santa María,** where you can rent a **horse** ($9 per hr.) and ride around the bay. Continuing south along the Punta Banda peninsula (take the paved road BCN 23, which splits west off Rte. 1 north of Maneadero), you'll find lonelier beaches along the stretch known as **Baja Beach.** Horses are available for rent, and you can swim anywhere along the clean, soft, white sand (remember, all beaches are public) in front of a quiet smattering of U.S. tourists in semi-permanent RV parks. To get to Baja Beach, walk down a dirt road after the sign, on the right hand side. By car, bear right at the first fork in the road after turning onto the peninsula. Proceed with caution; this road is very poorly maintained. Beautiful hiking spots are nearby (see **Near Ensenada: Hiking** below). You can also take a bus to La Bufadora (below) and ask the driver to let you off, but don't count on a ride back.

NEAR ENSENADA: HIKING

Breathtaking hikes on well-kept trails can be completed around the mountains of the Punta Banda peninsula near La Bufadora. Bring a snack, as there are some good spots with spectacular view of cliffs and never-ending blue sea to stop and picnic. Don't forget a bathing suit—when you reach the bottom, you can relieve your sweaty body with a dip amid the rocks in the chilly Pacific. Most of the trails consist of unmarked footpaths and dirt roads. Be sure to stay on a path once you've chosen it; trail blazing will damage the surrounding flora. The best spot to enter the trails is **Cerro de la Punta,** on the road to La Bufadora near the end of the Punta Banda peninsula. Turn right up a long driveway at the "Cerro de la Punta" sign (parking 10 pesos). You'll see a small clearing and a large house on the cliffs; here, you can hike up among the cacti to the top of the mountains for views or down beautiful trails on the oceanside.

Other stops earlier along the road to La Bufadora are equally scenic. The bus to La Bufadora (see below) will drop you off anywhere along this road, including Cerro de la Punta, but you may wait quite a while for the bus back. Hiking farther inland offers completely different terrain, ranging from deep lagoons to cactus forests to ponderosa pine. The rugged mountain range east of Ensenada is the solitary **Sierra de Juárez,** where the **Parque Nacional Constitución de 1857** is located. Be forewarned: you'll need an **all-terrain vehicle** or **pickup truck** to make the trek. To get there, follow **Highway 3** east from Av. Juárez in Ensenada all the way past **Ojos Negros.** At about km 58, turn left onto the dirt road leading into the park. Follow signs (or, better, ask a guide for help); after about one hour and 20 minutes, you will find yourself at **Laguna Hanson,** a little lake surrounded by basic camping spots. If you aren't wheeled, **Ecotur,** Espinoza 1251 (tel. 76 44 15), at Calle 9, offers excursions. Call at least three days in advance to book a tour.

NEAR ENSENADA: LA BUFADORA

La Bufadora, the largest geyser on the Pacific coast, is 30km south of Ensenada. On a good day, the "Blowhole" shoots water 40m into the air out of a water-carved cave. On a bad day, visitors will have to be satisfied with the beautiful view from the Bufadora peak. The area is crowded with droves of visitors, cheesy curio shops, and food vendors. In spite of the bustling buzz of the area, the geyser makes the trip worthwhile. Parking costs $1 or 8 pesos. To get there, drive south on the Transpeninsular Hwy. Head straight past exits for the airport, military base, and Playa Estero, and take a right after about 20 minutes at the sign marked "La Bufadora." Continue on that road until its end. Alternatively, you can take a yellow mini-bus from Ensenada to **Maneadero** (3 pesos) and a connecting bus to La Bufadora (2 pesos).

VALLE DE SAN QUINTÍN

Occupying the lonely mid-Pacific coast of northern Baja, San Quintín Valley (pop. 30,000) is the lifeblood of the peninsula's agricultural production. Driving south from Ensenada on Route 1 (the Transpeninsular Highway) for 180 kilometers (113mi.), you'll encounter a series of small, bland towns bordered by the ocean on the west and the mountains on the east—farmland lies everywhere in between. The valley's settlement is made up of numerous ranches belonging to gallant *vaqueros* (cowboys) and three tiny towns (listed north to south): **San Quintín, Lázaro Cárdenas** (not to be confused with its same-named neighbor only about 100km to the northeast), and **El Eje del Papaloto.** What brings most people here, however, is the superb fishing off the small *bahía.* Americans and other foreigners are hard to find in the area's main strip (as is virtually everything). The summer morning fogs and the cool bay breezes of the old port area give way to hot afternoon sun and vistas of desert and cacti. Above all, the town makes a good rest stop on the way to points farther south, or a convenient place to stock up on supplies for a camping excursion to the nearby **Parque Nacional Sierra San Pedro Mártir** (see p. 513).

ORIENTATION AND PRACTICAL INFORMATION. All three towns border **Route 1,** Mexico's **Transpeninsular Highway.** Small streets off the highway have neither street signs nor common-use names. Addresses are designated by highway location. The beaches are all west of the highway, off small dirt and sand roads. Coming from the north, San Quintín is the first town, Cárdenas (as it is known in the region) is second, and little Eje comes last. The Valle de San Quintín **tourist office** (tel. 6 27 28) actually comes before the towns themselves at km 178 in Col. Vicente Guerrero; look for signs. The friendly staff will provide plenty of info about the valley and the surrounding area (open M-F 8am-5pm, Sa-Su 10am-3pm). To **exchange currency** and traveler's checks, head to **BITAL,** the Valle's bank, in Lázaro Cárdenas behind the PEMEX station (open M-F 8am-7pm, Sa 9am-2:30pm). **Emergency:** dial 134. **Police:** in Cárdenas, east of the highway. **Farmacia Baja California:** (tel. 5 24 38) in Cárdenas, Rte.1 at km 195 (open daily 8am-10pm). **Clínica Santa María:** (tel. 75 22 63 or 75 22 12) in San Quintín, on a dirt road off Rte. 1 at km 190. **Post office:** a gray building next to the Farmaciá Baja California in Cárdenas (open M-F 8am-3pm). **Postal code:** 22930. **LADATELs** are in all three towns and a **caseta** is in Cárdenas. **Phone code:** 616.

ACCOMMODATIONS AND FOOD. Sleeping arrangements in the Valle are minimal but, for the most part, comfortable. In San Quintín, **Hotel Chavez** (tel. 5 20 05), on Rte. 1 at km 194 just before the bridge, offers large, airy rooms, soft beds, and cable TV in the main lobby (singles 180 pesos; doubles 240 pesos; call ahead for reservations). In Lázaro Cárdenas, **Motel Romo** (tel. 5 23 96), at km 196 on the west side of Rte. 1, has almost-new carpeted rooms. Clean bathrooms border on Art Deco and large windows let in the sunlight. Singles 110 pesos; doubles 130 pesos. About three kilometers down a dirt road just south of Lázaro Cárdenas lies **Motel San Carlos** (follow signs for the Old Mill). Situated near the old pier on San Quintín Bay, its carpeted rooms with baths offer guests a nightly serenade of wind and waves lapping at the shore. Singles $20; doubles $25. Cheap eats aren't tough to find in San Quintín. Small *loncherías* along both sides of Rte. 1 serve tacos for 9 pesos. Enjoy a *bistec milanesa* (49 pesos) among framed portraits of John Wayne, Clint Eastwood, and other *vaqueros* in the air-conditioned **Asadero El Alazán** in San Quintín, at km 190 on Rte. 1.

SIGHTS AND ENTERTAINMENT. San Quintín is best known for the fishing off the San Quintín Bay. You can drive out to the **Molino Viejo** (Old Pier) and to the **Old Mill Hotel** (619-428-2779 or 800 479-7962), where you can get a fishing permit, hire a boat for the day, and catch a glimpse of some original mill machinery of the failed 19th-century English colony. The Old Mill itself is a semi-permanent American expat community. To get there, turn west on a sand and dirt road on km 198 and head down about four kilometers (2½mi.) (signs will point you in the right direction). Or, if you'd like something a little different, check out the salt lakes formed on the edge of the sea, west of Cárdenas. To get there, turn left at the corner of the military base. Head down a dirt and sand road for approximately 8.2 kilometers (5mi.). You don't need an all-terrain-vehicle, but follow the sand paths very carefully. Although San Quintín's nightlife is hardly hoppin', those in search of spirits can wet their whistle at **Bar Romo** (tel. 5 23 96), on Rte. 1 in Cárdenas, where *mariachis* and local singers are cheered on by catcalls until the late hours. In San Quintín, grab a chilly *cerveza* (about 12 pesos) or margarita (20 pesos) at the friendly tourist-oriented **Restaurant Bar San Quintín** (tel. 5 23 76) on Rte. 1 next to Hotel Chavez. The well-stocked bar and weekend *mariachis* will help you strum a buzz in no time. (Open daily 7:30am-1am.)

NEAR VALLE DE SAN QUINTÍN: PARQUE NACIONAL SIERRA SAN PEDRO MÁRTIR

Although the trippy towns of the Valle de San Quintín appeal mostly to anglers, the nearby **Parque Nacional Sierra San Pedro Mártir** has enough canyons, peaks, and waterfalls to satisfy the urges of the most zealous land lover. Founded in 1947, the park occupies the highest zone on the peninsula and is home to **Picacio del Diablo** (also known as **Cerro de la Encantada** or **La Providencia**), the highest peak in Baja at 3086 meters (9300ft.) above sea level. From its peak on a clear day, you can admire the aquamarine waters of the Sea of Cortés, turn around, and check out the vast Pacific Ocean. The climb to the peak is rated three to five and is said to be one of the most challenging climbs in Mexico. For those uninterested in scaling mountains, the park has three canyons to explore as well as the San Pedro Mártir Falls, an 800-meter (½mi.) fall accessible only with an authorized guide. Check out the tourist office in San Quintín or contact **Ecotur.** The park is situated on a plateau, and because of its elevation, it has considerably more rainfall than its lowland desert surroundings—it even snows in the winter here. As a result, the park is beautifully shaded by evergreens (pines and junipers abound) and is host to a vast array of wildlife including deer, puma, eagles, not-so-wild cows, and the Nelson rainbow trout (a species endemic to the region). The park's isolated location makes it one of the least-visited parks in Mexico and a prime destination for backpackers and hikers who wish to be alone to commune with nature. There are several tent site locations, but none for trailer or car camping. A few trails leading to viewpoints and wilderness campsites are nominally maintained and can be accessed off the park's only road. See a ranger at the entrance to the park for information and help with orientation.

The park is also home to Mexico's **National Observatory.** Founded in 1967, the observatory is one of the most important in all of Latin America; it houses both reflecting telescopes and a new state-of-the-art telescope that utilizes infrared technology. The observatory lies at the end of the road leading into the park and tours are given on Saturdays from 11am to 1pm upon arrangement with the administration.

GETTING THERE. The road leading to the park and observatory lies approximately 51km north of San Quintín and runs east of the highway for 100 kilometers (62½mi.). Be forewarned—this road is not for the faint of heart. The ride to the park is approximately 2½ hours on a poorly maintained dirt road (due to heavy rainfall, the road may be temporarily closed). You can make the trek in a passenger vehicle, but it is highly recommended to go with four-wheel-drive. Be careful of oncoming traffic as the road is narrow and the cliffs steep. Also watch out for cattle; local *vaqueros* use the road to herd their cows to greener pastures. In spite of the dangerous curves, the views from the road are unparalleled—breathtaking vistas of canyons and hills tinted yellow and red by wildflowers are some of the best in all of Baja. The trails in the park are not well-marked, and it is advisable to bring a compass and, for some trails, mandatory to bring along an authorized guide. If you plan on backpacking or spending the night in the park, bring plenty of safe drinking water.

LA PAZ

The eclectic and beautiful capital of Baja California Sur, La Paz (pop. 140,000) is part port, part party town, and part peaceful paradise. Home to 10 tranquil beaches along the Sea of Cortés, this is where Mexicans vacation, leaving the honky-tonk Cabos to U.S. tourists. In a past life, La Paz was a quiet fishing village, frequently harassed by pirates for the iridescent white spheres concealed in the oysters off its coast; John Steinbeck's *The Pearl* depicted the town as a tiny, unworldly treasure chest. La Paz's hour of reckoning came in the 1940s, when the oysters got sick and died, wiping out the town's pearl industry. Within two decades, the institution of Baja ferries and the completion of the Transpeninsular

Highway in the late 1960s spurred La Paz's rebirth. Now, the row of nightclubs along the beach and snorkel stores may make La Paz (The Peace) feel sheepish about its name. No worries, though: the days are still hot and nonchalant, and the fishermen are still friendly. At night, despite the big bass beats issuing from semi-gringoized dance clubs, pelicans still skip along the lamp-lit water, and a merciful breeze ruffles the hair of couples strolling along the rocky beach and the serene boardwalk pier at sunset.

ORIENTATION

La Paz lies 1496 kilometers (935mi.) southeast of Tijuana, on the Transpeninsular Hwy. (Rte. 1), overlooks the **Bahía de la Paz** on Baja's east coast. The city's main street, and loveliest lane for a stroll, is **Avenida Obregón,** more commonly known as the **Malecón,** which runs along alternately sandy and rocky shore. Activity centers around the area delineated by **Constitución, Ocampo, Serdán,** and the shore. The **municipal bus system** in La Paz serves the city sporadically (approximately every 30min. 6am-10pm, 3-3.50 pesos). Flag buses down anywhere, or wait by the stop on Revolución and Degollado, next to the market. From the station, try to convince your driver to drop you off in the *centro.* If you're in the center of activity, you need not worry about the buses; it's all easily navigable on foot.

CROSSING THE GULF

Ferries leave from the suburb of **Pichilingue;** they're the best way to get from La Paz to the Mexican mainland. Buy tickets at the **Sematur Company office** (tel. 5 46 66), at 5 de Mayo and Prieto (open M-F 8am-6pm, Sa-Su 8am-4pm). Ferries go to **Mazatlán** (15hr.; daily at 3pm; 209-831 pesos, cars 2243 pesos, motorcycles 396 pesos) and **Topolobampo,** a suburb of Los Mochis (9hr.; daily 10pm except for "cargo only" days—call for precise info; *salón* (3rd-class) 123 pesos, cars 1089 pesos, motorcycles 242 pesos). The dock office is open daily from 8am to 10pm.

In order to secure a ticket, be sure to get to the Sematur main office early, ideally right after it opens. During holidays, competition for ferry tickets is fierce. A travel agency might be the most trouble-free way to make reservations—it costs the same and allows you to pick up the tickets at the agency instead of having to wait in the long lines at the ferry office. **Turismo Express Aventuras** (tel. 5 63 10), on Obregón, in the same building as the tourist office (open M-F 8am-8pm, Sa 9am-8pm, Su 9am-2pm), and **Operadora de Mar de Cortés** (tel. 5 22 77; fax 5 85 99), on Bravo at Ortega, a 15-minute walk from the center, will sell you a ticket. Tickets can be picked up from 4 to 6pm the day before departure.

In order to get a vehicle on the ferry, you will need (at the very least) proof of Mexican insurance (or a major credit card with the car owner's name on it), car registration, permission for the importation of a car into Mexico, a tourist card, and **three photocopies** of each. You can get a permit at **Banjército** (tel. 2 11 16), at the ferry stop in Pichilingue, or through **AAA** in the U.S. Regardless of whether you have a car or not, you will need to obtain a **tourist card (FMT)** if you entered Mexico via Baja and are mainland-bound; get one from **Servicios Migratorios** (see p. 515). Clear all of the paperwork before purchasing the ticket; otherwise, Sematur will deny you a spot whether or not you hold reservations.

You need not hike 17km to the ferry dock in Pichilingue—**Autotransportes Aguila** buses run between the dock and the downtown terminal on Obregón, between Independencia and 5 de Mayo (M-F 9:30am and every hr. 11:30am-5:30pm, 15 pesos). When you get off the ferry, hurry to catch the 9:30am bus to the *centro;* otherwise you'll have to wait for two hours. A taxi from dock to downtown, or vice versa, will set you back a good 100 pesos.

PRACTICAL INFORMATION

TRANSPORTATION

Airport: West of La Paz, accessible only by taxi (80 pesos). If heading from the airport to the center, buy taxi tickets inside to avoid being swindled. Served by **Aerocalifornia** (tel. 4 62 88), between Ocampo and Bravo, and **Aeroméxico** (tel. 4 62 88), at Obregón, between Hidalgo and Morelos. Open M-F 8:45am-7pm, Sa 9am-2pm.

Buses: There are 3 stations. The **main station** is on Jalisco and Independencia, about 25 blocks southeast of downtown. Two municipal buses, "Central Camionera" and "Urbano," head to the terminal; catch them near the public market at Degollado and Revolución. Taxis cost 30 pesos. Aguila and ABC (tel. 2 42 70) provide service to points north, including: **Loreto** (5hr., 8 per day 9am-10pm, 137 pesos); **Mulegé** (7hr., 8 per day 9am-10pm, 197 pesos); **Santa Rosalía** (8hr., 8 per day 9am-10pm, 213 pesos); **San Ignacio** (9hr., 5 per day 10am-10pm, 278 pesos); **Ensenada** (19½hr., 4 per day 10am-10pm, 592 pesos); **Tijuana** (21hr., 4 per day 10am-10pm, 649 pesos); and **Mexicali** (24½hr., 4pm, 746 pesos). A bus from the **Aguila Malecón station** (tel. 2 78 98), on Independencia at Obregón, is the best way to get to nearby beaches. Buses run to: **El Carmancito, El Coramuel, Playas Palmira, Tesoro,** and **Pichilingue** (up to 30min., 11 per day 7am-7:30pm, 6-11 pesos), and to **Playas Balandras** and **Tecolote** (45min., Sa-Su only, every hr. 8am-6pm, 15 pesos). The last bus back to La Paz leaves Tecolote 7pm weekdays only and Pichilingue at 6pm weekdays, 7pm weekends; but, be sure to ask the driver before you get off the bus. The new **Enlaces Terrestres station** (tel. 3 31 80), on Degollado at Serdán, is more convenient for heading south. Buses run to: **Todos Santos** (2hr., 9 per day 7am-8pm, 35 pesos); **Cabo San Lucas** (3hr., 7 per day 6:30am-7pm, 72 pesos); and **San José del Cabo** (3½hr., 7 per day 6:30am-7pm, 82 pesos).

TOURIST AND FINANCIAL SERVICES

Visitor Information: (tel. 2 59 39), Obregón at 16 de Septiembre, in a pavilion on the water. Excellent city maps and information about Baja Sur, especially Los Cabos. English-speaking staff. Open M-F 8am-8pm.

Tourist Police: Fabulous folks recognizable by their starched white uniforms and big grins. Their job is "protection and orientation," but they will also give recommendations for hiking, beaches, hotels, restaurants, and barbers.

Immigration Office: Servicios Migratorios, Obregón 2140 (tel. 5 34 93; fax 2 04 29), between Juárez and Allende. You must stop here to obtain a tourist card if you entered Mexico via Baja and are mainland-bound. Open M-F 9am-6pm. After hours, head to the airport outpost outside of town (tel. 4 63 49), open daily 7am-11pm.

LOCAL SERVICES

Currency Exchange: Bancomer (tel. 5 42 48), on 16 de Septiembre, half a block from the waterfront has a 24hr. **ATM.** Open for exchange M-F 8:30am-2:30pm, Sa 9am-2:30pm. **BITAL,** 5 de Mayo (tel. 2 22 89), at Madero, has a 24hr. **ATM** and talking doors. Open for exchange M-Sa 8am-7pm.

American Express: (tel. 2 86 66), 5 de Mayo at Domínguez. Open daily 8am-8pm.

Laundromat: Lavandería Yoli (tel. 2 10 01), 5 de Mayo at Rubio, across the street from the stadium. Wash and dry a big load 18 pesos. Open M-Sa 7am-9pm, Su 8am-3pm.

EMERGENCY AND COMMUNICATIONS

Emergency: Dial 060 or 080.

Police: (tel. 2 07 81) on Colima at México. Open 24hr.

Red Cross: Reforma 1091 (tel. 2 12 22), between Isabel la Católica and Félix Ortega. Open 24hr.

Pharmacy: Farmacia Bravo (tel. 2 69 33), next to the hospital. Open 24hr.

Hospital: Salvatierra (tel. 2 14 96 or 2 14 97), on Bravo at Verdad, between Domínguez and the Oncological Institute.

Post Office: (tel. 2 03 88 or 5 23 58) on Revolución at Constitución. Open M-F 8am-3pm, Sa 9am-1pm. **Postal Code:** 23000.

Fax: TELECOM (tel. 2 67 07; fax 5 08 09), upstairs from the post office. Open M-Sa 8am-7pm, Su 8:30am-11:30pm.

Internet: Baja Net Cafe Internet, Madero 430 (tel. 5 93 80), between Hidalgo and Constitución. Enjoy free coffee and A/C. 20-30 pesos per 30min. Open M-Sa 8am-8pm.

Telephones: Sexy young **LADATELs,** as well as older, more mature payphones, pepper the downtown area and *zócalo*.

AREA CODE	The area code for La Paz is 112.

ACCOMMODATIONS

The city is full of inexpensive establishments bound to satisfy even the most finicky of travelers. The cluttered artistic look, however, seems to be making a resurgence in the budget hotels of La Paz. A student of Mexican folk art could skip the Museo Antropológico and tour the lobbies of these hotels instead. Many economical lodgings cluster in the downtown area.

Hotel Yeneka, Madero 1520 (tel. 5 46 88), between 16 de Septiembre and Independencia. Quite possibly the most unique hotel in all of Baja. Doubles as a museum of eccentric items, including a 1916 Model-T Ford, a pet hawk, and a stuffed monkey. Each Tarzan-hut room has been remodeled in matching twig furniture and painted with rainbow colors. You can see the painted handprints of the owner's little son on the walls and the green hallways are a labor of love. All rooms come with fans and foam mattresses laid on concrete frames. Laundry, fax, bike rentals, and a restaurant are but a few of the services this budget bunkhouse offers. Singles 160 pesos; doubles 230 pesos; triples 300 pesos.

Pensión California Casa de Huéspedes (tel. 2 28 96), on Degollado at Madero. Bungalow rooms have concrete floors and concrete-slab beds. You can't help but admire the plastic turtle sculpture, sea shells, washing machine, picture mural of past guests, and unique shower-toilet-sink combo. Prices include use of the communal kitchen and TV. Bring your own blanket and towel. Padlocks on the doors provide security. Singles 100 pesos; doubles 130 pesos; triples 160 pesos. **Hostería del Convento** (tel. 2 35 08), across the street, which is under the same ownership, has almost an identical setup at a lower cost. Singles 85 pesos.

Hotel Posada San Miguel, B. Domínguez 1510 (tel. 5 88 88), just off 16 de Septiembre. Step back in time as you enter the beautiful fountained courtyard. Oversized framed black-and-white photographs of La Paz in its early days, tiled arches, and wrought-iron scrollwork on windows and railings help to create a feeling of an earlier, simpler time. Cubical rooms with sinks and large, comfortable beds. Singles 100 pesos; doubles 120 pesos; triples 140 pesos.

FOOD

On the waterfront you'll find decor, menus, and prices geared toward peso-spewing tourists. Move inland a few blocks and watch the prices plunge. Seafood meals are generally fresh. The **public market,** at Degollado and Revolución, offers a cheap selection of fruits, veggies, and fresh fish.

Restaurante El Quinto Sol (tel. 2 16 92), on B. Domínguez at Independencia is one of the few vegetarian joints in Baja. Menu includes sausage à la soybean, as well as an assortment of juices. Luscious yogurt smoothie with fruit 15 pesos; vegetarian steak 45 pesos; tasty pastries 12 pesos. Open M-Sa 7am-10pm.

Restaurant Palapa Adriana (tel. 2 83 29), on the beach, off Obregón at Constitución. Not just on the water, but practically in the water. *Huachinango* (red snapper) 50 pesos; *pollo con mole* 35 pesos; *pulpo al ajo* 60 pesos. Great view and sea breeze *gratis.* Open daily 10am-10pm.

La Luna Bruja, on Playa Pichilingue, the second *cabana* on shore, farthest from the ferry dock. Defying the stereotype of the overpriced beachfront *palapa,* this quiet restaurant offers amazing seafood at good prices. *Tostados de ceviche* 30 pesos; fish about 50 pesos. Ice-cold beer 15 pesos (or buy a 40 oz. for 25 pesos)–a real deal when it's hand-delivered to you on the beach. Open daily 12-10pm.

La Fuente, on Obregón at Bañuelos, across from the big arch. What better way to battle the heat than with a few scoops of ice cream? This local *nevería* is always buzzing–during the day with little kids, at night with eager clubgoers. Open daily 8am-midnight.

BEACH AND SIGHTS

Instead of curving around long expanses of wave-washed sand, the beaches of La Paz snuggle into small coves sandwiched between cactus-studded hills and calm, transparent water. This is prime windsurfing territory. But be careful—La Paz lifeguards make appearances only on weekends and at popular beaches.

The best beach near La Paz is **Playa Tecolote** (Owl Beach), 25 kilometers northeast of town. A quiet extension of the Sea of Cortés laps against this gorgeous stretch of gleaming white sand near tall, craggy mountains. Even though there are no bathrooms, Tecolote is terrific for **camping.** Several spots on the eastern side of the beach along the road to the more secluded **Playa El Coyote** come equipped with a stone barbecue pit. **Actividades Aquatica,** on Tecolote, rents **snorkeling** gear (50 pesos per day), **kayaks,** and **paddle boats** and organizes trips to **Isla Espiritu Santo** (300 pesos per person, min. 4 people). The snorkeling off **Playa Balandra,** just south of Tecolote, is excellent. Balandra is actually a cove with almost no view of the sea; it resembles a big blue swimming pool with rocky hills instead of cement walls. Because facilities are sparse and sporadically open, it is best to rent equipment either in the city or at nearby Pichilingue or Tecolote. You may not be able to reach Tecolote or Balandra weekdays without a car; **Autotransportes Aguila** buses get you there from the mini-station on Obregón and Independencia (spring break and July-Aug. daily, in the low season Sa-Su only; 12 pesos).

Plenty of other beaches are easily accessible by taking the "Pichilingue" bus up the coast (10 pesos). Be forewarned that neither of these buses run back to La Paz after 6:30 or 7pm. The "Pichilingue" bus goes as far as the ferry dock, at which point you need to walk one kilometer farther on the paved road to **Playa de Pichilingue.** This beach is the most crowded and a favorite among the teen set, who splash in the shallow waters and ride **paddleboats** in the winter (30 pesos per hr.). Unfortunately, the view from Pichilingue is corrupted by the ferry docks and the nearby power plant. Along the same bus route lies **Playa El Coromuel,** near La Concha Hotel, where visitors and locals congregate on weekends. All of the above beaches are out of walking distance from the city center, though a short ride away. The farther you venture from La Paz, the prettier and more secluded the beaches.

The aquatic fun in this city doesn't stop at the shoreline; many popular dive spots are located around La Paz. North of La Paz is **Salvatierra Wreck,** a dive spot where a 100 meter boat sank in 1976. Also popular is the huge **Cerraluo Island,** east of La Paz. This popular destination promises reefs, huge fish, and untouched wilderness. Both of these destinations (and many others) require guides because of strong currents, fluctuating weather conditions, and inaccessibility.

Baja Diving and Service, Obregón 1665 (tel. 2 18 26; fax 2 86 44), between 16 de Septiembre and Callejón La Paz, organizes daily scuba and snorkeling trips to nearby reefs, wrecks, and islands, where you can mingle with hammerheads, manta rays, giant turtles, and other exotica (scuba trips $77 per day without equipment, US$15 extra for equipment, snorkeling $40 per day). Trips leave at 7am and return before 5pm. Nearby, **Sea & Scuba** (tel. 3 52 33), at the corner of Obregón and Ocampo, offers similar activities and rates. Forty-five kilometers south of La Paz along the transpeninsular highway is **El Triunfo,** an abandoned mining town. Marked by a huge tower/chimney, this lonely desert town offers lovely views, solitude, and a chance to see local artwork done in shell or stone.

ENTERTAINMENT

Structure (tel. 2 45 44), Obregón and Ocampo, 3 blocks east of the center, is a new, hoppin' disco with a dim interior and loud, terrific techno. Some Thursdays feature live karate and sporting events while young couples drink beer (15 pesos) and watch Mexico's version of MTV on scattered screens. Cover F men 70 pesos, women 30 pesos, includes open bar; Sa 2-for-1 specials. Open Th-Su 10pm-late.

La Cabaña, Obregón 1570, on the 2nd fl. of Hotel Perla, is a bit more mature. Live bands croon favorite Mexican ballads to a dressy over-35 crowd. This joint is bizarre, kitschy, and rockin'. Catch Wednesday boxing matches, and on Sunday nights you can two-step to good ol' country tunes. Cover F-Sa 30 pesos. Open W-Su 9pm-3am.

Carlos 'n' Charlie's/La Paz-Lapa, Obregón and 16 de Septiembre, is central and noticeable. Huge margaritas (32 pesos) form a staple of gringo nightlife. Patrons go buck-wild at the La Paz-Lapa, an outdoor booze and rockfest. U.S. and Mexican teens get down and sing along to Aerosmith amid giant palm trees and an imposing bar. Tongue-in-cheek signs like "Do not dive from balcony" turn into real warnings after 3am. Cover and drink prices vary. Women usually pay less; sometimes before 10pm they can enter and drink free. Cover Th men 40 pesos; includes open bar. Open daily 10:30pm-late.

INDEX

INDEX

M

N

INDEX

T

INDEX

ABOUT LET'S GO

FORTY YEARS OF WISDOM

As a new millennium arrives, *Let's Go: Europe*, now in its 40th edition and translated into seven languages, reigns as the world's bestselling international travel guide. For four decades, travelers criss-crossing the Continent have relied on *Let's Go* for inside information on the hippest backstreet cafes, the most pristine secluded beaches, and the best routes from border to border. In the last 20 years, our rugged researchers have stretched the frontiers of backpacking and expanded our coverage into Asia, Africa, Australia, and the Americas. We're celebrating our 40th birthday with the release of *Let's Go: China*, blazing the traveler's trail from the Forbidden City to the Tibetan frontier; *Let's Go: Perú & Ecuador*, spanning the lands of the ancient Inca Empire; *Let's Go: Middle East*, with coverage from Istanbul to the Persian Gulf; and the maiden edition of *Let's Go: Israel*.

It all started in 1960 when a handful of well-traveled students at Harvard University handed out a 20-page mimeographed pamphlet offering a collection of their tips on budget travel to passengers on student charter flights to Europe. The following year, in response to the instant popularity of the first volume, students traveling to Europe researched the first full-fledged edition of *Let's Go: Europe*, a pocket-sized book featuring honest, practical advice, witty writing, and a decidedly youthful slant on the world. Throughout the 60s and 70s, our guides reflected the times. In 1969 we taught travelers how to get from Paris to Prague on "no dollars a day" by singing in the street. In the 80s and 90s, we looked beyond Europe and North America and set off to all corners of the earth. Meanwhile, we focused in on the world's most exciting urban areas to produce in-depth, fold-out map guides. Our new guides bring the total number of titles to 48, each infused with the spirit of adventure and voice of opinion that travelers around the world have come to count on. But some things never change: our guides are still researched, written, and produced entirely by students who know first-hand how to see the world on the cheap.

HOW WE DO IT

Each guide is completely revised and thoroughly updated every year by a well-traveled set of over 250 students. Every spring, we recruit over 180 researchers and 70 editors to overhaul every book. After several months of training, researcher-writers hit the road for seven weeks of exploration, from Anchorage to Adelaide, Estonia to El Salvador, Iceland to Indonesia. Hired for their rare combination of budget travel sense, writing ability, stamina, and courage, these adventurous travelers know that train strikes, stolen luggage, food poisoning, and marriage proposals are all part of a day's work. Back at our offices, editors work from spring to fall, massaging copy written on Himalayan bus rides into witty, informative prose. A student staff of typesetters, cartographers, publicists, and managers keeps our lively team together. In September, the collected efforts of the summer are delivered to our printer, which turns them into books in record time, so that you have the most up-to-date information available for your vacation. Even as you read this, work on next year's editions is well underway.

WHY WE DO IT

We don't think of budget travel as the last recourse of the destitute; we believe that it's the only way to travel. Living cheaply and simply brings you closer to the people and places you've been saving up to visit. Our books will ease your anxieties and answer your questions about the basics—so you can get off the beaten track and explore. Once you learn the ropes, we encourage you to put *Let's Go* down now and then to strike out on your own. You know as well as we that the best discoveries are often those you make yourself. When you find something worth sharing, please drop us a line. We're Let's Go Publications, 67 Mount Auburn St., Cambridge, MA 02138, USA (email: feedback@letsgo.com). For more info, visit our website, http://www.letsgo.com.

READER QUESTIONNAIRE

Name: ____________________

Address: ____________________

City: ____________ **State:** _____ **Country:** ____________

ZIP/Postal Code: __________ **E-mail:** ______________ **How old are you?** ____

And you're...? in high school in college in graduate school employed retired between jobs

Which book(s) have you used? ____________________

Where have you gone with Let's Go? ____________________

Have you traveled extensively before? yes no

Had you used Let's Go before? yes no **Would you use it again?** yes no

How did you hear about Let's Go? friend store clerk television review bookstore display ad/promotion internet other: __________

Why did you choose Let's Go? reputation budget focus annual updating wit & incision price other: __________

Which guides have you used? Fodor's Footprint Handbooks Frommer's $-a-day Lonely Planet Moon Guides Rick Steve's Rough Guides UpClose other: __________

Which guide do you prefer? Why? ____________________

Please rank the following in your Let's Go guide: (1=needs improvement, 5=perfect)

packaging/cover	1 2 3 4 5	food	1 2 3 4 5	maps	1 2 3 4 5
cultural introduction	1 2 3 4 5	sights	1 2 3 4 5	directions	1 2 3 4 5
"Essentials"	1 2 3 4 5	entertainment	1 2 3 4 5	writing style	1 2 3 4 5
practical info	1 2 3 4 5	gay/lesbian info	1 2 3 4 5	budget resources	1 2 3 4 5
accommodations	1 2 3 4 5	up-to-date info	1 2 3 4 5	other: ________	1 2 3 4 5

How long was your trip? one week two wks. three wks. a month 2+ months

Why did you go? sightseeing adventure travel study abroad other: __________

What was your average daily budget, not including flights? __________

Do you buy a separate map when you visit a foreign city? yes no

Have you used a Let's Go Map Guide? yes no **If you have, which one?** __________

Would you recommend them to others? yes no

Have you visited Let's Go's website? yes no

What would you like to see included on Let's Go's website? __________

What percentage of your trip planning did you do on the web? __________

What kind of Let's Go guide would you like to see? recreation (e.g., skiing) phrasebook spring break adventure/trekking first-time travel info Europe altas

Which of the following destinations would you like to see Let's Go cover? Argentina Brazil Canada Caribbean Chile Costa Rica Cuba Morocco Nepal Russia Scandinavia Southwest USA other: __________

Where did you buy your guidebook? independent bookstore college bookstore travel store Internet chain bookstore gift other: __________

Please fill this out and return it to **Let's Go, St. Martin's Press,** 175 Fifth Ave., New York, NY 10010-7848. All respondents will receive a free subscription to ***The Yellowjacket***, the Let's Go Newsletter. You can find a more extensive version of this survey on the web at http://www.letsgo.com.

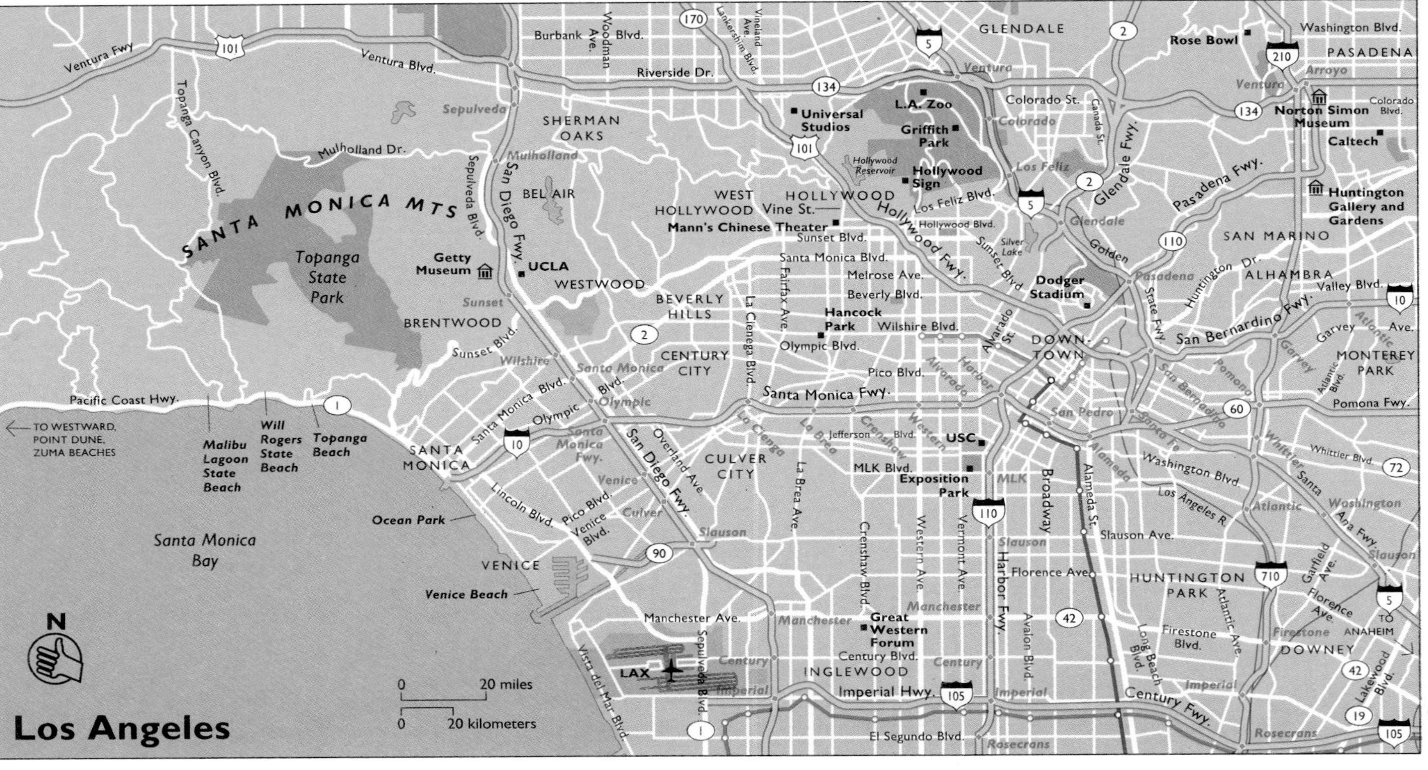
Los Angeles
N
0 20 miles
0 20 kilometers
Ventura Fwy
Ventura Blvd.
Burbank Blvd.
Woodman Ave.
Riverside Dr.
Lankershim Blvd.
Vineland Ave.
GLENDALE
Rose Bowl
Washington Blvd.
PASADENA
Arroyo
Colorado St.
Colorado Blvd.
Norton Simon Museum
Caltech
Huntington Gallery and Gardens
Topanga Canyon Blvd.
Sepulveda
SHERMAN OAKS
Universal Studios
L.A. Zoo
Griffith Park
Hollywood Reservoir
Hollywood Sign
Canada St.
Glendale Fwy.
Pasadena Fwy.
Mulholland Dr.
Mulholland
Sepulveda Blvd.
San Diego Fwy.
BEL AIR
WEST HOLLYWOOD
HOLLYWOOD
Vine St.
Los Feliz Blvd.
Los Feliz
Mann's Chinese Theater
Hollywood Blvd.
Hollywood Fwy.
Silver Lake
Glendale
Golden
SAN MARINO
SANTA MONICA MTS
Topanga State Park
Getty Museum
UCLA
WESTWOOD
Sunset Blvd.
Santa Monica Blvd.
Melrose Ave.
Beverly Blvd.
Sunset Blvd
Dodger Stadium
Pasadena
State Fwy.
Huntington Dr.
ALHAMBRA
Valley Blvd.
BEVERLY HILLS
BRENTWOOD
Sunset
Hancock Park
Wilshire Blvd.
Alvarado St.
DOWNTOWN
San Bernardino Fwy.
Garvey Ave.
Atlantic
MONTEREY PARK
Atlantic Blvd.
Wilshire
Santa Monica
CENTURY CITY
La Cienega Blvd.
Fairfax Ave.
Olympic Blvd.
Pico Blvd.
Alvarado
Harbor
Garvey
Pomona
San Bernardino
Pomona Fwy.
Pacific Coast Hwy.
Olympic
Santa Monica Fwy.
San Pedro
Santa Fe
TO WESTWARD, POINT DUNE, ZUMA BEACHES
Malibu Lagoon State Beach
Will Rogers State Beach
Topanga Beach
SANTA MONICA
Overland Ave.
La Brea
Crenshaw
Jefferson Blvd.
Western
USC
Alameda
Washington Blvd.
Whittier Blvd.
Whittier
Santa Ana Fwy.
CULVER CITY
La Brea Ave.
MLK Blvd.
Exposition Park
Broadway
Alameda St.
Los Angeles R
Washington
Atlantic
Venice
Lincoln Blvd.
Pico Blvd.
Venice Blvd.
Culver
Slauson
Crenshaw Blvd.
Western Ave.
Vermont Ave.
Harbor Fwy.
MLK
Slauson Ave.
Ocean Park
Santa Monica Bay
VENICE
Venice Beach
Florence Ave.
Avalon Blvd.
HUNTINGTON PARK
Atlantic Ave.
Garfield Ave.
Florence Ave.
Manchester Ave.
Manchester
Great Western Forum
Century Blvd.
INGLEWOOD
Firestone Blvd.
Long Beach Blvd.
Firestone
TO ANAHEIM
DOWNEY
LAX
Vista del Mar Blvd.
Sepulveda Blvd.
Century
Imperial
Imperial Hwy.
Century Fwy.
Lakewood Blvd.
El Segundo Blvd.
Rosecrans

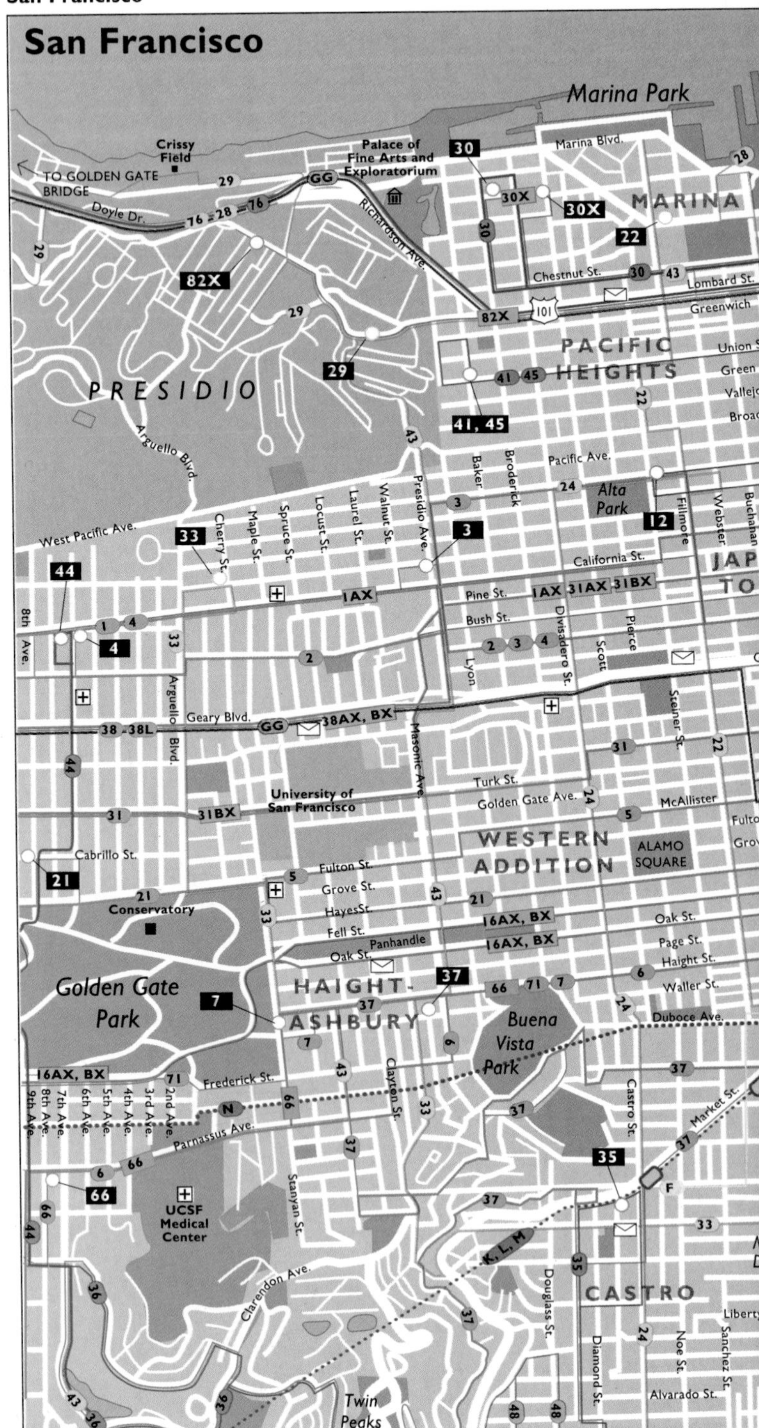
San Francisco
Marina Park
Crissy Field
TO GOLDEN GATE BRIDGE
Palace of Fine Arts and Exploratorium
Marina Blvd.
MARINA
Doyle Dr.
Richardson Ave.
Chestnut St.
Lombard St.
Greenwich
PACIFIC HEIGHTS
PRESIDIO
Arguello Blvd.
Pacific Ave.
Alta Park
West Pacific Ave.
Cherry St.
Maple St.
Spruce St.
Locust St.
Laurel St.
Walnut St.
Presidio Ave.
Baker
Broderick
Fillmore
Webster
Buchanan
California St.
Pine St.
Bush St.
Divisadero St.
Scott
Pierce
Lyon
Steiner St.
Geary Blvd.
Masonic Ave.
Turk St.
Golden Gate Ave.
McAllister
University of San Francisco
Cabrillo St.
WESTERN ADDITION
ALAMO SQUARE
Fulton St.
Grove St.
Hayes St.
Fell St.
Oak St.
Panhandle
Page St.
Haight St.
Waller St.
Duboce Ave.
Conservatory
Golden Gate Park
HAIGHT-ASHBURY
Buena Vista Park
Frederick St.
Clayton St.
Castro St.
Market St.
9th Ave.
8th Ave.
7th Ave.
6th Ave.
5th Ave.
4th Ave.
3rd Ave.
2nd Ave.
Parnassus Ave.
Stanyan St.
UCSF Medical Center
Clarendon Ave.
Douglass St.
CASTRO
Diamond St.
Noe St.
Sanchez St.
Alvarado St.
Liberty
Twin Peaks

TO ALCATRAZ
Fisherman's Wharf
Pier 39
200 yards
200 meters
N
San Francisco Bay
TELEGRAPH HILL
Coit Tower
NORTH BEACH
RUSSIAN HILL
CHINATOWN
JACKSON SQUARE
Ferry Building
Transamerica Pyramid
NOB HILL
UNION SQUARE
Transbay Terminal
Tourist Info
SOMA
China Basin
CHINA BASIN
Central Basin
SF General
Jefferson
North Point
Columbus Ave.
Leavenworth
Mason
Powell St.
Stockton
Grant
Jones
Taylor St.
Filbert
Kearny St.
Montgomery St.
Sansome
Battery
Front
Davis
The Embarcadero
Drumm
Clay St.
Sacramento
Sutter
Post
Geary St.
Market St.
Stuart St.
Spear
Main St.
Beale St.
Fremont St.
1st St.
2nd St.
3rd St.
4th St.
5th St.
6th St.
Larkin
Hyde St.
Turk St.
Mission St.
Howard St.
8th St.
Folsom St.
Harrison St.
9th St.
10th St.
11th St.
12th St.
Brannan St.
Townsend
King St.
7th St.
Owens St.
China Basin St.
Treat Ave.
San Bruno Ave.
Potrero St.
Hampshire St.
Mariposa St.
Missouri St.
Texas St.
Mississippi St.
Pennsylvania St.
IndianaSt.
Minnesota St.
Alabama St.
Florida St.
Bryant St.
York St.
Harrison St.
Vermont St.
Kansas St.
Rhode Island St.
De Haro St.
Carolina St.
Wisconsin St.
Arkansas St.
Connecticut St.
Tennessee St.
3rd St.
Illinois St.
Capp St.
Shotwell St.
Folsom St.
S. Van Ness Ave.
Mission St.
80
280

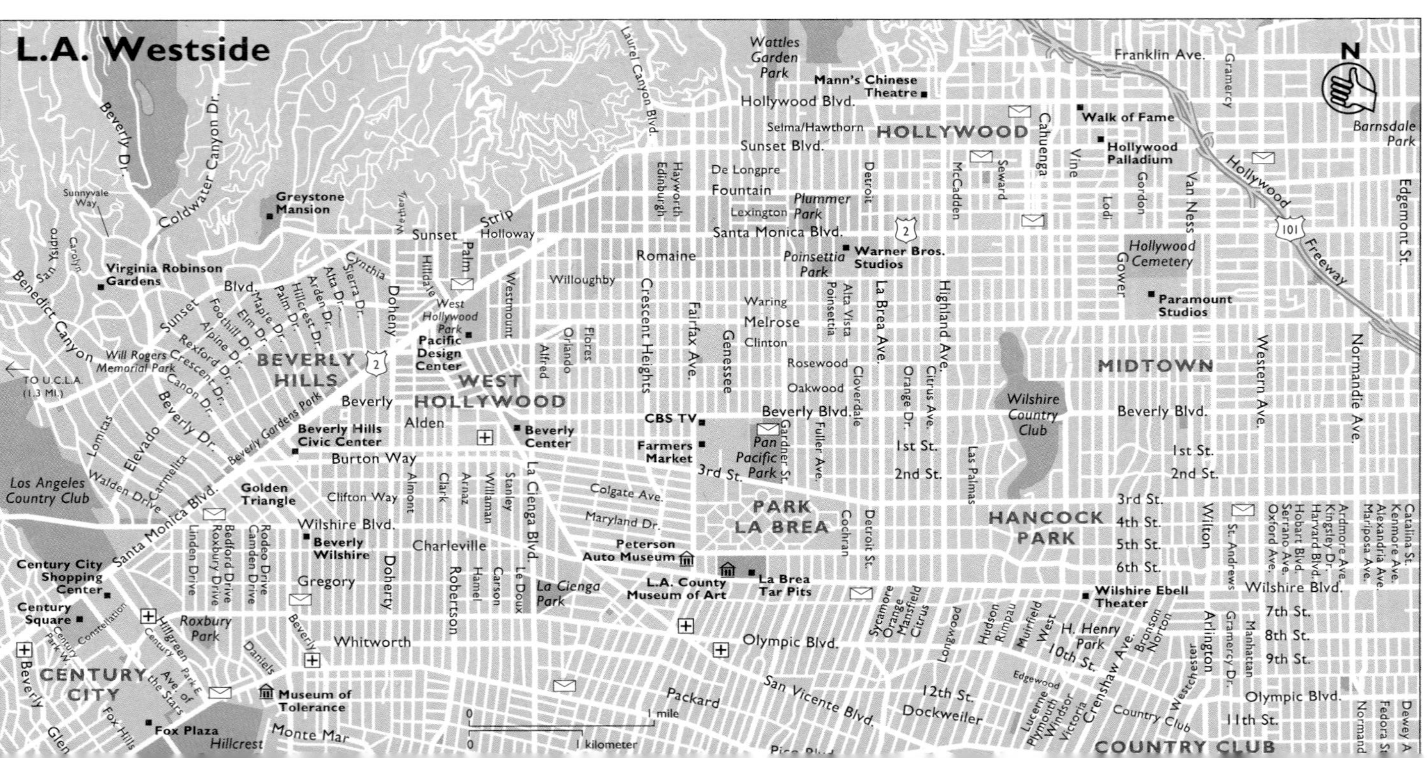

L.A. Westside
N
Beverly Dr.
Coldwater Canyon Dr.
Sunnyvale Way
San Ysidro
Carolyn
Benedict Canyon
Virginia Robinson Gardens
Greystone Mansion
Wetherly
Sunset
Strip
Holloway
Sunset Blvd.
Foothill Dr.
Elm Dr.
Maple Dr.
Palm Dr.
Hillcrest Dr.
Arden Dr.
Alta Dr.
Sierra Dr.
Cynthia
Doheny
Hilldale
Palm
West Hollywood Park
Pacific Design Center
Westmount
Willoughby
Alpine Dr.
Rexford Dr.
Crescent Dr.
Canon Dr.
Beverly Dr.
Will Rogers Memorial Park
TO U.C.L.A (1.3 MI.)
BEVERLY HILLS
2
Beverly
WEST HOLLYWOOD
Alden
Beverly Gardens Park
Beverly Hills Civic Center
Burton Way
Beverly Center
Lomitas
Elevado
Carmelita
Walden Drive
Los Angeles Country Club
Santa Monica Blvd.
Golden Triangle
Clifton Way
Almont
Clark
Arnaz
Willaman
Stanley
La Cienga Blvd.
Wilshire Blvd.
Beverly Wilshire
Charleville
Linden Drive
Roxbury Drive
Bedford Drive
Camden Drive
Rodeo Drive
Gregory
Doherty
Robertson
Hamel
Carson
Le Doux
La Cienga Park
Century City Shopping Center
Century Square
Constellation
Century Park W.
Hillgreen
Century Park E.
Roxbury Park
Beverly
Daniels
Whitworth
CENTURY CITY
Ave. of the Stars
Fox Hills
Glen
Fox Plaza
Hillcrest
Museum of Tolerance
Monte Mar
0
1 mile
1 kilometer
Laurel Canyon Blvd.
Hayworth
Edinburgh
Romaine
Crescent Heights
Orlando
Alfred
Flores
Fairfax Ave.
Genessee
Wattles Garden Park
Mann's Chinese Theatre
Hollywood Blvd.
Selma/Hawthorn
Sunset Blvd.
De Longpre
Fountain
Lexington
Plummer Park
Santa Monica Blvd.
Poinsettia Park
Warner Bros. Studios
Waring
Melrose
Clinton
Poinsettia
Alta Vista
Rosewood
Oakwood
Cloverdale
La Brea Ave.
Detroit
CBS TV
Farmers Market
3rd St.
Pan Pacific Park
Gardner St.
Fuller Ave.
Beverly Blvd.
Orange Dr.
Citrus Ave.
Highland Ave.
1st St.
2nd St.
Las Palmas
Colgate Ave.
Maryland Dr.
Peterson Auto Museum
PARK LA BREA
Cochran
Detroit St.
L.A. County Museum of Art
La Brea Tar Pits
Sycamore
Orange
Mansfield
Citrus
Longwood
Hudson
Rimpau
Muirfield
West
H. Henry Park
10th St.
Olympic Blvd.
Packard
San Vicente Blvd.
12th St.
Dockweiler
Edgewood
Lucerne
Plymouth
Windsor
Victoria
Crenshaw Ave.
Country Club
COUNTRY CLUB
HOLLYWOOD
McCadden
Seward
Cahuenga
Vine
Walk of Fame
Hollywood Palladium
Lodi
Gordon
Gower
Hollywood Cemetery
Paramount Studios
Van Ness
Franklin Ave.
Gramercy
Hollywood Freeway
101
Barnsdale Park
Edgemont St.
MIDTOWN
Wilshire Country Club
Beverly Blvd.
1st St.
2nd St.
Western Ave.
Normandie Ave.
HANCOCK PARK
3rd St.
4th St.
5th St.
6th St.
Wilton
St. Andrews
Oxford Ave.
Serrano Ave.
Hobart Blvd.
Harvard Blvd.
Kingsley Dr.
Ardmore Ave.
Mariposa Ave.
Alexandria Ave.
Kenmore Ave.
Catalina St.
Wilshire Ebell Theater
Wilshire Blvd.
Bronson
Norton
Westchester
Arlington
Gramercy Dr.
Manhattan
7th St.
8th St.
9th St.
Olympic Blvd.
11th St.
Normand
Fedora St
Dewey A